Ethical Obligations and Decision Making in Accounting

Text and Cases

Fourth Edition

Steven M. Mintz, DBA, CPA
Professor of Accounting
California Polytechnic State University,
San Luis Obispo

Roselyn E. Morris, Ph.D., CPA
Professor of Accounting
Texas State University–San Marcos

ETHICAL OBLIGATIONS AND DECISION MAKING IN ACCOUNTING: TEXT AND CASES,
FOURTH EDITION

Published by McGraw-Hill Education, 2 Penn Plaza, New York, NY 10121. Copyright © 2017 by McGraw-Hill Education. All rights reserved. Printed in the United States of America. Previous editions © 2014, 2011 and 2008. No part of this publication may be reproduced or distributed in any form or by any means, or stored in a database or retrieval system, without the prior written consent of McGraw-Hill Education, including, but not limited to, in any network or other electronic storage or transmission, or broadcast for distance learning.

Some ancillaries, including electronic and print components, may not be available to customers outside the United States.

This book is printed on acid-free paper.

1 2 3 4 5 6 QVS 20 19 18 17 16

ISBN 978-1-259-25419-2
MHID 1-259-25419-4

Senior Vice President, Products & Markets: *Kurt L. Strand*
Vice President, General Manager, Products & Markets: *Marty Lange*
Vice President, Content Design & Delivery: *Kimberly Meriwether David*
Managing Director: *Tim Vertovec*
Senior Brand Manager: *Natalie King*
Director, Product Development: *Rose Koos*
Director of Digital Content: *Patricia Plumb*
Lead Product Developer: *Kristine Tibbetts*
Senior Product Developer: *Rebecca Mann*
Marketing Manager: *Kyle Burdette*
Senior Digital Product Analyst: *Xin Lin*
Senior Director, Content Design & Delivery: *Linda Avenarius*
Program Manager: *Daryl Horrocks*
Content Project Manager: *Angela Norris*
Buyer: *Jennifer Pickel*
Designer: *Tara McDermott*
Content Licensing Specialists: *Jacob Sullivan / Melissa Homer*
Cover Image: *(c) Olaser/Getty Images*
Compositor: *SPi Global*
Typeface: STIX Mathjax Main 10/12
Printer: *Quad/Graphics*

All credits appearing on pages or at the end of the book are considered to be an extension of the copyright page.

Library of Congress Cataloging-in-Publication Data
Names: Mintz, Steven M., author. | Morris, Roselyn E., author.
Title: Ethical obligations and decision making in accounting : text and cases
 / Steven M. Mintz, DBA, CPA, Professor of Accounting California
 Polytechnic State University, San Luis Obispo, Roselyn E. Morris, Ph.D.,
 CPA, Professor of Accounting Texas State University-San Marcos.
Description: Fourth Edition. | New York, NY : McGraw-Hill Education, 2016. |
 Revised edition of the authors' Ethical obligations and decision making in
 accounting, 2014.
Identifiers: LCCN 2015044426 | ISBN 9781259543470 (alk. paper)
Subjects: LCSH: Accountants--Professional ethics--United States--Case
 studies.
Classification: LCC HF5616.U5 M535 2016 | DDC 174/.4--dc23 LC record available at
http://lccn.loc.gov/2015044426

2013011582

The Internet addresses listed in the text were accurate at the time of publication. The inclusion of a Web site does not indicate an endorsement by the authors or McGraw-Hill Education, and McGraw-Hill Education does not guarantee the accuracy of the information presented at these sites.

mheducation.com/highered

Dedication

"Educating the mind without educating the heart is no education at all."

Aristotle

What Aristotle meant by this statement is intelligence that is not informed by our hearts--by compassion--is not really intelligent at all. We strive in this book not only to educate accounting students to be future leaders in the accounting profession but to stimulate your ethical perception and cultivate virtue thereby awakening your sense of duty and obligation to the public interest.

About the Authors

Steven M. Mintz, DBA, CPA, is a professor of accounting in the Orfalea College of Business at the California Polytechnic State University–San Luis Obsipo. Dr. Mintz received his DBA from George Washington University. His first book, titled *Cases in Accounting Ethics and Professionalism,* was also published by McGraw-Hill. Dr. Mintz has recently been acknowledged by accounting researchers as one of the top publishers in accounting ethics and in accounting education. He was selected for the 2014 Max Block Distinguished Article Award in the "Technical Analysis" category by The CPA Journal. Dr. Mintz received the 2015 Accounting Exemplar Award of the Public Interest Section of the American Accounting Association. He also has received the Faculty Excellence Award of the California Society of CPAs. Dr. Mintz writes two popular ethics blogs under the names "ethicssage" and "workplaceethicsadvice."

Roselyn E. Morris, Ph.D., CPA, is a professor of accounting in the Accounting Department at the McCoy College of Business, Texas State University–San Marcos. Dr. Morris received her Ph.D. in business administration from the University of Houston. She is a past president of the Accounting Education Foundation and chair of the Qualifications Committee of the Texas Board of Public Accountancy. Dr. Morris has received the Outstanding Educator Award from the Texas Society of CPAs.

Both Professors Mintz and Morris have developed and teach an accounting ethics course at their respective universities.

Preface

Ethical Obligations and Decision Making in Accounting was written to guide students through the minefields of ethical conflict in meeting their responsibilities under the professions' codes of conduct. Our book is devoted to helping students cultivate the ethical commitment needed to ensure that their work meets the highest standards of integrity, independence, and objectivity. An expanded discussion of professional judgment highlights the challenges to ethical decision-making for internal accountants and auditors, and external auditors. We hope that this book and classroom instruction will work together to provide the tools to help students to make ethical judgments and carry through with ethical actions.

The fourth edition of *Ethical Obligations and Decision Making in Accounting: Text and Cases* incorporates a behavioral perspective into ethical decision-making that encourages students to get in touch with their values and learn how to voice them in the workplace when conflicts arise and ethical dilemmas exist. We build on traditional philosophical reasoning methods by taking the process one step further, that is, to convert ethical intent into ethical action. The "Giving Voice to Values" (GVV) approach provides this link. If accounting professionals are successful in voicing values in a way that encourages doubters and detractors to join the effort, then there may be no need for whistle-blowing. We also connect many of the issues discussed in the book with a new final chapter on "Ethical Leadership."

Several states now require their accounting students to complete an ethics course prior to being licensed as a CPA. This book has been designed to meet the guidelines for accounting ethics education including:

- encouraging students to make decisions in accordance with prescribed values, attitudes, and behaviors
- providing a framework for ethical reasoning, knowledge of professional values and ethical standards
- prescribing attributes for exercising professional skepticism and behavior that is in the best interest of the investing and consuming public and the profession.

What's New in the 4th Edition?

In response to feedback and guidance from numerous accounting ethics faculty, the authors have made many important changes to the fourth edition of *Ethical Obligations and Decision Making in Accounting: Text and Cases,* including the following:

- **Connect is available for the first time** with assignable cases, test bank assessment material, and SmartBook. **SmartBook** is an excellent way to ensure that students are reading and understanding the basic concepts in the book and it prepares them to learn from classroom discussions. Several of the **Chapter Cases** are available in an auto-graded format to facilitate grading by instructors. The purpose of using the digital format is to better prepare students ahead of class to free up instructors to discuss a broader range of topics in their lectures and in the give-and-take between teacher and student. **Connect Insight Reports** will also give the instructor a better view into the overall class's understanding of core topics prior to class, to appropriately focus lectures and discussion. The **Connect Library** also offers materials to support the efforts of first-time and seasoned instructors of accounting ethics, including a comprehensive Instructor's Manual, Test Bank, Additional Cases, and PowerPoint presentations.
- **Learning Objectives** have been added and linked to specific content material in each chapter.
- **Giving Voice to Values (GVV)** approach is explained in Chapter 2 and used throughout the text. GVV is an innovative pedagogical method that complements the traditional philosophical reasoning

approaches to ethical decision-making by emphasizing developing the capacity to express one's values in a way that positively influences others. The technique is used post-decision-making and is based on developing and fine-tuning an action plan using scripting and rehearsal. It is ideal for role-playing exercises.

- **International** auditing and ethics issues are incorporated into existing chapters.
- Added five new **Discussion Questions** to each chapter as well as revised questions with more current topics and issues.
- Replaced many of the **cases** with more current and topical issues. Eighteen of the 76 cases have been specifically developed to enable students to practice the "Giving Voice to Values" technique in the context of the decision-making model.
- **Expanded the discussion of whistleblowing obligations** of accounting professionals in Chapter 3 including guidelines for reporting under Dodd-Frank and the AICPA rules of conduct.
- Added a comprehensive section on **professional judgment** in accounting and auditing to Chapter 4 and models for making judgments and exercising professional skepticism.
- Updated Chapter 4 to incorporate the **Revised AICPA Code of Professional Conduct**.
- **Expanded** the discussion of the PCAOB inspection process in Chapters 5 and 6 for audits of companies listing stock in the U.S., including Chinese companies and audit deficiencies noted in inspections of U.S. companies.
- Updated case examples used throughout the text to describe **earnings management** techniques with expanded coverage in Chapter 7.
- New Chapter 8 on **"Ethical Leadership"** that ties together many of the topics in the chapters in the text. Ethical leadership is explored in the context of making ethical decisions and judgments in the performance of professional accounting services.
- Improved and expanded the scope of major cases that can be used as an end-of-course project to enhance the experiences of upper-division undergraduates and graduate students.
- Revised and greatly enhanced **Instructor's Resource Materials** and supplements.

Chapter 1

- **New** discussion of the use of social networks and social media communications, personal responsibility, and workplace ethics.
- Expanded discussion of moral philosophies and implications for ethical reasoning in accounting and auditing.
- Expanded discussion of the Principles of the AICPA Code of Professional Conduct, the public interest obligation, and regulation in the accounting profession.

Chapter 2

- **New** discussion of moral intensity and influence on ethical decision making.
- **New** discussion of Kidder's Ethical Checkpoints and link to moral action.
- Expanded discussion of Behavioral Ethics and cognitive development.
- **New** and comprehensive discussion of the **GVV** technique that provides a mechanism for students to act on ethical intent. Chapter 2 discusses the foundation of the approach including examples on applying the methodology. There are **five cases** in the chapter to engage students in discussions of the **GVV** approach to ethical action. Subsequent chapters also contain cases with a **GVV** dimension.

Chapter 3

- **New** section on "Organizational Ethics and Leadership."
- **New** discussion of "Character and Leadership in the Workplace."
- Updated results from the National Business Ethics Survey, Association of Certified Fraud Examiners Global Survey, and KPMG Integrity Survey.
- Expanded discussion of financial statement fraud schemes.
- **New** discussion of the morality of whistleblowing.
- Added discussion of major whistleblower case of *Anthony Menendez v. Halliburton, Inc.*
- Expanded discussion of Dodd-Frank provisions for whistleblowing by internal accountants and auditors, and external auditors including when external auditors can blow the whistle on their audit firms.
- Expanded discussion of subordination of judgment rules and their application to whistleblowing.

Chapter 4

- **Extensive new discussion** of professional judgment in accounting.
- Added an explanation of KPMG Professional Judgment Framework.
- Expanded discussion of professional skepticism.
- **New** discussion of professionalism and commercialism.
- **Comprehensive** discussion of the **Revised AICPA Code of Professional Conduct** including: Conceptual Framework for Members in Public Practice and Conceptual Framework for Members in Business.
- **New** discussion of ethical conflict requirements and decision-making model under the Revised Code.
- Expanded discussion of AICPA Conceptual Framework for Independence Standards.
- Expanded discussion of integrity and subordination of judgment rules.
- **New** discussion of confidentiality and disclosing fraud.
- Expanded discussion of ethics in tax practice.
- Expanded discussion of "Insider Trading" cases against CPAs.
- **New** discussion of Global Code of Ethics.

Chapter 5

- Expanded discussion of errors, illegal acts, and fraud.
- **New** discussion of Private Securities Litigation Reform Act and reporting requirements to the SEC; fraud and confidentiality issues explored.
- Discussion of **Professional Skepticism Scale** that measures traits conducive to developing a questioning mind and informed judgment.
- Discussion of findings of the Center for Audit Quality of audit deficiencies.
- Expanded discussion of PCAOB audit inspection process and high rate of deficiencies of audit firms.

Chapter 6

- **New** cases that explore in depth legal obligations of accountants and auditors.
- Expanded discussion of auditor legal liabilities.
- Expanded section on legal liabilities under Sarbanes-Oxley.
- **New** discussion of International Financial Reporting Standards and international enforcement.
- **New** discussion of principles versus rules-based standards and SEC position on objectives-oriented standards.
- **New** section on "Compliance and Management by Values."
- **New** section on "Global Ethics, Fraud, and Bribery" and the Foreign Corrupt Practices Act.
- Expanded discussion on regulatory issues and PCAOB inspections.

Chapter 7

- **New** section on "Non-Financial Measures of Earnings."
- Expanded discussion of earnings management and professional judgment.
- Expanded discussion of the use of accruals and earnings management.
- Introductory discussion of new revenue recognition standard.
- Detailed examples of financial statement restatements of Hertz Corporation and Cubic Corporation, and CVS-Caremark merger.

Chapter 8 – New Chapter on Ethical Leadership

Chapter 8 links back to discussions in Chapters 1 through 7 by incorporating material on "Ethical Leadership." The purpose is to leave students with a positive message of the importance of being a leader and ethical leadership in building organizational ethics. Leadership in decision-making in accounting, auditing, tax, and advisory services engagements is addressed. The chapter includes 20 discussion questions and 6 new cases. The chapter includes the following major topics:

- Discussion of moral decision-making and leadership.
- Exploring different types of leaders: authentic leaders, transformational leadership, followership and leadership, and how social learning theory influences leadership.
- Revisiting moral intensity in the context of ethical leadership.
- Ethical leadership and internal audit function.
- Ethical leadership and tax practice.
- Gender influences in leadership.
- Causes of leadership failures.
- Case studies on ethical leadership.
- Implications of ethical leadership for whistleblowing activities.
- Values-based leadership.
- Ethical leadership and the GVV technique.
- Ethical leadership competence.

McGraw-Hill Connect®
Learn Without Limits

Connect is a teaching and learning platform that is proven to deliver better results for students and instructors.

Connect empowers students by continually adapting to deliver precisely what they need, when they need it, and how they need it, so your class time is more engaging and effective.

Course outcomes improve with Connect.

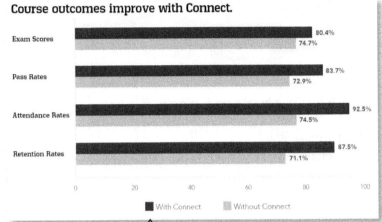

88% of instructors who use **Connect** require it; instructor satisfaction **increases** by 38% when **Connect** is required.

Using **Connect** improves passing rates by **10.8%** and retention by **16.4%**.

Analytics

Connect Insight®

Connect Insight is Connect's new one-of-a-kind visual analytics dashboard—now available for both instructors and students—that provides at-a-glance information regarding student performance, which is immediately actionable. By presenting assignment, assessment, and topical performance results together with a time metric that is easily visible for aggregate or individual results, Connect Insight gives the user the ability to take a just-in-time approach to teaching and learning, which was never before available. Connect Insight presents data that empower students and help instructors improve class performance in a way that is efficient and effective.

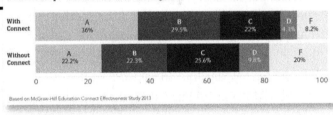

Students can view their results for any **Connect** course.

Adaptive

More students earn **A's** and **B's** when they use McGraw-Hill Education **Adaptive** products.

SmartBook®

Proven to help students improve grades and study more efficiently, SmartBook contains the same content within the print book, but actively tailors that content to the needs of the individual. SmartBook's adaptive technology provides precise, personalized instruction on what the student should do next, guiding the student to master and remember key concepts, targeting gaps in knowledge and offering customized feedback, and driving the student toward comprehension and retention of the subject matter. Available on smartphones and tablets, SmartBook puts learning at the student's fingertips—anywhere, anytime.

Over **4 billion questions** have been answered, making McGraw-Hill Education products more intelligent, reliable, and precise.

www.learnsmartadvantage.com

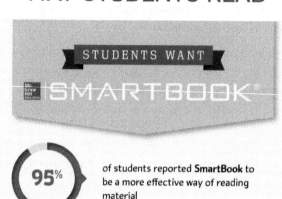
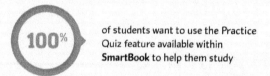
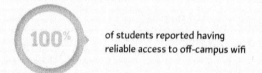
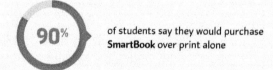
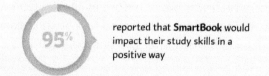

Acknowledgments

The authors want to express their sincere gratitude to these reviewers for their comments and guidance. Their insights were invaluable in developing this edition of the book.

- Donald Ariail, *Southern Polytechnic State University*
- Stephanie Bacik, *Wake Tech Community College*
- Charles Bunn, Jr., *Wake Tech Community College*
- Kevin Cabe, *Indiana Wesleyan University*
- Rick Crosser, *Metropolitan State University of Denver*
- Denise Dickins, *East Carolina University*
- Dennis L. Elam, *Texas A&M University–San Antonio*
- Rafik Elias, *California State University–Los Angeles*
- Athena Jones, *University of Maryland University College*
- Patrick Kelly, *Providence College*
- Lorraine S. Lee, *University of North Carolina–Wilmington*
- Stephen McNett, *Texas A&M University–Central Texas*
- Kenneth Merchant, *University of Southern California*
- Michael Newman, *University of Houston*
- Robin Radtke, *Clemson University*
- John Sennetti, *NOVA Southeastern University*
- Edward Smith, *St. John's University*
- Dale Wallis, *University of California–Los Angeles Extension*

We also appreciate the assistance and guidance given us on this project by the staff of McGraw-Hill Education, including Tim Vertovec, managing director; Natalie King, senior brand manager; Kyle Burdette, marketing manager; Rebecca Mann, senior product developer; Daryl Horrocks, program manager; Angela Norris, content project manager; Jacob Sullivan and Melissa Homer, content licensing specialists; and Jennifer Pickel, buyer. We greatly appreciate the efforts of Deborah Pfeiffer, copyeditor of the book.

Finally, we would like to acknowledge the contributions of our students, who have provided invaluable comments and suggestions on the content and use of these cases.

If you have any questions, comments, or suggestions concerning *Ethical Obligations and Decision Making in Accounting,* please send them to Steve Mintz at smintz@calpoly.edu.

Case Descriptions

Case #	Case Name/Description

1-1 Harvard Cheating Scandal
Student cheating at Harvard raises questions about responsibilities of instructors and student personal responsibilities.

1-2 Giles and Regas
Dating relationship between employees of a CPA firm jeopardizes completion of the audit.

1-3 NYC Subway Death: Bystander Effect or Moral Blindness
Real-life situation where onlookers did nothing while a man was pushed to his death off a subway platform.

1-4 Lone Star School District
Failure to produce documents to support travel expenditures raises questions about the justifiability of reimbursement claims.

1-5 Reneging on a Promise
Ethical dilemma of a student who receives an offer of employment from a firm that he wants to work for, but only after accepting an offer from another firm.

1-6 Capitalization versus Expensing
Ethical obligations of a controller when pressured by the CFO to capitalize costs that should be expensed.

1-7 Eating Time
Ethical considerations of a new auditor who is asked to cut down on the amount of time that he takes to complete audit work.

1-8 Shifty Industries
Depreciation calculations and cash outflow considerations in a tax engagement.

1-9 Cleveland Custom Cabinets
Ethical and professional responsibilities of an accountant who is asked to "tweak" overhead to improve reported earnings.

1-10 Better Boston Beans
Conflict between wanting to do the right thing and a confidentiality obligation to a coworker.

Case #	Case Name/Description

2-1 A Team Player (a GVV case)
Ethical dilemma for audit staff member who discovers a deficiency in inventory procedures but is unable to convince the group to report it. Application of Giving Voice to Values approach.

2-2 FDA Liability Concerns (a GVV case)
Conflict between a chef and CFO over reporting bacteria found in food and FDA inspection results. Application of GVV approach.

2-3 The Tax Return (a GVV case)
Tax accountant's ethical dilemma when asked by her supervisor to ignore reportable lottery winnings. Application of GVV approach.

2-4 A Faulty Budget (a GVV case)
Ethical and professional responsibilities of an accountant after discovering an error in his sales budget. Application of GVV approach.

2-5 Gateway Hospital (a GVV case)
Behavioral ethics considerations in developing a position on unsubstantiated expense reimbursement claims. Application of GVV approach.

2-6 LinkedIn and Shut Out
Small business owner's inability to gain support from LinkedIn after a contact in his professional network scams him out of $30,000.

2-7 Milton Manufacturing Company
Dilemma for top management on how best to deal with a plant manager who violated company policy but at the same time saved it $1.5 million.

4-4 **Commercialism and Professionalism (a GVV case)**
Ethical considerations in an alternative practice structure due to threats to independence; using GVV to resolve conflict.

4-5 **Han, Kang & Lee, LLC**
Pressure between audit partner who wants the client to write down inventory and other partners that want to keep the client happy.

4-6 **Tax Shelters**
Ethical dilemma of tax accountant in deciding whether to participate in tax shelter transactions targeted to top management of a client entity in light of cultural influences within the firm.

4-7 **M&A Transaction**
Ethical issues concerning a decision to provide merger and acquisition advisory services for an audit client.

4-8 **Valley View Hospital**
Ethical obligations of CPA in deciding whether to report a hospital/client for improper Medicare payments to the government because of a faulty Medicare accounting system.

4-9 **AOL-Time Warner**
Fall out after CFO of AOL blows the whistle on improper round-trip accounting procedures in AOL-Time Warner merger and is investigated himself for his part in the fraud by the SEC.

4-10 **Navistar International**
Confidentiality issues that arise when Navistar management questions the competency of Deloitte & Touche auditors by referring to PCAOB inspection reports and fraud at the company.

Case # **Case Name/Description**

5-1 **Loyalty and Fraud Reporting (a GVV case)**
Employee who embezzles $50,000 seeks out the help of a friend to cover it up. Application of the fraud triangle and GVV.

5-2 **ZZZZ Best**
Fraudster Barry Minkow uses fictitious revenue transactions from nonexistent business to falsify financial statements.

5-3 **Imperial Valley Community Bank**
Role of professional skepticism in evaluating audit evidence on collectability of loans and going concern assessment.

5-4 **Busy Season Planning**
Role of review partner in planning an audit.

5-5 **Tax Inversion**
Questions about the use of IFRS in a consolidation with an Irish entity motivated by tax inversion benefits.

5-6 **Rooster, Hen, Footer, and Burger**
Ethical obligations of a CPA following the discovery of an unreported related party transaction and push back by client entity.

5-7 **Diamond Foods: Accounting for Nuts**
Application of the fraud triangle to assess corporate culture and analysis of fraud detection procedures.

5-8 **Bill Young's Ethical Dilemma**
Options of a friend of an auditor advising the auditor following his inappropriate downloading of client information that shows bribery of foreign officials.

5-9 **Royal Ahold N.V. (Ahold)**
U.S. subsidiary of a Dutch company that used improper accounting for promotional allowances to meet or exceed budgeted earnings targets and questions about professional judgment by auditors.

5-10 **Groupon**
Competitive pressures on social media pioneer leads to internal control weakness and financial restatements.

Case # Case Name/Description

6-1 Advanced Battery Technologies: Reverse Merger
Application of legal standards to assess auditor liability following a reverse merger transaction by a Chinese company.

6-2 Heinrich Müller: Big Four Whistleblower? (a GVV case)
Ethical dilemma of tax accountant after finding confidential files of a client engaged in tax avoidance transactions in Liechtenstein in view of a culture of strict loyalty to the firm.

6-3 Richards & Co: Year-end Audit Engagement
Questions about audit procedures used to assess client's improper use of a credit received from a client to prop up revenue in one year while agreeing to repay the supplier in the following year.

6-4 Anjoorian et al.: Third-Party Liability
Application of the foreseeability test, near-privity, and the Restatement approach in deciding negligence claims against the auditor.

6-5 Vertical Pharmaceuticals Inc. et al. v. Deloitte & Touche LLP
Fiduciary duties and audit withdrawal considerations when suspecting fraud at a client.

6-6 Kay & Lee LLP
Auditor legal liability when foreseen third party relies on financial statement.

6-7 Getaway Cruise Lines: Questionable Payments to do Business Overseas (a GVV case)
Ethical dilemma of Director of International Accounting in voicing her values with respect to a dispute within the company over how to report "questionable payments" made to a foreign government.

6-8 Con-way Inc.
Auditor legal and audit responsibilities to assess facilitating payments and internal control requirements under the FCPA.

6-9 Satyam: India's Enron
Questions about corporate culture and fraud risk assessment surrounding CEO's falsification of financial information and misuse of corporate funds for personal purposes.

6-10 Autonomy
Investigations by U.S. SEC and UK Serious Fraud Office into accounting for an acquisition of a British software maker by Hewlett-Packard (HP).

Case # Case Name/Description

7-1 Nortel Networks
Use of reserves and revenue recognition techniques to manage earnings.

7-2 Solutions Network, Inc. (a GVV case)
Ethical challenges of a controller in voicing values when the company uses round-trip transactions to meet earnings targets.

7-3 GE: "Imagination at Work"
Assessing whether GE used earnings management techniques to accelerate revenue and meet financial analysts' earnings expectations.

7-4 Harrison Industries (a GVV case)
Challenges faced by first-year accountant in voicing values upon questioning the appropriateness of recording an accrued expense.

7-5 Dell Computer
Use of "cookie-jar" reserves to smooth net income and meet financial analysts' earnings projections.

7-6 Tier One Bank
Failure of KPMG to exercise due care and proper professional judgment in gathering supporting evidence for loan loss estimates.

7-7 Sunbeam Corporation
Use of cookie-jar reserves and "channel stuffing" by a turnaround artist to manage earnings.

7-8 Sino-Forest: Accounting for Trees
Failure of Ernst & Young to follow generally accepted auditing standards and lapses in professional ethics related to Chinese company's nonexistent forestry assets; cultural considerations of doing business in China.

7-9 The North Face, Inc.
Questions about revenue recognition on barter transactions and the role of Deloitte & Touche in its audit of the client.

7-10 Beazer Homes
Use of cookie jar reserves to manage earnings and meet EBIT targets.

Case # Case Name/Description

8-1 Research Triangle Software Innovations (a GVV case)
Advisory services staff member recommends the software package of an audit client to another client and deals with push back from her supervisor who is pushing the firm's package; issues related to leadership and application of GVV in resolving the matter.

8-2 Cumberland Lumber
Difference of opinion between chief internal auditor and aggressive CFO about recording year-end accruals.

8-3 Parmalat: Europe's Enron
Fictitious accounts at Bank of America and the use of nominee entities to transfer debt off the books by an Italian company led to one of Europe's largest fraud cases.

8-4 KPMG Tax Shelter Scandal
Major tax shelter scandal case involving KPMG that explores ethical standards in tax practice and in developing tax positions on tax shelter products in a culture that promoted making sales at all costs.

8-5 Krispy Kreme Doughnuts, Inc.
Questions about ethical leadership and corporate governance at Krispy Kreme, and audit by PwC, with respect to the company's use of round-trip transactions to inflate revenues and earnings to meet or exceed financial analysts' EPS guidance.

8-6 Rhody Electronics: A Difficult Client (a GVV case)
Conflict between audit manager and controller over audit planning and execution and implications for ethical leadership.

Major Cases

Case # Case Name/Description

1 Adelphia Communications Corporation
SEC action against Deloitte & Touche for failing to exercise the proper degree of professional skepticism in examining complex related-party transactions and contingencies that were not accounted for in accordance with GAAP.

2 Royal Ahold N.V. (Ahold)
Court finding that Deloitte & Touche should not be held liable for the efforts of the client to deprive the auditors of accurate information needed for the audit and masking the true nature of other evidence.

3 Madison Gilmore's Ethical Dilemma (a GVV case)
Distinguishing between operational and accounting earnings management and efforts of controller to voice values and convince the CFO about inappropriateness of recoding revenue on a bill-and-hold transaction.

4 Cendant Corporation
SEC action against Cendant for managing earnings through merger reserve manipulations and improper accounting for membership sales, and questions about the audit of Ernst & Young.

5 Vivendi Universal
Improper adjustments to EBITDA and operating free cash flow by a French multinational company to meet ambitious earnings targets and conceal liquidity problems.

6 Waste Management
Failure of Andersen auditors to enforce agreement with the board of directors to adopt proposed adjusting journal entries that were required in restated financial statements.

Brief Contents

Table of Contents

Chapter 1

Ethical Reasoning: Implications for Accounting

Learning Objectives

After studying Chapter 1, you should be able to:

LO 1-1 Explain how integrity enables a CPA to withstand pressures and avoid subordination of judgment.

LO 1-2 Discuss the relationship between one's values and ethics, and legal obligations.

LO 1-3 Describe how the pillars of character support ethical decision making.

LO 1-4 Differentiate between moral philosophies and their effect on ethical reasoning in accounting.

LO 1-5 Explain the concept of the public interest in accounting.

LO 1-6 Discuss the Principles section of the AICPA Code of Professional Conduct.

LO 1-7 Apply the IMA Statement of Ethical and Professional Practice to a case study.

Ethics Reflection

Penn State Child Abuse Scandal: A Culture of Indifference

What motivates an otherwise ethical person to do the wrong thing when faced with an ethical dilemma? Why does a good person act wrongly in a particular situation? These are the ethical questions that arise from the Penn State scandal. Football head coach Joe Paterno and administrators at Penn State University looked the other way and failed to act on irrefutable evidence that former assistant coach Jerry Sandusky had molested young boys, an offense for which Sandusky currently is serving a 30- to 60-year sentence. According to the independent report by Louis Freeh that investigated the sexual abuse, the top administrators at Penn State and Joe Paterno sheltered a child predator harming children for over a decade by concealing Sandusky's activities from the board of trustees, the university community, and authorities. They exposed the first abused child to additional harm by alerting Sandusky, who was the only one who knew the child's identity, of what assistant coach Mike McQueary saw in the shower on the night of February 9, 2001.[1] McQueary testified at the June 2012 trial of Sandusky that he observed the abuse[2] and informed Paterno, who reported the incident to his superiors but did not confront Sandusky or report the incident to the board of trustees or the police.[3]

Reasons for Unethical Actions

The report gives the following explanations for the failure of university leaders to take action:

- The desire to avoid the bad publicity
- The failure of the university's board of trustees to have reporting mechanisms in place to ensure disclosure of major risks
- A president who discouraged discussion and dissent
- A lack of awareness of the Clery Act, which requires colleges and universities participating in federal financial aid programs to keep and disclose information about crimes committed on and near their campuses
- A lack of whistleblower policies and protections
- A culture of reverence for the football program that was ingrained at all levels of the campus community

Explanations for Unethical Actions

Former Penn State president Graham Spanier, who was fired by the board of trustees in November 2011, is quoted as discussing in an interview with Jeffrey Toobin of the *New Yorker* about how the university worked that "honesty, integrity, and always doing what was in the *best interests of the university* [italics added] was how everyone agreed to operate and . . . we've always operated as a family. Our personal and social and professional lives were all very intertwined."[4]

A culture that fosters organizational interests to the exclusion of others explains what happened at Penn State, and it happens in other organizations as well, such as Enron and WorldCom. The culture of an organization should be built on ethical values such as honesty, integrity, responsibility, and accountability. While Penn State may have claimed to follow such principles, the reality was that its actions did not match these behavioral norms.

Postscript

The Penn State case just does not seem to go away. Here is a list of actions subsequent to the initial case:

- As of the summer 2015, at least seven civil cases as well as criminal complaints against three former Penn State administrators have been pending.
- In January 2015, the National Collegiate Athletic Association (NCAA) agreed to restore 111 of former head coach Joe Paterno's wins between 1998–2011, making Paterno once again the winningest coach in major college football.
- The Paterno family brought a lawsuit to contest the consent decree's statement that the head coach covered for Sandusky to protect the school's football program.
- The statue of Paterno that was tore down will be replaced by a projected $300,000 life-sized bronze sculpture downtown, about two miles from the original site, after Pennsylvanians overwhelmingly voted to support the school putting the statue out again by a margin of 59 to 25.

Ethical Blind Spots

Leaders of organizations who may be successful at what they do and see themselves as ethical and moral still cultivate a collection of what Max Bazerman and Ann Trebrunsel call *blind spots*.[5] Blind spots are the gaps between who you want to be and the person you actually are. In other words, most of us want to do the right thing—to act ethically—but internal and external pressures get in the way.

As you read this chapter, think about the following questions: (1) What would you have done if you had been in Joe Paterno's position, and why? (2) Which ethical reasoning methods can help me to make ethical decisions in accounting? (3) What are my ethical obligations to the public?

Have the courage to say no. Have the courage to face the truth. Do the right thing because it is right. These are the magic keys to living your life with integrity.

W. Clement Stone (1902–2002)

This quote by William Clement Stone, a businessman, philanthropist, and self-help book author, underscores the importance of integrity in decision making. Notice that the quote addresses integrity in one's personal life. That is because one has to act with integrity when making personal decisions in order to be best equipped to act with integrity on a professional level. Integrity, indeed all of ethics, is not a spigot that can be turned on or off depending on one's whims or whether the matter at hand is personal or professional. As the ancient Greeks knew, we learn how to be ethical by practicing and exercising those virtues that enable us to lead a life of excellence.

Joe Paterno and other university leaders did not act with integrity. They let external considerations of reputation and image dictate their internal actions. Ironically, the very factor—reputation—that they guarded so closely was the first to be brought down by the disclosure of a cover-up in the sex scandal case.

In accounting, internal accountants and auditors may be pressured by superiors to manipulate financial results. The external auditors may have to deal with pressures imposed on them by clients to put the best face on the financial statements regardless of whether they conform to generally accepted accounting principles (GAAP). It is the ethical value of integrity that provides the moral courage to resist the temptation to stand by silently while a company misstates its financial statement amounts.

Integrity: The Basis of Accounting

LO 1-1
Explain how integrity enables a CPA to withstand pressures and avoid subordination of judgment.

According to Mintz (1995), "Integrity is a fundamental trait of character that enables a CPA to withstand client and competitive pressures that might otherwise lead to the subordination of judgment."[6] A person of integrity will act out of moral principle and not expediency. That person will do what is right, even if it means the loss of a job or client. In accounting, the public interest (i.e., investors and creditors) always must be placed ahead of one's own self-interest or the interests of others, including a supervisor or client.

Integrity means that a person acts on principle—a conviction that there is a right way to act when faced with an ethical dilemma. For example, assume that your tax client fails to inform you about an amount of earned income for the year, and you confront the client on this issue. The client tells you not to record it and reminds you that there is no W-2 or 1099 form to document the earnings. The client adds that you will not get to audit the company's financial statements anymore if you do not adhere to the client's wishes. Would you decide to "go along to get along"? If you are a person of integrity, you should not allow the client to dictate how the tax rules will be applied in the client's situation. You are the professional and know the tax regulations best, and you have an ethical obligation to report taxes in accordance with the law. If you go along with the client and the Internal Revenue Service (IRS) investigates and sanctions you for failing to follow the IRS Tax Code, then you may suffer irreparable harm to your reputation. An important point is that a professional must never let loyalty to a client cloud good judgment and ethical decision making.

Worldcom: Cynthia Cooper: Hero and Role Model

Cynthia Cooper's experience at WorldCom illustrates how the internal audit function should work and how a person of integrity can put a stop to financial fraud. It all unraveled in April and May 2002 when Gene Morse, an auditor at WorldCom, couldn't find any documentation to support a claim of $500 million in computer expenses. Morse approached Cooper, the company's director of internal auditing and Morse's boss, who instructed Morse to "keep going." A series of obscure tips led Morse and Cooper to suspect that WorldCom was cooking the books. Cooper formed an investigation team to determine whether their hunch was right.

In its initial investigation, the team discovered $3.8 billion of misallocated expenses and phony accounting entries.[7] Cooper approached the chief financial officer (CFO), Scott Sullivan, but was dissatisfied with his explanations. The chief executive officer (CEO) of the company, Bernie Ebbers, had already resigned under pressure from WorldCom's board of directors, so Cooper went to the audit committee. The committee interviewed Sullivan about the accounting issues and did not get a satisfactory answer. Still, the committee was reluctant to take any action. Cooper persisted anyway. Eventually, one member of the audit committee told her to approach the outside auditors to get their take on the matter. Cooper gathered additional evidence of fraud, and ultimately KPMG, the firm that had replaced Arthur Andersen—the auditors during the fraud—supported Cooper. Sullivan was asked to resign, refused to do so, and was fired.[8]

One tragic result of the fraud and cover-up at WorldCom is the case of Betty Vinson. It is not unusual for someone who is genuinely a good person to get caught up in fraud. Vinson, a former WorldCom mid-level accounting manager, went along with the fraud because her superiors told her to do so. She was convinced that it would be a one-time action. It rarely works that way, however, because once a company starts to engage in accounting fraud, it feels compelled to continue the charade into the future to keep up the appearance that each period's results are as good as or better than prior periods. The key to maintaining one's integrity and ethical perspective is not to take the first step down the proverbial *ethical slippery slope.*

Vinson pleaded guilty in October 2002 to participating in the financial fraud at the company. She was sentenced to five months in prison and five months of house arrest. Vinson represents the typical "pawn" in a financial fraud: an accountant who had no interest or desire to commit fraud but got caught up in it when Sullivan, her boss, instructed her to make improper accounting entries. The rationalization by Sullivan that the company had to "make the numbers appear better than they really were" did nothing to ease her guilty conscience. Judge Barbara Jones, who sentenced Vinson, commented that "Ms. Vinson was among the least culpable members of the conspiracy at WorldCom. . . . Still, had Vinson refused to do what she was asked, it's possible this conspiracy might have been nipped in the bud."[9]

Accounting students should reflect on what they would do if they faced a situation similar to the one that led Vinson to do something that was out of character. Once she agreed to go along with making improper entries, it was difficult to turn back. The company could have threatened to disclose her role in the original fraud and cover-up if Vinson then acted on her beliefs. From an ethical (and practical) perspective it is much better to just do the right thing from the very beginning, so that you can't be blackmailed or intimidated later.

Vinson became involved in the fraud because she had feared losing her job, her benefits, and the means to provide for her family. She must live with the consequences of her actions for the rest of her life. On the other hand, Cynthia Cooper, on her own initiative, ordered the internal investigation that led to the discovery of the $11 billion fraud at WorldCom. Cooper did all the right things to bring the fraud out in the open. Cooper received the Accounting Exemplar Award in 2004 given by the American Accounting Association and was inducted into the American Institute of Certified Public Accountants (AICPA) Hall of Fame in 2005.

Cooper truly is a positive role model. She discusses the foundation of her ethics that she developed as a youngster because of her mother's influence in her book *Extraordinary Circumstances: The Journey of a Corporate Whistleblower.* Cooper says: "Fight the good fight. Don't ever allow yourself to be intimidated. . . . Think about the consequences of your actions. I've seen too many people ruin their lives."[10]

Religious and Philosophical Foundations of Ethics

Virtually all the world's great religions contain in their religious texts some version of the Golden Rule: "Do unto others as you would wish them to do unto you." In other words, we should treat others the way we would want to be treated. This is the basic ethic that guides all religions. If we believe honesty is important, then we should be honest with others and expect the same in return. One result of this ethic is the concept that every person shares certain inherent human rights, which will be discussed later in this chapter. Exhibit 1.1 provides some examples of the universality of the Golden Rule in world religions provided by the character education organization Teaching Values.[11]

EXHIBIT 1.1 The Universality of the Golden Rule in the World Religions

Religion	Expression of the Golden Rule	Citation
Christianity	All things whatsoever ye would that men should do to you, Do ye so to them; for this is the law and the prophets.	Matthew 7:1
Confucianism	Do not do to others what you would not like yourself. Then there will be no resentment against you, either in the family or in the state.	Analects 12:2
Buddhism	Hurt not others in ways that you yourself would find hurtful.	Uda–navarga 5,1
Hinduism	This is the sum of duty, do naught onto others what you would not have them do unto you.	Mahabharata 5, 1517
Islam	No one of you is a believer until he desires for his brother that which he desires for himself.	Sunnah
Judaism	What is hateful to you, do not do to your fellowman. This is the entire Law; all the rest is commentary.	Talmud, Shabbat 3id
Taoism	Regard your neighbor's gain as your gain, and your neighbor's loss as your own loss.	Tai Shang Kan Yin P'ien
Zoroastrianism	That nature alone is good which refrains from doing to another whatsoever is not good for itself.	Dadisten-I-dinik, 94, 5

Integrity is the key to carrying out the Golden Rule. A person of integrity acts with truthfulness, courage, sincerity, and honesty. Integrity means to have the courage to stand by your principles even in the face of pressure to bow to the demands of others. As previously mentioned, integrity has particular importance for certified public accountants (CPAs), who often are pressured by their employers and clients to give in to their demands. The ethical responsibility of a CPA in these instances is to adhere to the ethics of the accounting profession and not to subordinate professional judgment to the judgment of others. Integrity encompasses the whole of the person, and it is the foundational virtue of the ancient Greek philosophy of virtue.

The origins of Western philosophy trace back to the ancient Greeks, including Socrates, Plato, and Aristotle. The ancient Greek philosophy of virtue deals with questions such as: What is the best sort of life for human beings to live? Greek thinkers saw the attainment of a good life as the *telos,* the end or goal of human existence. For most Greek philosophers, the end is *eudaimonia,* which is usually translated as "happiness." However, the Greeks thought that the end goal of happiness meant much more than just experiencing pleasure or satisfaction. The ultimate goal of happiness was to attain some objectively good status, the life of excellence. The Greek word for excellence is *arete,* the customary translation of which is "virtue." Thus for the Greeks, "excellences" or "virtues" were the qualities that made a life admirable or excellent. They did not restrict their thinking to characteristics we regard as moral virtues, such as courage, justice, and temperance, but included others we think of as nonmoral, such as wisdom.[12]

Modern philosophies have been posited as ways to living an ethical life. Unlike virtue theory that relies on both the characteristics of a decision and the person making that decision, these philosophies rely more on methods of ethical reasoning, and they, too, can be used to facilitate ethical decision making. We review these philosophies later in the chapter.

What Is Ethics?

LO 1-2
Discuss the relationship between one's values and ethics, and legal obligations.

The term *ethics* is derived from the Greek word *ethikos,* which itself is derived from the Greek word *ethos,* meaning "custom" or "character." Morals are from the Latin word *moralis,* meaning "customs," with the Latin word *mores* being defined as "manners, morals, character."

In philosophy, ethical behavior is that which is "good." The Western tradition of ethics is sometimes called "moral philosophy." The field of ethics or moral philosophy involves developing, defending, and recommending concepts of right and wrong behavior. These concepts do not change as one's desires and motivations change. They are not relative to the situation. They are immutable.

In a general sense, ethics (or moral philosophy) addresses fundamental questions such as: How should I live my life? That question leads to others, such as: What sort of person should I strive to be? What values are important? What standards or principles should I live by?[13] There are various ways to define the concept of ethics. The simplest may be to say that ethics deals with "right" and "wrong." However, it is difficult to judge what may be right or wrong in a particular situation without some frame of reference.

In addition, the ethical standards for a profession, such as accounting, are heavily influenced by the practices of those in the profession, state laws and board of accountancy rules, and the expectations of society. Gaa and Thorne define ethics as "the field of inquiry that concerns the actions of people in situations where these actions have effects on the welfare of both oneself and others."[14] We adopt that definition and emphasize that it relies on ethical reasoning to evaluate the effects of actions on others—*the stakeholders.*

Difference between Ethics and Morals

Ethics and morals relate to "right" and "wrong" conduct. While they are sometimes used interchangeably, they are different: ethics refer to rules provided by an external source, such as codes of conduct for a group of professionals (i.e., CPAs), or for those in a particular organization. Morals refer to an individual's own principles regarding right and wrong and may be influenced by a religion or societal mores. Ethics tend to be more practical than morals, conceived as shared principles promoting fairness in social and business interactions. For example, a CEO involved in a sex scandal may involve a moral lapse, while a CEO misappropriating money from a company she is supposed to lead according to prescribed standards of behavior is an ethical problem. These terms are close and often used interchangeably, and both influence ethical decision making. In this text we oftentimes use the terms synonymously while acknowledging differences do exist.

Another important distinction can be thought of this way: When we form a moral judgment, we are employing moral standards—principles against which we compare what we see in order to form a conclusion. Such judgments might be about particular conduct, which includes a person's actions, or it might be about a person's character, which includes their attitudes and beliefs. Ethics, on the other hand, involve the study and application of those standards and judgments which people create or are established by organizations. So, we could say that ethics are the operational side of morality.

Norms, Values, and the Law

Ethics deal with well-based standards of how people _ought_ to act, does _not_ describe the way people _actually_ act, and is prescriptive, not descriptive. Ethical people always strive to make the right decision in all circumstances. They do not rationalize their actions based on their own perceived self-interests. Ethical decision making entails following certain well-established norms of behavior. The best way to understand ethics may be to differentiate it from other concepts.

Values and Ethics

Values are basic and fundamental beliefs that guide or motivate attitudes or actions. In accounting, the values of the profession are embedded in its codes of ethics that guide the actions of accountants and auditors in meeting their professional responsibilities.

Values are concerned with how a person behaves in certain situations and is predicated on personal beliefs that may or may not be ethical, whereas ethics is concerned with how a moral person should behave to act in an ethical manner. A person who values prestige, power, and wealth is likely to act out of self-interest, whereas a person who values honesty, integrity, and trust will typically act in the best interests of others. It does not follow, however, that acting in the best interests of others always precludes acting in one's own self-interest. Indeed, the Golden Rule prescribes that we should treat others the way we want to be treated.

The Golden Rule requires that we try to understand how our actions affect others; thus, we need to put ourselves in the place of the person on the receiving end of the action. The Golden Rule is best seen as a consistency principle, in that we should not act one way toward others but have a desire to be treated differently in a similar situation. In other words, it would be wrong to think that separate standards of behavior exist to guide our personal lives but that a different standard (a lower one) exists in business.

Laws versus Ethics

Being ethical is not the same as following the law. Although ethical people always try to be law-abiding, there may be instances where their sense of ethics tells them it is best not to follow the law. These situations are rare and should be based on sound ethical reasons.

> Assume that you are driving at a speed of 45 miles per hour (mph) on a two-lane divided roadway (double yellow line) going east. All of a sudden, you see a young boy jump into the road to retrieve a ball. The boy is close enough to your vehicle so that you know you cannot continue straight down the roadway and stop in time to avoid hitting him. You quickly look to your right and notice about 10 other children off the road. You cannot avoid hitting 1 or more of them if you swerve to the right to avoid hitting the boy in the middle of the road. You glance to the left on the opposite side of the road and notice no traffic going west or any children off the road. What should you do?
>
> **Ethical Perspective**
>
> If you cross the double yellow line that divides the roadway, you have violated the motor vehicle laws. We are told never to cross a double yellow line and travel into oncoming traffic. But the ethical action would be to do just that, given that you have determined it appears to be safe. It is better to risk getting a ticket than hit the boy in the middle of your side of the road or those children off to the side of the road.

Laws and Ethical Obligations

Benjamin Disraeli (1804–1881), the noted English novelist, debater, and former prime minister, said, "When men are pure, laws are useless; when men are corrupt, laws are broken." A person of goodwill honors and respects the rules and laws and is willing to go beyond them when circumstances warrant. As indicated by the previous quote, such people do not need rules and laws to guide their actions. They always try to do the right thing. On the other hand, the existence of specific laws prohibiting certain behaviors will not stop a person who is unethical (e.g., does not care about others) from violating those laws. Just think about a Ponzi scheme such as the one engaged in by Bernie Madoff, whereby he duped others to invest with him by promising huge returns that, unbeknownst to each individual investor, would come from additional investments of scammed investors and not true returns.

Laws create a minimum set of standards. Ethical people often go beyond what the law requires because the law cannot cover every situation a person might encounter. When the facts are unclear and the legal issues uncertain, an ethical person should decide what to do on the basis of well-established standards of ethical behavior. This is where moral philosophies come in and, for accountants and auditors, the ethical standards of the profession.

Ethical people often do less than is permitted by the law and more than is required. A useful perspective is to ask these questions:

- What does the law require of me?
- What do ethical standards of behavior demand of me?
- How should I act to conform to both?

The Gray Area

When the rules are unclear, an ethical person looks beyond his / her own self-interest and evaluates the interests of the stakeholders potentially affected by the action or decision. Ethical decision making requires that a decision maker be willing, at least sometimes, to take an action that may not be in his / her best interest. This is known as the "moral point of view."

Sometimes people believe that the ends justify the means. In ethics it all depends on one's motives for acting. If one's goals are good and noble, and the means we use to achieve them are also good and noble, then the ends do justify the means. However, if one views the concept as an excuse to achieve one's goals through any means necessary, no matter how immoral, illegal, or offensive to others the means may be, then that person is attempting to justify the wrongdoing by pointing to a good outcome regardless of ethical considerations such as how one's actions affect others. Nothing could be further from the truth. The process you follow to decide on a course of action is more important than achieving the end goal. If this were not true from a moral point of view, then we could rationalize all kinds of actions in the name of achieving a desired goal, even if that goal does harm to others while satisfying our personal needs and desires.

Imagine that you work for a CPA firm and are asked to evaluate three software packages for a client. Your boss tells you that the managing partners are pushing for one of these packages, which just happens to be the firm's internal software. Your initial numerical analysis of the packages based on functionality, availability of upgrades, and customer service indicates that a competitor's package is better than the firm's software. Your boss tells you, in no uncertain terms, to redo the analysis. You know what she wants. Even though you feel uncomfortable with the situation, you decide to "tweak" the numbers to show a preference for the firm's package. The end result desired in this case is to choose the firm's package. The means to that end was to alter the analysis, an unethical act because it is dishonest and unfair to the other competitors (not to mention the client) to change the objectively determined results. In this instance, ethical decision making requires that we place the client's interests (to get the best software package for his needs) above those of the firm (to get the new business and not upset the boss.

Ethical Relativism

Ethical relativism is the philosophical view that what is right or wrong and good or bad is not absolute but variable and relative, depending on the person, circumstances, or social situation. Ethical relativism holds that morality is relative to the norms of one's culture. That is, whether an action is right or wrong depends on the moral norms of the society in which it is practiced. The same action may be morally right in one society but be morally wrong in another. For the ethical relativist, there are no universal moral standards—standards that can be universally applied to all peoples at all times. The only moral standards against which a society's practices can be judged are its own. If ethical relativism is correct, then there can be no common framework for resolving moral disputes or for reaching agreement on ethical matters among members of different societies.

Most ethicists reject the theory of ethical relativism. Some claim that while the moral practices of societies may differ, the fundamental moral principles underlying these practices do not. For example, there was a situation in Singapore in the 1990s where a young American spray-painted graffiti on several cars. The Singaporean government's penalty was to "cane" the youngster by striking him on the buttocks four times. In the United States, some said it was cruel and unusual punishment for such a minor offense. In Singapore, the issue is that to protect the interests of society, the government treats harshly those who commit relatively minor offenses. After all, it does send a message that in Singapore, this and similar types of behavior will not be tolerated. While such a practice might be condemned in the United States, most people would agree with the underlying moral principle—the duty to protect the safety and security of the public (life and liberty concerns). Societies, then, may differ in their application of fundamental moral principles but agree on the principles.

Moral Relativism in Accounting

Accountants record and report financial truths. Their conduct is regulated by state boards of accountancy, professional codes of behavior, and moral conventions directed towards fairness and accountability. However, moral dilemmas and conflicts of interest inevitably arise when determining how best to present financial information. Betty Vinson is a case in point. She rationalized that in her circumstances going along with the improper accounting was justified because if Scott Sullivan, one of the foremost chief financial officers in the country, thought the accounting was all right, who was she to question it. After all, ethical judgments can be subjective and, perhaps, this was one of those situations. Clearly, Vinson suffered from moral blindness because she failed to consider the negative effects on shareholders and other stakeholders and moral failings of Sullivan's position. There was a gap between the person she truly was and how she acted in the WorldCom fraud brought about by pressures imposed on her by Sullivan.

Situation Ethics

Situation ethics, a term first coined in 1966 by an Episcopalian priest, Joseph Fletcher, is a body of ethical thought that takes normative principles—like the virtues, natural law, and Kant's categorical imperative that relies on the universality of actions—and generalizes them so that an agent can "make sense" out of one's experience when confronting ethical dilemmas. Unlike ethical relativism that denies universal moral principles, claiming the moral codes are strictly subjective, situational ethicists recognize the existence of normative principles but question whether they should be applied as strict directives (i.e., imperatives) or, instead, as guidelines that agents should use when determining a course of ethical conduct. In other words, situationists ask: Should these norms, as generalizations about what is desired, be regarded as intrinsically valid and universally obliging of all human beings? For situationists, the circumstances surrounding an ethical dilemma can and should influence an agent's decision-making process and may alter an agent's decision when warranted. Thus, situation ethics holds that "what in some times and in some places is ethical can be in other times and in other places unethical."[15] A problem with a situation ethics perspective is that it can be used to rationalize actions such as those in the Penn State scandal.

Student Cheating

Another danger of situational ethics is it can be used to rationalize cheating. Cheating in general is at epidemic proportions in society. The *2012 Report Card on the Ethics of American Youth,* conducted by the Josephson Institute of Ethics, found that of 43,000 high school students surveyed, 51 percent admitted to having cheated on a test during 2012, 55 percent admitted to lying, and 20 percent admitted to stealing.[16]

Cheating in college is prevalent as well. The estimates of number of students engaging in some form of academic dishonesty at least once ranges from 50 to 70 percent.[17] In 1997, McCabe and Treviño surveyed 6,000 students in 31 academic institutions and found contextual factors, such as peer influence, had the most effect on student cheating behavior.[18] Contextual appropriateness, rather than what is good or right, suggests that situations alter cases, thus changing the rules and principles that guide behavior.[19]

It used to be that professors only had to worry about students copying from each other during exams and on assignments handed in, as well as bringing "notes" to an exam that are hidden from view. Plagiarizing also has been a concern. In extreme cases, students might gain unauthorized access to exams. A persistent problem has been access to past exams that some professors use over again. Here, the individual professor needs to take responsibility for changing exams and not blame students for behaviors that, while unethical, could be prevented by actions of the professor.

Now, with the advent of electronic access to a variety of online resources, term papers can be acquired or other people found to write them for a student. A disturbing trend is the availability of the solutions manual and test bank questions online. Instructors have historically relied on these resources to assess student learning. All that may be assessed now is whether an otherwise unproductive student has suddenly become productive as a result of acquiring instructor's resource materials or accessing previous exams. Here, students are to blame for irresponsible behavior and basically cheat themselves out of learning materials needed in the workplace and for the CPA Exam.

Other forms of e-cheating include using cell phones to store data and cameras to zoom in and take pictures of test questions and then posting them on Web sites where other students can access the questions for later testing. Programmable calculators have been used for awhile to store information pertinent to potential test questions. In a study of cheating in business schools, of the 40 percent of students who indicated they used various electronic methods of cheating, 99 percent indicated from occasional use up to half the time.[20]

A comprehensive study of 4,950 students at a small southwestern university identified neutralizing techniques to justify violations of accepted behavior. In the study, students rationalized their cheating behavior without challenging the norm of honesty. The most common rationale was denial of responsibility (i.e., circumstances beyond their control, such as excessive hours worked on a job, made cheating okay in that instance). Then, they blamed the faculty and testing procedures (i.e., exams that try to trick students rather than test knowledge). Finally, the students appealed to a higher loyalty by arguing that it is more important to help a friend than to avoid cheating. One student blamed the larger society for his cheating: "In America, we're taught that results aren't achieved through beneficial means, but through the easiest means." The authors concluded that the use of these techniques of neutralization conveys the message that students recognize and accept cheating as an undesirable behavior but one that can be excused under certain circumstances, reflecting a situational ethic.[21]

Student Cheating at the University of North Carolina

If you're a sports fan, by now you have heard about the paper-class scandal that we call "Tar Heel Gate" in which 3,100 student-athletes at the University of North Carolina in Chapel Hill (UNC) were essentially allowed to take classes without attending classes and given grades good enough to keep them eligible to play men's football and basketball during a 20-year period.

For five years, UNC had insisted the paper classes were the doing of one rogue professor: the department chair of the African-American studies program, Julius Nyang'oro. However, an independent report found that five counselors actively used paper classes, calling them "GPA boosters," and that at least two counselors suggested to a professor the grade an athlete needed to receive to be able to continue to play.

Many of the academic-athletic staff who were named and implicated were also named by university learning specialist Mary Willingham. Willingham said that she had worked with dozens of athletes who came to UNC and were unable to read at an acceptable level, with some of them reading on par with elementary schoolchildren. She also said there were many members of the athletic staff who knew about the paper classes, and her revelations contradicted what UNC had claimed for years—that Nyang'oro acted alone in providing the paper classes.

Willingham went public with detailed allegations about paper classes and, after an assault on her credibility by the university, filed a whistleblower lawsuit. In March 2015, UNC announced it would pay Willingham $335,000 to settle her suit.

In an unusual twist to the story, the director of UNC's Parr Center for Ethics, Jeanette M. Boxill, was accused of steering athletes into fake classes to help them maintain their eligibility with the NCAA. Moreover, she covered up her actions after the fact. Boxill violated the most basic standards of academic integrity.

Although different in kind, Tar Heel Gate and the abuse scandal at Penn State have one common element: protecting the sports programs. At UNC, the goal was to keep student athletes eligible so that the sports programs would continue to excel and promote and publicize the school, not to mention earn millions of dollars in advertising. The NCAA investigation of the program is ongoing. In June 2015, five charges were leveled against UNC including a lack of institutional control for poor oversight of an academic department popular with athletes and the counselors who advised them. In August 2015, UNC notified the NCAA's enforcement staff that it identified two new pieces of information regarding NCAA violations, including a lack of institutional control when it allowed athletes to participate in years' worth of phony paper courses.

The university's own report on the matter is highly critical of a program that knowingly steered about 1,500 athletes toward no-show courses that never met and were not taught by any faculty members, and in which the only work required was a single research paper that received a high grade no matter the content. Still, the only sanction imposed by the board of Southern Association of Colleges and Schools' Commission on Colleges was a one-year probation. The board stopped short of imposing the harshest penalty, which would have blocked the country's oldest public university from receiving federal funds, including student loan proceeds. We believe this is a slap on the wrist for such gross violations and the accrediting agency should be ashamed.

The violations of ethics by UNC raise many important questions. How could such a reputable college sports program get away with the behavior for 20 years? Who was responsible for keeping a watchful eye out for violations of NCAA rules? Where were the managers of the affected sport programs; what did they know; when did they know it; what actions, if any, did they take?

UNC suffered from ethical blindness. It failed to see the ethical violations of its actions in establishing a route for student-athletes to remain academically eligible. It acted in its own self-interest regardless of the impact of its behavior on the affected parties. The blind spots occurred because of a situational ethic whereby those who perpetrated the fraud and covered it up came to believe their actions were for the greater good of those involved in the athletic program and the UNC community, much like at Penn State, but failed to see the effects of their actions on other stakeholders including other colleges that were at a competitive disadvantage. Honesty was ignored, integrity was not in the picture, and the athletes were not provided with the education they deserved. Ironically, in the end the very stakeholders who allegedly would benefit the greatest from student-athletes taking paper classes suffered the most.

Student Cheating and Workplace Behavior

Some educators feel that a student's level of academic integrity goes hand in hand with a student's ethical values on other real-world events that present ethical challenges.[22] In other words, developing a sound set of ethical standards in one area of decision making, such as personal matters, will carry over and affect other areas such as workplace ethics.

Some educators believe that ethics scandals in the business world can be attributed to the type of education that graduates of MBA programs obtained in business schools.[23] In 2006, McCabe, Butterfield, and Treviño reported on their findings regarding the extent of cheating among MBA students compared to nonbusiness graduate students at 32 universities in the United States and Canada. The authors found that 56 percent of business students admitted to cheating, versus 47 percent of nonbusiness students.[24]

Several researchers have examined student cheating in college and the tendency of those students to cheat in the workplace. Lawson surveyed undergraduate and graduate students enrolled in business schools and found a strong relationship between "students' propensity to cheat in an academic setting and their attitude toward unethical behavior in the business world."[25] Another study looked at the issue of graduate students cheating versus workplace dishonesty. Sims surveyed MBA students and found that students who engaged in behaviors considered severely dishonest in college also engaged in behaviors considered severely dishonest at work.[26]

If students who cheat in the university setting subsequently cheat in the workplace, then ethics education is all the more important. Once a student rationalizes cheating by blaming others or circumstances, it is only a small step to blaming others in the workplace for one's inability to get things done or unethical behavior.

Social Networkers and Workplace Ethics

The Ethics Resource Center conducted a survey of social networkers in 2012 to determine the extent to which employees use social networking on the job. The survey points out that social networking is now the norm and that a growing number of employees spend some of their workday connected to a social network. More than 10 percent are "active social networkers," defined as those who spend at least 30 percent of their workday linked up to one or more networks.[27]

One concern is whether active social networkers engage in unethical practices through communications and postings on social media sites. Survey respondents say they think about risks before posting online and consider how their employers would react to what they post. But, they do admit to discussing company information online: 60 percent would comment on their personal sites about their company if it was in the news; 53 percent share information about work projects once a week or more; greater than one-third say they often comment, on their personal sites, about managers, coworkers, and even clients. The survey concludes that nothing is secret anymore and, unlike in Las Vegas, management must assume that what happens at work does not stay at work and may become publicly known.

An interesting result of the survey is active social networkers are unusually vulnerable to risks because they witness more misconduct and experience more retaliation as a result when they report it than their work colleagues. A majority (56 percent) of active social networkers who reported misdeeds experienced retaliation compared to fewer than one in five (18 percent) of other employee groups.

An encouraging result is that effective training on the use of social networks and an ongoing commitment to an ethical culture in which employees act with integrity can mitigate the risks presented by social networking at work. The survey found that in companies with both social networking policies and training, employees are more aware of what they post, think more carefully about the implications of online activity, and spend less of their worktime online. Moreover, where policies are in place, half of the social networkers say it is unacceptable to publicly post comments about their company even when they do not identify it. Without policies, only 40 percent say such posts are unacceptable. In companies with social networking policies, 88 percent consider their employer's reaction before making work-related posts, compared to the 76 percent in companies without such policies.[28]

Our conclusion about using social networking sites at work is that the burden falls both on the employees, who should know better than to discuss company business online where anyone can see it, and employers who have the responsibility to establish a culture that discourages venting one's feelings about the employer online for all to see. Organizational codes of ethics need to be expanded to create policies for the use of social networking sites, training to reinforce those policies, and consequences for those who violate the policies.

Cultural Values

Between 1967 and 1973, Dutch researcher Geert Hofstede conducted one of the most comprehensive studies of how values in the workplace are influenced by culture. Using responses to an attitude study of approximately 116,000 IBM employees in 39 countries, Hofstede identified four cultural dimensions that can be used to describe general similarities and differences in cultures around the world: (1) individualism, (2) power distance, (3) uncertainty avoidance, and (4) masculinity.[29] In 2001, a fifth dimension, long-term orientation—initially called Confucian dynamism—was identified.[30] More recently, a sixth variable was added—indulgence versus restraint—as a result of Michael Minkov's analysis of data from the World Values Survey.[31] Exhibit 1.2 summarizes the five dimensions from Hofstede's work for Japan, the United Kingdom, and the United States, representing leading industrialized nations; and the so-called BRIC countries (Brazil, Russia, India, and China), which represent four major emerging economies.[32]

EXHIBIT 1.2 Hofstede's Cultural Dimensions[*]

Cultural Variables	Countries/Scores						
	Brazil	Russia	India	China	Japan	U.K.	U.S.
Power Distance (PDI)	69	93	77	80	54	35	40
Individualism (IDV)	38	39	48	20	46	89	91
Masculinity (MAS)	49	36	56	66	95	66	62
Uncertainty Avoidance (UAI)	76	95	40	30	92	35	46
Long-Term Orientation (LTO)	65	N/A	61	118	80	25	29

* High scores indicate a propensity toward the cultural variable; low scores indicate the opposite.

Individualism (IDV) focuses on the degree that the society reinforces individual or collective achievement and interpersonal relationships. In individualist societies (high IDV), people are supposed to look after themselves and their direct family, while in collectivist societies (low IDV), people belong to "in-groups" that take care of them in exchange for loyalty. Imagine, for example, you are the manager of workers from different cultures and cheating/unethical behavior occurs in the workplace. A work group with collectivist values such as China and Japan (low IDV) might be more prone to covering up the behavior of one member of the group in order to "save face", whereas in the United Kingdom and United States (high IDV), there is a greater likelihood of an individual blowing the whistle.

Uncertainty Avoidance (UAI) is another cultural value that has important implications for workplace behavior, as it describes the tolerance for uncertainty and ambiguity within society. A high UAI ranking indicates that a country has a low tolerance of uncertainty and ambiguity. Such a society is likely to institute laws, rules, regulations, and controls to reduce the amount of uncertainty. A country such as Russia has a high UAI, while the United States and United Kingdom have lower scores (low UAI), indicating more tolerance for a variety of opinions. One implication is the difficulty of doing business in a country like Russia, which has strict rules and regulations about what can and cannot be done by multinational enterprises.

Other variables have important implications for workplace behavior as well, such as the Power Distance index (PDI), which focuses on the degree of equality between people in the country's society. A high PDI indicates inequalities of wealth and power have been allowed to grow within society, as has occurred in China and Russia as they develop economically. Long-term orientation (LTO) versus short-term orientation has been used to illustrate one of the differences between Asian cultures, such as China and Japan, and the United States and United Kingdom. In societies like China and Japan, high LTO scores reflect the values of long-term commitment and respect for tradition, as opposed to low-LTO countries, such as the United Kingdom and United States, where change can occur more rapidly. Time can often be a stumbling block for Western-cultured organizations entering the China market. The length of time it takes to get business deals done in China can be two or three times that in the West. One final point is to note that Brazil and India show less variability in their scores than other countries, perhaps reflecting fewer extremes in cultural dimensions.

Our discussion of cultural dimensions is meant to explain how workers from different cultures *might* interact in the workplace. The key point is that cultural sensitivity is an essential ingredient in establishing workplace values and may affect ethical behavioral patterns.

The Six Pillars of Character

LO 1-3
Describe how the pillars of character support ethical decision making.

It has been said that ethics is all about how we act when no one is looking. In other words, ethical people do not do the right thing because someone observing their actions might judge them otherwise, or because they may be punished as a result of their actions. Instead, ethical people act as they do because their "inner voice" or conscience tells them that it is the right thing to do. Assume that you are leaving a shopping mall, get into your car to drive away, and hit a parked car in the lot on the way out. Let's also assume that no one saw you hit the car. What are your options? You could simply drive away and forget about it, or you can leave a note for the owner of the parked car with your contact information. What would you do and why? Your actions will reflect the character of your inner being.

According to "virtue ethics," there are certain ideals, such as excellence or dedication to the common good, toward which we should strive and which allow the full development of our humanity. These ideals are discovered through thoughtful reflection on what we as human beings have the potential to become.

Virtues are attitudes, dispositions, or character traits that enable us to be and to act in ways that develop this potential. They enable us to pursue the ideals we have adopted. Honesty, courage, compassion, generosity, fidelity, integrity, fairness, self-control, and prudence are all examples of virtues in Aristotelian ethics. A quote attributed to Aristotle is, "We are what we repeatedly do. Therefore, excellence is not an act. It is a habit."[33]

The Josephson Institute of Ethics identifies Six Pillars of Character that provide a foundation to guide ethical decision making. These ethical values include trustworthiness, respect, responsibility, fairness, caring, and citizenship. Josephson believes that the Six Pillars act as a multilevel filter through which to process decisions. So, being trustworthy is not enough—we must also be caring. Adhering to the letter of the law is not enough; we must accept responsibility for our actions or inactions.[34]

Trustworthiness

The dimensions of trustworthiness include being honest, acting with integrity, being reliable, and exercising loyalty in dealing with others.

Honesty

Honesty is the most basic ethical value. It means that we should express the truth as we know it and without deception. In accounting, the full disclosure principle supports transparency and requires that the accounting professional disclose all the information that owners, investors, creditors, and the government need to know to make informed decisions. To withhold relevant information is dishonest. Transparent information is that which helps one understand the process followed to reach a decision. In other words it supports an ethical ends versus means belief.

Let's assume that you are a member of a discussion group in your Intermediate Accounting II class, and in an initial meeting with all members, the leader asks whether there is anyone who has not completed Intermediate I. You failed the course last term and are retaking it concurrently with Intermediate II. However, you feel embarrassed and say nothing. Now, perhaps the leader thinks that this point is important because a case study assigned to your group uses knowledge gained from Intermediate I. You internally justify the silence by thinking: Well, I did complete the course, albeit with a grade of F. This is an unethical position. You are rationalizing silence by interpreting the question in your own self-interest rather than in the interests of the entire group. The other members need to know whether you have completed Intermediate I because the leader may choose not to assign a specific project to you that requires the Intermediate I prerequisite knowledge.

Integrity

The integrity of a person is an essential element in trusting that person. MacIntyre, in his account of Aristotelian virtue, states, "There is at least one virtue recognized by tradition which cannot be specified except with reference to the wholeness of a human life—the virtue of integrity or constancy."[35] A person of integrity takes time for self-reflection, so that the events, crises, and challenges of everyday living do not determine the course of that person's moral life. Such a person is trusted by others because that person is true to her word.

Ultimately, integrity means to act on principle rather than expediency. If my superior tells me to do something wrong, I will not do it because it violates the ethical value of honesty. If my superior pressures me to compromise my values just this one time, I will not agree. I have the courage of my convictions and am true to the principles of behavior that guide my actions.

Going back to the previous example, if you encounter a conflict with another group member who pressures you to plagiarize a report available on the Internet that the two of you are working on, you will be acting with integrity if you refuse to go along. You know it's wrong to plagiarize another writer's material. Someone worked hard to get this report published. You would not want another person to take material you had published without permission and proper citation. Why do it to that person, then? If you do it simply because it might benefit you, then you act out of self-interest, or egoism, and that is wrong.

Reliability

The promises that we make to others are relied on by them, and we have a moral duty to follow through with action. Our ethical obligation for promise keeping includes avoiding bad-faith excuses and unwise commitments. Imagine that you are asked to attend a group meeting on Saturday and you agree to do so. That night, though, your best friend calls and says he has two tickets to the basketball game between the Dallas Mavericks and San Antonio Spurs. The Spurs are one of the best teams in basketball and you don't get this kind of opportunity very often, so you decide to go to the game instead of the meeting. You've broken your promise, and you did it out of self-interest. You figured, who wouldn't want to see the Spurs play? What's worse, you call the group leader and say that you can't attend the meeting because you are sick. Now you've also lied. You've started the slide down the proverbial ethical slippery slope, and it will be difficult to climb back to the top.

Loyalty

We all should value loyalty in friendship. After all, you wouldn't want the friend who invited you to the basketball game to telephone the group leader later and say that you went to the game on the day of the group meeting.

Loyalty requires that friends not violate the confidence we place in them. In accounting, loyalty requires that we keep financial and other information confidential when it deals with our employer and client. For example, if you are the in-charge accountant on an audit of a client for your CPA firm-employer and you discover that the client is "cooking the books," you shouldn't telephone the local newspaper and tell the story to a reporter. Instead, you should go to your supervisor and discuss the matter and, if necessary, go to the partner in charge of the engagement and tell her. Your ethical obligation is to report what you have observed to your supervisor and let her take the appropriate action. However, the ethics of the accounting profession allow for instances whereby informing those above your supervisor is expected, an act of internal whistleblowing, and in rare circumstances going outside the organization to report the wrongdoing. Whistleblowing obligations will be discussed in Chapter 3.

There are limits to the confidentiality obligation. For example, let's assume that you are the accounting manager at a publicly owned company and your supervisor (the controller) pressures you to keep silent about the manipulation of financial information. You then go to the CFO, who tells you that both the CEO and board of directors support the controller. Out of a misplaced duty of loyalty in this situation, you might rationalize your silence as did Betty Vinson. Ethical values sometimes conflict, and loyalty is the one value that should never take precedence over other values such as honesty and integrity. Otherwise, we can imagine all kinds of cover-ups of information in the interest of loyalty or friendship.

While attending a Josephson Institute of Ethics training program for educators, one of the authors of this book heard Michael Josephson make an analogy about loyal behavior that sticks with him to this day. Josephson said: "Dogs are loyal to their master, while cats are loyal to the house." How true it is that dogs see their ultimate allegiance to their owner while cats get attached to the place they call home—their own personal space. Now, in a business context, this means that a manager should try to encourage "cat" behavior in the organization (sorry, dog lovers). In that way, if a cover-up of a financial wrongdoing exists, the "cat loyalty" mentality incorporated into the business environment dictates that the information be disclosed because it is not in the best interests of the organization to hide or ignore it. If we act with "dog loyalty," we will cover up for our supervisor, who has a say about what happens to us in the organization. Recall our discussion of cultural values, and that someone from a country or group with a low score on individualism (a collectivist society) is more likely to hide a damaging fact out of loyalty to the controller and her superiors, while someone from a more individualistic society is more likely to come forward with information about the wrongdoing. A cover-up may be an understandable position because of internal pressures that work against voicing one's concerns and acting on one's values, but it is unethical all the same. Moreover, once we go along with the cover-up, we have started the slide down the ethical slippery slope, and there may be no turning back. In fact, our supervisor may come to us during the next period and expect us to go along with the same cover-up in a similar situation. If we refuse at that point, the first instance may be brought up and used as a threat against us because we've already violated ethical standards once and don't want to get caught. It is important to emphasize that we should not act ethically out of fear of the consequences of hiding information. Instead, we should act ethically out of a positive sense that it is the right way to behave.

Often when we cover up information in the present, it becomes public knowledge later. The consequences at that time are more serious because trust has been destroyed. We have already discussed the Penn State scandal and forfeiture of trust by Joe Paterno for failing to take steps to stop child abuse. Another example is Lance Armstrong, who for years denied taking performance-enhancing drugs while winning seven Tour de France titles. In 2012, he finally admitted to doing just that, and as a result, all those titles were stripped away by the U.S. Anti-Doping Agency. Or consider former president Richard Nixon, who went along with the cover-up in the Watergate break-in only to be forced to resign the presidency once the cover-up became public knowledge.

Respect

All people should be treated with dignity. We do not have an ethical duty to hold all people in high esteem, but we should treat everyone with respect, regardless of their circumstances in life. In today's slang, we might say that respect means giving a person "props." The Golden Rule encompasses respect for others through notions such as civility, courtesy, decency, dignity, autonomy, tolerance, and acceptance.[36]

By age 16, George Washington had copied by hand 110 *Rules of Civility & Decent Behavior in Company and Conversation*. They are based on a set of rules composed by French Jesuits in 1595. While many of the rules seem out of place in today's society, Washington's first rule is noteworthy: "Every Action done in Company, ought to be with Some Sign of Respect, to those that are Present."[37]

Washington's vernacular was consistent with the times as indicated by the last of his rules: "Labour to keep alive in your Breast that Little Spark of Celestial fire Called Conscience."[38] We have found many definitions of conscience, but the one we like best is the universal lexical English WordNet used for research and developed by the Cognitive Sciences Laboratory at Princeton University. The definition is: "Motivation deriving logically from ethical or moral principles that govern a person's thoughts and actions."[39]

As a member of the case discussion group in the previous example, it would be wrong to treat another member with discourtesy or prejudice because you have drawn conclusions about that person on the basis of national origin or some other factor rather than her abilities and conduct. You would not want to be disrespected or treated unfairly because of how you dress or walk or talk, so others should not be judged based on similar considerations. We should judge people based on their character.

Responsibility

Josephson points out that our capacity to reason and our freedom to choose make us morally responsible for our actions and decisions. We are accountable for what we do and who we are.[40]

The judgments we make in life reflect whether we have acted responsibly. Eleanor Roosevelt, the former first lady, puts it well: "One's philosophy is not best expressed in words; it is expressed in the choices one makes...and the choices we make are ultimately our responsibility."[41]

A responsible person carefully reflects on alternative courses of action using ethical principles. A responsible person acts diligently and perseveres in carrying out moral action. Imagine if you were given the task by your group to interview five CPAs in public practice about their most difficult ethical dilemma, and you decided to ask one person, who was a friend of the family, about five dilemmas that person faced in the practice of public accounting. Now, even if you made an "honest" mistake in interpreting the requirement, it is clear that you did not exercise the level of care that should be expected in this instance in carrying out the instructions to interview five different CPAs. The due care test is whether a "reasonable person" would conclude that you had acted with the level of care, or diligence, expected in the circumstance. The courts have used this test for many years to evaluate the actions of professionals.

Responsibility for accounting professionals means to meet one's ethical and professional obligations when performing services for an employer or client. Professional accountants in business often find themselves at the front line of protecting the integrity of the financial reporting process. Public accountants should approach audit services with an inquiring mind and be skeptical of what the client says and the information provided. As discussed later on, in the final analysis, the ultimate obligation of accounting professionals is to meet their public interest responsibilities. The public (i.e., investors and creditors) relies on the ethics of accountants and auditors and trusts they will act in the name of the public good.

Fairness

A person of fairness treats others equally, impartially, and openly. In business, we might say that the fair allocation of scarce resources requires that those who have earned the right to a greater share of corporate resources as judged objectively by performance measures should receive a larger share than those whose performance has not met the standard.

Let's assume that your instructor told the case study groups at the beginning of the course that the group with the highest overall numerical average would receive an A, the group with second highest a B, and so on. At the end of the term, the teacher gave the group with the second-highest average—90.5—an A and the group with the highest average—91.2—a B. Perhaps the instructor took subjective factors into account in deciding on the final grading. You might view the instructor's action as unfair to the group with the highest average. It certainly contradicts his original stated policy and is capricious and unfair, especially if the instructor does not explain his reason for doing this. As Josephson points out, "Fairness implies adherence to a balanced standard of justice without relevance to one's own feelings or inclinations."[42]

Fairness in accounting can be equated with objectivity. Objectivity means the financial and accounting information needs to presented free from bias, that is, consistent with the evidence and not based solely on one's opinion about the proper accounting treatment. Objectivity helps to ensure that financial statements are reliable and verifiable. The purpose of objectivity is to make financial statements more useful to investors and end users.

Caring

The late Edmund L. Pincoffs, a philosopher who formerly taught at the University of Texas at Austin, believed that virtues such as caring, kindness, sensitivity, altruism, and benevolence enable a person who possesses these qualities to consider the interests of others.[43] Josephson believes that caring is the "heart of ethics and ethical decision making."[44]

The essence of caring is empathy. *Empathy* is the ability to understand, be sensitive to, and care about the feelings of others. Caring and empathy support each other and enable a person to put herself in the position of another. This is essential to ethical decision making.

Let's assume that on the morning of an important group meeting, your child comes down with a temperature of 103 degrees. You call the group leader and say that you can't make it to the meeting. Instead, you suggest that the meeting be taped and you will listen to the discussions later that day and telephone the leader with any questions. The leader reacts angrily, stating that you are not living up to your responsibilities. Assuming that your behavior is not part of a pattern and you have been honest with the leader up to now, you would have a right to be upset with the leader, who seems uncaring. In the real world, emergencies do occur, and placing your child's health and welfare above all else should make sense in this situation to a person of rational thought. You also acted diligently by offering to listen to the discussions and, if necessary, follow up with the leader.

Putting yourself in the place of another is sometimes difficult to do because the circumstances are unique to the situation. For example, what would you do if a member of your team walked into a meeting all bleary-eyed? You might ignore it, or you might ask that person if everything is all right. If you do and are informed that the person was up all night with a crying baby, then you might say something like, "If there's anything I can do to lighten the load for you today, just say the word."

A person who can empathize seems to know just what to say to make the other person feel better about circumstances. On the other hand, if you have never been married and have not had children, you might not be able to understand the feelings of a mother who has just spent the night trying to comfort a screaming child.

Citizenship

Josephson points out that "citizenship includes civic virtues and duties that prescribe how we ought to behave as part of a community."[45] An important part of good citizenship is to obey the laws, be informed about the issues, volunteer in your community, and vote in elections. During his presidency, Barack Obama called for citizens to engage in some kind of public service to benefit society as a whole.

Accounting professionals are part of a community with specific ideals and ethical standards that govern behavior. These include responsibilities to one another to advance the profession and not bring discredit on oneself or others. As citizens of a community, accountants and auditors should strive to enhance the reputation of the accounting profession.

It might be said that judgments made about one's character contribute toward how another party views that person's reputation. In other words, what is the estimation in which a person is commonly held, whether favorable or not? The reputation of a CPA is critical to a client's trusting that CPA to perform services competently and maintain the confidentiality of client information (except for certain whistleblowing instances). One builds "reputational capital" through favorable actions informed by ethical behavior.

Expectations of Millennials

Universum, the global employer branding and research company, annually surveys college undergraduate and MBA students. In 2014, it surveyed about 60,000 U.S. college students from 311 institutions to find out what they were looking for as they enter the world of work, as well as their views on the attractiveness of specific employers. The results of the survey reflect a desire to join an organization that respects its people, provides a supportive environment, recognizes performance, provides development and leadership opportunities, challenges one intellectually, fosters a work/life balance, and serves the public good.[46]

Students were asked to identify up to three career goals. The top five goals (with percentages of students who selected them) were:

1. Work/life balance (79 percent)
2. Job security (50 percent)
3. Be a leader or manager of people (43 percent)
4. Be competitively or intellectually challenged (43 percent)
5. Dedicated to a cause or feel I am serving a greater good (36 percent)

It also asked students to identify the most important "attractors" an employer could offer. The responses provided by at least 40 percent of students were:

1. Leaders who will support my development (49 percent)
2. Respect for its people (46 percent)
3. Creative and dynamic work environment (43 percent)
4. Recognizing performance (meritocracy) (43 percent)
5. Friendly work environment (42 percent)

These results are interesting in that Millennials clearly recognize motivating factors other than money in selecting a career. Their values appear in many ways to be consistent with the Six Pillars of Character including respect, responsibility, fairness, and civic virtue. Moreover, they were concerned about a prospective employer's reputation and image, and 39 percent found ethical standards to be an attractive attribute in a prospective employer, second only to financial strength (40 percent). Other civic virtue issues of importance included corporate social responsibility (21 percent) and environmental sustainability (13 percent).

How did the accounting profession fare with respect to the most desirable businesses to work for? Perhaps not surprisingly, Google was the most desirable employer to work for (21 percent), followed by Walt Disney Company (14 percent) and then Apple (13 percent). Of the Big-4 international professional accounting firms, Ernst & Young (EY) was the highest rated (13 percent), followed by Deloitte (11 percent), PricewaterhouseCoopers (PwC) (10 percent), and KPMG (7 percent). We caution students not to make too much of the rank ordering of CPA firms because more prestigious surveys such as the 2015 survey conducted by Fortune Magazine of the top 500 companies to work for has KPMG at the top while another survey conducted by Vault in 2015 ranks PwC the highest. Consulting Magazine's 2014 survey lists Deloitte Consulting as the best firm to work for followed by EY. These surveys generally are based on quality of life issues and development opportunities.

Reputation

It might be said that judgments made about one's character contribute toward how another party views that person's reputation. In other words, what is the estimation in which a person is commonly held, whether favorable or not? The reputation of a CPA is critical to a client's trusting that CPA to perform services competently and maintain the confidentiality of client information (except for whistleblowing instances). One builds "reputational capital" through favorable actions informed by ethical behavior.

All too often in politics and government, a well-respected leader becomes involved in behavior that, once disclosed, tears down a reputation earned over many years of service. The example of former senator and presidential candidate John Edwards shows how quickly one's reputation can be destroyed—in this case because of the disclosure of an extramarital affair that Edwards had with a 42-year-old campaign employee, Rielle Hunter, that Edwards covered up.

In 2006, Edwards's political action committee (PAC) paid Hunter's video production firm $100,000 for work. Then the committee paid another $14,086 on April 1, 2007. The Edwards camp said the latter payment from the PAC was in exchange for 100 hours of unused videotape Hunter shot. The same day, the Edwards presidential campaign had injected $14,034.61 into the PAC for a "furniture purchase," according to federal election records.

Edwards, a U.S. senator representing North Carolina from 1998 until his vice presidential bid in 2004, acknowledged in May 2009 that federal investigators were looking into how he used campaign funds. Edwards was accused of soliciting nearly $1 million from wealthy backers to finance a cover-up of his illicit affair during his 2008 bid for the White House.

Edwards admitted to ABC News[47] in an interview with Bob Woodruff in August 2009 that he repeatedly lied about having an affair with Hunter. Edwards strenuously denied being involved in paying the woman hush money or fathering her newborn child, admitted the affair was a mistake in the interview, and said: "Two years ago, I made a very serious mistake, a mistake that I am responsible for and no one else. In 2006, I told Elizabeth [his wife] about the mistake, asked her for her forgiveness, asked God for His forgiveness. And we have kept this within our family since that time." Edwards said he told his entire family about the affair after it ended in 2006, and that his wife Elizabeth was "furious" but that their marriage would survive. On January 21, 2010, he also finally admitted to fathering Hunter's child, Quinn (and since the girl was born in 2008, that indicates pretty clearly that Edwards's statement that the affair ended in 2006 was less than truthful).

On May 31, 2012, a jury found him not guilty on one of six counts in the campaign-finance trial and deadlocked on the remaining charges; the Department of Justice decided not to retry him on those charges. On the courthouse steps, Edwards acknowledged his moral shortcomings.

Edwards violated virtually every tenet of ethical behavior and destroyed his reputation. He lied about the affair and attempted to cover it up, including allegations that he fathered Hunter's baby. He violated the trust of the public and lied after telling his family about the affair in 2006. He even had the audacity to run for the Democratic nomination for president in 2008. One has to wonder what it says about Edwards's ethics that he was willing to run for president of the United States while hiding the knowledge of his affair, without considering what might happen if he had won the Democratic nomination in 2008, and then the affair became public knowledge during the general election campaign. His behavior is the ultimate example of ethical blindness and the pursuit of one's own self-interests to the detriment of all others. Perhaps the noted Canadian-American chemist and author Orlando Aloysius Battista (1917–1995), said it best: "An error doesn't become a mistake until you refuse to correct it." In other words, when you do something wrong, admit it, take responsibility for your actions, accept the consequences, promise never to do it again, and move on. Unfortunately, most adulterers like Edwards go to great lengths to cover up their moral failings and don't admit to them until they have been caught.

Civility, Ethics, and Workplace Behavior

Can there be any doubt that incivility in society is on the rise? Not according to one of your authors. Mintz opines in his blog about incivility that daily we witness instances of inconsiderate, "in your face" behavior in communications and other forms of rudeness. There are many causes of incivility, many of which are social media–driven. The sometimes anonymous feel of posts on Twitter and other social media sites makes it relatively easy to use impersonal forms of communication to vent one's feelings without the immediate consequences of face-to-face discussions. One inappropriate Twitter rant begets another and eventually we see a further erosion of ethics in society.

Civility is not peripheral to ethics, dealing merely with manners, proper etiquette, and politeness. It runs much deeper and requires restraint, respect, and responsible action both in one's personal behavior and professional activities. Remember, ethics deals in broad terms with how we treat others.

Two pertinent questions are: Can you be civil and not entirely ethical? Can you be ethical and not terribly civil? The answer to the first is a qualified "yes." You can be well behaved and gracious to others but still be motivated by non-ethical values such as greed. The problem is you may wind up using others to advance your self-interests. The answer to the second is "no." Treating others badly and with disrespect means you have not committed to act in accordance with the pillars of character.

Taken to its extreme, uncivil behavior could manifest itself in meanness toward others, bullying, and cyberbullying. Such behaviors fly in the face of caring and empathy for others. Fair treatment is replaced by biased behaviors against others who somehow are seen as different, inferior, or just not worthy of respect. Civility should be taught in our schools at the earliest possible age. Benjamin Franklin said that "the purpose of the high school shall be to teach civility, because without civility democracy will fail."

Just as one's social networking practices in personal matters can influence workplace behavior including critical postings about fellow employees or the company, uncivil behavior in personal affairs might translate into incivility in the workplace. This may be company driven if employees feel mistreated or under extreme pressure to produce results. The result could be a lack of organizational commitment and loyalty issues that lead one to vent frustrations on social media. Of course, one's propensity to act disrespectfully toward others can translate into workplace incivility including bullying behavior.

Incivility in the workplace can lead to tangible costs for a business. In a survey of 800 managers and employees in 17 industries published in *Harvard Business Review*, Porath and Pearson report that workers who had experienced incivility indicated that they lost work time worrying about the incident (80 percent), their commitment to the organization declined (78 percent), performance declined (66 percent), lost work time avoiding the offender (63 percent), and intentionally decreased their work effort (48 percent).[48]

Civility in accounting manifests itself in the way accounting professionals market and promote their services and in their interactions with clients. The AICPA Code of Professional Conduct prohibits acts that might bring the profession into disrepute or do harm to current or prospective clients. For example, advertising of professional services and solicitation of new clients should not be made in a false, fraudulent, misleading, or deceptive manner. CPAs should not make promises in their communications that may not be kept such as to create unjustified expectations of favorable results.

Professionalism and work ethic are important qualities of accounting professionals. Professionalism is generally defined as the strict adherence to courtesy, honesty, and responsibility when dealing with individuals or other companies in business and clients in public accounting. For CPAs, this means to act in accordance with personal and professional values such as trustworthiness, integrity, transparency, and the pursuit of excellence. A strong work ethic includes completing assignments in a timely manner, diligently, and with the highest quality possible. Ethics and professionalism in accounting also means to always place the public interest ahead of one's self-interests, the interests of an employer, and the client's interests. The public expects accounting and auditing professionals to be selfless in the pursuit of the public good.

Modern Moral Philosophies

LO 1-4
Differentiate between moral philosophies and their effect on ethical reasoning in accounting.

The ancient Greeks believed that reason and thought precede the choice of action and that we deliberate about things we can influence with our decisions. In making decisions, most people want to follow laws and rules. However, rules are not always clear, and laws may not cover every situation. Therefore, it is the ethical foundation that we develop and nurture that will determine how we react to unstructured situations that challenge our sense of right and wrong. In the end, we need to rely on moral principles to guide our decision making. However, the ability to reason out ethical conflicts may not be enough to assure ethical decision making occurs in accounting. This is because while we believe that we should behave in accordance with core values, we may wind up deviating from these values that trigger ethical reasoning in accounting because of internal pressures from supervisors and others in top management. In the end, a self-interest motive may prevail over making a decision from an ethical perspective, and unethical behavior may result. This is the moral of the story of Betty Vinson's role in the WorldCom fraud. Moreover, even if we know what the right thing to do is, we still may be unable to act on our beliefs because others in the organization provide reasons and rationalizations to deviate from those beliefs and may establish barriers to ethical action. This occurred in the WorldCom fraud when Scott Sullivan, the CFO, attempted to divert Cynthia Cooper from her goal to reveal the accounting fraud.

The noted philosopher James Rest points out that moral philosophies present guidelines for "determining how conflicts in human interests are to be settled for optimizing mutual benefit of people living together in groups." However, there is no single moral philosophy everyone accepts. Notably, moral philosophies have been used to defend a particular type of economic system and individuals' behavior within these systems.[49]

Adam Smith's seminal work, *An Inquiry Into the Nature and Causes of the Wealth of Nations (1776),* outlined the basis for free-market capitalism. Capitalism *laissez-faire* philosophies, such as minimizing the role of government intervention and taxation in the free markets, and the idea that an "invisible hand" guides supply and demand are key elements of his political philosophy. These ideas reflect the concept that each person, by looking out for his or her self-interest, inadvertently helps to create the best outcome for all. "It is not from the benevolence of the butcher, the brewer, or the baker, that we can expect our dinner, but from their regard to their own interest," Smith wrote.[50]

Even before Smith wrote *The Wealth of Nations* he produced a treatise on moral philosophy. *The Theory of Moral Sentiments* (1759) makes the case that business should be guided by the morals of good people. Smith sets forth a theory of how we come to be moral, of how morality functions on both individual and societal levels, and of what forces are likely to corrupt our sense of morality, which is derived from our capacity to sympathize directly and indirectly with other people. This occurs by feeling what others actually feel in their circumstances. We are able to achieve this moral perspective because of our consciences, which allow us to envision our own actions just as a disinterested observer might.[51]

Moral norms therefore express the feelings of an impartial spectator. A feeling, whether on the part of a person motivated to take action or on the part of a person who has been acted upon by others, is worthy of moral approval if and only if an impartial observer would sympathize with that feeling. When achieving a morally right feeling is difficult, we call that achievement "virtuous"; otherwise, we describe people as acting or failing to act within the bounds of "propriety." In the end, moral norms and ideals, and the judgments by which we guide ourselves towards those norms and ideals, arise out of the process by which we try to achieve mutual sympathy.

Smith distinguishes two kinds of normative guides to action: rules and virtues. Moral rules bar certain types of egregious behavior, such as murder, theft, and rape. They provide a basis for shared expectations of society and are essential to justice, without which societies could not survive. Virtue, on the other hand, requires more than simply following moral rules. Our emotional tendencies not only affect the sentiments of the impartial observer but we adopt those sentiments so that we identify with and become the impartial spectator to the extent possible. If we are truly virtuous, a submission to certain rules will constrain everything we do, but within that framework we can operate without rules by adopting dispositions such as kindness, empathy, patience, endurance, and courage.[52]

Moral philosophies provide specific principles and rules that we can use to decide what is right or wrong in specific instances. They can help a business decision maker formulate strategies to deal with ethical dilemmas and resolve them in a morally appropriate way. There are many such philosophies, but we limit the discussion to those that are most applicable to the study of accounting ethics, including teleology, deontology, justice, and virtue ethics. Our approach focuses on the most basic concepts needed to help you understand the ethical decision-making process in business and accounting that we outline in Chapter 2. We do not favor any one of these philosophies because there is no one correct way to resolve ethical issues in business. Instead, we present them to aid in resolving ethical dilemmas in accounting. Exhibit 1.3 summarizes the basis for making ethical judgments for each of the major moral philosophies. The discussion that follows elaborates on these principles and applies them to a common situation in accounting. One word of caution. Even though you may know what the right thing to do is, that does not mean you will act in the same way as your thoughts and feelings. Distractions occur and reasons and rationalizations are provided, making it more difficult to "give voice to your values," as will be discussed in Chapter 2.

Teleology

Recall that *telos* is the Greek word for "end" or "purpose." In teleology, an act is considered morally right or acceptable if it produces some desired result such as pleasure, the realization of self-interest, fame, utility, wealth, and so on. Teleologists assess the moral worth of behavior by looking at its consequences, and thus moral philosophers often refer to these theories as consequentialism. Two important teleological philosophies that typically guide decision making in individual business decisions are egoism and utilitarianism.

Egoism and Enlightened Egoism

Egoism defines right or acceptable behavior in terms of its consequences for the individual. *Egoists* believe that they should make decisions that maximize their own self-interest, which is defined differently by each individual. In other words, the individual should "[d]o the act that promotes the greatest good for oneself."[53] Many believe that egoistic people and companies are inherently unethical, are short-term-oriented, and will take advantage of others to achieve their goals. Our *laissez-faire* economic system enables the selfish pursuit of individual profit, so a regulated marketplace is essential to protect the interests of those affected by individual (and corporate) decision making.

There is one form of egoism that emphasizes more of a direct action to bring about the best interests of society. Enlightened egoists take a long-range perspective and allow for the well-being of others because they help achieve some ultimate goal for the decision maker, although their own self-interest remains paramount. For example, enlightened egoists may abide by professional codes of ethics, avoid cheating on taxes, and create safe working conditions. They do so not because their actions benefit others, but because they help achieve some ultimate goal for the egoist, such as advancement within the firm.[54]

Let's examine the following example from the perspectives of egoism and enlightened egoism. The date is Friday, January 17, 2016, and the time is 5:00 p.m. It is the last day of fieldwork on an audit, and you

EXHIBIT 1.3   Ethical Reasoning Method Bases for Making Ethical Judgments

	Teleology			Deontology	Justice	Virtue Ethics
	Egoism	**Enlightened Egoism**	**Utilitarianism**	**Rights Theory**		
Ethical Judgments	Defines "right" behavior by consequences for the decision maker	Considers well-being of others within the scope of deciding on a course of action based on self-interest.	Evaluates consequences of actions (harms and benefits) on stakeholders *Act* Evaluate whether the intended *action* provides the greatest net benefits. *Rule* Select the action that conforms to the correct *moral rule* that produces the greatest net benefits	Considers "rights" of stakeholders and related duties to them. Treats people as an end and not merely as a means to an end. *Universality Perspective:* Would I want others to act in a similar manner for similar reasons in this situation?	Emphasizes rights, fairness, and equality. Those with equal claims to justice should be treated equally; those with unequal claims should be treated unequally.	Only method where ethical reasoning methods—"virtues" (internal traits of character)—apply both to the *decision maker* and the *decision* Judgments are made not by applying rules, but by possessing those traits that enable the decision maker to act for the good of others. Similar to Principles of AICPA Code and IMA Standards.
Problems with Implementation	Fails to consider interests of those affected by the decision	Interests of others are subservient to self-interest.	Can be difficult to assign values to harms and benefits.	Relies on moral absolutes—no exceptions; need to resolve conflicting rights	Can be difficult to determine the criteria to distinguish equal from unequal claims.	Virtues may conflict, requiring choices to be made.

are the staff auditor in charge of receivables. You are wrapping up the test of subsequent collections of accounts receivable to determine whether certain receivables that were outstanding on December 31, 2015, and that were not confirmed by the customer as being outstanding, have now been collected. If these receivables have been collected and in amounts equal to the year-end outstanding balances, then you will be confident that the December 31 balance is correct and this aspect of the receivables audit can be relied on. One account receivable for $1 million has not been collected, even though it is 90 days past due. You go to your supervisor and discuss whether to establish an allowance for uncollectibles for part of or the entire amount. Your supervisor contacts the manager in charge of the audit, who goes to the CFO to discuss the matter. The CFO says in no uncertain terms that you should not record an allowance of any amount. The CFO does not want to reduce earnings below the current level because that will cause the company to fail to meet financial analysts' estimates of earnings for the year. Your supervisor informs you that the firm will go along with the client on this matter, even though the $1 million amount is material. In fact, it is 10 percent of the overall accounts receivable balance on December 31, 2015.

The junior auditor faces a challenge to integrity in this instance. The client is attempting to circumvent GAAP. The ethical obligation of the staff auditor is not to subordinate judgment to others' judgment, including that of top management of the firm.

If you are an egoist, you might conclude that it is in your best interests to go along with the firm's position, to support the client's presumed interests. After all, you do not want to lose your job. An enlightened egoist would consider the interests of others, including the investors and creditors, but still might reason that it is in her long-run interests to go along with the firm's position to support the client because she may not advance within the firm unless she is perceived to be a "team player."

Utilitarianism

Utilitarians follow a relatively straightforward method for deciding the morally correct course of action for any particular situation. First, they identify the various courses of action that they could perform. Second, they determine the utility of the consequences of all possible alternatives and then select the one that results in the greatest net benefit. In other words, they identify all the foreseeable benefits and harms (consequences) that could result from each course of action for those affected by the action, and then choose the course of action that provides the greatest benefits after the costs have been taken into account.[55] Given its emphasis on evaluating the benefits and harms of alternatives on stakeholders, utilitarianism requires that people look beyond self-interest to consider impartially the interest of all persons affected by their actions.

The utilitarian theory was first formulated in the eighteenth century by the English writer Jeremy Bentham (1748–1832) and later refined by John Stuart Mill (1806–1873). Bentham sought an objective basis that would provide a publicly acceptable norm for determining what kinds of laws England should enact. He believed that the most promising way to reach an agreement was to choose the policy that would bring about the greatest net benefits to society once the harms had been taken into account. His motto became "the greatest good for the greatest number." Over the years, the principle of utilitarianism has been expanded and refined so that today there are many different variations of the principle. Modern utilitarians often describe benefits and harms in terms of satisfaction of personal preferences or in purely economic terms of monetary benefits over monetary costs.[56]

Utilitarians differ in their views about the kind of question we ought to ask ourselves when making an ethical decision. Some believe the proper question is: What effect will my doing this action in this situation have on the general balance of good over evil? If lying would produce the best consequences in a particular situation, we ought to lie.[57] These act-utilitarians examine the specific action itself, rather than the general rules governing the action, to assess whether it will result in the greatest utility. For example, a rule in accounting such as "don't subordinate judgment to the client" would serve only as a general guide for an act-utilitarian. If the overall effect of giving in to the client's demands brings net utility to all the stakeholders, then the rule is set aside.

Rule-utilitarians, on the other hand, claim that we must choose the action that conforms to the general rule that would have the best consequences. For the rule-utilitarian, actions are justified by appealing to rules such as "never compromise audit independence." According to the rule-utilitarian, an action is selected because it is required by the correct moral rules that everyone should follow. The correct moral rules are those that maximize intrinsic value and minimize intrinsic disvalue. For example, a general rule such as "don't deceive" (an element of truthfulness) might be interpreted as requiring the full disclosure of the possibility that the client will not collect on a material, $1 million receivable. A rule-utilitarian might reason that the long-term effects of deceiving the users of financial statements are a breakdown of the trust that exists between the users and preparers and auditors of financial information.

In other words, we must ask ourselves: What effect would everyone's doing this kind of action (subordination of judgment) have on the general balance of good over evil? So, for example, the rule "to always tell the truth" in general promotes the good of everyone and therefore should always be followed, even if lying would produce the best consequences in certain situations. Notwithstanding differences between act- and rule-utilitarians, most hold to the general principle that morality must depend on balancing the beneficial and harmful consequences of conduct.[58]

While utilitarianism is a very popular ethical theory, there are some difficulties in relying on it as a sole method for moral decision making because the utilitarian calculation requires that we assign values to the benefits and harms resulting from our actions. But it is often difficult, if not impossible, to measure and compare the values of certain benefits and costs. Let's go back to our receivables example. It would be difficult to quantify the possible effects of going along with the client. How can a utilitarian measure the costs to the company of possibly having to write off a potential bad debt after the fact, including possible higher interest rates to borrow money in the future because of a decline in liquidity? What is the cost to one's reputation for failing to disclose an event at a point in time that might have affected the analysis of financial results? On the other hand, how can we measure the benefits to the company of *not* recording the allowance? Does it mean the stock price will rise and, if so, by how much?

Deontology

The term *deontology* is derived from the Greek word *deon*, meaning "duty." *Deontology* refers to moral philosophies that focus on the rights of individuals and on the intentions associated with a particular behavior, rather than on its consequences. *Deontologists* believe that moral norms establish the basis for action. Deontology differs from rule-utilitarianism in that the moral norms (or rules) are based on reason, not outcomes. Fundamental to deontological theory is the idea that equal respect must be given to all persons.[59] In other words, individuals have certain inherent rights and I, as the decision maker, have a duty (obligation, commitment, or responsibility) to respect those rights.

Philosophers claim that rights and duties are correlative. That is, my rights establish your duties and my duties correspond to the rights of others. The deontological tradition focuses on duties, which can be thought of as establishing the ethical limits of my behavior. From my perspective, duties are what I owe to others. Other people have certain claims on my behavior; in other words, they have certain rights against me.[60]

As with utilitarians, deontologists may be divided into those who focus on moral rules and those who focus on the nature of the acts themselves. In *act deontology*, principles are or should be applied by individuals to each unique circumstance allowing for some space in deciding the right thing to do. *Rule deontologists* believe that general moral principles determine the relationship between the basic rights of the individual and a set of rules governing conduct. It is particularly appropriate to the accounting profession, where the Principles of the AICPA Code support the rights of investors and creditors for accurate and reliable financial information and the duty of CPAs to act in accordance with the profession's rules of conduct to meet their obligations to the users of the financial statements. Rule deontologists believe that conformity to general moral principles based on logic determines ethicalness. Examples include Kant's categorical imperative, discussed next, and the Golden Rule of the Judeo-Christian tradition: "Do unto others as you would have them do unto you." Unlike act deontologists, who hold that actions are the proper basis on which to judge morality or ethicalness and treat rules only as guidelines in the decision-making process, rule deontologists argue there are some things we should never do.[61] Similarly, unlike act-utilitarians, rule deontologists argue that some actions would be wrong regardless of utilitarian benefits. For example, rule deontologists would consider it wrong for someone who has no money to steal bread, because it violates the right of the store owner to gain from his hard work baking and selling the bread. This is the dilemma in the classic novel *Les Misérables* by Victor Hugo. The main character, Jean Valjean, serves a 19-year sentence at hard labor for stealing a loaf of bread to feed his starving family.

Rights Principles

A *right* is a justified claim on others. For example, if I have a right to freedom, then I have a justified claim to be left alone by others. Turned around, I can say that others have a duty or responsibility to leave me alone.[62] In accounting, because investors and creditors have a right to accurate and complete financial information, I have the duty to ensure that the financial statements "present fairly" the financial position, results of operations, and changes in cash flows.

Formulations of *rights theories* first appeared in the seventeenth century in writings of Thomas Hobbes and John Locke. One of the most important and influential interpretations of moral rights is based on the work of Immanuel Kant (1724–1804), an eighteenth-century philosopher. Kant maintained that each of us has a worth or dignity that must be respected. This dignity makes it wrong for others to abuse us or to use us against our will. Kant expressed this idea as a moral principle: Humanity must always be treated as an end, not merely as a means. To treat a person as a mere means is to use her to advance one's own interest. But to treat a person as an end is to respect that person's dignity by allowing each the freedom to choose for himself.[63]

An important contribution of Kantian philosophy is the so-called categorical imperative: "Act only according to that maxim by which you can at the same time will that it should become universal law."[64] The "maxim" of our acts can be thought of as the intention behind our acts. The maxim answers the question: What am I doing, and why? In other words, moral intention is a prerequisite to ethical action, as we discuss more fully in the next chapter.

Kant tells us that we should act only according to those maxims that could be universally accepted and acted on. For example, Kant believed that truth telling could be made a universal law, but lying could not. If we all lied whenever it suited us, rational communication would be impossible. Thus, lying is unethical. Imagine if every company falsified its financial statements. It would be impossible to evaluate the financial results of one company accurately over time and in comparison to other companies. The financial markets might ultimately collapse because reported results were meaningless, or even misleading. This condition of universality, not unlike the Golden Rule, prohibits us from giving our own personal point of view special status over the point of view of others. It is a strong requirement of impartiality and equality for ethics.[65]

One problem with deontological theory is that it relies on moral absolutes—absolute principles and absolute conclusions. Kant believed that a moral rule must function without exception. The notions of rights and duties are completely separate from the consequences of one's actions. This could lead to making decisions that might adhere to one's moral rights and another's attendant duties to those rights, but which also produce disastrous consequences for other people. For example, imagine if you were the person hiding Anne Frank and her family in the attic of your home and the Nazis came banging at the door and demanded, "Do you know where the Franks are?" Now, a strict application of rights theory requires that you tell the truth to the Nazi soldiers. However, isn't this situation one in which an exception to the rule should come into play for humanitarian reasons?

Whenever we are confronted with a moral dilemma, we need to consider whether the action would respect the basic rights of each of the individuals involved. How would the action affect the well-being of those individuals? Would it involve manipulation or deception—either of which would undermine the right to truth that is a crucial personal right? Actions are wrong to the extent that they violate the rights of individuals.[66]

Sometimes the rights of individuals will come into conflict, and one has to decide which right has priority. There is no clear way to resolve conflicts between rights and the corresponding moral duties to respect those rights. One of the most widely discussed cases of this kind is taken from William Styron's novel *Sophie's Choice*. Sophie and her two children are at a Nazi concentration camp. A guard confronts Sophie and tells her that one of her children will be allowed to live and one will be killed. Sophie must decide which child will be killed. She can prevent the death of either of her children, but only by condemning the other to be killed. The guard makes the situation even more painful for Sophie by telling her that if she chooses neither, then both will be killed. With this added factor, Sophie has a morally compelling reason to choose one of her children. But for each child, Sophie has an equally strong reason to save him or her. Thus, the same moral precept gives rise to conflicting obligations.[67]

Now, we do not face such morally excruciating decisions in accounting (thank goodness). The ultimate obligation of accountants and auditors is to honor the public trust. The public interest obligation that is embedded in the profession's codes of ethics requires that if a conflict exists between the obligations of a decision maker to others, the decision maker should always decide based on protecting the public's right (i.e., investors and creditors), such as in the receivables example, to receive accurate and reliable financial information about uncollectibles.

Justice

Justice is usually associated with issues of rights, fairness, and equality. A just act respects your rights and treats you fairly. Justice means giving each person what she or he deserves. *Justice* and *fairness* are closely related terms that are often used interchangeably, although differences do exist. While *justice* usually has been used with reference to a standard of rightness, *fairness* often has been used with regard to an ability to judge without reference to one's feelings or interests.

Justice as Fairness

John Rawls (1921–2002) developed a conception of justice as fairness using elements of both Kantian and utilitarian philosophy. He described a method for the moral evaluation of social and political institutions this way.

Imagine that you have set for yourself the task of developing a totally new social contract for today's society. How could you do so fairly? Although you could never actually eliminate all of your personal biases and prejudices, you would need to take steps at least to minimize them. Rawls suggests that you imagine yourself in an original position behind a veil of ignorance. Behind this veil, you know nothing of yourself and your natural abilities, or your position in society. You know nothing of your sex, race, nationality, or individual tastes. Behind such a veil of ignorance all individuals are simply specified as rational, free, and morally equal beings. You do know that in the "real world," however, there will be a wide variety in the natural distribution of natural assets and abilities, and that there will be differences of sex, race, and culture that will distinguish groups of people from each other.

Rawls says that behind the veil of ignorance the only safe principles will be fair principles, for you do not know whether you would suffer or benefit from the structure of any biased institutions. The safest principles will provide for the highest minimum standards of justice in the projected society.

Rawls argues that in a similar manner, the rational individual would only choose to establish a society that would at least conform to the following two rules:

1. *Each person is to have an equal right to the most extensive basic liberty compatible with similar liberty for others.*

2. *Social and economic inequalities are to be arranged so that they are both:*

    (a) reasonably expected to be to everyone's advantage and
    (b) attached to positions and offices open to all.

The first principle—often called the *Liberty Principle*—is very Kantian in that it provides for basic and universal respect for persons as a minimum standard for all just institutions. But while all persons may be morally equal, we also know that in the "real world" there are significant differences between individuals that under conditions of liberty will lead to social and economic inequalities.

The second principle—called the *Difference Principle*—permits such inequalities and even suggests that it will be to the advantage of all (similar to the utility principle), but only if they meet the two specific conditions. Thus the principles are not strictly egalitarian, but they are not laissez-faire either. Rawls is locating his vision of justice in between these two extremes.

When people differ over what they believe should be given, or when decisions have to be made about how benefits and burdens should be distributed among a group of people, questions of justice or fairness inevitably arise. These are questions of *distributive justice.*[68]

The most fundamental principle of justice, defined by Aristotle more than 2,000 years ago, is that "equals should be treated equally and unequals unequally." In other words, individuals should be treated the same unless they differ in ways that are relevant to the situation in which they are involved. The problem with this interpretation is in determining which criteria are morally relevant to distinguish between those who are equal and those who are not. It can be a difficult theory to apply in business if, for example, a CEO of a company decides to allocate a larger share of the resources than is warranted (justified), based on the results of operations, to one product line over another to promote that operation because it is judged to have more long-term expansion and income potential. If I am the manager in charge of the operation getting fewer resources but producing equal or better results, then I may believe that my operation has been (I have been) treated unfairly. On the other hand, it could be said that the other manager deserves to receive a larger share of the resources because of the long-term potential of that other product line. That is, the product lines are not equal; the former deserves more resources because of its greater upside potential.

Justice as fairness is the basis of the objectivity principle in the AICPA Code that establishes a standard of providing unbiased financial information. In our discussion of ethical behavior in this and the following chapters, questions of fairness will be tied to making objective judgments. Auditors should render objective judgments about the fair presentation of financial results. In this regard, auditors should act as impartial arbiters of the truth, just as judges who make decisions in court cases should. The ethical principle of objectivity requires that such judgments be made impartially, unaffected by pressures that may exist to do otherwise. An objective auditor with knowledge about the failure to allow for the uncollectible receivables would not stand idly by and allow the financial statements to be materially misleading.

For purposes of future discussions about ethical decision making, we elaborate on the concept of *procedural justice.* Procedural justice considers the processes and activities that produce a particular outcome. For example, an ethical organization environment should positively influence employees' attitudes and behaviors toward work-group cohesion. When there is strong employee support for decisions, decision makers, organizations, and outcomes, procedural justice is less important to the individual. In contrast, when employees' support for decisions, decision makers, organizations, or outcomes is not very strong, then procedural justice becomes more important.[69] Consider, for example, a potential whistleblower who feels confident about bringing her concerns to top management because specific procedures are in place to support that person. Unlike the Betty Vinson situation, an environment built on procedural justice supports the whistleblower, who perceives the fairness of procedures used to make decisions.

Virtue Ethics

Virtue considerations apply both to the decision maker and to the act under consideration by that party. This is one of the differences between virtue theory and the other moral philosophies that focus on the act. To make an ethical decision, I must internalize the traits of character that make me an ethical (virtuous) person, such as the Six Pillars of Character. This philosophy is called *virtue ethics,* and it posits that what is moral in a given situation is not only what conventional morality or moral rules require but also what a well-intentioned person with a "good" moral character would deem appropriate.

Virtue theorists place less emphasis on learning rules and instead stress the importance of developing *good habits of character,* such as benevolence. Plato emphasized four virtues in particular, which were later called *cardinal virtues:* wisdom, courage, temperance, and justice. Other important virtues are fortitude, generosity, self-respect, good temper, and sincerity. In addition to advocating good habits of character, virtue theorists hold that we should avoid acquiring bad character traits, or vices, such as cowardice, insensibility, injustice, and vanity. Virtue theory emphasizes moral education because virtuous character traits are developed in one's youth. Adults, therefore, are responsible for instilling virtues in the young.

The philosopher Alasdair MacIntyre states that the exercise of virtue requires "a capacity to judge and to do the right thing in the right place at the right time in the right way." Judgment is exercised not through a routinizable application of the rules, but as a function of possessing those dispositions (tendencies) that enable choices to be made about what is good for people and by holding in check desires for something other than what will help achieve this goal.[70]

At the heart of the virtue approach to ethics is the idea of "community." A person's character traits are not developed in isolation, but within and by the communities to which he belongs, such as the Principles in the AICPA Code that pertain to standards of acceptable behavior in the accounting profession (its community).

MacIntyre relates virtues to the internal rewards of a practice (i.e., the accounting profession). He differentiates between the external rewards of a practice (such as money, fame, and power) and the internal rewards, which relate to the intrinsic value of a particular practice. MacIntyre points out that every practice requires a certain kind of relationship between those who participate in it. The virtues are the standards of excellence (i.e., AICPA Code principles) that characterize relationships within the practice. To enter into a practice is to accept the authority of those standards, obedience to the rules, and commitment to achieve the internal rewards. Some of the virtues that MacIntyre identifies are truthfulness, trust, justice, courage, and honesty.[71]

Mintz points out that the accounting profession is a practice with inherent virtues that enable accountants to meet their ethical obligations to clients, employers, the government, and the public at large. For instance, for auditors to render an objective opinion of a client's financial statements, they must be committed to perform such services without bias and to avoid conflicts of interest. Impartiality is an essential virtue for judges in our judicial system. CPAs render judgments on the fairness of financial statements. Therefore, they should act impartially in carrying out their professional responsibilities.[72]

The virtues enable accounting professionals to resolve conflicting duties and loyalties in a morally appropriate way. They provide accountants with the inner strength of character to withstand pressures that might otherwise overwhelm and negatively influence their professional judgment in a relationship of trust.[73] For example, if your boss, the CFO, pressures you to overlook a material misstatement in financial statements, the virtues of honesty and trustworthiness will lead you to place your obligation to investors and creditors ahead of any perceived loyalty obligation to your immediate supervisor or other members of top management. The virtue of integrity enables you to withstand the pressure to look the other way. Now, in the real world, this is easier said than done. You may be tempted to be silent because you fear losing your job. However, the ethical standards of the accounting profession obligate accountants and auditors to bring these issues to the attention of those in the highest positions in an organization, including the audit committee of the board of directors, as Cynthia Cooper did in the WorldCom fraud.

We realize that for students, it may be difficult to internalize the concept that, when forced into a corner by one's supervisor to go along with financial wrongdoing, you should stand up for what you know to be right, even if it means losing your job. However, ask yourself the following questions: Do I even want to work for an organization that does not value my professional opinion? If I go along with it this time, might the same demand be made at a later date? Will I begin to slide down that ethical slippery slope where there is no turning back? How much is my reputation for honesty and integrity worth? Would I be proud if others found out what I did (or didn't do)? To quote the noted Swiss psychologist and psychiatrist, Carl Jung: "You are what you do, not what you say you'll do."

The Public Interest in Accounting

LO 1-5
Explain the concept of the public interest in accounting.

Following the disclosure of numerous accounting scandals in the early 2000s at companies such as Enron and WorldCom, the accounting profession, professional bodies, and regulatory agencies turned their attention to examining how to rebuild the public trust and confidence in financial reporting. Stuebs and Wilkinson point out that restoring the accounting profession's public interest focus is a crucial first step in recapturing the public trust and securing the profession's future.[74] Copeland believes that in order to regain the trust and respect the profession enjoyed prior to the scandals, the profession must rebuild its reputation on its historical foundation of ethics and integrity.[75]

In the United States, the state boards of accountancy are charged with protecting the public interest in licensing candidates to become CPAs. The behavior of licensed CPAs and their ability to meet ethical and professional obligations is regulated by the state boards. Regulatory oversight is based on the statutorily defined scope of practice of public accountancy. There are 54 state boards including four U.S. territories. The National Association of State Boards of Accountancy (NASBA) provides a forum for discussion of the different state board requirements to develop an ideal set of regulations in the Uniform Accountancy Act.

The accounting profession is a community with values and standards of behavior. These are embodied in the various codes of conduct in the professional bodies, including the American Institute of Certified Public Accountants (AICPA). The AICPA is a voluntary association of CPAs with more than 400,000 members in 145 countries, including CPAs in business and industry, public accounting, government, and education; student affiliates; and international associates. CPA state societies also exist in the United States.

The Institute of Management Accountants (IMA), with a membership of more than 70,000, is the worldwide association for accountants and financial professionals working in business. We discuss ethics standards of the IMA later in this chapter. The Institute of Internal Auditors (IIA) is an international professional association representing the internal audit profession with more than 180,000 members. The IIA also has a code of ethics for its professionals.

On an international level, the largest professional accounting association is the Institute of Chartered Accountants [equivalent to CPAs] in England and Wales (ICAEW) that has over 142,000 members worldwide. A truly global professional association is the International Federation of Accountants (IFAC). IFAC is a global professional body dedicated to serve the public interest with over 175 members and associate members in 130 countries representing approximately 2.5 million accountants.

Typically, licensed CPAs work for public accounting firms, and in business, government, and education. It is important to note that state board rules and statutory regulations always supersede rules of professional associations, such as the AICPA, so that when the rules conflict a licensed CPA should follow the state board rules. A good example is when a licensed CPA has possession of client records while performing professional services. Under Rule 501.76 of the Texas State Board of Public Accountancy, a licensee must not withhold client records, including workpapers that constitute client records, once a demand has been made for them regardless of whether fees due to the licensee are outstanding for services already provided. However, under Rule 501 (Section 1.400.200) of the AICPA Code of Professional Conduct (AICPA Code), members of the AICPA can withhold member work product if there are fees due for the specific work product. In this instance, the more restrictive requirement of the Texas State Board must be followed.

Regulation of the Accounting Profession

Professions are defined by the knowledge, skills, attitudes, behaviors, and ethics of those in the (accounting) profession. Regulation of a profession is a specific response to the need for certain standards to be met by the members of the profession. The accounting profession provides an important public service through audits and other assurance services and those who choose to join the community pledge to act in the public interest.

According to IFAC Policy Position Statement 1, a number of reasons exist why regulation might be necessary to ensure that appropriate quality is provided in the market for professional accounting services. These include compliance with ethics, technical, and professional standards and the need to represent the interests of users of those services (i.e., investors and creditors).[76]

Regulations exist to address the knowledge imbalance between the client and the provider of services, who has professional expertise. Regulation also helps when there are significant benefits or costs from the provision of accountancy services that accrue to third parties, other than those acquiring and producing the services.

Effective regulation is predicated on serving the interests of those who are the beneficiaries of professional accounting services. To meet the public interest, regulation must be objectively determined, transparent, and implemented fairly and consistently. The benefits of regulation to the economy and society should outweigh the costs of that regulation.

While regulation is important, it is a necessary but insufficient condition to ensure ethical and professional behavior. Regulations should be designed to promote and achieve this behavior. It is the ethical behavior of the professional accountant that is the ultimate guarantee of good service and quality.

AICPA Code of Conduct

LO 1-6
Discuss the Principles section of the AICPA Code of Professional Conduct.

Given the broader scope of membership in the AICPA and the fact that state boards of accountancy generally recognize its ethical standards in state board rules of conduct, we emphasize the AICPA Code in most of this book. The Principles section of the AICPA Code, which mirrors virtues-based principles, are discussed next. We discuss the rules of conduct that are the enforceable provisions of the AICPA Code in Chapter 4. Later in this chapter, we explain the IMA Statement of Ethical Professional Practice to apply a framework of professional values along with ethical reasoning to a dilemma faced by management accountants.

The Principles of the AICPA Code are aspirational statements that form the foundation for the Code's enforceable rules. The Principles guide members in the performance of their professional responsibilities and call for an unyielding commitment to honor the public trust, even at the sacrifice of personal benefits. While CPAs cannot be legally held to the Principles, they do represent the expectations for CPAs on the part of the public in the performance of professional services. In this regard, the Principles are based on values of the profession and traits of character (virtues) that enable CPAs to meet their obligations to the public.

The Principles include (1) Responsibilities, (2) The Public Interest, (3) Integrity, (4) Objectivity and Independence, (5) Due Care, and (6) Scope and Nature of Services.[77]

The umbrella statement in the Code is that the overriding responsibility of CPAs is to exercise sensitive professional and moral judgments in all activities. By linking professional conduct to moral judgment, the AICPA Code recognizes the importance of moral reasoning in meeting professional obligations.

The second principle defines the public interest to include "clients, credit grantors, governments, employers, investors, the business and financial community, and others who rely on the objectivity and integrity of CPAs to maintain the orderly functioning of commerce." This principle calls for resolving conflicts between these stakeholder groups by recognizing the primacy of a CPA's responsibility to the public as the way to best serve clients' and employers' interests. In discharging their professional responsibilities, CPAs may encounter conflicting pressures from each of these groups. According to the public interest principle, when conflicts arise, the actions taken to resolve them should be based on integrity, guided by the precept that when CPAs fulfill their responsibilities to the public, clients' and employers' interests are best served.

As a principle of CPA conduct, integrity recognizes that the public trust is served by (1) being honest and candid within the constraints of client confidentiality, (2) not subordinating the public trust to personal gain and advantage, (3) observing both the form and spirit of technical and ethical standards, and (4) observing the principles of objectivity and independence and of due care.

Objectivity requires that all CPAs maintain a mental attitude of impartiality and intellectual honesty and be free of conflicts of interest in meeting professional responsibilities. Objectivity pertains to all CPAs in their performance of all professional services. Independence applies only to CPAs who provide attestation services (i.e., auditing and other assurance services), not tax and advisory services. The reason lies in the scope and purpose of an audit. When conducting an audit of a client's financial statements, the CPA gathers evidence to support an opinion on whether the financial statements present fairly, in all material respects, the client's financial position and the results of operations and cash flows in accordance with GAAP. The audit opinion is relied on by investors and creditors (external users), thereby triggering the need to be independent of the client entity to enhance assurances. In tax and advisory engagements, the service is provided primarily for the client (internal user) so that the CPA might become involved in some relationships with the client that might otherwise impair audit independence but do not come into play when providing nonattest services; nonattest services do require objectivity in decision making and the exercise of due care to protect the public interest.

Independence is required both in fact and in appearance. Because it is difficult to determine independence in fact inasmuch as it involves identifying a mindset, CPAs should avoid relationships with a client entity that may be seen as impairing objective judgment by a "reasonable" observer. The foundational standard of independence is discussed in the context of the audit function in Chapter 4.

The due care standard (diligence) calls for continued improvement in the level of competency and quality of services by (1) performing professional services to the best of one's abilities, (2) carrying out professional responsibilities with concern for the best interests of those for whom the services are performed, (3) carrying out those responsibilities in accordance with the public interest, (4) following relevant technical and ethical standards, and (5) properly planning and supervising engagements. A key element of due care is professional skepticism, which means to have a questioning mind and critical assessment of audit evidence.

The importance of the due care standard is as follows. Imagine if a CPA were asked to perform an audit of a school district and the CPA never engaged in governmental auditing before and never completed a course of study in governmental auditing. While the CPA or CPA firm may still obtain the necessary skills to perform the audit—for example, by hiring someone with the required skills—the CPA/firm would have a hard time supervising such work without the proper background and knowledge.

The due care standard also relates to the scope and nature of services performed by a CPA. The latter requires that CPAs practice in firms that have in place internal quality control procedures to ensure that services are competently delivered and adequately supervised and that such services are consistent with one's role as a professional. Also, CPAs should determine, in their individual judgments, whether the scope and nature of other services provided to an audit client would create a conflict of interest in performing an audit for that client.

A high-quality audit features the exercise of professional judgment by the auditor and professional skepticism throughout the planning and performance of the audit. Professional skepticism is an essential attitude that enhances the auditor's ability to identify and respond to conditions that may indicate possible misstatement of the financial statements. Professional judgment is a critical component of ethical behavior in accounting. The qualities of behavior that enable professional judgment come not only from the profession's codes of conduct, but also the virtues and ability to reason through ethical conflicts using ethical reasoning methods.

Virtue, Character, and CPA Obligations

Traits of character such as honesty, integrity, and trustworthiness enable a person to act with virtue and apply the moral point of view. Kurt Baier, a well-known moral philosopher, discusses the moral point of view as being one that emphasizes practical reason and rational choice.[78] To act ethically means to incorporate ethical values into decision making and to reflect on the rightness or wrongness of alternative courses of action. The core values of integrity, objectivity, and independence; attitudes for exercising professional skepticism; and a framework for ethical reasoning all underlie virtue-based decision making in accounting.

Aristotle believed that deliberation (reason and thought) precedes the choice of action and we deliberate about things that are in our power (voluntary) and can be realized by action. The deliberation that leads to the action always concerns choices, not the ends. We take the end for granted—a life of excellence or virtue—and then consider in what manner and by what means it can be realized. In accounting, we might say that the end is to gain the public trust and serve the public interest, and the means to achieve that end is by acting in accordance with the profession's ethical standards.

Aristotle's conception of virtue incorporates positive traits of character that enable reasoned judgments to be made, and in accounting, they support integrity—the inner strength of character to withstand pressures that might otherwise overwhelm and negatively influence their professional judgment. A summary of the virtues is listed in Exhibit 1.4.[79]

EXHIBIT 1.4   Virtues and Ethical Obligations of CPAs

Aristotle's Virtues	Ethical Standards for CPAs
Trustworthiness, benevolence, altruism	Integrity
Honesty, integrity	Truthfulness, non-deception
Impartiality, open-mindedness	Objectivity, independence
Reliability, dependability, faithfulness	Loyalty (confidentiality)
Trustworthiness	Due care (competence and prudence)

Application of Ethical Reasoning in Accounting

LO 1-7
Apply the IMA Statement of Ethical and Professional Practice to a case study.

In this section, we discuss the application of ethical reasoning in its entirety to a common dilemma faced by internal accountants and auditors. The case deals with the classic example of when pressure is imposed on accountants by top management to ignore material misstatements in financial statements.

Many internal accountants, such as controllers and CFOs, are CPAs and members of the IMA. The IMA's Statement of Ethical Professional Practice[80] is presented in Exhibit 1.5. Other than independence, which is a specific ethical requirement of an external audit, the standards of the IMA are similar to the Principles of Professional Conduct in the AICPA Code. Most important, read through the "Resolution of Ethical Conflict" section, which defines the steps to be taken by members when they are pressured to go along with financial statement improprieties. Specific steps to be taken include discussing matters of concern with the highest levels of the organization, including the audit committee.

DigitPrint Case Study

DigitPrint was formed in March 2015 with the goal of developing an outsource business for high-speed digital printing. The company is small and does not yet have a board of directors. The comparative advantage of the company is that its founder and president, Henry Higgins, owned his own print shop for several years before starting DigitPrint. Higgins recently hired Liza Doolittle to run the start-up business. Wally Wonderful, who holds the Certified Management Accountant (CMA) certification from the IMA, was hired to help set up a computerized system to track incoming purchase orders, sales invoices, cash receipts, and cash payments for the printing business.

EXHIBIT 1.5 Institute of Management Accountants Statement of Ethical Professional Practice

Members of IMA shall behave ethically. A commitment to ethical professional practice includes overarching principles that express our values, and standards that guide our conduct.

Principles

IMA's overarching ethical principles include: Honesty, Fairness, Objectivity, and Responsibility. Members shall act in accordance with these principles and shall encourage others within their organizations to adhere to them.

Standards

A member's failure to comply with the following standards may result in disciplinary action.

I. Competence

Each member has a responsibility to:

1. Maintain an appropriate level of professional expertise by continually developing knowledge and skills.
2. Perform professional duties in accordance with relevant laws, regulations, and technical standards.
3. Provide decision support information and recommendations that are accurate, clear, concise, and timely.
4. Recognize and communicate professional limitations or other constraints that would preclude responsible judgment or successful performance of an activity.

II. Confidentiality

Each member has a responsibility to:

1. Keep information confidential except when disclosure is authorized or legally required.
2. Inform all relevant parties regarding appropriate use of confidential information. Monitor subordinates' activities to ensure compliance.
3. Refrain from using confidential information for unethical or illegal advantage.

III. Integrity

Each member has a responsibility to:

1. Mitigate actual conflicts of interest, regularly communicate with business associates to avoid apparent conflicts of interest. Advise all parties of any potential conflicts.
2. Refrain from engaging in any conduct that would prejudice carrying out duties ethically.
3. Abstain from engaging in or supporting any activity that might discredit the profession.

IV. Credibility

Each member has a responsibility to:

1. Communicate information fairly and objectively.
2. Disclose all relevant information that could reasonably be expected to influence an intended user's understanding of the reports, analyses, or recommendations.
3. Disclose delays or deficiencies in information, timeliness, processing, or internal controls in conformance with organization policy and/or applicable law.

Resolution of Ethical Conduct

In applying the Standards of Ethical Professional Practice, you may encounter problems identifying unethical behavior or resolving an ethical conflict. When faced with ethical issues, you should follow your organization's established policies on the resolution of such conflict. If

(Continued)

these policies do not resolve the ethical conflict, you should consider the following courses of action:

1. Discuss the issue with your immediate supervisor except when it appears that the supervisor is involved. In that case, present the issue to the next level. If you cannot achieve a satisfactory resolution, submit the issue to the next management level. If your immediate superior is the chief executive officer or equivalent, the acceptable reviewing authority may be a group such as the audit committee, executive committee, board of directors, board of trustees, or owners. Contact with levels above the immediate superior should be initiated only with your superior's knowledge, assuming he or she is not involved. Communication of such problems to authorities or individuals not employed or engaged by the organization is not considered appropriate, unless you believe there is a clear violation of the law.

2. Clarify relevant ethical issues by initiating a confidential discussion with an IMA Ethics Counselor or other impartial advisor to obtain a better understanding of possible courses of action.

3. Consult your own attorney as to legal obligations and rights concerning the ethical conflict.

DigitPrint received $2 million as venture capital to start the business. The venture capitalists were given an equity share in return. From the beginning, they were concerned about the inability of the management to bring in customer orders and earn profits. In fact, only $200,000 net income had been recorded during the first year. Unfortunately, Wonderful had just discovered that $1 million of accrued expenses had not been recorded at year-end. Had that amount been recorded, the $200,000 net income of DigitPrint would have changed to an $800,000 loss.

Wonderful approached his supervisor, Doolittle, with what he had uncovered. She told him in no uncertain terms that the $1 million of expenses and liabilities could not be recorded, and warned him of the consequences of pursuing the matter any further. The reason was that the venture capitalists might pull out from financing DigitPrint because of the reduction of net income, working capital, and the higher level of liabilities. Wonderful is uncertain whether to inform Higgins. On one hand, he feels a loyalty obligation to go along with Doolittle. On the other hand, he believes he has an ethical obligation to the venture capitalists and other financiers that might help fund company operations.

We provide a brief analysis of ethical reasoning methods based on the following. First, consider the ethical standards of the IMA and evaluate potential actions for Wonderful. Then, use ethical reasoning with reference to the obligations of an accountant to analyze what you think Wonderful should do.

IMA Standards

Wonderful is obligated by the competence standard to follow relevant laws, regulations, and technical standards, including GAAP, in reporting financial information. Of particular importance is his obligation to disclose all relevant information, including the accrued expenses, that could reasonably be expected to influence an intended user's understanding (i.e., venture capitalists) of the financial reports. Doolittle has refused to support his position and told him in no uncertain terms not to pursue the matter. At this point, Wonderful should follow the Resolution of Ethical Conduct procedures outlined in the IMA Standards and take the matter up the chain of command. Typically, in a public corporation, this would mean to go as far as the audit committee of the board of directors. However, DigitPrint is a small company without a board, so Henry Higgins, the founder and president, is the final authority. If Higgins backs Doolittle's position of nondisclosure, then Wonderful should seek outside advice from a trusted adviser, including an attorney, to help evaluate legal obligations and rights concerning the ethical conflict. The danger for Wonderful would be if he goes along with the improper accounting for the accrued expenses, and the venture capitalists find out about the material misstatement in the financial statements at a later date, then Wonderful would be blamed both by the company and the venture capitalists.

Utilitarianism

Wonderful should attempt to identify the harms and benefits of the act of recording the transactions versus not recording them. The consequences of failing to inform the venture capitalists about the accrued expenses are severe, not only for Wonderful but also for DigitPrint. These include a possible lawsuit, investigation by regulators for failing to record the information, and, most important, a loss of reputational capital in the marketplace. The primary benefit to Wonderful is acceptance by his superiors, and he can be secure in the knowledge that he'll keep his job. Utilitarian values are difficult to assign to each potential act. Still, Wonderful should act in accordance with the moral rule that honesty requires not only truth telling, but disclosing all the information that another party has a need (or right) to know.

Rights Theory

The venture capitalists have an ethical right to know about the higher level of payables, the lower income, and the effect of the unrecorded transactions on working capital; the company has a duty to the venture capitalists to record the information. Wonderful should take the necessary steps to support such an outcome. The end goal of securing needed financing should not cloud Wonderful's judgment about the means chosen to accomplish the goal (i.e., nondisclosure). Wonderful should ask whether he believes that others in a similar situation should cover up the existence of $1 million in accrued expenses. Assuming that this is not the case, he shouldn't act in this way.

Justice

In this case, the justice principle is linked to the fairness of the presentation of the financial statements. The omission of the $1 million of unrecorded expenses means that the statements would not "present fairly" financial position and results of operations. It violates the rights of the venture capitalists to receive accurate and reliable financial information. As previously explained, a procedural justice perspective applied to the case means to assess the support for employee decisions on the part of the company. As a new employee, Wonderful needs to understand the corporate culture at DigitPrint.

Virtue Considerations

Wonderful is expected to reason through the ethical dilemma and make a decision that is consistent with virtue considerations. The virtue of integrity requires Wonderful to have the courage to withstand the pressure imposed by Doolittle and not subordinate his judgment to hers. Integrity is the virtue that enables Wonderful to act in this way. While he has a loyalty obligation to his employer, it should not override his obligation to the venture capitalists, who expect to receive truthful financial information. A lie by omission is dishonest and inconsistent with the standards of behavior in the accounting profession.

What Should Wonderful Do?

Wonderful should inform Doolittle that he will take his concerns to Higgins. That may force Doolittle's hand and cause her to back off from pressuring Wonderful. As president of the company, Higgins has a right to know about the situation. After all, he hired Doolittle because of her expertise and, presumably, based on certain ethical expectations. Higgins may decide to disclose the matter immediately and cut his losses because this is the right thing to do. On the other hand, if Higgins persists in covering up the matter, then, after seeking outside/legal advice, Wonderful must decide whether to go outside the company. His conscience may move him in this direction. However, the confidentiality standard requires that he not do so unless legally required.

A Message for Students

As you can tell from the DigitPrint case, ethical matters in accounting are not easy to resolve. On one hand, the accountant feels an ethical obligation to his employer or the client. On the other hand, the profession has strong codes of ethics that require accountants and auditors to place the public interest ahead of all other interests. Accounting professionals should analyze conflicting situations and evaluate the ethics by considering professional standards and the moral principles discussed in this chapter. A decision should be made after careful consideration of these factors and by applying logical reasoning to resolve the dilemma.

Keep in mind that you may be in a position during your career where you feel pressured to remain silent about financial wrongdoing. You might rationalize that you didn't commit the unethical act, so your hands are clean. That's not good enough, though, as your ethical obligation to the public and the profession is to do whatever it takes to prevent a fraud from occurring and, if it does, take the necessary steps to correct the matter. We hope that you will internalize the ethical standards of the accounting profession, and look at the bigger picture when pressured by a superior to go along with financial wrongdoing. The road is littered with CFOs/CPAs who masterminded (or at least directed) financial frauds at companies such as Enron, WorldCom, and Tyco. The result of their trials was a jail sentence for Andy Fastow of 10 years, Scott Sullivan of 5 years, and Mark Swartz of 8 1/3 to 25 years. Most important is they lost their livelihood, as well as the respect of the community. A reputation for trust takes a long time to build, but it can be destroyed in no time at all.

Scope and Organization of the Text

The overriding philosophy of this text is that the obligations of accountants and auditors are best understood in the context of ethical and professional responsibilities and organizational ethics. Ethical leadership is a critical component of creating the kind of ethical organization environment that supports ethical decision making.

Ethical decision making in accounting is predicated on moral reasoning. In this chapter, we have attempted to introduce the complex philosophical reasoning methods that help to fulfill the ethical obligations of accounting professionals. In Chapter 2, we address behavioral ethics issues and cognitive development to lay the groundwork for discussions of professional judgment and professional skepticism that form the basis of a sound audit. We introduce a decision-making model that provides a framework for ethical decision making and can be used to help analyze cases presented at the end of each chapter. A critical component of ethical behavior is to go beyond knowledge of what the right thing to do is and translate such knowledge into action. Cognitive development theories address this issue. We also explain the "Giving Voice to Values" methodology that has become an integral part of values-based decision making. In Chapter 3, we transition to the culture of an organization and how processes and procedures can help to create and sustain an ethical organization environment, including effective corporate governance systems. We also address whistleblowing considerations for accounting professionals and the confidentiality requirement.

The remainder of this book focuses more directly on accounting ethics. Chapter 4 addresses the AICPA Code and provisions that establish standards of ethical behavior for accounting professionals. In Chapter 5, we address fraud in financial statements, including the Fraud Triangle, and the obligations of auditors to assess the risk of material misstatements in the financial statements. We also address the PCAOB inspection process.

Auditors can be the target of lawsuits because of business failures and deficient audit work. In Chapter 6, we look at legal liability issues and regulatory requirements. The techniques used to manipulate earnings and obscure financial statement items are discussed in the context of earnings management in Chapter 7. These "financial shenanigans" threaten the reliability of the financial reports and can lead to legal liabilities for accountants and auditors. Finally, in Chapter 8, we look at ethical leadership, the heart and soul of an ethical organization. Leadership in the accounting profession is examined from the perspective of auditor and firm behavior. This chapter ties together much of the discussion in this book and discusses challenges to ethical decision making in the accounting profession going forward.

Concluding Thoughts

Our culture seems to have morphed toward exhibitionist tendencies where people do silly (stupid) things just to get their 15 minutes of fame through a YouTube video and with the promise of their own reality television show. Think about the "balloon boy" incident in October 2009, when the whole world watched a giant balloon fly through the air as a tearful family expressed fears that their six-year-old boy could be inside, all the while knowing the whole thing was staged. The messages sent by some reality programs is anti-ethics, such as MTV's "16 and Pregnant." Then there is the Canadian-based online dating service and social networking service, Ashley Madison. Its tacky Web site aims to facilitate cheating (Slogan: "Life is short. Have an affair.")

When was the last time you picked up a newspaper and read a story about someone doing the right thing because it was the right thing to do? It is rare these days. We seem to read and hear more about pursuing one's own selfish interests, even to the detriment of others. It might be called the "What's in it for me?" approach to life. Nothing could be more contrary to leading a life of virtue, and, as the ancient Greeks knew, benevolence is an important virtue.

In a classic essay on friendship, Ralph Waldo Emerson said: "The only reward of virtue is virtue; the only way to have a friend is to be one."[81] In other words, virtue is its own reward, just as we gain friendship in life by being a friend to someone else. In accounting, integrity is its own reward because it builds trust in client relationships and helps honor the public trust that is the foundation of the accounting profession.

We want to conclude on a positive note. Heroes in accounting do exist: brave people who have spoken out about irregularities in their organizations, such as Cynthia Cooper from WorldCom, whom we have already discussed. Another such hero is David Walker, who served as comptroller general of the United States and head of the Government Accountability Office from 1998 to 2008. Walker appeared before an appropriations committee of the U.S. Senate in 2008 and spoke out about billions of dollars in waste spent by the U.S. government, including on the Iraqi war effort. Then there was auditor Joseph St. Denis, who spoke out about improper accounting practices at his former company, AIG, which received a $150 billion bailout from the U.S. government during the financial crisis of 2008. All three received the Accounting Exemplar Award from the Public Interest Section of the American Accounting Association and serve as role models in the profession.

Discussion Questions

1. A common ethical dilemma used to distinguish between philosophical reasoning methods is the following. Imagine that you are standing on a footbridge spanning some trolley tracks. You see that a runaway trolley is threatening to kill five people. Standing next to you, in between the oncoming trolley and the five people, is a railway worker wearing a large backpack. You quickly realize that the only way to save the people is to push the man off the bridge and onto the tracks below. The man will die, but the bulk of his body and the pack will stop the trolley from reaching the others. (You quickly understand that you can't jump yourself because you aren't large enough to stop the trolley, and there's no time to put on the man's backpack.) Legal concerns aside, would it be ethical for you to save the five people by pushing this stranger to his death? Use the deontological and teleological methods to reason out what you would do and why.

2. Another ethical dilemma deals with a runaway trolley heading for five railway workers who will be killed if it proceeds on its present course. The only way to save these people is to hit a switch that will turn the trolley onto a side track, where it will run over and kill one worker instead of five. Ignoring legal concerns, would it be ethically acceptable for you to turn the trolley by hitting the switch in order to save five people at the expense of one person? Use the deontological and teleological methods to reason out what you would do and why.

3. The following two statements about virtue were made by noted philosophers/writers:

   a. MacIntyre, in his account of Aristotelian virtue, states that integrity is the one trait of character that encompasses all the others. How does integrity relate to, as MacIntrye said, "the wholeness of a human life"?

   b. David Starr Jordan (1851–1931), an educator and writer, said, "Wisdom is knowing what to do next; virtue is doing it." Explain the meaning of this phrase as you see it.

4. a. Do you think it is the same to act in your own self-interest as it is to act in a selfish way? Why or why not?

   b. Do you think "enlightened self-interest" is a contradiction in terms, or is it a valid basis for all actions? Evaluate whether our laissez-faire, free-market economic system does (or should) operate under this philosophy.

5. In this chapter, we have discussed the Joe Paterno matter at Penn State. Another situation where a respected individual's reputation was tarnished by personal decisions is the resignation of David Petraeus, former U.S. military general and head of the Central Intelligence Agency (CIA). On November 9, 2012, Petraeus resigned from the CIA after it was announced he had an extramarital affair with a biographer, Paula Broadwell, who wrote a glowing book about his life. Petraeus acknowledged that he exercised poor judgment by engaging in the affair. When Federal Bureau of Investigation (FBI) agents investigated the matter because of concerns there may have been security leaks, they discovered a substantial number of classified documents on her computer. Broadwell told investigators that she ended up with the secret military documents after taking them from a government building. No security leaks had been found. In accepting Petraeus's resignation, President Obama praised Petraeus's leadership during the Iraq and Afghanistan wars and said: "By any measure, through his lifetime of service, David Petraeus has made our country safer and stronger." Should our evaluation of Petraeus's lifetime of hard work and Petraeus's success in his career be tainted by one act having nothing to do with job performance?

6. One explanation about rights is that there is a difference between what we have the right to do and

what the right thing to do is. Explain what you think is meant by this statement. Do you believe that if someone is rude to you, you have a right to be rude right back?

7. Steroid use in baseball is an important societal issue. Many members of society are concerned that their young sons and daughters may be negatively influenced by what apparently has been done at the major league level to gain an advantage and the possibility of severe health problems for young children from continued use of the body mass enhancer now and in the future. Mark McGwire, who broke Roger Maris's 60-home-run record, initially denied using steroids. He has never come close to the 75 percent positive vote to be in the Hall of Fame. Unfortunately for McGwire, his approval rating has been declining each year since he received 23.7 percent of the vote in 2010 and only 10 percent of the sportscasters voted in 2015 to elect him into the Hall. Some believe that Barry Bonds and Roger Clemens, who were the best at what they did, should be listed in the record books with an asterisk after their names and an explanation that their records were established at a time when baseball productivity might have been positively affected by the use of steroids. Some even believe they should be denied entrance to the baseball Hall of Fame altogether. The results for Bonds (36.8 percent) and Clemens (37.5 percent) in their third year of eligibility (2015) were not close to meeting the 75 percent requirement, and that led some to question whether these superstars would ever be voted into the Hall.[82] Evaluate whether Bonds and Clemens should be elected to the Hall of Fame from a situational ethics point of view.

8. Your best friend is from another country. One day after a particularly stimulating lecture on the meaning of ethics by your instructor, you and your friend disagree about whether culture plays a role in ethical behavior. You state that good ethics are good ethics, and it doesn't matter where you live and work. Your friend tells you that in her country it is common to pay bribes to gain favor with important people. Comment on both positions from a relativistic ethics point of view. What do you believe and why?

9. Hofstede's Cultural Dimensions in Exhibit 1.2 indicate that China has a score of only 20 in Individualism, while the U.S. score is 91. How might the differences in scores manifest itself when the public interest is threatened by harmful actions taken by a member of management who has direct control over an employee's standing within the organization? Should cultural considerations in this instance influence ethical behavior?

10. a. What is the relationship between the ethical obligation of honesty and truth telling?

    b. Is it ever proper to not tell someone something that he or she has an expectation of knowing? If so, describe under what circumstances this might be the case. How does this square with rights theory?

11. Is there a difference between cheating on a math test, lying about your age to purchase a cheaper ticket at a movie theater, and using someone else's ID to get a drink at a bar?

12. Do you think it is ethical for an employer to use social media information as a factor when considering whether to hire an employee? What about monitoring social networking activities of employees while on the job? Use ethical reasoning in answering these questions.

13. In a 2014 segment of *Shark Tank,* Trevor Hiltbrand, the founder of nootropic supplement maker Cerebral Success, sought funding from the "Sharks" to introduce a line of nootropic shots to be sold on college campuses in Five Hour Energy-style containers, but encountered some pushback from some of the Sharks who questioned the ethics of marketing to stressed-out, sleep-deprived college students anxious to get good grades. Should it matter if Hiltbrand was trying to capitalize on the need to gain a competitive edge in college by selling something that may not have received FDA approval?

14. According to Adam Smith's *The Wealth of Nations,* when it comes to government oversight in the free market and regulations, the less intervention, the better. Does the government play an important

role in encouraging businesses to behave in an ethical manner? Explain the basis for your answer. What role do environmental laws have in a capitalistic system?

15. According to the 2011 National Business Ethics Survey conducted by the Ethics Resource Center, *Generational Differences in Workplace Ethics*,[83] a relatively high percentage of Millennials consider certain behaviors in the workplace ethical when compared with their earlier counterparts. These include:

- Use social networking to find out about the company's competitors (37%),
- "Friend" a client or customer on a social network (36%),
- Upload personal photos on a company network (26%),
- Keep copies of confidential documents (22%),
- Work less to compensate for cuts in benefits or pay (18%),
- Buy personal items using a company credit card (15%),
- Blog or tweet negatively about a company (14%), and
- Take a copy of work software home for personal use (13%).

The report further concludes that younger workers are significantly more willing to ignore the presence of misconduct if they think that behavior will help save jobs.

a. Choose one or more behaviors and explain why Millennials might view the behavior as ethical.

b. Choose one or more behaviors and explain why you think it is unethical.

Use ethical reasoning to support your points of view.

16. How should an accounting professional go about determining whether a proposed action is in the public interest?

17. Distinguish between ethical rights and obligations from the perspective of accountants and auditors.

18. Using the concept of justice, evaluate how an auditor would assess the equality of interests in the financial reporting process.

19. Why is it important for a CPA to promote professional services in an ethical manner? Do you believe it would be ethical for a CPA to advertise professional services using testimonials and endorsements? Why or why not?

20. Do you think it would be ethical for a CPA to have someone else do for her that which she is prohibited from doing by the AICPA Code of Professional Conduct? Why or why not? Do you think a CPA can justify allowing the unethical behavior of a supervisor by claiming, "It's not my job to police the behavior of others?"

21. Assume in the DigitPrint case that the venture capitalists do not provide additional financing to the company, even though the accrued expense adjustments have not been made. The company hires an audit firm to conduct an audit of its financial statements to take to a local bank for a loan. The auditors become aware of the unrecorded $1 million in accrued expenses. Liza Doolittle pressures them to delay recording the expenses until after the loan is secured. The auditors do not know whether Henry Higgins is aware of all the facts. Identify the stakeholders in this case. What alternatives are available to the auditors? Use the AICPA Code of Professional Conduct and Josephson's Six Pillars of Character to evaluate the ethics of the alternative courses of action.

22. In the discussion of loyalty in this chapter, a statement is made that "your ethical obligation is to report what you have observed to your supervisor and let her take the appropriate action." We point out that you may want to take your concerns to others. The IMA Statement of Ethical Professional

Practice includes a confidentiality standard that requires members to "keep information confidential except when disclosure is authorized or legally required.

23. Do you think there are any circumstances when you should go outside the company to report financial wrongdoing? If so, to what person/organization would you go? Why? If not, why would you not take the information outside the company?

24. Assume that a corporate officer or other executive asks you, as the accountant for the company, to omit or leave out certain financial figures from the balance sheet that may paint the business in a bad light to the public and investors. Because the request does not involve a direct manipulation of numbers or records, would you agree to go along with the request? What ethical considerations exist for you in deciding on a course of action?

25. Sir Walter Scott (1771–1832), the Scottish novelist and poet, wrote: "Oh what a tangled web we weave, when first we practice to deceive." Comment on what you think Scott meant by this phrase.

26. Assume you are preparing for an interview with the director of personnel and you are considering some of the questions that you might be asked. Craft a response that you would feel comfortable giving for each one.

- Describe an experience in the workplace when your attitudes and beliefs were ethically challenged. Use a personal example if you have not experienced a workplace dilemma.

- What are the most important values that would drive your behavior as a new staff accountant in a CPA firm?

- Describe your ethical expectations of the culture in an accounting firm.

- What would you do if your position on an accounting issue differs from that of firm management?

Endnotes

1. Freeh, Sporkin, and Sullivan, LLP, *Report of the Special Investigative Counsel Regarding the Actions of The Pennsylvania State University Related to the Child Sexual Abuse Committed by Gerald A. Sandusky,* July 12, 2012, Available at: www.thefreehreportonpsu.com/REPORT_FINAL_071212.pdf.

2. Graham Winch, "Witness: I Saw Sandusky Raping Boy in Shower," June 12, 2012, Available at: www.hlntv.com/article/2012/06/12/witness-i-saw-sandusky-raping-child.

3. Eyder Peralta, "Paterno, Others Slammed In Report For Failing To Protect Sandusky's Victims," July 12, 2012, Available at: www.npr.org/blogs/thetwo-way/2012/07/12/156654260/was-there-a-coverup-report-on-penn-state-scandal-may-tell-us.

4. Jeffrey Toobin, "Former Penn State President Graham Spanier Speaks," the *New Yorker* online, August 22, 2012, Available at: www.newyorker.com/online/blogs/newsdesk/2012/08/graham-spanier-interview-on-sandusky-scandal.html#ixzz2PQ326lkq.

5. Max H. Bazerman and Ann E. Trebrunsel, *Blind Spots: Why We Fail to Do What's Right and What to Do about It* (Princeton, NJ: Princeton University Press, 2011).

6. Steven M. Mintz, "Virtue Ethics and Accounting Education," *Issues in Accounting Education* 10, no. 2 (Fall 1995), p. 257.

7. Susan Pulliam and Deborah Solomon, "Ms. Cooper Says No to Her Boss," *The Wall Street Journal,* October 30, 2002, p. A1.

8. Lynne W. Jeter, *Disconnected: Deceit and Betrayal at WorldCom* (Hoboken, NJ: Wiley, 2003).

9. Securities Litigation Watch, *Betty Vinson Gets 5 Months in Prison,* Available at: http://slw.issproxy.com /securities_litigation_blo/2005/08/betty_vinson_ge.html.

10. Cynthia Cooper, *Extraordinary Circumstances* (Hoboken, NJ: Wiley, 2008).

11. Teaching Values, *The Golden Rule in World Religions,* Available at: www.teachingvalues.com/ goldenrule.html.

12. William J. Prior, *Virtue and Knowledge: An Introduction to Ancient Greek Ethics* (London: Routledge, 1991).

13. William H. Shaw and Vincent Barry, *Moral Issues in Business* (Belmont, CA: Wadsworth Cengage Learning, 2010), p. 5.

14. James C. Gaa and Linda Thorne, "An Introduction to the Special Issue on Professionalism and Ethics in Accounting Education," *Issues in Accounting Education* 1, no. 1 (February 2004), p. 1.

15. Joseph Fletcher, *Situation Ethics: The New Morality* (Louisville: KY: Westminster John Knox Press), 1966.

16. Josephson Institute of Ethics, *2012 Report Card on the Ethics of American Youth's Values and Actions,* Available at: http://charactercounts.org/programs/reportcard/2012/index.html.

17. Eric G. Lambert, Nancy Lynee Hogan, and Shannon M. Barton, "Collegiate Academic Dishonesty Revisited: What Have They Done, How Often Have They Done It, Who Does It, and Why Do They Do It?" *Electronic Journal of Sociology,* 2003, Available at: www.sociology.org/content/vol7.4 /lambert_etal.html.

18. Donald L. McCabe and Linda Klebe Treviño, "Individual and Contextual Influences on Academic Dishonesty: A Multicampus Investigation," *Research in Higher Education* 38, no. 3, 1997.

19. Paul Edwards, ed., *The Encyclopedia of Philosophy,* Vol. 3 (New York: Macmillan Company and Free Press, 1967).

20. Brenda Sheets and Paula Waddill, "E-Cheating Among College Business Students," *Information Technology, Learning, and Performance Journal,* Fall 2009, Volume 25, Issue 2, p. 4.

21. Emily E. LaBeff, Robert E. Clark, Valerie J. Haines, and George M. Diekhoff, "Situational Ethics and College Student Cheating," *Sociological Inquiry* 60, no. 2 (May 1990), pp. 190–197.

22. See, for example: Donald L. McCabe, Kenneth D. Butterfield, and Linda Klebe Treviño, "Academic Dishonesty in Graduate Business Programs: Prevalance, Causes, and Proposed Action," *Academy of Management Learning & Education* 5 (2006): 294–305.

23. See, for example, Kathy Lund Dean and Jeri Mullins Beggs, "University Professors and Teaching Ethics: Conceptualizations and Expectations," *Journal of Management Education* 30, no. 1 (2006), pp. 15–44.

24. McCabe, Butterfield, and Treviño.

25. Raef A. Lawson, "Is Classroom Cheating Related to Business Students' Propensity to Cheat in the 'Real World'?" *Journal of Business Ethics* 49, no. 2, (2004), pp. 189–199.

26. Randi L. Sims, "The Relationship between Academic Dishonesty and Unethical Business Practices," *Journal of Education for Business* 68, no. 12, (1993), pp. 37–50.

27. Ethics Resource Center, 2013 National Business Ethics Survey of Social Networkers, Available at: http://www.ethics.org/nbes/key-findings/social-networking/.

28. Ethics Resource Center, 2013 National Business Ethics Survey of Social Networkers, Available at: http://www.ethics.org/nbes/key-findings/social-networking/, pp. 8–10.

29. Geert Hofstede, *Culture's Consequences: International Differences in Work-Related Values* (London: Sage, 1980).

30. Geert Hofstede, *Culture's Consequences: Comparing Values, Behaviours, Institutions, and Organizations* (Thousand Oaks, CA: Sage, 2001), p. 359.

31. Michael Minkov, *What Makes Us Different and Similar: A New Interpretation of the World Values Survey and Other Cross-Cultural Data* (Sofia, Bulgaria: Klasika y Stil Publishing House, 2007).

32. The results are published on a Web site devoted to Hofstede's work: http://geert-hofstede.com /countries.html.

33. Aristotle, *Nicomachean Ethics,* trans. W. D. Ross (Oxford, UK: Oxford University Press, 1925).

34. Michael Josephson, *Making Ethical Decisions,* rev. ed. (Los Angeles: Josephson Institute of Ethics, 2002).

35. Alasdair MacIntyre, *After Virtue,* 2nd ed. (Notre Dame, IN: University of Notre Dame Press, 1984).

36. Josephson.

37. George Washington, *George Washington's Rules of Civility and Decent Behavior in Company and Conversation* (Bedford, ME: Applewood Books, 1994), p. 9.

38. Washington.

39. Cognitive Sciences Laboratory at Princeton University, *WordNet,* Available at: http://wordnet.princeton.edu.

40. Josephson.

41. Amy Anderson, "Profiles in Greatness - Eleanor Roosevelt," Success, December 1, 2008, http://www.success.com/article/profiles-in-greatness-eleanor-roosevelt.

42. Josephson.

43. Edmund L. Pincoffs, *Quandaries and Virtues against Reductivism in Ethics* (Lawrence: University Press of Kansas, 1986).

44. Josephson.

45. Josephson.

46. Michigan Technological University/Business, Universum Student Survey 2014, University Report/ US Edition, Available at: http://www.mtu.edu/career/employers/partner/2014/presentations/usss 2014 university report - ug - business - michigan technological university.pdf.

47. Rhonda Schwartz, Brian Ross, and Chris Francescani, "Edwards Admits Sexual Affair; Lied as Presidential Candidate" (Interview with "Nightline"), August 8, 2008.

48. Christine Porath and Christine Pearson, "The Price of Incivility," *Harvard Business Review,* January–February 2013, Available at: https://hbr.org/2013/01/the-price-of-incivility.

49. James R. Rest, *Moral Development: Advances in Research and Theory* (NY: Praeger, 1986).

50. Adam Smith, *An Inquiry into the Nature and Causes of the Wealth of Nations* (1776), eds. R. H. Campbell, A. S. Skinner, and W. B. Todd (Oxford: Oxford University Press, 1976).

51. Adam Smith, *The Theory of Moral Sentiments* (1759), eds. D. D. Raphael and A. L. Macfie (Oxford: Oxford University Press, 1976).

52. Samuel Fleischacker, "Adam Smith's Moral and Political Philosophy," *The Stanford Encyclopedia of Philosophy* (Spring 2013 Edition), ed. Edward N. Zalta, Available at: http://plato.stanford.edu/archives /spr2013/entries/smith-moral-political/.

53. O. C. Ferrell, John Fraedrich, and Linda Ferrell, *Business Ethics: Ethical Decision Making and Cases,* 9th ed. (Mason, OH: South-Western, Cengage Learning, 2011), p. 157.

54. Ferrell et al., p. 157.

55. Ferrell et al., p. 158.

56. Manuel Velasquez, Claire Andre, Thomas Shanks, and Michael J. Meyer, "Calculating Consequences: The Utilitarian Approach to Ethics," *Issues in Ethics* 2, no. 1 (Winter 1989), Available at: www.scu.edu/ethics.

57. Velasquez et al., 1989.

58. Velasquez et al., 1989.

59. Velasquez et al., 1989

60. Velasquez et al., 1989.

61. Ferrell et al., pp. 160–161.

62. Claire Andre and Manuel Velasquez, "Rights Stuff," Markkula Center for Applied Ethics' *Issues in Ethics* 3, no. 1 (Winter 1990), Available at: www.scu.edu/ethics/publications/iie/v3n1/.

63. Velasquez et al., 1990.

64. Immanuel Kant, *Foundations of Metaphysics of Morals,* trans. Lewis White Beck (New York: Liberal Arts Press, 1959), p. 39.

65. Velasquez et al., 1990.

66. Velasquez, et al. 1990.

67. William Styron, *Sophie's Choice* (London: Chelsea House, 2001).

68. Manuel Velasquez, Claire Andre, Thomas Shanks, and Michael J. Meyer, "Justice and Fairness," *Issues in Ethics* 3, no. 2 (Spring 1990).

69. Ferrell et al., p. 165.

70. MacIntyre, pp. 187–190.

71. MacIntyre, pp. 190–192.

72. Mintz, 1995.

73. Mintz, 1995.

74. Martin Stuebs and Brett Wilkinson, "Restoring the Profession's Public Interest Role," *The CPA Journal* 79, no. 11, (2009) pp. 62–66.

75. James E. Copeland, Jr., "Ethics as an Imperative," *Accounting Horizons* 19, no. 1 (2005), pp. 35–43.

76. International Federation of Accountants (IFAC), *IFAC Policy Position Statement 1,* September 2011, Available at: http://www.ifac.org/system/files/publications/files/PPP1-Regulation-of-the-Accountancy-Profession.pdf.

77. American Institute of Certified Public Accountants, *Code of Professional Conduct* at June 1, 2012 (New York: AICPA, 2012); Available at: www.aicpa.org/Research/Standards/CodeofConduct/Pages/default.aspx.

78. Kurt Baier, *The Rational and Moral Order: The Social Roots of Reason and Morality* (Oxford, U.K.: Oxford University Press, 1994).

79. Steven M. Mintz, "Virtue Ethics and Accounting Education," *Issues in Accounting Education* 10, no. 2 (1995), p. 260.

80. IMA—The Association of Accountants and Financial Professionals in Business, *IMA Statement of Ethical Professional Practice*, Available at: www.imanet.org/pdfs/statement%20of%20Ethics_web.pdf.

81. Ralph Waldo Emerson, *Essays: First and Second Series* (New York: Vintage Paperback, 1990).

82. See: www.espn.go.com/mlb/story/_/id/8828339/no-players-elected-baseball-hall-fame-writers.

83. Ethics Resource Center, Generational Differences in Workplace Ethics: A Supplemental Report of the 2011 National Business Ethics Survey, Available at: http://www.ethics.org/files/u5/2011 GenDiffFinal_0.pdf.

Chapter 1 Cases

Case 1-1 Harvard Cheating Scandal

Yes. Cheating occurs at the prestigious Harvard University. In 2012, Harvard forced dozens of students to leave in its largest cheating scandal in memory, but the institution would not address assertions that the blame rested partly with a professor and his teaching assistants. The issue is whether cheating is truly cheating when students collaborate with each other to find the right answer—in a take-home final exam.

Harvard released the results of its investigation into the controversy, in which 125 undergraduates were alleged to have cheated on an exam in May 2012.[1] The university said that more than half of the students were forced to withdraw, a penalty that typically lasts from two to four semesters. Many returned by 2015. Of the remaining cases, about half were put on disciplinary probation—a strong warning that becomes part of a student's official record. The rest of the students avoided punishment.

In previous years, students thought of Government 1310 as an easy class with optional attendance and frequent collaboration. But students who took it in spring 2012 said that it had suddenly become quite difficult, with tests that were hard to comprehend, so they sought help from the graduate teaching assistants who ran the class discussion groups, graded assignments, and advised them on interpreting exam questions.

Administrators said that on final-exam questions, some students supplied identical answers (right down to typographical errors in some cases), indicating that they had written them together or plagiarized them. But some students claimed that the similarities in their answers were due to sharing notes or sitting in on sessions with the same teaching assistants. The instructions on the take-home exam explicitly prohibited collaboration, but many students said they did not think that included talking with teaching assistants.

The first page of the exam contained these instructions: "The exam is completely open book, open note, open Internet, etc. However, in all other regards, this should fall under similar guidelines that apply to in-class exams. More specifically, students may not discuss the exam with others—this includes resident tutors, writing centers, etc."

Students complained about confusing questions on the final exam. Due to "some good questions" from students, the instructor clarified three exam questions by e-mail before the due date of the exams.

Students claim to have believed that collaboration was allowed in the course. The course's instructor and the teaching assistants sometimes encouraged collaboration, in fact. The teaching assistants—graduate students who graded the exams and ran weekly discussion sessions—varied widely in how they prepared students for the exams, so it was common for students in different sections to share lecture notes and reading materials. During the final exam, some teaching assistants even worked with students to define unfamiliar terms and help them figure out exactly what certain test questions were asking.

Some have questioned whether it is the test's design, rather than the students' conduct, that should be criticized. Others place the blame on the teaching assistants who opened the door to collaboration outside of class by their own behavior in helping students to understand the questions better.

An interesting part of the scandal is that, in March 2013, administrators searched e-mail accounts of some junior faculty members, looking for the source of leaks to the news media about the cheating investigation, prompting much of the faculty to protest what it called a breach of trust.

Harvard adopted an honor code on May 6, 2014. The goal is to establish a culture of academic integrity at the university.

---

[1] The facts of this case are taken from Richard Perez-Peña," Students Disciplined in Harvard Scandal," February 1, 2013, Available at www.nytimes.com/2013/02/02/education/harvard-forced-dozens-to-leave-in-cheating-scandal.html?_r=0.

Answer the following questions about the Harvard cheating scandal.

1. Using Josephson's Six Pillars of Character, which of the character traits (virtues) apply to the Harvard cheating scandal and how do they apply with respect to the actions of each of the stakeholders in this case?

2. Who is at fault for the cheating scandal? Is it the students, the teaching assistants, the professor, or the institution? Use ethical reasoning to support your answer.

3. Do you think Harvard had a right to search the e-mail accounts of junior faculty, looking for the source of leaks to the news media? Explain.

4. What is meant by the culture of an organization? Can an honor code establish a culture of academic integrity in an institution such as Harvard University?

Case 1-2 Giles and Regas

Ed Giles and Susan Regas have never been happier than during the past four months since they have been seeing each other. Giles is a 35-year-old CPA and a partner in the medium-sized accounting firm of Saduga & Mihca. Regas is a 25-year-old senior accountant in the same firm. Although it is acceptable for peers to date, the firm does not permit two members of different ranks within the firm to do so. A partner should not date a senior in the firm any more than a senior should date a junior staff accountant. If such dating eventually leads to marriage, then one of the two must resign because of the conflicts of interest. Both Giles and Regas know the firm's policy on dating, and they have tried to be discreet about their relationship because they don't want to raise any suspicions.

While most of the staff seem to know about Giles and Regas, it is not common knowledge among the partners that the two of them are dating. Perhaps that is why Regas was assigned to work on the audit of CAA Industries for a second year, even though Giles is the supervising partner on the engagement.

As the audit progresses, it becomes clear to the junior staff members that Giles and Regas are spending personal time together during the workday. On one occasion, they were observed leaving for lunch together. Regas did not return to the client's office until three hours later. On another occasion, Regas seemed distracted from her work, and later that day, she received a dozen roses from Giles. A friend of Regas's who knew about the relationship, Ruth Revilo, became concerned when she happened to see the flowers and a card that accompanied them. The card was signed, "Love, Poochie." Regas had once told Revilo that it was the nickname that Regas gave to Giles.

Revilo pulls Regas aside at the end of the day and says, "We have to talk."

"What is it?" Regas asks.

"I know the flowers are from Giles," Revilo says. "Are you crazy?"

"It's none of your business," Regas responds.

Revilo goes on to explain that others on the audit engagement team are aware of the relationship between the two. Revilo cautions Regas about jeopardizing her future with the firm by getting involved in a serious dating relationship with someone of a higher rank. Regas does not respond to this comment. Instead, she admits to being distracted lately because of an argument that she had with Giles. It all started when Regas had suggested to Giles that it might be best if they did not go out during the workweek because she was having a hard time getting to work on time. Giles was upset at the suggestion and called her ungrateful. He said, "I've put everything on the line for you. There's no turning back for me." She points out to Revilo that the flowers are Giles's way of saying he is sorry for some of the comments he had made about her.

Regas promises to talk to Giles and thanks Revilo for her concern. That same day, Regas telephones Giles and tells him she wants to put aside her personal relationship with him until the CAA audit is complete in two weeks. She suggests that, at the end of the two-week period, they get together and thoroughly examine the possible implications of their continued relationship. Giles reluctantly agrees, but he conditions his acceptance on having a "farewell" dinner at their favorite restaurant. Regas agrees to the dinner.

Giles and Regas have dinner that Saturday night. As luck would have it, the controller of CAA Industries, Mark Sax, is at the restaurant with his wife. Sax is startled when he sees Giles and Regas together. He wonders about the possible seriousness of their relationship, while reflecting on the recent progress billings of the accounting firm. Sax believes that the number of hours billed is out of line with work of a similar nature and the fee estimate. He had planned to discuss the matter with Herb Morris, the managing partner of the firm. He decides to call Morris on Monday morning.

"Herb, you son of a gun, it's Mark Sax."

"Mark. How goes the audit?"

"That's why I'm calling," Sax responds. "Can we meet to discuss a few items?"

"Sure," Morris replies. "Just name the time and place."

"How about first thing tomorrow morning?" asks Sax.

"I'll be in your office at 8:00 a.m.," says Morris.

"Better make it at 7:00 a.m., Herb, before your auditors arrive."

Sax and Morris meet to discuss Sax's concerns about seeing Giles and Regas at the restaurant and the possibility that their relationship is negatively affecting audit efficiency. Morris asks whether any other incidents have occurred to make him suspicious about the billings. Sax says that he is only aware of this one instance, although he sensed some apprehension on the part of Regas last week when they discussed why it was taking so long to get the audit recommendations for adjusting entries. Morris listens attentively until Sax finishes and then asks him to be patient while he sets up a meeting to discuss the situation with Giles. Morris promises to get back to Sax by the end of the week.

Questions

1. Analyze the behavior of each party from the perspective of the Six Pillars of Character. Assess the personal responsibility of Ed Giles and Susan Regas for the relationship that developed between them. Who do you think is mostly to blame?
2. If Giles were a person of integrity but just happened to have a "weak moment" in starting a relationship with Regas, what do you think he will say when he meets with Herb Morris? Why?
3. Assume that Ed Giles is the biggest "rainmaker" in the firm. What would you do if you were in Herb Morris's position when you meet with Giles? In your response, consider how you would resolve the situation in regard to both the completion of the CAA Industries audit and the longer-term issue of the continued employment of Giles and Regas in the accounting firm.

Case 1-3 NYC Subway Death: Bystander Effect or Moral Blindness

On December 3, 2012, a terrible incident occurred in the New York City subway when Ki-Suck Han was pushed off a subway platform by Naeem Davis. Han was hit and killed by the train, while observers did nothing other than snap photos on their cell phones as Han was struggling to climb back onto the platform before the oncoming train struck him. Davis was arraigned on a second-degree murder charge and held without bail in the death of Han.

One of the most controversial aspects of this story is that of R. Umar Abbasi, a freelance photographer for the *New York Post,* who was waiting for a train when he said he saw a man approach Han at the Times Square station, get into an altercation with him, and push him into the train's path. He too chose to take pictures of the incident, and the next day, the *Post* published the photographer's handiwork: a photo of Han with his head turned toward the approaching train, his arms reaching up but unable to climb off the tracks in time.

Abbasi told NBC's "Today" show that he was trying to alert the motorman to what was going on by flashing his camera. He said he was shocked that people nearer to the victim didn't try to help in the 22 seconds before the train struck. "It took me a second to figure out what was happening . . . I saw the lights in the distance. My mind was to alert the train," Abbasi said. "The people who were standing close to him . . . they could have moved and grabbed him and pulled him up. No one made an effort."

In a written account Abbasi gave the *Post,* he said that the crowd took videos and snapped photos on their cell phones after Han's mangled body was pulled onto the platform. He said that he shoved the onlookers back while a doctor and another man tried to resuscitate the victim, but Han died in front of them.

Some have attributed the lack of any attempt by those on the subway platform to get involved and go to Han's aid as the bystander effect. The term *bystander effect* refers to the phenomenon in which the greater the number of people present, the less likely people will be to help a person in distress. When an emergency situation occurs, observers are more likely to take action if there are few or no other witnesses. One explanation for the bystander effect is that each individual thinks that others will come to the aid of the threatened person. But when you are alone, either you will help, or no one will.

Questions

1. Do you think the bystander effect was at work in the subway death incident? What role might situational ethics have played in Abbasi's response? How might the bystander effect translate to a situation where members of a work group observe financial improprieties committed by one of their group that threatens the organization? In general, do you think that someone would come forward?

2. Another explanation for the inaction in the subway incident is a kind of *moral blindness,* where a person fails to perceive the existence of moral issues in a particular situation. Do you believe moral blindness existed in the incident? Be sure to address the specific moral issues that give rise to your answer.

3. What would you have done if you were in Abbasi's place and why?

Case 1-4 Lone Star School District

Jose and Emily work as auditors for the state of Texas. They have been assigned to the audit of the Lone Star School District. There have been some problems with audit documentation for the travel and entertainment reimbursement claims of the manager of the school district. The manager knows about the concerns of Jose and Emily, and he approaches them about the matter. The following conversation takes place:

Manager: Listen, I've requested the documentation you asked for, but the hotel says it's no longer in its system.

Jose: Don't you have the credit card receipt or credit card statement?

Manager: I paid cash.

Jose: What about a copy of the hotel bill?

Manager: I threw it out.

Emily: That's a problem. We have to document all your travel and entertainment expenses for the city manager's office.

Manager: Well, I can't produce documents that the hotel can't find. What do you want me to do?

Questions

1. Assume that Jose and Emily are CPAs and members of the AICPA. What ethical standards in the Code of Professional Conduct should guide them in dealing with the manager's inability to support travel and entertainment expenses?

2. Using Josephson's Six Pillars of Character as a guide, evaluate the statements and behavior of the manager.

3. a. Assume that Jose and Emily report to Sharon, the manager of the school district audit. Should they inform Sharon of their concerns? Why or why not?

   b. Assume that they don't inform Sharon, but she finds out from another source. What would you do if you were in Sharon's position?

Case 1-5 Reneging on a Promise

Part A

Billy Tushoes recently received an offer to join the accounting firm of Tick and Check LLP. Billy would prefer to work for Foot and Balance LLP but has not received an offer from the firm the day before he must decide whether to accept the position at Tick and Check. Billy has a friend at Foot and Balance and is thinking about calling her to see if she can find out whether an offer is forthcoming.

Question

1. Should Billy call his friend? Provide reasons why you think he should or should not. Is there any other action you suggest Billy take prior to deciding on the offer of Tick and Check? Why do you recommend that action?

Part B

Assume that Billy calls his friend at Foot and Balance and she explains the delay is due to the recent merger of Vouch and Trace LLP with Foot and Balance. She tells Billy that the offer should be forthcoming. However, Billy gets nervous about the situation and decides to accept the offer of Tick and Check. A week later, he receives a phone call from the partner at Foot and Balance who had promised to contact him about the firm's offer. Billy is offered a position at Foot and Balance at the same salary as Tick and Check. He has one week to decide whether to accept that offer. Billy is not sure what to do. On one hand, he knows it's wrong to accept an offer and then renege on it. On the other hand, Billy hasn't signed a contract with Tick and Check, and the offer with Foot and Balance is his clear preference because he has many friends at that firm.

Questions

1. Identify the stakeholders in this case. Evaluate the alternative courses of action for Billy using ethical reasoning. What should Billy do? Why?
2. Do you think it is ever right to back out of a promise that you gave to someone else? If so, under what circumstances? If not, why not?

Case 1-6 Capitalization versus Expensing

Gloria Hernandez is the controller of a public company. She just completed a meeting with her superior, John Harrison, who is the CFO of the company. Harrison tried to convince Hernandez to go along with his proposal to combine 12 expenditures for repair and maintenance of a plant asset into one amount ($1 million). Each of the expenditures is less than $100,000, the cutoff point for capitalizing expenditures as an asset and depreciating it over the useful life. Hernandez asked for time to think about the matter. As the controller and chief accounting officer of the company, Hernandez knows it's her responsibility to decide how to record the expenditures. She knows that the $1 million amount is material to earnings and the rules in accounting require expensing of each individual item, not capitalization. However, she is under a great deal of pressure to go along with capitalization to boost earnings and meet financial analysts' earnings expectations, and provide for a bonus to top management including herself. Her job may be at stake, and she doesn't want to disappoint her boss.

Questions

Assume both Hernandez and Harrison hold the CPA and CMA designations.

1. What are the loyalty obligations of both parties in this case?
2. Assume that you were in Gloria Hernandez's position. What would motivate you to speak up and act or to stay silent? Would it make a difference if Harrison promised this was a one-time request?
3. What would you do and why?

Case 1-7 Eating Time

Kevin Lowe is depressed. He has been with the CPA firm Stooges LLP for only three months. Yet the partners in charge of the firm—Bo Chambers and his brother, Moe—have asked for a "sit-down." Here's how it goes:

"Kevin, we asked to see you because your time reports indicate that it takes you 50 percent longer to complete audit work than your predecessor," Moe said.

"Well, I am new and still learning on the job," replied Lowe.

"That's true," Bo responded, "but you have to appreciate that we have fixed budgets for these audits. Every hour over the budgeted time costs us money. While we can handle it in the short run, we will have to bill the clients whose audit you work on a larger fee in the future. We don't want to lose clients as a result."

"Are you asking me to cut down on the work I do?" Lowe asked.

"We would never compromise the quality of our audit work," Moe said. "We're trying to figure out why it takes you so much longer than other staff members."

At this point, Lowe started to perspire. He wiped his forehead, took a glass of water, and asked, "Would it be better if I took some of the work home at night and on weekends, completed it, but didn't charge the firm or the client for my time?"

Bo and Moe were surprised by Kevin's openness. On one hand, they valued that trait in their employees. On the other hand, they couldn't answer with a yes. Moe looked at Bo, and then turned to Kevin and said, "It's up to you to decide how to increase your productivity on audits. As you know, this is an important element of performance evaluation."

Kevin cringed. Was the handwriting on the wall in terms of his future with the firm?

"I understand what you're saying," Kevin said. "I will do better in the future—I promise."

"Good," responded Bo and Moe. "Let's meet 30 days from now and we'll discuss your progress on the matters we've discussed today and your future with the firm."

In an effort to deal with the problem, Kevin contacts Joyce, a friend and fellow employee, and asks if she has faced similar problems. Joyce answers "yes" and goes on to explain she handles it by "ghost-ticking." Kevin asks her to explain. "Ghost-ticking is when we document audit procedures that have not been completed." Kevin, dumbfounded, wonders, what kind of a firm am I working for?

Questions

1. Kevin is not a CPA yet. What are his ethical obligations in this case?
2. Given the facts in the case, evaluate using deontological and teleological reasoning whether Kevin should take work home and not charge it to the job. What about engaging in ghost-ticking?
3. What would you do if you were Kevin and why? How would you explain your position to Bo and Moe when you meet in 30 days?

Case 1-8 Shifty Industries

Shifty Industries is a small business that sells home beauty products in the San Luis Obispo, California, area. The company has experienced a cash crunch and is unable to pay its bills on a timely basis. A great deal of pressure exists to minimize cash outflows such as income tax payments to the Internal Revenue Service (IRS) by interpreting income tax regulations as liberally as possible.

You are the tax accountant and a CPA working at the company and you report to the tax manager. He reports to the controller. You are concerned about the fact that your supervisor has asked you to go along with an improper treatment of section 179 depreciation on the 2015 tax return so you can deduct the $100,000 full cost of eligible equipment against taxable income. The problem as you see it is the 2014 limitation of $500,000, which would have been fine for 2015 had Congress extended it, was rolled back to a maximum of $25,000. Therefore, your supervisor is planning to allow Shifty to deduct $75,000 more than allowed by law. Using a 35 percent tax rate it means the company is "increasing" its cash flow by $26,250.

Answer the following questions to prepare for a meeting you will have tomorrow morning with the tax manager.

Questions

1. What values are most important to you in deciding on a course of action? Why?

2. Who are the stakeholders in this case and how might they be affected by your course of action?

3. What would you do and why, assuming your approach will be based on the application of the ethical reasoning methods discussed in the chapter?

Case 1-9 Cleveland Custom Cabinets

Cleveland Custom Cabinets is a specialty cabinet manufacturer for high-end homes in the Cleveland Heights and Shaker Heights areas. The company manufactures cabinets built to the specifications of homeowners and employs 125 custom cabinetmakers and installers. There are 30 administrative and sales staff members working for the company.

James Leroy owns Cleveland Custom Cabinets. His accounting manager is Marcus Sims, who reports to the director of finance. Sims manages 15 accountants. The staff is responsible for keeping track of manufacturing costs by job and preparing internal and external financial reports. The internal reports are used by management for decision making. The external reports are used to support bank loan applications.

The company applies overhead to jobs based on direct labor hours. For 2016, it estimated total overhead to be $4.8 million and 80,000 direct labor hours. The cost of direct materials used during the first quarter of the year is $600,000, and direct labor cost is $400,000 (based on 20,000 hours worked). The company's accounting system is old and does not provide actual overhead information until about four weeks after the close of a quarter. As a result, the applied overhead amount is used for quarterly reports.

On April 10, 2016, Leroy came into Sims's office to pick up the quarterly report. He looked at it aghast. Leroy had planned to take the statements to the bank the next day and meet with the vice president to discuss a $1 million working capital loan. He knew the bank would be reluctant to grant the loan based on the income numbers in Exhibit 1. Without the money, Cleveland could have problems financing everyday operations.

EXHIBIT 1 Cleveland Custom Cabinets

Net Income for the Quarter Ended March 31, 2016	
Sales	$6,400,000
Cost of goods sold	4,800,000
Gross margin	$1,600,000
Selling and administrative expenses	1,510,000
Net income	$ 90,000

Leroy asked Sims to explain how net income could have gone from 14.2 percent of sales for the year ended December 31, 2015, to 1.4 percent for March 31, 2016. Sims pointed out that the estimated overhead cost had doubled for 2016 compared to the actual cost for 2015. He explained to Leroy that rent had doubled and the cost of utilities skyrocketed. In addition, the custom-making machinery was wearing out more rapidly, so the company's repair and maintenance costs also doubled from 2015.

Leroy wouldn't accept Sims's explanation. Instead, he told Sims that the quarterly income had to be at least the same percentage of sales as at December 31, 2015. Sims looked confused and reminded Leroy that the external auditors would wrap up their audit on April 30. Leroy told Sims not to worry about the auditors. He would take care of them. Furthermore, "as the sole owner of the company, there is no reason not to 'tweak' the numbers on a one-time basis. I own the board of directors, so no worries there." He went on to say, "Do it this one time and I won't ask you to do it again." He then reminded Sims of his obligation to remain loyal to the company and its interests. Sims started to soften and asked Leroy just how he expected the tweaking to happen. Leroy flinched, held up his hands, and said, "I'll leave the creative accounting to you."

Questions

1. Do you agree with Leroy's statement that it doesn't matter what the numbers look like because he is the sole owner? Even if it is true that Sims "owns" the board of directors, what should be their role in this matter? What about the external auditors? Should Sims simply accept Leroy's statement that he would handle them?

2. a. Assume that Sims is a CPA and holds the CMA. Put yourself in Sims's position. What are your ethical considerations in deciding whether to tweak the numbers?

    b. Assume you do a utilitarian analysis to help decide what to do. Evaluate the harms and benefits of alternative courses of action. What would you do? Would your analysis change if you use a rights theory approach?

3. Think about how you would actually implement your chosen action. What barriers could you face? How would you overcome them? Is it worth jeopardizing your job in this case? Why or why not?

Case 1-10 Better Boston Beans

Better Boston Beans is a coffee shop located in the Faneuil Hall Marketplace near the waterfront and Government Center in Boston. It specializes in exotic blends of coffee, including Sumatra Dark Roast Black, India Mysore "Gold Nuggets," and Guatemala Antigua. It also serves a number of blended coffees, including Reggae Blend, Jamaican Blue Mountain Blend, and Marrakesh Blend. For those with more pedestrian tastes, the shop serves French Vanilla, Hazelnut, and Hawaiian Macadamia Nut varieties. The coffee of the day varies, but the most popular is Colombia Supremo. The coffee shop also serves a variety of cold-blended coffees.

Cyndie Rosen has worked for Better Boston Beans for six months. She took the job right out of college because she wasn't sure whether she wanted to go to graduate school before beginning a career in financial services. Cyndie hoped that by taking a year off before starting her career or going on to graduate school, she would experience "the real world" and find out firsthand what it is like to work a 40-hour week. (She did not have a full-time job during her college years because her parents paid for the tuition and books.)

Because Cyndie is the "new kid on the block," she is often asked to work the late shift, from 4 p.m. to midnight. She works with one other person, Jeffrey Levy, who is the assistant shift supervisor. Jeffrey has been with Boston Beans for three years but recently was demoted from shift supervisor. Jeffrey reports to Sarah Hoffman, the new shift supervisor. Sarah reports to David Cohen, the owner of the store.

For the past two weeks, Jeffrey has been leaving before 11 p.m., after most of the stores in the Marketplace close, and he has asked Cyndie to close up by herself. Cyndie feels that this is wrong and it is starting to concern her, but she hasn't spoken to Jeffrey or anyone else. Basically, she is afraid to lose her job. Her parents have told her that financially she is on her own. They were disappointed that Cyndie did not go to graduate school or interview for a professional position after graduating from college.

Something happened that is stressing Cyndie out and she doesn't know what to do about it. At 11 p.m. one night, 10 Japanese tourists came into the store for coffee. Cyndie was alone and had to rush around and make five different cold-blended drinks and five different hot-blended coffees. While she was working, one of the Japanese tourists, who spoke English very well, approached her and said that he was shocked that such a famous American coffee shop would only have one worker in the store at any time during the workday. Cyndie didn't want to ignore the man's comments, so she answered that her coworker had to go home early because he was sick. That seemed to satisfy the tourist.

It took Cyndie almost 20 minutes to make all the drinks and also field two phone calls that came in during that time. After she closed for the night, she reflected on the experience. Cyndie realized that it could get worse before it gets better because Jeffrey was now making it a habit to leave work early.

At this point, Cyndie realizes that she either has to approach Jeffrey about her concerns or speak to Sarah. She feels much more comfortable talking to Sarah because, in Cyndie's own words, "Levy gives me the creeps."

Questions

1. Do you think it was right for Cyndie to tell the Japanese tourist that "her coworker had to go home early because he was sick?"

2. Cyndie decided to speak with Jeffrey. From an ethical perspective, do you think Cyndie made the right decision as opposed to speaking directly with either Sarah Hoffman or David Cohen? Would you have done the same thing? Why or why not?

3. During their discussion, Jeffrey tells Cyndie that he has an alcohol problem. Lately, it's gotten to him really bad. That's why he's left early—to get a drink and calm his nerves. Jeffrey also explains that this is the real reason he was demoted. He had been warned that if one more incident occurred, David would fire him. He pleaded with Cyndie to work with him through these hard times. How would you react to Jeffrey's request if you were Cyndie? Would your answer change if Jeffrey was a close personal friend instead of someone who gave you the creeps? Why or why not?

4. Assume that Cyndie keeps quiet. The following week, another incident occurs. Cyndie gets into a shouting match with a customer who became tired of waiting for his coffee after 10 minutes. Cyndie felt terrible about it, apologized to the customer after serving his coffee, and left work that night wondering if it was time to apply to graduate school. The customer was so irate that he contacted David and expressed his displeasure about both the service and Cyndie's attitude. David asks to meet with Jeffrey, Sarah, and Cyndie the next day. What are Cyndie's ethical responsibilities at this point?

Chapter 2

Cognitive Processes and Ethical Decision Making in Accounting

Learning Objectives

After studying Chapter 2, you should be able to:

LO 2-1 Describe Kohlberg's stages of moral development.

LO 2-2 Explain the components of Rest's model and how it influences ethical decision making.

LO 2-3 Describe the link between moral intensity and ethical decision making.

LO 2-4 Explain how moral reasoning and virtue influence ethical decision making.

LO 2-5 Apply the steps in the Integrated Ethical Decision-Making Model to a case study.

LO 2-6 Analyze the thought process involved in making decisions and taking ethical action.

LO 2-7 Describe the "Giving Voice to Values" technique and apply it to a case study.

Ethics Reflection

Arthur Andersen and Enron

One event more than any other that demonstrates the failure of professional judgment and ethical reasoning in the period of accounting frauds of the late 1990s and early 2000s is the relationship between Enron and its auditors, Arthur Andersen. Bazerman and Tenbrunsel characterize it as *motivated blindness,* a term that describes the common failure of people to notice others' unethical behavior when seeing that behavior would harm the observer.[1] In 2000, Enron paid Andersen a total of $52 million: $25 million in audit fees and $27 million for consulting services. This amount was enough to make Enron Andersen's second largest account and the largest client in the Houston office. Andersen's judgment was compromised by this relationship and led to moral blindness with respect to Enron's accounting for so-called special-purpose entities (SPEs)—entities set up by the firm and kept off the balance sheet. When Enron declared bankruptcy, there was $13.1 billion in debt on the company's books, $18.1 billion on its nonconsolidated subsidiaries' books, and an estimated $20 billion more off the balance sheets.[2] Barbara Toffler pinpoints Andersen's failures in *Final Accounting,* her book about the rise and fall of Andersen,[3] noting that *The Powers Report* denounced Andersen for failing to fulfill its professional and ethical obligations in connection with its auditing of Enron's financial statements, as well as to bring to the attention of Enron's board of directors concerns about Enron's internal controls over these related-party transactions.

The possibility of an accounting fraud at Enron was first raised in an article by two *Fortune* magazine reporters, Bethany McLean and Peter Elkind, who in 2004 wrote a book that became the basis for a movie of the same name, titled *The Smartest Guys in the Room,*[4] in which they criticized Andersen for failing to use the professional skepticism that requires that an auditor approach the audit with a questioning mind and a critical assessment of audit evidence.

Andersen's ethics were called into question shortly after Enron disclosed that a large portion of the 1997 earnings restatement consisted of adjustments that the auditors had proposed at the end of the 1997 audit but had allowed to go uncorrected. Congressional investigators wanted to know why Andersen tolerated $51 million of known misstatements during a year when Enron reported only $105 million of earnings. Andersen chief executive officer (CEO) Joseph Berardino explained that Enron's 1997 earnings were artificially low due to several hundred million dollars of nonrecurring expenses and write-offs. The proposed adjustments were not material, Berardino testified, because they represented less than 8 percent of "normalized" earnings.[5]

The Enron-Andersen relationship illustrates how a CPA firm can lose sight of its professional obligations. While examining Enron's financial statements, the auditors at Andersen knew that diligent application of strict auditing standards required one decision, but that the consequences for the firm were harmful to its own business interests. It placed the client's interests ahead of its own and the public interest.

Some Andersen auditors paid a steep price for their ethical failings: Their licenses to practice as CPAs in Texas were revoked. David Duncan was charged with failing to exercise due care and professional skepticism in failing to conduct an audit in accordance with generally accepted auditing standards (GAAS) and acting recklessly in issuing unqualified opinions on the 1998–2000 audits, thus violating Section 10(b) of the Securities and Exchange Act.[6]

In this chapter, we explore the process of ethical decision making and how it influences professional judgment. Ethical decision making relies on the ability to make moral judgments using the reasoning methods discussed in Chapter 1. However, the ability to reason ethically does not ensure that ethical action will be taken. The decision maker must follow up ethical intent with ethical action. That may be more difficult than it sounds because the accountant may encounter resistance from those who have a vested interest in the outcome and provide reasons and rationalizations for deviating from sound ethical decisions in a particular instance. In such cases, the decision maker needs to find a way to give "voice" to values -- express one's beliefs and act on them. Think about the following questions as you read this chapter: (1) What are the cognitive processes that guide ethical decision making? (2) What would you do if your attitudes and beliefs conflict with your intended behavior? (3) If you encounter resistance to ethical action, ask yourself: Who can I speak to, what can I say, and what actions can I take to act in accordance with my values?

As we practice resolving dilemmas we find ethics to be less a goal than a pathway, less a destination than a trip, less an inoculation than a process.

Ethicist Rushworth Kidder (1944–2012)

Kidder believed that self-reflection was the key to resolving ethical dilemmas, and a conscious sense of vision and deep core of ethical values provide the courage to stand up to the tough choices.

Kohlberg and the Cognitive Development Approach

LO 2-1
Describe Kohlberg's stages of moral development.

Cognitive development refers to the thought process followed in one's moral development. An individual's ability to make reasoned judgments about moral matters develops in stages. The psychologist Lawrence Kohlberg concluded, on the basis of 20 years of research, that people develop from childhood to adulthood through a sequential and hierarchical series of cognitive stages that characterize the way they think about ethical dilemmas. Moral reasoning processes become more complex and sophisticated with development. Higher stages rely upon cognitive operations that are not available to individuals at lower stages, and higher stages are thought to be "morally better" because they are consistent with philosophical theories of justice and rights.[7] Kohlberg's views on ethical development are helpful in understanding how individuals may internalize moral standards and, as they become more sophisticated in their use, apply them more critically to resolve ethical conflicts.

Kohlberg developed his theory by using data from studies on how decisions are made by individuals. The example of Heinz and the Drug, given here, illustrates a moral dilemma used by Kohlberg to develop his stage-sequence model.

Heinz and the Drug

In Europe, a woman was near death from a rare type of cancer. There was one drug that the doctors thought might save her. It was a form of radium that a druggist in the same town had recently discovered. The drug was expensive to make, but the druggist was charging 10 times what the drug cost him to make: It cost $200 for the radium, and he charged $2,000 for a small dose of the drug. The sick woman's husband, Heinz, went to everyone he knew to borrow the money, but he could get together only about $1,000—half the cost. He told the druggist that his wife was dying and asked him to sell it cheaper or let him pay later. But the druggist said, "No, I discovered the drug and I'm going to make money from it." Heinz got desperate and broke into the man's store to steal the drug for his wife.

Should the husband have done that? Was it right or wrong? Most people say that Heinz's theft was morally justified, but Kohlberg was less concerned about whether they approved or disapproved than with the reasons they gave for their answers. Kohlberg monitored the reasons for judgments given by a group of 75 boys ranging in age from 10 to 16 years and isolated the six stages of moral thought. The boys progressed in reasoning sequentially, with most never reaching the highest stages. He concluded that the universal principle of justice is the highest claim of morality. Kohlberg's justice orientation has been criticized by Carol Gilligan, a noted psychologist and educator.[8] Gilligan claims that because the stages were derived exclusively from interviews with boys, the stages reflect a decidedly male orientation and they ignore the care-and-response orientation that characterizes female moral judgment. For males, advanced moral thought revolves around rules, rights, and abstract principles. The ideal is formal justice, in which all parties evaluate one another's claims in an impartial manner. But this conception of morality, Gilligan argues, fails to capture the distinctly female voice on moral matters. Gilligan believes that women need more information before answering the question: Should Heinz steal the drug? Females look for ways of resolving the dilemma where no one—Heinz, his wife, or the druggist—will experience pain. Gilligan sees the hesitation to judge as a laudable quest for nonviolence, an aversion to cruel situations where someone will get hurt. However, much about her theories has been challenged in the literature. For example, Kohlberg considered it a sign of ethical relativism, a waffling that results from trying to please everyone (Stage 3). Moreover, Gilligan's beliefs seem to imply that men lack a caring response when compared to females. Rest argues that Gilligan has exaggerated the extent of the sex differences found on Kohlberg's scale.[9]

The dilemma of Heinz illustrates the challenge of evaluating the ethics of a decision. Table 2.1 displays three types of responses.[10]

TABLE 2.1	Three Sample Responses to the Heinz Dilemma
A:	It really depends on how much Heinz likes his wife and how much risk there is in taking the drug. If he can get the drug in no other way and if he really likes his wife, he'll have to steal it.
B:	I think that a husband would care so much for his wife that he couldn't just sit around and let her die. He wouldn't be stealing for his own profit; he'd be doing it to help someone he loves.
C:	Regardless of his personal feelings, Heinz has to realize that the druggist is protected by the law. Since no one is above the law, Heinz shouldn't steal it. If we allowed Heinz to steal, then all society would be in danger of anarchy.

Kohlberg considered how the responses were different and what problem-solving strategies underlie the three responses. Response A (Preconventional) presents a rather uncomplicated approach to moral problems. Choices are made based on the wants of the individual decision maker (egoism). Response B (Conventional) also considers the wife's needs. Here, Heinz is concerned that his actions should be motivated by good intentions (i.e., the ends justify the means). In Response C (Postconventional), a societywide perspective is used in decision making. Law is the key in making moral decisions[11] (for example, rule utilitarianism; justice orientation).

The examples in Table 2.2 demonstrate the application of Kohlberg's model of cognitive development to possible decision making in business.

TABLE 2.2 Kohlberg's Stages of Moral Development

Level 1—Preconventional

At the preconventional level, the individual is very self-centered. Rules are seen as something external imposed on the self.

Stage 1: Obedience to Rules; Avoidance of Punishment

At this stage, what is right is judged by one's obedience to rules and authority.

Example: A company forbids making payoffs to government or other officials to gain business. Susan, the company's contract negotiator, might justify refusing the request of a foreign government official to make a payment to gain a contract as being contrary to company rules, or Susan might make the payment if she believes there is little chance of being caught and punished.

Stage 2: Satisfying One's Own Needs—Egoism

In Stage 2, rules and authority are important only if acting in accordance with them satisfies one's own needs (egoism).

Example: Here, Susan might make the payment even though it is against company rules if she perceives that such payments are a necessary part of doing business. She views the payment as essential to gain the contract. Susan may believe that competitors are willing to make payments, and that making such payments are part of the culture of the host country. She concludes that if she does not make the payment, it might jeopardize her ability to move up the ladder within the organization and possibly forgo personal rewards of salary increases, bonuses, or both. Because everything is *relative,* each person is free to pursue her individual interests.

Level 2—Conventional

At the conventional level, the individual becomes aware of the interests of others and one's duty to society. Personal responsibility becomes an important consideration in decision making.

Stage 3: Fairness to Others

In Stage 3, an individual is not only motivated by rules but seeks to do what is in the perceived best interests of others, especially those in a family, peer group, or work organization. There is a commitment to loyalty in the relationship.

Example: Susan wants to be liked by others. She might be reluctant to make the payment but agrees to do so, not because it benefits her interests, but in response to the pressure imposed by her supervisor, who claims that the company will lose a major contract and employees will be fired if she refuses to go along.

Stage 4: Law and Order

Stage 4 behavior emphasizes the morality of law and duty to the social order. One's duty to society, respect for authority, and maintaining the social order become the focus of decision making.

Example: Susan might refuse to make the illegal payment, even though it leads to a loss of jobs in her company (or maybe even the closing of the company itself), because she views it as her duty to do so in the best interests of society. She does not want to violate the law.

(Continued)

Level 3—Postconventional
Principled morality underlies decision making at this level. The individual recognizes that there must be a societywide basis for cooperation. There is an orientation to principles that shape whatever laws and role systems a society may have.

Stage 5: Social Contract

In Stage 5, an individual is motivated by upholding the basic rights, values, and legal contracts of society. That person recognizes in some cases that legal and moral points of view may conflict. To reduce such conflict, individuals at this stage base their decisions on a rational calculation of benefits and harms to society.

Example: Susan might weigh the alternative courses of action by evaluating how each of the groups is affected by her decision to make the payment. For instance, the company might benefit by gaining the contract. Susan might even be rewarded for her action. The employees are more secure in their jobs. The customer in the other country gets what it wants. On the other hand, the company will be in violation of the Foreign Corrupt Practices Act (FCPA), which prohibits (bribery) payments to foreign government officials. Susan then weighs the consequences of making an illegal payment, including any resulting penalties, against the ability to gain additional business. Susan might conclude that the harms of prosecution, fines, other sanctions, and the loss of one's reputational capital are greater than the benefits.

Stage 6: Universal Ethical Principles

Kohlberg was still working on Stage 6 at the time of his death in 1987. He believed that this stage rarely occurred. Still, a person at this stage believes that right and wrong are determined by universal ethical principles that everyone should follow. Stage 6 individuals believe that there are inalienable rights, which are universal in nature and consequence. These rights, laws, and social agreements are valid not because of a particular society's laws or customs, but because they rest on the premise of universality. Justice and equality are examples of principles that are deemed universal. If a law conflicts with an ethical principle, then an individual should act in accordance with the principle.

An example of such a principle is Immanuel Kant's categorical imperative, the first formulation of which can be stated as: "Act only according to that maxim [reason for acting] by which you can at the same time will that it would become a universal law."[12] Kant's categorical imperative creates an absolute, unconditional requirement that exerts its authority in all circumstances, and is both required and justified as an end in itself.

Example: Susan would go beyond the norms, laws, and authority of groups or individuals. She would disregard pressure from her supervisor or the perceived best interests of the company when deciding what to do. Her action would be guided only by universal ethical principles that would apply to others in a similar situation.

Let's return to the receivables example in Chapter 1 that applies ethical reasoning to the methods discussed in Exhibit 1.3 (Ethical Reasoning Method Bases for Making Ethical Judgments). In the receivables example, an auditor who reasons at Stage 3 might go along with the demands of a client out of loyalty or because she thinks the company will benefit by such inaction. At Stage 4, the auditor places the needs of society and abiding by the law (GAAP, in this instance) above all else, so the auditor will insist on recording an allowance for uncollectibles.

An auditor who reasons at Stage 5 would not want to violate the public interest principle embedded in the profession's ethical standards, which values the public trust above all else. Investors and creditors have a right to know about the uncertainty surrounding collectibility of the receivables. At Stage 6, the auditor would ask whether she would want other auditors to insist on providing an allowance for the uncollectibles if they were involved in a similar situation. This creates an objective standard for determining the right decision. The auditor reasons that the orderly functioning of markets and a level playing field require that financial information should be accurate and reliable, so another auditor should also decide that the allowance needs to be recorded. The application of virtues such as objectivity and integrity enables her to carry out the ethical action and act in a responsible manner.

Kohlberg's model suggests that people continue to change their decision priorities over time and with additional education and experience. They may experience a change in values and ethical behavior.[13] In the context of business, an individual's moral development can be influenced by corporate culture, especially ethics training.[14] Ethics training and education have been shown to improve managers' moral development. More will be said about corporate culture in Chapter 3.

Universal Sequence

Kohlberg maintains that his stage sequence is universal; it is the same in all cultures. This seems to run contrary to Geert Hofstede's five cultural dimensions discussed in Chapter 1. For example, we might expect those in a highly collectivist-oriented society to exhibit Stage 3 features more than in an individualistic one that reflects Stage 2 behavior.

William Crain addresses whether different cultures socialize their children differently, thereby teaching them different moral beliefs.[15] He points out that Kohlberg's response has been that different cultures do teach different beliefs, but that his stages refer not to specific beliefs, but to underlying modes of reasoning. We might assume, then, that in a collectivist society, blowing the whistle on a member of a work group would be considered improper because of the "family" orientation (Stage 3), while in a more individualistic one, it is considered acceptable because it is in the best interests of society (Stage 4). Thus, individuals in different cultures at the same stage-sequence might hold different beliefs about the appropriateness of whistleblowing but still reason the same because, from a fairness perspective, it is the right way to behave.

The Ethical Domain in Accounting and Auditing

Professions, such as accounting, are characterized by their unique expertise gained through education and training, a commitment to lifelong learning, service to society, a code of ethics, and an agreement to abide by the profession's code, and participation in the self-governance and monitoring of the profession.[16] A commitment to serve the public interest is the bedrock of the accounting profession. Snoeyenbos, Almeder, and Humber have described this as a "social contract," in which the professional discharges her obligation by operating with high standards of expertise and integrity. When the profession does not maintain these standards, the social contract is broken, and society may decide to limit the role or the autonomy of the profession. This occurred in the aftermath of the accounting scandals when Congress passed the Sarbanes-Oxley Act (SOX) and established the Public Company Accounting Oversight Board (PCAOB) to oversee the auditing, ethics, and independence practices of CPA firms that audit companies with stock listed on the New York Stock Exchange (NYSE) and NASDAQ. For nonpublicly-owned companies, the standards of the AICPA still apply.[17]

The ethical domain for accountants and auditors usually involves four key constituent groups, including (1) the client organization that hires and pays for accounting services; (2) the accounting firm that employs the practitioner, typically represented by the collective interests of the firm's management; (3) the accounting profession, including various regulatory bodies such as the Securities and Exchange Commission (SEC) and the PCAOB; and (4) the general public, who rely on the attestations and representations of the practitioner and the firm.[18] Responsibilities to each of these groups may conflict. For example, fees are paid by the client organization rather than by the general public, including investors and creditors who are the direct beneficiary of the independent auditing services, so the public interest may conflict with client interests. These conflicts might influence the cognitive development of auditors, thereby influencing their ethical reasoning.

The accounting profession's codes of conduct (i.e., the AICPA Code and IMA Ethical Standards) encourage the individual practitioner's ethical behavior in a way that is consistent with the stated rules and guidelines of the profession. These positive factors work in conjunction with an individual's attitudes and beliefs and ethical reasoning capacity to influence professional judgment and ethical decision making.

Kohlberg's theory of ethical development provides a framework that can be used to consider the effects of conflict areas on ethical reasoning in accounting. For example, if an individual accountant is influenced by the firm's desire to "make the client happy," then the result may be reasoning at Stage 3. The results of published studies during the 1990s by accounting researchers indicate that CPAs reason primarily at Stages 3 and 4. One possible implication of these results is that a larger percentage of CPAs may be overly influenced by their relationship with peers, superiors, and clients (Stage 3) or by rules (Stage 4). A CPA who is unable to apply the technical accounting standards and rules of conduct critically when these requirements are unclear is likely to be influenced by others in the decision-making process.[19] If an auditor reasons at the postconventional level, then that person may refuse to give in to the pressure applied by the supervisor to overlook the client's failure to follow GAAP. This is the ethical position to take, although it may go against the culture of the firm to "go along to get along."

Empirical studies have explored the underlying ethical reasoning processes of accountants and auditors in practice. Findings show that ethical reasoning may be an important determinant of professional judgment, such as the disclosure of sensitive information[20] and auditor independence.[21] Results also show that unethical and dysfunctional audit behavior, such as the underreporting of time on an audit budget, may be systematically related to the auditor's level of ethical reasoning.[22] In reviewing these and other works, Ponemon and Gabhart conclude that the results imply that ethical reasoning may be an important cognitive characteristic that may affect individual judgment and behavior under a wide array of conditions and events in extant professional practice.[23]

The role of an accountant is to tell a story—to make an account—of a series of business activities. This story can be told from a variety of perspectives (i.e., employer or client) and can therefore result in many accounts. It is the role of the accountant to determine the perspective that will fairly present the information in accordance with laws and accounting standards, but they contain options and ambiguities. A higher level of understanding is required to deal with these different perspectives, the options and ambiguities that exist within the standards, and the uncertainties of business life. This higher level of understanding is encapsulated in the postconventional level of reasoning.[24]

Moral Reasoning and Moral Behavior

Within the cognitive-developmental paradigm the most distinguishing characteristic of morality is the human capacity to reason. Moral judgment has long been regarded as the single most influential factor—and the only truly moral determinant—of a person's moral behavior.[25] By definition, morality requires that a person's actions be rational, motivated by purpose or intent, and carried out with autonomous free will. Kohlberg maintained that it is as a result of development in moral reasoning that one becomes truly a moral person, in both mind and deed.[26]

Kohlberg's work is not without its critics. Some philosophers complain it draws too heavily from Rawls's Theory of Justice and makes deontological ethics superior to other ethical perspectives. They note that the theory applies more to societal issues than to individual ethical decisions. A number of psychologists have challenged the notion that people go through "rigid" stages of moral reasoning, arguing instead that they can engage in many ways of thinking about a problem, regardless of their age.[27]

Although he later admitted to having underestimated the complexity of the relation between moral stage and action and revised his thinking to include two intervening cognitive functions to explain it—a prescriptive judgment of the moral right and a personal judgment of responsibility to act accordingly —Kohlberg still contended that it is the logic of a person's reasoning that most strongly influences her moral behavior. Thus, reason constitutes the essential core and strength of character of a person's moral maturity in Kohlberg's theory.[28]

Kohlberg's commitment to reason has been challenged by some who claim he disregarded other factors also associated with moral functioning, such as emotion[29] and traits of character.[30] Others have criticized Kohlberg's emphasis on reason without considering its interaction with other components of morality, and its link to moral behavior in particular.[31] Still others claim the over-reliance on dilemmas, such as Heinz and the Drug, to evaluate moral reasoning shortchanges the role of virtue ethics and its focus on the character of individuals and their overall approach to life.[32]

Noted moral psychologist James Rest attempted to address some of the problems that are recognized in Kohlberg's work, and in doing so has moved from the six-stage model to one with three levels of understanding: personal interest, maintaining norms, and postconventional. Rest focuses on the maintaining norms (similar to the conventional level) and postconventional schemas. By maintaining norms, Rest means recognizing the need for societywide norms; a duty orientation; the need for cooperation; uniform and categorical application of norms, laws, and rules; and that individuals will obey the norms and laws and expect others to do the same even though it may not benefit all affected parties equally.[33]

Rest's conception has particular appeal for accountants who at this level of moral development recognize the importance of various laws and standards, comply with them, understand that sometimes compliance would benefit them and sometimes not, but recognize that obeying these norms is important for society. Rest recognized that, while operating at this level would be ideal for an accountant, it does not ensure that the accountant can make good decisions when there are options and ambiguities within accounting and auditing standards, nor does it ensure that he will have the ability to make good decisions when business circumstances arise that are outside the current laws, norms, or standards.[34]

A higher level of understanding is needed to deal with these different perspectives. The postconventional schema integrates such issues by recognizing that accountants do not have to follow the norms but should seek the moral criteria behind the norms for guidance in action. In accounting this means the fair presentation of financial information in a way that benefits society—that is, the public interest.

Rest's Four-Component Model of Ethical Decision Making

LO 2-2
Explain the components of Rest's model and how it influences ethical decision making.

Cognitive-developmental researchers have attempted to understand the process of ethical decision making. In particular, Rest asserts that ethical actions are not the outcome of a single, unitary decision process, but result from a combination of various cognitive structures and psychological processes. Rest's model of ethical action is based on the presumption that an individual's behavior is related to her level of moral development. Rest built on Kohlberg's work by developing a four-component model of the ethical decision-making process. The four-component model describes the cognitive processes that individuals use in ethical decision making; that is, it depicts how an individual first identifies an ethical dilemma and then continues through to his intention and finally finds courage to behave ethically. Each component of the model must be present before the moral action will be undertaken.[35]

Rest built his four-component model by working backward. He started with the end product—moral action—and then determined the steps that produce such behavior. He concluded that ethical action is the result of four psychological processes: (1) moral sensitivity (recognition), moral judgment, (3) moral focus (motivation), and (4) moral character.

Moral Sensitivity

The first step in moral behavior requires that the individual interpret the situation as moral. Absent the ability to recognize that one's actions affect the welfare of others, it would be virtually impossible to make the most ethical decision when faced with a moral dilemma.

A good example of failing to spot the ethical issues is Dennis Kozlowski, the former CEO of Tyco International. On June 17, 2005, Kozlowski was convicted of crimes related to his receipt of $81 million in purportedly unauthorized bonuses, the purchase of art for his Manhattan apartment of $14.725 million, and the payment by Tyco of a $20 million investment banking fee to Frank Walsh, a former Tyco director. He also had Tyco pay the $30 million for his apartment, which included $6,000 shower curtains and $15,000 "dog umbrella stands," not to mention charging the company one-half of the $2 million, 40th birthday party for his wife held on the Italian island of Sardinia under the guise of having a board of directors meeting.

On September 19, 2005, Kozlowski was sentenced to serve from eight years and four months to twenty-five years in prison for his role in the scandal. On January 17, 2014, he was granted conditional release.

Kozlowski, commenting on his trial in a March 2007 interview with Morley Safer for "60 Minutes," said, "I am absolutely not guilty of the charges. There was no criminal intent here. Nothing was hidden. There were no shredded documents. All the information the prosecutors got was directly off the books and records of the company." He also claimed to have done nothing different from his predecessors. He invoked "ethical legalism" in his defense -- if it is legal, it is ethical.

Kozlowski was blinded by his ambition and never remotely thought about the ethics of his actions. He was not sensitive to these issues because of a desire to keep up with "The Masters of the Universe," by which he meant other CEOs who, at the time, were raking in hundreds of millions of dollars in executive compensation.

Our ability to identify an ethical situation enables us to focus on how alternative courses of action might affect ourselves and others. Kozlowski acted without reflecting on the ethics of the situation. He failed even the most basic test of ethical behavior, which is ethics is all about how we act when no one is looking.

Moral Judgment

An individual's ethical cognition of what "ideally" ought to be done to resolve an ethical dilemma is called *prescriptive reasoning*.[36] The outcome of one's prescriptive reasoning is his ethical judgment of the ideal solution to an ethical dilemma. Generally, an individual's prescriptive reasoning reflects his cognitive understanding of an ethical situation as measured by his level of moral development.[37] Once a person is aware of possible lines of action and how people would be affected by the alternatives, a process aided by the philosophical reasoning methods, a judgment must be made about which course of action is more morally justifiable (which alternative is just or right).

Moral judgment relates to developing moral reasoning abilities over time. Kohlberg argued that individuals progress through a series of moral stages just as they do physical stages. Each stage is more advanced than the one before. People engage in more complex reasoning as they progress up the stages and become less self-centered and develop broader definitions of morality. Rest added that developing moral judgment is a social and cognitive construct that progressed from a self-focused view of moral issues, through a group-based moral perspective, to a reliance on postconventional moral principles, and a primary factor in the understanding of moral actions and emotions.

Making moral judgments is crucial for moral behavior. Carpendale suggests that moral reasoning is viewed as a process of coordinating all perspectives involved in a moral dilemma. He contends that Kohlberg's stages entail a view of moral reasoning as the application of a moral principle or rule to a dilemma in order to generate a solution. Once an individual has internalized a moral principle or rule she would then be expected to apply it to all moral conflicts encountered. If reasoning consists of understanding and coordinating conflicting perspectives in a moral dilemma, consistency in reasoning across different situations should not be expected.[38]

Moral Motivation

After concluding what course of action is best, decision makers must be focused on taking the moral action and follow through with ethical decision making. Moral values may conflict with other values. Moral motivation reflects an individual's willingness to place ethical values (e.g., honesty, integrity, trustworthiness, caring, and empathy) ahead of nonethical values (e.g., wealth, power, and fame) that relate to self-interest. An individual's ethical motivation influences her intention to comply or not comply with her ethical judgment in the resolution of an ethical dilemma.

Sometimes individuals want to do the right thing but are overwhelmed by countervailing pressures that may overpower their ethical intentions because of perceived personal costs. The loss of a job or a client can be motivating factors that compromise integrity and block ethical action.

What would you do if the primary revenue-producing client in your tax practice threatens to fire you and take his bookkeeping work elsewhere unless you ignore a 1099 form showing a significant amount of income that is reportable to the IRS? We can imagine some tax accountants rationalizing not reporting income especially if the client makes a convincing, albeit unethical case to go along just this one time.

Emotions also play a part in moral motivation. Organizations should create ethically rewarding environments to increase moral motivation. To reduce the costs of behaving morally, policies and procedures should be instituted that make it easier to report unethical behavior, prevent retaliation, and create an ethical culture in the organization. Leaders have to inspire employees and build confidence that their ethical intentions are supported by organizational systems.

Moral Character

Individuals do not always behave in accordance with their ethical intention. An individual's intention to act ethically and her ethical actions may not be aligned because of a lack of ethical character. Individuals with strong ethical character will be more likely to carry out their ethical intentions with ethical action than individuals with a weak ethical character because they are better able to withstand any pressures (i.e., have courage and maintain integrity to do otherwise). Once a moral person has considered the ethics of the alternatives, she must construct an appropriate plan of action, avoid distractions, and maintain the courage to continue.

Executing a plan of action takes character. Moral agents have to overcome indifference and opposition, resist distractions, cope with fatigue, and develop tactics and strategies for reaching their goals. Johnson points out that this helps to explain why there is only a moderate correlation between moral judgment and moral behavior. Many times deciding does not lead to doing.[39]

The character traits and virtues discussed in this chapter contribute to ethical follow-through. Courage helps leaders implement their plans despite the risks and costs of doing so while prudence helps them choose the best course of action. Integrity encourages leaders to be true to themselves and their choices. Compassion and justice focus the attention of leaders on the needs of others rather than on personal priorities. Selflessness is the underlying virtue that, in accounting, enables an accounting professional to place the public interest ahead of those of one's employer or client.

The four components of Rest's model are processes that must take place for moral behavior to occur. Rest does not offer the framework as a linear decision-making model, suggesting instead that the components interact through a complicated sequence of "feed-back" and "feed-forward" loops. An individual who demonstrates adequacy in one component may not necessarily be adequate in another, and moral failure can occur when there is a deficiency in any one component.[40] For example, an individual who has good moral reasoning capacity, a skill that can be developed (Component 2), may fail to perceive an ethical problem because she does not clearly understand how others might feel or react—a lack of empathy (Component 1).

Moral Intensity

LO 2-3
Describe the link between moral intensity and ethical decision making.

The lack of research on the characteristics of a moral issue prompted Thomas Jones to develop the moral intensity model. He argued that the characteristics of the moral issue—what he collectively termed moral intensity—influence ethical decision making. Jones's model links moral intensity to Rest's Four-Component Model. The six dimensions are briefly explained below.[41]

Magnitude of Consequences refers to the degree to which an individual may be harmed or benefited by the decision maker's action. A greater degree of harm or benefit results in an increase in moral intensity.

Temporal Immediacy refers to the length of time between the action and its consequences. An action with immediate negative consequences will cause a greater increase in moral intensity than an action for which the consequences are delayed.

Social Consensus refers to the degree of agreement among a social group that an action is good or bad. This social group could be society as a whole (e.g., a fraudulent financial statement is not morally accepted by society because accounting rules and SEC laws prohibit it). A strong Social Consensus that an act is morally wrong increases moral intensity.

Proximity refers to the nearness of the decision maker to the individuals potentially affected by the consequences. An increase in proximity results in an increase of moral intensity. An auditor who becomes too close to a client and is dealing with fraudulent financial statements is likely to feel more pressure from the client because of their close relationship.

Probability of Effect refers to the likelihood that the predicted consequences and the expected level of harm/benefit will occur. Moral intensity increases with an action that has a high probability of occurrence and high likelihood of causing predicted harm. Pressures increase on auditors when harm to the public interest intensifies with the likelihood of fraudulent financial statements.

Concentration of Effect refers to the relationship between the number of people affected and the magnitude of harm. Moral intensity increases if the Concentration of Effect is great. Fraudulent financial statements issued by a publicly owned company that is also using the statements for a significant loan creates additional pressures on auditors to make the most ethical decision possible.[42]

Our contention is there is an important link between moral intensity and ethical decision making. As individuals face morally intense situations, their awareness of the moral dilemma, their judgments about choices and consequences, and their intention to act are significantly affected by specific characteristics of the moral situation. One study found that Social Consensus is significantly associated with moral awareness, judgment, and intention. As subjects in the study recognized a moral issue, formed a judgment, and decided on their intention to act, they were strongly affected by what they believed others within their social group considered morally right or wrong.[43]

The link between Social Consensus and ethical decision making makes sense in accounting because it is a community with shared values and beliefs and expectations for ethical actions. On the other hand, if the CPA firm has a culture of placing the client's interests ahead of the public interest, then intensity increases and moral action may not occur.[44]

Aligning Ethical Behavior and Ethical Intent: Virtue-Based Decision Making

LO 2-4
Explain how moral reasoning and virtue influence ethical decision making.

One question that arises from Rest's model is how to align ethical behavior with ethical intent. The answer is through the exercise of virtue, according to a study conducted by Libby and Thorne.[45] The authors point out that audit failures at companies such as Enron and WorldCom demonstrate that the rules in accounting cannot replace auditors' professional judgment. Transactions (i.e., special-purpose entities at Enron) can be structured around rules, and rules cannot be made to fit every situation. The rules may be unclear or nonexistent, in which case professional judgment is necessary for decisions to be made in accordance with the values of the profession as embodied in its codes of conduct. Professional judgment requires not only technical competence, but also depends on auditors' ethics and virtues.

Libby and Thorne surveyed members of the Canadian accounting community with the help of the Canadian Institute of Chartered Accountants (CICA), the equivalent of the AICPA in the United States, to develop a set of virtues important in the practice of auditing.[46] The authors divided the virtues into two categories: intellectual virtues, which indirectly influence an individual's intentions to exercise professional judgment; and instrumental virtues, which directly influence an individual's actions. The most important intellectual virtues were found to be integrity, truthfulness, independence, objectivity, dependability, being principled, and healthy skepticism. The most important instrumental virtues were diligence (i.e., due care) and being alert, careful, resourceful, consultative, persistence, and courageous. The authors concluded from their study that virtue plays an integral role in both the intention to exercise professional judgment and the exercise of professional judgment, and the necessity of possessing both intellectual and instrumental virtues for auditors.

Returning now to Rest's model, in her seminal paper on the role of virtue on auditors' ethical decision making, Thorne contends that the model fails to provide a theoretical description of the role of personal characteristics, except for level of moral development, in auditors' ethical decision processes. Thorne develops a model of individuals' ethical decision processes that integrates Rest's components with the basic tenets of virtue ethics theory. Her model relies on virtue-based characteristics, which tend to increase the decision maker's propensity to exercise sound ethical judgment. Thorne believes that virtue theory is similar to the approach advocated by the cognitive-developmental perspective in three ways. First, both perspectives suggest that ethical action is the result of a rational decision-making process. Second, both perspectives are concerned with an individual's ethical decision-making process. Third, both perspectives acknowledge the critical role of cognition in individuals' ethical decision making. Exhibit 2.1 presents Thorne's integrated model of the ethical decision-making process.[47]

EXHIBIT 2.1   Thorne's Integrated Model of Ethical Decision Making[*]

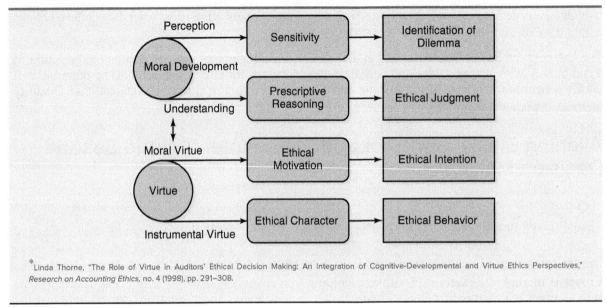

[*]Linda Thorne, "The Role of Virtue in Auditors' Ethical Decision Making: An Integration of Cognitive-Developmental and Virtue Ethics Perspectives," *Research on Accounting Ethics,* no. 4 (1998), pp. 291–308.

Exhibit 2.1 indicates that moral development and virtue are both required for ethical behavior. In her examination of the model, Armstrong suggests that moral development comprises sensitivity to the moral content of a situation or dilemma and prescriptive reasoning, or the ability to understand the issues, think them through, and arrive at an ethical judgment. Similarly, virtue comprises ethical motivation, which describes an individual's willingness to place the interests of others ahead of her own interest; and ethical character, which leads to ethical behavior.[48]

Even though virtue is a critical component of ethical behavior, other factors may get in the way of taking ethical action including situational pressures, business norms, and the moral intensity of the issue itself that influences ethical decision making. Also, one's strength of character deepens with experience, and reflection on ethical dilemmas can bolster one's resolve.

Ethical Decision-Making Models

LO 2-5
Apply the steps in the Integrated Ethical Decision-Making Model to a case study.

Dealing with moral issues can be perplexing. How, exactly, should we think through an ethical issue? What questions should we ask? What factors should we consider? The philosophical methods of moral reasoning suggest that once we have ascertained the facts, we should ask ourselves five questions when trying to resolve a moral issue:

- What benefits and what harms will each course of action produce, and which alternative will lead to the best overall consequences?

- What moral rights do the affected parties have, and which course of action best respects those rights?
- Which course of action treats everyone the same, except where there is a morally justifiable reason not to, and does not show favoritism or discrimination?
- Which course of action advances the common good?
- Which course of action develops moral virtues?

In commenting on the method, Velasquez points out that it does not provide an automatic solution to moral problems. It is not meant to. The method is merely meant to help identify most of the important ethical considerations. In the end, we must deliberate on moral issues for ourselves, keeping a careful eye on both the facts and on the ethical considerations involved.[49]

Virtue is not specifically recognized in the philosophical model, although it is implied by the considerations. It would be difficult to answer these questions in a morally appropriate way without being an honest, trustworthy person in evaluating these considerations and willing to act out of integrity in deciding on the preferred course of action.

Decision-making guidelines can help us make better ethical choices. Johnson points out that taking a systematic approach encourages teams and individuals to carefully define the problem, gather information, apply ethical standards and values, identify and evaluate alternative courses of action, and follow through on their choices. They are also better equipped to defend their decisions.

Kidder's Ethical Checkpoints

Ethicist Rushworth Kidder acknowledges that ethical issues can be "disorderly and sometimes downright confusing." They can arise suddenly, create complex issues, and have unexpected consequences. However, Kidder argues that there is an underlying structure to the ethical decision-making process.[50] Kidder suggests that nine steps or checkpoints can help bring order to otherwise confusing ethical issues. What follows is a brief summary of the major points.

1. *Recognize that there is a moral issue.* Similar to Rest's notion of ethical sensitivity, we must acknowledge that an issue deserves our attention and moral questions exist.

2. *Determine the actor.* Kidder distinguishes between involvement and responsibility. Because we are members of larger communities, we are involved in any ethical issue that arises in the group. Yet we are only responsible for dealing with problems that we can do something about. For example, I may be concerned that clients threaten to fire their auditors if they plan to give a negative opinion on the financial statements. However, there is little I can do about it unless it happens in my firm.

3. *Gather the relevant facts.* Adequate, accurate, and current information is important for making effective decisions of all kinds, including ethical ones. Consider the motives of affected parties, patterns of behavior, likely consequences if the problem persists, and likely outcome of one course of action or another.

4. *Test for right-versus-wrong issues.* Kidder suggests using four determinations including a *legal test.* If lawbreaking is involved (i.e., fraudulent financial statements), then the problem becomes a legal matter, not a moral one. The *smell test* relies on intuition. If you have an uneasy feeling about the decision or course of action, chances are it involves right-versus-wrong issues. The *front-page test* asks how you would feel if your decision made it to the front page of the local newspaper. If you feel uncomfortable about it, then you should consider choosing another alternative. The *mom test*

asks how you would feel if your mother or some other important role model became aware of your choice. If you have a queasy feeling, then it is best to reconsider your choice.

5. *Test for right-versus-right paradigms.* If an issue does not involve wrong behavior, then it likely pits two important positive values against each other. Kidder identified four such models: truth-telling versus loyalty to others and institutions; personal needs versus needs of the community; short-term benefits versus long-term negative consequences; and justice versus mercy. When an ethical dilemma pits two core values against each other, a determination should be made whether they are in conflict with one another in this situation.

6. *Apply the ethical standards and perspectives.* Consider which ethical principle is most relevant and useful to this specific issue. Is it utilitarianism? Kant's categorical imperative? Justice as fairness? Or, is it a combination of perspectives?

7. *Look for a third way.* Compromise is one way to reveal a new alternative that will resolve the problem or to develop a creative solution. A third way can also be the product of moral imagination. One's conception of the moral and ethical issues can change when considering different perspectives from a moral point of view. We may discover a better, economically viable, and morally justifiable solution.

8. *Make the decision.* At some point we have to make the decision. However, we may be mentally exhausted from wrestling with the problem, get caught up in analysis paralysis, or lack the necessary courage to come to a decision.

9. *Revisit and reflect on the decision.* Return to the decision later, after the issue has been resolved, to debrief. Reflect on the lessons to be learned. How can you apply them to future decisions? What ethical issues did it raise?

Johnson evaluates Kidder's approach to ethical decision making by pointing out it seems to cover all the bases, beginning with defining the issue all the way through to learning from the situation in the aftermath of the decision. He recognizes that some decisions involve deciding between two "goods" and leaves the door open for creative solutions. Making a choice is an act of courage, as Kidder points out, and we can apply lessons learned in one dilemma to future problems.[51]

On the flip side, Johnson points out that it is not easy to determine who has responsibility for solving a problem, the facts may not be available, or a time constraint prevents gathering all the relevant information, and decisions do not always lead to action. The model seems to equate deciding with doing and, as we saw in our earlier discussion of moral action, we can decide on a course of action but not follow through. Johnson concludes that Kidder is right to say that making ethical choices takes courage. However, it takes even more courage to put the choice into effect.

We believe that a decision-making process in accounting helps to organize one's thoughts about the ethical issues that accounting professionals face and can serve as a basis for analysis in many of the cases in this book. The integrated model explained below draws on Rest's Model and Kidder's Checkpoints to provide a basis for ethical decision making when accounting issues create ethical dilemmas. Consideration is given to moral intensity and how intellectual instrumental virtues enable ethical action to occur.

The integrated model links to Rest's framework as follows:

Integrated Ethical Decision-Making Process

1. Identify the ethical and professional issues (ethical sensitivity).

- *What are the ethical and professional issues in this case (i.e., GAAP and GAAS)?*
- *Who are the stakeholders (i.e., investors, creditors, employees, management, the organization)?*
- *Which ethical/professional standards apply (i.e., AICPA Code Principles, IMA Ethical Standards, and IFAC standards)?*

2. Identify and evaluate alternative courses of action (ethical judgment).

- *What legal issues exist?*
- *What can and cannot be done in resolving the conflict under professional standards?*
- *Which ethical reasoning methods apply to help reason through alternatives (i.e., rights theory, utilitarianism, justice, and virtue)?*

3. Reflect on the moral intensity of the situation and virtues that enable ethical action to occur (ethical intent).

- *Evaluate the magnitude of the consequences if specific actions are taken; likelihood of those consequences; ability to effect ethical responses by one's actions; consensus view within the profession about the appropriateness of the intended actions.*
- *Consider whether anyone's rights are at stake and how they manifest in the decision-making process*
- *Consider how virtue (i.e., intellectual virtues) motivates ethical actions.*

4. Take action (ethical behavior).

- *Decide on a course of action consistent with one's professional obligations.*
- *How can virtue (i.e., instrumental virtue) support turning ethical intent into ethical action?*
- *What steps can I take to strengthen my position and argument?*
- *How can I counter reasons and rationalizations that mitigate against taking ethical action? Who can I go to for support?*

Reflection would follow after the decision has been made. What was the outcome? How should it affect my approach to ethical decision making? How can I do better in the future?

Application of the Integrated Ethical Decision-Making Model: Ace Manufacturing

In order to illustrate the use of the model, a short case appears in Exhibit 2.2. The facts of the case and ethical issues are analyzed below using the Integrated Model. It is not our intention to cover all points; instead, it is to illustrate the application of the model and consideration of Rest's framework, moral intensity, and the virtues previously discussed and identified in Thorne's study.

Ace Manufacturing: Integrated Ethical Decision-Making Process

1. Identify the ethical and professional issues (ethical sensitivity).

GAAP

- Appears there may be fraud in the financial statements. Expense accounts were charged for personal withdrawals.

- Financial statements do not fairly present financial position and results of operations due to improper expensing of personal expenditures.
- Taxable income may be similarly misstated.

Stakeholders

- Owners including Jack Jones
- Paul Jones (son)
- Larry Davis (new accountant/CPA)
- IRS
- Banks that may be approached about the loan

Ethical/professional standards

- Objectivity: Davis should not permit bias or influence, because of his relationship with Paul, to interfere with making the right choice.
- Integrity: Don't subordinate judgment to Paul even though he is your boss.
- Due care: Professional skepticism has been exercised; carry through diligently and insist on supporting evidence for the recorded expenditures.

2.   Identify and evaluate alternative courses of action (ethical judgment).

Legal issues

- GAAP appears to be violated; financial statements are fraudulent. Legal liabilities may exist.
- Tax payments will be understated assuming the improper accounting carries over to taxable income.

Alternatives/ethical analysis

- Do nothing: Moral blindness is not a defense to unethical action; violates the rights of the owners of the business; Davis will have violated his ethical responsibilities under the AICPA Code.
- Confront Paul and insist on an explanation: (a) allow him to repay the amount if he agrees to do so, or (b) bring the matter to the attention of the owners regardless of what Paul says.
- Report the matter to Jack Jones—let Paul's dad deal with it: He may pay back the amounts for his son, which sweeps the ethical problem under the rug; he may read the riot act to his son.
- Report the matter to all of the owners: Davis may be fired; the other owners may be grateful and negate any negative action against Davis by Paul or his dad.

Prevailing ethical theories: Rule utilitarianism dictates that certain rules should never be violated regardless of any utilitarian benefits. Owners have a right to know about Paul's ethical lapse.

3.   Reflect on the moral intensity of the situation and virtues that enable ethical action to occur (ethical intent).

- Do I want to be responsible for getting Paul in trouble with his dad, possibly fired? Paul may be prosecuted for his actions. The consequences for Ace are severe so I need to be sure of my decision.

- I want to do the right thing but will my actions do irreparable harm to others? Should I be concerned about "caring about others" given the profession's standards?

- Can I ever trust Paul again? What he did is wrong and I shouldn't become a party to a cover-up.

- I am accountable for my actions; I need to maintain my integrity and not subordinate judgment to Paul.

4.   *Take action (ethical behavior).*

- Insist that steps be taken to correct the accounting; have the courage to stand up for my beliefs.

- I should give Paul an opportunity to explain why he did what he did, out of fairness, but be prepared to approach the other owners if his explanation and intended actions are not satisfactory.

Once I decide what to do and why, I need to assess how best to express myself and be true to my values. This entails considering how others may react to my decision. This is where a "Giving Voice to Values" framework comes in handy, as discussed below.

Traditional philosophical reasoning methods have limitations. We have already pointed out the need for a link between moral judgment, moral intent, and moral behavior. Beyond that, even if a decision maker has followed a sound ethical analysis, knows what to do, and has made the ethical choice, it still does not mean that her voice will be heard within the organization and it may require a different approach to make a real difference. In the Ace Manufacturing case, Larry Davis needs to prepare for what might happen when he meets with Paul. As explained later on, scripting responses is a sound way of ensuring that one's voice is heard in the resolution of the matter. This is where tools that are provided through behavioral ethics come into play.

EXHIBIT 2.2   Ace Manufacturing

Ace Manufacturing is a privately held company in Anytown, USA. There are three stockholders of the company—Joe Smith, Sue Williams, and Jack Jones. Jones manages the business including the responsibility for the financial statements. Smith and Williams are in charge of sales and marketing. Each owner has a one-third stake in the business.

Jones recently hired his son, Paul, to manage the office. Paul has limited managerial experience, but his father hopes Paul will take over in a few years when he retires, and this is a good opportunity for Paul to learn the business.

Paul is given complete control over payroll, and he approves disbursements, signs checks, and reconciles the general ledger cash account to the bank statement balance. Previously, the bookkeeper was the only employee with such authority. However, the bookkeeper recently left the company, and Jack Jones needed someone he could trust to be in charge of these sensitive operations. He did ask his son to hire someone as soon as possible to help with these and other accounting functions. Paul hired Larry Davis shortly thereafter based on a friend's recommendation. While Davis is relatively inexperienced, he did graduate with honors in Accounting from Anytown University and recently passed all parts of the CPA Exam.

On March 21, one year after hiring Davis, Paul discovered that he needed surgery. Even though the procedure was fairly common and the risks were minimal, Paul planned to take three weeks off after the surgery because of other medical conditions that might complicate the recovery. He told Davis to approve vouchers for payment and present them to his father during the four-week period for payment. Paul had previously discussed this plan with his father, and they both agreed that Davis was ready to assume the additional responsibilities. They did not, however, discuss the matter with either Smith or Williams.

(Continued)

The bank statement for March arrived on April 4. Paul did not tell Davis to reconcile the bank statement. In fact, he specifically told Davis to just put it aside until he returned. But Davis looked at the March statement while trying to trace a payment to a vendor who had billed the company for an invoice that Davis thought had already been paid. In the course of examining the bank statement, Davis noticed five separate payments to Paul, each for $2,000, during March. He became suspicious because Paul's salary was $3,950 per month. What's more, a check for that amount appeared on the statement.

Curiosity got the better of Davis and he decided to trace the checks paid to Paul to the cash disbursements journal. He looked for supporting documentation but couldn't find any. He noticed that the five checks were coded to different accounts including supplies, travel and entertainment, office expense, and two miscellaneous expenses. He then reviewed the banks statements for January and February and found five separate check payments each month to Paul each for $2,000.

Davis didn't know what to do at this point. He was quite certain there was no business justification for the $30,000 payments to Paul for the first three months of the year and he was concerned that if the same pattern continued unabated for the next three months, the total of $60,000 payments to Paul might threaten the ability of the company to secure a $100,000 loan for working capital.

What would you do if you were in the position of Larry Davis? Use the Integrated Ethical Decision-Making Model to craft your responses.

Behavioral Ethics

LO 2-6
Analyze the thought process involved in making decisions and taking ethical action.

The field of behavioral ethics emphasizes the need to consider how individuals actually make decisions, rather than how they would make decisions in an ideal world. Research in behavioral ethics reveals that our minds have two distinct modes of decision making— "System 1" and "System 2" thinking.[52] Daniel Kahneman, the Nobel Prize–winning behavioral economist, points out that System 1 thinking is our intuitive system of processing information: fast, automatic, effortless, and emotional decision processes; on the other hand, System 2 thinking is slower, conscious, effortful, explicit, and a more reasoned decision process. For example, System 1 thinking is detecting that one object is more distant than another, while an example of System 2 thinking is parking in a narrow space.[53]

Kahneman's fundamental proposition is that we identify with System 2, *"the conscious, reasoning self that has beliefs, makes choices and decides what to think about and what to do."* But the one that is really in charge is System 1 as it *"effortlessly originates impressions and feelings that are the main sources of the explicit beliefs and deliberate choices of System 2."*[54]

What follows is an example of using System 1 thinking instead of the more deliberate approach of System 2, and drawing the wrong conclusion as a result. To illustrate, answer the following question: A baseball bat and ball together cost $110. If the bat costs $100 more than the ball, how much does the ball cost? Most people say $10. They decide quickly, without doing the math or thinking through the question. However, it is the wrong answer. The ball actually cost $5, and the bat cost $105.

The broader point of this exercise is to explain how System 1 thinking can lead to snap decisions that make it more difficult to resolve an ethical dilemma in a morally appropriate way. It may occur because you lack important information regarding a decision, fail to notice available information, or face time and cost constraints. You don't have the time or inclination and fail to see the dangers of deciding too quickly.

Many decisions in business and accounting have ethical challenges. This is because of the impacts of those decisions and the fact that outcomes are likely to affect stakeholders in different ways and will express different ethical values. A decision-making model built on System 2 thinking can provide a more systematic analysis that enables comprehensible judgment, clearer reasons, and a more justifiable and defensible action than otherwise would have been the case.

One limitation of the philosophical reasoning approaches incorporated into decision-making models is that how we think we should behave is different from how we decide to behave. This creates a problem of *cognitive dissonance*, a term first coined by Leon Festinger in 1956. The inconsistency between our thoughts, beliefs, or attitudes and our behavior creates the need to resolve contradictory or conflicting beliefs, values, and perceptions.[54] Tompkins and Lawley point out that:

> This dissonance only occurs when we are "attached" to our attitudes or beliefs, i.e., they have emotional significance or consequences for our self-concept or sense of coherence about how the world works. The psychological opposition of irreconcilable ideas (cognitions) held simultaneously by one individual, create[s] a motivated force that [c]ould lead, under proper conditions, to the adjustment of one's beliefs to fit one's behavior instead of changing one's behavior to fit one's beliefs (the sequence conventionally assumed).[55]

Cognitive dissonance suggests that we have an inner drive to hold all our attitudes and beliefs in harmony and avoid disharmony. When there is inconsistency between attitudes or behaviors (dissonance), something must change to eliminate the dissonance. Festinger posits that dissonance can be reduced in one of three ways: (1) change one or more of the attitudes, behavior, or beliefs so as to make the relationship between the two elements a consonant one; (2) acquire new information that outweighs the dissonant beliefs; or (3) reduce the importance of the cognitions (beliefs, attitudes).[56]

The Betty Vinson situation at WorldCom, discussed in Chapter 1, is a case in point about the dangers of reducing dissonance by changing one's attitudes and behaviors. Vinson knew it was wrong to "cook the books." She felt it in her inner being, but she did not act on those beliefs. Instead, she followed the orders from superiors and later justified her behavior by rationalizing it as a one-time act and demanded by people who knew accounting better than herself. In a sense she reduced the importance of her own intuitions about the appropriateness of what she was asked to do.

Bazerman and Gino ask: What makes even good people cross ethical boundaries?[57] Wittmer asks: Do individuals in organizations always act and behave consistently with what they know or believe to be the right thing to do?[58] The behavioral approach to ethics leads to understanding and explaining moral and immoral behavior in systematic ways. In reality, whether behaviors are viewed legally or ethically, we hold individuals accountable for their behaviors and choices, at least in part because they *should have* known better. Even if we agree on what someone should ethically do in a given situation, our judgment is often clouded by other factors that cause us to act against our intuition of what good sense dictates.

Why did CEO Richard Scrushy certify HealthSouth Corporation's financial statements when he knew or was reckless in not knowing they were materially false and misleading? What influenced him to behave unethically? Once we start asking these questions, we shift our attention from inquiring about what the right thing to do is, or what a good person should do. Rather, we are attempting to understand why such an individual acted the way he did, trying to identify the factors that influenced or caused the behaviors. We have moved from a prescriptive framework, such as with the philosophical reasoning methods, to a more descriptive mode of analysis. Such a perspective is important in leading organizations toward more ethical behavior.[59]

Behavioral ethics looks at how human beings actually behave in moral contexts and describes the actual behavior of people, how situational and social forces influence it, and ways in which decisions can be nudged in a more ethical direction through simple interventions. This approach to ethics requires understanding and explaining moral and immoral behavior in systematic ways. It requires understanding the antecedents and consequences of both ethical and unethical actions. Finally, it requires identifying levers at both the individual and the institutional level to change ethically questionable behaviors when individuals are acting in unethical ways that they would not endorse with greater reflection.[60]

Giving Voice to Values

LO 2-7
Describe the "Giving Voice to Values" technique and apply it to a case study.

"Giving Voice to Values (GVV)" is a behavioral ethics approach that shifts the focus away from traditional philosophical reasoning to an emphasis on developing the capacity to effectively express one's values in a way that positively influences others by finding the levers to effectively voice and enact one's values.[61] The methodology asks the protagonist to think about the arguments others might make that create barriers to expressing one's values in the workplace and how best to counteract these "reasons and rationalizations."[62]

GVV links to ethical intent and ethical action in Rest's Model. An ethical decision maker should start by committing to expressing her values in the workplace. The intent is there, but it may fall short of the mark of taking ethical action unless a pathway can be found to express one's values in the workplace. It is the pathway that GVV addresses.

GVV is used post–decision making; that is, you have already decided what to do and have chosen to voice your values. In the Ace Manufacturing case, elaborated on below, Davis knows he must act and we assume he has decided to give Paul a chance to explain about the "personal" expenditures. Other decisions might be made by students, but we use the alternative of giving Paul a chance to explain his actions as the basis for the following discussion.

Davis wants to do what he thinks is right, but he needs to be prepared for the eventuality that Paul will pressure him to stay silent. Davis needs to find a way to communicate his values powerfully and persuasively in the face of strong countervailing organizational or individuals norms, reasons, and rationalizations. In other words, how can Davis find a way to effectively articulate his point of view so that others can be convinced of its rightness?

According to Mary Gentile who developed the GVV methodology, "It shifts the focus away from awareness and analysis to action by addressing a series of questions for protagonists after identifying the right thing to do," including: How can you get it done effectively and efficiently? What do you need to say, to whom, and in what sequence? What will the objections or pushback be and, then, what will you say next? What data and examples do you need to support your point of view?[63]

Kohlberg argued that higher moral development requires role-taking ability. Role-taking ability involves understanding the cognitive and affective (i.e., relating to moods, emotions, and attitudes) aspects of another person's point of view. Davis needs to consider how Paul might react; what he might say; and how Davis might counter those statements when he meets with Paul.

The underlying theme of GVV is that we can effectively voice values in the workplace if we have the proper tools to do so. GVV relies on developing arguments and action plans, and rehearsing how to voice/enact not just any values, but moral values specifically. For our purposes, the pillars of character and virtues discussed in this and the previous chapter are our target behaviors.

Reasons and Rationalizations

An important part of the GVV methodology is to develop ways to confront barriers we may encounter when value conflicts exist in the workplace. These barriers often appear in the form of "reasons and rationalizations" that can confound our best attempts to fulfill our sense of organizational and personal purpose. These are the objections one might hear from colleagues when attempting to point out an ethical problem in the way things are being done, as Cynthia Cooper experienced in the WorldCom case. Or, sometimes you do not hear them because they are the unspoken assumptions of the organization.[64]

GVV provides a framework to deal with the opposing points of view based on the following series of questions.[65]

- What are the main arguments you are trying to counter? That is, what are the *reasons and rationalizations* you need to address?
- What is at *stake* for the key parties, including those who disagree with you?
- What *levers* can you use to influence those who disagree with you?
- What is your most *powerful and persuasive response* to the reasons and rationalizations you need to address? To whom should the argument be made? When and in what context?

Gentile identifies the most frequent categories of argument or rationalization that we face when we speak out against unethical practice. Some of the most common arguments include:

Expected or Standard Practice: "Everyone does this, so it's really standard practice. It's even expected."

Materiality: "The impact of this action is not material. It doesn't really hurt anyone."

Locus of Responsibility: "This is not my responsibility; I'm just following orders here."

Locus of Loyalty: "I know this isn't quite fair to the customer, but I don't want to hurt my reports/team /boss/company."

An additional argument we include is:

Isolated Incident: "This is a one-time request; you won't be asked to do it again."

Basic Exercise in GVV

GVV Brief Exercise: Doing Good by Being Good

Matt and Becca volunteered to head up the Accounting Club efforts to organize volunteers for a clean-up effort and raise donations to help the students, faculty, and staff at the college affected by Hurricane Debits. Over 1,200 had been displaced from their homes, apartments, and dorm rooms due to the severe weather. Over the next month the 25 students of the club helped clean up debris left by the storm and donated over 2,000 hours of time. Matt set up a GoFundMe Web page and posted pictures of the devastation on Instagram. Donations from the community totaled $20,367. The relief agencies in town suggested the club purchase $100 Visa and MasterCard gift cards to be distributed to the affected community members. Matt purchased 200 such cards and Becca delivered them.

Later that afternoon at the Accounting Club meeting, Matt announced that $20,000 was raised for the GoFundMe program and 200 locals received a $100 gift card each. Becca, who was the club treasurer, quickly realized there was $367 unaccounted for. Matt tried to explain there were fees for processing the transactions.

Becca asked Matt: "Why didn't you go to the stores that agreed to waive the fees for the disaster relief recovery?"

"Becca, they waived most of the fees but the remaining fees totaled $400. I donated $33 to cover the balance."

"Do you have receipts for the balance?"

"Becca, don't you trust me?"

"Matt, do you recall what our Auditing professor said yesterday? Trust but verify? I need the receipt for the gift cards."

"Ok, Becca. I'll find it and get it to you soon."

Shortly after the meeting ended, Becca hears Matt telling another member about a trip he planned to see his girlfriend.

"Matt, last week you told me you had no money to go. How did you get it?"

"It's not such an expensive trip. It should cost about $400," Matt told David.

David was surprised to hear the amount was the same as the credit card fees but said nothing. Becca happened to overhear the conversation and immediately realized that 4 more victims could have been helped. She was suspicious of Matt's explanation, to say the least.

Becca knew she had to do something but wasn't sure of the approach she should take. She also knows Matt is a former president of the club, is graduating this year, and has a position with a Big Four accounting firm.

Answer the following questions to develop a script for Becca assuming she has decided to approach Matt about the $400.

Discussion Questions (brief talking points are provided for Becca).

1. **What are the main arguments you are trying to counter? That is, what are the reasons and rationalizations you need to address?**

- *Matt created a trust and loyalty defense (Locus of Loyalty).*
- *Matt is graduating and doesn't want anything to affect his position with the firm.*
- *Matt may say the $400 is a small amount and not worth arguing over (Materiality).*
- *Matt may say it was a one-time event and won't happen again (Isolated Incident).*

2. **What's at stake for the key parties, including those with whom you disagree?**

- *Matt's reputation is on the line.*
- *Becca may be concerned other club members would not support her and suggest she should let it go, given Matt's situation. (They might approach the dilemma from an egoistic point of view; Becca needs to emphasize enlightened egoism/Rights).*
- *Becca needs to consider what would happen if the club faculty advisor found out or members of the community become aware of the situation (Kidder's front page test).*

3.   What levers can you use to influence those with whom you disagree?

- *Becca could speak to David who also attended the meeting and develop a plan to approach Matt.*

- *Becca could tell Matt that she will go to the faculty advisor if he doesn't repay the $367.*

- *Becca could emphasize to Matt he is jeopardizing the respect that others have for him.*

4.   What is your most powerful and persuasive response to the reasons and rationalizations you need to address?

- *Becca could explain to Matt he is cheating the victims out of money that is rightly theirs. She could emphasize the lack of ethical standards in his action.*

- *Becca could explain to Matt if he had acted similarly while working for the Big Four firm, he would have violated the profession's ethical standards including due care and integrity.*

- *Becca could explain that her loyalty obligation is to the club and victims of the disaster.*

- *Becca could emphasize to Matt that he doesn't want to implicate David in any cover-up and needs to do the right thing.*

Students should think about other points they might make if faced with a similar ethical dilemma.

Ace Manufacturing: GVV Analysis

Building on the Ace Manufacturing case discussed earlier on, once Davis has decided what to do, which is to give Paul a chance to explain, he needs to consider how best to express his point of view; act on his beliefs; and convince Paul to take corrective action. He needs to anticipate the reasons and rationalizations Paul may provide and how to counter them. Using the GVV framework, what follows is a brief explanation of how such a meeting with Paul might go.

What are the main arguments you are trying to counter? That is, what are the reasons and rationalizations you need to address?

These could be addressed from the perspective of Paul trying to convince Davis to remain silent about the apparent misappropriation of company cash and/or offering to pay back the money.

- Davis was told to put bank statements aside and not to do reconciliations.

- Paul may explain that, because the company is privately owned, no one gets hurt by what he did.

- He may try to convince Davis that the use of company cash for personal purposes is a common practice in the company because it's not publicly owned. (*Expected or Standard Practice*)

- Paul may play the sympathy card and explain that he needed the money to pay for hospitalization costs.

- He may argue that the amount of money involved is not significant. (*Materiality*)

- He may rationalize that the reason for withdrawing cash is the low monthly salary for someone in his position; he's not being compensated adequately.

- He may explain it was a one-time event and won't happen again. (*Isolated Incident*)

- Paul may pressure Davis into staying silent by implying his dad knows about it and has approved the withdrawals.
- He may promise to pay the money back as soon as he gets out of the hospital (no harm, no foul).

What is at stake for the key parties, including those who disagree with you? (Moral intensity issues exist here.)

- Paul's reputation is on the line because he committed a fraud on the company.
- Jack Jones will feel embarrassed for himself and his son if Davis discloses what Paul has done to the other owners.
- The other owners have a right to know what has happened.
- Davis may lose his job if he confronts Paul even if he drops the matter later on.
- The ability of the company to secure the $100,000 loan is at stake.
- Davis' reputation for integrity is at stake.

What levers can you use to influence those who disagree with you?

- Davis can ask Paul for supporting documentation to back up the coding of expenses to different accounts; he can share with Paul his analysis of the bank statements. When faced with the evidence, Paul may agree to repay the amount and not do it again.
- Davis can try to convince Paul that his actions are harmful to the company and potentially very embarrassing for his dad; he needs to come forward sooner rather than later and correct the "mistake."
- He can try to convince Paul that he needs to look at the long-term effects of taking money from the company that has not been properly authorized, rather than focus on short-term gain.
- Davis can use the leverage of threatening to go to all the owners if Paul doesn't admit the mistake and take corrective action; his loyalty obligation is to the three owners, not Paul. They are the ones with the most at stake.
- Davis has an ethical responsibility to inform the owners; Smith and Williams might serve as supporters to help counteract the reasons and rationalizations provided by Paul for his actions.
- Davis' reputation is at stake. As a CPA, he cannot violate the ethics of the profession; the accounting is wrong and needs to be corrected; he needs to explain about his integrity obligation.

What is your most powerful and persuasive response to the reasons and rationalizations you need to address? To whom should the argument be made? When and in what context?

- Davis should explain to Paul that he was acting diligently when he looked at the bank statements because he didn't want to pay the same vendor twice and needed to see whether the first check had cleared the bank statement.
- He should explain that using company cash for personal purposes is never acceptable unless Paul can demonstrate that the other owners knew about it and approved it.
- He should stress to Paul that taking company funds without approval is wrong regardless of the amount involved; it violates ethical norms; there are no good reasons for doing so.

- Davis should challenge Paul's statement that his dad knows about it and approved it by suggesting they both go to Jack Jones and discuss the matter; he is calling Paul's bluff. Paul may back off at this point, which confirms the asset misappropriation.

- He should explain to Paul that it is not enough to simply pay the money back. Davis doesn't want to get caught up in a cover-up. He should ask himself: What if Paul persists in his actions even after repaying the $30,000? If he doesn't inform the owners now, he could be accused of being part of the problem, dismissed from his job, and the oversight authorities in the accounting profession may be contacted. While this may seem remote at the time, Davis should be skeptical of anything Paul tells him.

Responses to Reasons and Rationalizations: Ace Manufacturing Case

Assume that Larry Davis calls Paul Jones and they set a 2:00 p.m. meeting at Paul's home where he is convalescing. The meeting goes like this:

"Paul, how are you feeling?"

"OK, Larry. What's happening at work?"

"That's why I wanted to see you."

"Yeah, why's that?"

"I noticed $10,000 payments to you each month for the first three months of the year. I can't find any supporting documentation for these amounts."

Paul immediately becomes indignant. "I told you not to look at the bank statements. You ignored my orders and disrespected my position. Your job is on the line here."

Davis is taken aback. He hesitates at first but explains about the vendor billing and tells Paul he saved the company $40,000 by detecting the duplicate billing. Paul starts to get tired and stressed out so they agree to meet in Paul's office the following week when he returns to work.

Paul's final comment is, "Tell no one about this meeting!" Davis returns to the office and starts to reflect on the meeting. He is not sure what to do at this point. He is thinking about his options, including not waiting for the meeting with Paul before acting.

Based on the meeting between Paul and Davis and earlier considerations, what are the most powerful and persuasive responses to the reasons and rationalizations given by Paul in his defense that Davis needs to address?

Davis might seek out some advice at this point. Perhaps he has a trusted friend or adviser who can bring a fresh perspective to the situation? Davis has to be be true to his values, have the courage to act on his beliefs, and meet his ethical and professional obligations.

What would you do at this point if you were in Larry's position?

Concluding Thoughts

In this chapter we have progressed from describing Kohlberg's model of moral development to Rest's model of ethical decision making and considered issues of moral intensity and virtue in developing an Integrated Ethical Decision-Making Model. We intend the model to be used as a framework to guide ethical analysis by students and frame the debate in the classroom when ethical dilemmas are discussed. It is not necessary to consider every element of the model in every case. Instead, it should serve as a reminder to students of some of the most important points to consider when making ethical decisions.

Ethical decisions are not made in a vacuum. Pressures exist in the real world of business and accounting; cultures may support or work against ethical behavior; and individuals react differently to the reasons and rationalizations given for not taking the ethical path. Therefore, it is important to understand how best to make your case when faced with an ethical dilemma. As we have learned, knowing what to do is not the same as doing it. We need a way to overcome obstacles and deal with those who would distract us from our goal to be the best person we can be; to make the ethical choice; and to follow through with ethical action. This is where the GVV framework is most valuable.

The tendency when a book on ethics is written is to focus on negative behaviors whether by a CEO, CFO, or accounting professional who does not live up to her values. But we should not loose sight of the many heroes we have in accounting, some of which were named in our concluding thoughts to Chapter 1. There are many such people who on a daily basis stand up to their supervisors and clients who pressure them to go along with financial wrongdoing; clients want to tell their own story about the company's success rather than a truthful one. New whistleblowing laws and protections in SOX and the Dodd-Frank Financial Reform Act that will be discussed in Chapter 3 provide a mechanism for accounting professionals to speak out after they have made a good faith effort to change things albeit to no avail. However, application of the GVV methodology in the real world may serve to negate the need for whistleblowing. The protagonist may be successful in voicing her values in an effective manner and changing the ethical landscape.

The field of behavioral ethics holds great promise for helping students to better understand their motivations for action and learn how to speak up when wrongdoing exists. Speaking up when things go wrong and voicing one's beliefs is something that takes practice, which is why we discussed the GVV methodology in this chapter. We follow through with additional discussions in the rest of the book.

You will face dilemmas in the workplace; all of us do. You may make some mistakes, but in truth the only mistake is not trying to correct wrongdoing. Perhaps the least likely person to choose for our final inspirational quote in this chapter is Kristi Loucks, a cake designer and pastry chef who also writes books. Loucks famously said, "The road to success is littered with failures, but the lessons learned are crucial in plotting your course to success!"

Discussion Questions

Sometimes in life things happen that seem to defy logic, yet that may be a sign of the times we are living in today. The following story applies to questions 1 and 2:

On October 15, 2009, in Fort Collins, Colorado, the parents of a six-year-old boy, Falcon Heene, claimed that he had floated away in a homemade helium balloon that was shaped to resemble a silver flying saucer. Some in the media referred to the incident as "Balloon Boy." The authorities closed down Denver International Airport, called in the National Guard, and a police pursuit ensued. After an hour-long flight that covered more than 50 miles across three counties, the empty balloon was found near the airport. It was later determined that the boy was hiding in the house all along in an incident that was a hoax and motivated by publicity that might lead to a reality television show. The authorities blamed the father, Richard, for the incident and decided to prosecute him. Richard Heene pleaded guilty on November 13, 2009, to the felony count of falsely influencing authorities. He pleaded to protect his wife, Mayumi, a Japanese citizen, whom he believed may have been deported if Richard was convicted of a more serious crime. Richard also agreed to pay $36,000 in restitution.

1. Identify the stakeholders and how they were affected by Heene's actions using ethical reasoning. What stage of moral reasoning in Kohlberg's model is exhibited by Richard Heene's actions? Do you believe the punishment fit the crime? In other words, was justice done in this case? Why or why not?

2. In an example of art imitating life, 16-year-old playwright Billy Reece was inspired by the Balloon Boy incident to write a play that was first performed at the Thespian Festival at the University of Nebraska–Lincoln in 2014. *Balloon Boy: The Musical* was presented in the 2015 New York Musical Theater Festival Developmental Reading Series. It has been said that, "Art has the power to evoke the same emotions, thoughts, moral and ethical controversies, and conflicts that we experience in life." Plato was certain that art was nothing but a dangerous and shallow imitation of life that served only to draw humans far away from the Truth. Discuss these thoughts from your own perspective of emotions, thoughts, moral considerations, and what "truth" means to you.

3. In the debate over why good people do bad things, Tenbrunsel suggests that people are often blind to the ethical dimensions of a situation, a concept he refers to as "bounded ethicality." Craig Johnson addresses moral disengagement by saying: When others try to encourage you to bad behavior ("the dark side") realize that you are an independent agent, and that you have a personal responsibility to behave morally. Discuss what this means to you.

4. One reason otherwise good people may do bad things is what psychologists call scripts. This term refers to the procedures that experience tells us to use in specific situations. Unlike other forms of experience, scripts are stored in memory in a mechanical or rote fashion. Explain why a System 1 approach to decision making might create a script that leads us to make a questionable or unethical decision.

5. How do you assess at what stage of moral development in Kohlberg's model you reason at in making decisions? Do you believe your level of reasoning is consistent with what is expected of an accounting professional? How does the stage you indicate relate to the findings of research studies discussed in this chapter about moral reasoning in accounting?

6. Using the child abuse scandal at Penn State discussed in Chapter 1, explain the actions that would have been taken by Joe Paterno if he had been reasoning at each stage in Kohlberg's model and why.

7. In his research into the components of ethical decision making, Rest raised the following issue: Assuming someone possesses sound moral reasoning skills, "Why would they ever chose the moral alternative, especially if it involves sacrificing some personal value or suffering some hardship? What motivates the selection of moral values over other values?" How does Rest's model deal with such a question? How would you answer it from the point of view of an accounting professional?

8. In the text, we point out that Rest's model is not linear in nature. An individual who demonstrates adequacy in one component may not necessarily be adequate in another, and moral failure can occur when there is a deficiency in any one component. Give an example in accounting when ethical intent may not be sufficient to produce ethical behavior and explain why that is the case.

9. In teaching about moral development, instructors often point out the threefold nature of morality: It depends on emotional development (in the form of the ability to feel guilt or shame), social development (manifested by the recognition of the group and the importance of moral behavior for the group's existence), and cognitive development (especially the ability to adopt another's perspective). How does this perspective of morality relate to ethical reasoning by accountants and auditors?

10. Do you believe that our beliefs trigger our actions, or do we act and then justify our actions by changing our beliefs? Explain.

11. Do you believe that a person's stage of moral development and personal moral philosophy play a role in how values and actions are shaped in the workplace? Explain.

12. Explain why moral problems may be of greater intensity than nonmoral problems.

13. Michael just graduated with a degree in Accounting from State University. He worked hard in school but could only achieve a 2.95 GPA because he worked 40 hours a week to pay his own way through college. Unfortunately, Michael was unable to get a job because the recruiters all had a 3.0 GPA cut-off point. Michael stayed with his college job for another year but is anxious to start his public accounting career. One day he reads about a job opening with a local CPA firm. The entry-level position pays little but it's a way for Michael to get his foot in the door. However, he knows there will be candidates for the position with a higher GPA than his so he is thinking about using his overall GPA, which was 3.25 including two years of community college studies, rather than his major GPA and the GPA at State, even though the advertisement asks for these two GPAs. Michael asks for your opinion before sending in the resume. What would you say to Michael and why?

14. In this chapter, we discuss the study by Libby and Thorne of the association between auditors' virtue and professional judgment, done by asking members of the Canadian Institute of Chartered Accountants to rate the importance of a variety of virtues. The most important virtues identified were truthful, independent, objective, and having integrity. The authors note that the inclusion of these virtues in professional codes of conduct (such as the Principles of the AICPA Code of Professional Conduct) may account for their perceived importance. Explain how these virtues relate to an auditor's intention to make ethical decisions.

15. You are in charge of the checking account for a small business. One morning, your accounting supervisor enters your office and asks you for a check for $150 for expenses that he tells you he incurred entertaining a client last night. He submits receipts from a restaurant and lounge. Later, your supervisor's girlfriend stops by to pick him up for lunch, and you overhear her telling the receptionist what a great time she had at dinner and dancing with your supervisor the night before. What would you do and why?

16. According to a survey reported by the *Daily Mail* in the United Kingdom, one in eight women has bought expensive clothes, worn them on a night out, and then returned them the next day. Nearly half of those who did confess said they were motivated by money because they couldn't afford to keep the clothes given their current economic condition. But 18 percent said they did it because they enjoyed the "buzz." Those most likely to do it were 18- to 24-year-olds, 16 percent of whom admitted to returning worn clothes (http://www.dailymail.co.uk/femail/article-2157430 /How-women-wear-expensive-new-frock-shop.html#ixzz3ea5m2mo).

    Assume you are best friends with one such woman. She asks you to go shopping with her for a dress for the Senior Prom. She says the dress will be returned after the prom. You know what she does is wrong, but she is your best friend and don't want her to get in trouble. What would you do and why? How might you counter the likely reasons and rationalizations she will give for her actions?

17. Sharon is an intern with a local CPA firm. Prior to returning to school, her supervisor goes on sick leave and asks her to do some complicated reconciliation work for him. She is given what seems to her to be an unrealistic deadline. Sharon looks at the workpapers and supporting documentation and realizes she doesn't have the skills to complete the work without help. She contacts her supervisor who tells her to talk to Holly, a good friend of Sharon and former intern at the firm, for help. Holly returned to school one semester ago. What ethical considerations do you have in this matter? What would you do and why?

18. Identify the ethical issues in each of the following situations and what your ethical obligations are, assuming you are faced with the dilemma.

a. A consultant for a CPA firm is ordered by her superior to downgrade the ratings of one company's software package being considered for a client and increase the ratings for another company, which is run by the superior's wife. What would you do and why?

b. A tax accountant is told by his superior to take a position on a tax matter that is not supportable by the facts in order to make the client happy. This is a common practice in the firm and the likelihood of the IRS questioning it is remote. Would you go along with your supervisor?

c. An auditor for a governmental agency concluded a contractor's accounting system was inadequate; her supervisor changed the opinion to adequate in order to minimize the audit hours on the job and make the process seem more efficient. Would you go above your supervisor in this matter and bring your concerns to high-ups in the agency?

19. In a June 1997 paper published in the *Journal of Business Ethics,* Sharon Green and James Weber reported the results of a study of moral reasoning of accounting students prior to and after taking an auditing course. The study also compared the results between accounting and nonaccounting students prior to the auditing course. The authors found that (1) accounting students, after taking an auditing course that emphasized the AICPA Code, reasoned at higher levels than students who had not taken the course; (2) there were no differences in moral reasoning levels when accounting and nonaccounting majors were compared prior to an auditing course; and (3) there was a significant relationship between the students' levels of ethical development and the choice of an ethical versus unethical action.[66] Do you think that taking an Accounting Ethics course would affect your level of moral development and ability to reason through ethical issues? Why or why not?

20. Explain why the process of ethical decision making depends on a number of moral, social, psychological, and organizational factors.

21. Emotional self-awareness refers to understanding your own feelings, what causes them, and how they impact your thoughts and actions. It is widely known that ethical dilemmas involving other employees/managers are inherently emotional. Researchers have found that such strong negative emotions as sadness and anger influenced individuals to make less ethical decisions, and that emotional intelligent individuals were able to make ethical decisions against the biasing influence of those negative emotions. Explain how moods could influence the thought process and ethical decision making. Have you made a decision you later regretted based on your emotional response?

22. Windsor and Kavanagh propose in a research study that client management economic pressure is a situation of high moral intensity that sensitizes auditors' emotions and thus motivates their moral reasoning to make deliberative decisions either to resist or accede to client management wishes. Explain how you think such a process might work.

23. The nature of accountants' work puts them in a special position of trust in relation to their clients, employers, and the general public, who rely on their professional judgment and guidance in making decisions. Explain the link between professional judgment and ethical decision making in accounting.

24. Explain what you think each of the following statements means in the context of moral development.

a. How far are you willing to go to do the right thing?

b. How much are you willing to give up to do what you believe is right?

c. We may say that we would do the right thing, but when it requires sacrifice, how much are we willing to give up?

25. A major theme of this chapter is that our cognitive processes influence ethical decision making. Use the theme to comment on the following statement, which various religions claim as their own and has been attributed to Lao Tzu and some say the Dalai Lama:

"Watch your thoughts; they become your words.

Watch your words; they become your actions.

Watch your actions; they become your habits.

Watch your habits; they become your character.

Watch your character; it becomes your destiny."

Endnotes

1. Max H. Bazerman and Ann E. Trebrunsel, *Blind Spots: Why We Fail to Do What's Right and What to Do About It* (Princeton, NJ: Princeton University Press, 2011).

2. Wendy Zellner, "The Fall of Enron," *BusinessWeek,* December 17, 2001, p. 30.

3. Barbara Ley Toffler with Jennifer Reingold, *Final Accounting: Ambition, Greed, and the Fall of Arthur Andersen* (New York: Broadway Books, 2003), p. 217.

4. Bethany McLean and Peter Elkind, *The Smartest Guys in the Room: The Amazing Rise and Scandalous Fall of Enron* (New York: Penguin Group, 2003).

5. Paul M. Clikeman, *Called to Account: Fourteen Financial Frauds That Shaped the American Accounting Profession* (New York: Routledge, 2009).

6. Daniel Edelman and Ashley Nicholson, "Arthur Andersen Auditors and Enron: What Happened to Their Texas CPA Licenses?" *Journal of Finance and Accountancy*, http://www.aabri.com /manuscripts/11899.pdf.

7. Lawrence Kohlberg, "Stage and Sequence: The Cognitive Developmental Approach to Socialization," in *Handbook of Socialization Theory and Research,* ed. D. A. Goslin (Chicago: Rand McNally, 1969), pp. 347–480.

8. Carol Gilligan, *In a Different Voice: Psychological Theory and Womens Development* (Cambridge, MA: Harvard University Press, 1982).

9. James R. Rest and Darcia Narvaez, eds., *Moral Development in the Professions: Psychology and Applied Ethics* (New York: Psychology Press, 1994), p. 4.

10. Rest and Narvaez.

11. Rest and Narvaez.

12. Muriel J. Bebeau and S. J. Thoma, "Intermediate Concepts and the Connection to Moral Education," *Educational Psychology Review* 11, no. 4 (1999), p. 345.

13. O. C. Ferrell, John Fraedrich, and Linda Ferrell, *Business Ethics: Ethical Decision Making and Cases* (Mason, OH: South-Western, Cengage Learning, 2009 Update), pp. 162–163.

14. Clare M. Pennino, "Is Decision Style Related to Moral Development Among Managers in the U.S.?" *Journal of Business Ethics* 41 (December 2002), pp. 337–347.

15. William Crain, *Theories of Development: Concepts and Applications,* 6th ed. (Upper Saddle River, NJ, 2010).

16. Kay Plummer, "Improving Ethical Judgment through Deep Learning," in *Ethics and Auditing,* eds. Tom Campbell and Keith Houghton (Canberra, Australia: ANU-E Press, 2010).

17. Milton Snoeyenbos, Robert F. Almeder, and James M. Humber, *Business Ethics, Corporate Values and Society* (Buffalo, NY: Prometheus Books, 1983), pp. 239–264.

18. Lawrence A. Ponemon and David R. L. Gabhart, "Ethical Reasoning Research in the Accounting and Auditing Professions," in *Moral Development in the Professions: Psychology and Applied Ethics,* eds. James R. Rest and Darcia Narvaez (New York: Psychology Press, 1994), pp. 101–120.

19. See Michael K. Shaub, "An Analysis of the Association of Traditional Demographic Variables with the Moral Reasoning of Auditing Students and Auditors," *Journal of Accounting Education* (Winter 1994), pp. 1–26; and Lawrence A. Ponemon, "Ethical Reasoning and Selection Socialization in Accounting," *Accounting, Organizations, and Society* 17 (1992), pp. 239–258.

20. David Arnold and Larry Ponemon, "Internal Auditors' Perceptions of Whistle-Blowing and the Influence of Moral Reasoning: An Experiment," *Auditing: A Journal of Practice and Theory* (Fall 1991), pp. 1–15.

21. Larry Ponemon and David Gabhart, "Auditor Independence Judgments: A Cognitive Developmental Model and Experimental Evidence," *Contemporary Accounting Research* (1990), pp. 227–251.

22. Larry Ponemon, "Auditor Underreporting of Time and Moral Reasoning: An Experimental-Lab Study," *Contemporary Accounting Research* (1993), pp. 1–29.

23. Ponemon and Gabhart, 1994, p. 108.

24. Plummer, p. 244.

25. Lawrence Kohlberg, *Essays on Moral Development: Vol. II: The Psychology of Moral Development: The Nature and Validity of Moral Stages* (San Francisco: Harper & Row, 1984).

26. Mary Louise Arnold, "Stage, Sequence, and Sequels: Changing Conceptions of Morality, Post-Kohlberg," *Educational Psychology Review,* Vol. 12, No. 4, 2000, pp. 365–383.

27. James R. Rest, Darcia Narvaez, Muriel J. Bebeau, and Stephen J. Thoma, *Postconventional Moral Thinking: A Neo-Kohlbergian Approach* (Mahwah, NJ: Lawrence Erlbaum, 1999).

28. M. L. Arnold, pp. 367–368.

29. John C. Gibbs, "Toward an Integration of Kohlberg's and Hoffman's Moral Development Theories," *Human Development* 34, 1991, pp. 88–104.

30. Richard S. Peters, *Moral Development and Moral Education* (London: George Allen & Unwin, 1982).

31. Augusto Blasi, "Bridging Moral Cognition and Moral Action: A Critical Review of the Literature," *Psychological Bulletin,* Vol. 88, No. 1, 1980, pp. 1–45.

32. William Damon and Anne Colby, "Education and Moral Commitment," *Journal of Moral Education,* Vol. 25, No. 1, 1996, pp. 31–37.

33. Craig E. Johnson, *Organizational Ethics: A Practical Approach,* 3rd ed. (NY: Sage Publications, Inc., 2015).

34. Plummer, pp. 242–244.

35. James R. Rest, "Morality," in *Handbook of Child Psychology: Cognitive Development,* Vol. 3, series ed. P. H. Mussen and vol. ed. J. Flavell (New York: Wiley, 1983), pp. 556–629.

36. Lawrence Kohlberg, *The Meaning and Measurement of Moral Development* (Worcester, MA: Clark University Press, 1979).

37. Rest and Narvaez, p. 24.

38. Jeremy I. M. Carpendale, "Kohlberg and Piaget on Stages and Moral Reasoning," *Developmental Review,* Vol. 20, Issue 2, 2000, pp. 181–205.

39. Craig E. Johnson, *Meeting the Ethical Challenges of Leadership* (New York: Sage Publications, 2011).

40. Steven Dellaportas, Beverly Jackling, Philomena Leung, Barry J. Cooper, "Developing an Ethics Education Framework for Accounting," *Journal of Business Ethics Education*, 8, no.1 (2011), pp. 63–82.

41. Thomas Jones, "Ethical Decision Making by Individuals in Organizations: An Issue-Contingent Model," *Academy of Management Review* 16, pp. 366–395.

42. Jones, p. 379.

43. Sarah Hope Lincoln and Elizabeth K. Holmes, "Ethical Decision Making: A Process Influenced by Moral Intensity," *Journal of Healthcare, Science and the Humanities,* Vol. 1, No. 1, 2011, pp. 55–69.

44. Johnson.

45. Theresa Libby and Linda Thorne, "Virtuous Auditors: While Virtue Is Back in Fashion, How Do You Define It and Measure Its Importance to an Auditor's Role?" *CA Magazine,* November 2003, Available at: www.camagazine.com/archives/print-edition/2003/nov/regulars/camagazine24374.aspx.

46. Libby and Thorne.

47. Linda Thorne, "The Role of Virtue in Auditors' Ethical Decision Making: An Integration of Cognitive-Developmental and Virtue Ethics Perspectives," *Research on Accounting Ethics,* no. 4 (1998), pp. 293–294.

48. Mary Beth Armstrong, J. Edward Ketz, and Dwight Owsen, "Ethics Education in Accounting: Moving Toward Ethical Motivation and Ethical Behavior," *Journal of Accounting Education* 21 (2003), pp. 1–16.

49. Manuel Velasquez, Claire Andre, Thomas Shanks, and Michael J. Meyer, "Thinking Ethically: A Framework for Moral Decision Making," Available at: http://www.scu.edu/ethics/practicing/decision/thinking.html#sthash.zMGI3C7i.dpuf.

50. Rushworth M. Kidder, *How Good People Make Tough Choices* (NY: Simon & Schuster, 1995).

51. Johnson, 2011, pp. 249–250.

52. Richard F. West and Keith Stanovich, "Individual Differences in Reasoning: Implications for the Rationality Debate," *Behavioral & Brain Sciences* (2000), 23, pp. 645–665.

53. Daniel Kahneman, "A Perspective on Judgment and Choice: Mapping Bounded Rationality," *American Psychologist* (2003), 58, pp. 697–720.

54. Leon Festinger, *A Theory of Cognitive Dissonance* (Evanston, IL: Row & Peterson, 1957).

55. Penny Tompkins and James Lawley, "Cognitive Dissonance and Creative Tension—The Same or Different?" from presentation at The Developing Group, October 3, 2009, Available at: http://www.cleanlanguage.co.uk/articles/articles/262/0/Cognitive-Dissonance-and-Creative-Tension/Page0.html.

56. Festinger.

57. Max H. Bazerman and Francesca Gino, "Behavioral Ethics: Toward a Deeper Understanding of Moral Judgment and Dishonesty," *Annual Review of Law and Social Science* 8 (December 2012), pp. 85–104.

58. Dennis P. Wittmer, "Behavioral Ethics in Business Organizations: What the Research Teaches Us," in *Encyclopedia of Business Ethics and Society,* ed. Robert W. Kolb (NY: Sage Publications, 2008).

59. Wittmer, p. 62.

60. Bazerman and Gino.

61. The University of Texas uses a program, "Ethics Unwrapped," to teach GVV to its students. Videos are available on the following Web site: http://ethicsunwrapped.utexas.edu/

62. Materials to teach GVV and cases are available on the GVV Web site: http://www.babson.edu /Academics/teaching-research/gvv/Pages/curriculum.aspx

63. M.C. Gentile, *Giving Voice to Values: How to Speak Your Mind When You Know What's Right.* (New Haven, CT: Yale University Press, 2010).

64. Gentile.

65. Gentile.

66. Sharon Green and James Weber, "Influencing Ethical Development: Exposing Students to the AICPA Code of Conduct," *Journal of Business Ethics* 16, no. 8 (June 1997), pp. 777–790.

Chapter 2 Cases

Case 2-1 A Team Player? (a GVV case)

Barbara is working on the audit of a client with a group of five other staff-level employees. During the audit, Diane, a member of the group, points out that she identified a deficiency in the client's inventory system that she did not discover during the physical observation of the client's inventory. The deficiency was relatively minor, and perhaps that is why it was not detected at the time. Barbara suggests to Diane that they bring the matter to Jessica, the senior in charge of the engagement. Diane does not want to do it because she is the one who identified the deficiency and she is the one who should have detected it at the time of the observation. Three of the other four staff members agree with Diane. Haley is the only one, along with Barbara, who wants to inform Jessica.

After an extended discussion of the matter, the group votes and decides not to inform Jessica. Still, Barbara does not feel right about it. She wonders: What if Jessica finds out another way? What if the deficiency is more serious than Diane has said? What if it portends other problems with the client? She decides to raise all these issues but is rebuked by the others who remind her that the team is already behind on its work and any additional audit procedures would increase the time spent on the audit and make them all look incompetent. They remind Barbara that Jessica is a stickler for keeping to the budget and any overages cannot be billed to the client.

Questions

1. Discuss these issues from the perspective of Kohlberg's model of moral development. How does this relate to the established norms of the work group as you see it?

2. Assume you are in Barbara's position. What would you do and why? Consider the following in answering the question:

- How can you best express your point of view effectively?

- What do you need to say, to whom, and in what sequence?

- What do you expect the objections or pushback will be and, then, what would you say next?

Case 2-2 FDA Liability Concerns (a GVV case)

Gregory and Alex started a small business based on a secret-recipe salad dressing that got rave reviews. Gregory runs the business end and makes all final operational decisions. Alex runs the creative side of the business.

Alex's salad dressing was a jalapeno vinaigrette that went great with barbeque or burgers. He got so many requests for the recipe and a local restaurant asked to use it as the house special, that Alex decided to bottle and market the dressing to the big box stores. Whole Foods and Trader Joe's carried the dressing; sales were increasing every month. As the business grew, Gregory and Alex hired Michael, a college friend and CPA, to be the CFO of the company.

Michael's first suggestion was to do a five-year strategic plan with expanding product lines and taking the company public or selling it within five to seven years. Gregory and Alex weren't sure about wanting to go public and losing control, but expanding the product lines was appealing. Michael also wanted to contain costs and increase profit margins.

At Alex's insistence, they called a meeting with Michael to discuss his plans. "Michael, we hired you to take care of the accounting and the financial details," Alex said. "We don't understand profit margins. On containing costs, the best ingredients must be used to ensure the quality of the dressing. We must meet all FDA requirements for food safety and containment of food borne bacteria, such as listeria or e coli, as you develop cost systems."

"Of course," Michael responded. "I will put processes in place to meet the FDA requirements."

At the next quarterly meeting of the officers, Alex wanted an update on the FDA processes and the latest inspection. He was concerned whether Michael understood the importance of full compliance.

"Michael," Alex said, "the FDA inspector and I had a discussion while he was here. He wanted to make sure I understood the processes and the liabilities of the company if foodborne bacteria are traced to our products. Are we doing everything by the book and reserving some liabilities for any future recalls?"

Michael assured Alex and Gregory that everything was being done by the book and the accounting was following standard practices. Over the next 18 months, the FDA inspectors came and Michael reported everything was fine.

After the next inspection, there was some listeria found in the product. The FDA insisted on a recall of batch 57839. Alex wanted to recall all the product to make sure that all batches were safe.

"A total recall is too expensive and would mean that the product could be off the shelves for three to four weeks. It would be hard to regain our shelf advantage and we would lose market share," Michael explained.

Alex seemed irritated and turned to Gregory for support, but he was silent. He then walked over to where Michael was sitting and said, "Michael, nothing is more important than our reputation. Our promise and mission is to provide great-tasting dressing made with the freshest, best, organic products. A total recall will show that we stand by our mission and promise. I know we would have some losses, but don't we have a liability reserve for recall, like a warranty reserve?"

"The reserve will not cover the entire expense of a recall," Michael said. "It will be too expensive to do a total recall and will cause a huge loss for the quarter. In the next six months, we will need to renew a bank loan; a loss will hurt our renewal loan rate and terms. You know I have been working to get the company primed to go public as well."

Alex offered that he didn't care about going public. He didn't start the business to be profitable. Gregory, on the other hand, indicated he thought going public was a great idea and would provide needed funds on a continuous basis.

Alex told Michael that he needed to see all the FDA inspection reports. He asked, "What is the FDA requiring to be done to address the issue of listeria?"

"I'm handling it, Alex," Michael said. "Don't worry about it. Just keep making new salad dressings so that we can stay competitive."

"Well, Michael, just answer what the FDA is asking for."

"Just to sterilize some of our equipment, but it shouldn't be too bad."

"Michael, it's more than that," Alex responded. "The FDA contacted me directly and asked me to meet with them in three days to discuss our plans to meet the FDA requirements and standards. We will be fined for not addressing issues found in prior inspections. I want to see the past inspection reports so I can better understand the scope of the problem."

"Listen, Alex," Michael said. "I just completed a cost–benefit analysis of fixing all the problems identified by the FDA and found the costs outweighed the benefits. We're better off paying whatever fines they impose and move on."

"Michael, I don't care about cost–benefit analysis. I care about my reputation and that of the company. Bring me all the inspection reports tomorrow."

The three of them met the following day. As Alex reviewed the past inspection reports, he realized that he had relied on Michael too much and his assurances that all was well with the FDA. In fact, the FDA had repeatedly noted that more sterilization of the equipment was needed and that storage of the products and ingredients needed additional care. Alex began to wonder whether Michael should stay on with the company. He also was concerned about the fact that Gregory had been largely silent during the discussions. He wondered whether Gregory was putting profits ahead of safety and the reputation of the company.

Questions

Alex knows what the right thing to do is. As Alex prepares for a meeting on the inspection reports the next day, he focuses on influencing the positions of Michael and Gregory, both of whom will be involved in the meeting. Put yourself in Alex's position and answer the following questions.

1. What are the main arguments you are trying to counter? That is, what are the reasons and rationalizations you need to address? *safety + reputation > cost margins*
2. What is at stake for the key parties, including those who disagree with you?
3. What levers can you use to influence those who disagree with you? *long term*
4. What is your most powerful and persuasive response to the reasons and rationalizations you need to address? To whom should the argument be made? When and in what context?

Case 2-3 The Tax Return (a GVV case)

Brenda Sells sent the tax return that she prepared for the president of Purple Industries, Inc., Harry Kohn, to Vincent Dim, the manager of the tax department at her accounting firm. Dim asked Sells to come to his office at 9 a.m. on Friday, April 12, 2016. Sells was not sure why Dim wanted to speak to her. The only reason she could come up with was the tax return for Kohn.

"Brenda, come in," Vincent said.

"Thank you, Vincent," Brenda responded.

"Do you know why I asked to see you?"

"I'm not sure. Does it have something to do with the tax return for Mr. Kohn?" asked Brenda.

"That's right," answered Vincent.

"Is there a problem?" Brenda asked.

"I just spoke with Kohn. I told him that you want to report his winnings from the lottery. He was incensed."

"Why?" Brenda asked. "You and I both know that the tax law is quite clear on this matter. When a taxpayer wins money by playing the lottery, then that amount must be reported as revenue. The taxpayer can offset lottery gains with lottery losses, if those are supportable. Of course, the losses cannot be higher than the amount of the gains. In the case of Mr. Kohn, the losses exceed the gains, so there is no net tax effect. I don't see the problem."

"You're missing the basic point that the deduction for losses is only available if you itemize deductions," Vincent said. "Kohn is not doing that. He's using the standard deduction."

Brenda realized she had blown it by not knowing that.

Brenda didn't know what to say. Vincent seemed to be telling her the lottery amounts shouldn't be reported. But that was against the law. She asked, "Are you telling me to forget about the lottery amounts on Mr. Kohn's tax return?"

"I want you to go back to your office and think carefully about the situation. Consider that this is a one-time request and we value our staff members who are willing to be flexible in such situations. And, I'll tell you, other staff in the same situation have been loyal to the firm. Let's meet again in my office tomorrow at 9 a.m."

Questions

1. Analyze the alternatives available to Brenda using Kohlberg's six stages of moral development. Assume that Brenda has no reason to doubt Vincent's veracity with respect to the statement that it is "a one-time request." Should that make a difference in what Brenda decides to do? Why or why not?

2. Assume you have decided what your position will be in the meeting with Vincent but are not quite sure how to respond to the reasons and rationalizations provided by him to ignore the lottery losses. How might you counter those arguments? What would be your most powerful and persuasive responses?

3. Assume that Brenda decides to go along with Vincent and omits the lottery losses and gains. Next year a similar situation arises with winnings from a local poker tournament. Kohn now trusts Brenda and shared with her that he won $4,950 from that event. He tells you to not report it because it was below the $5,000 threshold for the payer to issue a form W-2G. If you were Brenda, and Vincent asked you to do the same thing you did last year regarding omitting the lottery losses and gains, what would you do this second year and why?

Case 2-4 A Faulty Budget (a GVV Case)

Jackson Daniels graduated from Lynchberg State College two years ago. Since graduating from college, he has worked in the accounting department of Lynchberg Manufacturing. Daniels was recently asked to prepare a sales budget for the year 2016. He conducted a thorough analysis and came out with projected sales of 250,000 units of product. That represents a 25 percent increase over 2015.

Daniels went to lunch with his best friend, Jonathan Walker, to celebrate the completion of his first solo job. Walker noticed Daniels seemed very distant. He asked what the matter was. Daniels stroked his chin, ran his hand through his bushy, black hair, took another drink of scotch, and looked straight into the eyes of his friend of 20 years. "Jon, I think I made a mistake with the budget."

"What do you mean?" Walker answered.

"You know how we developed a new process to manufacture soaking tanks to keep the ingredients fresh?"

"Yes," Walker answered.

"Well, I projected twice the level of sales for that product than will likely occur."

"Are you sure?" Walker asked.

"I checked my numbers. I'm sure. It was just a mistake on my part."

Walker asked Daniels what he planned to do about it.

"I think I should report it to Pete. He's the one who acted on the numbers to hire additional workers to produce the soaking tanks," Daniels said.

"Wait a second, Jack. How do you know there won't be extra demand for the product? You and I both know demand is a tricky number to project, especially when a new product comes on the market. Why don't you sit back and wait to see what happens?"

"Jon, I owe it to Pete to be honest. He hired me."

"You know Pete is always pressuring us to 'make the numbers.' Also, Pete has a zero tolerance for employees who make mistakes. That's why it's standard practice around here to sweep things under the rug. Besides, it's a one-time event—right?"

"But what happens if I'm right and the sales numbers were wrong? What happens if the demand does not increase beyond what I now know to be the correct projected level?"

"Well, you can tell Pete about it at that time. Why raise a red flag now when there may be no need?"

As the lunch comes to a conclusion, Walker pulls Daniels aside and says, "Jack, this could mean your job. If I were in your position, I'd protect my own interests first."

Jimmy (Pete) Beam is the vice president of production. Jackson Daniels had referred to him in his conversation with Jonathan Walker. After several days of reflection on his friend's comments, Daniels decided to approach Pete and tell him about the mistake. He knew there might be consequences, but his sense of right and wrong ruled the day. What transpired next surprised Daniels.

"Come in, Jack" Pete said.

"Thanks, Pete. I asked to see you on a sensitive matter."

"I'm listening."

"There is no easy way to say this so I'll just tell you the truth. I made a mistake in my sales budget. The projected increase of 25 percent was wrong. I checked my numbers and it should have been 12.5 percent. I'm deeply sorry; want to correct the error; and promise never to do it again."

Pete's face became beet red. He said, "Jack, you know I hired 20 new people based on your budget."

"Yes, I know."

"That means ten have to be laid off or fired. They won't be happy and once word filters through the company, other employees may wonder if they are next."

"I hadn't thought about it that way."

"Well, you should have." Here's what we are going to do…and this is between you and me. Don't tell anyone about this conversation."

"You mean not even tell my boss?"

"No, Pete said." Cwervo can't know about it because he's all about correcting errors and moving on. Look, Jack, it's my reputation at stake here as well."

Daniels hesitated but reluctantly agreed not to tell the controller, Jose Cwervo, his boss. The meeting ended with Daniels feeling sick to his stomach and guilty for not taking any action.

Questions

1. What are Daniels's options in this situation? Use ethical reasoning to identify the best alternative. What would you do if you were in Daniels' position?

2. Given that you have decided to take some action even though you had agreed not to do so, who would you approach to express your point of view and why?

3. What is at stake for the key parties?

4. What are the main arguments you are likely to encounter in making the strongest case possible?

5. What is your most powerful and persuasive response to the reasons and rationalizations you may need to address? To whom should the argument be made? When and in what context?

Case 2-5 Gateway Hospital (a GVV case)

Troy just returned from a business trip for health-care administrators in Orlando. Kristen, a relatively new employee who reports to him, also attended the conference. They both work for Gateway Hospital, a for-profit hospital in the St. Louis area. The Orlando conference included training in the newest reporting requirements in the health-care industry, networking with other hospital administrators, reports on upcoming legislation in health care, and the current status of regulations related to the Affordable Care Act. The conference was in late March and coincided with Troy's kids' spring break, so the entire family traveled to Orlando to check out Walt Disney World and SeaWorld.

The hospital's expense reimbursement policy is very clear on the need for receipts for all reimbursements. Meals are covered for those not provided as part of the conference registration fee, but only within a preset range. Troy has never had a problem following those guidelines. However, the trip to Orlando was more expensive than Troy expected. He did not attend all sessions of the conference, to enjoy time with his family. Upon their return to St. Louis, Troy's wife suggested that Troy submit three meals and one extra night at the hotel as business expenses, even though they were personal expenses. Her rationale was that the hospital policies would not totally cover the business costs of the trip. Troy often has to travel and misses family time that cannot be recovered or replaced. Troy also knows that his boss has a reputation of signing forms without reading or careful examination. He realizes the amount involved is not material and probably won't be detected.

Kristen is approached by Joyce, the head of the accounting department, about Troy's expenses, which seem high and not quite right. Kristen is asked about the extra night because she did not ask for reimbursement for that time. Kristen knows it can be easily explained by saying Troy had to stay an extra day for additional meetings, a common occurrence for administrators, although that was not the case. She also knows that the hospital has poor controls and a culture of "not rocking the boat," and that other employees have routinely inflated expense reports in the past.

Assume you, as Kristen, have decided the best approach, at least in the short run, is to put off responding to Joyce so that you can discuss the matter with Troy. Answer the following questions.

Questions

1. What are the main arguments you feel Troy will make and reasons and rationalizations you need to address?

2. What is at stake for the key parties in this situation?

3. What levers can you use to influence how Troy reacts to your position in this matter?

4. What is your most powerful and persuasive response to the reasons and rationalizations you need to address? To whom should the argument be made? When and in what context?

Case 2-6 LinkedIn and Shut Out

The facts of this case are fictional. Any resemblance to real persons, living or dead, is purely coincidental.

Kenny is always looking to make contacts in the business world and enhance his networking experiences. He knows how important it is to drive customers to his sports memorabilia business. He's just a small seller in the Mall of America in Bloomington, Minnesota.

Kenny decided to go on LinkedIn. Within the first few weeks, he received a number of requests that said, "I'd like to add you to my professional network." At first almost all of such requests came from friends and associates he knew quite well. After a while, however, he started to receive similar requests from people he didn't know. He would click on the "view profile" button, but that didn't provide much useful information so he no longer looked at profiles for every request. He simply clicked the "accept" button and the "You are now connected" message appeared.

One day Kenny received the following message with a request to "connect":

"I plan to come to your sports memorabilia store in the future so I thought I'd introduce myself first. I am a financial planner and have helped small business owners like yourself to develop financial plans that provide returns on their investments three times the average rate received for conventional investments. I'm confident I can do the same for you. As a qualified professional, you can trust my services."

Kenny didn't think much about it. It certainly sounded legitimate. Besides, he would meet the financial planner soon and could judge the type of person he was. So, Kenny linked with the planner.

A week later, the financial planner dropped by Kenny's store and provided lots of data to show that he had successfully increased returns for dozens of people. He even had testimonials with him. Kenny agreed to meet with him in his St. Paul office later that week to discuss financial planning.

The meeting took place and Kenny gave the financial planner a check for $30,000, which was most of Kenny's liquid assets. At first the returns looked amazing. Each of the first two quarterly statements he received from the planner indicated that he had already earned $5,000; a total of $10,000 in six months. Three months later Kenny did not receive a statement. He called the planner and the phone had been disconnected. He sent e-mails but they were returned as not valid. No luck with text messages.

Kenny started to worry whether he ever would see his money—at least the $30,000. He was at a loss what to do. A friend suggested he contact LinkedIn and see if it could help. His online contact led to the following response in an e-mail:

> As per our agreement with you, we are not liable to you or others for any indirect, incidental, special, consequential, or punitive damages, or any loss of data, opportunities, reputation, profits or revenues, related to the services of LinkedIn. In no event shall the liability of LinkedIn exceed, in the aggregate for all claims against us, an amount that is the lesser of (a) five times the most recent monthly or yearly fee that you paid for a premium service, if any, or (b) $1,000. This limitation of liability is part of the basis of the bargain between you and LinkedIn and shall apply to all claims of liability (e.g., warranty, tort, negligence, contract, law) and even if LinkedIn has been told of the possibility of any such damage, and even if these remedies fail their essential purpose. If disputes arise relating to this Agreement and/or the Services, both parties agree that all of these claims can only be litigated in the federal or state courts of Santa Clara County, California, USA, and we each agree to personal jurisdiction in those courts.

To say Kenny was distraught is an understatement. He felt like he had been shut out. While he did he not understand all the legalese, he knew enough that he would have to hire an attorney if he wanted to pursue the matter.

Questions

1. How would you characterize Kenny's thought process in the way he responded to requests to connect on LinkedIn?

2. Who is to blame for what happened to Kenny and why?

3. What would you do at this point if you were in Kenny's position and why?

Case 2-7 Milton Manufacturing Company

Milton Manufacturing Company produces a variety of textiles for distribution to wholesale manufacturers of clothing products. The company's primary operations are located in Long Island City, New York, with branch factories and warehouses in several surrounding cities. Milton Manufacturing is a closely held company, and Irv Milton is the president. He started the business in 2005, and it grew in revenue from $500,000 to $5 million in 10 years. However, the revenues declined to $4.5 million in 2015. Net cash flows from all activities also were declining. The company was concerned because it planned to borrow $20 million from the credit markets in the fourth quarter of 2016.

Irv Milton met with Ann Plotkin, the chief accounting officer (CAO), on January 15, 2016, to discuss a proposal by Plotkin to control cash outflows. He was not overly concerned about the recent decline in net cash flows from operating activities because these amounts were expected to increase in 2016 as a result of projected higher levels of revenue and cash collections. However, that was not Plotkin's view.

Plotkin knew that if overall negative capital expenditures continued to increase at the rate of 40 percent per year, Milton Manufacturing probably would not be able to borrow the $20 million. Therefore, she suggested establishing a new policy to be instituted on a temporary basis. Each plant's capital expenditures for 2016 for investing activities would be limited to the level of those capital expenditures in 2013, the last year of an overall positive cash flow. Operating activity cash flows had no such restrictions. Irv Milton pointedly asked Plotkin about the possible negative effects of such a policy, but in the end, he was convinced that it was necessary to initiate the policy immediately to stem the tide of increases in capital expenditures. A summary of cash flows appears in Exhibit 1.

EXHIBIT 1   Milton Manufacturing Company

Summary of Cash Flows
For the Years Ended December 31, 2015 and 2014 (000 omitted)

	December 31, 2015	December 31, 2014
Cash Flows from Operating Activities		
Net income	$ 372	$ 542
Adjustments to reconcile net income to net cash provided by operating activities	(2,350)	(2,383)
Net cash provided by operating activities	$ (1,978)	$ (1,841)
Cash Flows from Investing Activities		
Capital expenditures	$ (1,420)	$ (1,918)
Other investing inflows (outflows)	176	84
Net cash used in investing activities	$ (1,244)	$ (1,834)
Cash Flows from Financing Activities		
Net cash provided (used in) financing activities	$ 168	$ 1,476
Increase (decrease) in cash and cash equivalents	$ (3,054)	$ (2,199)
Cash and cash equivalents—beginning of the year	$ 3,191	$ 5,390
Cash and cash equivalents—end of the year	$ 147	$ 3,191

Sammie Markowicz is the plant manager at the headquarters in Long Island City. He was informed of the new capital expenditure policy by Ira Sugofsky, the vice president for operations. Markowicz told Sugofsky that the new policy could negatively affect plant operations because certain machinery and equipment, essential to the production process, had been breaking down more frequently during the past two years. The problem was primarily with the motors. New and better models with more efficient motors had been developed by an overseas supplier. These were expected to be available by April 2016. Markowicz planned to order 1,000 of these new motors for the Long Island City operation, and he expected that other plant managers would do the same. Sugofsky told Markowicz to delay the acquisition of new motors for one year, after which time the restrictive capital expenditure policy would be lifted. Markowicz reluctantly agreed.

Milton Manufacturing operated profitably during the first six months of 2016. Net cash inflows from operating activities exceeded outflows by $1,250,000 during this time period. It was the first time in two years that there was a positive cash flow from operating activities. Production operations accelerated during the third quarter as a result of increased demand for Milton's textiles. An aggressive advertising campaign initiated in late 2015 seemed to bear fruit for the company. Unfortunately, the increased level of production put pressure on the machines, and the degree of breakdown was increasing. A big problem was that the motors wore out prematurely.

Markowicz was concerned about the machine breakdown and increasing delays in meeting customer demands for the shipment of the textile products. He met with the other branch plant managers, who complained bitterly to him about not being able to spend the money to acquire new motors. Markowicz was very sensitive to their needs. He informed them that the company's regular supplier had recently announced a 25 percent price increase for the motors. Other suppliers followed suit, and Markowicz saw no choice but to buy the motors from the overseas supplier. That supplier's price was lower, and the quality of the motors would significantly enhance the machines' operating efficiency. However, the company's restrictions on capital expenditures stood in the way of making the purchase.

Markowicz approached Sugofsky and told him about the machine breakdowns and the concerns of other plant managers. Sugofsky seemed indifferent but reminded Markowicz of the capital expenditure restrictions in place and that the Long Island City plant was committed to keeping expenditures at the same level as it had in 2014. Markowicz argued that he was faced with an unusual situation and he had to act now. Sugofsky hurriedly left, but not before he said to Markowicz, "You and I may not agree with it, but a policy is a policy."

Markowicz reflected on his obligations to Milton Manufacturing. He was conflicted because he viewed his primary responsibility and that of the other plant managers to ensure that the production process operated smoothly. The last thing the workers needed right now was a stoppage of production because of machine failure.

At this time, Markowicz learned of a 30-day promotional price offered by the overseas supplier to gain new customers by lowering the price for all motors by 25 percent. Coupled with the 25 percent increase in price by the company's supplier, Markowicz knew he could save the company $1,500, or 50 percent of cost, on each motor purchased from the overseas supplier.

After carefully considering the implications of his intended action, Markowicz contacted the other plant managers and informed them that while they were not obligated to follow his lead because of the capital expenditure policy, he planned to purchase 1,000 motors from the overseas supplier for the headquarters plant in Long Island City.

Markowicz made the purchase at the beginning of the fourth quarter of 2016 without informing Sugofsky. He convinced the plant accountant to record the $1.5 million expenditure as an operating (not capital) expenditure because he knew that the higher level of operating cash inflows resulting from increased revenues would mask the effect of his expenditure. In fact, Markowicz was proud that he had "saved" the company $1.5 million, and he did what was necessary to ensure that the Long Island City plant continued to operate.

The acquisitions by Markowicz and the other plant managers enabled the company to keep up with the growing demand for textiles, and the company finished the year with record high levels of profit and net cash inflows from all activities. Markowicz was lauded by his team for his leadership. The company successfully executed a loan agreement with Second Bankers Hours & Trust Co. The $20 million borrowed was received on October 3, 2016.

During the course of an internal audit of the 2016 financial statements, Beverly Wald, the chief internal auditor (and also a CPA), discovered that there was an unusually high number of motors in inventory. A complete check of the inventory determined that $1 million worth of motors remained on hand.

Wald reported her findings to Ann Plotkin, and together they went to see Irv Milton. After being informed of the situation, Milton called in Sugofsky. When Wald told him about her findings, Sugofsky's face turned beet red. He told Wald that he had instructed Markowicz *not* to make the purchase. He also inquired about the accounting since Wald had said it was wrong.

Wald explained to Sugofsky that the $1 million should be accounted for as inventory, not as an operating cash outflow: "What we do in this case is transfer the motors out of inventory and into the machinery account once they are placed into operation because, according to the documentation, the motors added significant value to the asset."

Sugofsky had a perplexed look on his face. Finally, Irv Milton took control of the accounting lesson by asking, "What's the difference? Isn't the main issue that Markowicz did not follow company policy?" The three officers in the room nodded their heads simultaneously, perhaps in gratitude for being saved the additional lecturing. Milton then said he wanted the three of them to brainstorm some alternatives on how best to deal with the Markowicz situation and present the choices to him in one week.

Questions

Use the Integrated Ethical Decision-Making Process discussed in the chapter to help you assess the following:

1. Identify the ethical and professional issues of concern to Beverly Wald as the chief internal auditor and a CPA.
2. Who are the stakeholders in this case and what are their interests?

3. Identify alternative courses of action for Wald, Plotkin, and Sugofsky to present in their meeting with Milton. How might these alternatives affect the stakeholder interests?

4. If you were in Milton's place, which of the alternatives would you choose and why?

Case 2-8 Juggyfroot

"I'm sorry, Lucy. That's the way it is," Ricardo said. The client wants it that way.

"I just don't know if I can go along with it, Ricardo," Lucy replied.

"I know. I agree with you. But, Juggyfroot is our biggest client, Lucy. They've warned us that they will put the engagement up for bid if we refuse to go along with the reclassification of marketable securities," Ricardo explained.

"Have you spoken to Fred and Ethel about this?" Lucy asked.

"Are you kidding? They're the ones who made the decision to go along with Juggyfroot," Ricardo responded.

"I don't care, Ricardo. I expect more from you. I didn't join this firm to compromise my values."

The previous scene took place in the office of Deziloo LLP, a large CPA firm in Beverly Hills, California. Lucy Spheroid is the partner on the engagement of Juggyfroot, a publicly owned global manufacturer of pots and pans and other household items. Ricardo Rikey is the managing partner of the office. Fred and Ethel are the engagement review partners that make final judgments on difficult accounting issues, especially when there is a difference of opinion with the client. All four are CPAs.

Ricardo Rikey is preparing for a meeting with Norman Baitz, the CEO of Juggyfroot. Ricardo knows that the company expects to borrow $5 million next quarter and it wants to put the best possible face on its financial statements to impress the banks. That would explain why the company reclassified a $2 million market loss on a trading investment to the available-for-sale category so that the "loss" would now show up in stockholder's equity, not as a charge against current income. The result was to increase earnings in 2015 by 8 percent. Ricardo knows that without the change, the earnings would have declined by 2 percent and the company's stock price would have taken a hit. However, he is also very aware of his ethical and professional responsibilities.

In the meeting, Ricardo decides to overlook the recommendation by Fred and Ethel. Ricardo points out to Baitz that the investment in question was marketable, and in the past, the company had sold similar investments in less than one year. Ricardo adds there is no justification under generally accepted accounting principles (GAAP) to change the classification from trading to available-for-sale.

What happened next shocked Ricardo back to reality. The conversation between Baitz and Ricardo went this way.

"I hate to bring it up, Ricardo, but do you recall what happened last year at about the same time?"

"What do you mean?"

"You agreed that we could record $1 million as revenue for 2014 based on a sale of our product that we held at an off-site distribution warehouse until the client asked for delivery, which occurred in 2015."

Ricardo remembered all too well. It almost cost the firm the Juggyfroot account. "Are you going to throw that in my face?"

"No, Ricardo. Just a gentle reminder that you had agreed to go along with what we had asked at that time. We expect you to be loyal to our interests here as well."

The meeting broke up when Baitz received a confidential phone call. They agreed to continue it first thing in the morning.

Questions

1. Should Ricardo let what happened last year affect how he approaches the issue of the improper recording of marketable securities when he resumes his discussion with Baitz in the morning? Why or why not?

2. How would you handle the issue if you were in Ricardo's position? Develop an action plan to get your point of view across. What would you say? What do you expect the objections or pushback will be? How would you convince Baitz of the rightness of your position?

Case 2-9 Phar-Mor

The Dilemma

The story of Phar-Mor shows how quickly a company that built its earnings on fraudulent transactions can dissolve like an Alka-Seltzer.

One day, Stan Cherelstein, the controller of Phar-Mor, discovered cabinets stuffed with held checks totaling $10 million. Phar-Mor couldn't release the checks to vendors because it did not have enough cash in the bank to cover the amount. Cherelstein wondered what he should do.

Background

Phar-Mor was a chain of discount drugstores, based in Youngstown, Ohio, and founded in 1982 by Michael Monus and David Shapira. In less than 10 years, the company grew from 15 to 310 stores and had 25,000 employees. According to Litigation Release No. 14716 issued by the SEC,[1] Phar-Mor had cumulatively overstated income by $290 million between 1987 and 1991. In 1992, prior to disclosure of the fraud, the company overstated income by an additional $238 million.

The Cast of Characters

Mickey Monus personifies the hard-driving entrepreneur who is bound and determined to make it big whatever the cost. He served as the president and chief operating officer (COO) of Phar-Mor from its inception until a corporate restructuring was announced on July 28, 1992.

David Shapira was the CEO of both Phar-Mor and Giant Eagle, Phar-Mor's parent company and majority stockholder. Giant Eagle also owned Tamco, which was one of Phar-Mor's major suppliers. Shapira left day-to-day operations of Phar-Mor to Monus until the fraud became too large and persistent to ignore.

Patrick Finn was the CFO of Phar-Mor from 1988 to 1992. He brought Monus the bad news that, following a number of years of eroding profits, the company faced millions in losses in 1989.

John Anderson was the accounting manager at Phar-Mor. Hired after completing a college degree in accounting at Youngstown State University, Anderson became a part of the fraud.

Coopers & Lybrand, prior to its merger with Price Waterhouse, were the auditors of Phar-Mor. The firm failed to detect the fraud as it was unfolding.

How It Started

The facts of this case are taken from the SEC filing and a PBS *Frontline* episode called "How to Steal $500 Million." The interpretation of the facts is consistent with reports, but some literary license has been taken to add intrigue to the case.

Finn approached Monus with the bad news. Monus took out his pen, crossed off the losses, and then wrote in higher numbers to show a profit. Monus couldn't bear the thought of his hot growth company that had been sizzling for five years suddenly flaming out. In the beginning, it was to be a short-term fix to buy time while the company improved efficiency, put the heat on suppliers for lower prices, and turned a profit. Finn believed in Monus's ability to turn things around, so he went along with the fraud. Also, he thought of himself as a team player. Finn prepared the reports, and Monus changed the numbers for four months before turning the task over to Finn. These reports with the false numbers were faxed to Shapira and given to Phar-Mor's board. Basically, the company was lying to its owners.

The fraud occurred by dumping the losses into a "bucket account" and then reallocating the sums to one of the company's hundreds of stores in the form of increases in inventory amounts. Phar-Mor issued fake invoices for merchandise purchases and made phony journal entries to increase inventory and decrease cost of sales. The company overcounted and double-counted merchandise in inventory.

The fraud was helped by the fact that the auditors from Coopers observed inventory in only 4 out of 300 stores, and that allowed the finance department at Phar-Mor to conceal the shortages. Moreover, Coopers informed Phar-Mor in advance which stores they would visit. Phar-Mor executives fully stocked the 4 selected stores but allocated the phony inventory increases to the other 296 stores. Regardless of the accounting tricks, Phar-Mor was heading for collapse and its suppliers threatened to cut off the company for nonpayment of bills.

Stan Cherelstein's Role

Cherelstein, a CPA, was hired to be the controller of Phar-Mor in 1991, long after the fraud had begun. One day, Anderson called Cherelstein into his office and explained that the company had been keeping two sets of books—one that showed the true state of the company with the losses and the other, called the "subledger," that showed the falsified numbers that were presented to the auditors.

Cherelstein and Anderson discussed what to do about the fraud. Cherelstein asked Anderson why he hadn't done something about it. Anderson asked how could he? He was the new kid on the block. Besides, Pat (Finn) seemed to be disinterested in confronting Monus.

Cherelstein was not happy about the situation and felt like he had a higher responsibility. He demanded to meet with Monus. Cherelstein did get Monus to agree to repay the company for the losses from Monus's (personal) investment of company funds into the World Basketball League (WBL). But Monus never kept his word. In the beginning, Cherelstein felt compelled to give Monus some time to turn things around through increased efficiencies and by using a device called "exclusivity fees," which vendors paid to get Phar-Mor to stock their products. Over time, Cherelstein became more and more uncomfortable as the suppliers called more and more frequently, demanding payment on their invoices.

Accounting Fraud

Misappropriation of Assets

The unfortunate reality of the Phar-Mor saga was that it involved not only bogus inventory but also the diversion of company funds to feed Monus's personal habits. One example was the movement of $10 million in company funds to help start the WBL.

False Financial Statements

According to the ruling by the U.S. Court of Appeals that heard Monus's appeal of his conviction on all 109 counts of fraud, the company submitted false financial statements to Pittsburgh National Bank, which increased a revolving credit line for Phar-Mor from $435 million to $600 million in March 1992. It also defrauded Corporate Partners, an investment group that bought $200 million in Phar-Mor stock in June 1991. The list goes on, including the defrauding of Chemical Bank, which served as the placing agent for $155 million in 10-year senior secured notes issued to Phar-Mor; Westinghouse Credit Corporation, which had executed a $50 million loan commitment to Phar-Mor in 1987; and Westminster National Bank, which served as the placing agent for $112 million in Phar-Mor stock sold to various financial institutions in 1991.

Tamco Relationship

The early financial troubles experienced by Phar-Mor in 1988 can be attributed to at least two transactions. The first was that the company provided deep discounts to retailers to stock its stores with product. There was concern early on that the margins were too thin. The second was that its supplier, Tamco, was shipping partial orders to Phar-Mor while billing for full orders. Phar-Mor had no way of knowing this because it was not logging in shipments from Tamco.

After the deficiency was discovered, Giant Eagle agreed to pay Phar-Mor $7 million in 1988 on behalf of Tamco. Phar-Mor later bought Tamco from Giant Eagle in an additional effort to solve the inventory and billing problems. However, the losses just kept on coming.

Back to the Dilemma

Cherelstein looked out the window at the driving rain. He thought about the fact that he didn't start the fraud or engage in the cover-up. Still, he knew about it now and felt compelled to do something. Cherelstein thought about the persistent complaints by vendors that they were not being paid and their threats to cut off shipments to Phar-Mor. Cherelstein knew that, without any product in Phar-Mor stores, the company could not last much longer.

Questions

1. Evaluate the role of each of the stakeholders in this case from an ethical perspective. How do you assess blame for the Phar-Mor fraud?
2. Assume you are in Stan Cherelstein's position. Evaluate the moral intensity issues in the case. How do these issues relate to Rest's Four-Component Model of Ethical Decision Making? What are the challenges for Cherelstein in that regard?
3. Assume you decide to confront Monus. How would you counter the likely reasons and rationalizations you will hear from Monus? What levers do you have to influence Monus's behavior?
4. What is the ethical message of Phar-Mor? That is, explain what you think the moral of this story is.

Case 2-10 WorldCom

The WorldCom fraud was the largest in U.S. history, surpassing even that of Enron. Beginning modestly during mid-year 1999 and continuing at an accelerated pace through May 2002, the company—under the direction of Bernie Ebbers, the CEO; Scott Sullivan, the CFO; David Myers, the controller; and Buford Yates, the director of accounting—"cooked the books" to the tune of about $11 billion of misstated earnings. Investors collectively lost $30 billion as a result of the fraud.

The fraud was accomplished primarily in two ways:

1. Booking "line costs" for interconnectivity with other telecommunications companies as capital expenditures rather than operating expenses.
2. Inflating revenues with bogus accounting entries from "corporate unallocated revenue accounts."

During 2002, Cynthia Cooper, the vice president of internal auditing, responded to a tip about improper accounting by having her team do an exhaustive hunt for the improperly recorded line costs that were also known as "prepaid capacity." That name was designed to mask the true nature of the costs and treat them as capitalizable costs rather than as operating expenses. The team worked tirelessly, often at night and secretly, to investigate and reveal $3.8 billion worth of fraud.

Soon thereafter, Cooper notified the company's audit committee and board of directors of the fraud. The initial response was not to take action, but to look for explanations from Sullivan. Over time, Cooper realized that she needed to be persistent and not give in to pressure that Sullivan was putting on her to back off. Cooper even approached KPMG, the auditors that had replaced Arthur Andersen, to support her in the matter. Ultimately, Sullivan was dismissed, Myers resigned, Andersen withdrew its audit opinion for 2001, and the Securities and Exchange Commission (SEC) began an investigation into the fraud on June 26, 2002.

In an interview with David Katz and Julia Homer for *CFO Magazine* on February 1, 2008, Cynthia Cooper was asked about her whistleblower role in the WorldCom fraud. When asked when she first suspected something was amiss, Cooper said: "It was a process. My feelings changed from curiosity to discomfort to suspicion based on some of the accounting entries my team and I had identified, and also on the odd reactions I was getting from some of the finance executives."[1]

---

[1]David K. Katz and Julia Homer, "WorldCom Whistle-blower Cynthia Cooper," *CFO Magazine*, February 1, 2008. Available at: www.cfo.com/article.cfm/10590507.

Cooper did exactly what is expected of a good auditor. She approached the investigation of line-cost accounting with a healthy dose of skepticism and maintained her integrity throughout, even as Sullivan was trying to bully her into dropping the investigation.

When asked whether there was anything about the culture of WorldCom that contributed to the scandal, Cooper laid blame on Bernie Ebbers for his risk-taking approach that led to loading up the company with $40 billion in debt to fund one acquisition after another. He followed the same reckless strategy with his own investments, taking out loans and using his WorldCom stock as collateral. Cooper believed that Ebbers's personal decisions then affected his business decisions; he ultimately saw his net worth disappear, and he was left owing WorldCom some $400 million for loans approved by the board. Ebbers was sentenced to 25 years in jail for his offenses.

Betty Vinson, the company's former director of corporate reporting, was one of five former WorldCom executives who pleaded guilty to fraud. At the trial of Ebbers, Vinson said she was told to make improper accounting entries because Ebbers did not want to disappoint Wall Street. "I felt like if I didn't make the entries, I wouldn't be working there," Vinson testified. She said that she even drafted a resignation letter in 2000, but ultimately she stayed with the company. It was clear she felt uneasy with the accounting at WorldCom.

Vinson said that she took her concerns to Sullivan, who told her that Ebbers did not want to lower Wall Street expectations. Asked how she chose which accounts to alter, Vinson testified, "I just really pulled some out of the air. I used some spreadsheets."[2]

Her lawyer urged the judge to sentence Vinson to probation, citing the pressure placed on her by Ebbers and Sullivan. "She expressed her concern about what she was being directed to do to upper management, and to Sullivan and Ebbers, who assured her and lulled her into believing that all was well," he said. In the end, Vinson was sentenced to five months in prison and five months of house arrest.

Questions

1. Identify the stakeholders in the WorldCom case and how their interests were affected by the financial fraud.

2. Do you think Betty Vinson was a victim of "motivated blindness"? Are there steps should could have taken to stand up for what she believed? Explain.

3. In a presentation at James Madison University in November 2013, Cynthia Cooper said, "You don't have to be a bad person to make bad decisions." Discuss what you think Cooper meant and how it relates to our discussion of ethical and moral development in the chapter.

---

[2]Susan Pulliam, "Ordered to Commit Fraud, a Staffer Balked, Then Caved: Accountant Betty Vinson Helped Cook the Books at WorldCom," *The Wall Street Journal*, June 23, 2003. Available at: www.people.tamu.edu/˜jstrawser/acct229h/Current%20 Readings/E.%20WSJ.com%20-%20A%20Staffer%20 Ordered%20to%20Commit%20Fraud,%20Balked.pdf.

Chapter

3

Organizational Ethics and Corporate Governance

Learning Objectives

After studying Chapter 3, you should be able to:

LO 3-1 Describe the link between organizational climate and ethical leadership.

LO 3-2 Explain the link between organizational ethics, individual ethics, and corporate culture.

LO 3-3 Analyze why and how organizational culture is formed.

LO 3-4 Discuss the views of employees about ethics in their organizations.

LO 3-5 Describe the causes of fraud, detection methods, and preventative controls.

LO 3-6 Explain the components of corporate governance and their relationship to corporate culture.

LO 3-7 Analyze the moral basis for whistleblowing and accountants' obligations to whistle blow.

Ethics Reflection

Satyam: India's Enron

Corporate governance failures marked the business and accounting frauds of the early 2000s. The United States was not alone. Enron and WorldCom had their counterparts in the global arena. Italy had a massive fraud at Parmalat, and Satyam, sometimes referred to India's Enron, was a $1.4 billion fraud that triggered a reduction in share price of almost 99 percent.

Satyam Computer Services was the fourth-largest software exporter in India until January 2009, when the CEO and cofounder, Ramalinga Raju, confessed to inflating the company's profits and cash reserves over an eight-year period. The accounting fraud at Satyam involved dual accounting books, more than 7,000 forged invoices, and dozens of fake bank statements. The total amount of losses was 50 billion Rs (rupees) (equal to about $1.40 billion). This represented about 94 percent of the company's cash and cash equivalents. Raju stepped down in early January 2009. In April 2015, he was convicted of forging documents and falsifying accounts. He is currently serving a seven-year prison term.

The Satyam incident was investigated by India's "Serious Frauds" (seems a redundancy) Office that coordinated the investigations and the diversion of funds by promoters within and outside India and corporate governance failings.

Corporate Governance Failings

The legal complaints alleged that members of the audit committee of the Satyam board of directors—who were responsible for overseeing the integrity of the company's financial statements, the performance and compensation of the outside auditors from PricewaterhouseCoopers (PwC) India firms, and the adequacy and effectiveness of internal accounting and financial controls—were responsible for the publication of false and misleading public statements due to their extreme recklessness in discharging their duties and their resulting failure to discover and prevent the massive accounting fraud.

Effective corporate governance was missing at Satyam at all levels including:

- Lack of independent members of the board of directors; those not beholden to management.
- Audit committee failings to properly oversee financial reporting and internal controls.
- Questionable "ethical" tone at the top that worked against promoting ethical and competent behavior throughout the organization.
- External audits that were heavily influenced by conflicts of interest between PwC and management.

A unique aspect of the corporate governance system in India is the ownership of shares by outside promoters, multinational blockholder companies, and the state. Unlike in the United States where public ownership is high and transparency is key, the more closed system in India leads to a relative lack of full and fair disclosure.

Audit Failures by PwC and Resulting Legal Actions

The complaint asserted claims against PwC and its Indian partners and affiliates. Satyam's outside auditors from the PwC India firms allegedly were aware of the fraud but still certified the company's financial statements as accurate. The company's financial statements were signed off on by PwC on March 31, 2008.

PwC and its Indian affiliates initially hid behind "client confidentiality" and stated that it was "examining the contents of the statement." Realizing that this was not enough, PwC came up with a second statement claiming that "the audits were conducted in accordance with applicable auditing standards and were supported by appropriate audit evidence." This is somewhat troublesome because an audit in accordance with generally accepted auditing standards (GAAS) calls for examining the contents of the financial statements. Given that the firm did not identify the financial wrongdoing at Satyam, it would appear that the firm, at the very least, was guilty of professional negligence. At a minimum, the firm missed or failed to do the following:

- Fictitious invoices with customers were recorded as genuine.
- Raju recorded a fictional interest credit as income.
- The auditors didn't ask for a statement of confirmation of balance from banks (for cash balances) and debtors (for receivables), a basic procedure in an audit.

One ironic note about the Satyam fraud is in September 2008 the World Council for Corporate Governance honored the company with a "Golden Peacock Award" for global excellence in corporate governance. Once news of the fraud broke, the council rescinded the award, stating that the company failed to disclose material information.

As you read this chapter, reflect on the following questions: (1) What systems are necessary to ensure that a company runs efficiently and ethically? (2) What role does corporate culture and ethical leadership play in creating an ethical organization? (3) What are the components of an ethical control environment from an accounting and auditing perspective? (4) How do whistleblowing obligations of accounting professionals influence ethical behavior?

The thing I have learned at IBM is that culture is everything. Underneath all the sophisticated processes, there is always the company's sense of values and identity.

Louis V. Gerstner, Jr., former CEO, IBM

This statement by former IBM chief executive officer (CEO) Louis Gerstner highlights one of the themes of this chapter: The culture of an organization establishes the boundaries within which ethical decisions must be made. As we learned from previous chapters, it is one thing to know that you should behave in a certain way, but it is quite another to do it (or even want to do it) given the pressures that may exist from within the organization.

Organizational Ethics and Leadership

LO 3-1
Describe the link between organizational climate and ethical leadership.

Organizational ethics can be thought of as the generally accepted principles and standards that guide behavior in business and other organizational contexts. High ethical standards require both organizations and individuals to conform to sound moral principles. In organizations, a critical component of creating an ethical organization environment is the culture that includes shared values, beliefs, goals, norms, and problem solving mechanisms. The ethical climate of an organization plays an important role in organizational culture. Whereas an organization's overall culture establishes ideals that guide a wide variety of member behaviors, the ethical climate focuses specifically on issues of right and wrong.

Organizational ethical climate refers to the moral atmosphere of the work environment and the level of ethics practiced within a company. Leaders determine organizational climate and establish character and define norms. Character plays an important role in leadership. Leaders of good character have integrity, courage, and compassion. They are careful and prudent. Their decisions and actions inspire employees to think and act in a way that enhances the well-being of the organization, its people, and society in general. Ralph Waldo Emerson, the American essayist, poet, and philosopher, said, "Our chief want is someone who will inspire us to be what we know we could be."

Johnson points out that virtues are woven into the inner lives of leaders, shape the way they see and behave, operate independent of the situation, and help leaders to live more fulfilling lives. He identifies courage, temperance, wisdom, justice, optimism, integrity, humility, reverence, and compassion as underlying traits of character of effective leaders. Ethical leaders recognize that moral action is risky but continue to model ethical behavior despite the danger. They refuse to set their values aside to go along with the group, to keep silent when customers may be hurt, or to lie to investors. They strive to create ethical environments even when faced with opposition from their superiors and subordinates. Ethical leaders serve as role models for those within the organization and stakeholders that rely on it.[1]

There is no one size fits all for ethical climates. Johnson believes that an organization must first identify principles and practices that characterize positive ethical climates and then adapt them to a particular organization setting. He identifies key markers of highly ethical organizations including humility, zero tolerance for individual and collective destructive behaviors, justice, integrity, trust, a focus on process, structural reinforcement, and social responsibility. We add that an ethical climate is enhanced through a values-driven organization that encourages openness and transparency, and provides a supportive environment to voice matters of concern without fear of retribution or retaliation.[2]

Is there a difference between ethical decision making in general, as we discussed in Chapter 2, and ethical decision making in an organizational setting? We believe there are important differences that incorporate both individual and organizational factors into the process. Ferrell et al. describes a process that is depicted in Exhibit 3.1.[3] What follows is a brief explanation of the components of the framework.

Ethical Issue Intensity

Recall our previous discussion of Rest's Model and the first step of recognizing that an ethical issue exists. Ethical awareness requires that an individual or work group choose among several actions that various stakeholders inside or outside the firm will ultimately evaluate as right or wrong. The relative importance of the issue to the individual, work group and/or organization (intensity) is based on the values, beliefs, and norms involved and situational pressures in the workplace.

EXHIBIT 3.1   Framework for Understanding Ethical Decision Making in Business

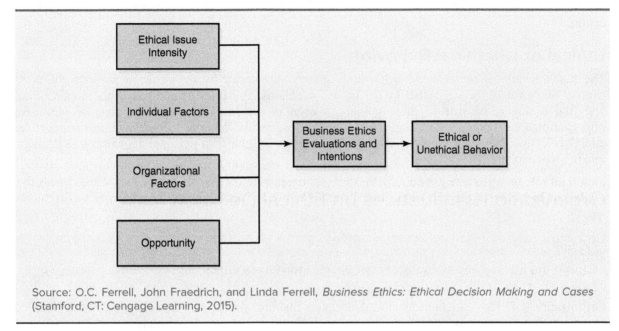

Source: O.C. Ferrell, John Fraedrich, and Linda Ferrell, *Business Ethics: Ethical Decision Making and Cases* (Stamford, CT: Cengage Learning, 2015).

Individual Factors

Values of individuals can be derived from moral philosophies, such as those discussed in Chapter 1. These provide principles or rules people use to decide what is right or wrong from a moral and personal perspective. Although an individual's intention to engage in ethical behavior relates to individual values, organizational and social forces also play an important role by shaping behavioral intentions and decision making.[4]

Organizational Factors

Research has established that in the workplace, the organization's values often have a greater influence on decisions than a person's own values.[5] Ethical decisions in the workplace are made jointly, in work groups or other organizational settings. The strength of personal values, the opportunities to behave unethically, and the exposure to others who behave ethically or unethically influence decision making. An alignment between an individual's own values and the values of the organization help create positive work environments and organizational outcomes.

Opportunity

Ferrell points out that opportunity describes the conditions in an organization that limit or permit ethical or unethical behavior.[6] Opportunity results from conditions that either provide internal or external rewards, or fail to erect barriers against unethical behavior. The opportunities that employees have for unethical behavior in an organization can be reduced or eliminated with aggressive enforcement of rules and codes of ethics.

Business Ethics Evaluations and Intentions

Ethical dilemmas involve problem-solving situations when the rules governing decisions are often vague or in conflict. The results of an ethical decision are often uncertain: It is not always immediately clear whether or not we made the right decision. Moreover, the decision we make may not always comport with the one we intended to make because of pressures within the organization. As discussed in Chapter 2, this is where giving voice to one's values becomes a critical component of taking ethical action.

Ethical or Unethical Behavior

The resulting ethical or unethical behavior is greatly influenced by the decision maker's ability to express one's values; be supported by the norms, standards, and rules of conduct in the organization; and find a way to be true to these guidelines even in the face of opposing points of view. An organizational ethical culture is shaped by effective leadership. Without top management support for ethical behavior, the opportunity for employees to engage in their own personal approaches to decision making will evolve.

Organizational Influences on Ethical Decision Making

LO 3-2
Explain the link between organizational ethics, individuals ethics, and corporate culture.

Organizational factors can impede ethical decision making. Smith and Carroll presented a detailed argument that organizational factors such as socialization processes, environmental influences, and hierarchical relationships collectively constitute a "stacked deck," which impedes moral behavior.[7] Organizational factors are likely to play a role in moral decision making and behavior at two points: establishing moral intent and engaging in moral behavior. Explicit organizational behaviors may cause unethical (or ethical) behavior to result despite good (or bad) intention.

Thomas Jones developed an explanatory model[8] that merged Rest's four-step moral reasoning model with Fiske and Taylor's work on social cognition to illustrate the ethical decision-making process of an individual who encounters an ethical dilemma within the context of work.[9] Of particular importance is the role that moral intensity plays in recognizing moral issues. Moral issues of high intensity will be more salient because the magnitude of consequences is greater, their effects stand out, and their effects involve significant others (greater social, cultural, psychological, or physical proximity).

While Jones's model illustrates the impact that moral intensity has on ethical choices and behavior and acknowledges that organizational factors influence the establishment of moral intent and behavior—the last two steps in Rest's model—the model fails to address what Burchard calls the cyclical, ongoing dynamic exchange between the individual and organization, which affects the development and sustaining of one's code of conduct in the organizational context.[10] It was left to Jones and Hiltebeitel to fill the gap when they conducted a study of organizational influence on moral decisions and proposed a model that demonstrated organizational influence on the moral decision-making process.[11] As Jones had done with his previous model, Jones and Hiltebeitel based their model on Rest's moral reasoning and Kohlberg's moral development theory.

The Jones-Hiltebeitel model looks at the role of one's personal code of conduct in ethical behavior within an organization. When an employee was called upon to perform routine tasks—those with no internal conflict or cognitive dissonance—the actions taken were almost automatic. However, when those tasks diverged from the routine, the employee would refer to her personal code of conduct for ethical cues. The implications for ethical behavior within the organization are significant because an unethical individual might act dishonestly in one case, while a virtuous person would act in a truthful, trustworthy manner.

According to the model, when one's personal code is insufficient to make the necessary moral decision, the individual will look at the factors that influenced the formation of the code, including professional and organizational influences to resolve the conflict. The influences that are strongest are the ones that determine the reformation of the individual's code of conduct. The implications for the culture of an organization are significant because an organization that values profits above all else might elicit one kind of response, such as to go along with improper accounting, while an organization that values integrity above all else might lead to questioning improper accounting and doing what one can to reverse false and misleading financial results.[12]

Ethical Dissonance Model

Burchard points out that the Jones-Hiltebeitel model and others like it pay too little attention to the examination of ethical person-organization fit upon the person-organization exchange, within each of the four potential fit options. Burchard presents what she calls the Ethical Dissonance Cycle Model to illustrate the interaction between the individual and the organization, based on the person-organization ethical fit at various stages of the contractual relationship in each potential ethical fit scenario.[13] The model is complex, so we restrict our coverage to the basics of the person-organization interchange and its implications for ethical behavior within organizations. This is an important consideration because the ethics of an individual influences the values that one brings to the workplace and decision making, while the ethics (through its culture) of an organization influences that behavior. To keep it simple, we adopt the idea that there can be a dissonance between what is considered ethical and what may actually be "best" for the subject inviting ethical consideration.

Of the four potential fit options, two possess high person-organization fit: (1) high organizational ethics, high individual ethics (High-High), and (2) low organizational ethics, low individual ethics (Low-Low); and two possess low person-organization fit: (1) high organizational ethics, low individual ethics (High-Low) and (2) low organizational ethics, high individual ethics (Low-High).[14]

Let's pause for a moment and consider the practical implications of this model. Imagine that you are interviewing for a position with a mid-sized company in your town. You can easily find out information about the company on the Internet to prepare for the interview, such as the scope of its operations, products and services, customer base, and geographical locations. However, it is less easy to find out about its reputation for ethics, although reports in the media about specific events might be of some use. Now, let's assume that you knew (and understood) what is meant by organizational fit and in this case the fit is Low-High. Would that affect whether you interview with the company? Might you ask questions to better understand why that fit exists? Would it affect your final decision whether to work for the company? The information you might gather during the process could be invaluable when you face ethical dilemmas in the workplace.

In two of the fit options (High-High and Low-Low), no ethical dissonance exists. Person-organization fit is optimal, and the organization is highly effective, either to constructive or destructive ends. The other two (High-Low and Low-High) demonstrate a lack of person-organization fit in the realm of ethics and values.[15]

High Organizational Ethics, High Individual Ethics (High-High)[16]

Assume that you know your values and beliefs are an ethical match for the company you work for. You are likely to continue to stay employed in the organization. The issue for us is how you might assess organizational ethics. Koh and Boo identified three distinct measures of organizational ethics: support for ethical behavior from top management, the ethical climate of the organization, and the connection between career success and ethical behavior.[17] These three factors relate to the culture of the organization and may have implications for actions such as whistleblowing, as discussed later on. Koh and Boo found that positive ethical culture and climate produces favorable organizational outcomes by setting down the ethical philosophy and rules of conduct and practices (i.e., code of ethics).

Low Organizational Ethics, Low Individual Ethics (Low-Low)[18]

When both the individual and organization possess low moral and ethical development, the fit is there, but it is turns in a negative direction. A culture of corruption is difficult to change, and for the employee, it takes more conscious effort to stop the corruption than to participate in it. You might say that the employee adopts the attitude of going along to get along. Padilla et al. contends that "dysfunctional leader behaviors and susceptible followers interacting in the context of a contributing environment produce negative organizational outcomes in which 'followers must consent to, or be unable to resist, a destructive leader.' "[19]

High Organizational Ethics, Low Individual Ethics (High-Low)[20]

According to Hamilton and Kelman, if the individual possesses lower ethics than that which is held by the organization, the discovery of an individual's lack of person-organization fit is often pointed out by socialized members within the ethical organization.[21] Those assimilated members of the organization may attempt to socialize the individual to the ways of the organization to alleviate the ethical dissonance. Once this dissonance is discovered, the likelihood that the mismatched employee will leave the company rises. The more the individual's personal decisions are seen to be in conflict with the ethical decisions that are perceived to be encouraged by the organization, the greater the discomfort of the individual. Imagine, for example, a newly hired employee thought there was nothing wrong with accepting free gifts from contractors doing business with one's employer, but the employer has a code of ethics forbidding such practices. The culture of the organization conflicts with the individual's low ethical standards in this instance, and others in the organization that identify with organizational values may attempt to resolve the dissonance and alter the employee's behavior. If the employee's behavior does not change, the employee may be let go for cause or insubordination.

Low Organizational Ethics, High Individual Ethics (Low-High)[22]

A reduction in job satisfaction is likely if an employee striving to be ethical perceives little top management support for ethical behavior, an unfavorable ethical climate in the organization, and/or little association between ethical behavior and job success.[23] Once this ethical dissonance is discovered, the likelihood of employee turnover rises. Sims and Keon found a significant relationship between the ethical rift between one's personal decisions and the perceived unwritten/informal policies of the organization, and the individual's level of comfort within the organization. The greater the difference between the decisions that the individual made and the decisions perceived as expected and reinforced by the organization, the greater levels of discomfort the individual would feel, and the more likely the individual would be to report these feelings of discomfort.[24] The case of Cynthia Cooper, discussed in Chapter 1, illustrates the low organizational, high individual ethics environment. Cooper reported her concerns to top management, and once she was convinced that nothing would be done to address the improper accounting for capitalized costs, she blew the whistle by going to the audit committee and external auditors.

Seven Signs of Ethical Collapse

In her book *The Seven Signs of Ethical Collapse,* Marianne Jennings analyzes the indicators of possible ethical collapse in companies and provides advice how to avoid impending disaster. She starts with a description of ethical collapse, saying that it "occurs when any organization has drifted from the basic principles of right and wrong," and she uses financial reporting standards and accounting rules as one area where this might occur. She points out that "not all companies that have drifted ethically have violated any laws."[25] Enron did not necessarily violate generally accepted accounting principles (GAAP) in treating the effects of *some* of its transactions with special-purpose entities off-balance-sheet. However, the company ignored conflicts of interest of Andy Fastow who managed some of the entities while wearing a second hat as CFO of Enron during the time the two entities had mutual dealings.

According to Jennings, "When an organization collapses ethically, it means that those in the organization have drifted into rationalizations and legalisms, and all for the purpose of getting the results they want and need at almost any cost." A good example is Dennis Kozlowski at Tyco International who misappropriated company resources for personal purposes without the approval of the board of directors and rationalized that he was just doing what those before him had done. Thus, he invoked one of the reasons and rationalizations that we discussed in giving voice to values—Expected or Standard Practice. Jennings links the rationalizations and legalisms to a culture that leads to behavior based on the notion "It's not a question of should we do it." It is a culture of "Can we do it legally?" This mentality occurs because of the combination of the seven factors working together to cloud judgment.[26]

Jennings identifies seven common ethical signs of moral meltdowns in companies that have experienced ethical collapse. The common threads she found that make good people at companies do really dumb things include (1) pressure to maintain numbers; (2) fear and silence; (3) young 'uns and a bigger-than-life CEO (i.e., loyalty to the boss); (4) weak board of directors; (5) conflicts of interest overlooked or unaddressed; (6) innovation like no other company; and (7) goodness in some areas atones for evil in others.[27] We briefly address four of the seven signs.

Pressure to Maintain the Numbers

Jennings points out that the tension between ethics and the bottom line will always be present. The first sign of a culture at risk for ethical collapse occurs when there is not just a focus on numbers and results, but an unreasonable and unrealistic obsession with meeting quantitative goals. This "financial results at all costs" approach was a common ethical problem at both Enron and WorldCom. At WorldCom, the mantra was that financial results had to improve in every quarter, and the shifting of operating expenses to capitalized costs was used to accomplish the goal regardless of the propriety of the accounting treatment. It was an "ends justifies means" culture that sanctioned wrongdoing in the name of earnings. Accountants like Betty Vinson got caught up in the culture and did not know how to extricate themselves from the situation.

Fear of Reprisals

Fear and silence characterizes a culture where employees are reluctant to raise issues of ethical concern because they may be ignored, treated badly, transferred, or worse. It underlies the whistleblowing process in many organizations where ethical employees want to blow the whistle but fear reprisals, so they stay silent. One aspect of such a culture is a "kill the messenger syndrome," whereby an employee brings bad news to higher-ups with the best intentions of having the organization correct the matter, but instead the messenger is treated as an outcast.

Loyalty to the Boss

Dennis Kozlowski, the dominant, larger-then-life CEO of Tyco, had an appetite for a lavish style of living. He surrounded himself with young people who were taken by his stature and would not question his actions. Kozlowski, who once spent $6,000 on a shower curtain for an apartment paid for by the company, made sure these "young 'uns" received all the trappings of success so they would be reluctant to speak up when ethical and legal issues existed for fear of losing their expensive homes, boats, and cars and the prestige that comes along with financial success at a young age. They were selected by the CEO for their positions based on their inexperience, possible conflicts of interest, and unlikelihood to question the boss's decisions. Of course, not all bigger-than-life CEOs are unethical (e.g., Steve Jobs and Warren Buffett).

Weak Board of Directors

A weak board of directors characterizes virtually all the companies with major accounting frauds in the early part of the 2000s. One example is HealthSouth, one of the largest healthcare providers in the United States specializing in patient rehabilitation services. Richard Scrushy surrounded himself with a weak board so that when he made decisions as CEO at HealthSouth that contributed to an accounting scandal where the company's earnings were falsely inflated by $1.4 billion, the board would go along, in part because of their interrelationships with Scrushy and HealthSouth that created conflicts of interest. Jennings identifies the following conflicts of interest:[28]

- One director earned $250,000 per year from a consulting contract with HealthSouth over a seven-year period.
- Another director had a joint investment venture with Scrushy on a $395,000 investment property.
- Another director's company was awarded a $5.6 million contract to install glass at a hospital being built by HealthSouth.
- MedCenter District, a hospital-supply company that was run online, did business with HealthSouth and was owned by Scrushy, six directors, and the wife of one of those directors.
- The same three directors had served on both the audit committee and the compensation committee for several years.
- Two of the directors had served on the board for 18 years.
- One director received a $425,000 donation to his favorite charity from HealthSouth just prior to his going on the board.

Stakeholder Orientation

In a business context, investors and shareholders, creditors, employees, customers, suppliers, governmental agencies, communities, and many others who have a "stake" or a claim in some aspect of a company's products, operations, markets, industry, and outcome are known as *stakeholders*. Business influences these groups, but these groups also have the ability to influence business; therefore, the relationship between companies and their stakeholders is a two-way street.

The well-known ethicist Archie Carroll points out that questions of right, wrong, fairness, and justice permeate an organization's activities as it attempts to interact successfully with major stakeholder groups. He believes that the principal task of management is not only to deal with the various stakeholder groups in an ethical fashion, but also to reconcile the conflicts of interest that occur between the organization and the stakeholder groups.[29]

Ferrell states that the degree to which an organization understands and addresses stakeholder demands can be referred to as a *stakeholder orientation*.[30] This orientation comprises three sets of activities: (1) the organization-wide generation of data about stakeholder groups and assessment of the firm's effects on these groups, (2) the distribution of this information throughout the firms, and (3) the responsiveness of the organization as a whole to this information.[31]

Generating data about stakeholders begins with identifying the stakeholders that are relevant to the firm followed by the concerns about the organization's conduct that each relevant stakeholder group shares. At this stage, the values and standards of behavior are used to evaluate stakeholder interests and concerns from an ethical perspective. The ethical reasoning methods previously discussed help to make the necessary judgments.

Stakeholder management requires that an individual consider issues from a variety of perspectives other than one's own or that of the organization. The case of the Ford Pinto illustrates how important stakeholder concerns can be left out of the decision-making process.

The Case of the Ford Pinto

The case of the Ford Pinto illustrates a classic example of how a company can make a fatal mistake in its decision making by failing to consider the interests of the stakeholders adequately. The failure was due to total reliance on utilitarian thinking instead of the universality perspective of rights theory, to the detriment of the driving public and society in general.

The Pinto was Ford Motor Company's first domestic North American subcompact automobile, marketed beginning on September 11, 1970. It competed with the AMC Gremlin and Chevrolet Vega, along with imports from makes such as Volkswagen, Datsun, and Toyota. The Pinto was popular in sales, with 100,000 units delivered by January 1971, and was also offered as a wagon and Runabout hatchback. Its reputation suffered over time, however, especially from a controversy surrounding the safety of its gas tank.

The public was shocked to find out that if the Pinto cars experienced an impact at speeds of only 30 miles per hour or less, they might become engulfed in flames, and passengers could be burned or even die. Ford faced an ethical dilemma: what to do about the apparently unsafe gas tanks that seemed to be the cause of these incidents. At the time, the gas tanks were routinely placed behind the license plate, so a rear-end collision was more likely to cause an explosion (whereas today's gas tanks are placed on the side of the vehicle). However, the federal safety standards at the time did not address this issue, so Ford was in compliance with the law. Ford's initial response was based on ethical legalism—the company complied with all the laws and safety problems, so it was under no obligation to take any action.

Eventually, Ford did use ethical analysis to develop a response. It used a risk–benefit analysis to aid decision making. This was done because the National Highway Traffic Safety Administration (NHTSA) excused a defendant from being penalized if the monetary costs of making a production change were greater than the "societal benefit" of that change. The analysis followed the same approach modeled after Judge Learned Hand's ruling in *United States v. Carroll Towing* in 1947 that boiled the theory of negligence down to the following: If the expected harm exceeded the cost to prevent it, the defendant was obligated to take the precaution, and if he (or it, in the case of a company) did not, liability would result. But if the cost was larger than the expected harm, the defendant was not expected to take the precaution. If there was an accident, the defendant would not be found guilty.[32] A summary of the Ford analysis follows.

Ford's Risk-Benefit Analysis[33]

Benefits of Fixing the Pintos

Savings: 180 burn deaths, 180 serious burn injuries, 2,100 burned vehicles

Unit cost: $200,000 per death (figure provided by the government); $67,000 per burn injury and $700 to repair a burned vehicle (company estimates)

Total benefits: $180 \times (\$200,000) + 180 \times (\$67,000) + 2,100 \times (\$700) = $ **$49.5 million**

Costs of Fixing the Pintos

Sales: 11 million cars, 1.5 million light trucks

Unit cost: $11 per car, $11 per light truck

Total cost: $11,000,000 \times (\$11) + 1,500,000 \times (\$11) = $ **$137 million**

Based on this analysis and other considerations, including not being required by law to change its product design, Ford decided not to change the placement of the fuel tank.

Ford's risk–benefit analysis relied only on act-utilitarian reasoning, an approach that ignores the rights of various stakeholders. A rule-utilitarian approach might have led Ford to follow the rule "Never sacrifice public safety." A rights theory approach would have led to the same conclusion, based on the reasoning that the driving public has an ethical right to expect that their cars will not blow up if there is a crash at low speeds.

The other danger of utilitarian reasoning is that an important factor may be omitted from the analysis. Ford did not include as a potential cost the lawsuit judgments that might be awarded to the plaintiffs and against the company. For example, in May 1972, Lily Gray was traveling with 13-year-old Richard Grimshaw when their Pinto was struck by another car traveling approximately 30 miles per hour. The impact ignited a fire in the Pinto, which killed Gray and left Grimshaw with devastating injuries. A judgment was rendered against Ford, and the jury awarded the Gray family $560,000 and Matthew Grimshaw, the father of Richard Grimshaw, $2.5 million in compensatory damages. The surprise came when the jury also awarded $125 million in punitive damages. This was subsequently reduced to $3.5 million.[34]

In the aftermath of the scandal, it is interesting to consider whether any of the Ford executives who were involved in the decision-making process would have predicted in advance that they would have made such an unethical choice. Dennis Gioia, who was in charge of recalling defective automobiles at Ford, did not advocate ordering a recall. Gioia eventually came to view his decision not to recall the Pinto as a moral failure—what De Cremer and Tenbrunsel call a failure to think outside his prevailing background narrative or script at the point of decision. "My own schematized (scripted) knowledge influenced me to perceive recall issues in terms of the prevailing decision environment and to unconsciously overlook key features of the Pinto case . . . mainly because they did not fit an existing script." While personal morality was very important to Gioia, he admits that the framing narrative of his workplace "did not include ethical dimension."[35] The moral mistake was that there were other, better choices that he could have made—albeit ones outside the purview of Gioia's framing narrative.

Lessons Learned?

Has the automobile industry learned a lesson from Ford's experience with the Pinto? Some observers thought not when, in February 1993, an Atlanta jury held the General Motors Corporation responsible for the death of a Georgia teenager in the fiery crash of one of its pickup trucks. At the trial, General Motors contended in its defense that when a drunk driver struck seventeen-year-old Shannon Moseley's truck in the side, it was the impact of the high-speed crash that killed Moseley. However, the jury was persuaded that Moseley survived the collision only to be consumed by a fire caused by his truck's defective fuel-tank design. Finding that the company had known that its "side-saddle" gas tanks which are mounted outside the rails of the truck's frame, are dangerously prone to rupture, the jury awarded $4.2 million in actual damages and $101 million in punitive damages to Moseley's parents.

What undoubtedly swayed the jury was the testimony of former GM safety engineer Ronald E. Elwell. Although Elwell had testified in more than 15 previous cases that the pickups were safe, this time he switched sides and told the jury that the company had known for years that the side-saddle design was defective but had intentionally hidden its knowledge and had not attempted to correct the problem. At the trial, company officials attempted to paint Elwell as a disgruntled employee, but his testimony was supported by videotapes of General Motors' own crash tests. After the verdict, General Motors said that it still stood behind the safety of its trucks and contended "that a full examination by the National Highway Traffic Safety Administration of the technical issues in this matter will bear out our contention that the 1973–1987 full-size pickup trucks do not have a safety-related defect."[36] Of course, that wasn't to be.

A stakeholder orientation adds to a corporation's reputation for being trustworthy. Many parties rely on the considerate, fair-minded, and ethical treatment of stakeholders. Gone are the days when only shareholder interests mattered. Too many groups rely on a corporation today for too many things for an ethical company to ignore those interests.

Establishing an Ethical Culture

LO 3-3
Analyze why and how organizational culture is formed.

Corporate culture is the shared beliefs of top managers in a company about how they should manage themselves and other employees, and how they should conduct their business(es). Southwest Airlines promotes a culture of a: (1) warrior spirit; (2) servant's heart; and (3) (fun-loving attitude). Most people who fly on Southwest see it as caring about the customer.[37]

An important element of ethical culture is the tone at the top. Tone at the top refers to the ethical environment that is created in the workplace by the organization's leadership. An ethical tone creates the basis for standards of behavior that become part of the code of ethics.

The tone set by managers influences how employees respond to ethical challenges and is enhanced by ethical leadership. When leaders are perceived as trustworthy, employee trust increases; leaders are seen as ethical and as honoring a higher level of duties. Employees identify with the organization's values and the likely outcome is high individual ethics; high organization ethics; and a lack of dissonance.[38]

If the tone set by management upholds ethics and integrity, employees will be more inclined to uphold those same values. However, if top management appears unconcerned about ethics and focuses solely on the bottom line, employees will be more prone to commit fraud, whether occupational (i.e., job-related), or participation in fraudulent financial reporting as occurred with Betty Vinson.

The culture at Tyco can be characterized as laissez-faire because Dennis Kozlowski was too preoccupied with his personal affairs to pay much attention to the company. Consequently, there was an absence of directions, standards, and expectations. With an absence of effective leadership, each department, in fact, each individual did whatever they wanted.

Corporate culture starts with an explicit statement of values, beliefs, and customs from top management. A code of ethics serves as a guide to support ethical decision making. It clarifies an organization's mission, values, and principles, linking them with standards of professional conduct.

Trust in Business

Trust in business is the cornerstone of relationships with customers, suppliers, employees, and others who have dealings with an organization. Trust means to be reliable and carry through words with deeds. Looking back at Rest's model, trust is gained when an employee follows through ethical intent with ethical action. Trust becomes pervasive only if the organization's values are followed and supported by top management. By modeling the organization's values, senior leaders provide a benchmark for all employees.

A good example of building trust in an organization is from Paul O'Neill, former CEO at Alcoa Inc., the world's third-largest producer of aluminum. O'Neill created a reputation for trust among his employees by setting strict ethical standards and carrying through with them. In an interview with "PBS Newshour" on July 9, 2002, O'Neill was asked by reporter Jim Lehrer why Alcoa was able to avoid the accounting scandals that infected so many companies in the late 1990s and early 2000s. He responded with the following statement: "When I went there [to Alcoa], I called the chief financial officer and the controller and I said to them, 'I don't want to ever be accused of or guilty of managing earnings,' that is to say making earnings that really aren't as a consequence of operations." O'Neill went on to express in the interview his dismay at the number of cases where employees of a company were told that these are the company's values, and then senior management totally ignored those same values.

Trust can be lost, even if once gained in the eyes of the public, if an organization no longer follows the guiding principles that helped to create its reputation for trust. A good example is what has happened with Johnson & Johnson. The company was a model of ethical behavior during the Tylenol incident but has come under intense scrutiny lately over questions about the safety of its other products.

Johnson & Johnson: Trust Gained

In addition to a statements of values, standards of business practices, and a code of ethics, some companies use a credo to instill virtue. A credo is an aspirational statement that encourages employees to internalize the values of the company. A good example of a corporate credo is that of Johnson & Johnson, which appears in Exhibit 3.2.

EXHIBIT 3.2   Johnson & Johnson Credo

We believe our first responsibility is to the doctors, nurses, and patients, to mothers and fathers and all others who use our products and services. In meeting their needs, everything we do must be of high quality. We must constantly strive to reduce our costs in order to maintain reasonable prices. Customers' orders must be serviced promptly and accurately. Our suppliers and distributors must have an opportunity to make a fair profit.

We are responsible to our employees, the men and women who work with us throughout the world. Everyone must be considered as an individual. We must respect their dignity and recognize their merit. They must have a sense of security in their jobs. Compensation must be fair and adequate, and working conditions clean, orderly, and safe. We must be mindful of ways to help our employees fulfill their family responsibilities. Employees must feel free to make suggestions and complaints. There must be equal opportunity for employment, development, and advancement for those qualified. We must provide competent management, and their actions must be just and ethical.

We are responsible to the communities in which we live and work, and to the world community as well. We must be good citizens—support good works and charities and bear our fair share of

(Continued)

taxes. We must encourage civic improvements and better health and education. We must maintain in good order the property we are privileged to use, protecting the environment and natural resources.

Our final responsibility is to our stockholders. Business must make a sound profit. We must experiment with new ideas. Research must be carried on, innovative programs developed, and mistakes paid for. New equipment must be purchased, new facilities provided, and new products launched. Reserves must be created to provide for adverse times. When we operate according to these principles, the stockholders should realize a fair return.

Source: *Johnson & Johnson Credo,* http://www.jnj.com/sites/default/files/pdf/jnj_ourcredo_english_us_8.5x11_cmyk.pdf.

The Johnson & Johnson credo clearly sets a positive tone. Notice how it emphasizes the company's primary obligations to those who use and rely on the safety of its products. The Johnson & Johnson credo implies that shareholders will earn a fair return if the company operates in accordance with its ethical values. Johnson & Johnson was credited with being an ethical organization in part because of the way it handled the Tylenol poisoning incidents in 1982. However, more recent events bring into question whether the company is suffering from a "Dr. Jekyll and Mr. Hyde" syndrome.

Tylenol Poisoning

In the fall of 1982, seven people in the Chicago area collapsed suddenly and died after taking Tylenol capsules that had been laced with cyanide. These five women and two men became the first victims ever to die from what came to be known as "product tampering."

McNeil Consumer Products, a subsidiary of Johnson & Johnson, was confronted with a crisis when it was determined that each of the seven people had ingested an Extra-Strength Tylenol capsule laced with cyanide. The news of this incident traveled quickly and was the cause of a massive, nationwide panic.

Tamara Kaplan, a professor at Penn State University, contends that Johnson & Johnson used the Tylenol poisonings to launch a public relations program immediately to preserve the integrity of both their product and their corporation as a whole. We find this to be a vacuous position, however. By Kaplan's own admission, "Johnson & Johnson's top management put customer safety first, before they worried about their company's profit and other financial concerns."[39] This hardly sounds like a company that used a catastrophic event to boost its image in the eyes of the public.

Johnson & Johnson's stock price dropped precipitously after the initial incident was made public. In the end, the stock price recovered because the company's actions gained the support and confidence of the public. Johnson & Johnson acted swiftly to remove all the product from the shelves of supermarkets, provide free replacements of Tylenol capsules with the tablet form of the product, and make public statements of assurance that the company would not sell an unsafe product. To claim that the company was motivated by a public relations agenda (even though in the end, its actions did provide a public relations boon for the company) is to ignore a basic point that Johnson & Johnson's management may have known all along: that is, good ethics is good business. But don't be fooled by this expression. It is good for the company if it benefits as a result of an ethical action. However, the main reason to make ethical decisions, as Johnson & Johnson did, is that it is the proper way to act. Much like Alcoa, Johnson & Johnson's credo instills a sense of pride for what the company stands for.

Johnson & Johnson: Trust Deficit

Johnson & Johnson learned the hard way that trust gained can easily be lost simply with one or two bad acts. The company learned that losing sight of one's values can cost. Johnson & Johnson announced in January 2012 that it recorded pretax charges and special items totaling $3.3 billion for the fourth quarter of 2011 in order to provide a reserve for probable losses from product liability lawsuits. The pending lawsuits are attributable to misleading marketing practices and manufacturing-quality lapses.

On November 4, 2013, Johnson & Johnson agreed to pay more than $2.2 billion in criminal and civil fines to settle accusations that it improperly promoted the antipsychotic drug Risperdal to older adults, children and people with developmental disabilities. The agreement is the third-largest pharmaceutical settlement in U.S. history and the largest in a string of recent cases involving the marketing of antipsychotic and anti-seizure drugs to older dementia patients. It is part of a decade-long effort by the federal government to hold the health care giant — and other pharmaceutical companies — accountable for illegally marketing the drugs as a way to control patients with dementia in nursing homes and children with certain behavioral disabilities, despite the health risks of the drugs.[40]

In another setback for the company, on February 24, 2015, a Philadelphia jury decided J&J must pay $2.5 million in damages for failing to warn that its Risperdal antipsychotic could cause gynecomastia, which is abnormal development of breasts in males. The lawsuit was brought by the family of an autistic boy who took the drug in 2002 and later developed size 46 DD breasts, according to a lawyer for the family. The case has drawn attention for a few reasons. For one, this was the first lawsuit claiming J&J hid the risks of gynecomastia to go to trial after a handful of cases were settled in recent years. The trial also served as a reminder that J&J had already paid $2.2 billion two years prior to resolve criminal and civil allegations of illegally marketing Risperdal to children and the elderly.[41]

Unfortunately, the problems for Johnson & Johnson go further back. Exhibit 3.3 provides a brief summary of the investigations against the company:

EXHIBIT 3.3 Johnson & Johnson's Product Liabilities

- On December 21, 2011, it was announced that Johnson & Johnson must defend a lawsuit claiming that it misled investors about quality control failures at manufacturing plants that led to recalls of the popular over-the-counter drug Motrin. Allegedly, top executives made misleading statements about details of the recalls, leading to stock losses after the true reasons for the recalls became public.

- Earlier in 2011, a lawsuit filed by a group of consumers alleging that Johnson & Johnson's baby shampoo includes potentially cancer-causing chemicals was allowed to go forward after evidence came out that the product contained a chemical ingredient called methylene chloride, which is banned by the U.S. Food and Drug Administration (FDA) for use in cosmetics.

- In January 2011, it was announced that Johnson & Johnson might have to pay up to $1 billion for lawsuits concerning its subsidiary DePuy Orthopaedics, which sold metal-on-metal hip implants that were found to shed minute metal particles into a patient's bloodstream over time. Lawsuits over the implants have piled up across the country, accusing DePuy of manufacturing a defective product, failing to warn patients and doctors of problems with the implant, and negligence in designing, manufacturing, and selling the product.

  It is worth noting that Johnson & Johnson raised its product-liability reserves to $570 million at the end of 2010 and allotted $280 million for medical costs of patients directly affected by the recalled hip implants. In November 2013, it was announced that Johnson & Johnson agreed to a settlement that could reach up to $4 billion to resolve thousands of lawsuits filed by patients injured by a flawed all-metal replacement hip.

- Women who have suffered serious injury and disfigurement filed lawsuits in 2012 against Johnson & Johnson subsidiary Ethicon, claiming that vaginal mesh manufactured by Ethicon caused them life-altering complications. Upon investigation, a number of doctors and scientists concluded that the Ethicon vaginal mesh and bladder slings did not meet reasonable safety standards. The FDA issued Public Health Notifications regarding the use of vaginal mesh products to treat pelvic organ prolapse and stress urinary incontinence in October 2008, in February 2009, and in July 2011.

(Continued)

In March 2015, The Lawsuit Settlement Funding Company announced that Johnson & Johnson's Ethicon subsidiary reached a settlement in their transvaginal mesh devices. The settlement came just one day after a $5.7 million verdict was reached against Johnson & Johnson's Ethicon by a California jury over their Gynecare TVT Abbrevo vaginal mesh device. Details of the latest settlement have not been disclosed.

Some might say that Johnson & Johnson made withdrawals from its "trust" bank in recent years. The company reacted slowly to a variety of crises, at first failing to admit any culpability and disclaiming financial liability. We can't escape the logical conclusion that "where there is smoke, there is fire." The disappointing fact is that these instances occurred as a result of management and internal actions and reflect a culture that has changed dramatically from the days of the Tylenol poisoning. Perhaps Johnson & Johnson is learning the hard way that it takes a long time to build a reputation for trust, but not very long to tear it down.

Ethics in the Workplace

LO 3-4
Discuss the views of employees about ethics in their organizations.

When we think about workplace ethics, the first thing that comes to mind is a code of conduct that influences the development of an ethical culture in the workplace. A code goes beyond what is legal for an organization and provides normative guidelines for ethical conduct. Support for ethical behavior from top management is a critical component of fostering an ethical climate. Employees who sense that top managers act unethically quickly lose trust in those managers. The result can be to become disillusioned with the goals of the organization and question whether the corporate culture is one that is consistent with individual, personal values and beliefs.

An ethical organization is one in which top managers establish a tone at the top that promotes ethical behavior including to raise questions when questionable behavior occurs. Here is a list of measures that should be taken to establish an ethical culture:

1. Establish clear policies on ethical conduct including a code of ethics.
2. Develop an ethics training program that instills a commitment to act ethically and explains code provisions.
3. Assign a top-level officer (i.e., Chief Ethics and Compliance Officer) to oversee compliance with ethics policies.
4. Use the internal auditors to investigate whether ethics policies have been followed in practice.
5. Establish strong internal controls to prevent and detect unethical behaviors, such as fraud.
6. Establish whistleblowing policies including reporting outlets.
7. Establish an ethics hotline where employees can discuss questionable behavior on an anonymous basis.
8. Have employees sign a statement that they have complied with ethics policies.
9. Enforce ethics policies fairly and take immediate action against those who violate the policies.
10. Reward ethical behavior by including it in the performance evaluation system.

Character and Leadership in the Workplace

"Character Counts" is the mantra of the Josephson Institute of Ethics whose Six Pillars of Character were discussed in Chapter 1. Characteristics of ethical behavior in leaders include: compassion, courage, diligence, fairness, honesty, inclusiveness, initiative, integrity, optimism, respect, responsibility, and trustworthiness. Good leaders have strong character and have a moral imperative underwrite their actions. Management guru, Warren Bennis, is quoted as saying, "Managers are people who do things right, and leaders are people who do the right thing."

Good character can be developed through experience and learning. Each situation we encounter presents a different experience and opportunity to learn and deepen character. Character becomes critical when managing a crisis, such as an ethical dilemma where stakeholder interests conflict.

Managers can set the right tone at the top and foster ethical leadership, both of which are necessary for ethical decision making, by following four simple rules:

1. *Consider how your actions affect others.* How will the stakeholders be affected by my intended actions? Here, a utilitarian analysis might help.
2. *Do no harm.* Your actions and decisions should not harm others. One exception is whistleblowing because of the need to emphasize "the greater good," which means the public interest in accounting.
3. *Make decisions that are universal.* Consistent with the categorical imperative, ask yourself whether you would want others to resolve the conflict by taking the same or similar action you are about to take. Universal decisions are those that respect the rights of others.
4. *Reflect before deciding.* As a final step, think about how you would feel if your actions and decisions appear on the front pages of the local newspaper. Would you be proud to defend them and comfortable explaining them?

Integrity: The Basis for Trust in the Workplace

Albert Camus, the French Nobel Prize winning author, journalist, and philosopher, said, "Integrity has no need of rules." People of integrity are self-driven to do the right thing. Leaders of integrity act on the knowledge that their actions are ethical and provide the basis for others in the workplace to follow their lead.

KPMG's *Integrity Survey 2013* provides an inside look at organizational misconduct based upon responses from more than 3,500 U.S. working adults. Key findings from the report include:[42]

- Nearly three out of four employees reported that they had observed misconduct within their organizations in the previous 12 months.
- More than half of employees reported that what they observed could potentially cause a significant loss of public trust if discovered.
- Some of the driving forces behind fraud and misconduct in the corporate environment include pressure to do "whatever it takes" to meet targets, not taking the code of conduct seriously, believing employees will be rewarded based upon results and not the means used to achieve them, and fear of losing one's job for not meeting performance targets.
- Nearly half of employees were uncertain that they would be protected from retaliation if they reported concerns to management. And more than half suggested a lack of confidence that they would be satisfied with the outcome.

- Ethics and compliance programs continue to have a favorable impact on employee perceptions and behaviors.

Employees were asked what they would do if they observed a violation of their organization's standards of conduct. The results were: 78 percent would notify their supervisor or another manager; 54 percent would try resolving the matter directly; 53 percent would call the ethics or compliance hotline; 26 percent would notify someone outside the organization; and 23 percent would look the other way or do nothing.

It's encouraging to learn that over three-fourths would inform their supervisor, in part because it is the generally recognized initial step in considering whether to blow the whistle. It is somewhat troubling that almost one-quarter of the workers would look the other way or do nothing. Perhaps they have not been given an opportunity to voice their values or have not discovered an effective means to do so.

The tone at the top set by top management is a determining factor in creating organizational commitment to high ethics and integrity. Employees were asked whether the chief executive officer and other senior executives exhibited characteristics attributable to personal integrity and ethical leadership. Approximately two-thirds of the employees agreed that their leaders set the right tone regarding the importance of ethics and integrity and served as positive role models for their organization, leaving one-third unsure or in disagreement.

Perhaps not surprisingly, a large percentage (64 percent) indicated that the root cause of misconduct was pressure to do "whatever it takes" to meet business objectives, while 59 percent said they believed they would be rewarded for results, not the means used to achieve them. In such instances, the corporate culture does not foster integrity or ethical behavior; instead, expedience and self-interest drive workplace behavior.

Employees Perceptions of Ethics in the Workplace

Going beyond the Integrity Survey, it is important to understand how employees view the ethics of the organizations they work for, in part to better understand corporate governance systems and whistleblowing. The *2013 National Business Ethics Survey* (NBES) conducted by the Ethics Resource Center provides interesting data about ethics in the workplace. The report is the eighth in a series. The 2013 survey provides information on the views of 6,579 respondents that represent a broad array of employees in the for-profit sector.[43] Exhibit 3.4 summarizes observed misconduct. It is encouraging that all such instances have declined between 2011 and 2013.

EXHIBIT 3.4 2013 NBES Survey of Reporting of Observed Misconduct

Type of Misconduct	2013	2011
Stealing or theft	64%	69%
Falsifying time reports or hours worked	49%	61%
Falsifying expense reports	48%	66%
Falsifying and/or manipulating financial reporting information	45%	62%
Falsifying invoices, books, and/or records	40%	N/A
Accepting inappropriate gifts or kickbacks from suppliers or vendors	36%	52%

The results of the NBES survey depicted in Exhibit 3.5, indicate a lessening of observed misconduct, virtually no change in reporting it, and a decline in pressure to compromise ethical standards from 2011 to 2013, which may reflect an improving corporate culture. This seems to be the case since the "weak-leaning" culture response went down by 6 points in the same time period. The results also show an increase in ethics training programs and the use of ethical conduct as a performance measure in employee evaluations.

EXHIBIT 3.5   Views of Employees on Ethics in the Workplace from the 2011 National Business Ethics Survey

Item	2013	2011	2009
Pressure to compromise ethical standards	9%	13%	8%
Weak/weak-leaning ethical culture	34%	40%	35%
Observed misconduct	41%	45%	55%
Reported observed misconduct	63%	65%	63%
Experienced retaliation after reporting (i.e., whistleblowing)	21%	22%	15%

The percentage of employees experiencing retaliation is up, indicating it still remains a problem in corporate America. Perhaps the new protections under SOX and Dodd-Frank will help to stem the rising tide.

One concern is that, while misconduct is down overall, a relatively high percentage of misconduct is committed by managers—the very people who should be establishing an ethical culture and providing ethical leadership. Workers reported that 60 percent of misconduct involved someone with managerial authority from the supervisory level up to top management. Nearly a quarter (24 percent) of observed misdeeds involved senior managers. Also, workers said that 26 percent of misconduct is ongoing within their organizations and about 12 percent of wrongdoing was reported to take place company-wide.

Perhaps not surprising, the results indicate that occupational fraud and financial statement fraud are of greatest concern because of their effects on the accuracy and reliability of the financial statements.

Fraud in Organizations

LO 3-5
Describe the causes of fraud, detection methods, and preventative controls.

Fraud can be defined as a deliberate misrepresentation to gain an advantage over another party. Fraud comes in many different forms, including fraud in financial statements, the misappropriation of assets (theft) and subsequent cover-up, and disclosure fraud. We introduce the concept of fraudulent financial statements in this chapter and discuss it more fully in Chapter 5. In this chapter, we will look at the results of the *2014 Global Fraud Survey: Report to the Nations on Occupational Fraud and Abuse,* conducted by the Association of Certified Fraud Examiners (ACFE).

Occupational Fraud

The 2014 ACFE survey is a follow-up to its *2012 Global Fraud Study.* The 2014 survey reports on 1,483 cases of occupational fraud that were reported by the Certified Fraud Examiners (CFEs) who investigated them. These offenses occurred in nearly 100 countries on six continents.[44]

The ACFE report focuses on *occupational fraud* schemes in which an employee abuses the trust placed in him by an employer for personal gain. The ACFE defines occupational fraud as "the use of one's occupation for personal enrichment through the deliberate misuse or misapplication of the employing organization's resources or assets."[45] A summary of the findings follows:

- Survey participants estimated that the typical organization loses 5 percent of its revenues to fraud each year. If applied to the 2013 estimated Gross World Product, this translates into a potential projected global fraud loss of nearly $3.7 trillion.
- The median loss caused by the occupational fraud cases studied was $145,000. Additionally, 22 percent of the cases involved losses of at least $1 million.
- The frauds reported lasted a median of 18 months before being detected.
- Asset misappropriation schemes were the most common type of occupational fraud, comprising 85 percent of the reported cases.
- Financial statement fraud schemes made up just 9 percent of the cases, but caused the greatest median loss at $1 million.
- Occupational fraud is more likely to be detected by a tip than by any other method—more than twice the rate of any other detection method. Employees accounted for nearly half of all the tips that led to the discovery of fraud.
- Organizations with hotlines were much more likely to catch fraud by a tip. These organizations also experienced frauds that were 41 percent less costly, and they detected frauds 50 percent more quickly.
- Corruption and billing schemes pose the greatest risks to organizations throughout the world.
- The presence of anti-fraud controls is correlated with significant decreases in the cost and duration of occupational fraud schemes.
- Perpetrators with higher levels of authority tend to cause much larger losses. Owners/executives only accounted for 19 percent of all cases, but they caused a median loss of $500,000. Employees, conversely, committed 42 percent of occupational frauds but only caused a median loss of $75,000. Managers ranked in the middle, committing 36 percent of frauds with a median loss of $130,000.

How Occupational Fraud Is Committed and Detected

Asset misappropriation schemes include when an employee steals or misuses resources, such as charging personal expenses to the company while traveling on business trips. Corruption schemes include misusing one's position or influence in an organization for personal gain, something that Dennis Kozlowski was known for doing. Kozlowski and chief financial officer (CFO) Mark Swartz were convicted on June 21, 2005, of taking bonuses worth more than $120 million without the approval of Tyco's directors, abusing an employee loan program, and misrepresenting the company's financial condition to investors to boost the stock price while selling $575 million in stock.

A surprising result is that a "tip" was the most common way of detecting fraud, at 42.2 percent in 2014. According to the ACFE report, detection by tip has been the most common method of initial detection since the first survey in 2002. It could be that tips are primarily provided by whistleblowers, but the study does not reach that conclusion. Exhibit 3.6 shows the frequency of detection methods as reported by survey respondents.

An important conclusion from these results is that controls such as management reviews and internal audits account for a significant percentage of detection methods (30 percent), and the external audit, at only 3 percent, does not seem to be a reliable method to detect fraud.

EXHIBIT 3.6 Initial Detection of Occupational Frauds from the *ACFE 2014 Global Survey: Report to the Nations on Occupational Fraud and Abuse*

Detection Method	Percentage Reported	Median Loss
Tip	42.2%	$149,000
Management Review	16.0%	$125,000
Internal Audit	14.1%	$100,000
By Accident	6.8%	$325,000
Account Reconciliation	6.6%	$75,000
Document Examination	4.2%	$220,000
External Audit	3.0%	$360,000
Surveillance/Monitoring	2.6%	$49,000
Notified by Law Enforcement	2.2%	$1,250,000
IT Controls	1.1%	$70,000
Confession	0.8%	$220,000
Other	0.5%	N/A

Frequency of Anti-Fraud Controls

The survey concludes that proactive fraud prevention and detection controls are a vital part in managing the risk of fraud. Respondents indicated that external audits were the most common control enacted by the victim organization, as they were present in 80 percent of the reported cases. It seems counterintuitive that only 3 percent of the frauds are detected by external audits. The answer lies in that an audit is not designed to detect fraud *per se;* instead it is to identify and detect risks of material misstatement of the financial statements due to error and fraud.

With more than 42 percent of frauds being detected by tips, hotlines should play an essential role in organizations' anti-fraud programs. However, only 54 percent had a hotline mechanism in place, and less than 11 percent provided rewards for whistleblowers. Exhibit 3.7 summarizes the frequency of anti-fraud controls.

EXHIBIT 3.7 Frequency of Anti-Fraud Controls: 2014 ACFE Global Fraud Survey

Anti-Fraud Control	Percentage Reported
External Audit of Financial Statements	81.4%
Code of Conduct	77.4%
Internal Audit Department	70.8%
Management Certification of Financial Statements	70.0%
External Audit of Internal Controls over Financial Reporting	65.2%
Management Review	62.6%
Independent Audit Committee	62.0%
Hotline	54.1%
Employee Support Programs	52.4%

(Continued)

Fraud Training for Managers/Executives	47.8%
Fraud Training for Employees	47.7%
Anti-Fraud Policy	45.4%
Dedicated Fraud Department, Function, or Team	38.6%
Proactive Data Monitoring/Analysis	34.8%
Formal Fraud Risk Assessments	33.5%
Surprise Audits	33.2%
Job Rotation/Mandatory Vacations	19.9%
Rewards for Whistleblowers	10.5%

Red-Flag Warnings of Fraud

The ACFE study found that most occupational fraudsters' crimes are motivated at least in part by some kind of financial pressure. In addition, while committing a fraud, an individual will frequently display certain behavioral traits associated with stress or a fear of being caught.[46] Overall, at least one red flag was identified in 92 percent of cases, and, in 64 percent of cases, the fraudster displayed two or more behavioral red flags. Approximately 44 percent of fraud perpetrators were living beyond their means while the fraud was ongoing, and 33 percent were experiencing known financial difficulties. These warning signs should alert internal auditors that trouble may lie ahead with respect to actual fraud. Exhibit 3.8 shows the fraud indicators identified in the study.

EXHIBIT 3.8   Behavioral Red Flags Displayed by Perpetrators: *ACFE 2014 Global Survey: Report to the Nations on Occupational Fraud and Abuse*

Behavioral Indicators of Fraud	Percentage Reported
Living Beyond Means	43.8%
Financial Difficulties	33.0%
Unusually Close Association with Vendor/Customer	21.8%
Control Issues, Unwillingness to Share Duties	21.1%
"Wheeler-Dealer" Attitude	18.4%
Divorce/Family Problems	16.8%
Instability, Suspiciousness, or Defensiveness	15.0%
Addiction Problems	11.8%
Complained about Inadequate Pay	9.4%
Past Employment-Related Problems	8.9%
Refusal to Take Vacations	8.8%
Excessive Pressure within Organization	8.4%
Social Isolation	7.4%
Complained about Lack of Authority	6.5%
Excessive Family/Peer Pressure for Success	6.0%
Instability in Life Circumstance	5.9%
Past Legal Problems	5.8%

The results of the survey clearly indicate that internal auditors should have their "eyes wide open" with respect to whether senior officers have adopted a lavish living style that creates the incentive to "cook the books" in a way that provides financial results to support their lifestyle. If earnings go up, stock prices often rise as well. Top managers typically own stock in their companies, so an incentive exists to boost earnings sometimes at any cost. A good example is the former CEO of HealthSouth, Richard Scrushy. Recall that we earlier identified the company as one that showed signs of ethical collapse because of its weak board of directors. Scrushy was behind the $2.7 billion earnings overstatement at HealthSouth.

Scrushy allegedly received $226 million in compensation over seven years, while HealthSouth was losing $1.8 billion during the same period. A skeptical auditor would have asked where all that money was going and would have looked for warnings that Scrushy might have been living beyond his means. Scrushy was charged with knowingly engaging in financial transactions using criminally derived property, including the purchase of land, aircraft, boats, cars, artwork, jewelry, and other items. At his trial, it become known that he had used money from his compensation for several residences in the state of Alabama and property in Palm Beach, Florida; a 92-foot Tarrab yacht called *Chez Soiree,* a 38-foot Intrepid Walkaround watercraft and a 42-foot Lightning boat; a 1998 Cessna Caravan 675, together with amphibious floats and other equipment, and a 2001 Cessna Citation 525 aircraft; diamond jewelry; several luxury automobiles, including a 2003 Lamborghini Murcielago, a 2000 Rolls Royce Corniche, and two 2002 Cadillac Escalades; and paintings by Pablo Picasso, Marc Chagall, Pierre-August Renoir, among others.

It is not just the internal auditors who wore blinders and the board that looked the other way. The external auditors did not detect the fraud either.

Internal Control Weaknesses

According to the Center for Audit Quality, internal control includes all of the processes and procedures that management puts in place to help make sure that its assets are protected and that company activities are conducted in accordance with the organization's policies and procedures.[47] For example, a bank reconciliation should be prepared regularly and by a person(s) with no responsibility for cash record keeping for the handling of cash. The bank reconciliation should be reviewed by an independent person and, in the case of a small business, by the owner. The ACFE survey found that cash-related fraud schemes accounted for almost 40 percent of all types of occupational fraud including skimming (14.1 percent)—the illegal practice of taking money from cash receipts for personal use; check tampering (13.7 percent); and cash larceny (10.7 percent)—the theft of cash after it has been recorded on the books.

An effective system of internal controls is critical to establish an ethical corporate culture that should be supported by the tone at the top. By examining Exhibit 3.7 we can see the importance of certain control mechanisms, including the external audit of financial statements (81.4 percent) and the external audit of the internal controls over financial reporting (65.2 percent). Also, the ACFE survey indicates that 32.2 percent of the internal control weaknesses are due to a lack of internal controls. While remaining at a high level, the 2014 results are 3.5 percent below the 2012 findings and 5.6 percent below 2010 findings. This may reflect a commitment by management to improve controls in view of the requirements in the Sarbanes-Oxley Act (SOX) of 2002.

As directed by Section 404 of SOX, the Securities Exchange Act of 1934 adopted a regulation that public companies have to include in their annual reports a report of management on the company's internal control over financial reporting. The internal control report must include a statement of management's responsibility for establishing and maintaining adequate internal control over financial reporting for the company; management's assessment of the effectiveness of the company's internal control over financial reporting as of the end of the company's most recent fiscal year; a statement identifying the framework used by management to evaluate the effectiveness of the company's internal control over financial reporting; and a statement that the registered public accounting firm that audited the company's financial statements included in the annual report has issued an attestation report on management's assessment of the company's internal control over financial reporting.

An internal control system, no matter how well conceived and operated, can provide only reasonable—not absolute—assurance to management and the board of directors regarding achievement of an entity's objectives. The likelihood of achievement is affected by a variety of factors including: judgments in decision making can be faulty; breakdowns can occur due to simple mistakes and errors in the application of controls; and controls can be circumvented by the collusion of two or more people. Management override of internal controls may be a problem as well similar to what happened at Enron and WorldCom. Indeed, 18.9 percent of respondents in the ACFE survey indicated that override of existing controls had occurred at victim organizations.

Example of Occupational Fraud

What follows is a description of a payroll fraud scheme. Payroll schemes accounted for 11.8 percent of of fraud techniques in the ACFE survey.

> The head of a department distributed paychecks to her employees on a weekly basis. Typically, the department head received the payroll checks each week from a payroll processing company and then distributed them to employees. One day another employee noticed the department head had locked his door after the checks were received and wondered about it. He became suspicious and reported it to his manager. A payroll audit discovered that several former employees were still receiving paychecks. It was discovered that the department head had the ability to access and edit electronic time keeping records for hourly employees and knew the passwords to the payroll system for their supervisors. He used this access to falsify hours, and thus paychecks, for previous employees. He then took the paychecks to check cashing companies to redeem them. The department head ultimately confessed to over 100 instances of payroll fraud over a 10-month period totaling almost $100,000.

In this case a lack of proper internal controls contributed to the fraud. The company lacked a proper separation of duties, did not regularly monitor payroll records for "ghost employees," did not require that employees regularly change their passwords, and allowed the department head who distributed the checks to also accept them from the payroll service. Perhaps a fraud hotline for employees to report suspicious behavior would have led to earlier reporting of the fraud.

Financial Statement Fraud

Financial statement fraud schemes occur because an employee—typically a member of top management —causes a misstatement or omission of material information in the organization's financial reports. Examples include recording fictitious revenues, understating reported expenses, artificially inflating reported assets, and failing to accrue expenses at the end of the year, such as what occurred in the DigitPrint case in Chapter 1.

A report by Ernst & Young, *Detecting Financial Statement Fraud: What Every Manager Needs to Know,*[48] provides examples of common methods to overstate revenue, understate expenses, and make improper asset valuations. Revenue overstatements include the following:

- Recording gross, rather than net, revenue.
- Recording revenues of other companies when acting as a "middleman."
- Recording sales that never took place.
- Recording future sales in the current period.

- Recording sales of products that are out on consignment.

Common methods of understating expenses include the following:

- Reporting cost of sales as a non-operating expense so that it does not negatively affect gross margin.
- Capitalizing operating costs, recording them as assets on the balance sheet instead of as expenses on the income statement (i.e., WorldCom).
- Not recording some expenses at all, or not recording expenses in the proper period.

Examples of improper asset valuations include the following:

- Manipulating reserves.
- Changing the useful lives of assets.
- Failing to take a write-down when needed.
- Manipulating estimates of fair market value.

One of the most bizarre examples of financial statement fraud involved Miniscribe, a manufacturer of computer hard drive disks that committed inventory fraud in the 1980s in the amount of $15 million. This was a mere pittance compared to the $11 billion fraud at WorldCom some 15 years later, but the efforts of Miniscribe's management to cover up the fraud were as audacious as any ever seen. Exhibit 3.9 summarizes this fraud.

EXHIBIT 3.9 Miniscribe Fraud

Miniscribe was a Colorado-based manufacturer of computer hard disk drives whose top officers were convicted of management fraud by covering up a multimillion-dollar inventory overstatement between December 1986 and January 1989, which falsely inflated Miniscribe's profits and accelerated its descent into bankruptcy.

Miniscribe went public in 1983, but it soon grew beyond its capacity. In 1985, a venture capital group, Hambrecht & Quist, invested $20 million in Miniscribe and gained control of its management.

Following its change in management, Quentin T. Wiles became the chair of the board and CEO. Wiles had a reputation as a successful, demanding executive who expected performance. Salaries and bonuses at Miniscribe often depended upon Miniscribe "making the numbers." Assisting Wiles was a management team consisting largely of CPAs. Patrick Schleibaum initially served as Miniscribe's CFO.

Despite reported growth and profitability, Miniscribe's financial position began to deteriorate early in 1987. In January 1987, Miniscribe conducted its annual inventory count to determine the value of inventory on hand. The accuracy of the inventory count was critical to the proper preparation of Miniscribe's 1986 year-end financial statements.

Management retained the independent accounting firm of Coopers & Lybrand (now PwC) to audit Miniscribe and verify the accuracy of its inventory count. The standard procedure for verifying a company's inventory count is through a test count—an inventory sampling deemed representative of the entire inventory. Problems arose when, unbeknownst to the auditors, management detected an inventory hole of between $2 million and $4 million. This inventory hole appeared because the actual inventory count, and thus dollar value of the inventory, was less than the value of the inventory recorded on Miniscribe's books. The overstatement of inventory led to the understatement of cost of goods sold and inflated earnings equal to the amount of the inventory overstatement.

(Continued)

At this point, Wiles was unaware of the inventory hole. Schleibaum properly decided to charge a portion of the hole against an emergency fund known as "inventory reserves." The remainder of the hole also should have been charged off or expensed as a cost of goods sold, with a corresponding reduction in profits. Schleibaum directed his subordinates to conceal the remainder of the inventory hole through improper means so that Miniscribe could continue to "make the numbers." This occurred by falsely inflating the inventory count. To hide the false count from the auditors, division managers broke into the auditors' work trunks at Miniscribe after business hours and altered the test count to match the inflated inventory count. The inflated numbers were then entered into Miniscribe's computer system and reflected as additional inventory. Schleibaum signed a management representation letter to the auditors indicating that Miniscribe's financial statements were accurate, including its inventory valuation. Miniscribe cleared the 1986 audit.

Miniscribe reported the false profits resulting from concealment of the inventory hole on its 1986 income statement and 1987 first-quarter earnings statement. Miniscribe disseminated this information to the public through its 1986 annual report and 1987 first-quarter financial report. Schleibaum signed the 1986 10-K report (annual report to the Securities and Exchange Commission) and 1987 first-quarter 10-Q report, which contained Miniscribe's false financial statements. Miniscribe filed the 10-K and 10-Q reports with the SEC as required by law. Miniscribe's reported success allowed the company to raise funds through a $97 million issue of debentures early in 1987.

In the spring of 1987, Wiles became concerned about Miniscribe's internal controls and financial strength. He worried that if an inventory problem actually existed, Miniscribe and its officers might be liable to those investors purchasing the debentures on the basis of the company's reported financial strength. Ultimately, a $15 million hole in inventory was discovered. Wiles had decided that Miniscribe could not afford to write off the inventory hole in 1987; instead, it had to cover it up to maintain investor confidence. Wiles planned to write off the inventory hole over six quarters, beginning with the first quarter of 1988.

In December 1987, independent auditors began preparing for Miniscribe's 1987 year-end audit. Miniscribe again faced the problem of clearing the independent audit. In mid-December, Miniscribe's management, with Wiles's approval and Schleibaum's assistance, engaged in an extensive cover-up, which included recording the shipment of bricks as in-transit inventory. To implement the plan, Miniscribe employees first rented an empty warehouse and procured 10 exclusive-use trailers. They then purchased 26,000 bricks.

On Saturday, December 18, 1987, Schleibaum and others gathered at the warehouse. Wiles did not attend. From early morning to late afternoon, those present loaded the bricks onto pallets, shrink-wrapped the pallets, and boxed them. The weight of each brick pallet approximated the weight of a pallet of disk drives. The brick pallets then were loaded onto the trailers and taken to a farm in Larimer County, Colorado.

Miniscribe's books, however, showed the bricks as in-transit inventory worth approximately $4 million. Employees at two of Miniscribe's buyers, CompuAdd and CalAbco, agreed to refuse fictitious inventory shipments from Miniscribe totaling $4 million. Miniscribe then added the fictitious inventory shipments to the company's inventory records.

Additionally, the officers employed other means to cover the inventory hole, including (1) recording the shipment of nonexistent inventory, (2) packaging scrap as inventory, (3) double-counting inventory, and (4) failing to record payables upon the receipt of materials. These various means distributed the inventory hole throughout Miniscribe's three facilities, making the problem more difficult for the independent auditors to detect.

Again, Schleibaum signed a management representation letter to the auditors stating that Miniscribe's 1987 financial reports were accurate and truthful, and Miniscribe cleared the independent audit. The result of the cover-up was that Miniscribe's book inventory and reported profits for 1987 were overstated by approximately $15 million and $22 million, respectively. These figures represented 17 percent of Miniscribe's inventory and 70 percent of its profits for the year.

(Continued)

Eventually, Miniscribe got caught up in its own fraud, as it became more and more difficult to cover the inventory hole and questions were asked about its accounting. The sharp decline in the stock market in October 1987 hastened the day when the house of cards that was Miniscribe collapsed. The company finally declared bankruptcy in 1990.

Source: *United States of America v. Quentin T. Wiles and Patrick J. Schleibaum,* Nos. 94-1592, 95-1022. United States Court of Appeals, Tenth Circuit, December 10, 1996 102 F.3d 1043.

Of particular note in the Miniscribe fraud is the unethical behavior at the highest levels of management that created a culture of blindness to what was right and wrong and led to the perpetuation of the fraud. It serves as an example of top management fraud, and an override of internal controls existed as well. The corporate governance system at Miniscribe failed because the company lacked independent members on its board of directors to serve as a check against excessive management behavior. To say the auditors were deficient in their procedures is an understatement. It is quite rare, to say the least, that auditors fail to adequately secure their working papers at the end of the day. These files should never be left at the client's office. Just imagine if electronic records were not password protected or flash drives were left on the premises.

Why Does Financial Statement Fraud Occur?

Why does financial statement fraud occur? This question has been examined since the 1980s when well-publicized financial statement frauds occurred at companies including ZZZZ Best, Miniscribe, Phar-Mor, Cendant, and Waste Management. Theoretically, there are three factors that appear to be present in every case of financial statement fraud that are addressed in auditing standards.[49] These are explored in detail in Chapter 5. We briefly summarize them here.

Situational pressure. Situational pressures may prompt an otherwise honest person to commit fraud. It typically occurs as a result of immediate pressure within either her internal or external environment. For example, financial analysts project earnings and companies feel the pressure to meet or exceed these amounts. An accountant may come to believe she has no option other than to go along with the fraud. The Betty Vinson situation at WorldCom is a case in point. She did not know how to effectively voice her values or where she could turn to for help.

Perceived opportunity. The opportunity to commit fraud and conceal it must exist. People do not normally commit fraud believing they will get caught. They do it because they believe they can get away with it (i.e., have access to the underlying financial information or override internal controls). The opportunity to commit fraud and conceal it often involves the absence of, or improper oversight by, the board of directors or audit committee, weak or nonexistent internal controls, unusual or complex transactions, accounting estimates that require sufficient subjective judgment by management, and ineffective internal audit staff.

Rationalization. People who commit financial statement fraud are able to rationalize the act. Being able to justify the act makes it possible. The individual must first convince herself that the behavior is temporary or is acceptable. She may believe it is in the best interest of the company to commit the fraud, perhaps because a needed loan will not be secured without financial statements to back it up. There is often the belief that everything will return to normal after the trigger event has passed.

Financial statement fraud does not occur in a vacuum. It is enabled by the absence of an ethical culture. Oftentimes, a culture is created and a tone at the top established that presents the image of a company willing to do whatever it takes to paint a rosy picture about financial results. Effective oversight and strong internal controls give way to greed, moral blindness, and inattentiveness to the important details that help to prevent and detect fraud. As with most situations in business, the desire to succeed crowds out ethical behavior. Those in the way are pressured to be team players; go along just this one time; and, in the end, compromise their values.

We end this section with a quote from Sophocles, the ancient Greek tragedian. He said, "I would prefer even to fail with honor than win by cheating." In other words, it is better to fail with one's morals and dignity intact than win by being dishonest.

Foundations of Corporate Governance Systems

An essential part of creating an ethical organization environment is to put in place effective corporate governance systems that establish control mechanisms to ensure that organizational values guide decision making and that ethical standards are being followed. The four pillars of corporate governance are accountability, fairness, transparency, and independence. *Accountability* means to ensure that management is accountable to the board and the board is accountable to the shareholders. *Fairness* means to protect shareholders rights, treat them equitably, and provide effective redress for violations. *Transparency* requires timely, accurate, disclosure on all material matters, including the financial situation, performance, ownership, and corporate governance. *Independence* means to have the procedures and structures in place to minimize, or avoid completely conflict of interest and to ensure that independent directors are free from the influence of others.[50]

Defining Corporate Governance

There is no single, accepted definition of *corporate governance*. A fairly narrow definition given by Shleifer and Vishny emphasizes the separation of ownership and control in corporations. They define corporate governance as dealing with "the ways in which the suppliers of finance to corporations assure themselves of getting a return on their investment."[51] Parkinson defines it as a process of supervision and control intended to ensure that the company's management acts in accordance with the interests of shareholders.[52]

The first corporate governance report, *Sir Adrian Cadbury's Report on the Financial Aspects of Corporate Governance* (1992), took a broader view in defining it as "the system by which companies are directed and controlled," and further explained that boards of directors are responsible for the governance of their companies, while the shareholders' role in governance is to appoint the directors and auditors, and to satisfy themselves that an appropriate governance structure is in place.[53]

The definition of corporate governance that we like the best is by Tricker, who says that governance is not concerned with running the business of the company *per se*, but with giving overall direction to the enterprise, with overseeing and controlling the executive actions of management, and with satisfying legitimate expectations of accountability and regulation by interests beyond the corporate boundaries.[54] In this regard, corporate governance can be seen as a set of rules that define the relationship between stakeholders, management, and board of directors of a company and influence how that company is operating. At its most basic level, corporate governance deals with issues that result from the separation of ownership and control. But corporate governance goes beyond simply establishing a clear relationship between shareholders and managers.

A corporate governance regime typically includes mechanisms to ensure that the agent (management) runs the firm for the benefit of one or more principals (shareholders, creditors, suppliers, clients, employees, and other parties with whom the firm conducts its business). The mechanisms include internal ones, such as the board of directors, its committees including the audit committee, executive compensation policies, and internal controls, and external measures, which include monitoring by large shareholders and creditors (in particular, banks), external auditors, and the regulatory framework of a securities exchange commission, the corporate law regime, and stock exchange listing requirements and oversight.

Views of Corporate Governance

Differences exist about the role of corporate governance in business. Some organizations take the view that as long as they are maximizing shareholder wealth and profitability, they are fulfilling their core responsibilities. Other firms take a broader view based on the stakeholder perspective.

The shareholder model of corporate governance is founded on classic economic precepts, including maximizing wealth for investors and creditors. In a public corporation, firm decisions should be oriented toward serving the best interests of investors. Underlying these decisions is a classic agency problem, in which ownership (investors) and control (managers) are separate. Managers act as the agents of the investors (principals), who expect those decisions to increase the value of the stock they own.[55] However, managers may have motivations beyond stockholder value such as increasing market share, or more personal ones including maximizing executive compensation. In these instances, decisions may be based on an egoist approach to ethical decision making that ignores the interests of others.

Because shareholder owners of public companies are not normally involved in the daily operations, the board of directors oversee the companies, and CEOs and other members of top management run them. Albrecht et al. points out that the principal-agent relationship involves a transfer of trust and duty to the agent, while also assuming that the agent is opportunistic and will pursue interests that are in conflict with those of the principal, thereby creating an "agency problem."[56] Because of these potential differences, corporate governance mechanisms are needed to align investor and management interests. A fundamental challenge underlying all corporate governance affairs dates back to the days of Adam Smith. In *The Wealth of Nations,* Smith said that "the directors of companies, being managers of other people's money, cannot be expected to watch over it with the same vigilance with which they watch over their own."

One traditional approach is for shareholders to give the CEO shares or options of stock that vest over time, thus inducing long-term behavior and deterring short-term actions that can harm future company value. When the interests of top management are brought in line with interests of shareholders, agency theory argues that management will fulfill its duty to shareholders, not so much out of any sense of moral duty to shareholders, but because doing what shareholders have provided incentives for maximizes their own utility.[57]

Jensen and Meckling demonstrate how investors in publicly traded corporations incur (agency) costs in monitoring managerial performance. In general, agency costs arise whenever there is an "information asymmetry" between the corporation and outsiders because insiders (the corporation) know more about a company and its future prospects than do outsiders (investors).[58]

Agency costs can occur if the board of directors fails to exercise due care in its oversight role of management. Enron's board of directors did not monitor the company's incentive compensation plans properly, thereby allowing top executives to "hype" the company's stock so that employees would add it to their 401(k) retirement plans. While the hyping occurred, often through positive statements about the company made by CEO Ken Lay, Lay himself sold about 2.3 million shares for $123.4 million.

The agency problem can never be perfectly solved, and shareholders may experience a loss of wealth due to divergent behavior of managers. Investigations by the SEC and U.S. Department of Justice of 20 corporate frauds during the Enron-WorldCom era indicate that $236 billion in shareholder value was lost between the time the public first learned of the first fraud and September 3, 2002, the measurement date.

An alternative to agency theory is stewardship theory. In this theory, managers are viewed as stewards of their companies, predominately motivated to act in the best interests of the shareholders. The theory holds that as stewards, managers will choose the interests of shareholders, perhaps psychologically identified as the best interests of "the company," over self-interests, regardless of personal motivations or incentives.[59]

Under stewardship theory, directors have a fiduciary duty to act as stewards of the shareholders' interest. Inherent in the concept of the company is the belief that directors can be trusted. Contrary to agency theory, stewardship theory believes that directors do not inevitably act in a way that maximizes their own personal interests: They can and do act responsibly with independence and integrity. Even though some will fail, it does not invalidate the theory.[60]

Stewardship advocates recognize that directors need to consider a broader range of interests, including employees, customers, suppliers, and other legitimate stakeholders, but under the law their first responsibility is to the shareholders. They argue that conflicts of interest between stakeholder groups and the company should be met by competitive pressures in free markets, backed by legislation and legal controls to protect various stakeholder interests (i.e., environmental law; health and safety law; employment discrimination law).

Other theories of management exist, including "resource dependency" and "managerial and class hegemony." However, our goal is not to address all such theories but to provide the framework within which control mechanisms exist to enhance behavior in accordance with laws and ethics.

Corporate Governance Regulation

Each state in the United States has its own companies law to regulate corporate activity within its boundaries. Federal laws are embodied in the SEC regulations. Over the years the SEC developed an extensive corporate governance regime for companies listed on stock exchanges, including the New York Stock Exchange (NYSE) and NASDAQ. The NYSE has issued extensive regulations as well.

Corporate governance regulation in the United States has been ratcheted up in the aftermath of passage of the Sarbanes-Oxley Act. SOX requires management certification of the internal controls over financial reporting (Section 302); that auditors attest to and report on management's assessment on the effectiveness of the internal control structure and procedures for financial reporting (Section 404); protections for whistleblowers (Section 806); and independent audit committees that oversee financial reporting.

One goal of SOX is to reduce the number of restatements of corporate financial reports, especially those that result from materially misleading financial statements. Have the corporate governance requirements of SOX made a differences in the level of financial statement restatements? After all, if this is not the case, then we must question the effectiveness of the act.

According to a study by Audit Analytics, the proportion of corporate financial restatements that had *no* impact on the bottom line was 59 percent in 2014. That brought the increase over the past four years to 22 percentage points, which suggests that the SOX corporate-governance law has succeeded in bolstering companies' internal controls over financial reporting. Among companies listed on major stock exchanges, there were 460 restatements in 2014 that had no effect on income statements, up slightly from a year earlier.[61]

KBR Inc. made the largest downward earnings restatement, with the engineering and construction company reducing its 2013 net income by $156 million. That was the smallest high for a downward adjustment since 2002; the largest during the period came in 2004, when Fannie Mae wiped $6.3 billion off its prior profits. The 2014 average downward net-income restatement was about $4.4 million, down from $6.6 million a year earlier.

These results are encouraging, although we are not convinced they will be sustained. The reason is, regardless of regulatory requirements under Section 404, the underlying consideration is good old-fashioned ethical behavior. Will egoistic CEOs and CFOs revert to self-interest–driven behavior, as occurred in the scandals of the early 2000s, or have they "seen the light"? If past history is used as a guide, we may be due for another round of corporate financial reporting scandals as seemingly have occurred every 10–15 years.

The takeaway from the results reported by Audit Analytics is it appears SOX is encouraging more ethical behavior on the part of top corporate executives, but the jury is still out whether it will have a long-lasting effect. Another concern is that, in accounting, it is only "material" restatements that are considered and the results of the study point to 59 percent as having "no impact" on the bottom line. What does that mean with respect to the size of the restatements and how was the materiality determined?

Executive Compensation

One of the most common approaches to the agency problem is to link managerial compensation to the financial performance of the corporation in general and the performance of the company's shares. Typically, this occurs by creating long-term compensation packages and stock option plans that tie executive wealth to an increase in the corporation's stock price. These incentives aim to encourage managers to maximize the market value of shares. One of the biggest issues that corporate boards of directors face is executive compensation. It has been found that most boards spend more time deciding how much to compensate top executives than they do ensuring the integrity of the company's financial reporting systems.[62]

Excessive Pay Packages

A problem arises when top management purposefully manipulates earnings amounts to drive up the price of stock so they can cash in more lucrative stock options. During the financial crisis of 2008–2009, Congress charged executives at some of the nation's largest companies with gaining pay packages in the millions while their companies suffered losses, and they may have even accepted funds from the government to keep them liquid. The Obama administration named a "compensation czar," Kenneth Feinberg, to set salaries and bonuses at some of the biggest firms at the heart of the economic crisis, as part of a broader government campaign to reshape pay practices across corporate America. The initiative reflected public uproar over executive compensation at companies such as American International Group (AIG), which received a $180 billion bailout from the government and decided to pay $165 million in bonuses to executives.

A 2014 study at the Harvard Business School found that Americans believe CEOs make roughly 30 times what the average worker makes in the United States, when in actuality they are making more than 340 times the average worker. On a global basis, this compares with a ratio of 148:1 in Switzerland, the nearest country, 84:1 in the United Kingdom, and 67:1 in Japan.

A troubling situation occurs when executives receive huge severance packages after leaving their organizations. The former CEO of CVS received a severance package worth $185 million when he left in early 2011, even though the company's net earnings had declined in the prior year. In 2014, the former chief operating officer of Yahoo, who was fired earlier in the year, received about $96 million in compensation for his 15 months on the job, including about $58 million in severance packages.

We do not know whether CEOs at top American companies are overpaid. After all, they have the daunting task of running multibillion-dollar companies in an increasingly globalized, competitive environment. However, it does give us pause when we read that, in 2013, the average CEO compensation was $15.2 million as compared with the average worker being paid about $52,100. From an ethical perspective, fairness issues do exist. Thomas Dunfee, a Wharton professor of legal studies and business ethics, puts it this way: Do executive compensation figures reflect an efficient market, or a failed one? Are pay levels adequately disclosed? Should shareholders have more say? Are there issues of fairness and justice?[63]

Backdating Stock Options

An executive compensation scandal erupted in 2006 when it was discovered that some companies had changed the grant dates of their options to coincide with a dip in the stock price, making the options worth more because less money would be needed to exercise them and buy stock. Although backdating was legal, it must be expensed and disclosed properly in the financial statements. Legalities aside, it is difficult to justify such a practice from an ethical perspective because it purposefully manipulates the option criteria that determine their value.

In the wake of this scandal, hundreds of companies conducted internal probes and the SEC launched investigations into more than 140 firms. The agency filed charges against 24 companies and 66 individuals for backdating-related offenses, and at least 15 people have been convicted of criminal conduct. An interesting case is that of Nancy Heinen, Apple Computer's general counsel until she left in 2006. She was investigated by the SEC for receiving backdated options and wound up agreeing to pay $2.2 million in disgorgement (return of ill-gotten gains), interest, and penalties. Steve Jobs, the former CEO of Apple, apologized on behalf of the company, stating that he did not understand the relevant accounting laws. Of course, ignorance of the law is no excuse for violating it—at least in spirit —especially by someone like Jobs, who presumably had dozens of accountants on staff to advise on these matters. Notably, SOX includes stricter reporting requirements that are supposed to cut down on such practices.

Clawbacks

The Dodd-Frank Wall Street Reform and Consumer Protection Act (H.R. 4173)[64] was signed into federal law by President Barack Obama on July 21, 2010. Passed as a response to the late-2000s recession, it brought the most significant changes to financial regulation in the United States since the regulatory reform that followed the Great Depression. Two areas where Dodd-Frank relates to corporate governance are in executive compensation and in whistleblowing procedures, which will be discussed later on.

Clawbacks have been on the regulatory radar screen in a big way since 2002, when SOX gave the SEC power to recover compensation and stock profits from CEOs and CFOs of public companies in the event of financial restatements caused by misconduct. Clawback policies among Fortune 100 companies were already on the rise before the financial crisis, jumping from 17.6 percent in 2006 to 42.1 percent in 2007. In 2010, the year Dodd-Frank was passed, 82.1 percent of the Fortune 100 had them. In 2012, 86.5 percent of the Fortune 100 firms had adopted publicly disclosed policies. Now, about 90 percent have such policies. The ethical justification for clawbacks is the breach of fiduciary duty owed by top management to shareholders and inequities when they benefit from their own wrongful acts.

On July 1, 2015, the SEC proposed rules directing U.S. stock exchanges to create listing standards requiring listed companies to implement policies to recover or "claw back" incentive-based compensation received by executive officers as a result of materially incorrect financial statements. These proposed rules are mandated by Section 954 of Dodd-Frank. Companies may need to comply with the proposed rules as early as the end of 2016, though this timing will depend on when the SEC's proposed rules are finalized, and will likely be in early 2017.

According to a PwC study, many companies have modified their clawback policies since enactment of SOX and Dodd-Frank, and others have indicated that their policies will likely change once the SEC issues its clawback rules. Of the 100 companies in the study, 90 percent have policies to recover compensation if there is a restatement of financial results. However, of those that claw back upon restatement, 73 percent require evidence that the employee caused or contributed to false or incorrect financial reporting, while 27 percent require repayment in the event of a restatement even without any personal accountability. In many cases, the clawback amount is only the excess of the amount paid over the payment determined based on the financial results after applying the restatement. We believe that, when designed properly, a policy allowing for clawback of pay from high-level executives is a significant mechanism for corporate accountability.

Say on Pay

Dodd-Frank includes "say-on-pay" provisions (Section 951) that require SEC-registered issuers to provide shareholders at least once every three calendar years a separate nonbinding say-on-pay vote regarding the compensation of the company's named executive officers (i.e., CEO and CFO) and the company's three other most highly compensated officers. Although the vote on compensation is nonbinding, the company must include a statement in the "Compensation Discussion and Analysis" of the proxy statement whether its compensation policies and decisions have taken into account the results of the shareholder-say-on-pay vote and, if so, how. The idea is for the vote of the shareholders to be taken seriously not only by the company, but also by other companies in the same marketplace.

In perhaps the most widely followed shareholder action, in April 2012, 55 percent of Citigroup's shareholders voted against CEO Vikram Pandit's $15 million compensation package for 2011, a year when the bank's stock tumbled. At the time of the vote, Pandit had received nearly $7 million in cash for 2011, with the remainder to be paid in restricted stock and cash over the next few years (and thus subject to possible restructuring by the board). Citigroup's shareholders expressed concerns that the compensation package lacked significant and important goals to provide incentives for improvement in the shareholder value of the institution. Soon after the vote, a shareholder filed a derivative lawsuit against the CEO, the board of directors, and other directors and executives for allegedly awarding excessive pay to its senior officers.

On April 29, 2015, the SEC proposed new rules requiring public companies to make it easier for investors to judge whether top executives' compensation is in step with the company's financial performance. The proposal aims to give investors greater clarity about the link between what corporate executives are paid each year and total shareholder return—the annual change in stock price plus reinvested dividends. If finalized, companies would have to include a new table in their annual proxy filings disclosing top executives' "actual pay." The new figure is based on the total compensation public companies already calculate for their five highest-paid executives, though it would exclude certain components of pay that officers do not actually take home, such as share grants that have yet to vest.

Questions raised by shareholders and others about the size of executive compensation packages and say-on-pay votes are designed to build equity into the compensation system. Issues with respect to whether CEOs are overpaid, as many have said, do bring up questions of fairness and justice. Without transparency, it is difficult to have accountability. Over the long haul, the question is whether these nonbinding referendums are likely to have any impact on the potential civil liability of directors for approving allegedly excessive executive compensation that the shareholders reject. According to Robert Scully, who analyzed the law in the January 2011 *The Federal Lawyer,* the answer is probably not. Scully maintains that Dodd-Frank does not preempt state fiduciary law or entirely occupy the field of director liability for excessive compensation. Instead, the act focuses on the process by which public company executive compensation is set, thereby enforcing the primacy of the business judgment rule in determining executive compensation.[65]

Corporate Governance Structures and Relationships

LO 3-6
Explain the components of corporate governance and their relationship to corporate culture.

In his book *Corporate Governance and Ethics,* Zabihollah Rezaee points out that corporate governance is shaped by internal and external mechanisms, as well as policy interventions through regulations. Internal mechanisms help manage, direct, and monitor corporate governance activities to create sustainable stakeholder value. Examples include the board of directors, particularly independent directors; the audit committee; management; internal controls; and the internal audit function. External mechanisms are intended to monitor the company's activities, affairs, and performance to ensure that the interests of insiders (management, directors, and officers) are aligned with the interests of outsiders (shareholders and other stakeholders). Examples of external mechanisms include the financial markets, state and federal statutes, court decisions, and shareholder proposals.[66] Three noteworthy points are: (1) independent directors enhance governance accountability; (2) separation of the duties of the CEO and board chair; and (3) separate meetings between the audit committee and external auditors strengthen control mechanisms.

Ethical and Legal Responsibilities of Officers and Directors

Duty of Care—Managers and Directors

Directors and officers are deemed fiduciaries of the corporation because their relationship with the corporation and its shareholders is one of trust and confidence. As fiduciaries, directors and officers owe ethical—and legal—duties to the corporation and to the shareholders. These fiduciary duties include the duty of care and the duty of loyalty.

The standard of *due care* provides that a director or officer act in good faith, exercise the care that an ordinarily prudent person would exercise in similar circumstances, and act in the way that she considers to be in the best interests of the corporation. Directors and officers who have not exercised the required duty of care can be held liable for the harms suffered by the corporation as a result of their negligence.

The duty of due care specifies the manner in which directors must discharge their legal responsibilities, not the substance of director decisions. Directors, due to their statutory responsibilities to direct the business and affairs of a corporation, also have a duty to monitor and oversee the business affairs of a corporation properly. Failure to do so may constitute a breach of the duty of care.

Duty of Loyalty

The duty of loyalty requires directors to act in the best interests of the corporation. *Loyalty* can be defined as faithfulness to one's obligations and duties. In the corporate context, the duty of loyalty requires directors and officers to subordinate their personal interests to the welfare of the organization. For example, directors must not use corporate funds or confidential corporate information for personal advantage. They must also refrain from self-dealing, such as when a director opposes a stock tender offer that is in the corporation's best interest simply because its acceptance may cost the director her position.

Duty of Good Faith

The obligation of good faith requires an honesty of purpose that leads to caring for the well-being of the constituents of the fiduciary. Vice Chancellor Leo Strine of the Delaware Chancery Court linked good faith to fiduciary analysis in the Enron fraud by suggesting that the Enron case might influence courts to look more carefully at whether directors have made a good faith effort to accomplish their duties. He connected good faith with directors' "state of mind." Strine identified certain kinds of director conduct that may call good faith into question. These include "a failure to monitor if [the directors'] laxity in oversight was so persistent and substantial that it evidences bad faith." It can also arise in situations where "committee members knew that their inadequate knowledge disabled them from discharging their responsibilities with fidelity."[67]

Business Judgment Rule

A corporate director or officer may be able to avoid liability to the corporation or to its shareholders for poor business judgments under the *business judgment rule.* Directors and officers are expected to exercise due care and to use their best judgment in guiding corporate management, but they are not insurers of business success. Honest mistakes of judgment and poor business decisions on their part do not make them liable to the corporation for resulting damages.

To obtain the business judgment rule's protection, directors must be independent and disinterested as to the matter acted upon. Directors must act with due care and good faith. The due care inquiry is process-oriented, and due care is measured by a standard of gross negligence, not simple negligence. The burden of proof is on the party challenging the board's decision, to establish facts rebutting the presumption in favor of upholding the decision. Unless a plaintiff succeeds in rebutting the rule, the court will not substitute its views for those of the board's if the latter's decision can be "attributed to any rational business purpose."

The business judgment rule generally immunizes directors and officers from liability for the consequences of a decision that is within managerial authority, as long as the decision complies with management's fiduciary duties and as long as acting on the decision is within the powers of the corporation. Therefore, if there is a reasonable basis for a business decision, it is unlikely that a court will interfere with that decision, even if the corporation suffers as a result.

Honest Services Fraud

Jeff Skilling, the former CEO of Enron, was originally sentenced to a 24-year jail sentence for fraud and insider trading. He has appealed the 19 out of 28 charges that he was sentenced for in 2006 all the way up to the U.S. Supreme Court. His lawyers challenged the ruling based on the instructions given to the jury, which asked them to consider whether he had deprived his company of "intangible honest services." The U.S. Supreme Court found on June 24, 2010, that he had not violated the honest services rule, as he had not solicited or accepted bribes or kickbacks; rather, he conspired to defraud Enron's shareholders by other means.

Honest services fraud refers to a ruling in *18 U.S.C. § 1346* that addresses any "scheme or artifice to defraud" designed to deprive another of the intangible right of honest services. The statute has been applied by federal prosecutors in cases of public corruption as well as in cases in which private individuals breached a fiduciary duty to another. In the former, the courts have been divided on the question of whether a state law violation is necessary for honest services fraud to have occurred. In the latter, the courts have taken differing approaches to determining whether a private individual has committed honest services fraud—a test based on reasonably foreseeable economic harm and a test based on materiality.

In *Skilling v. United States,* the U.S. Supreme Court said that one of Skilling's convictions was flawed when it sharply curtailed the use of the honest services fraud law. The high court ruled prosecutors can use the law only in cases where evidence shows the defendant accepted bribes or kickbacks, and because Skilling's misconduct entailed no such things, he did not conspire to commit honest services fraud. In the opinion, Justice Ginsburg wrote: "The Government charged Skilling with conspiring to defraud Enron's shareholders by misrepresenting the company's fiscal health to his own profit, but the Government never alleged that he solicited or accepted side payments from a third party in exchange for making these misrepresentations. Instead, he conspired to defraud Enron's shareholders by other means." The Supreme Court told a lower court to decide whether he deserved a new trial; the lower court said no.[68]

Perhaps the legal system is growing weary of dealing with Skilling's appeals because on May 8, 2013, it was announced by the U.S. Department of Justice that Skilling might be freed 10 years early. This means he would spend a total of 14 years in jail. In return for the lighter sentence, Skilling agreed to stop appealing his conviction. The agreement would also allow more than $40 million seized from him to be freed up for distribution to Enron fraud victims.

Relationships between Audit Committee, Internal Auditors, and External Auditors

Following the passage of SOX, the audit committee was seen as the one body that was (or at least should be) capable of preventing identified fraudulent financial reporting. The audit committee has an oversight responsibility for the financial statements. The internal auditors should have direct and unrestricted access to the audit committee so that they can take any matters of concern directly to that group without having to go through top management. The external auditors rely on the support and actions of the audit committee to resolve differences with management over proper financial reporting. The goal of such relationships should be to establish an ethical corporate culture that supports good corporate governance. **Exhibit 3.10** depicts the ideal relationship between the internal auditors and audit committee. The framework is identified in the Treadway Commission Report titled *Report of the National Commission on Fraudulent Financial Reporting*.

EXHIBIT 3.10   Internal Control Environment—"Corporate Culture"

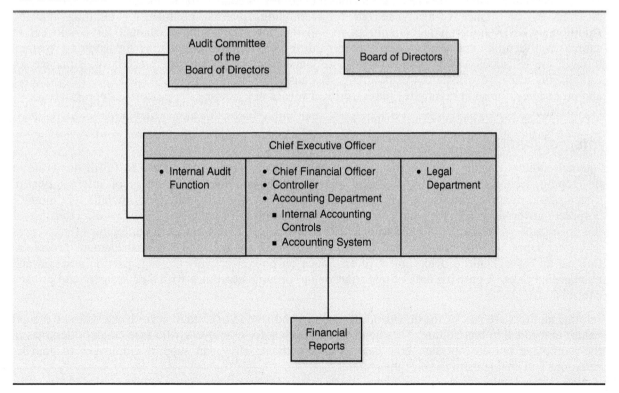

Audit Committee

In the accounting scandals of the early 2000s, the audit committee either didn't know about the fraud or chose to look the other way. A conscientious and diligent committee is an essential ingredient of an effective corporate governance system—one that takes its role in financial statement oversight to heart and follows basic principles of responsibility, accountability, and transparency. SOX requires that the audit committee of the board of directors should be completely independent of management and include at least three members, one of which should have "financial expertise."

An effective device to ensure audit committee independence is for the committee to meet separately with the senior executives, the internal auditors, and the external auditors. The perception of internal auditors as the "eyes and ears" of the audit committee suggests that the head of the internal audit department attend all audit committee meetings. Recall the role of Cynthia Cooper at WorldCom. She informed the audit committee every step of the way as her department uncovered the fraud, and ultimately she gained the support of the external auditors.

The audit committee's duties include: (1) monitor the integrity of the financial statements; (2) review any formal announcements relating to the company's financial performance; (3) review significant financial reporting judgments contained in the statements and performance statements; (4) review the company's internal financial controls and risk management procedures; (5) monitor the effectiveness of the company's internal audit function; (6) review the company's whistleblower processes and compliance program; and (7) review and monitor the external auditor's independence and objectivity and the effectiveness of the audit process.

The audit committee should also seek assurances from the CEO and CFO, as part of the CEO/CFO financial statement certification process under Section 302 of SOX, that they have put in place effective disclosure controls and procedures to ensure that all reports have been prepared and filed properly with the appropriate authorities in accordance with applicable requirements.

SOX calls on audit committees to create formal procedures to collect, track, and process hotline claims received by the issuer company related to accounting, internal controls, or auditing matters. Additionally, SOX holds audit committees responsible for establishing a channel for employees to submit confidential, anonymous concerns regarding questionable accounting or auditing matters through the whistleblower hotline. However, the legislation did not provide prescriptive guidance for establishing effective whistleblower programs. Because the SEC has not mandated specific processes and procedures, the audit committee plays a critical role in determining the processes appropriate for its organization.

Internal Auditors

Internal auditors interact with top management and, as such, should assist them to fulfill their role in developing accurate and reliable financial statements, ensure the effectiveness of internal control systems, and monitor compliance with laws and regulations. Specific obligations include: (1) monitor corporate governance activities and compliance with organization policies; (2) review effectiveness of the organization's code of ethics and whistleblower provisions; (3) assess audit committee effectiveness and compliance with regulations; and (4) oversee internal controls and risk management processes. Internal auditors should provide objective assurance on how effectively the organization assesses and manages its risks. A growing area of importance is to provide assurance with data security and privacy controls.

Internal auditors are part of the organization's culture and should operate in accordance with the ethical values embedded in that culture. They can serve as outlets for employees who face ethical dilemmas in the workplace but are not sure how best to handle them. They can support employees in conflict situations and enable them to voice their values.

External Auditors

External auditors have an obligation to the public interest that underlies their corporate governance responsibilities. One of the primary roles of external auditors in corporate governance is protecting the interests of shareholders. This is possible because external audits should be conducted independent of any influence of management or the board of directors of the company. External audits should be designed to introduce a measure of accountability into the financial reporting process.

Effective two-way communication between audit committees and external auditors is an integral part of the audit process. Such communications improve the ability of the audit committee to provide oversight and provide an opportunity for the auditors to discuss relevant matters with a forum other than management. These types of communications are essential to a high-quality audit.

The Public Company Accounting Oversight Board (PCAOB) has recognized the importance of this topic with the adoption of Auditing Standard No. 16, *Communications with Audit Committees* ("AS 16"). Required communications include:

- Matters relating to the company's accounting policies and practices including why certain accounting policies and practices are considered critical.
- Estimates made by management and the process used to develop these estimates including significant changes to the process used by management to develop estimates, reasons for the changes, and the effects on the financial statements.
- The auditor's judgment about the quality of the entity's financial reporting including the auditor's evaluation of and conclusions about the qualitative aspects of the company's significant accounting policies and practices. Auditors should also discuss significant unusual transactions and their opinion on the business rationale thereof.
- Whether the audit committee is aware of matters relevant to the audit including, but not limited to, violations or potential violations of laws or regulations including fraud risks.

While in the past communications between the external auditor and audit committee have been deemed an incidental part of the audit process, it is now recognized as an essential and required aspect of an effective and efficient audit. A company's audit committee is the primary link between the board of directors, management, and the independent auditors. Improving communication among these parties will play a vital role in improving the overall value of the audit for all stakeholders.

Internal Controls as a Monitoring Device

The internal controls that are established by management should help prevent and detect fraud, including materially false and misleading financial reports, asset misappropriations, and inadequate disclosures in the financial statements. These controls are designed to ensure that management policies are followed, laws are strictly adhered to, and ethical systems are built into corporate governance.

COSO Framework

The system of internal controls and whether it operates as intended enables the auditor to either gain confidence about the internal processing of transactions or create doubt for the auditor that should be pursued. *Internal Control—Integrated Framework,* published by the Committee of Sponsoring Organizations (COSO) of the Treadway Commission in 1992, establishes a framework that defines internal control as a process, effected by an entity's board of directors, management, and other personnel, designed to provide reasonable assurance regarding the achievement of the following objectives: (a) effectiveness and efficiency of operations; (b) reliability of financial reporting; and (c) compliance with applicable laws and regulations.[69]

The COSO report states that management should enact five components related to these objectives as part of the framework: (1) the control environment; (2) risk assessment; (3) control activities; (4) monitoring; and (5) information and communication.

1. The *control environment* sets the tone of an organization, influencing the control consciousness of its people. It is the foundation for all aspects of internal control, providing discipline and structure.
2. *Risk assessment* is the entity's identification and evaluation of how risk might affect the achievement of objectives.
3. *Control activities* are the strategic actions established by management to ensure that its directives are carried out.
4. *Monitoring* is a process that assesses the efficiency and effectiveness of internal controls over time.
5. *Information and communication* systems provide the information in a form and at a time that enables people to carry out their responsibilities.

The COSO framework emphasizes the roles and responsibilities of management, the board of directors, internal auditors, and other personnel in creating an environment that supports the objectives of internal control. One important contribution of COSO is in the area of corporate governance. COSO notes that if members of the board and audit committee do not take their responsibilities seriously, then the system will likely break down as occurred in Enron and WorldCom.

The results for a company can be devastating when internal controls fail or are overridden by management. A good example is what happened to Groupon after it announced a restatement in its financial statements on March 30, 2012, that resulted from a material weakness in its internal controls with respect to the inadequacy of its reserve for coupon returns. Exhibit 3.11 presents a summary of the facts surrounding the restatement. There can be no doubt that the company's fortunes changed on a dime after the announcement, as its IPO share price close of $26.11 on March 30, 2012, trended downward and continued going in the wrong direction declining to $4.14 as of November 30, 2012. The stock has not done much better since then, closing around the same level as recently as July 2015.

EXHIBIT 3.11 Internal Control Disaster at Groupon

Groupon, Inc., offers online retail services and provides daily deals on things to do, eat, see, and buy in more than 500 markets in 44 countries. It has offices across North America, Europe, Latin America, Asia, and other parts of the world.

On November 5, 2011, Groupon took its company public in an IPO with a buy-in price set at $20 per share. Groupon shares rose from their IPO price of $20 by 40 percent in early trading on NASDAQ and ended at the 4 p.m. market close at $26.11, up 31 percent. The closing price valued Groupon at $16.6 billion, making it more valuable than companies such as Adobe Systems and nearly the size of Yahoo.

Groupon employees broke out the champagne, as did Silicon Valley and Wall Street, as financial analysts took Groupon's stock market debut as a sign that investors are still willing to make risky bets on fast-growing but unprofitable young Internet companies, even as the IPO environment had shifted downward since the financial troubles that started in 2007.

At a size of up to $805 million, Groupon ranked as the third-largest Internet IPO sold in the United States in 2011, after a $1.4 billion issue by Russian search-engine operator Yandex NV in May and a $855 million issue by China social networking platform Renren, according to Dealogic. It was the ninth-largest ever, on a list topped by the $1.9 billion sale by Google in 2004.

Less than five months later, on March 30, 2012, Groupon announced that it had revised its financial results, an unexpected restatement that deepened losses and raised questions about its accounting practices. As part of the revision, Groupon disclosed a "material weakness" in its

(Continued)

internal controls, saying that it had failed to set aside enough money to cover customer refunds. The accounting issue increased the company's losses in the fourth quarter to $64.9 million from $42.3 million. The news that day sent shares of Groupon tumbling 6 percent, to $17.29. Shares of Groupon had fallen by 30 percent since it went public.

In its announcement of the restatement, Groupon explained that it had encountered problems related to certain assumptions and forecasts the company used to calculate its results. In particular, the company said that it underestimated customer refunds for higher-priced offers, such as laser eye surgery. Groupon collects more revenue on such deals, but it also sees a higher number of refunds. The company honors customer refunds for the life of its coupons, so these payments can affect its financials at various times. Groupon deducts refunds within 60 days from receiving revenue; after that, the company has to take an additional accounting charge related to the payments.

As Groupon prepared its financial statements for 2011, its independent auditor, Ernst & Young, determined that the company did not account accurately for the possibility of higher refunds. By the firm's assessment, that constituted a material weakness." Groupon said in its annual report, "We did not maintain effective controls to provide reasonable assurance that accounts were complete and accurate."

In an interesting twist, in response to the conclusion that the company's internal controls contained a material weakness, Groupon blamed Ernst & Young in part for not identifying the weakness. The auditors were at fault for not identifying problems with the financial controls earlier, said Herman Leung, a financial analyst at Susquehanna Financial Group in San Francisco. "This should have been highlighted by the auditors. The business is growing so fast that it sounds like they don't have the proper financial controls to deal with the growth."[70] In fact, it was management's assessment of the material weakness in internal controls over financial reporting that led to the disclosure. Ernst & Young had signed the fourth-quarter audit report included in Groupon's annual report, giving a clean (unmodified) opinion.

In a related issue, on April 3, 2012, a shareholder lawsuit was brought against Groupon, accusing the company of misleading investors about its financial prospects in its IPO and concealing weak internal controls. According to the complaint, the company overstated revenue, issued materially false and misleading financial results, and concealed how its business was not growing as fast and was not nearly as resistant to competition, such as from LivingSocial and Amazon, as it had suggested.

These claims bring up a gap in the sections of SOX that deal with companies' internal controls. There is no requirement to disclose a control weakness in a company's IPO prospectus. Groupon had no obligation to disclose the problem until it filed its first quarterly or annual report as a public company—which is what it did.

Liability for False Certifications

The SEC's increased focus on identifying and penalizing misstatements in public company financials came to light in April 2014 when Chairman Mary Jo White highlighted in prepared testimony before the U.S. House Financial Services Committee the SEC's new Financial Fraud Task Force and the strides it was taking to identify "both traditional and emerging financial fraud issues." The commission has been analyzing patterns of internal control problems even absent a restatement in the financials and holding "gatekeepers"—such as auditors and corporate officer—accountable for corporate misstatements.

The SEC's disclosure on July 30, 2014, of an enforcement action against two corporate executives of a small Florida-based computer equipment company exemplifies the type of emerging theory of fraud it is now pursuing. The commission went after both the CEO and CFO of Quality Services Group Inc. (QSGI) solely for alleged misrepresentations in public disclosures about the company's internal controls environment, which are required by SOX.

The SEC alleged that QSGI's CEO (Marc Sherman) and former CFO (Edward Cummings) knew of significant internal controls issues in the company's inventory practices that they failed to disclose to auditors and investors. Central to the SEC's theory of fraud is that Sherman and Cummings (1) signed Form 10-Ks with management reports on internal controls that falsely omitted issues and (2) signed certifications in which they falsely represented that they had evaluated the management report on internal controls and disclosed all significant deficiencies to auditors.[71]

What makes QSGI a unique case is that it did not arise from a restatement of the company's prior financial statements; indeed, there does not appear to have been any material mistakes in the company's reported financials. Here the SEC hinged its fraud claims on alleged unreported deficiencies in QSGI's internal controls over its accounting function.

From a legal perspective, this case may sound an end to the days where corporate officers may simply adopt a "no harm, no foul" approach to disclosure when a company identifies an immaterial accounting issue or otherwise fails to follow its accounting policies and practices.

The message of this case may be that transparency with the company's audit committee and with external auditors regarding evaluations of the company's internal controls will protect the company, its investors, and its officers.

Compliance Function

The Ethics and Compliance Officer Association (ECOA) has recognized its increased responsibilities resulting from SOX. The mission of ECOA is to promote "ethical business practices and [serve] as a global forum for the exchange of information and strategies among organizations and individuals responsible for ethics, compliance, and business conduct programs."[72] An important step in encouraging the reporting of wrongdoing is to appoint a trusted member of the management team to be the organization's ethics officer. This person should take the lead in ensuring that the organization is in compliance with the laws and regulations, including SEC securities laws, SOX, and Dodd-Frank. A chief compliance officer (CCO) should serve as a sounding board for management to try out new ideas to see if these ideas pass the ethics "smell" test. The ethics officer plays a critical role in helping create a positive ethical tone in organizations.

The 2012 State of Compliance study conducted by PwC found that oversight of the compliance function has been changing. Fewer compliance officers report to the general counsel on a daily basis (35 percent in 2012, compared to 41 percent in 2011), although the number reporting on a daily basis to the CEO held steady at 32 percent. On a formal basis, 32 percent of respondents report to the audit committee, almost as many as who report to the general counsel (33 percent).

Over the past decade, heightened regulations related to SOX and Dodd-Frank have elevated the importance and visibility of the chief compliance officer role. Now an official member of the C-suite, compliance leaders are tasked with building comprehensive and robust programs that not only address existing requirements, but also anticipate regulatory changes and their likely impact.

Has SOX Accomplished Its Intended Goal?

In virtually all the frauds of the late 1990s and early 2000s, the CEOs and CFOs knew about their companies' materially misstated financial statements. One important provision of SOX that helps protect the public against fraudulent financial statements is the requirement of Section 302 that the CEO and CFO must certify that to the best of their knowledge, there are no material misstatements in the financial statements.

A valid question, now that SOX is almost 15 years old, is whether its promise of holding CEOs and CFOs criminally responsible for fraud has been a success. The law states that, under Section 302, if top corporate executives knowingly sign off on a false financial report, they're subject to a prison term of up to 10 years and a fine of up to $1 million, with penalties escalating to 20 years and $5 million if their misconduct is willful. In practice, very few defendants have even been charged with false certification, and fewer still have been convicted.

Richard Scrushy, the former HealthSouth Corporation CEO, falsely certified the financial statements of the company but was not sent to jail for that crime. On the other hand, HealthSouth CFO Weston L. Smith was sentenced in 2005 to 27 months in prison for his role in the company's $2.7 billion accounting fraud. Smith had pleaded guilty to one count each of conspiracy to commit wire and securities fraud, falsely certifying a financial report, and falsifying a report to the SEC. In 2007, the former CFO of a medical equipment financing company called DVI pleaded guilty to mail fraud and false certification and was sentenced to 30 months in prison.

So, the question in the end is, why have there not been more prosecutions under Section 302? Frankel believes that the answer may lie partly in how corporations have responded to SOX. Most major corporations have implemented internal compliance systems that make it very difficult to show that the CEO or CFO knowingly signed a false certification. And when prosecutors have enough evidence to show that those internal systems failed and top executives knowingly engaged in wrongdoing, they often prefer, for strategic reasons, to charge crimes other than false certification.[73]

However, the tide may be turning against CFOs, who typically mastermind financial frauds. Emboldened by legislative expansions of liability for financial executives under SOX and Dodd-Frank, the SEC increasingly is pursuing claims against CFOs that do not allege actual wrongdoing. It does so by alleging that the CFO's subordinates violated securities laws and that the CFO either certified the resulting reports or failed to implement adequate internal safeguards.

Perhaps the most alarming of these cases was the prosecution of Craig Huff, CFO of Nature's Sunshine Products (NSP), in 2009. The SEC charged him as part of a Foreign Corrupt Practices Act allegation that a Brazilian subsidiary of the company bribed customs officials. The SEC alleged that a wholly owned Brazilian subsidiary of NSP made payments to customs agents to import unregistered products into Brazil.

Huff was not alleged to have participated in or even known about the bribery scheme, but he was charged under a theory of control-person liability for violations of the books-and-records and internal-controls provisions of the securities laws, because NSP did not disclose the payments to customs agents in its SEC filings. Huff paid a civil penalty of $25,000 to settle the case.

The SEC is also embracing its powers to seek disgorgement of bonuses and other compensation that CFOs received in years in which the company restated its financials. In 2007, the former CFO of Beazer Homes, James O'Leary, faced disgorgement of profits and bonuses from the SEC when Beazer Homes was found to have overstated its income while O'Leary was CFO. The SEC alleged that chief accounting officer Michael Rand directed the fraud by recording improper accounting reserves in order to decrease the company's net income and meet estimates of diluted earnings per share.

The SEC did not accuse O'Leary of any accounting misconduct, but it stated he received substantial compensation and stock-sale profits while Beazer was misleading investors and fraudulently overstating its income. He agreed to return $1.4 million in past bonuses and stock profits he received while the company was submitting false financial statements.

The jury is still out on whether SOX serves as an adequate deterrent to financial fraud. We should not be surprised if the answer is "no" because laws do not necessarily lead to ethical behavior. Any law—including SOX—establishes the rules of the game and how violators will be punished. As we have learned throughout these first three chapters, ethical behavior comes from within; it comes from a desire to do the right thing, not because we may be punished if we do not. In the end, it is a postconventional mindset that guides ethical reasoning when the chips are down, not a conventional one. Laws are needed, but they serve as only a minimum standard of ethical conduct. Codes of ethics are needed because they help to establish an ethical organization environment. But it is virtuous behavior that should guide corporate officers through the minefield of conflicts and pressures that exist in decision making.

Whistleblowing

LO 3-7
Analyze the moral basis for whistleblowing and accountants' obligations to whistle blow.

There is a symbiotic relationship between whistleblowing and an organization's culture. Effective internal whistleblowing processes are an important part of a healthy corporate culture. Internal auditors have a critical role to play in monitoring whistleblowing procedures, given the nature of internal control. The audit committee should ensure that matters of concern are raised through appropriate channels and promptly dealt with. Whistleblowing should be part of the internal control environment and an effective corporate governance system.

There is no one set definition of whistleblowing, although most definitions characterize the practice as disclosing to others in an organization an action that violates organizational norms or the law. Near and Miceli take a broad view of whistleblowing as "the disclosure by organization members (former or current) of illegal, immoral, or illegitimate practices under the control of their employers, to persons or organizations that may be able to effect action." This definition includes whistleblowers who use internal channels (e.g., a hotline or ombudsperson) or external channels (e.g., the external auditors or the SEC) to blow the whistle. They identify four elements of the whistleblowing process: the whistleblower, the whistleblowing act or complaint, the party to whom the complaint is made, and the organization against which the complaint is lodged. In discussing the act itself, they label it as an act of "dissidence" somewhat analogous to civil disobedience.[74] The term *organizational dissidence* fits in with our discussion of cognitive dissonance in Chapter 2, which emphasized the difference between our thoughts, beliefs or attitudes, and behavior.

Morality of Whistleblowing

Given that the act of whistleblowing is a personal choice, the key to whether an individual will blow the whistle on wrongdoing is whether the whistleblower perceives organizational policies are designed to encourage moral autonomy, individual responsibility, and organizational support for whistleblowers.

Moral agency is important for the determination of moral behavior and it enables the moral evaluation of the agent's behavior.[75] The basic characteristic of the philosophical concept of moral agency is autonomy and is viewed in the context of the ability or will to be one's own person. Autonomy plays an important role in conceptions of moral obligation and responsibility.[76]

Autonomous will means to act according to reasons and motives that are taken as one's own and not the product of organizational policies and external forces such as whistleblowing legislation. Autonomous will is the central value in the Kantian tradition of moral philosophy that moral requirements are based on the standard of rationality he called the Categorical Imperative.[77] The Categorical Imperative in Kant's ethical system is an unconditional moral law that applies to all rational beings and is independent of any personal motive or desire. Therefore, we could say that even if pressure exists in an organization to not report wrongdoing, a rational, moral person will withstand such pressure, regardless of perceived retaliation, because it is a moral requirement to do so. Kant argued that conformity to the Categorical Imperative, and hence to moral requirements themselves, is essential to rational agency.[78]

Rights and Duties

Researchers have posed the question of whether workplace whistleblowing is a right, and thus allows for responsible behavior, or whether it is an imposed corporate duty, thus resulting in liability of workers. If an organization institutes an internal whistleblowing policy, it is because it perceives moral autonomy to be weak. When businesses then implement the policy, it leads to the conclusion that moral autonomy is strong, and employees are expected to blow the whistle.[79] Therefore, if employees do not blow the whistle in accordance with corporate policy, they then become liable for not doing so, rendering the policy a tool that controls employee behavior. Responsibility for misdeeds then shifts from the organization to the individual, and employees are further stripped of the right to moral autonomy.[80]

Miceli and Near's research has shown that what whistleblowers hope and believe their speaking out will achieve is the correction of what they perceive as an organizational wrongdoing (e.g., fraudulent financial statements). This research also found that not everyone who perceives a wrongdoing acts upon that perception. In fact, only 42 percent stated they were ready to blow the whistle. Those who observe wrongdoing but would not do so identify a "retaliatory climate" in their organizations as the primary barrier to blowing the whistle on corporate wrongdoing, while those who say they would speak up about it were confident that they "would not experience managerial retaliation if they blew the whistle."[81] Recall that the National Business Ethics Survey found that 46 percent of employees did not blow the whistle for fear of retaliation, while 21 percent that reported misconduct said they faced some form of retribution.[82]

Whistleblowing regulations attempt to protect individuals when they behave responsibly toward society in light of irresponsible behavior by their organizations. This certainly is the motivation for the anti-retaliation provisions of both SOX and Dodd-Frank. The acknowledgement of the need for such protection, however, implies that moral agency, autonomy, and responsibility are problematic in organizations, or at the very least, that they do not come naturally and are not welcomed when they arrive. When organizations establish an ethical culture and anonymous channels to report wrongdoing, they create an environment that supports whistleblowing and whistleblowers while controlling for possible retaliation.[83]

Anthony Menendez v. Halliburton, Inc.[84]

Doing the right thing and blowing the whistle does not always pay off and can be an arduous task. A case in point is what happened to Anthony Menendez in his whistleblowing ordeal with Halliburton. One day in February 2006, he received an e-mail from Halliburton's chief accounting officer, Mark McCollum, that was addressed to much of the accounting department. It read, "The SEC has opened an inquiry into the allegations of Mr. Menendez." Everyone was told to retain their documents until further notice. Menendez had been outed. The facts of the case are summarized in Exhibit 3.12. (An expanded version of this case with multiple areas for discussion appears in Case 3-8).

EXHIBIT 3.12   Accountant Takes on Halliburton and Wins

The story begins less than one year earlier when Menendez was hired as the Director of Technical Accounting Research and Training at Halliburton. Only months before that, Halliburton had settled with the U.S. Securities and Exchange Commission (SEC) after a two-year accounting probe. It didn't take long for Menendez to realize the company was violating some very basic accounting revenue recognition rules.

Halliburton contracts with energy companies like Royal Dutch Shell and BP to find and exploit huge oil and gas fields. It sells services of its geologists and engineers who work intricate machinery that Halliburton built and sold to its customers. The company's accountants had been

(Continued)

allowing the company to count the full value of the equipment right away as revenue, sometimes even before it had assembled the equipment. But the customers could walk away in the middle of the contracts. Also, Menendez knew that if the equipment were damaged, Halliburton, not the customer, absorbed the loss.

Menendez recommended the company wait until the work was completed to record the equipment sales as revenue. Even though top Halliburton accounting executives, including Halliburton's chief accounting officer, Mark McCollum, agreed with Menendez's analysis, they didn't act to correct the accounting because of concern about its impact in slowing revenue growth. Later, an outside expert, Doug Carmichael, the former chief accountant of the Public Company Accounting Oversight Board (PCAOB), would agree with Menendez.

In meetings with an executive who worked for Menendez, James Paquette, the two agreed on the revenue recognition issue. But other groups in accounting were fighting them. Paquette was concerned what would happen even if they made a convincing case and still the other accountants and executives didn't budge. Menendez had replied that he hoped that wouldn't happen, but that there were "avenues for us to hold up our integrity."

On July 18, 2005, Menendez turned on a digital recorder, put it in the front pocket of his slacks. and walked into a meeting with McCollum. Even though McCollum had indicated that Menendez's position had merits, he told Menendez that the approach he was using and memo he had prepared on the matter was wrong. He was making his colleagues feel stupid and needed to be more collegial. He told Menendez that the Halliburton team, working with the external auditors from KPMG, had reached a different conclusion. He also offered that Menendez shouldn't put things in writing and had to be more "circumspect about the use of e-mail to communicate." He finished by telling Menendez that he wasn't asking him to compromise his ethics and compromise the position he felt so strongly about.

Menendez waited to see what would happen. Given that billions in equipment sales were involved, he knew this was no trivial matter. Finally, in the fall he realized nothing would happen. The company had justified its accounting treatment by indicating that the equipment sitting in Halliburton's warehouses was "customer-owned inventory." Menendez agonized and several days later filed a confidential complaint with the SEC in November 2005.

He spoke to the SEC about the matter and was told to go to the audit committee. Menendez assumed the SEC would take action, but nothing seemed to occur, until February 4, 2006, when he heard the SEC was poking around.

Unbeknownst to Menendez, his complaint went to the Halliburton legal department as well as the board committee, an apparent violation of company policy. The audit committee was supposed to keep such reports confidential. A few days later, the SEC notified the company that it had opened an investigation into the company's revenue recognition. Then, the e-mail from McCollum got distributed. Halliburton's general counsel said "the SEC is investigating Mr. Menendez's complaints" to the company's chief financial officer, KPMG, other top executives, and McCollum. McCollum had forwarded it to at least 15 of Menendez's colleagues in accounting. As far as Halliburton was concerned, they had a traitor in their ranks.

The ramifications were immediate. Menendez was stripped of his responsibilities and became a pariah at the firm. Halliburton contracted with an outside law firm to conduct an "investigation." Not surprisingly, it cleared the company. The SEC informed Halliburton it would not bring any enforcement action against it.

Menendez went back to the SEC to no avail. The commission wouldn't even accept the documents he had provided. Finally, he felt he had to leave Halliburton having been punished for blowing the whistle. He brought a claim under SOX in May 2006 based on retaliation, but the government would not take up his case. He brought separate lawsuits, but lost. He persisted even when others told him he had no chance of prevailing. No one would take his case. Finally, he decided to represent himself in the appeals process. It went on for three years. In September

(Continued)

2011, the administrative laws appeals panel had ruled. It overturned the original trial judge. After five years, Menendez had his first victory.

Halliburton appealed the reversal. Another two years went by and in April 2013, the appeals panel ruled that he had been retaliated against for blowing the whistle, just as he had argued all along.

Menendez acted on principle in his quest for the truth. He only wanted to be proven right so he had asked for a token sum. The panel, noting the importance of punishing retaliations against whistleblowers, awarded him $30,000.

Menendez ultimately got a job at General Motors based on a recommendation from the expert witness, Doug Carmichael. GM's chief accounting officer who hired Menendez was quoted as telling him it took a lot of courage to stand tall and the company needed people with high integrity who would work hard and were trustworthy.

Menendez still works at GM. Halliburton has thrived, never being penalized by the SEC. In 2014, the company generated $3.5 billion in profit on $33 billion in revenue.

Menendez's case was filed before Dodd-Frank became effective. It is interesting to contemplate what might have happened had he filed a whistleblower claim under the act. Would he have been rewarded for his efforts?

Obligation to Report Fraud

The foundation for making moral judgments in accounting is the public interest ideal. The provisions of Dodd-Frank allow for responsible behavior by describing a process for reporting unresolved differences between an auditor and the firm. The confidentiality obligation for CPAs not withstanding, whistleblowing in accounting is a duty when it is motivated by a desire to protect the public.

The reporting requirements for fraud are detailed in Section 10A of the Securities Exchange Act of 1934 and are based on the principles of integrity and acting in the public interest. The following steps are part of a prescribed process that should be followed in deciding whether to report fraud.

1. Determine whether the violations have a material effect, quantitatively or qualitatively, on the financial statements.
2. If yes, has management, or the board of directors, caused management to take remedial action, including reporting externally if necessary?
3. If no, then the auditor must make a formal report of its conclusions and provide the report to the board of directors. The board then has one business day to inform the SEC and provide a copy of the communication to the external auditor.

If the auditing firm does not receive a copy within one business day, then it has two choices:

a. Provide a copy of its own report to the SEC within one business day, or
b. Resign from the engagement and provide a copy of the report to the SEC within one business day of resigning.

Although external auditors might turn to whistleblowers against clients, in reality this is unlikely to occur until and unless the process prescribed under Section 10A has played out to first resolve the matter internally through the client's internal compliance system. However, if an internal resolution cannot be found, the auditor should consider any disclosure responsibilities to regulatory authorities. Furthermore, external auditors must follow the process described in Interpretation 102-4 when an auditor contemplates blowing the whistle on the client or audit firm.

Dodd-Frank Provisions

The Dodd-Frank Wall Street Reform and Consumer Protection Act (Dodd-Frank) was adopted by Congress on January 5, 2010, and became effective on August 12, 2011.[85] It changes the regulatory landscape for internal accountants and auditors, and external auditors and auditing firms, by protecting whistleblowers that "voluntarily" provide the SEC with "original information" about a violation of federal securities laws that leads to a successful enforcement proceeding. Under the United States Code (US Code), the enforcement action must result in monetary sanctions of more than $1 million.[86]

Dodd-Frank defines a whistleblower as any individual who provides information to the SEC relating to a violation of the securities laws that has occurred, is ongoing, or is about to occur. *Voluntarily* means the whistleblower has provided information prior to the government, a self-regulatory organization, or the PCAOB asking for it directly from the whistleblower. Original information must be based upon the whistleblower's independent knowledge or independent analysis, not already known to the SEC and not derived exclusively from an allegation made in a judicial or administrative hearing or a governmental report, hearing, audit, or investigation (HR 4173).[87]

Section 922 of Dodd-Frank provides an award for whistleblowers (who meet certain criteria) of "not less than 10 percent and not more than 30 percent, in total, of what has been collected of the monetary sanctions imposed in the section." Kastiel believes the award incentivizes whistleblowing and provides a payment for disclosing the relevant information to the SEC.[88]

The "incentivization" provision of Dodd-Frank has been referred to as a "bounty hunter" program. Is it ethical to provide financial incentives to motivate employees to come forward and report financial wrongdoing? This is not an easy question to answer.

One major concern with this new provision is that it may cause would-be whistleblowers to go external with the information rather than internal using the organization's prescribed reporting mechanisms. Employees have a loyalty obligation to their employers that include maintaining confidentiality and not doing anything to harm their employers. However, as discussed in Chapter 1, the loyalty obligation should never be used to mask one's ethical obligation to maintain integrity and protect the public interest. Assuming the internal reporting process has played out and nothing has been done to correct for the wrongdoing, we believe from an ethical perspective external whistleblowing is the proper course of action especially if it is the *only* way for the public to know. An employee should not fall victim to the bystander effect and assume others will report it. Along with knowledge comes the responsibility to correct wrongdoings, which is in the best long-term interests of the organization.

Internal Accountants' Eligibility

Under Dodd-Frank, internal accountants are excluded from receiving whistleblower awards because of their pre-existing legal duty to report securities violations.[89] This includes individuals with internal compliance or audit responsibilities at an entity who receive information about potential violations since it is part of their job responsibilities to report suspicion of illegal acts and fraud to management.

Under certain circumstances, internal accountants are eligible to become Dodd-Frank whistleblowers in three situations: (1) Disclosure to the SEC is needed to prevent "substantial injury" to the financial interest of an entity or its investors; (2) the whistleblower "reasonably believes" the entity is impeding investigation of the misconduct (e.g., destroying documents or improperly influencing witnesses); or (3) the whistleblower has first reported the violation internally and at least 120 days have passed with no action.

The substantial injury provision does not require the whistleblower to reasonably believe that the entity might commit a "material violation"; rather, the whistleblower will generally only need to demonstrate that responsible management or governance personnel at the entity were aware of an "imminent violation" and were not taking steps to prevent it. The 120-day "look-back" period begins after the internal accountant or auditor either provided information of a possible violation to the relevant entity's management (i.e., audit committee, chief legal officer, or chief compliance officer), or at least 120 days have elapsed since the whistleblower received the information, if the whistleblower received it under circumstances indicating that these people were already aware of the information. The internal accountant cannot become eligible for a whistleblower award by learning of possible misconduct, realizing that those responsible for the entity's compliance are not aware of the possible misconduct, failing to provide the information to them, waiting for the 120-day period to run, and then reporting the information to the SEC (SEC 2010).[90]

External Auditor Eligibility

External auditors are generally prohibited from blowing the whistle on their clients because the information gained during a mandated audit would not be considered to derive from an individual's independent knowledge or analysis. The Dodd-Frank Act prohibits an external auditor who is already obligated to report information to the SEC from personally profiting from reporting that same information as a whistleblower. However, for auditors and their firms the whistleblower rules allow the auditor or an employee associated with the auditor to make a whistleblower submission alleging that the firm failed to assess, investigate, or report wrongdoing in accordance with Section 10A, or that the firm failed to follow other professional standards. If the whistleblower makes such a submission, the whistleblower will be able to obtain an award not only from a successful enforcement action against the auditing firm, but also from any successful action against the firm's engagement client. In allowing such claims, the goal of the SEC is to "help insure that wrongdoing by the [accounting] firm (or its employees) is reported on a timely fashion." According to the SEC, this goal is paramount "because of the important gatekeeper role that auditors play in the securities markets."[91]

The disclosure of confidential information about clients raises questions about a possible violation of Rule 301 of the AICPA Code (AICPA 2013, ET Section 301) and of state privilege laws.[92] The external disclosure of confidential information can, under certain circumstances, be treated as an exception to the rule if disclosure is linked to compliance with applicable laws and government regulations, which include the Dodd-Frank. The act defines the circumstances under which the disclosure of confidential information by external auditors will not violate confidentiality and entails a good faith effort to get the company or client to alter the accounting that triggers the concern.

Rosenthal and Smith point out that several members of the public accounting profession, including KPMG, Ernst & Young, PricewaterhouseCoopers and the Center for Audit Quality, believe that permitting CPAs to obtain monetary rewards for blowing the whistle on their own firms' performance of services for clients could create several significant problems including: (1) undermining the ethical obligations of CPAs not to divulge confidential client information by providing a financial reward for whistleblowing; (2) harming the quality of external audits because client management might restrict access to client information for fear the financial incentive for whistleblowing could lead to reporting client-specific information to the SEC; (3) overriding the firms' internal reporting mechanisms for audit-related disagreements; and (4) incentivizing an individual to bypass existing programs to report disagreements including hotlines.[93]

Integrity Considerations

Rule 102 of the AICPA Code requires that "In the performance of any professional service, a member shall maintain objectivity and integrity, shall be free of conflicts of interest, and shall not knowingly misrepresent facts or subordinate his or her judgment to others."[94] Interpretation 102-4 was revised effective August 31, 2013, to provide additional guidelines as to the scope and application of Rule 102 with respect to extending the subordination of judgment provision to include not only differences of opinion between an internal accountant and his or her supervisor but differences between an external auditor and the audit firm.

Assume that an auditor does not believe the audit firm has done everything that it can to resolve differences with the client over proper accounting and the firm has decided to accept the client's position on the matter. The auditor knows the audit firm's decision violates the rights of the investors and creditors who expect auditors to act in their best interests. It is the integrity standard that establishes the basis for moral action and to avoid subordinating judgment. Integrity is a critical component of choosing the means necessary to report wrongdoing even if it leads to blowing the whistle on an employer and in the face of possible retaliation for one's action. Interpretation 102-4 forms the basis of the ethical obligations of external auditors to meet the requirements of Dodd-Frank prior to blowing the whistle and becoming eligible for a whistleblower award. The process to follow is depicted in Exhibit 3.13.

EXHIBIT 3.13   Ethical Responsibilities of CPAs to Avoid Subordination of Judgment*

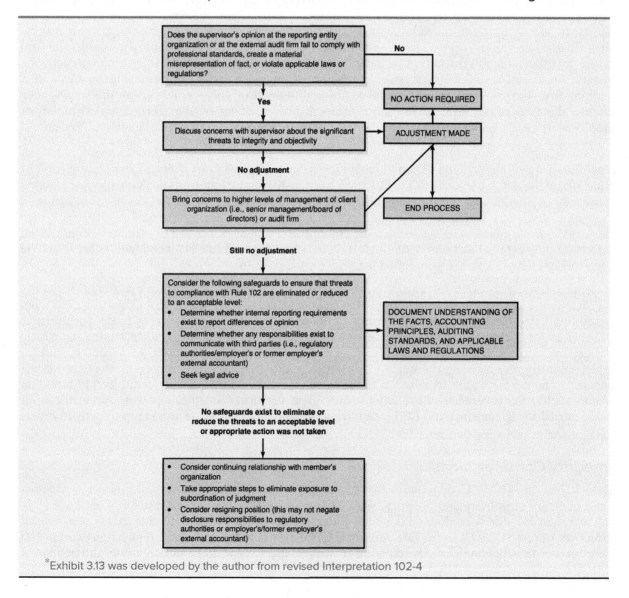

*Exhibit 3.13 was developed by the author from revised Interpretation 102-4

Under Interpretation 102-4, when differences of opinion exist on how best to handle disagreements with the client and the firm refuses to make the required adjustments, then the external auditor should consider whether safeguards exist to ensure that threats to compliance with Rule 102 are eliminated or reduced to an acceptable level. In doing so, the external auditor should determine whether internal reporting requirements exist within the firm to report differences of opinion and any responsibilities that may exist to communicate with third parties, such as regulatory authorities. In that regard, the CPA is advised to seek legal advice on the matter.

If the external auditor concludes that safeguards cannot eliminate or reduce the threats to integrity and objectivity to an acceptable level or other appropriate action was not taken, then the auditor should consider whether the relationship with the organization should be terminated including possibly resigning one's position. These steps are necessary to prevent subordination of judgment.

Nothing in Interpretation 102-4 precludes an external auditor from resigning from the audit firm; however, resignation does not negate the auditor's disclosure responsibilities to the SEC. As previously discussed, the confidentiality requirement of Rule 301 does not prohibit an auditor from complying with applicable laws and government regulations such as Dodd-Frank. As Taylor and Thomas (2013) point out, there are times when CPAs might choose to report internal disputes over accounting issues to an external party in order to maintain professional integrity.[95]

The Morality of Whistleblowing

Whistleblowing always involves an actual or at least declared intention to prevent something bad that would otherwise occur. It always involves information that would not ordinarily be revealed. Most ethicists agree whistleblowing is an ethical action. According to the "standard theory" on whistleblowing of Michael Davis, whistleblowing is morally required when it is required at all; people have a moral obligation to prevent serious harm to others if they can do so with little costs to themselves. Thus, a utilitarian analysis might be used to evaluate the ethics of whistleblowing, keeping in mind that the application of a rule-utilitarian perspective could lead to the conclusion that a categorical imperative exists to do whatever it takes to stop fraudulent behavior regardless of whether a particular action might bring more harm than good to the stakeholders.[96]

DeGeorge analyzes when whistleblowing is a moral act. His starting position is based on the universal ethical principle that "corporations have a moral obligation not to harm." DeGeorge identifies five criteria when whistleblowing is morally permitted. Briefly, (1) the firm's actions will do serious and considerable harm to others; (2) the whistleblowing act is justifiable once the employee reports it to her immediate supervisor and makes her moral concerns known; (3) absent any action by the supervisor, the employee should take the matter all the way up to the board, if necessary; (4) documented evidence must exist that would convince a reasonable and impartial observer that one's views of the situation is correct and that serious harm may occur; and (5) the employee must reasonably believe that going public will create the necessary change to protect the public and is worth the risk to oneself.[97]

DeGeorge's criteria establish the foundation for moral behavior to occur when contemplating whistleblowing. He rejects the position that external whistleblowing is *always* morally justifiable, and also rejects the position that external whistleblowing is *never* morally justifiable. Basically his position is that the whistleblower should have a moral motivation to engage in the act (i.e., to expose unnecessary harm, and illegal or immoral actions). In this way DeGeorge's propositions meet Rest's conditions for ethical decision making and have a virtues-based dimension to them.

Whistleblowing Experiences

Since its inception in 2011, the SEC's whistleblower program has paid more than $50 million to 16 whistleblowers who provided the SEC with unique and useful information that contributed to a successful enforcement action.

On August 29, 2014, the SEC announced a whistleblower award of more than \$300,000, 20 percent of the \$1.5 million settlement, to a company employee who performed audit and compliance functions and reported wrongdoing (insider trading and numerous securities violations) to the SEC after the company failed to take action within 120 days after the employee reported it internally. It was the first award for a whistleblower with an audit or compliance function at a company. The SEC mistakenly released the reference number of the case for which the whistleblower received the award, resulting in the indirect release of that individual's name. The SEC quickly redacted the reference number but it still violated the confidentiality requirement to protect the identity of the whistleblower.

On April 22, 2015, the SEC announced its second award of more than a million dollars to a compliance professional. The award involves a compliance officer who had a reasonable basis to believe that disclosure to the SEC was necessary to prevent imminent misconduct from causing substantial financial harm to the company or investors.

While we believe the whistleblowing program is the right thing to do to protect the public interest, we are concerned about two things:

1. A self-interested and opportunistic person may be induced to reveal company information to the SEC after following the prescribed internal compliance process, that led to no action by the company, with inadequate safeguards as to the quality of the information provided, and
2. Permitting compliance officers to become whistleblowers merely because of the passage of time (i.e., 120 days), rather than on a case-specific consideration of whether the company adequately addressed the underlying compliance issues in good faith, can erode corporate culture and trust in compliance officials; the result may be to subvert the overarching objectives of preventing, detecting, and remediating corporate misconduct on an enterprise-wide basis.[98]

We agree with others who have pointed out that, by reporting through the internal compliance process, others in the organization become informed of the facts and become potential whistleblowers.[99] As a practical matter, there may be no way around widening the circle of those in the know, but organizations should, at a minimum, take steps to protect the identity of the whistleblower.

Concluding Thoughts

Our journey in this chapter leads us to conclude that organizations should take reasonable steps to ensure that they develop an ethical culture, including instilling ethical values within the firm's policies, procedures, and practices; develop a code of ethics that is enhanced through training; establish a hotline for the anonymous reporting of alleged wrongdoing; develop whistleblowing guidelines; appoint a chief ethics and compliance officer; monitor ethical behavior and compliance with applicable regulations;, and create an ethical tone at the top, all of which should occur with ethical leadership at the helm and strong internal controls. Research supports the proposition that "strong ethical cultures" diminish organizational misconduct and thereby the need for employees to blow the whistle internally or externally.[100]

Creating an ethical culture is a necessary but insufficient condition to ensure that ethical behavior occurs. Individuals within the organization may attempt to subvert the systems and pressure others to look the other way or go along with wrongdoing under the guise of being a team player or accepting a one-time fix to a perceived problem. In these situations, outlets should exist for employees to voice their values when they believe unethical or fraudulent behavior has occurred. Just imagine how Anthony Menendez's experiences would have changed had Halliburton created such a supportive environment.

Discussion Questions

1. In her book *The Seven Signs of Ethical Collapse,* Jennings explains: "When an organization collapses ethically, it means that those in the organization have drifted into rationalizations and legalisms, and all for the purpose of getting the results they want and need at almost any cost." Discuss what you think Jennings meant by this statement in the context of the giving voice to values discussions in Chapter 2.

2. Have you ever been faced with a personal dilemma whether to blow the whistle on wrongdoing? What did you do and why? How did elements of the giving voice to values framework influence your decision?

3. Identify a company that you believe has an ethical culture. Explain why you selected that company.

4. One way of analyzing whether National Security Agency (NSA) whistleblower Edward Snowden's actions were justified in leaking classified materials exposing the breadth of the U.S. government's surveillance activities is by weighing personal morality against the morality that comes with one's adopted professional role. Using this perspective, do you believe Snowden's act was ethical?

5. How does employee perceptions of commitment, integrity, and transparency in the workplace contribute toward creating an ethical corporate culture?

6. It has been said that recent graduates from a business school majoring in accounting and just entering the profession are especially vulnerable to ethical missteps because they are often naive and may not see the ethical aspects of situations they confront. Explain the various dimensions of such alleged ethical challenges in the workplace.

7. Explain how "groupthink" might lead a person to ignore moral and ethical duty in an organization.

8. Do you believe that employees who observe more occupational fraud in their organizations are more likely to engage in occupational fraud themselves?

9. The following questions are about corporate governance and executive compensation:

    (a) How does agency theory address the issue of executive compensation?

    (b) How might stakeholder theory argue against the current model of executive compensation in the United States?

    (c) What is meant by the statement, "Compensation systems always become in part *end* and not simply *means*"?

10. The issue of the size of executive compensation packages is explored in the text. The highest paid CEO in 2014 was David Zaslav, the CEO of Discovery Communications, whose total executive compensation package was $156.1 million, the vast majority of which was from stock awards. Critics claim that CEOs receive excessive executive compensation packages when compared with the average worker. Consider that NBA basketball star LeBron James took in $64.8 million in 2014, the majority of which was from endorsements, while radio and TV entertainer Howard Stern earned $95 million? Are the top paid corporate executives overpaid when compared to top entertainers? Why or why not?

11. Five months before the new 2002 Lexus ES hit showroom floors, the company's U.S. engineers sent a test report to Toyota City in Japan: The luxury sedan shifted gears so roughly that it was "not acceptable for production." Days later, another Japanese executive sent an e-mail to top managers saying that despite misgivings among U.S. officials, the 2002 Lexus was "marginally acceptable for production." The new ES went on sale across the nation on October 1, 2001.

In years to come, thousands of Lexus owners discovered that some of the vehicles had transmission problems, which caused it to hesitate when motorists hit the gas or lurch forward unintentionally. The 2002–2006 ES models would become the target of lawsuits, federal safety investigations, and hundreds of consumer complaints, including claims of 49 injuries.

In an August 15, 2005, memo explaining the company's position, a staff attorney wrote, "The objective will be to limit the number of vehicles to be serviced to those owners who complain and to limit the per-vehicle cost."

In 2010, Toyota was fined a record $16.4 million for delays in notifying U.S. federal safety officials about defects that could lead to sudden acceleration.

Do you believe national culture might have played a role in how Toyota handled the matter? What about corporate culture? What are the similarities between the Toyota case and the Ford and GM situations discussed in the chapter?

12. The 2011 National Business Ethics Survey defines "active social networkers" as people who spend more than 30 percent of the workday participating on social networking sites. According to the results of the survey, active social networkers air company linen in public. Sixty percent would comment on their personal sites about their company if it was in the news, 53% say they share information about work projects once a week or more, and more than a third say they often comment, on their personal sites, about managers, coworkers, and even clients. What are the dangers of such behavior for the employee and employer?

13. Brief and Motowidlo define prosocial behavior within the organizational setting as "behavior which is (a) performed by a member of an organization, (b) directed toward an individual, group, or organization with whom she interacts while carrying out her organizational role, and (c) performed with the intention of promoting the welfare of the individual, group, or organization toward which it is directed."[101]

    The researchers on whistleblowing using this model have generally argued that stages 5 and 6 represent cognitive moral development consistent with prosocial behavior. Discuss why stages 5 and 6 of Kohlberg's model are more likely to be associated with prosocial behavior than lower stages of moral development.

14. What is the link between the internal control environment and accountability?

15. The Committee of Sponsoring Organizations (COSO) explains the importance of the control environment to internal controls by stating that it sets the tone of an organization, influencing the control consciousness of its people. It is the foundation for all aspects of internal control, providing discipline and structure. Explain what is meant by this statement.

16. It has been argued that an organization that does not support those that whistle-blow because of violation of professional standards is indicative of a failure of organizational ethics. Explain what you think this statement means from the perspective of corporate culture.

17. Evaluate the ethics of the practice of whistleblowing from the perspectives of virtue, rights theory, and utilitarianism.

18. Just because a person has a right to blow the whistle, does that mean she has a duty to blow the whistle? How might we make that determination?

19. How do the concepts of cognitive dissonance and organizational/ethical dissonance relate to whether an accountant might choose to blow the whistle on corporate wrongdoing?

20. Explain how we might evaluate auditors' whistleblowing intentions? Why would this be important to do?

21. Explain how internal auditors' sensitivity to ethical dilemmas might be influenced by corporate governance mechanisms.

22. On October 24, 2013, the Second Circuit Court of Appeals ruled that a tipster who provided information to the SEC about illegal payments to foreign government officials by Stryker Corporation under the Foreign Corrupt Practices Act (FCPA) was not eligible to receive a Dodd-Frank award because his information was provided before the act went into effect in 2010. Stryker had made those payments between August 2003 and February 2008. The commission ruled the company had incorrectly described the unlawful payments in its books and records and failed to devise and maintain an adequate system of internal accounting controls, as required under the FCPA. Stryker was fined $13.3 million: $7.5 million in disgorgement; $2.3 million in prejudgment interest; and a $3.5 million civil penalty. Do you believe the court's opinion was ethical from a fairness perspective? From a rights perspective? Explain.

23. The following relates to the Menendez–Halliburton situation described in the text.

    (a) How would you characterize Halliburton's accounting for revenue from ethical and professional perspectives?

    (b) Once KPMG learned that Menendez had provided a complaint to Halliburton's audit committee highlighting questionable accounting and auditing practices, the KPMG audit partner instructed the audit team members to avoid communications with Menendez. How would you characterize those actions ethically and professionally?

24. "Give me the 'McFacts,' ma'am, nothing but the McFacts!" So argued the defense attorney for McDonald's Corporation as she questioned Stella Liebeck, an 81-year-old retired sales clerk, two years after her initial lawsuit against McDonald's claiming that it served dangerously hot coffee. Liebeck had bought a 49-cent cup of coffee at the drive-in window of an Albuquerque McDonald's, and while removing the lid to add cream and sugar, she spilled the coffee and suffered third-degree burns of the groin, inner thighs, and buttocks. Her suit claimed that the coffee was "defective." During the trial, it was determined that testing of coffee at other local restaurants found that none came closer than 20° to the temperature at which McDonald's coffee is poured (about 180°F). The jury decided in favor of Liebeck and awarded her compensatory damages of $200,000, which they reduced to $160,000 after determining that 20 percent of the fault belonged with Liebeck for spilling the coffee. The jury then found that McDonald's had engaged in willful, reckless, malicious, or wanton conduct, the basis for punitive damages. It awarded $2.7 million in punitive damages. That amount was ultimately reduced by the presiding judge to $480,000. The parties then settled out of court for an unspecified amount reported to be less than the $480,000.

    For its part, McDonald's had suggested that Liebeck may have contributed to her injuries by holding the cup between her legs and not removing her clothing immediately. The company also argued that Liebeck's age may have made the injuries worse than they might have been in a younger individual, "since older skin is thinner and more vulnerable to injury."

    Who is to blame for the McSpill? Be sure to support your answer with a discussion of personal responsibility, corporate accountability, and ethical reasoning.

25. Is business ethics an oxymoron?

Endnotes

1. Craig E. Johnson, *Meeting the Ethical Challenges of Leadership: Casting Light or Shadow* (New York: Sage Publications, 2015).

2. Johnson, pp. 321–323.

3. O.C. Ferrell, John Fraedich, and Linda Ferrell, *Business Ethics: Ethical Decision Making and Cases*, 9th ed. (Mason, OH: South-Western, 2011).

4. O.C. Ferrell, John Fraedrich, and Linda Ferrell, *Business Ethics: Ethical Decision Making and Cases* (Stamford, CT: Cengage Learning, 2015), pp. 128–146.

5. O.C. Ferrell and Linda Ferrell, "Role of Ethical Leadership in Organizational Performance," *Journal of Management Systems* 13, (2001), pp. 64–78.

6. Ferrell et al.

7. H. R. Smith and Archie B. Carroll, "Organizational Ethics: A Stacked Deck," *Journal of Business Ethics*, Vol. 3, No. 2 (May 1984), pp. 95–100.

8. Thomas M. Jones, "Ethical Decision Making by Individuals in Organizations: An Issue-Contingent Model," *Academy of Management Review,* Vol. 16, No. 2 (1991), pp. 366–395.

9. Susan E. Fiske and Shelley E. Taylor, *Social Cognition* (NY: McGraw-Hill, 1991).

10. MaryJo Burchard, "Ethical Dissonance and Response to Destructive Leadership: A Proposed Model," *Emerging Leadership Journeys*, 4, no. 1, pp. 154–176.

11. Scott K. Jones and Kenneth M. Hiltebeitel, "Organizational Influence in a Model of the Moral Decision Process of Accountants," *Journal of Business Ethics* 14, no. 6 (1995), pp. 417–431.

12. Jones.

13. Burchard.

14. Burchard, pp. 158–159.

15. Lawrence A. Pervin, "Performance and Satisfaction as a Function of Individual-Environment Fit," *Psychological Bulletin* 69, no. 1 (January 1968), pp. 56–68.

16. Burchard, pp. 162–163.

17. Hian Chye Koh and El'fred H. Y. Boo, "Organizational Ethics and Job Satisfaction and Commitment," *Management Decision* 4, nos. 5 and 6 (2004), pp. 677–693.

18. Burchard, pp. 163–164.

19. Art Padilla, Robert Hogan, and Robert B. Kaiser, "The Toxic Triangle: Destructive Leaders, Susceptible Followers, and Conducive Environments," *Leadership Quarterly* 18 (3), (2007), pp. 176–194.

20. Burchard, pp. 164–165.

21. V. Lee Hamilton and Herbert Kelman, *Crimes of Obedience: Toward a Social Psychology of Authority and Responsibility* (New Haven, CT: Yale University Press, 1989).

22. Burchard, pp. 163–164.

23. Koh and Boo.

24. Randi L. Sims and Thomas L. Keon, "The Influence of Ethical Fit on Employee Satisfaction, Commitment, and Turnover," *Journal of Business Ethics* 13, no. 12 (1994), pp. 939–948.

25. Marianne M. Jennings, *The Seven Signs of Ethical Collapse: How to Spot Moral Meltdowns in Companies Before It's Too Late* (New York: St. Martin's Press, 2006).

26. Jennings.

27. Jennings.

28. Jennings, pp. 138–139.

29. Archie B. Carroll and Ann K. Buchholtz, *Business & Society: Ethics and Stakeholder Management* (Mason, OH: Cengage Learning, 2009).

30. Ferrell et al, p. 35.

31. Isabelle Maignan and O. C. Ferrell, "Corporate Social Responsibility: Toward a Marketing Conceptualization," *Journal of the Academy of Marketing Science* 32 (2004), pp. 3–19.

32. *United States v. Carroll Towing,* 159 F.2d 169 (2d Cir. 1947).

33. Douglas Birsch and John H. Fiedler, *The Ford Pinto Case: A Study in Applied Ethics, Business, and Technology* (Albany: State University of New York, 1994).

34. *Grimshaw v. Ford Motor Co.,* 1 19 Cal.App.3d 757, 174 Cal. Rptr. 348 (1981).

35. David De Cremer and Ann E. Tenbrunsel, *Behavioral Business Ethics: Shaping an Emerging Field* (New York: Routledge, 2012).

36. *General Motors v. Moseley,* 213 Ga. App. 875 (1984).

37. Jay W. Lorsch, "Managing Culture: The Invisible Barrier to Strategic Change," *California Management Review* 28 (1986), pp. 95–109.

38. Cam Caldwell, Linda A. Hayes, and Do Tien Long, "Leadership, Trustworthiness, and Ethical Stewardship," *Journal of Business Ethics* 96 (2010), pp. 497–512.

39. Tamara Kaplan, "The Tylenol Crisis: How Effective Public Relations Saved Johnson & Johnson," Pennsylvania State University. Available here: http://www.aerobiologicalengineering.com/wxk116/TylenolMurders/crisis.html.

40. Katie Thomas, "J. & J. to Pay $2.2 Billion in Risperdal Settlement," November 4, 2013, Available at: http://www.nytimes.com/2013/11/05/business/johnson-johnson-to-settle-risperdal-improper-marketing-case.html.

41. Ed Silverman, "Johnson & Johnson Loses Trial Over Risperdal And Male Breasts," February 24, 2015, Available at: http://blogs.wsj.com/pharmalot/2015/02/24/johnson-johnson-loses-trial-over-risperdal-and-male-breasts/tab/print/.

42. *KPMG Integrity Survey 2013.*

43. Ethics Resource Center (ERC), *2013 National Business Ethics Survey (NBES) of the U.S. Workforce.*

44. Association of Certified Fraud Examiners, *2012 Global Fraud Study: Report to the Nations on Occupational Fraud and Abuse,* www.acfe.com/uploadedFiles/ACFE_Website/Content/rttn/2012-report-to-nations.pdf.

45. ACFE, p. 6.

46. ACFE, p. 57.

47. Center for Audit Quality, *Guide to Internal Control over Financial Reporting*, 2013.

48. Ernst & Young, *Detecting Financial Statement Fraud: What Every Manager Needs to Know,* October 2010, Center for Audit Quality.

49. AICPA Professional Standards, *Consideration of Fraud in a Financial Statement Audit* (AU-C Section 240), (NY: AICPA, 2014).

50. Ferrell et al., p. 42.

51. Andrei Shleifer and Robert Vishny, "A Survey of Corporate Governance," *Journal of Finance* (1997).

52. J. E. Parkinson, *Corporate Power and Responsibility* (Oxford, UK: Oxford University Press, 1994).

53. Bob Tricker, *Corporate Governance: Principles, Policies, and Practices,* 3rd ed., (Oxford, UK: Oxford University Press, 2015).

54. Tricker.

55. O.C. Ferrell, John Fraedrich, and Linda Ferrell, *Business Ethics: Ethical Decision Making and Cases* (Stamford, CT: Cengage Learning, 2015, p. 44).

56. W. Steve Albrecht, Conan C. Albrecht, and Chad O. Albrecht, "Fraud and Corporate Executives: Agency, Stewardship, and Broken Trust," *Journal of Forensic Accounting* 5 (2004), pp. 109–130.

57. Lex Donaldson and James H. Davis, "Stewardship Theory," *Australian Journal of Management* 16, no. 1 (June 1991).

58. Michael Jensen and William H. Meckling, "Theory of the Firm: Managerial Behavior, Agency Costs, and Ownership Structure," *Journal of Financial Economics* (1976), pp. 305–360.

59. Chamu Sundaramurthy and Marianne Lewis, "Control and Collaboration: Paradoxes and Government," *Academy of Management Review* 28, Issue 3 (July 2003), pp. 397–416.

60. Tricker, pp. 65–71.

61. Michael Murphy, "Restatements Affect Bottom Line Less Often," *The CFO Journal,* April 21, 2015.

62. John A. Byrne with Louis Lavelle, Nanette Byrnes, Marcia Vickers, and Amy Borrus, "How to Fix Corporate Governance," *BusinessWeek,* May 6, 2002, pp. 69–78.

63. "Current Controversies in Executive Compensation: 'Issues of Justice and Fairness,'" Knowledge@Wharton, May 2, 2007, Available at: http://knowledge.wharton.upenn.edu/article/current-controversies-in-executive-compensation-issues-of-justice-and-fairness/.

64. Dodd-Frank Wall Street Reform and Consumer Protection Act (H.R. 4173), www.sec.gov/about/laws/wallstreetreform-cpa.pdf.

65. Robert E. Scully, Jr. "Executive Compensation, the Business Judgment Rule, and the Dodd-Frank Act: Back to the Future for Private Litigation?" *The Federal Lawyer,* January 2011.

66. Zabihollah Rezaee, *Corporate Governance and Ethics* (New York: Wiley, 2009).

67. Leo L. Strine, Jr., "Derivative Impact? Some Early Reflections on the Corporation Law Implications of the Enron Debacle," *57 Business Lawyer,* 1371, 1373 (2002).

68. *Skilling v. United States,* 561 U.S. 358, 130 S. Ct. 2896, 177 L. Ed. 2d 619, 8 EXC 59 (2010).

69. Committee of Sponsoring Organizations of the Treadway Commission (COSO), 2013 *Internal Control—Integrated Framework,* Report Available at: http://www.coso.org/documents/Internal%20Control-Integrated%20Framework.pdf.

70. Available at: http://www.bloomberg.com/news/articles/2012-04-02/groupon-revisions-highlight-new-model-s-risks.

71. Securities and Exchange Commission, "SEC Charges Company CEO and Former CFO With Hiding Internal Controls Deficiencies and Violating Sarbanes-Oxley Requirements," July 30, 2014.

72. Ethics and Compliance Officer Association (ECOA), www.theecoa.org.

73. Alison Frankel, "Sarbanes-Oxley's Lost Promise: Why CEOs Haven't been Prosecuted," *Reuters.com On the Case* blog, July 27, 2012, Available at: www.blogs.reuters.com/alison-frankel/2012/07/27/sarbanes-oxleys-lost-promise-why-ceos-havent-been-prosecuted/.

74. Janet P. Near and Marcia P. Miceli, "Organizational Dissidence: The Case of Whistle-blowing," *Journal of Business Ethics* 4 (1985), pp. 1–16.

75. Eva Tsahuridu and Wim Vandekerchove, "Organizational Whistleblowing Policies: Making Employees Responsible or Liable?" *Journal of Business Ethics* 82 (2008), pp. 107-118.

76. Alan Wolfe, *Whose Keeper? Social Science and Moral Obligation*(Berkeley, CA: University of California Press, 1991).

77. Immanuel Kant, *Foundations of Metaphysics of Morals*, trans. Lewis White Beck (New York: Liberal Arts Press, 1959), p. 39.

78. Tsahuridu & Vandekerchove, 2008.

79. Marion Mogielnicki, "Hunting for 'Bounty' and Finding 'Moral Autonomy': The Dodd-Frank Act Expansion of Whistle Blower Protections,"*Academy of Business Research*, Vol. 2, (2011), pp. 74-84.

80. Tsahuridu & Vandekerchove, 2008.

81. Miceli and Near, pp. 698-699.

82. Ethics Resource Center (ERC), 2013 National Business Ethics Survey (NBES) of the U.S. Workforce.

83. Tsahuridu & Vandekerchove, 2008.

84. Jesse Eisinger, "The Whistleblower's Tale: How an Accountant took on Halliburton and Won," *Pro Publica,* April 21, 2015.

85. Dodd-Frank Wall Street Reform and Consumer Protection Act (H.R. 4173), www.sec.gov/about/laws/wallstreetreform-cpa.pdf.

86. SEC, "Implementation of the Whistleblower Provisions of Section 21F of the Securities Exchange Act of 1934," Available at: https://www.sec.gov/rules/final/2011/34-64545.pdf.

87. Dodd-Frank Wall Street Reform and Consumer Protection Act (H.R. 4173), www.sec.gov/about/laws/wallstreetreform-cpa.pdf.

88. Kobi Kastiel, "Elements of an Effective Whistleblower Hotline," *Harvard Law School Forum on Corporate Governance and Financial Regulation*, October 25, 2014. Available at: http://corpgov.law.harvard.edu/2014/10/25/elements-of-an-effective-whistleblower-hotline/.

89. SEC, "Implementation of the Whistleblower Provisions of Section 21F of the Securities Exchange Act of 1934," Available at: https://www.sec.gov/rules/final/2011/34-64545.pdf.

90. SEC, "Implementation of the Whistleblower Provisions of Section 21F of the Securities Exchange Act of 1934," Available at: https://www.sec.gov/rules/final/2011/34-64545.pdf.

91. SEC, "Implementation of the Whistleblower Provisions of Section 21F of the Securities Exchange Act of 1934," Available at: https://www.sec.gov/rules/final/2011/34-64545.pdf.

92. AICPA, *Code of Professional Conduct and Bylaws*, June 1, 2011, Available at: https://www.aicpa.org/research/standards/codeofconduct/downloadabledocuments/2011june1codeofprofessionalconduct.pdf

93. Jason Rosenthal, Esq. and Lesley Smith, Esq, "Should CPAs be Financially Rewarded As Whistleblowers?" *CPA Insider*, 2011, Available at: https://www.cpa2biz.com/Content/media/PRODUCER_CONTENT/Newsletters/Articles_2011/CPA/Jul/Whistleblowers.jsp.

94. AICPA, *Code of Professional Conduct and Bylaws*, June 1, 2011, Available at: https://www.aicpa.org/research/standards/codeofconduct/downloadabledocuments/2011june1codeofprofessionalconduct.pdf

95. Eileen Z. Taylor and Jordan A. Thomas, "Enhanced Protections for Whistleblowers under the Dodd-Frank Act," *The CPA Journal* (2013) pp. 66-71.

96. Michael Davis, "Some Paradoxes of Whistleblowing," *Business & Professional Ethics Journal*, Vol. 15, No. 1 (1996), pp.147-155.

97. Richard T. De George, *Business Ethics,* 7th ed. (NY: Prentice-Hall, 2010).

98. Philip Stamatakos and Ted Chung, "Dodd-Frank's Whistleblower Provisions and the SEC's Rule: Compliance and Ethical Considerations," *Corporate Governance Advisor*, September/October 2011.

99. Daniel Hurson, "United States: Ten 'Rules' For Becoming A Successful SEC Whistleblower," September 11, 2013, Available at: http://www.mondaq.com/unitedstates/x/261844/Corporate+Commercial+Law/The+New+Rules+For+Becoming+A+Successful+SEC+Whistleblower.

100. Mark S. Schwartz, "Developing and Sustaining an Ethical Corporate Culture: The Core Elements," *Business Horizons* 56 (2013), pp. 39–50.

101. Arthur P. Brief and Stephan J. Motowidlo, "Prosocial Organizational Behaviors," *The Academy of Management Review*, Vol. 11, No. 4 (Oct., 1986), pp. 710-725.

Chapter 3 Cases

Case 3-1 The Parable of the Sadhu

Bowen H. McCoy

Reprinted with permission from "The Parable of the Sadhu," by Bowen H. McCoy, *Harvard Business Review.* Copyright © Harvard Business Publishing.

Last year, as the first participant in the new six-month sabbatical program that Morgan Stanley has adopted, I enjoyed a rare opportunity to collect my thoughts as well as do some traveling. I spent the first three months in Nepal, walking 600 miles through 200 villages in the Himalayas and climbing some 120,000 vertical feet. My sole Western companion on the trip was an anthropologist who shed light on the cultural patterns of the villages that we passed through.

During the Nepal hike, something occurred that has had a powerful impact on my thinking about corporate ethics. Although some might argue that the experience has no relevance to business, it was a situation in which a basic ethical dilemma suddenly intruded into the lives of a group of individuals. How the group responded holds a lesson for all organizations, no matter how defined.

The Sadhu

The Nepal experience was more rugged than I had anticipated. Most commercial treks last two or three weeks and cover a quarter of the distance we traveled.

My friend Stephen, the anthropologist, and I were halfway through the 60-day Himalayan part of the trip when we reached the high point, an 18,000-foot pass over a crest that we'd have to traverse to reach the village of Muklinath, an ancient holy place for pilgrims.

Six years earlier, I had suffered pulmonary edema, an acute form of altitude sickness, at 16,500 feet in the vicinity of Everest base camp—so we were understandably concerned about what would happen at 18,000 feet. Moreover, the Himalayas were having their wettest spring in 20 years; hip-deep powder and ice had already driven us off one ridge. If we failed to cross the pass, I feared that the last half of our once-in-a-lifetime trip would be ruined.

The night before we would try the pass, we camped in a hut at 14,500 feet. In the photos taken at that camp, my face appears wan. The last village we'd passed through was a sturdy two-day walk below us, and I was tired.

During the late afternoon, four backpackers from New Zealand joined us, and we spent most of the night awake, anticipating the climb. Below, we could see the fires of two other parties, which turned out to be two Swiss couples and a Japanese hiking club.

To get over the steep part of the climb before the sun melted the steps cut in the ice, we departed at 3.30 a.m. The New Zealanders left first, followed by Stephen and myself, our porters and Sherpas, and then the Swiss. The Japanese lingered in their camp. The sky was clear, and we were confident that no spring storm would erupt that day to close the pass.

At 15,500 feet, it looked to me as if Stephen was shuffling and staggering a bit, which are symptoms of altitude sickness. (The initial stage of altitude sickness brings a headache and nausea. As the condition worsens, a climber may encounter difficult breathing, disorientation, aphasia, and paralysis.) I felt strong—my adrenaline was flowing—but I was very concerned about my ultimate ability to get across. A couple of our porters were also suffering from the height, and Pasang, our Sherpa sirdar (leader), was worried.

Just after daybreak, while we rested at 15,500 feet, one of the New Zealanders, who had gone ahead, came staggering down toward us with a body slung across his shoulders. He dumped the almost naked, barefoot body of an Indian holy man—a sadhu—at my feet. He had found the pilgrim lying on the ice, shivering and suffering from hypothermia. I cradled the sadhu's head and laid him out on the rocks. The New Zealander was angry. He wanted to get across the pass before the bright sun melted the snow. He said, "Look, I've done what I can. You have porters and Sherpa guides. You care for him. We're going on!" He turned and went back up the mountain to join his friends.

I took a carotid pulse and found that the sadhu was still alive. We figured he had probably visited the holy shrines at Muklinath and was on his way home. It was fruitless to question why he had chosen this desperately high route instead of the safe, heavily traveled caravan route through the Kali Gandaki gorge. Or why he was shoeless and almost naked, or how long he had been lying in the pass. The answers weren't going to solve our problem.

Stephen and the four Swiss began stripping off their outer clothing and opening their packs. The sadhu was soon clothed from head to foot. He was not able to walk, but he was very much alive. I looked down the mountain and spotted the Japanese climbers, marching up with a horse.

Without a great deal of thought, I told Stephen and Pasang that I was concerned about withstanding the heights to come and wanted to get over the pass. I took off after several of our porters who had gone ahead.

On the steep part of the ascent where, if the ice steps had given way, I would have slid down about 3,000 feet, I felt vertigo. I stopped for a breather, allowing the Swiss to catch up with me. I inquired about the sadhu and Stephen. They said that the sadhu was fine and that Stephen was just behind them. I set off again for the summit.

Stephen arrived at the summit an hour after I did. Still exhilarated by victory, I ran down the slope to congratulate him. He was suffering from altitude sickness—walking 15 steps, then stopping, walking 15 steps, then stopping. Pasang accompanied him all the way up. When I reached them, Stephen glared at me and said, "How do you feel about contributing to the death of a fellow man?"

I did not completely comprehend what he meant. "Is the sadhu dead?" I inquired.

"No," replied Stephen, "but he surely will be!"

After I had gone, followed not long after by the Swiss, Stephen had remained with the sadhu. When the Japanese had arrived, Stephen had asked to use their horse to transport the sadhu down to the hut. They had refused. He had then asked Pasang to have a group of our porters carry the sadhu. Pasang had resisted the idea, saying that the porters would have to exert all their energy to get themselves over the pass. He believed they could not carry a man down 1,000 feet to the hut, reclimb the slope, and get across safely before the snow melted. Pasang had pressed Stephen not to delay any longer.

The Sherpas had carried the sadhu down to a rock in the sun at about 15,000 feet and pointed out the hut another 500 feet below. The Japanese had given him food and drink. When they had last seen him, he was listlessly throwing rocks at the Japanese party's dog, which had frightened him.

We do not know if the sadhu lived or died.

For many of the following days and evenings, Stephen and I discussed and debated our behavior toward the sadhu. Stephen is a committed Quaker with deep moral vision. He said, "I feel that what happened with the sadhu is a good example of the breakdown between the individual ethic and the corporate ethic. No one person was willing to assume ultimate responsibility for the sadhu. Each was willing to do his bit just so long as it was not too inconvenient. When it got to be a bother, everyone just passed the buck to someone else and took off. Jesus was relevant to a more individualistic stage of society, but how do we interpret his teaching today in a world filled with large, impersonal organizations and groups?"

I defended the larger group, saying, "Look, we all cared. We all gave aid and comfort. Everyone did his bit. The New Zealander carried him down below the snow line. I took his pulse and suggested we treat him for hypothermia. You and the Swiss gave him clothing and got him warmed up. The Japanese gave him food and water. The Sherpas carried him down to the sun and pointed out the easy trail toward the hut. He was well enough to throw rocks at a dog. What more could we do?"

"You have just described the typical affluent Westerner's response to a problem. Throwing money—in this case, food and sweaters—at it, but not solving the fundamentals!" Stephen retorted.

"What would satisfy you?" I said. "Here we are, a group of New Zealanders, Swiss, Americans, and Japanese who have never met before and who are at the apex of one of the most powerful experiences of our lives. Some years the pass is so bad no one gets over it. What right does an almost naked pilgrim who chooses the wrong trail have to disrupt our lives? Even the Sherpas had no interest in risking the trip to help him beyond a certain point."

Stephen calmly rebutted, "I wonder what the Sherpas would have done if the sadhu had been a well-dressed Nepali, or what the Japanese would have done if the sadhu had been a well-dressed Asian, or what you would have done, Buzz, if the sadhu had been a well-dressed Western woman?"

"Where, in your opinion," I asked, "is the limit of our responsibility in a situation like this? We had our own well-being to worry about. Our Sherpa guides were unwilling to jeopardize us or the porters for the sadhu. No one else on the mountain was willing to commit himself beyond certain self-imposed limits."

Stephen said, "As individual Christians or people with a Western ethical tradition, we can fulfill our obligations in such a situation only if one, the sadhu dies in our care; two, the sadhu demonstrates to us that he can undertake the two-day walk down to the village; or three, we carry the sadhu for two days down to the village and persuade someone there to care for him."

"Leaving the sadhu in the sun with food and clothing—where he demonstrated hand-eye coordination by throwing a rock at a dog—comes close to fulfilling items one and two," I answered. "And it wouldn't have made sense to take him to the village where the people appeared to be far less caring than the Sherpas, so the third condition is impractical. Are you really saying that, no matter what the implications, we should, at the drop of a hat, have changed our entire plan?"

The Individual versus the Group Ethic

Despite my arguments, I felt and continue to feel guilt about the sadhu. I had literally walked through a classic moral dilemma without fully thinking through the consequences. My excuses for my actions include a high adrenaline flow, a superordinate goal, and a once-in-a-lifetime opportunity—common factors in corporate situations, especially stressful ones.

Real moral dilemmas are ambiguous, and many of us hike right through them, unaware that they exist. When, usually after the fact, someone makes an issue of one, we tend to resent his or her bringing it up. Often, when the full import of what we have done (or not done) hits us, we dig into a defensive position from which it is very difficult to emerge. In rare circumstances, we may contemplate what we have done from inside a prison.

Had we mountaineers been free of stress caused by the effort and the high altitude, we might have treated the sadhu differently. Yet isn't stress the real test of personal and corporate values? The instant decisions that executives make under pressure reveal the most about personal and corporate character.

Among the many questions that occur to me when I ponder my experience with the sadhu are: What are the practical limits of moral imagination and vision? Is there a collective or institutional ethic that differs from the ethics of the individual? At what level of effort or commitment can one discharge one's ethical responsibilities?

Not every ethical dilemma has a right solution. Reasonable people often disagree; otherwise there would be no dilemma. In a business context, however, it is essential that managers agree on a process for dealing with dilemmas.

Our experience with the sadhu offers an interesting parallel to business situations. An immediate response was mandatory. Failure to act was a decision in itself. Up on the mountain, we could not resign and submit our résumés to a headhunter. In contrast to philosophy, business involves action and implementation—getting things done. Managers must come up with answers based on what they see and what they allow to influence their decision-making processes. On the mountain, none of us but Stephen realized the true dimensions of the situation we were facing.

One of our problems was that, as a group, we had no process for developing a consensus. We had no sense of purpose or plan. The difficulties of dealing with the sadhu were so complex that no one person could handle them. Because the group did not have a set of preconditions that could guide its action to an acceptable resolution, we reacted instinctively as individuals. The cross-cultural nature of the group added a further layer of complexity. We had no leader with whom we could all identify and in whose purpose we believed. Only Stephen was willing to take charge, but he could not gain adequate support from the group to care for the sadhu.

Some organizations do have values that transcend the personal values of their managers. Such values, which go beyond profitability, are usually revealed when the organization is under stress. People throughout the organization generally accept its values, which, because they are not presented as a rigid list of commandments, may be somewhat ambiguous. The stories people tell, rather than printed materials, transmit the organization's conceptions of what is proper behavior.

For 20 years, I have been exposed at senior levels to a variety of corporations and organizations. It is amazing how quickly an outsider can sense the tone and style of an organization and, with that, the degree of tolerated openness and freedom to challenge management.

Organizations that do not have a heritage of mutually accepted, shared values tend to become unhinged during stress, with each individual bailing out for himself or herself. In the great takeover battles we have witnessed during past years, companies that had strong cultures drew the wagons around them and fought it out, while other companies saw executives—supported by golden parachutes—bail out of the struggles.

Because corporations and their members are interdependent, for the corporation to be strong, the members need to share a preconceived notion of correct behavior, a "business ethic," and think of it as a positive force, not a constraint.

As an investment banker, I am continually warned by well-meaning lawyers, clients, and associates to be wary of conflicts of interest. Yet if I were to run away from every difficult situation, I wouldn't be an effective investment banker. I have to feel my way through conflicts. An effective manager can't run from risk either; he or she has to confront risk. To feel "safe" in doing that, managers need the guidelines of an agreed-upon process and set of values within the organization.

After my three months in Nepal, I spent three months as an executive-in-residence at both the Stanford Business School and the University of California at Berkeley's Center for Ethics and Social Policy of the Graduate Theological Union. Those six months away from my job gave me time to assimilate 20 years of business experience. My thoughts turned often to the meaning of the leadership role in any large organization. Students at the seminary thought of themselves as antibusiness. But when I questioned them, they agreed that they distrusted all large organizations, including the church. They perceived all large organizations as impersonal and opposed to individual values and needs. Yet we all know of organizations in which people's values and beliefs are respected and their expressions encouraged. What makes the difference? Can we identify the difference and, as a result, manage more effectively?

The word *ethics* turns off many and confuses more. Yet the notions of shared values and an agreed-upon process for dealing with adversity and change—what many people mean when they talk about corporate culture—seem to be at the heart of the ethical issue. People who are in touch with their own core beliefs and the beliefs of others and who are sustained by them can be more comfortable living on the cutting edge. At times, taking a tough line or a decisive stand in a muddle of ambiguity is the only ethical thing to do. If a manager is indecisive about a problem and spends time trying to figure out the "good" thing to do, the enterprise may be lost.

Business ethics, then, has to do with the authenticity and integrity of the enterprise. To be ethical is to follow the business as well as the cultural goals of the corporation, its owners, its employees, and its customers. Those who cannot serve the corporate vision are not authentic businesspeople and, therefore, are not ethical in the business sense.

At this stage of my own business experience, I have a strong interest in organizational behavior. Sociologists are keenly studying what they call corporate stories, legends, and heroes as a way organizations have of transmitting value systems. Corporations such as Arco have even hired consultants to perform an audit of their corporate culture. In a company, a leader is a person who understands, interprets, and manages the corporate value system. Effective managers, therefore, are action-oriented people who resolve conflict, are tolerant of ambiguity, stress, and change, and have a strong sense of purpose for themselves and their organizations.

If all this is true, I wonder about the role of the professional manager who moves from company to company. How can he or she quickly absorb the values and culture of different organizations? Or is there, indeed, an art of management that is totally transportable? Assuming that such fungible managers do exist, is it proper for them to manipulate the values of others?

What would have happened had Stephen and I carried the sadhu for two days back to the village and become involved with the villagers in his care? In four trips to Nepal, my most interesting experience occurred in 1975, when I lived in a Sherpa home in the Khumbu for five days while recovering from altitude sickness. The high point of Stephen's trip was an invitation to participate in a family funeral ceremony in Manang. Neither experience had to do with climbing the high passes of the Himalayas. Why were we so reluctant to try the lower path, the ambiguous trail? Perhaps because we did not have a leader who could reveal the greater purpose of the trip to us.

Why didn't Stephen, with his moral vision, opt to take the sadhu under his personal care? The answer is partly because Stephen was hard-stressed physically himself and partly because, without some support system that encompassed our involuntary and episodic community on the mountain, it was beyond his individual capacity to do so.

I see the current interest in corporate culture and corporate value systems as a positive response to pessimism such as Stephen's about the decline of the role of the individual in large organizations. Individuals who operate from a thoughtful set of personal values provide the foundation for a corporate culture. A corporate tradition that encourages freedom of inquiry, supports personal values, and reinforces a focused sense of direction can fulfill the need to combine individuality with the prosperity and success of the group. Without such corporate support, the individual is lost.

That is the lesson of the sadhu. In a complex corporate situation, the individual requires and deserves the support of the group. When people cannot find such support in their organizations, they don't know how to act. If such support is forthcoming, a person has a stake in the success of the group and can add much to the process of establishing and maintaining a corporate culture. Management's challenge is to be sensitive to individual needs, to shape them, and to direct and focus them for the benefit of the group as a whole.

For each of us, the sadhu lives. Should we stop what we are doing and comfort him, or should we keep trudging up toward the high pass? Should I pause to help the derelict I pass on the street each night as I walk by the Yale Club en route to Grand Central Station? Am I his brother? What is the nature of our responsibility if we consider ourselves to be ethical persons? Perhaps it is to change the values of the group so that it can, with all its resources, take the other road.

Questions

1. Throughout *The Parable of the Sadhu,* Bowen McCoy refers to the breakdown between the individual and corporate ethic. Explain what he meant by that and how, if we view the hikers on the trek up the mountain in Nepal as an organization, the ethical person-organization fit applied to the decisions made on the climb.
2. Using the various ethical discussions in the first three chapters as your guide, evaluate the actions of McCoy, Stephen, and the rest of the group from an ethical perspective.
3. What role did leadership and culture play in this case?
4. What is the moral of the story of the sadhu from your perspective?

Case 3-2 Rite Aid Inventory Surplus Fraud

Occupational fraud comes in many shapes and sizes. The fraud at Rite Aid is one such case. On February 10, 2015, the U.S. Attorney's Office for the Middle District of Pennsylvania announced that a former Rite Aid vice president, Jay Findling, pleaded guilty to charges in connection with a $29.1 million dollar surplus inventory sales/kickback scheme. Another former vice president, Timothy P. Foster, pleaded guilty to the same charges and making false statements to the authorities. Both charges are punishable by up to five years' imprisonment and a $250,000 fine.

The charges relate to a nine-year conspiracy to defraud Rite Aid by lying to the company about the sale of surplus inventory to a company owned by Findling when it was sold to third parties for greater amounts. Findling would then kick back a portion of his profits to Foster.

Findling admitted he established a bank account under the name "Rite Aid Salvage Liquidation" and used it to collect the payments from the real buyers of the surplus Rite Aid inventory. After the payments were received,

Findling would send lesser amounts dictated by Foster to Rite Aid for the goods, thus inducing Rite Aid to believe the inventory had been purchased by J. Finn Industries, not the real buyers. The government alleged Findling received at least $127.7 million from the real buyers of the surplus inventory but, with Foster's help, only provided $98.6 million of that amount to Rite Aid, leaving Findling approximately $29.1 million in profits from the scheme. The government also alleged that Findling kicked back approximately $5.7 million of the $29.1 million to Foster.

Foster admitted his role during the guilty plea stage of the trial. He voluntarily surrendered $2.9 million in cash he had received from Findling over the life of the conspiracy. Foster had stored the cash in three 5-gallon paint containers in his Phoenix, Arizona, garage.

Assume you are the director of internal auditing at Rite Aid and discover the surplus inventory scheme. You know that Rite Aid has a comprehensive corporate governance system that complies with the requirements of Sarbanes-Oxley and the company has a strong ethics foundation. Moreover, the internal controls are consistent with the COSO framework. Explain the steps you would take to determine whether you would blow the whistle on the scheme applying the requirements of AICPA Interpretation 102-4 that are depicted in Exhibit 3.13. In that regard, answer the following questions.

Questions

1. What steps must you take to be eligible to blow the whistle to the SEC under the Dodd-Frank Financial Reform Act?

2. Would you inform the external auditors about the fraud? Explain.

3. Assume you met all the requirements to blow the whistle under Dodd-Frank. Would you do so? Why or why not?

Case 3-3 United Thermostatic Controls (a GVV case)

United Thermostatic Controls is a publicly owned company that engages in the manufacturing and marketing of residential and commercial thermostats. The thermostats are used to regulate temperature in furnaces and refrigerators. United sells its product primarily to retailers in the domestic market, with the company headquartered in Detroit. Its operations are decentralized according to geographic region. As a publicly owned company, United's common stock is listed and traded on the NYSE. The organization chart for United is presented in Exhibit 1.

EXHIBIT 1   United Thermostatic Controls Organization Chart

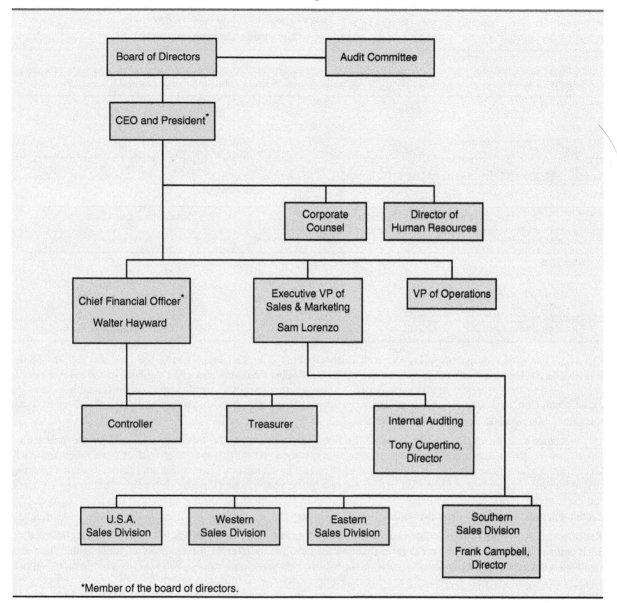

*Member of the board of directors.

Frank Campbell is the director of the Southern sales division. Worsening regional economic conditions and a reduced rate of demand for United's products have created pressures to achieve sales revenue targets set by United management nonetheless. Also, significant pressures exist within the organization for sales divisions to maximize their revenues and earnings for 2015 in anticipation of a public offering of stock early in 2016. Budgeted and actual sales revenue amounts, by division, for the first three quarters in 2015 are presented in Exhibit 2.

EXHIBIT 2   United Thermostatic Controls—Sales Revenue, 2015 (1st 3Qs)

Budgeted and Actual Sales Revenue

First Three Quarters in 2015

	U.S.A. Sales Division			Western Sales Division		
Quarter Ended	**Budget**	**Actual**	**% Var.**	**Budget**	**Actual**	**% Var.**
March 31	$ 632,000	$ 638,000	.009%	$ 886,000	$ 898,000	.014%
June 30	640,000	642,000	.003	908,000	918,000	.011
September 30	648,000	656,000	.012	930,000	936,000	.006
Through September 30	$1,920,000	$1,936,000	.008%	$2,724,000	$2,752,000	.010%

	Eastern Sales Division			Southern Sales Division		
Quarter Ended	**Budget**	**Actual**	**% Var.**	**Budget**	**Actual**	**% Var.**
March 31	$ 743,000	$ 750,000	.009%	$ 688,000	$ 680,000	(.012)%
June 30	752,000	760,000	.011	696,000	674,000	(.032)
September 30	761,000	769,000	.011	704,000	668,000	(.051)
Through September 30	$2,256,000	$2,279,000	.010%	$2,088,000	$2,022,000	(.032)%

Campbell knows that actual sales lagged even further behind budgeted sales during the first two months of the fourth quarter. He also knows that each of the other three sales divisions exceeded their budgeted sales amounts during the first three quarters in 2015. He is very concerned that the Southern division has been unable to meet or exceed budgeted sales amounts. He is particularly worried about the effect this might have on his and the division managers' bonuses and share of corporate profits.

In an attempt to improve the sales revenue of the Southern division for the fourth quarter and for the year ended December 31, 2015, Campbell reviewed purchase orders received during the latter half of November and early December to determine whether shipments could be made to customers prior to December 31. Campbell knows that sometimes orders that are received before the end of the year can be filled by December 31, thereby enabling the division to record the sales revenue during the current fiscal year. It could simply be a matter of accelerating production and shipping to increase sales revenue for the year.

Reported sales revenue of the Southern division for the fourth quarter of 2015 was $792,000. This represented an 18.6 percent increase over the actual sales revenue for the third quarter of the year. As a result of this increase, reported sales revenue for the fourth quarter exceeded the budgeted amount by $80,000, or 11.2 percent. Actual sales revenue for the year exceeded the budgeted amount for the Southern division by $14,000, or 0.5 percent. Budgeted and actual sales revenue amounts, by division, for the year ended December 31, 2015, are presented in Exhibit 3.

During the course of their test of controls, the internal audit staff questioned the appropriateness of recording revenue of $150,000 on two shipments made by the Southern division in the fourth quarter of the year. These shipments are described as follows:

1. United shipped thermostats to Allen Corporation on December 31, 2015, and billed Allen $85,000, even though Allen had specified a delivery date of no earlier than February 1, 2016, to take control of the product. Allen intended to use the thermostats in the heating system of a new building that would not be ready for occupancy until March 1, 2016.

2. United shipped thermostats to Bilco Corporation on December 30, 2015, in partial (one-half) fulfillment of an order. United recorded $65,000 revenue on that date. Bilco had previously specified that partial shipments would not be accepted. Delivery of the full shipment had been scheduled for February 1, 2016.

EXHIBIT 3   United Thermostatic Controls—Sales Revenue, 2015 (4 Qs)

	Budgeted and Actual Sales Revenue in 2015					
	U.S.A. Sales Division			Western Sales Division		
Quarter Ended	**Budget**	**Actual**	**% Var.**	**Budget**	**Actual**	**% Var.**
March 31	$ 632,000	$ 638,000	.009%	$ 886,000	$ 898,000	.014%
June 30	640,000	642,000	.003	908,000	918,000	.011
September 30	648,000	656,000	.012	930,000	936,000	.006
December 31	656,000	662,000	.009	952,000	958,000	.006
2015 Totals	$2,576,000	$2,598,000	.009%	$3,676,000	$3,710,000	.009%

	Eastern Sales Division			Southern Sales Division		
Quarter Ended	**Budget**	**Actual**	**% Var.**	**Budget**	**Actual**	**% Var.**
March 31	$ 743,000	$ 750,000	.009%	$ 688,000	$ 680,000	(.012)%
June 30	752,000	760,000	.011	696,000	674,000	(.032)
September 30	761,000	769,000	.011	704,000	668,000	(.051)
December 31	770,000	778,000	.010	712,000	792,000	.112
2015 Totals	$3,026,000	$3,057,000	.010%	$2,800,000	$2,814,000	.005%

During their investigation, the internal auditors learned that Campbell had pressured United's accounting department to record these two shipments early to enable the Southern division to achieve its goals with respect to the company's revenue targets. The auditors were concerned about the appropriateness of recording the $150,000 revenue in 2015 in the absence of an expressed or implied agreement with the customers to accept and pay for the prematurely shipped merchandise. The auditors noted that, had the revenue from these two shipments not been recorded, the Southern division's actual sales for the fourth quarter would have been below the budgeted amount by $70,000, or 9.8 percent. Actual sales revenue for the year ended December 31, 2015, would have been below the budgeted amount by $136,000, or 4.9 percent. The revenue effect of the two shipments in question created a 5.4 percent shift in the variance between actual and budgeted sales for the year. The auditors felt that this effect was significant with respect to the division's revenue and earnings for the fourth quarter and for the year ended December 31, 2015. The auditors decided to take their concerns to Tony Cupertino, director of the internal auditing department. Cupertino is a licensed CPA.

Cupertino discussed the situation with Campbell. Campbell informed Cupertino that he had received assurances from Sam Lorenzo, executive vice president of sales and marketing, that top management would support the recording of the $150,000 revenue because of its strong desire to meet or exceed budgeted revenue and earnings amounts. Moreover, top management is very sensitive to the need to meet financial analysts' consensus earnings estimates. According to Campbell, the company is concerned that earnings must be high enough to meet analysts' expectations because any other effect might cause the stock price to go down. In fact, Lorenzo has already told Campbell that he did not see anything wrong with recording the revenue in 2015 because the merchandise had been shipped to the customers before the end of the year and the terms of shipment were FOB shipping point.

At this point, Cupertino is uncertain whether he should take his concerns to Walter Hayward, the CFO, who is also a member of the board of directors, or take them directly to the audit committee. Cupertino knows that the majority of the members of the board, including those on the audit committee, have ties to the company and members of top management. Cupertino is not even certain that he should pursue the matter any further because of the financial performance pressures that exist within the organization. However, he is very concerned about his responsibilities as a CPA and obligations to work with the external auditors who will begin their audit in a few weeks. It is at this point that Cupertino learns from Campbell that the CFO of Bilco agreed to accept full shipment when the goods arrive in return for a 20 percent discount on the total price that would be paid on February 1, 2016. Cupertino asked Campbell how he had found out. It seems Campbell took the initiative to help solve the revenue problem by going directly to the Bilco CFO.

Questions

1. Identify the stakeholders in this case and their interests.
2. Describe the ethical and professional responsibilities of Tony Cupertino.
3. Assume you are in Cupertino's position and know you have to do something about the improper accounting in the Southern sales division. Consider the following in crafting a plan how best to voice your values and take appropriate action:

   - How can you get it done effectively and efficiently?
   - What do you need to say, to whom, and in what sequence?
   - What will the objections or pushback be, and then,
   - What would you say next? What data and other information do you need to make your point and counteract the reasons and rationalizations you will likely have to address?

Case 3-4 Franklin Industries' Whistleblowing (a GVV Case)

Natalie got the call she had been waiting for over six long months. Her complaint to the human resources department of Franklin Industries had been dismissed. It was HR's conclusion that she was not retaliated against for reporting an alleged embezzlement by the Accounting Department manager. In fact, HR ruled there was no embezzlement at all. Natalie had been demoted from assistant manager of the department to staff supervisor seven months ago after informing Stuart Masters, the controller, earlier in 2015, about the embezzlement. Her blood started to boil as she thought about all the pain and agony she'd experienced these past six months without any level of satisfaction for her troubles.

Natalie Garson is a CPA who works for Franklin Industries, a publicly owned company and manufacturer of trusses and other structural components for home builders throughout the United States. Six months ago she filed a complaint with HR after discussing a sensitive matter with her best friend and coworker, Roger Harris. Natalie trusted Harris, who had six years of experience at Franklin. The essence of the discussion was that Natalie was informed by the accounting staff of what appeared to be unusual transactions between Denny King, the department manager, and an outside company no one had never heard of before. The staff had uncovered over $5 million in payments, authorized by King, to Vic Construction. No one could find any documentation about Vic, so the staff dug deeper and discovered that the owner of Vic Construction was Victoria King. Further examination determined that Victoria King and Denny King were siblings.

Once Natalie was convinced there was more to the situation than meets the eye, she informed the internal auditors, who investigated and found that Vic Construction made a $5 million electronic transfer to a separate business owned by Denny King. One thing lead to another, and it was determined by the internal auditors that King had funneled $5 million to Vic Construction, which, at a later date, transferred the money back to King. It was a $5 million embezzlement from Franklin Industries.

Natalie met with Roger Harris that night and told him about the HR decision that went against her. She was concerned whether the internal auditors would act now in light of that decision. She knew the culture at Franklin was "don't rock the boat." That didn't matter to her. She was always true to her values and not afraid to act when a wrongdoing had occurred. She felt particularly motivated in this case—it was personal. She felt the need to be vindicated. She hoped Roger would be supportive.

As it turned out, Roger cautioned Natalie about taking the matter any further. He had worked for Franklin a lot longer than Natalie and knew the board of directors consisted mostly of insider directors. The CEO of Franklin was also the chair of the board. It was well known in the company that whatever the CEO wanted to do, the board rubber-stamped it.

Natalie left the meeting with Roger realizing she was on her own. She knew she had to act but didn't know the best way to go about it. Even though Roger cautioned against going to the CEO or board, Natalie didn't dismiss that option.

Questions

Assume you are in Natalie's position. Answer the following questions.

1. Consider the following assuming you have decided to act on your values:

   - What are the main arguments you are trying to counter? That is, what are the reasons and rationalizations you need to address?
   - What is at stake for the key parties, including those who disagree with you?
   - What levers can you use to influence those who disagree with you?
   - What is your most powerful and persuasive response to the reasons and rationalizations you need to address? To whom should the argument be made? When and in what context?

2. Assume you decide not to follow the script outlined in question 1 to bring the matter to the attention of others in the organization for fear of being fired. Do you think you have sufficient standing to file a whistleblower claim with the SEC under the Dodd-Frank Act? Explain.

Case 3-5 Walmart Inventory Shrinkage (a GVV Case)

The facts of this case are from the Walmart shrinkage fraud discussed in an article in *The Nation* on June 11, 2014. "Literary license" has been exercised for the purpose of emphasizing important issues related to organizational ethics at Walmart. Any resemblance to actual people and events is coincidental.[1]

Shane O'Hara always tried to do the right thing. He was in touch with his values and always tried to act in accordance with them, even when the going got tough. But, nothing prepared him for the ordeal he would face as a Walmart veteran and the new store manager in Atomic City, Idaho.

In 2013, Shane was contacted by Jeffrey Cook, the regional manager, and told he was being transferred to the Atomic City store in order to reduce the troubled store's high rate of "shrinkage"—defined as the value of goods that are stolen or otherwise lost—to levels deemed acceptable by the company's senior managers for the region. As a result of fierce competition, profit margins in retail can be razor thin, making shrinkage a potent—sometimes critical—factor in profitability. Historically, Walmart had a relatively low rate of about 0.8 percent of sales. The industry average was 1 percent.

Prior to his arrival at the Atomic City store, Shane had heard the store had shrinkage losses as high as $2 million or more—a sizable hit to its bottom line. There had even been talk of closing the store altogether. He knew the pressure was on to keep the store open, save the jobs of 40 people, and cut losses so that the regional manager could earn a bonus. It didn't hurt that he would qualify for a bonus as well, so long as the shrinkage rate was cut by more than two-thirds.

Shane did what he could to tighten systems and controls. He managed to convince Cook to hire an "asset-protection manager" for the store. The asset-protection program handles shrink, safety, and security at each of its stores. The program worked. Not only did shrinkage decline but other forms of loss, including changing price tags on items of clothing, were significantly reduced.

However, it didn't seem to be enough to satisfy Cook and top management. During the last days of August 2013, Shane's annual inventory audit showed a massive reduction in the store's shrinkage rate that surprised even him:

[1]Spencer Woodman, "Former Managers Allege Pervasive Inventory Fraud at Walmart: How Deep Does the Rot Go?" *The Nation,* June 11, 2014.

down to less than $80,000 from roughly $800,000 the previous year. He had no explanation for it, but was sure the numbers had been doctored in some way.

During the remainder of 2013, a number of high-level managers departed from the company. Cindy Rondel, the head of Walmart's Idaho operations, retired; so did her superior, Larry Brooks. Walmart's regional asset-protection manager for Idaho, who was intimately involved with inventory tracking in the state, was fired as well. Shane wondered if he was next.

Shane decided to contact Cook to discuss his concerns. Cook explained why the shrinkage rate had shrunk so much by passing it off as improper accounting at the Atomic City store that had been corrected. He told Shane that an investigation would begin immediately and he was suspended with pay until it was completed. Shane was in shock. He knew the allegations weren't true. He sensed he might become the fall guy for the fraud.

Shane managed to discretely talk about his situation with another store manager in the Atomic City area. That manager said she had been the target of a similar investigation the year before. In her case, she had discovered how the fraud was carried out and the numbers were doctored, but she had told no one—until now.

She explained to Shane that the fraud involved simply declaring that missing items were not in fact missing. She went on to say you could count clothing items in the store and if the on-hand count was off—as in, you were supposed to have 12 but you only had 10—you could explain that the other 2 were in a bin where clothing had been tried on by customers, not bought, and left in the dressing room often with creases that had to be cleaned before re-tagging the clothing for sale. So, even though some items may have been stolen, they were still counted as part of inventory. There was little or no shrinkage to account for.

At this point Shane did not know what his next step should be. He needed to protect his good name and reputation. But what steps should he take? That was the question.

Questions

Assume you are in Shane O'Hara's position. Answer the following questions.

1. Who are the stakeholders in this case and what are the ethical issues?
2. What would you do next and why? Consider the following in crafting your response.
   - How should the organizational culture at Walmart influence your actions?
   - What do you need to say, to whom, and in what sequence?
   - What are the reasons and rationalizations you are likely to hear from those who would try to detract you from your goal?
   - How can you counteract those pressures? What is your most powerful and persuasive response to these arguments? To whom should you make them? When and in what context?

Case 3-6 Bennie and the Jets (a GVV Case)

Bennie Gordon graduated with a master's in accounting two years ago and now works as an accounting manager at the division level at Jet Energy Company, a company headquartered in Winston-Salem, North Carolina. Jet Energy is a utility company regulated by the state and provides electricity to 7 million customers in southern states. Jet Energy is allowed a maximum rate of return on operating income of 12.5 percent on electricity it sells. If the company is earning more than that, regulators can cut the rate that it charges its customers.

Gordon reports to Sarah Higgins, the controller of the division. Higgins reports to Sam Thornton, the chief financial officer. Thornton reports to Vanessa Jones, the CEO of the company. Joan Franks is the chief compliance officer. The company has an audit committee of three members, all of whom sit on the board of directors.

Gordon has identified irregular accounting entries dealing with the reclassification of some accounting items to make the company's returns lower so state regulators would not cut rates. One example is that Jet Energy often gets rebates from insurers of its nuclear plants, based on safety records. Although the cost of the premiums is expensed to the electricity business, the rebates—approximately $26 million to $30.5 million each—were not booked back to the same accounts. On a number of occasions, they were booked below operating income in a non-operating account. The moves kept Jet Energy from exceeding its allowable returns and kept the states from reducing electricity rates.

After two years of being silent, Gordon decided it was time to address the issue. He knows his options include to report the matter to top management and/or the North Carolina Utilities Commission.

Questions

1. What process would you recommend Bennie Gordon follow in bringing his concerns out in the open? Do these include whistleblowing?
2. Assume you are Bennie's best friend and he asks you for advice. Consider the following in putting together a plan of action for Bennie to follow.

   - What are the ethical values that should be front and center in deciding how best to advise Bennie on what to do?
   - What reasons and rationalizations do you anticipate may be lodged by stakeholders based on the advice you might give? How would you counter them?
   - What levers can Bennie use to influence those that might disagree with him?
   - What is your final advice to Bennie and why?

Case 3-7 Olympus

Summary of the Case *

On September 25, 2012, Japanese camera and medical equipment maker Olympus Corporation and three of its former executives pleaded guilty to charges related to an accounting scheme and cover-up in one of Japan's biggest corporate scandals. Olympus admitted that it tried to conceal investment losses by using improper accounting under a scheme that began in the 1990s.

The scandal was exposed in 2011 by Olympus's then-CEO, Michael C. Woodford. As the new president of Olympus, he felt obliged to investigate the matter and uncovered accounting irregularities and suspicious deals involving the acquisition of U.K. medical equipment manufacturer Gyrus. He called the company's auditors, PwC, to report it. The firm examined payments of £1.1 billion (US$687) related to financial advice on the acquisition paid to a non-existent Cayman Islands firm. A fraud of $1.7 billion emerged, including an accounting scandal to hide the losses. Along the way, the Japanese way of doing business came under attack by Woodford.

Olympus initially said that it fired Woodford, one of a handful of foreign executives at top Japanese companies, over what it called his aggressive Western management style. Woodford disclosed internal documents to show he was dismissed after he raised questions about irregular payouts related to mergers and acquisitions. Without any serious attempt by management to investigate, he went behind the board's back and commissioned a report by PwC into the Gyrus deal, including the unusually high advisory fee and apparent lack of due diligence. On October 11, 2011, he circulated the report to the board and called on the chair of the board, Tsuyoshi Kikukawa, and executive vice president Hisashi Mori to resign. Three days later, the board fired Woodford.

Ultimately, the accounting fraud was investigated by the Japanese authorities. "The full responsibility lies with me, and I feel deeply sorry for causing trouble to our business partners, shareholders, and the wider public," Kikukawa told the Tokyo district court. "I take full responsibility for what happened."

---

* The facts of this case are drawn from: Michael Woodford, *Exposure: Inside the Olympus Scandal: How I Went from CEO to Whistleblower* (NY: Penguin Books, 2012).

Prosecutors charged Kikukawa, Mori, and a former internal auditor, Hideo Yamada, with inflating the company's net worth in financial statements for five fiscal years up to March 2011 due to accounting for risky investments made in the late-1980s bubble economy. The three former executives had been identified by an investigative panel, commissioned by Olympus, as the main suspects in the fraud. In December 2011, Olympus filed five years' worth of corrected financial statements plus overdue first-half results, revealing a $1.1 billion hole in its balance sheet.

An Olympus spokesman said the company would cooperate fully with the investigative authorities. It is under investigation by law enforcement agencies in Japan, Britain, and the United States. On April 2, 2015, Olympus reached an ¥11 billion ($92 million) out-of-court settlement in Japan with institutional investors over allegations of accounting fraud.

Olympus Spent Huge Sums on Inflated Acquisitions, Advisory Fees to Conceal Investment Losses

Olympus's cover-up of massive losses has shed light on several murky methods that some companies employed to clean up the mess left after Japan's economic bubble burst. Many companies turned to speculative investments as they suffered sluggish sales and stagnant operating profits. The company used "loss-deferring practices" to make losses look smaller on the books by selling bad assets to related companies.

To take investment losses off its books, Olympus spent large sums of money to purchase British medical equipment maker Gyrus Group PLC and three Japanese companies and paid huge consulting fees. Olympus is suspected of having deliberately acquired Gyrus at an inflated price, and in the year following the purchase, it booked impairment losses as a result of decreases in the company's value.

To avert a rapid deterioration of its financial standing, Olympus continued corporate acquisitions and other measures for many years, booking impairment losses to improve its balance sheet. Losses on the purchases of the three Japanese companies amounted to $34.5 billion. With money paid on the Gyrus deal included, Olympus may have used more than $62.5 billion in funds for past acquisitions to conceal losses on securities investments.

The previous method that recorded stocks and other financial products by book value—the price when they were purchased—was abolished. The new method listed them by market value (mark-to-market accounting). Under this change, Olympus had to report all the losses in its March 2001 report. However, Olympus anticipated this change a year in advance and posted only about $10.6 billion of the nearly $62.5 billion as an extraordinary loss for the March 2000 settlement term. The company did not post the remainder as a deficit; rather, it deferred it using questionable measures.

Olympus's Tobashi Scheme

At the heart of Olympus's action was a once-common technique to hide losses called *tobashi*, which Japanese financial regulators tolerated before clamping down on the practice in the late 1990s. *Tobashi,* translated loosely as "to blow away," enables companies to hide losses on bad assets by selling those assets to other companies, only to buy them back later through payments, often disguised as advisory fees or other transactions, when market conditions or earnings improve.

Tobashi allows a company with the bad assets to mask losses temporarily, a practice banned in the early 2000s. The idea is that you pay off the losses later, when company finances are better.

Olympus appears to have pushed to settle its *tobashi* amounts from 2006 to 2008, when the local economy was picking up and corporate profits were rebounding, in an effort to "clean up its act." Business was finally strong enough to be able to withstand a write-down. It was during those years that the company engineered the payouts that came under scrutiny: $687 million in fees to an obscure financial adviser over Olympus's acquisition of Gyrus in 2008, a fee that was roughly a third of the $2 billion acquisition price, more than 30 times the norm. Olympus also acquired three small Japanese companies from 2006 to 2008 with little in common with its core business for a total of $773 million, only to write down most of their value within the same fiscal year.

Olympus Scandal Raises Questions about the "Japan Way" of Doing Business

The scandal rocked corporate Japan, not least because of the company's succession of firings, denials, admissions, and whistleblowing. It also exposed weaknesses in Japan's financial regulatory system and corporate governance.

"This is a case where Japan's outmoded practice of corporate governance remained and reared its ugly head," according to Shuhei Abe, president of Tokyo-based Sparx Group Company. "With Olympus's case, it will no longer be justifiable for Japan Inc. to continue practicing under the excuse of the 'Japan way of doing things.'"

On the surface, Olympus seemed to have checks on its management. For example, it hired directors and auditors from outside the company, as well as a British president who was not tied to corporate insiders. In reality, however, the company's management was ruled by former chairman Kikukawa and a few other executives who came from its financial sections.

The company's management is believed to have been effectively controlled by several executives who had a background in financial affairs, including Kikukawa and Mori, both of whom were involved in the cover-up of past losses. Olympus's board of auditors, which is supposed to supervise the board of directors, included full-time auditor Hideo Yamada, who also had financial expertise.

After Woodford made his allegations, he was confronted by a hostile board of directors that acted based on the premise that whistleblowing offended their corporate culture. Subsequently, the board fired him saying that he had left because of "differences in management styles." Employees were warned not to speak to him or jeopardize their careers.

One problem with corporate governance in Japan is truly independent non-executive directors are unusual. Many Japanese do not see the need for such outside intervention. They question how outsiders can know enough about the company to make a valuable contribution. Moreover, how could they be sensitive to the corporate culture? They could even damage the credibility of the group.

Accounting Explanations

Olympus hid a $1.7 billion loss through an intricate array of transactions.

A one-paragraph summary of what it did appears in the investigation report:

> The lost disposition scheme is featured in that Olympus sold the assets that incurred loss to the funds set up by Olympus itself, and later provided the finance needed to settle the loss under the cover of the company acquisitions. More specifically, Olympus circulated money either by flowing money into the funds by acquiring the entrepreneurial ventures owned by the funds at the substantially higher price than the real values, or by paying a substantially high fee to the third party who acted as the intermediate in the acquisition, resulting in recognition of a large amount of goodwill, and subsequently amortized goodwill recognized impairment loss, which created substantial loss.

Here is a more understandable version of the event:

> Olympus indirectly loaned money to an off-the-books subsidiary and then sold the investments that had the huge losses to the subsidiary at historical cost, eventually paying a huge premium to buy some other small companies and writing off the underwater investments as if they were goodwill impairments.

A more detailed bookkeeping analysis of the complicated transactions appears in Exhibit 1.

Auditor Responsibilities

Arthur Andersen was the external auditor through March 31, 2002, after which Andersen closed its doors for good in the post-Enron era. Then KPMG AZSA LLC was the auditor through March 31, 2009. The 2010 and 2011 fiscal years were audited by Ernst & Young ShinNihon LLC.

The investigative report noted that the fraud was hidden quite well. Three banks were involved in hiding information from the auditors. The summary report said that all three of them agreed not to tell auditors the information that would normally be provided on an audit confirmation.

KPMG did come across one of the *tobashi* schemes carried out through one of the three different routes that had been set up. According to the investigative report:

Not everything was going smoothly. The report said that in 1999, Olympus's then-auditor, KPMG AZSA LLC, came across information that indicated the company was engaged in *tobashi,* which recently had become illegal in

Japan. Mori and Yamada initially denied KPMG's assertion, but the auditor pushed them that same year to admit to the presence of one fund and unwind it, booking a loss of $10.5 billion. The executives assured KPMG that that was the only such deal, the report said. However, the schemes expanded, without detection, for another six years or so and was in place, without detection, until the last component was unwound at the end of fiscal year 2010.

Olympus Finally Had Enough of the Deception

The last part of the bad investments was finally written off in March 2011. That was the last month of the fiscal year, when Ernst & Young took over the audit from KPMG. Mori and Yamada had finally decided to unwind and write off the underwater financial assets and repay the loans that Olympus had made through its unconsolidated subsidiary. Of course, by then, the financial press had gotten wind of what was going on at Olympus.

EXHIBIT 1 Detailed Bookkeeping Analysis of Olympus's Accounting Fraud*

PHASE 1

Transaction 1:

This is a summary of a complex move—it involved purchasing a certificate of deposit (CD) at several banks that were asked to loan the money back to an unrelated entity, with the CD as collateral, so the subsidiary can buy investments from Olympus.

Note: According to the investigative committee's report, three banks were involved through the course of the whole project: Commerzbank, LGT, and Société Générale. The committee's report indicates that all three banks agreed to Olympus's request not to tell the auditors about the CDs being collateral for a loan.

(Olympus books)

DR Certificate of deposit
CR Cash
   (CD purchase at banks; banks loan it to unconsolidated subsidiary)

(Unconsolidated subsidiary books)

DR Cash
CR Note payable to banks
   (Cash from banks; collateralized by Olympus)

Transaction 2:

(Olympus books)

DR Cash
CR Financial assets (Investments)
   (Proceeds from selling underwater investments to unconsolidated subsidiary; may have triggered gain on sale)

(Unconsolidated subsidiary books)

DR Financial assets (Investments)
CR Cash
   (To buy underwater investments from Olympus)

PHASE 2

Eventually the CDs would have to be rolled over and brought back. In addition, the unrealized losses would have to be written down eventually, so the second phase was launched.

*"Olympus Scandal: $1.5 billion in Losses Hidden in Dodgy Acquisitions," Available at http://factsanddetails.com/japan.php?itemid=2305&catid=24&subcatid=157.

(Continued)

Transaction 3:

Olympus bought some tiny (startup) companies. It paid significantly more than they were worth and paid large amounts for consultants for their service as finders and intermediaries.

(Olympus books)
DR Investments (startup subsidiary)
DR Goodwill—(cash paid less fair market value of subsidiary net assets)
CR Cash
    (Investments in new subsidiaries)

Note: The investment in the consolidated subsidiary shows a large amount of goodwill, which could then be written down.

(Entries by the newly formed consolidated subsidiary)
DR Cash
CR Common stock
    (Cash investment from Olympus)

Transaction 4:

The effect of these transactions was to transfer money into the newest consolidated subsidiary, which used the money to buy the bad investments from the older, unconsolidated subsidiary. The unconsolidated subsidiary then repaid the note payable to the bank and Olympus liquidated its CD.

(Entries by the newly formed consolidated subsidiary)
DR Financial assets (Investments)
CR Cash
    (Buy underwater investments from unconsolidated subsidiary at book value)

(Unconsolidated subsidiary books)

DR Cash (from consolidated subsidiary)
CR Financial assets (Investments)
    (Proceeds received from consolidated subsidiary from sale of underwater investments)
DR Note payable to banks
CR Cash
    (Repay loan to banks)

Entries by Olympus
DR Cash
CR Certificate of deposit
    (CD liquidated)

Questions

1. Does it seem reasonable that Olympus engaged in an accounting fraud for so long and the auditors did not detect it? Were the transactions in question and accounting for them something that should have been detected earlier through proper auditing procedures? What caused the failure of the auditors to act on the fraud? Explain.

2. Evaluate the corporate culture at Olympus including corporate governance. What were the shortcomings and what do you think caused them?

3. Do you believe Michael Woodford did the right thing by blowing the whistle on accounting irregularities? Were there other options open to him? Once he was fired, could he have made a whistleblower's claim with the SEC under Dodd-Frank? Why or why not?

Case 3-8 Accountant takes on Halliburton and Wins!

The whistleblowing aspects of this case were first discussed in the text. What follows is a more comprehensive discussion of accounting and auditing issues.

In 2005, Tony Menendez, a former Ernst & Young LLP auditor and director of technical accounting and research training for Halliburton, blew the whistle on Halliburton's accounting practices. The fight cost him nine years of his life. Just a few months later in 2005, Menendez received an e-mail from Mark McCollum, Halliburton's chief accounting officer, and a top-ranking executive at Halliburton, that also went to much of the accounting department. "The SEC has opened an inquiry into the allegations of Mr. Menendez," it read. Everyone was to retain their documents until further notice.

What happened next changed the life of Menendez and brought into question how such a large and influential company could have such a failed corporate governance system. Further, the role of the auditors, KPMG, with respect to its handling of accounting and auditing matters, seemed off, and independence was an issue. Exhibit 1 summarizes some of the relevant accounting and auditing issues in the case.

EXHIBIT 1   Issues Related to the Sarbanes-Oxley Act, SEC, and KPMG

Tony Menendez contacted Halliburton's audit committee because he believed it was in the best interest of the employees and shareholders if he made himself available to the committee in its efforts to investigate the questionable accounting and auditing practices and properly respond to the SEC. It was discovered that Halliburton did not have in place, as required by Section 301 of the Sarbanes-Oxley Act (SOX), a process for "(1) the receipt and treatment of complaints received by the issuer regarding accounting, internal controls, or auditing matters; and (2) the confidential, anonymous submission of employees of the issuer of concerns regarding questionable accounting or auditing matters."

After waiting for the company to take action to no avail, Menendez felt there was no alternative to blowing the whistle and on November 4, 2005, he contacted the SEC and PCAOB stating in part:

"As a CPA and the Director of Technical Accounting Research and Training for Halliburton, I feel it is my duty and obligation to report information that I believe constitutes both a potential failure by a registered public accounting firm, KPMG, to properly perform an audit and the potential filing of materially misleading financial information with the SEC by Halliburton."

Two weeks later, at the agencies' request, he met with SEC enforcement staff at their Fort Worth office. On November 30, 2005, he· approached members of top management of Halliburton. On February 4, 2006, Menendez provided what he believed would be a confidential report to Halliburton's audit committee, giving the company yet another opportunity for self-examination. However, on the morning of February 6, 2006, Menendez's identity was disclosed to Mark McCollum, Halliburton's chief accounting officer, and less than an hour after finding out that Menendez had reported the questionable accounting and auditing practices to the SEC, McCollum distributed information about Menendez's investigation and identity.

The disclosure was followed by a series of retaliatory actions. Halliburton management stripped Menendez of teaching and researching responsibilities, ordered subordinates to monitor and report on his activity, excluded him from meetings and accounting decisions, and ordered financial and accounting personnel to pre-clear any conversations about accounting issues before discussing them with Menendez.

In May 2005, Menendez filed a civil whistleblower complaint under SOX. In July 2006, Halliburton told the Department of Labor committee handling the case that KPMG had insisted that Menendez be excluded from a meeting concerning accounting for a potential joint venture arrangement called "RTA." Halliburton indicated it acceded to KPMG's demand and excluded Menendez from the meeting. SOX prohibits an employer from discriminating against an employee, contractor, or agent and from prohibiting such party from engaging in activity protected under the Act, and the SEC

(Continued)

stated that the assertion by the company that KPMG's presence was mandatory was misleading. In fact, the SEC opined that KPMG's presence was not even advisable since KPMG was supposed to be an independent auditor in both appearance and in fact.

The RTA meeting was scheduled to determine whether or not Halliburton would be required to consolidate the proposed joint venture. Senior management explicitly stated that the division management would not receive approval to proceed unless Halliburton could both avoid consolidation and maintain control over the joint venture activities. Earlier in the development of the accounting position regarding this joint venture, KPMG told management that it would allow the company to avoid consolidation and FIN 46R's Anti-Abuse criteria on the basis that the determination required professional judgment, and indicated that KPMG would be willing to support a conclusion that Halliburton was not significantly involved in the joint venture activities, when clearly the facts and circumstances did not support such a conclusion. Menendez had vehemently objected to KPMG and management's proposed conclusion on the basis that such a position was absurd.

According to the SEC, given KPMG's previous guidance to the company regarding RTA, and its willingness to accommodate unsupportable conclusions, continued input by KPMG on RTA was inappropriate and, once again, put KPMG in the position of auditing its own recommendations and advice. In the end, the concerted failures of management and the external auditor underscored the lack of independence between company and KPMG, which was a root cause of the accounting violations Menendez fought to correct and, at last, had to report.

Nature of Halliburton's Revenue Transactions in Question

During the months following the "leaked" e-mail, Menendez waited and watched to see if Halliburton would act on his claims that the company was cooking the books. The issue was revenue recognition as discussed following.

Halliburton enters into long-term contracts with energy giants like Royal Dutch Shell or BP to find and exploit huge oil and gas fields. It sells services—the expertise of its geologists and engineers. Halliburton also builds massive and expensive machinery that its professionals use to provide those services. Then, the company charges its customers for that equipment, which has particularly high profit margins. At the crux of the matter, the company's accountants had been allowing the company to count the full value of the equipment right away as revenue, sometimes even before it had assembled the equipment. But the customers could walk away in the middle of the contracts. Menendez realized that if the equipment were damaged, Halliburton, not the customer, was on the hook.

Menendez accused Halliburton of using so-called bill-and-hold techniques that distort the timing of billions of dollars in revenue and allowed Halliburton to book product sales before they occurred.

Menendez explained Halliburton's accounting this way:

> For example, the company recognizes revenue when the goods are parked in company warehouses, rather than delivered to the customer. Typically, these goods are not even assembled and ready for the customer. Furthermore, it is unknown as to when the goods will be ultimately assembled, tested, delivered to the customer, and, finally, used by the company to perform the required oilfield services for the customer.

Based on Menendez's claims, Halliburton's accounting procedures violated generally accepted accounting principles. For companies to recognize revenue before delivery, "the risks of ownership must have passed to the buyer," the SEC's staff wrote in a 2003 accounting bulletin. There also "must be a fixed schedule for delivery of the goods" and the product "must be complete and ready for shipment" among other things.

Shortly after joining Halliburton in March 2005, Menendez said he discovered a "terribly flawed" flow chart on the company's in-house Web site, called the Bill and Hold Decision Tree. The flow chart, a copy of which Menendez included in his complaint, walks through what to do in a situation where a "customer has been billed for completed inventory which is being stored at a Halliburton facility."

First, it asks: Based on the contract terms, "has title passed to customer?" If the answer is no—and here's where it gets strange—the employee is asked: "Does the transaction meet all of the 'bill-and-hold' criteria for revenue recognition?" If the answer to that question is yes, the decision tree says to do this: "Recognize revenue." The decision tree didn't specify what the other criteria were.

In other words, Halliburton told employees to recognize revenue even though the company still owned the product. Ironically, the accelerated revenue for financial statement purposes led to higher income taxes paid to the IRS.

"The policy in the chart is clearly at odds with generally accepted accounting principles," said Charles Mulford, a Georgia Institute of Technology accounting professor, who reviewed the court records. "It's very clear cut. It's not gray."

According to the accounting rules, it is possible to use bill-and-hold and comply with the rules. But it's hard. The customer, not the seller, must request such treatment. The customer also must have a compelling reason for doing so. Customers rarely do.

Top Halliburton accounting executives had agreed with Menendez's analysis, including McCollum, the company's chief accounting officer. But according to Menendez, they dragged their feet on implementing a change that was certain to slow revenue growth. In an e-mail response to detailed questions, a Halliburton spokeswoman wrote, "The accounting allegations were made by Mr. Menendez almost nine years ago and were promptly reviewed by the company and the Securities and Exchange Commission. The company's accounting was appropriate and the SEC closed its investigation." This seems curious when we examine the SEC's own rules for recognition.

Hocus Pocus Accounting: Bill-and-Hold Schemes

The proper accounting for Halliburton's bill-and-hold transactions was not lost on its external auditors, KPMG. In fact, in early 2005, KPMG published an article entitled: *Bill and Hold Transactions in the Oilfield Services Industry,* which made it clear that oilfield services companies had to comply with all four criteria of SEC Staff Accounting Bulletin (SAB 101) to recognize revenue early. These include:

- Persuasive evidence of an arrangement exists;
- Delivery has occurred or services have been rendered;
- The seller's price to the buyer is fixed or determinable; and
- Collectibility is reasonably assured.

KPMG went on to recognize that it would be rare for an oilfield services company to actually meet the necessary criteria. The impact to Halliburton was highlighted by KPMG's recognition that bill-and-hold transactions for oilfield services companies were "common" and "involve very large and complex products and equipment that carry significant amounts of economic value." KPMG went on to state that "perhaps no area of revenue recognition has received as much scrutiny as bill-and-hold."

Menendez's Complaint to the DOL

Menendez's allegations are part of a 54-page complaint he filed against Halliburton with a Department of Labor (DOL) administrative-law judge in Covington, Louisiana, who released the records to Menendez in response to a Freedom of Information Act request. Menendez claimed Halliburton retaliated against him in violation of the Sarbanes-Oxley Act's whistleblower provisions after he reported his concerns to the SEC and the company's audit committee.

According to a company spokesperson, Halliburton's audit committee "directed an independent investigation" and "concluded that the allegations were without merit." She declined to comment on bill-and-hold issues, and Halliburton's court filings in the case don't provide any details about its accounting practices.

Menendez filed his complaint shortly after a DOL investigator in Dallas rejected his retaliation claim. His initial claim was rejected by the court and subsequently appealed after many years, and the decision was ultimately overturned, but not until after he and his family had endured a nine-year ordeal during which time he was an outcast at Halliburton.

The Final Verdict Is In: Accountant Takes on Halliburton and Wins!

The appeals process went on for three years. In September 2011, the administrative-law appeals panel ruled. It overturned the original trial judge. After five years, Menendez had his first victory.

But it wasn't over. Halliburton appealed to the Fifth Circuit Court of Appeals. There were more legal filings, more hours of work, more money spent.

Finally, in November 2014, almost nine years after Menendez received "The E-mail," he prevailed. The appeals panel ruled that he indeed had been retaliated against for blowing the whistle, just as he had argued all along.

Because he had wanted only to be proven right, he'd asked for a token sum. The administrative-law panel, noting the importance of punishing retaliations against whistleblowers, pushed for an increase and Menendez was awarded $30,000.

To say that the outcome stunned experts is something of an understatement. "Accountant beats Halliburton!'' said Thomas, the attorney and expert on whistleblower law. "The government tries to beat Halliburton and loses."

Post-Decision Interview about Whistleblowing

In an interview with a reporter, Menendez offered that Halliburton had a whistleblower policy prior to this incident as required under Sarbanes-Oxley. It was required to be confidential, and although Halliburton's policy promised confidentiality, at the same time it discouraged anonymous complaints on the basis that if you didn't provide your identity, the company might not be able to properly investigate your concern. Menendez added that confidentiality was absolutely central to his case and he relied on this policy but it was Halliburton that blatantly ignored its own policy and betrayed his trust.

He was asked how the whistleblowing policy of the SEC might be improved. He said that all too often it is almost impossible for a whistleblower to prevail and that there needs to be more protections and a more balanced playing field. "It shouldn't take nine years and hundreds of thousands of dollars to even have a remote chance of prevailing," he said.

The Human Aspect of the Case

Menendez felt he had to leave Halliburton because of the retaliation and how everyone treated him differently after the e-mail. During the appeals process, as Menendez and his wife waited for vindication and money got tight, he finally caught a break. Through the accounting experts he had met during his legal odyssey, he heard that General Motors was looking for a senior executive.

He agonized over whether to tell interviewers about his showdown with Halliburton. Ultimately, he figured they would probably find out anyway. When he flew up to Detroit and met with Nick Cypress, GM's chief accounting officer and comptroller, he came clean. Cypress had heard good things about Menendez from Doug Carmichael, the accounting expert who had been Menendez's expert witness at trial.

After telling him, Menendez asked Cypress, "Does this bother you?"

"Hell no!" the GM executive replied.

This was not the typical reaction top corporate officers have to whistleblowers. The interviewer asked Cypress about it: "I was moved by it," he explained. "It takes a lot of courage to stand tall like that, and I needed that in the work we were doing. I needed people with high integrity who would work hard who I could trust" to bring problems directly to senior management.

Today, Menendez still works at GM. His job is overseeing how GM recognizes about $100 billion worth of revenue, the very issue underlying his struggle with Halliburton. In the meantime, Halliburton has thrived. The SEC never levied any penalty for the accounting issue raised by Menendez. In 2014, the company generated $3.5 billion in profit on $33 billion in revenue. It's not possible to tell if the company maintains the same revenue recognition policy from its public filings, says GT professor Mulford. But since the SEC passed on an enforcement action on the issue, the company likely feels it is in accordance with accounting rules. (Mulford believes that Menendez was right back then and that the SEC should have looked harder at the issue initially.)

Many of the Halliburton and KPMG officials involved in the accounting issue or the retaliation have continued to prosper in the corporate ranks. One is now Halliburton's chief accounting officer. McCollum is now the company's executive vice president overseeing the integration of a major merger. The KPMG executive who disagreed with Menendez is now a partner at the accounting firm.

Menendez did not tell his friends and family of his legal victory. He's more cautious than he used to be. "I changed a lot. It was almost 10 years where everything was in question. Wondering what would people think of you."

He and his wife still worry that disaster could arrive in the next e-mail. "It can really weaken a soul and tear apart a family or a marriage, if you aren't careful. Because of the enormous powers of a company," said his wife. If people asked her advice, she said, "I'd probably say don't do it."

Recently, Menendez finally explained the story to his son, Cameron, who is now 13 and old enough to understand. Cameron's response: "You should have asked for more money, Dad," the teenager said. "We could use it."

Years ago, Menendez and his wife bought a bottle of champagne to celebrate his eventual victory. They still haven't opened it.

Questions

1. Describe the inadequacies in the corporate governance system at Halliburton.
2. Consider the role of KPMG in the case with respect to the accounting and auditing issues. How did the firm's actions relate to the ethical and professional expectations for CPAs by the accounting profession?
3. Some critics claim that while Menendez's actions may have been courageous, he harmed others along the way. His family was in limbo for many years and had to deal with the agony of being labeled a whistleblower and disloyal to Halliburton. The company's overall revenue did not change; a small amount was merely shifted to an earlier period. Halliburton didn't steal any money, cheat the IRS, or cheat their customers or their employees. In fact, it lessened its cash flows by paying out taxes earlier than it should have under the rules.

   How do you respond to these criticisms?

Case 3-9 Bhopal, India: A Tragedy of Massive Proportions

We are citizens of the world. The tragedy of our times is that we do not know this.
Woodrow T. Wilson (1856–1924), 28th president of the United States

At five past midnight on December 3, 1984, 40 tons of the chemical methyl isocynate (MIC), a toxic gas, started to leak out of a pesticide tank at the Union Carbide plant in Bhopal, India. The leak was first detected by workers about 11:30 p.m. on December 2, 1984, when their eyes began to tear and burn. According to AcuSafe,[1] "in 1991 the official Indian government panel charged with tabulating deaths and injuries counted more than 3,800 dead and approximately 11,000 with disabilities." However, estimates now range as high as 8,000 killed in the first three days and over 120,000 injured.[2] There were 4,000 deaths officially recorded by the government, although 13,000 death claims were filed with the government, according to a United Nations report, and hundreds of thousands more claim injury as a result of the disaster.[3] On June 7, 2010, an Indian court convicted eight former senior employees of Union Carbide's Indian subsidiary to two years in jail each for causing "death by negligence" over their part in the Bhopal gas tragedy in which an estimated 15,000 people died more than 25 years ago. While the actual numbers may be debatable, there can be no doubt that the Bhopal incident raises a variety of interesting ethical questions, including:

[1] AcuSafe is an Internet resource for safety and risk management information that is a publication of AcuTech, a global leader in process safety and security risk management located in Houston, Texas; see www.acusafe.com/Incidents/Bhopal1984/incidentbhopal1984.htm.

[2] According to CorpWatch, www.corpwatch.org/.

[3] United Nations, *United Nations University Report (UNU Report) on Toxic Gas Leak*, Available at: www.unu.edu/unupress/unupbooks/uu21le/uu211eOc.htm.

- What were the values that motivated the response of Union Carbide to the Bhopal disaster?
- Did the company wittingly or unwittingly do a utilitarian analysis of the potential harms and costs of fixing the problems at the Bhopal plant and benefits of doing so?
- Do the actions of management at Union Carbide reflect failed leadership?

You make up your own mind as you read about the tragedy that is Bhopal.

In the Beginning

On May 4, 1980, the first factory exported from the West to make pesticides using MIC began production in Bhopal, India. The company planned to export the chemicals from the United States to make the pesticide Sevin. The new CEO of Union Carbide came over from the United States especially for the occasion.[4]

As you might expect, the company seemed very concerned about safety issues. "Carbide's manifesto set down certain truths, the first being that 'all accidents are avoidable provided the measures necessary to avoid them are defined and implemented.'" The company's slogan was "Good safety and good accident prevention practices are good business."

Safety Measures

The Union Carbide plant in Bhopal was equipped with an alarm system with a siren that was supposed to be set off whenever the "duty supervisor in the control room" sensed even the slightest indication that a possible fire might be developing "or the smallest emission of toxic gas." The "alarm system was intended to warn the crews working on the factory site." Even though thousands of people lived in the nearby *bustees* (shantytowns), "none of the loudspeakers pointed outward" in their direction. Still, they could hear the sirens coming from the plant. The siren went off so frequently that it seemed as though the population became used to it and wasn't completely aware that one death and several accidental poisonings had occurred before the night of December 2, and there was a "mysterious fire in the alpha-naphtol unit."

In May 1982, three engineers from Union Carbide came to Bhopal to evaluate the plant and confirm that everything was operating according to company standards. However, the investigators identified more than 60 violations of operational and safety regulations. An Indian reporter managed to obtain a copy of the report that noted "shoddy workmanship," warped equipment, corroded circuitry, "the absence of automatic sprinklers in the MIC and phosgene production zones," a lack of pressure gauges, and numerous other violations. The severest criticism was in the area of personnel. There was "an alarming turnover of inadequately trained staff, unsatisfactory instruction methods, and a lack of rigor in maintenance reports."

The reporter wrote three articles proclaiming the unsafe plant. The third article was titled "If You Refuse to Understand, You Will Be Reduced to Dust." Nothing seemed to matter in the end because the population was assured by Union Carbide and government representatives that no one need be concerned because the phosgene produced at the plant was not a toxic gas.

The Accident

The accident occurred when a large volume of water entered the MIC storage tanks and triggered a violent chain reaction. Normally, water and MIC were kept separate, but on the night of December 2, "metal barriers known as slip blinds were not inserted and the cleaning water passed directly into the MIC tanks." It is possible that additional water entered the tanks later on in the attempts to control the reaction. Shortly after the introduction of water, "temperatures and pressures in the tanks increased to the point of explosion."

The report of consultants that reviewed the facts surrounding the accident indicates that workers made a variety of attempts to save the plant, including:[5]

---

[4]Dominique LaPierre and Javier Moro, *Five Past Midnight in Bhopal* (New York: Warner Books, 2002).

[5]Ron Graham, "FAQ on Failures: Union Carbide Bhopal," Barrett Engineering Consulting, www.tcnj.edu/rgraham/failures/UCBhopal.html.

- They tried to turn on the plant refrigeration system to cool down the environment and slow the reaction, but the system had been drained of coolant weeks before and never refilled as a cost-saving measure.
- They tried to route expanding gases to a neighboring tank, but the tank's pressure gauge was broken, indicating that the tank was full when it was really empty.
- They tried other measures that didn't work due to inadequate or broken equipment.
- They tried to spray water on the gases and have them settle to the ground, but it was too late as the chemical reaction was nearly completed.

The Workers and Their Reaction

It was reported that the maintenance workers did not flush out the pipes after the factory's production of MIC stopped on December 2. This was important because the pipes carried the liquid MIC produced by the plant's reactors to the tanks. The highly corrosive MIC leaves chemical deposits on the lining of tanks that can eventually get into the storage tanks and contaminate the MIC. Was it laziness, as suggested by one worker?

Another worker pointed out that the production supervisor of the plant left strict instructions to flush the pipes, but it was late at night and neither worker really wanted to do it. Still, they followed the instructions for the washing operation, but the supervisor had omitted the crucial step to place solid metal discs at the end of each pipe to ensure hermetically sealed tanks.

The cleansing operation began when one worker connected a hosepipe to a drain cock on the pipework and turned on the tap. After a short time, it was clear to the worker that the injected water was not coming out of two of the four drain cocks. The worker called the supervisor, who walked over to the plant and instructed the worker to clean the filters in the two clogged drain cocks and turn the water back on. They did that, but the water did not flow out of one drain. After informing the supervisor, who said to just keep the water flowing, the worker left for the night. It would now be up to the night shift to turn off the tap.

The attitude of the workers as they started the night shift was not good as Union Carbide had started to cut back on production and lay off workers. They wondered if they might be next. The culture of safety that Union Carbide tried to build up was largely gone, as the workers typically handled toxic substances without protective gear. The temperature readings in the tanks were made less frequently, and it was rare that anyone checked the welding on the pipework in the middle of the night.

Even though the pressure gauge on one of the tanks increased beyond the "permitted maximum working pressure," the supervisor ignored warnings coming from the control room because he was under the impression that Union Carbide had built the tanks with special steel and walls thick enough to resist even greater pressures. Still, the duty head of the control room and another worker went to look directly at the pressure gauge attached to the three tanks. They confirmed the excessive pressure in one tank.

The duty head climbed to the top of that tank, examined the metal casing carefully, and sensed the stirring action. The pressure inside was increasing quickly, leading to a popping sound "like champagne corks." Some of the gas then escaped, and a brownish cloud appeared. The workers returned to where the pipes had been cleaned and turned off the water tap. They smelled the powerful gas emissions, and they heard the fizzing, which sounded as if someone was blowing into an empty bottle. One worker had a cool enough head to sound the general alarm, but it was too late for most of the workers and many of those living in the shantytowns below the plant.

The Political Response

Union Carbide sent a team to investigate the catastrophe, but the Indian government had seized all records and denied the investigators access to the plant and the eyewitnesses. The government of the state of Madhya Pradesh (where the plant was located) tried to place the blame squarely on the shoulders of Union Carbide. It sued the company for damages on behalf of the victims. The ruling Congress Party was facing national parliamentary elections three weeks after the accident, and it "stood to lose heavily if its partners in the state government were seen to be implicated, or did not deal firmly with Union Carbide."[6]

6United Nations, *United Nations University Report (UNU Report) on Toxic Gas Leak.*

The government thwarted early efforts by Union Carbide to provide relief to the victims to block the company's attempt to gain the goodwill of the public. The strategy worked: The Congress Party won both the state legislative assembly and the national parliament seats from Madhya Pradesh by large margins.

Economic Effects

The economic impact of a disaster like the one that happened in Bhopal is staggering. The $25 million Union Carbide plant in Bhopal was shut down immediately after the accident, and 650 permanent jobs were lost. The loss of human life meant a loss of future earning power and economic production. The thousands of accident victims had to be treated and in many cases rehabilitated. The closure of the plant had peripheral effects on local businesses and the population of Bhopal. It is estimated that "two mass evacuations disrupted commercial activities for several weeks, with resulting business losses of $8 to $65 million."

In the year after the accident, the government paid compensation of about $800 per fatality to relatives of the dead persons. About $100 apiece was awarded to 20,000 victims. Beginning in March 1991, new relief payments were made to all victims who lived in affected areas, and a total of $260 million was disbursed. Overall, Union Carbide agreed to pay $470 million to the residents of Bhopal. By the end of October 2003, according to the Bhopal Gas Tragedy Relief and Rehabilitation Department, compensation had been awarded to 554,895 people for injuries received and 15,310 survivors of those killed. The average amount that families of the dead received was $2,200.

Union Carbide's Response

Shortly after the gas release, Union Carbide launched what it called "an aggressive effort to identify the cause." According to the company, the results of an independent investigation conducted by the engineering consulting firm Arthur D. Little were that "the gas leak could only have been caused by deliberate sabotage. Someone purposely put water in the gas storage tank, causing a massive chemical reaction. Process safety systems had been put in place that would have kept the water from entering the tank by accident."[7]

A 1993 report prepared by Jackson B. Browning, the retired vice president of Health, Safety, and Environmental Programs at Union Carbide Corporation, stated that he didn't find out about the accident until 2:30 a.m. on December 3. He claims to have been told that "no plant employees had been injured, but there were fatalities—possibly eight or twelve—in the nearby community."

A meeting was called at the company's headquarters in Danbury, Connecticut, for 6 a.m. The chair of the board of directors of Union Carbide, Warren M. Anderson, had received the news while returning from a business trip to Washington, DC. He had a "bad cold and a fever," so Anderson stayed at home and designated Browning as his "media stand-in" until Anderson could return to the office.[8]

At the first press conference called for 1:00 p.m. on December 3, the company acknowledged that a disaster had occurred at its plant in Bhopal. The company reported that it was sending "medical and technical experts to aid the people of Bhopal, to help dispose of the remaining [MIC] at the plant and to investigate the cause of the tragedy." Notably, Union Carbide halted production at its only other MIC plant in West Virginia, and it stated its intention "to convert existing supplies into less volatile compounds."

Anderson traveled to India and offered aid of $1 million and the Indian subsidiary of Union Carbide pledged the Indian equivalent of $840,000. Within a few months, the company offered an additional $5 million in aid that was rejected by the Indian government. The money was then turned over to the Indian Red Cross and used for relief efforts.

The company continued to offer relief aid with "no strings attached." However, the Indian government rejected the overtures, and it didn't help the company to go through third parties. Union Carbide believed that the volatile

---

[7]After the leak, Union Carbide started a Web site, www.bhopal.com, to provide its side of the story and details about the tragedy. In 1998, the Indian state government of Madhya Pradesh took over the site.

[8]Jackson B. Browning, *The Browning Report*, Union Carbide Corporation, 1993, Available at: www.bhopal.com/pdfs/browning.pdf.

political situation in India—Prime Minister Indira Gandhi had just been assassinated in October—hindered its relief efforts, especially after the election of Rajiv Gandhi on a government reform platform shortly after the assassination. It appeared to the company that Union Carbide was to be made an example of as an exploiter of Indian natural resources, and it suspected that the Indian government may have wanted to "gain access to Union Carbide's financial resources."

Union Carbide had a contingency plan for emergencies, but it didn't cover the "unthinkable." The company felt compelled to show its "commitment to employee and community safety and, specifically, to reaffirm the safety measures in place at their operation." Anderson went to West Virginia to meet with the employees in early February 1985. At that meeting, as "a measure of the personal concern and compassion of Union Carbide employees," the workers established a "Carbide Employees Bhopal Relief Fund and collected more than $100,000 to aid the tragedy's victims."[9]

Analysis of Union Carbide's Bhopal Problems

Documents uncovered in litigation[10] and obtained by the Environmental Working Group of the Chemical Industry Archives, an organization that investigates chemical company claims of product safety, indicate that Union Carbide "cut corners and employed untested technologies when building the Bhopal Plant." The company went ahead with the unproven design even though it posed a "danger of polluting subsurface water supplies in the Bhopal area." The following excerpt is from a document numbered UCC 04206 and included in the Environmental Working Group Report on Bhopal, India.[11] It also reveals the indifferent attitude of the Indian government toward environmental safety:

> The systems described have received provisional endorsement by the Public Health Engineering Office of the State of Madhya Pradesh in Bhopal. At present, there are no state or central government laws and/or regulations for environmental protection, though enactment is expected in the near future. It is not expected that this will require any design modifications.

Technology Risks

> The comparative risk of poor performance and of consequent need for further investment to correct it is considerably higher in the [Union Carbide–India] operation than it would be had proven technology been followed throughout. . . . [T]he MIC-to-Sevin process, as developed by Union Carbide, has had only a limited trial run. Furthermore, while similar waste streams have been handled elsewhere, this particular combination of materials to be disposed of is new and, accordingly, affords further chance for difficulty. In short, it can be expected that there will be interruptions in operations and delays in reaching capacity or product quality that might have been avoided by adoption of proven technology.

> [Union Carbide–India] finds the business risk in the proposed mode of operation acceptable, however, in view of the desired long-term objectives of minimum capital and foreign exchange expenditures. So long as [Union Carbide–India] is diligent in pursuing solutions, it is their feeling that any shortfalls can be mitigated by imports. Union Carbide concurs.

As previously mentioned, there were one death and several accidental poisonings at the Bhopal plant before December 3, 1984. The International Environmental Law Research Center prepared a Bhopal Date Line showing that the death occurred on December 25, 1981, when a worker was exposed to phosgene gas. On January 9, 1982, 25 workers were hospitalized as a result of another leak. On October 5, 1982, another leak from the plant led to the hospitalization of hundreds of residents.[12]

---

[9] *The Browning Report*, p. 8.

[10] *Bano et al. v. Union Carbide Corp & Warren Anderson, 99cv11329 SDNY*, filed on 11/15/99.

[11] Environmental Working Group, *Chemical Industry Archives*, www.chemicalindustryarchives.org/dirtysecrets/bhopal/index.asp.

[12] S. Muralidhar, "The Bhopal Date Line," International Environmental Law Research Centre, Available at: www.ielrc.org/content/n0409.htm.

It is worth noting that the workers had protested unsafe conditions after the January 9, 1982, leak, but their warning went unheeded. In March 1982, a leak from one of the solar evaporation ponds took place, and the Indian plant expressed its concern to Union Carbide headquarters. In May 1982, the company sent its U.S. experts to the Bhopal plant to conduct the audit previously mentioned.

Union Carbide's reaction to newspaper allegations that Union Carbide–India was running an unsafe operation was for the plant's works manager to write a denial of the charges as baseless. The company's next step was, to say the least, bewildering. It rewrote the safety manuals to permit switching off of the refrigeration unit and a shutdown of the vent gas scrubber when the plant was not in operation. The staffing at the MIC unit was reduced from 12 workers to 6. On November 29, 1984, three days before the disaster, Union Carbide completed a feasibility report and the company had decided to dismantle the plant and ship it to Indonesia or Brazil.

India's Position

The Indian government has acknowledged that 521,262 persons, well over half the population of Bhopal at the time of the toxic leak, were "exposed" to the lethal gas. In the immediate aftermath of the accident, most attention was devoted to medical recovery. The victims of the MIC leak suffered damage to lung tissue and respiratory functions. The lack of medical documentation affected relief efforts. The absence of baseline data made it difficult to identify specific medical consequences of MIC exposure and to develop appropriate medical treatment. Another problem was that a lot medical expenses had to paid by Indians because funding was not sufficient.[13]

In his paper, Ungarala analyzed the *Browning Report* and characterized the company's response as one of public relations. He noted that the report identified the media and other interested parties such as customers, shareholders, suppliers, and other employees as the most important to pacify. Ungarala criticized this response for its lack of concern for the people of Bhopal and the Indian people in general. Instead, the corporation saw the urgency to assure the people of the United States that such an incident would not happen here.[14]

Browning's main strategy to restore Union Carbide's image was to distance the company from the site of the disaster. He points out early in the document that Union Carbide had owned only 50.9 percent of the affiliate, Union Carbide–India Ltd. He notes that all the employees in the company were Indians and that the last American employee had left two years before the leak.

The report contended that the company "did not have any hold over its Indian affiliate." This seems to be a contentious issue because while "many of the day-to-day details, such as staffing and maintenance, were left to Indian officials, the major decisions, such as the annual budget, had to be cleared with the American headquarters." In addition, according to both Indian and U.S. laws, a parent company (United Carbide in this case) holds full responsibility for any plants that it operates through subsidiaries and in which it has a majority stake. Ungarala concluded that Union Carbide was trying to avoid paying the $3 billion that India demanded as compensation and was looking to find a "scapegoat" to take the blame.[15]

After the government of Madhya Pradesh took over the information Web site from Union Carbide, it began to keep track of applications for compensation. Between 1985 and 1997, over 1 million claims were filed for personal injury. In more than half of those cases, the claimant was awarded a monetary settlement.[16]

The total amount disbursed as of March 31, 2003, was about $345 million. An additional $25 million was released through July 2004, at which time the Indian Supreme Court ordered the government to pay the victims and families of the dead the remaining $330 million in the compensation fund.

[13]Dr. Madabhushi Sridhar, "The Present And Continuous Disaster Of Bhopal: Environmental Dimensions," Available at: http://www.legalservicesindia.com/articles/bhopal.htm.

[14]Pratima Ungarala, *Bhopal Gas Tragedy: An Analysis*, Final Paper HU521/Dale Sullivan 5/19/98, Available at: www.hu.mtu.edu/hu_dept/tc@mtu/papers/bhopal.htm.

[15]Ungarala.

[16]Madhya Pradesh Government, Bhopal Gas Tragedy Relief and Rehabilitation Department, Available at: www.mp.nic.in/bgtrrdmp/facts.htm.

Lawsuits

The inevitable lawsuits began in December 1984 and March 1985, when the government of India filed against Union Carbide–India and the United States, respectively. Union Carbide asked for the case filed in the Federal District Court of New York to be moved to India because that was where the accident had occurred and most of the evidence existed. The case went to the Bhopal District Court—the lowest-level court that could hear such a case. During the next four years, the case made "its way through the maze of legal bureaucracy" from the state high court up to the Supreme Court of India.

The legal disputes were over the amount of compensation and the exoneration of Union Carbide from future liabilities. The disputes were complicated by a lack of reliable information about the causes of the event and its consequences. The government of India had adopted the "Bhopal Gas Leak Disaster Ordinance—a law that appointed the government as sole representative of the victims." It was challenged by victim activists, who pointed out that the victims were not consulted about legal matters or settlement possibilities. The result was, in effect, to dissolve "the victims' identity as a constituency separate and differing from the government."[17]

In 1989, India had another parliamentary election, and it seemed a politically opportune time to settle the case and win support from the voters. It had been five years since the accident and the victims were fed up with waiting. By that time, many of the victims had died and more had moved out of the gas-affected neighborhoods. Even though the Indian government had taken Union Carbide to court asking for $3 billion, the company reached a settlement with the government in January 1989 for $470 million; the agreement gave Union Carbide immunity from future prosecution.

In October 1991, India's Supreme Court upheld the compensation settlement but cancelled Union Carbide's immunity from criminal prosecution. The money had been held in a court-administered account until 1992 while claims were sorted out. By early 1993, there were 630,000 claims filed, of which 350,000 had been substantiated on the basis of medical records. The numbers are larger than previously mentioned because the extent of health problems grew continuously after the accident and hundreds of victims continued to die. Despite challenges by victims and activists to the settlement with Union Carbide, at the beginning of 1993, the government of India began to distribute the $470 million, which had increased to $700 million as a result of interest earned on the funds.[18]

What Happened to Union Carbide?

Not surprisingly, the lawsuits and bad publicity affected Union Carbide's stock price. Before the disaster, the company's stock traded between $50 and $58 a share. In the months immediately following the accident, it traded at $32 to $40. In the latter half of 1985, GAF Corporation of New York made a hostile bid to take over Union Carbide. The ensuing battle and speculative stock trading ran up the stock price to $96, and it forced the company into financial restructuring.

The company's response was to fight back. It sold off its consumer products division and received more than $3.3 billion for the assets. It took on additional debt and used the funds from the sale and borrowing to repurchase 38.8 million of its shares to protect the company from further threats of a takeover.

The debt burden had accounted for 80 percent of the company's capitalization by 1986. At the end of 1991, the debt levels were still high—50 percent of capitalization. The company sold its Linde Gas Division for $2.4 billion, "leaving the company at less than half its pre-Bhopal size."

The Bhopal disaster "slowly but steadily sapped the financial strength of Union Carbide and adversely affected" employee morale and productivity. The company's inability to prove its sabotage claim affected its reputation. In 1994, Union Carbide sold its Indian subsidiary, which had operated the Bhopal plant, to an Indian battery manufacturer. It used $90 million from the sale to fund a charitable trust that would build a hospital to treat victims in Bhopal.

[17]Michael R. Reich, *Toxic Politics: Responding to Chemical Disasters* (Ithaca, NY: Cornell University Press, 1991).

[18]*United Nations Report.*

Two significant events occurred in 2001. First, the Bhopal Memorial Hospital and Research Centre opened its doors. Second, Dow Chemical Company purchased Union Carbide for $10.3 billion in stock and debt, and Union Carbide became a subsidiary of Dow Chemical.

Subsequent to the initial settlement with Union Carbide, the Indian government took steps to right the wrong and its aftereffects caused by the failure of management and the systems at Union Carbide in Bhopal. On August 8, 2007, the Indian government announced that it would meet many of the demands of the survivors by taking legal action on the civil and criminal liabilities of Union Carbide and its new owner, Dow Chemical. The government established an "Empowered Commission" on Bhopal to address the health and welfare needs of the survivors, as well as environmental, social, economic, and medical rehabilitation.

On June 26, 2012, Dow Chemical Co. won dismissal of a lawsuit alleging polluted soil and water produced by its Union Carbide chemical plant in Bhopal, India, had injured area residents, one of at least two pending cases involving the facility known for the 1984 disaster that killed thousands.

U.S. District Judge John Keenan in Manhattan ruled that Union Carbide and its former chairman, Warren Anderson, weren't liable for environmental remediation or pollution-related claims made by residents near the plant, which had been owned and operated by a former Union Carbide unit in India.

Questions

1. Characterize the values illustrated by management at Union Carbide in the way it handled the Bhopal disaster.
2. Identify the ethical issues that arise from the facts of the case. How do you assess stakeholder responsibilities?
3. Compare the decision-making process used by Union Carbide to deal with its disaster with that of Ford Motor Co. in the Pinto case and Johnson & Johnson in the Tylenol incident as described in this chapter. Evaluate management decision making in these cases from an ethical reasoning perspective.
4. The document uncovered by the Environmental Working Group Report refers to the acceptable "business risk" in the Bhopal operation due to questions about the technology. Is it ethical for a company to use business risk as a measure of whether to go ahead with an operation that may have safety problems? How would you characterize such a thought process from the perspective of ethical reasoning?

Case 3-10 Accountability of Ex-HP CEO in Conflict of Interest Charges

How could a CEO and chairperson of the board of directors of a major company resign in disgrace over a personal relationship with a contractor that led to a sexual harassment charge and involved a conflict of interest, a violation of the code of ethics? It happened to Mark Hurd on August 6, 2010. Hurd was the former CEO for Hewlett-Packard (HP) for five years and also served as the chair of the board of directors for four years. On departure from HP, Hurd said he had not lived up to his own standards regarding trust, respect, and integrity.

The board of directors of HP began an investigation of Hurd in response to a sexual harassment complaint by Jodie Fisher, a former contractor, who retained lawyer Gloria Allred to represent her. While HP did not find that the facts supported the complaint, they did reveal behavior that the board would not tolerate. Subsequent to Hurd's resignation, a severance package was negotiated granting Hurd $12.2 million, COBRA benefits, and stock options, for a total package of somewhere between $40 and $50 million.

In a letter to employees of HP on August 6, interim CEO Cathie Lesjak outlined where Hurd violated the "Standards of Business Conduct" and the reasons for his departure.[1] Lesjak wrote that Hurd "failed to maintain accurate expense reports, and misused company assets." She indicated that each was a violation of the standards and "together they demonstrated a profound lack of judgment that significantly undermined Mark's credibility and his ability to effectively lead HP." The letter reminded employees that everyone was expected to adhere strictly to the standards in all business dealings and relationships and senior executives should set the highest standards for professional and personal conduct.

The woman who brought forward the sexual harassment complaint was a "marketing consultant" who was hired by HP for certain projects, but she was never an employee of HP. During the investigation, inaccurately documented expenses were found that were claimed to have been paid to the consultant for her services. Falsifying the use of company funds violated the HP Standards of Business Conduct.

As for the sexual harassment claim, Allred alleged in the letter that Hurd harassed Fisher at meetings and dinners over a several year period during which time Fisher experienced a number of unwelcome sexual advances from Hurd including kissing and grabbing. Fisher said that this continual sexual harassment made her uncertain about her employment status.

In August 2013, HP and former CEO, Mark Hurd, won dismissal of a lawsuit that challenged the computer maker's public commitment to ethics at a time when Hurd was allegedly engaging in sexual harassment.

HP did not violate securities laws despite making statements such as a commitment to be "open, honest, and direct in all our dealings" because such statements were too vague and general, U.S. District Judge Jon Tigar in San Francisco wrote.

As a result, shareholders led by a New York City union pension fund could not pursue fraud claims over Hurd's alleged violations of HP's standards of business conduct, the judge ruled.

"Adoption of the plaintiff's argument (would) render every code of ethics materially misleading whenever an executive commits an ethical violation following a scandal," Tigar wrote.

Shareholders led by the Cement & Concrete Workers District Council Pension Fund of Flushing, New York, claimed in their lawsuit that the share price had been fraudulently inflated because of Hurd's alleged activities.

They also claimed that HP's statements about its rules of conduct implied that Hurd was in compliance, and that Hurd ignored his duty to disclose violations.

At most, Tigar said, such statements "constitute puffery—if the market was even aware of them."

Tigar also said Hurd's alleged desire to keep his dealings with Fisher secret did not by itself give rise to a fraud claim.

"Nothing suggests that Hurd thought that he could mislead investors with the statements the court finds were immaterial," the judge wrote.

Questions

1. When he was CEO, Hurd wrote in the Standards of Business Conduct at HP that "We want to be a company known for its ethical leadership...." His message in the preface continued: "Let us commit together, as individuals and as a company, to build trust in everything we do by living our values and conducting business consistent with the high ethical standards embodied within our SBC."

   What is the role of trust in business? How does trust relate to stakeholder interests? How does trust engender ethical leadership? Evaluate Mark Hurd's actions in this case from an ethical and professional perspective.

2. Despite hundreds of pages of policies, codes of ethics, organizational values, and carefully defined work environments and company culture, lapses in workplace ethics occur every day. Explain why you think these lapses occur and what steps might be taken by an organization to ensure that its top executives live up to values it espouses.

3. Leo Apotheker, the former CEO of HP who succeeded Mark Hurd, resigned in September 2011, after just 11 months on the job—but he left with a $13.2 million severance package. Hurd left with a package between $40 million and $50 million. Do you think executives who resign from their positions or are fired because of unethical actions should be forced to give back some of those amounts to the shareholders to make them whole? Why or why not?

Chapter 4

Ethics and Professional Judgment in Accounting

Learning Objectives

After studying Chapter 4, you should be able to:

LO 4-1 Explain how professional judgment and skepticism influences ethical decision making.

LO 4-2 Discuss how the public interest may be affected by commercial activities of CPAs.

LO 4-3 Explain the threats and safeguards approach to independence.

LO 4-4 Discuss how nonattest services can impair audit independence.

LO 4-5 Describe the process to resolve ethical conflicts that affect integrity and objectivity.

LO 4-6 Explain the rules of conduct in the AICPA Code.

LO 4-7 Discuss ethics in tax practice.

Ethics Reflection

Professional judgment plays an integral role in ethical decision making in accounting. Underlying professional judgment are core values and attitudes such as objectivity, integrity, due care including professional skepticism, and an independent mindset that leads the auditor to question choices that have been made by management in applying generally accepted accounting principles. Professional judgment is a necessary but insufficient condition to ensure that moral decisions are made. As we learned in Chapters 2 and 3, ethical action and courage, and a willingness to voice one's values when the going gets tough, are essential to following up ethical judgments with ethical behavior.

Audit failures at companies like Enron and WorldCom were due in part to a lapse in professional judgment. Enron auditors failed to ask probing questions about the company's use of special-purpose entities and a lack of supporting evidence to validate their purpose. Accountants at WorldCom allowed their judgment to be compromised by pressures applied by top management to put the best face possible on the financial statements.

The Center for Audit Quality (CAQ) studied SEC sanctions against auditors over the period 1998–2010 that related to instances of fraudulent financial reporting by U.S. publicly traded companies.[1] During that time period, there were 87 separate instances where the SEC imposed such sanctions. CAQ summarized the auditor deficiencies noted by the SEC in these cases. In six of the cases, bogus audits were allegedly conducted. In the other 81, the SEC issued sanctions against individual auditors in 80 cases, and sanctions against audit firms in 26 of the cases.

The underlying causes of the deficiencies noted and number of relevant cases include:

- Failure to gather sufficient competent audit evidence (73%)
- Failure to exercise due professional care (67%)
- Insufficient level of professional skepticism (60%)
- Failure to obtain adequate evidence related to management representations (54%)
- Failure to express and appropriate audit opinion (47%)

Professional skepticism is an important component of objectivity and due care, and it an essential ingredient in gathering the evidence necessary to support audit judgments. Professional judgments are based on the information gathered and probing questions of management. These judgments cannot be adequately assessed without a strong foundation in ethics. That foundation consists of ethical values, moral reasoning skills, and a commitment to act ethically even in the face of countervailing pressures. On a professional level, the AICPA Code of Professional Conduct provides a sound basis to help accountants and auditors make the right choice.

As you read the chapter, reflect on the following:

- What are the underlying behavioral characteristics of good judgment?

- What is the link between moral reasoning methods and making professional judgments?
- How does cognitive dissonance influence professional judgment?
- What is the role of professional judgment in making ethical decisions?
- How does the AICPA Code address issues of professional judgment?

PCAOB Staff Audit Practice Alert No. 10, *Maintaining and Applying Professional Skepticism in Audits,* notes that while powerful incentives and pressures exist that can impede professional skepticism, professional skepticism is essential to an effective audit especially given the increasing judgment and complexity in financial reporting and environmental issues.[2] Auditors and audit firms need to remember that their overriding duty is to put the interests of investors first. Appropriate application of professional skepticism is key to fulfilling the auditor's duty to investors as pointed out by the U.S. Supreme Court.

By certifying the public reports that collectively depict a corporation's financial status, the independent auditor assumes a public responsibility transcending any employment responsibility with the client. The independent public accountant performing this special function owes ultimate allegiance to the corporation's creditors and stockholders, as well as to the investing public. This "public watchdog" function demands that the accountant maintain total independence from the client at all times and requires complete fidelity to the public trust.

Chief Justice Warren Burger, writing the unanimous opinion of the Supreme Court in United States v. Arthur Young & Co.

This important ruling of the U.S. Supreme Court reminds us that the independent audit provides the foundation for the existence of the accounting profession in the United States. Even though independent audits were common before the passage of the landmark legislation of the Securities Act of 1933 and the Securities Exchange Act of 1934, there is no doubt that CPAs derive their franchise as a profession from these two pieces of legislation, which require independent audits of publicly owned companies.

The Burger Court opinion emphasizes the trust that the public places in the independent auditor. The accounting profession is the only profession where one's public obligation supersedes that to a client. The medical profession recognizes the primacy of the physician's responsibility to a patient. The legal profession emphasizes the lawyer's responsibility to the client. The Public Interest Principle in the AICPA Code of Professional Conduct states, "In discharging their professional responsibilities, members (of the AICPA) may encounter conflicting pressures from each of these groups [clients, employers . . .]. In resolving those conflicts, members should act with integrity, guided by the precept that when members fulfill their responsibility to the public, clients' and employers' interests are best served." Professional judgment enables CPAs to meet their professional obligations to resolve conflicts in a morally appropriate way.

What is Professional Judgment in Accounting?

LO 4-1
Explain how professional judgment and skepticism influences ethical decision making.

Link between Attitudes, Behaviors, and Judgment

Professional judgment is influenced by personal behavioral traits (i.e., attitudes and ethical values) as well as one's knowledge of the accounting and auditing issues in question. Theoretical models of ethical decision making, such as that of Hunt and Vitell, include personal values in their theory as one of several personal characteristics that potentially influence all ethical decision processes.[3] The role of personal values (i.e., virtues) in auditor ethical decision making was discussed in Chapters 1 and 2.

Personal values link to ethical sensitivity and judgment. Ethical awareness of an ethical dilemma is a mediator on the personal factors and ethical judgment relationship, as recognized by Rest in his model of ethical decision making. It is unlikely that an accountant making a judgment on an employer's application of generally accepted accounting principles (GAAP) would make the best choice without realizing that the decision will affect others through its consequences. Likewise, objectivity and due care are attitudes and behaviors that enable that choice to be made. For an auditor, professional skepticism is essential in making professional judgments. It helps to frame auditors' mindset of independent thought.

KPMG Professional Judgment Framework

KPMG developed a framework of the elements of professional judgment in its monograph, *Elevating Professional Judgment in Auditing and Accounting: The KPMG Professional Judgment Framework*. It starts with a common definition of judgment: *Judgment is the process of reaching a decision or drawing a conclusion where there are a number of possible alternative solutions.*[4]

Judgment occurs in a setting of uncertainty, risk, and often conflicts of interest. We can see the link between judgment and decision making not only in Rest's model but the Integrated Model of Ethical Decision Making described in Chapter 2. The evaluation of alternatives links to ethical intent, which leads to ethical action. Professional judgment follows a similar path with pressures along the way imposed by one's supervisor, top management, or CPA firm management that might lead to compromising judgment.

The KPMG framework identifies five components of professional judgment that revolve around one's mindset. The components are: (1) clarify issues and objectives; (2) consider alternatives; (3) gather and evaluate information; (4) reach conclusion; and (5) articulate and document rationale. The framework recognizes that influences and biases might affect the process as could one's knowledge of professional standards.

The framework is prescriptive. In the real world we may deviate from the process because of pressures, time constraints, and limited capacity. These constraints, influences, and biases threaten good judgment. For example, let's assume on the last day of an audit you determine that copies of documents for equipment purchases were provided by the client rather than original ones. You realize that fraudulent alteration of documents can occur more readily than if the documents are original. However, to ask the client to provide originals at the eleventh hour means extra time and budget pressures for the firm. Indeed, your supervisor wants to wrap up the audit at the end of the day. Since the firm has never had a problem with this client, you decide to let it go. The process then becomes altered at step three because of our biases and influences.

At the very center of the KPMG framework is *mindset*. Auditors should approach matters objectively and independently, with inquiring and incisive minds. Professional skepticism is required by auditing standards. It requires an objective attitude that includes a questioning mind and critical assessment of audit evidence. In the previous example, professional skepticism was sacrificed for expedience.

Professional skepticism is not the same as professional judgment, but it is an important component of professional judgment. It is a frame of reference to guide audit decisions and enhances ethical decision making.

As decision makers navigate through the professional judgment framework, judgment traps and tendencies can lead to bias. One common judgment trap is the tendency to want to immediately solve a problem by making a quick judgment. The auditor in the previous example may choose to shortcut the process by accepting copies of original documents rather than spending the time to convince the client of why originals are needed.

Link between KPMG Framework and Cognitive Processes

Each of us have our own biases that may cloud decision making and alter our final choices. We may be easy going and avoid conflicts at all costs, which would not make for a very good auditor, who needs to have a questioning mind and be willing to critically assess audit data. We also need to be deliberative about our thought processes and consider both the why and the how we make decisions.

Recall our discussion in Chapter 2 about System 1 and System 2 thinking. System 1 thinking is fast, automatic, effortless, and difficult to control or modify. It is instinctive whereas System 2 is slower, effortful, and a more deliberative process. The auditor in our previous example may act quickly and dismiss any attempt to engage in a thoughtful process that critically analyzes the reasons for and against examining additional documents to gather reliable evidence about the supportability of the expenditures.

Our intuitive judgments can fall prey to cognitive traps and biases that negatively influence our judgments. Three common judgment traps are groupthink, a rush to solve a problems, and "judgment triggers." Groupthink finds a home in stage 3 of Kohlberg's model. We become influenced by the expectations of the group and, consequently, we subjugate our own beliefs and thought process. We may do so to avoid conflicts or save time. In an audit, this means the team might accept copies of documents if the majority of members convince the others that the client can be trusted and the group doesn't want to bust the budget.

Defining the problem correctly begins with ethical awareness and then the application of ethical reasoning to identify stakeholder interests; how our intended actions may affect them; an ethical analysis of harms and benefits and stakeholder rights; and our professional obligations given the dynamics of the situation. This is a System 2 thought process that is inconsistent with attempting to "rush to judgment," and is facilitated by ethical decision-making models such as those discussed in Chapter 2.

Judgment triggers can lead to accepting a solution to the problem before it is properly identified and evaluated. Biased judgments might be made because of judgment tendencies. KPMG identifies four common judgment tendencies that are most applicable and important for audit professionals: the availability tendency, the confirmation tendency, the overconfidence tendency, and the anchoring tendency. The first two triggers are most important for our purposes.

The *availability tendency* may lead to judgments based on the accessibility of information rather than a deliberative analysis of how the facts of the current situation differ from prior ones. Also, an auditor may rely on past procedures in the current audit even though that approach may not be relevant to the current situation. The auditor in our previous example may take the easy way out and just accept the copies of documents since she already has them.

The tendency for decision makers to put more weight on information that is consistent with their initial beliefs or preferences is the *confirmation tendency*. The auditor trusts the client based on past experiences and is more willing to accept the copies. However, in many instances, we cannot know something to be true unless we explicitly consider how and why it may be false. Confirmation bias in auditing may occur when auditors over-rely on management's explanations for a significant difference between the auditor's expectation and management's recorded value, even when the client's explanation is inadequate.

Briefly, the *overconfidence tendency* is when decision makers overestimate their own abilities to perform tasks or to make accurate diagnoses or other judgments and decisions, as may be the case when estimating outcomes or likelihoods. The *anchoring tendency* relates to starting from an initial numerical value and then adjusting insufficiently away from it in forming a final judgment as when the auditor becomes anchored to management's estimate.

Given the increasing judgment and complexity in financial reporting, it is essential that auditors exercise sound professional judgment and control for biases and tendencies. The SEC's Advisory Committee on Improvements to Financial Reporting (CIFiR), developed a framework for accounting judgments consisting of two components, (1) a critical and good faith thought process and (2) documentation. We discuss the first component in this chapter in the context of professional, ethical standards and leave the second to the next chapter, which addresses audit evidence gathering, evaluation, fraud considerations, and professional judgment.[5]

The proposed CIFiR framework aims to improve the quality of auditors' judgments and allow for consistent evaluation of such judgments. The process entails a "critical and reasoned evaluation made in good faith" including the pros and cons of all reasonable accounting alternative methods. The goal is to improve the quality of auditors' judgments and increase auditors' propensity to curb aggressive reporting even when faced with less precise accounting standards.

The audit of financial statements has always required auditors to exercise their professional judgment, but the use and importance of these judgments continues to grow as the overall complexity and estimation uncertainty inherent in financial statements increases. In an effort to facilitate auditors' use of sound professional judgment, audit firms have turned to developing professional judgment frameworks, such as the one provided by KPMG, to promote a rigorous, thoughtful, and deliberate judgment process to guide making reasonable accounting judgments.[6]

Role of Professional Skepticism

Glover and Prawitt authored the monograph *Enhancing Auditor Professional Skepticism* for the Standards Working Group of the Global Policy Committee (comprising BDO, Deloitte, Ernst & Young, Grant Thornton, KPMG, and PricewaterhouseCoopers). The purpose of the monograph is to develop a common understanding of professional skepticism, how it should be applied, the threats to professional skepticism and the safeguards that may be cost-effective. It begins by defining professional skepticism by linking back to the Greek word *skeptikos,* meaning "inquiring or reflective." To inquire is "to seek information by questioning." The characteristics commonly associated with being a skeptic include questioning and careful observation, probing reflection, looking beyond the obvious, and suspension of belief.[7]

Professional skepticism links to professional judgment through the ethical standards of independent thought, objectivity, and due care, which are incorporated in the AICPA Code of Professional Conduct. Professional skepticism links to ethical values such as the virtues identified in the Libby and Thorne study discussed in Chapter 2. They identified instrumental virtues of being diligent, alert, careful, resourceful, consultative, persistent, and courageous. Auditors need to internalize these virtues to meet the requirements of professional skepticism.

Professional skepticism is part of the skill set auditors should have and is closely interrelated to the fundamental concepts of auditor independence and professional judgment, which contribute to audit quality.[8] According to Arnold Schilder, chairman of the International Auditing and Assurance Standards Board (IAASB), auditor independence, technical proficiency, and professional judgment collectively enable an auditor to maintain a skeptical mindset in planning and executing an audit.

To promote the application of professional skepticism, CPA-firm management should set an appropriate tone that emphasizes a questioning mind throughout the audit and the exercise of professional skepticism in gathering and evaluating evidence. More will be said about the application of professional skepticism in audits of financial statements in Chapter 5.

The firm's leadership and the examples it sets significantly influence the internal culture of the firm. The tone at the top and continual reinforcement of the importance of professional skepticism on audit engagements are important influences on individuals' behavior.

According to the International Standard on Quality Control 1 issued by IAASB, to establish a quality-oriented internal culture, the firm's leadership should set clear, consistent, and frequent actions and messages about the importance of professional skepticism in building quality audits.[9]

Accountability can be thought of as the requirement to justify one's judgments to others. Absent a healthy dose of professional skepticism, it would be difficult for the auditor to justify having made judgments in accordance with the ethical standards of the accounting profession. These standards exist to protect the public interest and honor the public trust.

The Public Interest in Accounting

LO 4-2
Discuss how the public interest may be affected by commercial activities of CPAs.

Professional judgment is what makes an accountant a professional and it underlies the fundamental obligation to protect the public interest. The profession's codes of ethics call for independent judgments and to not subordinate professional judgment to a supervisor or client. Professional accountants make judgments about specific accounting treatments, such as fair value measurement and revenue recognition, and in determining the nature, timing, and scope of necessary audit procedures. Professional judgment is essential to evaluating the risks of material misstatements in the financial statements. When professional judgment is compromised by taking shortcuts or allowing biases and pressures imposed by others to taint decision making, the public loses trust in the accounting profession.

Following the disclosure of numerous accounting scandals during the dark days of Enron, the accounting profession and professional bodies turned their attention to examining how to rebuild the public trust and confidence in financial reporting. The International Federation of Accountants (IFAC) addresses the public interest dimension in its Policy Position Paper #4, entitled *A Public Interest Framework for the Accountancy Profession*. The framework is designed to enable IFAC and other professional bodies to better evaluate whether the public interest is being served through actions of the profession and its institutions. IFAC considers the "public interest" to represent the common benefits derived by stakeholders of the accounting profession through sound financial reporting. It links these benefits to responsibilities of professional accountants, including the application of high standards of ethical behavior and professional judgment.

Public interest obligations are explicitly accepted by the accounting profession in national jurisdictions and internationally. The IFAC-published *Handbook of the Code of Ethics for Professional Accountants*

(2015), which has greatly influenced national codes, recognizes that "A distinguishing mark of the accounting profession is the acceptance of its responsibility to act in the public interest." The Code describes a conceptual framework that identifies threats to fundamental principles of behavior that relies on professional judgment to evaluate the significance of those threats.[10] More will be said about the threats later on.

The fundamental principles of professional ethics for professional accountants identified by the International Ethics Standards Board for Accountants (IESBA) include integrity, objectivity, professional competence and due care, confidentiality, and professional behavior including compliance with laws and regulations. These principles are similar to those in the AICPA Code, state board of accountancy rules in the United States, and the codes of conduct in the United Kingdom and Australia, as well as most of the developed world.[11]

In the United States, the AICPA Code of Professional Conduct was restructured with certain parts revised as of December 31, 2014 and others were fully revised as of December 15, 2015. It continues to be built upon the premise that "A distinguishing mark of a profession is acceptance of its responsibility to the public." The public interest in accounting includes clients, credit grantors, governments, employers, investors, the business and financial community, and others who rely on the objectivity and integrity of CPAs in carrying out their professional responsibilities. The Public Interest Principle in the AICPA Code recognizes that conflicts may exist between stakeholder interests, and it calls for fulfilling responsibilities to the public as a way of also serving clients' and employers' interests.[12]

Professionalism versus Commercialism

Boyce points out that whether or not it has been broadly recognized, the accounting profession has always been characterized, to differing degrees, both by the pursuit of professional self-interest and the public interest. Increasingly, professional firms, particularly the Big Four international firms, have turned their attention to deliver business and client-focused service that threatens the public's confidence in the profession.[13] The perception that auditors may not be and may not act independent of the client's interests has taken a hit in recent years as commercialism has once again bumped up against professionalism.

Alarm bells went off in October 2013, when PwC announced it was acquiring the consulting giant Booz & Company. Back in 2002, PwC had sold its previous consulting business to IBM for $3.5 billion, as a response to restrictions created by the Sarbanes-Oxley Act (SOX) on providing consulting services for audit clients. As a result of its acquisition of Booz, PwC added $9.2 billion in global consulting revenue and increased its consulting group's share of total global firm revenue of $32.1 billion to 28.5 percent, up from 21.7 percent in 2009. Lynn Turner, the former SEC chief accountant, raised an important question about the merger when he asked, "Are the auditors going to serve management, or are they going to serve the best interests of the investing public?"[14]

Not to be outdone, on April 13, 2015, KPMG announced that it had entered into an agreement to acquire substantially all of the assets of Beacon Partners, Inc., a provider of management consulting services to hospitals, physician groups, and other health-care providers. KPMG is trying to leverage its foothold in the health-care industry in light of the growth in services as a result of the Affordable Care Act (Obamacare). In June 2014, it bought Zanett Commercial Solutions, a consulting firm with a significant focus on health care.

According to a survey by Monadnock Research, advisory revenue for the Big Four firms surged $36 billion in 2013 for their global networks, a rate four times the 3.4 percent gain in audit fees.[15] The PCAOB is concerned that consulting may take the firms' focus away from core auditing responsibilities. Unlike audits that are conducted primarily to satisfy the public interest, consulting services satisfy the client's interest and do not require independence from the client.

The growth in consulting services raises questions about any conflict of interest that might arise between consulting and auditing. For example, when examining activities of the client that result from the firm's consulting services, a reasonable person may conclude that the auditor could not be independent of the client in performing audit services because of the consulting relationship. Just imagine if the auditor determined that the consulting work done was deficient or led to financial problems for the client. Can the auditor still be independent when conducting the audit? The fact is it does not matter whether the auditor is independent because as long as the appearance of independence has been tainted by the consulting relationship, the independence standard would be compromised.

In examining whether professionalism and commercialism can coexist in CPA firms, Love points out that the profession will lose its *raison d'etre* if the public believes that CPAs are not independent due to the type of, or amount of fees received for, advisory services performed for clients upon which they render any assurance opinion.[16] We would like to think that the profession learned its lesson from Enron where Andersen received $27 million for tax and consulting services and $25 million for auditing. Unfortunately, this may be an instance of going "back to the future" as the profession has been investigated over and over again since 1977 for certain practices that threaten the public interest, including providing consulting services for audit clients.

Investigations of the Profession: Where Were the Auditors?

The auditing profession in the United States has come under periodic scrutiny from Congress during the past 40 years. The questions that are consistently asked are: Where were the auditors? Why didn't auditing firms detect and report the many frauds that occurred during this time period? Was it a matter of bending to the wishes of the client that hires (and can fire) the firm, and pays its fee? Were these failures due to inadequate and sometimes sloppy audits by firms that may have been trying to cut corners because they lowballed their audit fees to lure clients, with the hope of gaining lucrative tax advice and consulting fees down the road? In the case of Andersen's treatment of Enron, it seems all of the factors were present, as well as the cozy relationship that the auditor had with Enron that influenced the firm's ability to be independent in making decisions regarding the audits.

The rules of conduct in the AICPA Code are best understood in light of the investigations of the accounting profession that followed high-profile frauds during the past 40 years. Congressional concern was that auditors were not living up to their ethical and professional responsibilities (as stated in the Burger Court opinion). The major themes of these investigations were (1) whether nonauditing services impair auditor independence, (2) the need for management to report on internal controls, (3) the importance of developing techniques to prevent and detect fraud, and (4) the need to strengthen the role of the audit committee and communications between the auditor and audit committee.

Metcalf Committee and Cohen Commission: 1977–1978

As CPA firms have become global entities, the profession's concern about ethics and regulation has grown. In 1977, a major study examined the relationship between auditors and clients and the provision of nonauditing services for those clients. The Metcalf (Moss) Report was the first real investigation of the accounting profession since the 1930s. An investigation was conducted between 1975 and 1977 by Senator Lee Metcalf (D-MT) and, on the House side, Representative John Moss (D-CA). The Metcalf Report issued four recommendations, two of which are described here. The report did not lead to any new legislation at the time, although in the aftermath of the frauds at Enron and WorldCom, changes were made to enhance audits and financial reporting.

The first recommendation of the Metcalf Committee was to establish a self-regulatory organization of firms that audit publicly owned companies. It led to the AICPA's formation of a two-tier voluntary peer review program in 1977: one for firms with public-company clients and one for smaller firms with only private-company clients. In 2004, the Public Company Accounting Oversight Board (PCAOB) assumed the AICPA's responsibilities relating to firms that audit public clients, ending the period of self-regulation by the profession, at least for public companies. PCAOB instituted a mandatory quality inspection program for CPA firms that audit public companies. The AICPA continued its two-tier program to assist firms in meeting state licensing and AICPA membership requirements.

The second recommendation of the Metcalf Committee was to limit types of management services to those relating directly to accounting. The accounting profession was upset at the implication that the provision of management consulting services somehow tainted the audit. It was left to the profession's own Cohen Commission to conduct an in-depth study of the issue. The report included an instance that demonstrates the potential conflict when providing nonauditing services for an audit client. It was discovered that the audit of Westec Corporation had been compromised because of a consulting project.

The Cohen Commission examined a variety of issues that are still debated today, including the auditor's responsibility for detecting fraud and the expectation gap that exists between the profession's goals for the audit and what the public expects an audit to accomplish. Beyond that, the commission recommended that management report on its internal controls to the users of the financial statements and that the auditor should evaluate management's report. This recommendation was ultimately enacted into legislation as part of SOX.

The events that eventually led to change were two rounds of major scandals—one in the 1980s that included the failures of savings and loan institutions, and the second in the late 1990s and early 2000s, led by Enron and WorldCom. After Enron and WorldCom, the profession agreed to go along with change in the form of the provisions passed by SOX and the creation of PCAOB, which will be discussed later on.

Practices such as providing lucrative advisory services for audit clients and opinion shopping have contributed over the years to a shift in the environment of professionalism that has existed in the accounting profession to one emphasizing commercial interests. Most people believe that these practices became less prevalent after the passage of SOX. However, the Big Four firms' recent thirst for consulting services has opened that door once again.

House Subcommittee on Oversight and Investigations: 1986

Representative Ron Wyden (D-OR) had introduced a bill in May 1986 to hold the accounting profession responsible for the detection of fraud in light of the failure at ESM Government Securities and bank failures in the early 1980s at Continental Illinois National Bank and Trust and Penn Square Bank. Even though Continental Illinois had received a $4.5 billion federal bailout, the company ultimately was liquidated by the Federal Deposit Insurance Corporation (FDIC) just four months after receiving an unqualified opinion on its audit by Peat Marwick (now KPMG). This was the first time we heard the refrain in Congress, "Where were the auditors?"

Representative John Dingell (D-MI) was chair of both the House Committee on Energy and Commerce and its Subcommittee on Oversight and Investigations. In January and February 1988, the subcommittee held two hearings concerning the failure of ZZZZ Best Company, a corporation that had "created" 80 percent or more of its total revenue in the form of fictitious revenue from the restoration of carpets, drapes, and other items in office buildings after fires and floods. Chair Dingell characterized the fraud as follows:

> The fact that auditors and attorneys repeatedly visited make-believe job sites and came away satisfied does not speak well for the present regulatory system. The fact that the auditing firm discovering the fraud resigned the engagement without telling enforcement authorities is even more disturbing. . . . Cases such as ZZZZ Best demonstrate vividly that we cannot afford to tolerate a system that fails to meet the public's legitimate expectations in this regard.

Savings and Loan Industry Failures: Late 1980s–Early 1990s

By the late 1980s, the savings and loan (S&L) industry failures became the focus of congressional hearings as a $300 million failure at Beverly Hills Savings & Loan and a $250 million failure at Sunrise Savings, a Florida S&L, engulfed Deloitte & Touche. Arthur Young, the firm that was to merge with Ernst & Whinney to form Ernst & Young, had run into deep trouble in its S&L audits. In particular, it certified the financial statements of the Western Savings Association in 1984 and 1985, which were overstated by $400 million. If Arthur Young had not merged with Ernst & Whinney, the firm may have been forced out of business. Eventually the firm paid the federal government $400 million to settle claims that the company's auditors failed to warn of disastrous financial problems that caused some of the nation's biggest thrift failures.

Perhaps the most publicized failure is that of Lincoln Savings & Loan. Thousands of California retirees lost their life savings after buying uninsured subordinated debentures issued by Lincoln's parent company, American Continental, and sold through Lincoln branches. Arthur Young, the auditors of American Continental, issued unqualified opinions on the entity's financial statements for fiscal years 1986 and 1987. The audit opinions were part of the annual reports of American Continental that were furnished to prospective buyers of the worthless debentures.

The cost to the public to clean up 1,043 failed thrift institutions with total assets of over $500 billion during the 1986–1995 period was reported to be $152.9 billion, including $123.8 billion of U.S. taxpayer losses. The balance was absorbed by the thrift industry itself. It was the greatest collapse of U.S. financial institutions since the Great Depression. Little did we know that 20 years later banks and financial institutions would be embroiled in a scandal that involved risky investments, including derivatives and worthless mortgage-backed securities, and some institutions would need federal bailout funds to stay in business, while others would be taken over by the government or other institutions.

The accounting issues in failed S&Ls centered on three issues: (1) the failure to provide adequate allowances for loan losses, (2) the failure to disclose dubious deals between the S&Ls and some of their major customers, and (3) the existence of inadequate internal controls to prevent these occurrences. The profession was already considering ways to address the large number of business failures in the 1980s when the S&L debacle occurred. The profession's response to deal with this new pressure was to form the Treadway Commission, and its work was given a new sense of urgency.

Treadway Commission Report

The National Commission on Fraudulent Financial Reporting, referred to as the Treadway Committee after its chair James C. Treadway, was formed in 1985 to study and report on the factors that can lead to fraudulent financial reporting. The Committee of Sponsoring Organizations (COSO) of the Treadway Commission was established as a result of the commission's work and turned its attention to corporate culture.

As discussed in Chapter 3, COSO emphasizes the need to change corporate culture and establish the systems necessary to prevent fraudulent financial reporting. It starts with the tone at the top and relies on a strong system of internal controls built on a foundation of ethics. Its lasting legacy is the development of an integrated framework for internal control that serves as the foundation for companies to build effective internal control systems. The systems are evaluated annually by management and a report prepared, as required by SOX. Auditors then do their own independent review and issue their own assessment. The framework was first identified in 1992 and since has been updated with the most recent version issued in 2013, "The 2013 COSO Framework and SOX Compliance."

The Role of the Accounting Profession in the Financial Crisis of 2007–2008

The financial crisis that started in 2007 and accelerated in 2008 ushered in a period of reflection about how the United States could have been pushed into a recession brought on by excessive risk taking and a mortgage meltdown. Some have blamed moral hazard as a major contributing factor. *Moral hazard* occurs where one party is responsible for the interests of another, but has an incentive to put its own interests first. Research by Atif Mian and Amir Sufi of the University of Chicago's business school provides hard evidence that securitization of mortgages fostered moral hazard among mortgage originators, which led them to issue loans to uncreditworthy borrowers. They were motivated to do so by moral hazard effects, in that the securitized assets were sold off to unsuspecting investors and so the risk of default transferred to these parties, not the originating banks.

For two and a half years, the U.S. Senate focused on the role of financial institutions in the financial crisis of 2007–2008 that started with the failure of Lehman Brothers. A bankruptcy examiner's report issued on April 12, 2011, shed light on the role of auditing firms in the financial meltdown. The report was written by Jenner & Block Chairman Anton Valukas. The details of Lehman's financial activities that vaulted the company into bankruptcy are too complicated to discuss in detail, but we provide a summary in Exhibit 4.1.

EXHIBIT 4.1 Lehman's Financial Transactions and Accounting Disclosures

Despite the profession's efforts to control for risk and improve corporate culture, the United States experienced its worst recession that began in 2007 in part due to risky financial activities and improper accounting practices. It started when the investment banking firm of Lehman Brothers failed because it was unable to retain the confidence of its lenders and counterparts and because it did not have sufficient liquidity to meet its current obligations. Lehman engaged in a series of business decisions and transactions using a device known as "Repo 105" that had left it with heavy concentrations of illiquid assets with deteriorating values such as residential and commercial real estate.

Confidence eroded when Lehman reportedly had two consecutive quarters of huge reported losses, $2.8 billion in the second quarter of 2008 and $3.9 billion in the third quarter of that year.

The business decisions that had brought Lehman to its crisis of confidence may have been in error but were deemed by the bankruptcy examiner to be largely within the business judgment rule. But the decision not to disclose the effects of those judgments created a valid claim against the senior officers who oversaw and certified misleading financial statements. Legal claims of failing to meet professional responsibilities were charged against Lehman's CEO, Richard Fuld, and its CFOs, Christopher O'Meara, Erin M. Callan, and Ian Lowitt. A valid claim also existed against its external auditor, Ernst & Young, for its failure to question and challenge improper or inadequate disclosures in those financial statements, among other things.

Lehman had used an accounting device (known within Lehman as "Repo 105") to manage its balance sheet by temporarily removing approximately $50 billion of assets from the balance sheet at the end of the first and second quarters of 2008.

In an ordinary "repo," Lehman raised cash by selling assets with a simultaneous obligation to repurchase them the next day or several days later; such transactions were accounted for as financings, and the assets remained on Lehman's balance sheet. In a Repo 105 transaction, Lehman did exactly the same thing, but because the assets were 105 percent or more of the cash received, accounting rules permitted the transactions to be treated as sales rather than financings, so that the assets could be removed from the balance sheet. With Repo 105

(Continued)

transactions, Lehman's reported net leverage was 12.1 at the end of the second quarter of 2008, but if Lehman had used ordinary repos, net leverage would have been reported at 13.9.

Lehman did not disclose its use—or the significant magnitude of its use—of Repo 105 to the federal government, to the rating agencies, to its investors, or to its own board of directors. Ernst & Young was aware of its use but did not question it or the nondisclosure of the Repo 105 accounting transactions. It took Lehman until September 2008, several months into the financial meltdown, to publicly disclose the liquidity issues. On September 10, 2008, the company announced that it was projecting a $3.9 billion loss for the third quarter of 2008. By the close of trading on September 12, its stock price had declined to $3.65 a share, a 94 percent drop from the $62.19 price on January 2, 2008.

Over the weekend of September 12–14, 2008, a series of meetings were held by U.S. Treasury Secretary Henry Paulson, president of the Federal Reserve Bank of New York Timothy Geithner, SEC chairman Christopher Cox, and the chief executives of leading financial institutions. The government made a decision that many believe ushered in the financial crisis. It refused to fund a solution to the Lehman problem, stating that it did not have the legal authority to make a direct capital investment in Lehman, and Lehman's assets were insufficient to support a loan large enough to avoid its collapse.

As an alternative to government intervention, Lehman approached Barclays, a British bank, and it appeared a deal had been reached on September 14 that would save Lehman from collapse, but later that day, the deal fell apart when it was learned that the Financial Services Authority, the United Kingdom's bank regulator, refused to waive U.K.-shareholder-approval requirements. Clearly, that would take too long. Meanwhile, Lehman could no longer fund its operations. The bank collapsed on September 15, when it filed for bankruptcy protection. The filing remains the largest bankruptcy filing in U.S. history, with Lehman holding over $600 billion in assets.

At the Senate Banking Committee hearings on the Lehman failure and subsequent financial crisis, Valukas spoke about the general principle that auditors play a critical role in the proper functioning of public companies and financial markets. He said:

> Boards of directors and audit committees are entitled to rely on external auditors to serve as watchdogs—to be important gatekeepers who provide an independent check on management. And the investing public is entitled to believe that a "clean" report from an independent auditor stands for something. The public has every right to conclude that auditors who hold themselves out as independent will stand up to management and not succumb to pressure to avoid rocking the boat. I found that [valid] claims exist against Lehman's external auditor in connection with Lehman's issuance of materially misleading financial reports.

Reflecting on the years of investigations after business and audit failures and important changes in the landscape of audit regulations, we would like to think the profession has learned its lesson. Yet, the recent trend of expanding the scope and nature of consulting services provided to audit clients gives us great pause. At times we have had to shake our heads in bewilderment at some of the arrangements. A good example is what Ernst & Young did when it lobbied congressional staff on behalf of two audit clients. The SEC charged the firm with violations of auditor independence rules that require firms to maintain their objectivity and impartiality with clients. The firm agreed to pay more than $4 million to settle the charges in 2014. While the investigations of the profession previously discussed raised the question "Where were the auditors?" In this case we have to ask "What were they thinking?"

AICPA Code: Independence Considerations for Members in Public Practice

LO 4-3

Explain the threats and safeguards approach to independence.

Introduction to Revised Code

On June 1, 2014, the AICPA issued a codification of the principles, rules, and interpretations and rulings in the AICPA Code of Professional Conduct (Revised Code) that simplifies the identification of topics that are now contained in designated areas, whereas a CPA used to have to wade through actual rules, interpretations, and rulings to be knowledgeable about all aspects of an ethical situation. A major improvement of the Revised Code is the creation of three sections, one each for members in public practice, members in business, and other members. This simplifies identifying how the rules apply to practitioners in the performance of their professional services.[17]

The most significant change is the incorporation of two broad conceptual frameworks, one for members in public practice and another for CPAs in business.[18] These conceptual frameworks incorporate a "threats and safeguards" approach and are designed to assist users in analyzing relationships and circumstances that the code does not specifically address.

A significant improvement is the new section on "Ethical Conflicts" that arise from obstacles to following the appropriate course of action due to internal or external pressures and/or conflicts in applying relevant professional standards or legal standards. The ethical conflicts provision is used in combination with the conceptual framework to determine whether specific rules of conduct have been violated. The Revised Code was transitioned in and became fully effective on December 15, 2015.

The numbering in the Revised Code can be confusing and we have kept it at a minimum in order to focus on the important material that students should know. The Principles in the Code (Section 0.300) were discussed in Chapter 1. They are now categorized in the Revised Code as follows:

- Responsibilities (0.300.020)
- The Public Interest (0.300.030)
- Integrity (0.300.040)
- Objectivity and Independence (0.300.050)
- Due Care (0.300.060)
- Scope and Nature of Services (0.300.070)

In the discussions below, we refer to the Revised Code as the "Code" to simplify matters.

Three important points about the applicability of the Code are as follows: (1) It applies to CPAs in the performance of all professional services except when the wording of the rule indicates otherwise; (2) it is a violation of the rules for a CPA to permit others acting on their behalf from engaging in behavior that, had the CPA done so, it would have violated the rules; and (3) when differences exist between AICPA rules and those of the licensing state board of accountancy, the CPA should follow the state board's rules.

Members in Public Practice

Section 1.000.010 describes a conceptual framework that applies to members in public practice and provides a foundation to evaluate whether threats to the CPA's compliance with the rules of conduct are at an acceptable level or whether safeguards should be developed to prevent a violation of the rules. Under the Code, in the absence of an interpretation of a specific rule of conduct that addresses a particular relationship or circumstance, a CPA should evaluate whether that relationship or circumstance would lead a reasonable and informed third party who is aware of the relevant information to conclude a threat exists to the CPA's compliance with the rules that is not at an acceptable level. In some circumstances no safeguards can reduce a threat to an acceptable level. For example, a CPA cannot subordinate professional judgment to others without violating the "Integrity and Objectivity" Rule.

Conceptual Framework for AICPA Independence Standards

The conceptual framework approach is used to evaluate independence matters in Section 1.210. The Code uses a risk-based approach to assess whether a CPA's relationship with a client would pose an unacceptable risk. Risk is unacceptable if the relationship would compromise (or would be perceived as compromising by an informed third party knowing all the relevant information) the CPA's professional judgment when rendering an attest service to the client (i.e., audit, review, or attestation engagement). Key to that evaluation is identifying and assessing the extent to which a threat to the CPA's independence exists, and if it does, whether it would be reasonable to expect that the threat would compromise the CPA's professional judgment and, if so, whether it can be effectively mitigated or eliminated. Under the risk-based approach, steps are taken to prevent circumstances that threaten independence from compromising the professional judgments required in the performance of an attest engagement.

The risk-based approach involves the following steps:

1. Identifying and evaluating threats to independence.
2. Determining whether safeguards already eliminate or sufficiently mitigate identified threats and whether threats that have not yet been mitigated can be eliminated or sufficiently mitigated by safeguards.
3. If no safeguards are available to eliminate an unacceptable threat or reduce it to an acceptable level, independence would be considered impaired.

Threats to Independence

Independence in fact is defined as the state of mind that permits the performance of an attest service without being affected by influences that compromise professional judgment, thereby allowing an individual to act with integrity and professional skepticism. To *appear to be independent,* the CPA should avoid circumstances that might cause an informed third party to reasonably conclude that the integrity, objectivity, or professional skepticism of a firm or member of the audit (attest) engagement team has been compromised.

Threats to independence include a self-review threat, advocacy threat, adverse interest threat, familiarity threat, undue influence threat, financial self-interest threat, and management participation threat. A brief description of each threat follows, and Exhibit 4.2 provides examples of each threat.

Self-Review Threat

A self-review threat occurs when a CPA reviews evidence during an attest engagement that is based on her own or her firm's nonattest work. An example would be preparing source documents used to generate the client's financial statements.

EXHIBIT 4.2 Examples of Threats to Independence

Threat	Example
Self-Review Threat	Preparing source documents used to generate the client's financial statements.
Advocacy Threat	Promoting the client's securities as part of an initial public offering or representing a client in U.S. tax court.
Adverse Interest Threat	Commencing, or the expressed intention to commence, litigation by either the client or the CPA against the other.
Familiarity Threat	A CPA on the attest engagement team whose spouse is the client's CEO.
Undue Influence Threat	A threat to replace the CPA or CPA firm because of a disagreement with the client over the application of an accounting principle.
Financial Self-Interest Threat	Having a loan from the client, from an officer or director of the client, or from an individual who owns 10 percent or more of the client's outstanding equity securities.
Management Participation Threat	Establishing and maintaining internal controls for the client.

Advocacy Threat

An advocacy threat occurs when a CPA promotes an attest client's interests or position in such a way that objectivity may be, or may be perceived to be, compromised. These are of particular concern when performing tax services.

Adverse Interest Threat

An adverse interest threat occurs when a CPA takes actions that are in opposition to an attest client's interests or positions.

Familiarity Threat

A familiarity threat occurs when a close relationship is formed between the CPA and an attest client or its employees, members of top management, or directors of the client entity, including individuals or entities that performed nonattest work for the client (i.e., tax or consulting services).

Undue Influence Threat

An undue influence threat results from an attempt by the management of an attest client or other interested parties to coerce the CPA or exercise excessive influence over the CPA.

Financial Self-Interest Threat

A financial self-interest threat occurs when there is a potential benefit to a CPA from a financial interest in, or from some other financial relationship with, an attest client. It goes beyond simple situations where independence would be impaired, such as directly owning shares of stock of the client or having material indirect financial interest. Financial self-interest threats can also arise from business relationships with a client or a member of management that creates a mutual self-interest.

Management Participation Threat

A management participation threat occurs when a CPA takes on the role of client management or otherwise performs management functions on behalf of an attest client.

Safeguards to Counteract Threats

Safeguards are controls that eliminate or reduce threats to independence. These range from partial to complete prohibitions of the threatening circumstance to procedures that counteract the potential influence of a threat. The nature and extent of the safeguards to be applied depend on many factors, including the size of the firm and whether the client is a public interest entity. To be effective, safeguards should eliminate the threat or reduce to an acceptable level the threat's potential to impair independence.

There are three broad categories of safeguards. The relative importance of a safeguard depends on its appropriateness in light of the facts and circumstances.

1. *Safeguards created by the profession, legislation, or regulation.* For example, continuing education requirements on independence and ethics and external review of a firm's quality control system.

2. *Safeguards implemented by the client,* such as a tone at the top that emphasizes the attest client's commitment to fair financial reporting and a governance structure, such as an active audit committee, that is designed to ensure appropriate decision making, oversight, and communications regarding a firm's services.

3. *Safeguards implemented by the firm,* including policies and procedures to implement professional and regulatory requirements.

Exhibit 4.3 categorizes examples by source of the safeguard. It applies to the conceptual framework for independence and the Integrity and Objectivity Rule.

EXHIBIT 4.3   Examples of Safeguards in Applying the Conceptual Framework

Source of the Safeguard	Examples of Safeguards
Created by the profession, legislation, or regulation	Professional resources, such as hotlines, for consultation on ethical issues.
Implemented by the client	The client has personnel with suitable skill, knowledge, or experience who make managerial decisions about the delivery of professional services and makes use of third-party resources for consultation as needed.
	The tone at the top emphasizes the client's commitment to fair financial reporting and compliance with the applicable laws, rules, regulations, and corporate governance policies.
	Policies and procedures are in place to achieve fair financial reporting and compliance with the applicable laws, rules, regulations, and corporate governance policies.
	Policies and procedures are in place to address ethical conduct.
	Policies are in place that bar the entity from hiring a firm to provide services that do not serve the public interest or that would cause the firm's independence or objectivity to be considered impaired.
Implemented by the firm	Policies and procedures addressing ethical conduct and compliance with laws and regulations.

Notice how many of the safeguards relate to organizational ethics processes discussed in Chapter 3.

Global Code of Ethics

The International Federation of Accountants (IFAC) is comprised of more than 175 members and associates in 130 countries and jurisdictions, representing approximately 2.5 million accountants around the world. IFAC is not a regulatory authority, but it does serves to represent the public interest in the global arena.

IFAC established the International Ethics Standards Board for Accountants (IESBA) to develop and issue high-quality ethical standards and other pronouncements for professional accountants for use around the world. The result was the issuance of the IESBA Handbook, Code of Ethics for Professional Accountants (IFAC Code), which establishes ethical requirements for professional accountants performing services in the global business arena. A member body of IFAC or a firm from its country may not apply less stringent standards than those stated in the IFAC Code. However, if a member body or firm is prohibited from complying with certain parts of this Code by national law or regulation, they should be governed by their country's requirements but comply with all other parts of the Code.

The 2015 IFAC Code becomes effective on April 15, 2016. For the most part, the IFAC Code is similar to the AICPA Code. In fact, the AICPA Code was revised to incorporate the more principles-based approach under the IFAC Code that relies on the conceptual framework to evaluate all issues that may arise when specific rules do not address a matter. It also follows the threats and safeguards approach we discussed above.[19]

IFAC's "Fundamental Principles" of professional behavior differ slightly from the AICPA Code. The principles also describe the basic standards somewhat differently. The principles include:

Integrity. To be straightforward and honest in all professional and business relationships.

Objectivity. To not allow bias, conflict of interest, or undue influence of others to override professional or business judgment.

Professional Competence and Due Care. To maintain knowledge and skill at the level required to ensure that a client or employer receives competent professional service based on current developments in practice, legislation, and techniques and act diligently and in accordance with applicable technical and professional standards.

Confidentiality. To respect the confidentiality of information acquired as a result of professional and business relationships and therefore not disclose any such information to third parties without proper and specific authority, unless there is a legal or professional right or duty to disclose, nor use the information for the personal advantage of the professional accountant or third parties.

Professional Behavior. To comply with relevant laws and regulations and avoid any actions that discredits the profession.

The AICPA Code has converged with many of the IESBA's ethical standards in the IFAC Code. It is not surprising that ethics provisions have been moving toward convergence on a global level similar to auditing standards, and the convergence of International Financial Reporting Standards (IFRS) and U.S. GAAP.

Relationships That May Impair Independence

A variety of relationships have the potential to impair audit independence because of conflicts of interest that may arise. Some of these potential conflicts arise from financial relationships, while others occur when providing nonattest services for an attest client or being employed by a former attest client. Some of the trickiest relationships today arise from the different forms of organization in which traditional CPA firm services are provided to clients.

Financial Relationships

The ownership of stock in a client creates a financial self-interest threat to independence. The problem with owning direct and material indirect financial interests is that these arrangements might create the impression in the mind of an outside observer that the CPA cannot make decisions without being influenced by the stock ownership, even if that is not the case for any specific CPA. The logical conclusion is that the auditor's opinion would be tainted by the existence of these relationships.

Another example of a financial self-interest threat is when a CPA becomes involved in a loan transaction to or from a client, including home mortgage loans from financial institution clients. This type of loan is prohibited under the Code. It provides that independence is considered to be impaired if, during the period of the professional engagement, a covered member, such as a CPA on the attest engagement team or an individual in a position to influence the attest engagement team, has any loan to or from a client, any officer or director of the client, or any individual owning 10 percent or more of the client's outstanding equity securities or other ownership interests.

Examples of permitted loans include automobile loans and leases collateralized by the automobile, loans fully collateralized by cash deposits at the same financial institution (e.g., "passbook loans"), and aggregate credit card balances from credit cards and overdraft reserve accounts that are reduced to $10,000 or less on a current basis, taking into consideration the payment due and any available grace period.

Perhaps no other situation illustrates the danger of a CPA accepting loans from a client more than that of Jose Gomez, the lead partner of Alexander Grant (now Grant Thornton) during its audit of ESM Government Securities from 1977 to 1984. Over the eight-year period, ESM committed fraud and, in the process, used its leverage against Gomez from $200,000 in loans to him so he would keep silent about the fact that ESM's financial statements did not present fairly financial position and the results of operations. Top management of ESM also threatened to pull the audit from Gomez's firm if he spoke out about the fraud. Gomez compromised his integrity, and the event ruined his reputation. Ultimately, Gomez was sentenced to a 12-year prison term and served 4½ years, and the firm paid approximately $175 million in civil payments.

The Independence Rule also extends to certain family members of the CPA. The detailed provisions are beyond the scope of this book, but we do want to emphasize two points to provide examples of familiarity threats to independence. First, when a CPA is part of the attest engagement team, which includes employees and contractors directly involved in an audit and those who perform concurring and second partner reviews, the rules extend to that CPA's immediate family members and close relatives. Immediate family members include the CPA's spouse, spousal equivalent, and dependents (whether or not they are related). The rules also extend to the CPA's close relatives, including parents, siblings, or nondependent children, if they hold a key position with the client (that is, one that involves direct participation in the preparation of the financial statements or a position that gives the CPA the ability to exercise influence over the contents of the financial statements). Close relatives are subject to the Independence Rule if they own a financial interest in the client that is material to that person's net worth and of which the CPA has knowledge, or if they own a financial interest in the client that enables the close relative to exercise significant influence over the client. The potential danger in these family relationships is that the family member's financial or employment relationship with the client might influence the perception that the CPA can be independent in fact or appearance. One problem with the rule is that the CPA might feign ignorance of the ownership interest even though he is aware of it—an unethical act.

There are other relationships that will bring a CPA under the Independence rules, including when a partner or manager provides 10 hours or more of nonattest services to the attest client. The problem is it may appear to an outside observer that the partner or manager may be able to influence the attest work because of the significant number of hours devoted to the nonattest services.

Let's stop at this point and consider that the Independence Rule is a challenging standard for the CPA and family members to meet, and it might present some interesting dilemmas. For example, imagine that a CPA knows that her father owns a financial interest in a client entity but does not know if that interest is material to the father's net worth. Should the CPA contact the father to find out? Or, might the CPA reason that it is better not to know because the Independence Rule applies only if the CPA has knowledge of the extent of the father's financial interest in the client? From an ethical perspective, the CPA should make a good-faith effort to determine the extent of her father's financial interest in the client entity.

Employment or Association with Attest Clients

It is not unusual for a CPA who has worked on an engagement for a client to be offered a position with that client. If the client has confidence in the abilities of the CPA and trusts that party, then the client may seek to hire the professional, for example, as the controller or CFO. The rules establish that independence may be impaired when a partner or professional employee leaves the firm and is subsequently employed by or associated with the client in a key position unless the following conditions are met:

- Amounts due to the former partner/professional are not material to the firm.
- The former partner/professional is not in a position to influence the accounting firm's operations or financial policies.
- The former partner/professional employee does not participate in or appear to participate in or is not associated with the firm once the relationship with the client begins.

An example of participating in the firm is continuing to consult for it or have one's name included in firm literature, which implies a relationship still exists.

Providing Nonattest Services to an Attest Client

As previously mentioned, concern exists in Congress and the SEC about a possible impairment of audit independence when the firm also provides nonaudit services for the client. An example of a prohibited activity under AICPA and SEC rules is that a CPA should not perform management functions or make management decisions for an attest client. The relationship creates a management participation threat that places the CPA in the compromising position of making decisions for the client and then auditing those decisions. On the other hand, the CPA may provide advice, research materials, and recommendations to assist the client's management in performing its functions and making decisions.

The Code establishes requirements that must be met during the period covered by the financial statements and the period of the attest engagement by the CPA in order to conduct nonattest services for the client without impairing audit independence. Under Code Section 1.295, individual nonattest services may be permitted because adequate safeguards are provided by the Interpretation. However, when performing multiple services there may be unacceptable threats (i.e, management participation, self-review) to independence.

General requirements exist for the attest client when a CPA performs nonattest services, including:

- Assume all management responsibilities.
- Oversee the service, by designating an individual, preferably within senior management, who possesses suitable skill, knowledge, and/or experience.
- Evaluate the adequacy and results of the services performed.
- Accept responsibility for the results of the service.

Other requirements exist, including to clearly establish the objectives of the engagement, services to be performed, client's acceptance of its responsibilities, member's responsibilities, and any limitations of the engagement.

Nontraditional Forms of Ownership

Other restrictions exist because of the variety of forms of organization that exist today for providing professional accounting services to clients. For example, a traditional CPA firm may be acquired by a public company that will provide nonattest services to clients, while, at the same time, a spin-off of the original firm provides the attest services. The arrangement is necessary because only firms that are majority owned by CPAs can perform attest services. The problem with these so-called "alternative practice structures" is that the managers of the public company may attempt to exert pressure over those in the CPA firm because of their ownership leverage and because their ethical requirements are not likely to be as high as the ones for the CPAs. In these cases the CPAs remain responsible, financially and otherwise, for all the attest work performed.

One of the largest entities providing professional accounting services through an alternative practice structure is CBIZ. CBIZ offers traditional accounting services, business tax services, and consulting. CBIZ is associated with Mayer Hoffman McCann P.C., a national, independent CPA firm. Through this association, CBIZ advertises that it offers audit and attest services. Together, the two entities rank as one of top national accounting providers.

One of the problems with these associations is the potential for objectivity to be compromised because of the relationship. For example, just imagine if CBIZ prepares the tax returns for a client that is also serviced by Mayer Hoffman for its audit needs. The danger is the managers at CBIZ might attempt to influence the auditors from Mayer Hoffman on behalf of the client. While holding the auditors responsible for their own work is a necessary provision that is included in the Code, it may not be a sufficient one to eliminate biases that are created by the relationship. The appearance may be that the audit work could be tainted by the relationship.

Other forms of organization also provide ethical challenges for CPAs, including network firms where CPA firms join larger groups, which typically are membership associations that are legal separate entities otherwise unrelated to their members. Another is when the affiliate of a financial statement attest client is subject to the Independence Rule in the Code.

We expect new forms of organization will come into being as CPAs/CPA firms attempt to quench their seemingly never-ending thirst for more business and a broadened scope of professional services. This would not necessarily be a bad thing, in part because clients come to trust their auditors/audit firms. However, with the hiring of non-CPAs to service these clients, a legitimate question to raise is whether the CPA side of the practice can exercise restraint on the behavior of the non-CPAs when warranted.

SEC Position on Auditor Independence

LO 4-4
Discuss how nonattest services can impair audit independence.

Publicly owned companies have been obligated to follow SEC rules since the passage of the Securities Act of 1933 and the Securities and Exchange Act of 1934. The PCAOB has taken some of that responsibility away from the SEC, while at the same time requiring the SEC to adopt final rules on auditor independence.

The SEC approach to independence emphasizes independence in fact and appearance in three ways: (1) proscribing certain financial interests and business relationships with the audit client, (2) restricting the provision of certain nonauditing services to audit clients, and (3) subjecting all auditor conduct to a general standard of independence. The general standard of independence is stated as follows: "The Commission will not recognize an accountant as independent, with respect to an audit client, if the accountant is not, or a reasonable investor with knowledge of all relevant facts and circumstances would conclude that the accountant is not, capable of exercising objective and impartial judgment on all issues encompassed within the accountant's engagement."

The general standard of independence is evaluated by applying four principles that are similar to the AICPA's conceptual framework and that indicate when auditor independence may be impaired by a relationship with the audit client. If a situation results in any of the following, the auditor's independence may be impaired: (1) creates a mutual or conflicting interest between an accountant and his audit client, (2) places an accountant in the position of auditing her own work, (3) results in an accountant acting as management or an employee of the audit client, or (4) places an accountant in a position of being an advocate for the audit client.

The SEC believes that these principles are "general guidance and their application may depend on particular facts and circumstances . . . [but they do] provide an appropriate framework for analyzing auditor independence issues." To provide further guidance on implementing the principles, the SEC identified three basic overarching principles that underlie auditor independence: (1) an auditor cannot function in the role of management, (2) an auditor cannot audit her own work, and (3) an auditor cannot serve in an advocacy role for his client.[20]

SEC Actions Against Big Four CPA Firms

Over the years, the SEC has brought actions against auditing firms for violating the independence rules. The cases are instructive and illustrate the failure of the auditing profession to adhere to both the form and the spirit of the independence rules, and therefore violate the public trust. All firms become targets of the SEC sooner or later because of the threats to independence. We have selected one such independence violation for each of the Big Four.

Avon and Pinnacle: Nonaudit Services Influence PwC's Audit Work

On July 18, 2002, PwC agreed to settle charges that it violated SEC's independence rules in its audit of two clients, Avon and Pinnacle. The cases are somewhat complicated but boil down to the firm's approval of improper accounting of expenses. The actions against PwC for its audits of Avon and Pinnacle are particularly significant because they suggest that the firm may have been swayed in its audit by fees it was paid for nonaudit services.

According to the SEC, Avon hired PwC to help put together a complex software system in the late 1990s and then terminated the project before it was completed in April 1999. Instead of writing off the full cost of the project, about $42 million, Avon wrote down only $15 million and recorded the rest of the money spent, which consisted largely of fees to PwC, as a capital expense. PwC approved the flawed accounting. This accounting treatment delayed the effect of the failed project on Avon's earnings. The company took an additional charge of $24 million in the third quarter of 2001. Avon restated its financial statements for the first three months of 1999 and for the full year 2001.[21]

In Pinnacle's case, PwC approved improper treatment of about $8.5 million as a capital expense—including $6.8 million in fees to the firm for nonaudit services—after Pinnacle bought a network of towers serving cellular telephones from Motorola in 1999. PwC also improperly approved Pinnacle's accounting of more than $24 million in reserves related to the acquisition. Pinnacle restated its accounting of that transaction.[22]

Stephen Cutler, the SEC's Division of Enforcement director, said the cases demonstrate the heightened risk of an audit failure when an accounting firm assists in and approves the accounting treatment of its own consulting fees. "Faced with that situation, PwC lacked the objectivity and impartiality required of an independent auditor," he said.

PeopleSoft and Ernst & Young: Mutuality of Interests

On April 16, 2004, the SEC sanctioned EY because it was not independent in fact or appearance when it audited the financial statements of PeopleSoft for fiscal years 1994–1999. The SEC's sanctions included a six-month suspension from accepting new SEC audit clients, disgorgement of audit fees (more than $1.6 million), an injunction against future violations, and an independent consultant report on its independence and internal quality controls.

The SEC found independence violations arising from EY's business relationships with PeopleSoft while auditing the company's financial statements. These relationships created a mutuality of interests between the firm and PeopleSoft, resulting in a financial self-interest threat.

The basic facts are EY's Tax Group created a Global Expatriate Management System (EY/GEMS) as an in-house software program for assisting clients with the tax consequences of managing employees with international assignments. The EY/GEMS system was enhanced with the use of PeopleTools, a software product created by EY's audit client, PeopleSoft. A business relationship was created whereby a license to use PeopleTools was granted to EY in return for a payment to PeopleSoft of 15 percent of each licensee fee that EY received from outside customers purchasing the new software, 30 percent of each license renewal fee, and a minimum royalty of $300,000, payable in 12 quarterly payments of $25,000 each.

The licensing agreement provided that EY would make PeopleSoft a third-party beneficiary of each sublicense. PeopleSoft agreed to assist EY's efforts by providing technical assistance for a $15,000 quarterly fee. The agreement provided that EY could not distribute the derivative software to PeopleSoft's direct competitors. The agreement permitted EY to use PeopleSoft trademarks and trade names in marketing materials. PeopleSoft maintained a degree of control over the product by restricting EY's distribution rights and requiring the firm to work closely with PeopleSoft to ensure the quality of the product.

The SEC found that EY and PeopleSoft had a "symbiotic relationship" engaging in joint sales and marketing efforts and sharing considerable proprietary and confidential business information, and that EY partnered with PeopleSoft to accomplish increased sales and boost consulting revenues for EY. The findings of the SEC indicate that EY and PeopleSoft acted together to promote the product so that a reasonable investor with knowledge of all the facts would conclude that EY was closely identified in fact and appearance with its audit client. Brenda P. Murray, the chief administrative law judge at the SEC, wrote in her opinion that "Ernst's day-to-day operations were profit-driven and ignored considerations of auditor independence."

KPMG Gets Slammed for Independence Violations

KPMG LLP agreed to pay $8.2 million on January 24, 2014, to settle charges by the SEC that the firm violated auditor independence rules by providing certain nonaudit services to affiliates of companies whose books KPMG was auditing. In audit reports, KPMG repeatedly represented that it was independent despite providing services at various times from 2007 to 2011 to three audit clients.[23]

"The prohibited services included restructuring, corporate finance, and expert services—to an affiliate of one company that was an audit client," the SEC stated. KPMG provided such prohibited nonaudit services as bookkeeping and payroll to affiliates of another audit client. These relationships created a self-review threat to independence.

In a separate instance, KPMG hired an individual who had recently retired from a senior position at an affiliate of an audit client. KPMG then loaned him back to that affiliate to do the same work he had done as an employee of that affiliate, which resulted in the professional acting as a manager, employee, and advocate for the audit client. An SEC investigation also revealed some KPMG personnel owned stock in companies or affiliates of companies that were KPMG audit clients, further violating auditor independence rules.

The SEC noted that—without admitting or denying the findings—KPMG agreed to pay $5,266,347 in disgorgement of fees received from the three clients plus prejudgment interest of $1,185,002 and an additional penalty of $1,775,000. In addition, KPMG agreed to implement internal changes to educate firm personnel and monitor the firm's compliance with auditor independence requirements for nonaudit services and that an independent consultant would evaluate these changes.

Deloitte Consulting's Business Relationship with Audit Client Management

On July 1, 2015, the SEC charged Deloitte & Touche LLP with violating auditor independence rules when its consulting affiliate kept a business relationship with a trustee serving on the boards and audit committees of three funds Deloitte audited. Deloitte agreed to pay more than $1 million to settle the charges. Deloitte also disgorged to the SEC audit fees of nearly $500,000 plus prejudgment interest of about $116,000, and it paid a penalty of $500,000.[24]

Deloitte violated its own policies by failing to conduct an independence consultation before starting a new business relationship with trustee Andrew C. Boynton. Deloitte failed to discover that the required initial independence consultation was not performed until nearly five years after the independence-impairing relationship had been established between Deloitte Consulting and Boynton, who was paid consulting fees for his external client work.

Deloitte compromised its independence because the relationship made it appear that the firm may not be objective and impartial in conducting its audit of the three funds. Deloitte represented in audit reports that it was independent of the three funds while Boynton simultaneously served on their boards and audit committees.

These cases against the Big Four raise the red flag about consulting services and possible impairments of audit independence. CPA firms have to be more attentive to possible impairments of audit independence as they increase the nature and scope of nonaudit services provided to audit clients. Biases can creep into the decision making in a subtle way and compromise independent judgment.

Insider Trading Cases

What possesses an audit partner to trade on inside information or give tips about it to others and violate the accounting profession's most sacred ethical standard of audit independence? Is it carelessness, greed, or ethical blindness? In the cases of Thomas Flannigan and Scott London, it appears all were involved.

Insider Trading: Thomas Flannigan, Deloitte & Touche

In 2010, Deloitte and Touche found itself involved in an SEC investigation of repeated insider trading by Thomas P. Flanagan, a former management advisory partner and a vice chairman at Deloitte. Flanagan traded in the securities of multiple Deloitte clients on the basis of inside information that he learned through his duties as a Deloitte partner. The inside information concerned market-moving events such as earnings results, revisions to earnings guidance, sales figures and cost cutting, and an acquisition. Flanagan's illegal trading resulted in profits of more than $430,000.

Flanagan also tipped his son, Patrick, to certain of this material nonpublic information. Patrick then traded based on that information. Patrick's illegal trading resulted in profits of more than $57,000. The

SEC charges included: (1) Between 2003 and 2008, Flanagan made 71 purchases of stock and options in the securities of Deloitte audit clients. Flanagan made 62 of these purchases in the securities of Deloitte audit clients while serving as the advisory partner on those audits; and (2) on at least nine occasions between 2005 and 2008, Flanagan traded on the basis of material nonpublic information of Deloitte clients, including Best Buy, Motorola, Sears, and Option Care.

Insider Trading: Scott London, KPMG

In the case of Scott London, the former partner in charge of the KPMG's Southern California's regional audit practice, it seems greed and stupidity were the underlying causes of insider trading. On April 11, 2013, the SEC charged London with leaking confidential information to his friend, Brian Shaw, about Skechers, and Herbalife. Shaw, a jewelry store owner and country club friend of London, repaid London with $50,000 in cash and a Rolex watch, according to legal filings.

After federal regulators froze Shaw's investment account because of suspicious activity, the jeweler fully confessed, paid back nearly $2 million in illegally gained profits and fines to the SEC, and cooperated in the investigation against London.

London was sentenced to 14 months in a federal prison and forced to pay a $100,000 fine. He also was fired from his $900,000-a-year job as an auditor for KPMG in 2012, and the company was forced to redo several of London's prior audits. The audit opinions signed by London on Skechers and Herbalife had to be withdrawn by the firm.

The leaking of confidential financial information about a company to anyone prior to its public release affects the level playing field that should exist with respect to personal and business contacts of an auditor and the general public. It violates the fairness doctrine in treating equals equally, and it violates basic integrity standards. Such actions cut to the core values of integrity and trust—the foundation of the public interest obligation of CPAs.

These insider trading cases illustrate the risk to audit independence when audit engagement team members, including partners, trade on information that is not publicly available. Beyond that, the use of sensitive financial information about a client for personal reasons violates the independence requirement because it creates a financial self-interest relationship between the partner and the client.

Non–Big Four Firms Not Immune to Independence Violations

In what appears to be a common problem, at least for non–Big Four firms, on December 8, 2014, the SEC sanctioned eight firms and the PCAOB separately sanctioned seven others for violating auditor independence rules when they prepared the financial statements of brokerage firms that were their audit clients. The PCAOB said its enforcement actions grew out of information gathered by the board's inspection program. "The bedrock of audit quality is independence," said PCAOB chairman James Doty in a statement. "When an auditor's independence is impaired, the auditor's responsibility to exercise professional skepticism, and to serve the public trust, is also put at risk. Adhering to independence requirements is critically important."[25]

In the SEC action, the agency found that during audits the eight firms relied on data from financial statements and notes that the audit firms themselves had prepared for the clients. That meant the audit firms were auditing their own work, thereby creating a self-review threat to independence, and they inappropriately aligned themselves more closely with the interests of clients' management teams in helping prepare the books rather than strictly auditing them.

"Operation Broken Gate"

In October 2013, the SEC announced the launch of "Operation Broken Gate"—an initiative to identify auditors who neglect their duties and the required auditing standards. Operation Broken Gate is the

SEC's effort to hold gatekeepers accountable. Around the same time, the SEC announced its "focus on auditors" program to increase its efforts to identify independence violations. The trigger event was the filing of multiple auditor independence cases whereby the firms loaned staff to their audit clients, similar to the KPMG case above. Technically, an independent auditor may loan staff to its client and clearly the auditor may provide tax services to its client. But if the loaned staff looks like a client employee, regardless of the services provided, the SEC may conclude the arrangement violates the independence rules.

The SEC's concerns go beyond independence violations. The underlying conduct that motivated Operation Broken Gate centers on a failure to comply with the pertinent professional standards. Cases have been filed against CPAs/CPA firms for a lack of due care, failure to obtain sufficient competent evidential matter, failure to properly assess audit risk, insufficient documentation of audit procedures in work papers, failure to properly assess internal controls, failure to perform an engagement quality review, and failure to communicate certain information with the audit committee. The possibility that audit firms are doing sloppy work is concerning. We hope the firms are not going "back to the future" again by low-balling audit bids to win clients with the hope to provide lucrative consulting work in the future. Low bids can cause reduced audit work, assigning less experienced auditors to an engagement, reducing supervision of audits, and failing to provide quality review services.

AICPA Code: Ethical Conflicts

LO 4-5
Describe the process to resolve ethical conflicts that affect integrity and objectivity.

Under the Revised Code, when evaluating whether a CPA in public practice is in compliance with the rules, a CPA should assess whether an ethical conflict exists. Ethical Conflicts (1.000.020) create challenges to ethical decision making because they present barriers to meeting the requirements of the rules of conduct. An ethical conflict may exist, for example, if a CPA in public practice suspects a fraud may have occurred, but reporting the suspected fraud would violate the confidentiality obligation. Recall that in Chapter 3 we discussed Interpretation 102-4 (in the previous code) that applies to subordination of judgment situations and whistleblowing. These rules are now covered in Section 1.130.020 of the Revised Code and will be discussed later on.

Exhibit 4.4 identifies the major considerations for CPAs in assessing the risk that ethical conflicts may lead to a violation of the rules of conduct. Briefly, the CPA should consider whether any departures exist to the rules, laws, or regulations and how they will be justified in order to ensure that conflicts are resolved in a way that permits compliance with these requirements. Resolution of the conflict may call for consulting with others in the entity or others, including legal counsel. Any unresolved conflicts can lead to a violation of the rules of conduct, which, in turn, should focus the CPA's attention on any continuing relationship with the engagement team, specific assignment, client, firm, or employer.

Integrity and Objectivity

We first discussed Integrity and Objectivity in Chapter 1. The Revised Code addresses the Integrity and Objectivity Rule (1.100.001) by linking it to challenges from conflict of interest situations and subordination of judgment. In the absence of an interpretation that addresses a particular relationship or circumstance, the CPA should apply the conceptual framework approach to evaluate threats and safeguards. Guidance under the ethical conflicts framework also should be considered (Exhibit 4.4) when addressing such obstacles to ensure proper handling of internal or external pressures that create barriers to following the professional or legal standards, or both.

EXHIBIT 4.4   **Ethical Conflicts and Compliance with the Rules of Conduct for Members in Public Practice and Business***

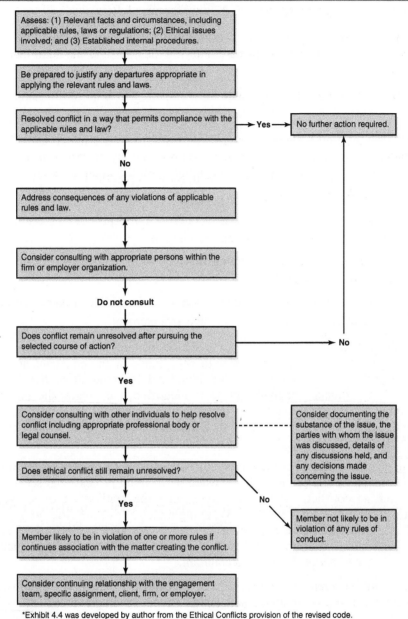

*Exhibit 4.4 was developed by author from the Ethical Conflicts provision of the revised code.

Conflicts of Interest

Conflicts of interest (1.110.010) for members in public practice occur when a professional service, relationship, or specific matter creates a situation that might impair objective judgment. Determinations are made through the application of professional judgment in order to evaluate whether a reasonable and informed third party who is aware of the relevant information would conclude that a conflict of interest exists.

A conflict of interest creates adverse and self-interest threats to integrity and objectivity. For example, threats may occur when the CPA/CPA firm provides a professional service related to a particular matter involving two or more clients whose interests are in conflict, or the firm's interest and that of the client are in conflict.

Illustrations of conflicts are given in the rules. A few examples follow.

- Providing corporate finance services to a client seeking to acquire an audit client of the firm, when the firm has obtained confidential information during the course of the audit that may be relevant to the transaction.

- Advising two clients at the same time who are competing to acquire the same company when the advice might be relevant to the parties' competitive positions.

- Providing services to both a vendor and a purchaser who are clients of the firm in relation to the same transaction.

- Advising a client to invest in a business in which, for example, the immediate family member of the CPA has a financial interest in the business.

- Providing forensic investigation services to a client for the purpose of evaluating or supporting contemplated litigation against another client of the firm.

- Providing tax or personal financial planning services for several members of a family whom the CPA knows have opposing interests.

- Referring a personal financial planning or tax client to an insurance broker or other service provider, which refers clients to the CPA under an exclusive arrangement.

To identify possible conflicts of interest, the CPA should examine situations that may create threats to compliance with integrity and objectivity prior to acceptance of the engagement and throughout the term of the relationship. This includes matters identified by external parties including current or potential clients. The earlier a potential conflict is identified, the greater the likelihood of applying safeguards to eliminate or reduce significant threats to an acceptable level. If the threat has not been eliminated or reduced to an acceptable level, then appropriate safeguards should be applied to ensure acting with objectivity and integrity.

Examples of safeguards include: (1) implementing mechanisms to prevent unauthorized disclosure of confidential information of one or more clients when performing professional services for two or more clients whose interests conflict; (2) regularly reviewing the application of safeguards by a senior individual not involved in the engagements; (3) having a member of the firm not involved in providing the services or otherwise affected by the conflict review the work performed to assess whether key judgments and conclusions are appropriate; and (4) consulting with third parties, such as a professional body, legal counsel, or another professional accountant.

In cases where identified threats are so significant that no safeguards will eliminate them or reduce them to an acceptable level, or adequate safeguards cannot be implemented, the CPA should either decline to perform the service that would result in the conflict of interest, or terminate the relevant relationship or dispose of the relevant interests to eliminate the threat or reduce it to an acceptable level.

When a conflict of interest exists, the CPA should disclose the nature of the conflict to clients and other appropriate parties affected by the client and obtain their consent to perform professional services even if threats are at an acceptable level. If consent is not received, then the CPA should either cease performing the services or take action to eliminate or reduce the threat to an acceptable level.

An example of a potential conflict of interest is when a CPA offers gifts to clients or accepts gifts or entertainment from a client. Threats need to be evaluated as well as the significance of any such threats and safeguards that might mitigate their effects. Such situations may create self-interest, familiarity, or undue influence threats to compliance with the Integrity and Objectivity Rule.

Generally, gifts are differentiated from entertainment by whether the client participates in the activity with the firm. For example, giving tickets to a sporting event for the client to use would be considered a gift versus attending the event with the client, which would be considered entertainment. The determining factor as to whether the threats created by the gifts are at an acceptable or unacceptable level is the reasonableness of the circumstances, taking into consideration the nature of the gift or entertainment, occasion for which it is provided, cost or value, whether the entertainment was associated with the active conduct of business directly before, during, or after the entertainment, and the individuals from the client and the CPA's firm who participated in the entertainment.

Let's assume your client comes to your office one day. You are the partner in charge of the audit for the client. The client wants to show his appreciation for the audit engagement team's completion of the audit one week early and under budget. He gives you a dozen tickets for the baseball game between the Los Angeles Angels of Anaheim and L.A. Dodgers. It is just a regular, inter-league game and has no significance beyond that. Can you accept the gift?

If the audit is completed, the first question is whether the acceptance of the gift might make it appear to a reasonable observer that the gift is intended to influence the audit opinion. If so, that would create an undue influence threat and compromise integrity and objectivity. Also, it could be perceived as an advance payoff for future audit opinions. The influence does not have to be immediate. Beyond that, the first issue to consider is: Would acceptance violate any laws, regulations, or firm policies? If so, acceptance would create a threat that cannot be reduced or eliminated through any safeguards. If not, consider the following:

- What is the nature, value, and intent of the gift?
- Is it more than clearly inconsequential?
- Is it reasonable in the circumstances?
- Is it standard practice to accept or reject such gifts?
- Does the client expect a "quid pro quo?"

From an ethical perspective, the best way to approach the issue is to, first, apply the smell test. Second, evaluate whether acceptance is consistent with your values and those of the firm. Third, ask whether you would be comfortable explaining why you agreed to accept the gifts if you were questioned by a superior or a newspaper reporter?

It is never wise to potentially compromise your reputation and the trust others place in you, so the safe way to deal with such gifts is to decline them. Thus, you will not have to explain them away at a later date.

Subordination of Judgment

The Integrity Rule prohibits a CPA from knowingly misrepresenting facts or subordinating one's judgments when performing professional services for a client or employer. The Subordination of Judgment (1.130.020) interpretation addresses differences of opinion between a CPA and that person's supervisor or others within the organization. The interpretation had been restricted to matters between internal accountants and supervisors but was revised and now it also applies to external CPA auditors when differences of opinion exist between external auditors and senior management of the firm. The rule recognizes that pressures may be imposed by superiors in an accounting firm on an engagement team member because firm management is unaware of, unable to, or unwilling to reexamine its own conclusions regarding an accounting position that would result in a materially different financial statement presentation or footnote disclosure than that which the engagement team member believes accords with professional standards.

Differences of opinion on accounting matters can raise whistleblowing considerations, as was discussed in Chapter 3. Exhibit 3.13 describes the steps that should be taken by accounting professionals when faced with situations where differences of opinion exist in order to avoid subordinating judgment. A summary of the steps and related considerations follow.

- Consider any threats to integrity and objectivity including self-interest, familiarity, and undue influence threats and assess their significance.

- Evaluate the significance of threats to determine if they are at an acceptable level: Significance relates to whether the result of the position taken by the supervisor or other person fails to comply with applicable professional standards, creates a material misrepresentation of fact, or may violate applicable laws or regulations.

- If threats are at an acceptable level, discuss the conclusion with the person taking the position; if not at an acceptable level, bring concerns to supervisor.

- If differences of opinion are not resolved, discuss the matter with higher levels of management (i.e., supervisor's immediate superior, senior management, and those charged with governance).

- If appropriate action is not taken, consider the following safeguards to ensure that the threats are reduced to an acceptable level to avoid subordination of judgment:

  - Determine whether the organization's internal policies and procedures have any additional requirements for reporting differences of opinion.

  - Determine any reporting responsibilities to third parties, if applicable, and whether communication of confidentiality to the internal accountant/auditor employer or organization's external accountant are required.

  - Consult with legal counsel regarding responsibilities.

  - Document understanding of facts, accounting principles, auditing or other professional standards involved or applicable laws or regulations, and the conversations and parties with whom such matters were discussed.

- If the CPA concludes that no safeguards can eliminate or reduce the threats to an acceptable level or that appropriate action was not taken, then consider whether to continue the relationship with the organization and take steps to eliminate exposure to any subordination of judgment.

- Consider resigning from the organization, but that would not relieve the CPA from any reporting responsibilities to third parties, such as regulatory authorities or the employer's (former employer's) external accountant.

The threats and safeguards approach also applies to nonattest services performed for an attest client because they may cause an impairment of independence. These threats include self-review, management participation, and advocacy. When significant independence threats exist during the period of the professional engagement or the period covered by the financial statements, independence will be impaired unless the threats are reduced to an acceptable level and any other requirements are met as previously discussed. One final note, the rules recognize that, while one kind of nonattest service may not be significant enough individually to impair independence because adequate safeguards exist, the cumulative effect of multiple nonattest services can increase the significance of these threats as well as other threats to independence.

The broad scope of the threats and safeguards approach also reaches to tax services provided to an attest client. These services include preparation of a tax return and the transmittal of the return and any related payment to the taxing authority in paper or electronic form. Self-review and management participation threats to compliance with the Independence Rule may exist.

Threats would be at an acceptable level and independence would not be impaired, provided the CPA does not have custody or control over the attest client's funds or assets and the individual designated by the client to oversee the tax services reviews and approves the return and related tax payment and, if required, signs the tax return prior to the CPA's transmitting it to the taxing authority.

Professional judgment is essential in applying the conceptual framework to independence, integrity, and objectivity situations through evaluations of the significance of threats, whether they can be reduced to an acceptable level, and the steps to be taken to resolve differences of opinion on accounting issues with management of the employer or one's CPA firm. In making these determinations, the CPA must not only apply the rules of conduct but should also consider ethical judgments of right and wrong in light of the public interest principle.

AICPA Code: Conceptual Framework for Members in Business

The Revised Code includes new material for CPAs in business to evaluate whether relationships may exist between the CPA and the employing organization that create threats to compliance with the Integrity and Objectivity Rule. The conceptual framework for members in business (2.000.010) applies to integrity and objectivity, as well as other rules of conduct, but not Independence, because CPAs in business do not provide attest services to clients that require complete independence.

Similar to the guidance for CPAs in public practice, the threats and safeguards approach for CPAs in business identifies a variety of threats to compliance with the Integrity and Objectivity Rule that create the need for safeguards to reduce the threat to an acceptable level or eliminate it. These threats and safeguards are different than those for CPAs in public practice. The examples below illustrate the differences.

Threats and Safeguards

Adverse interest threat. These threats to objectivity arise because the CPA's interests may be opposed to the interests of the employing organization. For instance, a CPA may have charged, or expressed an intention to charge, the employing organization with violations of law. The threat that arises is the result of the ethical conflict. An example would be if a CPA made a whistleblowing charge against the employer under Sarbanes-Oxley or Dodd-Frank. Other threats may exist because a CPA's or the CPA's immediate family or close relative has a financial or other relationship with a vendor, customer, competitor, or potential acquisition of the employing organization and when a CPA has sued or expressed an intention to sue the employing organization or its officers, directors, or employees.

Advocacy threat. Advocacy threats exist because a CPA may promote an employing organization's interests or position to the point that her objectivity is compromised. This would be the case if obtaining favorable financing or additional capital is dependent upon the accuracy of information included in or excluded from a prospectus, an offering, a business plan, a financing application, or a regulatory filing.

Familiarity threat. A familiarity threat arises from a long or close relationship with a person or an employing organization that causes a CPA to become too sympathetic to the latter's interests or too accepting of the person's or employing organization's product or service. Some examples include when a CPA uses an immediate family member's or a close relative's company as a supplier to the employing organization and when a CPA regularly accepts gifts or entertainment from a vendor or customer of the employing organization.

Self-interest threat. The existence of a self-interest threat means that a CPA could benefit, financially or otherwise, from an interest in or relationship with the employing organization or persons associated with the employing organization, such as when a CPA holds a financial interest in the employing organization and the value of that financial interest is directly affected by the CPA's decisions, as would be the case if the financial interest is in the form of shares or share options.

Self-review threat. A self-review threat may occur when a CPA is unable to appropriately evaluate the results of a previous judgment made or service performed or supervised by the CPA, or an individual in the employing organization, and the CPA relies on that service in forming a judgment as part of another service. An example is when performing an internal audit procedure, an internal auditor accepts work that she previously performed in a different position.

Undue influence threat. These threats occur because a CPA subordinates her judgment to that of an individual associated with the employing organization or any relevant third party due to that individual's position, reputation or expertise, aggressive or dominant personality, or attempts to coerce or exercise excessive influence over the CPA. An example is when a CPA is pressured to become associated with misleading information or to change a conclusion regarding an accounting or tax position.

The safeguards to reduce the threats to compliance with the rules for CPAs in business, or reduce them to an acceptable level, are different from those for CPAs in public practice. For CPAs in business, the safeguards are implemented by the employing organization not the firm, and client safeguards are not applicable.

Safeguards implemented by the employing organization include:

1. a tone at the top that emphasizes a commitment to fair financial reporting and compliance with applicable laws, rules, regulations, and corporate governance policies;
2. policies and procedures addressing ethical conduct and compliance with laws, rules, and regulations;
3. an audit committee charter, including independent audit committee members;
4. internal policies and procedures requiring disclosure of identified interests or relationships among the employing organization, its directors or officers, and vendors, suppliers, or customers;
5. dissemination of corporate ethical compliance policies and procedures, including whistleblower hotlines, the reporting structure, dispute resolution, or similar policies, to promote compliance with laws, rules, regulations, and other professional requirements;
6. policies and procedures for implementing and monitoring ethical practices;
7. a reporting structure whereby the internal auditor does not report to the financial reporting group;
8. policies and procedures that do not allow an internal auditor to monitor areas where the internal auditor has operational or functional responsibilities;
9. policies for promotion, rewards, and enforcement of a culture of high ethics and integrity; and
10. use of the third-party resources for consultation as needed on significant matters of professional judgment.

Ethical Conflicts

Similar to CPAs in public practice, ethical conflicts (2.000.020) for CPAs in business may arise that create threats to compliance with some or all of the rules of conduct. An ethical conflict occurs when obstacles to following an appropriate course of action exists due to internal or external pressures and/or conflicts exist in applying relevant professional and legal standards. Steps should be taken to best achieve compliance with the rules and laws by weighing the following factors: relevant facts and circumstances, ethical issues involved, and established internal procedures. CPAs in business must be prepared to justify any departures they believe may be appropriate in applying the relevant rules and laws. The failure to resolve the conflict in a way that permits compliance with the applicable rules and laws should lead the CPA to address the consequences of any violations. Beyond that, the process is similar to that for CPAs in public practice: consulting with appropriate persons within the organization; considering contacting an appropriate professional body or legal counsel for advice; documenting the findings and discussions; and, if necessary, considering whether to remain with the employer. Exhibit 4.4 describes the steps to be taken to deal with ethical conflicts and avoid violating the rules.

Integrity and Objectivity/Conflicts of Interest

The Integrity and Objectivity Rule (2.100.001) is similar to that for CPAs in public practice. It requires avoidance of conflicts of interest and not subordinating judgment to others as might be the case if a controller were pressured by a CFO to go along with misstated financial statements. The threats and safeguards framework is used when the rules or interpretations do not specifically address an issue.

When conflicts of interest exist, the CPA should use professional judgment to resolve it, taking into account whether a reasonable and informed third party who is aware of the relevant information would conclude that a conflict exists.

A conflict of interest (2.000.020) creates adverse interest and self-interest threats to compliance with the Integrity and Objectivity Rule. Examples include:

- Undertaking a professional service related to a particular matter involving two or more parties whose interests with respect to that matter are in conflict; or

- Interests of the CPA with respect to the particular matter and the interests of a party for whom the services are undertaken related to that matter are in conflict.

Conflicts may exist because of a relationship with the employing organization, a vendor, a customer, a lender, a shareholder, or other party. An example of a situation in which conflicts of interest may arise is acquiring confidential information from one employing organization that could be used by the CPA to the advantage or disadvantage of the other employing organization.

When a conflict of interest has been identified, the CPA should evaluate the significance of the threat to determine if it is at an acceptable level by evaluating the significance of relevant interests or relationships and the significance of the threats created by undertaking the professional service or services. In general, the more direct the connection between the CPA and the matter causing the conflict, the more significant the threat to compliance with integrity and objectivity will be.

When a conflict of interest exists, the CPA should disclose the nature of the conflict to the relevant parties, including the appropriate levels within the employing organization and obtain their consent to undertake the professional service. This should be done even if the threat is at an acceptable level.

Threats to compliance with the Integrity and Objectivity Rule would not be at an acceptable level and could not be reduced to an acceptable level by the application of safeguards, and the CPA would be considered to have knowingly misrepresented facts in violation of the rule if the CPA:

- Makes, or permits or directs another party to make, materially false and misleading entries in an entity's financial statements or records;

- Fails to correct an entity's financial statements or records that are materially false and misleading when the CPA has the authority to record the entries; or

- Signs, or permits or directs another to sign, a document containing materially false and misleading information.

Subordination of Judgment

The Integrity and Objectivity Rule prohibits a CPA from knowingly misrepresenting facts or subordinating judgment when performing professional services for an employer. Self-interest, familiarity, and undue influence threats to compliance with the rule may exist when a CPA and the supervisor, or any other person within the organization, have a difference of opinion relating to the application of accounting principles; auditing standards; or other relevant standards, including standards applicable to tax and consulting services or applicable laws or regulations. The process to follow to resolve the difference is similar to that previously discussed for CPAs in public practice. These matters can lead to whistleblowing outcomes under Dodd-Frank, which are addressed in Exhibit 3.13.

The Integrity and Objectivity Rule also requires the CPA in business to be candid when dealing with the employer's external accountant and not knowingly misrepresent facts or knowingly fail to disclose material facts. This would include, for example, responding to specific inquiries for which the employer's external accountant requests written representation.

Link between Conceptual Framework and Giving Voice to Values

The conceptual framework approach that underlies the ethical standards for CPAs in public practice and business is consistent with the thought process of the Giving Voice to Values methodology. For example, in bringing one's concerns to higher-ups in the organization, the goal should be to convince the appropriate party(ies) that the position taken is the best one from both ethical and professional perspectives. In deciding what to say, how to say it, and to whom the discussion should be directed, the CPA should consider what the likely objections and pushbacks might be and how they can effectively be counteracted. Similarly, to meet one's professional responsibilities under the Integrity and Objectivity Rule, the CPA must convince others of the most ethical action.

Let's look at an example. Carl Kilgore is a CPA and the assistant controller of a public company. He oversees the accounting for construction jobs for his company. One job has just been completed and the bill was prepared by the accounting department. Before Carl can even see it, the controller (Jack Long), who is also a CPA, drops by and tells Carl to pad the bill by 50 percent. It seems this particular client never scrutinizes the bills from your company because of a long-standing relationship of trust. In fact, this is the first time to your knowledge that any such padding has occurred. What would you do if you were Carl Kilgore and why?

Carl's an ethical guy and he doesn't want to get caught up in a fraud or cover-up so he carefully considers how best to make the case that the padding is wrong. Application of the conceptual framework calls for discussing the threat to integrity and objectivity with his supervisor, who is Jack Long, and trying to convince him to eliminate the padding. This may be a futile attempt, but, still, Carl should reason out his options because he can use it to bring the matter to those above Carl, if necessary. Carl reflects on the following:

- What are the main arguments by Jack you are trying to counter?
- What is at stake for the key parties, including those who disagree with you?
- What levers can you use to influence those who disagree with you?
- What is your most effective response to the reasons and rationalizations you need to address? To whom should the argument be made? When and in what context?

Carl's most persuasive position is based on the fraudulent accounting. Ethically, Jack should be reminded that objectivity and Carl's integrity would be compromised if he goes along with the fraud. If necessary, Carl can go to the CFO and CEO and remind them of their responsibility to certify the accuracy of the financial statements under SOX. The point is the GVV framework can help formulate a game plan to deal with such conflicts in an ethically acceptable way. Hopefully, Carl has the option of using a hotline to report any unresolved differences. Carl's ultimate goal is to present the most convincing case in order to avoid the need to blow the whistle externally, either to the outside auditors or the regulatory authorities.

SOX: Nonaudit Services

Similar to AICPA and SEC rules, SOX prohibits CPAs and CPA firms from providing certain nonattest services for public company attest clients. The potential for a conflict of interest exists because of a self-review threat to independence that occurs when a CPA reviews, as part of an attest engagement, evidence that results from the CPA's own nonattest services.

Section 201 of SOX provides that the following nonattest services may not be performed for attest clients in addition to bookkeeping or other services related to the accounting records or financial statements of the audit client:

1. Financial information systems design and implementation.
2. Appraisal or valuation services, fairness opinions, or contribution-in-kind reports.
3. Actuarial services.
4. Internal audit outsourcing services.
5. Management functions or human resources.
6. Broker or dealer, investment adviser, or investment banking services.
7. Legal services and expert services unrelated to the audit.
8. Any other service that the board of directors determines, by regulation, is impermissible.

SOX allows an accounting firm to "engage in any nonaudit service, including tax services," that is not listed above, only if the activity is preapproved by the audit committee of the issuer company. The preapproval requirement is waived if the aggregate amount of all such nonaudit services provided to the issuer constitutes less than 5 percent of the total amount of revenues paid by the issuer to its auditor.

The rules do not give CPAs definitive guidance on how audit committees should determine whether a tax service is an allowable activity requiring preapproval or is a prohibited service that even preapproval cannot save other than saying that tax compliance, planning, and advice are acceptable once approved. It is generally understood that the SEC allows the provision of tax-minimization services to audit clients, except for transactions that have no business purpose other than tax avoidance (i.e., tax shelters).

The issue of whether a CPA firm should be allowed to do permitted tax services for audit clients can be evaluated ethically from a utilitarian perspective. The question is whether the benefits of auditor-provided tax services outweigh the risks that the audit will not be performed with the level of objectivity necessary to ensure the independence standard is met. An argument to allow permitted tax services is that the insight learned from providing tax services can enhance audit effectiveness and, in turn, the client's financial reporting quality. The argument against it would be that it creates a self-review threat and could lead to an advocacy relationship between the tax accountants and audit client, whichc creates a threat to independence that cannot be reduced or eliminated by any safeguards.

Rules of Professional Practice

LO 4-6
Explain the rules of conduct in the AICPA Code.

The remaining sections of the Code address ethics rules dealing with the performance of professional services for clients or one's employer. The standards for CPAs in public practice and those in business are similar with a few exceptions noted below. Given the broad scope of these rules, we limit coverage to the provisions most important for students to understand. The rules are as follows:

- General Standards (1.300)
- Acts Discreditable (1.400)
- Fees and Other Types of Remuneration (1.500)
- Advertising and Other Forms of Solicitation (1.600)
- Confidential Information (1.700)
- Form of Organization and Name (1.800)

The conceptual framework applies to these rules in order to identify threats and safeguards when specific interpretations do not address a particular situation. If the CPA cannot demonstrate that safeguards were applied and eliminated or reduced threats to an acceptable level, then there would be a violation of the rules.

General Standards Rule (1.300.001)

The General Standards Rule establishes requirements for competence, compliance with professional standards, and adherence to accounting principles.

Competence (1.300.010)

Competence means having the appropriate technical qualifications to perform professional services and proper supervision and evaluation of the quality of work performed. While a reasonable care standard exists, CPAs are not expected to be infallible of knowledge or judgment.

One interpretation of the competence standard establishes the requirements for the use of a third-party service provider (i.e., outsourcing). This occurs most often with bookkeeping services, tax preparation, or consulting services, including related clerical or data entry functions. The interpretation requires:

- Verifying that the third-party service provider has the required professional qualifications, technical skills, and other resources before engaging their services.
- Adequately planning and supervising the provider's services to ensure they are performed with competence and due care.
- Threats to compliance with the Integrity and Objectivity Rule should be considered.
- Confidentiality of client information must be secured.

To meet the competency standard, CPAs must be sensitive to situations when one's capabilities are limited and the conservative action may be to recommend another practitioner to perform the services. For example, a CPA or CPA firm should not undertake an audit of a school district without sufficient knowledge of generally accepted government accounting and auditing standards. Think of it this way:

An accounting student who works on a group project with other students to develop a business plan might feel comfortable working on the financial plan, but presumably that student would not want to be responsible for developing the marketing plan. He would expect a marketing student to assume that responsibility.

The competence standard for CPAs in business includes a requirement that when a CPA who is a stockholder, partner, director, officer, or employee of an entity prepares or submits the entity's financial statements to third parties, the CPA should clearly communicate, preferably in writing, the CPA's relationship to the entity and should not imply that she is independent of the entity. In addition, if the communication states affirmatively that the financial statements are presented in conformity with the applicable financial reporting framework, the CPA should comply with the Accounting Principles Rule. It is important for CPAs in business to take note of these requirements because from time to time they may be asked to prepare and submit financial statements to support a loan request of the employer.

Compliance with Standards

A variety of professional standards establish rules of conduct related to specific services including Statements on Auditing Standards (SAS), Statements on Standards for Accounting and Review Services (SSARS), Statements on Standards for Consulting Services (SSCS), and Statements on Standards for Tax Services (SSTS).

The Accounting Principles Rule obligates CPAs to ensure that the financial statements are prepared in accordance with GAAP and assess whether any material modifications to those statements are needed. If a CPA believes a departure from GAAP is justified to avoid misleading statements due to unusual circumstances, then the CPA can still comply with the rule by describing the departure; its approximate effects, if practicable; and the reasons why compliance with the principle would result in a misleading statement.

Of particular note is that the rule does not prohibit a CPA from preparing or reporting on financial statements based on other financial reporting frameworks such as International Financial Reporting Standards (IFRS)[26] promulgated by the International Accounting Standards Board (IASB) or statutory financial reporting requirements for an entity that are required by law or a U.S. or foreign governmental regulatory body to whose jurisdiction the entity is subject.

Acts Discreditable (1.400.001)

Acts Discreditable covers a broad number of actions that may bring discredit to the profession including discrimination and harassment in employment practices, solicitation or disclosure of CPA examination questions and answers, failure of a CPA/CPA firm to file and pay income taxes, negligence in the preparation of financial statements or records, and standards relating to governmental accounting and auditing.

Confidentiality of Information Gained through Employment

A confidentiality requirement exists for employees of firms that precludes disclosing confidential employer information obtained as a result of an employment relationship, such as discussions with the employer's vendors, customers, or lenders. An example where confidential information is generally protected is customer lists, target clients, costs, and marketing strategies that might afford competitive advantages. Perhaps the most dangerous situation is when an employee leaves the company, by choice or force, and decides to use confidential information for personal gain.

Situations exist where a CPA is permitted or may be required to disclose confidential employer information under the law, such as occurs with whistleblowing disclosures when the conditions for doing so under Dodd-Frank have been met, as discussed in Chapter 3. Disclosure also may be required to comply with a validly issued and enforceable subpoena or summons.

A professional responsibility exists to disclose confidential information under the following conditions unless prohibited by law.

- Initiate a complaint, or respond to any inquiry made by, the Professional Ethics Division or trial board of the AICPA or state CPA society, or state board of accountancy;
- Protect the CPA's professional interests in legal proceedings;
- Comply with professional standards and other ethics requirements; or
- Report potential concerns regarding questionable accounting, auditing, or other matters to the employer's confidential complaint hotline or those charged with governance.

Disclosure is also permitted on behalf the employer to:

- Obtain financing with lenders;
- Communicate with vendors, clients, customers; or
- Communicate with the employer's external accountant, attorneys, regulators, and other business professionals.

Records Request

The records request rule is somewhat complicated and relies on basic definitions as explained below.

- *Client-provided records* are accounting or other records belonging to the client that were provided to the member [CPA] by or on behalf of the client, including hard-copy or electronic reproductions of such records.
- *Member-prepared records* are accounting or other records that the member was not specifically engaged to prepare and that are not in the client's books and records or are otherwise not available to the client, with the result that the client's financial information is incomplete. Examples include adjusting, closing, combining, or consolidating journal entries (including computations supporting such entries) and supporting schedules and documents that are proposed or prepared by the member as part of an engagement (e.g., an audit).
- *Member's work products* are deliverables as set forth in the terms of the engagement, such as tax returns.
- *Member's working papers* are all other items prepared solely for purposes of the engagement and include items prepared by the CPA, such as audit programs, analytical review schedules, and statistical sampling results and analyses.

The rules are summarized as follows.

1. Client-provided records in the custody or control of the member (CPA) should be returned to the client at the client's request.
2. Unless a CPA and the client have agreed to the contrary, when a client makes a request for member-prepared records, or a member's work products that are in the custody or control of the member or the member's firm and that have not previously been provided to the client, the member should respond to the client's request as follows:

   a. Member-prepared records relating to a completed and issued work product should be provided to the client, except that such records may be withheld if there are fees due to the member for the specific work product.

b. Member's work products should be provided to the client, except that such work products may be withheld in any of the following circumstances:

- If there are fees due to the member for the specific work product.
- If the work product is incomplete.
- For purposes of complying with professional standards (for example, withholding an audit report due to outstanding audit issues).
- If threatened or outstanding litigation exists concerning the engagement or member's work.

State board rules on these matters can be confusing. The New York State Rules of the Board of Regents provide that certain information should be provided to a client upon request, including copies of tax returns and reports, or other documents that were previously issued to or for such client; copies of information that are contained in the accountant's working papers, if the information would ordinarily constitute part of the client's books and records and is not otherwise available to the client; and copies of client-owned records or records that the licensee receives from a client, and any records, tax returns, reports, or other documents and information that are contained in an accountant's working papers that were prepared for the client by the accountant and for which the accountant *has received payment from the client.* This implies that information can be withheld if payment has not been received. On the other hand, Texas State Board Rule 501.76 provides that a person's workpapers (to the extent that such workpapers include records that would ordinarily constitute part of the client's or former client's books and records and are not otherwise available to the client or former client) *should be furnished to the client within a reasonable time* (promptly, not to exceed 20 business days) after the client has made a request for those records. The person can charge a reasonable fee for providing such workpapers. The question is whether a "reasonable fee" precludes withholding working papers that constitute client books and records due to nonpayment of *client service fees.* As the saying goes, a word to the wise should be sufficient. Check with your state board rules on these matters once you become a licensed CPA.

The complexities of work-product privilege were brought to the forefront in a U.S. Supreme Court decision on May 24, 2010. In *United States v. Textron Inc.,* the Supreme Court declined to review a lower court opinion and let stand the decision by the First Circuit Court of Appeals that a corporation's tax accrual workpapers were not protected from an IRS summons by the work-product privilege. Exhibit 4.5 summarizes the facts of this case.

EXHIBIT 4.5   Supreme Court Declines To Hear *Textron* Work-product Privilege Case

The case results from an IRS administrative summons for Textron's tax accrual workpapers with respect to the company's 1998–2001 tax returns. The workpapers were spreadsheets prepared by persons (some of whom were lawyers) in Textron's tax department to support Textron's calculation of its tax reserves for its audited financial statements. Textron refused to supply the workpapers to the IRS, and the dispute ended up in litigation.

In district court, Textron argued that its tax accrual workpapers were protected by either the attorney-client privilege, the tax practitioner privilege, or the work-product privilege. Textron acknowledged at trial that the documents' primary purpose was to support its reserve amounts for contingent tax liabilities, but it argued that they also analyzed the prospects for litigation over individual tax positions. The district court rejected Textron's attorney-client and tax practitioner privilege claims, saying that Textron waived those privileges by showing the documents to its outside accountants; however, it held that Textron's tax accrual workpapers were protected by the work-product privilege (*Textron Inc. v. United States*, 507 F. Supp. 2d 138 [D.R.I. 2007]).

(Continued)

A contentious issue in the case was whether Textron created the workpapers "in anticipation of litigation," because the work-product privilege does not protect documents prepared in the ordinary course of business. The district court concluded that although Textron undeniably created the workpapers to satisfy its financial audit requirements, but for the prospect of litigation, the documents would not have been created at all, and therefore they were protected by the work-product privilege.

On appeal, a three-judge panel of the First Circuit affirmed the district court. The court then granted an IRS petition to hear the case. The full court reversed the district court and held that the work-product privilege did not apply to Textron's tax accrual workpapers because the documents sought were prepared not for litigation, but for a statutorily required purpose of financial reporting, and so were prepared in the ordinary course of business; therefore, they were not protected by the privilege.

The Supreme Court decided not to review the case by denying a writ of certiorari.

Contingent Fees (1.510.001)   *conditioned on the outcome of a service.*

Years ago in the accounting profession, it was a violation of the rules of conduct for a CPA to accept a contingent fee for services performed for a client or for recommending a product or service to the client. These forms of payment were thought to be "unprofessional" and could potentially compromise the CPA's professional judgment. Over the years, however, professional accountants have become more involved in performing nonattest services that do not require independence and are largely provided to satisfy the client's interest, not the public interest. Thus, there is no third-party reliance on the work of the accountant. Moreover, CPAs who provide these nonattest services to clients are now competing with non-CPAs who perform similar services and are not bound by a professional code of conduct such as the AICPA Code. The result has been a loosening of the rules to permit the acceptance of contingent fees and commissions when performing advisory-type services for a nonattest client. Certain restrictions do apply, as discussed next.

Under the rule, a CPA is prohibited from performing for a contingent fee any professional services for, or to receive such a fee from, a client for whom the CPA or CPA firm performs any of the following services: (1) an audit or review of a financial statement; (2) a compilation of a financial statement when the CPA expects, or reasonably might expect, that a third party will use the financial statement, and the compilation report does not disclose a lack of independence; (3) an examination of prospective financial information; or (4) preparation of an original or amended tax return or claim for tax refund for a contingent fee for any client.

The danger of accepting a contingent fee for services provided to an attest client is it creates a financial self-interest threat to independence that may not be reduced or eliminated by any safeguards. Imagine if an accounting firm and audit client were to agree that the firm would receive 30 percent of any tax savings to the client resulting from tax advice provided by the firm. In this case, the fee is dependent on the outcome of the service. The fact that a government agency might challenge the amount of the client's tax savings, and thereby alter the final amount of the fee paid to the firm, heightens rather than lessens the mutuality of interest between the firm and client.

Exceptions do exist in tax practice where a contingent fee can be accepted including: (1) if the fee is fixed by courts or other public authorities, (2) if the fee is determined based on the results of judicial proceedings or the findings of governmental agencies, (3) when filing an amended state or federal tax return claiming a tax refund based on a tax issue that is the subject of a tax case involving a different taxpayer or with respect to which the taxing authority is developing a position, or (4) when filing an amended federal or state income tax return (or refund claim) claiming a tax refund in an amount greater than the threshold for review by the Joint Committee on Internal Revenue Taxation ($1 million at March 1991) or state taxing authority.

Commissions and Referral Fees (1.520.001)

The commission and referral fees rule is similar to that for contingent fees. Unlike a contingent fee, which is conditioned on the outcome of a service, a commission is typically paid to a CPA for recommending or referring to a client any product or service of another party, such as an investment product whereby the CPA receives a commission from the investment company if the client purchases the product. A similar arrangement exists when a CPA, for a commission, recommends or refers any product or service to be supplied by a client to another party. The restricted services identified under the contingent fees rule applies equally to the commissions rule. The same independence concerns exist because of the financial self-interest.

Imagine, for example, that a CPA is engaged to perform financial planning services for a client and to recommend a financial product or products based on the service. Now, if one of three products pays a commission to the CPA, assuming that the client purchases the product, while the other two do not, it may appear that the CPA can no longer be independent with respect to providing audit or other attest services for the client. The key point is that it doesn't matter if the CPA can, in fact, make independent decisions. The perception may be in the mind of a reasonable observer that such an independent mindset is no longer possible because of the commission arrangement. What if, for example, during the course of the audit and valuation of the investment product, the CPA discovers a flaw in the logic used to recommend the commission-based product to the client? Would the CPA disclose that fact to the client?

One requirement under the commission and referral fee rule that does not exist for contingent fees is to disclose permitted commissions and referral fees to any person or entity to whom the CPA recommends or refers a product or service to which the commission relates. In other words, the act of disclosing meets the CPA's ethical obligation under the AICPA Code. A protection beyond disclosure is that requirements for due care and adherence to the Objectivity and Integrity Rule applies in making product and service recommendations.

State board rules on these matter may differ from the AICPA rule, so it is important to understand and follow the state board rule that may have more restrictive guidelines. For example, the Texas State Board of Public Accountancy's commissions rule requires that a "person [licensed CPA] who receives, expects or agrees to receive, pays, expects, or agrees to pay other compensation in exchange for services or products recommended, referred, or sold by him shall, no later than the making of such recommendation, referral, or sale, disclose to the client in writing the nature, source, and amount, or an estimate of the amount when the amount is not known, of all such other compensation." In Washington State the rule also includes a requirement to specify the CPA's role as the client's advisor.

In California, Section 5061 of the California Accountancy Act *prohibits* the acceptance or payment of a *referral fee* as follows: (a) Except as expressly permitted by this section (applies only to commissions), a person engaged in the practice of public accountancy shall not: (1) pay a fee or commission to obtain a client or (2) accept a fee or commission for referring a client to the products or services of a third party.

Advertising and Other Forms of Solicitation (1.600.001)

The advertising and solicitations rule establishes guidelines when and how a CPA can promote professional services or solicit clients. While advertising and solicitation is permitted, these forms of communication cannot be done in a manner that is false, misleading, or deceptive. Solicitation by the use of coercion, overreaching, or harassing conduct is prohibited under the rule.

Advertising and solicitation practices of CPAs should never cross the line, as might occur if they (1) create false or unjustified expectations of favorable results; (2) imply the ability to influence any court, tribunal, regulatory agency, or similar body or official; (3) contain a representation that specific professional services in current or future periods will be performed for a stated fee, estimated fee, or fee range when it was likely at the time of the representation that such fees would be substantially increased and the prospective client was not advised of that likelihood; and (4) contain any other representations that would be likely to cause a reasonable person to misunderstand or be deceived.

Given the new ways to engage current and future clients using social media outlets, it is fair to say the AICPA rules on advertising and solicitation lack specificity. Perhaps the AICPA believes its rules provide sufficient blanket coverage on all forms of practice. Still, some state boards provide clearer guidance such as Louisiana, which has issued a "Statement of Position" on Advertising and Communications that clarifies the advertising rule applies to licensees' Web sites, e-mails, and other electronic or Internet marketing, as well as all other forms of advertising, marketing, and public communications. In recent years, like so many professional service providers, CPAs have increasingly used the Internet and developed CPA firm Web sites. Prior to the advent of the Internet and universal access to marketing and advertising information, such information may have been in brochures or other printed material. Traditionally, such material was disseminated only by hand or mail and was not as available for general reference or scrutiny. Now, the information is available with one click, so the rules need to catch up with the technology.

Confidential Information (1.700.001)

The general requirement to maintain client confidentiality is that a CPA should not disclose confidential client information without the specific consent of the client. Confidentiality issues can be tricky from a legal perspective so CPAs are best served when when they consult with legal counsel prior to disclosing, or determining whether to disclose, confidential client information.

Permitted Disclosure of Confidential Information

Client permission to discuss confidential issues generally is granted when there is a change of auditor and the successor auditor approaches the client for permission to discuss matters related to the audit with the predecessor. This step is required by GAAS. Of course, the client can always deny permission and cut off any such contact, in which case the successor auditor probably should run in the opposite direction of the client as quickly as possible. In other words, the proverbial "red flag" will have been raised. The CPA should be skeptical and wonder why the client may have refused permission.

The rule also permits the CPA to discuss confidential client information without violating the rule in the following situations: (1) in response to a validly issued subpoena or summons, or to adhere to applicable laws and government regulations (i.e, Dodd-Frank); (2) to provide the information necessary for a review of the CPA's professional practice (inspection/quality review) under PCAOB, AICPA, state CPA society, or board of accountancy authorization; and (3) to provide the information necessary for one's defense in an investigation of the CPA in a disciplinary matter.

Confidentiality and Disclosing Fraud

Warning outsiders of client fraud is an area where CPAs need to be especially wary. Cashell and Fuerman point out that, based on prior court cases, CPAs generally do not have an obligation to inform outsiders of fraud unless by remaining silent they themselves become culpable. In any situation, the decision to blow the whistle is risky. If an accountant notifies third parties that a client's financials are fraudulent and that claim proves to be false, the accountant could be sued for defamation and also for breach of the professional obligation of confidentiality. Because of the potential legal ramifications associated with both disclosure and nondisclosure of client fraud, it is advisable to seek legal counsel guidance when confronted with such a decision.[27]

Exhibit 4.6 summarizes key cases that deal with the accountant's obligation to report fraud committed by a client to outsiders. All of these cases occurred before Dodd-Frank so rulings today presumably would be different as long as the Act's reporting requirements are met. These cases have one common element, which is the auditors were not hired to find fraud so reporting it was much more problematic.

EXHIBIT 4.6   Disclosing Fraud and Confidentiality

There have been several cases that support the CPA's lack of obligation to disclose fraud to outsiders. One common characteristic in these cases is that the CPA either was not engaged to, or did not, report on the fraudulent financial information. Two such cases of note are *Fischer v. Kletz* and *Gold v. DCL*.

In *Fischer v. Kletz* (1966), Peat, Marwick, Mitchell & Co. (KPMG), subsequent to issuing its audit report on the 1963 annual financial statements of Yale Express System, Inc., discovered that they were substantially false and misleading. The firm also discovered that several 1964 interim statements, with which it was not associated, were also false and misleading. The firm delayed disclosing its findings to the SEC and the public until May 1965.

One of the plaintiff's claims against KPMG was that it aided and abetted Yale's scheme to defraud with respect to the interim statements. The court reasoned that there was no basis in law for imposing a duty upon the firm to disclose its knowledge of the misleading interim statements because it was not associated with the statements.

In the second case, *Gold v. DCL Inc.* (1973), Price Waterhouse & Co. (PwC) informed DCL in December 1971 that it intended to qualify its audit report on DCL's 1971 financial statements. DCL was in the business of leasing computers, and the firm believed that DCL's ability to recover its computer equipment costs was impaired due to the impending release of a new line of more powerful computers by IBM. On February 8, 1972, DCL announced earnings without mentioning PwC's concern, and on February 15, prior to issuing its opinion, the firm was replaced. In this case, the plaintiff claimed PwC failed to inform the public that the financial information released by DCL on February 8 was, in its opinion, incomplete and misleading. The court, in dismissing this claim, ruled that there is no basis in principle or authority for extending an auditor's duty to disclose beyond cases where the auditor is giving or has given some representation or certification, and the silence and inaction of the defendant auditors did not make them culpable. In holding that the auditors had no duty to disclose, the court reasoned that because the auditors had issued no public opinion, rendered no certification, and in no way invited the public to rely on their financial judgment, there was no special relationship that imposed a duty of disclosure.

Even where the intent has been to warn others of pending financial harm, the courts have held that CPAs must not divulge client information. In *Wagenheim v. Alexander Grant & Co.* (AG) (1983),[28] the court ruled AG improperly divulged confidential information about its client, Consolidated Data Services, Inc. (CDS), to other clients. CDS, an audit client of AG, performed payroll services for several of AG's other clients. Upon discovery that CDS was having financial difficulty, AG warned its other clients to stop doing business with CDS. AG argued the other clients would suffer financial damage without the warning. In ruling against AG, the court stated there was no proof that CDS was "irretrievably" insolvent and, therefore, AG had no legal right to alert third parties of CD's financial problems. In its discussion, however, the court indicated that AG's actions might have been justified if CDS either intended fraud by not disclosing its insolvency or did not intend to fulfill its contractual obligations with AG's clients.

Form of Organization and Name (1.800.001)

Ethics rules apply not only to individual CPAs who are licensed by state boards but also to accounting firms and certain members of alternative practice structures, networks, and affiliate firms. The forms of organization used by CPA firms over the years have changed to recognize the importance of nonattest services to the revenue flow of firms and competition with non-CPA firms in providing such services. Years ago, CPAs had to own 100 percent of a firm's equity interests. Today, most states simply require a majority ownership in the hands of licensed CPAs.

Clearly, the rules now accommodate non-CPA owners who perform a variety of advisory services and want a partial ownership interest in the firm. Toffler, in her book on the demise of Arthur Andersen,[29] laid blame on the proliferation of nonattest services at Andersen and non-CPA consultants, who operated under a less strict culture of ethical behavior than their CPA-attest colleagues. She claims that corners were cut and decisions were made that were in the interests of the client and firm, at the sacrifice of the public interest, as a result of compromises to independence and objectivity in audit services so as not to upset clients and possibly lose lucrative consulting services.

State boards need to have regulatory authority over practice units as well as CPAs because the members of a CPA firm might pressure an individual CPA within that firm to do something unethical. The firm should be sanctioned for the inappropriate behavior, and so should the CPA if she gives in to the pressure. Let's assume that you are working for a CPA firm in your hometown and your supervisor-CPA tells you to ignore a material sales return at year-end and wait to record it as a reduction of revenue until the first of next year. It seems that the client needs to record the revenue to meet targeted amounts and trigger bonuses to top management. If you go along with your supervisor, then you, the supervisor, and the firm itself can be cited for violating the ethics rules.

The rules provide that CPAs may practice public accounting only in a form of organization permitted by state law or regulation. The AICPA and virtually all state board rules prohibit the use of a firm name that is false, misleading, deceptive and/or may imply the ability to provide services not justified. Imagine, for example, if the firm name is Maximum Refunds, LLP.

Most states have rules far more extensive than the AICPA rule because of regulatory issues. For example, in North Carolina, the rules specify that non-CPA owners must be active participants in the business; the business must be the primary occupation of the non-CPA owners; and non-CPA owners must be of good moral character. Further, the name of a non-CPA owner may not be used in the name of the CPA firm.

An interesting question is whether the board of accountancy has any recourse against non-CPA owners even if they are registered with the board. In North Carolina, the board does not have any authority to discipline non-CPA owners of the CPA firm for violations of the state board rules on professional ethics and conduct. However, the rules do specify that the CPA partner who has been designated as the supervising partner of the CPA firm is held accountable for the non-CPA owners' compliance with the board's rules of conduct.

Commercialism and the Accounting Profession

We previously addressed whether commercialism and professionalism can coexist given the re-emergence of advisory services as a mainstay of CPA firm professional services. The culture of consulting is different than that of auditors, who have a public interest obligation.

The recent growth in consulting services has been fueled by acquiring strategy firms, such as PwC's acquisition of Booz & Company. Deloitte's acquisition of Monitor, a strategy firm that had gone bust, vaulted it into the leading firm by revenue in 2014. The numbers in billions of dollars in revenue are as follows: (1) Deloitte ($34.2); (2) PwC ($33.95); (3) EY ($27.37); and (4) KPMG ($24.82), for a whopping total of $120 billion. Compare these numbers to 2012, when total global revenue for the Big Four was $94 billion, and we see an almost 30 percent increase in two years. What's more telling is the 2012 numbers were 7 percent off from the previous record high in 2008, of $101 billion. It would seem that reaction to the new regulations under SOX and heightened scrutiny of the profession in Congress in the aftermath of Enron and WorldCom led the profession to pull back—but not for long. It seems to have resumed its old ways.

We are not raising the red flag solely because of the size of these firms. We are concerned about the mix of cultures and the firms' expansion into an ever-growing array of consulting services that brush up against the strict independence requirement for auditors and overriding mandate to protect the public interest even at the sacrifice of client or self-interest.

Ethics and Tax Services

LO 4-7
Discuss ethics in tax practice.

Students who graduate from college and take positions with accounting firms might end up providing tax services for a client at some time in their careers. Tax services include tax compliance, where much of the service is derived from audited financial records, tax consulting, tax planning, and tax shelters.

The AICPA explicitly recognizes the tax professional's dual obligations to the client to act as an advocate and to foster integrity in the tax system by honestly and fairly administering the tax laws. While client advocacy is an acceptable standard in tax practice, the tax accountant remains obligated to act objectively, with integrity, exercise due care, and follow the Statements on Standards for Tax Services (SSTS) issued by the AICPA. In addition, the CPA must place the public interest ahead of those of the client and self-interests.

In the performance of tax services for an audit client, the tax CPA is expected to consider whether any threats to independence exist that cannot be reduced or eliminated by safeguards and how such matters will be handled to avoid a violation of audit independence. Providing some tax services for audit clients can create a conflict of interests that threatens independence. Barrett points out that when auditors review the items for accrued taxes payable on the balance sheet and income tax expense on the income statement, they must reach conclusions about the validity of these amounts before they can express an opinion as to whether the financial statements fairly present the entity's financial condition and operating results in accordance with GAAP. As a result, auditors must examine the entity's tax returns and assess so-called "tax reserves" or "tax provisions" to evaluate tax expense for the current period and to determine whether any material unrecorded or undisclosed tax liabilities exist.[30] Here, a self-review threat may exist that cannot be reduced or eliminated by any safeguards.

Statements on Standards for Tax Services (SSTS)

The AICPA has issued seven Statements on Standards for Tax Services (SSTS) that explain CPAs' responsibilities to their clients and the tax systems in which they practice. The statements demonstrate a CPA's commitment to tax practice standards that balance advocacy and planning with compliance.

The statements establish required ethics rules for tax practitioners. Given the complexity of this area, we limit our discussion to the "realistic possibility" standard under *SSTS No. 1* and issues related to taking a tax position and tax planning.

SSTS No. 1—Tax Return Positions

This statement sets forth the applicable standards for CPAs when recommending tax return positions or preparing or signing tax returns (including amended returns, claims for refund, and information returns) filed with any taxing authority. The following definitions apply:

- A *tax return position* is a position reflected on a tax return on which a CPA has specifically advised a taxpayer, or a position about which a CPA has knowledge of all material facts and, on the basis of those facts, has concluded whether the position is appropriate.

- A *taxpayer* is a client, a CPA's employer, or any other third-party recipient of tax services.

The statement addresses a CPA's obligation to advise a taxpayer of relevant tax return disclosure responsibilities and potential penalties. In addition to the AICPA and IRS tax regulations, various taxing authorities at the federal, state, and local levels may impose specific reporting and disclosure standards with regard to recommending tax return positions or preparing or signing a tax return. A CPA should determine and comply with the standards, if any, that are imposed by the applicable taxing authority with respect to recommending a tax return position, or preparing or signing a tax return. If the applicable taxing authority has no written standards in this regard, then the following standards will apply.

A CPA should not recommend a tax return position or prepare or sign a tax return taking a position unless he has a good-faith belief that the position has at least a realistic possibility of being sustained administratively or judicially on its merits if challenged. This is known as the *realistic possibility of success* standard under *SSTS Interpretation No. 101-1*. It requires that the tax return position should not be recommended unless the position satisfies applicable reporting and disclosure standards.

Notwithstanding the previous statement, a CPA may recommend a tax return position if he concludes that there is a reasonable basis for the position and advises the taxpayer to disclose that position appropriately. An interesting aspect of the standard is the prohibition against recommending a tax return position or preparing or signing a tax return reflecting a position that the CPA knows exploits the "audit selection process of a taxing authority," or serves as a mere arguing position advanced solely to obtain leverage in a negotiation with a taxing authority. The former refers to the fact that a tax practitioner might recommend an overly aggressive position to a client hoping that the IRS does not choose to examine the client's tax return. Clearly, that would be a violation of basic ethical standards, including honesty (nondeceptiveness) and integrity.

SSTS Interpretation No. 1-1—Realistic Possibility Standard

SSTS No. 1-1 applies to CPAs when providing tax services that involve tax planning. A CPA can still recommend a nonfrivolous position provided appropriate disclosure is recommended. Tax planning includes recommending or expressing an opinion on a tax return position or a specific tax plan developed by the CPA, or a third party, that relates to prospective or completed transactions. The basic standards include:

- Establish the relevant background facts.
- Consider the reasonableness of the assumptions and representations.
- Apply the pertinent authorities to the relevant facts.
- Consider the business purpose and economic substance of the transaction, if relevant to the tax consequences of the transaction.
- Arrive at a conclusion supported by the authorities.

In conducting the required due diligence to establish a tax position, the CPA needs to decide whether to rely on the assumptions concerning facts rather than other procedures to support the advice or a representation from the taxpayer or another person. The CPA also should consider whether the tax advice provided will be communicated to third parties, particularly if those third parties may not be knowledgeable or may not be receiving independent tax advice with respect to a transaction.

When engaged in tax planning, the CPA should understand the business purpose and economic substance of the transaction when relevant to the tax consequences. The business purpose for the transaction should be described and if the business reasons are relevant to the tax consequences, it is insufficient to merely assume that a transaction is entered into for valid business reasons without specifying what those reasons are.

Examples are provided in *SSTS No. 1-1* to assist in the application of the standards to fact situations. One such example is described in Exhibit 4.7.

EXHIBIT 4.7 **Application of the Realistic Possibility Standard**

Facts: The relevant tax regulation provides that the details (or certain information regarding) a specific transaction are required to be attached to the tax return, regardless of the support for the associated tax position (for example, if there is substantial authority or a higher level of comfort for the position). While preparing the taxpayer's return for the year, the CPA is aware that the attachment is required.

Conclusion: In general, if the taxpayer agrees to include the attachment required by the regulation, the CPA may sign the return if the CPA concludes that the associated tax return position satisfies the realistic possibility standard. However, if the taxpayer refuses to include the attachment, the CPA should not sign the return, unless the CPA concludes the associated tax return position satisfies the realistic possibility standard and there are reasonable grounds for the taxpayer's position with respect to the attachment.

Tax Shelters

A listed transaction is defined by the IRS as a transaction that is the same as or substantially similar to one of the types of transactions that the IRS has determined to be a tax avoidance transaction. Such actions are identified by notice, regulation, or other form of published guidance as listed transactions. Tax avoidance transactions are sometimes labeled *tax shelters*. It is complicated, but basically the term *prohibited tax shelter transaction* means listed transactions, transactions with contractual protection, or confidential transactions.

The IRS guidelines for listed transactions identify participation in any of the following:

- A tax return reflects tax consequences or a tax strategy described in published guidance that lists the transaction.
- The CPA knows or has reason to know that tax benefits reflected on the tax return are derived directly or indirectly from such tax consequences or tax strategy.
- The client is in a type or class of individuals or entities that published guidance treats as participants in a listed transaction.

In other words, under IRS rules, any transaction that is the same or "substantially similar" to a transaction identified as a tax avoidance transaction by IRS notice, regulation, or other published guidance is a reportable transaction—it must be reported to the IRS.

One of the most controversial aspects of the Enron collapse was the alleged involvement of Andersen in marketing aggressive tax planning ideas that the IRS and the courts subsequently found to be abusive. After the Enron scandal, the accounting profession received a second serious blow in 2005, when KPMG settled a criminal tax case with the Department of the Treasury and the IRS for $456 million to prevent the firm's prosecution over tax shelters sold between 1996 and 2002. This is the largest criminal tax case ever filed.

The creation of tax shelter investments to help wealthy clients avoid paying taxes has been part of tax practice for many years. The difference in the KPMG case, according to the original indictment, is that tax professionals in the firm prepared false documents to deceive regulators about the true nature of the tax shelters. There appeared to be a clear intent to deceive the regulators, and that makes it fraud.

The indictment claimed that the tax shelter transactions broke the law because they involved no economic risk and were designed solely to minimize taxes. The firm had collected about $128 million in fees for generating at least $11 billion in fraudulent tax losses, and this resulted in at least $2.5 billion in tax evaded by wealthy individuals. On an annual basis, KPMG's tax department was bringing in for the firm nearly $1.2 billion of its $3.2 billion total U.S. revenue. Ultimately, the $128 million in fees were forfeited as part of the $456 million settlement.

Perhaps the most interesting aspect of the KPMG tax shelter situation is the culture that apparently existed in the firm's tax practice during the time the shelters were sold. In 1998, the firm had decided to accelerate its tax services business. The motivation probably was the hot stock market during the 1990s and the increase in the number of wealthy taxpayers. The head of the KPMG's tax department, Jeffrey M. Stein, and its CFO, Richard Rosenthal, created an environment that treated those who didn't support the "growth at all costs" effort as not being team players. From the late 1990s, KPMG established a telemarketing center in Fort Wayne, Indiana, that cold-called potential clients from public lists of firms and companies. KPMG built an aggressive marketing team to sell tax shelters that it created with names like Blips, Flip, Opis, and SC2.

In an unusual move, the Justice Department brought a lawsuit against two former KPMG managers on 12 counts of tax evasion using illegal tax shelters. On April 1, 2009, John Larson, a former senior tax manager, was sentenced to more than 10 years and ordered to pay a fine of $6 million. Robert Plaff, a former tax partner at KPMG, was sentenced to more than 8 years and fined $3 million. A third person convicted in the case, Raymond J. Ruble, a former partner at the law firm Sidley Austin, was sentenced to 6 years and 7 months. In handing down the ruling in the U.S. District Court in Manhattan, Judge Lewis A. Kaplan stated, "These defendants knew they were on the wrong side of the line," adding later that they had cooked up "this mass-produced scheme to cheat the government out of taxes for the purposes of enriching themselves." The losses through the scheme were estimated at more than $100 million.

In a more recent case that illustrates the danger for CPAs of developing tax shelter arrangements for their clients, on June 18, 2012, BDO USA LLP (BDO), the seventh-largest U.S. accounting firm, agreed to pay a civil penalty of $34.4 million to the IRS and forfeit $15.6 million to the U.S. government as part of a deferred prosecution agreement. BDO admitted that it helped U.S. citizens evade about $1.3 billion in income taxes from 1997 to 2003 by failing to register various tax shelters, as required by law, in an effort to conceal them from the IRS. Some of these tax shelters were deemed abusive and fraudulent.

The settlement and payment resulted from the determinations described in Exhibit 4.8, according to the IRS:

EXHIBIT 4.8 BDO Tax Shelter Arrangements

- Between 1997 and 2003, BDO violated federal tax laws concerning the registration and maintenance and turning over to the IRS of tax shelter investor lists involving abusive and fraudulent tax shelters.

- Primarily through a group within the firm known as the Tax Solutions Group, BDO developed, marketed, sold, and implemented fraudulent tax shelter products to high-net-worth individuals, who had, or expected to have, reportable income or gains in excess of $5 million.

- These fraudulent tax shelters, although designed to appear to the IRS to be investments, in fact were a series of preplanned steps that assisted BDO's high-net-worth clients to evade individual income taxes of approximately $1.3 billion.

- The fraudulent tax shelters were sometimes known under the following names: SOS, Short Sale, BEST, BEDS, Spread Options, Currency Option Investment Strategy (COINS), Digital Options, G-1 Global Fund, FC Derivatives, Distressed Asset Debt, POPS, OPIS, Roth IRA, and OID Bond.

In November 2014, the PCAOB announced it was scrutinizing PwC over tax-saving strategies it provided to audit client Caterpillar, Inc., to determine whether a conflict of interest existed that could compromise PwC's ability to perform a tough audit of the company. The PCAOB's review results from a request by Senator Carl Levin (D-Michigan) after he received information that Caterpillar had deferred or avoided $2.4 billion in taxes under strategies devised by PwC. The tax shelter allegedly involved shifting profits to Switzerland from the United States, which saved Caterpillar more than $2.4 billion. Neither PwC nor Caterpillar had been charged with any wrongdoing as of August 2015.

Senator Levin also asked the PCAOB to review whether its rules should be strengthened to prohibit an auditor from auditing a company's tax obligations when those obligations rely on the tax strategy developed by the same firm. The danger is when a firm provides tax strategies to a company for which it also serves as the independent auditor, it could end up auditing its own work, thereby creating a self-review threat that cannot be reduced or eliminated by any safeguards.

In deciding tax shelter cases, the courts have mostly relied on the economic substance doctrine, which provides that transactions designed to yield tax benefits, but which do not change the taxpayer's economic position independent of those benefits, will not be respected. The common law doctrine normally requires the application of two separate tests—an objective test that focuses on the realistic potential of the transaction to generate a profit, and a subjective test focusing on the taxpayer's nontax business purpose in engaging in the transaction.

On March 30, 2010, the economic substance doctrine was codified in the Internal Revenue Code [IRC section 7701(o)]. It provides that, with respect to a transaction (or series of transactions) in which the common law economic substance doctrine is relevant, the transaction is treated as having economic substance only if the following tests are met:

- The transaction affects the taxpayer's economic position in a meaningful way, apart from any federal income tax effect; *and,*

- The taxpayer has a substantial purpose for engaging in the transaction, apart from any federal income tax effect.

The problem with the economic substance doctrine, much as with that of the realistic possibility of success standard, is it is ambiguous and subject to interpretation. In his analysis of the KPMG tax shelters, Stuebs points out that applying these legal standards requires and relies on judgment based on underlying fairness principles in taxation and wealth redistribution and its use to assess the validity of tax shelter laws. In contrast, ethical analysis relies on the duties, responsibilities, and obligations resulting from moral incentives to guide judgment. He notes that ethical duties are responsibilities or obligations owed by members of society to each other and the challenge is to identify specific ethical duties and to whom these duties are owed.[31] In tax practice this is a daunting task because the objectives of the tax client may be counter to society's goals, and the public interest obligation of CPAs may be shifted into the background.

PCAOB Rules

The PCAOB has issued a variety of standards that pertain to ethics and independence. We briefly review them below.

Rule 3520—Auditor Independence

Rule 3520 establishes the requirement for the accounting firm to be independent of its audit client throughout the audit and professional engagement period, as a fundamental obligation of the auditor. Under Rule 3520, a registered public accounting firm or an associated person's independence obligation with respect to an audit client that is an issuer encompasses not only an obligation to satisfy the independence criteria set out in the rules and standards of the PCAOB, but also an obligation to satisfy all other independence criteria applicable to the engagement, including the independence criteria set out in the rules and regulations of the commission under the federal securities laws.

Rule 3521—Contingent Fees

Rule 3521 treats registered public accounting firms as not independent of their audit clients if the firm, or any affiliate of the firm, during the audit and professional engagement period, provides any service or product to the audit client for a contingent fee or a commission, or receives from the audit client, directly or indirectly, a contingent fee or commission. This rule mirrors Rules 1.510 and 1.520 of the AICPA Code that prohibit contingent fees, commissions, and referral fees for any service provided to an attest client.

Rule 3522—Tax Transactions

Under Rule 3522, a rule that was issued in the aftermath of the tax shelter transactions, a registered public accounting firm is not independent of its audit client if the firm, or any affiliate of the firm, during the audit and professional engagement period, provides any nonauditing service to the audit client related to marketing, planning, or opining in favor of the tax treatment of either a confidential transaction or an "aggressive tax position" transaction. An aggressive tax position transaction is one that was initially recommended, directly or indirectly, by the registered public accounting firm and a significant purpose of which is tax avoidance, unless the proposed tax treatment is at least more likely than not to be allowable under applicable tax laws.

Rule 3523—Tax Services for Persons in Financial Reporting Oversight Roles

Rule 3523 treats a registered public accounting firm as not independent if the firm provides tax services to certain members of management who serve in *financial reporting oversight roles* at an audit client or to immediate family members of such persons unless any of the following apply:

1. The person is in a financial reporting oversight role at the audit client only because she serves as a member of the board of directors or similar management or governing body of the audit client.

2. The person is in a financial reporting oversight role at the audit client only because of the person's relationship to an affiliate of the entity being audited:

    a. Whose financial statements are not material to the consolidated financial statements of the entity being audited.
    b. Whose financial statements are audited by an auditor other than the firm or an associated person of the firm.

3. The person was not in a financial reporting oversight role at the audit client before a hiring, promotion, or other change in employment and the tax services are provided pursuant to an engagement in process before the hiring, promotion, or other change in employment completed not after 180 days after the hiring or promotion event.

We are skeptical of ethics rules that build in exceptions, such as for members of the board of directors. From an ethical perspective, a practice is wrong if it violates certain standards of behavior, and it doesn't matter if the relationship with the other party is not deemed to be significant. After all, members of the board of directors at most companies today have ratcheted-up responsibilities under SOX and NYSE listing requirements. There does not appear to be a reasonable basis to exclude board members from the rule that prohibits providing tax services for persons in financial reporting oversight roles.

Rule 3524—Audit Committee Preapproval of Certain Tax Services

In connection with seeking audit committee preapproval to perform for an audit client any permissible tax service, a registered public accounting firm should do all of the following:

1. Describe, in writing, to the audit committee of the issuer:

    a. The scope of the service, the fee structure for the engagement, and any side letter or other amendment to the engagement letter, or any other agreement (whether oral, written, or otherwise) between the firm and the audit client, relating to the service.
    b. Any compensation arrangement or other agreement, such as a referral agreement, a referral fee, or a fees-sharing arrangement, between the registered public accounting firm (or an affiliate of the firm) and any person (other than the audit client) with respect to the promoting, marketing, or recommending of a transaction covered by the service.

2. Discuss with the audit committee of the issuer the potential effects of the services on the independence of the firm.

3. Document the substance of its discussion with the audit committee of the issuer.

Rule 3525—Audit Committee Preapproval of Nonauditing Services Related to Internal Control over Financial Reporting

Rule 3525 provides that, when seeking audit committee preapproval to perform for an audit client any permissible nonauditing service related to internal control over financial reporting, a registered public accounting firm should describe, in writing, to the audit committee the scope of the service, discuss with the committee the potential effects of the service on the independence of the firm, and document the substance of its discussion with the audit committee of the issuer.

Rule 3526—Communication with Audit Committees Concerning Independence

Rule 3526 establishes guidelines when an accounting firm should discuss with the audit committee of the client information with respect to any relationships between the firm and the entity that might bear on auditor independence. Under the rule, a registered public accounting firm must do the following:

1. Prior to accepting an initial engagement, pursuant to the standards of the PCAOB, describe in writing, to the audit committee of the issuer, all relationships between the registered public accounting firm or any affiliates of the firm and the potential audit client or persons in financial reporting oversight roles at the potential audit client that, as of the date of the communication, may reasonably be thought to bear on independence.
2. Discuss with the audit committee the potential effects of the relationships on the independence of the firm, should it be appointed as the entity's auditor.
3. Document the substance of its discussion with the audit committee.

These requirements would also apply annually subsequent to being engaged as the auditor. An additional requirement annually is to affirm to the audit committee of the issuer of the communication that the registered public accounting firm is still independent in compliance with Rule 3520.

An important issue is whether the PCAOB has made a difference in reducing audit failures. Perhaps the most valuable part of the PCAOB's work has been in the audit inspections of registered auditing firms. Prior to establishing the PCAOB under SOX, these inspections were conducted as part of the accounting profession's own peer review program. Once it was determined that firms such as Andersen that conducted audits at companies like Enron and WorldCom had been given clean reviews by other public accounting firms, the SEC realized that the inspection process had to be carried out by an independent body such as the PCAOB. The success of the PCAOB is open to question, although we have observed that the process seems to be more rigorous and is helping to identify deficient audit procedures at CPA firms, as will be discussed in Chapter 5. For now, suffice it to say the PCAOB takes its responsibilities seriously and has been quite critical of the auditing profession, especially the Big Four firms. For example, the PCAOB found deficiencies in 23 of the KPMG LLP audits it evaluated in its 2013 annual inspection. The 23 deficient audits were out of 50 audits or partial audits conducted by KPMG that the PCAOB evaluated—a deficiency rate of 46 percent.[32] In the previous year's inspection, the PCAOB found deficiencies in 17 of 50 KPMG audits inspected, or 34 percent.

The 23 deficiencies were significant enough that it appeared KPMG hadn't obtained sufficient evidence to support its audit opinions that a company's financial statements were accurate or that it had effective internal controls, the PCAOB said. One word of caution is that a deficiency in the audit doesn't mean a company's financial statements were wrong, however, or that the problems found haven't since been addressed.

Still, the report spotlights the PCAOB's continuing concerns about audit quality. Overall, 39 percent of audits inspected in the latest evaluations of the Big Four firms were found to have deficiencies, compared with 37 percent the previous year.

Concluding Thoughts

Professional judgment is more important today for auditors than ever before. Complex financial transactions and the broad application of fair value measurements require judgment. Technical skills are important but so are ethical reasoning abilities. Professional and ethical judgment skills can help to express one's views and "give voice to values." Virtue-based decision making is an important component because it depends on "practical wisdom," or the ability to see the right thing to do in circumstances.

A systematic process needs to be identified and followed to make sure the auditor adequately addresses issues such as data gathering and evaluation, stakeholder considerations, ethical analysis, and ethical decision making. The process relies on professional skepticism to ensure that a mindset exists whereby auditors act independent of any biases and management pressures, and make objective judgments. At the end of the process, auditors should ask: *How would you justify a judgment or decision?* and *Are you comfortable moving ahead with the judgment process?*

The AICPA Revised Code supports the formal judgment process outlined in Chapter 2 and discussed in this chapter. The underlying foundation of the process in the Code is a conceptual framework to assess whether independence, integrity, and objectivity may be compromised as a result of threats that exist making it more difficult to follow the rules of conduct. Safeguards can be put into place to reduce or eliminate such threats, although nothing can substitute for ethical intent and ethical action. The desire to do the right thing and act in accordance with the profession's ethical standards is a critical component of ethical behavior and influences professional judgment. Integrity is required to carry through intent with ethical action, and to be prepared to respond to reasons and rationalizations given by others that are intended to negatively influence ethical decisions.

The accounting profession is in danger of losing sight of its mandate to protect the public interest because of increased commercial tendencies. Firms have been transitioning away from compliance-oriented services into more lucrative advisory services. On the one hand, we see this as a natural expansion in the scope of professional services and may very well benefit the client in more ways than one. Knowledge and expertise are important hallmarks of the profession. Clients benefit when trusted advisers provide services that otherwise might have been provided by professionals who have a lesser set of technical skills and lower ethical standards.

The problem is the expansion of nonattest services may threaten to alter the ethical culture of a firm, as Andersen found out with Enron. Consultants may have a different mindset than the objective judgment required of auditors. Biases can creep into decision making if firms do not build in the quality controls necessary to ensure independent decision making. Also, increased opportunities to establish business relationships with clients and client management present a threat, and auditors must take care not to get too cozy with their clients.

We are concerned about the nature and scope of audit deficiencies identified by PCAOB in its inspections of the Big Four CPA firms. A "failure" rate of almost 40 percent is unacceptable. Perhaps it is just a matter of time before the public trust that CPAs have fought so hard to regain in the aftermath of Enron and other accounting scandals will be questioned once again. We hope not. We do believe the profession needs to pivot and work on developing the judgment skills so essential in today's complex accounting environment. Certainly, ethics education has an important role to play in this regard.

Discussion Questions

1. In our discussion of the KPMG professional judgment framework, we pointed out that biased judgments can be made because of judgment tendencies. One such tendency that was not included in the framework is self-serving bias. Explain what you think this means and how it might influence audit judgment.

2. Explain the threats to professional skepticism that might influence audit judgment.

3. Explain the safeguards that can be used to reduce or eliminate threats to audit independence.

4. It has been said that independence is the cornerstone of the accounting profession. Explain what this means. What does it mean to say that auditors have special and critical gatekeeping duties?

5. Is independence impaired when an auditor is hired, paid, and fired by the same corporate managers whose activities are the subject of the audit? Does it matter that in most companies the audit

committee hires, evaluate, fires (if appropriate), and determines the fees of the external auditor with minimal input from senior management?

6. How might financial incentives in the form of client services unconsciously introduce auditor bias into the independent audit function? Are there any solutions to the conflict?

7. Do you believe the internal audit activity should be independent? Explain.

8. Do you believe that the SEC should prohibit auditors from providing *all* nonaudit services for audit clients? Use ethical reasoning to support your answer.

9. Assume that a CPA serves as an audit client's business consultant and performs each of the following services for the client. Identify the threats to independence. Do you believe any safeguards can be employed to reduce the threat to an acceptable level? Explain.

   a. Advising on how to structure its business transactions to obtain specific accounting treatment under GAAP.

   b. Advising and directing the client in the accounting treatment that the client employed for numerous complex accounting, apart from its audit of the client's financial statements.

   c. Selecting the audit client's most senior accounting personnel by directly interviewing applicants for those positions.

10. What are the dangers of creeping commercialism in the accounting profession?

11. Can a CPA auditor be independent without being objective? Can a CPA auditor be objective without being independent? Explain.

12. What is the problem with an auditor overrelying on management's representations on the financial statements?

13. Andy Simmons is a CPA with his own accounting and tax practice. He occasionally does an audit for small business clients. One day an audit client shows Andy a letter from the local Property Tax Assessor's office. It seems the client inquired about the process to be followed to appeal the 20 percent increase in his property taxes. He already wrote an appeal letter and was denied. The letter said that most folks who appeal those decisions hire a CPA to represent them before the administrative board in property tax assessment hearings. If your client asks you to represent him in the appeal process, can you do so under the AICPA Code? Explain.

14. You're struggling in your new accounting practice to tap into a potential client base. You have tried traditional advertising and marketing tools to no avail. Your friend tells you to use social media as a tool to reach potential customers. You're not sure about it. Your concern is one of ethics. The last thing you want to do is violate the ethical standards of the accounting profession. Identify the ethical issues that should be of concern to you in deciding whether and how to use social media for advertising and solicitation of new clients.

15. You have decided to leave your CPA firm. Using the AICPA rules as a guide, answer the following questions: (1) Can you post some negative comments about your former employer on Twitter? (2) Can you call your former clients and tell them that you are leaving? (3) Can you take their files with you when you go?

16. You previously worked for the Department of Revenue, a governmental agency in your town. You cut all ties with the agency after you left two years ago to start your own tax accounting business. One day you receive a call from the agency asking you to conduct a tax audit of taxpayers in the town. You do not conduct a financial statement audit of any of these clients. Assume the proposed arrangement is to pay you 25 percent of additional amounts collected following your audits of property tax returns plus 50 percent of all first-year tax penalties. What ethical issues exist for you in deciding whether to accept the engagement? Would you accept it? Explain.

17. You were engaged to file the 2015 individual and corporate tax returns for a client. The client provided her records and other tax information on March 1, 2016, to help prepare the 2015 tax return. Your client paid you $12,000 in advance to prepare those returns. On April 1 after repeated requests to return her records, you informed the client that her tax returns for 2015 would be completed by April 15, and all of the records would be returned at that time. However, you failed to complete the return. The client paid another accountant $15,000 to complete the returns after the deadline and incurred tax penalties. Do you believe that you violated any of the rules of conduct in the AICPA Code? Did you violate any ethical standards beyond the Code? Explain.

18. In January 2008, it was discovered that William Borchard, who handled due diligence for clients of PwC interested in mergers and acquisitions, divulged controversial plans to Gregory Raben, an auditor at the firm, and Raben used the information to buy stock ahead of a series of corporate takeovers. The SEC found the two guilty of insider trading, a violation of the law. Assume none of the clients were audit clients. What are the ethical issues involved in engaging in such transactions? Were any of the AICPA rules of conduct violated? Explain.

19. Assume that the CPA firm of Packers & Vikings audits Chi Bears Systems. The controller of Chi Bears, a CPA, happens to be a tax expert. During the current tax season, Packers & Vikings gets far behind in reviewing processed tax returns. It does not want to approach clients and ask permission to file for an extension to the April 15 deadline so the firm approaches the controller and offers him a temporary position as a consultant for the tax season. Was it ethical for the firm to make the offer? Would it be ethically acceptable for the controller to accept the position? Explain.

20. Assume you are the senior in charge of the audit of a client in New York who offers you two tickets to the Super Bowl between the New York Giants and the Denver Broncos. The opportunity to see the Manning brothers square off against each other is appealing. How would you decide whether to accept the tickets for the game?

21. In recent years the move by accounting firms to offshore tax and consulting work has grown and expanded into audit work. What are the ethical concerns that might be raised about the practice of electronically transmitting audit information to offshore centers like those in India that provide accounting professionals to audit U.S. corporations' financial statements?

22. According to SOX rules that mandate auditor rotation, the lead audit partner on an engagement is prohibited from providing those services for a client for greater than five consecutive years. The purpose of the rule is to encourage professional skepticism. Discuss the costs and benefits of auditor rotation as you see it. Do you think audit firms should be rotated periodically?

23. In August 2008, EY agreed to pay more than $2.9 million to the SEC to settle charges that it violated ethics rules by co-producing a series of audio CDs with a man who was also a director at three of EY's audit clients. According to the SEC, EY collaborated with Mark C. Thompson between 2002 and 2004 to produce a series of audio CDs called *The Ernst & Young Thought Leaders Series.* Thompson served on the boards at several of EY's clients during the period when the CDs were produced. What threats to independence existed in the relationship between EY and Thompson? From an ethical perspective, would it have mattered if it was not an audit client but one for whom advisory services only were performed?

24. On May 20, 2014, the SEC settled an investigation of James T. Adams, the former chief risk officer at Deloitte, for causing violations of the auditor independence rules. It seems that Adams accepted tens of thousands of casino markers while he was the advisory partner on a Deloitte casino gaming client. Review the facts of the case and explain how Adams's actions compromised his independence under the AICPA Code.

25. Is accounting a trustworthy profession? How would you know whether it is or is not?

Endnotes

1. Steven M. Glover and Douglas F. Prawitt, *Enhancing Auditor Professional Skepticism,* Center for Audit Quality, November 2013, Available at: http://www.thecaq.org/docs/research /skepticismreport.pdf.

2. PCAOB, Staff Practice Alert No. 10: Maintaining and Applying Professional Skepticism in Audits, December 4, 2012, Available at: http://pcaobus.org/standards/qanda/12-04-2012_sapa_10.pdf.

3. Shelby D. Hunt and Scott Vitell, "A General Theory of Marketing Ethics," *Journal of Macromarketing,* Spring 1986, 6, pp. 5–16.

4. Steven Glover and Douglas Prawitt, "Elevating Professional Judgment in Auditing and Accounting: The KPMG Professional Judgment Framework," Available at: https://www.researchgate.net /publication/258340692_Elevating_Professional_ Judgment_in_Auditing_and_Accounting_The_KPMG_Professional_Judgment_Framework.

5. PCAOB, Panel Discussion—CIFir Proposal Relating to Judgments made by Financial Statement Preparers and Auditors, February 27, 2008.

6. B. E. Christensen, S. M. Glover, and D. A. Wood, "Extreme Estimation Uncertainty in Fair Value Estimates: Implications for Audit Assurance," *Auditing: A Journal of Practice and Theory,* Vol. 31, No. 1 (2012), pp. 127–146.

7. Glover and Prawitt.

8. Kathy Hurtt, "Development of a Scale to Measure Professional Skepticism," *Auditing: A Journal of Theory and Practice,* May 2012, Vol. 29, No. 1, pp. 149–171.

9. IAASB, "International Standard on Quality Control 1," *Quality Control for Firms that Perform Audits and Reviews of Financial Statements, and Other Assurance and Related Services Engagements,* Effective as of December 15, 2009, Available at: http://www.ifac.org/system/files /downloads/a007-2010-iaasb-handbook-isqc-1.pdf.

10. International Ethics Standards Board for Accountants, *Handbook of the Code of Ethics for Professional Accountants,* IFAC, 2015, Available at: http://www.ethicsboard.org/iesba-code.

11. The International Ethics Standards Board for Accountants® (IESBA®) is an independent standard-setting body that serves the public interest by setting robust, internationally appropriate ethics standards, including auditor independence requirements, for professional accountants worldwide. These are compiled in the *Code of Ethics for Professional Accountants.*

12. AICPA, *Code of Professional Conduct,* As of December 14, 2014, Available at: http://www.aicpa.org/Research/Standards/CodeofConduct/DownloadableDocuments /2014December14CodeofProfessionalConduct.pdf.

13. Gordon Boyce, "Professionalism, the Public Interest, and Social Accounting," *Accounting for the Public Interest: Perspectives on Accountability, Professionalism and Role in Society,* ed. Steven Mintz (NY: Springer Dordrecht Heidelberg, 2014).

14. Ira Sager, "Arthur Levitt on PwC's Deal to Buy Booz: 'We Are Slipping Back,'" *Bloomberg Businessweek,* October 30, 2013, Available at: http://www.bloomberg.com/bw/articles/2013-10-30 /arthur-levitt-on-pricewaterhousecoopers-deal-to-buy-booz-we-are-slipping-back.

15. Francine McKenna, "Exclusive From Monadnock Research: Big Four Fiscal 2013 Advisory Practice Ranking and Conflict Risk Metrics," March 18, 2014, Available at: http://retheauditors.com/2014/03/18/exclusive-from-monadnock-research-big-four-fiscal-2013-advisory-practice-rankings-and-conflict-risk-metrics/.

16. Vincent J. Love, "Can Professionalism and Commercialism Coexist in CPA Firms?" *The CPA Journal,* February 2015, pp. 6–9.

17. Steven Mintz, "Revised AICPA Code of Professional Conduct: Analyzing the Ethical Responsibilities for Members in Public Practice and Members in Business," *The CPA Journal,* December 2014, pp. 62–71.

18. Ellen Goria, "Revised AICPA Code of Ethics . . . What's the Fuss?," *Journal of Accountancy,* February 2014, pp. 42–45.

19. IFAC, *Handbook of the Code of Ethics for Professional Accountants,* 2015 Edition, (NY: IFAC, 2015).

20. SEC, *Final Rule: Revision of the Commission's Auditor Independence Requirements,* February 5, 2001, Available at: www.sec.gov/rules/final/33-7919.htm.

21. "PwC Pays for Audit Violation," *Accountancy Live,* August 1, 2002, Available at: https://www.accountancylive.com/pwc-pays-audit-violation.

22. Jason Bramwell, "KPMG Settles SEC Charges Over Violating Auditor Independence Rules," Accounting Web, January 24, 2014, Available at: http://www.accountingweb.com/practice/practice-excellence/kpmg-settles-sec-charges-over-violating-auditor-independence-rules.

23. Sarah N. Lynch, "Deloitte to Pay $1mln to Resolve SEC Auditor Independence Rule Charges," *Reuters Business News,* July 1, 2015.

24. Michael Cohn, "SEC and PCAOB Discipline Firms for Violating Auditor Independence Rules," *Accounting Today,* December 8, 2014, Available at: http://www.accountingtoday.com/news/auditing /sec-pcaob-discipline-firms-violating-auditor-independence-rules-72953-1.html.

25. Michael Cohn, "SEC and PCAOB Discipline Firms for Violating Auditor Independence Rules," *Accounting Today,* December 8, 2014, Available at: http://www.accountingtoday.com /news/auditing/sec-pcaob-discipline-firms-violating-auditor-independence-rules-72953-1.html.

26. IFRS has become widely adopted by countries for financial reporting, which includes the requirement for all companies operating in the European Union. Approximately 120 nations and reporting jurisdictions require IFRS to one extent or another.

27. James D. Cashell and Ross D. Fuerman, "The CPA's Responsibility for Client Information," *The CPA Journal,* September 1995, Available at: http://www.cpajournal.com/1995/SEP95/aud0995.htm.

28. *Wagenheim v. Alexander Grant & Co.* (AG) (1983), Nos. 82AP-1039 and -1040. 19 Ohio App. 3d 7 (1983), Available at: http://www.leagle.com/decision/19832619OhioApp3d7_125.xml /WAGENHEIM%20v.%20ALEXANDER%20GRANT%20&%20CO.

29. Matthew J. Barrett, "'Tax Services' is a Trojan Horse in the Auditor's Independence Provisions of Sarbanes-Oxley," *Michigan State Law Review* (2004), Available at: http://papers.ssrn.com /sol3/papers.cfm?abstract_id=813226.

30. Barbara Ley Toffler with Jennifer Reingold, *Final Accounting: Ambition, Greed, and the Fall of Arthur Andersen* (New York: Broadway Books, 2003).

31. Martin Stuebs, "Moral Confrontation: Companion to Moral Imagination," *Research on Professional Responsibility and Ethics in Accounting,* Volume 14 (2010), pp. 57–78.

32. Michael Rapoport, "KPMG Audits had 46% Deficiency Rate in PCAOB Inspections," October 23, 2014, Available at: http://www.wsj.com/articles/kpmg-audits-had-46-deficiency-rate-in-pcaob-inspection-1414093002.

Chapter 4 Cases

Case 4-1 KBC Solutions

The audit of KBC Solutions by Carlson and Smith, CPAs, was scheduled to end on February 28, 2016. However, Rick Carlson was uncertain whether it could happen. As the review partner, he had just completed going over the work paper files of the senior auditor in charge of the engagement, Grace Sloan, and had way too many questions to wrap things up by the end of the week. Rick called Grace into his office and asked her about some questionable judgments she had made. He hoped her explanations would be satisfactory and he could move on with completing the audit.

1. Why did you approve the accounting for new acquisitions of plant and equipment that were not supported by adequate underlying documentation?
2. Why did you accept the client's determinations of accrued expenses rather than make your own independent judgments?
3. How can you justify relying on last year's work papers to determine the proper allowance for uncollectibles one year later?

To say Grace was stressed out would be an understatement. This was her first engagement as a senior and she wondered whether it would be her last. Grace knew she had to make a convincing case for her judgments or suffer the consequences. She responded to each point as follows.

1. The client had problems with their systems and had to contact the vendor for a duplicate copy of the relevant invoices. She expects the copy within two days.
2. The client seemed to have a reasonable basis for those judgments so she saw no reason to delay completion of the audit over the accrued expenses.
3. Although the confirmation rate on the receivables was slightly below expected norms, there was no reason not to accept the client's explanation for those not confirmed as being correct in amount and due date.

Grace knew her answers would not completely satisfy Rick. She did, however, believe there were extenuating circumstances she felt compelled to explain even though it might reflect negatively on her leadership abilities. She explained that the audit team pressured her to let certain matters go because they were behind schedule in completion of the audit. She was convinced by the majority to trust the client on outstanding issues, which included the three raised by Rick.

Rick was not very happy with the explanation. He wondered about the professional judgments exercised by Grace and what her future with the firm should be.

Questions

1. Critically evaluate the judgments made by Grace as the senior by using the KPMG Professional Judgment Framework.
2. Did Grace violate any rules of conduct in the AICPA Code? Explain.
3. Does Rick have any ethical obligations in this matter? What should he do about signing off on the audit and why?

Case 4-2 Beauda Medical Center

Lance Popperson woke up in a sweat, with an anxiety attack coming on. Popperson popped two anti-anxiety pills, lay down to try to sleep for the third time that night, and thought once again about his dilemma. Popperson is an associate with the accounting firm of Hodgins and Gelman LLP. He recently discovered, through a "water cooler" conversation with Brad Snow, a friend of his on the audit staff, that one of the firm's clients managed by Snow recently received complaints that its heart monitoring equipment was malfunctioning. Cardio-Systems Monitoring, Inc. (CSM), called for a meeting of the lawyers, auditors, and top management to discuss what to do about the complaints from health-care facilities that had significantly increased between the first two months of 2015 and the last two months of that year. Doctors at these facilities claimed that the systems shut off for brief periods, and in one case, the hospital was unable to save a patient who went into cardiac arrest.

Popperson tossed and turned and wondered what he should do about the fact that Beauda Medical Center, his current audit client, planned to buy 20 units of Cardio-Systems heart monitoring equipment for its brand-new medical facility in the outskirts of Beauda.

Questions

Assume that both Popperson and Snow are CPAs. Do you think Snow violated his confidentiality obligation under the AICPA Code by informing Popperson about the faulty equipment at CSM? Explain.

Assume that Popperson informs the senior auditor in charge of the Beauda Medical audit, and the senior informs the manager, Kelly Kim. A meeting is held the next day with all parties in the office of Ben Smith, the managing partner of the firm. Here's how it goes:

Ben: If we tell Beauda about the problems at CSM, we will have violated our confidentiality obligation as a firm to CSM. Moreover, we may lose both clients.

Kelly: Lance, you are the closest to the situation. How do you think Beauda's top hospital administrators would react if we told them?

Lance: They wouldn't buy the equipment.

Ben: Once we tell them, we're subject to investigation by our state board of accountancy for violating confidentiality. We don't want to alert the board and have it investigate our actions. What's worse, we may be flagged for the confidentiality violation in our next peer review.

Kelly: Who would do that? I mean, CSM won't know about it, and the Beauda people are going to be happy we prevented them from buying what may be faulty equipment.

Senior: I agree with Kelly. They are not likely to say anything.

Ben: I don't like it. I think we should be silent and find another way to warn Beauda Medical without violating confidentiality.

Lance: What should we do? I need to be clear about my ethical responsibilities and the firm's as well.

Analyze the dilemma using the discussion in the chapter about conflicts of interest. Explain the threats in this situation and evaluate the steps to be taken to deal with those threats so as not to violate the rules of conduct. What do you think the firm should do and why?

Case 4-3 Family Games, Inc.

Family Games, Inc., is a publicly owned company with annual sales of $50 million from a variety of wholesome electronic games that are designed for use by the entire family. However, during the past two years, the company reported a net loss due to cost-cutting measures that were necessary to compete with overseas manufacturers and distributors.

"Yeah, I know all of the details weren't completed until January 2, 2016, but we agreed on the transaction on December 30, 2015. By my way of reasoning, it's a continuation transaction and the $12 million revenue belongs in the results for 2015. What's more, the goods are on the delivery truck waiting to be shipped after the New Year."

This comment was made by Carl Land, the CFO of Family Games, to Helen Strom, the controller of Family Games, after Strom had expressed her concern that because the lawyers did not sign off on the transaction until January 2, 2016, because of the holiday, the revenue should not be recorded in 2015. Land felt that Strom was being hyper-technical. He had seen it before from Helen and didn't like it. She needed to learn to be a team player.

"Listen, Helen, this comes from the top," Land said. "The big boss said we need to have the $12 million recorded in the results for 2015."

"I don't get it," Helen said to Land. "Why the pressure?"

"The boss wants to increase his performance bonus by increasing earnings in 2015. Apparently, he lost some money in Vegas over the Christmas weekend and left a sizable IOU at the casino," Land responded.

Helen shook her head in disbelief. She didn't like the idea of operating results being manipulated based on the personal needs of the CEO. She knew that the CEO had a gambling problem. This sort of thing had happened before. The difference this time was that it had the prospect of affecting the reported results, and she was being asked to do something that she knows is wrong.

"I can't change the facts," Helen said.

"All you have to do is backdate the sales invoice to December 30, when the final agreement was reached," Land responded. "As I said before, just think of it as a revenue-continuation transaction that started in 2015 and, but for one minor technicality, should have been recorded in that year. Besides, you know we push the envelope around here."

"You're asking me to 'cook the books,'" Helen said. "I won't do it."

"I hate to play hardball with you, Helen, but the boss authorized me to tell you he will stop reimbursing you in the future for child care costs so that your kid can have a live-in nanny 24-7 unless you go along on this issue. I promise, Helen, it will be a one-time request," Land said.

Helen was surprised by the threat and dubious "one-time-event" explanation. She sat down and reflected on the fact that the reimbursement payments for her child care were $35,000, 35 percent of her annual salary. As a single working mother, Helen knew there was no other way that she could afford to pay for the full-time care needed by her autistic son.

Questions

1. Explain the nature of the dilemma for Helen using the AICPA Code as a guide. What steps should she take to resolve the issue?

2. What would you do if you were in Helen's position? How would you attempt to convince Carl Land of the rightness of your position and give voice to your values?

Case 4-4 Commercialism versus Professionalism (a GVV case)

One area of concern for the accounting profession for the past 20 years has been the proliferation of alternative practice structures. Potential problems exist because the audit side of the business may be influenced by the public entity that controls it. One such situation involves K&B, CPA Associates, and Cryden Business and Tax Services.

Billy Kamen, CPA, has been a partner of K&B for more than 30 years. He thought he had seen it all in the accounting profession. The rules of conduct slowly have been eaten away because of growing commercial interests. First it was competitive bidding, which used to be against the rules but has become the standard way to gain new clients. Next, it was advertising and soliciting new clients. He reflected on the good old days when all CPAs could do was use their professional designation on business cards or in yellow pages advertisements. That was it! No media advertising and certainly no cold calls to potential clients. Then, the commissions and contingent fees rules were amended to allow such practices for nonaudit clients. The final rule to be changed was the 100 percent CPA-ownership requirement for a firm to "hold out" as a CPA firm. It now requires only majority licensed CPA ownership. Billy had thought about early retirement after Cryden bought out K&B, but decided to stay on.

This is the way the arrangement works. K&B provides all of the audit and other attest-related services and is 100 percent owned by CPAs. Cryden, on the other hand, provides accounting (i.e., bookkeeping), tax compliance, and consulting services (i.e., financial planning) often to the same audit clients of K&B. The owners of K&B are also employees of Cryden and, from time to time, do tax planning work and some consulting services for clients of Cryden who may also be audit clients of K&B. The rest of the employees of Cryden are employees of the company only, and some of them hold the CPA designation.

There is an administrative services agreement between the two entities, stipulating that support and personnel staff are made available to the CPA firm by Cryden. Cryden also provides office space, equipment, and recordkeeping for K&B.

On his first audit under the new structure, an issue arose where Billy faced an ethical dilemma. He wasn't sure what to do. He has been involved in the audit of Hall Technologies, a large company that researched and developed new software products and had been serviced by K&B CPAs for 15 years. Billy has been the lead engagement partner on the audit during that time. One day Billy was sitting in his office reflecting on a meeting he just had with Chad Cryden where Chad told Billy he had to accept Hall's accounting for a new R&D program whereby the company had spent $1 million to date on pre-development costs basically testing out the product to ensure technological feasibility. Billy had already decided those costs should be expensed immediately, but Chad had told him the costs would benefit future periods so they should be amortized over 5 years.

It turns out that Hall Industries was a tax client of Cryden as well as an audit client of K&B, and Frederick Hall had pressured Chad to exert influence over Billy to accept the company's accounting for the software development expenses. That is why Chad had come to see Billy.

Billy wasn't sure how to proceed. He knew the accounting was wrong, but he also knew the CPA firm was trying to do everything possible to make the new arrangement work. K&B had been a middle-market firm before Cryden acquired it, and may have been forced to go out of business because it no longer could meet the demands for capital to meet technology requirements and because of the difficulty the firm was having attracting and retaining talented young professionals.

Questions

1. Discuss the issue of commercialism versus professionalism in the accounting profession with respect to the changes in the rules of conduct described in the case. Do you think these changes are good or bad for the profession? For the public? Explain.

2. What are the threats to compliance with the rules of conduct that arise as a result of the alternative practice structure in this case? Why are they threats?

3. What safeguards might be established to ensure the threats have been eliminated or reduced to acceptable levels?

4. What would you do if you were Billy? Consider the following:

- How can you get it done effectively and efficiently?

- What do you need to say and to whom?

- What can you expect the pushback to be and how might you counteract any reasons and rationalizations?

Case 4-5 Han, Kang & Lee, LLC

Joe Kang is an owner and audit partner for Han, Kang & Lee, LLC. As the audit on Frost Systems was reaching its concluding stages on January 31, 2016, Kang met with Kate Boller, the CFO, to discuss the inventory measurement of one its highly valued products as of December 31, 2015. Kang told Boller that a write-down of 20 percent had to be made because the net realizable value of the inventory was 20 percent less than the original cost recorded on its books. That meant the earnings for the year would be reduced by $2 million and the client would show a loss for the year. In a heated exchange with Boller, Kang was told to use the January 31, 2016, value, which reflected a full recovery of the market amount. Boller suggested that subsequent values were acceptable under GAAP. Besides, she said, that was the method the previous auditors had used. She went on to explain that the market value for this product was known to be volatile and a smoothing effect was justified in the accounting procedures.

Kang was under a great deal of pressure from the other partners of the firm to keep Boller happy. It seems Frost Systems was about to embark on a variety of projects, on which it was considering having the firm provide consulting assistance, advice, and recommendations. The revenue from these arrangements could turn out to be twice the audit fees. Kang called a meeting of the other partners. While the three of them had different points of view on the issue, the final vote was 2-1 to accept the client's accounting.

Questions

1. Do you think the client's accounting approach to the market valuation of the inventory was acceptable under GAAP? Include in your discussion a brief explanation of why fair value measurements are difficult.

2. Evaluate the professional judgment used by Kang and the firm in assessing the client's accounting and reaching its own decision to accept it.

3. Would independence be impaired if the firm were offered, and accepted, the consulting arrangements? Consider whether any threats to independence would exist and, if so, how they might be reduced to an acceptable level.

4. What would you do at this point if you were Joe Kang and why?

Case 4-6 Tax Shelters

You are a tax manager and work for CPA firm that that performs audits, advisory services, and tax planning for wealthy clients in a large Midwestern city. You just joined the tax department after five years as a tax auditor for the county government. During the first six months in tax, you found out that the firm is aggressively promoting tax shelter products to top management officials of audit clients. Basically the company developed a product and then looked for someone in management to sell it to, rather than the more conventional method whereby an officer might approach the firm asking it to identify ways to shelter income.

The way these products work is the firm would offer an opinion letter to the taxpayer to provide cover in case the IRS questioned the reasonableness of the transaction. The opinion would say that the firm "reasonably relied on a person who is qualified to know," and that would support the contention that the opinion was not motivated out of any intention to play the audit lottery. It also would protect the taxpayer against penalties in the event the firm is not correct and does not prevail in a tax case.

As time goes on, it becomes clear that the culture of the tax department is shifting from client service to maximization of tax revenues. It is the most lucrative type of service for all big firms and the competition in the industry is fierce in this area of practice. You become concerned, however, when you discover the firm did not register the tax shelter products, as required under the law.

One day you are approached by the tax partner you report to and asked to participate in one of the tax shelter transactions, with the end result being you would recommend to the tax partner whether he should sign off before presenting the product to the client. You feel uncomfortable with the request based on what you have learned about these products. You make an excuse about needing to complete three engagements that are winding down, and buy some time.

The first thing you do is look for completed tax shelter arrangements with clients that had been reviewed and approved by the tax quality control engagement partner. What you find makes you more suspicious about the products. Several are marked "restricted" on the cover page without any further details. You then call a friend who is a manager in the audit department and set up a time to meet and discuss your concerns.

What you learn only heightens your concerns. Your friend confided there is a culture in the tax department where business rationality sometimes displaces professional norms, a process accelerated by a conformist culture. Your friend also confided that the audit managers and partners are jealous of their tax peers because the tax managers and partners earn almost twice what the auditors earn because of the higher level of client revenues. It was clear your friend harbors ill feelings about the whole situation.

The following week the tax partner comes back and presents you with another tax shelter opportunity for the firm and all but demands that you oversee it. He implies in a roundabout way that your participation is a rite of passage to partnership in the firm. You manage to stall and put off the final decision a few days.

Questions

1. Evaluate the ethics of the tax shelter transactions, including your concerns about the practices.

2. Who are the stakeholders in this case, and what are your professional responsibilities?

3. What are the options available to you in this matter?

4. What would you do and why?

Case 4-7 M&A Transaction

Yardley, Inc., is a mid-size company in Oklahoma City. It has been struggling the past few years because chemical products it uses in its agricultural production process increasingly have been deemed environmentally unsafe. Yardley's primary reliance on the agricultural industry for sales and profits has begun to take its toll. Cash flow is down and the company needs a quick infusion if it is to survive much longer.

One positive trend for the company is its growing bioscience business. Yardley's revenues in this sector have doubled in three years, which may enable the company to return to profitability within another three years.

Mikan, Inc., is a regional company in Denver, Colorado, that has been in the bioscience and biotechnology industry for years. It is well established and has as its goal further regional and national expansion and, ultimately, a global reach. Mikan has been buying up smaller companies with bioscience services and now has its sights set on Yardley.

Pettit & Schayes, LLP, provides audit and advisory services to Mikan from its Denver office. The firm was recently contacted by Jenna Golden, the chair of the board of directors of Mikan, with the idea of acquiring

Yardley because of its growing bioscience business. It wasn't lost on Jenna that Pettit & Schayes provides audit and tax services for Yardley through its Oklahoma City office and the knowledge gained should be quite helpful to Mikan going forward.

Kelly Rogers is the partner in charge of merger and acquisition (M&A) services at Pettit & Schayes. Jenna asks Kelly to attend a board meeting of Mikan where the acquisition issue will be discussed. The board members make a convincing case to proceed with the transaction. Kelly knows it will bring in a lot of additional revenue for the Denver office and open the door to more M&A services down the line and bonuses for M&A staff. She expresses a keen interest on the part of the firm to move forward and asks the board for two weeks to present an engagement plan to conduct the due diligence work for the acquisition.

Questions

1. What are the ethical issues that should be of concern to Kelly Rogers and Pettit & Schayes in deciding whether the firm should perform the transaction advisory services for Mikan?

2. Do you believe one party or the other in the proposed transaction would have an advantage if Pettit & Schayes is hired to perform the due diligence and advise both clients on the arrangement?

3. Would your concerns be any different if Pettit & Schayes were not the auditor of Yardley but instead a different firm audited its financial statements? Explain.

Case 4-8 Valley View Hospital

Sue Kolb has been associated with Valley View Hospital in Highlands Ranch, a small town in Colorado. Kolb is a CPA licensed in Colorado and handles the hospital's financial affairs; she climbed the ladder to CFO after 10 years in the accounting department.

In 2015, Valley View's board of trustees hired Denver-based Bronco Resources, Inc., to manage the hospital's operations. Bronco, formerly a division of Hospital Corporation of America (HCA), claimed that it could maximize the federal government's reimbursement for hospital expenses.

Kolb found out that Bronco was using a secret accounting system devised by HCA to cheat the government out of Medicare payments. Bronco, and similar companies around the country, had been keeping two sets of accounting records for reporting the health-care costs of Medicare patients. One set inflated the costs that were charged to the federal government. The other set, for internal use, listed the actual costs of hospital operations.

Kolb questioned the company's accounting methods and threatened not to go along with the fraud. She was told by the CEO that she would be fired if she followed through on the threat.

Questions

1. Who are the stakeholders in this case, and what are their interests?

2. What are Kolb's ethical obligations with respect to the Medicare fraud and her reporting it within Valley View under the AICPA Code of Professional Conduct?

3. What would you do at this point if you were Sue Kolb, and why?

Case 4-9 AOL-Time Warner[1]

How does one go from whistleblower to being charged by the SEC for participating in a scheme from mid-2000 to mid-2002 to overstate online revenue through round-trip transactions over two years while being the CFO of the America Online (AOL) Division of Time Warner? Just ask Joseph A. Ripp. Ripp consented to a final judgment with the SEC on May 19, 2008, permanently preventing him from future violations of the Securities Exchange Act of 1934 Section 13(b)(2)(A) and ordering him to pay disgorgement of $130,000 and pay a civil penalty of $20,000.

The Warning Letter from Ripp

Our story starts on May 14, 2001, when Joseph A. Ripp, the newly appointed CFO of AOL, faxed a letter to the Las Vegas offices of Arthur Andersen informing it that an AOL business partner, and Andersen client, had forged a signature on a contract and booked several million dollars of sham revenue.

That letter set off a chain of events that culminated in the accounting scandal that followed Time Warner's merger with AOL, including huge fines and criminal convictions. Ripp was called one of the "white hats" in the whole affair by the Justice Department.

But, on May 19, 2008, the SEC, after nearly six years of investigating accounting at AOL, filed a civil lawsuit against former executives alleging financial fraud. Seven were AOL executives before the merger; the eighth was Ripp. The SEC had charged Ripp with being a participant in the fraud and making public statements to investors that were part of the release of the fraudulent financial statements. To say his former colleagues at Time Warner were shocked is an understatement. Gerald Levin, the former CEO of Time Warner, said of Ripp, "This is precisely the type of guy you'd want to manage your financial group."

In addition to Ripp, two CPAs were charged with misleading the external auditor (Andersen) about the fraudulent transactions: J. Michael Kelly was the CFO of AOL and Mark Wovsaniker, former head of accounting policy.

In another twist to the story, on September 23, 2011, a New York federal judge stripped claims from the SEC lawsuit against two AOL-Time Warner executives on engineering the online scheme, citing a recent U.S. Supreme Court decision, because two parties to the lawsuit—Wovsaniker and Steven Rindner, former CEO in the company's business affairs unit—did not have ultimate authority over the misleading financial statements.

Fraudulent Round-Trip Transactions to Inflate Online Advertising Revenue

The following is taken from the SEC's ruling in the case against the former AOL-Time Warner officials.

Beginning in mid-2000, stock prices of Internet-related businesses declined precipitously as, among other things, sales of online advertising declined and the rate of growth of new online subscriptions started to flatten. Beginning at this time, and extending through 2002, AOL employed fraudulent round-trip transactions that boosted its online advertising revenue to mask the fact that it also experienced a business slow-down. The round-trip transactions enabled AOL to effectively fund its own online advertising revenue by giving the counterparties the means to pay for advertising that they would not otherwise have purchased. To conceal the true nature of the transactions, AOL typically structured and documented round-trips as if they were two or more separate, bona fide transactions, conducted at arm's length and reflecting each party's independent business purpose. AOL delivered mostly untargeted, less desirable, remnant online advertising to the round-trip advertisers, and the round-trip advertisers often had little or no ability to control the quantity, quality, and sometimes even the content of the online advertising they received. Because the round-trip customers effectively were paying for the online advertising with AOL's funds, the customers seldom, if ever, complained.

Several of the counterparties to the round-trip transactions were publicly traded companies. Three of these counterparties—Homestore, Inc., PurchasePro.com, Inc., and a California software company—improperly

---

[1] Tim Arango, "From a Whistle-Blower to a Target," *The New York Times*, June 9, 2008, Available at: http://www.nytimes.com/2008/06/09/business/media/09aol.html?pagewanted=print.

recognized revenue on the round-trip transactions and reported materially misstated financial results to their own investors. As a consequence, the company aided and abetted the frauds of three public companies.

The company also artificially inflated the number of AOL subscribers in the second, third, and fourth quarters of 2001 so it could report to the investment community that it had met its new subscriber targets, an important metric the market used to evaluate AOL (both before and after its merger with Time Warner). Specifically, the company counted members from "bulk subscription sales" to corporate customers (for distribution to their employees) when the company knew that the memberships had not, and mostly would not, be activated. In at least one instance, the company entered into round-trip arrangements to fund the corporate customers' purchases of bulk subscriptions. Additionally, in last-minute efforts to meet the quarterly targets, the company on at least four occasions shipped nonconforming bulk subscription membership kits to the customers prior to quarter-end with the understanding that it would turn around and replace them at a later date with conforming kits, but it nonetheless counted new subscribers from these sales as of the quarter-end.

Questions

1. The role of Joseph Ripp in the accounting fraud at AOL is one of whether a CFO who seemingly goes along with an accounting fraud and then is responsible for uncovering it should be viewed as a hero or villain. How should we view Joseph Ripp in this case: a participant in the fraud or an innocent bystander? A hero or a villain? Explain.

2. Two of the officers—J. Michael Kelly, the former CFO of AOL, and Mark Wovsaniker, former head of accounting policy—consented to the charges of the SEC that they misled the external auditors about the fraudulent transactions. What were the ethical responsibilities of Kelly and Wovsaniker in this matter in general, and specifically with respect to their relationship with the external auditors? Did they violate those standards?

3. Do you think the decision to reverse the charges against Wovsaniker because he did not have ultimate authority over the misleading financial statements was the "right" decision from an ethical perspective? Include in your discussion how that decision accords with the rules of conduct in the AICPA Code.

Case 4-10 Navistar International

In a bizarre twist to a bizarre story, on October 22, 2013, Deloitte agreed to pay a $2 million penalty to settle civil charges—brought by the Public Company Accounting Oversight Board (PCAOB)—that the firm violated federal audit rules by allowing its former partner to continue participating in the firm's public company audit practice, even though he had been suspended over other rule violations. The former partner, Christopher Anderson, settled with the PCAOB in 2008 by agreeing to a $25,000 fine and a one-year suspension for violating rules during a 2003 audit of the financial statements for a unit of Navistar International Corp. According to the charges, "Deloitte permitted the former partner to conduct work precluded by the Board's order and put investors at risk."[1]

After he settled the case and agreed to a one-year suspension, the PCAOB said Deloitte placed Anderson into another position that still allowed him to be involved in the preparation of audit opinions. Allowing a suspended auditor to continue working in that capacity is a violation of PCAOB rules, unless the SEC gives the firm permission. During the suspension, Anderson rendered advice on assignments involving three other Deloitte clients, according to the PCAOB. Deloitte said that it had

---

[1] *Navistar Intern. Corp. v. Deloitte & Touche LLP*, 837 F.Supp.2d 926 (2011), Available at: No. 11 C 3507, http://www.leagle.com /decision/In%20FDCO%2020111028F31/NAVISTAR%20INTERN.%20CORP.%20v.%20DELOITTE%20&%20TOUCHE%20LLP.

taken "several significant actions to restrict the deployment" of Anderson. "However, we recognize more could have been done at that time to monitor compliance with the restrictions we put in place."[2]

In January 2013, Deloitte had settled a lawsuit alleging it committed fraud and negligence, forcing Navistar to restate earnings between fiscal year 2002 and the first nine months of 2005. Deloitte was dropped by Navistar in 2006, and the company was delisted by the New York Stock Exchange.

One (of the many) unusual aspects of this case was the claim by Navistar that Deloitte lied about its competency to provide audit services. "Deloitte lied to Navistar and, on information and belief, to Deloitte's other audit clients, as to the competency of its audit and accounting services," Navistar alleged in its complaint. "Navistar feels compelled, more than five years later [2010], to sue Deloitte for, fraud, fraudulent concealment, negligent misrepresentation, deceptive business practices, and breach of fiduciary duty arising from the accounting advice, audit services and internal controls advice that Deloitte provided to Navistar relating to Navistar's financial statements from 2003 to 2005."[3]

Deloitte spokesman Jonathan Gandal expressed the firm's position as follows:

> "A preliminary review shows it to be an utterly false and reckless attempt to try to shift responsibility for the wrongdoing of Navistar's own management. Several members of Navistar's past or present management team were sanctioned by the SEC for the very matters alleged in the complaint."[4]

Early in the fraud, Navistar denied wrongdoing and said the problem was with "complicated" rules under SOX. Cynics reacted by saying it is hard to see how the law can be blamed for Navistar's accounting shortcomings, including management having secret side agreements with its suppliers who received "rebates;" improperly booking income from tooling buyback agreements, while not booking expenses related to the tooling; not booking adequate warranty reserves; or failing to record certain project costs.

It is clear that Navistar employees committed fraud and actively took steps to avoid discovery by the auditors. The auditors did not discover the fraud, according to Navistar, and in retrospect, the company wanted to hold the auditors responsible for that failure. Deloitte maintained that in each case, the fraudulent accounting scheme was nearly impossible to detect because the company failed to book items or provide information about them to the auditors.

It took Navistar five years to sue Deloitte. That seems like an unusually long period of time and raises suspicions whether the company waited until its own problems were resolved with the SEC. Perhaps Navistar thought if it had sued Deloitte while the SEC investigated, it might be misconstrued by the SEC as an admission of guilt.

Deloitte may have been guilty of failing to consider adequately the risks involved in the Navistar audit. After SOX was passed in mid-2002, all the large audit firms did some major cleanup of their audit clients and reassessed risk, an assessment that should have been done more carefully at the time of accepting the client. Big Four auditors, in particular, wanted to shed risky clients to protect themselves

---

[2]Steven R. Straher, "Deloitte fined $2 million for letting suspended exec work on audit," *October 23, 2013*, Available at: http://www.chicagobusiness.com/article/20131023/NEWS04/131029905/deloitte-fined-2-million-for-letting-suspended -exec-work-on-audit.

[3]*Navistar Intern. Corp. v. Deloitte & Touche LLP.*
Michigan State Law Review (2004), Available at: http://papers.ssrn.com/sol3/papers.cfm?abstract_id=813226.

[4]"Navistar Sues Its Former Auditor Deloitte & Touche," April 26, 2011, Available at: http://www.bloomberg.com/news/articles /2011-04-26/navistar-sues-ex-auditor-deloitte-for-500-million-over-malpractice-claim.

from new liability. Interestingly, to accomplish that goal with Navistar, Deloitte brought in a former Arthur Andersen partner to replace the engagement partner who might have become too close to Navistar and its management, thereby adjusting to the client's culture.

Whether because of his experience with Andersen's failure, fear of personal liability, a "not on my watch" attitude, or possibly a heads-up on interest by the SEC in some of Navistar's accounting, this new partner cleaned house. Many prior agreements between auditor and client and many assumptions about what could or could not be gotten away with were thrown out.

One problem for Navistar was that it was too dependent on Deloitte to hold its hand in all accounting matters, even after the SOX prohibited that reliance. According to Navistar's complaint, "Deloitte provided Navistar with much more than audit services. Deloitte also acted as Navistar's business consultant and accountant. For example, Navistar retained Deloitte to advise it on how to structure its business transactions to obtain specific accounting treatment under GAAP . . . Deloitte advised and directed Navistar in the accounting treatments Navistar employed for numerous complex accounting issues apart from its audits of Navistar's financial statements, functioning as a *de facto* adjunct to Navistar's accounting department. . . . Deloitte even had a role in selecting Navistar's most senior accounting personnel by directly interviewing applicants."[5]

The audit committee's role is detailed in the 2005 10-K filed in December 2007:

> "The audit committee's extensive investigation identified various accounting errors, instances of intentional misconduct, and certain weaknesses in our internal controls. The audit committee's investigation found that we did not have the organizational accounting expertise during 2003 through 2005 to effectively determine whether our financial statements were accurate. The investigation found that we did not have such expertise because we did not adequately support and invest in accounting functions, did not sufficiently develop our own expertise in technical accounting, and as a result, we relied more heavily than appropriate on our then outside auditor. The investigation also found that during the financial restatement period, this environment of weak financial controls and under-supported accounting functions allowed accounting errors to occur, some of which arose from certain instances of intentional misconduct to improve the financial results of specific business segments."

The complaint against Deloitte also references audit discrepancies cited in PCAOB inspections of Deloitte. Navistar believed the discrepancies related to Deloitte's audit of the company. However, the names of companies in PCAOB inspections are not made publicly available due to confidentiality and proprietary information concerns.

Questions

1. Use the Six Pillars of Character and ethical reasoning to assess the ethical values and decisions made by Navistar and Deloitte in the case.

2. Evaluate the deficiencies in internal controls and corporate governance at Navistar. Do you believe external auditors should be expected to discover fraud when a company, such as Navistar, is so poorly run that its personnel did not have the necessary training and expertise, its internal controls were deficient, and it relied too heavily on Deloitte to determine GAAP compliance? Explain.

3. Discuss the deficiencies in the work done by Deloitte for Navistar with respect to the AICPA Code of Professional Conduct.

---

[5]*United States Securities Exchange Commission v. Navistar International Corp.,* In the United States District Court for the Northern District of Illinois, January 22, 2015, Available at: https://www.sec.gov/litigation/litreleases/2015/court-filing23183.pdf.

Chapter

5

Fraud in Financial Statements and Auditor Responsibilities

Learning Objectives

After studying Chapter 5, you should be able to:

LO 5-1 Distinguish between audit requirements for errors, fraud, and illegal acts.

LO 5-2 Explain the components of the Fraud Triangle.

LO 5-3 Describe fraud risk assessment procedures.

LO 5-4 Explain the standards for audit reports.

LO 5-5 Discuss the characteristics of professional skepticism.

LO 5-6 Explain PCAOB auditing standards.

LO 5-7 Describe the PCAOB inspection process.

Ethics Reflection

A disconnect sometimes exists between a CPA's professional responsibility for detecting fraud and the public's perception of a CPA's duties in this regard. The "expectations gap" is one of understanding the actual role and responsibility of the external auditor with respect to detecting financial reporting fraud, and the public's perception with respect to the auditor's role therein. In an attempt to close the gap, the AICPA recently revised its audit reports to provide more information in the report and clarify its purpose for the investing public.

Audits are designed to look for fraud, using the "Fraud Triangle," and detecting material misstatements in the financial statements due to error and fraud. Unfortunately, the reality is, according to the *2014 Global Fraud Study* published by the Association of Certified Fraud Examiners (ACFE),[1] external audits are among the least effective controls in combating fraud, with only 3 percent of the fraud cases detected in this way. Perhaps more troubling is the median financial statement fraud lasts 24 months. A lot of damage can be done in that time period.

Financial statement fraud undermines the reliability, quality, transparency, and integrity of the financial reporting process and jeopardizes the integrity and objectivity of auditors and auditing firms. Financial statement fraud diminishes the confidence of the capital markets, as well as market participants, in the reliability of financial information and, as a consequence, makes the capital markets less efficient. It causes devastation in the normal operations and performance of alleged companies and erodes public confidence and trust in the accounting and auditing professions. Ultimately, financial statement fraud translates to massive stockholder losses and debts to creditors, not to mention emotional trauma to employees who lose their jobs and retirement funds.

For a while it appeared that financial statement fraud was on the decline. From 2008–2013, there were year-over-year decreases in SEC enforcement cases. However, for 2014 the SEC filed 99 accounting-fraud enforcement actions, a 46 percent increase from its 68 actions in the previous year. New investigations were up about 30 percent from the previous year.

One danger is once the heated stock market that has existed since the financial recession ended cools down, disclosure of financial fraud may come to light, since accounting fraud historically flourishes in such markets and often is exposed only after stock values turn lower. We warned about a new period of financial statement fraud and new round of Congressional investigations in Chapter 4. We hope to be proven wrong but are not confident that will occur.

Students need to understand the causes of fraud and how best to evaluate their potential effects on the financial statements. Without a clear understanding of the elements of fraud, it is highly unlikely an auditor will detect fraud as evidenced by the ACFE study. Students also should understand the nature and scope of an audit because the professional and ethical responsibilities of auditors are directly linked to the proper conduct of an audit. As you read this chapter, reflect on the following: (1) What are the red flags that are indicators fraud may exist? (2) What are the auditor's responsibilities to detect and report fraud? (3) Will the revised audit report provide any tangible benefits with respect to increasing its informational value, usefulness, and relevance to the investing public? (4) Can the audit firms enhance professional skepticism in light of deficiencies in audit reports identified in PCAOB inspections?

The true standards of audit practice are found within the auditor's character: honesty, integrity, self control and high ethical values. The printed standards are merely guidelines for trying to make the art of auditing into a profession.

Michael L.Piazza

This quote from Michael L. Piazza, director and producer of AuditWisdom.com, harkens back to our discussion of professional ethics in Chapter 4. Regardless of the existing standards for audit practice discussed in this chapter, it comes down to one's sense of right and wrong and willingness to voice values to positively impact auditor responsibilities to detect and report fraud.

Fraud in Financial Statements

LO 5-1
Distinguish between audit requirements for errors, fraud, and illegal acts.

According to the AICPA audit standard on fraud, *Consideration of Fraud in a Financial Statement Audit* (AU-C Section 240), the primary responsibility for the prevention and detection of fraud rests with both those charged with governance of the entity and management. A strong emphasis should be placed on fraud prevention, which may reduce opportunities for fraud to take place, and fraud deterrence, which could persuade individuals not to commit fraud because of the likelihood of detection and punishment.[2] As we discussed in Chapter 3, this involves a commitment to creating a culture of ethical behavior, tone at the top, and reinforcement through governance structures.

An auditor conducting an audit in accordance with generally accepted auditing standards (GAAS) is responsible for obtaining reasonable assurance that the financial statements as a whole are free from material misstatements, whether caused by fraud or error. Due to the inherent limitations of an audit, an unavoidable risk exists that some material misstatements of the financial statements may not be detected, even though the audit was conducted in accordance with those standards.[3]

The auditing profession recognizes its obligation to look for fraud by being alert to certain red flags, assessing the control environment of the organization, passing judgment on internal controls, and considering audit risk and materiality when performing an audit. However, this is a far cry from guaranteeing that fraud will be detected, especially when top management goes to great lengths to hide it from the auditors.

Audits involve a great deal of professional judgment with respect to the nature and scope of transactions examined, assessment of internal controls, and evaluation of estimates and judgments made by management. These determinations are aided by professional skepticism throughout the audit, recognizing the possibility that a material misstatement due to fraud could exist, notwithstanding the auditor's past experience of the honesty and integrity of management and those charged with governance within the entity.

When the financial statements are materially misstated, the auditor should not give an *unmodified* opinion but should modify the opinion as either qualified because of that matter or adverse opinion if the material misstatement leads to the conclusion that the financial statements, taken as a whole, do not present fairly the financial position, results of operations, and cash flows. This language relates to the statements on auditing standards issued by the AICPA Auditing Standards Board (ASB). The PCAOB uses the term "unqualified" rather than "unmodified." The AICPA's standards switched from "unqualified" to "unmodified" in 2012, to align terminology with *International Standards on Auditing* issued by the International Federation of Accountants.

Fraudulent financial reporting involves either intentional misstatements or omissions of amounts or disclosures in financial statements that are intended to deceive financial statement users. Fraudulent financial reporting generally occurs in one of three ways: (1) Deception such as manipulation, falsification, or alteration of accounting records or supporting documents from which the financial statements are prepared; (2) misrepresentation in, or intentional omission from, the financial statements of events, transactions, or other significant information; and (3) intentional misapplication of accounting principles relating to measurement, recognition, classification, presentation, or disclosure. Accountants and auditors who go along with the fraud fail in their ethical obligation to place the public interest above all else. Because fraud involves an intentional act, the perpetrator of the falsehood knows, or should know, that what she proposes to do is wrong. Once financial statements have been falsified, the trust relationship between an auditor and the public breaks down.

Nature and Causes of Misstatements

Misstatements in the financial statements can result from errors or fraud and may consist of any of the following:

1. An inaccuracy in gathering or processing data from which financial statements are prepared.
2. A difference between the amount, classification, or presentation of a reported financial statement element, account, or item and the way that it should have been reflected under GAAP.
3. The omission of a financial statement element, account, or item.
4. A financial statement disclosure that is not presented in conformity with GAAP.
5. The omission of information required to be disclosed in conformity with GAAP.
6. An incorrect accounting estimate due to oversight, misrepresentation of facts, or fraud.
7. Management's judgments concerning an accounting estimate or the selection or application of accounting policies that the auditor may consider unreasonable or inappropriate.

Misstatements also can exist when transactions are recorded without economic substance. Transactions should not be recorded in such a manner as to hide the true intent of the transaction, which would mislead the users of the financial statements. Substance over form issues can arise when a transaction is extremely complex, which makes it difficult to ascertain what the substance of the transaction is. For example, Enron sought to hide debt by setting up special-purpose-entities that executed financing transactions that ultimately benefited Enron but were left off its books.

External auditors examine client transactions to ensure that the substance over form criterion is being followed. The issue is an important one for auditors, since they are required to attest to the fairness of presentation of a set of financial statements, and fairness of presentation and the substance over form concept are essentially the same thing.

Errors, Fraud, and Illegal Acts

Material errors, fraud, and illegal acts represent situations where the financial statements should be restated. Exhibit 5.1 describes the auditors' obligations to detect and report each of these events. The following briefly describes the nature and effects of such acts.

EXHIBIT 5.1   Auditors' Responsibility to Detect Errors, Illegal Acts, and Fraud

	Responsible for Detection		Required to Communicate Findings	
	Material	**Immaterial**	**Material**	**Immaterial**
Errors	Yes	No	Yes (audit committee)	No
Illegal acts	Yes (direct effect)	No	Yes (audit committee)	Yes (one level above)
Fraud	Yes	No	Yes (audit committee)	Yes (by low-level employee, to one level above) (by management-level employee, to audit committee)

Errors

An *error* can occur due to unintentional misstatements or omissions of amounts or disclosures in the financial statements. Errors may involve mistakes in gathering or processing data, unreasonable accounting estimates arising from oversight or misinterpretation of facts, or mistakes in the application of GAAP. Auditors are responsible for detecting errors that have a material effect on the financial statements and reporting their findings to the audit committee. Errors are typically recorded by adjusting the opening balance of retained earnings for the prior period adjustment to net income.

Fraud

Auditors should be sensitive to red flags that warn fraud is possible, if not likely. Fraud, whether fraudulent financial reporting or misappropriation of assets, involves incentive or pressure to commit fraud, a perceived opportunity to do so, and some rationalization of the act. The intentional act of fraud occurs when an individual(s) in management, those charged with governance, employees or third parties, use deception in a way that results in a material misstatement in the financial statements. In its most common form, management fraud involves top management's deceptive manipulation of financial statements.

In an "Analysis of Alleged Auditor Deficiencies in SEC Fraud Investigations: 1998–2010" conducted for the Center for Audit Quality, it was determined that the failure to exercise due professional care and appropriate levels of professional skepticism resulted in auditors' inability to detect fraud. Being more attuned to the red flags that fraud may exist is an essential component of enhanced professional judgment.[4]

The intent of management determines whether the misapplication of GAAP is an error in judgment or a deliberate decision to manipulate earnings. In a court of law, it typically comes down to the credibility of the CFO and CEO who are charged with fraud. Absent a "smoking gun," the court might look for parallel actions by these top officers, such as selling their own shares of corporate stock after the fraudulent act but before it becomes public knowledge, as occurred at Enron and WorldCom.

Illegal Acts

Illegal acts are violations of laws or governmental regulations. For example, a violation of the Foreign Corrupt Practices Act (FCPA) that prohibits bribery constitutes an illegal act. Illegal acts include those attributable to the entity whose financial statements are under audit or as acts by management or employees acting on behalf of the entity. Such acts expose the company to both legal liability and public disgrace. The auditor's responsibility is to determine the proper accounting and financial reporting treatment of a violation once it has been determined that a violation has in fact occurred.

The auditor's responsibility is to detect and report misstatements resulting from illegal acts that have a direct and material effect on the determination of financial statement amounts (i.e., they require an accounting entry). The auditors' responsibility for detecting direct and material effect violations is greater than their responsibility to detect illegal acts arising from laws that only indirectly affect the client's financial statements. An example of the former would be violations of tax laws that affect accruals and the amount recognized as income tax liability for the period. Tax law would be violated, triggering an adjustment in the current period financial statements if, say, a company, for tax purposes, were to expense an item all in one year that should have been capitalized and written off over three years. Examples of items with an indirect effect on the statements include the potential violation of other laws such as the FCPA, occupational safety and health regulations, environmental protection laws, and equal employment regulations. The events are due to operational, not financial, matters and their financial statement effect is indirect, such as a possible contingent liability that should be disclosed in the notes to the financial statements.

The auditor's obligation when she concludes that an illegal act has or is likely to have occurred is first to assess the impact of the actions on the financial statements, including materiality considerations. This should be done regardless of any direct or indirect effect on the statements. The auditor should consult with legal counsel and any other specialists in this regard. Illegal acts should be reported to those charged with governance such as the audit committee. The auditor should consider whether the client has taken appropriate remedial action concerning the act. Such remedial action may include taking disciplinary actions, establishing controls to safeguard against recurrence, and, if necessary, reporting the effects of the illegal acts in the financial statements. Ordinarily, if the client does not take the remedial action deemed necessary by the auditor, then the auditor should withdraw from the engagement. This action on the part of the auditor makes clear that she will not be associated in any way with illegal activities.

Reporting Fraud/Illegal Acts

The auditor should assure herself that the audit committee is informed as soon as practicable and prior to the issuance of the auditor's report with respect to illegal acts that come to the auditor's attention. The auditor need not communicate matters that are clearly inconsequential and may reach agreement in advance with the audit committee on the nature of such matters to be communicated. The communication should describe the act, the circumstances of its occurrence, and the effect on the financial statements.

The standards for reporting fraud and illegal acts seem to err on the side of protecting the auditor's position in a legal matter rather than strict honesty because certain items can be ignored even though they violate the law. Honesty requires that we should express the truth as we know it and without deception. By leaving out truthful (inconsequential) information in auditor communications, the standards sanction unethical behavior. Some may view our perspective as being too harsh given the perceived lack of a material monetary effect on the financial statements. Others may find it impractical given the realities of auditing. But we believe that it is a slippery slope once distinctions are made as to whether acts that are inherently wrong by their nature are not reported. Moreover, even inconsequential items can become consequential if the pattern of misstatement persists.

The Private Securities Litigation Reform Act (PSLRA) of 1995

The Private Securities Litigation Reform Act (PSLRA) of 1995 places additional requirements upon public companies registered with the SEC and their auditors when (1) the illegal act has a material effect on the financial statements, (2) senior management and the board of directors have not taken appropriate remedial action, and (3) the failure to take remedial action is reasonably expected to warrant departure from a standard (i.e., unmodified audit report) or to warrant resignation.

When the auditor believes that fraud or the illegal act has a material effect on the financial statements and the matter has been reported to the client, the board of directors has one business day to inform the SEC under the requirements of Section 10A(b) of the Securities Exchange Act of 1934 ("Required Responses to Audit Discoveries"). If the board decides not to inform the SEC, the auditor must provide the same report to the SEC within one business day or resign from the engagement within one business day. In either case, the ethical obligation of confidentiality is waived so that the auditor can provide the necessary information and the SEC can live up to its responsibility to protect investor interests. If auditors do not fulfill this legal obligation, the SEC can impose a monetary fine on them.

A good example of the application of Section 10A is the litigation in the Xerox fraud. The accounting issues are discussed in Chapter 7; here, we look at the reporting requirements for fraud and illegal acts and whether KPMG met those standards with regard to its client, Xerox.

In *SEC v. KPMG LLP, Joseph T. Boyle, Michael A. Conway, Anthony P. Dolanski, and Ronald A. Safran*, the SEC alleged, among other claims, violations of Section 10A by KPMG and four of its partners.[5] On January 29, 2003, the SEC filed an action against the firm and its partners, claiming as follows:

> "Defendants KPMG . . . and certain KPMG partners permitted Xerox Corporation to manipulate its accounting practices and fill a $3 billion "gap" between actual operating results and results reported to the investing public from 1997 through 2000. Instead of putting a stop to Xerox's fraudulent conduct, the KPMG defendants themselves engaged in fraud by falsely representing to the public that they had applied professional auditing standards to their review of Xerox's accounting, that Xerox's financial reporting was consistent with GAAP and that Xerox's reported results fairly represented the financial condition of the company. . . . Section 10(A) of the Exchange Act requires a public accountant conducting an audit of a public company such as Xerox to: (1) determine whether it is likely that an illegal act occurred and, if so, (2) determine what the possible effect of the illegal act is on the financial statements of the issuer, and (3) if the illegal act is not clearly inconsequential, inform the appropriate level of management and assure that the Audit Committee of the client is adequately informed about the illegal act detected. If neither management nor the Audit Committee takes timely and appropriate remedial action in response to the auditor's report, the auditor is obliged to take further steps, including reporting the likely illegal act to the Commission."

In November 2004, KPMG reached a settlement with the SEC. KPMG consented to a finding that it violated Section 10(A) of the Securities Exchange Act of 1934; to pay disgorgement of $9,800,000, plus prejudgment interest; to pay a civil penalty of $10 million; and to implement a number of internal reforms. A final judgment against KPMG was issued on April 20, 2005.

Confidentiality Obligation

Recall that Section 1.700 of the AICPA Code of Professional Conduct prohibits CPAs from directly disclosing information to outside parties, including illegal acts, unless the auditors have a legal duty to do so. Therefore, it does permit the CPA to discuss confidential client information without violating the rule to adhere to applicable laws and government regulations. Compliance with the Private Securities Litigation Reform Act (PSLRA) of 1995 would qualify as an exception to the bar on disclosing confidential client information, as would compliance with SOX and Dodd-Frank provisions. Auditors are also required to communicate illegal acts in other situations. When illegal activities cause the auditors of a public company to lose faith in the integrity of senior management, they should resign, and a Form 8-K, which discloses the reasons for the auditors' resignation, should be filed with the SEC by management. The auditors must file a response to the filing indicating whether they agree with management's reasons and providing the details when they disagree.

Notwithstanding the reporting obligations described above, disclosure of fraud and an illegal act to parties other than the client's senior management and its audit committee or board of directors is not ordinarily part of the auditor's responsibility, and such disclosure would be precluded by the auditor's ethical or legal obligation of confidentiality, unless the matter affects his opinion on the financial statements. The auditor should recognize, however, that in the following circumstances, a duty to notify parties outside the client may exist:

- When the entity reports an auditor change under the appropriate securities law on Form 8-K.
- To a successor auditor when the successor makes inquiries in accordance with *Terms of Engagement* (AU-C Section 210).
- In response to a subpoena.
- To a funding agency or other specified agency in accordance with requirements for the audits of entities that receive financial assistance from a government agency.

Because potential conflicts with the auditor's ethical and legal obligations for confidentiality may be complex, the auditor should always consider consulting with legal counsel before discussing illegal acts with parties other than the client.

The Fraud Triangle

LO 5-2
Explain the components of the Fraud Triangle.

Donald R. Cressey, a noted criminologist, is mostly credited with coming up with the concept of a Fraud Triangle. Albrecht points out that, while researching his doctoral thesis in the 1950s, Cressey developed a hypothesis of why people commit fraud. He found that trusted persons become trust violators when they conceive of themselves as having a financial problem that is nonsharable, are aware that this problem can be secretly resolved by violation of the position of financial trust, and are able to apply to their contacts in that situation verbalizations which enable them to adjust their conceptions of themselves as users of the entrusted funds or property.[6]

Edwin Sutherland, another criminologist, argued that persons who engage in criminal behavior have accumulated enough feelings and *rationalizations* in favor of law violation that outweigh their pro-social definitions. Criminal behavior is learned and will occur when perceived rewards for criminal behavior exceed the rewards for lawful behavior or *perceived opportunity*. So, while not directly introducing the Fraud Triangle, Sutherland did introduce the concepts of rationalizations and opportunities. It is interesting to think about how Sutherland's thesis relies on a utilitarian analysis of harms and benefits of criminal behavior.[7]

The Fraud Triangle in auditing is discussed in AU-C Section 240. The deception that encompasses fraudulent financial reporting is depicted in Exhibit 5.2.[8]

Three conditions generally are present when fraud occurs. First, management or other employees have an incentive or are under pressure, which provides the motivation for the fraud. Second, circumstances exist that provide an opportunity for a fraud to be perpetrated. Examples include the absence of, or ineffective, internal controls and management's override of internal controls. Third, those involved are able to rationalize committing a fraudulent act.

EXHIBIT 5.2 The Fraud Triangle

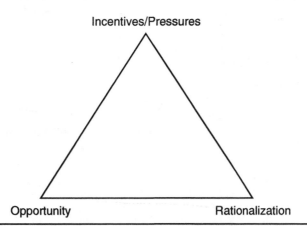

As noted in the auditing standard, some individuals possess an attitude, character, or set of ethical values that allow them to commit a dishonest act knowingly and intentionally. For the most part, this is the exception rather than the rule. However, even honest individuals can commit fraud in an environment that imposes sufficient pressure on them. The greater the incentive or pressure, the more likely that an individual will be able to rationalize the acceptability of committing fraud.[9]

It is important for students to understand the link between elements of the Fraud Triangle and our earlier discussions about cognitive development. The disconnect between one's values and actions may be attributable to motivations and incentives to act unethically, perhaps because of a perceived gain or as a result of pressures imposed by others who might try to convince us it is a one-time request or standard practice, or to be loyal to one's supervisor or the organization. These also become rationalizations for unethical actions invoked by the perpetrator of the fraud.

Incentives/Pressures to Commit Fraud

The incentive to commit fraud typically is a self-serving one. Egoism drives the fraud in the sense that the perpetrator perceives some benefit by committing the fraud, such as a higher bonus or promotion. The fraud may be caused by internal budget pressures or financial analysts' earnings expectations that are not being met. Personal pressures also might lead to fraud if, for example, a member of top management is deep in personal debt or has a gambling or drug problem. In a "60 Minutes" interview with Dennis Kozlowski, the former CEO of Tyco, Kozlowski said his motivation to steal from the company was to keep up with "the masters of the universe." This meant keeping up with other CEOs of large and successful companies that had pay packages in the hundreds of millions. Kozlowski was generous with his lieutenants because he thought they would be loyal to the boss. In 2005, a jury found that Kozlowski and ex-CFO Marc Swartz stole about $137 million from Tyco in unauthorized compensation and made $410 million from the sale of inflated stock.

Opportunity to Commit Fraud

The second side of the Fraud Triangle connects the pressure or incentive to commit fraud with the opportunity to carry out the act. Employees who have access to assets such as cash and inventory should be monitored closely through an effective system of internal controls that helps safeguard assets. For example, the company should segregate cash processing responsibilities, including the opening of mail that contains remittance advices, along with checks for the payment of services; the recording of the receipts as cash and a reduction of receivables; the depositing of the money in the bank; and the reconciling of the balance in cash on the books with the bank statement balance. Obviously, when the fraud is perpetrated by the CEO and CFO, as was the case with Tyco, access is a given. Then, it is just a matter of circumventing the controls or overriding them or, in the case of Kozlowski, enlisting the aid of others in the organization to hide what was going on.

Rationalization for the Fraud

Fraud perpetrators typically try to explain away their actions as acceptable. For corporate executives, rationalizations to commit fraud might include thoughts such as "We need to protect our shareholders and keep the stock price high," "All companies use aggressive accounting practices," "It's for the good of the company," or "The problem is temporary and will be offset by future positive results." In the Tyco case, Kozlowski stated in his "60 Minutes" interview that he wasn't doing anything different from what was done by his predecessor. He took the low road of ethical behavior and rationalized his actions by essentially claiming that everyone (at least at Tyco) did what he did by misappropriating company resources for personal purposes. The fact is he established the culture that condoned such behavior.

Other rationalizations might include "My boss doesn't pay me enough," or "I'll pay the money back before anyone notices it's gone." The underlying motivation for the fraud in these instances may be dissatisfaction with the company and/or personal financial need. AU-C Section 240 (AU-C 240) provides an extensive list of risk factors that can contribute to the likelihood that fraudulent financial reporting will occur. These are presented in Exhibit 5.3.

EXHIBIT 5.3	Risk Factors Relating to Misstatements Arising from Fraudulent Financial Reporting

Incentives/Pressures

a. *Incentives* exist because financial stability or profitability is threatened by economic, industry, or entity operating conditions, such as (or as indicated by):

- High degree of competition or market saturation, accompanied by declining margins.
- High vulnerability to rapid changes, such as changes in technology, product obsolescence, or interest rates.
- Significant declines in customer demand and increasing business failures in either the industry or overall economy.
- Operating losses making the threat of bankruptcy, foreclosure, or hostile takeover imminent.
- Recurring negative cash flows from operations and an inability to generate cash flows from operations while reporting earnings and earnings growth.
- Rapid growth or unusual profitability, especially compared to that of other companies in the same industry.
- New accounting, statutory, or regulatory requirements.

b. Excessive *pressure* exists for management to meet the requirements or expectations of third parties due to the following:

- Profitability or trend level expectations of investment analysts, institutional investors, significant creditors, or other external parties (particularly expectations that are unduly aggressive or unrealistic), including expectations created by management in, for example, overly optimistic press releases or annual report messages.
- Need to obtain additional debt or equity financing to stay competitive—including financing of major research and development or capital expenditures.

(Continued)

- Marginal ability to meet exchange listing requirements or debt repayment or other debt covenant requirements.
- Perceived or real adverse effects of reporting poor financial results on significant pending transactions, such as business combinations or contract awards.

c. Information available indicates that management's or those charged with governance's personal financial situation is threatened by the entity's financial performance arising from the following:

- Significant financial interests in the entity.
- Significant portions of their compensation (for example, bonuses, stock options, and earn-out arrangements) being contingent upon achieving aggressive targets for stock price, operating results, financial position, or cash flow.
- Personal guarantees of debts of the entity.

d. Excessive pressure on management or operating personnel to meet financial targets set up by those charged with governance or management, including sales or profitability incentive goals.

Opportunities

a. The nature of the industry or the entity's operations provides opportunities to engage in fraudulent financial reporting that can arise from the following:

- Significant related-party transactions not in the ordinary course of business or with related entities not audited or audited by another firm.
- A strong financial presence or ability to dominate a certain industry sector that allows the entity to dictate terms or conditions to suppliers or customers that may result in inappropriate or non-arm's-length transactions.
- Assets, liabilities, revenues, or expenses based on significant estimates that involve subjective judgments or uncertainties that are difficult to corroborate.
- Significant, unusual, or highly complex transactions, especially those close to period end that pose difficult "substance over form" questions.
- Significant operations located or conducted across international borders in jurisdictions where differing business environments and cultures exist.
- Significant bank accounts or subsidiary or branch operations in tax-haven jurisdictions for which there appears to be no clear business justification.

b. There is ineffective monitoring of management as a result of the following:

- Domination of management by a single person or small group (in a nonowner-managed business) without compensating controls.
- Ineffective oversight over the financial reporting process and internal control by those charged with governance.

c. There is a complex or unstable organizational structure, as evidenced by the following:

- Difficulty in determining the organization or individuals that have controlling interest in the entity.
- Overly complex organizational structure involving unusual legal entities or managerial lines of authority.
- High turnover of senior management, counsel, or board members.

d. Internal control components are deficient as a result of the following:

- Inadequate monitoring of controls, including automated controls and controls over interim financial reporting (where external reporting is required).

(Continued)

- High turnover rates or employment of ineffective accounting, internal audit, or information technology staff.
- Ineffective accounting and information systems, including situations involving significant deficiencies or material weaknesses in internal control.

Attitudes/Rationalizations

Risk factors reflective of attitudes/rationalizations by those charged with governance, management, or employees that allow them to engage in and/or justify fraudulent financial reporting, may not be susceptible to observation by the auditor. Nevertheless, the auditor who becomes aware of the existence of such information should consider it in identifying the risks of material misstatement arising from fraudulent financial reporting. For example, auditors may become aware of the following information that may indicate a risk factor:

- Ineffective communication, implementation, support, or enforcement of the entity's values or ethical standards by management or the communication of inappropriate values or ethical standards.
- Nonfinancial management's excessive participation in or preoccupation with the selection of accounting principles or the determination of significant estimates.
- Known history of violations of securities laws or other laws and regulations, or claims against the entity, its senior management, or board members alleging fraud or violations of laws and regulations.
- Excessive interest by management in maintaining or increasing the entity's stock price or earnings trend.
- A practice by management of committing to analysts, creditors, and other third parties to achieve aggressive or unrealistic forecasts.
- Management failing to correct known significant deficiencies or material weaknesses in internal control on a timely basis.
- An interest by management in employing inappropriate means to minimize reported earnings for tax-motivated reasons.

Source: AICPA's AU-C Section 240.

Tyco Fraud

The corporate governance system at Tyco completely broke down, thereby creating the opportunity for fraud to occur and thrive. Most members of Tyco's board of directors benefited personally as a result of Tyco's practices. For example, one board member worked for a law firm that "just happened" to receive as much as $2 million in business from Tyco. This person's pay at the law firm was linked to the amount of work that he helped bring in from Tyco. Another director received a $10 million payment for help in engineering an acquisition for Tyco. The problem here was (1) Tyco board members did business with the company, (2) directors and officers borrowed money from the company, and (3) related-party disclosures were not made in the financial statements. Clearly, board members lacked independence from management and the company, and their own greed contributed to the lax oversight at Tyco.

Exhibit 5.4 applies the Fraud Triangle to Tyco. Notice how the opportunities to commit fraud because of lax oversight and the complicity of those in corporate governance enabled the fraud. The Tyco fraud serves as a shocking example of what can happen when all systems involved in the governance of a corporation fail at the same time. Kozlowski sold $258 million of Tyco stock back to the company, on top of salary and other compensation valued near $30 million. By the time Kozlowski quit under indictment for sales tax fraud in 2002, $80 billion of Tyco's shareholder wealth had evaporated. In the end, Kozlowski had no problem coming up with every excuse imaginable to rationalize the fraud and accepted no responsibility for his actions.

EXHIBIT 5.4 **Application of the Fraud Triangle to Tyco**

Incentive	Pressure	Opportunity	Rationalization
Pursuit of self-interest: Keeping up with the "masters of the universe."	Keep up with Wall Street expectations that were enamored with Kozlowski's aggressive management style.	There was lack of internal controls to support growth.	Claimed to need to "push the company," to continue to grow without putting into place the infrastructure to support some of that growth.
Pursuit of self-interest: Use of corporate funds for personal purposes.		Kozlowski was in a position to sign off on home purchases and elaborate use of corporate funds for personal purposes.	Victim of "Enronitis" and the jury's alleged distaste for the $100 million man; actions did not negatively affect employees as was the case with Enron's share price decline in 401(k) employee retirement funds.
Pursuit of self-interest: What's in it for me?	Mark Swartz (CFO) wanted in on the action.	Swartz benefited from the misuse of corporate assets for personal purposes so one element of oversight was compromised.	Did everything the way the "programs" were authorized to operate; did the same things as his predecessors.
Pursuit of self-interest: What's in it for me?	Concessions to get the board to buy into the fraud.	Members of the board also benefited; some misused corporate resources for personal purposes, thereby compromising this element of governance.	Did everything the way the "programs" were authorized to operate.
Pursuit of self-interest: Go along to get along.	Auditors didn't want to lose Tyco as a client.	Auditors failed to assess the culture at Tyco (control environment) properly.	Activities were approved at the top management and board level.

Ethical relativism is what drove Kozlowski's actions. He created his own rules and governed his own ethics. We believe that this is why he never saw anything wrong with the things that he was doing. Even to the end, he maintained that he didn't do anything wrong. Kozlowski was judging himself by his own standard, which was created by him, and because he thought that he had not broken any of the pre-established rules, he felt innocent.

All systems failed at Tyco. Kozlowski bought off the board of directors by providing personal favors. The audit committee was irrelevant. The company and its top officers violated its duty of care and were loyal to Kozlowski's interests, not the shareholders. The external auditors for their part either didn't look too hard to find the fraud or looked the other way when it should have been detected.

On August 13, 2003, the SEC issued a cease-and-desist order against Richard P. Scalzo, the PwC engagement partner for the firm's audits of Tyco's financial statements for fiscal years 1997 through

2001. The commission's order found that Scalzo recklessly violated the antifraud provisions of the federal securities laws and engaged in improper professional conduct. On July 7, 2007, PwC agreed to pay $225 million to settle audit malpractice claims arising from the criminal misdeeds of top executives at Tyco, marking the largest single legal payout ever made by that firm and one of the biggest ever by an auditor.

PwC's audit of Tyco is striking in its failure to exercise a degree of due care and professional skepticism warranted by audit standards and the ethics rules of conduct. Unfortunately, the culture in the accounting profession during those years was all too often to look the other way or not insist too hard for the documentation that would support questionable transactions.

Fraud Considerations and Risk Assessment

LO 5-3
Describe fraud risk assessment procedures.

Fraud considerations in an audit require that the auditor should evaluate the risk of fraud, including the effectiveness of internal controls, and communicate with those charged with governance responsibilities about fraud.

Fraud Risk Assessment

Most of the requirements of AU-C 240 call for the auditor to engage in risk assessment during the audit. Actually, the assessment of risk starts with an evaluation of evidence about the potential client before agreeing to do the audit. One important step is to communicate with the predecessor auditor to find out the reasons for the firing or the reasons for no longer servicing the client. Of particular importance is assessing the integrity of the top management and key accounting personnel. The successor auditor also should clarify with the predecessor whether there were any differences of opinion with management over the application of accounting principles and how these were handled, including the role of the audit committee.

Fraud risk assessment depends in large part on maintaining professional skepticism when evaluating the reliability of audit evidence obtained and assessing whether a material misstatement due to fraud exists. In making the assessment, of course, the auditor should not approach the audit with an attitude toward management of "You are crooks. Prove me wrong." Instead, a healthy attitude is one that informs management in word and deed that the auditor's responsibility is to ask the tough questions, thoroughly examine relevant documentation, and probe to determine whether the organization culture promotes ethical decision making and whether there is support for financial statement amounts and disclosures.

AU-C 240 identifies the broad goals of fraud risk assessment as to (1) make inquiries of management and others within the organization to obtain their views about the risks of fraud and how they are addressed; (2) consider any unusual or unexpected relationships that have been identified in performing analytical procedures (i.e., financial statement comparisons over time and ratio analysis) in planning the audit; (3) consider whether one or more fraud risk factors exist; and (4) consider other information (i.e., interim financial results and factors associated with the acceptance of the client) that may be helpful in identifying risks of material misstatement due to fraud.

Internal Control Assessment

The risk that internal controls will not help prevent or detect a material misstatement in the financial statements is a critical evaluation to provide reasonable assurance. The system of internal controls and whether it operates as intended enables the auditor to gain either confidence about the internal processing of transactions, which is fine, or doubt, which the auditor should pursue.

Recall our discussion in Chapter 3 about the five components of internal control under the COSO framework: (1) the control environment; (2) risk assessment; (3) control activities; (4) monitoring; and (5) information and communication.

Control Environment

Because of its importance to effective internal control over financial reporting, the auditor must evaluate the control environment at the company. As part of evaluating the control environment, the auditor should assess:

- Whether management's philosophy and operating style promote effective internal control over financial reporting;

- Whether sound integrity and ethical values, particularly of top management, are developed and understood; and

- Whether the board or audit committee understands and exercises oversight responsibility over financial reporting and internal control.

A direct relationship exists between the degree of risk that a material weakness could exist in a particular area of the company's internal control over financial reporting and the amount of audit attention that should be devoted to that area. In addition, the risk that a company's internal control over financial reporting will fail to prevent or detect misstatement caused by fraud usually is higher than the risk of failure to prevent or detect error. The auditor should focus more of his or her attention on the areas of highest risk.

COSO sponsored a study, *Fraudulent Financial Reporting: 1998–2007,* to provide a comprehensive analysis of fraudulent financial reporting occurrences investigated by the SEC during that time period. Some of the important findings include:

- There were 347 alleged cases of public company fraudulent reporting during 1998–2007, versus 294 cases from 1987 to 1997.

- The total cumulative misstatement or misappropriation was nearly $120 billion.

- The SEC named the CEO and/or CFO for some level of involvement in 89 percent of the fraud cases, up from 83 percent in the 1987–1997 period.

- The most common fraud technique involved improper revenue recognition, followed by the overstatement of existing assets or capitalization of expenses.

- Twenty-six percent of the fraud firms changed auditors between the last clean financial statements and the last fraudulent financial statements, whereas only 12 percent of the no-fraud firms switched auditors during the same time. Sixty percent of the fraud firms that changed auditors did so during the fraud period, while the remaining 40 percent changed in the fiscal period just before the fraud began.

Enterprise Risk Management—Integrated Framework

In 2001, COSO initiated a project to develop a framework that would be readily usable by managements to evaluate and improve their organizations' enterprise risk management (ERM). The framework incorporates internal control principles that enhance corporate governance and risk management. *ERM* is defined as a process, effected by an entity's board of directors, management, and other personnel and applied in strategy settings and across the enterprise, designed to identify potential events that may affect the entity and to manage risk within its risk appetite.

According to COSO, ERM encompasses six elements:[10]

1. *Aligning risk appetite and strategy.* Risk appetite is considered by management in evaluating strategic alternatives, setting related objectives, and developing mechanisms to manage related risks.

2. *Enhancing risk response decisions.* ERM provides the discipline to identify and select among alternative risk responses—risk avoidance, reduction, sharing, and acceptance.

3. *Reducing operational surprises and losses.* ERM provides the capability to identify potential events and establish responses, reducing surprises and associated costs or losses.

4. *Identifying and managing multiple and cross-enterprise risks.* ERM facilitates effective responses to interrelated aspects of risk that affect different parts of the organization, and integrated responses to multiple risks.

5. *Seizing opportunities.* ERM allows management to consider a full range of potential events, positioning it to identify and proactively realize opportunities.

6. *Improving deployment of capital.* The risk information provided by ERM enables management to assess effectively overall capital needs and enhance capital allocation.

COSO's ERM is designed to help an entity get where it wants to go and avoid pitfalls and surprises along the way. ERM adds a number of strategic issues, including objective setting by management, identification of risks and opportunities affecting achievement of an entity's objectives, and risk responses selected by management to align risk tolerance and risk appetite.

In 2009, COSO issued *Guidance on Monitoring Internal Control Systems,* an integral part of its framework. Monitoring should be done to assess the quality of internal control performance over time. To provide reasonable assurance that an entity's objectives will be achieved, management should monitor controls to determine whether they are operating effectively and whether they need to be redesigned when risks change.

According to COSO's *Guidance,* effective monitoring involves (1) establishing a baseline for control effectiveness, (2) designing and executing monitoring procedures that are based on the significance of business risks relative to the entity's objectives, and (3) assessing and reporting results, including follow-up on corrective actions.

Monitoring can be done through ongoing activities or separate evaluations that are built into the normal, recurring activities of the entity and include regular management and supervisory activities. Management can use internal auditors or personnel performing similar functions to monitor the operating effectiveness of internal control. For example, management might review whether bank reconciliations are being prepared on a timely basis and reviewed by the internal auditors.

The success of COSO's efforts to strengthen internal controls and ERM systems depends on changing the culture of most organizations. Shifting employees' attitudes about risk management will happen only after they see senior management and the board of directors adopting the procedures. As the risk management culture develops throughout the organization, each aspect of the ERM framework can be incorporated efficiently into day-to-day operations. To create a risk management culture requires a commitment to integrity and ethical values in all aspects of an entity's operations.

The ERM framework represents the accounting profession's response to the increased need to manage risk in the aftermath of the accounting scandals and business failures that caused substantial harm to investors, company personnel, and other stakeholders. The framework adopts the position that management should determine its risk appetite and align it with strategic objectives. Unfortunately,

ERM seems to place emphasis in the wrong areas by focusing on risk appetite. The usefulness of the ERM framework in establishing an ethical culture can be questioned because it does not place any emphasis on the ethical dimensions of making strategic decisions. Instead, the focus is on the company's "hunger" for risk in terms of its strategic objectives.

Audit Committee Responsibilities for Fraud Risk Assessment

The audit committee should evaluate management's identification of fraud risks, implementation of antifraud measures, and creation of the appropriate tone at the top. Active oversight by the audit committee can help reinforce management's commitment to create a culture with "zero tolerance" for fraud. An entity's audit committee also should ensure that senior management (in particular, the CEO and CFO) implements appropriate fraud deterrence and prevention measures to better protect investors, employees, and other stakeholders.

The audit committee's evaluation and oversight not only helps ensure that senior management fulfills its responsibility, but also can serve as a deterrent to senior management engaging in fraudulent activity (that is, by ensuring an environment is created whereby any attempt by senior management to involve employees in committing or concealing fraud would lead promptly to reports from such employees to appropriate persons, including the audit committee).

The audit committee also plays an important role in helping those charged with governance fulfill their oversight responsibilities with respect to the entity's financial reporting process and the system of internal control. In exercising this oversight responsibility, the audit committee should consider the potential for management override of controls or other inappropriate influence over the financial reporting process. Some examples follow:

- The audit committee should solicit the views of the internal auditors and independent auditors with respect to management's involvement in the financial reporting process and, in particular, the ability of management to override information processed by the entity's financial reporting system (for example, the ability of management or others to initiate or record nonstandard journal entries).
- The audit committee should consider reviewing the entity's reported information for reasonableness compared with prior or forecasted results, as well as with peers or industry averages.
- Information received in communications from the independent auditors can assist the audit committee in assessing the strength of the entity's internal control and the potential for fraudulent financial reporting.

As part of its oversight responsibilities, the audit committee should encourage management to provide a mechanism for employees to report concerns about unethical behavior, actual or suspected fraud, or violations of the entity's code of conduct or ethics policy. The committee should then receive periodic reports describing the nature, status, and eventual disposition of any fraud or unethical conduct. A summary of the activity, follow-up, and disposition also should be provided to all of those charged with governance.

Auditor's Communication with Those Charged with Governance

Whenever the auditor has determined that there is evidence that fraud may exist, the matter should be brought to the attention of the appropriate level of management. AU-C 240 requires such communication even if the matter might be considered inconsequential, such as a minor misappropriation by an employee. Fraud (whether caused by senior management or other employees) that causes a material misstatement of the financial statements should be reported directly to those charged with governance. In addition, the auditor should reach an understanding with those charged with governance regarding the nature and extent of communications with them about misappropriations perpetrated by lower-level employees.

AU-C Section 260 identifies the auditor's communication responsibilities. In that regard, audit committees are a key element in communicating with those charged with governance.[11] Good governance principles suggest that:

- The auditor has access to the audit committee as necessary.
- The chair of the audit committee meets with the auditor periodically.
- The audit committee meets with the auditor without management at least annually unless prohibited by law or regulation.

Given the importance of an independent audit in detecting fraud in financial statements, the auditor should discuss with the audit committee relationships that create threats to auditor independence and the related safeguards that have been applied to eliminate or reduce those threats to an acceptable level.

Another important area for communication is about accounting estimates. Certain accounting estimates are particularly sensitive because of their significance to the financial statements and because of the possibility that future events affecting them may differ significantly from management's current judgments. In communicating with those charged with governance about the process used by management in formulating sensitive estimates, including fair value estimates, and about the basis for the auditor's conclusions regarding the reasonableness of those estimates, the auditor should consider the following:

- The nature of significant assumptions;
- The degree of subjectivity involved in the development of the assumptions; and
- The relative materiality of the items being measured to the financial statements as a whole.

If the auditor, as a result of the assessment of the risks of material misstatement, has identified such risks due to fraud that have continuing control implications, the auditor should consider whether these risks represent significant deficiencies or material weaknesses in the entity's internal control that should be communicated to management and those charged with governance. The auditor should also consider whether the absence of or deficiencies in controls to prevent, deter, and detect fraud represent significant deficiencies or material weaknesses that should be communicated to management and those charged with governance.

Management Representations and Financial Statement Certifications

The responsibility for preventing and detecting fraud rests with the management of entities. The auditor has a responsibility to plan and perform the audit to obtain reasonable assurance about whether the financial statements are free of material misstatement, whether caused by error or fraud. The auditor should communicate with management and inquire whether any significant fraud or error has been detected, in part to adjust audit procedures accordingly. However, the auditor faces the inevitable risk that some significant errors will not be detected, even if the audit is planned and done properly. Management can override internal controls and create deceptive accounting for transactions that makes identifying fraud difficult at best.

One way to deal with the problem, although not foolproof, is to obtain written representations (also known as management representations or client representations) to confirm certain matters and support other evidence obtained during the audit. The representations are made by the CEO, the CFO, and other appropriate officers. The management letter generally includes:

- A statement that the client has provided access to all known information that bears on the fair presentation of the financial statements.
- Confirmation that management has performed an assessment of the effectiveness of internal control over financial reporting based on criteria established in the Internal Control—Integrated Framework issued by COSO.
- Conclusions as to whether the company has maintained an effective internal control over financial reporting.
- Disclosure of any deficiencies in the design or operation of internal control over financial reporting.

Under Section 302 of the Sarbanes-Oxley Act (SOX), all quarterly (10-Q) and annual (10-K) filings with the SEC are required to include certifications from the CEO and CFO related to the fairness of the financial statements and the effectiveness of the internal control over financial reporting. In addition to the statements made in traditional management representations as explained above, Section 302 requires a statement whether the report contains any material untrue statements or material omission or be considered misleading.

Audit Report and Auditing Standards

LO 5-4
Explain the standards for audit reports.

Background

The free market for stocks and bonds can only exist if there is sharing of reliable financial information, strengthened by information that is transparent and unbiased. The external audit is intended to enhance the confidence that users can place on the financial statements that have been prepared by management. Since 1926 the New York Stock Exchange (NYSE) has required an auditor's report with public companies' financial statements. Then the Securities Exchange Act of 1934, which is discussed further in Chapter 6, required all public companies to have an independent auditor's report on annual financial statements. Presently, the PCAOB oversees public companies' audits since the Sarbanes-Oxley Act of 2002. The Auditing Standards Board (ASB) of the AICPA oversees the audits of nonpublic companies. For both public and nonpublic entities, the auditor's report on financial statements and related disclosures provides (or disclaims) an opinion on whether the entity's financial statements and related disclosures are presented in accordance with generally accepted accounting principles (GAAP). The opinion is based on the test of controls and substantive procedures that have been performed during the audit engagement.

Audit Report

The auditors' unmodified or standard report for nonpublic companies under the AICPA requirements is presented in Exhibit 5.5. The auditors' unmodified or standard report for public companies under the PCAOB requirements is presented in Exhibit 5.6.

EXHIBIT 5.5 Unmodified Opinion for Nonpublic Companies

Independent Auditors' Report
To the Board of Directors and Stockholders, XYZ Company
Introductory Paragraph

We have audited the accompanying consolidated financial statements of XYZ Company and its subsidiaries, which comprise the consolidated balance sheets as of December 31, 2015, and 2014, and the related consolidated statements of income, changes in stockholders' equity, and cash flows for the years then ended, and the related notes to the financial statements.

Management's Responsibility for the Financial Statements

Management is responsible for the preparation and fair presentation of these consolidated financial statements in accordance with accounting principles generally accepted in the United States of America; this includes the design, implementation, and maintenance of internal control relevant to the preparation and fair presentation of consolidated financial statements that are free from material misstatement, whether due to fraud or error.

Auditor's Responsibility

Our responsibility is to express an opinion on these consolidated financial statements based on our audits. We conducted our audits in accordance with auditing standards generally accepted in the United States of America. Those standards require that we plan and perform the audit to obtain reasonable assurance about whether the consolidated financial statements are free of material misstatement.

An audit involves performing procedures to obtain audit evidence about the amounts and disclosures in the consolidated financial statements. The procedures selected depend on the auditor's judgment, including the assessment of the risks of material misstatement of the consolidated financial statements, whether due to fraud or error. In making those risk assessments, the auditor considers internal controls relevant to the entity's preparation and fair presentation of the consolidated financial statements in order to design audit procedures that are appropriate in the circumstances, but not for the purpose of expressing an opinion on the effectiveness of the entity's internal controls. Accordingly, we express no such opinion. An audit also includes evaluating the appropriateness of accounting policies used and the reasonableness of significant accounting estimates made by management, as well as evaluating the overall presentation of the consolidated financial statements.

We believe that the audit evidence we have obtained is sufficient and appropriate to provide a basis for our audit opinion.

Opinion

In our opinion, the consolidated financial statements referred to above present fairly, in all material respects, the financial position of XYZ Company and its subsidiaries as of December 31, 2015, and 2014, and the results of its operations and its cash flows for the years then ended in accordance with accounting principles generally accepted in the United States of America.

Optional Paragraph

Report on Other Legal and Regulatory Requirements *[This section usually won't apply unless the auditor has other reporting responsibilities. If so, then the opening paragraph after the salutation should be titled Report on the Financial Statements]*

[Auditor's signature]

[Auditor's city and state]

[Date of the auditor's report]

EXHIBIT 5.6   The Auditors' Unmodified or Unqualified Report for Public Companies

Report of Independent Registered Public Accounting Firm

To the Board of Directors and Stockholders of ABC Public Company:

We have audited the accompanying consolidated balance sheets of ABC Public Company as of December 31, 2015, and 2014, and the related consolidated statement of income stockholders' equity, and cash flows for each of the two years in the period ended December 31, 2015. These financial statements are the responsibility of the Company's management. Our responsibility is to express an opinion on these financial statements based on our audits.

We conducted our audits in accordance with the standards of the Public Company Accounting Oversight Board (United States). Those standards require that we plan and perform the audit to obtain reasonable assurance about whether the financial statements are free of material misstatements. An audit includes examining, on a test basis, evidence supporting the amounts and disclosures in the financial statements. An audit also includes assessing the accounting principles used and significant estimates made by management, as well as evaluating the overall financial statement presentation. We believe that our audits provide a reasonable basis for our opinion.

In our opinion, the financial statements referred to herein present fairly, in all material respects, the consolidated financial position of ABC Public Company at December 31, 2015, and 2014, and the consolidated results of its operations and its cash flows for each of the two years in the period ended December 31, 2015, in conformity with U.S. generally accepted accounting principles.

We also have audited, in accordance with the standards of the Public Company Accounting Oversight Board (United States), ABC Public Company's internal control over financial reporting as of December 31, 2015, based on criteria established in the *Internal Control—Integrated Framework* issued by the Committee of Sponsoring Organizations of the Treadway Commission, and our report dated February 9, 2016, expressed an unqualified opinion thereon.

[Auditor's signature]*

New York, New York

February 9, 2016

*Section ISA 700 of the *International Standards on Auditing* allows the signature to be that of the audit firm, the personal name of the auditor who directed the audit, or both, as appropriate for the particular jurisdiction. For audits of years ending after December 15, 2016, the personal name of the auditor who directed the audit will ordinarily be required. Also effective for audits of periods ending after December 15, 2016, the International Auditing and Assurance Standards Board will require audit reports of public companies to include a "key audit matters" section. Key audit matters are those matters that were of the most significance in the audit, in the auditor's professional judgment. Similar disclosures in audit reports are being considered by the ASB and PCAOB.

There are differences between the unmodified report used for nonpublic companies' audits and the PCAOB audit report. The primary differences include:

- The PCAOB report is titled Report of Independent Registered Public Accounting Firm, and the ASB report is titled Independent Auditor's Report.
- The PCAOB report does not include section headings.

- The PCAOB includes less detailed descriptions of management's and auditor's responsibilities.
- The PCAOB report references standards of the PCAOB rather than generally accepted auditing standards.
- The PCAOB includes an additional paragraph indicating that the auditors have also issued a report on the client's internal control over financial reporting.

Students should understand the auditing process and how audit opinions might change based on material differences with the client on accounting and financial reporting issues. Given that many students may have already completed an auditing course, we focus on the most important conceptual issues here.

Audit Opinions

Auditors can express an unmodified opinion, a qualified opinion, an adverse opinion, or a disclaimer. An auditor also can withdraw from the engagement under restricted circumstances. The qualified opinion, adverse opinion, or disclaimer of opinion is a "modified" opinion.

Opinion Paragraph – Unmodified or Unqualified

An auditor should give an unmodified or unqualified opinion when the financial statements "present fairly" financial position, results of operations, and cash flows. Certain situations may call for adding an additional paragraph: either an emphasis-of-matter or other-matter paragraph.

An emphasis-of-matter paragraph is a paragraph in the auditor's report that refers to a matter appropriately presented or disclosed in the financial statements (e.g., going concern, litigation uncertainty, subsequent events, etc.). It is added when, in the auditor's professional judgment, the item is of such importance that it is fundamental to users' understanding of the financial statements. Some emphasis-of-matter paragraphs are required by recently Clarified Statements on Auditing Standards (SASs) or by the PCAOB, and others are added at the discretion of the auditor.

An other-matter paragraph is a paragraph included in the auditor's report that refers to a matter other than those presented or disclosed in the financial statements that, in the auditors' professional judgment, is relevant to users' understanding of the audit, the auditor's responsibilities, or the auditor's report (e.g., supplemental information).

An emphasis-of-matter or other-matter paragraph follows the opinion paragraph and has a section heading of "Emphasis-of-Matter" or "Other-Matter" for the ASB report.

Opinion Paragraph—Modified (Qualified) (Adverse)

Recall that Rule 203 of the AICPA Code of Professional Conduct precludes rendering an opinion that states that the financial statements have been prepared in accordance with GAAP, or any statement that the auditor is not aware of any material modifications that should be made to such statements or data to make them conform with GAAP, if such statements or data contain any departure from an accounting principle that has a material effect on the statements or data taken as a whole. The result would be the issuance of a modified opinion on the matter that creates a deviation from GAAP.

The auditor should modify the opinion in the auditor's report when (1) the auditor concludes, based on the audit evidence obtained, the financial statements as a whole are materially misstated; or (2) the auditor is unable to obtain sufficient appropriate audit evidence to conclude that the financial statements as a whole are free from material misstatement. The circumstances when each opinion is proper are discussed next.

A qualified opinion would be appropriate when (1) the auditor, having obtained sufficient appropriate audit evidence, concludes that misstatements, individually or in the aggregate, are material but not pervasive to the financial statements; or (2) the auditor is unable to obtain sufficient appropriate audit evidence on which to base the opinion, but the auditor concludes that the possible effects on the financial statements of undetected misstatements, if any, could be material but not pervasive.

2) An adverse opinion is proper when the auditor, having obtained sufficient appropriate audit evidence, concludes that misstatements, individually or in the aggregate, are both material and pervasive to the financial statements. Pervasive is a term used in the context of misstatements to describe the effects on the financial statements of misstatements, if any that are undetected due to an inability to obtain sufficient appropriate audit evidence. Pervasive effects on the financial statements require professional judgment by the auditor and are not generally confined to specific elements, accounts, or items of the financial statements, but if they are, they would represent or could represent a substantial proportion of the financial statements.

3) A disclaimer of opinion is warranted when the auditor is unable to obtain sufficient appropriate audit evidence on which to base the opinion, and the auditor concludes that the possible effects on the financial statements of undetected misstatements, if any, could be both material and pervasive.

The auditor should include a separate paragraph in the audit report that describes the matter giving rise to the modification. This paragraph should be placed immediately before the opinion paragraph in the auditor's report and include a heading such as "Basis for Qualified Opinion," "Basis for Adverse Opinion," or "Basis for Disclaimer of Opinion," as appropriate for the ASB report.

Exhibit 5.7 includes a summary of various paragraphs that can be included in the standard audit report and modified opinions. Students should consult an auditing text to the exact wording of these different opinions.

EXHIBIT 5.7   **Examples of Paragraphs in the Audit Report**

Type of Report/Opinion	Management's Responsibility	Auditor's Responsibility	Opinion	Emphasis-of-Matter OR Other-Matter
Unmodified Opinion	Standard	Standard	Standard	
Emphasis-of-Matter				
Going Concern Issue	Standard	Standard	Standard	Description
Consistent GAAP Application	Standard	Standard	Standard	Description
Modified Opinions				
Qualified	Standard	Include departure from GAAP or scope limitation	"Except for the [GAAP departure or effects of scope limitation] . . . the financial statements present fairly . . ."	

(Continued)

Adverse	Standard	Include substantial reasons for adverse opinion	"... the financial statements do not present fairly ..."
Disclaimer	Omitted	Omitted	Changed to indicate that an opinion cannot be expressed on the financial statements and why

Withdrawal from the Engagement

From time to time, an auditor might consider withdrawing from an engagement. Withdrawal generally is not appropriate because an auditor is hired by the client to do an audit and render an opinion, not walk away from one's obligations when the going gets tough. However, if a significant conflict exists with management or the auditor decides that management cannot be trusted, then a withdrawal may be justified. Factors that affect the auditor's conclusion include the implication of the involvement of a member of management or those charged with governance in any misconduct. Trust issues are a matter of ethics. Once pressure builds up in the auditor–client relationship and it boils over, the auditor must consider whether the breakdown in the relationship has advanced to the point that any and all information provided by the client is suspect. An auditor should not allow himself to be in the position of questioning the client's motives with every statement made and piece of evidence gathered. Withdrawal triggers the filing of the SEC's 8-K form by management.

Limitations of the Audit Report

Three phrases in the audit report are critical to understanding the limits of the report: (1) *reasonable assurance,* (2) *material,* and (3) *present fairly.* These expressions are used to signal the reader about specific limitations of the audit report.

Reasonable Assurance

The term *reasonable* is often used in law to define a standard of behavior to decide legal issues. For example, an auditor should exercise a *reasonable* level of care (due care) to avoid charges of negligence and possible liability to the client. The *reasonable* (prudent) person standard typically is used to judge whether an uninvolved individual looking at the behavior of an auditor, perhaps in relation to independence and client relationships, can conclude that the auditor has maintained the appearance of independence. This appearance standard is used because oftentimes it is difficult to know whether the auditor truly is independent in fact in making audit decisions because independence in fact relies on what was in the mind of the auditor at the time she decided to either include or exclude certain audit evidence.

Reasonable assurance is not an absolute guarantee that the financial statements are free of material misstatement. Auditors do not examine all of a company's transactions. The transactions selected for examination are determined based on materiality considerations and risk assessment. Even then, only a small percentage of transactions are selected, often by statistical sampling techniques. Professional judgment is critical in making these determinations.

The auditor uses professional judgment to decide whether available evidence is sufficient to justify an opinion. If the auditor fails to follow GAAS in making that decision, then an allegation of negligence is supportable. If the auditor was to ignore purposefully justified audit procedures or evidence that, for example, has negative implications for the client, then a charge of constructive fraud or fraud may be sustained in a court of law. These charges can be brought by clients as well as third parties, as will be discussed in Chapter 6.

Materiality

The concept of *materiality* recognizes that some matters are important to the fair presentation of financial statements, while others are not. The materiality concept is fundamental to the audit because the audit report states that an audit is performed to obtain reasonable assurance about whether the financial statements are free of material misstatement.

Materiality judgments require the use of professional judgment and are based on management and auditor perceptions of the needs of a reasonable person who will rely on the financial statements. *Materiality* is defined in the glossary of Statement of Financial Accounting Concepts (SFAC) 2, Qualitative Characteristics of Accounting Information,[12] as: *The magnitude of an omission or misstatement of accounting information that, in the light of surrounding circumstances, makes it probable that the judgment of a reasonable person relying on the information would have been changed or influenced by the omission or misstatement.*

The concept of materiality is perhaps one of the most challenging in accounting. The application of professional judgment to the surrounding circumstances in which materiality is at issue provides the setting to assess whether an item or event is either quantitatively or qualitatively significant enough to warrant financial reporting or disclosure.

Materiality in the context of an audit reflects the auditor's judgment of the needs of users in relation to the information in the financial statements and the possible effect of misstatements on user decisions as a group. Materiality is judged by assessing whether the omissions or misstatements of items in the statements could, individually or collectively, influence the economic decisions of users taken on the basis of financial statements. Materiality depends on the size and nature of the omission or misstatement judged in the surrounding circumstances.

Typically, an auditor might use a percentage for the numerical threshold, such as 5 percent. Materiality is then judged by comparing an item in question to some amount such as total assets or net income. If the questionable item is equal to or greater than 5 percent of the comparison amount, then it is material and must be reported in the financial statements.

Assume that a company has one item in inventory that cost $400,000. The auditor believes the current market value is $381,000, or $19,000 (4.75 percent) below cost. Under the 5 percent rule, the item may be judged immaterial and the write-down ignored. However, what if the net income for the year is only $300,000? Then the $19,000 write-down becomes material because it equals 6.33 percent of net income.

One unintended consequence of the accounting profession's approach to materiality is that a controller—knowing the 5 percent rule is in effect—may attempt to decrease expenses or increase revenues by an amount less than 5 percent to increase earnings by an amount that will not be challenged by the auditor. It is somewhat ironic that the auditor can let the difference go unchallenged, even though it may be due to the misapplication of GAAP, simply because it is not "material" in amount. A good example is at North Face Inc. where the company engaged in barter transactions in the late 1990s. The CFO knew the materiality criteria used by the auditors, Deloitte & Touche, and he structured a transaction to produce gross profit ($800,000) below the materiality amount. The auditors had recommended an adjustment for that amount, which was part of a $1.64 million revenue transaction. The auditors passed on the adjustment using materiality as the explanation.

Staff Accounting Bulletin (SAB) 99,[13] issued by the SEC, clarifies that the exclusive use of a percentage materiality criteria to assess material misstatements in the financial statements has no basis in law and is unacceptable. The commission did state that the use of a percentage as a numerical threshold, such as 5 percent, may provide the basis for a preliminary assumption that, without considering all relevant circumstances, a deviation of less than the specified percentage with respect to a particular item on the registrant's financial statements is unlikely to be material. However, the SEC ruled that both qualitative and quantitative factors must be considered when assessing materiality. Materiality judgments in lawsuits against accountants rely on the "reasonable person" standard, that "a substantial likelihood that the . . . fact would have been viewed by the reasonable investor as having significantly altered the 'total mix' of information made available." If an item is material, it should be disclosed in the body of the financial statements or footnotes.

Materiality is judged both by the relative amount and by the nature of the item. For example, even a small theft by the president of a company is material because it raises doubts about the trustworthiness of the president, may indicate that other misappropriations have occurred, and brings into question the tone set from the top.

The SEC lists some of the qualitative factors that may cause quantitatively small misstatements to become material in SAB 99, including:

- It arises from an item capable of precise measurement.
- It arises from an estimate and, if so, the degree of imprecision inherent in the estimate.
- It masks a change in earnings or other trends.
- It hides a failure to meet analysts' consensus expectations for the enterprise.
- It changes a loss into income or vice versa.
- It concerns a segment or other portion of the registrant's business that has been identified as playing a significant role in the registrant's operations or profitability.
- It affects the registrant's compliance with regulatory requirements.
- It affects the registrant's compliance with loan covenants or other contractual requirements.
- It has the effect of increasing management's compensation—for example, by satisfying the requirements for the award of bonuses or other forms of incentive compensation.
- It involves concealment of an unlawful transaction.

Auditors should be on the alert for these red flags, which signal that qualitatively material items may not have been recorded and disclosed in accordance with GAAP.

What Is Meant by "Present Fairly"?

Without an understanding of the term *present fairly,* the users of a financial statement would be unable to assess its reliability. For the purposes of our discussion about fair presentation, we will proceed with the following guideline: that the auditor's assessment of fair presentation depends on whether (1) the accounting principles selected and applied have general acceptance; (2) the accounting principles are appropriate in the circumstances; (3) the financial statements, including the related notes, are informative of matters that may affect their use, understanding, and interpretation; (4) the information presented in the statements is classified and summarized in a reasonable manner—that is, neither too detailed nor too condensed; and (5) the financial statements reflect transactions and events within a range of reasonable limits.

The assessment of "fair presentation" in the financial statements is made in the context of the applicable financial reporting framework. A *financial reporting framework* is a set of criteria (such as U.S. GAAP and International Financial Reporting Standards [IFRS]) used to determine the measurement, recognition, presentation, and disclosure of all material items appearing in the financial statements.

The term *fair presentation framework* is used to refer to a financial reporting framework that requires compliance with the requirements of the framework and (1) acknowledges explicitly or implicitly that, to achieve fair presentation of the financial statements, it may be necessary for management to provide disclosures beyond those specifically required by the framework; or (2) acknowledges explicitly that it may be necessary for management to depart from a requirement of the framework to achieve a fair presentation of the financial statements. Such departures are expected to be necessary only in extremely rare circumstances.

We wonder how the term *fair* in *fair presentation* relates to the traditional ethics notion of fairness as justice. Does this mean that financial statements that present fairly are just statements? We think not, because justice means, in part, to treat equals equally and unequals unequally. There is no such distinction in accounting to provide a different level of information for different user groups that might have different needs for information to assist decision making.

Outside the United States, in European and other countries that have adopted IFRS, the term *true and fair view* replaces *fair presentation*. Historically, the former is associated with a higher degree of professional judgment, while the latter is more rules-based. However, determinations of fair presentation have moved more to the professional judgment arena as standards in the United States evolve to better accord with the International Standards on Auditing (ISA). Evidence of the movement toward increased professional judgment and professional skepticism can be seen in frameworks such as the KPMG Professional Judgment Framework discussed in Chapter 4.

Generally Accepted Auditing Standards (GAAS)

The whole of GAAS are comprehensive and more detailed than we need to focus on for our purposes. Instead, we address matters that pertain to professional judgment and professional skepticism in keeping with one of the themes in Chapter 4.

An independent auditor plans, conducts, and reports the results of an audit in accordance with GAAS. *Auditing standards* provide a measure of audit quality and the objectives to be achieved in an audit. Auditing standards differ from auditing procedures because the procedures are steps taken by the auditor during the course of the audit to comply with GAAS. The application of auditing standards entails making judgments with regard to the nature of audit evidence, sufficiency, competency, and reliability. Materiality considerations also are important to assess whether the audit opinion should be modified.

The PCAOB requires the 10 basic standards developed by the ASB of the AICPA and now incorporated into its "clarified" auditing standards.

General Standards

There are three general standards that relate to the quality of the professionals who perform the audit. These include (1) adequate technical training and proficiency, (2) independence in mental attitude, and (3) due care in the performance of the audit and preparation of the report. As discussed in Chapter 4, to be independent means to avoid all appearances that one's judgment may be clouded by events and relationships. Due care in performing an audit is also included in the Code; it requires diligence and competence in making professional judgments, including to exercise professional skepticism.

Standards of Fieldwork

Standards of fieldwork establish the criteria for judging whether the audit has met quality requirements. The standards include (1) to adequately plan the audit work and supervise assistants so that the audit is more likely to detect a material misstatement; (2) to obtain a sufficient understanding of the entity and its internal control, to assess the risk of material misstatement of the financial statements, whether due to error or fraud, and to plan effectively the nature, timing, and extent of further audit procedures; and (3) to gather sufficient competent evidential matter through audit procedures including inspection, observation, inquiries, and confirmations to provide a reasonable basis (support) for an opinion regarding the financial statements under audit.

Standards of Reporting

There are three reporting standards that guide auditors in rendering an audit report and in determining the degree of responsibility that the auditor is taking with respect to the expression of an opinion of the financial statements. They include (1) determination of whether the statements have been prepared in conformity with GAAP, (2) identification of situations where the accounting principles have not been observed consistently in the current period in relation to the preceding period, and (3) discussion in the report of any situation identified in the footnotes to the financial statements where informative disclosures are inadequate. In each case, professional judgments are necessary to meet the requirements of these standards.

Audit Evidence

Gathering and objectively evaluating audit evidence requires the auditor to consider the competency and sufficiency of the evidence. Representations from management, while part of the evidential matter the auditor obtains, are not a substitute for the application of those auditing procedures necessary to afford a reasonable basis for an opinion regarding the financial statements under audit.

Audit risk and materiality need to be considered together in determining the nature, timing, and extent of auditing procedures and in evaluating the results of those procedures. According to AU-C 315, the auditor should consider audit risk and materiality both in (a) planning the audit and designing auditing procedures and (b) evaluating whether the financial statements taken as a whole are presented fairly, in all material respects, in conformity with GAAP.[14]

The auditor's response to the risks of material misstatement due to fraud involves the application of professional skepticism when gathering and evaluating audit evidence. Examples of the application of professional skepticism in response to the risks of material misstatement due to fraud are obtaining additional corroboration of management's explanations or representations concerning material matters, such as through third-party confirmation, the use of a specialist, analytical procedures, examination of documentation from independent sources, or inquiries of others within or outside the entity. The independent auditor's direct personal knowledge, obtained through physical examination, observation, computation, and inspection, is more persuasive than information obtained indirectly.

Audit procedures are specific acts performed by the auditor to gather evidence about whether specific assertions are being met. For example, the client may state that the inventory value is $1 million. That is a specific assertion. The auditor then uses the procedure of observing the physical count of inventory to assess inventory quantity and traces certain year-end purchases and sales of inventory to invoices and other documentation as part of the cutoff process to determine whether year-end transactions should be part of the inventory. Typically, the auditor also tests the pricing of the inventory to assess the application of methods such as first-in, first-out (FIFO); last-in, first-out (LIFO); and the weighted average methods. The current market value of the inventory also has to be assessed.

Audit procedures help obtain an understanding of the entity and its environment, including its internal controls, to assess the risks of material misstatements. Audit procedures also test the operating effectiveness of controls in preventing or detecting material misstatements.

Professional skepticism plays an important role in gathering audit evidence and evaluating its usefulness. Recall that the term means to have a questioning mind and make a critical assessment of audit evidence. However, these requirements are somewhat ambiguous and leave open to interpretation what constitutes appropriate levels of questioning and critical assessment, and how such behavior is demonstrated and can be documented.[15]

Professional Skepticism

LO 5-5
Discuss the characteristics of professional skepticism.

Professional skepticism plays a fundamentally important role in the audit by facilitating professional judgment, particularly regarding decisions about:

- The nature, timing, and extent of audit procedures to performed to reduce the risk of material misstatements to an appropriate level;
- Whether sufficient, competent, and relevant evidence has been obtained and whether additional evidence needs to be gathered to support risk analyses;
- The evaluation of management's judgments and estimates used in recording transactions and financial statement presentations;
- Considerations of fraud in the audit; and
- The conclusions reached based on the audit evidence obtained.

An important concern is, given that professional skepticism is a state of mind, it may be difficult to document all such assessments throughout the audit. Nevertheless, audit documentation remains critical in evidencing professional skepticism because it provides evidence that the audit was planned and performed in accordance with GAAS. Here are some steps that can be taken by the auditor:[16]

- Document the thought process, alternative views considered, judgments made, and how they collectively influence audit evidence gathered and support the final conclusion.
- Document challenges to management's views and assumptions, not just how they were accepted.
- Document the basis for unusual, one-time transactions and related business rationale.
- Include a complete and comprehensive record of discussions with management, particularly in the areas of uncertainty.
- Document assessments of the reliability of the source of documents, specifically those prepared by the entity.
- Document professional skepticism in significant matters.

Nelson suggests that the lack of skepticism can either be the result of a failure in problem recognition (lack of skeptical judgment) or a failure to act on a problem recognized (lack of skeptical action).[17] Hurtt et al. (hereinafter referred to as "the authors") develop a framework of judgment based on Nelson's foundational components. Skeptical judgment occurs when an auditor recognizes that a potential issue may exist and that more work or effort is necessary. Skeptical action occurs when an auditor changes her behavior based on the skeptical judgment. Both are essential to the audit, with skeptical judgment being a necessary condition for skeptical action.[18]

Skeptical judgment relies on being able to recognize an issue and formulate a skeptical judgment, considering its impact on the audit and, ultimately, the users of the financial statements. An auditor may have the necessary knowledge, experience, or traits to recognize an issue and be able to formulate a skeptical judgment, but may choose not to do so because of pressures during the audit. In other words, the auditor may not have the capacity to effectively and ethically deal with those pressures and carry through skeptical judgment with skeptical action.

The authors defines traits as individual characteristics that enable auditors to determine when evidence does not "add up," or the traits that allow auditors to exercise skeptical judgment.[19] Hurtt developed a Professional Skepticism Scale that measures trait skepticism using a scale composed of six characteristics: (1) questioning mind, (2) suspension of judgment, (3) search for knowledge, (4) interpersonal understanding, (5) autonomy, and (6) self-esteem. Other studies use scales designed to measure trust and have equated a lower score with skepticism. Overall, research into individual differences in traits has demonstrated that auditors with higher levels of trait skepticism (as measured by the Professional Skepticism Scale) or lower levels of trust tend to exhibit more skeptical judgments.[20]

Research has indicated that the impact of experience on skeptical judgment (or lack thereof) is derived from a number of factors, such as the level of knowledge of the client's business and industry, the number of years one works as an auditor, and task-specific experience with more complex audit tasks.[21] One concern is, regardless of training and experience, auditors still may make biased judgments, as discussed in Chapter 4. What is needed is for auditors to be aware of their thought processes or the unconscious biases affecting their judgments, so they may begin to engage in more skeptical thinking. Bazerman et al. note, "What's needed is education that helps auditors understand the unconscious errors they make and the reasons they make them, so that they can begin to change the conduct of accounting to prevent the conflicts of interest that promote bias."[22]

Motivation and its relationship to skeptical judgment links to our earlier discussions of moral intent and moral action. Bazerman and Tenbrunsel suggest that when employees are not making skeptical judgments, one should examine audit-firm goals and reward incentives. They discuss the cognitive effects that "people see what they want to see and easily miss contradictory information when it's in their interest to remain ignorant," an idea we discussed in Chapter 2 as *motivated blindness*. They also note the link between skeptical judgment and action and how that relates to the reward structure in auditing: "Many managers are guilty of rewarding results rather than high-quality decisions. An employee may make a bad decision that turns out well and be rewarded or a good decision that turns out poorly and be punished" and further "laws often punish bad outcomes more aggressively than bad intentions.[23]

Based on their analysis of research into professional skepticism and judgment, the authors conclude that auditors may not feel extrinsically motivated to make skeptical judgments because incentive systems do not reward them for the process of making skeptical judgments, but only reward them when the judgments result in a favorable outcome for the firm. They also believe that the firm's philosophy and operating style is an important antecedent for creating incentives and motivating auditors to become more skeptical. However, they note that the personality traits the individual auditor brings to the firm are also very important determinants of whether the auditor exhibits an appropriate level of skepticism. In other words, diligence, thoroughness, objectivity, and reliability all are traits that can foster professional skepticism. Skepticism does not happen in a vacuum. It relies on individual traits of character supported by firm systems and an organizational culture that respects skeptical judgment backed by firm leadership that sets the proper tone.[24]

Another important antecedent to skeptical judgment is the influence of the external environment. The authors identify these influences as the individual auditor's interaction with her firm through accountability to reviewers, the impact of accountability to regulators, and the impact of more difficult risk assessments. They note that these influences represent powerful incentives that can motivate skeptical judgment in either a positive or negative manner. Accountability to reviewers and regulators serves as a lever that impacts both skeptical judgment and skeptical action. Clearly, the PCAOB in its inspection process described later on looks for adequate judgments and skepticism when reviewing the audit reports of registered public companies.[25]

PCAOB Standards and Inspections

We discussed PCAOB ethics and independence standards in Chapter 4 and GAAS earlier in this chapter. PCAOB also issues audit standards for public companies. Most of those standards address issues that do not directly link to matters of ethics and corporate governance so we restrict our coverage to those topics. We also briefly address audit evidence and analyses issues because many of the deficiencies cited in PCAOB inspection reports deal with these matters.

PCAOB Standards

LO 5-6

Explain PCAOB auditing standards.

AS No. 5: An Audit of Internal Control over Financial Reporting That Is Integrated with an Audit of Financial Statements

AS No. 5 establishes requirements and provides direction that applies when an auditor is engaged to perform an audit of management's assessment of the effectiveness of internal control over financial reporting. It provides that "effective internal control over financial reporting [ICFR] provides reasonable assurance regarding the reliability of financial reporting and the preparation of financial statements for external purposes. If one or more material weaknesses exist, the company's ICFR cannot be considered effective." The standard emphasizes that the general standards are applicable to an audit of ICFR. Those standards require technical training and proficiency as an auditor, independence, and the exercise of due professional care, including professional skepticism. The standard also establishes fieldwork and reporting standards applicable to an audit of ICFR.

The audit of ICFR should be integrated with the audit of financial statements. While the objectives of the audits are not identical, the auditor must plan and perform the work to achieve the objectives of both audits. In an integrated audit, the auditor should design testing procedures for internal controls to accomplish the objectives of both audits simultaneously: (1) to obtain sufficient evidence to support the auditor's opinion on ICFR at year-end, and (2) to obtain sufficient evidence to support the auditor's control risk assessments for purposes of the auditing of financial statements.

AS No. 5 standards include obtaining reasonable assurance about whether the financial statements are free of material misstatement, whether caused by error or fraud, and whether management's assessment of the effectiveness of the company's ICFR is fairly stated in all material respects. Accordingly, there is some risk that a material misstatement of the financial statements or a material weakness in internal control over financial reporting would remain undetected. Although not absolute, reasonable assurance is, nevertheless, a high level of assurance. Also, an integrated audit is not designed to detect error or fraud that is immaterial to the financial statements or deficiencies in internal control over financial reporting that, individually or in combination, are less severe than a material weakness. If, for any reason, the auditor is unable to complete the audit or is unable to form or has not formed an opinion, she may decline to express an opinion or decline to issue a report as a result of the engagement.

AS No. 7—Engagement Quality Review[26]

Engagement quality reviews are required and often provide a picture of how an audit has been conducted and the firm's own quality control procedures, both of which are scrutinized by the PCAOB in its inspection process. The qualities of the reviewer include competence, independence, integrity, and objectivity.

Most of the standard deals with the responsibilities of the engagement reviewer to evaluate significant judgments made by the engagement team, including assessment of significant risks of material misstatements and fraud, and the related conclusions reached in forming an overall conclusion on the engagement and in preparing the engagement report. Risk assessment is an important component of the PCAOB's inspection process and oftentimes directly influences its findings.

An interesting issue addressed in the standard is the requirement for a two-year "cooling-off" period for an engagement partner that steps down from an engagement and becomes the engagement quality reviewer. The PCAOB included the cooling-off period because it believed that it would be harder for an engagement partner who has had overall responsibility for the audit for at least a year to perform the review with the proper level of objectivity.

The inclusion of the two-year period has been criticized by some smaller firms as imposing an undue hardship on them given the limited number of partners. To address this issue, the PCAOB decided to follow the SEC's exemption from partner rotation requirements for its cooling-off period requirement for firms with fewer than five issuer clients and fewer than 10 partners.

The SEC independence rules allow engagement partners and concurring partners to serve for five consecutive years, after which they may not serve in either role for another five-year period. Within the five-year period, the rules do not impose a cooling-off period before the engagement partner can serve as the concurring partner. So, an engagement partner might serve for three years and then immediately serve as the review partner for two additional years under SEC rules.

On April 1, 2015, the PCAOB censured two CPAs for violating its partner rotation/cooling-off period requirements.[27] In the first case the PCAOB censured Dustin M. Lewis, a partner at L.L. Bradford & Company LLC, for violating independence with respect to five issuer audit clients because he served as either lead partner or concurring partner on those audits for a combined period of more than five consecutive years. The censure notice points out that Lewis failed to properly evaluate the significant judgments made by the audit engagement team.

The PCAOB also censured Eric S. Bullinger, a partner in the same CPA firm, because he served as lead partner on four issuer audits for more than five years and either lead or concurring partner on two audits for a combined period of more than five consecutive years. Bullinger also served as engagement quality reviewer immediately after serving as the engagement partner without satisfying the mandatory two-year cooling-off period.

AS No. 14—Evaluating Audit Results

This standard establishes requirements regarding the auditor's evaluation of audit results and determination of whether the auditor has obtained sufficient appropriate audit evidence. The evaluation process set forth in this standard includes, among other things, evaluation of misstatements identified during the audit; the overall presentation of the financial statements, including disclosures; and the potential for management bias in the financial statements.

In forming an opinion on whether the financial statements are presented fairly, in all material respects, in conformity with the applicable financial reporting framework, the auditor should take into account all relevant audit evidence, regardless of whether it appears to corroborate or to contradict the assertions in the financial statements.

In the audit of financial statements, the auditor's evaluation of audit results should include the following:

- The results of analytical procedures performed in the overall review of the financial statements ("overall review").
- Misstatements accumulated during the audit, including, in particular, uncorrected misstatements.
- The qualitative aspects of the company's accounting practices.
- Conditions identified during the audit that relate to the assessment of the risk of material misstatement due to fraud ("fraud risk").
- The presentation of the financial statements, including disclosures.
- The sufficiency and appropriateness of the audit evidence obtained.

AS No. 15—Audit Evidence

This standard explains what constitutes audit evidence and establishes requirements for designing and performing audit procedures to obtain sufficient appropriate audit evidence to support the opinion expressed in the auditor's report. *Audit evidence* is all information, whether obtained from audit procedures or other sources, that is used by the auditor in arriving at the conclusions on which the auditor's opinion is based. It consists of both information that supports and corroborates management's assertions regarding the financial statements or internal control over financial reporting and information that contradicts such assertions.

The auditor must plan and perform audit procedures to obtain sufficient appropriate audit evidence to provide a reasonable basis for her opinion. Sufficiency is the measure of the quantity of audit evidence. The quantity of audit evidence needed is affected by the following:

- *Risk of material misstatement (in the audit of financial statements) or the risk associated with the control (in the audit of internal control over financial reporting).* As the risk increases, the amount of evidence that the auditor should obtain also increases. For example, ordinarily more evidence is needed to respond to significant risks.

- *Quality of the audit evidence obtained.* As the quality of the evidence increases, the need for additional corroborating evidence decreases. Obtaining more of the same type of audit evidence, however, cannot compensate for the poor quality of that evidence.

Appropriateness is the measure of the quality of audit evidence (i.e., its relevance and reliability). To be appropriate, audit evidence must be both relevant and reliable in providing support for the conclusions on which the auditor's opinion is based.

AS No. 16—Communications with Audit Committees[28]

AS No. 16 requires the auditor to communicate with the company's audit committee regarding certain matters related to the conduct of an audit and to obtain certain information from the audit committee relevant to the audit.

The auditor should communicate to the audit committee the following matters:

1. *Significant accounting policies and practices.* Significant accounting policies include management's initial selection of, or changes in, significant accounting policies or the application of such policies in the current period and the effect on financial statements or disclosures of

significant accounting policies in controversial areas or areas for which there is a lack of authoritative guidance or consensus, or diversity in practice.

2. *Critical accounting policies and practices.* All critical accounting policies and practices to be used should be communicated to the audit committee, including the reasons certain policies and practices are considered critical and how current and future events might affect the determination of whether certain policies are considered critical.

3. *Critical accounting estimates.* A description of the process management used to develop critical accounting estimates should be communicated, along with management's significant assumptions used in critical accounting estimates that have a high degree of subjectivity. Additional communications include any significant changes that management made to the processes used to develop critical accounting estimates or significant assumptions, a description of management's reasons for the changes, and the effects of the changes on the financial statements.

4. *Significant unusual transactions.* Significant unusual transactions include those that are outside the normal course of business for the company or that otherwise appear to be unusual due to their timing, size, or nature; and the policies and practices management used to account for significant unusual transactions.

The auditor should communicate to the audit committee a variety of matters dealing with the quality of the company's financial reporting. This includes:

- Qualitative aspects of significant accounting policies and practices, including situations in which the auditor identified bias in management's judgments about the amounts and disclosures in the financial statements.
- The results of the auditor's evaluation of the differences between estimates best supported by the audit evidence and estimates included in the financial statements, which are individually reasonable but that indicate a possible bias on the part of the company's management.
- The auditor's assessment of management's disclosures related to the critical accounting policies and practices, along with any significant modifications to the disclosure of those policies and practices proposed by the auditor that management did not make.
- The basis for the auditor's conclusions regarding the reasonableness of the critical accounting estimates.
- The auditors' understanding of the business rationale for significant unusual transactions.
- The results of the auditor's evaluation of whether the presentation of the financial statements and the related disclosures are in conformity with the applicable financial reporting framework, including the auditor's consideration of the form, arrangement, and content of the financial statements (including the accompanying notes), encompassing matters such as the terminology used, the amount of detail given, the classification of items, and the bases of amounts set forth.
- Situations in which, as a result of the auditor's procedures, the auditor identified a concern regarding management's anticipated application of accounting pronouncements that have been issued but are not yet effective and might have a significant effect on future financial reporting.
- Alternative treatments permissible under the applicable financial reporting framework for policies and practices related to material items that have been discussed with management, including the ramifications of the use of such alternative disclosures and treatments and the treatment preferred by the auditor.

The auditor should communicate to the audit committee matters that are difficult or contentious for which the auditor consulted outside the engagement team and that the auditor reasonably determined are relevant to the audit committee's oversight of the financial reporting process. The auditor also should communicate to the audit committee, when applicable, the following matters relating to the auditor's evaluation of the company's ability to continue as a going concern:

- If the auditor believes there is substantial doubt about the company's ability to continue as a going concern for a reasonable period of time, the conditions and events that the auditor identified that, when considered in the aggregate, indicate that there is substantial doubt.
- If the auditor concludes, after consideration of management's plans, that substantial doubt about the company's ability to continue as a going concern is alleviated, the basis for the auditor's conclusion, including elements the auditor identified within management's plans that are significant to overcoming the adverse effects of the conditions and events.
- If the auditor concludes, after consideration of management's plans, that substantial doubt about the company's ability to continue as a going concern for a reasonable period of time remains, then the effects, if any, on the financial statements and adequacy of related disclosures should be communicated, along with the effects on the auditor's report.

The auditor should communicate to the audit committee the following matters related to the auditor's report:

- When the auditor expects to modify the opinion in the auditor's report, the reasons for the modification, and the wording of the report.
- When the auditor expects to include explanatory language or an explanatory paragraph in the auditor's report (i.e., emphasis of matter), the reasons for the explanatory language or paragraph, and the wording of the explanatory language or paragraph.

The auditor should communicate to the audit committee any disagreements with management about matters, whether or not satisfactorily resolved, that individually or in the aggregate could be significant to the company's financial statements or the auditor's report. Disagreements with management do not include differences of opinion based on incomplete facts or preliminary information that are later resolved by the auditor obtaining additional relevant facts or information prior to the issuance of the auditor's report.

The auditor should communicate to the audit committee any significant difficulties encountered during the audit. Significant difficulties encountered during the audit include, but are not limited to:

- Significant delays by management, the unavailability of company personnel, or an unwillingness by management to provide information needed for the auditor to perform her audit procedures.
- An unreasonably brief time within which to complete the audit.
- Unexpected extensive effort required by the auditor to obtain sufficient appropriate audit evidence.
- Unreasonable management restrictions encountered by the auditor on the conduct of the audit.
- Management's unwillingness to make or extend its assessment of the company's ability to continue as a going concern when requested by the auditor.

Audit committee communications are an essential part of an effective governance system and a key ingredient in creating an ethical organization environment. Open communications between the auditor and audit committee are essential to supporting the financial reporting oversight role assigned to the audit committee under SOX. The audit committee plays a critical role in resolving differences between the auditor and management and supporting the goal of a fair presentation of the financial statements and efficient and effective internal controls over financial reporting.

AS No. 18—Related-Party Transactions[29]

Related-party transactions and relationships pose an increased risk of material misstatement due to fraud, conflict of interest, or error. The auditor should perform procedures to obtain an understanding of the company's relationships and transactions with its related parties that might reasonably be expected to affect the risks of material misstatement of the financial statements by:

- Obtaining an understanding of the nature of these transactions and relationships;
- Performing inquiries of management to clarify issues; and
- Communicating with the audit committee.

The auditor's inquiry of management should include:

- The nature of any relationships, including ownership structure, between the company and its related parties;
- The transactions entered into, modified, or terminated, with its related parties during the period under audit and the terms and business purposes (or the lack thereof) of such transactions;
- Any related-party transactions that have not been authorized and approved in accordance with the company's established policies or procedures regarding the authorization and approval of transactions with related parties; and
- The auditor's evaluation of whether the company has properly identified its related parties and relationships and transactions with related parties.

The auditor should also consider the internal controls over these relationships and whether they have been undisclosed in the past. The auditor must evaluate whether related-party transactions have been properly accounted for and disclosed in the financial statements. This includes evaluating whether the financial statements contain the information regarding relationships and transactions with related parties essential for a fair presentation in conformity with the applicable financial reporting framework.

If the financial statements include a statement by management that transactions with related parties were conducted on terms equivalent to those prevailing in an arm's-length transaction, the auditor should determine whether the evidence obtained supports or contradicts management's assertion. If the auditor is unable to obtain sufficient appropriate audit evidence to substantiate management's assertion, and if management does not agree to modify the disclosure, the auditor should express a qualified or adverse opinion.

The auditor should communicate to the audit committee the auditor's evaluation of the company's identification of, accounting for, and disclosure of its relationships and transactions with related parties. The auditor also should communicate other significant matters arising from the audit regarding the company's relationships and transactions with related parties including, but not limited to:

- The identification of related parties or relationships or transactions with related parties that were previously undisclosed to the auditor;
- The identification of significant related-party transactions that have not been authorized or approved in accordance with the company's established policies or procedures;
- The identification of significant related-party transactions for which exceptions to the company's established policies or procedures were granted;
- The inclusion of a statement in the financial statements that a transaction with a related party was conducted on terms equivalent to those prevailing in an arm's-length transaction and the evidence obtained by the auditor to support or contradict such an assertion; and
- The identification of significant related-party transactions that appear to the auditor to lack a business purpose.

Related-party transactions can be particularly troublesome for auditors because management may not want the auditors to know about such relationships, especially if they create conflicts of interest and mask significant transactions that may not have been conducted aboveboard. A healthy dose of skepticism is needed to ferret out these matters and ensure they are properly recorded and disclosed in the financial statements.

Audit Deficiencies—SEC Actions

The findings of a study of audit deficiencies for the Center for Audit Quality that covered the years from 1998 to 2010 indicate that the SEC imposed sanctions on audit firms in 87 separate instances.[30] These deficiencies persist today and cover the following areas:

- Failure to gather sufficient competent evidence (73 percent).
- Failure to exercise due care (67 percent).
- Insufficient level of professional skepticism (60 percent).
- Failure to obtain adequate evidence related to management representations (54 percent).
- Failure to express an appropriate audit opinion (47 percent).

How does a Big Four firm fail so miserably in its audit of a company? The Satyam case referred to in our ethics reflection in Chapter 3 demonstrates how significant deficiencies in audit procedures can lead to such results. PwC's India firm had to inform the SEC that its audit reports issued for the 2005–2008 accounting fraud years could no longer be relied on.

PwC was sanctioned because of a lack of due care, including the exercise of professional skepticism, by, in part, accepting evidence provided by management that was less than persuasive. The firm also was cited for failing to report likely illegal acts that have a material effect on Satyam's financial statements and failing to perform the necessary procedures to identify such problems.

The quality review conducted within PwC was severely criticized by the SEC.[31] In its enforcement action against the firm, the commission pointed to PW India's failure to conduct procedures to confirm Satyam's cash and cash equivalent balances or its accounts receivables, including to properly execute third-party confirmation procedures that resulted in the fraud at Satyam going undetected for years. PW India's failures in auditing Satyam "were indicative of a quality control failure throughout PW India" because PW India staff "routinely relinquished control of the delivery and receipt of cash confirmations entirely to their audit clients and rarely, if ever, questioned the integrity of the confirmation responses they received from the client by following up with the banks."

After the fraud at Satyam came to light, PW India replaced virtually all senior management responsible for audit matters. The affiliates suspended its Satyam audit engagement partners from all work and removed from client service all senior audit professionals on the former Satyam audit team. These are extraordinarily harsh measures that clearly indicate a failure of quality controls and leadership at PW India and the firm itself.

PCAOB Inspections Program

LO 5-7
Describe the PCAOB inspection process.

In addition to authorizing the PCAOB to inspect and set professional standards for public accounting firms, SOX conferred broad discretion on the board to investigate and discipline firms and their "associated persons" for violations of the federal securities laws governing the preparation and issuance of audit reports, as well as other professional standards. SOX did so, however, without curtailing the existing enforcement authority of the SEC over public-company auditors.

Enforcement Proceedings

Under SOX and the board's rules, PCAOB enforcement proceedings are nonpublic unless (1) the parties consent to a public hearing, (2) the board has imposed sanctions and the time to file an appeal with the SEC has expired, or (3) the SEC, on appeal, issues an order regarding the sanctions imposed. Because a respondent in a PCAOB proceeding has little incentive to consent to a public hearing, and the appeals process can take years to complete, there are enforcement actions brought by the PCAOB that are not yet—and may never be—known to the public. Moreover, if a formal or informal investigation is conducted but no disciplinary proceeding is instituted, or if a disciplinary proceeding is instituted but no sanctions are imposed by a hearing officer (or, on appeal, by the board), the public is unlikely to learn of the existence of the investigation or the proceeding.

The PCAOB made public 25 enforcement proceedings in 2014, an increase from 17 in 2013. The types of cases that the board made public in 2014 were similar to those that have been the standard fare of the Enforcement Division's caseload since the PCAOB's inception.[32] The information made public is sometimes startling, such as PCAOB-registered firms or their personnel improperly interfering with board inspections or investigations by taking improper steps to modify, supplement, or backdate audit work papers.

Taken as a whole, the proceedings demonstrate that most PCAOB enforcement actions involve serious failures by smaller firms with limited experience with PCAOB standards to comply with the board's auditing standards and other requirements, but also reflect the board's willingness to sanction more seasoned auditors who fail to demonstrate sufficient professional skepticism or to respond appropriately to potential "red flags."

Inspections and Audit Deficiencies

A significant issue addressed in many enforcement actions against audit firms is a lack of professional skepticism and due care. PCAOB *Staff Audit Practice Alert 10, Maintaining and Applying Professional Skepticism in Audits,* notes continued concerns about whether auditors consistently and diligently apply professional skepticism. PCAOB points out that certain circumstances can impede the appropriate application of professional skepticism and allow unconscious biases to prevail, including incentives and pressures resulting from certain conditions inherent in the audit environment, scheduling and workload demands, or an inappropriate level of confidence or trust in management.[33]

The PCAOB Alert notes that firms' quality controls systems can enhance professional skepticism of engagement teams by setting a proper tone at the top that emphasizes the importance of skepticism by, for example, challenging management representations. A critical assessment of audit evidence and challenging mindset is also beneficial in assessing the risks of material misstatements and internal control assessments.

Professional skepticism is an integral part of due care and a critical component for auditors in evaluating significant management estimates and judgments about recorded transactions and financial statement presentations. Biases and tendencies to accept management's statements on these issues compromise auditor objectivity and violate the profession's ethical standards.

Auditors sometimes develop an unwarranted level of trust in management because of failings in their professional skepticism. Moreover, certain conditions inherent in the audit environment can create incentives and pressures that can impede the appropriate application of professional skepticism and allow unconscious bias to exist. The PCAOB Alert identifies the following examples that can inhibit professional skepticism:

- Incentives and pressures to build or maintain a long-term audit engagement;
- Incentives and pressures to avoid significant conflicts with management;
- Desire to achieve high client satisfaction ratings;
- Desire to keep audit costs low; and
- Desire to cross-sell services to client.

The PCAOB's experience with audit inspections of Big Four CPA firms is disconcerting. The results of inspections of 2013 audits indicated an average audit failure rate of 39 percent, an increase above the 37 percent rate in the previous year. Deloitte was at the low end at 28 percent, while EY hit a staggering 50 percent failure rate. PwC's rate was 32 percent, while KPMG came in at a 46 percent failure rate.

In EY's inspection report, the PCAOB found fault with 28 of the 57 audits inspected, and 27 of the 28 failed audits contained problems in the audit of internal control over financial reporting. The report says EY most often stumbled in selecting controls to test, testing the design of effectiveness of controls, and testing operating effectiveness. The PCAOB said in the report that each of the deficiencies described represents situations where the firm failed to obtain adequate audit evidence to support its opinion on financial statements and internal control. Many of the deficiencies involved a lack of professional care and professional skepticism.[34]

EY, as a firm and firm management, needs to deal with these disappointing results. Its failure rate has gone from 22 percent in 2010, to 36 percent in 2011, to 48 percent in 2012, and now one-half of its audits are deficient. EY has said all the right things in its letter that accompanied the report. "The PCAOB's inspection process assists us in identifying areas where we can continue to improve audit quality," wrote Stephen Howe, managing partner, and Frank Mahoney, vice chair of assurance services. "We respect and benefit from this process as it aids us in fulfilling our responsibilities to investors, other stakeholders, and the capital markets generally."[35] We do have to wonder about its long-term commitment to perform quality audits given the persistently high deficiency rate.

In the PCAOB's inspection report on KPMG audits, the Board said some of the firm's personnel had failed to sufficiently evaluate "contrary evidence" that seemed to contradict its audit conclusions. It also chided KPMG for not acting quickly enough to fix quality-control problems.[36]

There is some good news for the firms. In its first statement based on inspections of 2014 audit reports, the PCAOB said that the firms have shown real improvements in their internal control audits. Deloitte was the first firm to have its report released and showed just 21 percent of its audits had deficiencies.[37]

PCAOB Inspections of Chinese Firms

An increasingly controversial matter is the reluctance of foreign-based entities operating under the banner of Big Four U.S. international CPA firms to cooperate with the PCAOB in its inspections of audits conducted by foreign entities that list stocks on U.S. exchanges. In China, the matter has boiled over into a dispute between the PCAOB and Chinese authorities, which find the disclosure about Chinese companies to non-Chinese regulators to be unacceptable. Chinese law forbids companies from handing over documents to the SEC, thereby stifling the PCAOB's inspection process. On January 23, 2014, the SEC came down hard on Chinese units of Big Four firms ruling that these units should be barred from auditing U.S.-traded companies for six months. The ruling was stayed while the regulators worked out a deal.

The dilemma for U.S. regulators is the growing number of Chinese companies listing stock on U.S. exchanges that are found to have engaged in financial fraud. The SEC has been investigating a variety of Chinese companies listed in the United States and has filed 25 enforcement cases against Chinese firms and their executives. A good example is at Longtop Financial. The company, based in Xiamen, China, makes software for Chinese financial services companies. Its auditor, Deloitte Touche Tohmatsu, resigned after Longtop said that its chief financial officer offered to resign.

Here are the reasons provided by Deloitte for its resignation from the audit of Longtop Financial: (1) the recently identified falsity of the group's financial records in relation to cash at bank and loan balances; (2) the deliberate interference by the management in Deloitte's audit process; and (3) the unlawful detention of Deloitte's audit files. "These recent developments undermine our ability to rely on the representations of the management which is an essential element of the audit process; hence our resignation." Deloitte added that "we are no longer able to place reliance on management representations in relation to prior-period financial reports. Accordingly, we request that the Company take immediate steps to make the necessary 8-K filing [to the SEC] to state that continuing reliance should no longer be placed on our audit reports on the previous financial statements and moreover that we decline to be associated with any of the Company's financial communications during 2010 and 2011.[38]

On February 6, 2015, it was announced that the Chinese affiliates of the Big Four firms agreed to pay $500,000 each to settle the dispute with the SEC over their reluctance to give the agency documents about Chinese companies under investigation. The settlement also allowed the firms to avoid a temporary suspension of their right to audit U.S.-traded firms. Under the $2 million agreement, the Chinese arms of PricewaterhouseCoopers, Deloitte Touche Tohmatsu, KPMG, and Ernst & Young also agreed to follow procedures designed to ensure that the SEC is able to obtain audit documents from them in the future.

The settlement follows a judge's ruling in 2014 that the accounting firms had violated U.S. law when they refused to give the SEC the audit workpapers about some Chinese clients the SEC was investigating. Even though the clients' securities traded in the United States, the firms had argued they were prevented from sharing the workpapers by strict Chinese laws that treat such documents as akin to state secrets. Many of the documents were later turned over to the SEC after they were routed from the firms through the China Securities Regulatory Commission (CSRC), the equivalent to the U.S. SEC.

On June 29, 2015, the PCAOB announced it was planning its first-ever inspection of an audit firm in China under a pilot program agreed to with the CSRC, marking a step toward resolution of a stalemate over accounting oversight of Chinese firms listed on U.S. markets. The inspection was expected to take place at the end of 2015, subject to final agreements.

The contentious nature of the relationship between the PCAOB and the CSRC highlights our concern about the quality and reliability of Big Four audits done for U.S.-quoted Chinese companies. A series of investigations into financial fraud and attempts by Chinese management to block auditors' access to needed audit information raises serious questions about the trustworthiness of the audits and brings into question whether the best interests of U.S. investors are being adequately protected.

Concluding Thoughts

Financial statement fraud threatens the foundation of the financial reporting process and jeopardizes the integrity of the auditing function. Signposts that fraud may exist need to be ingrained in the DNA of auditors. Influences that might bias their approach to an audit and their evaluation of audit evidence must be controlled through an ethical approach that emphasizes objectivity, due care, and the exercise of professional skepticism.

Financial statement fraud problems continue to persist. The COSO study identified an increasing trend in the number of cases, including greater CEO and CFO involvement. Auditor changes by fraud firms occurred in more than 25 percent of the cases during the fraud period. Auditors seem to be lacking in due care and professional skepticism in many of these cases, accepting management's representations rather than challenging them.

Audit standards have come a long way in the last 20 years. In particular, the standards today provide a framework to evaluate internal controls and assess audit risk, and they do a better job of identifying the red flags indicating that fraud may be present. The Fraud Triangle provides a framework to evaluate risks of fraud and better understand how to prevent and detect it from occurring. A strong corporate governance system, including an independent audit committee, effective internal controls over financial reporting, and audit risk assessment procedures, is the best way to prevent fraud.

It is disturbing that such a high percentage of audits by Big Four CPA firms that have been examined by the PCAOB indicate deficiencies in internal control over financial reporting and failures of professional judgment. Overreliance on management's representations seems to be the culprit once again, causing many of the audit deficiencies. As the saying goes, "trust but verify" should be the mantra of a sound audit.

We believe the firms should recommit to the public interest ideal that is the foundation for the accounting profession. This can be done through greater scrutiny of management's intentions, being alert to internal pressures within the company, and asking probing questions during audits. Skeptical judgment and skeptical action is a good place to start to improve the quality of audits.

Discussion Questions

1. What are the objectives of audit risk assessment, and why is it important in assessing the likelihood that fraud may occur? Explain why risk assessment performed during audit planning sets the tone for the entire audit engagement.

2. Distinguish between an auditor's responsibilities to detect and report errors, illegal acts, and fraud. What role does materiality have in determining the proper reporting and disclosure of such events?

3. AU-C 240 points to three conditions that enable fraud to occur. Briefly describe each condition. How does one's propensity to act ethically, as described by Rest's model of morality, influence each of the three elements of the Fraud Triangle?

4. What is the ethical value of applying the Fraud Triangle to assess the risk of material misstatements in the financial statements?

5. All companies are vulnerable to fraud, but small businesses are particularly vulnerable. Why do you think this may be the case? What signs of possible fraud may be more pronounced in small businesses when compared to larger ones?

6. Explain the content of each section of the AICPA audit report. Evaluate the importance of each section with respect to the users of financial reports.

7. Give one example each of when an auditor might render an unmodified opinion and include an emphasis-of-matter paragraph and an other-matter paragraph. What is the value of such paragraphs in the audit report?

8. The following statement expresses the conclusion of XYZ auditors with respect to the company's investment in ABC. Assume that all amounts are material. What type of audit opinion should be rendered given this statement? Explain the reasoning behind your answer.

   XYZ's investment in ABC, a foreign subsidiary acquired during the year and accounted for by the equity method, is carried at $120,000 on the statement of financial position as at December 31, 2015, and XYZ's share of ABC's net income of $20,000 is included in XYZ's income for the year then ended. We were unable to obtain sufficient appropriate audit evidence about the

> carrying amount of XYZ's investment in ABC as at December 31, 2015, and XYZ's share of ABC's net income for the year because we were denied access to the financial information, management, and the auditors of ABC. Consequently, we were unable to determine whether any adjustments to these amounts were necessary.

9. Rationalization for fraud can fall under two categories: "no harm" and "no responsibility." Assume an employee is directed by management to reduce recorded expenses at year-end by insignificant amounts individually, but which are material in total. How might the employee justify her actions if questioned by the auditor with respect to no harm and no responsibility? What stage of moral development in Kohlberg's model is best illustrated by the employee's actions? Why?

10. What do you think is meant by the term ethical auditing with respect to the principles and rules of professional conduct in the AICPA Code?

11. Some criticize the accounting profession for using expressions in the audit report that seem to be building in deniability should the client commit a fraudulent act. What expressions enable the CPA to build a defense should the audit wind up in the courtroom? Do you see anything wrong with these expressions from an ethical point of view?

12. Do you think the concept of materiality is incompatible with ethical behavior? Consider in your answer how materiality judgments affect risk assessment in an audit of financial statements.

13. According to GAAS, the auditor must evaluate the control deficiencies that he has become aware of to determine whether those deficiencies, individually or in combination, are significant deficiencies or material weaknesses. What is the purpose of the auditor's evaluation of internal controls in these contexts with respect to conducting an audit in accordance with established auditing standards?

14. Mr. Arty works for Smile Accounting Firm as a senior accountant. Currently, he is doing a review of rental property compliance testing of rental receipts and expenses of the property owned by the client. He determines that the staff accountants tested only two tenants per property, instead of the three required by the audit program based on materiality considerations. However, to request more information from the client would cause massive delays, and the manager on the engagement is pressing hard for the information now. The manager did approach the client, who stated that she "needed the report yesterday." The manager reminds Arty that no problems were found from the testing of the two properties, in past years the workpapers called for just two properties to be reviewed, the firm has never had any accounting issues with respect to the client, and he is confident the testing is sufficient. Explain the relationship between the manager's explanations and the judgment tendencies discussed in Chapter 4.

15. Auditing standards require that a "brainstorming" session should be held at the beginning of each audit to help identify steps to assess the possibility that material misstatements/fraud in the financial statements exist. Discuss how brainstorming sessions might enhance audit judgments, professional skepticism, and decision making. Consider the groupthink dimension in your discussion.

16. Discuss the link between skeptical judgment and skeptical action and Rest's Four-Component Model of Ethical Decision Making.

17. What are the auditor's responsibilities to communicate information to the audit committee under PCAOB standards? If the auditor discovers that the audit committee routinely ignores such communications especially when they are critical of management's use of GAAP in the financial statements, what step(s) might the auditor take at this point?

18. Evaluate the costs and benefits of having a two-year "cooling-off" period for engagement partners.

19. Explain how PCAOB inspections can lead to improvements in audit engagement quality.

20. Discuss the cultural factors that create barriers for the Chinese units of Big Four firms to receiving support from the Chinese authorities to share audit information with the PCAOB to aid its inspection process.

21. In its report prepared for audit committees and other stakeholders in December 2014, "Our Commitment to Audit Quality," EY acknowledges that recent PCAOB findings indicate the need for improving audits of internal control over financial reporting (ICFR), increasing the focus on controls over the use of electronic audit evidence (EAE), scoping multi-location audits, auditing management's estimates, and performing substantive analytical procedures. In its opening letter in the report, the firm states: "At EY, the delivery of quality audits is central to our purpose, values, management processes...Our reputation is based on providing quality audit services objectively, independently, and with appropriate skepticism." Given the 50 percent audit deficiency rate cited by the PCAOB in its inspection of EY audits, would you conclude that the firm failed in its role to adequately protect the public interest?

22. The International Auditing and Assurance Standards Board has issued a new standard effective December 15, 2016, requiring that engagement partners physically sign the audit report with their names instead of the name of the firms, as is done in the United States. What value do you believe this new requirement might bring to the end-user of the audit report? Is it a necessary provision? Explain.

23. Do you agree that a professional accountant providing professional services to a client *that is not an audit client* of the firm or a network firm, who is unable to escalate a matter pertaining to an illegal act within the client, should be required to disclose the suspected illegal act to the entity's external auditor? If not, why not and what action should be taken? What about informing the SEC? Under what circumstances, if any, should the auditor consider a whistleblowing action against the client and/or the firm under Dodd-Frank?

24. Audit morality includes moral sensitivity, moral judgment, moral motivation, and moral character. Explain how audit morality plays a key role in determining best audit practices that influence audit performance.

25. Dennis just got hired after not working for two years following his reporting of financial statement fraud by his previous employer. Dennis was treated as an outcast and ultimately fired after the company "trumped up" some unsubstantiated claims of poor performance. Dennis fought the dismissal in court as wrongful termination but lost. It was two difficult years during which time his marriage broke up. In order to get hired for the new job, Dennis felt compelled to shade the truth about why he left the job. Here is what Dennis told the recruiter when asked whether he had left the company because of any differences:

    "I didn't feel as though there was a good growth path and that it didn't make sense to stay somewhere that wasn't going to work out for me."

    Did Dennis do the right thing? Explain.

Endnotes

1. Association of Certified Fraud Examiners (ACFE), *2014 Global Fraud Study: Report to the Nation on Occupational Fraud and Abuse,* Available at: http://www.acfe.com/rttn/docs/2014-report-to-nations.pdf.

2. American Institute of Certified Public Accountants (AICPA), *Consideration of Fraud in a Financial Statement Audit* (AU-C Section 240).

3. AICPA, AU-C Section 240.

4. *Securities and Exchange Commission v. KPMG LLP,* Joseph T. Boyle, Michael A. Conway, Anthony P. Dolanski, and Ronald A. Safaran, Civil Action No. 03-CV-0671 (DLC), Available at: www.sec.gov/litigation/complaints/comp17954.htm.

5. Mark S. Beasley, Joseph V. Carcello, Dana R. Hermanson, and Terry L. Neal, "An Analysis of Alleged Auditor Deficiencies in SEC Fraud Investigations: 1998–2010," Center for Audit Quality (2013).

6. W. Steve Albrecht, "Iconic Fraud Triangle Endures," *Fraud Magazine,* July–August 2014, Available at: http://www.fraud-magazine.com/article.aspx?id=4294983342.

7. Albrecht.

8. AICPA, AU-C Section 240.

9. AU-C Section 240.

10. COSO, *Enterprise Risk Management–Integrated Framework* (NY: AICPA, September 2004).

11. American Institute of Certified Public Accountants (AICPA), *The Auditor's Communication with those Charged with Governance* (AU-C Section 260).

12. Financial Accounting Standards Board (FASB), *Statement of Financial Accounting Standards* (Stamford, CT: FASB, November 1977).

13. SEC, Staff Accounting Bulletin 99: Materiality, Available at: https://www.sec.gov/interps/account/sab99.htm.

14. American Institute of Certified Public Accountants (AICPA), *Understanding the Entity and its Environment and Assessing the Risks of Material Misstatement* (AU-C Section 315).

15. Steven M. Glover and Douglas F. Prawitt, "Enhancing Auditor Professional Skepticism: The Professional Skepticism Continuum," *Current Issues in Auditing,* Vol. 8, No. 2 (2014), pp. 1–10.

16. "Applying Professional Skepticism," Available at: http://www.oag-bvg.gc.ca/internet/methodology/performance-audit/manual/1041.shtm.

17. Mark W. Nelson, "A Model and Literature Review of Professional Skepticism in Auditing," *Auditing: A Journal of Practice & Theory,* Vol. 28, No. 2 (2009), pp. 1–34.

18. R. Kathy Hurtt, Helen Brown-Liburd, Christine E. Earley, and Ganesh Krishnamoorthy, "Research on Auditor Professional Skepticism: Literature Synthesis and Opportunities for Future Research," *Auditing: A Journal of Practice & Theory,* Vol. 32, Supplement 1 (2013), pp. 45–97.

19. Hurtt et al., pp. 50–53.

20. R. Kathy Hurtt, "Development of a Scale to Measure Professional Skepticism," *Auditing: A Journal of Practice & Theory,* Vol. 29, No. 1 (2010), pp. 149–171.

21. Hurtt et al., pp. 52–53.

22. Max H. Bazerman, Geoge Lowenstein, and Don A. Moore, "Why Good Accountants do Bad Audits," *Harvard Business Review,* April 2011, pp. 58–65.

23. Max H. Bazerman and Ann E. Tenbrunsel, "Good People Often Let Bad Things Happen," *Harvard Business Review,* November 2002, pp. 97–102.

24. Hurtt et al., pp. 55–56.

25. Hurtt et al., pp. 61–65.

26. PCAOB, *Auditing Standard 7, Engagement Quality Review,* December 15, 2009, Available at: http://pcaobus.org/Standards/Auditing/pages/auditing_standard_7.aspx.

27. PCAOB, "Order Instituting Disciplinary Proceedings, Making Findings and Imposing Sanctions: In the Matter of Dustin M. Lewis, CPA, and Eric S. Bullinger, CPA," *PCAOB Release No. 105-2015-005,* April 1 , 2015, Available at: http://pcaobus.org/Enforcement/Decisions/Documents/Lewis_and_Bullinger.pdf.

28. PCAOB, *Auditing Standard 16, Communications with Audit Committee,* December 15, 2012, Available at: http://pcaobus.org/Standards/Auditing/Pages/Auditing_Standard_16.aspx.

29. PCAOB, *Auditing Standard 18, Related Parties,* December 15, 2015, Available at: http://pcaobus.org/Standards/Auditing/Pages/Auditing_Standard_18.aspx.

30. Beasley et al., pp. 2–5.

31. *SEC Charges India-Based Affiliates of PwC for Role in Satyam Accounting Fraud,* April 5, 2011, Available at: https://www.sec.gov/news/press/2011/2011-82.htm.

32. Law360, "Spotlight on PCAOB's 2014 Enforcement Program," Available at: http://www.law360.com/articles/628875/spotlight-on-pcaob-s-2014-enforcement-program.

33. PCAOB, *Staff Audit Practice Alert No. 10: Maintaining and Applying Professional Skepticism in Audits,* December 4, 2012, Available at: http://pcaobus.org/standards/qanda/12-04-2012_sapa_10.pdf.

34. Tammy Whitehouse, "PCAOB Report on EY Hammers Hard on Internal Control," *Compliance Week,* August 29, 2014, Available at: https://www.complianceweek.com/blogs/accounting-auditing-update/pcaob-report-on-ey-hammers-hard-on-internal-control#.Vbpgdvkuzlw.

35. Whitehouse.

36. Michael Rapoport, "KPMG Audits Had 46% Deficiency Rate in PCAOB Inspection," *The Wall Street Journal,* August 23, 2014, Available at: http://www.wsj.com/articles/kpmg-audits-had-46-deficiency-rate-in-pcaob-inspection-1414093002.

37. Emily Chasan, "Big Firms Getting Better Grades on Internal Control Audits: PCAOB," *The Wall Street Journal,* June 4, 2015, Available at: http://blogs.wsj.com/cfo/2015/06/04/big-firms-getting-better-grades-on-internal-control-audits-pcaob/.

38. Reuters, "SEC Investigating Longtop Financial of China," May 23, 2011, Available at: http://www.nytimes.com/2011/05/24/business/24longtop.html.

Chapter 5 Cases

Case 5-1 Loyalty and Fraud Reporting (a GVV case)

Assume Vick and Ethan are CPAs. Ethan Lester was seen as a "model employee" who deserved a promotion to CFO, according to Kelly Fostermann, the CEO of Fostermann Corporation, a Maryland-based, largely privately held company that is a prominent global designer and marketer of stereophonic systems. Kelly considered Lester to be an honest employee based on performance reviews and his unwillingness to accept the promotion, stating that he wasn't ready yet for the position. Little did she know that Lester was committing a $50,000 fraud during 2015 by embezzling cash from the company. In fact, no one seemed to catch on because Lester was able to override internal controls. However, the auditors were coming in and to solidify the deception, he needed the help of Vick Jensen, a close friend who was the accounting manager. Lester could "order" Jensen to cover up the fraud but hoped he would do so out of friendship and loyalty. Besides, Lester knew Jensen had committed his own fraud two years ago and covered it up by creating false journal entries for undocumented sales, returns, transactions, and operating expenses.

Lester went to see Jensen and explained his dilemma. He could see Jensen's discomfort in hearing the news. Jensen had thought he had turned the corner on being involved in fraud after he quietly paid back the $20,000 he had stolen two years ago. Here is how the conversation went.

"Vick, I need your help. I blew it. You know Mary and I split up 10 months ago."

"Yes," Vick said.

"Well, I got involved with another woman who has extravagant tastes. I'm embarrassed to say she took advantage of my weakness and I wound up taking $50,000 from company funds."

"Ethan, what were you thinking?"

"Don't get all moral with me. Don't you recall your own circumstances?"

Vick was quiet for a moment and then asked, "What do you want me to do?"

"I need you to make some entries in the ledger to cover up the $50,000. I promise to pay it back, just as you did. You know I'm good for it."

Vick reacted angrily, saying, "You told me to skip the bank reconciliations—that you would do them yourself. I trusted you."

"I know. Listen, do this one favor for me, and I'll never ask you again."

Vick grew increasingly uneasy. He told Ethan he needed to think about it … his relationship with the auditors was at stake.

Questions

1. Analyze the facts of the case using the Fraud Triangle. Include a discussion of the weaknesses in internal controls.

2. Which rules of professional conduct should Vick consider in deciding on a course of action? Explain. What are Vick's ethical obligations in this matter?

3. Use the "Giving Voice to Values" framework to help Vick decide on his next course of action. Why do you recommend it?

Case 5-2 ZZZZ Best[1]

The story of ZZZZ Best is one of greed and audaciousness. It is the story of a 15-year-old boy from Reseda, California, who was driven to be successful, regardless of the costs. His name is Barry Minkow. Although this case dates back over 30 years, it does serve as an example of what can happen when auditors do not look too hard to find fraud.

Minkow had high hopes to make it big—to be a millionaire very early in life. He started a carpet cleaning business in the garage of his home. Minkow realized early on that he was not going to become a millionaire cleaning other people's carpets, but that he could in the insurance restoration business. In other words, ZZZZ Best would contract to do carpet and drapery cleaning jobs after a fire or flood. Because the damage from the fire or flood probably would be covered by insurance, the customer would be eager to have the work done, and perhaps not be all that concerned with how much it would cost. The only problem with Minkow's insurance restoration idea was that it was all a fiction. Allegedly, over 80 percent of his revenue was from this work. In the process of creating the fraud, Minkow was able to dupe the auditors, Ernst & Whinney (now EY), into thinking the insurance restoration business was real. The auditors never caught on until it was too late.

How Barry Became a Fraudster

Minkow wrote a book, *Clean Sweep: A Story of Compromise, Corruption, Collapse, and Comeback,*[2] that provides some insights into the mind of a 15-year-old kid who was called a "wonder boy" on Wall Street until the bubble burst. He was trying to find a way to drum up customers for his fledgling carpet cleaning business. One day, while he was alone in his garage-office, Minkow called Channel 4 in Los Angeles. He disguised his voice so he wouldn't sound like a teenager and told a producer that he had just had his carpets cleaned by the 16-year-old owner of ZZZZ Best. He sold the producer on the idea that it would be good for society to hear the success story about a high school junior running his own business. The producer bought it lock, stock, and carpet cleaner. Minkow gave the producer the phone number of ZZZZ Best and waited. It took less than five minutes for the call to come in. Minkow answered the phone and when the producer asked to speak with Mr. Barry Minkow, Minkow said, "Who may I say is calling?" Within days, a film crew was in his garage shooting ZZZZ Best at work. The story aired that night, and it was followed by more calls from radio stations and other television shows wanting to do interviews. The calls flooded in with customers demanding that Barry Minkow personally clean their carpets.

As his income increased in the spring of 1983, Minkow found it increasingly difficult to run the company without a checking account. He managed to find a banker that was so moved by his story that the banker agreed to allow an underage customer to open a checking account. Minkow used the money to buy cleaning supplies and other necessities. Even though his business was growing, Minkow ran into trouble paying back loans and interest when due.

Minkow developed a plan of action. He was tired of worrying about not having enough money. He went to his garage—where all his great ideas first began—and looked at his bank account statement, which showed that he had more money than he thought he had based on his own records. Minkow soon realized it was because some checks he had written had not been cashed by customers, so they didn't yet show up on the bank statement. Voilá! Minkow started to kite checks between two or more banks. He would write a check on one ZZZZ Best account and deposit it into another. Because it might take a few days for the check written on Bank #1 to clear that bank's records (back then, checks weren't always processed in real time the way they are today), Minkow could pay some bills out of the second account and Bank #1 would not know—at least for a few days—that Minkow had written a check on his account when, in reality, he had a negative balance. The bank didn't know it because some of the checks that Minkow had written before the visit to Bank #2 had not cleared his account in Bank #1.

It wasn't long thereafter that Minkow realized he could kite checks big time. Not only that, he could make the transfer of funds at the end of a month or a year and show a higher balance than really existed in Bank #1 and carry it onto the balance sheet. Because Minkow did not count the check written on his account in Bank #1 as an outstanding check, he was able to double-count.

---

[1] The facts are derived from a video by the ACFE, *Cooking the Books: What Every Accountant Should Know about Fraud,* Available at: http://www.acfe.com/selfstudy.aspx?id=2590&terms=(video+cooking+the+books)+.

[2] Barry Minkow, *Clean Sweep: A Story of Compromise, Corruption, Collapse, and Comeback* (Nashville, TN: Thomas Nelson, 1995).

Time to Expand the Fraud

Over time, Minkow moved on to bigger and bigger frauds, like having his trusted cohorts confirm to banks and other interested parties that ZZZZ Best was doing insurance restoration jobs. Minkow used the phony jobs and phony revenue to convince bankers to make loans to ZZZZ Best. He had cash remittance forms made up from nonexistent customers with whatever sales amount he wanted to appear on the document. He even had a co-conspirator write on the bogus remittance form, "Job well done." Minkow could then show a lot more revenue than he was really making.

Minkow's phony financial statements enabled him to borrow more and more money and expand the number of carpet cleaning outlets. However, Minkow's personal tastes had become increasingly more expensive, including purchasing a Ferrari with the borrowed funds and putting a down payment on a 5,000-square-foot home. So, the question was: How do you solve a perpetual cash flow problem? You go public! That's right, Minkow made a public offering of stock in ZZZZ Best. Of course, he owned a majority of the stock to maintain control of the company.

Minkow had made it to the big leagues. He was on Wall Street. He had investment bankers, CPAs, and attorneys all working for him—the now 19-year-old kid from Reseda, California, who had turned a mom-and-pop operation into a publicly owned corporation.

Barry Goes Public

Pressured to get a big-time CPA firm to do his audit by the underwriting firm selling his stock, Minkow hired Ernst & Whinney to perform the April 30, 1987, fiscal year-end audit. Minkow continued to be one step ahead of the auditors—that is, until the Ernst & Whinney auditors insisted on going to see an insurance restoration site. They wanted to confirm that all the business—all the revenue—that Minkow had said was coming in to ZZZZ Best was real.

The engagement partner drove to an area in Sacramento, California, where Minkow did a lot of work—supposedly. He looked for a building that seemed to be a restoration job. Why he did that isn't clear, but he identified a building that seemed to be the kind that would be a restoration job in progress.

Earlier in the week, Minkow had sent one of his cohorts to find a large building in Sacramento that appeared to be a restoration site. As luck would have it, Minkow's associate picked out the same site as had the partner later on. Minkow's cohorts found the leasing agent for the building. They convinced the agent to give them the keys so that they could show the building to some potential tenants over the weekend. Minkow's helpers went up to the site before the arrival of the partner and placed placards on the walls that indicated ZZZZ Best was the contractor for the building restoration. In fact, the building was not fully constructed at the time, but it looked as if some restoration work was going on at the site.

Minkow was able to pull it off in part due to luck and in part because the Ernst & Whinney auditors did not want to lose the ZZZZ Best account. It had become a large revenue producer for the firm, and Minkow seemed destined for greater and greater achievements. Minkow was smart and used the leverage of the auditors not wanting to lose the ZZZZ Best account as a way to complain whenever they became too curious about the insurance restoration jobs. He would even threaten to take his business from Ernst & Whinney and give it to other auditors. To get on their good side, he would wine and dine the auditors and even invite them to his house.

Minkow also took a precaution with the site visit. He had the auditors sign a confidentiality agreement that they would not make any follow-up calls to any contractors, insurance companies, the building owner, or other individuals involved in the restoration work. This prevented the auditors from corroborating the insurance restoration contracts with independent third parties.

The Fraud Starts to Unravel

It was a Los Angeles housewife who started the problems for ZZZZ Best that would eventually lead to the company's demise. Because Minkow was a well-known figure and flamboyant character, the *Los Angeles Times* did a story about the carpet cleaning business. The Los Angeles housewife read the story about Minkow and recalled that ZZZZ Best had overcharged her for services in the early years by increasing the amount of the credit card charge for its carpet cleaning services.

Minkow had gambled that most people don't check their monthly statements, so he could get away with the petty fraud. However, the housewife did notice the overcharge and complained to Minkow, and eventually he returned the overpayment. She couldn't understand why Minkow would have had to resort to such low levels back then if he was as successful as the *Times* article made him out to be. So she called the reporter to find out more, and that ultimately led to the investigation of ZZZZ Best and future stories that weren't so flattering.

Because Minkow continued to spend lavishly on himself and his possessions, he always seemed to need more and more money. It got so bad over time that he was close to defaulting on loans and had to make up stories to keep the creditors at bay, and he couldn't pay his suppliers. The complaints kept coming in, and eventually the house of cards that was ZZZZ Best came crashing down.

During the time that the fraud was unraveling, Ernst & Whinney decided to resign from the ZZZZ Best audit. It had started to doubt the veracity of Minkow and his business at ZZZZ Best. Of course, by then it mattered little because the firm had been a party to the cover-up for some time.

Legal Liability Issues

The ZZZZ Best fraud was one of the largest of its time. ZZZZ Best reportedly settled a shareholder class action lawsuit for $35 million. Ernst & Whinney was sued by a bank that had made a multimillion-dollar loan based on the financial statements for the three-month period ending July 31, 1986. The bank claimed that it had relied on the review report issued by Ernst & Whinney in granting the loan to ZZZZ Best. However, the firm had indicated in its review report that it was not issuing an opinion on the ZZZZ Best financial statements. The judge ruled that the bank was not justified in relying on the review report because Ernst & Whinney had expressly disclaimed issuing any opinion on the statements. The firm lucked out in that the judge understood that a review engagement only provides limited assurance rather than the reasonable assurance of the audit.

Barry Minkow was charged with engaging in a $100 million fraud scheme. He was sentenced to a term of 25 years.

Questions

1. Do you believe that auditors should be held liable for failing to discover fraud in situations such as ZZZZ Best, where top management goes to great lengths to fool the auditors? Explain.

2. Discuss the red flags that existed in the ZZZZ Best case and evaluate Ernst & Whinney's efforts with respect to fraud risk assessment. Criticize the firm's approach to the audit from a professional judgment perspective.

3. These are selected numbers from the financial statements of ZZZZ Best for fiscal years 1985 and 1986:

	1985	1986
Sales	$1,240,524	$4,845,347
Cost of goods sold	576,694	2,050,779
Accounts receivable	0	693,773
Cash	30,321	87,014
Current liabilities	2,930	1,768,435
Notes payable—current	0	780,507

   a. What is the purpose of performing analytical review procedures in an audit performed under GAAS? What calculations or analyses would you make with these numbers that might help you assess whether the financial relationships are "reasonable"?

   b. Given the facts of the case, what inquiries might you make of management based on your analysis?

Barry: The Afterlife

After being released from jail in 1997, Minkow became a preacher and a fraud investigator, and he spoke at schools about ethics. He had established a reputation of trust as a pastor in the Community Bible Church in San

Diego that he had served after being released from prison. However, over time his greedy nature got the better of him. He admitted that he tricked a widower into making a $75,000 donation for a hospital in Sudan to honor his wife after she died of cancer. Only there was no hospital, and Minkow pocketed the money. Minkow also admitted, among others things, that he stole $300,000 from a widowed grandmother who was trying to raise her teenage granddaughter. In addition, Minkow confessed to diverting church member donations for his own benefit and embezzling money intended as church donations. In all, Minkow admitted stealing—and concealing from the IRS—at least $3 million from church parishioners and lenders. As described in court documents, Minkow's conduct continued for over a decade. On April 28, 2014, he was sentenced to five years in prison for his crimes that will be tacked on to the five-year term in the Lennar scheme, described below.

Soon after his arrival at Community Bible Church, a church member asked him to look into a money management firm in nearby Orange County. Suspecting something was not right, Minkow used his "fraud-sniffing" abilities to alert federal authorities, who discovered the firm was a $300 million pyramid scheme. This was the beginning of the Fraud Discovery Institute, a for-profit investigative firm. Minkow managed to dupe the investment community again; several Wall Street investors liked what they saw and sent him enough money to go after bigger targets. By Minkow's estimate, he had uncovered $1 billion worth of fraud over the years.

Once again, Barry's true self got the better of him and in 2009, he issued a report accusing the major homebuilder Lennar of massive fraud. Minkow claimed that irregularities in Lennar's off-balance-sheet debt accounting were evidence of a massive Ponzi scheme. He accused Lennar of not disclosing enough information about this to its shareholders, and also claimed that a Lennar executive took out a fraudulent personal loan. Minkow denounced Lennar as "a financial crime in progress" and "a corporate bully." From January 9, 2009 (when Minkow first made his accusations), to January 22, 2009, Lennar's stock tumbled from $11.57 a share to only $6.55. Minkow issued the report after being contacted by Nicholas Marsch, a San Diego developer who had filed two lawsuits against Lennar for fraud. One of Marsch's suits was summarily thrown out of court, while the other ended with Marsch having to pay Lennar $12 million in counterclaims.

Lennar responded by adding Minkow as a defendant in a libel-and-extortion suit against Marsch. According to court records, Minkow had shorted Lennar stock, buying $20,000 worth of options in a bet that the stock would fall. Minkow also forged documents alleging misconduct on Lennar's part. He went forward with the report even after a private investigator he had hired for the case could not substantiate Marsch's claims. (In an unrelated development, it was also revealed that Minkow operated the Fraud Discovery Institute out of the offices of his church and even used church money to fund it—something which could have potentially jeopardized his church's tax-exempt status.)

On December 27, 2010, Florida circuit court judge Gill Freeman issued terminating actions against Minkow in response to a motion by Lennar. Freeman found that Minkow had repeatedly lied under oath, destroyed or withheld evidence, concealed witnesses, and deliberately tried to "cover up his misconduct." According to Freeman, Minkow had even lied to his own lawyers about his behavior. Freeman determined that Minkow had perpetuated "a fraud on the court" that was so egregious that letting the case go any further would be a disservice to justice. In her view, "no remedy short of default" was appropriate for Minkow's lies. She ordered Minkow to reimburse Lennar for the legal expenses it incurred while ferreting out his lies. Lennar estimates that its attorneys and investigators spent hundreds of millions of dollars exposing Minkow's lies.

On March 16, 2011, Minkow announced through his attorney that he was pleading guilty to one count of insider trading. Prosecutors had charged that Minkow and Marsch conspired to extort money from Lennar by driving down its stock. According to his lawyer, Minkow had bought his Lennar options using "nonpublic information." The complaint also revealed that Minkow had sent his allegations to the FBI, IRS, and SEC, and that the three agencies found his claims credible enough to open a formal criminal investigation into Lennar's practices. Minkow then used confidential knowledge of that investigation to short Lennar stock, even though he knew he was barred from doing so. Minkow opted to plead guilty to the conspiracy charge rather than face charges of securities fraud and market manipulation, which could have sent him to prison for life.

Minkow resigned his position as senior pastor, saying in a letter to his flock that because he was no longer "above reproach," he felt that he was "no longer qualified to be a pastor."

Questions *(continued)*

4. Why do you think Minkow was able to pull off the fraud at the church for so long and not be detected?

Case 5-3 Imperial Valley Community Bank

Bill Stanley, of Jacobs, Stanley & Company, started to review the working paper files on his client, Imperial Valley Community Bank, in preparation for the audit of the client's financial statements for the year ended December 31, 2016. The bank was owned by a parent company, Nuevo Financial Group, and it serviced a small western Arizona community near Yuma that reached south to the border of Mexico. The bank's preaudit statements are presented in Exhibit 1.

EXHIBIT 1   Imperial Valley Community Bank

Balance Sheet (preaudit) December 31, 2016	
Assets	
Cash and cash equivalents	$1,960,000
Loans receivable	6,300,000
Less: Reserve for loan losses	(25,000)
Unearned discounts and fees	(395,000)
Accrued interest receivable	105,000
Prepayments	12,000
Real property held for sale	514,000
Property, plant, and equipment	390,000
Less: Accumulated depreciation	(110,000)
Contribution to Thrift Guaranty Corp.	15,000
Deferred start-up costs	44,000
Total assets	$8,810,000
Liabilities & Equity	
Liabilities	
Regular and money market savings	$2,212,000
T-bills and CDs	5,180,000
Accrued interest payable	190,000
Accounts payable and accruals	28,000
Total liabilities	$7,610,000
Equity	
Capital stock	$ 700,000
Additional paid-in capital	1,120,000
Retained earnings (deficit)	(620,000)
Total equity	$1,200,000
Total liabilities and equity	$8,810,000

(Continued)

Statement of Operations (preaudit) for the Year Ended December 31, 2016

Revenues

Interest earned	$ 820,000
Discount earned	210,000
Investment income	82,000
Fees, charges, and commissions	78,000
Total revenues	$1,190,000

Expenses

Interest expense	$ 815,000
Provision for loan losses	180,000
Salary expense	205,000
Occupancy expense including depreciation	100,000
Other administrative expense	160,000
Legal expense	12,000
Thrift Guaranty Corp. payment	48,000
Total expenses	$1,520,000
Net loss for the year	$(330,000)

Background

Bill Stanley knew there were going to be some problems to contend with during the course of the audit, so he decided to review the planning memo that he had prepared about two months earlier. This memo is summarized in Exhibit 2.

EXHIBIT 2   Planning Memo

1. The firm of Jacobs, Stanley & Co. succeeded the firm of Nelson, Thomas & Co. as auditors for Imperial Valley Community Bank. The prior auditors conducted the 2014 and 2015 audits. Jacobs, Stanley & Co. communicated in writing with Nelson, Thomas & Co. prior to accepting the engagement. In addition, authorization was given by the client for a review of the predecessor auditors' working papers. The findings of these inquiries are summarized in item 6 below and the internal office communication.

2. Imperial Valley Community Bank was incorporated in Arizona on June 12, 2000. It is a wholly owned subsidiary of Nuevo Financial Group, S.A., a Mexican corporation. As a community bank with maximum asset limitations, it is restricted to certain types of business, including making real estate and consumer loans and certain types of commercial loans.

3. Imperial Valley accepts deposits in the form of interest-bearing passbook accounts and certificates of deposit. Most of the depositors are of Spanish descent. The client primarily services the Spanish-speaking community in the Imperial Valley of southern Arizona, which is a rural community located on the Mexican border.

4. The principal officers of Imperial Valley are Jose Ortega and his brother, Arturo. They serve as the CEO and the CFO, respectively. Two cousins serve as the chief operating officer (COO) and chief ethics and compliance officer (CECO).

(Continued)

5. Imperial Valley is subject to the regulations of the Arizona Community Bank Law and is examined by the Department of Corporations. It was last examined in December 2015 and was put on notice as "capital impaired." Additional capital was being sought from local investors.

6. Based on review of the prior auditors' working papers, the following items were noted:

   a. The client's lack of profitability was due to a high volume of loan losses resulting from poor underwriting procedures and faulty documentation.

   b. Imperial Valley has a narrow net interest margin due to the fact that all deposits are interest bearing and it pays the highest interest rates in the area.

   c. Due to the small size of the client and its focus on handling day-to-day operating problems, the internal controls are marginal at best. There were material weaknesses in its loan underwriting procedures and documentation, as well as in compliance with regulatory requirements.

   d. There are no reports issued by management on the internal controls.

   e. Audit evidence was frequently unavailable to the prior auditors, and they expressed their concerns about this matter in an internal memo.

The next item he reviewed was an internal office communication on potential audit risks. This communication described three areas of particular concern:

1. The client charged off $420,000 in loans in 2015 and had already charged off $535,000 through July 31, 2016. Assuming that reserve requirements by law are a minimum of 1.25 percent of loans outstanding, this statutory amount probably would not be large enough for the loan loss reserve. This, in combination with the prior auditors' concerns about proper loan underwriting procedures and documentation, indicates that the audit engagement team should carefully review loan quality.

2. The audit report issued on the 2015 financial statements contained an unmodified opinion with an emphasis-of-matter paragraph describing the uncertainty about the client's ability to continue as a going concern. The concern was caused by the "capital impairment" declaration by the Arizona Department of Corporations.

3. The client had weak internal controls according to the prior auditors. Some of the items to look out for, in addition to proper loan documentation, were whether the preaudit financial statement information provided by the client was supported by the general ledger, whether the accruals were appropriate, and whether all transactions were properly authorized and recorded on a timely basis.

Audit Findings

Jacobs, Stanley & Company conducted the audit of the financial statements for the year ended December 31, 2016, and the following were the areas of greatest concern to Stanley:

1. **Adequacy of Loan Collateral.** A review of 30 loan files representing $2,100,000 of total loans outstanding (33.3 percent of the portfolio) indicated that much of the collateral for the loans was in the form of second or third mortgages on real property. This gave the client a potentially unenforceable position due to the existence of very large senior liens. For example, if foreclosure became necessary to collect Imperial Valley's loan, the client would have to pay off these large senior liens first. Other collateral often consisted of personal items such as jewelry and furniture. In the case of jewelry, often there was no effort made by the client after granting the loan to ascertain whether the collateral was still in the possession of the borrower. The jewelry could have been sold without the client's knowledge. It was difficult to obtain sufficient audit evidence about these amounts.

2. **Collectibility of Loans.** Many loans were structured in such a way as to require interest payments only for a small number of years (two or three years), with a balloon payment for principal due at the end of this time. This structure made it difficult to evaluate the payment history of the borrower properly. Although the annual interest payments may have been made for the first year or two, this was not necessarily a good indication that the borrower would come up with the cash needed to make the large final payment, and the financial statements provided no additional disclosures about this matter.

3. **Weakness in Internal Controls.** Internal control weaknesses were a pervasive concern. The auditors recomputed certain accruals and unearned discounts, confirmed loan and deposit balances, and reconciled the preaudit financial information provided by the client to the general ledger. Some adjustments had to be made as a result of this work. A material weakness in the lending function was identified. Loans were too frequently granted merely because the borrowers were well known to Imperial Valley officials, who believed that they could be counted on to repay their outstanding loans. An ability to repay these loans was based too often on "faith" rather than on clear indications that the borrowers would have the necessary cash available to repay their loans when they came due. This was of great concern to the auditors, especially in light of the inadequacy of the loan reserve, as detailed in item 5 that follows.

4. **Status of Additional Capital Infusion.** The audit engagement team is working under the assumption that under Arizona regulatory requirements, a community bank must maintain a 6:1 ratio of "thrift certificates" to net equity capital. Based on the financial information provided by Imperial Valley, the capital deficiency was only $32,000 below capital requirements (preaudit), as follows:

Thrift certificates	$\dfrac{\$7,392,000}{6}$
Net equity capital required	$1,232,000
Net equity capital reported	$1,200,000
Deficiency	$ 32,000

Audit adjustments explained in Exhibit 3 increased the capital deficiency to $622,000, as follows:

Net equity capital required	$1,232,000
Net equity capital (postaudit)	$ 610,000
($1,200,000–$590,000)	
Deficiency	$ 622,000

EXHIBIT 3   Audit Adjustments

AJE #1	Reserve for loan losses	$ 200,000	
	Loans receivable		$ 200,000
	To write down loans to net realizable value		
AJE #2	Reserve for loan losses	$ 300,000	
	Unearned discounts & fees	80,000	
	Loans receivable		$ 380,000
	To write off loans more than 180 days past due in compliance with statutes		
AJE #3	Provision for loan losses	$ 590,000	
	Reserve for loan losses		$ 590,000

(Continued)

To increase the reserve balance to 2 percent of outstanding loans as follows: Reserve balance (preaudit)		$ (25,000)
Less adjusting entry		
#1	$ 200,000	
#2	300,000	
		$ 500,000
Subtotal		$ 475,000
Add: Desired balance		
Loan balance (preaudit)	$ 6,300,000	
Less: AJE #1	(200,000)	
#2	(380,000)	
Loan balance (postaudit)	$ 5,720,000	
Reserve requirement	2%	
Desired balance (approx.)		115,000
Adjustment required		$ 590,000

There was a possibility that the parent company, Nuevo Financial Group, would contribute the additional equity capital. Also, management had been in contact with a potential outside investor about the possibility of investing $600,000. This investor, Manny Gonzalez, has strong ties to the Imperial Valley community and to the family ownership of Imperial Valley.

5. **Adequacy of General Reserve Requirement.** The general reserve requirement of 1.25 percent had not been met. Based on the client's reported outstanding loan balance of $6,300,000, a reserve of $78,750 would be necessary. However, audit adjustments for the charge-off of uncollectible loan amounts significantly affected the amount actually required. In addition, the auditors felt that a larger percentage would be necessary because of the client's history of problems with loan collections; initially, a 5 percent rate was proposed. Management felt this was much too high, arguing that the company had improved its lending procedures in the last few months and that it expected to have a smaller percentage of charge-offs in the future. A current delinquent report showed only two loans from 2016 still on the past due list. The auditors agreed to a 2 percent reserve, and an adjusting entry (AJE #3, shown in Exhibit 3) was made.

Regulatory Environment

Imperial Valley Community Bank was approaching certain regulatory filing deadlines during the course of the audit. Stanley had a meeting with the regulators at which representatives of management were present. Gonzalez also attended the meeting because he had expressed some interest in possibly making a capital contribution. There was a lot of discussion about the ability of Imperial Valley to keep its doors open if the loan losses were recorded as proposed by the auditors. This was a concern because the proposed adjustments would place the client in a position of having net equity capital significantly below minimum requirements.

The regulators were concerned about the adequacy of the 2 percent general reserve because of the prior collection problems experienced by Imperial Valley. The institution's solvency was a primary concern. At the time of the meeting, the regulators were quite busy trying to straighten out problems caused by the failure of two other community banks in Arizona. Many depositors had lost money as a result of the failure of these banks. Also, the regulators were unable to make a thorough audit of the company on their own, so they relied quite heavily on the work of Jacobs, Stanley & Company. In this sense, the audit was used as leverage on the institution to get more money in as a cushion to protect depositors. The regulators viewed this as essential in light of the other bank failures and the fact that the insurance protection mechanism for thrift and loan depositors was less substantial than depository insurance available through the Federal Deposit Insurance Corporation (FDIC) in commercial banks and in savings and loans (S&Ls).

Summary of the Client's Position

The management of Imperial Valley Community Bank placed a great deal of pressure on the auditors to reduce the amount of the loan write-offs. It maintained that the customers were "good for the money." Managers pointed out the payments to date on most of the loans had been made on a timely basis. The client felt that the auditors did not fully understand the nature of its business. Managers contended that a certain amount of risk had to be accepted in their business because they primarily made loans that commercial banks did not want to make. "We are the bank of last resort for many of our customers," commented bank president Eddie Salazar. Salazar then commented that the auditors' inability to understand and appreciate this element of the thrift and loan business was the main reason why the auditors were having trouble evaluating the collectibility of the outstanding loans. Management informed the auditors that they vouched for the collectibility of the outstanding loans.

Outstanding Loans

The auditors' contended that the payments to date, which were mostly annual interest amounts, were not necessarily a good indication that timely balloon principal payments would be made. They felt it was very difficult to evaluate the collectibility of the balloon payments adequately, primarily because the borrowers' source of cash for loan repayment had not been identified. They could not objectively audit or support borrowers' good intentions to pay or undocumented resources as represented by client management.

To ensure that they were not being naïve about the community bank, the auditors checked with colleagues in another office of the firm who knew more about this type of business. One professional in this office explained that the real secret of this business was to follow up ruthlessly with any nonpayer. The auditors certainly did not believe that this was being done by Imperial Valley management.

The auditors knew that Manny Gonzalez was a potential source of investment capital for Imperial Valley. They believed it was very important to give Gonzalez an accurate picture because if a rosier picture were painted than actually existed, and Gonzalez made an investment, then the audit firm would be a potential target for a lawsuit.

Board of Trustees

The auditors approached the nine-member board of trustees that oversaw the operations of Imperial Valley, three of whom also served on the audit committee. Of the nine board members, four were officers with the banks and five were "outsiders." All members of the audit committee were outsiders. The auditors had hoped to solicit the support of the audit committee in dealing with management over the audit opinion issue, as detailed in the next section. However, the auditors were concerned about the fact that all five outsiders had loans outstanding from Imperial Valley that carried 2 percent interest payments until the due date in two years. Perhaps not coincidentally, all five had supported management with respect to the validity of collateral and loan collectibility issues with customers.

Auditor Responsibilities

The management of Imperial Valley was pressuring the auditors to give an unmodified opinion. If the auditors decided to modify the opinion, then, in the client's view, this would present a picture to their customers and the regulators that their financial statements were not accurate. The client maintained that this would be a blow to its integrity and would shake depositors' confidence in the institution.

On one hand, the auditors were very cognizant of their responsibility to the regulatory authority, and they were also concerned about providing an accurate picture of Imperial Valley's financial health to Manny Gonzalez or other potential investors. On the other hand, they wondered whether they were holding the client to standards that were too strict. After all, the audit report issued in the preceding year was unmodified with an emphasis-of-matter paragraph on the capital impairment issue. They also wondered whether the doors of the institution would be closed by the regulators if they gave a qualified or adverse opinion. What impact could this action have on the depositors and the economic health of the community? Bill Stanley wondered whose interests they were really representing—depositors, shareholders, management, the local community, or regulators, or all of these.

Stanley knew that he would soon have to make a recommendation about the type of audit opinion to be issued on the 2016 financial statements. Before approaching the engagement review partner on the engagement, Stanley drafted the following memo to file.

Memo: Going-Concern Question

The question of the going-concern status of Imperial Valley Community Bank is being raised because of the client's continuing operating losses and high level of loan losses that has resulted in a "capital impairment" designation by the Arizona Department of Corporations. The client lost $920,000 after audit adjustments in 2016. This is in addition to a loss of $780,000 in 2015. Imperial Valley has also reported a loss of $45,000 for the first two months of 2017.

Imperial Valley is also out of compliance with regulatory capital requirements. After audit adjustments, the client has net equity capital of $610,000 as of December 31, 2016. The Arizona Department of Corporations requires a 6:1 ratio of thrift certificates to capital. As of December 31, 2016, these regulations would require net equity capital of $1,232,000. Imperial Valley was therefore undercapitalized by $622,000 at that date, and no additional capital contributions have been made subsequent to December 31. It is possible, however, that either the parent company, Nuevo Financial Group, or a private investor, Manny Gonzalez, will contribute additional equity capital.

We have been unable to obtain enough support for the value of much of the collateral backing outstanding loans. We also have concluded that there is a substantial doubt about the bank's ability to continue in business. The reasons for this conclusion include the following:

- The magnitude of losses, particularly loan losses, implies that Imperial Valley is not well managed.
- The losses are continuing in 2017. Annualized losses to date, without any provision for loan losses, are $270,000.
- Additional equity capital has not been contributed to date, although Gonzalez has $600,000 available.
- Our review of client loan files and lending policies raises an additional concern that loan losses may continue. If this happens, it would only exacerbate the conditions mentioned herein.

We also believe that it is not possible to test the liquidation value of the assets at this time should Imperial Valley cease to operate. The majority of client assets are loans receivable. These would presumably have to be discounted in order to be sold. In addition, there is some risk that the borrowers will simply stop making payments.

In conclusion, it is our opinion that a going-concern question exists for Imperial Valley Thrift & Loan at December 31, 2016.

Questions

1. What is the role of professional skepticism in auditing financial statements? Do you think that the auditors were skeptical enough in evaluating the operations of Imperial Valley? Explain.
2. What is the role of assessing risk including materiality in an audit? Do you think the auditors did an adequate job in this regard? Explain.
3. Assume that the auditors decide to support management's position and reduce the amount of loan write-offs. The decision was made in part because of concerns that regulators might force the bank to close its doors, and then many customers would have nowhere else to go to borrow money. Evaluate the ethics of the auditors' decision.

4. Assume that you were asked to review the information in this case as the engagement review partner on the audit of Imperial Valley Community Bank. How would you assess the quality of the audit? Include an assessment of internal controls in your analysis.

Case 5-4 Busy Season Planning

Romello Accounting LLP is a small CPA firm consisting of three partners and seven other professional staff. The firm offers full attestation and assurance services. Most of the work is for small and medium-sized nonpublic companies. The firm is registered with the PCAOB and does audits of about 30 penny stock or pink sheet companies and broker-dealers each year.

Tony Romello, the managing partner of the firm, has been the review partner on all audits for the last several years. Unfortunately, Tony encountered major health concerns in the last month and will not be available for the upcoming busy season. Michelle Thompson and Max King, the two remaining partners, are discussing staffing during the busy season.

"I am sorry that Tony is so ill, but I am concerned about our staff needs over the next three months. With two senior auditors and five staff auditors, we are all going to be very busy. I guess it is too late to hire experienced staff and get them trained quickly," Michelle stated.

"Don't forget that we will need a review partner," Max mused. "Hey, I could be the review partner for your audits and you can be review partner on my audits."

"I almost forgot that," Michelle said. "But don't we need to get a review partner who hasn't worked on the audits the last two years? That would exclude both of us, since we are switching off audits every five years. . . . Hey, maybe we can get Tom Mullins, CPA, to be our review partner on a contract basis?"

Max immediately objected. "You know that, as a retired Big Four audit partner, he would eat up our slim profits with his contract rate. Let's just make do this year and start planning to have a new partner by this time next year."

"We can't do that," Michelle countered. "When we have the PCAOB inspections, we will get penalized. We would also be cited in our peer reviews. No, no, I'm not comfortable thinking of not having a review partner. Also, without Tony this year, you and I will be busy supervising the staff without the added responsibilities of being review partner."

"Oh brother, you are such a rule follower!"

Questions

Consider the staffing of audits in responding to the following questions.

1. Identify the stakeholders of audits and their interests. Is there a difference between stakeholders and interests of public versus nonpublic companies?
2. What are a firm's considerations in having review partners? Does it really matter from a professional judgment perspective whether review partners rotate off after a prescribed number of years? Explain.
3. Assume Max convinces Michelle to let him serve as the review partner for all audits and Michelle will serve as the engagement partner on all audits. Do you see any problems with this approach from an ethical perspective?

Case 5-5 Tax Inversion (a GVV case)

Jamie Keller was pleased with his new job position as director of international consolidation for Gamma Enterprises. Gamma Enterprises was a consolidation of high-tech gaming companies, with subsidiaries of Alpha, Beta, Gamma, Delta, and Epsilon. This past year Gamma had completed a tax inversion with Epsilon, which is headquartered in Ireland, becoming the parent company. Gamma was the oldest company of the group and the only subsidiary with material inventory.

Jamie was preparing for a meeting with Jason Day, the CFO of the group, as well as the senior manager on the audit of Gamma. The discussion was planning for the year-end and issues with the tax inversion and consolidation with Epsilon as the parent company.

Jamie and Jason were in the conference room when Thomas Stein, the senior auditor, arrived. Jamie was surprised as Thomas was an accounting classmate from State University.

"Thomas, what a surprise! I did not know that we would be working together on the annual financial statements. Long time, no see," Jamie said.

"Yes, it's good to see you. We did many a team project together in school. Congratulations on your new position. Jason told me what a great job you were doing."

Jason cleared his throat and said, "I see we all know each other. Let's get started as I think there are a lot of year-end issues with this tax inversion. First, the company will keep the corporate physical headquarters here in Philadelphia, but many of the governance meetings will be at Epsilon headquarters in Dublin, Ireland. Jamie, I need you to prepare a study for the board to consider at the next meeting as to whether all the subsidiaries should change to IFRS for the consolidation or not. Thomas, can you briefly explain the issues with such a change?"

"Under IFRS most assets will be revalued to fair market values. That will increase the values on the balance sheet. The biggest drawback will be the taxes the company will owe with changing from LIFO to weighted average for Gamma's inventory," Thomas began.

"Hold on, a minute," Jason jumped in. "This tax inversion is to be a tax savings or tax-neutral situation, particularly this year when the stockholders are expecting profits. The U.S. government has allowed LIFO inventory for tax and financial reporting purposes so that is what Gamma is going to do."

Jamie asked, "Are you suggesting that Gamma continue using U.S. GAAP while the other subsidiaries change to the IFRS basis? If I remember correctly from school, a company must pick one financial reporting format and follow the principles in those standards. Besides, LIFO is not acceptable under IFRS."

"I don't see why it is a big deal to use IFRS for all but Gamma's inventory, Jason said. Thomas, what do you think?"

"I'm sure something can be worked out," Thomas replied.

The discussion changed to other issues. After the meeting, Jamie and Thomas went to lunch to catch up on old times. At lunch, Jamie commented, "Thomas, do you really mean to let Jason and Gamma Enterprises pick and choose which accounting standards to follow, using a mixed-bag approach?"

"No, you were right, Jamie. However, I could see that the issue was upsetting Jason. It may take time to convince him."

"I was just surprised that you seemed open to it at all. Aren't the auditors suppose to be the watchdogs of business?"

"Jamie, I am up for partner this next year. I need to keep Gamma as a happy client. The pressure to keep revenues coming into the accounting firm is a big weight on my shoulders."

"Well, just don't forget your values."

Questions

Assume you are Thomas's position and know that you have to let Jason know the correct way to convert to IFRS accounting.

- What will be the objections or pushback from Jason?
- What would you say next? What data and other information do you need to make your point and counteract the reasons and rationalizations you will likely have to address?

Consider whether Jamie and Thomas could work together to convince Jason (and the board) to change accounting methods. Identify the stakeholders in this case and their interests in addressing the following questions.

- What are the main arguments you are trying to counter? That is, what are the reasons and rationalizations you need to address?
- What is at stake for the key parties, including those who disagree with you?
- What levers can you use to influence those who disagree with you?
- What is your most powerful and persuasive response to the reasons and rationalizations you need to address? To whom should the argument be made? When and in what context?

Case 5-6 Rooster, Hen, Footer, and Burger

Barry Yellen, CPA, is a sole practitioner. The largest audit client in his office is Rooster Sportswear. Rooster is a privately owned company in Chicken Heights, Idaho, with a 12-person board of directors.

Barry is in the process of auditing Rooster's financial statements for the year ended December 31, 2016. He just discovered a related-party transaction that has him worried. For one thing, the relationship has existed for the past two years, but Barry did not discover it. What's just as troubling is that the client hid it from him.

Rooster bought out Hen Sportswear two years ago but still operates it as a separate entity, and since then has systematically failed to disclose to the private investors related-party transactions involving the CEO of Rooster, Frank Footer. It seems that Footer is borrowing money from Hen and is deeply in debt to the CEO of that company, who is his brother-in-law. Also, Hen has hired relatives of Footer, most of whom are unqualified for their jobs, and pays them an above-market salary. This has been hidden from Barry as well.

Barry was informed by an anonymous tipster that Rooster operates a secret off-balance-sheet cash account to pay for cash bonuses to senior officers, travel and entertainment expenses and an apartment rental for Footer, and cash and noncash gifts to local government officials to "grease the wheels" when permits need to be expedited in favor of Rooster. Barry doesn't know what to make of it, because he is too focused right now on the related-party transactions with Hen Sportswear.

Barry is in the process of questioning Hans Burger, CPA, who is the CFO of Rooster, about these transactions. Burger explains that he had raised these issues with Footer but was instructed in no uncertain terms to leave them alone. He did just that. Burger told Barry he needed this job and wouldn't jeopardize it out of a sense of "ethics."

Barry is in his office back at the firm and reflecting on how best to handle this matter.

Questions

1. What are related-party transactions and the obligations of Barry as the auditor of Rooster Sportswear? Why are related-party transactions a particularly sensitive area?
2. What are Barry's ethical obligations in this matter? Include in your discussion the issues of concern from an audit perspective and why they should be of concern to Barry in deciding what to do.

3. Assume you are Barry's best friend and he asks for your advice. What would you tell Barry and ethical reasoning in developing the advice.

Case 5-7 Diamond Foods: Accounting for Nuts[1]

Diamond Foods, based in Stockton, California, is a premium snack food and culinary nut company with diversified operations. The company had a reputation of making bold and expensive acquisitions. Due to competition within the snack food industry, Diamond developed an aggressive company culture that placed high emphasis upon performance. The company's slogan was "Bigger is better." However, without strong ethical oversight, questionable behavior started to persist at Diamond Foods in 2009. Serious allegations of fraud against top management led to a restructuring of leadership. Here is the story we dub: "Accounting for Nuts."

On November 14, 2012, Diamond Foods Inc. disclosed restated financial statements tied to an accounting scandal that reduced its earnings during the first three quarters of 2012 as it took significant charges related to improper accounting for payments to walnut growers. The restatements cut Diamond's earnings by 57 percent for FY2011, to $29.7 million, and by 46 percent for FY2010, to $23.2 million. By December 7, 2012, Diamond's share price had declined 54 percent for the year.

Diamond Foods, long-time maker of Emerald nuts and subsequent purchaser of Pop Secret popcorn (2008) and Kettle potato chips (2010), became the focus of an SEC investigation after The Wall Street Journal raised questions about the timing and accounting of Diamond's payments to walnut growers. The case focuses on the matching of costs and revenues. At the heart of the investigation was the question of whether Diamond senior management adjusted the accounting for the grower payments on purpose to increase profits for a given period.

The case arose in September 2011, when Douglas Barnhill, an accountant who is also a farmer of 75 acres of California walnut groves, got a mysterious check for nearly $46,000 from Diamond. Barnhill contacted Eric Heidman, the company's director of field operations, on whether the check was a final payment for his 2010 crop or prepayment for the 2011 harvest. (Diamond growers are paid in installments, with the final payment for the prior fall's crops coming late the following year.) Though it was September 2011, Barnhill was still waiting for full payment for the walnuts that he had sent Diamond in 2010. Heidman told Barnhill that the payment was for the 2010 crop, part of FY2011, but that it would be "budgeted into the next year." The problem is under accounting rules, you cannot legitimately record in a future fiscal year an amount for a prior year's crop. That amount should have been estimated during 2010 and recorded as an expense against revenue from the sale of walnuts.

An investigation by the audit committee in February 2012 found payments of $20 million to walnut growers in August 2010 and $60 million in September 2011 that were not recorded in the correct periods. The disclosure of financial restatements in November 2012 and audit committee investigation led to the resignation of former CEO Michael Mendes, who agreed to pay a $2.74 million cash clawback and return 6,665 shares to the company. Mendes's cash clawback was deducted from his retirement payout of $5.4 million. Former CFO Steven Neil was fired on November 19, 2012, and did not receive any severance. The SEC brought a lawsuit against Diamond Foods, Mendes and Neil. It settled with the company and Mendes on January 9, 2014. In a separate action Neil settled charges that he had directed the effort to fraudulently underreport money paid to walnut growers by delaying the recording of payments into later fiscal periods.

As a result of the audit committee investigation and the subsequent analysis and procedures performed, the company identified material weaknesses in three areas: control environment, walnut grower accounting, and accounts payable timing recognition. The company announced efforts to remediate these areas of material weakness, including enhanced oversight and controls, leadership changes, a revised walnut cost estimation policy, and improved financial and operation reporting throughout the organization.

An interesting aspect of the case is the number of red flags, including unusual timing of payments to growers, a leap in profit margins, and volatile inventories and cash flows. Moreover, the company seemed to push hard on

[1] Stanford University, United States District Court Northern District of California San Francisco Division: Case No. 11-cv-05386, *In Re: Diamond Foods, Inc. Securities Litigation Consolidated Complaint Class Action,* Available at: http://securities.stanford.edu/filings-documents/1048/DMND00_01/2012730_r01c_11CV05386.pdf.

every lever to meet increasingly ambitious earnings targets and allowed top executives to pull in big bonuses, according to interviews with former Diamond employees and board members, rivals, suppliers and consultants, in addition to reviews of public and nonpublic Diamond records.

Nick Feakins, a forensic accountant, noted the relentless climb in Diamond's profit margins, including an increase in net income as a percent of sales from 1.5 percent in FY2006 to more than 5 percent in FY2011. According to Feakins, "no competitors were improving like that; even with rising Asian demand." Reuters did a review of 11 companies listed as comparable organizations in Diamond's regulatory filings and found that only one, B&G Foods, which made multiple acquisitions, added earnings during the period.

Another red flag was that while net income growth is generally reflected in operating cash flow increases, at Diamond, the cash generation was sluggish in FY2010, when earnings were strong. This raises questions about the quality of earnings. Also, in September 2010, Mendes had promised EPS growth of 15 percent to 20 percent per year for the next five years. In FY2009, FY2010, and FY2011, $2.6 million of Mendes's $4.1 million in annual bonus was paid because Diamond beat its EPS goal, according to regulatory filings.

Diamond Foods fraudulent actions also stretched to falsely disclosing its strong overall financial performance in conference calls with financial analysts. In its call for the third quarter FY 2011, Mendes said: "Earnings per share had increased 73 percent to 52 cents, exceeding the top end of the company's guidance range. Strong operating cash flow for the period helped fund a significant increase in new product and advertising investment as EBITDA [Earnings before interest, taxes, depreciations and amortization] of $31 million was more than double the same period in the prior year."

As for the role of Deloitte in the fraud, the SEC charged that Neil misled them by giving false and incomplete information to justify the unusual accounting treatment for the payments. The SEC's order against Mendes found that he should have known that Diamond's reported walnut cost was incorrect because of information he received at the time, and he omitted facts in certain representations to Deloitte about the special walnut payments. One problem was Neil did not document accounting policies or design the process for which walnut grower payments and the walnut cost estimates were determined. This was exacerbated by the fact that management did not communicate the intent of the payments effectively.

Questions

1. Use the fraud triangle to analyze the business and audit risks that existed at Diamond Foods during the period of its accounting fraud.
2. Answer the following:
   a. Did Diamond Foods commit an illegal act? Explain.
   b. Evaluate the control environment at Diamond Foods.
3. Based on the facts of the case, do you think the auditors from Deloitte could have done more to identify the fraud at Diamond Foods? Were there any apparent deficiencies in their audit procedures and evaluation of the risk of material misstatement in the financial statements of Diamond Foods? Explain.

Case 5-8 Bill Young's Ethical Dilemma

Bill Young felt uneasy but good about downloading hundreds of pages of documents about Infant Products Inc., an audit client of his former CPA firm, Rogers & Autry, which involved the bribery of foreign government officials to gain favored treatment—a crime under the Foreign Corrupt Practice Act. He had stumbled upon the information while looking for other files online. Bill had already decided to quit his job and was in the process of cleaning up his office and boxing personal items. He thought about it but did not see anything wrong with the downloading. Besides, the bribery case involved selling tainted infant formula in China. Payments were made to government officials to look the other way.

Bill pondered what his options were. Should he inform management of the company even though he had handed in his official resignation letter? Should he disclose the matter to an investigative reporter who had been sniffing around the company for months following up on a tip he had received about improper foreign payments by the company? Or should he report the matter to the authorities? He also considered remaining silent. Bill carefully weighed these options by reflecting on the harms and benefits of his alternative courses of action.

Questions

1. You are Bill's best friend. Assume he asks for your advice about what he should do. What would you say and why? Support your answer with reference to relevant auditing and/or ethics requirements.

2. Bill is at home now having already spoken to you about the matter. He decides to carefully consider the consequences of his actions. What are the harms and benefits of the alternatives identified by Bill?

3. Assume Bill decides not to follow your advice but calls you again to let you know about his decision. If you sense an opportunity to provide additional input during the conversation, what would your advice be to Bill at this point and why?

Case 5-9 Royal Ahold N.V. (Ahold)

Ahold is a publicly held company organized in the Netherlands with securities registered with the SEC pursuant to Section 12(B) of the Exchange Act. Ahold's securities trade on the NYSE and are evidenced by American Depositary Receipts (ADRs).[1] Today its common shares are sold on NYSE Euronext.

As a foreign issuer, Ahold prepared its financial statements pursuant to Dutch accounting rules and included, in its filings with the commission, a reconciliation to U.S. GAAP and condensed financial statements prepared pursuant to U.S. GAAP.[2] Those were the rules at that time. However, today foreign companies listed on U.S. stock exchanges are allowed to submit their financial statements to the U.S. SEC using International Financial Reporting Standards (IFRS).

U.S. Foodservice (USF), a food service and distribution company with headquarters in Columbia, Maryland, is a wholly owned subsidiary of Ahold. USF was a publicly held company with securities registered with the SEC pursuant to Section 12(B) of the Exchange Act prior to being acquired by Ahold in April 2000.

Summary of the Charges against Ahold

On October 13, 2004, the SEC charged Royal Ahold N.V. (Ahold) with multiple violations of Section 17(A) of the Securities Act, Section 10(B) of the Exchange Act, and Exchange Act Rule 10(B-5). Charges were also filed against three former top executives: Cees van der Hoeven, the former CEO and chair of the executive board; A. Michael Meurs, the former CFO and executive board member; and Jan Andreae, the former executive vice president and executive board member. The commission also filed a related administrative action charging Roland

---

[1] An ADR represents ownership in the shares of a non-U.S. company and trades in U.S. financial markets. The stocks of many non-U.S. companies trade on U.S. stock exchanges through the use of ADRs. ADRs enable U.S. investors to buy shares in foreign companies without the hazards or inconveniences of cross-border and cross-currency transactions. ADRs carry prices in U.S. dollars, pay dividends in U.S. dollars, and can be traded like the shares of U.S.-based companies.

[2] Starting in 2005, members of the European Union (EU), including the Netherlands, adopted IFRS as the only acceptable standards for EU companies when filing statements with securities commissions in the European Union. Subsequent to the adoption, the SEC in the United States announced it would accept IFRS-based financial statement filings for foreign companies listing their stock on the NYSE and NASDAQ without reconciliation to U.S. GAAP. The United States has not adopted IFRS, although the SEC has established a method known as "condorsement" that calls for IFRS to be examined for conformity with U.S. GAAP and determination whether to endorse IFRS as a part of GAAP. These issues are discussed in Chapter 8.

Fahlin, a former member of Ahold's supervisory board and audit committee, with causing violations of the reporting, books and records, and internal control provisions of the securities laws.[3]

As a result of two frauds and other accounting errors and irregularities that are described in the following text, Ahold made materially false and misleading statements in SEC filings and in other public statements for at least fiscal years 1999 through 2001 and for the first three quarters of 2002. The company failed to adhere to the requirements of the Exchange Act and related rules that require each issuer of registered securities to make and keep books, records, and accounts that, in reasonable detail, accurately and fairly reflect the business of the issuer. The company also failed to devise and maintain a system of internal controls sufficient to provide reasonable assurances that, among other things, transactions are recorded as necessary to permit preparation of financial statements and to maintain the accountability of accounts.

The SEC's complaints, filed in the U.S. District Court for the District of Columbia, alleged that, as a result of the fraudulent inflation of promotional allowances at USF, the improper consolidation of joint ventures through fraudulent side letters, and other accounting errors and irregularities, Ahold's original SEC filings for at least fiscal years 2000 through 2002 were materially false and misleading. For fiscal years 2000 through 2002, Ahold overstated net sales by approximately $30 billion. Ahold overstated its operating income and net income by approximately $3.3 billion and $829 million, respectively, in total for fiscal years 2000 and 2001 and the first three quarters of 2002.

Ahold agreed to settle the commission's action, without admitting or denying the allegations in the complaint, by consenting to the entry of a judgment permanently enjoining the company from violating the antifraud and other provisions of the securities laws. Various officers of the company also settled charges, without admitting or denying the allegations in the complaint, by consenting to permanent injunctions and officer and director bars.

Statement of Facts

The following summarizes the main facts of the case with respect to transactions between Ahold and USF.

Budgeted Earnings Goals

From the time that it acquired USF in April 2000, Ahold and USF budgeted annual earnings goals for USF. Compensation for USF executives was based on, among other things, USF's meeting or exceeding budgeted earnings targets. USF executives each received a substantial bonus in early 2002 because USF purportedly satisfied earnings goals for FY2001. USF executives were each eligible for a substantial bonus if USF met earnings targets for FY2002. Certain USF executives engaged in or substantially participated in a scheme whereby USF reported earnings equal to or greater than the targets, regardless of the company's true performance.

Promotional Allowances

A significant portion of USF's operating income was based on payments by its vendors, referred to in various ways such as "promotional allowances," "rebates," "discounts," and "program money" (referred to below only as "promotional allowances"). During at least FY2001 and FY2002, USF made no significant profit on most of its end sales to its customers. Instead, the majority of USF's operating income was derived from promotional allowances.

In a typical promotional allowance agreement, USF committed to purchasing a minimum volume from a vendor. The vendor in turn paid USF a per-unit rebate of a portion of the original price that it charged USF, according to an agreed-upon payment schedule.

Sometimes the volume-based promotional allowances were paid as they were earned, but it was a common practice for the vendor to "prepay" on multiyear contracts at least some portion of the amounts that would be due if USF met all the projected purchase volume targets in the contract. Promotional allowances were critical to USF's financial results—without them, USF's operating income for FY2001 and FY2002 would have been materially reduced.

---

[3] U.S. Securities and Exchange Commission, Litigation Release No. 18929, October 13, 2004, Available at: www.sec.gov/litigation/litreleases/lr18929.htm.

False Confirmations and Statements

USF executives engaged in or substantially participated in a scheme whereby USF reported earnings equal to or greater than its earnings targets, regardless of the company's true performance. The primary method used to carry out this fraudulent scheme to "book to budget" was to inflate USF's promotional allowance income improperly. USF executives booked to budget by, among other things, causing USF to record completely fictitious promotional allowances that were sufficient to cover any shortfall to budgeted earnings.

USF executives covered up the false earnings by making it appear that the inflated promotional allowance income had been earned by (1) inducing vendors to confirm false promotional allowance income, payments, and receivable balances; (2) manipulating the promotional allowance accounts receivable from vendors and manipulating and misapplying cash receipts; and (3) making false and misleading statements and material omissions to the company's independent auditors, other company personnel, and/or Ahold personnel.

USF executives falsely represented to the company's independent auditors that there were no written promotional allowance contracts for the vast majority of promotional allowance agreements when in fact they knew, or were reckless in not knowing, that such written contracts existed. These executives falsely represented that USF had only handshake deals with its vendors that a USF executive would renegotiate at the end of each year to arrive at a mutually agreed-upon final amount due from each vendor for the year. They knew, or were reckless in not knowing, that these representations were false when they were made.

Interaction with Deloitte Auditors

Because USF lacked an internal auditing department, Ahold hired Deloitte to perform internal auditing services at USF, a practice permitted for the same external audit firm prior to SOX. Deloitte reported to the internal audit director of the company. In auditing the promotional allowances and internal control processes, a number of documents were requested from USF management, including the vendor contracts. Management refused to produce many of the requested documents. Several members of management refused to meet with the internal auditors, making the completion of internal audit objectives virtually impossible.

Deloitte conducted confirmations of the promotional allowances to verify income. Management had already induced vendors to falsely report promotional allowances to income amounts and receivables to the auditors and had concealed the existence of written contracts with USF vendors. Deloitte accepted confirmation letters via fax and from brokers and sales executives instead of financial officers.

For each vendor subject to the confirmation process, USF executives prepared a schedule purportedly reflecting the promotional allowances earned by USF for the year, the amount paid by the vendor, and the balance due. USF executives grossly inflated the figures contained in these schedules. The schedules were used both by USF to support the related amounts recorded in its financial statements and by its auditors to perform the year-end audit.

USF had no comprehensive, automated system for tracking the amounts owed by the vendors pursuant to the promotional allowance agreements. Instead, USF, for purposes of interim reporting, purported to estimate an overall "promotional allowance rate" as a percentage of sales and recorded periodic accruals based on that rate. Information provided by USF executives caused the estimated rate to be inflated. The intended and actual result of inflating USF's promotional allowance income was that USF, and Ahold, materially overstated their operating incomes. Deloitte did not detect this in its audit.

Fraudulent Acts by Management

As previously noted, USF executives contacted or directed subordinates to contact vendors to alert them that they would receive confirmation letters and to ask them to sign and return the letters without objection. If a vendor balked at signing the fraudulent confirmation, USF executives pressed the vendor by, for example, falsely representing that the confirmation was just "an internal number" and that USF did not consider the receivable reflected in the confirmation to be an actual debt that it would seek to collect. USF executives sent, or directed subordinates to send, side letters to vendors who continued to object to the fraudulent confirmations. The side letters assured the vendors that they did not, in fact, owe USF amounts reflected as outstanding in the confirmation letters.

USF executives attempted to prevent the discovery of the fraudulent scheme by making accounting entries that unilaterally deducted material amounts from the balances that USF owed to certain vendors for the products USF had purchased, and simultaneously credited the promotional allowance receivable balance for the amount of such deductions. These "deductions" were made at the end of the year and had the net effect of making it appear that USF had made material progress in collecting promotional allowance payments allegedly due.

The large year-end deductions facilitated the fraudulent recording of promotional allowance income because these deductions made it appear that the amounts recorded had been earned and paid. The USF executives concealed the fact that the deductions were not authorized nor legitimate and that a substantial percentage of the deductions were reversed in the early part of the following fiscal year.

USF executives also knew, or were reckless in not knowing, that the amounts paid by some vendors included prepayments on multi-year contracts. But they falsely represented to USF personnel, Ahold personnel, and/or the company's independent auditors that none of the promotional allowance agreements included such prepayments. As a result, USF treated the prepayments by vendors as if they were payments for currently owed promotional allowances. This made it falsely appear that USF was making material progress in collecting the inflated promotional allowance income that it had recorded.

Financial Statement Misstatements and Restatements

As a result of the schemes already described, USF materially overstated its operating income during at least FY2001 and FY2002. On February 24, 2003, Ahold announced that it would issue restated financial statements for previous periods and would delay filing its consolidated 2002 financial statements as a result of an initial internal investigation based, in part, on the overstatement of income at USF. Ahold announced in May 2003 that USF's income had been overstated by more than $800 million since April 2000. Ahold's stock price plummeted from approximately $10.69 per share to $4.16 per share.

Deloitte & Touche had been Ahold's group (the consolidated entity) auditor since the company went public. A few years after Ahold had acquired USF and the accounting fraud surfaced, investors sued the firm for engaging in deceptive conduct and recklessly disregarding misstatements in Ahold's financial statements. The charges were dismissed because it was concluded that Deloitte was being deceived by Ahold executives, many of whom went to great lengths to conceal the fraud.

Questions

1. Evaluate the facts and circumstances of the case using the Fraud Triangle. Discuss how auditors perform an audit and assess risk when red flags exist that the financial statements may be materially misstated.
2. Evaluate the role of Deloitte from the perspective of professional judgment by referring to the discussions in Chapters 4 and 5. Do you think Deloitte compromised its professional responsibilities in accepting evidence and explanations provided by the client for the joint venture and promotional allowance transactions? Explain.
3. The court ruled that Deloitte was not responsible for the fraud at Ahold because its management deceived the auditors and hid information from the firm. Do you think Deloitte compromised its ethical responsibilities in this case? Identify any such deficiencies and why you believe compromises existed.

Case 5-10 Groupon

The Groupon case was first discussed in Chapter 3. Here, we expand on the discussion of internal controls and the risk of material misstatement in the financial statements.

Groupon is a deal-of-the-day recommendation service for consumers. Launched in 2008, Groupon—a fusion of the words *group* and *coupon*—combines social media with collective buying clout to offer daily deals on products, services, and cultural events in local markets. Promotions are activated only after a certain number of people in a given city sign up.

Groupon pioneered the use of digital coupons in a way that created an explosive new market for local business. Paper coupon use had been declining for years. But when Groupon made it possible for online individuals to obtain deep discounts on products in local stores using e-mailed coupons, huge numbers of people started buying. Between June 2009 and June 2010, revenues grew to $100 million. Then, between June 2010 and June 2011, revenues exploded tenfold, reaching $1 billion. In August 2010, *Forbes* magazine labeled Groupon the world's fastest growing corporation. And that did not hurt the company's valuation when it went public in November 2011.

On November 5, 2011, Groupon took its company public with a buy-in price of $20 per share. Groupon shares rose from that IPO price of $20 by 40 percent in early trading on NASDAQ, and at the 4 p.m. market close, it was $26.11, up 31 percent. The closing price valued Groupon at $16.6 billion, making it more valuable than companies such as Adobe Systems and nearly the size of Yahoo. However, after disclosures of fraud and increased competition from the likes of AmazonLocal and LivingSocial, its value had dropped to about $6 billion.

Less than five months after its IPO on March 30, 2012, Groupon announced that it had revised its financial results, an unexpected restatement that deepened losses and raised questions about its accounting practices. As part of the revision, Groupon disclosed a "material weakness" in its internal controls saying that it had failed to set aside enough money to cover customer refunds. The accounting issue increased the company's losses in the fourth quarter to $64.9 million from $42.3 million. These amounts were material based on revenue of $500 million in the prior year. The news that day sent shares of Groupon tumbling 6 percent, to $17.29. Shares of Groupon had fallen by 30 percent since it went public, and the downward trend continues today.

In its announcement of the restatement, Groupon explained that it had encountered problems related to certain assumptions and forecasts that the company used to calculate its results. In particular, the company said that it underestimated customer refunds for higher-priced offers such as laser eye surgery.

Groupon collects more revenue on such deals, but it also carries a higher rate of refunds. The company honors customer refunds for the life of its coupons, so these payments can affect its financials at various times. Groupon deducts refunds within 60 days from revenue; after that, the company has to take an additional accounting charge related to the payments.

Groupon's restatement is partially a consequence of the "Groupon Promise" feature of its business model. The company pledges to refund deals if customers aren't satisfied. Because it had been selling those deals at higher prices—which leads to a higher rate of returns—it needed to set aside larger amounts to account for refunds, something it had not been doing.

The financial problems escalated after Groupon released its third-quarter 2012 earnings report, marking its first full-year cycle of earnings reports since its IPO. While the net operating results showed improvement year-to-year, the company still showed a net loss for the quarter. Moreover, while its revenue had been increasing in fiscal 2012, its operating profit had declined over 60 percent. This meant that its operating expenses were growing faster than its revenues, a sign that trouble might be lurking in the background. The company's stock price on NASDAQ went from $26.11 per share on November 5, 2011, the end of the IPO day, to $4.14 a share on November 30, 2012, a decline of more than 80 percent in one year. The company did not meet financial analysts' expectations for the third quarter of 2012.

There had been other oddities with Groupon's accounting that reflected a culture of indifference toward GAAP and its obligations to the investing public.

- It reported a 1,367 percent increase in revenue for the three months ending March 31, 2011 versus the same period in 2010

- It admitted to recognizing as revenue commissions received on sales of coupons/gift certificates, but also recognized the total value of the coupons and gift certificates at the date of sale.

As Groupon prepared its financial statements for 2011, its independent auditor, Ernst & Young (EY), determined that the company did not accurately account for the possibility of higher refunds. By the firm's assessment, that constituted a "material weakness." Groupon said in its annual report, "We did not maintain effective controls to provide reasonable assurance that accounts were complete and accurate." This meant that other transactions could be at risk because poor controls in one area tend to cause problems elsewhere. More important, the internal control problems raised questions about the management of the company and its corporate governance. But Groupon blamed EY for the admission of the internal control failure to spot the material weakness.

In a related issue, on April 3, 2012, a shareholder lawsuit was brought against Groupon accusing the company of misleading investors about its financial prospects in its IPO and concealing weak internal controls. According to the complaint, the company overstated revenue, issued materially false and misleading financial results, and concealed the fact that its business was not growing as fast and was not nearly as resistant to competition as it had suggested. These claims identified a gap in the sections of SOX that deal with companies' internal controls. There is no requirement to disclose a control weakness in a company's IPO prospectus.

The red flags had been waving even before the company went public in 2011. In preparing its IPO, the company used a financial metric that it called "Adjusted Consolidated Segment Operating Income." The problem was that that figure excluded marketing costs, which make up the bulk of the company's expenses. The net result was to make Groupon's financial results appear better than they actually were. In fact, a reported $81.6 million profit would have been a $98.3 million loss had the marketing costs been included. After the SEC raised questions about the metric—which *The Wall Street Journal* called "financial voodoo"—Groupon downplayed the formulation in its IPO documents.

Groupon reported the weakness in its internal controls through a Section 302 provision in SOX that requires public companies' top executives to evaluate each quarter whether their disclosure controls and procedures are effective. The company seems to have concluded that the internal control shortcoming was serious enough to treat as an overall deficiency in disclosure controls rather than pointing it out in its report on internal controls that is required under Section 404. EY expressed no opinion on the company's internal controls in its audit report, which makes us wonder whether it was willing to stand up to Groupon's management on the shortcomings in its internal controls and governance. In fact, the firm signed clean audit opinions for four years.

Questions

1. Prompted by frauds such as at Groupon, which was carried out in part by creating a metric that is not recognized in the accounting literature, although not specifically prohibited either, the PCAOB has issued a release requesting comments on a proposal to include either in the audit report or as a separate document an *Auditor's Discussion and Analysis (AD&A)*. It would be an analog of the management's discussion and analysis (MD&A) currently required in certain filings under the federal securities laws. The idea is to give users a more detailed view both of the auditor's work and impressions and concerns about the entity being audited.

   Do you think the AD&A is a good idea? Should it comment on the audit, the company's financial statements, or both? Should it comment on any other information? Explain.

2. The role of Ernst & Young in the Groupon fraud is somewhat unclear. The firm did render unmodified opinions for four years. Do you believe it is possible that an audit firm can render an unmodified opinion and have no responsibility for detecting and reporting a financial fraud? Explain in general and specifically with reference to the fraud at Groupon.

3. According to a 2012 survey of 192 U.S. executives conducted by Deloitte & Touche LLP and Forbes Insights, social media was identified as the fourth-largest risk on par with financial risk.[1] This ranking derives from social media's capacity to accelerate to other risks, such as financial risk associated with disclosures in violation of SEC rules, for example. Other risks inherent to social media include information leaks, reputational damage to brand, noncompliance with regulatory requirements, third-party, and governance risks.

---

[1]Deloitte & Forbes Insight, Aftershock: Adjusting to the New World of Risk Management, Available at: http://deloitte.wsj.com/cfo/files/2012/10/Aftershock_Adjusting-to-the-new-world-of-risk-management.pdf

a. Why is it important for a firm such as EY, in a case such as Groupon, to fully understand the nature of risk when a company conducts its business online?

b. What role can internal auditors play in dealing with such risks?

c. How should external auditors adapt their risk assessment procedures for social media/networking clients?

Chapter

Legal, Regulatory, and Professional Obligations of Auditors

Learning Objectives

After studying Chapter 6, you should be able to:

LO 6-1 Distinguish between common-law rulings and auditors' legal liability.

LO 6-2 Explain the basis for auditors' statutory legal liability.

LO 6-3 Discuss auditors' legal liabilities under SOX.

LO 6-4 Explain the provisions of the FCPA.

LO 6-5 Describe the cultural and professional constraints on adopting IFRS.

LO 6-6 Distinguish between legal compliance and management by values.

LO 6-7 Discuss the factors that promote global ethics, and prevent global fraud and bribery.

Ethics Reflection

Auditors are potentially liable for both criminal and civil offenses. Auditors can be found liable in cases where they have breached their responsibilities to perform work with professional competence and due care and to act independently of their clients. Their legal liabilities stem from the fact that audit failures harm parties that have suffered as a result (i.e., shareholders). Third-parties also may be harmed as a result of the failure (i.e., banks and other financial institutions). Those harmed can sue for damages if they can show knowledge of the falsehood on the part of the auditors and reliance on the materially misleading financial statements by third parties to their detriment.

On April 20, 2015, PricewaterhouseCoopers (PwC) agreed to pay $65 million to settle claims over its audits of the failed investment company MF Global. According to the original complaint filed in U.S. District Court Southern District of New York, MF Global charged PwC with professional malpractice, breach of contract, and unjust enrichment in connection with its advice concerning, and approval of, the company's off-balance-sheet accounting for its investments.

The decision notes that:

> "But for PwC's erroneous accounting advice, MF Global Holdings could not have—and would not have—invested heavily in European sovereign debt to generate immediate revenues and would not have suffered the massive damages that befell the company in 2011. Had PwC met its duty to provide accounting advice and auditing services consistent with the professional standards of ordinary skill, prudence, and diligence, it would have advised MF Global Holdings that the transactions had to be recorded on the company's consolidated financial statements as secured financings and not as sales. In that circumstance, the company would never have amassed the enormous Euro exposure it did, nor would it have suffered massive damages as a direct and proximate result of PwC's negligence and malpractice."

The brokerage firm collapsed in October 2011 after former New Jersey Governor and Senator Jon Corzine took over as chairman and CEO in 2010 and pushed the firm to invest about $6.3 billion in risky sovereign debt from troubled countries in the Eurozone. MF Global had employed questionable transactions known as repo-to-maturity, using the sovereign debt bonds as collateral for the loans it took out, while earning money from the spread between the rate on the bonds and the rate it paid to the counterparty on the financing.[1]

MF Global agreed to pay $200 million in civil fines. The firm's shareholders had sued PwC for its audits of MF Global in 2010 and 2011 that failed to detect problems with the firm's financial statements. The shareholders had contended that PwC's audits gave MF Global a clean bill of health even though the accounting firm knew or should have known that the firm's financial statements were erroneous and its internal controls weren't effective.

PwC settled the lawsuit without admitting wrongdoing. As is typical of the disclaimer in this kind of lawsuit, a PwC spokesperson, Caroline Nolan, said, "PwC is pleased to resolve this matter and avoid the cost and distraction of prolonged securities litigation. The firm stands behind its audit work and its opinions on MF Global's financial statements."

The PwC settlement was the second in the course of one week in 2015 in which a Big Four accounting firm settled claims about its work for a major securities firm that later collapsed. Ernst & Young (EY) agreed to pay $10 million to settle allegations from the New York Attorney General's office that it turned a blind eye to problems at its client Lehman Brothers Holdings Inc. before Lehman's 2008 collapse.[2]

Back in 2001, Lehman Brothers bankers dreamed up a scheme that they named "Repo 105" to temporarily "sell" bad debts on condition that they would repurchase them a week to 10 days later. The term *repo* is derived from "repossess" and 105 referred to the 5 percent premium it paid for the service, as opposed to the usual 2 percent. With the worst deals taken off its balance sheet, the bank appeared more financially healthy than it actually was.

"If auditors issue opinions that are unreliable or provide cover for their clients by helping to hide material information, that harms the investing public, our economy, and our country," Eric Schneiderman, attorney general of New York State, said in a public statement issued after the settlement with EY. "Auditors will be held accountable when they violate the law, just as they are supposed to hold the companies they audit accountable."[3]

As you read this chapter, think about the following questions: (1) What is the link between professional ethics and legal liability? (2) What are the standards of practice that underlie potential legal liability? (3) When can legal liability exist in global operations?

"Accountants must be prepared to compensate all foreseeable victims whose economic losses are proximately caused by the accountants' negligent statements."

U.S. Supreme Court Justice Benjamin Cardozo

In the first major U.S. Supreme Court ruling on accountants' legal liability (*Ultramares v. Touche*, 1933), Justice Benjamin Cardozo expressed his deep concern for the future of the developing public accounting profession. His statement above created the first common-law legal liability standard for auditors, known as the privity/near privity rule. This standard would ultimately be accompanied by others that addressed third-party liability as more and more lawsuits were filed against auditors for negligence/gross negligence and fraud. The first part of this chapter addresses those standards and applies them in a variety of cases where auditors were sued for their failure to follow GAAP and GAAS, exercise due care, and approach the audit with the requisite professional skepticism. Later on we address global regulatory issues.

Legal Liability of Auditors: An Overview

LO 6-1
Distinguish between common-law rulings and auditors' legal liability.

Zoe-Vonna Palmrose, a former professor at the University of Southern California and now at the University of Washington, identifies the four general stages in an audit-related dispute: (1) the occurrence of events that result in losses for users of the financial statements, (2) the investigation by plaintiff attorneys before filing, to link the user losses with allegations of material omissions or misstatements of financial statements, (3) the legal process, which commences with the filing of the lawsuit, and (4) the final resolution of the dispute.[4] The first stage comes about as a result of some loss-generating event, including client bankruptcy, fraudulent financial reporting, and the misappropriation of assets.

Auditors can be sued by clients, investors, creditors, and the government for failure to perform services adequately and in accordance with the profession's ethics standards. Auditors can be held liable under two classes of law: (1) common law and (2) statutory law. Common-law liability evolves from legal opinions issued by judges in deciding a case. These opinions become legal principles that set a precedent and guide judges in deciding similar cases in the future. Statutory law reflects legislation passed at the state or federal level that establishes certain courses of conduct that must be adhered to by covered parties.[5]

Exhibit 6.1 summarizes the types of liability and auditors' actions that result in liability.

EXHIBIT 6.1 Summary of Types of Liability and Auditors' Actions Resulting in Liability

Types of Liability	Auditors' Actions Resulting in Liability
Common law—clients	Breach of contract (privity relationship)
	Negligence
	Gross negligence/constructive fraud
	Fraud
Common law—third parties	Negligence
	Gross negligence/constructive fraud
	Fraud
Federal statutory law—civil liability	Negligence
	Gross negligence/constructive fraud
	Fraud
Federal statutory law—criminal liability	Willful violation of federal statutes

Source: William F. Messier Jr., Steven M. Glover, and Douglas F. Prawitt, *Auditing and Assurance Services: A Systematic Approach* (New York: McGraw-Hill Irwin, 2012), p. 664.

Common-Law Liability

Common-law liability requires the auditor to perform professional services with due care. Evidence of having exercised due care exists if the auditor can demonstrate having performed services with the same degree of skill and judgment possessed by others in the profession. Typically, an auditor would cite adherence to generally accepted auditing standards as evidence of having exercised due care in conducting the audit. Due care includes exercising the degree of professional skepticism expected in the audit of financial statements.

Breach of contract is a claim that accounting and auditing services were not performed in a way consistent with the terms of a contract. Although auditors may have contractual relationships with third parties, cases involving breach of contract are brought most frequently against auditors by their clients.[6]

Tort actions (for wrongdoings) cover other civil complaints (e.g., fraud, deceit, and injury) arising from auditors' failure to exercise the appropriate level of professional care sometimes referred to as substantiated performance. Clients or users of financial statements can bring tort actions against auditors.[7]

Lawsuits for damages under common law usually result when someone suffers a financial loss after relying on financial statements later found to be materially misstated. Plaintiffs in legal actions involving auditors, such as clients or third-party users of financial statements, generally assert all possible causes of action, including breach of contract, tort, deceit, fraud, and anything else that may be relevant to the claim. These cases are often referred to as "audit failures" in the financial press.

Liability to Clients—Privity Relationship

An accountant has a contractual obligation to the client that creates a *privity relationship*. A client can bring a lawsuit against an accountant for failing to live up to the terms of the contract, asserting breach of contract, and other tort actions. When privity exists, plaintiffs must demonstrate all of the following:[8]

1. They suffered an economic loss.

2. Auditors did not perform in accordance with the terms of the contract, thereby breaching that contract.

3. Auditors failed to exercise the appropriate level of professional care related to tort actions.

4. The breach of contract or failure to exercise the appropriate level of care caused the loss.

In addition to breach of contract, auditors may be liable to clients for tort liability that ranges from simple ordinary negligence to the more serious case of fraud. In the case of ordinary negligence, the auditor failed to exercise due care or the standard of care that other accountants would have done in similar situations. Notice the link to ethical responsibilities of accountants and auditors through the due care ethics rule and the *universality perspective*. The legal interpretation of the due care rule is linked to what accountants would have done in similar situations (for similar reasons) through the *categorical imperative* (Kantian Rights) ethical reasoning method. Finally, legal liability between the ordinary negligence responsibility and fraud includes gross negligence or constructive fraud that represents an extreme or reckless departure from professional standards of care.

Ultramares v. Touche

In the 1933 landmark case, *Ultramares v. Touche,* that was referred to in the opening quote, the New York State Court of Appeals held that a cause of action based on negligence could not be maintained by a third party who was not in contractual privity. The court did leave open the possibility that a third party could successfully sue for gross negligence that constitutes fraud and fraud.[9]

Ultramares had lent $100,000 to Fred Stern & Company. Before making the loan, the company had asked Stern to provide an audited balance sheet, and Stern had its auditor, Touche Ross & Co. (now Deloitte & Touche), do so. The firm issued an unqualified audit report. Subsequently, the company went bankrupt, and it was alleged that false accounting entries had been made to conceal the company's problems. Ultramares alleged that Touche had been both negligent and fraudulent in its audit of Stern. Because the privity relationship did not exist for Ultramares and Stern, the fraud charges against Touche were dismissed. However, the jury ruled that Touche had been negligent and awarded Ultramares about $186,000 in damages.

The importance of the *Ultramares* decision is that third parties (i.e., Ultramares) without privity could sue if negligence was so great as to constitute gross negligence. The opinion of the New York Court of Appeals was written by Judge Benjamin Cardozo:

If a liability for negligence exists, a thoughtless slip or blunder, the failure to detect a theft or forgery beneath the cover of deceptive entries, may expose accountants to a liability in an indeterminate amount for an indeterminate time to an indeterminate class [third parties]. The hazards of a business on these terms are so extreme as to [raise] doubt whether a flaw may not exist in the implication of a duty that exposes to these circumstances.

The *Ultramares* decision was the first of three different judicial approaches to deciding the extent of an accountant's liability to third parties. The other two are the *Restatement (Second) of the Law of Torts* approach and the foreseeable third-party approach. Both are described in the following text.

Liability to Third Parties

Near-Privity Relationship

While the *Ultramares* decision established a strict privity standard, a number of subsequent court decisions in other states moved away from this standard over time. Following years of broadening the auditor's liability to third parties to include those that were "foreseen"and "reasonably foreseeable" (which we will discuss shortly), in a 1985 decision, the court seemed to move the pendulum back in favor of limiting the liability of accountants to third parties based on the privity standard. The New York Court of Appeals expanded the privity standard in the case of *Credit Alliance v. Arthur Andersen & Co.*[10] to include a *near-privity relationship* between third parties and the accountant. In the case, Credit Alliance was the principal lender to the client and demonstrated that Andersen had known Credit Alliance was relying on the client's financial statements prior to extending credit. The court also ruled that there had been direct communication between the lender and the auditor regarding the client.

The *Credit Alliance* case establishes the following tests that must be satisfied for holding auditors liable for negligence to third parties: (1) knowledge by the accountant that the financial statements are to be used for a particular purpose; (2) the intention of the third party to rely on those statements; and (3) some action by the accountant linking him or her to the third party that provides evidence of the accountant's understanding of intended reliance. The 1992 New York Court of Appeals decision in *Security Pacific Business Credit, Inc. v. Peat Marwick Main & Co.*[11] sharpens the last criterion in its determination that the third party must be known to the auditor, who directly conveys the audited report to the third party or acts to induce reliance on the report.

Actually Foreseen Third Parties

The "middle ground" approach followed by the vast majority of states (and federal courts located within those states) expands the class of third parties that can sue successfully an auditor for negligence beyond near-privity to a person or limited group of persons whose reliance is (*actually*) *foreseen,* even if the specific person or group is unknown to the auditor.[12]

The courts have deviated from the *Ultramares* principle through a variety of decisions. For example, a federal district court in Rhode Island decided a case in 1968, *Rusch Factors, Inc. v. Levin,*[13] that held an accountant liable for negligence to a third party that was not in privity of contract. In that case, Rusch Factors had requested financial statements prior to granting a loan. Levin audited the statements, which showed the company to be solvent when it was actually insolvent. After the company went into receivership, Rusch Factors sued, and the court ruled that the *Ultramares* doctrine was inappropriate. In its decision, the court relied heavily on the *Restatement (Second) of the Law of Torts.*

Restatement (Second) of the Law of Torts

The Restatement (Second) of the Law of Torts approach, sometimes known as Restatement 552,[14] expands accountants' legal liability exposure for negligence beyond those with near privity (actually foreseen) to a small group of persons and classes who are or *should be* foreseen by the auditor as relying on the financial information. This is known as the *foreseen third-party* concept because even though there is no privity relationship, the accountant knew that that party or those parties would rely on the financial statements for a specified transaction.

Section 552 states: "The liability . . . is limited to loss (a) suffered by the person or one of the persons for whose benefit and guidance he or she intends to supply the information, or knows that the recipient [client] intends to supply it; and (b) through reliance upon it in a transaction which he or she intends the information to influence, or knows that the recipient so intends." For example, assume that a client asks an accountant to prepare financial statements and the accountant knows that those statements will be used to request a loan from one or more financial institutions. The accountant may not know the specific bank to be approached, but he or she does know the purpose for which the statements will be used. Thus, the third parties as a class of potential users can be foreseen.

A majority of states now use the modified privity requirement imposed by Section 552 of the *Restatement (Second) of the Law of Torts*. The *Restatement* modifies the traditional rule of privity by allowing nonclients to sue accountants for negligent misrepresentation, provided that they belong to a "limited group" and provided that the accountant had actual knowledge that his or her professional opinion would be supplied to that group. In some state court decisions, a less restrictive interpretation of Section 552 has been made. For example, a 1986 decision by the Texas Court of Appeals in *Blue Bell, Inc. v. Peat, Marwick, Mitchell & Co.* (now KPMG) held that if an accountant preparing audited statements knows or should know that such statements will be relied upon, the accountant may be held liable for negligent misrepresentation.[15]

Reasonably Foreseeable Third Parties

A third judicial approach to third-party liability expands the legal liability of accountants well beyond *Ultramares*. The *reasonably foreseeable third-party* approach results from a 1983 decision by the New Jersey Supreme Court in *Rosenblum, Inc. v. Adler*.[16] In that case, the Rosenblum family agreed to sell its retail catalog showroom business to Giant Stores, a corporation operating discount department stores, in exchange for Giant common stock. The Rosenblums relied on Giant's 1971 and 1972 financial statements, which had been audited by Touche. When the statements were found to be fraudulent and the stock was deemed worthless, the investors sued Touche. The lower courts did not allow the Rosenblums' claims against Touche on the grounds that the plaintiffs did not meet either the *Ultramares* privity test or the *Restatement* standard. The case was taken to the New Jersey Supreme Court, and it overturned the lower courts' decision, ruling that auditors can be held liable for ordinary negligence to all *reasonably foreseeable third parties* who are recipients of the financial statements for routine business purposes. In finding for Rosenblum on certain motions, the Court held, "Independent auditors have a duty of care to all persons whom the auditor should reasonably foresee as recipients of the statements from the company for proper business purposes, provided that the recipients rely on those financial statements. It is well recognized that audited financial statements are made for the use of third parties who have no direct relationship with the auditor. Auditors have responsibility not only to the client who pays the fee but also to investors, creditors, and others who rely on the audited financial statements."

Another important case that followed this approach was *Citizens State Bank v. Timm, Schmidt, & Company*.[17] In this case, the bank sued the public accounting firm after relying on financial statements for one of its debtors that had been audited by Timm. The Wisconsin court used a number of reasons for extending auditors' liability beyond privity. The following quote from the case demonstrates the court's rather liberal leanings with respect to auditor legal liability to third parties: "If relying third parties, such as creditors, are not allowed to recover, the cost of credit to the general public will increase because creditors will either have to absorb the cost of bad loans made in reliance on faulty information or hire independent accountants to verify the information received."

Since 1987, no state high court has adopted this foreseeability approach to accountants' legal liability, while a large number have approved or adopted one of the narrower standards.[18] For example, in its 1992 ruling in *Bily v. Arthur Young,* the California Supreme Court expressly rejected the foreseeability approach in favor of the *Rusch Factors* or *Restatement* standard. The court gave a number of reasons for rejecting the *Rosenblum* foreseeability approach, including that the foreseeability rule exposes auditors to potential liability in excess of their proportionate share and the sophisticated plaintiffs have other ways to protect themselves from the risk of inaccurate financial statements (e.g., they can negotiate improved terms or hire their own auditor).[19]

However, in its 2003 ruling in *Murphy v. BDO Seidman, LLP,* the California Court of Appeals ruled that "grapevine plaintiffs," who alleged indirect reliance based on what others (e.g., stockholders and stockbrokers) told them about the financial statements, had legal claims for ordinary negligence against the auditors so long as the auditor would have reasonably foreseen that stockholders or stockbrokers would tell other people of the content of the financial statements and that the other people would rely upon the misrepresentations in purchasing the corporate stock. The court ruled that nothing in the *Bily* decision precludes indirect reliance.[20]

The *Murphy* ruling seems to stretch auditors' legal liability to third parties beyond reasonable bounds. Imagine, for example, that you are watching Jim Cramer's television show "Mad Money" on CNBC, and Cramer recommends a stock that you then purchase online. Shortly thereafter, news breaks of an accounting fraud. You sue the auditors based on your belief that the auditors should have known the public would buy the stock after Cramer recommended it. It makes little sense to conclude that a plaintiff may be successful in a lawsuit against the auditors based on a claim of ordinary negligence in this situation, given that auditors cannot control every use of audit information.

The conflicting common-law rulings can be confusing in trying to apply legal precedent to current court cases. To assist students, we have developed a summary in Exhibit 6.2 of the primary legal issues and guiding principles addressed in important court cases in deciding the auditor's liability to third parties.

EXHIBIT 6.2 **Auditor Legal Liability to Third Parties**

Legal Approach	Case	Legal Principle	Legal Liability to Third Parties
Ultramares	*Ultramares v. Touche*	Privity (only clients can sue)	Possibly gross negligence that constitutes (constructive) fraud
Near-privity relationship	*Credit Alliance*	Three-pronged approach: knowledge of accountant that the statements will be used for a particular purpose; intention of third party to rely on those statements; some action by third party that provides evidence of the accountant's understanding of intended reliance	Ordinary negligence

(Continued)

Restatement (Second) of the Law of Torts	Rusch Factors	Actually foreseen third-party users	Ordinary negligence beyond near-privity
Foreseeable third party	Rosenblum	Reasonably foreseeable third-party users	Ordinary negligence with reliance on the statements

Liability for fraud is not restricted to cases where the auditor had knowledge of the deceit. Some courts have interpreted gross negligence (i.e., constructive fraud) as an instance of fraud. Such fraud occurs when the auditor acts so carelessly in the application of professional standards that it implies a reckless disregard for the standards of due care. Examples are if the auditor failed to observe the physical count of inventory at year-end or to confirm accounts receivable.

The legal liability of accountants is not limited to audited statements. In the 1967 case *1136 Tenants Corp. v. Max Rothenberg & Co.,*[21] an accounting firm was sued for negligent failure to discover embezzlement by the managing agent who had hired the firm to "write up" the books, which did not include any audit procedures. The firm was held liable for failure to inquire or communicate about missing invoices, despite a disclaimer on the financial statements informing users that "No independent verification were undertaken thereon." The firm moved to dismiss the case, but the court denied the motion and held that even if a CPA "acted as a robot, merely doing copy work," there was an issue as to whether there were suspicious circumstances relating to missing invoices that imposed a duty on the firm to warn the client. When the case went to trial, the court found there to be an engagement to audit and entered a judgment for more than $237,000 despite the firm's oral evidence that it was employed for $600 annually to write up the books.

SSARS and Engagement Letters

The *1136* case affected auditing standards in two notable areas. First, the engagement letter was developed to clarify the responsibilities of accountants and auditors in performing professional services. The engagement letter formalizes the relationship between the auditor and the client. It serves as a contract detailing the responsibilities of the accountant or auditor and expectations for management.

A second result was that the Accounting and Review Services Committee of the AICPA, a senior technical committee, was formed to formulate standards to be followed by accountants who perform two levels of service—a compilation and a review. A *review* provides limited assurance that the financial statements are free of material misstatements (a lower standard than the reasonable assurance requirement in the audit), while a *compilation* provides no assurance because the only services provided are of a bookkeeping nature.

Engagement letters are used for audit engagements; however, the clarified auditing standards are not definitive with respect to whether engagement letters are required for a compilation or review. If auditors do not use the engagement letter, they should have a good reason for not having one, have that reason documented in writing in the workpapers, document in the workpapers their understanding with the client for the services to be provided in the engagement, and document in the workpapers why they are sure there's no misunderstanding between them and their client.[22]

Under Statements on Standards for Accounting and Review Services (SSARS) 21, the documentation for a compilation and review should include an engagement letter. When the word *should* appears, it identifies a presumptively mandatory requirement. That means compliance is required anytime the situation exists which is covered by that requirement. The only exception is when the workpapers document the reason for the departure and how alternative procedures have accomplished the same objective. The purpose of an engagement letter is to make it clear what services will be provided during the engagement and to make sure that there is no misunderstanding with the client. A written engagement letter accomplishes that purpose.[23]

Auditor Liability to Third Parties

Plaintiff Claims for Action

Common-law liability for fraud is available to third parties in any jurisdiction. The plaintiff (third party) must prove (1) a false representation by the accountant, (2) knowledge or belief by the accountant that the representation was false, (3) that the accountant intended to induce the third party to rely on false representation, (4) that the third party relied on the false representation, and (5) that the third party suffered damages.[24]

Courts have held that fraudulent intent or scienter may be established by proof that the accountant acted with knowledge of the false representation. However, liability for fraud is not limited to cases where the auditor was knowingly deceitful. Some courts have interpreted gross negligence or constructive fraud as an instance of fraud. An important case in this area is *State Street Trust Co. v. Ernst.*[25] In this case, the auditors issued an unqualified opinion on their client's financial statements, knowing that State Street Trust Company was making a loan based on those financial statements. A month later, the auditors sent a letter to the client indicating that receivables had been overstated. The auditors, however, did not communicate this information to State Street, and the client subsequently went bankrupt. The New York court ruled that the auditor's actions appeared to be grossly negligent and that "reckless disregard of consequences may take the place of deliberate intention." In such cases, while fraudulent intent may not be present, the court "constructs" fraud due to the grossness of the negligence.[26]

In *Phar-Mor v. Coopers & Lybrand,* (now PricewaterhouseCoopers) the auditors were found guilty of fraud under both common and statutory law, even though the plaintiffs acknowledged that the auditors had no intent to deceive. Instead, the plaintiff successfully argued reckless disregard for the truth (i.e., gross negligence or constructive fraud), which gives rise to an inference of fraud. An important part of this ruling is that plaintiffs who are barred from suing for ordinary negligence because they lack a privity relationship or are not foreseen users can choose to sue the auditor for fraud because to find an auditor guilty of fraud, the plaintiffs need only prove gross negligence.[27]

In more recent cases, the court ruled in *Houbigant, Inc. v. Deloitte & Touche LLP* [28] and *Reisman v. KPMG Peat Marwick LLP*[29] that for an auditor to be found guilty of fraud, the plaintiffs must prove only that the auditor was aware that its misrepresentations might reasonably be relied upon by the plaintiff, not that the auditor intended to induce the detrimental reliance. The court referred to recent audit failures in its *Houbigant* decision: "It should be sufficient that the complaint contains some rational basis for inferring that the alleged misrepresentation was knowingly made. Indeed, to require anything beyond that would be particularly undesirable at this time, when it has been widely acknowledged that our society is experiencing a proliferation of frauds perpetrated by officers of large corporations . . . unchecked by the 'impartial' auditors they hired."[30]

Auditor Defenses

The auditor's defense against third-party lawsuits for negligence that claim the auditor did not detect a misstatement or fraud requires proof that (1) the auditor did not have a duty to the third party, (2) the third party was negligent, (3) the auditor's work was performed in accordance with professional standards, (4) the third party did not suffer a loss, (5) any loss to the third party was caused by other events, or (6) the claim is invalid because the statute of limitations has expired.[31] Here are examples of the various defenses that an auditor can use:

1. Auditors can defend a common-law action by presenting arguments and evidence to rebut third-party plaintiffs' claims and evidence. Once a plaintiff has demonstrated an economic loss and materially misstated financial statements, defenses available to auditors against third parties include the following:[32] The third party lacked standing to sue in a particular jurisdiction, as would be the case when bringing a lawsuit for ordinary negligence; and the appropriate relationship between the auditor and third party did not exist (i.e., a privity relationship).

2. The third party's loss was due to events other than the financial statements and auditors' examination, as might be the case if poor business practices or stock market declines caused the loss.

3. Auditors' work was performed in accordance with accepted auditing standards (e.g., AICPA or PCAOB standards), which is generally interpreted to mean that auditors were not negligent (ordinary negligence).

Grant Thornton LLP v. Prospect High Income Fund, et al.

A Texas Supreme Court decision in 2010 in the case of *Grant Thornton LLP v. Prospect High Income Fund, et al.* has strengthened defenses available to auditors brought by third parties for negligent misrepresentation and fraud. The Court overruled what had been a broader standard for establishing liability in negligent misrepresentations when financial failings of their clients exist. The ruling also sets new limitations on "holder" claims, wherein investors contend that they were put at a disadvantage because they held securities based on an auditor's report that they otherwise would have sold.[33] Given the potential importance of the case, we present a summary of the ruling in Exhibit 6.3.

EXHIBIT 6.3   *Grant Thornton LLP v. Prospect High Income Fund, et al.*

Background

Epic Resorts, a timeshare operator, issued $130 million in corporate bonds in 1998 and sold them in the open market. Epic was required to make semiannual interest payments of $8.45 million to bondholders. To secure the interest payments, it was also required to maintain $8.45 million in an escrow account at U.S. Trust, which served as both the indenture trustee and escrow agent, for the benefit of the bondholders. Epic was required to provide annual audited financial statements, as well as a negative assurance statement from its auditors confirming that Epic was in compliance with the financial conditions of the indenture and related agreements.

Grant Thornton was engaged as Epic's auditor in March 2000, and subsequently audited Epic's financial statements for both 1999 and 2000. In the course of its 1999 audit, Grant discovered that Epic did not have the minimum required amount in the U.S. Trust account. Despite this deficiency, in April 2000, Grant issued an unqualified opinion on Epic's 1999 financial statements and confirmed in its negative assurance letter that Epic was in compliance with the escrow requirement. Grant's opinion and negative assurance were based, in part, upon representations from Epic that it was allowed to use more than one account to meet its escrow responsibilities, and the combined balances of escrow funds that it held never totaled less than the required minimum. U.S. Trust never objected to the lack of sufficient funds in the account that it maintained. In April 2001, Grant issued an unqualified opinion on Epic's 2000 financial statements, despite a continuing shortfall of funds in the U.S. Trust account, but it did not issue a negative assurance letter to the trustee.

The plaintiffs in this case were hedge funds that over several years purchased Epic bonds. Prospect had made three purchases before Grant was hired to perform its first audit. Thereafter, Highland Capital Management Corporation and its portfolio manager, Davis Deadman, began managing

(Continued)

Prospect's investments and, as a result, became familiar with Epic's bonds. Deadman, on behalf of the Cayman Fund, a second fund, purchased more Epic bonds in December 2000, two days before Epic made its semiannual interest payment. At about the same time, Epic's primary lender, Prudential, told Epic that it would not renew its credit arrangement. This credit was critical to Epic's survival and its ability to meet its obligations to bondholders. Deadman learned of Prudential's decision sometime in the first quarter of 2001 but continued to buy Epic bonds throughout the spring of 2001.

In June 2001, Epic defaulted on its interest payment to bondholders, claiming that Prudential's failure to renew the credit arrangement forced the timeshare operator to use that money to fund operations. Four days after this default, the hedge funds purchased more bonds and forced Epic into bankruptcy. The hedge funds then sued Grant Thornton, alleging that the audit reports misrepresented the status of the escrow account.

Procedural History

The plaintiff hedge funds sued Grant for negligent misrepresentation, direct negligence, fraud, conspiracy to commit fraud, aiding and abetting fraud, and third-party beneficiary breach of contract. They sought damages equal to the par value of the bonds, plus five years' interest. The trial court, two months before trial in August 2004, granted summary judgment to Grant Thornton on all counts. In October 2006, the Dallas Court of Appeals affirmed the judgment on certain claims, but reversed the judgment on the negligent misrepresentation, fraud, conspiracy, and aiding and abetting claims, finding genuine issues as to material facts.

Grant Thornton filed its petition for review with the Texas Supreme Court in January 2007. The petition argued that the Court of Appeals erred in not holding the following: (1) there was no evidence of a causal connection between Grant's alleged misrepresentation and the funds' alleged injury; (2) there was no evidence of actual and justifiable reliance; and (3) liability for fraudulent misrepresentations runs only to those whom the auditor knows and intends to influence, all of which was not present. The hedge funds responded that Grant's misrepresentations caused them to fail to take action to protect themselves earlier and to refrain from selling their bonds ("holder" claims). The petition was granted in August 2008. In a victory for the auditing profession, in July 2010, the Texas Supreme Court ruled the law does not impose on auditors an obligation to provide an accurate accounting to anyone who reads and relies upon an audit report.

The good news for accountants and other defendants is that this ruling sets forth a strong defense to the otherwise difficult-to-defend claim that "if I had known, I would have sold or taken other action to protect myself." Up until now, defendants have had little ability to defend holder claims because there is rarely any proof other than the plaintiff's testimony of what he did not do or would have done. This unfairness was recognized by the U.S. Supreme Court when it refused to allow holder claims under Rule 10(B-5), but that decision left open the possibility that there could be state law causes of action. *Prospect* significantly closes that door. The decision could influence other courts to deny the open-ended holder claims.

Statutory Liability

LO 6-2
Explain the basis for auditors' statutory legal liability.

Auditors may have legal liability under the Securities Act of 1933 and the Securities Exchange Act of 1934. These statutory liabilities may lead to convictions for crimes, provided their conduct was "willful." Given the centrality of the concept of "willfulness" in our criminal jurisprudence and the fact that numerous individuals have been prosecuted, convicted, and imprisoned for "willfully" violating the federal securities laws, we might expect that the standard for when a "willful" violation has occurred would by now be well settled. There is, however, a surprising paucity of case law interpreting the willfulness standard in the securities arena, and those courts that have addressed the issue have not always been uniform in defining a standard for when conduct proscribed by the statutes is criminal.

The term "willful" and its application in criminal securities law cases often is influenced by the context of the situation. Section 32(a) of the Securities Exchange Act of 1934 provides that any person who "willfully" violates any provision of the Act can be charged with a crime, while Section 15(b)(4) authorizes the SEC to seek civil administrative penalties against any person who "willfully" violates certain provisions of the securities laws.

In 1970, the first Court of Appeals addressed the "willfulness" issue in *United States* v.*Peltz,* 433 F.2d 48.[34] In that decision the court held that, in order to sustain a criminal conviction, the prosecution had to establish "a realization on the defendant's part that he was doing a wrongful act."

In 1972, the Court of Appeals in *United States* v. *Schwartz,* 464 F.2d 499,[35] under a different panel of judges, addressed the meaning of the term "willfully" and stated that a criminal conviction under Section 32(a) for willfully violating a provision of the Exchange Act would be sustained upon "satisfactory proof . . . that the defendant intended to commit the act prohibited."

Other cases have led to somewhat different decisions in the same way that legal rulings involving the civil liability of auditors to third parties for ordinary negligence has changed over time.

Securities Act of 1933

The Securities Act of 1933 regulates the disclosure of information in a registration statement for a new public offering of securities (i.e., IPO). Companies must file registration statements (S-1, S-2, and S-3 forms) and prospectuses that contain financial statements that have been audited by an independent CPA. Accountants who assist in the preparation of the registration statement are civilly liable if the registration statement (1) contains untrue statements of material facts, (2) omits material facts required by statute or regulation, or (3) omits information that if not given makes the facts stated misleading.[36]

Section 11 of the Securities Act of 1933 imposes a liability on issuer companies and others, including auditors, for losses suffered by third parties when false or misleading information is included in a registration statement. Any purchaser of securities may sue: The purchaser generally must prove that (1) the specific security was offered through the registration statements, (2) damages were incurred, and (3) there was a material misstatement or omission in the financial statements included in the registration statement. The plaintiff need not prove reliance on the financial statements unless the purchase took place after one year of the offering.

If items (2) and (3) are proven, it is a *prima facie* case (sufficient to win against the CPA unless rebutted) and shifts the burden of proof to the accountant, who may escape liability by proving the following: (1) after reasonable investigation, the CPA concludes that there is a reasonable basis to believe that the financial statements were true and there was no material misstatement (the materiality defense); (2) a "reasonable investigation" was conducted (the due diligence defense); (3) the plaintiff knew that the financial statements were incorrect when the investment was made (the knowledge of falsehood defense); or (4) the loss was due to factors other than the material misstatement or omission (the lack of causation defense).

Materiality Defense

An accountant might argue that the false or misleading information is not material and thus should not have had an impact on the purchaser's decision-making process. The SEC and the courts have attempted to define materiality. The term *material* describes the kind of information that an average prudent investor would want to have so that he can make an intelligent, informed decision whether or not to buy the security. Thus, it is linked to objectivity. A material fact is one that, if correctly stated or disclosed, would have deterred or tended to deter the average prudent investor from purchasing the securities in question. The term does not cover minor inaccuracies or errors in matters of no interest to investors. Facts that tend to deter a person from purchasing a security are those that have an important bearing upon the nature or condition of the issuing corporation or its business.[37]

Due Diligence Defense

To establish a due diligence defense, the defendant must prove that a reasonable investigation of the financial statements of the issuer and controlling persons was conducted. As a result, there was no reason to believe any of the information in the registration statement or prospectus was false or misleading. To determine whether a reasonable investigation has been made, the law provides that the standard of *reasonableness* is that required of a prudent person in the management of his own property. The burden of proof is on the defendant, and the test is as of the time the registration became effective. The due diligence defense, in effect, requires proof that a party was not guilty of fraud or negligence.[38]

The due diligence defense available to the auditor under Section 11 requires that the auditor has made a reasonable investigation of the facts supporting or contradicting the information included in the registration statement. The test is whether a "prudent person" would have made a similar investigation under similar circumstances.

Key Court Decisions

Two court decisions illustrate the application of Section 11 to securities registration matters: *Escott v. BarChris Construction Corp.* and *Bernstein v. Crazy Eddie, Inc.* These cases are summarized in Exhibits 6.4 and 6.5, respectively.

EXHIBIT 6.4 *Escott v. BarChris Construction Corp.*

In *Escott v. BarChris Construction Corp.*, the company issued a registration statement in 1961 in connection with its public offering of convertible bonds. The statements included audited financial statements by Peat, Marwick, Mitchell & Co. The financial statements included material overstatements of revenues, current assets, gross profit, and backlog of sales orders and material understatements of contingent liabilities, loans to company officers, and potential liability for customer delinquencies. BarChris's worsening financial position resulted in a default on interest payments and the company eventually declared bankruptcy. Barry Escott and other investors sued BarChris's executive officers, directors, and the auditors under Section 11 of the Securities Act, citing a lack of appropriate professional care during the conduct of the audit. The judge ruled that the auditor's actions in reviewing events subsequent to the balance sheet date were not conducted with due diligence because the senior auditor in charge of reviewing these events had not spent sufficient time and accepted unconvincing answers to key questions. The court determined that there had been sufficient warning signs that further investigation was necessary. The auditors' failure to perform a reasonable investigation of subsequent events did not satisfy Section 11(b) and resulted in their liability to investors in BarChris's bonds.[39]

EXHIBIT 6.5 *Bernstein v. Crazy Eddie, Inc.*

New Yorkers were taken in by the television commercials of an electronics company called Crazy Eddie that aired during the mid- and late-1980s. The former chair and CEO, Eddie Antar, advertised that his prices were lower than the competition. An actor would come on the screen, act like a madman, and scream, "Our prices are insane." In the aftermath of the fraud at Crazy Eddie, cynics might claim that Eddie Antar was insane.

Crazy Eddie made several public offerings of securities from 1984 through 1987, during which time the prospectuses wrongly gave the impression that the company was a growing concern. The financial statements had been misstated by a number of schemes, including inflated inventory and net income. The plaintiffs in the case were purchasers of the company's stock prior to the disclosure of the fraudulent financial statements. They sued Peat Marwick, the board of directors, and others, alleging that the accounting firm had violated GAAS and GAAP by failing to uncover the company's fraudulent and fictitious activities. The plaintiffs were able to show that they suffered a loss and that the certified financial statements in the registration statements and prospectuses had been false and misleading, in violation of Sections 11 and 12 of the Securities Acts of 1933. The court decided the plaintiffs did not have to prove fraud or gross negligence, only that any material misstatements in the registration statements were misleading and that they had suffered a loss. In this case, the auditor was unable to prove that they had exercised appropriate due professional care to rebut the claim.[40]

Securities Exchange Act of 1934

The Securities Exchange Act of 1934 regulates the ongoing reporting by companies whose securities are listed and traded on stock exchanges. The Act requires ongoing filing of quarterly (10-Q) and annual (10-K) reports and the periodic filing of an 8-K form whenever a significant event takes place affecting the entity, such as a change in auditors. Entities having total assets of $10 million or more and 500 or more stockholders are required to register under the Securities Exchange Act. The form and content of 10-K and 10-Q filings are governed by the SEC through Regulation S-X (which covers annual and interim financial statements) and Regulation S-K (which covers other supplementary disclosures).[41]

In addition to these two regulations, auditors must be familiar with Financial Reporting Releases (FRRs), which express new rules and policies about disclosure, and Staff Accounting Bulletins (SABs), which provide unofficial, but important, interpretations of Regulations S-X and S-K. Taken together, these four pronouncements provide the authoritative literature for information that must be filed with the SEC.[42]

Section 18 of the Act imposes liability on any person who makes a material false or misleading statement in documents filed with the SEC. The auditor's liability can be limited if the auditor can show that she "acted in good faith and had no knowledge that such statement was false or misleading." However, a number of cases have limited the auditor's good-faith defense when the auditor's action has been judged to be grossly negligent.[43]

The liability of auditors under the act often centers on Section 10 and Rule 10b-5. These provisions make it unlawful for a CPA to (1) employ any device, scheme, or artifice to defraud; (2) make an untrue statement of material fact or omit a material fact necessary in order to make the statement made, in the light of the circumstances under which they were made, not misleading; or (3) engage in any act, practice, or course of business to commit fraud or deceit in connection with the purchase or sale of the security.[44]

Once a plaintiff has established the ability to sue under Rule 10b-5, the following elements must be proved: (1) a material, factual misrepresentation or omission, (2) reliance by the plaintiff on the financial statements, (3) damages suffered as a result of reliance on the financial statements, and (4) the intent to deceive, manipulate, or defraud (scienter).[45]

Reliance by Plaintiff

The first element can include materially misleading information or the omission of material information. Reliance cannot be established if the damages or loss suffered by the plaintiff would have occurred regardless of whether the audited financial statements were misstated. A good example of the failure to establish direct causation between the audited financial statements, reliance thereon, and damages to the plaintiff is the court ruling in *Maxwell v. KPMG LLP*. In this case, the court ruled that even if the other elements necessary to sue under Rule 10b-5 could be established, Maxwell's alleged reliance on the audited financial statements of an acquiring entity was irrelevant, as the business model of that entity was bound to fail because of the dot.com collapse, and thus Maxwell's harm was not caused by KPMG's audit.[46]

This ruling stands as an example of non-accounting events that are the proximate cause of a failed business being given more weight than audited statements. The necessary conditions for the demise of the audit client (Whittman-Hart) were first, its decision to buy US Web, and second, the precipitate decline of the dot.com business. The decision to buy US Web was not influenced by KPMG's approving Whittman-Hart's accounting decisions, and neither were the dot.com troubles. U.S. Web's agreement to be bought may have been influenced by KPMG's advice to Whittman-Hart, but that is irrelevant because US Web was doomed by the coming collapse of its market and thus was not harmed by the advice.

Intent to Deceive or Defraud (Scienter)

Under Rule 10b-5, auditor liability is linked to scienter, or the intent to deceive, manipulate, or defraud. It is not enough to assert the failure to exercise the appropriate level of care to cause liability. The *Hochfelder* case that appears in Exhibit 6.6 illustrates the need for purchasers and sellers of securities to prove scienter on the part of the auditors and confirm the inability for these parties to bring suit against auditors for ordinary negligence. The case was also significant in providing exposure for auditors in cases of gross negligence, even in the absence of scienter.

EXHIBIT 6.6　*Ernst & Ernst v. Hochfelder*

An important case that strengthens the scienter requirement is the 1976 U.S. Supreme Court reversal in *Ernst & Ernst v. Hochfelder*. The U.S. Court of Appeals had ruled in favor of Hochfelder and reversed the lower court opinion. The court decision includes this statement: "One who breaches a duty of inquiry and disclosure owed another is liable in damages for aiding and abetting a third party's violation of Rule 10b-5 if the fraud would have been discovered or prevented but for the breach, and that there were genuine issues of fact as to whether [Ernst] committed such a breach, and whether inquiry and disclosure would have led to discovery or prevention of the . . . fraud."[47]

The *Hochfelder* case involves the president of a brokerage firm who induced Hochfelder to invest in "escrow" accounts that the president represented would yield a high rate of return. The president converted those funds to personal use. The fraud came to light after the president committed suicide, leaving a note that described the brokerage as bankrupt and the escrow accounts as "spurious." Hochfelder's cause of action rested on a theory of negligent nonfeasance. The premise was that Ernst had failed to utilize "appropriate auditing procedures" in its audits of the brokerage, thereby failing to discover internal practices of the firm said to prevent an effective audit. The

(Continued)

practice principally relied on the president's rule that only he could open mail addressed to him or to his attention at the brokerage, even if it arrived in his absence. Hochfelder argued that had Ernst conducted a proper audit, it would have discovered this "mail rule."

The U.S. Supreme Court reversed the decision, ruling that a private cause of action for damages does not come under Rule 10b-5 in the absence of any allegation of scienter. The Court cited the language in Section 10 that it is unlawful for any person to use or employ any manipulative or deceptive device or contrivance in contravention of SEC rules. The Court ruled that the use of those words clearly shows that it was intended to prohibit a type of conduct quite different from negligence. The term *manipulative* connotes intentional or willful conduct designed to deceive or defraud investors, a type of conduct that did not exist in the case.

In a footnote to the decision, the Court recognized that in certain areas of the law, recklessness is considered to be a form of intentional conduct for the purpose of imposing liability for some act, thereby providing potential exposure to auditors for gross negligence under the Securities Exchange Act.

Court Decisions and Auditing Procedures

From time to time, court decisions lead to establishing new audit standards, policies, and procedures in reaction to a court ruling. The cases described below illustrate the point: McKesson & Robbins (Exhibit 6.7) and Equity Funding (Exhibit 6.8).

EXHIBIT 6.7 *United States v. McKesson & Robbins*

The *McKesson & Robbins* case in 1939 was the first instance in which auditing practices were subject to significant public scrutiny. The case involved a conspiracy to defraud the company, by its former president, Donald Coster. Coster and his brothers undertook an elaborate scheme that included dummy trading companies, fictitious warehouses, and forged documents. A cynic might contend that Coster's actions served as a (negative) role model for Barry Minkow in ZZZZ Best some 40-plus years later.

A 1939 investigation by the SEC revealed that Coster and his confidants had stolen around $2.9 million of McKesson & Robbins's cash in the previous 12 years. However, due to the lack of two "then-not-required" audit procedures, physical observation of inventory and direct confirmation of accounts receivable, Price Waterhouse failed to detect $19 million nonexistent assets (out of total assets of over $87 million) and $1.8 million gross profit on fictitious sales of $18 million that were included in McKesson's 1937 certified financial statements.[48]

Up until 1940, the auditor was allowed to rely on the representations of management concerning the accuracy of physical quantities and the costs of its inventory. The SEC criticized the accountants for inaccuracies in the corporation's audited financial statements and set forth several findings in the *McKesson & Robbins* case:[49]

1. The accounting firm "failed to employ that degree of vigilance, inquisitiveness, and analysis of the evidence available that is necessary in a professional undertaking and is recommended in all well-known and authoritative works on auditing."
2. Although the accounting profession claims that the auditor is not a guarantor and should not be liable for fraud, the SEC ruled that "the discovery of gross overstatements in the accounts is a major purpose of such an audit even though it [may] be conceded that [the audit] might not disclose every minor defalcation."
3. The SEC advised the accounting profession to take physical inventories and to require confirmations of accounts and notes receivable.

(Continued)

4. The SEC recommended that the board of directors nominate the auditors and that the activities of management be included in the audit.

The SEC made additional recommendations to the AICPA, including to distinguish auditing "standards" from auditing "procedures." Also, the auditor's certificate should state whether "the audit was made in accordance with generally accepted auditing standards applicable in the circumstances." Subsequently, the AICPA adopted these procedures and eventually codified them in the *Statement on Auditing Standards.*

EXHIBIT 6.8 *Equity Funding Corporation of America Securities Litigation*

The *Equity Funding* case changed the way that CPA firms audited clients, and it brought attention to the red flags that might indicate fraud. Equity Funding's principal line of business was to create "funding programs" that included the sale of life insurance combined with mutual fund investment. Equity Funding derived its income from commissions on the sales. The fraud started just prior to the company's going public, and it was motivated by an attempt to increase the earnings of the company. Equity Funding inflated its earnings by recording fictitious commissions from the sale of its product that the company called "reciprocals." The company also borrowed funds without recording them as liabilities; instead, the cash was recorded as payments on the loans receivable by participants in the program. By reducing the loans receivable, Equity Funding could record more fictitious commissions. The last part of the fraud involved creating fictitious insurance policies, which were then reinsured with other insurance companies. This enabled the company to obtain additional cash to pay premiums on policies, which in turn required that more fictitious policies be created on its books.[50]

Equity Funding collapsed in 1973 when a former employee disclosed the existence of the massive fraud. During the period of the fraud, Equity Funding was audited first by Wolfson Weiner, which ultimately was taken over by the CPA firm Seidman & Seidman. A lengthy audit by Touche during the bankruptcy proceedings disclosed that the company had generated more than $2 billion of fictitious insurance policies.

On November 1, 1973, a federal grand jury in California indicted 22 executives and employees of Equity Funding, including Stanley Goldblum, the chair and CEO of the company. According to the indictment, Goldblum wanted to achieve a level of growth that was not attainable through legitimate business operations. He arranged for various officers and employees to make fictitious bookkeeping entries to inflate the company's income and assets. He also directed employees to create fictitious insurance policies. On November 2, 1970, an employee was instructed to write a computer program creating fictitious policies with a face value of $430 million and a total yearly premium of $5.5 million. In 1971, some phony policies were reinsured, and some employees were instructed to create death claims on the policies.[51]

Creating phony accounting entries is relatively easy, but creating the documentation for 64,000 phony policies was a big challenge, even at Equity Funding. Management wanted to be able to satisfy the auditors, who would ask to see a sample of policies for review. The auditors would examine the policies' documentation on file, and then cross-check for premium receipts and reserve policy information. However, in all but a handful of cases, there were no policy files available. To solve this problem, management created an in-house institution—the "forgery party."

At Equity Funding, policy files the auditors requested would often be "temporarily unavailable." Employees would work at night to forge the missing files to have them ready for auditor review the next day. The fact that the auditors were duped was the least of their embarrassment. One night when an auditor left his briefcase unlocked, an Equity Funding executive, in full sight of others, opened the case and took the audit plan and was able to anticipate next steps. Another time, an

(Continued)

auditor wanted to send out policy confirmations to a sample of policyholders. Equity Funding officials, eager to help, did some clerical chores for the auditor. The result was letters addressed to branch sales managers and agents, who dutifully filled out the forms for the fictitious policyholders.[52]

The McKesson & Robbins case involved audit failings in the area of accounts receivable and inventory, while the Equity Funding case addressed the inspection of assets and confirming customer insurance policies. In both cases, the auditors failed to exercise the level of care required in audit examinations.

An AICPA committee studied the Equity Funding scandal and concluded that "customary audit procedures properly applied" would have reasonably ensured detection of the fraud. There is no way to know if this is true. However, we can examine some of the ethical issues confronting the auditors at Equity Funding including independence and professional skepticism.

The auditors at Equity Funding compromised their independence in a number of instances. For example, one of the auditors earned $130,000 to $150,000 a year, largely because this company was his firm's largest client. Equity Funding paid the auditing firm $300,000 in 1970, more than twice the amount paid by the firm's next three largest clients. The second auditor was given 300 shares of Equity Funding in 1965, which he kept in his wife's former name until he sold them in 1967. The third auditor received a $2,000 loan from an Equity Funding officer. Finally, these auditors (who were subsequently found guilty of fraudulent activities) were allowed to continue auditing Equity Funding—at the insistence of Stanley Goldblum—when another accounting firm bought out their firm.[53]

When auditors allow management extended periods of time to pull the records needed for the audit, it allows management to selectively choose the records, add data that didn't exist, clear out data that is harmful, and generally sanitize the information going to the auditors. Professional skepticism should lead auditors to conclude that delays in providing requested audit documentation is a red flag that records may have been created to satisfy the auditors.

Another red flag that the auditors did not seem to pursue was the rapidly increasing revenue and accounts receivable accounts. The auditors missed the ongoing fraud, not because they lacked technical know-how, but because they did not follow the basics of auditing. Beyond analytical reviews and examining documentation, a fundamental tenet of auditing is to verify the existence of the asset. If the auditors missed 64,000 phony insurance policies, $25 million in counterfeit bonds, and $100 million in missing assets, they simply weren't doing their job.

An interesting aspect of the Equity Funding scandal was the abuse of information technology—to falsify accounting data and hide a fraud, the first time information technology was used to hide a fraud. At the time, auditors believed that the computer was a black box and it did not really matter what went on inside. Audit managers who believed the computer was irrelevant to the audit began to take more seriously the implications of using electronic data processing (EDP) in accounting.

The popular press treated the fraud as a computer fraud, but it really was not—it was a management fraud. Still, the fact is that Equity Funding management probably could not have perpetrated the fraud without the use of computers. The public's perception of the part that the computer played in the fraud caused a new wave of interest in audit procedures where computers were a component of the accounting system. The prevailing belief at this time was that traditional audits (those that audited around the computer) were sufficient to detect the existence of material and significant frauds, such as the Equity Funding fraud. Others, primarily EDP auditors, had espoused the need for auditing through the computer. These people were now receiving attention from accountants, auditors, and management.[54]

Private Securities Litigation Reform Act (PSLRA)

The Private Securities Litigation Reform Act (PSLRA) of 1995 amends the Securities Exchange Act of 1934 by adding Section 10A, "Audit Requirements," which specified that each independent auditor of an issuer under the Act must include "Procedures designed to provide reasonable assurance of detecting illegal acts that would have a direct and material effect on the determination of financial statements amounts." The Act also includes in federal law the auditor's responsibility to detect fraud and requires auditors to promptly notify the audit committee and board of directors of illegal acts. Recall that we had discussed the reporting requirements of illegal acts in Chapter 5.

The PSLRA imposed a new, more stringent pleading standard regarding plaintiffs seeking relief under federal securities laws even before discovery may commence. The Act requires all securities plaintiffs to plead scienter—intent to defraud—through "facts giving rise to a strong inference that the defendant acted with the required state of mind." It also imposed a new sanctions provision applying a loser-pays rule to such plaintiffs, thereby addressing one of the perceived unfair aspects of previous law that had established a joint-and-several liability for auditors.[55]

Proportionate Liability

The attempts to reform auditor liability in the United States focused on the argument that the tort system was out of control, partly as a consequence of the 1933 Securities Act, which placed auditors under a joint-and-several liability regime and made them, not the plaintiffs, carry the burden of proof. The accounting profession had fought over time to effectuate this change because of what the profession perceived to be frivolous lawsuits that included the auditors as defendants primarily because the plaintiffs counted on out-of-court settlement by the auditors who had "deep pockets"; auditors also carry large amounts of professional liability insurance for such matters. The senior partners in the large firms argued that SEC Rule 10-b permits class action claims against companies and auditors where share prices have fallen. Because there is no provision in U.S. law for recovery of costs by successful defendants, auditors felt compelled to settle even meritless legal claims in order to avoid high costs of litigation. Prior to enactment of the PSLRA in 1995, the average claim in 1991 was $85 million; the average settlement was $2.6 million, with legal costs of $3.5 million. The audit firms claimed that legal costs represented 9 percent of their revenues in 1991.[56]

The PSLRA changes the legal liability standard of auditors from joint-and-several liability to proportionate liability. The Act adopts proportionate liability for all unknowing securities violations under the Exchange Act. (It adopts the same rule for non-officer directors under Section 11 of the Securities Act.) This provision is particularly important for underwriters, venture capital firms, outside directors, accounting firms, and others pulled into securities cases as deep-pocketed defendants. Plaintiffs will no longer have the hammer of joint-and-several liability to coerce peripheral defendants into settlements because the risk to those defendants of defending the action is unacceptable and they fear being charged with the entire responsibility for the fraud rather than only their share of it. Only those whom the trier of fact finds to have committed "knowing" securities fraud—that is, had actual knowledge that (1) a statement was false and/or that an omission led to a misleading statement, and (2) investors were reasonably likely to rely on the misrepresentation or omission—will suffer joint-and-several liability.

One of the most influential (and confusing) cases involving application of the PSLRA was *Tellabs, Inc. v Makor Issues & Rights*. Several plaintiffs brought a class action securities fraud lawsuit against Tellabs, a manufacturer of equipment for fiber optic cable networks. The plaintiffs alleged that Tellabs had misrepresented the strength of its products and earnings in order to conceal the declining value of the company's stock. In this case it was ruled that plaintiffs did not meet the "strong inference" standard. The District Court dismissed the complaints. The court held that the plaintiff's allegations were too vague to establish a "strong inference" of scienter on the part of Tellabs.[57]

On appeal, the U.S. Court of Appeals for the Seventh Circuit reversed one of the lower court's dismissals. The Seventh Circuit court ruled that a plaintiff need only allege "acts from which, if true, a reasonable person could infer that the defendant acted with the required intent." The Court of Appeals decided to consider only the plausibility of the inference of a guilty mental state, and not any competing inferences of an innocent mental state. This decision was due in part to the court's concern that weighing competing inferences was more properly the task of a jury. The Seventh Circuit's ruling conflicted with those of other Courts of Appeals, which required plaintiffs to show that the inference of scienter supported by the alleged facts was more plausible than any competing inference of innocent intent.

The case went to the U.S. Supreme Court where Justice Ruth Bader Ginsburg wrote the opinion for the Court, which held that the Seventh Circuit's more relaxed standard was not strong enough to comport with Congress's intent in PSLRA to limit securities fraud litigation. "The strength of an inference cannot be decided in a vacuum. The inquiry is inherently comparative [...]," the Court ruled. A court must consider each plausible inference of intent, both fraudulent and nonfraudulent, and then decide whether a reasonable person would consider the guilty inference "at least as strong as any opposing inference."[58]

"Particularity" Standard

One goal of the PSLRA was to harmonize the previous holdings of the courts of appeal that led to varying standards of auditor legal liability. The strong inference standard has been interpreted by the Second and Third Court of Appeals to allow scienter to be pled through "particularized" allegations establishing either (1) strong circumstantial evidence of conscious misbehavior or recklessness, or (2) facts showing that the defendant had both the motive and opportunity to commit securities fraud. With respect to these standards, the Second and Third Circuit Courts continue to apply a definition of "recklessness" and "motive and opportunity" very similar to the ones pre-PSLRA.[59]

While the legal standards appear not to have changed as a result of the PSLRA, legal rulings have better defined the concept of "motive." To establish motive a plaintiff must allege facts demonstrating a "concrete and personal benefit" that could be realized through the alleged fraud, and motives that generally are possessed by most corporate insiders, such as to keep the stock price high, are insufficient as a matter of law.

As is typical of legal rulings, the Ninth Circuit took a divergent view post-PSLRA insofar as pleading scienter is concerned. It rejected "motive and opportunity." Instead, a plaintiff alleging securities fraud must plead, at a minimum, detailed facts constituting strong circumstantial evidence of "deliberate recklessness." The Court defines the standard as consisting of "facts that come closer to demonstrating 'intent,' as opposed to more motive and opportunity."

Application of the PSLRA seems to rely as much on scienter after the passage of the Act as it did before. The key is for plaintiffs to establish a degree of recklessness sufficient to establish knowledge of the falsehood. Additionally, courts have sided with auditors, in some instances, when they successfully assert the fraud was hidden from them by management or when internal controls are overridden by management. A good example is the ruling in Doral Financial Corporation against PwC, which is summarized in Exhibit 6.9.

EXHIBIT 6.9 PricewaterhouseCoopers Escapes Liability in Doral Litigation[60]

In a 2010 decision with potential implications for securities fraud claims against accounting firms, the U.S. Court of Appeals for the Second Circuit upheld a lower court's dismissal of securities fraud claims by shareholders of Doral Financial Corporation (Doral) against Doral's auditor, PricewaterhouseCoopers (PwC). The litigation arose after Doral, a financial services company that engages in mortgage and commercial banking, restated its financial statements for the years 2000 through 2004. The restatements showed that Doral had overstated its pre-tax income by $920 million and understated its debt by $3.3 billion.

(Continued)

The plaintiffs alleged that Doral engaged in at least two substantial frauds involving the securitization of mortgages. First, the plaintiffs claimed that Doral engaged in "side deals and oral agreements" that essentially turned the "sales" of the securities into secured borrowings, resulting in the overstatement of earnings and an understatement of debt. Second, the plaintiffs claimed that Doral improperly valued the interest-only strips (IO Strips) that it retained as part of the securitizations by using "manufactured" assumptions to conceal losses in its IO Strip portfolio. With respect to PwC, the plaintiffs claimed that the firm's audit reports and its report on Doral's internal controls were materially false and allowed Doral to conceal and perpetuate its frauds. On this basis, the plaintiffs claimed that PwC, like Doral, violated Section 10(b) of the Securities and Exchange Act of 1934 and Rule 10b-5 thereunder.

Judge Jed Rakoff of the U.S. District Court for the Southern District of New York had dismissed the claims against PwC in 2009, holding that the plaintiffs failed to allege the requisite scienter under the Private Securities Litigation Reform Act (PSLRA). In a summary order issued on September 3, 2009, the Second Circuit agreed. Citing the U.S. Supreme Court's 2007 decision in Tellabs, Inc. v. Makor Issues & Rights, Ltd., the Second Circuit noted that, under the PSLRA, a plaintiff must "state with particularity facts giving rise to a strong inference" of scienter, or an intent to "deceive, manipulate or defraud." The inference of scienter must be such that a reasonable person would deem it "cogent and at least as compelling as any opposing inference one could draw" from the same alleged facts. The court stated that this burden could be met by alleging facts showing that the defendant had "both motive and opportunity to commit the fraud," or constituting "strong circumstantial evidence of conscious misbehavior or recklessness." However, in determining whether the alleged facts were sufficient to raise a "strong inference" of scienter, the court was required to "take into account plausible opposing inferences," even if neither party had raised them.

The court acknowledged that the plaintiffs raised "numerous allegations of carelessness" by PwC, but concluded that the allegations failed to create a strong inference of recklessness. The plaintiffs alleged, for instance, that PwC recklessly failed to uncover the side agreements that altered the terms of the mortgage sales. However, the plaintiffs also alleged that the side agreements were a "tightly-held secret," known only to a few individuals within Doral's management. The court therefore held that it was more plausible that PwC failed to discover the side deals because Doral's management hid them from PwC.

The court also held that PwC's failure to identify problems with Doral's system of internal controls was insufficient to establish recklessness. It noted that the plaintiffs had alleged that Doral overrode several of its internal controls, which further undermined any inference of recklessness by PwC.

The court closed by stating that the plaintiffs' allegations of PwC's recklessness might be "plausible" under the general pleading standards established by the Supreme Court in Bell Atlantic Corp. v. Twombly and Ashcroft v. Iqbal. The court continued, however, that "the PSLRA requires . . . more than mere plausibility." Because the "competing inference" that Doral deceived PwC was stronger than the inference that PwC was reckless, it was proper to dismiss the claims. Indeed, it is not uncommon for securities fraud claims to allege that the individuals within a company who perpetuated an alleged fraud took steps to conceal their actions and ignored or circumvented the company's system of internal controls. Following the court's rationale, allegations of this nature would give rise to a strong "competing inference" that the auditor, like the plaintiffs themselves, was a victim of the fraud, and therefore should not be held liable for it.

It should be noted that the competing inference prevailed even though, as the District Court noted, the plaintiffs alleged that PwC personnel were "regularly present" at Doral and had "unlimited access" to information regarding its operations, and that PwC violated GAAP and GAAS in conducting its audits. The District Court held that these allegations were insufficient to establish scienter unless accompanied by some evidence of "corresponding fraudulent intent." The same

(Continued)

was true of the plaintiff's allegations that PwC had a financial incentive to ignore the fraud because it collected over $6 million in fees from Doral and provided non-audit services to Doral during the relevant period. The Second Circuit did not offer another opinion on these conclusions.

In effect, the decisions by the District Court and the Second Circuit require allegations of facts rising to the level of deliberate or willful ignorance of misconduct (if not conscious knowledge or active participation) in order to hold an auditor liable under Section 10(b) and Rule 10b-5. Indeed, the District Court framed the issue in these terms when it discussed and dismissed allegations based on information allegedly provided by a former Doral internal auditor that PwC personnel attended meetings of the Doral Audit Committee at which questions about the company's internal controls were raised: "At most, [the former internal auditor's] information may raise an inference the PwC was negligent in not following up on such discussions, but it certainly does not show the conscious turning away from the true facts required for recklessness."

We believe not much has changed, in reality, with respect to auditors' legal liability and what we are experiencing is different interpretations by different courts, in somewhat different circumstances. The intent standard still should provide the legal basis, at least for fraud determination.

SOX and Auditor Legal Liabilities

LO 6-3
Discuss auditors' legal liabilities under SOX.

Major developments in auditor liability have occurred as a result of the Sarbanes-Oxley Act. SOX was passed to increase the transparency of financial reporting by enhancing corporate disclosure and governance practices and to foster an ethical climate.[61] SOX increases auditor liability to third parties by specifying or expanding the scope of third parties to whom an auditor owes a duty of care. SOX also increases auditor liability to third parties because it requires accounting firms to review and assess management's report on internal controls and issue its own report.

Section 404. *Internal Control over Financial Reporting*

Traditionally, because auditors had no duty to disclose control weaknesses or their effects on substantive audit testing in the audit report, courts deemed control irregularities immaterial for deciding auditors' liability under Section 11 of the Securities Exchange Act of 1933. The case of *Monroe v. Hughes* (1991) illustrates the current law.[62] In that case, the auditor found internal control irregularities, conferred with management and expanded the scope of its financial audit by performing more elaborate substantive testing. The auditor issued an unqualified audit report, but did not disclose the control irregularities in the audit report. In the following year, the auditor found significant deterioration in internal controls and was unable to issue an unqualified financial statement opinion for that year. The client collapsed and investors sued the auditor under Section 11, claiming that the auditor should have disclosed in its audit opinion the internal control irregularities it discovered. The *Monroe* court (and others facing similar questions) rejected the investors' argument, citing Section 11's due diligence defense, negligence standard, and observing that good faith compliance with GAAS discharges an auditor's professional obligation to act with reasonable care. No legal or accounting authority required auditors to disclose control irregularities.[63]

PCAOB *Auditing Standard No. 5* has for all intents and purposes reversed this rule, since it imposes duties on auditors to disclose and explain in their reports material control weaknesses and their effect on the overall audit process. That is, auditors must plan their audit to detect all material weaknesses in the client's control structure and operational effectiveness. Failing to disclose detected material weaknesses exposes them to Section 11 liability. Given the emphasis on internal control assessments by external auditors under *AS No. 5* and Section 404 of SOX, it is somewhat puzzling that the results of PCAOB inspections to date have shown that auditors' opinions on internal controls are inadequate in many cases.

Section 302. *Corporate Responsibility for Financial Reports*

Section 302 requires the certification of periodic reports filed with the SEC by the CEO and CFO of public companies. The certification states that "based on the officer's knowledge, the report does not contain any untrue statement of a material fact or omit to state a material fact necessary in order to make the statements, in light of the circumstances under which such statements were made, not misleading."

The early cases set the tone for SEC's expectations with respect to Section 302 certifications. The first reported case was *Higginbotham v. Baxter Int'l.,* in 2005. The plaintiffs argued that the 302 certifications concerning the adequacy of the company's internal controls were false, and accordingly, the court could infer that Section 10(b)'s scienter requirement was met as to the individuals signing those certifications. The *Higginbotham* court rejected this argument because plaintiffs provided " no specific allegations as to what the deficiencies in the controls were, nor [did they provide] any specific allegations as to [the certifying executives'] awareness of those deficiencies."[64] The ruling does not mean that a false statement with regard to internal controls is not an actionable offense. Instead, the conclusion to be drawn is that claims of scienter require more than just an assertion; specific proof of such knowledge must exist.

The next such case was *In re Lattice Semiconductor Corp.* In *Lattice Semiconductor,* plaintiffs alleged a series of accounting errors that resulted in materially misstated financial statements. In this case, plaintiffs argued that false 302 certifications raised a strong inference that the CEO and CFO were, at a minimum, deliberately reckless, thereby satisfying Section 10(b)'s scienter requirement. Defendants responded by arguing that if "these certifications raised a strong inference of *scienter,* every corporate officer who signed a certification for a Form 10-Q or 10-K filing that was later found to be incorrect would be subject to a securities fraud action."[65]

The *Lattice Semiconductor* court sided with plaintiffs, holding that the 302 certifications in that case did, in fact, give rise to an inference of scienter "because they provide evidence either that defendants knew about the improper journal entries and unreported sales credits that led to the over-reporting of revenues (because of the internal controls they said existed) or, alternatively, knew that the controls they attested to were inadequate."

Soon after *Lattice Semiconductor,* the court in *In re WatchGuard Secs. Litig.* considered allegedly false 302 certifications in the context of a private Section 10(b) action. In *WatchGuard,* plaintiffs alleged that the defendant company had made material misstatements about interest expenses and revenue recognition in its financial statements. Plaintiffs also contended that WatchGuard's quarterly 302 certifications were themselves actionable misstatements on which they could base a Section 10(b) and Rule 10b-5 claim. Plaintiffs also argued that the certifications demonstrated scienter under the "deliberate recklessness" standard because the certifying individual defendants either knew about WatchGuard's revenue recognition problems or were "deliberately reckless in not obtaining the information or conducting the investigations described in their certifications prior to publishing the false financial statements."[66]

The *WatchGuard* court rejected plaintiffs' arguments, holding that the individual defendants' 302 certifications were, by themselves, inadequate to support a strong inference of scienter. In so holding, the court stressed that the failure of plaintiffs to plead scienter adequately is what doomed their 302 argument. "In a case like this one, however, where the court finds no strong inference that any defendant was at least deliberately reckless in issuing corporate earnings statements, the court has no basis for a strong inference that the Sarbanes-Oxley certifications were culpably false."[67]

It is safe to say the courts are still finding their way with respect to legal liability issues and alleged violations of SOX under Section 302. However, based upon the reported private securities cases thus far, it appears that that Section 302 certifications that turn out to be inaccurate do not give rise to independent private claims under the securities laws, nor do they appear to alter the fundamental standards that are applied in Section 10(b) actions. Rather, they are viewed by courts in the overall context of a case and bear on civil liability only when other pleaded facts create a strong inference of scienter against the 302 certifier.[68]

Perspective on Accomplishments of SOX

SOX is sometimes faulted for not preventing the financial crisis and the great recession. But defenders argue that it wasn't designed to do more than ensure that accounting rules were followed. "If you've got employees who are stealing stuff out the back door of the warehouse, [SOX] would tell you whether you have inventory controls in place, not whether the door is locked," according to Gary Kabureck, vice president and chief accounting officer (CAO) at Xerox Corp.

One consolation, says Lynn Turner, former chief accountant for the SEC, is that SOX no doubt mitigated the force of the financial crisis, which could have been worse. "We didn't see the huge rash of fraudulent reporting like we saw in the 1996–2002 time period," he says. "So that would tell you, 'Yes, the legislation did accomplish its goal.' "

As described in Chapter 4, the history of accounting frauds is as old as the SEC's tenure. The "bottom line" may be that the government will not be successful in its effort to control fraud because you cannot legislate ethics. This is no surprise, because being ethical comes from one's desire to do the right thing and courage to carry out an ethical action in the face of pressure and resistance from one's superiors. Still, a set of civil and criminal deterrents is an important part of a healthy securities regulatory system.

Foreign Corrupt Practices Act (FCPA)

LO 6-4
Explain the provisions of the FCPA.

In addition to the PSLRA and SOX, other laws have influenced audit procedures, legal liability, requirements for internal controls over financial reporting, and ethics requirements under the due care principle. The law with the greatest effect in the U.S. is the Foreign Corrupt Practices Act (FCPA).

The Foreign Corrupt Practices Act (FCPA) establishes standards for the acceptability of payments made by U.S. multinational entities or their agent to foreign government officials. The act was motivated when, during the period of 1960 to 1977, the SEC cited 527 companies for bribes and other dubious payments that were made to win foreign contracts. Lockheed Corporation was one of the companies caught in this scandal. It was determined that Lockheed had made about $55 million in illegal payments to foreign governments and officials. One such payment, $1.7 million to Japanese premier Kukuei Tanaka, led to his resignation in disgrace in 1974.

The FCPA makes it a crime to offer or provide payments to officials of foreign governments, political candidates, or political parties for the purpose of obtaining or retaining business. It applies to all U.S. corporations, whether they are publicly or privately held, and to foreign companies filing with the SEC. The Department of Justice (DOJ) is responsible for all criminal enforcement and for civil enforcement of the antibribery provisions with respect to domestic entities and foreign companies and nationals. The SEC is responsible for civil enforcement of the antibribery provisions with respect to registrants.

Under the FCPA, a corporation that violates the law can be fined up to $1 million, while its officers who directly participated in violations of the act or had "reason to know" of such violations can be fined up to $10,000, imprisoned for up to five years, or both. The act also prohibits corporations from indemnifying fines imposed on directors, officers, employees, or agents. FCPA does not prohibit "grease payments" (i.e., *permissible facilitating payments*) to foreign government employees whose duties are primarily ministerial or clerical because such payments are sometimes required to persuade recipients to perform their normal duties.[69]

As a result of the criticisms of the antibribery provisions of the 1977 FCPA, Congress amended the act as part of the Omnibus Trade and Competitiveness Act of 1988 to clarify when a payment is prohibited, as follows:[70]

1. A payment is defined as illegal if it is intended to influence a foreign official to act in a way that is incompatible with the official's legal duty.

2. The "reason to know" standard is replaced by a "knowing" standard, so that criminal liability for illegal payments to third parties applies to individuals who "knowingly" engage in or tolerate illegal payments under the act.

3. The definition of "grease" payments is expanded to include payments to any foreign official that facilitates or expedites securing the performance of a routine governmental action.

4. Examples of acceptable payments include (1) obtaining permits, licenses, and the official documents to qualify a person to do business in a foreign country; (2) processing governmental papers, such as visas or work orders; (3) providing police protection, mail pickup, and delivery, or scheduling inspections associated with contract performance or inspections related to the transit of goods across country; (4) providing telephone service, power, and water, unloading and loading cargo, or protecting perishable product or commodities from deterioration; and (5) performing actions of a similar nature.

Two affirmative defenses for those accused of violating the act are that the payment is lawful "under the written laws" of the foreign country, and that the payment can be made for "reasonable and bona fide expenditures." These include lodging expenses incurred by or for a foreign official to promote products or services or execute the performance of a contract.

Individuals can be prosecuted under the 1988 amendment even if the company for which they work is *not* guilty. Penalties for violations were raised to $2 million for entities and $100,000 for individuals. The maximum term of imprisonment is kept at five years. A $10,000 civil penalty also was enacted.

The health-care industry has been under increased SEC and DOJ scrutiny for a number of years now for potential FCPA violations. What has been described as an "industry sweep" has focused primarily on medical device and pharmaceutical companies. Exhibit 6.10 summarizes one of the most comprehensive FCPA actions taken by the SEC and DOJ, against Pfizer on August 7, 2012.

EXHIBIT 6.10 The SEC Case Against Pfizer

The allegations by the SEC against Pfizer Inc. illustrate the vast global nature of foreign bribery. On August 7, 2012, the SEC charged Pfizer Inc. with violating the FCPA when its subsidiaries bribed doctors and other health-care professionals employed by foreign governments in order to win business.[71]

(Continued)

The SEC alleged that employees and agents of Pfizer's subsidiaries in Bulgaria, China, Croatia, Czech Republic, Italy, Kazakhstan, Russia, and Serbia made improper payments to foreign officials to obtain regulatory and formulary approvals, sales, and increased prescriptions for the company's pharmaceutical products. They tried to conceal the bribery by improperly recording the transactions in accounting records as legitimate expenses for promotional activities, marketing, training, travel and entertainment, clinical trials, freight, conferences, and advertising.

The SEC separately charged another pharmaceutical company that Pfizer acquired a few years ago—Wyeth LLC—with its own FCPA violations. Pfizer and Wyeth agreed to separate settlements in which they will pay more than $45 million combined to settle their respective charges. In a parallel action, the DOJ announced that Pfizer H.C.P. Corporation, an indirectly wholly-owned subsidiary of Pfizer, agreed to pay a $15 million penalty to resolve the investigation of its potential FCPA violations.

"Pfizer subsidiaries in several countries had bribery so entwined in their sales culture that they offered points and bonus programs to improperly reward foreign officials who proved to be their best customers," said Kara Brockmeyer, chief of the SEC Enforcement Division's FCPA Unit. "These charges illustrate the pitfalls that exist for companies that fail to appropriately monitor potential risks in their global operations."

According to the SEC's complaint against Pfizer filed in U.S. District Court for the District of Columbia, the misconduct dated back as far as 2001. Employees of Pfizer's subsidiaries authorized and made cash payments and provided other incentives to bribe government doctors to use Pfizer products. In China, for example, Pfizer employees invited "high-prescribing doctors" in the Chinese government to clublike meetings that included extensive recreational and entertainment activities to reward doctors' past product sales or prescriptions. Pfizer China also created various "point programs," under which government doctors could accumulate points based on the number of Pfizer prescriptions they wrote. The points were redeemed for various gifts ranging from medical books to cell phones, tea sets, and reading glasses.

The SEC further alleged that Wyeth subsidiaries engaged in FCPA violations primarily before but also after the company's acquisition by Pfizer in late 2009. Starting at least in 2005, subsidiaries marketing Wyeth nutritional products in China, Indonesia, and Pakistan bribed government doctors to recommend their products to patients by making cash payments or, in some cases, providing BlackBerrys and cell phones or travel incentives. They often used fictitious invoices to conceal the true nature of the payments. In Saudi Arabia, Wyeth's subsidiary made an improper cash payment to a customs official to secure the release of a shipment of promotional items used for marketing purposes. The promotional items were held in port because Wyeth Saudi Arabia had failed to secure a required Saudi Arabian Standards Organization Certificate of Conformity. (This could have been deemed a facilitating payment under FCPA.)

Following Pfizer's acquisition of Wyeth, Pfizer undertook a risk-based FCPA due diligence review of Wyeth's global operations and voluntarily reported the findings to the SEC staff. Pfizer diligently and promptly integrated Wyeth's legacy operations into its compliance program and cooperated fully with SEC investigators.

Pfizer consented to the entry of a final judgment ordering it to pay disgorgement of $16,032,676 in net profits, as well as prejudgment interest of $10,307,268, for a total of $26,339,944. Wyeth also is required to report to the SEC on the status of its remediation and implementation of compliance measures over a two-year period, and is permanently enjoined from further violations of Sections 13(b)(2)(A) and 13(b)(2)(B) of the Securities Exchange Act of 1934.

The enforcement action against Pfizer arose in part out of improper payments, including hospitality and travel expenses, made to doctors and health-care professionals employed by government-controlled or owned health-care providers in countries such as Bulgaria, Croatia, Kazakhstan, Italy, China, Serbia, and Russia.

In a speech on compliance in the pharmaceutical industry on March 3, 2015, Andrew Ceresney, SEC's Director of the Division of Enforcement, pointed out that the best way for a company to avoid FCPA violations is to have a robust FCPA compliance program that includes compliance personnel, extensive policies and procedures, training, vendor reviews, due diligence on third-party agents, expense controls, escalation of red flags, and internal audits to review compliance.[72] An effective compliance program also includes performing risk assessments and monitoring internal controls over financial reporting.

In discussing the importance of internal controls and its relevance to FCPA reporting, Ceresny noted that the number of enforcement actions the SEC brought in the financial reporting area increased by over 40 percent in fiscal year 2014 compared to 2013, and the number of new financial reporting investigations opened increased by about 30 percent in the same period. "Many of these cases are focused on issuers and their executives and financial personnel. But we also are looking closely at gatekeepers, who play a critical role in ensuring accurate and reliable financial reporting. In every financial reporting investigation, we look at the work of the auditors to determine whether their audits were performed in accordance with professional standards."[73]

The FCPA violations at Pfizer clearly illustrate the importance of an effective system of internal controls, strong corporate governance, and a tone at the top that filters throughout the organization and strengthens compliance with regulations and ethical behavior. FCPA compliance is important for accountants and auditors who are charged with disclosing illegal acts and evaluating internal controls.

Internal Accounting Control Requirements

The FCPA requires all SEC registrants to maintain internal accounting controls to ensure that all transactions are authorized by management and recorded properly. The FCPA requires public company issuers to maintain adequate books and records that, in reasonable detail, accurately and fairly reflect an issuer's transactions and disposition of assets. In addition, public companies must maintain internal controls to ensure transparency in the financial condition of the company, the relevant risk to the company, and the transactions conducted by the company.

Michael Volkov, an expert in corporate corruption and compliance, believes that the SEC's case against Oracle Corporation, that was settled on August 16, 2012, is the most significant for books and records and internal control violations. Oracle paid $2 million for secretly "parking" a portion of the proceeds from certain sales to the Indian government between 2005 and 2007, during which time the company structured transactions so that $2.2 million was held by Oracle's distributors and kept off the company's books. Oracle did not accurately record these funds and failed to maintain a system of effective internal controls to prevent improper side funds. The notable point is that the SEC was unable to establish that any of these funds were used for any illegal bribery payments under the FCPA, and instead relied on the fact that Oracle's violations increased the risk of bribery payments.[74]

In the Oracle case, the SEC faulted the U.S. parent corporation for not auditing local distributors hired by its Indian subsidiary, without alleging FCPA violations. It would seem that the decision reflects the SEC's expansive enforcement of the FCPA's internal controls provision, and its enforcement as a strict liability statute that means whatever the SEC says it means (after the fact). One concern is that the SEC might bring an FCPA enforcement action even if the company was not aware of any internal control weaknesses at the time.

A Summary of DOJ and SEC FCPA Enforcement Actions

The law firm of Gibson Dunn reports enforcement actions of the DOJ and SEC. The following is a summary of such actions during the 10-year period of 2005–2014.[75]

TABLE 6.1 Doj and Sec Fcpa Enforcement Actions

Date	DOJ	SEC	Total Enforcement Actions
2005	7	5	12
2006	7	8	15
2007	18	20	38
2008	20	13	33
2009	26	14	40
2010	48	26	74
2011	23	25	48
2012	11	12	23
2013	19	8	27
2014	17	9	26

The spike during 2009 through 2011 reflects actions taken in the wake of the financial recession and fallout from Congress's investigations in the aftermath of Enron and WorldCom. It appears that enforcement actions have now settled at the rate of about 25 per year.

During the reported time period, approximately three out of every five corporate FCPA resolutions have required some form of ongoing reporting or monitoring of the company's compliance program during a post-resolution period. But the frequency and mix of the various types of reporting obligations (or lack thereof) has changed substantially over time. From 2005 to 2009, it was more common for companies to escape an FCPA resolution without any form of post-resolution supervision. But in those cases where supervision was imposed, it was nearly always in the form of an independent compliance monitor. The compliance undertakings DOJ requires of settling companies also have increased dramatically over time. In its earliest manifestations, standard post-resolution undertakings typically numbered nine. In more recent settlements, DOJ has imposed 18 separate post-settlement requirements, including "periodic reviews and testing of [the company's] anti-corruption compliance code, policies, and procedures . . . taking into account relevant developments in the field and evolving international and industry standards." In effect, the 18 articulated requirements serve as DOJ's template for an effective anti-corruption compliance program.[76]

FCPA violations are troubling because they result from bribery of foreign government officials. If bribery occurs in a company, we can only wonder what other ethical transgressions exist. It is rare when a company violates a law, oftentimes very blatantly, and toes the line in other areas of operations. The violations always reflect a failure of the corporate governance system and unethical tone at the top. As for the auditors, we have to wonder how they can miss FCPA violations given the heightened ethical requirements when operating in the global arena where different cultures establish different standards of ethical conduct.

Regulatory and Professional Issues: An International Perspective

LO 6-5
Describe the cultural and professional constraints on adopting IFRS.

Given the increased pace of globalization of business and accounting, we briefly review regulatory and professional issues in this section. The purpose is to make you aware of ethical and professional responsibilities when performing audit and other services in countries and regions around the world where laws are different, cultural factors affect accounting and financial reporting, and issues related to fraud and global bribery present difficult challenges due to cultural considerations and regulatory requirements.

Restoring the Public Trust

Enron, WorldCom, Royal Dutch Shell (U.K.-Netherlands), Parmalat (Italy), and Satyam (India), all were involved in major financial statement frauds in the early 2000s that led to legal liabilities for the auditors. A lack of internal controls, ineffective internal audits, and inattentive boards of directors all share blame for these frauds, as did the external audit failures. To address these issues, in 2003 the International Federation of Accountants (IFAC) issued a research report, *Rebuilding Public Confidence in Financial Reporting: An International Perspective,* which examined ways of restoring the credibility of financial reporting and corporate disclosure from an international perspective. The report identifies several key weaknesses in corporate governance from a number of corporate failures worldwide. The findings of the study include a recommendation for more effective corporate ethics codes as well as the provision of training and support for individuals within organizations to better prepare them to deal with ethical dilemmas.

IFAC addresses the public interest dimension in its Policy Position Paper # 4 entitled *A Public Interest Framework for the Accountancy Profession.* The framework is designed to enable IFAC and other professional bodies to better evaluate whether the public interest is being served through actions of the profession and its institutions. IFAC considers the "public interest" to represent the common benefits derived by stakeholders (i.e., investors and creditors) of the accounting profession through sound financial reporting. It links these benefits to responsibilities of professional accountants, including the application of high standards of ethical behavior and professional judgment.[77]

International Financial Reporting

The Influence of Culture on International Financial Reporting

We addressed Hofstede's cultural values in Chapter 1, and now link them to financial reporting in the international environment. Research suggests that cultural differences cause accountants in different countries to interpret and apply accounting standards differently. This research reveals that two accounting values directly influenced by national culture are *conservatism* and *secrecy,* which affect the measurement and disclosure of financial information in financial reports and have the greatest potential to affect cross-border financial statement comparability.

Tsakumis et al. points out that cultural values that exist in a country influence a country's accounting values (e.g., accountants' levels of conservatism and secrecy), which influence how financial reporting standards are applied. They depict the relationship as follows:[78]

Cultural Values > Accounting Values > Application of Financial Reporting Standards[79]

Gray uses Hofstede's values to identify four widely recognized accounting values that can be used to define a country's cultural foundation with respect to financial reporting:

1. Professionalism (preference for professional judgment) versus statutory control (compliance-driven prescriptive legal requirements).
2. Uniformity (consistency across companies in the use of accounting practices) versus flexibility (choice of accounting practice in accordance with the perceived circumstances of individual companies).
3. Conservatism (a cautious approach to measurement to deal better with the uncertainty of future events) versus optimism (following a more hands-off, risk-taking approach).
4. Secrecy (preference for confidentiality and restrictions on disclosures) versus transparency (open and public accountability).

From an accounting perspective, high conservatism implies a tendency to defer the recognition of assets and items that increase net income while reserving for possible future declines in earnings. Within Hofstede's framework, higher levels of conservatism are most closely linked with countries that have higher *uncertainty avoidance* and lower *individualism.* High secrecy implies a tendency to restrict the disclosure of relevant information to outside parties. Higher levels of secrecy within a culture are associated with higher *uncertainty avoidance* and *power distance* and with lower *individualism.*

International Financial Reporting Standards (IFRS)

Cultural factors and national regulations influence financial reporting around the world. The international community has been trying since 1973 to bring together the various global accounting standards into one set of International Financial Reporting Standards. One common set of accounting standards should go a long way toward increasing transparency and the understandability of international financial reports.

The convergence effort was given a big boost in 2005, when the European Union adopted IFRS for all companies doing business in the European Zone. Around the same time, an increasing number of lesser-developed countries adopted IFRS as they moved toward a more capitalistic system. About 120 countries have now adopted IFRS for financial reporting purposes.

What about the United States? Historically, listing rules required that non-U.S. companies must reconcile their financial statements prepared under home country standards to U.S. GAAP. This is a tedious exercise and, unless you believe that U.S. GAAP better reflects financial position and results of operations than IFRS, the cost of reconciliation probably exceeds any benefits derived. The SEC now permits foreign companies to use IFRS without reconciliation to U.S. GAAP.

To say the United States has been reluctant to embrace IFRS is an understatement. The current approach is dubbed "condorsement." This approach is in essence an *endorsement approach* that would share characteristics of the incorporation approaches with other jurisdictions that have incorporated or are incorporating IFRS into their financial reporting systems. However, during the undefined transitional period, the framework would employ aspects of the *convergence approach* to address existing differences between IFRS and U.S. GAAP. The framework would retain a U.S. standard setter and would facilitate the transition process by incorporating IFRSs into U.S. GAAP over some defined period of time. At the end of this period, the objective would be that a U.S. issuer compliant with U.S. GAAP should also be able to represent that it is compliant with IFRS as issued by the International Accounting Standards Board.

The condorsement approach has essentially stalled. The SEC has placed it on the back burner. A great deal of concern has existed in the United States over whether IFRS is better than U.S. GAAP. One undeniable fact is the principles-based approach of IFRS that relies on broad concepts for the application of financial reporting standards has increasingly been influencing standards in the United States, although the rules-based system still provides the basic framework for financial reporting.

The effectiveness of IFRS adoption may be hampered by differences, across countries, in the institutional setting in which financial reporting occurs. Brown et al. study different legal regimes and IFRS compliance and note that IFRS use a range of legal system proxies to capture country differences, but the proxies are deficient in that they seldom focus explicitly on factors that affect how compliance with accounting standards is promoted through external audit and the activities of independent enforcement bodies. The most widely used proxies focus on the nature of legal systems and the extent of legal protection of shareholder and creditor rights, This is important because it highlights the need for a common set of ethical standards to deal with such differences.[80]

A significant event occurred in 1983 when the International Organization of Securities Commissions (IOSCO) was formed. The international body brings together the world's securities regulators and is recognized as the global standard setter for the securities sector. Its membership regulates more than 95 percent of the world's securities markets in more than 115 jurisdictions. IOSCO develops, implements, and promotes adherence to internationally recognized standards for securities regulation. It has issued 30 principles of securities regulation based on the following objectives: the protection of investors; ensuring that markets are fair, efficient, and transparent; and the reduction of systemic risk.

A look at the objectives of IOSCO sheds light on ways in which cross-border financial statements might be regulated, even though IOSCO has no specific enforcement powers. Short of creating an "international SEC," which is unlikely to happen any time soon, "enforcement" of international financial reports falls on the regulatory agencies in each country. Still, international enforcement remains problematic given legal differences and cultural considerations.

Principles- versus Rules-Based Standards

The debate over whether the IFRS principles-based standards are "better" than the rules-based system in U.S. GAAP has been going on for a long time. One lesser-known provision of SOX is for a study to be conducted of the need to adopt a principles-based approach to standard setting to replace the more rules-based system in the United States. A study by the SEC notes that imperfections exist when standards are established on either a rules-based or a principles-only basis. Principles-only standards may present enforcement difficulties because they provide little guidance or structure for exercising professional judgment by preparers and auditors. Thus, our discussions about professional judgment in Chapter 4 take on a whole new meaning when dealing with the more principles-based international accounting standards.

The SEC study recommends that those involved in the standard-setting process more consistently develop standards on a principles-based or objectives-oriented basis. Such standards should have the following characteristics:[81]

- Be based on an improved and consistently applied conceptual framework.
- State clearly the accounting objective of the standard.
- Provide sufficient detail and structure so that the standard can be operationalized and applied on a consistent basis.
- Minimize exceptions from the standard.
- Avoid use of percentage tests (bright lines) that allow structuring of financial transactions to achieve technical compliance with the standard while evading the intent of the standard.

In contrast to objectives-oriented standards, rules-based standards can provide a basis for avoidance of the accounting objectives inherent in the standards. Internal inconsistencies, exceptions, and bright-line tests reward those willing to engineer their way around the intent of standards. This can result in financial reporting that is not representationally faithful to the underlying economic substance of transactions and events. In a rules-based system, financial reporting may well come to be seen as an act of compliance rather than an act of communication. In addition, because multiple exceptions exist that could lead to internal inconsistencies, significant judgment is needed in determining where an accounting transaction falls within the myriad of possible exceptions.

At the other extreme, a principles-only approach typically provides insufficient guidance to make the standards reliably operational. As a consequence, principles-only standards require preparers and auditors to exercise significant judgment in applying overly broad standards to more specific transactions and events, and often do not provide a sufficient structure to frame the judgment that must be made. The result of principles-only standards can be a significant loss of comparability among reporting entities. Furthermore, under a principles-only standard-setting regime, the increased reliance on the capabilities and judgment of preparers and auditors could increase the likelihood of retrospective disagreements on accounting treatments. In turn, this could result in increased litigation with regulators for both companies and auditors.

From a corporate governance perspective, outside the United States it is common to have a two-tier system of governance with the management board of directors overseeing the financial reporting of the company and a supervisory board that oversees the management board. A unitary system exists in the United States. We like the two-tier approach as it builds in an extra layer of oversight and reduces management's role in the financial reporting process, thereby addressing one of the issues under agency theory.

The concept of "true and fair" was created in Great Britain in 1844, when corporations were expected to fulfill the requirement of "full and fair" in the balance sheet. The audit reports in most countries that have adopted IFRS use the term "true and fair view" in lieu of the U.S. "present fairly." A true and fair view is the governing criterion by which financial statements are to be judged. It relies on the notion of placing the economic substance of a transaction ahead of its legal form. In that way it mirrors a principles-based approach to decision making.

Exhibit 6.11 presents the authors' conceptual view of the major ingredients of a principles-based approach to making accounting judgments. Notice how, in a principles-based environment, virtue-based considerations (e.g., objectivity and integrity) form the basis to evaluate representational faithfulness and to make professional judgments about the economic substance of transactions and the assessment of a true and fair view.

EXHIBIT 6.11 Conceptual Framework of a Principles-Based Approach to Decision Making

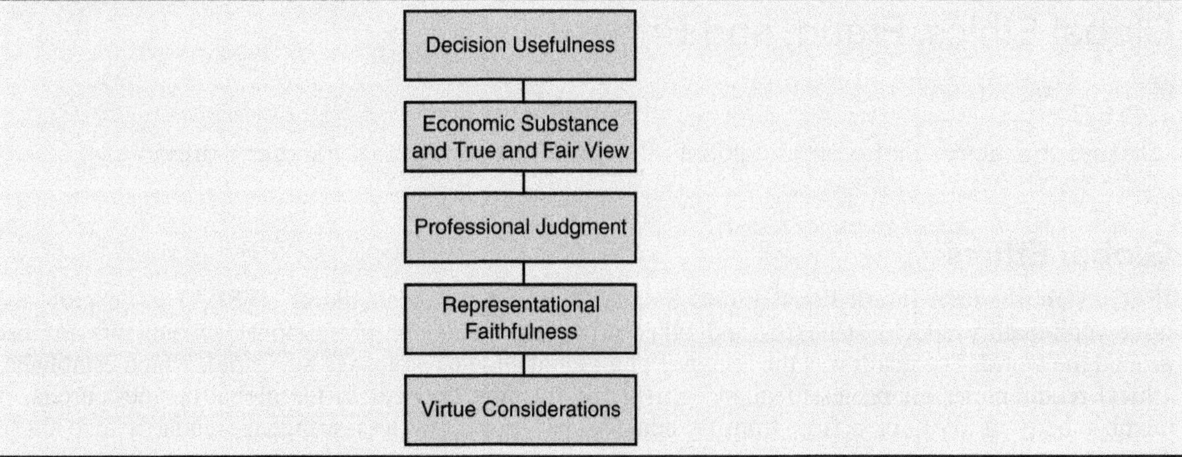

Compliance and Ethical Issues

LO 6-6
Distinguish between legal compliance and management by values.

The Treviño et al. study of specific characteristics of legal compliance programs has implications for the international environment. The authors found that such programs mattered less than broader perceptions of the program's orientation toward values and ethical aspirations. They discovered that what helped the most are consistency between policies and actions as well as dimensions of the organization's ethical climate such as ethical leadership, fair treatment of employees, and open discussion of ethics. On the other hand, what hurts the most is an ethical culture that emphasizes self-interest and unquestioning obedience to authority, and the perception that legal compliance programs exist only to protect top management from blame.[82]

With respect to the issues of ethical leadership, Collins examined the character traits of effective business leaders in the culture of 11 companies that transformed themselves from good solid businesses into great companies that produced phenomenal and sustained returns for their stockholders. Every one of the companies he profiled during the critical period in which it was changing from good to great has what he termed "Level 5" leadership, which was his top ranking for executive capabilities. Leaders in all companies exhibited the traits of fanatical drive and workerlike diligence, but Level 5 leaders were also people of integrity and conscience who put the interest of their stockholder and their employees ahead of their own self-interest.[83]

Kirk O. Hanson, the executive director of the Markkula Center for Applied Ethics at Santa Clara University, points out that global companies today manage by compliance or values. He discusses a compliance mentality as focusing on meeting the minimum standards and exact wording of a global code of ethics rather than the true meaning and purpose of the code. While he acknowledges the likelihood of a "management by values" approach being more public interest oriented, it does create implementation challenges.[84]

The problem of a compliance approach in implementing global standards is that it can result in achieving compliance formally without actually changing corporate behavior. Moreover, achieving compliance without considering ethical consequences can lead to the problem of ethical legalism. The laws can't cover every situation so a sound set of values backed by an ethical tone at the top is just as important in global operations, maybe even more so, than for U.S. domestic companies. As we have discussed before, adherence to the law is a minimal standard for ethical behavior.

Global Ethics, Fraud, and Bribery

LO 6-7
Discuss the factors that promote global ethics, and prevent global fraud and bribery.

Global Ethics

IFAC established the International Ethics Standards Board for Accountants (IESBA) to develop and issue high-quality ethical standards and other pronouncements for professional accountants for use around the world. The result was the issuance of a global code of ethics (IFAC Code), which establishes ethical requirements for professional accountants performing services in the global business arena. A member body of IFAC or a firm from its country may not apply less stringent standards than those stated in the IFAC Code. However, if a member body or firm is prohibited from complying with certain parts of this Code by national law or regulation, they should be governed by their country's requirements but comply with all other parts of the Code.

The 2012 IFAC Code contains provisions virtually identical to those embodied in the AICPA Code of Professional Conduct. The following is a brief list of similarities:[85]

1. To act in accordance with the public interest.

2. To identify threats to independence (i.e., self-interest threats, advocacy threats, self-review threats, familiarity threats, and intimidation threats) and develop safeguards to mitigate such threats.

3. To be independent in fact, meaning having a state of mind that permits the expression of a conclusion without being affected by influences that compromise professional judgment, allowing an individual to act with integrity, and exercising objectivity and professional skepticism.

4. To maintain the appearance of independence, meaning the avoidance of facts and circumstances that are so significant that a reasonable and informed third party, having knowledge of all relevant information, including safeguards applied, would reasonably conclude that a firm's or a member of the assurance team's integrity, objectivity, or professional skepticism had been compromised.

5. To adhere to standards related to integrity, objectivity, professional competence and due care, confidentiality, and professional behavior.

Global Fraud

The seventh annual Global Fraud Survey prepared by Kroll in conjunction with the Economist Intelligence Unit provides insight and helps guide businesses around the world facing the challenge of fighting fraud. According to the survey, following a decrease in 2012, fraud is on the rise again, and so are the costs involved in managing it. These factors are in turn driving up companies' sense of vulnerability. Every kind of fraud covered in the survey saw an increase in incidence, with vendor, supplier, or procurement fraud, and management conflict of interest seeing the biggest growth.[86]

Awareness of fraud is up, regardless of whether it's related to cybercrime, information theft, outsourcing, or expansion into new and riskier markets. Yet measures to guard against fraud continue to be constrained by budgets and corporate policy. One finding is that fraud remains an inside job. Companies that suffered fraud and knew who was responsible reported that 32 percent had experienced at least one crime where a leading figure was in senior or middle management, 42 percent where it was a junior employee, and 23 percent where it was an agent or intermediary.

The Global Fraud Survey findings were compared with Transparency International's Corruption Perceptions Index (CPI). The CPI measures the perceived levels of public-sector corruption as seen by business people and country analysts, ranging between 10 (very clean) and 0 (highly corrupt). The comparison clearly demonstrates that fraud and corruption frequently go hand in hand.

Global Bribery

In some countries, corruption is part of the country's culture, so fraud, bribery, and kickbacks are a way of doing business. Whether you call it "grease payments" (United States), *baksheesh* (Middle East), *mordida* (Latin America), or *ghoos* (India), these payments are designed to speed up "routine governmental action," such as processing papers, issuing permits, and other actions of an official, in order to expedite performance of duties of a nondiscretionary nature (i.e., which they are already bound to perform). The payment is not intended to influence the outcome of the official's action, only its timing. These facilitation payments are one of the few exceptions to anti-bribery prohibitions of the FCPA.

In 2010, the United Kingdom passed the U.K. Bribery Act that bans facilitating payments. It defines such payments as "Small unofficial payments made to secure or expedite the performance of a routine or necessary action to which the payer has legal or other entitlement."[87] In other words, the act bans what the FCPA permits. The jury is out whether the tougher U.K. anti-bribery law will hurt U.K. multinationals as they compete with companies in countries that allow facilitating payments. It should be noted that international anti-corruption treaties also ban facilitation payments.

The act includes a new corporate criminal offense of failure to prevent bribery. The company may be guilty of a criminal offense unless they can demonstrate that they had adequate procedures in place to deal with bribery, including facilitation payments. Similar defensive procedures exist in the United States under the Federal Sentencing Guidelines for Organizations.

In November 2011, the U.K. Serious Fraud Office (SFO) provided guidance as to what the agency deems to be corruption indicators, or "red flags" of corruption. While not exhaustive, the list helps to clarify those business practices that the SFO deems to be questionable:

- Abnormal cash payments.
- Pressure exerted for payments to be made urgently or ahead of schedule.
- Payments being made through a third-party country; for example, goods or services are supplied to country A, but payment is made to a shell company in country B.
- Private meetings with public contractors or companies hoping to tender for contracts.
- Lavish gifts.
- Agreement to contracts not favorable to the organization, either with terms or time period.
- Unexplained preference for certain contractors during the tendering period.

The SFO has found that, to date, U.K. companies appear to be addressing the Bribery Act's requirements and reducing potential risks by ensuring that they have adequate procedures in place to prevent bribery. As part of their decision making, companies are increasingly reviewing existing policies and contracts to make sure that they comply with the law's requirements.

The U.K. Bribery Act has a potentially wide territorial reach. A non-U.K. corporation will commit an offense of offering or accepting a bribe or of bribing a foreign public official under the Bribery Act if an act that forms part of that offense takes place in the United Kingdom. Even if the relevant act takes place outside the U.K., proceedings for the offense may still be brought in the U.K. if the person who does that act has a "close connection" with the U.K. The Bribery Act provides an exhaustive list of people who will be considered to have a "close connection" with the United Kingdom, which includes British citizens and British nationals living overseas.

For an offense to arise, the briber must be "associated" with the commercial organization, a term that applies to the organization's agents, employees, and subsidiaries. A foreign corporation which "carries on a business, or part of a business" in the U.K. may therefore be guilty of the U.K. offense even if, for example, the relevant acts were performed by the corporation's agent outside the U.K. The Bribery Act does not expand on what will constitute the carrying on of "part of a business" in the U.K., so this will be an issue for the courts to decide. However, the guidance on adequate procedures suggests that having a U.K. subsidiary or securities listed in the United Kingdom will not, of itself, be sufficient.[88]

In a recent survey of compliance, over half of all corruption incidents were identified from "tips" when a whistleblowing hotline was available, showing that having a hotline increases reporting and internal detection. Interestingly, 86 percent of respondents claim to be prepared to report potential breaches of the Bribery Act, even though 44 percent of respondents do not have, or are not aware of, clearly defined procedures for reporting Bribery Act contraventions.[89]

Global companies need to realize that preventing corruption is fundamentally a matter of corporate culture. Procedures, policies, rules, and systems won't work unless they are supported by a culture that is truly geared toward doing the right thing. Culture is a very powerful force. A good perspective is to assess the way things really happen in the company. What is most rewarded? How are conflicting priorities reconciled? What happens when short-term business objectives run counter to company values? When people see something wrong, do they come forward or hold back in fear?

PCAOB Inspections of Chinese Companies

A troubling issue faced by U.S. regulators is the challenge of getting Chinese authorities to cooperate with the PCAOB inspections of U.S. audit firms operating in China, as first discussed in Chapter 5. Cultural factors impede the ability of the regulators to gain access to sensitive audit information related to the examination of the financial statements of Chinese companies listing their shares on U.S. stock exchanges. The lack of transparency does not bode well for global cooperation on audit inspections, which arguably is the most important measure of compliance with national laws and serves as a proxy for international enforcement.

Fraud and audit failure can occur in any country, but China is a special case because the authorities there seem to be less than fully committed to getting to the bottom of scandals whose victims have been American, Canadian, or other foreign investors. The Longtop Financial case discussed in Chapter 5 is just one example.

The SEC has long sought the cooperation of the Chinese government to share audit workpapers with other regulators. The Chinese insist they would provide documents only if the SEC promises not to use them in an enforcement proceeding without Chinese permission. Clearly, that defeats the purpose of getting that information.

Before we attack China for its seemingly combative approach to cooperating with regulators outside China, we need to understand that in addition to cultural differences, the Chinese government is the major stockholder in many "public" companies. China's state-owned enterprises present unique challenges for regulators in the United States and elsewhere because the auditors are asking government shareholders to provide financial data on government-controlled entities. This is a challenge, to say the least.

Chinese companies listing shares in the United States have largely fallen through a regulatory loophole, partly because U.S. audit inspectors at the PCAOB have not been allowed inside China where the audits are done. The SEC has to work through the China Securities Regulatory Commission (CSRC). In the Longtop Financial case, the PCAOB had asked Deloitte to turn over its working papers because Longtop had allegedly committed fraud. After months of discussion, the SEC received a substantial volume of documents called for by its subpoena, including Deloitte audit workpapers and certain other documents related to Longtop. The production was made by the CSRC in January 2014, in response to the SEC's request for assistance in August 2012. The CSRC produced the documents to the SEC after obtaining them from Deloitte, thereby eliminating any claims that it had violated confidentiality in regards to its Chinese client.

Auditors have resisted handing over records for fear of violating China's state secrets law. Dozens of Chinese companies have raised billions of dollars in the past decade listing their shares on U.S. and foreign exchanges. Accuracy, reliability, and transparency concerns have led to share price reductions in some of those companies amid questions about their bookkeeping and financial disclosures. From an ethical perspective, it is an issue of trust and representational faithfulness in the financial reporting. Can foreign investors trust the financial reports produced by accountants in China and audited by the Big Four CPA firms to faithfully represent what they purport to represent, thereby enhancing the usefulness of such reports? Can we really trust that the CSRC turns over all relevant information? Time will tell whether the Chinese authorities allow the PCAOB direct access to Big Four and other firms auditing Chinese companies. We can only hope that Chinese regulators gain an appreciation for full and fair transparency of financial information.

Concluding Thoughts

Auditor legal liability follows from the failure to adhere to prescribed ethical and professional standards embodied in the AICPA Code, GAAP, and GAAS. The history of litigation against auditors shows that due care and the exercise of professional skepticism are the underpinnings of an audit conducted in accordance with prescribed standards. In the post-SOX period, auditors have to be particularly sensitive to their assessment of management's report on internal controls.

At the end of the day, it is the ethical standards, professionalism, and practices embedded in the culture of individual auditors and audit firms that will protect them when difficult situations arise, conflicts exist with management over an accounting or financial reporting issue, or management just wants to test the waters and see how far they can push the envelope. The public interest requires that auditors act with integrity and in accordance with the profession's ethical standards. When auditors fall short in this regard, lawsuits that are filed by clients and third parties alleging negligence, constructive fraud, and fraud are more likely to be successful against those auditors, and legal liabilities can include steep financial penalties, suspension from practice, and even jail time for the offenses.

On an international level, ethical standards require that global companies must go beyond simple compliance with the laws because laws can never address all situations. Thus, a strong set of ethical values should be embedded in the corporate culture and inform all aspects of global operations. An ethical culture works best to ward off temptations to engage in global fraud or bribery.

The moral of our story is fairly simple: When a company's ethical compass is pointing true north, everything else falls into line, and legal liability issues are controlled. This isn't to say that companies with great ethics don't fail. But it does seem to indicate that companies without good ethics are far more likely to fail because they fail to nurture an environment of honesty, trustworthiness, responsibility, accountability, and integrity.

Discussion Questions

1. As discussed in the opening reflection, MF Global filed a complaint charging PwC with professional malpractice, breach of contract, and unjust enrichment in connection with its advice concerning, and approval of, the company's off-balance-sheet accounting for its investments. The court's decision points out that absent PwC's advice, MF Global Holdings would not have invested heavily in European sovereign debt to generate immediate revenues and would not have suffered the massive damages that befell the company in 2011. Do you believe that auditors should be held legally liable when they advise clients on matters related to the company's finances that turn out to be wrong? Explain with reference to legal and professional standards.

2. Distinguish between common-law liability and statutory liability for auditors. What is the basis for the difference in liability?

3. Is there a conceptual difference between an error and negligence from a reasonable care perspective? Give examples of each in your response.

4. Distinguish between the legal concepts of actually foreseen third-party users and reasonably foreseeable third-party users. How does each concept establish a basis for an auditor's legal liability to third parties?

5. Do you think that the provision of nonaudit services for a client with a failed audit is evidence of negligence? Explain.

6. Explain the legal basis for a cause of action against an auditor. What are the defenses available to the auditor to rebut such charges? How does adherence to the ethical standards of the accounting profession relate to these defenses?

7. Assume a third party such as a successor audit firm quickly discovers a fraud that the predecessor external auditor has overlooked for years. Do you think this provides evidence supporting scienter? Explain.

8. What are the legal requirements for a third party to sue an auditor under Section 10 and Rule 10b-5 of the Securities Exchange Act of 1934? How do these requirements relate to the *Hochfelder* decision?

9. Valley View Manufacturing Inc. sought a $500,000 loan from First National Bank. First National insisted that audited financial statements be submitted before it would extend credit. Valley View agreed to do so, and an audit was performed by an independent CPA who submitted her report to Valley View. First National, upon reviewing the audited statements, decided to extend the credit desired. Certain ratios used by First National in reaching its decision were extremely positive indicating a strong cash flow. It was subsequently learned that the CPA, despite the exercise of reasonable care, had failed to discover a sophisticated embezzlement scheme by Valley View's chief accountant. Under these circumstances, what liability might the CPA have?

10. Nixon & Co., CPAs, issued an unmodified opinion on the 2015 financial statements of Madison Corp. These financial statements were included in Madison's annual report and Form 10-K filed with the SEC. Nixon did not detect material misstatements in the financial statements as a result of negligence in the performance of the audit. Based upon the financial statements, Harry Corp. purchased stock in Madison. Shortly thereafter, Madison became insolvent, causing the price of the stock to decline drastically. Harry has commenced legal action against Nixon for damages based upon Section 10(b) and Rule 10b-5 of the Securities Exchange Act of 1934. What would be Nixon's best defense to such an action? Explain.

11. The following pertains to auditor legal liability standards under the PSLRA:

    a. The Reform Act requires that, in any private securities fraud action in which the plaintiff is alleging a misleading statement or omission on the part of the defendant, "the complaint shall specify each statement alleged to have been misleading, the reason or reasons why the statement is misleading, and, if an allegation regarding the statement or omission is made on information and belief, the complaint shall state with particularity all facts on which that belief is formed."[90]

       Do you believe this standard better protects auditors from legal liability than the standards which existed before the PSLRA? Explain.

    b. Do you believe the change in standards for auditors' liability under the PSLRA from joint-and-several to proportional liability was a good thing? Explain.

12. Some auditors claim that increased exposure under Section 404 of SOX creates a litigation environment that is unfairly risky for auditors. Do you think that the inability of auditors to detect a financial statement misstatement due to gross deficiencies in internal controls over financial reporting should expose auditors to litigation? Why or why not? Include reference to appropriate ethical standards in your response.

13. Assume a U.S. company operates overseas and is approached by foreign governments officials with a request to provide family members with student internships with the company. The company does business in that country with foreign customers and is negotiating for a contract with one such customer to provide services. Under what circumstances might such a request violate the FCPA?

14. Has the accounting profession created a situation in which auditors' ethical behavior is impaired by their professional obligations? How does the profession's view of such obligations relate to how courts tend to view the legal liability of auditors?

15. Consider the following statement and explain the relationship between legal compliance on a global level and ethical responsibilities of accountants and auditors: "Ethical values and legal principles are usually closely related, but ethical obligations typically exceed legal duties."

16. Business ethics is about managing ethics in an organizational context and involves applying principles and standards that guide behavior in business conduct. According to IFAC, "The decisions and behaviors of accountants should reinforce good governance and ethical practices, develop and promote an ethical culture, foster trust and transparency, bring credibility and value to decision making, and present a faithful picture of organizational health to stakeholders." Explain how accountants and auditors can meet these expectations in a global environment and protect the public interest.

17. How do Gray's accounting values establish a basis for financial reporting in countries with different cultural systems?

18. What are the costs and benefits of establishing one set of accounting standards (i.e., IFRS) around the world? How do cultural factors, legal systems, and ethics influence your answer? Apply a utilitarian approach in making the analysis.

19. The Institute of Chartered Accountants in England and Wales (ICAEW) has adopted a code of ethics based on the IFAC Code. In commenting on the principles-based approach used in these codes, the ICAEW states that a principles approach "focuses on the spirit of the guidance and encourage responsibility and the exercise of professional judgment, which are key elements of professions."[91] Explain how factors underlying professional judgment that were discussed in Chapter 4 come into play in the global environment.

20. Consider the practice of making "facilitating payments" to foreign officials and others as part of doing business abroad in the context of the following statement: International companies are confronted with a variety of decisions that create ethical dilemmas for the decision makers. "Right-wrong" and "just-unjust" derive their meaning and true value from the attitudes of a given culture. Some ethical standards are culture-specific, and we should not be surprised to find that an act that is considered quite ethical in one culture may be looked upon with disregard in another. Explain how culture interacts with the acceptability of making facilitating payments in a country. Use rights theory and justice reasoning to analyze the ethics of allowing facilitating payments such as under the FCPA in the United States and prohibiting them as under the U.K. Bribery Act.

21. One provision of the U.K. Bribery Act is that it applies to bribes that occur anywhere in the world by non-U.K. companies that conduct any part of their business in the United Kingdom. For example, the Bribery Act would cover a company that has a few employees working in the United Kingdom or that simply sells its goods or services in the United Kingdom. Evaluate this policy from an ethical perspective using ethical reasoning. In particular, do you think the policy is fair? Is it right?

22. What is the purpose of having a two-tier system of boards of directors in countries such as Germany? How does the dual-board approach ameliorate the potential conflicts in the principal-agent relationship between investor and manager?

23. In discussing the benefits of the Global Code of Ethics, Richard George, chairperson of the International Ethics Standards Board for Accountants, said, "Strong and clear independence standards are vital to investor trust in financial reporting. The increase in trust and certainty that flow from familiarity with standards, including a common understanding of what it means to be independent when providing assurance services, will contribute immeasurably to a reduction in barriers to international capital flows."[92] Explain the link between auditor independence and facilitating international capital flows from the public interest perspective.

24. What are the unique challenges to the global internal audit function?

25. In this chapter, we discuss problems encountered by the PCAOB in gaining access to inspect workpapers of auditors in U.S. international accounting firms that have Chinese company clients that list their stock in the United States. Explain why these problems exist from a cultural and legal perspective. How might shareholder interests be compromised by the arrangement between the PCAOB and CSRC that was struck in the Longtop Financial case discussed in this chapter?

Endnotes

1. JS 44/C/SDNY, REV. 2/2014, Available at: http://go.bloomberg.com/assets/content/uploads/sites/2/2014/03/3-28-14-8.pdf.

2. Karen Freifeld, "Ernst & Young Settles with N.Y. for $10 million over Lehman Auditing," *Reuters,* April 15, 2015, Available at: http://www.reuters.com/article/2015/04/15/us-ernst-lehman-bros-idUSKBN0N61SM20150415.

3. Michael Rapaport, "PwC Settles MF Global Lawsuit for $65 Million," *The Wall Street Journal,* April 17, 2015, Available at: http://www.wsj.com/articles/pwc-to-pay-65-million-to-settle-lawsuit-over-mf-global-1429302372.

4. Zoe-Vonna Palmrose, *Empirical Research in Auditor Litigation: Considerations and Data, Studies in Accounting Research No. 33* (Sarasota, FL: American Accounting Association,1999).

5. William F. Messier Jr., Steven M. Glover, and Douglas F. Prawitt, *Auditing and Assurance Services: A Systematic Approach* (New York: McGraw-Hill Irwin, 2012).

6. Timothy J. Louwers, Robert J. Ramsay, David H. Sinason, Jerry R. Strawser, and Jay C. Thibodeau, *Auditing and Assurance Services* (New York: McGraw-Hill Irwin, 2013).

7. Louwers et al., p. 637.

8. Louwers et al., pp. 637–638.

9. *Ultramares v. Touche,* 174 N.E. 441 (N.Y. 1931).

10. *Credit Alliance v. Arthur Andersen & Co.,* 483 N.E. 2d 100 (N.Y. 1985).

11. *Security Pacific Business Credit v. Peat Marwick Main & Co.,* 165 A.D.2d 622 (N.Y. App. Div. 1991), Available at: https://casetext.com/case/security-pacific-v-peat-marwick.

12. Messier et al., pp. 692–693.

13. *Rusch Factors, Inc. v. Levin,* 284. F.Supp. 85, 91.

14. *Restatement (Second) of the Law of Torts,* Section 552A–E (1997), www.tomwbell.com/NetLaw /Ch05/R2ndTorts.html.

15. *Blue Bell, Inc. v. Peat, Marwick, Mitchell & Co.,* 715 S.W. 2d 408 (Dallas 1986).

16. *Rosenblum, Inc. v. Adler,* 93 N.J. 324 (1983).

17. *Citizens State Bank v. Timm, Schmidt & Company* (1983), Available at: www.wisbar.org/res /capp/2007/2006ap002290.htm.

18. Dan M. Goldwasser and Thomas Arnold, *Accountants' Liability* (New York: Practising Law Institute, 2009).

19. *Bily v. Arthur Young,* 834 P. 2d 745 (Cal. 1992).

20. Richard Mann and Barry Roberts, *Essentials of Business Law and the Legal Environment,* (Boston, MA: Cengage Learning, 2015).

21. *1136 Tenants Corp. v. Max Rothenberg & Co.,* 27 App. Div. 2d 830, 277 NYS 2d 996 (1967).

22. Attestation Update—A&A for CPAs, Available at: http://attestationupdate.com/2011/01 /18/engagement-letters-required-for-a-compilation-or-review/.

23. AICPA, AR Section 60: Framework for Performing and Reporting on Compilation and Review Engagements, Available at: http://www.aicpa.org/Research/Standards/CompilationReview /DownloadableDocuments/AR-00060.pdf.

24. Messier et al., p. 705.

25. *State Street Trust Co. v. Ernst,* Court of Appeals, N.Y. (1938), 278 N.Y. 104. 15 N.E.2d 416.

26. Messier et al., p. 705.

27. *Phar-Mor v. Coopers & Lybrand,* Available at: www.cases.justia.com/us-court-of-appeals/F3/22 /1228/579478/.

28. Supreme Court, New York County, *Water St. Leasehold LLC v Deloitte & Touche, Llp,* Available at: http://law.justia.com/cases/new-york/other-courts/2004/2004-51260.html.

29. Howard Reisman & others vs. KPMG Peat Marwick LLP, 57 Mass. App. Ct. 100, April 10, 2002 - January 15, 2003, November 24, 2003, Available at: http://masscases.com/cases/app/57 /57massappct100.html.

30. *Houbigant, Inc. v. Deloitte & Touche LLP.*

31. Louwers et al., pp. 641–642.

32. Louwers et al., pp. 642–643.

33. *Grant Thornton LLP v. Prospect High Income Fund, et al.,* July 2, 2010, Available at: http://www.txcourts.gov/media/819887/OpinionsFY2010.pdf.

34. *United States v. Philip Peltz, 433 F. 2d 48, September 17, 1970*, Available at: https://bulk.resource.org/courts.gov/c/F2/433/433.F2d.48.141.34578_1.html.

35. *United States v. Robert Schwartz, 464 F. 2d 499, July 17, 1972*, Available at: https://bulk.resource.org/courts.gov/c/F2/464/464.F2d.499.71-1871.456.html.

36. Securities Exchange Act of 1934, Title 15 of the U.S. Code.

37. O. Lee Reed, Marisa Anne Pagnattaro, Daniel R. Cahoy, Peter J. Shedd, and Jere W. Morehead, *The Legal and Regulatory Environment of Business* (New York: McGraw-Hill Irwin, 2013).

38. Reed et al.

39. *Escott v. BarChris Construction Corp.*, U.S. District Court for the Southern District of New York, 1968, 283 F.Supp. 643.

40. *Securities and Exchange Commission v. Eddie Antar, Sam E. Antar, Mitchell Antar, Isaac Kairey, David Panoff, Eddie Gindi, and Kathleen Morin*, Civil Action No. 89-3773 (JCL), Litigation Release 15251, February 10, 1997, Available at: www.sec.gov/litigation/litreleases/lr15251.txt.

41. Securities Exchange Act of 1934, Title 15 of the U.S. Code.

42. Louwers et al., p. 648.

43. Messier et al., p. 709.

44. Messier et al., p. 709.

45. Securities Exchange Act of 1934.

46. Jean Braucher (Editor), John Kidwell (Editor), William C Whitford (Editor), *Revisiting the Contracts Scholarship of Stewart Macaulay: On the Empirical and the Lyrical (International Studies in the Theory of Private Law)*, (Oxford: UK, Hart Publishing, 2013.

47. *Ernst & Ernst v. Hochfelder*, 425 U.S. 185 (1976).

48. *United States of America Before the Securities and Exchange Commission in the Matter of McKesson and Robbins, Inc. (Accountancy in Transition)* (New York: Garland Publishing,1982).

49. *United States v. McKesson & Robbins, Inc.*, 351 U.S. 305 (1956)

50. *In re Equity Funding Corporation of America Securities Litigation*, 603 F. 2d 1353 (1979).

51. *In re Equity Funding.*

52. David R. Hancox, "Equity Funding: Could It Happen Again?" Available at: www.davehancox.com/hancox---sulem---public-speaking/publications/equity-funding.

53. Steven M. Davidoff, "In Insider and Enron Cases, Balancing Lies and Thievery," Available at: http://dealbook.nytimes.com/2012/06/19/in-insider-and-enron-cases-balancing-lies-and-thievery/?_r=0.

54. Institute of Internal Auditors, "Fundamentals of the Internal Auditing Function," Available at: https://www.theiia.org/bookstore/media/pdf/6019_Excerpt.pdf.

55. 15 U.S.C. § 78 u-4(b)(1) (2012), Available at: https://www.law.cornell.edu/uscode/text/15/78u-4.

56. HR 3763: Sarbanes-Oxley Act in full, Available at: www.sec.gov/about/laws/soa2002.pdf.

57. U.S. Court of Appeals for the Seventh Circuit, Tellabs Inc. v. Makor Issues & Rights, Docket No. 06-484, Available at: http://www.oyez.org/cases/2000-2009/2006/2006_06_484.

58. U.S. Supreme Court, Tellabs Inc. v. Makor Issues & Rights, Ltd. et al., Available at: http://www.oyez.org/cases/2000-2009/2006/2006_06_484.

59. Robert W. Perrin, Brian T. Glennon, and Julie R. F. Gerchik, "The State of Scienter: A Comparative Survey Ten Years After the Enactment of the Private Securities Litigation Reform Act," Securities Litigation Report, December–January 2006 Vol. 3, No. 1.

60. American Bar Association, "Second Circuit Affirms Dismissal of Securities Fraud Claims Against PricewaterhouseCoopers in Doral Litigation," Available at: https://apps.americanbar.org/litigation/committees/professional/casenotes/0110_doral.html.

61. Lawrence A. Cunningham, Stephen Kwaku, and Arnold Wright, "The Sarbanes-Oxley Act: Legal Implications and Research Opportunities," *Research in Accounting Regulation,* Vol. 19, 2006.

62. *Monroe v. Hughes,* 860 F. Supp. 733 (1991), Available at: http://law.justia.com/cases/federal/district-courts/FSupp/860/733/2159100/.

63. Cunningham et al.

64. *Higginbotham v. Baxter Int'l.,* 2005 WL 1272271 (N.D. Ill. May 25, 2005).

65. *In re Lattice Semiconductor Corp. Secs. Litig.,* 2006 U.S. Dist. LEXIS 262 (Jan. 3, 2006 Dist. Ore.).

66. *In re WatchGuard Secs. Litig.,* 2006 U.S. Dist. LEXIS 272717 (W.D.Wash., April 21, 2006).

67. *In re WatchGuard Secs. Litig.*

68. Timothy P. Harkness, Celiza P. Bragança and John Bessonnette, *Minding Your 302s: Assessing Potential Civil, Administrative, and Criminal Liability for False Financial Statement Certifications.* Available at: www.pli.edu/emktg/compliance_coun/Minding_302s_CC_34.pdf.

69. *United States v. Richard Scrushy,* Available at: www.justice.gov/archive/dag/cftf/chargingdocs/scrushyindictment.pdf.

70. Richard D. Ramsey and A. F. Alkhafaji, "The 1977 Foreign Corrupt Practices Act and the 1988 Omnibus Trade Bill," *Management Decision* 29, no. 6., pp. 22–39.

71. U.S. Securities and Exchange Commission, "SEC Charges Pfizer with FCPA Violations," Available at: http://www.sec.gov/News/PressRelease/Detail/PressRelease/1365171483696.

72. Andrew Ceresny, "FCPA, Disclosure, and Internal Controls Issues Arising in the Pharmaceutical Industry," Remarks at CBI's Pharmaceutical Compliance Congress, Washington, D.C., March 3, 2015, Available at: http://www.sec.gov/news/speech/2015-spch030315ajc.html.

73. Ceresny.

74. Michael Volkov, "A Closer Look at Internal Controls Enforcement," Available at: http://www.law360.com/articles/641956/a-closer-look-at-internal-controls-enforcement.

75. Gibson Dunn, *2014 Year-End FCPA Update,* January 5, 2015, Available at: http://www.gibsondunn.com/publications/pages/2014-Year-End-FCPA-Update.aspx.

76. Gibson Dunn.

77. International Federation of Accountants (IFAC), *Rebuilding Public Confidence in Financial Reporting: An International Perspective* (New York: IFAC, 2003).

78. George T. Tsakumis, "The Influence of Culture on Accountants' Application of Financial Reporting Rules," *Abacus*, Vol. 43, No. 1, pp. 27-44.

79. Sidney J. Gray, "Towards a Theory of Cultural Influence on the Development of Accounting Systems Internationally," *Abacus*, March 1988, pp. 1–15.

80. Philip Brown, John Preiato, and Ann Tarca, "Measuring Country Differences in Enforcement of Accounting Standards: An Audit and Enforcement Proxy," FIRN Research Paper, December 10, 2013, Available at SSRN: http://ssrn.com/abstract=2286029 or http://dx.doi.org/10.2139/ssrn.2286029.

81. SEC, *Study Pursuant to Section 108(d) of the Sarbanes-Oxley Act of 2002 on the Application by the U.S. Financial Reporting System of a Principles-Based Accounting System, 2003*, submitted to the Committee on Banking, Housing, and Urban Affairs of the U.S. Senate and Committee on Financial Services of the U.S. House of Representatives, Available at: https://www.sec.gov/news/studies/principlesbasedstand.htm.

82. Linda Klebe Treviño, Gary R. Weaver, David G. Gibson, and Barbara Ley Toffler, "Managing Ethics and Legal Compliance: What Works and What Hurts," *California Management Review*, Vol. 41, No. 2, pp 131–151.

83. Jim Collins, *Good to Great: Why Some Companies Make the Leap ... and Others Don't* (New York: Harper Collins Publications, 2001).

84. Kirk O. Hanson, "Beyond Compliance: Globalization Demands More Effective Programs," Available at: http://www.scu.edu/ethics/practicing/focusareas/business/beyond-compliance.html.

85. International Federation of Accountants (IFAC), International Ethics Standards Board for Accountants, *Handbook of the Code of Ethics for Professional Accountants, 2012 Edition*, Available at: www.ifac.org.

86. Kroll, *2013/2014 Global Fraud Report*, Available at: http://fraud.kroll.com/wp-content/uploads/2013/10/GlobalFraudReport_2013-14_WEB.pdf.

87. U.K. Ministry of Justice, *UK Bribery Act 2010*, Available at: http://www.justice.gov.uk/downloads/legislation/bribery-act-2010-guidance.pdf.

88. Sam Rubenfeld, "Companies Show Little Concern about UK Bribery Act Enforcement," *The Wall Street Journal* blog post, June 25, 2012, Available at: http://blogs.wsj.com/corruption-currents/2012/06/25/companies-show-little-concern-about-uk-bribery-act-enforcement/.

89. *UK Bribery Act 2010*.

90. 15 U.S. Code § 78u–4 - Private securities litigation, Available at: https://www.law.cornell.edu/uscode/text/15/78u-4.

91. Institute of Chartered Accountants in England and Wales (ICAEW), *ICAEW Code of Ethics*, Available at: http://www.icaew.com/en/technical/ethics/icaew-code-of-ethics/icaew-code-of-ethics.

92. "New Code will Facilitate Global Convergence," August 28, 2009, Available at: http://www.accountingweb.com/practice/practice-excellence/new-code-of-ethics-will-facilitate-global-convergence.

Chapter 6 Cases

Case 6-1 Advanced Battery Technologies: Reverse Merger

Auditors are not always found guilty of negligence, gross negligence, and fraud when lawsuits are filed against them. And they do not always settle lawsuits to avoid costly, protracted litigation. A good example is legal action taken against three accounting firms in *In re Advanced Battery Technologies, Incorporated and Ruble Sanderson v. Bagell, Josephs, Levine & Co., LLC, Friedman LLP, and EFP Rothenberg, LLP.* For purposes of this case, Advanced Battery is referred to as *ABAT* and the three accounting firms simply as "the auditors."

On March 25, 2015, the Second Circuit and Eleventh Circuit Courts of Appeal affirmed dismissals of securities fraud claims filed against the auditors that audited Chinese reverse-merger companies because the plaintiffs did not adequately plead scienter under the heightened pleading standard imposed by the Private Securities Litigation Reform Act of 1995.[1] Under the PSLRA, plaintiffs must "state with particularity facts giving rise to a strong inference that the defendant acted with the required state of mind" with respect to each act or omission of the defendant that is alleged to violate the securities laws.

The Second Circuit's opinion in *ABAT* stated that to allege scienter on a recklessness theory against an independent audit firm under Section 10(b) of the Securities Exchange Act of 1934 and Rule 10b-5, a plaintiff must allege facts showing that the audit firm's auditing practices were so deficient as to amount to "no audit at all" or that the audit firm disregarded signs of fraud that were "so obvious" that the audit firm must have been aware of them.

The *ABAT* ruling is significant because it is the first federal appellate case to expressly reject scienter arguments based on the alleged discrepancy between a company's filings with the U.S. SEC and with China's State Administration of Industry and Commerce (SAIC), a regulatory agency to which Chinese companies must submit financial statements as part of an annual examination. The decision reflects a growing trend of courts rejecting securities fraud claims filed against independent audit firms in the context of Chinese reverse-merger companies.

In *ABAT*, the plaintiffs alleged that the auditors falsely represented that they performed their audits in accordance with professional standards and that ABAT's financial statements were fairly presented. An amended complaint upon appeal of the lower court decision against ABAT alleged that the audit firms were reckless and committed an "extreme departure from the reasonable standards of care" by failing to identify several purported "red flags," including: (1) conflicts between ABAT's financial statements filed with China's SAIC and with the SEC; and (2) the unreasonably high profits that ABAT reported in its SEC filings, in contrast to the significant losses that it reported in its SAIC filings. The district court denied leave to amend, and the Second Circuit affirmed.[2]

The Second Circuit agreed with the district court that the proposed amended complaint, like the previous complaint, failed to adequately plead the audit firms' scienter under the theory of recklessness and that amendment would be futile. The appellate court explained that the plaintiff was required to allege conduct "that is highly unreasonable, representing an extreme departure from the standards of ordinary care," such that the conduct "must, in fact, approximate an actual intent to aid in the fraud being perpetrated by the audited company as, for example, when a defendant conducts an audit so deficient as to amount to no audit at all, or disregards signs of fraud so obvious that the defendant must have been aware of them."[3]

---

[1] A reverse merger occurs when a privately-held Chinese company goes public in the U.S. by merging with U.S. publicly-traded "shell companies." The reverse merger trend was initially fueled by the difficulties of going public in China. Reverse mergers are often described as an inexpensive "back-door" way of taking a company public, but they have a sketchy history in the U.S. One reason is the publicly held shell company has virtually no assets or business of its own. Many shell companies are the remnants of failed companies, though some are created from scratch for the single purpose of merging with an existing private company.

[2] In re *Advanced Battery Technologies, Incorporated and Ruble Sanderson v. Bagell, Josephs, Levine & Co., LLC, Friedman LLP, and EFP Rothenberg, LLP,* 14-1410-cv, March 25, 2015, Available at: http://caselaw.findlaw.com/us-2nd-circuit/1695335.html.

[3] "2 cases audit firm defendants can rely on," *Law360*, New York, April 9, 2015, Available at: http://www.law360.com/articles/640875/2-cases-audit-firm-defendants-can-rely-on.

Much of the Second Circuit's analysis focused on the plaintiff's argument that the audit firms acted recklessly by failing to inquire about or review ABAT's financial filings with China's SAIC. In rejecting these arguments, the court noted that none of the "standards on which [the lead plaintiff] relies—the Generally Accepted Auditing Standards, Statements on Auditing Standards, or GAAP [generally accepted accounting principles]—specifically requires an auditor to inquire about or review a company's foreign regulatory filings."

The court declined to adopt the general rule, urged by the plaintiff, that allegations of an audit firm's failure to inquire about or review such foreign filings are adequate to plead recklessness under the PSLRA. Although the court noted that "such a legal duty could arise under certain circumstances" (which it did not explain), it concluded that those circumstances were not pled here. In addition, the Second Circuit held that ABAT's report of high profit margins in its SEC filings triggered, at most, a duty to perform a more rigorous audit of those filings, not of the company's SAIC-China filings. The court declined to infer recklessness from the allegations that one of the audit firms had access to, and "presumably relied" on, the financial data underlying ABAT's SAIC filings but failed to see that the data contradicted the company's SEC filings. Instead, the court found another inference more compelling—that ABAT maintained different sets of data for its Chinese and U.S. regulators and provided the audit firm with false data.

The *ABAT* opinion is significant because it illustrates the high burden plaintiffs face in pleading recklessness in Section 10(b) cases against independent audit firms. Notably, since under the PSLRA the plaintiffs filing suit must plead with particularity facts alleging that the audit firm's work was so deficient as to amount to no audit at all, the historical legal standards for auditor liability seem to have turned in favor of the auditors. Also, the Second Circuit's determination that allegations that an audit firm failed to review AIC filings is not sufficient to meet this high burden for pleading scienter is significant, as such allegations are frequently pled in matters involving audits of the financial statements of Chinese companies listed on U.S. securities exchanges.

Questions

1. Do you believe the legal standards of allegations with "particularity sufficient facts" and of "no audit at all" cited in *ABAT* under Section 10(b) of the Securities Exchange Act of 1934 are too strict, too lenient, or just about right with respect to auditors' legal liability in cases similar to *ABAT*? Explain.

2. In *ABAT*, the plaintiffs alleged that the auditors falsely represented that they performed their audits in accordance with professional standards and that ABAT's financial statements were fairly presented. The amended complaint alleged that the audit firms were reckless and committed an "extreme departure from the reasonable standards of care" by failing to identify several purported "red flags." Do you believe the failure to identify red flags should be sufficient in a court of law to successfully allege gross negligence? Include in your discussion the purpose of auditors looking to detect red flags as part of their audits in accordance with GAAS.

3. Do you believe that auditors should be held legally liable when their filings to the SEC are [overly] optimistic while filings with Chinese regulatory agencies are [unduly] pessimistic? Explain using ethical reasoning to craft your answer.

Case 6-2 Heinrich Müller: Big Four Whistleblower? (a GVV case)

The facts of this case and names of main characters have been changed to focus on specific ethical and professional obligations.

Heinrich Müller had always been a team player. His many years at one of the Big Four firms taught him to be loyal, even to a fault. The German culture expected nothing less. However, stumbling across details of thousands of firm-arranged tax avoidance deals has changed his mind. He is sitting in his office wondering whether to blow the whistle on his firm. This is how the situation developed.

The case takes place in Liechtenstein where tax avoidance deals are not unheard of. In fact, the country is known to be a tax haven. Müller's information encompasses the political class in the tiny European country and elsewhere in the European Union (EU). He has 28,000 pages of documents from his firm that reveal how companies in the EU funneled money through Liechtenstein to lower their tax bills to as little as 1 percent.

At the time of the case, Müller was a senior tax accountant at the firm. He came across the confidential tax files in 2015 while searching for training documents on a shared drive. At first, it wasn't clear that the arrangements were illegal under Liechtenstein law, but further digging on his part made it clear that they were. Müller believed the public has a right to know about the deals. The fact that he had become disillusioned with his firm's auditing certainly played into his dilemma. He already had been contemplating whether to quit his job, make a clean break of it, and find employment elsewhere. That is when he discovered the incriminating files. He knew his boss was aware of the details so he decided to discuss the matter with her. Greta Von Hildenberg had always been a straight shooter so he felt comfortable discussing the matter with her.

Prior to the meeting, Müller took a copy of an internal folder containing the confidential tax agreements between Liechtenstein and some of the largest multinational companies in the world. He knew Von Hildenberg could not refute the fact that the firm was complicit in developing the deals that lowered taxable income and cheated the citizens of the EU out of tax money rightfully due to them.

At the time for the meeting, he knocked on Von Hildenberg's door. Much to his surprise, Gunther Kross was in her office. Kross was the head of the tax practice. He welcomed Müller and asked him to sit down. The ensuing conversation went this way.

"Heinrich, Greta tells me you have something to discuss with her."

Müller wasn't sure how to respond. He was still recovering from the shock of seeing Kross at the meeting. Finally he offered, "Yes."

"Well, what is it, Heinrich?" Kross asked. Müller hesitated but then disclosed what he had found in the tax filings and expressed his concerns about the matter.

"I don't see the problem, Heinrich. We both know this goes on all the time," Kross said.

"Perhaps, but the scope of it is alarming."

"What do you mean, Heinrich?"

"We're talking about $20 million euros ($20 million) of tax avoidance transactions."

"I see you have some files with you."

Müller's skin became flushed. He simply nodded his head.

"That's stealing confidential client information, do you know that, Heinrich?"

Müller felt he hadn't done anything with the files as yet so he answered by saying he only took the files for purposes of the meeting, even though he had already considered going public with the information. "I have no such intentions, I assure you Mr. Kross."

At this point Kross had to leave the meeting so it continued on between Heinrich and Von Hildenberg. Heinrich wondered why Von Hildenberg had been silent during the meeting. He asked her about it. She said that she followed orders and he should as well. Heinrich knew what she meant. The company had strict lines of communication, a loyalty oath that all employees had to sign, and a reputation of treating "traitors" to the cause harshly.

After a brief conversation, Heinrich was dismissed and he returned to his office to think through what his next step should be. Shortly thereafter, a German journalist from *Der Spiegel,* a popular German newspaper, called and asked to meet with Heinrich. Heinrich asked what it was about. The reporter didn't want to discuss it over the phone, but said he had received some disturbing information about tax transactions that affected the firm and heard Heinrich could be a valuable source of information. Reluctantly, Heinrich agreed to meet with the reporter later in the week.

Questions

1. Evaluate Heinrich's actions from an ethical perspective.

2. Assume you are in Heinrich's position and trying to decide among the following alternatives: (1) meet the reporter without discussing it with the firm; (2) meet with the reporter after first discussing it with the firm; (3) skipping a follow-up meeting altogether. What would you do and why?

3. Assume you have decided to meet with the firm first. Consider the following in developing a game plan on what you are going to say, who you are going to say it to, and why.

- What are the key values that inform your intended actions?
- What are the main arguments you are trying to counter? That is, what are the reasons and rationalizations you need to address?
- What is at stake for the key parties, including those who disagree with you?
- What levers can you use to influence those who disagree with you?
- What is your most powerful and persuasive response to the reasons and rationalizations you need to address? To whom should the argument be made? When and in what context?

4. In an ideal world, what do you hope the outcome of this situation will be after you meet with the firm? Explain.

Case 6-3 Richards & Co: Year-end Audit Engagement

Paul Lewis is the quality review partner on the Richards & Co. engagement. He was reviewing the workpapers prior to the December 31, 2015, annual audit when he came across transactions that caused him a great deal of concern. He wondered if the firm's auditors had handled them properly. The following information appeared in a memo to the file that prompted his concern.

Memo to File: Supplier Credits for Returned Product

For the last three quarters of the year, Richards has engaged in last-minute transactions that are questionable. The facts are, according to the client, that Richards received credits from a cellular phone supplier and promised to repay the supplier by purchasing cellular telephone and repair services at inflated prices in the subsequent quarter. The client has been unable to produce any supporting documents with respect to the promised purchases, and we have not been able to trace any such payments to cash disbursements.

The client has produced credit memos in the amount of $10 million, $7 million, and $4 million for December 31, 2015, September 30, 2015, and June 30, 2015, respectively, which is about 15 percent of the reported net income for 2015. The memos are marked to indicate that the credit was being provided in connection with defective telephone components. However, we could not identify any shipping documents to confirm that the components were returned to the supplier. Exhibit 1 shows the reported net income amounts by quarter and what they would have been without the credits.

EXHIBIT 1 Net Income Amounts

	Quarters for 2015			
	March 31	June 30	September 30	December 31
Reported net income	$36 million	$32 million	$33 million	$34 million
Net income w/o credits	$36 million	$28 million	$26 million	$24 million
Difference	-----$0-----	$ 4 million	$ 7 million	$10 million
Percentage		**14.3%**	**26.9%**	**41.7%**

We have filed 10-Q quarterly reports to the SEC based on the reported net income. We recommend, however, the firm conduct due diligence prior to publishing the 10-K annual report.

The client assures us that the promised purchases will be made and the only reason for not doing so is a cash flow problem. We are relying on management's representations in that regard. Richards is currently negotiating a loan for $20 million.

Questions

1. Does it seem from the limited data that the credit memo transactions can be justified as adjustments to reported net income amounts? Explain.

2. From an audit perspective, do you think the firm followed generally accepted auditing standards? Explain.

3. Based on the limited facts presented, do you think the firm violated any provisions of the Securities Exchange Act of 1934? Explain with reference to the auditors' legal liability.

Case 6-4 *Anjoorian et al.:* **Third-Party Liability**

In the 2007 case of *Paul V. Anjoorian v. Arnold Kilberg & Co., Arnold Kilberg, and Pascarella & Trench,* the Rhode Island Superior Court ruled that a shareholder can sue a company's outside accounting firm for alleged negligence in the preparation of the company's financial statements even though the accountant argued it had no duty of care to third parties like the shareholder, with whom it never engaged in a direct financial transaction. Judge Michael A. Silverstein disagreed, saying an accountant owes a duty to any individual or group of people who are meant to benefit from or be influenced by the information the accountant provides. Silverstein relied on the *Restatement (Second) of the Law of Torts:* "The Restatement approach strikes the appropriate balance between compensating victims of malpractice and limiting the scope of potential liability for those who certify financial statements. While it remains to be proved that [the firm] actually did foresee that [its] financial statements would be used by the shareholders [in the manner alleged], the absence of a particular financial transaction does not preclude the finding of a duty in this case."[1]

The facts of the case are described in Exhibit 1.

EXHIBIT 1 *Anjoorian Et Al.:* Third-party Liability

Facts of the Case

The defendants Pascarella and Trench, general partners of the accounting firm Pascarella & Trench (P&T), asked the court for summary judgment in their favor with respect to plaintiff Anjoorian's claim that P&T committed malpractice in the preparation of financial statements, and that the plaintiff (Anjoorian) suffered pecuniary harm as a result.

Anjoorian formerly owned 50 percent of the issued shares of Fairway Capital Corporation (FCC), a Rhode Island corporation. The other 50 percent of the shares were held by the three children of Arnold Kilberg. Kilberg himself owned no stock in the corporation, but he served as the day-to-day manager of the company. FCC was in the business of making and servicing equity loans to small businesses under the regulation of the U.S. Small Business Administration (SBA), and was capitalized by loans from the SBA and a $1.26 million investment by Anjoorian.

Beginning in 1990, P&T provided accounting services to FCC. The firm audited FCC's annual financial statements following the close of each calendar year between 1990 and 1994. In its representation letter (similar to the current Section 302 requirement under SOX), P&T stated that FCC was "responsible for the fair presentation in the financial statements of financial position." P&T's responsibility was to perform an audit in accordance with GAAS and to "express an opinion on the financial statements" based on the firm's audit. The first page of each financial statement contained the auditor's opinion that "the financial statements referred to above present fairly, in all material respects, the financial position of FCC in conformity with generally accepted accounting principles." Each report is addressed to "The Board of Directors and Shareholders." The 1990–1994 statements indicate that "it is management's opinion that all accounts presented on the balance sheet are collectible." In addition, the 1991–1994 statements indicate that "all loans are fully collateralized" according to the board of directors.

(Continued)

---

[1] Paul V. Anjoorian v. Arnold Kilberg & Co., Arnold Kilberg, and Pascarella & Trench by and through its general partners, Stephen E. Pascarella and John J. Trench, Available at: http://law.justia.com/cases/rhode-island/superior-court/2006/97-1013.html.

On March 2, 1994, Anjoorian filed a complaint and motion for a temporary restraining order seeking the dissolution of FCC on various grounds. P&T was not a party to that suit. As a result of that action, the three Kilberg children exercised their right to purchase the plaintiff's shares of the corporation. The court appointed an appraiser to determine the value of Anjoorian's shares, which the other shareholders would have to pay. The bulk of FCC's assets comprised its right to receive payment for the loans that it had made. The appraiser determined that the value of the corporation was $2,395,000, plus a payroll adjustment of $102,000, and minus a "loss reserve" adjustment to account for the fact that 10 of FCC's 30 outstanding loans were delinquent. The loss reserve adjustment reduced the total appraised value of the corporation by $878,234. Consequently, Anjoorian's 50 percent interest in the corporation was reduced accordingly by $439,117. He ultimately received a judgment for $809,382.85 against the other shareholders in exchange for the buyout of his shares.

In 1997, Anjoorian brought the lawsuit against Kilberg, Kilberg's company, and P&T. He claimed that P&T was negligent in preparing the annual financial statements for FCC because it did not include an accurate loan loss reserve in the statements. Anjoorian argued that he relied on the financial statements prepared by the defendants, and that if the statements had included a loan loss reserve, he would have sought dissolution of the corporation much earlier than 1994, when his shares would have been more valuable. Anjoorian submitted an appraisal suggesting that the appropriate loan loss reserve figure would have been much less—and, therefore, his share value much higher—in the years 1990 and 1991. He alleged that he lost over $300,000 in share value between 1990 and March 2, 1994. Nine years later, the defendants moved for summary judgment on the grounds that P&T owed no duty to Anjoorian as a shareholder.

Accountants' Liabilities to Third Parties

Silverstein observed that while the question of accountant liability to third parties was unsettled in Rhode Island, the Rhode Island Supreme Court had identified three competing interpretations. The first interpretation was the "foreseeability test," under which an auditor has a duty to all foreseeable recipients of information he provides. "This rule gives little weight to the concern for limiting the potential liability for accountants and is not widely adopted," Silverstein noted.

The second interpretation, the judge continued, was the "privity test," requiring a contractual relationship to exist between an accountant or auditor and another party.

Finally, the *Restatement* test, found in §522 of the *Restatement (Second) of Torts,* states an accountant who does not exercise reasonable care "is only liable to intended persons or classes of persons, and only for intended transactions or substantially similar transactions," said Silverstein. "[This approach] applies not only [to] specific persons and transactions contemplated by the accountant, but also specific classes of persons and transactions." Silverstein settled on the *Restatement* rule.[2]

Applying the rule, Silverstein denied summary judgment for the accounting firm, concluding there was a genuine issue of material fact on whether the accounting firm could be liable.

"This court would have no difficulty finding a duty in this case, in the absence of a specific financial transaction, if it can be shown that [the defendant] intended the shareholders to rely on the financial statements for the purpose of evaluating the financial health of the company, and therefore, their investment in the company," wrote Silverstein.[3]

Case Analysis

The court found that the addressing of the reports to the shareholders, while not conclusive, is a strong indication that P&T intended the shareholders to rely upon them. Therefore, the court concluded that genuine issues of fact exist as to whether P&T intended for Anjoorian to rely on these financial statements. Perhaps the court would have reached a different conclusion for a widely held public corporation with a potentially unlimited number of

[2] Eric T. Berkman, "Shareholder can sue accounting firm," January 26, 2007. Available at: http://newenglandinhouse.com/2007/01/26/shareholder-can-sue-accounting-firm/.

[3] Berkman.

shareholders whose identities change regularly. Here, however, FCC was a close corporation with only four shareholders, giving greater significance to the fact that the financial statements were addressed "to the shareholders."

The defendants also argued that, in order to find a duty to third parties, an accountant must have contemplated a specific transaction for which the financial statement would be used and that no such transaction was contemplated here.[4] The court found this argument unconvincing, stating that the case is unusual in that the alleged malpractice did not arise from a specific financial transaction. The typical case involves a person whose reliance on a defective financial statement induces the person to advance credit or invest new equity into the corporation.[5] When the investment is lost, or the loan unpaid, the person sues the accountant. In this case, however, Anjoorian had already invested his capital in the corporation when P&T was hired, and he alleged that he used the financial statements as a tool to evaluate the value of that investment. The alleged malpractice did not result in his advancing new value to the corporation and then losing his investment, but instead resulted in Anjoorian failing to withdraw his capital from the corporation while its value was higher.

The court opined that it would have no difficulty finding a duty in this case, in the absence of a specific financial transaction, if it could be shown that P&T intended the shareholders to rely on the financial statements for the purpose of evaluating the financial health of the company and, therefore, their investment in the company. In this case, the "particular transaction" contemplated by the *Restatement* relates to the purpose for which the financial statements would be used—the shareholders' decision whether to withdraw capital or not. While it remains to be proved that P&T actually did foresee that its financial statements would be used by the shareholders in this manner, the absence of a particular financial transaction does not preclude the finding of a duty in this case. Because the value of the shareholders' investment was limited to the amounts reflected in the company balance sheets, any loss from malpractice was an insurable risk for which accounting professionals can plan.[6]

The defendants argued that the plaintiff's theory of damages was speculative and against public policy. Anjoorian based his damage claims on the assertion that he relied on four annual audited financial statements to evaluate the status of his $1.26 million investment in FCC. Because the statements failed to include a loan loss reserve figure, he argued that the statements overstated the value of the corporation at the end of each year from 1990 to 1993. When Anjoorian sought dissolution in 1994, the value he obtained for his shares was significantly less than his expectation. He contended that if he had accurate financial information, he would have liquidated his investment earlier when his shares were more valuable. At issue was the existence and amount of the loan loss reserve. An appraiser of the value of the corporation in the dissolution action determined that the inclusion of a loan loss reserve in the financial statements was proper, and that created a genuine issue as to whether a breach of the duty of care occurred. The defendant had questioned the computation of the loan loss reserve but the court disagreed. (A detailed analysis of the amount of loan loss reserve has been omitted.)

Questions

1. The court found that the addressing of audit reports to the shareholders, while not conclusive, is a strong indication that P&T intended the shareholders to rely upon them. Do you agree, in general, that addressing the reports to a class of owners should be sufficient to hold an auditor legally liable to any shareholder who can demonstrate a lack of reasonable care? What about in applying the facts of this case? Would your conclusion change? Explain.

2. Judge Silverstein relied on the *Restatement (Second) of the Law of Torts* for his ruling. Assume he had relied on the "near-privity relationship" ruling in *Credit Alliance,* and evaluate the legal liability of the auditors using that standard.

3. The court decision refers to the importance of the auditors' knowing about third-party usage of the audited financial statements. What role does such knowledge play in enabling auditors to meet their professional and ethical responsibilities?

---

[4] Jenny Steele, *Tort Law: Text, Cases, and Materials,* 2nd edition (2010) (Oxford, UK: Oxford University Press).

[5] *Rusch Factors, Inc. v. Levin, 284 F. Supp. 85 (D.R.I. 1968).* U.S. District Court for the District of Rhode Island - 284 F. Supp. 85 (D.R.I. April 17, 1968), Available at: http://law.justia.com/cases/federal/district-courts/FSupp/284/85/1815507/.

[6] *Rusch Factors, Inc. v. Levin, 284 F. Supp. 85 (D.R.I. 1968).*

Case 6-5 *Vertical Pharmaceuticals Inc. et al. v. Deloitte & Touche LLP*[1]

On December 13, 2012, Vertical Pharmaceuticals Inc. and an affiliated company sued Deloitte & Touche LLP in New Jersey state court for alleged accountant malpractice, claiming the firm's false accusations of fraudulent conduct scrapped a public company's plans to acquire Vertical for more than $50 million.

Vertical is a privately owned company that sells niche prescription drugs geared toward women's health and pain management. Trigen Laboratories (TLI) sells and markets generic drugs. Deloitte was auditing the 2011 financial statements of Vertical and TLI, which are owned by the same three partners, when it abruptly suspended that review because of supposedly troubling items that two whistleblowers brought to the firm's attention, according to the complaint, which was filed November 21 in Morris County Superior Court.

Deloitte insisted that Vertical hire independent counsel and conduct an internal investigation with a forensic audit, the complaint said. Vertical agreed to those steps, but Deloitte eventually notified Vertical that it was resigning rather than finishing its work, according to the complaint.

"As a forensic audit later discovered—no money was being pilfered from the company. No partner was stealing money from another. No improper conduct was taking place," the complaint said.

The revelation that Deloitte resigned from the 2011 audit and the allegations of potential criminal conduct and financial improprieties that the auditor passed on to the audit committee left the acquisition for dead, the complaint said. The public company found another pharmaceutical company to acquire.

The deal would have helped rapidly grow Vertical's business and established a revenue stream for the company of more than $500 million, the complaint contended. "Deloitte knew the deal would be final once the 2011 audit was completed. Without Deloitte's interference in concocting a series of false, negligent statements regarding Vertical's financials, the 2011 audit would have been issued and the deal completed."

Vertical has asked for $200 million or more in damages on multiple counts, including accounting malpractice and breach of fiduciary duty. Deloitte also demanded and received $120,000 for all of its invoiced services before resigning, according to the complaint, which seeks back those funds as well.

Deloitte's allegedly slanted statements involved accusations that Vertical was pilfering company funds through two LLCs, inappropriately paying company employees through car allowances, committing fraud by having an owner's father as tax auditor, and paying an owner's wife off the books, according to the complaint.

The firm also falsely claimed Vertical's books were in terrible shape and that its management was unreliable, the complaint said. "A subsequent forensic audit initially to assuage Deloitte was ultimately completed . . . which found: None of these items had merit nor did they consider any resolution items justified to engender Deloitte's resignation; that Deloitte was well aware of the nature prior to its supposed whistleblower disclosures of the items; and that many of these items were in the process of being resolved based on advice provided by Deloitte as early as May 2011," the complaint said.

Questions

1. Do you believe Deloitte & Touche breached its fiduciary duty to Vertical Pharmaceuticals in this case? Explain.

2. Do you believe Deloitte was guilty of malpractice as alleged by Vertical? Use the discussion in this chapter to answer the question.

3. Do you think it was ethical for Deloitte to resign from the engagement without waiting for the results of the investigation and forensic audit that was conducted at Deloitte's insistence? Use ethical reasoning to support your belief.

---

[1] The case is Vertical Pharmaceuticals Inc. et al v. Deloitte & Touche LLP, case number L-2852-12, filed on December 13, 2012, in the Superior Court of New Jersey, Morris County.

Case 6-6 *Kay & Lee, LLP*

Kay & Lee LLP was retained as the auditor for Holligan Industries to audit the financial statements required by prospective banks as a prerequisite to extending a loan to the client. The auditor knows whichever bank lends money to the client is likely to rely on the audited statements.

After the audit report is issued, the bank that ultimately made the loan discovers that the client's inventory and accounts receivable were overstated. The client subsequently went bankrupt and defaulted on the loan. The bank alleged that the auditor failed to communicate about the inadequacy of the client's internal recordkeeping and inventory control. Moreover, the bank claims that the auditors were grossly negligent in not discovering the overvaluation of inventory and accounts receivable.

The auditors asserted that there was no way for them to know that the client included in the inventory account $1 million of merchandise in transit to a customer on December 31, 2015. The shipping terms were unclear so the auditors accepted management's representations in that regard (FOB Destination). As for the receivables, the auditors claimed the client falsified confirmations by sending them to a post office address, retrieving them, and then confirming the stated balances.

Questions

1. What would the bank have to prove to successfully bring a lawsuit against Kay & Lee?

2. What defenses might the auditors use to rebut any charges made about their (deficient) audit?

3. Critically evaluate the auditors' statements about the inventory and receivables with respect to generally accepted auditing standards and the firm's ethical responsibilities.

Case 6-7 Getaway Cruise Lines: Questionable Payments to do Business Overseas (a GVV case)

Kirsten had her dream job, combining her love of accounting with traveling. She'd just had a big promotion to Director of International Accounting for Getaway Cruise Lines. As the director in the Houston office, she was currently overseeing final contracts accounting for the docking of two small cruise ships during the 2016 Olympics in Rio de Janeiro, Brazil.

The idea behind using a luxury cruise ship as a hotel choice for the sporting events was based upon high-end travelers wanting luxury, individualized attention, and security in a high crime–ridden city. The marketing for the cruise lodging included secure transportation to and from the ship to the sport venues each day and for evening entertainment. The ship also offered onboard fine dining and nightclubs. Being smaller in size, the ships would be able to dock at a pier in the Rio harbor. The cruise line was offering private security for the guests who wanted the protection and would have guards on the pier at all times.

The last contracts were proving to be the thorniest and had the most difficult set of problems. The latest contract received from Bob Regan, Getaway's representative in the Brazil office, noted that the Getaway line needed to pay an additional $25,000 per ship to facilitate the applications. Additionally, the line would need to provide Rio with its surplus electricity and potable water. Kirsten knew that cruise lines used reversed osmosis to treat wastewater back into potable water and often sold the surplus at the different ports-of-call. Bob stated that Brazil was experiencing a severe drought, which was affecting the country's electricity supply and causing rolling blackouts, making it a requirement for any ships in the harbor to share a certain amount of their electricity and potable water. The final documents, fees, and other agreements were to be signed at Getaway headquarters and returned in two days. As Kirsten reviewed the final contract, she was troubled by the $25,000 fee and the requirement to provide surplus electricity and water.

Kirsten called headquarters in Miami, Florida, to talk to her boss, Matt Davies, about the issues of concern to her and directions on how to handle them. She wondered if the additional requirements from Bob were legal payments.

Matt returned her call within the hour, but the conversation was not encouraging. He seemed in a hurry and impatient with the request for guidance on the problems.

"Kirsten, I do not understand your concerns over the paperwork and fees required. This is part of your job and why you were hired. I expect you to handle these details and the accounting without a lot of hand-holding."

"I know that I am to handle the final paperwork and accounting for all permits and other payments. The $25,000 fee request for each application surprised me. Also, the requirement for the ship to share its electricity and potable water seemed a bit odd and a little heavy-handed. Does share mean donate or does it mean sell?"

"Now, don't get too excited yet. I'm sure that all of these fees and requests for electricity and water are just a normal way of doing business in Rio. Are you sure you understood Regan correctly? Maybe you should use our translator and have the contracts re-translated so that the details of the request are clear and there are not any miscommunications. I'm sure the translator will show you that this is all just a misunderstanding. Use the water and electricity pricing sheet and make sure that the contract states that any sales of water and electricity are on a surplus basis, after the needs of our guests are met."

"Matt, I do not mind using the translator; I am very concerned about the possibility of making improper payments and the unease I feel about this. Maybe…"

"Kirsten, trust that all will be fine. Now I must go!"

"What is your availability tomorrow, if I need you?"

Matt told Kirsten to handle it. She was worried about the issues even though he had dismissed her concerns. In fact, she wondered why he didn't take it more seriously. Maybe she was reading too much into the situation, but her intuition was normally right on the money. Now she had to tackle the problems and see if they had reasonable solutions.

Kirsten decided she needed a little moral support from friends and family. She called her longtime friend John Fox. Fox was always a good listener and helped her to keep her moral compass in the right direction. Fox was able to listen and give feedback to Kirsten.

"John, can you see why this situation has me so stressed? Do you think I am overacting?"

"You do have a sticky situation on your hands. You were the one that spoke with Regan. I know that your intuition has been spot-on in the past and you should not ignore it in this situation. Say, didn't you mention that the CEO of Getaway had set a high ethical tone at the company as a top goal of the line? If you feel the fees and sale of electricity and water are improper, and if it doesn't look like Davies will take a stand on it, can you contact the CEO? Don't you think the CEO would want to know if the company was about to make questionable payments or engage in corruption?"

"You make a good point. I can always count on objective advice from you. I'll call Davies tomorrow and try to clarify his position. I would really hate to break the chain of command and go right to the top. I'll have to try and convince him that these payments may cross the line and seem to be improper to me."

"You could explain how bribery is against the law of the United States."

"I think I will have to start with how it is dishonest and unfair to other companies. I will have to think on this, but you have given me support and hope that this might turn out all right. I'll call you in a few days to give you an update. I really owe you!"

The next morning Kirsten felt calm and confident that she could confront any prospect of bribery with integrity. First, Kirsten met with the translator to get a new translation of the contracts. Then she had a conference call with Bob Regan in the Rio office.

Bob was as overbearing as Kirsten remembered. He stressed how the "facilitation fees," as he called them, must be paid within a week or the ships would not be allowed to dock in the Rio harbor. Kirsten asked more about the facilitation fees, whether a standard pricing list for the fees was available, why he was requesting the amount for three ships when only two would be docking, and more details on the sale of surplus electricity and water from the ship.

"Bob, let's settle the sale of the electricity and water to the city of Rio first. I have our standard contract for the sale of surplus utilities with the pricing list here." Kirsten explained. "The contract is for a set amount each week. The city has stressed that as guests in the harbor the line should want to donate it as a sign of mutual cooperation and leadership in the tourism industry."

"That's right," Bob replied.

"But Bob, the ship can only sell its utilities after needs of our guests are met. Our first obligation is to meet the needs of our guest."

"It's not that simple, Kirsten. Due to ongoing drought the city's needs must come before any other organization's needs. Besides, the providing of the utilities can be considered an additional rental cost of docking at the pier."

"But the docking fees were agreed to in principle two years ago. Are you saying that amount has increased?"

"No, no, you misunderstand. Of course, the docking fees have not changed. The basic contract is the same, but it has been updated for current circumstances. The situation has changed and now utilities need to be donated as well as the docking fees."

"But our obligations to our guests…"

"Yes, but if we do not help with utilities, the line will have to pay a fine of $100,000 a week for not sharing the utilities."

"But that was not part of the agreement."

"It is now a requirement for the ships to be allowed to dock in the harbor."

"How does this fit in with the facilitation fees?"

"Those fees are also part of whether the ships can dock or not."

"Are these additional requirements bribes to do business in Brazil even when the company has an existing contract? That would not be honest nor in keeping with the company's policies or U.S. laws."

"I do not think these requirements are bribes but rather the cost of doing business in Rio."

"I think I understand, Bob, but still feel uneasy about the situation. I need to consult with Matt Davies at headquarters. I have finished the paperwork and have no authority to renegotiate any contract revisions. I will get back to you soon."

Bob reminded Kirsten that the company had to meet the deadline or its ships couldn't dock nor could there be boarding or deboarding from the ship if there were any outstanding fees or fines due.

Kirsten thought about how she would present the issues to Matt and wondered about the future and alternatives open to her. After a brief period of reflection, she dialed Miami and asked to speak with him. Matt was in a meeting, so she left an urgent voice mail and another message with his assistant. While she waited for him to call back, she considered what might happen to her if Matt was adamant about the cruise line making the requested payments. What about her future with the line? Then she returned to the most important point, which was to be true to her values.

Questions

1. Do you think the two payments are facilitation payments or bribes? Explain.

2. How might Kristen best explain her point of view to Matt while being true to her values?

3. What are the likely reasons and rationalizations Matt will give for making the payments discussed in the case?

4. Are there any levers that Kirsten can use to counteract the reason and rationalizations and persuade Matt about the right thing to do?

Case 6-8 Con-way Inc.

Summary of Findings

Con-way is a Delaware corporation headquartered in San Mateo, California. It is an international freight transportation and logistics services company that conducts operations in a number of foreign jurisdictions. During the relevant period, the company was named CNF, Inc.; it changed its name to Con-way in April 2006. Con-way's common stock is registered with the SEC pursuant to Section 12(b) of the Exchange Act and is listed on the NYSE.[1]

Menlo Worldwide Forwarding, Inc. (Menlo Forwarding), was a wholly owned U.S-based subsidiary of Con-way that Con-way purchased in 1989. During the relevant period, Menlo Forwarding was headquartered in Redwood City, California, and had a 55 percent voting interest in Emery Transnational (Emery). Con-way sold Menlo Forwarding to United Parcel Service of America, Inc. (UPS), in December 2004.

California-based Con-way Inc., a global freight forwarder, was charged by the SEC with making payments that violated the FCPA. The company paid a $300,000 penalty and accepted a cease-and-desist order to settle the FCPA enforcement action. Con-way's FCPA violations were caused by a Philippines-based subsidiary, Emery Transnational. It made about $244,000 in improper payments between 2000 and 2003 to officials at the Philippines Bureau of Customs and the Philippine Economic Zone Area, and $173,000 in improper payments to officials at 14 state-owned airlines. In connection with the improper payments, Con-way failed to record these payments accurately on the company's books and records and knowingly failed to implement or maintain a system of effective internal accounting controls.

Lack of Oversight over Emery Transnational

During the relevant period, Con-way and Menlo Forwarding engaged in little supervision or oversight over Emery. Neither Con-way nor Menlo Forwarding took steps to devise or maintain internal accounting controls concerning Emery, to ensure that it acted in accordance with Con-way's FCPA policies, or to make certain that its books and records were detailed or accurate.

During the relevant period, Con-way and Menlo Forwarding only required that Emery periodically report back to Menlo its net profits, from which Emery then paid Menlo a yearly 55 percent dividend. Menlo incorporated the yearly 55 percent dividend into its financial results, which were then consolidated in Con-way's financial statements. Neither Con-way nor Menlo asked for or received any other financial information from Emery. Accordingly, neither Con-way nor Menlo maintained or reviewed any of the books and records of Emery—including the records of operating expenses, which should have reflected the illicit payments made to foreign officials.

Payments to Philippine Customers Officials

Emery made hundreds of small payments to foreign officials at the Philippines Bureau of Customs and the Philippine Economic Zone Area between 2000 and 2003 in order to obtain or retain business. These payments were made to influence the acts and decisions of these foreign officials and to secure a business advantage or economic benefit. By these payments, foreign officials were induced to (1) violate customs regulations by allowing Emery to store shipments longer than otherwise permitted, thus saving the company transportation costs related to its inbound shipments; (2) improperly settle Emery's disputes with the Philippines Bureau of Customs, or (3) reduce or not enforce otherwise legitimate fines for administrative violations.

To generate funding for these payments, Emery employees submitted a *Shipment Processing and Clearance Expense Report* to Emery's finance department. These reports requested cash advances to complete customs processing. The cash advances were then issued via checks made payable to Emery employees, who cashed the checks and paid the money to designated foreign officials. Unlike legitimate customs payments, the payments at issue were not supported by receipts from the Philippines Bureau of Customs and the Philippine Economic Zone Area. Emery did not identify the true nature of these payments in its books and records. From 2000 to 2003, these payments totaled at least $244,000.

---

[1]Securities and Exchange Commission, In the Matter of Con-way Inc., Accounting and Auditing Enforcement Release No. 2867, August 27, 2008,, Available at: www.sec.gov/litigation/admin/ 2008/34-58433.pdf.

Payments to Officials of Majority State-Owned Airlines

To obtain or retain business, Emery also made numerous payments to foreign officials at 14 state-owned airlines that did business in the Philippines between 2000 and 2003. These payments were made with the intent of improperly influencing the acts and decisions of these foreign officials and to secure a business advantage or economic benefit. Emery Transnational made two types of payments. The first type was known as "weight-shipped" payments, which were made to induce airline officials to reserve space for Emery on the airplanes improperly. These payments were valued based on the volume of the shipments the airlines carried for Emery. The second type were known as "gain shares" payments, which were paid to induce airline officials to falsely underweigh shipments and to consolidate multiple shipments into a single shipment, resulting in lower shipping charges. Emery paid the foreign officials 90 percent of the reduced shipping costs.

Both types of payments to foreign airline officials were paid in cash by members of Emery's management team. Checks reflecting the amount of the weight-shipped and gain shares payments were issued to these managers, who cashed the checks and personally distributed the cash payments to the foreign airline officials. Emery Transnational did not characterize these payments in its books and records as bribes. During the 2000–2003 period, these payments totaled at least $173,000. Neither Con-way nor Menlo requested or received any records of these payments or any of Emery's expenses during this period.

Discovery of Improper Payments and Internal Investigation

Con-way discovered potential FCPA issues in early 2003. Starting in January 2003, Menlo initiated steps to increase Emery's internal reporting requirements, including requiring Emery to begin reporting its income and expenses, in addition to its net profits. As a result, in reviewing Emery's records, Menlo employees noticed unusually high customs and airline-related expenditures.

Menlo conducted an internal investigation of the suspicious payments at Emery and determined that Emery employees had been making regular cash payments to customs officials and employees of majority state-owned airlines. Based on Menlo's investigation, Con-way conducted a broader review of all of Menlo foreign businesses and voluntarily disclosed the existence of possible FCPA violations to the staff. After completing its internal investigation, Con-way imposed heightened financial reporting and compliance requirements on Emery. Menlo terminated a number of the Emery employees involved in the misconduct, and Con-way provided additional FCPA training and education to its employees and strengthened its regulatory compliance program. In December 2004, Con-way sold Emery to UPS.

Legal Analysis

The FCPA, enacted in 1977, added Exchange Act Section 13(b)(2)(A) to require public companies to make and keep books, records, and accounts that, in reasonable detail, accurately and fairly reflect the transactions and dispositions of the assets of the issuer, and added Exchange Act Section 13(b)(2)(B) to require such companies to devise and maintain a system of internal accounting controls sufficient to provide reasonable assurances that (1) transactions are executed in accordance with management's general or specific authorization; and (2) transactions are recorded as necessary to permit preparation of financial statements in conformity with generally accepted accounting principles or any other criteria applicable to such statements, and to maintain accountability for assets.

As already detailed, Con-way's books, records, and accounts did not properly reflect the illicit payments made by Emery to Philippine customs officials and to officials of majority state-owned airlines. As a result, Con-way violated SEC Exchange Act Section 13(b)(2)(A). Con-way also failed to devise or maintain sufficient internal controls to ensure that Emery Transnational complied with the FCPA and to ensure that the payments it made to foreign officials were accurately reflected on its books and records. As a result, Con-way violated Section 13(b)(2)(B) of the Act.

Securities Exchange Act Section 13(b)(5) prohibits any person or company from knowingly circumventing or knowingly failing to implement a system of internal accounting controls as described in Section 13(b)(2)(B), or knowingly falsifying any book, record, or account as described in Section 13(b)(2)(A). By knowingly failing to implement a system of internal accounting controls concerning Emery Transnational, Con-way also violated Exchange Act Section 13(b)(5).

According to the SEC's complaint, none of Emery's improper payments were reflected accurately in Con-way's books and records. Also, Con-way knowingly failed to implement a system of internal accounting controls concerning Emery that would both ensure that Emery complied with the FCPA and require that the payments that it made to foreign officials were reflected accurately on its books and records.

Questions

1. The FCPA distinguishes between so-called facilitating payments and more serious activities. Do you think such a distinction and the related penalties for violations under the Act make sense from an ethical perspective? Use the utilitarian analysis to support your position.

2. Assume the auditors of Con-way knew about the accounting for FCPA payments in the books and records of the company. Do you think the auditors would be guilty of: (1) ordinary negligence; (2) gross negligence; or (3) fraud? Explain.

3. Given that the FCPA permits facilitating payments, do you believe it is ethically appropriate for companies to deduct such payments from their income taxes? Why or why not? What about outright bribery payments? What does the law require in each instance with respect to tax deductibility?

Case 6-9 Satyam: India's Enron

Satyam Computer Services, now Mahindra Satyam, is an India-based global business and information technology services company that specializes in consulting, systems integration, and outsourcing solutions. The company was the fourth-largest software exporter in India until January 2009, when the CEO and cofounder, Ramalinga Raju, confessed to inflating the company's profits and cash reserves over an eight-year period. The accounting fraud at Satyam involved dual accounting books, more than 7,000 forged invoices, and dozens of fake bank statements. The total amount of losses was Rs (rupees) 50 billion (equal to about $1.04 billion). This represented about 94 percent of the company's cash and cash equivalents. The global scope of Satyam's fraud led to the labeling of it as "India's Enron." Ironically, the name "Satyam" is derived from the Sanskrit word *satya,* which translates to "truth."

Although headquartered in Hyderabad, India, Satyam's stock was listed on the NYSE since 2001. When the news of the fraud broke, Satyam's stock declined almost 90 percent in value on both the U.S. and Indian stock exchanges. Several top managers either resigned or were fired and jail terms were given to Raju, the co-founder and CEO, and Sirinivas Vadlamani, the CFO. The auditors—PricewaterhouseCoopers (PwC)—were also implicated in the fraud.

Fraudulent Actions by Raju

Raju stepped down in early January 2009, admitting to falsifying financial figures of the company with respect to nonexistent cash and bank balances. Stunning his well-wishers and investors, Raju revealed the real motive behind the December 16 bid to acquire Maytas companies for $1.6 billion: to swap the fictitious cash reserves of Satyam built over years with the Maytas assets. Raju thought that the payments to Maytas could be delayed once Satyam's problem was solved. What had started as a marginal gap between actual operating profit and the one reflected in the books continued to grow over the years. It had attained unmanageable proportions as the size of the company's operations grew over the years. One lie led to another. The problem further worsened as the company had to carry additional resources and assets to justify a higher level of operations, leading to increased costs.

As things got out of hand, Raju was forced to raise Rs 1.23 billion (approximately $25.58 million) more by pledging the family-owned shares to keep the operations going. His woes were compounded with amounts due to vendors, fleet operators, and construction companies. The offloading of the pledged shares by IL&FS Trust Company, a Mumbai-based financial institution, and others brought down the promoters' stake from 8.65 percent to a fragile 3.6 percent. By the end of the day, Raju was left facing charges from several sides. The Ministry of Corporate Affairs, the state government, and the market regulator, SEBI, decided to probe the affairs of the company and Raju's role, as well as corporate governance issues.

Going by his confessional statement to the board of Satyam in January 2009, what Raju had done over the years appears to be rather simple manipulation of revenues and earnings to show a superior performance than what was actually the case. For this, he resorted to the time-tested practice of creating fictitious billings for services that were never rendered. The offset was either an inflation of receivables or the cash in bank balance. The following is a summary of the way financial statement amounts were manipulated:

- 94 percent (Rs 5.04 billion/approximately $10.5 million) of the cash in bank account balance in the September 30, 2008, balance sheet was inflated, due largely to exaggerated profits and fictitious assets.
- An accrued interest of Rs 376 million (approximately $7.82 million) was nonexistent.
- An understated liability of Rs 1.23 billion (approximately $25.58 million) resulting from Raju's infusion of personal funds into the company was recorded as revenue.
- Inflated revenues of Rs 588 million (approximately $12.23 million) went straight to the bottom line.

Acquisition of Maytas Properties and Maytas Infrastructure

In December 2008, Raju tried to buy two firms owned by his sons, Maytas Properties and Maytas Infrastructure (Satyam spelled backward is Maytas) for $1.6 billion. Raju tried to justify the purchase by stating that the company needed to diversify by incorporating the infrastructure market to augment its software market. However, many investors thought that the purchases of two firms were intended to line the pockets of the Raju family. Raju owned less than 10 percent of Satyam, whereas Raju's family owned 100 percent of the equity in Maytas Properties and about 40 percent of Maytas Infrastructure. Stock prices plunged dramatically after the announcement, so Raju rescinded his offer to buy the two companies.

With the prices of Satyam stock and the health of the company declining, four members of the board of directors of Satyam resigned within one month. In his confession, Raju took full responsibility for the accounting fraud and stated that the board knew nothing about the manipulation of financial statements. He indicated a willingness to accept the legal consequences of his actions.

An important question is how independently did the "independent" directors of Satyam act in the now highly questioned and failed decision to acquire the Maytas companies? One board member, M. Rammohan Rao, dean of the prestigious Indian School of Business (ISB) with campuses in Hyderabad and Mohali, claimed that the board had taken an independent view and raised concerns about the unrelated diversification, valuation, and other issues. Two views emerged. The first was, why not stick to our core competencies and why venture into a risky proposition? The second issue was related to the valuation of the companies. Maytas Properties was valued much higher than $1.3 billion, the amount that Satyam's management came up with for the acquisition price. When asked whether the fact that the target companies—Maytas Properties and Maytas Infrastructure—were led by Raju's two sons made any difference to the board, Rao said, "We felt the valuation proposed by the Satyam management was lower and conservative, despite the family ties. We took an independent view on this."[1]

When asked if the board had taken into consideration the possible impact of the purchase of the two companies on shareholders' interests and the market reaction, the ISB dean responded, "There were concerns on these grounds as well, especially the market reaction for such an unrelated diversification." However, according to Rao, there was no way that they could gauge the market reaction at first, so they decided to take a risk. But the way the market reacted was a bit unanticipated, he added.

Questions can be raised about corporate governance with respect to the failed acquisition of the Maytas companies. A conflict of interest arose when Satyam's board agreed to invest $1.6 billion to acquire a 100 percent stake in Maytas Properties and a 51 percent stake in Maytas Infrastructure. The Raju family, which ran the Maytas companies, also invited family or close friends to serve on the board of directors. These bonds created independence issues and questions about whether directors would be confrontational with top management when warranted.

Litigation in the United States

Securities fraud class action lawsuits were filed on behalf of a class of persons and entities who purchased or acquired the American Depositary Shares (ADSs)[1] of Satyam on the NYSE and/or were investors residing in the United States who purchased or acquired Satyam common stock traded on Indian exchanges between January 6, 2004, and January 6, 2009 (the class period).

---

[1]An American Depositary Share (ADS) is a U.S. dollar-denominated equity share of a foreign-based company available for purchase on an American stock exchange. ADSs are issued by depository banks in the U.S. under agreement with the issuing foreign company; the entire issuance is called an American Depositary Receipt (ADR) and the individual shares are referred to as ADSs.

The complaint alleged that Satyam, certain of its directors and officers, and the company's outside auditors (PwC) made false and misleading public statements regarding Satyam's financial condition and performance, which artificially inflated the stock price. On January 7, 2009, Satyam's chair, Ramalinga Raju, sent a letter to the company's board confessing to a massive accounting fraud. Raju admitted that the company's balance sheet and other public disclosures contained numerous false statements. For example, Raju wrote that, as of September 30, 2008, the company overstated revenue by approximately 22 percent and reported cash and bank balances of Rs 53.61 billion (approximately $1.1 billion), of which Rs 50.4 billion (over $1 billion) did not exist.[2]

Reports issued since the January 7 confession indicate that Raju likely understated the scope of the fraud, and that he and members of his family engaged in widespread theft of Satyam's funds through a complex web of intermediary entities.

The complaint also asserted claims against PricewaterhouseCoopers International Ltd. and its Indian partners and affiliates including Price Waterhouse Bangalore, PricewaterhouseCoopers Private Limited, and Lovelock & Lewes (PW India firms). Satyam's outside auditors from the PW India firms were aware of the fraud but still certified the company's financial statements as accurate. A document (the charge sheet) filed in a Hyderabad court by the Indian Central Bureau of Investigation (the equivalent of the U.S. Federal Bureau of Investigation), detailing charges against numerous Satyam employees and two partners of PW India firms, alleged that the auditors received documentation from Satyam's banks that showed that the company's disclosed assets were greatly overstated. The charge sheet further alleged that these auditors received fees from Satyam that were exorbitantly higher than the fees similarly situated Indian companies paid to their outside auditors; the Central Bureau of Investigation cited these fees as evidence of a "well-knit criminal conspiracy" between Satyam and the auditors.

The complaint asserted claims against other defendants as well. In particular, the complaint alleged that members of the audit committee of the Satyam board of directors—who were responsible for overseeing the integrity of the company's financial statements, the performance and compensation of the outside auditors from PW India firms, and the adequacy and effectiveness of internal accounting and financial controls—were responsible for the publication of false and misleading public statements due to their extreme recklessness in discharging their duties and their resulting failure to discover and prevent the massive accounting fraud. The complaint also alleged that Maytas Infrastructure and Maytas Properties and Raju's two sons were responsible for the false and misleading public statements. The Raju sons' false and misleading statements concerning Satyam's financial condition and performance artificially inflated the prices of the company's publicly traded securities during the class period, and caused significant damages to investors when the prices of the company's securities both in the United States and in India experienced severe declines as a direct result of disclosures regarding Satyam's true condition.

Actions Against PwC

PwC and its Indian affiliates initially hid behind "client confidentiality" and stated that it was "examining the contents of the statement." Realizing that this was not enough, PwC came up with a second statement claiming that "the audits were conducted in accordance with applicable auditing standards and were supported by appropriate audit evidence." This is somewhat troublesome because an audit in accordance with generally accepted auditing standards (GAAS) calls for examining the contents of the financial statements. Given that the firm did not identify the financial wrongdoing at Satyam, it would appear that the firm, at the very least, was guilty of professional negligence as follows.

- Fictitious invoices with customers were recorded as genuine.
- Raju recorded a fictional interest credit as income.
- The auditors didn't ask for a statement of confirmation of balance from banks (for cash balances) and debtors (for receivables), a basic procedure in an audit.

On January 24, 2009, Indian police arrested two partners of the Indian arm of PwC on charges of criminal conspiracy and cheating in connection with the fraud investigation at Satyam. Furious Indian investors had pressured the authorities to take such an action in light of the more than $1 billion fraud. Investors couldn't understand how a reported $1 billion in cash was really only $78 million, and how it wasn't detected by PwC. The company's financial statements were signed off by PwC on March 31, 2008.[3]

[2] Madan Mhasin, "Corporate Accounting Fraud: A Case Study of Satyam Computers Limited," *Open Journal of Accounting,* November 2012, Vol. 3 No. 10.

[3] Harichandan Arakali and Saikat Chatterjee, "Price Waterhouse Auditors Arrested in Satyam Inquiry (Update1)," January 24, 2009, Available at: http://www.bloomberg.com/apps/news?pid=newsarchive&sid=ar6hB_Hr347E.

Eventually, PwC agreed to pay $25.5 million to settle investor class-action allegations that its audits failed to stop a large accounting fraud at Satyam.

Questions

1. Madan Bahsin concludes in her research paper that examined the fraud at Satyam that "the scandal brought to light the importance of ethics and its relevance to corporate culture."[4] Explain what you believe Bahsin meant by linking the ethical reasoning methods discussed in the text to corporate governance, using the Satyam fraud to illustrate your points.

2. Hofstede's cultural values that were discussed in Chapter 1 reflect the following scores with respect to India and the United States.

Cultural Dimension	India	U.S.
Individualism (IDV)	48	91
Power Distance (PDI)	77	40
Uncertainty Avoidance (UAI)	40	46
Masculinity (MAS)	56	62
Long-term Orientation (LTO)	61	29

Do you believe these differences in cultural values and the discussion in this chapter about corporate governance in India can be used to explain the nature and scope of the fraud at Satyam including the involvement of Raju in the acquisition of two companies owned by his sons? What checks and balances might have existed in the United States to deal with the fraud in a more effective manner?

3. Briefly discuss the audit failures of PwC and its affiliates with respect to the accounting issues raised in the case including fraud risk assessment. What rules of professional conduct in the AICPA Code that was discussed in Chapter 4 were violated?

Case 6-10 Autonomy

Background

On November 20, 2012, Hewlett-Packard (HP) disclosed that it discovered an accounting fraud and has written down $8.8 billion of the value of Autonomy, the British software company that it bought in 2011 for $11.1 billion, after discovering that Autonomy misrepresented its finances. In May 2012, HP had fired former Autonomy CEO, Dr. Michael Lynch, citing poor performance by his unit.

According to HP, its internal probe and forensic review had uncovered that the majority of the impairment charge, over $5 billion, is linked to serious accounting improprieties, disclosure failures, and outright misrepresentations discovered by HP's internal investigation into Autonomy's practices prior to and in connection with the acquisition.

The investigation began after an unnamed "senior member" of Autonomy's leadership alleged there had been a "series of questionable accounting and business practices" prior to the acquisition. HP said that the whistleblower gave "numerous details" that HP previously had no "knowledge or visibility" of. HP said it has discovered "extensive evidence" that an unspecified number of former employees of Autonomy had cooked the books prior to HP's $11.1 billion acquisition of the software company.

The probe determined that Autonomy was "substantially overvalued at the time of its acquisition" due to misstatements of financial performance, including revenue, core growth rate, and gross margins.

So what is alleged to have happened? For one thing, Autonomy, as HP tells it, was selling some hardware at a loss. During a period of about eight quarters prior to HP's acquisition, Autonomy sold some hardware products that had

[4]Madan Bahsin, "Corporate Accounting Frauds: A Case Study of Satyam Computers Limited," International Journal of Contemporary Business Studies, Available at: http://akpinsightijcbs.webs.com/2.%20IJCBS%20Vol%203%20,No%20 10%20%20OCt%20%202012%20Madan.pdf.

a very low margin or on which it may have even taken a loss. It then allegedly turned around and booked those hardware sales as high-margin software sales and booked some of the cost as marketing expense.

There's a second piece of the puzzle, where HP says that Autonomy was selling software to value-added resellers—the middlemen in so many technology transactions—in which there are ultimately no end users. That, too, inflated apparent revenue.

Third, there were some long-term hosting deals—essentially, Autonomy hosting applications for its customers on a subscription basis—that were converted to short-term licensing deals. Future revenue for software subscriptions—that should have been deferred or recorded as coming in the future but not yet booked—were stripped out and booked all at once.

In a statement, former CEO, Leo Apotheker said he is both "stunned and disappointed to learn" of the alleged accounting improprieties, and the developments "are a shock to the many who believed in the company, myself included."

Apotheker said the due diligence process was "meticulous and thorough" and "it's apparent that Autonomy's alleged accounting misrepresentations misled a number of people over time—not just HP's leadership team, auditors, and directors."

Autonomy's Position

A spokeswoman for fired CEO Lynch told Reuters that the HP allegations are "false" and Autonomy's management was "shocked to see" the fraud charges. Lynch said that HP's due diligence was intensive and the larger company's senior management was "closely involved with running Autonomy for the past year."

Lynch further commented that[1]

- HP was using this as a ruse to distract investors from its bigger problems: "People certainly realize I'm not going to be used as Hewlett-Packard's scapegoat when it's got itself in a mess."
- HP's numbers didn't add up. It's questioning about $100 million in revenues, yet blaming $5 billion of the write-off on fishy accounting.
- He wanted HP to explain in detail how it came up with the $5 billion in write-offs from alleged fraud.
- He not only denied all wrongdoing, but he had backup because Autonomy was audited quarterly and every invoice over €100,000 euros ($129,000) was approved by auditors.

Lynch also said that some of the accusations are misleading because Autonomy was following IFRS, as British companies do, not the GAAP standard used by HP, which means it recognizes revenue differently in certain situations from U.S. practices. Finally, Lynch said that Autonomy's auditor, Deloitte, was aware of every transaction that had been questioned, and approved Autonomy's accounting methods.

Exhibit 1 contains statements made by HP and Lynch in the Autonomy matter.

EXHIBIT 1   Statements by HP and Dr. Michael Lynch at Autonomy

HP's Official Statement

HP has initiated an intense internal investigation into a series of accounting improprieties, disclosure failures, and outright misrepresentations that occurred prior to HP's acquisition of Autonomy. We believe we have uncovered extensive evidence of a willful effort on behalf of certain former Autonomy employees to inflate the underlying financial metrics of the company in order to mislead investors and potential buyers.

The matter is in the hands of the authorities, including the U.K. Serious Fraud Office (SFC), the U.S. Securities and Exchange Commission's Enforcement Division and the U.S. Department of Justice, and we will defer to them as to how they wish to engage with Dr. Lynch. In addition, HP will take legal action against the parties involved at the appropriate time.

(Continued)

[1]Poornima Gupta and Nicola Leske, "HP accuses Autonomy of wrongdoing, takes $8.8 billion charge," November 21, 2012, Available at: http://www.reuters.com/article/2012/11/21/us-hp-results-idUSBRE8AJ0OB20121121.

While Dr. Lynch is eager for a debate, we believe the legal process is the correct method in which to bring out the facts and take action on behalf of our shareholders. In that setting, we look forward to hearing Dr. Lynch and other former Autonomy employees answer questions under penalty of perjury.

For his part, Lynch offered a decidedly different narrative in a letter to HP's board that he released publicly on November 27, 2012.

To: The Board of Directors of Hewlett-Packard Company

I utterly reject all allegations of impropriety.

Autonomy's finances, during its years as a public company and including the time period in question, were handled in accordance with applicable regulations and accounting practices. Autonomy's accounts were overseen by independent auditors Deloitte LLC, who have confirmed the application of all appropriate procedures including those dictated by the International Financial Reporting Standards used in the U.K.

Having no details beyond the limited public information provided last week, and still with no further contact from you, I am writing today to ask you, the board of HP, for immediate and specific explanations for the allegations HP is making. HP should provide me with the interim report and any other documents which you say you have provided to the SEC and the SFO so that I can answer whatever is alleged, instead of the selective disclosure of non-material information via background discussions with the media.

I believe it is in the interest of all stakeholders, and the public record, for HP to respond to a number of questions that I have about the allegations.

- Many observers are stunned by HP's claim that these allegations account for a $5 billion write down and fail to understand how HP reaches that number. Please publish the calculations used to determine the $5 billion impairment charge. Please provide a breakdown of the relative contribution for revenue, cash flow, profit, and write-down in relation to:

    a. The alleged "mischaracterization" of hardware that HP did not realize Autonomy sold, as I understand this would have no effect on annual top or bottom lines and a minor effect on gross margin within normal fluctuations and no impact on growth, assuming a steady state over the period;

    b. The alleged "inappropriate acceleration of revenue recognition with value-added resellers" and the "[creation of] revenue where no end-user customer existed at the time of sale," given their normal treatment under IFRS; and

    c. The allegations of incorrect revenue recognition of long-term arrangements of hosted deals, again given the normal treatment under IFRS.

- In order to justify a $5 billion accounting write-down, a significant amount of revenue must be involved. Please explain how such issues could possibly have gone undetected during the extensive acquisition due diligence process and HP's financial oversight of Autonomy for a year from acquisition until October 2012 (a period during which all of the Autonomy finance reported to HP's CFO Cathie Lesjak).

- Can HP really state that no part of the $5 billion write-down was, or should be, attributed to HP's operational and financial mismanagement of Autonomy since the acquisition?

- How many people employed by Autonomy in September 2011 have left or resigned under the management of HP?

- HP raised issues about the inclusion of hardware in Autonomy's IDOL Product revenue, notwithstanding this being in accordance with proper IFRS accounting practice. Please confirm that Ms. Whitman and other HP senior management were aware of Autonomy's hardware sales before 2012. Did Autonomy, as part of HP, continue to sell third-party hardware of materially similar value after acquisition? Was this accounted for by HP and was this reported in the Autonomy segment of [its] accounts?

- Were Ms. Whitman and Ms. Lesjak aware that Paul Curtis (HP's Worldwide Director of Software Revenue Recognition), KPMG, and Ernst & Young undertook in December 2011 detailed studies of Autonomy's software revenue recognition with a view to optimizing for U.S. GAAP?
- Why did HP senior management apparently wait six months to inform its shareholders of the possibility of a material event related to Autonomy?

Hewlett-Packard is an iconic technology company, which was historically admired and respected all over the world. Autonomy joined forces with HP with real hopes for the future and in the belief that together there was an opportunity to make HP great again. I have been truly saddened by the events of the past months, and am shocked and appalled by the events of the past week.

I am placing this letter in the public domain in the interests of complete transparency.

Yours faithfully,

Dr. Mike Lynch

Accounting and Auditing Issues

Interviews in California and England with former Autonomy employees, business partners, and attorneys close to the case paint a picture of a hard-driving sales culture shaped by Lynch's desire for rapid growth. They describe him as a domineering figure, who on at least a few occasions berated employees he believed weren't measuring up.

Along the way, these people say, Autonomy used aggressive accounting practices to make sure revenue from software licensing kept growing—thereby boosting the British company's valuation. The firm recognized revenue upfront that under U.S. accounting rules would have been deferred, and struck "round-trip transactions"—deals where Autonomy agreed to buy a client's products or services while at the same time the client purchased Autonomy software, according to these people.

"The rules aren't that complicated," said Dan Mahoney of the accounting research business organization Center for Financial Research and Analysis (CFRA),[2] who covered Autonomy until it was acquired. He said that Autonomy had the hallmarks of a company that recognized revenue too aggressively. He said neither U.S. nor international accounting rules would allow companies to recognize not-yet-collected revenue from customers that might be at risk.

In a statement issued on November 30, 2012, HP said its ongoing investigation into the activities of certain former Autonomy employees had uncovered numerous transactions clearly designed to inflate the underlying financial metrics of the company before its acquisition. The company said it is confident the deals are improper even under the international accounting standards Lynch cites.

In an interview with the British publication, *The Guardian,* on April 10, 2013,[3] Meg Whitman said that the board, which approved the Autonomy transaction, relied on audited information from Deloitte & Touche and additional auditing from KPMG, though she said that she's not blaming the accountants.

"Neither of them saw what we now see after someone came forward to point us in the right direction," Whitman said.

Deloitte, which served as Autonomy's auditor in the United Kingdom, and KPMG, which performed the acquisition work for HP, have been under fire for allegedly failing to detect the accounting issues.

---

[2]Association of Certified Financial Crime Specialists, "HP-Autonomy debacle shines light on auditors, lawyers in financial crime cases," December 4, 2012, Available at: http://www.acfcs.org/hp-autonomy-debacle-shines-light-on-auditors-lawyers-in-financial-crime-cases/.

[3]Juliette Garside, "HP's Meg Whitman: 'we had to be straight' on Autonomy," The Guardian, April 10, 2013, Available at: http://www.guardian.co.uk/business/2013/apr/10/hp-autonomydeal-meg-whitman.

Deloitte said in a statement that it cannot comment further on this matter due to client confidentiality and that it will cooperate with the relevant authorities with any investigations into the allegations."[4]

Post-Legal Filings

An interesting issue is that, after Deloitte lost the Autonomy audit to Ernst & Young and reportedly £5.422 million (about $6 million) for Autonomy's audits during the four years prior to 2012, the firm was then free to engage in previously prohibited consulting activities that were banned for audit firm clients under Sarbanes-Oxley.

According to filings, Deloitte earned an additional £4.44 million (about $5 million) from Autonomy in those four years for services such as tax compliance, due diligence for acquisitions, and other services "pursuant to legislation." HP's auditor Ernst & Young started doing everything tax related for Autonomy after the acquisition. However, Deloitte was free to team with Autonomy and all of its technology products as an alliance partner for systems integration engagements. That could be worth billions in consulting revenue for Deloitte's U.K. firm.

In April 2015, HP filed a lawsuit against Michael Lynch and former CFO Sushovan Hussain for $5.1 billion. The two former executives have vowed to countersue, calling HP's statements "false and negligent" and the entire thing a "smear campaign."

In 2012, HP had turned the matter over to the U.S. SEC and DOJ, as well as the U.K.'s Serious Fraud Office. The latter recently ended its probe after failing to find sufficient evidence for conviction and left everything in the hands of U.S. officials, which are still investigating.

It is worth noting that, if there really were accounting fraud, you'd think the auditors might in some way be liable and we believe that Deloitte and KPMG, which also did some auditing, would have way deeper pockets than Lynch and Hussain. HP has talked about suing Deloitte but has yet to follow through on its previous threats.

Questions

1. In an analysis by the Association of Certified Financial Crime Specialists (ACFCS) about the Autonomy merger with HP, the following statement is made: "The scandal is prompting questions about who is to blame for the soured merger. As details emerge, the case is spotlighting the difficulties that accountants and lawyers face in complex mergers and acquisitions and business deals. The case also raises the issue of what responsibility these professionals have for detecting potentially fraudulent business records where the line between accounting discrepancies and financial crime is blurred."[5] Given the facts of the case, do you believe Deloitte met its obligations with regard to due care and professional judgment? Explain.

2. Meg Whitman is quoted in the case as saying that the board, which approved the Autonomy transaction, relied on audited information from Deloitte & Touche and additional auditing from KPMG. Given that auditing standards and legal requirements dictate that auditors are responsible for detecting material fraud in the financial statements of audit clients, would you blame the auditors for failing to uncover the improper accounting for revenue at Autonomy? Which audit and ethical standards are critical in making that determination?

3. Do you believe a conflict of interest exists when audit firms earn about as much money from nonaudit services as audit services, given they are expected to make independent judgments on the financial transactions and financial reporting of their audit clients? Explain by using the Autonomy case as one such example of a possible conflict.

---

[4] Francine McKenna, "Hewlett-Pckard's Allegations: A Material Writedown and all Four Audit Firms on the Spot," November 20, 2012. Available at: www.forbes.com/sites/francinemckenna/2012/11/20/hewlett-packards-autonomy-allegations-a-materialwritedown-puts-all-four-audit-firms-on-the-spot/.

Chapter 7

Earnings Management

Learning Objectives

After studying Chapter 7, you should be able to:

LO 7-1 Describe the motivation for earnings management.

LO 7-2 Explain what earnings management seeks to accomplish.

LO 7-3 Discuss how earnings management judgments are made.

LO 7-4 Describe the devices used to manage earnings.

LO 7-5 Explain the workings of financial shenanigans.

LO 7-6 Explain the causes and effects of financial restatements.

Ethics Reflection

Financial statement "restatements" include corrections of errors in published financial statements; unintentional mistakes in the application of GAAP, IFRS, or foreign accounting principles, which most financial statement restatements fall into; and financial fraud that leads to restatements caused by the intentional manipulation of data or by misappropriation of assets. The latter case is most troubling because it raises questions about the integrity of management, and the overall health of the company.

According to a study by the Center for Audit Quality (CAQ) for the 2003–2012 period, the number of restatement announcements peaked at 1,784 in 2006, soon after the implementation of Sarbanes-Oxley (SOX) Section 404 internal control reporting, and subsequently declined rapidly. By 2009, 711 restatements were announced, and the number remained near that level through 2012. The overall severity of restatements decreased: Restatement periods are shorter in duration. Somewhat surprisingly, fraud was identified as a factor in relatively few restatements: only 2 percent during the reporting time period.[1]

According to SEC rules, a financial statement restatement occurs if the company or its auditors conclude that "the company's previously issued financial statements . . . no longer should be relied upon because of an error in such financial statements. . . ." The rule also mandates that companies report such a restatement on Form 8-K, and it created Item 4.02 specifically for the disclosure of these restatements. Because the prior statements are unreliable, a company must file corrected reports on Form 10-K/A and/or Form 10-Q/A.[2]

In April 2015, Audit Analytics reported that, for the sixth consecutive year, "revision restatements," or those that do not undermine reliance on past financials, rose to 76 percent of all restatements reported. On the other hand, "reissuance restatements," which require disclosure in Item 4.02 of an 8-K and are more likely to have a negative market reaction, decreased. Consistent with recent trends, the severity of restatements remained low including: (1) those with a negative impact on net income; (2) the average cumulative impact on net income per restatement; (3) the percentage of restatements with no impact on income statements; (4) the average number of days restated; and (5) the average number of issues identified in restatements.[3]

Corporate governance failures, internal control deficiencies, risk assessment issues, and inadequate compliance systems—each might be a factor that creates the likelihood of financial statement restatements. Auditors must look for the red flags that these kinds of problems might lie ahead. Challenges to ethical standards and professional judgment of CPAs often come about because of complex financial transactions and pressures imposed by an employer, client, and/or members of top management. Auditors must exercise the appropriate level of care and develop a mindset that values professional skepticism in order to meet their professional and legal obligations.

DeZoort points to seven causes and effects of restatements: (1) complexity of accounting standards and/or transactions; (2) weak financial governance and controls; (3) increased auditor and audit committee conservatism—i.e., increased regulation, legal exposure for auditors, and audit committee responsibilities; (4) broad application of materiality; (5) earnings management, which occurs out of a desire to meet financial expectations; (6) lack of transparency; and (7) fraud.[4]

We focus attention in this chapter on earnings management and the techniques used to alter earnings in a way that misleads users of the financial statements and may be fraudulent. Many definitions of this term exist, which are discussed below. For now, we consider it to occur when managers use judgment in financial reporting and in structuring transactions to bring about a desired level of reported earnings.

Financial statement restatements are indicators that previous years' financial statements contained material misstatements. Historically, the most common reason for companies to restate their financial statements or be subject to SEC enforcement actions due to fraud has been the way in which they have recognized revenue. The higher the number in the income statement (i.e., sales revenue), the greater the effect on other profit numbers in the statement (i.e., gross profit and operating income) all the way down to net income. And within revenue recognition, the most prevalent form is premature recognition, or booking sales before prices have been fixed, contracts have been finalized, or goods or services have been delivered to customers.

In a famous 1998 speech titled "The Numbers Game," former SEC chairman Arthur Levitt used an epicurean analogy to describe the practice of improperly booking revenues. "Think about a bottle of wine," he said. "You wouldn't pop the cork on that bottle before it was ready. But some companies are doing this with their revenue—recognizing it before a sale is complete, before the product is delivered to a customer, or at a time when the customer still has options to terminate, void or delay the sale."[5]

As you read this chapter, reflect on the numerous ways in which financial statements can be manipulated, thereby sacrificing quality, and how accountants and auditors might do a better job looking for the red flags that signal fraud may be up ahead. Also, consider whether auditors are adequately meeting their ethical obligations and protecting the public interest with regard to identifying "financial shenanigans" and assessing earnings management.

Increasingly, I have become concerned that the motivation to meet Wall Street earnings expectations may be overriding common sense business practices. Too many corporate managers, auditors, and analysts are participants in a game of nods and winks. In the zeal to satisfy consensus earnings estimates and project a smooth earnings path, wishful thinking may be winning the day over faithful representation.

Arthur Levitt

This quote by former SEC chair Arthur Levitt from "The Numbers Game" links the practice of "earnings management" to an excessive zeal to project smoother earnings from year to year that casts a pall over the quality of the underlying numbers. Levitt identifies the cause as a "culture of gamesmanship" in business rooted in the emphasis on achieving short-term results such as meeting or exceeding financial analysts' earnings expectations.[6]

Warren Buffett once said that, "Earnings can be as pliable as putty when a charlatan heads the company reporting them." The quote emphasizes the importance of having an ethical person at the head of a company because a CEO who practices fraud can twist earnings to make them look better than they really are, thereby deceiving the users of the financial statements.

The accounting scandals at companies such as Enron, WorldCom, and Tyco involved the use of inside information by top management to sell shares owned at a relatively favorable current price compared to future prices. Presumably, the executives knew the earnings had been manipulated, and either the manipulation could no longer be sustained or the bubble was about to burst. While the executives sold their shares and typically enhanced their wealth, thousands of employees lost millions of dollars of accumulated wealth in stock ownership and 401-k plans. If the company failed, employees lost their jobs as well. Typically, managers acted without due regard for their fiduciary obligations to the shareholders and in violation of securities laws. It was the old story: Managers act out of self-interest and greed; greed begets more greed. It was a classic example of egoistic behavior motivated by a sense that they would never be caught.

Companies manage earnings when they ask, "How can we best report desired results?" rather than "How can we best report economic reality (the actual results)?" Levitt attributes the practice of earnings management to the pressure on Wall Street to "make the numbers." He identifies a pattern created by earnings management whereby "companies try to meet or beat Wall Street earnings projections in order to grow market capitalization and increase the value of stock options." He notes that on the one hand, auditors are under pressure to retain clients by the firm, and on the other, they are under pressure by management "not to stand in the way."

An important quality of useful information is *representational faithfulness*. To represent the transactions and events faithfully in the financial statements, the effects of transactions and events should be reported on the basis of economic substance of the transactions instead of legal form of the transaction. For example, if a company sells an asset but is still responsible for maintaining it or has other risks of "ownership," then reporting this transaction as a sale instead of secured loan does not faithfully represent the transaction and thus would distort the effect of the transaction on reported amounts and may have the potential to mislead the users of the statements.

Motivation for Earnings Management

LO 7-1
Describe the motivation for earnings management.

What motivates a manager to record transactions in a way that achieves a desired level of financial results even if the accounting treatment is not supportable by the facts? Is it simply to meet budget expectations? Does the manager want to put the best face possible on the financial statements? Or is the manager trying to deceive others about the true nature of the financial results—that is, fraud?

Earnings Guidance

During the 1990s and early 2000s, meeting or beating analysts' earnings expectations emerged as an important earnings benchmark. Bartov et al. found that the stock market has been found to award firms that meet or beat analysts' forecasts and punish firms that miss earnings targets.[7] Meeting or beating earnings through earnings and expectations management has drawn concerns over the integrity of managers. For instance, an analysis of Nortel Networks Corporation by Fogarty et al. (separate from Case 7-1 later in this chapter) reveals that earnings expectations management is tied to many other missteps of managers that collectively contributed to the downfall of the giant telecommunications firm.[8] Consistent with Fuller and Jensen, this suggests that earnings expectations management sets in motion a variety of organizational behaviors that often end up damaging the firm.[9] Erhard et al. suggest that meeting or beating earnings by manipulating earnings and analysts' earnings expectations is indicative of low integrity in relations with the capital markets, resulting in calls for boards of directors to take accountability for integrity of the entire corporate system.[10] Graham et al. also advocate changes in the culture of boards of directors by focusing on long-term strategic goals and shielding managers from the short-term pressure from the capital markets.[11] Taken collectively, the arguments suggest that, while managing earnings expectations may help the firm avoid missing earnings targets and market penalties, it can be detrimental to the long-term value of the firm and the capital markets, point out Liu et al.[12] These behaviors link to Burchard's Ethical Dissonance Model described in Chapter 3 with low organizational ethics in the person-organization fit, and if accompanied by low individual ethics, the ethical culture of the organization is more likely to lead to unethical choices than any other fit.

In addition to maximizing bonuses, the value of stock options, and meeting investors' earnings expectations, another objective of earnings management is to avoid the consequences of violation of debt covenants. Covenants in a long-term lending contract, such as required debt-to-equity ratio or minimum working capital requirements, exist to protect the lender from the potentially adverse actions of managers. Earnings management can serve as motivation to steer managers away from violating the terms of a debt contract, because such a violation would be highly costly to the manager and could affect her ability to operate the firm freely. Earnings management gives a manager the flexibility to choose those accounting policies that avoid a close proximity to covenant violation.

While some earnings management techniques may be perfectly acceptable under generally accepted accounting principles (GAAP), others are not. It is important to understand that firms and managers engaged in accounting manipulations, when discovered, bear substantial legal penalties. The legal costs not only include substantial monetary penalties, but also violations of securities laws.

An example of a company that provided false earnings guidance and was investigated by the SEC is Waste Management. The SEC's enforcement release against Waste Management Inc. describes its earnings guidance strategy as follows:[13]

> WMI violated the antifraud provisions in June 1999 when its management publicly projected results for the company's second quarter. The June forecast was a reiteration of second quarter projections made earlier in the year. Although the earlier projections may have had a reasonable basis when first disseminated, by at least the time when the reiteration occurred, WMI was aware of significant adverse trends in its business which made its continued public support of its previously announced forecasts unreasonable.

Research results on whether firm-provided earnings guidance leads to more or less earnings management is mixed. Kasznik found that firms issuing long-term, annual earnings forecasts make income-increasing choices when, *ex post,* earnings fall below their own forecasts.[14] However, recent research suggests that firms have very different incentives when issuing long-term annual earnings forecasts versus short-term (i.e., forecasts of quarterly earnings) guidance.[15]

We might expect that short-term earnings guidance issued by a company would almost always lead to a higher level of earnings management than if no such guidance were provided. However, at least one study did not show these results. In fact, Call et al. found strong and consistent evidence that the issuance of short-term quarterly earnings guidance is associated with less, rather than more, earnings management. They also found that regular guiders exhibit less earnings management than do less regular guiders. The authors used both "abnormal" accruals and "discretionary" revenues to measure earnings management.[16]

It could be that companies have become more conservative with their earnings guidance, at least for short-term periods. Perhaps we are experiencing a heightened sensitivity to making realistic projections in light of Sarbanes-Oxley and post-Enron sensibilities. It could be that companies have been on their best behavior during this period, which is supported by the lower level of restatements. The question is whether it will last especially if economic conditions worsen and pressures mount on CEOs and CFOs to produce consistently positive results similar to what we have seen during the recovery from the great recession.

Green Mountain Coffee Roasters

An interesting aspect of the Green Mountain case—*Employees' Retirement System, et al. v. Green Mountain Coffee Roasters, et al.*[17]—is that conference calls that provided earnings guidance to shareholders and analysts were used to mask a financial fraud. The facts of the case are discussed below.

Green Mountain manufactures the Keurig single-cup brewing system and many varieties of the associated "K-Cup" portion packs to brew single servings of coffee and other related products. The company operates on a razor/razor blade model—selling brewing machines but making its real money on the K-Cups. Between February 2, 2011, and November 9, 2011 (the "class period"), plaintiffs purchased or otherwise acquired Green Mountain common stock. A class-action lawsuit was brought against the company alleging fraud based on materially misleading statements made to deceive [with *scienter*] shareholders about the inventory levels and earnings of the company. The original district court decision went against the plaintiff-shareholders but it was appealed and the decision was remanded for further trial. In the end, the shareholders prevailed against Green Mountain.

During the class period, defendants represented to investors, including plaintiffs, that it was straining to meet consumer demand for its Keurig and K-Cup products and that the company was ramping up production without accumulating excess inventory. Accordingly, Green Mountain's stock price soared to record highs during the class period, from $32.96 per share on February 2, 2011, to a high of $111.62 per share on September 19, 2011.

News of a possible inventory fraud leaked out by third parties who make a living analyzing the financials of companies they feel may be playing fast and loose with the accounting rules. The plaintiff-shareholders brought a lawsuit claiming Green Mountain had represented to them that demand for its coffee makers (Keurig) was so high that it was increasing production without accumulating excess inventory. However, a number of confidential witnesses alleged that within the company excess inventory was piling "up to the rafters" and was being stored out of sight of the auditors from PricewaterhouseCoopers. There were allegations that the company claimed to ship 500,000 coffee brewers to customers, such as QVC, the home shopping channel, but the facts showed that the alleged shipments were never made. Indeed, most of the brewers never even left the dock and were instead taped off with a note saying "not to inventory." After the auditors left, the entire order was "put back in stock."

Other allegations included that, on numerous occasions before an inventory count or audit, "bags and bags of coffee would be loaded onto trucks" that would either leave temporarily or just sit behind the facility filled with product. When employees escorted auditors through the facility, they were not permitted "beyond a point blocked off by black plastic."

Throughout the class period, Green Mountain defendants continuously reassured investors that its business was booming. For example, Green Mountain held a conference call with investors on February 2, 2011, to discuss first quarter 2011 results. Green Mountain stated that "we remain focused on increasing production to fulfill unmet demand and achieving and maintaining optimum inventory levels." During its second quarter conference call on May 3, 2011, Green Mountain stated "we are not building any excess inventories at all at retail." On July 27, 2011, in another conference call to discuss third quarter results, defendant Frances Rathke—CFO, secretary, and treasurer of Green Mountain—stated that during the third quarter, "we got back into a place where we knew we had appropriate inventory levels." Lawrence Blanford, president, CEO, and director of the company, emphasized a need to increase production in 2012 to meet anticipated high consumer demand. When investors expressed concern about over-producing, Blanford reiterated that "we're at appropriate inventory levels."

In fact, Green Mountain was accumulating a significant overstock of expiring and unsold product. The complaint includes observations from numerous confidential witnesses ("CWs")—Green Mountain employees from different tiers of the company—detailing the company's increasing inventory buildup.

The conference calls providing earnings guidance and other communications to the public about how well Green Mountain was doing seemed to raise red flags for some who follow such announcements. In fact, the initial class action lawsuit that was filed in October 2011 came after a high-profile presentation by hedge fund manager David Einhorn who, in a stock bet against Green Mountain, accused the company of misleading auditors and inflating its results. Einhorn raised questions about the company's future prospects and its accounting procedures. Wall Street took notice as the stock price started to decline.

Sam Antar, former CFO of Crazy Eddie, a massive fraud in the 1980s that was discussed in Chapter 6, became a fraud investigator of sorts after serving jail time for his role in the Crazy Eddie fraud. Antar pointed to suspected inventory manipulation early on that, he alleged, fraudulently inflated Green Mountain's earnings. Of course, he turned out to be right. It is understandable that he would know about such things having been part of the inventory fraud at Crazy Eddie.

Antar provided some wisdom about auditing inventory when he explained that even when auditors confirm the existence of inventory in a company's warehouse, fraud is still possible. Inventory can be moved from location to location as auditors are making their rounds, and the same inventory can therefore be counted multiple times. This inflates the inventory on the balance sheet. Of course, in the case of Green Mountain, the company was counting the overstock inventory as ending inventory and inflating earnings while, at the same time, hiding the overstocked amounts from PwC. We're not quite sure why the firm did not catch on to the fraud; it was not prosecuted by the SEC.

Antar's analysis is important because it illustrates how analytical procedures can help to spot red flags about inventory fraud. If there is inventory growth that is higher than revenue growth over extended periods of time combined with declining inventory turnover trends, this can be considered a red flag that ending inventory is inflated, thereby overstating earnings.

According to Antar's analysis, Green Mountain inventory levels had been increasing much faster than revenue during a seven-quarter period in 2010–2012. Thus, the inventory turnover rate was declining, and it was taking Green Mountain longer to sell its products than in the past.

Antar provides the following numbers, straight from Green Mountain's SEC filings. Notice that revenue is increasing at a much slower rate than inventory is increasing.[18]

TABLE 7.1	Green Mountain Coffee Roasters					
			Fiscal Year 2012 vs. 2011 ($ in 000s)			
Quarter Ended	Reported Revenues: Fiscal Year 2012	Reported Revenues: Fiscal Year 2011	Change	Inventory at End of Current Quarter in 2012	Inventory at End of Previous Year Comparable Quarter in 2011	Increase in Inventory
6/23/2012	$869,194	$717,210	21%	$667,005	$417,496	60%
3/24/2012	$885,052	$647,658	37%	$602,121	$300,760	100%
12/24/2011	$1,158,216	$574,148	102%	$606,679	$269,132	125%

(Continued)

Fiscal Year 2011 vs. 2010 ($ in 000s)						
Quarter Ended	Reported Revenues: Fiscal Year 2011	Reported Revenues: Fiscal Year 2010	Change	Inventory at End of Current Quarter in 2011	Inventory at End of Previous Year Comparable Quarter in 2010	Increase in Inventory
9/24/2011	$711,883	$373,087	91%	$672,248	$262,478	156%
6/25/2011	$717,210	$316,583	127%	$417,496	$186,262	124%
3/26/2011	$647,658	$321,953	101%	$300,760	$109,929	174%
12/25/2010	$575,027	$345,152	67%	$269,132	$117,009	130%

Note: Revenues for the quarter ended 12/25/10 were later revised by Green Mountain Coffee from $575.027 million to $574.148 million after this blog reported discrepanies in ints numbers.

Ironically, the Green Mountain fraud mirrors what happened at Crazy Eddie. An ever increasing amount of inventory was on hand to sell relatively less product.

Taking the analysis further, Antar showed that the inventory turnover was 102.04 days (to sell inventory) in the quarter ended in June 2012 versus only 72.12 days in the quarter ended in June 2011. Green Mountain claimed in SEC filings it was increasing inventory to meet holiday demand. The same explanation was given in a conference call by CFO Fran Rathke. Of course, that was just a smokescreen to hide the fraud.

The Green Mountain case is instructive because it illustrates that a company does not need to financially structure transactions and engage in a sophisticated accounting fraud, as did Enron, to pull the wool over the eyes of shareholders and auditors. A simple phone call can set the scheme in motion, as happened at Green Mountain. This raises an interesting question: Should auditors monitor conference calls with investors, analysts, and even the financial press to determine whether something is said that could be false, fraudulent, or deceptive? It seems to us it may be the right time for the audit profession to look at developing procedures to assess these and other communications, such as those on social media, which have the potential to mislead the public.

Using Social Media to Report Earnings Guidance and Financial Results

In a ruling that portends changes to how companies communicate with investors, the SEC said on April 2, 2013, that postings on sites such as Facebook and Twitter are just as good as news releases and company Web sites as long as the companies have told investors which outlets they intend to use. The ruling permits companies to use social media channels to announce financial and other key information and post earnings information to the investing public in compliance with Regulation Fair Disclosure (Regulation FD).

The move was sparked by an investigation into a Facebook posting from Netflix Inc. Chief Executive Reed Hastings, who boasted on the social media site that the streaming-video company had exceeded 1 billion hours in a month for the first time, sending the firm's shares higher. The SEC opened the investigation in December 2012, to determine if the post had violated rules that bar companies from selectively disclosing information.

"An increasing number of public companies are using social media to communicate with their shareholders and the investing public," the SEC said. "We appreciate the value and prevalence of social media channels in contemporary market communications, and the commission supports companies seeking new ways to communicate."[19]

The SEC guidelines on these matters are under the fair disclosure rule that requires companies to disseminate information in a way that wouldn't be expected to give an advantage to one group of investors over another. The SEC has said that filing a form, known as an 8-K, or holding an earnings call are both ways to ensure compliance with the regulation.

In 2008, the SEC said that companies could use their corporate home pages, under certain circumstances, to disseminate sensitive information. Now, the agency says social media sites would also suffice—in some circumstances. It blessed sites as long as companies make clear to investors they plan to use them. It also suggested a corporate executive's personal Facebook page wasn't as likely as a company's social media page to be a channel through which companies would be allowed to make important announcements.

Given the SEC's openness to using social media for company communications about financial matters, we can only observe: Students, it is a brave new world out there, and one you all should thrive in.

Nonfinancial Measures of Earnings

Verschoor notes that the constant pressure to report favorable earnings performance motivates many companies to report income numbers that exclude unusual events that almost always seem to be costly and depress earnings. These non-GAAP numbers were, for many years, used to reflect a level of earnings that might put a positive spin on what otherwise might be not such good results under GAAP. In an effort to "eliminate the manipulative or misleading use of non-GAAP financial measures and, at the same time, enhance the comparability associated with the use of that information," the Sarbanes-Oxley Act directed the SEC to adopt new rules to address public companies' disclosure or release of certain financial information that is calculated and presented on the basis of methodologies other than in accordance with GAAP. The result was the adoption of Regulation G in January 2003, "Conditions for the Use of Non-GAAP Financial Measures."[20]

Regulation G requires public companies that disclose or release such non-GAAP financial measures to include, in that disclosure or release, a presentation of the most directly comparable GAAP financial measure and a reconciliation of the disclosed non-GAAP financial measure to the most directly comparable GAAP financial measure. The GAAP presentation must have equal or greater prominence. Management must disclose the reasons why the non-GAAP measure provides useful information to investors and offer a statement of additional purposes for which the non-GAAP measure is used. Only GAAP financial information can be presented directly on the face of a company's financial statements.

An example of a non-GAAP financial measure would be a measure of operating income that excludes one or more expense or revenue items that are identified as "nonrecurring." Another example would be non-GAAP financial measures including earnings before interest, taxes, depreciation, and amortization (EBITDA). EBITDA could be calculated using elements derived from GAAP financial presentations but, in any event, is not presented in accordance with GAAP.

Verschoor observes that "one danger of using non-GAAP measures is, even though current accounting standards may be imprecise, it is too easy for companies to turn poor GAAP earnings into great earnings by simply designing their own performance measures that can readily be adjusted to unethically report successful accomplishment of the goals created using those same measures." He believes that non-GAAP earnings reporting should be strictly limited and permitted in cases where current GAAP doesn't clearly reflect economic reality.[21] We agree and believe auditors should be tasked with at least reviewing this information as part of their annual audit requirements. Currently, the external auditor's opinion does not cover non-GAAP financial measures because they are not included in the financial statements.

The following information in Exhibit 7.1 illustrates how EBITDA measures might be calculated. It comes from Rackspace Hosting (RAX), a provider of cloud computing services, managing Web-based information technology systems for small and medium-sized businesses as well as large enterprises. The data appeared in the February 19, 2009, Form 8-K filed with the SEC.

EXHIBIT 7.1 — Rackspace Hosting (RAX) 8-K Form February 19, 2009[22] Adjusted EBITDA (Non-GAAP financial measure)

We use Adjusted EBITDA as a supplement measure to review and assess our performance. We define Adjusted EBITDA as Net Income, less Total Other Income (Expense), plus Income Taxes, Depreciation and Amortization, and non-cash charges for share-based compensation.

Adjusted EBITDA is a metric that is used in our industry by the investment community for comparative and valuation purposes. We disclose this metric in order to support and facilitate the dialogue with research analysts and investors.

Note that Adjusted EBITDA is not a measure of financial performance under accounting principles generally accepted in the United States (GAAP) and should not be considered a substitute for operating income, which we consider to be the most directly comparable GAAP measure. Adjusted EBITDA has limitations as an analytical tool, and when assessing our operating performance, you should not consider Adjusted EBITDA in isolation, or as a substitute for net income or other consolidated income statement data prepared in accordance with GAAP. Other companies may calculate Adjusted EBITDA differently than we do, limiting its usefulness as a comparative measure. See our Adjusted EBITDA reconciliation below.

	Years Ended December 31,		
(In thousands)	2006	2007	2008
Net income	$ 19,820	$ 17,829	$ 21,703
Less: Total other (income) expense	$ 523	$ 2,815	$ 7,461
Plus: Income taxes	$ 10,900	$ 9,965	$ 10,985
Plus: Depreciation and amortization	$ 32,335	$ 56,476	$ 90,172
Plus: Share-based compensation expense	$ 1,090	$ 4,252	$ 15,017
Adjusted EBITDA	$ 64,668	$ 91,337	$ 145,338

We believe these numbers clearly point to the dangers for users of financial statements when companies report non-GAAP measures. What should the "average investor" make of the fact that Adjusted EBITDA is 226 percent, 412 percent, and 570 percent of net income in 2006, 2007, and 2008, respectively? Doesn't the high level of, at least, depreciation indicate that the company needs to have adequate funds available to modernize and replace property, plant, and equipment as it wears out? Is this something that can safely be ignored by users? Perhaps, but at a minimum the variability in EBITDA and net income is confusing.

Income Smoothing

Levitt talks about another motivation to manage earnings: to smooth net income over time. The ideal pattern of earnings for a manager is a steady increase each year over a period of time. The results make it appear that the company is growing and doing better than it really is, and the manager should be given credit for the positive results. The market reacts by bidding up the price of the stock, and the manager is rewarded for the results by a performance bonus and stock options with a prospective value that increases over time because of income smoothing that triggers stock price increases.

Income smoothing occurs through the use of accounting techniques to level out net income fluctuations from one period to the next. Companies indulge in this practice because investors are generally willing to pay a premium for stocks with steady and predictable earnings streams, compared with stocks whose earnings are subject to wild fluctuations.

Levitt concludes that "these practices lead to erosion in the quality of earnings and, therefore, the quality of financial reporting." The notion that accounting information should represent what it purports to represent, or representational faithfulness,[23] would be distorted in these cases by the use of devices such as accelerating the recognition of revenue (i.e., channel stuffing), delaying the recognition of an expense, and creating "cookie-jar reserves" to smooth net income.

Sometimes a company will record overly aggressive accruals of operating expenses and create liability accounts in an effort to reduce future year operating expenses. It is an accounting practice in which a company uses generous reserves from good years against losses that might be incurred in bad years. During the late 1990s and early 2000s, these reserve practices were given the moniker of cookie-jar reserves because a company set aside some reserves to be taken out of the jar and used when needed to prop up earnings. Auditors must be sensitive to these transactions, most of which occur at year-end and are decided upon based on reported operating results. In other words if a manager does not like the reported results, she can increase or decrease the reserve account to draw out or inflate operating results.

A classic case of the use of cookie-jar reserves to manipulate income was at HealthSouth. The SEC investigated the practice and deemed it to be fraudulent. According to the SEC, the company fraudulently reduced contractual adjustments to increase revenue by more than $2.2 billion.[24] The contractual allowances represented the amount of the health-care billing not expected to be reimbursed. During the second quarter of 1996, HealthSouth began what was to become a systematic practice of reducing contractual adjustments—that is, narrowing the gap between standard health-care charges and anticipated reimbursements—even though the applicable contractual adjustments had not actually changed and there was otherwise no support for the reductions. This practice continued without interruption in every reporting period through mid-2002. At the same time, the company improperly reclassified a number of operating expenses to make it appear as if the expenses never occurred.

The contractual allowance account was a perfect tool to manipulate earnings from year to year to present a smoothing or increasing trend in earnings. The company historically had accounted for the provision of health-care services by recording both its standard charge for the service and a contractual adjustment. The first entry essentially is a constant, unaffected by the amount actually to be paid by or on behalf of a patient. The second is a variable, representing the company's estimate of a discount from the standard charge which it does not expect to collect. The amount of the variable—*the contractual adjustment*—is based on the source of payment, since different payors may reimburse different amounts for the same service. The difference between the standard charge and the contractual adjustment, frequently a significant amount, represents the company's net operating revenue.

One industry that routinely uses allowances to smooth net income over time is banking. Rivard et al. studied income smoothing techniques by banks and found them to be more aggressive in using loan-loss reserves as a tool of income smoothing. The provision for loan losses is a noncash accounting expense for banks. In theory, this expense represents expected future losses, which will eventually occur on loans extended during the previous period. These expenses accumulate on the bank's balance sheet in the loan-loss reserve account. When a loan is charged off, this reserve account is debited. Because banks have considerable flexibility in determining the size of the annual provision for loan losses, and because this is a noncash expense, it is an excellent tool for income smoothing. During periods of lower-than-normal earnings, the bank may understate its expected future loan loss and thus increase earnings. When profits are abnormally high, the opposite occurs. Over an extended period of time, the loan-loss reserve balance is maintained at the desired level and average earnings are unaffected. However, the variability of the earnings stream over that period is less than it would otherwise be. As the authors point out, income smoothing reduces not only earnings, but also tax liabilities in high-income years, and increases them in low-income years.[25]

Characteristics of Earnings Management

LO 7-2
Explain what earnings management seeks to accomplish.

Gaa and Dunmore point out that earnings may be managed in many different ways, but they all boil down to two basic possibilities. One is to alter the numbers already in the financial records by using discretionary accruals and other adjustments, and the other is to create or structure real transactions for the purpose of altering the reported numbers. There are also two kinds of motivations for altering the financial reports through disclosure decisions. Management may either intend to influence stakeholders' beliefs and behavior or to influence how contracts are performed.[26]

Earnings management occurs when companies artificially inflate (or deflate) their revenues or profits, or earnings per share (EPS) figures. Well-publicized ways of managing earnings during the period of financial fraud in the early 2000s were: (1) by using aggressive accounting techniques such as capitalizing costs that should have been expensed (e.g., WorldCom accounted for its line costs as capital expenditures rather than expensing them against revenue); and (2) by establishing or altering the elements of an estimate to achieve a desired goal (e.g., Waste Management's lengthening of the useful lives on trash hauling equipment to slow down depreciation each year).

Another perspective on earnings management is to divide the techniques into two categories: operating earnings management and accounting earnings management. Operating earnings management deals with altering operating decisions to affect cash flows and net income for a period such as easing credit terms to increase sales. Accounting earnings management deals with using the flexibility in accounting standards to alter earnings numbers.[27]

Generally, the end result of earnings management is to distort the application of GAAP, thereby bringing into question the quality of earnings. The question to be answered is whether the distortion is the result of appropriate decision making given that choices exist in the application of GAAP, or if it is motivated by a conscious effort to manipulate earnings for one's advantage, which is fraud.

While some authors distinguish between earnings manipulation and earnings management, we believe earnings manipulation is a form of earnings management. For example, Hopwood et al. believe that earnings management is management's routine use of nonfraudulent accounting and economic discretion, while earnings manipulation can refer either to the legitimate or aggressive use, or fraudulent abuse, of discretion. By their reckoning, earnings management is legitimate, while earnings manipulation can be legitimate, marginally ethical, unethical, or illegal, depending on its extent.[28] The problem with this distinction is ethics relates to one's intent. If one intends to manipulate earnings through smoothing or other techniques, it is unethical because it is designed to deceive another party; if not, why engage in the practice?

Definition of Earnings Management

There are a variety of definitions of earnings management. Schipper defines it as a "purposeful intervention in the external reporting process, with the intent of obtaining some private gain (as opposed to, say, merely facilitating the neutral operation of the process)."[29] Healy and Wahlen define it as "when managers use judgment in financial reporting and in structuring transactions to alter financial reports to either mislead some stakeholders about the underlying economic performance of the company, or to influence contractual outcomes that depend on reported accounting numbers."[30]

Dechow and Skinner note the difficulty of operationalizing earnings management based on the reported accounting numbers because they center on managerial intent, which is unobservable. Dechow and

Skinner offer their own view that a distinction should be made between making choices in determining earnings that may comprise aggressive, but acceptable, accounting estimates and judgments, as compared to fraudulent accounting practices that are clearly intended to deceive others.[31] These authors provide a link between earnings management and Rest's Model of how ethical decisions take place that was discussed in Chapter 2. Rest identifies ethical intent as an essential ingredient in making moral decisions. It is the first step that can lead to executing ethical decisions. Absent ethical intent, a decision maker may be motivated to skew earnings in her favor or that of the company.

Schipper views earnings management as a purposeful act by management as might be the case when earnings are manipulated to get the stock price up in advance of cashing in stock options. Healy and Wahlen focus on management's intent to deceive the stakeholders by using accounting devices to influence reported earnings positively. The underlying motivation for such actions according to the authors is the pursuit of self-interest rather than the interests of shareholders and other stakeholders.

Thomas E. McKee wrote a book on earnings management from the executive perspective. He defines *earnings management* as "reasonable and legal management decision making and reporting intended to achieve stable and predictable financial results." McKee believes earnings management reflects a conscious choice by management to smooth earnings over time and it does not include devices designed to "cook the books." He criticizes Schipper, Healy and Wahlen, and Dechow and Skinner for taking "unnecessarily negative view[s] of earnings management." McKee contends that a more positive definition is needed that portrays managers' motives in a positive light rather than the negative view adopted by others.[32]

Ethics of Earnings Management

The authors of this book believe that the acceptability of earnings management techniques should be judged using the ethics framework established earlier in the book. Virtue ethics examines the reasons for actions taken by the decision maker as well as the action itself. McKee's definition is self-serving from a management perspective and does not reflect virtues such as honesty (full disclosure) and dependability (reliable numbers). The definition also ignores the rights of shareholders and other stakeholders to receive fair and accurate financial information. McKee's explanation that earnings management is good because it creates a more stable and predictable earnings stream by smoothing net income cannot overcome the fact that a smooth net income by choice does not reflect what investors and creditors need or want to know because it masks true performance. Further, McKee's explanation for the "goodness" of earnings management is nothing more than a rationalization for an unethical act. Hopwood et al. provide cover for their view of the ethics of earnings management by stating that "the ethics issue might possibly be mitigated by clearly disclosing aggressive accounting assumptions in the financial statement disclosures."[33] We disagree with this characterization because disclosure should not be used to mask the ills of improper accounting that tests the limits of what does and does not present fairly financial position, results of operations, and cash flows. A disclosure may be nothing more than a rationalization for an unethical action with respect to earnings management, thereby closing the Fraud Triangle.

One might be able to rationalize the ethics of earnings management from an act-utilitarian perspective. Under this view, a decision about how to account for and report a financial transaction could be made by weighing the benefits to management and the company of using a particular technique (to smooth net income) versus the costs of providing potentially misleading information to the shareholders. Under a rule-utilitarian perspective, however, financial statements should never be manipulated to put a rosier face on the financials or for personal gain regardless of any utilitarian benefits.

Needles points out that the difference between an ethical and an unethical accounting choice is often merely the degree to which the choice is carried out. Needles believes the problem with many accounting judgments is that there is no clear limit beyond which a choice is obviously unethical. Thus, a perfectly routine accounting decision, such as expense estimation, may be illegal if the estimated amount is extreme, but it is perfectly ethical if it is reasonable. He provides an interesting example of how a manager might use the concept of an earnings continuum to decide whether to record the expense amount at the conservative end or aggressive end.[34]

Needles's example is based on a rather modest difference in estimate from $6,000 to $30,000 (1.0 percent to 5.0 percent of net sales). Exhibit 7.2 shows a difference of $0.24 per share ($1.70–$1.94) or approximately 12–14 percent of EPS (assuming 100,000 shares outstanding). We recognize that judgment is an essential part of deciding when a difference is and is not material. Needles's continuum illustrates a possible basis for such judgments and how an auditor might go about deciding whether or not to accept management's position on the issue.

EXHIBIT 7.2 Where Do You Draw the Line? The Earnings Management Continuum of Ethical Financial Reporting

Questionable Conservative	Conservative	Neutral	Aggressive	Fraudulent

2a: The Earnings Management Continuum of Ethical Financial Reporting.

$1.70	$1.76	$1.82	$1.88	$1.94

Violates GAAP   Within GAAP   Violates GAAP

2b: Overly Aggressive Earnings on the Continuum

Highly Conservative	Overly Conservative	Neutral	Overly Aggressive	Fraudulent
$1.70	$1.76	$1.82	$1.88	$1.94

Violates GAAP   Within GAAP   Violates GAAP

Source: Copyright © 2011. Reprinted with permission of the author, Belverd E. Needles, Jr.

How Managers and Accountants Perceive Earnings Management

Elias conducted a study of corporate ethical values and earnings management ethics. He defined corporate ethical values as a composite of the individual values of managers and both the formal and informal policies on the ethics of the organization. The tone at the top signals whether ethics policies are taken seriously by management and is, therefore, very important to create an ethical corporate environment. The study clearly shows that accountants in organizations with high ethical values perceived earnings management actions as more unethical. Certified public accountants (CPAs) in industry occupations were significantly less likely than those in public accounting to perceive high ethical values in their organizations.[35] This may be attributable to the greater pressure internally to meet financial analysts' earnings projections and provide bonuses and stock options for top management.

In a case study by Phillips and Zvinakis, it was determined that managers deceive shareholders by manipulating their companies' receivables, inventories, loss contingencies, and capital asset depreciation. In the past, audit committees have often failed to protect shareholders by inadequately monitoring and controlling the accounting judgments made by management.[36]

Anna and Jacob Rose investigated whether financial knowledge and trust influences audit committee members' judgment concerning client explanation for their accounting judgments. They found that audit committee members with less financial knowledge are more likely to accept insufficient client explanations for accounting judgment and are also more likely to reject sufficient client explanations for accounting judgments than more knowledgeable audit committee members. These results imply that the requirement by SOX to have three independent members of the board, one with financial expertise, on the audit committee should help to alleviate the disconnect between auditor obligations and trust.[37]

An early first survey of about how managers view the ethics of earnings management was conducted in 1990 by Bruns and Merchant. They found that managers disagreed considerably on whether earnings management is ethically acceptable. They also found that, in general, the respondents thought manipulating earnings via operating decisions (e.g., purposefully delaying making needed repairs to a subsequent year) was more ethically acceptable than manipulation by accounting methods. The authors were disturbed by these findings. They were concerned that these practices could be misleading to users of the information and, over time, reduce the credibility of accounting numbers, thereby damaging the reputation of the accounting profession.[38]

Rosenzweig and Fischer followed up on the Bruns and Merchant survey in 1995 by asking accounting professionals about factors causing earnings management. Two of these factors involve accounting manipulation, and two involve operating decisions designed to influence reported earnings. The accounting factors include actions that influence earnings by changing accounting methods. Examples include recording an expense in the wrong year or changing an inventory valuation in order to influence earnings. Examples of operating decision manipulations are deferring necessary expenditures to a subsequent year or offering unusually attractive terms to customers at year-end to include next year's sales into the current year.[39]

In a 2006 survey, Akers, Giacomino, and Bellovary surveyed accounting students and practitioners about their views of earnings management. With respect to accounting practitioners, the results show that accounting manipulation is much less acceptable ethically than operating decision manipulation. This finding parallels the attitude that Bruns and Merchant found among managers.[40] Generally, the practitioners had few ethical qualms about operating decision manipulation, with scores indicating an average rating between (fully) ethical and questionable. The practitioners, however, generally felt that operating decisions that influenced expenses were somewhat more suspect than those that influenced revenues.

The results of the survey by Akers et al. indicates that none of the 20 practices asked about were rated as "Totally Unacceptable." Additional findings include that (1) only 5 of the 20 practices were rated as a "Serious Infraction," (2) 10 practices were rated as a "Minor Infraction," (3) 4 practices were rated as a "Questionable Practice," and (4) 1 action was rated as an "Ethical Practice"—painting a capital asset ahead of schedule.

The five most serious infractions were (1) bury "scrap costs" in other expenses—no (operating) income effect; (2) request deferred billing from the supplier; (3) raise the return forecast (on purchases) from 22 to 35 percent, with actuals of 22 percent; (4) accelerate delivery to customers by 42 days; and (5) defer supply expenses by delaying recording the invoice. It is interesting to note that the most serious infraction did not even affect net income.[41] Instead, the action to bury scrap costs in other expenses shifts an operating expense into a nonoperating category, thereby increasing operating income, an amount on the income statement often considered to be a more important gauge of earnings than "bottom-line" net income. Other actions are clearly designed to manage earnings by either accelerating the recording of earnings or delaying the recording of operating expenses.

As to the 10 practices rated as minor infractions, the ethical significance of each is as follows: (1) reduce reserve for obsolescence to meet budget target; (2) increase reserve for obsolescence and reduce income; (3) accelerate delivery to the customer by 28 days; (4) defer expenses to meet the annual budget; (5) raise the return forecast from 22 to 35 percent; (6) request deferred billing from the supplier; (7) accelerate delivery to the customer by 16 days; (8) reduce reserve for obsolescence to continue work; (9) defer expenses to meet the quarterly budget; and (10) prepay expenses to reduce income by $60,000.[42]

One unexpected result is that the second most unacceptable minor infraction leads to a *decrease* in income. Students may wonder why a manager might choose to reduce reported income by increasing a reserve account with an offset that increases expenses (i.e., debit: estimated loss due to obsolescence of inventory; credit: reserve for obsolescence). A good example is the case of Sunbeam Corporation, where the newly hired CEO, Al Dunlap, directed the accountants to create a reserve account during his first few months as CEO based on the belief that increasing the expenses and showing an even larger net loss would work to his advantage in the long run because, in future periods, the company could restore the reserves to increase income making it appear that Dunlap had worked his magic in turning the company around. In other words, the increase in expenses in the current period when earnings were way below expectations (and there may even be a loss), creates a cookie-jar effect, while portraying the company as looking worse than it really is. Dunlap's use of cookie-jar reserves to further increase losses in a down year after he was hired and reversing it into income in subsequent years became known as "big-bath accounting." Dunlap figured he could blame the poor performance on the previous CEO, and it would make him look much better in future years.

Earnings Quality

On October 10, 2012, Dichev et al. released the results of a study of earnings quality taken from a survey of 169 CFOs of public companies and in-depth interviews of 12 CFOs and two standard setters. The results relate to the prevalence, magnitude, and detection of earnings management.[43]

Their key findings fall into three broad categories. The first includes results related to the definition, characteristics, and determinants of earnings quality. On definition, CFOs believe that earnings are high quality when they are sustainable and backed by actual cash flows. More specific quality characteristics include consistent reporting choices over time and avoidance of long-term estimates. Consistent with this view, current earnings are considered to be high quality if they serve as a good guide to the long-run profits of the firm.

The second set of results relates to how standard setting affects earnings quality. CFOs believe that reporting discretion has declined over time, and that current GAAP standards are somewhat of a constraint in reporting high-quality earnings. CFOs would like standard setters to issue fewer rules and to converge U.S. GAAP with International Financial Reporting Standards (IFRS) to improve earnings quality. Further, they believe that earnings quality would improve if reporting choices were to evolve at least partly from practice rather than being mandated from standards. As one consequence of such inflexible rules, CFOs say that the accounting standards sometimes drive operational decisions, rather than the other way around. CFOs also feel that the rules orientation of the Financial Accounting Standards Board (FASB) has centralized the audit function, depriving local offices of discretion in dealing with clients, and stunting the development of young auditing professionals. Overall, CFOs have come to view financial reporting largely as a compliance activity, rather than as a vehicle of innovation designed to inform stakeholders and lower the cost of capital.

The third set of results relies on observable GAAP earnings and a clear definition of earnings management, asking for within-GAAP manipulation that misrepresents performance (i.e., the researchers rule out outright fraud and performance-signaling motivations). The CFOs estimate that, in any given period, roughly 20 percent of firms manage earnings and the typical misrepresentation for such firms is about 10 percent of reported EPS. CFOs believe that 60 percent of earnings management is income-increasing, and 40 percent is income-decreasing, somewhat in contrast to the expected heavy emphasis on income-increasing results but consistent with the intertemporal setting up of accruals in settings like cookie-jar reserves and big baths. A large majority of CFOs feel that earnings misrepresentation occurs most often in an attempt to influence stock price, because of outside and inside pressure to hit earnings benchmarks, and to avoid adverse compensation and career consequences for senior executives. Finally, while CFOs caution that earnings management is difficult to unravel from the outside, they suggest a number of red flags that point to potential misrepresentation. The three most common flags are persistent deviations between earnings and the underlying cash flows, deviations from industry and other peer experience, and large and unexplained accruals and changes in accruals. There are also a number of red flags that relate to the role of the manager's character and the firm's culture, which allow and perhaps even encourage earnings management.

Accruals and Earnings Management

Accruals are needed on the balance sheet because when cash flows are examined within a limited time frame, they suffer from matching and timing problems and therefore often give the wrong picture of the period's performance. By measuring performance with earnings, the matching and timing problems inherent in cash flows are decreased through the use of the revenue recognition and matching principles.[44] The revenue recognition principle states that revenues should be recognized when the firm has delivered a product or has produced a substantial portion of it, and the cash receipt is reasonably certain. Over the lifetime of the firm, cash flows and earnings are the same, but when accounting principles are applied over finite time periods, cash flows have to be adjusted to produce the earnings number as is done in the operating section of a cash flow statement. These adjustments are made with accruals on the balance sheet, and thus, earnings are the sum of a period's change in accruals and its cash flows.

Accruals provide an opportunity for management to manage earnings through aggressive estimations or more conservative ones. The fraud at Waste Management is instructive in illustrating how estimates can be used to manipulate earnings. During the investigation of the fraud by the audit committee, it was determined that certain material items were incorrectly reported. Most restatements in the financial statements were related to aggressive calculations of vehicle, equipment, and container depreciation expense and capitalized interest. By increasing depreciation and salvage value assumptions for vehicle and container assets, Waste Management was postponing and avoiding depreciation expenses, effectively raising current income.

The matters reflected in prior-period restatements include earlier recognition of asset value impairments (primarily related to land, landfill, and recycling investments) and environmental liabilities (primarily landfill closure and postclosure expense accruals). It was also determined that capitalized interest relating to landfill construction projects had been miscalculated. When a company begins a construction project, so long as the project is not earning revenues, it is able to accrue the interest expense related to the project and record it as part of the cost of construction (asset account, not an expense). Basically the interest expense on construction becomes part of the constructed assets and can be depreciated over the useful life of the project. This is a common practice, but if interest expenses for construction projects are overstated, then expenses are being understated and capitalized interest is overstated.

A fertile area for earnings management is through the use of discretionary accruals. *Discretionary accruals* are items that management has full control over and is able to delay or eliminate. *Nondiscretionary accruals* are items that are estimated based on changes in the fundamental economic performance of the firm, and management has no control over them. Dividing commitments into optional and non-optional confirms that total commitments are applied to offering better information for financial statements.

Unlike nondiscretionary accruals, which arise from transactions that can be considered "normal" for a firm (i.e., recording an accrual for unbilled services that have been provided), a discretionary accrual is a nonmandatory expense that is recorded within the accounting system but has yet to be realized. An example of this would be an anticipated management bonus. Discretionary accruals are those that arise from managerial discretion and are generally interpreted as indicative of managed earnings. By recognizing accruals at a "convenient" time, companies can smooth earnings and better meet or exceed analysts' earnings projections.

Earnings Management Judgments

LO 7-3
Discuss how earnings management judgments are made.

A fertile area for earnings management is through the use of discretionary accruals. Management might use discretionary accruals to produce an earnings amount close to the amount forecast. Also, discretionary accruals might be used to smooth earnings and make it appear that results are consistent or growing over time.

Acceptability of Earnings Management from a Materiality Perspective

Materiality Judgments

The principle of materiality underscores the concept that some financial transactions are so insignificant that they are not worth measuring and reporting with exact precision. For example, some companies may define an item as material only if it affects earnings by more than 5 percent to 10 percent. This principle allows for some judgment and flexibility in financial reporting. It can be linked to Needles's idea of a continuum of ethical and unethical financial reporting through earnings management. However, the materiality principle can be misused by companies that seek to do so. For instance, a company could manipulate revenues or expenses deliberately, and yet do so within an established maximum percentage of acceptability and claim that the misstatement is not material.

In 1999, W. R. Grace & Company settled an earnings manipulation case with the SEC. The SEC alleged that Grace & Company violated GAAP by establishing an all-purpose reserve fund to "smooth" earnings from 1991 to 1995 by hiding profits in good years and using them to disguise slower earnings in later years. Internal company and audit-firm documents revealed that Grace's auditor, Andersen, discovered the buildup of earnings in the early 1990s and repeatedly warned company executives that what they were doing was improper. However, even after Grace began shifting money into earnings in 1993 and 1994, the outside auditors continued to give the company a favorable audit opinion on their financial statements. The accounting firm based its decision on the grounds that it did not view the improprieties as "material."[45]

The argument that the impact of distortions leading to a smoothing of earnings is too small to matter brings into question the reason why a company would work so hard to bring this about. In today's markets, missing an earnings projection by a few cents can lead to the loss of millions of dollars in the market value of a company's securities. The SEC clearly viewed the distortions by Grace & Company as material and therefore as a violation of GAAP, as well as a violation of securities laws.

Materiality and Legal Decisions

The concept of "materiality" is important in securities law. Whether in a registration statement, or in a filing under the 1934 Act, or in providing information to the trading markets, a company will be liable for any material misstatement, or any material omission of facts necessary to make other statements "not misleading."

This standard is most often encountered in fraud litigation brought under Section 10(b) and Rule 10b-5 under the 1934 Act, but also constitutes the linchpin standard for liabilities arising under Section 11 (false registration statements), Section 12 (false prospectuses), Section 15 (liability of controlling persons), and Section 17 (criminal fraud in securities sales) under the Securities Act of 1933. The fundamental disclosure requirements contained in the two statutes are premised upon a prohibition of material misstatement or omission.

Tests of the materiality standard occur periodically in court proceedings. One such case, *Matrixx Initiatives, Inc., v. Siracusano,* occurred in 2011.[46] The petitioners had suggested that there should be a bright-line test for materiality in a securities fraud suit. The Supreme Court adopted the position of the SEC— the "total mix" of information as viewed by a reasonable investor standard of materiality articulated earlier in *TSC Industries, Inc. v. Northway, Inc.*[47]

In the *Matrixx* case, the shareholder complaint claimed that the company made false statements about its key product, Zicam, a cold remedy nasal spray. In 2003, the company made statements touting the success of Zicam. At one point, Matrixx increased its earnings guidance based on Zicam sales.

The company, however, had received information that Zicam could cause a loss of smelling ability. The data came from several medical researchers, as well as individuals. The product liability suits were filed. Nevertheless, Matrixx continued to maintain that Zicam was safe and that none of the clinical trials supported a claim that the nasal spray caused a loss of smelling ability. Reports to the contrary were simply denied. A negative report of an investigation by the U.S. Food and Drug Administration (FDA) was followed by a drop in Matrixx's share price.

The district court dismissed the complaint, concluding that the adverse product reports were not material. It held that a pharmaceutical company need not disclose such reports unless they are statistically significant. The Ninth Circuit Court reversed. It rejected the statistically significant test, concluding that it was contrary to a ruling in *Basic Inc. v. Levinson.*[48] The Supreme Court affirmed. The court held that "the materiality of adverse event reports cannot be reduced to a bright-line rule.

"Although in many cases reasonable investors would not consider reports of adverse events to be material information, respondents have alleged facts plausibly suggesting that reasonable investors would have viewed these particular reports as material."[49]

The *Matrixx* decision illustrates how difficult materiality determinations can be and why auditors struggle with it when assessing what is a material misstatement in the financial statements. Additional information about the *Matrixx* case appears in Exhibit 7.3.

EXHIBIT 7.3   *Matrixx Initiatives, Inc., v. Siracusano*

In U.S. District Court, Matrixx moved to dismiss the class action for failure to plead properly that any misstatement or omission was "material" and failure to plead requisite scienter (intent to deceive). The court threw out the suit, but the Ninth Circuit reversed, applying the *Basic Inc. v. Levinson* standard for materiality.

The Supreme Court accepted certiorari in the case, presumably because of a conflict between the Ninth Circuit opinion and case law from the Second Circuit.

The court applied *Basic's* "total mix" standard and refused to develop a bright-line rule requiring that "statistically significant data" must be shown to establish materiality. Such a rigid rule would exclude from evidence information that "would otherwise be considered significant to the trading decision of a reasonable investor."

The court stated that medical experts and the FDA often consider a variety of factors in assessing causation

(Continued)

and don't require that these factors rise to a level of "statistical significance." The key test is whether the evidence is suggestive, not categorical, proof.

The court noted that, in 2009, the FDA issued a warning to Matrixx concerning possible health risks of its drug; it cited various reports of anosmia and suggestive scientific literature, none of which rose to a level of "statistical significance."

If medical experts and the FDA infer possible causation from such data, a reasonable investor might well reach the same conclusion. In addition, medical researchers reach conclusions in cases in which statistically significant data is not always available.

The SEC filed an amicus brief supportive of the Ninth Circuit. The court also relied upon an amicus brief filed by a group of law professors, stating that the law concerning materiality as articulated in *Basic* had proven to be an effective standard in litigation since 1988.

The holding in *Matrixx* does not mean that reports of adverse events necessarily mandate disclosure. Companies have to consider the context, content, and source of the reports. But a plaintiff does not have to produce "statistically significant evidence" to prove the necessary 10b-5 element of scienter; pleaded facts may give a strong inference of an intent to deceive, defraud, or manipulate, even without specific showing of statistical significance.

Materiality Considerations in Evaluating Internal Control Deficiencies Under SOX

SOX increased demands on management to prevent and detect material control weaknesses. To develop the controls, SOX requires that CPAs need to be able to identify key control exceptions and apply a materiality concept to determine the financial impact of such exceptions. In this regard, Vorhies identifies four perspectives to help CPAs meet their responsibilities under SOX, including (1) the actual financial statement misstatement or error, (2) an internal control deficiency caused by the failure in design or operation of a control, (3) a large variance in an accounting estimate compared with the actual determined amount, and (4) financial fraud by management or other employees to enhance a company's reported financial position and operating results.[50]

Under Section 302 of SOX, companies are required to (1) review their disclosure controls and procedures quarterly, (2) identify all key control exceptions and determine which are internal control deficiencies, (3) assess each deficiency's impact on the fair presentation of their financial statements, and (4) identify and report significant control deficiencies or material weaknesses to the audit committee of the board of directors and to the company's independent auditor.

Examples of misstatements or errors include incorrectly recorded financial statement amounts and financial statement amounts that should have been recorded but were not. Any internal control failure could be a control deficiency. Such deficiencies usually are the result of a failure in control design or operation. A design failure occurs when management fails to establish a sufficient level of internal control or control activities to achieve a control objective; an operating failure is when an adequately designed control does not operate properly. Because estimation processes are evaluated based on their adequacy, an accounting estimation generally would not result in a control deficiency or an uncorrected/unrecorded misstatement if it was reasonable given the available technology and the process was "normal" for the industry, and if the company's independent auditor reviewed and approved it. Estimating financial events and balances is a necessary evil given the accrual accounting system and need to report on the income and the state of assets at artificial points in time. So long as the estimation process is reasonable, CPAs cannot conclude that a control deficiency exists when the actual amount is compared with the estimate regardless of the size of the variance. If the estimation process is flawed, broken, or unreasonable, a control deficiency exists. An uncorrected/unrecorded misstatement also may exist—the difference between the estimate calculated and recorded in error versus what the correct estimate should have been.

Gemstar–TV Guide International, Inc.

The danger of relying on only a quantitative analysis to make materiality judgments can be seen in the audit by KPMG of Gemstar–TV Guide International, Inc. *Accounting and Auditing Enforcement Release (AAER) 2125,* issued by the SEC, concludes that $364 million of revenue was reported improperly and that certain disclosure policies were inconsistent with Gemstar's accounting for revenue, did not comply with GAAP disclosure requirements, or both. *AAER 2125* found that the KPMG auditors concurred in Gemstar's accounting for overstated revenue from licensing and advertising transactions in March 2000, December 2000, December 2001, and March 2002. Also, KPMG did not object to Gemstar's disclosure and issued audit reports stating that KPMG had conducted its audits in conformity with generally accepted accounting standards (GAAS) and that the financial statements fairly presented its results in conformity with GAAP. In reaching these conclusions, the KPMG auditors unreasonably relied on representations by Gemstar management, unreasonably determined that the revenues were immaterial to Gemstar's financial statements, or both. The KPMG auditors' materiality determinations were unreasonable in that they considered only quantitative materiality factors (i.e., that the amount of revenue was not a large percentage of Gemstar's consolidated financial results) and failed to also consider qualitative materiality (i.e., that the revenue related to business lines that were closely watched by securities analysts and had a material effect on the valuation of Gemstar stock).

The SEC complaint reads like a "what's what" in earnings management; it provides insight into the techniques that some companies use to manage earnings. The complaint alleges that Gemstar materially overstated its revenues by nearly $250 million through the following means:[51]

- Recording revenue under expired, disputed, or nonexistent agreements, and improperly reporting this as licensing and advertising revenue.

- Recording revenue from a long-term agreement on an accelerated basis in violation of GAAP and Gemstar's own policies, which required recording and reporting such revenue ratably over the terms of the agreement (consistent with the matching theory).

- Inflating advertising revenue by improperly recording and reporting revenue amounts from multiple-element transactions.

- Engaging in "round-trip" transactions, whereby Gemstar paid money to a third party to advertise its services and capitalized that cost while the third party used the funds received from Gemstar to buy advertising that Gemstar recorded 100 percent as revenue in the period of the transaction.

- Failing to disclose that it had structured certain settlements for the purpose of creating cookie-jar reserves of advertising revenue to smooth net income.

- Improperly recording advertising revenue from nonmonetary and barter transactions even though Gemstar could not establish the advertising's fair value properly.

Accrual accounting is not an exact science. A variety of assumptions and accounting estimates are used in arriving at the final earnings figures. These assumptions and estimates require sound judgment to protect against unacceptable forms of earnings management. Using the conception of earnings management by Healy and Wahlen, "earnings management" occurs when managers use judgment in financial reporting and in structuring transactions to alter financial reports to either mislead some stakeholders about the underlying economic performance of a company or influence contractual outcomes that depend on reported accounting numbers.[52]

IFRS—Principles- vs. Rules-Based Judgments

One concern about a principles-based system is whether an economic substance-over-form concept might lead preparers of financial statements to try and justify a specific accounting outcome with reference to commercial drivers in an attempt to manage earnings. To determine if there was a difference in the magnitude of earnings management in a principles-based versus rules-based environment, Mergenthaler examined the factors that executives consider when deciding to manage earnings. He contends that the probability of being penalized for earnings management and the penalty imposed on executives who manage are factors that influence executives' estimate of the expected cost of earnings management. Mergenthaler found a positive association between rules-based characteristics and the dollar magnitude of earnings management. He argues that this is because the expected cost of managing earnings is lower in a rules-based environment. The SEC study of principles-based standards seems to support Mergenthaler's contention. The commission expressed its concern that, in a principles-based system, there may be "a greater difficulty in seeking remedies against 'bad actors' either through enforcement or litigation."[53]

French authors Thomas Jeanjean and Herve Stolowy examined the effect of IFRS conversion on earnings quality—specifically on management manipulation of earnings to avoid recognition of losses. Their work examined more than 1,100 firms in three countries to determine whether the earnings management appeared to increase or decrease after implementation of IFRS. The authors measured financial reporting quality as a reduction in earnings management. Earnings management was assessed as the frequency of small profits compared to small losses, a technique used in past studies. Australia, France, and the United Kingdom were selected for examination, as these three countries were unable to adopt IFRS before the 2005 mandatory transition date, thus eliminating any early adoption benefits. According to their research, earnings management remained consistent in Australia and the United Kingdom after IFRS adoption. However, in France, earnings management appeared to increase, suggesting that earnings quality was not improved overall by adopting IFRS.[54]

A frequent question asked is whether principles-based accounting standards increase or decrease earnings informativeness. As outlined in the SEC study and the FASB report[55] on the principles-based approach, some argue that earnings are more informative when standards are principles-based. They contend that principles-based standards do not have bright-line thresholds or exceptions that allow managers to structure transactions that technically comply with a standard while circumventing its intent. On the other hand, some argue (e.g., Herz) that principles-based standards provide more opportunities for managers to use their discretion to obfuscate earnings, thereby reducing earnings informativeness.[56] This argument suggests that rules-based standards provide guidelines that prevent management from abusing GAAP to manipulate earnings.

In a study of principles-based standards and earnings effects, Folsom et al. examined whether the reliance on principles-based standards affects the informativeness of earnings. They defined principles-based standards as standards that have fewer rules-based characteristics than rules-based standards, as evidenced by fewer bright-line thresholds, scope and legacy exceptions, large volumes of implementation guidance, and high levels of detail. The authors found that firms that rely more on principles-based standards have a stronger relation between earnings and returns. They also found that earnings map better to future cash flows and are more persistent when the firm relies on principles-based standards. Overall, these findings suggest that managers use the discretion provided by principles-based standards to convey information better to investors.[57]

Earnings Management Techniques

LO 7-4
Describe the devices used to manage earnings.

In his remarks entitled "The Numbers Game," referred to in the beginning of the chapter, former SEC chairman Arthur Levitt described five techniques of "accounting hocus-pocus" that summarized the most glaring abuses of the flexibility inherent to accrual accounting: big-bath charges, creative acquisition accounting, cookie-jar reserves, materiality, and revenue recognition:[58]

- **Big-bath charges:** One example is when a company resorts to taking a one-time large restructuring charge/write-down, as opposed to appropriately recording the losses over several fiscal years. This is to avoid a succession of years of earnings decline that would have otherwise made the company financial health look bad in the eyes of stakeholders. To make it more difficult for companies to abuse "big-bath charges," in 1998, the FASB adopted *SFAS 144* on impairment losses and *SFAS 146* on the timing of the recognition of restructuring obligations. Another example occurred at Sunbeam Corporation that was discussed previously and in Case 7-7. Sunbeam had huge losses in the late 1990s. The company fired its CEO and brought in Al Dunlap. Dunlap wanted to look like a turnaround artist so he established and purposefully overstated cookie-jar-reserves to make it look as though the losses in the year he took over were higher than reported. Dunlap then could reverse the overstated expenses and increase income in future years to make him look better.

- **Creative acquisition accounting:** This is when, following a business acquisition, the acquirer allocates the bulk of the total purchase price to the acquiree's in-process research and development (R&D), as opposed to its long-lived assets as mandated by GAAP, thus recording a huge expense during the year of acquisition so that earnings in future years wouldn't be significantly affected by the acquisition costs. Since 1998, however, *SFAS Nos. 141* and *142* have been adopted to provide clearer guidelines on how the purchase price in a business acquisition should be allocated.

- **Cookie-jar reserves:** The objective of using cookie-jar-reserves is to smooth net income over time. This can take place in two ways. In the first scenario, a company with record revenues overstates its bad debt expense in quarter/year 1 so as to record little bad debt expense in subsequent quarters/years when it expects to achieve below-average revenues. The Lucent case that is discussed later shows the reverse treatment where the company reduced previously recorded allowances to inflate earnings in a low earnings year. In the second scenario, a company understates revenues by inflating unearned revenues in quarter/year 1 to pad revenue figures in subsequent quarters/years should they fall below market expectations. Since 1998, the SEC has released *SAB 101,* which outlines with more clarity when deferring revenue is permissible.

- **Materiality:** The concept of materiality is a gray area of accounting; consequently, it is subject to different interpretations, as previously discussed. Sometimes publicly traded companies resort to questionable accounting practices with seemingly immaterial monetary effects, but that practice allows the company to meet or beat analysts' earnings expectations, thereby creating a qualitatively material effect. In this type of situation, Levitt recommends that the misstatement be considered material because it is very likely that the company's stock price would have declined if the misstatement had been corrected.

- **Revenue recognition:** Some companies accelerate the recording of revenues to help meet analysts' earnings projections, increase year-end bonuses, improve the share price of stock and stock options owned by top executives, or all of them. The HealthSouth case discussed earlier in this chapter illustrates how contractual allowances can be manipulated to show higher revenues, earnings, and EPS, all of which led to higher share prices.

CVS Caremark Acquisition of Longs Drugstores

CVS Caremark used an acquisition technique that enabled it to manage earnings in a blatantly fraudulent way. The acquisition of Longs Drugstores by CVS on October 20, 2008, illustrates what can happen when experts allow client management to make the call on how to account for a transaction. CVS called the shots and the firm that conducted the valuation of assets of Longs went along with unsubstantiated reductions in asset values even though its independent analysis showed otherwise. As for the auditors, they uncritically accepted management's representations about these and other amounts. The auditors did not exercise the level of due care or professional skepticism warranted by the facts. However, the SEC did not file an action against either party, choosing instead to go after CVS and Laird Daniels, CPA, the retail controller for CVS during the fraud period. The discussion below is drawn from the SEC's legal settlement with Daniels.[59]

The SEC charged Daniels with accounting violations, saying he "orchestrated" the improper accounting adjustments by:

- Making untrue or misleading statements of material fact in violation of the Securities Exchange Act of 1934 Section 10(b).
- Directly or indirectly falsifying CVS's books and records.
- Aiding and abetting and causing CVS's violations of the Exchange Act, which require an issuer to file accurate quarterly reports with the SEC and require those reports to contain such further material information as is necessary to make the required statements in the reports not misleading.

CVS was accused of manipulating the accounting for its October 2008 purchase of Longs. The SEC said the changes improperly boosted profit by as much as 11.7 cents per share for the third quarter of 2009, enabling CVS to exceed rather than miss analyst forecasts. "CVS broke faith with investors," Andrew Ceresney, director of the SEC enforcement division, said in a statement. "The intentional misconduct by CVS breached the core principle of fair and accurate reporting of financial performance."[60]

On April 8, 2014, it was announced that CVS Caremark would pay $20 million to settle a variety of charges including making improper accounting adjustments that overstated the financial results in 2009 for its retail pharmacy line of business.

What follows is a brief summary of the facts of the case. Exhibit 7.4 contains a complete timeline of events.

On January 27, 2009, the valuation firm submitted a draft report applying a "continued use" premise—that CVS would retain and continue using all of the Longs stores' property, plant, and equipment (except for stores to be closed, as identified by CVS). The firm valued the Longs stores' property, plant, and equipment at more than $1.2 billion, including $937 million of real property and $229 million of personal property. The valuation results were included in CVS's audited financial statements for the fiscal year ended December 31, 2008, which were incorporated by reference in the annual report on Form 10-K that CVS filed with the SEC on February 27, 2009.

In its third quarter 2009 10-Q, CVS adjusted the value of certain fixed assets associated with the Longs stores from $229.3 million to $39.6 million. The difference was reallocated to goodwill, thus reducing the company's depreciation expense going forward and allowing CVS to reverse $49 million in depreciation expenses already incurred. The adjustment boosted adjusted EPS for the quarter by 17 percent and allowed CVS to beat analyst expectations.

The SEC concluded that the revision was not in compliance with GAAP. According to the SEC's *Accounting and Auditing Enforcement Release No. 71896:*[61]

> "The Longs PPA [purchase price accounting] adjustments did not comply with generally accepted accounting principles ("GAAP") on "Business Combinations," specifically *Statement of Financial Accounting Standards 141 (SFAS 141),* because: (1) they did not reflect the expected future use of the Longs personal property as of the acquisition date in October 2008; (2) they did not reflect information that CVS knew or had arranged to obtain as of the acquisition date; and (3) they did not account for CVS's use of the assets to generate revenue after the acquisition date. The failure to comply with GAAP had a material impact on the company's third-quarter 2009 financial results."[62]

EXHIBIT 7.4   Timeline of CVS Acquisition of Longs Drugstores

With the exception of *SFAS 141,* the following discussion is taken from the SEC's legal action against former CVS Retail Controller Laird Daniels, CPA. *(In the Matter of Laird Daniels, CPA, Respondent, Accounting and Auditing Enforcement Release No. 3548,* April 8, 2014).

October 20, 2008

CVS acquires Longs chain of approximately 525 drugstores on October 20, 2008. CVS hires a major accounting firm to prepare a valuation for the Longs purchase price accounting (PPA) under *Statement of Financial Accounting Standards (SFAS) 141* ("Business Combinations"). SFAS 141 was superseded by SFAS 141R as of December 2008—two months after the Longs acquisition. (NOTE 26)

The Original Purchase Price Allocation for the Longs Acquisition

November 2008

The engagement letter with the valuation firm specifies that, applying *SFAS 141,* the firm would determine the "fair value" of the Longs assets "as part of a 'going concern in continued use,'" and that "this valuation premise presupposes the continued utilization of the assets in connection with all other assets as the highest and best use."

December 15, 2008

The real estate finance director provides the valuation firm with a list indicating that CVS plans to close 36 stores right away, relocate 19 stores within one year, operate 123 stores with the intent to relocate them within three years (if possible), and operate 349 stores for the long-term.

The valuation firm's approach to determining the "fair value" of the tangible assets in the Longs stores depends on CVS's intended use of each store.

a. For assets in the stores to be operated for more than one year, the firm will apply a "continued use" premise.

b. For the assets in the stores to be closed within one year, the firm will determine the "orderly liquidation value" using data from the CVS real estate group indicating that approximately 35 percent of the assets would have liquidation value.

December 23, 2008

(Continued)

The valuation firm sends draft schedules of the real property that is valued at $937.2 million and the personal property valued at $229.3 million. The retail controller forwards the schedules to CVS's outside auditors.

January 30, 2009

After submitting its draft report, the valuation firm waits for comments from CVS's outside auditors so it can prepare its final report. On January 30, the retail controller tells the firm: "[The auditors] completed their review of the draft valuation report and had no comments. Please issue your report in final form as soon as you can." The firm responds that it will send a draft management representation letter for CVS to sign, as well as "a final invoice for our work."

In connection with the year-end 2008 audit, CVS's outside auditors review the valuation firm's approach to valuing tangible assets and concludes that the firm's methodology is reasonable. While the outside auditors work on the 2008 audit, CVS does not disclose anything about its plans to remodel any Longs stores, and so the auditors do not review the Longs valuation report for any potential impact of the remodeling.

CVS includes the values from the January draft valuation report in its audited financial statements for 2008, which were included in its annual report to shareholders for 2008 and are incorporated by reference in the annual report on Form 10-K that it files with the Commission on February 27. Note 2 to the audited financial statements, entitled "Business Combinations," indicated that CVS had acquired Longs for approximately $2.6 billion. Note 3, entitled "Goodwill and Other Intangibles," stated that "goodwill increased primarily due to the Longs Acquisition" and that the increase in amortizable intangible assets "was primarily due to the preliminary purchase price allocations. The audited financial statements did not contain any indication that the valuation of Longs' tangible assets such as personal property was not final.

February 27, 2009

The real estate finance director asks the valuation firm about potential adjustments to the value of assets in the Longs stores to be closed. He writes: "It seems there have been several changes in individual store strategies over the past few weeks, and I would guess these have not been picked up by you guys or [the retail controller]. I would like to talk about how these changes and future changes should be handled with respect to these value adjustments."

Minutes later, a senior manager at the valuation firm responds with a warning: "Keep in mind that any changes in strategy that were not known as of the acquisition date cannot be reflected in the valuation. The valuation was as of October 30, 2008. So the valuation can only reflect the strategies in place at that time—which I believe we accurately reflected. Any changes after the valuation date would have to be discussed with your audit team."

March 2009

The CVS fixed asset group adjusts the depreciation being taken on Longs PP&E (property, plant, and equipment) and technology assets by lengthening the remaining useful lives beyond the time period that the valuation firm used.

April 2009

The CVS property accounting group identifies a discrepancy between the depreciation on Longs' assets built into the 2009 budget and the actual depreciation being taken on those assets. On April 30, the corporate controller complains to the retail controller and to Daniels, who was then vice president for corporate budgeting, that the CVS fixed asset group has apparently made decisions about the remaining useful lives of Longs' assets that are inconsistent with the valuation firm's draft report, and the result is an unfavorable variance of $20 million per month.

May 2009

The controller fires the retail controller. Daniels becomes the retail controller and takes charge of working with the valuation firm on the Longs valuation.

On May 13, Daniels tells the valuation firm during a conference call that:

a. CVS is remodeling the Longs stores that are going to be operated for the long-term, and as part of the remodeling process, CVS is gutting the stores and discarding all the personal property; and

(Continued)

b. CVS is not receiving any value for the assets being discarded.

Daniels also tells the valuation firm that, as of the acquisition date on October 20, 2008, CVS intends to throw out all that personal property in the Longs stores.

On May 19, a senior manager at the valuation firm warns Daniels that it appears CVS is improperly changing its real estate strategy after the acquisition date.

On May 26, Daniels has a conference call with the valuation firm. Prior to the call, Daniels provided the firm with CVS's current real estate strategy for the Longs stores. The strategy list indicates that CVS plans to: (1) close 71 stores within one year; (2) operate 124 stores with the intent to relocate them within three years (if possible); and (3) operate 333 stores for the long-term. The valuation firm's internal manual on *SFAS 141* states that PPA adjustments are appropriate only if "the necessary information was determinable at the time the preliminary allocation was reported," as when, for example, the acquiring entity has commissioned an appraisal of plant and equipment that is not complete by the acquisition date.

June 3, 2009

The valuation firm tells Daniels that the personal property in the Longs drugstores are now valued at $49.6 million (compared with $229.3 million as of May 8). The firm reduces the value of personal property by $179.7 million based on the supposedly correct information provided by Daniels in May—that, as of the acquisition date on October 20, 2008, CVS intends to discard the assets in the stores to be remodeled, and that the discarded assets have no liquidation value.

October 1, 2009

The valuation firm sends Daniels a "final draft" of its valuation report. The value of personal property in the Longs drugstores has been further reduced—from $50.8 million to $39.6 million. The total reduction in the value of personal property in the Longs drugstores since the firm's January 27, 2009, draft report is approximately $189 million (from $229.3 million to $39.6 million).

CVS's Outside Auditors Accept the $189 Million Reduction in the Valuation of the Longs Stores Personal Property

Until the spring of 2009, CVS's outside auditors were not aware that CVS planned to discard almost all of the Longs stores personal property. In early June 2009, Daniels tells the outside auditors that CVS has finalized its strategy for which Longs stores will be closed, relocated, or remodeled, and that the adjustments to the valuation of the Longs stores could be larger than expected, because CVS was going to scrap all personal property in the stores being remodeled. This is the first time the outside auditors hear about the write-off of assets in stores being remodeled. The coordinating partner tells the engagement partner that he is a "little worried about what he [Daniels] may be trying to do."

June 19, 2009

Daniels tells a member of the Longs remodeling team at CVS:

I'm close to completing the valuation work with [the valuation firm] for Longs. The final step I have is getting the auditors comfortable with the changes. Our auditors were hoping they could see a summary of what we are spending on the resets [remodels] that have been completed. Is it possible to get a summary (with some detail) for the 4 stores that are done? Since we are writing off a lot of the assets, they would feel more comfortable seeing that were spending a fair amount per store to reset them.

September 25, 2009

The manager of property accounting provides Daniels with a spreadsheet listing the amount spent on remodeling for: (1) each Longs location whose assets had been written down to zero, and (2) each Longs location whose assets were included in the residual valuation of $50 million.

October 5, 2009

The outside auditors' senior manager alerts others members of the audit team about the upcoming finalization of the Longs PPA (prior period adjustment): "The biggest change is that PP&E went from $229 million in the initial valuation to $50 million (and the final one is expected to be $39 million). The reason

(Continued)

behind this as it has been explained to us is that CVS was either resetting / relocating / closing a number of the stores that was never communicated to [the valuation firm] and therefore an asset value was assigned that was way too high."

October 14, 2009

The valuation firm's senior manager provides Daniels with answers to questions from the outside auditors about the revised valuation. Daniels forwards the valuation firm's response to the outside auditors. Daniels never provides the outside auditors with any documents specifically confirming that CVS was gutting all the "full remodel" stores. Instead, when they accepted the PPA adjustments, the outside auditors relied on: (1) the representations by Daniels that CVS had always intended to scrap all assets in the Longs stores to be remodeled; and (2) the data identifying the amount of capital expenditures at each store.

November 5, 2009

CVS's Form 10-Q for the third quarter of 2009 includes adjustments to the Longs PPA. Compared to the valuation firm's January 2009 draft report, the value of Longs tangible assets is reduced by $212 million and goodwill is increased by the same amount. The reduction of tangible assets resulted primarily from the $189 million decrease in the value of personal property in the Longs drugstores reflected in the firm's "final draft" valuation report dated October 1.

CVS makes a one-time catch-up adjustment by reversing $49 million of the depreciation taken on Longs assets from the closing in October 2008 through June 2009. In addition, CVS does not take $19 million of depreciation that would otherwise have been taken on Longs' assets in the third quarter. The $49 million one-time depreciation reversal increases third-quarter 2009 EPS by 2.4¢.

Daniels Caused CVS to Make Improper Accounting Adjustments

The Longs' PPA adjustments did not comply with GAAP. Under *SFAS 141*, an acquiring entity should allocate the cost of the acquired entity to the assets and liabilities assumed "based on their estimated fair values at [the] date of acquisition." Plant and equipment "should be valued at "current replacement cost ... unless the expected future use of the assets indicates a lower value."

Under *SFAS 141*, an "allocation period" may be needed "to identify and measure the fair value" of the assets and liabilities. The allocation period "is intended to differentiate between amounts that are determined as a result of the identification and valuation process ... and amounts that are determined because information that was not previously obtainable becomes obtainable." The allocation period "ends when the acquiring entity is no longer waiting for information that it has arranged to obtain and that is known to be available or obtainable." In other words, a PPA adjustment is valid only if it is based on information that the acquiring entity "has arranged to obtain" and that was "known to be available or obtainable" on the acquisition date.

Under *SFAS 141*, CVS could only make adjustments to the Longs PPA based on information that was known or knowable as of the acquisition date on October 20, 2008. Given the facts set forth above, the PPA adjustments in the third quarter of 2009 (writing off $189 million of personal property in the Longs stores) were not proper under *SFAS 141* because:

a. They did not reflect CVS's intended future use of those assets as of the acquisition date on October 20, 2008;
b. They did not reflect information that was known or knowable to CVS as of October 20, 2008; and
c. They did not account for CVS's use of the assets to generate revenue after October 20, 2008.

The conclusion that the write-off of assets supposedly discarded during the remodeling process should not have been treated as a PPA adjustment is consistent with CVS's prior acquisitions, in which: (1) CVS did not write off the assets in stores being remodeled; and (2) subsequent decisions about which stores to close (not which stores to remodel) were the primary reason for changes to the PPA.

With proper accounting, current-period expenses in the third quarter of 2009 would have been as much as $189 million higher than was actually reported. For the quarter, the failure to recognize as much as $189 million of current-period expenses overstated operating profit by as much as 13.7 percent, overstated income from continuing operations by as much as 12.5 percent, overstated net income by as much as 12.5 percent, and overstated EPS by as much as 17 percent (as much as 9.3¢).

Definition of "Revenue Recognition"

Given the prominence of revenue recognition techniques in earnings management cases, we discuss some of the criteria for determining proper revenue, some of which are addressed in this chapter.

Generally, revenue is recognized only when a specific event has occurred and the amount of revenue is measurable. For example, income is recognized as revenue whenever the company delivers or performs its product or service and receives payment for it. Of course sometimes it is not that simple because uncertainties exist about collectibility, side agreements are made, and/or multiple elements exist in a revenue transaction that need to be separately valued.

The bedrock revenue recognition principles are explained in SEC Staff Accounting Bulletin 101 (SAB 101), "Revenue Recognition in Financial Statements." The basic guidelines provide that revenue generally is realized or realizable and earned when all of the following criteria are met:[63]

1. Persuasive evidence of an arrangement exists.
2. Delivery has occurred or services have been rendered,
3. The seller's price to the buyer is fixed or determinable.
4. Collectibility is reasonably assured.

Because of the difficulty of identifying when revenue should be recognized in certain situations (i.e., "selling" a product where a customer has an unlimited right of return), some companies choose to manipulate revenue recognition to make their financial figures look better. For example, if XYZ Corp. wants to hide the fact that it is having a bad year in sales, it may choose to recognize income that has not yet been earned in order to boost its sales revenue for the year. In other cases, facts may be obscured to manage earnings by, for example, backdating revenue transactions.

Here are some common revenue recognition devices that have been used to manage earnings.

Multiple Deliverables

Vendors often provide multiple products or services to their customers as part of a single arrangement or a series of related arrangements. These deliverables may be provided at different points in time or over different time periods. As a simple example, a vendor may enter into an arrangement with a customer to deliver and install a tangible product along with providing one year of maintenance services. In this arrangement, there are three deliverables: (1) the product, (2) installation, and (3) maintenance services. Issues often arise regarding how and whether to separate these deliverables and how to allocate the overall arrangement consideration. Subtopic 605-25, *Revenue Recognition—Multiple-Element Arrangements*, of the Financial Accounting Standards Board's Accounting Standards Codification (ASC) provides the guidance that should be followed in accounting for this and many other revenue arrangements with multiple deliverables.[64]

Channel Stuffing

Channel stuffing is a deceptive business practice used by a company to inflate its sales and earnings figures by deliberately sending retailers along its distribution channel more products than they are able to sell to the public. The goal is to beef up receivables and accelerate revenue into a period earlier than would normally be expected given the company's revenue cycle. One problem is concessions may need to be made to get customers to buy before they are ready to do so and/or receive the product. Another is that customers may return excess product at a later date, which may not be so bad for the vendor given it still recognizes a higher level of revenue when it wants; however, these kinds of transactions have a way of blowing up in your face when customers say "no" in the future. Moreover, the snow-ball effect makes it harder each year to maintain the charade.

The legality of channel stuffing comes into question because these transactions may not meet the "economic substance" test. The *economic substance* of transactions and events must be recorded in the financial statements rather than just their *legal form* in order to present fairly financial position, results of operations, and cash flows. One issue of concern is: What if a company cannot estimate future sales returns or, at net, if the channel stuffing transactions substantially reduce future revenues?

Round-Tripping

Global Crossing and Qwest were two telecommunications companies that engaged in "round-trip" transactions in the early 2000s. What happened is the companies were round-tripping revenues by recording a series of last-minute deals with other carriers, in which the contracts were for nearly identical amounts, for routes that had yet to be specified or, in some cases, on routes that had not yet been built. In a 2001 transaction between Global Crossing and Qwest, Global Crossing signed a $100 million contract only to "round-trip" the cash by purchasing a similar amount of undefined capacity from Qwest. Global Crossing would book the incoming contract as a large chunk of revenue, and then book the outgoing contract as a capital expense. To an objective observer, these capacity swaps appear to be a transaction solely for the purpose of boosting revenues. Hence, it fails the economic substance test.

Bill and Hold

In a traditional bill-and-hold scheme, such as engaged in by Sunbeam, a legitimate sales order is received, processed, and ready for shipment. The customer, however, is not ready for the shipment. The seller holds the goods in its facility or ships them to a different location, such as a third-party warehouse, for storage until the customer is ready to accept shipment. The seller then recognizes revenue immediately upon shipment to the warehouse. Since the risk of ownership has not passed to the buyer, the recording of revenue is not justified.

In a new twist on bill-and-hold transactions, in August 2014, the SEC brought charges against Newport Beach, California, telecommunications equipment maker AirTouch Communications Inc., former president and CEO Hideyuki Kanakubo, and former CFO Jerome Kaiser, for orchestrating a fraudulent revenue recognition scheme that violated GAAP by recognizing revenue on inventory that was shipped to a Florida warehouse, but never sold. They are also accused of defrauding an investor from whom they secured a $2 million loan for the company based on misstatements and omissions associated with the shipments.[65]

When AirTouch reported net revenues of a little more than $1.03 million in its report for the third quarter of 2012, it included approximately $1.24 million in inventory that had been shipped to a company in Florida that agreed to warehouse AirTouch's products in anticipation of future sales. The Florida company had not purchased the inventory, and AirTouch had not sold the inventory to any of its customers.

New Revenue Recognition Standard

The Financial Accounting Standards Board (FASB) and the International Accounting Standards Board (IASB) jointly issued a new revenue recognition standard, *Revenue from Contracts with Customers,* in May 2014 to converge the revenue recognition rules of both bodies. The new standard is effective for public companies for annual and interim periods beginning after December 15, 2017. Earlier application is permitted only as of annual reporting periods beginning after Dec. 15, 2016. All other entities are required to apply the guidance to annual reporting periods beginning after Dec. 15, 2018, and interim reporting periods within annual reporting periods beginning after Dec. 15, 2019. The new standard provides guidance for helping companies recognize revenue under both U.S. GAAP and IFRS. The new standard provides a single, comprehensive accounting model for revenue recognition. The standard is complex so we limit the discussion to the very basics here.

Under the new standard, companies under contract to provide goods or services to a customer will be required to follow a five-step process to recognize revenue:[66]

1. Identify contract(s) with a customer.

2. Identify the separate performance obligations in the contract.

3. Determine the transaction price.

4. Allocate the transaction price to the separate performance obligations.

5. Recognize revenue when the entity satisfies each performance obligation.

The new standard is more principles-based and may result in financial reporting that, in some cases, is more reflective of the underlying economics. The rule's expanded disclosure requirements will help financial statement users understand the nature, amount, timing, and uncertainty of revenue and cash flows arising from contracts with customers.

According to Prabhakar "PK" Kalavacherla, partner in the Audit Quality and Professional Practice group at KPMG LLP, companies that sell products and services in a bundle, or those engaged in major projects—in such industries as telecommunications, software, engineering, construction, and real estate —could see significant changes to the timing of revenue recognition. For telecommunications or cable companies, their current practice of recognizing revenue only to the extent of the cash received will be replaced by a requirement to estimate a stand-alone selling price for free or discounted goods or services (such as a wireless handset or free premium channel services for a limited time).[67] It remains to be seen whether a company can make reliable estimates of stand-alone selling prices that represent management's best estimate considering observable inputs. However, it could be more challenging if goods or services are not sold independently by the company or others.

The new standard requires extensive disclosures including disaggregation of total revenue; information about performance obligations; changes in contract asset and liability account balances between periods; and key judgments and estimates. Our concern is the devil is in the details and those can be quite complicated with revenue recognition. We'll reserve final comment until the standard goes into effect and any "tweaking" that is necessary is made.

Earnings Management: One More Thing

While earnings management is not necessarily the result of an intentional fraud, but the culmination of a series of aggressive interpretations of the accounting rules and aggressive operating activities, it still should be considered unethical if the primary motive for managing earnings is to deceive users of the true results of operations or reflect the economic substance. In many cases, earnings management is carried out by otherwise honest people who are motivated to tell the company's side of the story rather than strictly adhere to GAAP. The end result is misstatement of the financial results that oftentimes builds pressure to do the same in subsequent periods. One aggressive interpretation leads to another until the quality of the financial information is in doubt.

McGregor explains earnings manipulation as follows:

> The typical case of earnings manipulation begins with a track record of success. The company or division has posted significant sales and earnings growth over recent years. [Its] stock price trades at a high price earnings multiple as the market rewards its stellar growth. Unfortunately, it is becoming more difficult for the company to maintain the sales and earnings growth that analysts have grown to expect. Sales are behind target this quarter, so management runs special incentives for its sales force to accelerate sales and uses overtime to ship out its products. It works and the firm meets expectations.

The next quarter, the analyst expectations are higher. However, sales still have not picked up to the level required, so the firm provides additional incentives to its sales force, uses overtime to boost shipments but now has additional expenses to contend with (incentives and overtime), so it does not fully accrue all its consulting expenses. The following quarter rolls around and sales still haven't recovered, but the analysts keep raising the bar. This time the operating tactics are not enough, so management pressures the CFO to make the numbers. The CFO is aggressive in the interpretation of installment sales and expense accruals, and the company again meets expectations. The expectations keep rising, as does the firm's stock price. As the fourth quarter comes around, sales still are not at expectations. The CFO creates sales and under-accrues expenses all to meet expectations. The company has gone from aggressive operating practices to financial fraud.[68]

Earnings management techniques have come to be known as "financial shenanigans." Financial shenanigans are actions or omissions of information or financial structuring of transactions intended to hide or distort the real financial performance or financial condition of an entity. They range from minor deceptions to more serious misapplications of accounting principles. We discuss these techniques in the next section.

Financial Shenanigans

LO 7-5
Explain the workings of financial shenanigans.

Financial Statement Effects

Financial shenanigans can be broadly classified into two types: (a) schemes that overstate revenues and profits, which are designed to enhance reported results and earnings per share and (b) schemes that understate revenues and profits that are typically done to smooth out net income over time periods and make it appear less volatile.

Companies have numerous avenues to engage in financial shenanigans if they so desire. These include recognizing revenues prematurely, recording sales made to an affiliate or recording sales of unshipped items, capitalizing rather than expensing research and development costs, reclassifying balance sheet items to create income, amortizing costs or depreciating assets at a slower pace, setting up special-purpose vehicles to hide debt or mask ownership, and so on. In most instances of far-reaching and complex fraud, financial shenanigans were not detected even by a company's auditors.

Howard Schilit wrote a book that has become a classic in understanding the common types of financial shenanigans. We explain the basic financial shenanigan techniques,[69] with the number of examples in each category limited to the three most common techniques. We also use Schilit's framework to discuss earnings manipulations at two companies charged by the SEC with accounting fraud—Xerox and Lucent.

1. Recording Revenue Too Soon or of Questionable Quality

This may be the most common technique because many opportunities arise to accomplish it, including recording revenue before the earnings process has been completed or before an unconditional exchange has occurred. Examples of this shenanigan include:

- Recording revenue when future services remain to be provided.
- Recording revenue before shipment or before the customer's unconditional acceptance.
- Recording revenue even though the customer is not obligated to pay.

The Xerox case discussed later in this chapter illustrates how a company can move earnings into an earlier period by allocating more of the revenue in a multiyear contract to earlier years than justified given continuing servicing under the contract.

2. Recording Bogus Revenue

Typically, bogus revenue transactions lead to fictitious revenue. Examples include:

- Recording sales that lack economic substance.
- Recording as revenue supplier rebates that are tied to future required purchases.
- Releasing revenue that was held back improperly before a merger.

The ZZZZ Best case assignment in Chapter 5 illustrates how a master of deception like Barry Minkow can create nonexistent revenue by creating fictitious invoices for unperformed work.

3. Boosting Income with One-Time Gains

The gains (and losses) from the sale of operating and investment assets that should be recorded in another (e.g., miscellaneous) income account can be classified in other ways if the intent is to boost operating income. These include:

- Boosting profits by selling undervalued assets.
- Including investment income or gains as part of operating revenue.
- Including investment income or gains as a reduction in operating expenses.

IBM used the net proceeds from the sale of an operating unit ($300 million) to lower its operating costs, rather than accounting for it as a nonrecurring, one-time gain. We consider it fraud because it is a deliberate attempt to mislead users of the financial statements into thinking that operating income is larger than it really is. Financial analysts tend to put more emphasis on operating income than net income because of the miscellaneous, non-operating items recorded below the line of operating income to get net income.

4. Shifting Current Expenses to a Later or Earlier Period

A common approach to shifting expenses to a later period is by capitalizing a cost in the current period and expensing it over a period of time, rather than expensing the item completely in the current period. This was the technique used by WorldCom to inflate earnings by between $11 billion and $13 billion.

Additional examples include:

- Changing accounting policies and shifting current expenses to an earlier period.
- Failing to write down or write off impaired assets.
- Reducing asset reserves.

WorldCom capitalized its line costs that provided telecommunications capacity on other companies' systems rather than expense those costs as they were incurred. The effects on reported income were dramatic and illustrate how earnings management techniques can lead to reporting earnings when a loss has actually occurred. The following table illustrates just how that was done.

Form Filed with the Commission	Reported Line Cost Expenses	Reported Income (before Taxes and Minority Interests)	Actual Line Cost Expenses	Actual Income (before Taxes and Minority Interests)
10-Q, 3rd Q. 2000	$ 3.867 billion	$1.736 billion	$ 4.695 billion	$ 908 million
10-K, 2000	$15.462 billion	$7.568 billion	$16.697 billion	$6.333 billion
10-Q, 1st Q. 2001	$ 4.108 billion	$ 988 million	$ 4.879 billion	$ 217 million
10-Q, 2nd Q. 2001	$ 3.73 billion	$ 159 million	$ 4.29 billion	$ 401 million **loss**
10-Q, 3rd Q. 2001	$ 3.745 billion	$ 845 million	$ 4.488 billion	$ 102 million
10-K, 2001	$14.739 billion	$2.393 billion	$17.754 billion	$ 622 million **loss**
10-Q, 1st Q. 2002	$ 3.479 billion	$ 240 million	$ 4.297 billion	$ 578 million **loss**

5. Failing to Record or Improperly Reducing Liabilities

The liability account is often used to manipulate earnings because when liabilities that should be recorded are not, the expenses also are understated. When liabilities are reduced improperly, the same effect on expenses occurs. The result is to overstate earnings. Some examples include:

- Failing to record expenses and related liabilities when future obligations remain.
- Releasing questionable reserves (cookie-jar reserves) into income.
- Recording revenue when cash is received, even though future obligations remain.

The recording of discretionary accruals that was previously discussed is one application of the technique. The Lucent Technologies example discussed later in this chapter illustrates a variety of these techniques.

6. Shifting Current Revenue to a Later Period

Some companies act to delay the recording of revenue when the amount is relatively high in a given year. In a sense, this action sets up a "rainy day" reserve that can be used to restore earnings in low-earnings years. One way to accomplish this is to create a cookie-jar reserve with the excess revenues and release it back into the income stream at a later date, when it can do more good for the bottom line. Another method is through the use of deferred revenue. Examples include:

- Deliberately overstating the allowance for uncollectible accounts thereby understating current revenue and adjusting the allowance downward in future years to increase revenue.
- Deferring revenue recognition on a year-end service transaction that was completed by December 31 and then transferring it to earned revenue in subsequent years.
- Deliberately overstating the estimated sales returns account and adjusting it downward in future years.

As previously mentioned, in the 1990s the SEC brought a lawsuit against W. R. Grace & Co. for manipulating earnings to meet Wall Street's expectations. The SEC alleged that senior Grace executives deferred reporting some 1991 and 1992 income from National Medical Care, then the main Grace health-care unit. Grace assigned $10 million to $20 million of this unexpected profit to "corporate reserves," which it then used to increase the reported earnings of both the health-care unit and the company between 1993 and 1995, the SEC said.[70]

The actual earnings of the unit and its parent company sometimes fell short of analysts' expectations during this period, the suit alleged. Thus, Grace misled shareholders by reporting results buttressed by the reserves. The only problem was that Grace deferring reporting income by increasing or establishing reserves was not in conformity with GAAP. In fact, it smacks of using secret reserves to achieve a "cookie-jar reserve" effect.

7. Shifting Future Expenses to the Current Period as a Special Charge

A company might choose to accelerate discretionary expenses, such as repairs and maintenance, into the current period if the current year's revenue is relatively high in relation to expected future revenue or if future expenses are expected to be relatively high. The motivation to shift future expenses to the current period might be to smooth net income over time.

The delay in recording repairs and maintenance is a technique that McKee would probably categorize as appropriate, given the goal of providing smooth and predictable earnings. Recall that in the reported studies on earnings management, the idea of managing earnings through operating decisions was not perceived to be as big a problem as altering revenue amounts. However, the decision to delay needed repairs raises several ethical issues with respect to the company's operating decisions because it creates a risk that assets such as machinery and equipment may break down prematurely. The ethical issues and consequences are (1) the quality of product may suffer, leading to extra quality control and rework costs; (2) production slows and fails to meet deadlines, thereby risking customer goodwill; and (3) the costs to repair the machines can be greater than they would have been had maintenance been completed on a timely basis. Imagine, for example, that you fail to change the oil in your car on a regular basis. The result may be serious, costly repairs to the engine later on.

Red Flags of Earnings Management

Auditors need to be attuned to the red flags that fraud may exist because of overly aggressive accounting and outright manipulation of earnings. The following are some of the signs that trouble may lie ahead:

- Growth in the market share that seems unbelievable.
- Frequent acquisitions of businesses.
- Management growth strategy and emphasis on earnings and/or EPS.
- Reliance on income sources other than core business.
- One-time sources of income.
- Growth in revenue that doesn't line up well with receivables or inventory.
- Unexpected increase in accounts receivable.
- Slowdown of inventory turnover.
- Reduction in reserves.
- Not reserving for possible future losses.
- Reduction in discretionary costs at year-end (i.e., advertising; R&D).

- Unusual increase in borrowings; short-term borrowing at year-end.
- Extension of trade payables longer than normal credit.
- Change in members of top management, especially the CFO.
- Change in auditors.
- Changes in accounting policies toward more liberal applications.

Sometimes, a forensic accountant is brought into a case to find suspected fraudulent activity or can be called in after the fraud has been detected to assess the magnitude of the fraudulent activity. These days we believe audit firms should have at least one forensic accountant on each audit to help identify the signs that something is amiss and prevent earnings management from getting started, and stopping it in its track once under way.

Examples of Shenanigans

In this section, we describe the financial shenanigans that occurred at Xerox, Lucent, and Enron. We chose these companies because the techniques used to manage earnings vary from the relatively simple (recording revenue too soon) to the more exotic (using special-purpose entities to hide debt and inflate earnings).

The Case Of Xerox

Motivation for Fraudulent Scheme of Top Management

On June 3, 2003, the SEC filed a civil fraud injunctive action in the U.S. District Court for the Southern District of New York charging six former senior executives of Xerox Corporation, including its former CEOs Paul Allaire and G. Richard Thoman, and its former CFO Barry D. Romeril, with securities fraud and aiding and abetting Xerox's violations of the reporting, books and records, and internal control provisions of the federal securities laws. The complaint charged the former executives with engaging in a fraudulent scheme that lasted from 1997 to 2000 and misled investors about Xerox's earnings to "polish its reputation on Wall Street and to boost the company's stock price."[71]

The quality of the financial reports came into question as Xerox failed to disclose GAAP violations that led to acceleration in the recognition of approximately $3 billion in equipment revenues and an increase in pretax earnings by approximately $1.4 billion in Xerox's 1997–2000 financial results. The executives agreed to pay over $22 million in penalties, disgorgement, and interest without admitting or denying the SEC's allegations.

The tone at the top was one that viewed business success with meeting short-term earnings targets. Romeril directed or allowed lower-ranking defendants in Xerox's financial department to make accounting adjustments to results reported from operating divisions to accelerate revenues and increase earnings. These individuals used accounting methods to meet earnings goals and predictions of outside securities analysts. Allaire and Thoman then announced these results to the public through meetings with analysts and in communications to shareholders, celebrating that Xerox was enjoying substantially greater earnings growth than the true operating results warranted.

A description of two selected fraudulent accounting devices follows.

Fraudulent Lease Accounting

Xerox sold copiers and other office equipment to its customers for cash, but it more frequently entered into long-term lease agreements in which customers paid a single negotiated monthly fee in return for the equipment, service, supplies, and financing. Xerox referred to these arrangements as "bundled leases." We previously discussed the revenue recognition issues as "multiple deliverables."

The leases met the criteria under *SFAS 13* to be accounted for as "sales-type" leases, whereby the fair value of the equipment leased would be recognized as income in the period the lease is delivered, less any residual value the equipment was expected to retain once the lease expired. GAAP permits the financing revenue portion of the lease to be recognized only as it is earned over the life of the lease. *SFAS 13* also specifies that the portion of the lease payments that represents the fee for repair services and copier supplies be prorated over the term of the lease, matching it against the financing income.

Until the mid-1990s, Xerox followed satisfactory procedures for revenue recognition. However, the company encountered growing copier sales competition around the world and perceived a need to continue reporting record earnings. The management told KPMG that it was no longer able to reasonably assign a fair value to the equipment as it had in the past. The company abandoned the value determinations made at the lease inception, for public financial reporting purposes, but not for internal operating purposes, and substituted a formula that management could manipulate at will. Xerox did not test the value determinations to assess the reliability of the original method or if the new method did a better job of accurately reflecting the fair value of copier equipment.[72]

Xerox's "topside" lease accounting devices consistently increased the amount of lease revenues that Xerox recognized at the inception of the lease and reduced the amount it recognized over the life of the lease. One method was called *return on equity (ROE),* which pulled forward a portion of finance income and recognized it immediately as equipment revenue. The second, called *margin normalization,* pulled forward a portion of service income and recognized it immediately as equipment revenue. These income acceleration methods did not comply with GAAP because there was no matching of revenue with the period during which (1) financing was provided, (2) copier supplies were provided, and (3) repairs were made to the leased equipment.

"Cushion" Reserves

From 1997 through 2000, Xerox violated GAAP through the use of approximately $496 million of reserves to close the gap between actual results and earnings targets. Xerox had created reserves through charges to income prior to 1997. These cookie-jar reserves were released into income to make the numbers look better than they really were. The result was a smoothing of net income over time. This practice violated *SFAS 5, Accounting for Contingencies,* which allows a company to establish reserves only for identifiable, probable, and estimable risks and precludes the use of reserves, including excess reserves, for general or unknown business risks because they do not meet the accrual requirements of *SFAS 5.*

Sanctions by the SEC on KPMG

The SEC issued a cease-and-desist order against KPMG on April 19, 2005, for its role in auditing the financial statements of Xerox from 1997 through 2000. *AAER 2234* details KPMG's consent to institute a variety of quality control measures, which included providing oversight of engagement partner changes of audit personnel and related independence issues.[73]

On February 22, 2006, the SEC announced that all four remaining KPMG staff members in the commission's action in connection with the $1.2 billion fraudulent earnings manipulation scheme by Xerox from 1997 through 2000 had agreed to settle the charges against them. Three KPMG partners agreed to permanent injunctions, payment of $400,000 in penalties, and suspensions from practice before the commission. Four partners were charged with filing materially false and misleading financial statements with the SEC and aiding and abetting Xerox's filing of false financial reports. The SEC charged that the partners knew or should have known about improper "topside adjustments" that resulted in $3 billion of the restated revenues and $1.2 billion of the restated earnings.[74]

The concurring review partner on the audit engagement team was cited because the adjustments enabled Xerox to change the allocations of revenues that it received from leasing photocopiers and other types of office equipment. The partner agreed to a censure from the SEC for failing to exercise due care and professional skepticism, and adhere to GAAS.

On April 20, 2005, KPMG settled with the SEC over the financial fraud at Xerox, agreeing to pay $10 million in penalties, in addition to disgorging nearly $10 million in audit fees and paying another $2.7 million in interest.

The Case of Lucent Technologies

On May 20, 2004, the SEC charged Lucent Technologies, Inc., with securities fraud and violations of the reporting, books and records, and internal control provisions of the federal securities laws. The commission also charged current and former Lucent officers, executives, and employees with securities fraud and aiding and abetting Lucent's violations of federal securities laws. The SEC complaint alleged that Lucent fraudulently and improperly recognized approximately $1.148 billion of revenue and $470 million in pretax income during the fiscal year 2000.

The Lucent case is typical of the frauds that occurred in the late 1990s and early 2000s. The company's accounting techniques violated GAAP and were motivated by its drive to realize revenue, meet internal sales targets, and obtain sales bonuses. The internal controls were either violated or circumvented by top management. The board of directors and audit committee were either not involved or turned away from their obligations.

According to *AAER 2016,* Lucent officers improperly granted and/or failed to disclose various side agreements, credits, and other incentives (extracontractual commitments) made to induce Lucent's customers to purchase the company's products. The premature recognition of revenue occurred by "selling" $135 million in software to a customer that could choose from a software pool by September 29, 2001, and Lucent recognized $135 million in revenue in its fiscal year ending September 30, 2000. The parties reached an agreement to document separately additional elements of the software pool transaction that would give the customer more value in the form of side agreements. Top management postdated three letters documenting the side agreements with fictitious dates in October 2000. The effect of the postdated letters was to create the appearance that the side agreements were reached after September 30, 2000, and were not connected to the software pool agreement.[75] The accounting for these transactions enabled Lucent to manage earnings in a way that smoothed net income over time.

Lucent's story as a separate entity began in April 1996, when AT&T spun off the company. By 1999, operating income had reached $5.4 billion, tripling in two years. Net income had grown more than tenfold during that time period. These remarkable increases over a relatively short period of time should have raised a red flag for KPMG, but it did not. Exhibits 7.5 and 7.6 present the comparative amounts during the two-year period ended September 30, 1999.[76]

EXHIBIT 7.5   Lucent Technologies, Inc.: Comparative Sales and Income

Item	Sales and Income Amounts (in billions)		
	September 1999	September 1998	September 1997
Sales	$48.3	$31.8	$27.6
Operating income	5.4	2.6	1.6
Net income	4.8	1.0	0.4

EXHIBIT 7.6 Lucent Technologies, Inc.: Percentage Change in Sales and Income

	Percentage Changes in Sales and Income Amounts	
	September 1998 to September 1999	September 1997 to September 1998
Sales	52%	15%
Operating income	104	63
Net income	380	150

Schilit points out that Lucent's stock price increased from a low of about $14 per share on January 1, 1997, to a high of about $78 by September 1999. The stock price began to decline after that, to a low of about $7 per share on January 1, 2002, as the fraud unfolded.

Exhibit 7.7 takes Lucent's earnings management techniques and classifies them into Schilit's financial shenanigan categories.

EXHIBIT 7.7 Lucent Technologies, Inc.: Financial Shenanigans

Technique	Description	Shenanigan Number
Recorded revenue too soon	Lucent restated year 2000 earnings, removing $679 million of improperly included revenue.	No. 1
Boosted income with one-time gains	During fiscal 1998, Lucent recorded $558 million of pension income—over 50 percent of earnings for the year.	No. 3
Failed to write down impaired assets	Lucent reduced the allowance for doubtful accounts and released the previous reserves despite an increase in receivables of 32 percent.	No. 4
Shifted current expenses to a later period	Lucent reduced the allowance for inventory obsolescence although the inventory balance increased.	No. 4
Reduced liabilities by changing accounting assumptions	Lucent modified its accounting approach and assumptions for pensions.	No. 5
Released reserves into income	Lucent released $100 million of a previously recorded restructuring reserve, boosting operating income.	No. 5
Created new reserves from 10 acquisitions	Lucent wrote off $2.4 billion (58 percent of the cumulative purchase price) as an in-process R&D. This new reserve could be released into earnings later.	No. 7

The Story of Enron

The uniqueness of the decisions and manipulations at Enron and its link to the passage of SOX warrants a detailed discussion. Also, Enron has become a household name and synonymous with accounting fraud. The story of Enron is one of structuring financial transactions to keep debt off the books and report higher earnings. The failure of its corporate governance systems is the poster child for needed changes under SOX.

In the Beginning . . .

Enron was created in 1985 through Omaha-based InterNorth Inc.'s takeover of Houston Natural Gas Corporation. InterNorth paid a huge premium for Houston Natural Gas, creating $5 million in debt. The company's debt payments of $50 million a month quickly led to the selloff of billions of dollars' worth of assets. Its debt load was so high that it forced the company into financing projects with borrowings that were kept off the balance sheet.

Former Enron CEO Jeff Skilling suggested that Enron's problem were due to a fluid market for natural gas; the industry needed long-term supply contracts. But prices were volatile, and contracts were available only for 30-day spot deals. Producers were unwilling to commit to the long term, always believing the price could go up.

Skilling's "Gas Bank" Idea

Enron needed to find a way to bridge the gap between what the producers and big gas users wanted. Skilling discussed ways to pool the investments in gas-supply contracts and then sell long-term deals to utilities through a Gas Bank. The Gas Bank called for Enron to write long-term contracts that enabled it to start accounting for those contracts differently. Traditionally, accounting would book revenue from a long-term contract when it came in. But Skilling wanted Enron to book all anticipated revenue immediately, as if it was writing up a marketable security. The technique lends itself to earnings management because of the subjectivity involved in estimating future market value.

Counting all expected profits immediately meant a huge earnings kick for a company that was getting deeply in debt. But it also put Enron on a treadmill: To keep growing, it would have to book bigger and bigger deals every quarter. The result was to shift focus from developing economically sound partnerships to doing deals at all costs.

The marketplace didn't seem to like the Enron deals. The initial Gas Bank plan hadn't persuaded gas producers to sell Enron their reserves. To entice the producers, the company needed to offer them money up-front for gas that would be delivered later. The problem was where to get the cash.

Fastow's Special-Purpose Entities

In 1991, to revitalize the Gas Bank, Enron's CFO, Andy Fastow, began creating a number of partnerships. The first series of deals was called Cactus. The Cactus ventures eventually took in money from banks and gave it to energy producers in return for a portion of their existing gas reserves. That gave the producers money up-front and Enron gas over time.

Fastow worked to structure ventures that met the conditions under GAAP to keep the partnership activities off Enron's books and on the separate books of the partnership. To do so, the equity financing of the partnership venture had to include a minimum of 3 percent outside ownership. Control was not established through traditional means, which was the ownership of a majority of voting equity and combining of the partnership entity into the sponsoring organization (Enron), as is done with parent and subsidiary entities in a consolidation. Instead, the independent third parties were required to have a controlling and substantial interest in the entity. Control was established by the third-party investors exercising management rights over the entity's operations. There were a lot of "Monday morning quarterbacks" in the accounting profession who questioned the economic logic of attributing even the possibility of control to those who owned only 3 percent of the capital.

Bethany McLean and Peter Elkind are two *Fortune* magazine reporters credited with prompting the inquiries and investigations that brought down the Enron house of cards. McLean had written a story posing the simple question: "How, exactly, does Enron make its money?" Well, in the go-go years of the 1990s, all too often no one asked these kinds of questions (or, perhaps, did not want to know the answers).

According to McLean and Elkind, a small group of investors were pulled together, known internally as the Friends of Enron. When Enron needed the 3 percent of outside ownership, it turned to the friends. However, these business associates and friends of Fastow and others were independent only in a technical sense. Though they made money on their investment, they didn't control the entities or the assets within them. "This, of course, was precisely the point," McLean and Elkind say.[77]

The 3 percent investments triggered a "special-purpose vehicle or special-purpose entity (SPE)." The advantage of the independent partnership relationship was that the SPE borrowed money from banks and other financial institutions that were willing to loan money to it with an obligation to repay the debt. The SPE enabled Enron to keep debt off its books while benefiting from the transfer and use of the cash borrowed by the SPE. The money borrowed by the SPE was often "transferred" to Enron in a sale of an operating asset no longer needed by Enron. The sale transaction typically led to a recorded gain because the cash proceeds exceeded the book value of the asset sold. The result was increased cash flow and liquidity and inflated earnings. The uniqueness of the transactions engaged in by Enron was that they initially didn't violate GAAP. Instead, Enron took advantage of the rules to engineer transactions that enabled it to achieve its goals for enhanced liquidity and profitability.

Exhibit 7.8 depicts the typical transaction between Enron and the SPE.

EXHIBIT 7.8   Enron Corporation's SPEs

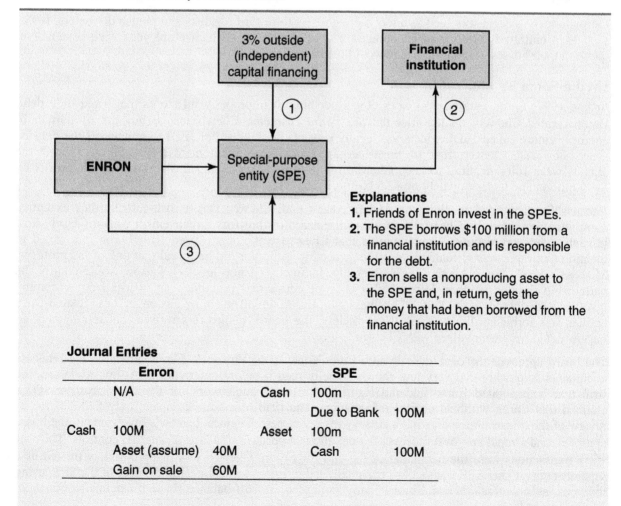

Explanations
1. Friends of Enron invest in the SPEs.
2. The SPE borrows $100 million from a financial institution and is responsible for the debt.
3. Enron sells a nonproducing asset to the SPE and, in return, gets the money that had been borrowed from the financial institution.

Journal Entries

Enron			SPE		
N/A			Cash	100m	
			Due to Bank		100M
Cash	100M		Asset	100m	
	Asset (assume)	40M	Cash		100M
	Gain on sale	60M			

The Growth of Special-Purpose Entities

Eventually, Enron would grow addicted to these arrangements because they hid debt. Not only did the company turn to its "friends," but increasingly, it had to borrow from banks and financial institutions that it did business with. These entities did not want to turn down a company like Enron, which was, at its peak, the seventh largest corporation in the United States. But Enron let the risk-shifting feature of the partnerships lapse, thus negating their conformity to GAAP. Over time, the financial institutions that were involved in providing the 3 percent for the SPEs became skeptical of the ability of the SPEs to repay the interest when due. These institutions asked Enron to relieve the risk of the SPEs' failure to repay the investments. Later, partnership deals were backed by promises of Enron stock. Thus, if something went wrong, Enron would be left holding the bag. Therefore, there was no true transfer of economic risk to the SPE, and according to GAAP, the SPE should have been consolidated into Enron's financial statements.

The Culture at Enron

The tension in the workplace grew with employees working later and later—first until 6 p.m. and then 11 p.m., and sometimes even into the next morning. Part of the pressure resulted from Skilling's new employee-evaluation policy. Workers called it "rank and yank." Employees were evaluated in groups, with each person rated on a scale of 1 to 5. The goal was to remove the bottom 15 percent of each group every year.

Ultimately, the system was seen as a tool for managers to reward loyalists and punish dissenters. It was seen as a cutthroat system and encouraged a "yes" culture, in which employees were reluctant to question their bosses—a fear that many would later come to regret.

Let the Force Be with You

In late 1997, Enron entered a number of partnerships to improperly inflate earnings and hide debt. Enron created Chewco, named after the *Star Wars* character, Chewbacca, to buy out its partner in another venture called JEDI, which was legally kept off the books. For JEDI to remain off the balance sheet, however, Chewco had to meet certain accounting requirements. But Enron skirted the already-weak rules required to keep Chewco off its books. JEDI helped overstate Enron's profits by $405 million and understate debt by $2.6 billion.

Because Enron needed to close the deal by year's end, Chewco was a rush job. Enron's executive committee presented the Chewco proposal to the board of directors on November 5. But CFO Fastow left out a few key details. He maintained that Chewco was not affiliated with Enron, but failed to mention that there was virtually no outside ownership in it. Nor did he reveal that one of his protégés, Michael Kopper, was managing the partnership. Indirectly (if not directly), Fastow would control the partnership through Kopper. Enron had a code of ethics that prohibited an officer from becoming involved with another entity that did business with Enron. Involvement by Fastow in these related-party entities was forbidden by the code. Nevertheless, the board of directors waived that requirement so Fastow could become involved with Chewco.

The board approved the deal, even though Enron's law firm, Vinson & Elkins, prepared the requisite documents so quickly that very few people actually read it before approving it. Arthur Andersen, the firm that both audited Enron and did significant internal audit work for the company (pre-SOX), claimed that Enron withheld critical information. The firm billed the company only $80,000 for its review of the transaction, indicating a cursory review at best. Chewco, Fastow's involvement, the board approval, and a rapid approval process all were allowed because of a lack of internal controls. The *Star Wars* transactions were the beginning of the end for Enron. Chewco was inappropriately treated as a separate entity. Other SPE transactions eventually led to Enron's guaranteeing the debt of the SPE, using its stock as collateral. When Enron finally collapsed, its off-balance-sheet financing stood at an estimated $17 billion.

Enron Just Keeps on Going

The greatest pressures were in Fastow's finance group. In 1999, he constructed two partnerships called LJM Cayman and LJM2 that readily passed through the board, the lawyers, and the accountants. They were followed by four more, known as the Raptors. They did it once—it worked—and then they did it again. It didn't take long to blur the lines between what was legal and what was not. When asked by a student during an interview for a position with Enron what he did at the company, one Enron employee in the finance group answered by saying, "I remove numbers from our balance sheet and inflate earnings."

As Enron pushed into new directions—wind power, water, high-speed Internet, paper, metals, data storage, advertising, etc.—it became a different company almost every quarter. Entrepreneurship was encouraged; innovation was the mantra. The quarter-by-quarter scramble to post ever-better numbers became all-consuming. Enron traders were encouraged to use "prudence reserves"—to essentially put aside some revenue until another quarter when it might be needed. Long-term energy contracts were evaluated using an adjustable curve to forecast energy prices. When a quarter looked tight, analysts were told to simply adjust the curve in Enron's favor.

Executive Compensation

Enron's goal of setting its executive pay in the 75th percentile of its peer group—including companies like Duke Energy, Dynegy, and PG&E, which it compared itself with to assess overall corporate performance—was easily exceeded. In 2000, Enron exceeded the peer group average base salary by 51 percent. In bonus payments, it outdistanced its peers by 383 percent. The stock options granted in 2000—valued at the time at $86.5 million—exceeded the number granted by peers by 484 percent. Top management became accustomed to the large payouts, and the desire for more became a part of the culture of greed at Enron.

While Enron was the first player into the new energy market, enabling it to score huge gains, competitors caught on over time, and profit margins shrank. Skilling began looking for new pastures, and in 1996, he set his sights on electricity. Enron would do for power what it had done for natural gas. The push into electricity only added to the pressures mounting inside Enron. Earlier in 1996, Ken Lay, Enron's CEO before Skilling took over, had predicted that the company's profits would double by 2000. This was a statement that would come back to haunt Lay in his civil trial in 2006, which alleged that he hyped Enron's stock to keep funds flowing, even though he knew the company was coming apart at the seams.

Lay pushed on as if nothing was wrong. Enron instituted a stock-option plan that promised to double employee salaries after eight years. Fresh off a $2.1 billion takeover of Portland General Corporation, an electric utility, Lay said his goal was nothing less than to make Enron the "world's greatest energy company."

Growth at all costs was the mantra at Enron. It encouraged executives to buy into this philosophy by giving out stock options that would provide cash over time and added the sweetener that if profits and the stock price went up enough, the schedule for those options would be sharply accelerated. It provided the incentive to find ways of increasing profits and improving stock price. It looked the other way when questions about ethics came up. Clearly, Enron and its officers pursued their self-interests to the detriment of all other interests and created a culture of greed. The environment at Enron reminds us of the famous quote by Gordon Gekko in the 1987 movie *Wall Street:* "Greed is good. Greed captures the essence of the evolutionary spirit."

Congressional Investigation and Skilling's Departure

In 2000, Skilling was granted 867,880 options to buy shares, in addition to his salary and bonus that totaled $6.45 million. In that year, he exercised and sold over 1.1 million shares from options he received from prior years, and he pocketed $62.48 million. Skilling testified before Congress that he did not dump Enron shares as he told others to buy because he knew or suspected that the company was in financial trouble. Skilling's holdings of Enron shares increased because his number of options increased. Even under Enron's option plan, in which options vested fully in three years (an unusually quick rate), Skilling wound up holding many Enron shares that he couldn't legally sell.

Lay and Skilling used as their defense in the 2006 civil trial that Enron was a successful company brought down by a crisis of confidence in the market. The government contended that Enron appeared successful but actually hid its failures through dubious, even criminal accounting tricks. In fact, Enron by most measures wasn't particularly profitable—a fact obscured by its share price until late in its history. But there was one area in which it succeeded like few others: executive compensation.

As the stock market began to decline in the late 1990s, Enron's stock followed the downward trend. The never-ending number of deals, even as business slowed, gave Wall Street pause. By April 2001, concerns mounted whether the company was disclosing financial information from its off-balance-sheet financing transactions adequately.

The pressure continued both internally and externally from a slowing economy, competition from other entities that were catching on to Enron's gimmicks, and stock market declines. Differences of opinion exist why he made the decision, but on August 14, 2001, Skilling, who just six months prior had been named the CEO of Enron, resigned. He gave as his public reason the ever-popular "I need to spend more time with my family."

Sherron Watkins's Role

But Enron executive Sherron Watkins was dubious, and she sent an anonymous letter to Ken Lay, the chair of the board of directors, warning him of an impending scandal. It said in part, "Has Enron become a risky place to work? For those of us who didn't get rich over the last few years, can we afford to stay?" She described in detail problems with Enron's partnerships, problems that the letter claimed would cause huge financial upheavals at the company in as little as a year. "I am incredibly nervous that we will implode in a wave of accounting scandals," Watkins wrote. "Skilling is resigning for 'personal reasons,' but I think he wasn't having fun, looked down the road, and knew this stuff was unfixable and would rather abandon ship now than resign in shame in two years."[78]

Lay took a copy of the letter to James V. Derrick Jr., Enron's general counsel, who agreed that it needed to be investigated. They decided to assign the task to Vinson & Elkins—which had helped prepare some of the legal documents for some of the partnerships. Enron wanted answers fast, seemingly regardless of due diligence, and the company instructed the outside lawyers not to spend time examining the accounting treatment recommended by Arthur Andersen—although that was at the heart of the letter's warnings.

Powers Committee Report

Vinson & Elkins began its investigation. Even while it investigated Fastow's role, the conflicts mounted. Kopper, who had sold his Chewco assets to Enron to deflect criticisms of Fastow's role, made a profit on the sale and then insisted that Enron cover the $2.6 million tax liability from the sale. The Powers Committee, formed by the audit committee to investigate the failure of Enron, concluded on this matter that "there is credible evidence that Fastow authorized Enron's payment to Chewco," adding that the payment—done against the explicit instructions of Enron's general counsel—was "one of the most serious issues we identified in connection with the Chewco buyout."[79]

Three days after beginning their investigation, the Vinson & Elkins lawyers investigating Watkins's warnings reported their findings to Lay and Derrick that there was no reason for concern. Everything in Fastow's operation seemed to be on the level. They promised a written report in a matter of weeks. By then, though, it would be too late.

The Final Days

In November 2001, Enron announced it had overstated earnings by $586 million since 1997. In December 2001, Enron made the largest bankruptcy filing ever at that time. By January 2002, the U.S. Department of Justice (DOJ) confirmed an investigation of Enron. The very next day, Andersen admitted to shredding documents related to its audit of Enron, an act of obstructing justice that would doom the firm following a DOJ lawsuit. It hardly mattered what the outcome of the lawsuit would be; Enron's clients started to abandon the firm in droves after the announcement of the lawsuit. Ultimately, the jury decided that the firm had obstructed justice, a decision that would be overturned later due to a technicality.

The Lay-Skilling Criminal Trial

Following the unanimous jury verdict on May 26, 2006, that found both Lay and Skilling guilty of fraud and conspiracy, Lay was quoted as saying, "Certainly we're surprised," and Skilling commented, "I think it's more appropriate to say we're shocked. This is not the outcome we expected."[80]

Skilling was convicted of 19 counts of fraud, conspiracy, and insider trading. Lay was convicted on 6 counts in the joint trial and four charges of bank fraud and making false statements to banks in a separate nonjury trial before U.S. District Judge Sam Lake related to Lay's personal finances. The sentencing for Lay and Skilling in the case, somewhat ironically, was set for September 11, 2006. Skilling faced a maximum of 185 years in prison. For Lay, the fraud and conspiracy convictions carried a combined maximum punishment of 45 years. The bank fraud case added 120 years, 30 years for each of the four counts. However, Ken Lay passed away just weeks after the verdict.

Skilling's Efforts to Overturn the Verdict

On October 23, 2006, Skilling was sentenced to 24 years and 4 months in prison, and fined $45 million. As discussed in Chapter 6, Skilling has fought to overturn that sentence almost from the beginning. On June 21, 2013, it was announced by the U.S. Department of Justice that Skilling will be freed 10 years early. This means he would spend a total of 14 years in jail. Skilling is eligible for parole in 2017.

Enron: A Review of Important Accounting Issues

The fraud at Enron was caused by a variety of factors, including these:

- Improperly failing to consolidate the results of an SPE (Chewco) with Enron. Consolidation was warranted because Chewco lacked the necessary independence from Enron's management because Andy Fastow had direct or indirect control over it.
- Failing to disclose adequately the related-party relationship between Enron and the SPEs, especially those that were independent of the company under GAAP.
- Overstating earnings from using mark-to-market accounting for investments in long-term gas contracts that relied on estimates of future market value to record unrealized gains.

The quality of financial reports was poor for the following reasons:

- Failure to disclose adequately the related-party transactions made it impossible for investors and creditors to know the full extent of these transactions, and loans were made to Enron based on vastly understated debt.
- The sale of assets to SPEs in return for the transfer of borrowed funds from the SPE, with the

subsequent recording of a gain, masked Enron's true earnings and made it appear that the company was doing better than it really was.

- The use of reserves and failure to explain the basis for creation made it impossible to judge the acceptability of these transactions.
- The failure to disclose Fastow's dual role with the SPEs and as CFO of Enron made it impossible for investors and creditors to gain the information they had an ethical right to know in order to evaluate the legitimacy of off-balance-sheet transactions and their effect on the financial statements.

Enron managed earnings through the following techniques (Schilit's shenanigan numbers are indicated in parentheses):

- Used reserves to increase earnings when reported amounts were too low (#5).
- Used mark-to-market estimates to inflate earnings in violation of GAAP (#1).
- Selected which operating assets to "sell" to the SPEs, thereby affecting the amount of the gain on transfer and earnings effect (#3).

The lack of strong controls contributed to the fraud as evidenced by the following:

- Top management overrode or ignored internal controls in the approval process for Chewco, the LJM SPEs, and the Raptors.
- Oversight by the board of directors was either negligent, as was the case with the waiving of the ethics code for Fastow, or nonexistent.
- A culture was established to make the deals at any cost, thereby diluting the due diligence process that should have raised red flags on some of the transactions.
- A culture of fear was created within Enron with its "rank or yank" policy and cutthroat competition.

FASB Rules on SPEs

While it may seem that the GAAP rules on SPEs are naïve, there are legitimate reasons for establishing the concept that an entity could isolate a business operation or some corporate assets. The idea was to control risk in a project such as investing in a new oil refinery. By following the rules to set up an SPE, an oil company could keep the large amount of debt off the books while using the funds from the SPE to construct the refinery. The off-balance-sheet effect helps control risk if the project fails. The original motivation by FASB was to establish a mechanism to encourage companies to invest in needed assets while keeping the related debt off their books.

The "creativity" of Andy Fastow was in using a less-well-known technique under GAAP to satisfy Enron's unique needs. Enron became the leader of structured transactions designed to meet specific goals rather than to present accurately its financial position and the results of its operations. These are nothing more than elaborate attempts to manage earnings.

FASB Interpretation 46(R)

After much debate about how to fix the original SPE ownership percentage and consolidation rules, FASB issued on December 24, 2003, a revision of its proposed Interpretation: FASB Interpretation 46(R), Consolidation of Variable Interest Entities.[81] Basically, Interpretation 46(R) requires unconsolidated variable interest entities to be consolidated by their primary beneficiaries if the entities do not effectively disperse risk among parties involved. Variable-interest entities that effectively disperse risks would not be consolidated unless a single party holds an interest or combination of interests that recombines risks that were previously dispersed.

The new rules apply an economic reality test to the consolidation of a variable interest entity. No longer is there a percentage ownership test. Instead, it is the dispersion of risk that determines the consolidation status. By effectively dispersing risk, the primary beneficiary controls its own risk with respect to activities of the unconsolidated variable interest entity.

Enron's Role in the Creation and Passage of SOX

The Enron fraud was a direct cause, along with WorldCom's, of congressional passage of SOX and efforts to reform the accounting profession. The provisions of the act that were motivated by the Enron fraud include:

- Prohibiting the provision of internal audit services for audit clients. Andersen provided the major part of internal audit services for Enron. Overall, Andersen earned from Enron in its last full year as accountants $27 million from nonauditing services and $25 million from auditing services.
- Requiring that off-balance-sheet financing activities be disclosed in the notes to the financial statements. Enron's SPEs were never referred to as providing off-balance-sheet financing.
- Requiring that related-party transactions be disclosed in the notes. The activities with the SPEs qualify as related-party transactions. By some accounts, Enron had over 3,000 SPEs, yet the footnote disclosure in its last year before filing for bankruptcy was limited to one page.

Enron also suffered from the same lack of controls and inadequate corporate governance that infected so many other companies during the accounting scandals. For example, the board of directors did not act independently, and the audit committee members were not independent of management. The internal environment at Enron, especially the tone at the top, promoted a culture of making deals regardless of the risks.

The internal controls at Enron were either ignored or overridden by management (i.e., the board waived its ethics policy so that Andy Fastow could control Chewco indirectly while simultaneously serving as the CFO for Enron). This created a conflict of interest that enabled Fastow to enrich himself through control of Chewco at the expense of Enron. The result was a serious breach of fiduciary responsibilities and the failure of management to meet its obligation as an agent for the shareholders.

Lessons to Be Learned from Enron

What is the moral of the Enron story? Certainly, we could say that weak internal controls equate with possible fraud. Also, we could point to the need for an ethical tone at the top to help prevent fraud. At Enron, once the company developed an appetite for establishing SPEs and keeping these transactions off the books, the company became more and more addicted to the cash provided through the SPEs. Even if it wanted to stop the transactions, Enron and its top management had set the company on a course that was difficult to change. Enron had started to slide down the ethical slippery slope, and there was no turning back.

The bottom-line factor that kept the Enron fraud going well past the point of no return was greed. Skilling saw Fastow getting rich, Lay saw Skilling getting rich, all the Enron employees thought they saw Lay getting rich, and then Lay hyped Enron stock to the employees for their 401-ks as a way for them, eventually, to get rich.

Enron ethics means that business ethics is a question of organizational "deep" culture rather than of cultural vestiges such as ethics codes, ethics officers, and the like. At Enron, everything was done with set purposes in mind—to make the deal at any cost; to line one's pockets with ill-gotten gains; and to deceive the stakeholders—including the company's own employees—into thinking Enron was doing better than it really was. The Enron affair illustrates just how quickly a company can go from good to bad when those at the top respect only nonethical values, such as power, wealth, and fame, rather than the ethical values of honesty, integrity, and responsibility.

Financial Statement Restatements

LO 7-6
Explain the causes and effects of financial statement restatements.

Characteristics of Restatements

A *financial statement restatement* occurs when a company, either voluntarily or under prompting by its auditors or regulators, revises its public financial information that was previously reported. As mentioned in the Ethics Reflection, so-called *revision restatements* have been increasing while *reissuance restatements* have been declining. Given that reissuance restatements are more serious, the distinction made by companies is an important one. That is because revision restatements do not undermine reliance on past financials while reissued statements basically say to the shareholders not to rely on the past statements.

Audit Analytics released the results of its 2014 review of restatements and found, for the sixth consecutive year, that revision restatements increased as a percentage of the total from 65 percent (2012) to 76 percent (2014). In its review of restatements from 2005 to 2012, Audit Analytics noticed that financial restatements were increasingly leaving out the word in their disclosures: "restatement."[82] This concerns us because a restatement is exactly what these adjustments to prior years' financial statements are. It also coincides with the continuing increase in the percentage of revision restatements, the less concerning of the two.

To test its belief that the word restatement was being left out, Audit Analytics looked at the restatements and compiled the following information, shown in Exhibit 7.9.

EXHIBIT 7.9 **Count of Records that Contain "Restate"**

	Years 2006–2012							
	2006	2007	2008	2009	2010	2011	2012	Total
Count of records that contain word "restate"	806	567	336	238	239	203	176	2565
No reference of word "restate"	56	48	76	86	101	152	223	742
Total	862	615	412	324	340	355	399	3307
% without word restate	6.5%	7.8%	18.4%	26.5%	29.7%	42.8%	55.9%	22.4%

Note: The analysis is based on the text of restatement disclosures of NYSE, NASDAQ, and AMEX companies that filed corrected or restated financial statements in the years 2006–2012, as identified in the Audit Analytics Restatement Database. OTCBB companies and companies that went dark prior to filling restated financial statements were excluded from the analysis.

In 2006, over 93 percent of the companies used the word "restate," or some derivative of the word, in the text of their disclosure. By 2012, only 44 percent of disclosures correcting prior year results actually mentioned "restate" or a derivative. Audit Analytics also noticed an increase in nuance to these disclosures with more varied language to describe them. Some *revise* prior periods; others correct *immaterial errors*; still others record *prior period adjustments*, and there are quite a few that *modify their accounting* or identify *overstatements* of certain assets.[83] To say this is confusing to the users of financial statements is an understatement.

Another cause for concern continues to be the number of "stealth restatements." The SEC requires companies to disclose within four business days a determination that past financial statements should no longer be relied on. This disclosure must appear in an 8-K report. The SEC defines a stealth restatement as one that is disclosed only in periodic reports and not in the 8-K or amended periodic report such as a 10-K/A or 10-Q/A. The percentage of stealth restatements has hold steady at about 50 percent for the past few years. This is a troublesome development for the SEC, as the 8-K form is designed to be an early warning system so that the public knows immediately about the financial statement restatements and does not have to wait until the statements are filed with the SEC.

Hertz Accounting Restatements

On July 16, 2015, Hertz Global Holdings, Inc., (Hertz) announced that it had filed its annual report on Form 10-K for the fiscal year ending December 31, 2014, which includes the restated results for 2012 and 2013 as well as selected unaudited restated financial information for 2011. In addition, the company had filed its quarterly report on Form 10-Q for the period ending March 31, 2015.

Financial Restatement

As discussed in the Form 10-K filed with the SEC, Hertz identified accounting misstatements for the years 2011 through 2013. The following information in Exhibit 7.10 summarizes the impact of misstatements identified.[84]

EXHIBIT 7.10 Hertz Impact of Misstatements

(In millions)	Year Ended December 31, (Unaudited) Increase/(Decrease)*		
	2011	2012	2013
As originally filed			
GAAP pretax income	$324	$451	$663
GAAP net income attributable to Hertz	$176	$243	$346
Misstatements previously disclosed and included in the originally filed 10-K/A**			
GAAP pretax income	$(19)	$ (9)	N/A
GAAP net income attributable to Hertz	$(12)	$ (4)	N/A
Additional misstatements identified			
GAAP pretax income	$(54)	$(81)	$(72)
GAAP net income attributable to Hertz	$(19)	$(58)	$(51)
Cumulative misstatements (Misstatements previously revised in 10-K/A plus additional errors identified)***			
GAAP pretax income	$(73)	$(90)	$(72)
GAAP net income attributable to Hertz	$(31)	$(62)	$(51)
Cumulative misstatements as a %			
GAAP pretax income	(23)%	(20)%	(11)%
GAAP net income attributable to Hertz	(18)%	(26)%	(15)%

*Increase/Decrease associated with misstatements and impact to GAAP pre-tax and GAAP net income.

**Amounts recorded as a revision in the 2013 Form 10-K/A.

*** In addition, $114 and $87 in errors reducing GAAP pre-tax income and GAAP net income, respectively, related to periods prior to 2011 were 2011. Of these amounts, $7 and $5 GAAP pre-tax and GAAP net income, respectively, were recorded in the 2013 Form 10-K/A as a revision.

The Form 10-K contained audited restated financial information for 2012 and 2013, audited financial information for 2014, and unaudited restated selected financial information for 2011. The Form 10-K also contained quarterly information for the quarters in 2013, as restated, and 2014. The Form 10-Q contained quarterly information for the first quarter of 2015.

The company noted that the filing of its Form 10-K cures the filing deficiency notice from the New York Stock Exchange (NYSE) as reported on March 24, 2015, and brings Hertz back into compliance with the NYSE listing requirements.

Non-GAAP Financial Measures

In Exhibit 7.11, Hertz addresses the issue of non-GAAP financial measures including EBITDA and Corporate EBITDA, and explains how these amounts were calculated. By comparing the validity of these amounts to pretax GAAP income, Hertz is misleading the readers into thinking, at least going forward, that non-GAAP measures of earnings may be as reliable as GAAP amounts. Hertz seems to have gone out of its way to make this disclosure unintelligible to the average reader.

EXHIBIT 7.11 Hertz Non-GAAP Financial Measures

EBITDA, Corporate EBITDA, net corporate debt, net debt, and monthly depreciation per unit are non-GAAP financial measures. Management believes that EBITDA and Corporate EBITDA are useful in measuring the comparable results of the Company period-over-period. The GAAP measure most directly comparable to EBITDA and Corporate EBITDA is pretax income. Net corporate debt is calculated as total debt excluding fleet debt less cash and equivalents and corporate restricted cash. Corporate debt consists of our Senior Term Facility; Senior ABL Facility; Senior Notes; and certain other indebtedness of our domestic and foreign subsidiaries. Net corporate debt and net debt are important to management, investors, and ratings agencies as it helps measure our leverage. Net corporate debt also assists in the evaluation of our ability to service our non–fleet–related debt without reference to the expense associated with the fleet debt, which is fully collateralized by assets not available to lenders under the non–fleet debt facilities. Monthly depreciation per unit is important as depreciation of revenue earning equipment and lease charges is one of our largest expenses for the car rental business and monthly depreciation per unit is reflective of how we are managing the costs of our fleet. The GAAP measure most directly comparable to monthly depreciation per unit is depreciation of revenue earning equipment and lease charges, net.

The Company believes that there is a degree of volatility with respect to certain of the Company's GAAP measures, in the case of EBITDA and Corporate EBITDA, primarily related to fair value accounting for its financial assets (which includes the Company's derivative financial instruments), its income tax reporting, and certain adjustments made to arrive at the relevant non–GAAP measures, and in the case of monthly depreciation per unit primarily related to estimated residual values and fleet size and composition, which preclude the Company from providing accurate forecasted GAAP to non–GAAP reconciliations. Based on the above, the Company believes that providing estimates of the amounts that would be required to reconcile the range of the non–GAAP EBITDA or Corporate EBITDA to forecasted pretax income or non-GAAP monthly depreciation per unit to depreciation of revenue earning equipment and lease charges, net, would imply a degree of precision that would be confusing or misleading to investors for the reasons identified above.

"Hertz Completes Financial Restatement; Provides 2015 Business Outlook," July 16, 2015, http://ir.hertz.com /2015-07-16-Hertz-Completes-Financial-Restatement-Provides-2015-Business-Outlook

Internal Controls

What happened to Hertz? The company performed well for a long time and then things went south. The following discussion comes from an article about the Hertz accounting fraud written by Whitehouse.[85]

Whitehouse points out that the auto rental company first warned on June 6, 2014, of a massive financial restatement yet to come. In a Form 8-K filing, Hertz warned that its current quarterly filing would be late and that its financial statements for 2011 should no longer be relied upon. The company also disclosed it had identified at least one material weakness in internal control over financial reporting and that disclosure controls and procedures were ineffective as of December 31, 2013. Hertz identified $46.3 million in reporting errors. At the time, its outside auditors, PwC, said, according to Hertz's filing, the company fairly presented its results and that the company "maintained, in all material respects, effective internal control over financial reporting." Hertz said the chairman of its audit committee had discussed the matter with PwC, and that it "expects to receive an adverse opinion" from the firm on its internal controls over financial reporting as of December 31, 2013.

PwC's expected shift in opinion on Hertz's internal controls doesn't come as a surprise, given the restatement and revisions. The real question is whether Hertz's managers and PwC reasonably should have been aware of the problems earlier, and how those problems were discovered. Were they uncovered by Hertz and brought to PwC's attention, or did PwC's review—and potential change of opinion—prompt Hertz to get ahead of the problem?

PwC, which issued clean audit opinions on Hertz for years, has been faulted by the Public Company Accounting Oversight Board in inspection reports for not challenging clients' internal controls around allowances for doubtful accountings. Whether PwC was faulted specifically for Hertz or for some other client, however, is unclear, and the PCAOB has rapped all the other Big Four audit firms for the same issue anyway.

"Out-of-Period Errors"

Hertz foreshadowed the errors in its 2013 year-end Form 10-K, reporting that it had discovered in the fourth quarter "certain out-of-period errors" totaling $46.3 million. In its 10-K, Hertz said the errors were not material in any given period, but if aggregated to the fourth quarter of 2013 when discovered, would be material to that quarter. As such, the company would be reaching back to revise earlier periods.

Hertz's 10-K filing identified accounting errors in four areas: capitalization and timing of depreciation for certain non-fleet assets; allowances for doubtful accounts in Brazil; allowances for uncollectible amounts with respect to renter obligations for damaged vehicles; and restoration obligations at the end of facility leases. Of the four specific accounting issues that tripped up Hertz, some are more common themes in restatements than others, said Peter Bible, a partner with EisnerAmper. Doubtful accounts, uncollectible amounts, and future costs associated with restoring leased property are all areas steeped in estimates and uncertainty, he said, and as such are classic areas for error. The depreciation issue, however, is more straightforward. "Usually when you see an asset put into place and a depreciation method selected, that's something you don't see missed or not accounted for correctly very much," he said.[86]

Steve Hazel, a partner at RGL Forensics, said any investigation into possible intentional misstatement of the financials would focus on whether the former CFO somehow benefited personally from the mistakes. "There's a lot of estimation and guesswork here," he said. "There's probably some degree of concern whether there was intent to commit fraud or just bad estimation or a bad thought process. But there's not enough information in this case to make a judgment call on those things."[87]

In discussing the difficulty of making accurate estimates, Tom Selling, a financial analysis expert, said: "Estimating the cost of restoring leased property at the end of a lease term is another complicated area. When you build out a leased facility, you have to estimate how much it's going to cost to tear it down and add the present value of that cost estimate to the value of the asset. Over time, if you estimate correctly, you have an increase in depreciation and a component of interest cost. Companies might make mistakes in estimating the cost or the discount rate, either of which would skew the reported figures.[88]

Restatements generally fall into one of three areas: fraud, misapplication of accounting rules, or clerical or bookkeeping errors. It's too soon to say definitively in the Hertz case, but the facts so far likely suggest misapplication of accounting rules. In Hertz's defense, it is involved in complex estimates and judgments in preparing its financial reports. Still, that doesn't excuse any intentional misstatements or overly aggressive estimates and judgments that might be motivated more by earnings management and to put the best face possible on the financials rather than to present them fairly and in accordance with GAAP rules.

Restatements Due to Errors in Accounting and Reporting

An analysis of causes of restatement due to errors in accounting and reporting was made by Turner and Weirich. Results from their study with respect to the kinds of accounting errors that trigger restatements are particularly relevant to the discussion of earnings management. Exhibit 7.12 presents these results.[89]

EXHIBIT 7.12 Accounting Errors that Trigger Financial Statement Restatements

Category	Cause of Restatements
Revenue recognition	Improper revenue recognition, including questionable items and misreported revenue
Expense recognition	Improper expense recognition, including period of recognition, incorrect amounts; includes improper lease accounting
Misclassification	Improper classification on income statement, balance sheet, or cash flow statement; includes non-operating revenue in the operating category; cash outflow from operating activities in investment activities
Equity	Improper accounting for EPS; stock-based compensation plans, options, warrants, and convertibles
Other comprehensive income (OCI)	Improper accounting for OCI transactions, including unrealized gains and losses on investments in debt and equity securities, derivatives, and pension-liability adjustments
Capital assets	Improper accounting for asset impairments; asset-placed-in-service dates and depreciation
Inventory	Improper accounting for valuation of inventory, including market adjustments and obsolescence
Reserves/allowances	Improper accounting for bad debt reserves on accounts receivable, reserves for inventory, and provision for loan losses
Liabilities/contingencies	Improper estimation of liability claims, loss contingencies, litigation matters, commitments, and certain accruals

Restatements due to errors also occur when a company switches from non-GAAP to GAAP. A good example of this occurred at Cubic Corporation, with its "development contracts." Cubic announced on August 1, 2012, that the audit committee of the company's board of directors, after consultation with EY, its independent auditor, determined that Cubic's financial statements for the fiscal years ending September 30, 2011, 2010, and 2009, the quarters ended March 31, 2012, and December 31, 2011, and each of the prior quarters of 2011 and 2010 could no longer be relied upon as complying with GAAP. Accordingly, Cubic informed the SEC that it would restate the financial statements.[90]

Exhibit 7.13 provides additional information on how the restatements were identified and reported.

EXHIBIT 7.13 **Cubic Corporation Restatement of Financial Statements (August 1, 2012)**[91]

The Audit Committee's decision to restate these financial statements follows a recommendation by management that revenues in these previously issued financial statements should be adjusted due to errors in calculating revenues on certain long-term fixed-price development type contracts ("development contracts") and on certain long-term service contracts with non-U.S. Government customers ("service contracts").

Preliminary indications from the company's evaluation are that the changes described below will result in an increase in revenues and net income cumulatively over the period of the restatement and an increase in retained earnings as of March 31, 2012. Cubic Corporation is continuing to evaluate the total amount of the adjustments and the specific impact on each period covered by the restatement, which may result in an increase or decrease in previously reported amounts for individual periods.

Cubic has historically recognized sales and profits for development contracts using the cost-to-cost percentage-of-completion method of accounting, modified by a formulary adjustment. Under the cost-to-cost percentage-of-completion method of accounting, sales and profits are based on the ratio of costs incurred to estimated total costs at completion. Cubic has consistently applied a formulary adjustment to the percentage completion calculation for development contracts that had the effect of deferring a portion of the indicated revenue and profits on such contracts until later in the contract performance period.

Cubic believed that this methodology was an acceptable variation of the cost-to-cost percentage-of-completion method as described in Accounting Standards Codification ("ASC") 605-35. The company now believes that generally accepted accounting principles do not support the practice of using a formulary calculation to defer a portion of the indicated revenue and profits on such contracts. Instead, Cubic believes that sales and profits should have been recognized based on the ratio of costs incurred to estimated total costs at completion, without using a formulary adjustment. The company is in the process of evaluating the differences resulting from this change but has not yet completed this evaluation.

While evaluating its revenue recognition for development contracts, Cubic also evaluated its long-standing practice of using the cost-to-cost percentage-of-completion method to recognize revenues for many of its service contracts. Under the accounting literature the cost-to-cost percentage of completion method is acceptable for U.S. Government contracts but not for contracts with other governmental customers, whether domestic or foreign.

Errors in accounting and financial reporting that affect earnings are corrected through a prior period adjustment to retained earnings. The importance of such adjustments to users of the statements depend on materiality issues. In the context of potentially faulty financial statements, however, the process by which materiality is determined is complex and can be lengthy. Depending on the timing of the discovery of the error and its magnitude, this event can lead to negative effects with respect to share value.

The basic accounting standard for materiality judgments is in *Statement of Financial Accounting Concepts (SFAC) No. 8. SFAC No. 8* provides that: "The omission or misstatement of an item in a financial report is material if, in the light of surrounding circumstances, the magnitude of the item is such that it is probable that the judgment of a reasonable person relying upon the report would have been changed or influenced by the inclusion or correction of the item."[92]

It is important to note the trend that both FASB and the SEC want accountants and auditors to follow: the application of professional judgment in making materiality decisions. We agree with the SEC and reiterate that the application of professional judgment entails an ethical approach to decision making. The qualities of an ethical auditor of objectivity, integrity, due care, and professional skepticism are critical components of that judgment. The shift to more professional judgments should be accompanied by better training for auditors in the area of ethical decision making. We would like to see the SEC and PCAOB address this issue.

Concluding Thoughts

Earnings management is typically motivated by a desire to meet or exceed forecasted results, meet financial analysts' earnings estimates, inflate share price to make stock options more lucrative, and enhance bonuses. Techniques such as channel stuffing, bill-and-hold transactions, round-tripping, cookie-jar reserves, and delaying accruals and expense recognition are the "financial shenanigans" often used to manage earnings with the goal of making it look like the company is doing better than it really is.

While *revision restatements* are up and *reissuance restatements* are down, we have learned that it is not uncommon for companies to use language and characterize restatements in a way that may not be truthful. The public expects accountants and auditors to serve as a check on such behavior. All too often it has been let down by audit failures and auditors who got caught up in making the client happy rather than protecting the public trust.

We believe that when management manipulates earnings, the quality of such information suffers. It is hard enough for most readers of financial statements to understand the underlying accounting and financial reporting techniques used to develop the statements. When such methods are manipulated, or new ones developed to put a positive spin on company results, then there is a distortion effect that compromises the dependability of the statements. In the end it is the users of the statements that suffer.

At the end of the day, financial reporting needs to focus more on representational faithfulness, meaning that there should be a correspondence or agreement between the accounting measures or descriptions in financial reports and the economic events they purport to represent. The accounting profession seems to recognize that the traditional term "reliability" may be misunderstood and denote an exactness that does not, and cannot, exist, given a variety of choices of accounting principles and changes to them that may occur from year to year. *Statement of Financial Accounting Concepts No. 8* essentially replaces reliability as a qualitative characteristic of useful information with representational faithfulness.

Faithful representation does not mean accurate in all respects. Free from error means there are no errors or omissions in the description of the event, and the process used to produce the reported information has been selected and applied with no errors in the process. In other words, a representation of an estimate can be faithful if the amount is described clearly and accurately as being an estimate, the nature and limitations of the estimating process are explained, and no errors have been made in selecting and applying an appropriate process for developing the estimate.

Earnings management occurs when managers manipulate the earnings numbers reported to outside investors. Such manipulations may benefit someone in the short run but typically hurt the firm in the long run. Ethical companies should build systems to resist short-term pressures to manage earnings.

As we have learned throughout this book, organizational ethics and strong corporate governance provides a foundation to ward off the temptation to manipulate reported results. In virtually all of the financial frauds discussed in this chapter, compromises were made in these systems in order to achieve self-interest goals. Companies played fast and loose with the accounting rules and often were successful in deceiving the independent auditors.

What is lacking in virtually all cases of earnings management is ethical leadership. The tone at the top establishes the culture within an organization. An ethical culture is enhanced when top managers understand their responsibilities to shareholders, creditors, and the public at large. Ethical leadership entails a commitment to do what is right regardless of the consequences. It is not always an easy standard to achieve because of the inevitable pressures that build up in an organization to produce consistently better financial results. In the final chapter we will examine just how an organization can promote ethical leadership in the context of accounting decision making.

Discussion Questions

1. In Arthur Levitt's speech, referred to in the opening quote, he also said, "I fear that we are witnessing an erosion in the quality of earnings, and therefore, the quality of financial reporting. Managing may be giving way to manipulation; integrity may be losing out to illusion." Explain what you think Levitt meant by this statement. What role do financial analysts' earnings expectations play in the quality of earnings?

2. Are the use of non-GAAP financial measures ethical?

3. Relevance and faithful representation are the qualitative characteristics of useful information under *SFAC No. 8*.[93] How does ethical reasoning enter into making determinations about the relevance and faithful representation of financial information?

4. Evaluate earnings management from a utilitarian perspective. Can earnings management be an ethical practice? Discuss why or why not.

5. Evaluate the following statements from an ethical perspective:

   > "Earnings management in a narrow sense is the behavior of management to play with the discretionary accrual component to determine high or low earnings."

   > "Earnings are potentially managed, because financial accounting standards still provide alternative methods."

6. Comment on the statement that materiality is in the eye of the beholder. How does this statement relate to the discussion in this chapter of how to gauge materiality in assessing financial statement restatements? Is materiality inconsistent with the notion of representational faithfulness?

7. Needles talks about the use of a continuum ranging from questionable or highly conservative to fraud to assess the amount to be recorded for an estimated expense. Do you believe that the choice of an overly conservative or overly aggressive amount would reflect earnings management? Explain.

8. In 2010, LinkedIn reported trade payable obligations totaling $10.8 million in other accrued expenses within accrued liabilities instead of accounts payable. In 2011, note 2 in the 10-K financial statements described the use of accrued liabilities instead of accounts payable as a classification. Do you believe LinkedIn's accounting qualifies as a financial shenanigan?

9. Comment on the statement that what a company's income statement reveals is interesting, but what it conceals is vital.

10. Maines and Wahlen[94] state in their research paper on the reliability of accounting information: "Accrual estimates require judgment and discretion, which some firms under certain incentive conditions will exploit to report non-neutral accruals estimates within GAAP. Accounting standards can enhance the information in accrual estimates by linking them to the underlying economic constructs they portray." Explain what the authors meant by this statement with respect to the possible existence of earnings management.

11. Krispy Kreme was involved in an accounting fraud where the company reported false quarterly and annual earnings and falsely claimed that, as a result of those earnings, it had achieved what had become a prime benchmark of its historical performance, that is, reporting quarterly earnings per

share that exceeded its previously announced EPS guidance by 1¢. One method used to report higher earnings was to ship two or three times more doughnuts to franchisees than ordered in order to meet monthly quotas. Would you characterize what Krispy Kreme did as earnings management? Explain.

12. Safety-Kleen issued a major financial restatement in 2001. The next year, the company restated (reduced) previously reported net income by $534 million for the period 1997–1999. PwC withdrew its financial statement audit reports for those years. Do you believe that financial restatements and withdrawing an audit report are *prima facie* indicators that a failed audit has occurred? Explain.

13. Revenue recognition in the Xerox case called for determining the stand-alone selling price for each of the deliverables and using it to separate out the revenue amounts. Why do you think it is important to separate out the selling prices of each element of a bundled transaction? How do these considerations relate to what Xerox did to manage its earnings? Do you think the new revenue recognition standard will change the criteria in accounting for transactions like at Xerox?

14. Tinseltown Construction just received a $2 billion contract to construct a modern football stadium in the City of Industry, located in southern California, for a new National Football League (NFL) team called the Los Angeles Devils of Industry. The company estimates that it will cost $1.5 billion to construct the stadium. Explain how Tinseltown can make revenue recognition decisions each year that enable it to manage earnings over the three-year duration of the contract.

15. Explain how a company might use the accounting rules for impairment of long-lived assets to manage earnings.

16. The SEC's new rules on posting financial information on social media sites such as Twitter means that companies can now tweet their earnings in 140 characters or less. What are the problems that may arise in using a social media platform to report key financial data including the potential effects on shareholders and the company?

17. Do you agree with each of the following statements? Explain.

   - EBITDA makes companies with asset-heavy balance sheets look healthier than they may actually be.

   - EBITDA portrays a company's debt service ability— but only *some types of debt*.

   - EBITDA isn't a determinant of cash flow *at all*.

18. Critics of IFRS argue that the more principles-based standards are not as precise as, and therefore easier to manipulate than, the more rules-based GAAP. The reason for this is that IFRS requires more professional judgment from both auditors and corporate accountants with regard to the practical application of the rules. The application of professional judgment opens the door to increased opportunities for earnings management. Do you agree with these concerns expressed about principles-based IFRS? Relate your discussion to the research results discussed in this chapter.

19. In the Enron case, the company eventually turned to "back-door" guaranteeing of the debt of Chewco, one of its SPEs, to satisfy equity investors. Assume that a $16 million loan agreement required that Enron stock should not fall below $40 per share. If the share price did decline below that trigger amount, either the loan would be called by the bank or the bank could choose to increase the guaranteed number of Enron shares based on the new price (assume $32). If the bank decides to increase the number of shares guaranteed, what would be (1) the original number of shares in the guarantee and (2) the new number of shares? Why would it be important from an accounting and ethical perspective for Enron to disclose information about the guarantee in its financial statements?

20. In the study of earnings quality by Dichev et al.,[95] CFOs stated that "current earnings are considered to be high quality if they serve as a good guide to the long-run profits of the firm." Discuss how and why current earnings may *not* be a good barometer of the long-term profits of the firm.

21. The auditor of Beastie Company is reviewing the following client information for the prior year ended December 31, 2015, and all four quarters of 2016.

ESTIMATED ACCRUALS IN PRETAX EARNINGS (IN MILLIONS)						
	12/31/15	Quarter ended 3/31/16	Quarter ended 6/30/16	Quarter ended 9/30/16	Quarter ended 12/31/16	Totals
Accruals relating to employee vacation pay	(2.0)	(0.4)	(0.5)	(0.6)	(0.6)	(4.1)
Accruals for charitable contributions	(0.6)	(0.1)	(0.2)	(0.2)	(0.3)	(1.4)

Characterize the accruals as discretionary or nondiscretionary. What are the potential issues that the auditors should address given these numbers?

22. Explain the meaning of the following two statements and why each may be true:

   a. Where management does not try to manipulate earnings, there is a positive effect on earnings quality.

   b. The absence of earnings management does not, however, guarantee high earnings quality.

23. Big Pharma has been criticized for making deals that may bring harm to shareholder interests. Evaluate the following transaction from earnings management and ethical perspectives: A pharmaceutical drug company agreed to make payments to wholesalers if they bought drugs they did not need. The company paid $66 million to wholesalers who then "bought" $720 million of the company's drugs for which no customers existed.

24. In well-governed companies, a sense of accountability and ethical leadership create a culture that places organizational ethics above all else. What role does organizational culture play in preventing financial shenanigans from being used to manage earnings?

25. Evaluate the following statement: Do the ends of positive organizational consequences justify the means of earnings management?

Endnotes

1. Susan Scholz, *Financial Restatement: Trends in the United States: 2002–2012,* Center for Audit Quality, 2014, Available at: http://www.thecaq.org/docs/reports-and-publications/financial-restatement-trends-in-the-united-states-2003-2012.pdf?sfvrsn=2.

2. SEC, *SEC Advisory Committee on Improvements to Financial Reporting Subcommittee III: Audit Process and Compliance*, November 2, 2007, Available at: https://www.sec.gov/about/offices/oca/acifr/acifr-sc3-report.pdf.

3. Audit Analytics, *2014 Financial Restatements Review*, Available at: http://www.auditanalytics.com/blog/2014-financial-restatements-review/.

4. Todd Dezoort, "What are the Leading Causes of Financial Restatements?" *QFinance,* Available at: http://www.financepractitioner.com/contentFiles/QF02/g1xtn5q6/12/3/what-are-the-leading-causes-of-financial-restatements.pdf.

5. Arthur Levitt, "The Numbers Game," Remarks made by the former SEC chairman before the NYU Center for Law and Business, September 28, 1998, Available at: https://www.sec.gov/news/speech/speecharchive/1998/spch220.txt.

6. Levitt, "The Numbers Game."

7. Eli Bartov, Dan Givoly, and Carla Hayn, "The Rewards to Meeting or Beating Earnings Expectations," *Journal of Accounting & Economics* 33 (2002), pp. 173–204.

8. Timothy Fogarty, Michel Magnan, Garen Markarian, and Serge Bohdjalian, "Inside Agency: The Rise and Fall of Nortel," February 1, 2008, Available at: http://papers.ssrn.com/sol3/papers.cfm?abstract_id=1092288.

9. Joseph Fuller and Michael C. Jensen, "Just Say No to Wall Street: Putting a Stop to the Earnings Game," *Journal of Applied Corporate Finance* 14 (4), (Winter 2002) pp. 41–46.

10. Werner Erhard and Michael C. Jensen, "Beyond Agency Theory: The Hidden and Heretofore Inaccessible Power of Integrity (PDF of Keynote Slides) (August 31, 2012)," Harvard Business School NOM Unit Working Paper No. 10-068; Barbados Group Working Paper No. 10-02, Available at SSRN: http://ssrn.com/abstract=1552009 or http://dx.doi.org/10.2139/ssrn.1552009.

11. John R. Graham, Harvey R. Campbell, and Shiva Rajgopal, "The Economic Implications of Corporate Financial Reporting," *Journal of Accounting & Economics* 40 (1), (December 2005) pp. 3–73.

12. Yangseon Kim and Caixing Liu, and S. Ghon Rhee, "The Effect of Firm Size on Earnings Management," University of Hawaii Working Paper, Available at: http://www2.hawaii.edu/~fima/PDF/Finance_Seminar/EarningsMgmt.pdf.

13. U.S. Securities and Exchange Commission Litigation Release No. 18422/October 22, 2003; *Accounting and Auditing Enforcement Release No. 1904 (AAER No. 1904)/*October 22, 2003, Available at: www.sec.gov/litigation/litreleases/lr18422.htm.

14. Ron Kasznik, "On the Association between Voluntary Disclosure and Earnings Management," (1999), *Journal of Accounting Research*, Vol. 37, No. 1, pp. 57–81.

15. Joel F. Houston, Baruch Lev, and Jennifer Wu Tucker, "To guide or not to guide: Causes and consequences of stopping and subsequently resuming earnings guidance," 2010, Contemporary Accounting Research, Vol. 27, No. 1, pp. 143–185.

16. Andrew C. Call, Shuping Chen, Bin Miao, and Yen H. Tong, "Short-term Earnings Guidance and Accrual-Based Earnings Management," *Review of Accounting Studies*, May 18, 2013, Available at: http://papers.ssrn.com/sol3/papers.cfm?abstract_id=2327515.

17. *Employees' Retirement System, et al. v. Green Mountain Coffee Roasters, et al.,* United States Court of Appeals for the Second Circuit, July 24, 2015, Available at: http://caselaw.findlaw.com/us-2nd-circuit/1708736.html.

18. Green Mountain Coffee Roasters, Inc., *Annual Report on Form 10-K*, September 29, 2012, Available at: http://www.sec.gov/Archives/edgar/data/909954/000110465912080228/a12-21067_110k.htm.

19. Jessica Holzer and Greg Bensinger, "SEC Embraces Social Media," *The Wall Street Journal,* April 2, 2013, Available at: http://www.wsj.com/articles/SB10001424127887323611604578398862292997352.

20. Curtis C. Verschoor, "Is Non-GAAP Reporting Unethical?" *Strategic Finance*, April 2014, pp. 15–17.

21. Verschoor.

22. RAX 8-K filed February 19, 2009, Available at: http://www.wikinvest.com/stock/Rackspace_Hosting_%28RAX%29/Adjusted_Ebitda_Non-gaap_Financial_Measure.

23. Financial Accounting Standards Board, "Recognition and Measurement in Financial Statements of Business Enterprises," *Statement of Financial Accounting Concepts (SFAC) No. 5* (Stamford, CT: FASB, May 1986).

24. Available at: http://securities.stanford.edu/filings-documents/1008/HRC98/200482_r03c_031500.pdf.

25. Richard J. Rivard, Eugene Bland, and Gary B. Hatfield Morris, "Income Smoothing Behavior of U.S. Banks under Revised International Capital Requirements," *International Advances in Economic Research* 9 (4), (November 2003) pp. 288–294.

26. Jim Gaa and Paul Dunmore, "The Ethics of Earnings Management," *Chartered Accountants Journal*, 2007, pp. 60–62.

27. Kenneth A. Merchant, *Rewarding Results: Motivating Profit Center Managers* (Boston: Harvard Business School Press, 1989).

28. William S. Hopwood, Jay J. Leiner, and George R. Young, *Forensic Accounting and Fraud Examination* (New York: McGraw-Hill Irwin, 2012).

29. K. Schipper, "Commentary on Earnings Management," *Accounting Horizons,* December 1989, pp. 91–102.

30. P. M. Healy and J. M. Wahlen, "A Review of Earnings Management Literature and Its Implications for Standard Setting," *Accounting Horizons* 13 (1999), pp. 365–383.

31. P. M. Dechow and P. J. Skinner, "Earnings Management: Reconciling the Views of Accounting Academics, Practitioners, and Regulation," *Accounting Horizons* 14 (2001), pp. 235–250.

32. Thomas E. McKee, *Earnings Management: An Executive Perspective* (Mason, OH: Thompson Corporation, 2005).

33. Hopwood et al., p. 426.

34. Belverd E. Needles Jr., "The Role of Judgment in Ethical Financial Reporting," *Beta Alpha Psi Newsletter*, Vol. 2, Issue 4, Fall 2011, Available at: http://www.archive-org-2012.com/org/b/2012-12-04_831172_21/.

35. R. Z. Elias, "The Impact of Corporate Ethical Values on Perceptions of Earnings Management," *Managerial Auditing Journal* 19 (2004), pp. 84–98.

36. Frank Phillips and K. Zvinakis, "Baywatch International: A Case Linking Financial Reporting, Business, and User Decisions," *Issues in Accounting Education* 15 (2000), pp. 605–622.

37. Anna M. Rose and Jacob Rose, "Management Attempts to Avoid Accounting Disclosure Oversight: The Effects of Trust and Knowledge on Corporate Directors Governance Ability," *Journal of Business Ethics* 83 (2008), pp. 193–205.

38. William J. Bruns Jr. and Kenneth A. Merchant, "The Dangerous Morality of Managing Earnings," *Management Accounting,* August 1990, pp. 62–69.

39. K. Rosenzweig and M. Fischer, "Is Managing Earnings Ethically Acceptable?" *Management Accounting,* March 1994, pp. 44–51.

40. Michael D. Akers, Don E. Giacomino, and Jodi L. Bellovary, "Earnings Management and Its Implications: Educating the Accounting Profession," *The CPA Journal,* August 2007, pp. 33–39.

41. Akers et al.

42. Akers et al.

43. Ilia D. Dichev, John R. Graham, Campbell R. Harvey, and Shivaram Rajgopal, The Misrepresentation of Earnings (August 10, 2015). Financial Analysts Journal, Forthcoming. Available at SSRN: http://ssrn.com/abstract=2376408 or http://dx.doi.org/10.2139/ssrn.2376408.

44. Patricia M. Dechow, "Accounting Earnings and Cash Flows as Measures of Firm Performance: The Role of Accounting Accruals," *Journal of Accounting & Economics* 18 (1994), pp. 3–42.

45. SEC, *In the Matter of W. R. Grace & Co., Respondent, Accounting and Auditing Enforcement Release No. 1140,* June 30, 1999, Available at: https://www.sec.gov/litigation/admin/34-41578.htm.

46. Supreme Court of the United States, *Matrixx Initiatives et al. v. Siracusano et al.* Certiorari to the U.S. Court of Appeals for the Ninth Circuit, March 22, 2011, Available at: http://www.supreme court.gov/opinions/10pdf/09-1156.pdf.

47. *TSC Industries, Inc. v. Northway, Inc.,* 426 U.S. 438 (1976), Available at: www.supreme.justia.com/cases/federal/us/426/438/.

48. *Basic, Inc. v. Levinson,* 485 U.S. 224 (1988), Available at: www.supreme.justia.com/cases/federal /us/485/224/.

49. *Mattrix Initiatives et al. v. Siracusano et al.*

50. James Brady Vorhies, "The New Importance of Materiality," *Journal of Accountancy,* May 2005, Available at: http://www.journalofaccountancy.com/issues/2005/may/thenewimportanceofmateriality.html

51. SEC, *In the Matter of KPMG [v. Gemstar], Accounting and Auditing Enforcement Release No. 2125,* Available at: www.sec.gov/litigation/admin/34-550564.html.

52. Healy and Wahlen.

53. R. D. Mergenthaler, *Principles-Based versus Rules-Based Accounting Standards and Extreme Cases of Earnings Management,* a dissertation prepared for the University of Washington, 2008.

54. Thomas Jeanjean and Herve H. Stolowy, "Do Accounting Standards Matter? An Exploratory Analysis of Earnings Management Before and After IFRS Adoption," *Journal of Accounting and Public Policy* 27 (6) (2008), pp. 480–494.

55. Financial Accounting Standards Board, *Principles-Based Approach to Standard Setting,* 2002, Available at: www.fasb.org/news/nr102102.shtml.

56. R. H. Herz, "A Year of Challenge and Change for the FASB," *Accounting Horizons* 17 (2003), pp. 247–255.

57. David Folsom, Paul Hribar, Rick Mergenthaler, and Kyle Peterson, "Principles-Based Standards and Earnings Attributes," April 25, 2012, Available at: www.ssrn.com/abstract=2046190 or www.dx.doi.org/10.2139/ssrn.2046190.

58. Levitt, "The Numbers Game."

59. SEC, *In the Matter of Laird Daniels, CPA, Respondent, Accounting and Auditing Enforcement Release No. 3548,* April 8, 2014, Available at: https://www.sec.gov/litigation/admin/2014/33-9573.pdf.

60. Jonathan Stempel, "CVS to Pay $20 Million to Settle SEC Fraud Charges," *Reuters,* April 8, 2014, Available at: http://www.reuters.com/article/2014/04/08/us-cvscaremark-sec-settlement-idUSBREA371L020140408.

61. SEC, *Securities and Exchange Commission v. CVS Caremark Corp., Accounting and Auditing Enforcement Release No. 3549,* April 8, 2014, Available at: https://www.sec.gov/litigation/litreleases/2014/lr22968.htm.

62. Financial Accounting Standards Board (FASB), *Statement of Financial Accounting Standards (SFAS) 141*, December 2007, Available at: http://www.fasb.org/jsp/FASB/Document_C/DocumentPage?cid=1218220124931&acceptedDisclaimer=true.

63. SEC, Staff Accounting Bulletin: No. 101—Revenue Recognition in Financial Statements, Available at: https://www.sec.gov/interps/account/sab101.htm.

64. Financial Accounting Standards Board, "Multiple-Deliverable Revenue Arrangements: a Consensus of the FASB Emerging Issues Task Force, Financial Accounting Standards Update No. 2009-13, October 2009, Available at: https://asc.fasb.org/imageRoot/62/6844362.pdf.

65. SEC, "California-Based Telecommunications Equipment Firm and Two Former Executives Charged in Revenue Recognition Scheme," August 22, 2014, Available at: http://www.sec.gov/News/PressRelease/Detail/PressRelease/1370542732440.

66. Kathryn Yeaton, "A New World of Revenue Recognition," *The CPA Journal*, July 2015, pp. 50–53.

67. Jason Bramwell, "FASB, IASB Unveil Final Standard on Revenue Recognition," May 28, 2014, Available at: http://www.accountingweb.com/aa/standards/fasb-iasb-unveil-final-standard-on-revenue-recognition.

68. Scott McGregor, "Earnings Management Manipulation," Available at: http://webpage.pace.edu/pviswanath/notes/corpfin/earningsmanip.html.

69. Howard M. Schilit, *Financial Shenanigans: How to Detect Accounting Gimmicks and Fraud in Financial Reports,* 3rd ed. (New York: McGraw-Hill, 2010).

70. *W. R. Grace & Co.*

71. SEC, Litigation Release No. 18174, *Securities and Exchange Commission v. Paul A. Allaire, G. Richard Thoman, Barry D. Romeril, Philip D. Fishbach, Daniel S. Marchibroda, and Gregory B. Tayler,* June 5, 2003, *Accounting and Auditing Enforcement Release No. 1796,* Available at: www.sec.gov/litigation/litreleases/lr18174.html.

72. SEC, Litigation Release No. 17645, *Accounting and Auditing Enforcement Release No. 1542, Securities and Exchange Commission v. Xerox Corporation,* Civil Action No. 02-CV-2780 (DLC) (S.D.N.Y.), April 11, 2002.

73. SEC, *In the Matter of KPMG LLP, Accounting and Auditing Enforcement Release No. 2234,* April 19, 2005, Available at: www.sec.gov/litigation/admin/34-51574.pdf.

74. SEC, Litigation Release No. 19573, *Accounting and Auditing Enforcement Release No. 2379, SEC v. KPMG LLP et al.,* Civil Action No. 03-CV 0671 (DLC) (S.D.N.Y.), February 22, 2006.

75. SEC, Litigation Release No. 18715, *Accounting and Auditing Enforcement Release No. 2016, Securities and Exchange Commission v. Lucent Technologies, Inc., Nina Aversano, Jay Carter, A. Leslie Dorn, William Plunkett, John Bratten, Deborah Harris, Charles Elliott, Vanessa Petrini, Michelle Hayes-Bullock, and David Ackerman,* Civil Action No. 04-2315 (WHW) (D.N.J.), filed May 17, 2004, Available at: www.sec.gov/litigation/litreleases/lr18715.htm.

76. SEC, *Accounting and Auditing Enforcement Release No. 2380, In the Matter of Thomas J. Yoho, CPA, Respondent,* Administrative Proceeding File No. 3-12215, February 22, 2006.

77. Bethany McLean and Peter Elkind, *The Smartest Guys in the Room: The Amazing Rise and Scandalous Fall of Enron* (New York: Penguin Books, 2003).

78. Mimi Swartz and Sherron Watkins, *Power Failure: The Inside Story of the Collapse of Enron* (New York: Doubleday, 2003), pp. 275–276.

79. Report of Investigation by the Special Investigative Committee of the Board of Directors of Enron Corp., William C. Powers, Jr., Chair, Available at: http://picker.uchicago.edu/Enron/PowersReport%282-2-02%29.pdf.

80. Michael Gracyzk, "Lay Says He's 'Shocked at Enron Verdict,'" Available at: http://www.freerepublic.com/focus/news/1638839/posts.

81. FASB, FASB Interpretation 46(R), Consolidation of Variable Interest Entities, December 24, 2003 (Norwalk, CT: FASB, 2003).

82. Mercedes Erickson, "Latest Results Show Continuing Positive Restatement Trends," *Audit Analytics,* April 27, 2015, Available at: http://www.auditanalytics.com/blog/author/merickson/.

83. Olga Usvyatsky, "Restatements: What's in a Name?," *Audit Analytics*, March 13, 2014, Available at: http://www.auditanalytics.com/blog/restatements-whats-in-a-name/.

84. PR Newswire, "Hertz Completes Financial Restatement; Provides 2015 Business Outlook," July 16, 2015, Available at: http://www.stockhouse.com/news/press-releases/2015/07/16/hertz-completes-financial-restatement-provides-2015-business-outlook.

85. Tammy Whitehouse, "How Wheels Came Off of Hertz' Accounting," *Compliance Week*, June 20, 2104, Available at: http://www.rgl.com/pubs/xprPubDetail.aspx?xpST=PubDetail&pub=323.

86. "Errors In Previously Issued Financials? A 'Big P' Problem," *Law360,* January 16, 2015, Available at: http://www.law360.com/articles/610752/errors-in-previously-issued-financials-a-big-p-problem.

87. Whitehouse.

88. Whitehouse.

89. Lynn E. Turner and Thomas R. Weirich, "A Closer Look at Financial Statement Restatements: Analyzing the Reasons Behind the Trend," *The CPA Journal*, December 2006, pp. 33–39.

90. Available at: www.cubic.com/News/Press-Releases/ID/423/Cubic-Corporation-to-Restate-Financial-Statements.

91. Cubic Corp., "Cubic Corporation to Restate Financial Statements," Company Press Release, August 1, 2012, Available at: www.cubic.com/News/Press-Releases/ID/423/Cubic-Corporation-to-Restate-Financial-Statements.

92. FASB, *Statement of Financial Accounting Concepts No. 8, Conceptual Framework for Financial Reporting* (NY: FASB, 2010).

93. FASB, *Statement of Financial Accounting Concepts No. 8, Conceptual Framework for Financial Reporting—Chapter 1,* The Objective of General Purpose Financial Reporting, *and Chapter 3,* Qualitative Characteristics of Useful Financial Information (a replacement of FASB Concepts Statements No. 1 and No. 2), September 2010, Available at http://www.fasb.org/cs/BlobServer?blobkey=id&blobwhere=1175822892635&blobheader=application%2Fpdf&blobcol=urldata&blobtable=MungoBlobs.

94. Laureen A. Maines and James M. Wahlen, "The Nature of Accounting Information Reliability: Inferences from Archival and Experimental Research," November 3, 2003, Available at: http://repository.binus.ac.id/content/m0034/m003421831.pdf.

95. Ilia D. Dichev, John R. Graham, Campbell R. Harvey, and Shivaram Rajgopal, The Misrepresentation of Earnings (August 10, 2015). Financial Analysts Journal, Forthcoming. Available at SSRN: http://ssrn.com/abstract=2376408 or http://dx.doi.org/10.2139/ssrn.2376408.

Chapter 7 Cases

Case 7-1 Nortel Networks

Canada-based Nortel Networks was one of the largest telecommunications equipment companies in the world prior to its filing for bankruptcy protection on January 14, 2009, in the United States, Canada, and Europe. The company had been subjected to several financial reporting investigations by U.S. and Canadian securities agencies in 2004. The accounting irregularities centered on premature revenue recognition and hidden cash reserves used to manipulate financial statements. The goal was to present the company in a positive light so that investors would buy (hold) Nortel stock, thereby inflating the stock price. Although Nortel was an international company, the listing of its securities on U.S. stock exchanges subjected it to all SEC regulations, along with the requirement to register its financial statements with the SEC and prepare them in accordance with U.S. GAAP.

The company had gambled by investing heavily in Code Division Multiple Access (CDMA) wireless cellular technology during the 1990s in an attempt to gain access to the growing European and Asian markets. However, many wireless carriers in the aforementioned markets opted for rival Global System Mobile (GSM) wireless technology instead. Coupled with a worldwide economic slowdown in the technology sector, Nortel's losses mounted to $27.3 billion by 2001, resulting in the termination of two-thirds of its workforce.

The Nortel fraud primarily involved four members of Nortel's senior management as follows: CEO Frank Dunn, CFO Douglas Beatty, controller Michael Gollogly, and assistant controller Maryanne Pahapill. At the time of the audit, Dunn was a certified management accountant, while Beatty, Gollogly, and Pahapill were chartered accountants in Canada.

Accounting Irregularities

On March 12, 2007, the SEC alleged the following in a complaint against Nortel:[1]

- In late 2000, Beatty and Pahapill implemented changes to Nortel's revenue recognition policies that violated U.S. GAAP, specifically to pull forward revenue to meet publicly announced revenue targets. These actions improperly boosted Nortel's fourth quarter and fiscal 2000 revenue by over $1 billion, while at the same time allowing the company to meet, but not exceed, market expectations. However, because their efforts pulled in more revenue than needed to meet those targets, Dunn, Beatty, and Pahapill selectively reversed certain revenue entries during the 2000 year-end closing process.

- In November 2002, Dunn, Beatty, and Gollogly learned that Nortel was carrying over $300 million in excess reserves. The three did not release these excess reserves into income as required under U.S. GAAP. Instead, they concealed their existence and maintained them for later use. Further, Beatty, Dunn, and Gollogly directed the establishment of yet another $151 million in unnecessary reserves during the 2002 year-end closing process to avoid posting a profit and paying bonuses earlier than Dunn had predicted publicly. These reserve manipulations erased Nortel's *pro forma* profit for the fourth quarter of 2002 and caused it to report a loss instead.[2]

---

[1] U.S. District Court for the Southern District of New York, *U.S. Securities and Exchange Commission v. Frank A. Dunn, Douglas C. Beatty, Michael J. Gollogly, and Maryanne E. Pahapill,* Civil Action No. 07-CV-2058, www.sec.gov/litigation /complaints/ 2007/comp20036.pdf .

[2] Pro forma means literally as a matter of form. Companies sometimes report income to the public and financial analysts that may not be calculated in accordance with GAAP. For example, a company might report pro forma earnings that exclude depreciation expense, amortization expense, and nonrecurring expenses such as restructuring costs. In general, pro forma earnings are reported in an effort to put a more positive spin on a company's operations. Unfortunately, there are no accounting rules on just how pro forma should be calculated, so comparability is difficult at best, and investors may be misled as a result.

- In the first and second quarters of 2003, Dunn, Beatty, and Gollogly directed the release of at least $490 million of excess reserves specifically to boost earnings, fabricate profits, and pay bonuses. These efforts turned Nortel's first-quarter 2003 loss into a reported profit under U.S. GAAP, which allowed Dunn to claim that he had brought Nortel to profitability a quarter ahead of schedule. In the second quarter of 2003, their efforts largely erased Nortel's quarterly loss and generated a *pro forma* profit. In both quarters, Nortel posted sufficient earnings to pay tens of millions of dollars in so-called return to profitability bonuses, largely to a select group of senior managers.

- During the second half of 2003, Dunn and Beatty repeatedly misled investors as to why Nortel was conducting a purportedly "comprehensive review" of its assets and liabilities, which resulted in Nortel's restatement of approximately $948 million in liabilities in November 2003. Dunn and Beatty falsely represented to the public that the restatement was caused solely by internal control mistakes. In reality, Nortel's first restatement was necessitated by the intentional improper handling of reserves, which occurred throughout Nortel for several years, and the first restatement effort was sharply limited to avoid uncovering Dunn, Beatty, and Gollogly's earnings management activities.

The complaint charged Dunn, Beatty, Gollogly, and Pahapill with violating and/or aiding and abetting violations of the antifraud, reporting, and books and records requirements. In addition, they were charged with violating the Securities Exchange Act Section 13(b)(2)(B) that requires issuers to devise and maintain a system of internal accounting controls sufficient to provide reasonable assurances that, among other things, transactions are recorded as necessary to permit the preparation of financial statements in conformity with U.S. GAAP and to maintain accountability for the issuer's assets.

Dunn and Beatty were separately charged with violations of the officer certification provisions instituted by SOX under Section 302. The commission sought a permanent injunction, civil monetary penalties, officer and director bars, and disgorgement with prejudgment interest against all four defendants.

Specifics of Earnings Management Techniques

From the third quarter of 2000 through the first quarter of 2001, when Nortel reported its financial results for year-end 2000, Dunn, Beatty, and Pahapill altered Nortel's revenue recognition policies to accelerate revenues as needed to meet Nortel's quarterly and annual revenue guidance, and to hide the worsening condition of Nortel's business. Techniques used to accomplish this goal include:

1. *Reinstituting bill-and-hold transactions.* The company tried to find a solution for the hundreds of millions of dollars in inventory that was sitting in Nortel's warehouses and offsite storage locations. Revenues could not be recognized for this inventory because U.S. GAAP revenue recognition rules generally require goods to be delivered to the buyer before revenue can be recognized. This inventory grew, in part, because orders were slowing and, in June 2000, Nortel had banned bill-and-hold transactions from its sales and accounting practices. The company reinstituted bill-and-hold sales when it became clear that it fell short of earnings guidance. In all, Nortel accelerated into 2000 more than $1 billion in revenues through its improper use of bill-and-hold transactions.

2. *Restructuring business-asset write-downs.* Beginning in February 2001, Nortel suffered serious losses when it finally lowered its earnings guidance to account for the fact that its business was suffering from the same widespread economic downturn that affected the entire telecommunications industry. As Nortel's business plummeted throughout the remainder of 2001, the company reacted by implementing a restructuring that, among other things, reduced its workforce by two-thirds and resulted in a significant write-down of assets.

3. *Creating reserves.* In relation to writing down the assets, Nortel established reserves that were used to manage earnings. Assisted by defendants Beatty and Gollogly, Dunn manipulated the company's reserves to manage Nortel's publicly reported earnings, create the false appearance that his leadership and business acumen was responsible for Nortel's profitability, and pay bonuses to these three defendants and other Nortel executives.

4. *Releasing reserves into income.* From at least July 2002 through June 2003, Dunn, Beatty, and Gollogly released excess reserves to meet Dunn's unrealistic and overly aggressive earnings targets. When Nortel internally (and unexpectedly) determined that it would return to profitability in the fourth quarter of 2002, the reserves were used to reduce earnings for the quarter, avoid reporting a profit earlier than Dunn had publicly predicted, and create a stockpile of reserves that could be (and were) released in the future as necessary to

meet Dunn's prediction of profitability by the second quarter of 2003. When 2003 turned out to be rockier than expected, Dunn, Beatty, and Gollogly orchestrated the release of excess reserves to cause Nortel to report a profit in the first quarter of 2003, a quarter earlier than the public expected, and to pay defendants and others substantial bonuses that were awarded for achieving profitability on a *pro forma* basis. Because their actions drew the attention of Nortel's outside auditors, they made only a portion of the planned reserve releases. This allowed Nortel to report nearly break-even results (though not actual profit) and to show internally that the company had again reached profitability on a *pro forma* basis necessary to pay bonuses.

Siemens Reserve

During the fraud trial, former Nortel accountant Susan Shaw testified about one of the most controversial accounting provisions on the company's books, relating to a 2001 lawsuit filed against Nortel by Siemens AG. It was long-standing practice across Nortel to establish reserves on a "worst case" basis, which meant at an amount equal to the maximum possible exposure.

Nortel had created an accounting reserve on its books at the time the Siemens lawsuit was filed to provide for a settlement in the case, but it was alleged that a portion of the provision was arbitrarily left on Nortel's books long after the lawsuit was resolved in the fourth quarter of 2001. It became part of a group of extra head office, non-operating reserves that allegedly was reversed arbitrarily—and with no appropriate business trigger—to push the company into a profit in 2003 and earn "return to profitability" bonuses for executives.

The $4-million remaining Siemens provision was initially booked to be reversed into income in the first quarter of 2003, but then withdrawn, allegedly because it was not needed to push the company into a profitable position in the quarter. It was then booked to be used in the second quarter, and became the only head office non-operating reserve used in the quarter.

The contention was that the Siemens reserve was used in that quarter because Nortel needed almost exactly $4 million more income to reach the payout trigger for the company's restricted share unit plan at that time. However, lawyer David Porter argued the Siemens amount was triggered in the second quarter because that is when the company believed it was no longer needed and should appropriately be reversed.

In cross-examination, Porter showed Shaw a working document recovered from the files of Nortel's external auditors at Deloitte & Touche, showing the auditor reviewed Nortel's justifications for keeping the Siemens reserve on the books until that time and for reversing it in the second quarter of 2003. Deloitte's notes showed the auditor reviewed Nortel's detailed rationale for the reserve and concluded its release in the second quarter was "reasonable."[3]

The company said it was holding on to the reserve because the settlement with Siemens had been "rancorous" and Nortel wanted to be sure there would be no further claims made after the lawsuit was settled and $32 million was paid to Siemens in two installments in late 2001 and late 2002.

In its working notes, Deloitte recorded that Nortel felt it was "prudent" to keep the $4 million on the books until mid-2002. Shaw testified she felt the reserve was being reversed on schedule with the plan to keep it in place for the first two quarters of the year. Porter asked Shaw whether the auditors were satisfied at the time there was an appropriate triggering event to use the reserve in the second quarter of 2002, and she replied there was one.

However, the amount became part of a broad restatement of reserves announced at Nortel at the end of 2003. The company noted in the restatement that the Siemens reserve should have been reversed in the fourth quarter of 2001 when the lawsuit was settled.

Role of Auditors and Audit Committee

In late October 2000, as a first step toward reintroducing bill-and-hold transactions into Nortel's sales and accounting practices, Nortel's then controller and assistant controller asked Deloitte to explain, among other things, (1) "[u]nder what circumstances can revenue be recognized on product (merchandise) that has not been

---

[3] Janet McFarland, "Nortel Accounting Reserve Reversal Deemed 'Reasonable,'" *The Globe and Mail,* September 6, 2012, Available at: http://www.theglobeandmail.com/globe-investor/nortel-accounting-reserve-reversal-deemed-reasonable-by-auditors-court-told/article4171550/.

shipped to the end customer?" and (2) whether merchandise accounting can be used to recognized revenues "when installation is imminent" or "when installation is considered to be a minor portion of the contract"?[4]

On November 2, 2000, Deloitte presented Nortel with a set of charts that, among other things, explained the US GAAP criteria for revenues to be recognized prior to delivery (including additional factors to consider for a bill-and-hold transaction) and also provided an example of a customer request for a bill-and-hold sale "that would support the assertion that Nortel should recognize revenue" prior to delivery.

Nortel's earnings management scheme began to unravel at the end of the second quarter of 2003. On the morning of July 24, 2003, the same day on which Nortel issued its second Quarter 2003 earnings release, Deloitte informed Nortel's audit committee that it had found a "reportable condition" with respect to weaknesses in Nortel's accounting for the establishment and disposition of reserves. Deloitte went on to explain that, in response to its concerns, Nortel's management had undertaken a project to gather support and determine proper resolution of certain provision balances. Management, in fact, had undertaken this project because the auditor required adequate audit evidence for the upcoming year-end 2003 audit. Nortel concealed its auditor's concerns from the public, instead disclosing the comprehensive review.

Shortly after Nortel's announced restatement, the audit committee commenced an independent investigation and hired outside counsel to help it "gain a full understanding of the events that caused significant excess liabilities to be maintained on the balance sheet that needed to be restated," as well as to recommend any necessary remedial measures. The investigation uncovered evidence that Dunn, Beatty, and Gollogly and certain other financial managers were responsible for Nortel's improper use of reserves in the second half of 2002 and first half of 2003.

In March 2004, Nortel suspended Beatty and Gollogly and announced that it would "likely" need to revise and restate previously filed financial results further. Dunn, Beatty, and Gollogly were terminated for cause in April 2004.

On January 11, 2005, Nortel issued a second restatement that restated approximately $3.4 billion in misstated revenues and at least another $746 million in liabilities. All of the financial statement effects of the defendants' two accounting fraud schemes were corrected as of this date, but there remained lingering effects from the defendants' internal control and other nonfraud violations.

Nortel also disclosed the findings to date of the audit committee's independent review, which concluded, among other things, that Dunn, Beatty, and Gollogly were responsible for Nortel's improper use of reserves in the second half of 2002 and first half of 2003. The second restatement, however, did not reveal that Nortel's top executives had also engaged in revenue recognition fraud in 2000.

In May 2006, in its Form 10-K for the period ending December 31, 2005, Nortel admitted for the first time that its restated revenues in part had resulted from management fraud, stating that "in an effort to meet internal and external targets, the senior corporate finance management team . . . changed the accounting policies of the company several times during 2000," and that those changes were "driven by the need to close revenue and earnings gaps."

Throughout their scheme, the defendants lied to Nortel's independent auditor by making materially false and misleading statements and omissions in connection with the quarterly reviews and annual audits of the financial statements that were materially misstated. Among other things, each of the defendants submitted management representation letters to the auditors that concealed the fraud and made false statements, which included that the affected quarterly and annual financial statements were presented in conformity with U.S. GAAP and that they had no knowledge of any fraud that could have a material effect on the financial statements. Dunn, Beatty, and Gollogly also submitted a false management representation letter in connection with Nortel's first restatement, and Pahapill likewise made false management representations in connection with Nortel's second restatement.

The defendants' scheme resulted in Nortel issuing materially false and misleading quarterly and annual financial statements and related disclosures for at least the financial reporting periods ending December 31, 2000, through December 31, 2003, and in all subsequent filings made with the SEC that incorporated those financial statements and related disclosures by reference.

---

[4]*U.S. SEC v. Nortel Networks Corporation and Nortel Networks Limited,* Civil Action No. 07-CV-8851, October 15, 2007, Available at: https://www.sec.gov/litigation/complaints/2007/comp20333.pdf.

On October 15, 2007, Nortel, without admitting or denying the SEC's charges, agreed to settle the commission's action by consenting to be enjoined permanently from violating the antifraud, reporting, books and records, and internal control provisions of the federal securities laws and by paying a $35 million civil penalty, which the commission placed in a Fair Fund[5] for distribution to affected shareholders.[6] Nortel also agreed to report periodically to the commission's staff on its progress in implementing remedial measures and resolving an outstanding material weakness over its revenue recognition procedures.

On January 14, 2009, Nortel filed for protection from creditors in the United States, Canada, and the United Kingdom in order to restructure its debt and financial obligations. In June, the company announced that it no longer planned to continue operations and that it would sell off all of its business units. Nortel's CDMA wireless business and long-term evolutionary access technology (LTE) were sold to Ericsson, and Avaya purchased its Enterprise business unit.

The final indignity for Nortel came on June 25, 2009, when Nortel's stock price dropped to 18.5¢ a share, down from a high of $124.50 in 2000. Nortel's battered and bruised stock was finally delisted from the S&P/TSX composite index, a stock index for the Canadian equity market, ending a colossal collapse on an exchange on which the Canadian telecommunications giant's stock valuation once accounted for a third of its value.

Postscript

The three former top executives of Nortel Networks Corp. were found not guilty of fraud on January 14, 2013. In the court ruling, Justice Frank Marrocco of the Ontario Superior Court found that the accounting manipulations that caused the company to restate its earnings for 2002 and 2003 did not cross the line into criminal behavior.

Accounting experts said the case is sure to be closely watched by others in the business community for the message it sends about where the line lies between fraud and the acceptable use of discretion in accounting.

The decision underlines that management still has a duty to prepare financial statements that "present fairly the financial position and results of the company" according to a forensic accountant, Charles Smedmor, who followed the case. "Nothing in the judge's decision diminished that duty."

During the trial, lawyers for the accused said that the men believed that the accounting decisions they made were appropriate at the time, and that the accounting treatment was approved by Nortel's auditors from Deloitte & Touche. Judge Marrocco accepted these arguments, noting many times in his ruling that bookkeeping decisions were reviewed and approved by auditors and were disclosed adequately to investors in press releases or notes added to the financial statements.

Nonetheless, the judge also said that he believed that the accused were attempting to "manage" Nortel's financial results in both the fourth quarter of 2002 and in 2003, but he added he was not satisfied that the changes resulted in material misrepresentations. He said that except for $80 million of reserves released in the first quarter of 2003, the rest of the use of reserves was within "the normal course of business." Judge Marrocco said the $80 million release, while clearly "unsupportable" and later reversed during a restatement of Nortel's books, was disclosed properly in Nortel's financial statements at the time and was not a material amount. He concluded that Beatty and Dunn "were prepared to go to considerable lengths" to use reserves to improve the bottom line in the second quarter of 2003, but he said the decision was reversed before the financial statements were completed because Gollogly challenged it.

In a surprising twist, Judge Marrocco also suggested the two devastating restatements of Nortel's books in 2003 and 2005 were probably unnecessary in hindsight, although he said he understood why they were done in the context of the time. He said the original statements were arguably correct within a threshold of what was material for a company of that size.

---

[5]A Fair Fund is a fund established by the SEC to distribute "disgorgements" (returns of wrongful profits) and penalties (fines) to defrauded investors. Fair Funds hold money recovered from a specific SEC case. The commission chooses how to distribute the money to defrauded investors, and when completed, the fund terminates.

[6]Theresa Tedesco and Jamie Sturgeon, "Nortel: Cautionary Tale of a Former Canadian Titan," *Financial Post,* June 27, 2009.

Darren Henderson, an accounting professor at the Richard Ivey School of Business at the University of Western Ontario, said that a guilty verdict would have raised the bar for management to justify their accounting judgments. But the acquittal makes it clear that "management manipulation of financial statements is very difficult to prove beyond a reasonable doubt in a court of law," he said.

It is clear that setting up reserves or provisions is still subject to management discretion, Henderson said. "The message . . . is that it is okay to use accounting judgments to achieve desired outcomes, [such as] a certain earnings target."

Questions

1. Discuss Nortel's accounting for the following transactions and why they were not in conformity with GAAP:
   - Revenue recognition
   - Reserve accounting
   - Accounting for contingent liabilities

2. The following two statements are made in the case:
   - Accounting experts said the case is sure to be closely watched by others in the business community for the message it sends about where the line lies between fraud and the acceptable use of discretion in accounting.
   - Darren Henderson opined that "The message . . . is that it is okay to use accounting judgments to achieve desired outcomes, [such as] a certain earnings target."

   Evaluate these statements from the perspectives of representational faithfulness and fair presentation of the financial results reported by Nortel.

3. During the trial, lawyers for the accused said that the men believed that the accounting decisions they made were appropriate at the time, and that the accounting treatment was approved by Nortel's auditors from Deloitte & Touche. Judge Marrocco accepted these arguments. Marrocco added he was "not satisfied beyond a reasonable doubt" that the trio [i.e., Dunn, Beatty, and Gollogly] had "deliberately misrepresented" financial results. Given the facts of the case do you believe Judge Marrocco's decision was justified? Explain.

4. Does it appear from the facts of the case that the Deloitte auditors met their ethical and professional responsibilities in the audit of Nortel's financial statements?

Case 7-2 Solutions Network, Inc. (a GVV case)

"We can't recognize revenue immediately, Paul, since we agreed to buy similar software from DSS," Sarah Young stated.

"That's ridiculous," Paul Henley replied. "Get your head out of the sand, Sarah, before it's too late."

Sarah Young is the controller for Solutions Network, Inc., a publicly owned company headquartered in Sunnyvale, California. Solutions Network has an audit committee with three members of the board of directors that are independent of management. Sarah is meeting with Paul Henley, the CFO of the company on January 7, 2016, to discuss the accounting for a software systems transaction with Data Systems Solutions (DSS) prior to the company's audit for the year ended December 31, 2015. Both Young and Henley are CPAs.

Young has excluded the amount in contention from revenue and net income for 2015, but Henley wants the amount to be included in the 2015 results. Without it, Solutions Network would not meet earnings expectations. Henley tells Young that the order came from the top to record the revenue on December 28, 2015, the day the transaction with DSS was finalized. Young points out that Solutions Network ordered essentially the same software from DSS to be shipped and delivered early in 2016. Therefore, according to Young, Solutions Network should delay revenue recognition on this "swap" transaction until that time. Henley argues against Sarah's position, stating that title had passed from the company to DSS on December 31, 2015, when the software product was shipped FOB shipping point.

Background

Solutions Network, Inc., became a publicly owned company on March 15, 2011, following a successful initial public offering (IPO). Solutions Network built up a loyal clientele in the three years prior to the IPO by establishing close working relationships with technology leaders, including IBM, Apple, and Dell Computer. The company designs and engineers systems software to function seamlessly with minimal user interface. There are several companies that provide similar products and consulting services, and DSS is one. However, DSS operates in a larger market providing IT services management products that coordinate the entire business infrastructure into a single system.

Solutions Network grew very rapidly during the past five years, although sales slowed down a bit in 2015. The revenue and earnings streams during those years are as follows:

Year	Revenues (millions)	Net Income (millions)
2010	$148.0	$11.9
2011	175.8	13.2
2012	202.2	15.0
2013	229.8	16.1
2014	267.5	17.3

Young prepared the following estimates for 2015:

Year	Revenues (millions)	Net Income (millions)
2015 (projected)	$262.5	$16.8

The Transaction

On December 28, 2015, Solutions Network offered to sell its Internet infrastructure software to DSS for its internal use. In return, DSS agreed to ship similar software 30 days later to Solutions Network for that company's internal use. The companies had conducted several transactions with each other during the previous five years, and while DSS initially balked at the transaction because it provided no value added to the company, it did not want to upset one of the fastest-growing software companies in the industry. Moreover, Solutions Network might be able to help identify future customers for DSS's IT service management products.

The $15 million of revenue would increase net income by $1.0 million. For Solutions Network, the revenue from the transaction would be enough to enable the company to meet targeted goals, and the higher level of income would provide extra bonus money at year-end for Young, Henley, and Ed Fralen, the CEO.

Accounting Considerations

In her discussions with Henley, Young points out that the auditors will arrive on January 15, 2016; therefore, the company should be certain of the appropriateness of its accounting before that time. After all, says Sarah, "the auditors rely on us to record transactions properly as part of their audit expectations." At this point Henley reacts angrily and tells Young she can pack her bags and go if she doesn't support the company in its revenue recognition of the DSS transaction. Young is taken aback. Henley seems unusually agitated. Perhaps he was under a lot more pressure to "meet the numbers" than she anticipated. To defuse the matter, Sarah makes an excuse to end the meeting prematurely and asks if they could meet on Monday morning, after the weekend. Henley agrees.

Over the weekend, Sarah calls her best friend, Shannon McCollough, for advice. Shannon is a controller at another company and Sarah would often commensurate with Shannon over their mutual experiences. Shannon suggests that Sarah should explain to Paul exactly what her ethical obligations are in the matter. Shannon thinks it might make a difference because Paul is a CPA as well.

After the discussion with Shannon, Sarah considers whether she is being too firm in her position. On the one hand, she knows that regardless of the passage of title to DSS on December 31, 2015, the transaction is linked to Solutions Network's agreement to take the DSS product 30 days later. While she doesn't anticipate any problems in that regard, Sarah is uncomfortable with the recording of revenue on December 31 because DSS did not complete its portion of the agreement by that date. She has her doubts whether the auditors would sanction the accounting treatment.

On the other hand, Sarah is also concerned about the fact that another transaction occurred during the previous year that she questioned but, in the end, went along with Paul's accounting for this transaction. On December 28, 2014, Solutions Network sold a major system for $20 million to Laramie Systems but executed a side agreement with Laramie on that date which gave Laramie the right to return the product for any reason for 30 days. Even though Solutions Network recorded the revenue in 2014 and Sarah felt uneasy about it, she did not object because Laramie did not return the product; her acceptance was motivated by the delay in the external audit until after the 30-day period had expired. Now, however, Sarah is concerned that a pattern may be developing.

Questions

1. What are the main arguments Sarah is trying to counter? That is, what are the reasons and rationalizations she needs to address in deciding how to handle the meeting with Paul?

2. What is at stake for the key parties in this case? What are Sarah's ethical obligations to them?

3. Should Sarah follow Shannon's advice? What if she does and Paul does not back off? What additional levers can she use to influence Paul and make her values understood?

4. What is the most powerful and persuasive response to the reasons and rationalizations Sarah needs to address? To whom should the argument be made? When and in what context?

Case 7-3 GE: "Imagination at Work"

Back on January 16, 2003, after more than 23 years, General Electric (GE) Co. decided to dump its well-recognized slogan, "We Bring Good Things to Life," and decided to spend more than $100 million to launch a new campaign with the tagline, "Imagination at Work." A reasonable question is whether GE took its new slogan too seriously because the transactions it engaged in certainly relied on imagining the results of operations it desired and developing the techniques to accomplish that goal.

On August 9, 2009, GE came clean and settled accounting fraud charges with the SEC for allegedly misleading investors with improper hedge accounting and revenue recognition schemes. Specifically, GE was charged with violating accounting rules when it changed its original hedge documentation to avoid recording fluctuations in the fair value of interest rates swaps, which would have dragged down the company's reported earnings-per-share estimates.

In addition, the SEC charged GE with making up schemes to accelerate the recognition of revenue from its locomotive and aircraft spare parts business, to make the company's financial results appear healthier than they actually were.

Without admitting or denying guilt, GE paid a fine of $50 million, and agreed to remedial action related to internal control enhancements. "GE bent the accounting rules beyond the breaking point," noted Robert Khuzami, director of the SEC's Division of Enforcement, in a statement. The facts of the case are taken from the complaint filed by the SEC against GE.[1]

The SEC uncovered the violations after conducting "risk-based" investigations at GE, in which the government

---

[1] David Henry, "SEC Fines GE $50 Million for Accounting Misdeeds," August 4, 2009, Available at: http://www.businessweek.com/bwdaily/dnflash/content/aug2009/db2009084_567813.htm.

staffers identify a potential risk in an industry or at a particular company and develop a plan to test whether the problem actually exists. In the case of GE, the SEC identified potential misuse of hedge accounting as a possible risk area.

The SEC filed its complaint in the U.S. District Court for the District of Connecticut pointing out that GE met or exceeded analysts' consensus earnings-per-share expectations every quarter from 1995 through filing of its 2004 annual report. However, the SEC charged that during 2002 and 2003, high-level GE accounting executives or other finance personnel approved accounting that did not comply with GAAP in order to hit the EPS estimates.[2]

The complaint filed by the SEC provides details of the accounting treatments GE tried to pass off as GAAP compliant. For instance, during the periods under investigation, GE issued commercial paper to fund assets that had fixed, long-term interest rates. Because the rolling commercial paper program exposed GE to fluctuations in variable, short-term interest rates, the company sought to hedge its exposure with interest rate swaps. GE was intent on qualifying for hedge accounting, which is considered advantageous because gains and losses on derivatives—in this case the swaps—can be deferred until they mature.

But in early 2003, GE changed its hedge accounting to accomplish two goals: to avoid reporting a disclosure that might have led to the loss of hedge accounting for its entire commercial paper program, and avoid recording what GE estimated to be an approximately $200 million pretax charge to earnings.

According to court documents, days before GE's quarterly results were to be released in 2003, the company developed an entirely new approach that, when applied retroactively to transactions that occurred months before, allowed GE to obtain the desired accounting results. The new approach violated GAAP. As a result, GE overstated earnings in the fourth quarter of 2002 by more than 5 percent, and thereby met its revised consensus EPS estimates.

In the revenue recognition schemes, GE enlisted the use of a middleman to allow GE to record revenue before products were sold to the end user, according to the complaint. In the fourth quarters of 2002 and 2003, GE "improperly" booked revenue of $223 million and $158 million, respectively, for six locomotives reportedly sold to financial institutions, "with the understanding that the financial institutions would resell the locomotives to GE's railroad customers in the first quarters of the subsequent fiscal years."

The idea was that GE could book the sales made to the financial institution in the current year, while it allowed its railroad customers to purchase the locomotives at their convenience sometime in the future.

In the case of the locomotives, the SEC said it found that in 2002 and again in 2003 managers had created ways to book sales before the end of December even though their customers were unwilling to buy the equipment until the new calendar year was under way. Each time GE managers arranged so-called "bridge financing" transactions in which financial firms agreed to purportedly "purchase" the locomotives and then resell them to GE's customers in the next quarter.

In December 2002, GE stored the locomotives and kept them fueled and idling to protect them against the cold. In one case, GE went so far as to promise a customer that it would cover as much as $4 million of tax liabilities that might result from using the financial intermediary. The 2002 transactions covered 131 of the 191 locomotives GE originally said it sold in that fourth quarter and overstated the business unit's revenues and profits by more than 39 percent. The next year, managers used essentially the same scheme, overstating the unit's revenues and profits by more than 16 percent.

That was not the case with the interest-rate derivatives. The SEC's complaint describes internal e-mails in which a GE accountant worried about the "extraordinarily big deal" of possibly losing the right to use a loophole that sometimes allows companies to ignore losses in the fair value of assets. "We've got to fix this," the accountant declared. The problem stemmed from the fact that GE had effectively made bets on interest rates by writing more derivatives contracts than it needed to fix its interest expense from borrowing at floating rates. To remedy the accounting problem, a plan was proposed to retroactively change how the company accounted for derivatives.

When auditors said no, GE personnel altered the plan and then held a meeting, complete with a PowerPoint presentation reviewing the risks they were taking. They went ahead with the retroactive change, which allowed GE

---

[2] *Securities and Exchange Commission v. General Electric Company*, U.S. District Court District of Columbia, Available at: https://www.sec.gov/litigation/complaints/2009/comp21166.pdf.

to avoid reporting a $200 million pretax charge that would have caused it to miss its expected earnings by 1.5¢ in the final quarter of 2002.

Questions

1. Review the SEC's complaint against GE (see Note 1) and explain the specifics of the company's hedging transactions and why they violated GAAP.

2. Did GE violate the rules for revenue recognition (pre-2016-change) on the "sale" of its locomotives? Explain.

3. Did GE engage in earnings management? How would you make that determination given the facts of the case?

Case 7-4 Harrison Industries (a GVV case)

It's no fun accepting a position for your dream job and then red flags are raised that make you wonder about the culture of the company. Those are the thoughts of Donna Mason on January 18, 2016, as she prepares for a meeting with her accounting supervisor, Cheryl Miles. Mason graduated summa cum laude from State University six months ago. She is working as a staff accountant at Harrison Industries in Provo, Utah. Mason is one of three staff accountants. She reports to Cheryl Miles who, in turn, reports to Kelly Lang, the chief accounting officer. Lang reports to the CEO, Ken Harrison, and the third generation of owner-CEOs of the privately held company. Harrison is also the chair of the board of directors, which has five of nine independent members.

Mason's concern is that on January 15, 2016, she was approached by Miles and told to record an accrual for unpaid severance payments of $5 million to be included in the December 31, 2015, financial statements. Mason expressed her concern at the time because it was an unusually high amount. Miles informed Mason that the company planned to shut down the home appliance division in 2016 and the severance payments would be significant. This was the first Mason heard about a shutdown of any division, and she found it strange because the company's operating income in all divisions had set record levels in fiscal year 2015. Moreover, the severance amounts are five times the annual payroll of the division.

The numbers below show the operating income levels and accruals for 2013 through 2015:

	12/31/2013	12/31/2014	12/31/2015
Operating Income	$10 million	$12 million	$20 million (pre-adjusting entries)
Accrued bonus and severance	$ 1 million	$ 1.2 million	???

Mason took a firm stance at first and told Miles she needed some documentation to record the accrued severance liability. Miles instructed Mason to record the entry, that it wasn't her job to question orders. Miles made it clear in no uncertain terms that questioning directions from one's supervisor was a basis for termination. This occurred on January 15, 2016.

Mason knew she had three days before the next meeting with Miles to consider her options. The first step she took was to contact her mentor, Steve Hahn, who explained the culture of the company is to go along to get along. Hahn quickly added that it was a rare occurrence for an employee to be asked to go along with something not right, so he advised Mason to do what Miles had asked. He seemed to be saying that if Miles asked her to record the severance payments, then it must be supportable.

Mason did a lot of independent checking of the company's computer files between January 15 and January 18, 2016, and found no evidence of a planned shutdown of the division. In fact, the division's income had risen on average by 5 percent a year for three straight years. The income level for 2015 was the highest—8 percent. It exceeded projections by 3 percent.

Mason is trying to build a strategy to convince Miles of why the severance accrual is not justified. She realizes that Miles could be under orders from Kelly Lang and/or Ken Harrison. She wonders whether it would be wise to approach them about her concerns. After all, they interviewed Mason for the accounting position and ultimately made the decision to offer her the job. Mason felt good about working for them and Harrison Industries because organizational values and ethics were high, as is Mason's.

Questions

1. What are the real and anticipated arguments that could be made by those at Harrison Industries who may try to convince Donna to go along with the accounting for future severance payments? Include in your discussion the possible motivation for the accounting treatment.

2. What is at stake for the key parties? What are Donna's ethical obligations to them?

3. What is Donna's most powerful and persuasive response to the reasons and rationalizations she needs to address? To whom should the argument be made?

4. What is Donna's most effective approach to giving voice to her values? Explain.

Case 7-5 Dell Computer

Background

For years, Dell's seemingly magical power to squeeze efficiencies out of its supply chain and drive down costs made it a darling of the financial markets. Now we learn that the magic was at least partly the result of a huge financial illusion. On July 22, 2010, Dell agreed to pay a $100 million penalty to settle allegations by the SEC that the company had "manipulated its accounting over an extended period to project financial results that the company wished it had achieved."

According to the commission, Dell would have missed analysts' earnings expectations in every quarter between 2002 and 2006 were it not for its accounting shenanigans. This involved a deal with Intel, a big microchip maker, under which Dell agreed to use Intel's central processing unit chips exclusively in its computers in return for a series of undisclosed payments, locking out Advanced Micro Devices (AMD), a big rival. The SEC's complaint said that Dell had maintained cookie-jar reserves using Intel's money that it could dip into to cover any shortfalls in its operating results.

The SEC said that the company should have disclosed to investors that it was drawing on these reserves, but it did not. And it claimed that, at their peak, the exclusivity payments from Intel represented 76 percent of Dell's quarterly operating income, which is a shocking figure. The problem arose when Dell's quarterly earnings fell sharply in 2007 after it ended the arrangement with Intel. The SEC alleged that Dell attributed the drop to an aggressive product-pricing strategy and higher-than-expected component prices, when the real reason was that the payments from Intel had dried up.

The accounting fraud embarrassed the once-squeaky-clean Michael Dell, the firm's founder and CEO. He and Kevin Rollins, a former top official of the company, agreed to each pay a $4 million penalty without admitting or denying the SEC's allegations. Several senior financial executives at Dell also incurred penalties. "Accuracy and completeness are the touchstones of public company disclosure under the federal securities laws," said Robert Khuzami of the SEC's enforcement division when announcing the settlement deal. "Michael Dell and other senior Dell executives fell short of that standard repeatedly over many years."

In its statement on the SEC settlement the company played down Michael Dell's personal involvement, saying that his $4 million penalty was not connected to the accounting fraud charges being settled by the company, but was "limited to claims in which only negligence, and not fraudulent intent, is required to establish liability, as well as secondary liability claims for other non-fraud charges."[1]

---

[1] Facts of the case are available at http://www.economist.com/blogs/newsbook/2010/07/dells_sec_settlement.

Accounting Irregularities

The SEC charged Dell Computer with fraud for materially misstating its operating results from FY2002 to FY2005. In addition to Dell and Rollins, the SEC also charged former Dell chief accounting officer (CAO) Robert W. Davis for his role in the company's accounting fraud. The SEC's complaint against Davis alleged that he materially misrepresented Dell's financial results by using various cookie-jar reserves to cover shortfalls in operating results and engaged in other reserve manipulations from FY2002 to FY2005, including improper recording of large payments from Intel as operating expense-offsets. This fraudulent accounting made it appear that Dell was consistently meeting Wall Street earnings targets (i.e., net operating income) through the company's management and operations. The SEC's complaint further alleged that the reserve manipulations allowed Dell to misstate materially its operating expenses as a percentage of revenue—an important financial metric that Dell highlighted to investors.[2]

The company engaged in the questionable use of reserve accounts to smooth net income. Davis directed Dell assistant controller Randall D. Imhoff and his subordinates, when they identified reserved amounts that were no longer needed for bona fide liabilities, to check with him about what to do with the excess reserves instead of just releasing them to the income statement. In many cases, he ordered his team to transfer the amounts to an "other accrued liabilities" account. According to the SEC, "Davis viewed the 'Corporate Contingencies' as a way to offset future liabilities. He substantially participated in the 'earmarking' of the excess accruals for various purposes."

Beginning in the 1990s, Intel had a marketing campaign that paid its vendors certain marketing rebates to use their products according to a written contract. These were known as market developing funds (MDFs), which according to accounting rules, Dell could treat as reductions in operating expenses because these payments offset expenses that Dell incurred in marketing Intel's products. However, the character of these payments changed in 2001, when Intel began to provide additional rebates to Dell and a few other companies that were outside the contractual agreements.

Intel made these large payments to Dell from 2001 to 2006 to refrain from using chips or processors manufactured by Intel's main rival, AMD. Rather than disclosing these material payments to investors, Dell decided that it would be better to incorporate these funds into their component costs without any recognition of their existence. The nondisclosure of these payments caused fraudulent misrepresentation, allowing Dell to report increased profitability over these years.

These payments grew significantly over the years making up a rather large part of Dell's operating income. When viewed as a percentage of operating income, these payments started at about 10 percent in FY2003 and increased to about 76 percent in the first quarter of FY2007.

When Dell began using AMD as a secondary supplier of chips in 2006, Intel cut the exclusivity payments off, which resulted in Dell having to report a decrease in profits. Rather than disclose the loss of the exclusivity payments as the reason for the decrease in profitability, Dell continued to mislead investors.

Dell's Internal Investigation

On August 16, 2007, Dell announced it had completed an internal investigation, which had revealed a variety of accounting errors and irregularities, and that it would restate results for FY2003 through FY2006, and the first quarter of 2007. The restatement cited certain accounting errors and irregularities in those financial statements as the reasons the previously issued statements should no longer be relied upon.

Dell said that the investigation of accounting issues found that executives wrongfully manipulated accruals and account balances, often to meet Wall Street quarterly financial expectations in prior years. The company was forced to restate its earnings during that time period, which lowered its total earnings during that time by $50 million to $150 million.

---

[2]Securities and Exchange Commission, *Securities and Exchange Commission v. Robert W. Davis* , Civil Action No. 1:10-cv-01464 (D.D.C.) and *Securities and Exchange Commission v. Randall D. Imhoff*, Civil Action No. 1:10-cv-01465 (D.D.C.), *Accounting and Auditing Enforcement Release No. 3177 /* August 27, 2010. Available at: www.sec.gov/litigation /litreleases/2010/lr21634 .htm.

As result of the SEC's investigation, Dell took another hit to its bottom line. With the restatement, Dell's first quarter 2011 earnings looked like this: net income of $341 million and earnings of 17¢ per share. That's instead of the initially reported $441 million and 22¢ per share.

PriceWaterhouseCoopers (PwC)

PwC had been Dell's independent auditor since 1986 and had signed off on every one of Dell's financial statements that were on file with the SEC. From 2003 to 2007, Dell paid PwC more than $50 million to perform auditing and other services. PwC issued clean (unmodified) audit opinions for the 2003 to 2006 financial statements, saying that they fairly represented the financial position of Dell.

It was alleged that PwC had consistently approved the now-restated financial statements as prepared in accordance with generally accepted accounting principles and did not conduct an audit in accordance with generally accepted auditing standards. The argument was that the opinions that the financial statements fairly represented financial position were materially false and misleading. The court ruled that the restatement does not by itself satisfy the scienter (knowledge of the falsehood) requirement to hold the auditors legally liable for deliberate misrepresentation of material facts or actions taken with severe recklessness as to the accuracy of its audits or reports.

The legal standard for auditor liability under Section 10(b) of the Securities Exchange Act of 1934 and Rule 10b-5 requires that the plaintiff must show (1) a misstatement or omission, (2) of a material fact, (3) made with scienter, (4) on which the plaintiff relied, and (5) that proximately caused the injury. The court pointed out in its opinion that "the mere publication of inaccurate accounting figures, or failure to follow GAAP, without more, does not establish scienter." To establish scienter adequately, the plaintiffs must state with particularity facts giving rise to a strong inference that the party knew that it was publishing materially false information, or that it was severely reckless in publishing such information. The court ruled that the plaintiffs did not prove fraudulent intent.[3]

In a suit by shareholders against the firm, PwC was accused of a variety of charges, including not being truly independent and ignoring red flags. These charges were dismissed on a basis of lack of evidence to support the accusations.

Questions

1. How would you characterize Dell's accounting techniques described in the case? Was it a case of aggressive accounting? Was it earnings management? Link your discussion to the specific accounting methodology and GAAP rules.

2. Identify the red flags that should have alerted PwC that Dell may have been engaging in fraud. Given that Dell issued clean opinions during the fraud years, do you think it is possible that the firm conducted its audit in accordance with GAAS? What indicators would you look for to make that determination?

3. The court decision relied on the concept of scienter for not holding PwC legally liable for issuing clean opinions when the financial statements did not fairly present financial position. Would you reach the same conclusion from an ethical perspective? Explain.

---

[3] *In re Dell Inc., Securities Litigation, U.S. District Court for the Western District of Texas Austin Division*, Case No. A-06-CA-726-55, October 6, 2008, Available at: http://securities.stanford.edu/filings-documents/1036/DELL_01/2008107_r01o_0600726.pdf.

Case 7-6 TierOne Bank

It took a long time but the Securities and Exchange Commission finally acted and held auditors responsible for the fraud that occurred in banks during the financial recession. Surprisingly to some, the TierOne bank case explained below was the nation's first case brought by federal securities regulators against auditors of a company that went down in the multibillion-dollar financial crisis and real estate meltdown. Federal banking authorities had brought a handful of cases against auditors, but the SEC hadn't brought one until TierOne.

TierOne Corporation, a holding company for TierOne Bank, had $3 billion in assets when it collapsed in 2010. The facts of the case are drawn from the initial decision reached by the SEC, *In the Matter of John J. Aesoph, CPA, and Darren M. Bennett, CPA,* unless otherwise noted.[1]

TierOne was a regional bank headquartered in Lincoln, Nebraska, that originated and purchased loans, and loan participation interests, with its primary market area in Nebraska, Iowa, and Kansas. From 2002 to 2005, TierOne opened or acquired nine loan production offices (LPO) in Arizona, Colorado, Florida, Minnesota, Nevada, and North Carolina, the main purpose of which was to originate construction and land-development loans. Over time, TierOne increased its portfolio in these high-risk loans. By September 2008, TierOne closed the LPOs, in the wake of real estate market deterioration. By year-end 2008, TierOne had a total net loan portfolio of approximately $2.8 billion, with a quarter of its loans concentrated in the LPO states. In October 2008, TierOne's regulator, the Office of Thrift Supervision (OTS), issued a report following its June 2008 examination of the bank, in which it downgraded TierOne's bank rating; criticized management and loan practices; and found that the bank had collateral-dependent loans either without appraisals or with unsupported or stale appraisals. The bank was closed by OTS in 2010. TierOne Corp. filed for bankruptcy three weeks later.

Cast of Characters

According to the agreement reached on June 27, 2014, the SEC sanctioned KPMG auditors John J. Aesoph and Darren M. Bennett, in connection with their roles as engagement partner and manager of the audit of the 2008 financial statements of TierOne. The SEC found that the pair failed to identify "material weakness" in TierOne's financial reporting. Given the findings of the SEC, it is somewhat surprising that the only penalty was for the two auditors to be prohibited from practicing before the SEC for one year and for six months, respectively.

According to the SEC, Aesoph and Bennett "rubber stamped" in their auditing of TierOne's accounts. This made it impossible to detect the deliberate understatement of the bank's reported losses on loans to real estate developers and construction companies. That information misled TierOne's stock investors, who relied on the audited data. Hence, the SEC brought action against the auditors.

Aesoph and Bennett were charged with improper professional conduct in connection with the December 31, 2008, year-end audit of TierOne's financial statements. They failed to comply with Public Company Accounting Oversight Board (PCAOB) auditing standards because they failed to subject TierOne's loan loss estimates—one of the highest risk areas of a bank audit—to appropriate scrutiny. The SEC also said the pair "failed to obtain sufficient competent evidential matter to support their audit conclusions, and failed to exercise due professional care and appropriate professional skepticism."

The SEC alleged in the indictment that TierOne's executives hid loan losses as OTS repeatedly requested information. On December 10, 2014, Gilbert Lundstrom, the former chief executive officer of TierOne, was indicted for hiding the condition of the bank from regulators, investors, and auditors. Allegedly, Lundstrom conspired with others to hide the bank's problems as losses mounted on its loan portfolio. "Lundstrom is essentially charged with having two sets of books, with the books shown to regulators concealing tens of millions of dollars in delinquent loans," said Christy L. Romero, special inspector general for the U.S. Troubled Asset Relief Program, established during the financial meltdown.[2]

---

[1]SEC, *In the Matter of John J. Aesoph, CPA, and Darren M. Bennett, CPA,* Initial Decision Release No. Administrative Proceeding File No. 3-151658, Available at: https://www.sec.gov/alj/aljdec/2014/id624cff.pdf.

[2]SEC, *U.S. v. Lundstrom,* 14-cr-03136, U.S. District Court, District of Nebraska (Lincoln), Available at: http://www.justice.gov/criminal-vns/case/lundstromg.

The trigger for the fraudulent activities by TierOne management was that TierOne's core capital ratio had fallen below the 8.5 percent minimum threshold mandated by the OTS. Lundstrom and others caused the bank to issue false statements that it met or exceeded the ratio.

Lundstrom knew that the bank needed to increase its reserves to cover loan losses and didn't report this, according to the indictment. Lundstrom in 2012 settled a lawsuit brought by the SEC claiming he understated TierOne's loan losses and losses on real estate repossessed by the bank so that the bank would appear to meet its mandated regulatory capital requirements. Lundstrom, who didn't admit the allegations when settling, agreed to pay $500,921 in penalties.

Another former TierOne executive, Don Langford, the bank's chief credit officer, pleaded guilty for his role in what prosecutors called a scheme to defraud shareholders and regulators. Langford played a major role in developing an internal estimate of losses embedded in TierOne's loan portfolio, but did not disclose that estimate to auditors or regulators. Langford's initial analysis indicated the bank needed an additional $65 million in loan loss reserves; a refined analysis, entitled the "Best/Worst Case Scenario," showed losses ranging from a "best case" of $36 million to a "worst case" of $114 million. Langford did not share any of this analysis with the bank's accounting staff or external auditors. KPMG resigned when it learned the analysis had been withheld.

As the value of properties declined and defaults increased during 2008 and 2009, Lundstrom and others directed TierOne employees to forgo ordering new appraisals even when the old ones were stale or no longer accurate. In some cases, when appraisals were made and came in at lower values than recorded by TierOne, the new appraisals were rejected, at the direction of Lundstrom and other bank executives. They also restructured loan terms to disguise the borrowers' inability to make timely interest and principal payments. As a result, Lundstrom and others were allegedly able to hide millions of dollars in losses from regulators and investors.

KPMG

KPMG LLP (KPMG) audited TierOne's 2008 financial statements. In March 2009, KPMG issued an unqualified audit opinion on TierOne's consolidated financial statements and effectiveness of its internal controls over financial reporting as of year-end 2008; certified that the audit was conducted in accordance with PCAOB standards that required KPMG to plan and perform the audit to obtain reasonable assurance whether the financial statements were free of material misstatement; and opined that the financial statements reflected in TierOne's year-end 2008 Form 10-K presented fairly, in all material respects, the financial position of TierOne and the results of its operations and cash flows, in conformity with U.S. Generally Accepted Accounting Principles (GAAP).

Subsequently, TierOne recorded $120 million in losses relating to its loan portfolio after obtaining updated appraisals. In April 2010, when KPMG learned that TierOne had failed to disclose the document created by Langford showing an internal analysis of varying estimates of additional loan loss reserves higher than what had been disclosed during the audit, the firm resigned and withdrew its audit opinion. Citing risk of material misstatement, KPMG had also warned the audit committee that TierOne's financials were not to be relied upon by investors. The two items cited in the report to the audit committee were: (1) TierOne's year-end 2008 financial statements contained "material misstatements related to certain out-of-period adjustments for loan loss reserves," and (2) TierOne's internal controls could not be relied on "due to a material weakness in internal control over financial reporting related to the material misstatements."

According to the SEC's order instituting administrative proceedings against Aesoph and Bennett, the auditors failed to comply with professional auditing standards in their substantive audit procedures over the bank's valuation of loan losses resulting from impaired loans. They relied principally on stale appraisals and management's uncorroborated representations of current value despite evidence that management's estimates were biased and inconsistent with independent market data. Aesoph and Bennett failed to exercise the appropriate professional skepticism and obtain sufficient evidence that management's collateral value and loan loss estimates were reasonable.[3]

---

[3] "SEC Charges Two KPMG Auditors for Failed Audit of Nebraska Bank Hiding Loan Losses During Financial Crisis," Available at: http://www.sec.gov/News/PressRelease/Detail/PressRelease/1365171513624.

As for the internal controls, the SEC said that the controls over the allowance for loans and lease losses identified and tested by the auditing engagement team did not effectively test management's use of stale and inadequate appraisals to value the collateral underlying the bank's troubled loan portfolio. For example, the auditors identified TierOne's Asset Classification Committee as a key control. But there was no reference in the audit workpapers to whether or how the committee assessed the value of the collateral underlying individual loans evaluated for impairment, and the committee did not generate or review written documentation to support management's assumptions. Given the complete lack of documentation, Aesoph and Bennett had insufficient evidence from which to conclude that the bank's internal controls for valuation of collateral were effective. Robert Khuzami, director of the SEC's Division of Enforcement, said, "Aesoph and Bennett merely rubber-stamped TierOne's collateral value estimates and ignored the red flags surrounding the bank's troubled real estate loans."[4]

In his defense, Bennett contended that the SEC's interpretations of accounting principles and auditing standards contravened accepted interpretations within the profession, and a Rule 102(e) finding based on the Division of Enforcement's "novel interpretations" would amount to impermissible rulemaking by enforcement, violating his due process rights by depriving him of notice of the standards against which his professional conduct was to be judged. He stated that the SEC suggested in its closing argument that "fair value" measurements ought not to exclude the impact of disorderly sales in times of economic turmoil, which he argued contravened *Statement of Financial Accounting Standards (SFAS) 157.*

Additionally, Bennett took issue with statements made by the SEC that, he claimed, suggested that the auditors should be responsible for "auditing" each of TierOne's loan loss reserve estimates, whereas under PCAOB standards "[t]he auditor is responsible for evaluating the reasonableness of accounting estimates made by management in the context of the financial statements taken as a whole." The SEC, however, contended that in order to evaluate the reasonableness of the estimates in the context of the financial statements taken as whole, they were required to evaluate those estimates on a loan-by-loan basis.

Questions

1. Was TierOne's accounting for the loan loss reserve indicative of "managed earnings?" How would you make that determination?

2. What role does professional judgment have in auditing the adequacy of a loan loss reserve? Do you believe KPMG exercised a degree of care and professional skepticism that is consistent with the level of ethical and professional judgment expected by the accounting profession? What about the public?

3. Given the facts of the case with respect to audit work performed by Aesoph and. Bennett, do you believe the sanctions imposed by the SEC were appropriate? Explain.

Case 7-7 Sunbeam Corporation

One of the earliest frauds during the late 1990s and early 2000s was at Sunbeam. The SEC alleged in its charges against Sunbeam that top management engaged in a scheme to fraudulently misrepresent Sunbeam's operating results in connection with a purported "turnaround" of the company. When Sunbeam's turnaround was exposed as a sham, the stock price plummeted, causing investors billions of dollars in losses. The defendants in the action included Sunbeam's former CEO and chair Albert J. Dunlap, former principal financial officer Russell A. Kersh, former controller Robert J. Gluck, former vice presidents Donald R. Uzzi and Lee B. Griffith, and Arthur Andersen LLP partner Phillip Harlow.

The SEC complaint described several questionable management decisions and fraudulent actions that led to the manipulation of financial statement amounts in the company's 1996 year-end results, quarterly and year-end 1997

[4]SEC, "SEC Charges two KPMG Auditors for Failed Audit of Nebraska Bank Hiding Loan Losses During Financial Crisis," Available at: http://www.sec.gov/News/PressRelease/Detail/PressRelease/1365171513624.

results, and the first quarter of 1998. The fraud was enabled by weak or nonexistent internal controls, inadequate or nonexistent board of directors and audit committee oversight, and the failure of the Andersen auditor to follow GAAS. The following is an excerpt from the SEC's *AAER 1393,* issued on May 15, 2001:

> From the last quarter of 1996 until June 1998, Sunbeam Corporation's senior management created the illusion of a successful restructuring of Sunbeam in order to inflate its stock price and thus improve its value as an acquisition target. To this end, management employed numerous improper earnings management techniques to falsify the Company's results and conceal its deteriorating financial condition. Specifically, senior management created $35 million in improper restructuring reserves and other "cookie-jar" reserves as part of a year-end 1996 restructuring, which were reversed into income the following year. Also in 1997, Sunbeam's management engaged in guaranteed sales, improper "bill-and-hold" sales, and other fraudulent practices. At year-end 1997, at least $62 million of Sunbeam's reported income of $189 million came from accounting fraud. The undisclosed or inadequately disclosed acceleration of sales through "channel-stuffing" also materially distorted the Company's reported results of operations and contributed to the inaccurate picture of a successful turnaround.[1]

A brief summary of the case follows.[2]

Chainsaw Al

Al Dunlap, a turnaround specialist who had gained the nickname "Chainsaw Al" for his reputation of cutting companies to the bone, was hired by Sunbeam's board in July 1996 to restructure the financially ailing company. He promised a rapid turnaround, thereby raising expectations in the marketplace. The fraudulent actions helped raise the market price to a high of $52 in 1997. Following the disclosure of the fraud in the first quarter of 1998, the price of Sunbeam shares dropped by 25 percent, to $34.63. The price continued to decline as the board of directors investigated the fraud and fired Dunlap and the CFO. An extensive restatement of earnings from the fourth quarter of 1996 through the first quarter of 1998 eliminated half of the reported 1997 profits. On February 6, 2001, Sunbeam filed for Chapter 11 bankruptcy protection in U.S. Bankruptcy Court.

Accounting Issues

Cookie-Jar Reserves

The illegal conduct began in late 1996, with the creation of cookie-jar reserves that were used to inflate income in 1997. Sunbeam then engaged in fraudulent revenue transactions that inflated the company's record-setting earnings of $189 million by at least $60 million in 1997. The transactions were designed to create the impression that Sunbeam was experiencing significant revenue growth, thereby further misleading the investors and financial markets.

Sunbeam took a total restructuring charge of $337.6 million at year-end 1996.[3] However, management padded this charge with at least $35 million in improper restructuring and other reserves and accruals,[4] excessive write-downs, and prematurely recognized expenses that materially distorted the Company's reported results of operations for fiscal year 1996, and would materially distort its reported results of operations in all quarters of fiscal year 1997, as these improper reserves were drawn into income.

---

[1]SEC, *In the Matter of Sunbeam Corporation, Respondent, Accounting and Auditing Enforcement Release No. 1393,* May 15, 2001, Available at www.sec.gov/litigation/admin/33-7976.htm.

[2]SEC, Litigation Release 17001, *Securities and Exchange Commission v. Albert J. Dunlap, Russell A. Kersh, Robert J. Gluck, Donald R. Uzzi, Lee B. Griffith, and Phillip E. Harlow,* 01-8437-CIV-Dimitrouleas (S.D. Fla., May 15, 2001), Available at: www.sec.gov/litigation/litreleases/lr17001.htm.

[3]Unless otherwise indicated, numbers are given as approximations. "Income" refers to earnings from continuing operations before income taxes.

[4]"Big-bath" restructuring charges may provide a method for companies to manage earnings in later periods when excess reserves are taken into income.

The most substantial contribution to Sunbeam's improper reserves came from $18.7 million in 1996 restructuring costs that management knew or was reckless in not knowing were not in conformity with generally accepted accounting principles. Sunbeam also created a $12 million litigation reserve against its potential liability for an environmental remediation. However, this reserve amount was not established in conformity with GAAP and improperly overstated Sunbeam's probable liability in that matter by at least $6 million.

Channel Stuffing

Eager to extend the selling season for its gas grills and to boost sales in 1996, CEO Dunlap's "turnaround year," the company tried to convince retailers to buy grills nearly six months before they were needed, in exchange for major discounts. Retailers agreed to purchase merchandise that they would not receive physically until six months after billing. In the meantime, the goods were shipped to a third-party warehouse and held there until the customers requested them. These bill-and-hold transactions led to recording $35 million in revenue too soon. However, the auditors (Andersen) reviewed the documents and reversed $29 million.

In 1997, the company failed to disclose that Sunbeam's 1997 revenue growth was partly achieved at the expense of future results. The company had offered discounts and other inducements to customers to sell merchandise immediately that otherwise would have been sold in later periods, a practice referred to as "channel stuffing." The resulting revenue shift threatened to suppress Sunbeam's future results of operations.

Sunbeam either didn't realize or totally ignored the fact that, by stuffing the channels with product to make one year look better, the company had to continue to find outlets for their product in advance of when it was desired by customers. In other words, it created a balloon effect, in that the same amount or more accelerated amount of revenue was needed year after year. Ultimately, Sunbeam (and its customers) just couldn't keep up, and there was no way to fix the numbers.

Sunbeam's Shenanigans

Exhibit 1 presents an analysis of Sunbeam's accounting with respect to Schilit's financial shenanigans.

EXHIBIT 1   Sunbeam Corporation's Aggressive Accounting Techniques

Technique	Example	Shenanigan Number
Recorded bogus revenue	Bill-and-hold sales	2
Released questionable reserves into income	Cookie-jar reserves	5
Inflated special charges	Litigation reserve	7

Red Flags

Schilit points to several red flags that existed at Sunbeam but either went undetected or were ignored by Andersen, including the following:[5]

1. *Excessive charges recorded shortly after Dunlap arrived.* The theory is that an incoming CEO will create cookie-jar reserves by overstating expenses, even though it reduces earnings for the first year, based on the belief that increases in future earnings through the release of the reserves or other techniques make it appear that the CEO has turned the company around, as evidenced by turning losses into profits. Some companies might take it to an extreme and pile on losses by creating reserves in a loss year, believing that it doesn't matter whether you show a $1.2 million loss for the year or a $1.8 million loss ($0.6 million reserve). This is known as "big-bath accounting."

---

[5]Howard M. Schilit, *Financial Shenanigans: How to Detect Accounting Gimmicks and Fraud in Financial Reports,* 2nd ed. (New York: McGraw-Hill, 2002).

2. *Reserve amounts reduced after initial overstatement.* Fluctuations in the reserve amount should have raised a red flag because they evidenced earnings management as initially record reserves were restored into net income.

3. *Receivables grew much faster than sales.* A simple ratio of the increase in receivables to the increase in revenues should have provided another warning signal. Schilit provides the following for Sunbeam's operational performance in Exhibit 2 that should have created doubts in the minds of the auditors about the accuracy of reported revenue amounts in relation to the collectibility of receivables, as indicated by the significantly larger percentage increase in receivables compared to revenues.

EXHIBIT 2   Sunbeam Corporation's Operational Performance

	Operational Performance		
	9 months 9/97 ($ in millions)	9 months 9/96 ($ in millions)	% Change
Revenue	$830.1	$715.4	16%
Gross profit	231.1	123.1	86%
Operating revenue	132.6	4.0	3,215%
Receivables	309.1	194.6	59%
Inventory	290.9	330.2	12%
Cash flow from operations	(60.8)	(18.8)	N/A

4. *Accrual earnings increased much faster than cash from operating activities.* While Sunbeam made $189 million in 1997, its cash flow from operating activities was a negative $60.8 million. This is a $250 million difference that should raise a red flag, even under a cursory analytical review about the quality of recorded receivables. Accrual earnings and cash flow from operating activity amounts are not expected to be equal, but the differential in these amounts at Sunbeam seems to defy logic. Financial analysts tend to rely on the cash figure because of the inherent unreliability of the estimates and judgments that go into determining accrual earnings.

Quality of Earnings

No one transaction more than the following illustrates questions about the quality of earnings at Sunbeam. Sunbeam owned a lot of spare parts that were used to fix its blenders and grills when they broke. Those parts were stored in the warehouse of a company called EPI Printers, which sent the parts out as needed. To inflate profits, Sunbeam approached EPI at the end of December 1997, to sell it parts for $11 million (and book a $5 million profit). EPI balked, stating that the parts were worth only $2 million, but Sunbeam found a way around that. EPI was persuaded to sign an "agreement to agree" to buy the parts for $11 million, with a clause letting EPI walk away in January 1998. In fact, the parts were never sold, but the profit was posted anyway.

Along came Phillip E. Harlow, the Arthur Andersen managing partner in charge of the Sunbeam audit. He concluded the profit was not allowed under GAAP. Sunbeam agreed to cut it by $3 million but would go no further. Harlow could have said that if such a spurious profit were included, he would not sign off on the audit. But he took a different tack. He decided that the remaining profit was not material. Since the audit opinion says the financial statements "present fairly, in all material respects" the company financial position, he could sign off on them. The part that was not presented fairly was not material. And so it did not matter.

Dunlap tries to Quiet the Markets . . . and the Board

Paine Webber, Inc., analyst Andrew Shore had been following Sunbeam since the day Dunlap was hired.[6] As an analyst, Shore's job was to make educated guesses about investing clients' money in stocks. Thus, he had been scrutinizing Sunbeam's financial statements every quarter and considered Sunbeam's reported levels of inventory for certain items to be unusual for the time of year. For example, he noted massive increases in the sales of electric blankets in the third quarter of 1997, although they usually sell well in the fourth quarter. He also observed that sales of grills were high in the fourth quarter, which is an unusual time of year for grills to be sold, and noted that accounts receivable were high. On April 3, 1998, just hours before Sunbeam announced a first-quarter loss of $44.6 million, Shore downgraded his assessment of the stock. By the end of the day, Sunbeam's stock prices had fallen 25 percent.

Dunlap continued to run Sunbeam as if nothing had happened. On May 11, 1998, he tried to reassure 200 major investors and Wall Street analysts that the first quarter loss would not be repeated and that Sunbeam would post increased earnings in the second quarter. It didn't work. The press continued to report on Sunbeams's bill-and-hold strategy and the accounting practices that Dunlap had allegedly used to artificially inflate revenues and profits.

Dunlap called an unscheduled board meeting to address the reported charges on June 9, 1998. Harlow assured the board that the company's 1997 numbers were in compliance with accounting standards and firmly stood by the firm's audit of Sunbeam's financial statements. As the meeting progressed the board directly asked Sunbeam if the company would make its projected second quarter earnings. His response that sales were soft concerned the board. A comprehensive review was ordered and eventually Dunlap was fired.

Settlement with Andersen

Harlow authorized unqualified audit opinions on Sunbeam's 1996 and 1997 financial statements although he was aware of many of the company's accounting improprieties and disclosure failures. These opinions were false and misleading in that, among other things, they incorrectly stated that Andersen had conducted an audit in accordance with generally accepted auditing standards, and that the company's financial statements fairly represented Sunbeam's results and were prepared in accordance with generally accepted accounting principles. In 2002, the SEC resolved a legal action against Andersen when a federal judge approved a $141 million settlement in the case. Andersen agreed to pay $110 million to resolve the claims without admitting fault or liability. In the end, losses to Sunbeam shareholders amounted to about $4.4 billion, with job losses of about 1,700.[7]

Questions

1. How did pressures for financial performance contribute to Sunbeam's culture, where quarterly sales were manipulated to influence investors? To what extent do you believe the Andersen auditors should have considered the resulting culture in planning and executing its audit?

2. Why is it important for auditors to use analytical comparisons such as the ratios in the Sunbeam case to evaluate possible red flags that may indicate additional auditing is required? How does making such calculations enable auditors to meet their ethical obligations?

3. Assume you were the technical advisory partner for Andersen on the Sunbeam engagement and reported directly to Harlow. You have just reviewed all the workpapers on the audit including materiality judgments. You are concerned about what you have just seen. Further assume that you consider yourself to be a pragmatist, one who is concerned with your own material welfare, but also with moral ideals. Develop a plan of action for voicing your values to ensure you are heard by Harlow and others in the firm. Consider the following in developing the plan to do the right thing:

   - What do you need to say to Harlow?
   - What are the likely objections or pushback?
   - What would you say next? To whom, and in what sequence?

---

[6] "Sunbeam Corporation: 'Chainsaw Al,' Greed, and Recovery," Available at: http://danielsethics.mgt.unm.edu /pdf/Sunbeam%20Case.pdf.

[7] *Securities and Exchange Commission v. Albert J. Dunlap et al.*

Case 7-8 Sino-Forest: Accounting for Trees

A member of the audit team of Ernst & Young in Canada became concerned about the accounting for inventory by its Canadian client, Sino-Forest, a Chinese company in the forestry business and headquartered in Ontario province. He sent an e-mail to the manager: "How do we know the trees are trees owned by the company? They could show us trees anywhere and we wouldn't know the difference." The manager answered, "Yeah, it's possible."[1]

Background

Unless otherwise indicated, all quoted material in the case is drawn from an investigative article by Janet McFarland, Andy Hoffman, and Jeff Fray, "OSC Cracks Down on Sino-Forest Auditors."

Sino-Forest owned and managed tree plantations as well as other manufacturing operations in China. Based in Mississauga, in Southern Toronto, Canada, and headquartered in Hong Kong with operations in mainland China, Sino-Forest was once the largest forestry firm listed in Canada, boasting a market valuation in excess of $6 billion. Between 2003 and 2010, the company raised more than $3 billion from investors hoping to cash in on China's soaring economic growth through the timber sector. However, Sino-Forest's share price imploded in 2011 when short-seller Carson Block and his firm Muddy Waters LLC labeled the company a fraud in a research report, questioned the ownership of its forestry assets, and likened the company to a Ponzi scheme.

A *Toronto Globe and Mail* investigation raised serious questions about the company's operations and in March 2012, Sino-Forest was granted court protection from its creditors under the Companies' Creditors Arrangement Act. In May 2012, the Ontario Securities Commission (OSC) filed fraud allegations against the company and six of its top executives including co-founder and former chairman and CEO Allen Chan. The OSC alleged the company and some of its former executives were involved in a "complex . . . scheme to inflate the assets and revenue of Sino-Forest," made "materially misleading statements," and "falsified the evidence of ownership for the vast majority of its timber holdings by engaging in a deceitful documentation process." The scheme allegedly involved transactions between companies that Sino-Forest secretly controlled.[2]

In an e-mailed statement at the time of the investigation, Ernst & Young, which was Sino-Forest's auditor from 2007 to 2012, said it was confident it did its work in compliance with generally accepted auditing standards and met all professional standards. "The evidence we will present to the OSC will show that Ernst & Young Canada did extensive audit work to verify ownership and existence of Sino-Forest's timber assets," the statement said.[3]

On September 30, 2012, Ernst & Young admitted no wrongdoing in its audits of Sino-Forest Corp., but it did agree to pay an $8 million penalty to the Ontario Securities Commission (OSC), cooperate with the investigation, and change its internal policies on emerging markets. The OSC approved a $117 million settlement with Ernst & Young in 2013 to resolve allegations that it performed negligent work. A separate settlement was reached with former Sino-Forest chief financial officer David Horsley for $5.6 million.

On January 26, 2015, a group of big-name Bay Street financial institutions that underwrote stock and debt issues for Sino-Forest agreed to pay $32.5 million to burned investors. In the settlement deal filed with the OSC, the underwriters made no admissions of liability and denied any liability in the plaintiffs' claims. But the $32.5 million payment released them from needing to defend themselves in the class action.[4]

[1]Janet McFarland, Andy Hoffman, and Jeff Fray, "OSC cracks down on Sino-Forest auditors," December 3, 2012, Available at: http://www.theglobeandmail.com/globe-investor/osc-cracks-down-on-sino-forest-auditors/article5913025/.

[2]Ian Austen, "Sino-Forest Report Rejects Fraud Claims, With Caveats," November 15, 2011, Available at: http://dealbook.nytimes.com/2011/11/15/sino-forest-report-rejects-fraud-claims-with-caveats/?_r=0.

[3]Richard Blackwell, "Ernst & Young reaches $8-million settlement over Sino-Forest audit," September 30, 2014, Available at: http://www.theglobeandmail.com/report-on-business/ernst-young-reaches-8-million-settlement-over-sino-forest-audit/article20854668/.

[4]Jeff Gray, "Sino-Forest underwriters settle for $32.5-million," Available at: http://www.theglobeandmail.com/report-on-business/industry-news/the-law-page/sino-forest-underwriters-settle-for-325-million/article22638013/.

"Independent" Directors Report

In response to the criticism from Muddy Waters, Sino-Forest appointed an independent directors' committee to investigate.

The quoted information in this and the next section is taken from the independent directors' report as reported by Ian Austen in "Sino-Forest Report Rejects Fraud Claims, With Caveats."[5]

The central claim raised by Block and others was that the company had greatly overstated its revenue and its timber holdings in China. The report said they were able to confirm the vast majority of Sino-Forest's claimed timber holdings although they had challenges assessing the value placed upon them. But they also noted that the majority of the company's timber holdings relied on informal agreements with government-owned forestry agencies rather than clearly defined legal ownership. "Forestry bureau confirmations are not officially recognized documents and are not issued pursuant to a legislative mandate," the report stated. "It appears they were issued at the request of the company or its suppliers." The report also indicated that the unusual corporate structure of Sino-Forest, along with irregular activities like the deletion of computer files and the use of personal e-mail accounts for corporate business, complicated the assessment of its financial records.

Block pointed out that all three directors who oversaw the investigation were defendants in shareholder lawsuits, and one of them had resigned prior to the release of the report.

Structural issues were a problem at Sino-Forest as well with the company running much of its business through 58 holding companies incorporated in the British Virgin Islands, a tax haven; company names include Glory Billionaire International, Trillion Edge Limited, and Ace Supreme. The directors concluded that the arrangements, while unusual by Western standards, were an accepted way of avoiding bureaucratic delays in China.

While the report similarly cleared Sino-Forest's reliance on third-party companies to broker sales, its investigation of those firms encountered severe limitations. In most meetings between the brokers and the panel's investigators, the report said "no financial records were given, no copies of documents presented could be taken, and the interviewees were not prepared to discuss any aspect of any other companies that deal with Sino-Forest that they control."

The committee said that an audit by PricewaterhouseCoopers as part of the independent directors' investigation found that the deposits matched the cash amounts reported by the company in the accounts verified. However, the auditors were able to examine only 28 of the 267 accounts the company has in mainland China.

The report noted that there was incomplete or inadequate record creation and retention practices, no integrated accounting system, and employees conducted company business from time to time using personal devices and noncorporate e-mail addresses.

Business in China

The Sino-Forest case reveals that business is done in China through informal agreements with state or party officials, who grant access to licenses, resources, and markets only if they are paid under the table. There can be no official records of these payments. Typically, auditors are not allowed to see bank accounts, and transactions are muddied by a proliferation of secret arrangements through authorized intermediaries (AIs).

The main job of foreign managers in China is not business per se but the cultivation and maintenance of personal relationships with officials. If they play this game well, they win—as did Sino-Forest prior to these embarrassing disclosures.

Sino-Forest's earnings depend on how its management divides surpluses between the company and its Chinese patrons. If they become greedier and demand more generous payoffs, reported earnings suffer. In effect, confidential agreements and corruption determine earnings per share more than real business operations.

---

[5]Barbara Shecter, "Sino-Forest execs deny fraud, call OSC allegations a misinterpretation of Chinese business practices," September 2, 2014, Available at:http://business.financialpost.com/news/fp-street/osc-lays-out-road-map-for-fraud-case-against-sino-forest-executives.

Sino-Forest's annual report references the three key risk factors that an insider to Chinese business would understand, but outsiders would likely miss:

1. We rely on our relationships with local plantation land owners and/or plantation land use rights holders, authorized intermediaries, key customers, suppliers, and third-party service providers.

2. We are heavily dependent on the expertise of our senior management and the relationships cultivated by them with our major customers and others. This concentration of authority creates risk in terms of measurement and completeness of transactions, which may lead to the possibility of inaccurate financial reporting.

3. Violations of PRC laws or regulation could result in civil and criminal penalties, including the revocation of licenses required for our business.[6]

Cultural Issues

Lawyers for executives of collapsed Sino-Forest, once a high flyer on the Toronto Stock Exchange, said their clients never committed fraud but followed common business practices accepted in China. To refute such claims, Hugh Craig, an OSC lawyer, said: "It was a Canadian company. It raised money from Canadians in Canada. A culture of accountability must be recognized." But a lawyer for Allen Chan, as well as the legal representative for four other former senior executives, was quoted as saying Canadian regulators made the mistake of looking through "a North American lens" when interpreting Sino-Forest's timber ownership and sales contracts in China. "These events did not take place on Bay Street or even rural Ontario," Emily Cole, a lawyer for Mr. Chan, told a three-member panel of OSC commissioners. "The panel should not draw conclusions about them as if they did."

Cole explained that her witness, Dr. Randall Peerenboom, an American who had lived in China for more than 20 years, would explain how business practices viewed as surprising, if not shocking, to Canadian regulators were the only way to do business in China where money could not be exchanged freely and local bank accounts were impossible to get. She claimed the OSC's fraud accusations centered in part on Sino-Forest's practice of buying and selling timber assets without any cash passing through the company. Purchasers bypassed the company entirely by paying Sino-Forest's suppliers. Cole explained that the accusation presupposed they could have sent money to Sino-Forest, but that wasn't possible. "Keep an open mind about these differences in business and culture," she urged the OSC panel.

During the trial, Markus Koehnen, who was representing former senior Sino-Forest executives Alfred Hung, Albert Ip, George Ho, and Simon Yeung, spent more than two hours walking the panel through such concepts at *guanxi,* or relationship building. He said understanding the key component of Chinese business that goes well beyond networking would clear up concerns over declaring revenue based on agreements made in farmers' fields, and the perceived impropriety of a series of close business connections between Sino-Forest and key customers and suppliers. The OSC had alleged that Sino-Forest's top executives hid these relationships that helped perpetrate the fraud and included the fabrication of assets and revenue.

Charges against EY

The OSC alleged that Ernst & Young failed to properly understand the legal basis of Sino-Forest's claim to its assets and relied on an opinion prepared by the forestry company's legal firm Jingtian and Gongchen Attorneys at Law. The OSC also accused EY of inappropriately relying on the valuation work of Poyry Forest Industry Ltd., a company hired by Sino-Forest to prepare periodic valuations of its timber holdings.

The OSC alleged that EY failed to adequately review or question documentation related to Sino-Forest's ownership of standing timber reserves the company held in China. "The purported assets constituted the vast majority of Sino-Forest's assets and produced nearly all of its reported revenue," the OSC said in its statement of allegations. "Ernst & Young's lack of diligence in these areas therefore resulted in significant negative consequences for Sino-Forest's shareholders."

---

[6] Paul Roderick Gregory, "Chinese Stock Alarm? Sino-Forest May be the Best of the Bunch, November 27, 2011, Available at: http://www.forbes.com/sites/paulroderickgregory/2011/11/27/chinese-stock-alarm-sino-forest-may-be-the-best-of-the-bunch/.

The OSC stated it had found significant evidence that the firm did not go far enough to prove that Sino-Forest's stated timber holdings exist, pointing out that EY never obtained two key elements of Sino's purchase contracts: the villagers' letter of authorization and the certificate of forest proprietorship. The precise location of the forestry assets was also not described in the purchase contracts. "Both of these deficiencies should have prompted Ernst & Young to make further enquiries of Sino-Forest management and to perform further audit procedures," the OSC said.

In its statement of allegations, the OSC alleged that EY failed to verify the ownership and existence of Sino-Forest's most significant forestry assets. The OSC said the specific location of purchased assets was not delineated in purchase contracts, which should have raised questions by auditors. And the commission said EY did "very limited" site visits to inspect the firm's purported assets, which were widely scattered throughout China. The regulator said an internal e-mail between members of EY's audit team shows staff were asking questions about site visits, which were done along with third-party forestry consultants Poyry Forest Interest Ltd., hired by Sino-Forest.

OSC enforcement director Tom Atkinson said the OSC launched the case because investors rely on auditors, especially when foreign companies are listing in Canada. "If auditors fail to abide by Canadian auditing standards and securities laws, we will hold them accountable," he said in a release. Class-action lawyer Dimitri Lascaris at Siskinds LLP, who had represented Sino-Forest's shareholders, said he believed audit firms would now "exercise a higher degree of professional skepticism going forward." he said. "Any time you are confronting circumstances of this nature and a liability of this magnitude, you are going to have a very powerful economic incentive to be very careful."

The OSC maintained the company didn't show enough "professional skepticism" in conducting its audits. OSC lawyer Yvonne Chisholm told the settlement hearing that the accounting firm overlooked flaws in its clients' accounting and didn't conduct proper reviews. But she also said there is no evidence of "dishonest" conduct by the accounting firm. The OSC also expressed a concern about the audit team itself. It noted that several of the senior EY partners involved in the Sino-Forest audits did not speak Chinese, and the firm did not translate many of the key Sino-Forest documents into English.

EY's lawyer Linda Fuerst told the hearing that "the honesty and integrity of Ernst & Young and its people were never in question." She said the settlement avoids the time, expense, and uncertainty of what would have been lengthy hearings.

In addition to the financial payment, EY told the OSC that it put in place new policies for auditing companies that have significant operations in emerging markets, and it had done a "focused assessment" of audits on companies based in China.

Lascaris said the EY settlement reinforces his argument that individuals or organizations are not motivated to sign no-contest settlements because of a concern over follow-up civil suits. The real motivation for no-contest settlements, Lascaris said, is that firms and individuals want to protect their reputations, and their ability to generate new business.

Over all, the settlement should send a message to Ernst & Young, and other capital markets participants, that audits need to be conducted with proper levels of diligence. OSC vice-chairman James Turner, who approved the settlement, said it underlines the vital "gate keeping" role that auditors play, and that auditors need to show sufficient scrutiny, skepticism, and diligence.

"This is a wake-up call for the audit profession," said forensic accountant Charles Smedmor, who teaches accounting at Toronto's Seneca College. "It underlines the need to drill down to get sufficient appropriate audit evidence to support audit opinions," Smedmor said.

Questions

1. Should operational and cultural considerations play a role in determining whether Sino-Forest committed a fraud? Explain.

2. Did Sino-Forest manage earnings? Refer to the discussion in this chapter about different perspectives on earnings management in responding.

3. Critically evaluate the audit work of Ernst & Young from the perspective of generally accepted auditing standards and professional ethics. Was this a failed audit?

Case 7-9 The North Face, Inc.

The North Face, Inc. (North Face) is an American outdoor product company specializing in outerwear, fleece, coats, shirts, footwear, and equipment such as backpacks, tents, and sleeping bags. North Face sells clothing and equipment lines catered toward wilderness chic, climbers, mountaineers, skiers, snowboarders, hikers, and endurance athletes. The company sponsors professional athletes from the worlds of running, climbing, skiing, and snowboarding.

North Face is located in Alameda, California, along with an affiliated company, JanSport. These two companies manufacture about half of all small backpacks sold in the United States. Both companies are owned by VF Corporation, an American apparel corporation.

The North Face brand was established in 1968 in San Francisco. Following years of success built on sales to a high-end customer base, in the 1990s North Face was forced to compete with mass-market brands sold by the major discount retailers. It was at that point the company engaged in accounting shenanigans that led to it being acquired by VF Corporation.

Barter Transactions[1]

Consumer demand for North Face products was steadily growing by the mid-1980s and the higher levels of demand for production were causing the manufacturing facilities to be overburdened. Pressure existed to maintain the level of production that was required. As North Face continued to grow in sales throughout the 1980s and into the 1990s, the management team set aggressive sales goals. In the mid-1990s the team established the goal of reaching $1 billion in annual sales by the year 2003. The pressure prompted Christopher Crawford, the company's chief financial officer (CFO), and Todd Katz, the vice president of sales, to negotiate a large transaction with a barter company and then proceed to improperly account for it in the financial statements.[2]

North Face entered into two major barter transactions in 1997 and 1998. The barter company North Face dealt with typically bought excess inventory in exchange for trade credits. The trade credits could be redeemed by North Face only through the barter company, and most often the trade credits were used to purchase advertising, printing, or travel services.

North Face began negotiating a potential barter transaction in early December 1997. The basic terms were that the barter company would purchase $7.8 million of excess inventory North Face had on hand. In exchange for that inventory, North Face would receive $7.8 million of trade credits that were redeemable only through the barter company.

Before North Face finalized the barter transaction, Crawford asked Deloitte & Touche, North Face's external auditors, for advice on how to account for a barter sale. The auditors provided Crawford with the accounting literature describing GAAP relating to non-monetary exchanges. That literature generally precludes companies from recognizing revenue on barter transactions when the only consideration received by the seller is trade credits.

What Crawford did next highlights one of the many ways a company can structure a transaction to manage earnings and achieve the financial results desired rather than report what should be recorded as revenue under GAAP.

[1]The information in this case was taken from: Securities and Exchange Commission, A Civil Complaint filed in the United States District Court Northern District of California against Christopher F. Crawford and Todd F. Katz, February 20, 2003, www.sec.gov/litigation/complaints/comp17978.htm.

[2]"North Face Accounting Fraud," October 14, 2013, http://bethmichel.blogspot.com/2013/10/0-false-18-pt-18-pt-0-0-false-false.html.

Crawford structured the transaction to recognize profit on the trade credits. First, he required the barter company to pay a portion of the purchase price in cash. Crawford agreed that North Face would guarantee that the barter company would receive at least a 60 percent recovery of the total purchase price when it resold the product. In exchange for the guarantee, the barter company agreed to pay approximately 50 percent of the total purchase price in cash and the rest in trade credits. This guarantee took the form of an oral side agreement that was not disclosed to the auditors.

Second, Crawford split the transaction into two parts on two days before the year-end December 31, 1997. One part of the transaction was to be recorded in the fourth quarter of 1997, the other to be recorded in the first quarter of 1998. Crawford structured the two parts of the barter sale so that all of the cash consideration and a portion of the trade credits would be received in the fourth quarter of 1997. The barter credit portion of the fourth quarter transaction was structured to allow profit recognition for the barter credits despite the objections of the auditors. The consideration for the 1998 first quarter transaction consisted solely of trade credits.

On December 29, 1997, North Face recorded a $5.15 million sale to the barter company. The barter company paid $3.51 million in cash and issued $1.64 million in trade credits. North Face recognized its full normal profit margin on the sale. Just 10 days later on January 8, 1998, North Face recorded another sale to the barter company, this time for $2.65 million in trade credits, with no cash consideration. North Face received only trade credits from the barter company for this final portion of the $7.8 million total transaction. Again, North Face recognized its full normal profit margin on the sale.

Materiality Issues

Crawford was a CPA and knew all about the materiality criteria that auditors use to judge whether they will accept a client's accounting for a disputed transaction. He committed the fraud because he saw internal control weaknesses and believed no one would notice. Crawford realized that if he made sure the portion of the barter transaction recorded during the fourth quarter of fiscal 1997 was below a certain amount, the auditors would not look at it. He also believed that Deloitte & Touche would not challenge the profit recognized on the $3.51 million portion of the barter transaction because of the cash payment.

Crawford also realized that Deloitte would maintain that no profit should be recorded on the $1.64 million balance of the December 29, 1997, transaction with the barter company for which North Face would be paid exclusively in trade credits. However, Crawford was aware of the materiality thresholds that Deloitte had established for North Face's key financial statement items during the fiscal 1997 audit. He knew that the profit margin of approximately $800,000 on the $1.64 million portion of the December 1997 transaction fell slightly below Deloitte's materiality threshold for North Face's collective gross profit. As a result, he believed that Deloitte would propose an adjustment to reverse the $1.64 million transaction but ultimately "pass" on that proposed adjustment since it had an immaterial impact on North Face's financial statements. As Crawford expected, Deloitte proposed a year-end adjusting entry to reverse the $1.64 million transaction but then passed on that adjustment during the wrap-up phase of the audit.

In early January 1998, North Face recorded the remaining $2.65 million portion of the $7.8 million barter transaction. Crawford instructed North Face's accountants to record the full amount of profit margin on this portion of the sale despite being aware that accounting treatment was not consistent with the authoritative literature. Crawford did not inform the Deloitte auditors of the $2.65 million portion of the barter transaction until after the 1997 audit was completed.

The barter company ultimately sold only a nominal amount of the $7.8 million of excess inventory that it purchased from North Face. As a result, in early 1999, North Face reacquired that inventory from the barter company.

Audit Considerations

The auditors did not learn of the January 8, 1998, transaction until March 1998. Thus, when the auditors made the materiality judgment for the fourth quarter transaction, they were unaware that a second transaction had taken place and unaware that Crawford had recognized full margin on the second barter transaction.

In mid-1998 through 1999, the North Face sales force was actively trying to resell the product purchased by the barter company because the barter company was unable to sell any significant portion of the inventory. North Face finally decided, in January and February 1999, to repurchase the remaining inventory from the barter company. Crawford negotiated the repurchase price of $690,000 for the remaining inventory.

Crawford did not disclose the repurchase to the 1998 audit engagement team, even though the audit was not complete at the time of the repurchase.

During the first week of March 1999, the auditors asked for additional information about the barter transaction to complete the 1998 audit. In response to this request, Crawford continued to mislead the auditors by failing to disclose that the product had been repurchased, that there was a guarantee, that the 1997 and 1998 transactions were linked, and that the company sales force had negotiated almost all of the orders received by the barter company.

Crawford did not disclose any of this information until he learned that the auditors were about to fax a confirmation letter to the barter company that specifically asked if any of the product had been returned or repurchased. Crawford then called the chair of North Face's audit committee, to explain that he had withheld information from the auditors. A meeting was scheduled for later that day for Crawford to make "full disclosure" to the auditors about the barter transactions.

Even at the "full disclosure" meeting with the auditors, Crawford was not completely truthful. He did finally disclose the repurchase and the link between the 1997 and 1998 transactions. He did not, however, disclose that there was a guarantee, nor did he disclose that the company's employees had negotiated most of the orders for the product.

Deloitte & Touche

Richard Fiedelman was the Deloitte advisory partner assigned to the North Face audit engagement. Pete Vanstraten was the audit engagement partner for the 1997 North Face audit. Vanstraten was also the individual who proposed the adjusting entry near the end of the 1997 audit to reverse the $1.64 million barter transaction that North Face had recorded in the final few days of fiscal 1997. Vanstraten proposed the adjustment because he was aware that the GAAP rules generally preclude companies from recognizing revenue on barter transactions when the only consideration received by the seller is trade credits. Vanstraten was also the individual who "passed" on that adjustment after determining that it did not have a material impact on North Face's 1997 financial statements. Fiedelman reviewed and approved those decisions by Vanstraten.

Shortly after the completion of the 1997 North Face audit, Vanstraten transferred from the office that serviced North Face. In May 1998, Will Borden was appointed the new audit engagement partner for North Face. In the two months before Borden was appointed the North Face audit engagement partner, Richard Fiedelman functioned in that role.

Fiedelman supervised the review of North Face's financial statements for the first quarter of fiscal 1998, which ended on March 31, 1998. While completing that review, Fiedelman became aware of the $2.65 million portion of the $7.8 million barter transaction that Crawford had instructed his subordinates to record in early January 1998. Fiedelman did not challenge North Face's decision to record its normal profit margin on the January 1998 "sale" to the barter company. As a result, North Face's gross profit for the first quarter of 1998 was overstated by more than $1.3 million, an amount that was material to the company's first-quarter financial statements. In fact, without the profit margin on the $2.65 million transaction, North Face would have reported a net loss for the first quarter of fiscal 1998 rather than the modest net income it actually reported that period.

In the fall of 1998, Borden began planning the 1998 North Face audit. An important element of that planning process was reviewing the 1997 audit workpapers. While reviewing those workpapers, Borden discovered the audit adjustment that Vanstraten had proposed during the prior year audit to reverse the $1.64 million barter transaction. When Borden brought this matter to Fiedelman's attention, Fiedelman maintained that the proposed audit adjustment should not have been included in the prior year workpapers since the 1997 audit team had *not* concluded that North Face could *not* record the $1.64 million transaction with the barter company. Fiedelman insisted that, despite the proposed audit adjustment in the 1997 audit workpapers, Vanstraten had concluded that it was permissible for North Face to record the transaction and recognize the $800,000 of profit margin on the transaction in December 1997.

Borden accepted Fiedelman's assertion that North Face was entitled to recognize profit on a sales transaction in which the only consideration received by the company was trade credits. Borden also relied on this assertion during the 1998 audit. As a result, Borden and the other members of the 1998 audit team did not propose an adjusting entry to require North Face to reverse the $2.65 million sale recorded by the company in January 1998.

After convincing Borden that the prior year workpapers misrepresented the decision that Vanstraten had made regarding the $1.64 million barter transaction, Fiedelman began the process of documenting this revised conclusion in the 1997 working papers that related to the already issued financial statements for 1997. The SEC had concluded in its investigation that Deloitte personnel prepared a new summary memorandum and proposed adjustments schedule reflecting the revised conclusion about profit recognition, and replaced the original 1997 working papers with these newly created working papers.

SEC Actions against Crawford

In the SEC action against Crawford and Katz, the SEC charged that Crawford tried to conceal the true nature of the improperly reported transactions from North Face's accountants and auditors. He made, directly or indirectly, material misrepresentations and omissions to the auditors in an attempt to hide his misconduct. Katz also made, directly or indirectly, material misrepresentations and omissions to the accountants and auditors in an attempt to hide his misconduct.[3]

The commission charged that Crawford committed a fraud because his actions violated Section 10(b) of the Exchange Act of 1934, in that he knew or was reckless in not knowing that (1) it was a violation of GAAP to record full margin on the trade credit portion of the sale and (2) that the auditors would consider the amount of the non-GAAP fourth quarter profit recognition immaterial and would not insist on any adjusting entry for correction.

A second charge was that Crawford aided and abetted violations of Section 13(a) of the Exchange Act that requires every issuer of a registered security to file reports with the SEC that accurately reflect the issuer's financial performance and provide other information to the public.

A third charge dealt with record-keeping and alleged violations of Section 13(b) in that the Exchange Act requires each issuer of registered securities to make and keep books, records, and accounts that, in reasonable detail, accurately and fairly reflect the business of the issuer and to devise and maintain a system of internal controls sufficient to provide reasonable assurances that, among other things, transactions are recorded as necessary to permit preparation of financial statements and to maintain the accountability of accounts.

The SEC asked the U.S. District Court of the Northern District of California to enter a judgment:

- Permanently enjoining Crawford and the vice president of sales, Katz, from violating Sections 10(b) and 13(b)(5) of the Exchange Act;
- Ordering Crawford to provide a complete accounting for and to disgorge the unjust enrichment he realized, plus prejudgment interest thereon;
- Ordering Crawford and Katz to pay civil monetary penalties pursuant to Section 21(d)(3) of the Exchange Act; and
- Prohibiting Crawford and Katz from acting as an officer or director of a public company pursuant to Section 21(d)(2) of the Exchange Act.

Crawford agreed to the terms in a settlement with the SEC that included his suspension from appearing or practicing before the commission as an accountant for at least five years, after which time he could apply to the commission for reinstatement.

Questions

1. Use the fraud triangle to analyze the red flags that existed in the case and the role and responsibilities of the auditors at Deloitte & Touche in The North Face accounting fraud.
2. Identify the general principles that dictate when revenue should be recorded. How did North Face violate those rules?

---

[3]SEC, *In the matter of Christopher F. Crawford, Accounting and Auditing Enforcement Release No. 1751 (AAER No. 1751),* April 4, 2003, Available at: www.sec.gov/litigation/admin/34-47633.htm.

3. Evaluate the actions of Deloitte & Touche first proposing an audit adjustment on the $1.64 million balance of the December 29, 1997, transaction with the barter company and then passing on the adjustment based on it not having a material effect on the financial statements. In this regard, should auditors conceal materiality levels from audit clients?

Case 7-10 Beazer Homes

Beazer Homes is a home-building company headquartered in Atlanta, Georgia. Its stock is listed on the New York Stock Exchange. Beazer is required to file Form 10-Q and Form 10-K, as well as an 8-K form when certain changes occur, such as restating financial statements.

As a homebuilder, Beazer often builds "model homes" for prospective homebuyers to tour while the remainder of a neighborhood and its future homes are under construction. As one of the last homes to be sold, model homes often may not be sold to a homebuyer for years, and thus may not provide a homebuilder with revenue and income on their sale until years after construction.

What follows is a description of the SEC's agreement, in *SEC v. Michael T. Rand*, to resolve charges that Beazer engaged in fraudulent accounting that led to material noncompliance with federal securities laws by improperly inflating Beazer's income by reducing or eliminating previously established artificial reserves and improperly recognizing sales revenue and income in sale-leaseback transactions involving its model homes.[1]

Sale-Leaseback Scheme

Under its sales-leaseback program, Beazer sold its model homes to investors, typically at a discounted price, thereby permitting it to recognize revenue and income from the sales. Under the "leaseback" portion of the transaction, Beazer leased back from the investor/buyer the same model homes, which Beazer could then use to show prospective home buyers.

In December 2005, the chief accounting officer, Michael T. Rand, CPA, entered into a secret side-agreement with one or more GMAC Model Home Finance personnel under which: (a) Beazer would "sell" the model homes and recognize revenue and income from such sales; (b) the homes would be leased back to Beazer for its use; but (c) Beazer would secretly receive a share of any profits from any subsequent sale of the model homes to a third party at the end of the leases. Under GAAP, a seller is not permitted to recognize revenue and income from a sale in a sale-leaseback transaction if the seller retains a continuing interest in the property after it has been sold. Beazer's continuing and secret interest in a share of any profits from the ultimate sale of the models was such a continuing interest.

What follows is a table showing model homes sold and improper pretax income recognized from the sale-leaseback transactions in violation of GAAP.

Overstated Pretax Income from Sale-Leaseback Transactions		
Quarter Ended	**# Homes Sold**	**Overstated Pretax Income**
December 31, 2005	90	$8.0 million
March 31, 2006	79	$4.2 million
June 30, 2006	37	$1.6 million
September 30, 2006	140	$8.3 million

---

[1]*SEC v. Michael T. Rand*, U.S. District Court for the Northern District of Atlanta, Georgia, July 1, 2009, Available at: https://www.sec.gov/litigation/complaints/2009/comp21114.pdf.

Cookie-Jar Reserves

Prior to 2006, Rand and other Beazer employees engaged in an accounting scheme involving "cookie-jar accounting." Specifically, Rand improperly decreased Beazer's income by artificially establishing, increasing, and/or maintaining future anticipated expenses or "reserves." He executed this strategy by manipulating, among other accounts, Beazer's land development and house reserve accounts.

In fiscal year 2006, when Beazer was in jeopardy of not meeting analysts' expectations, Rand eliminated certain unnecessary excess reserves that had been built up, thereby improperly boosting Beazer's pretax income by over $27.5 million. Beazer's arbitrary elimination of reserves to boost income resulted in financial statements that were not compiled in accordance with GAAP.

Land Inventory Accounting

As part of its home building and sale operations, Beazer purchased parcels of land upon which it constructed houses to form subdivisions. Beazer recorded the acquired land, along with costs for the common development of the parcel, such as sewer systems and streets, as an asset on Beazer's balance sheet in the land inventory accounts. As subdivisions were built, Beazer allocated the costs accumulated in the land inventory accounts to individual home lots, which were then offered for sale. When the home sale was recorded in Beazer's books, all associated homebuilding costs, including allocated costs recorded in the land inventory accounts, were expensed as a cost of the sale, with a corresponding reduction, or credit, in the land inventory account.

Because Beazer sold houses within a subdivision as the development of that subdivision progressed, the land inventory expense recorded for any particular house sale was necessarily an estimate. The setting of inventory credits was done by each division based on estimates of costs to acquire, develop, and complete subdivisions plus an added amount for contingencies. Once established, divisions needed approval from Rand, who reviewed the reserves on a monthly basis, to make adjustments.

As additional houses in a subdivision were sold, the land inventory account continued to be decreased (credited) by amounts representing the land acquisition and development costs allocated to each individual house. If costs had been allocated properly, then, shortly after the final house in a development had been sold, the balance in the land inventory account should have been at or near zero.

What follows is a table showing the overstatement in land inventory costs between 2001 and 2005.

Overstatement of Land Inventory Costs				
	Quarter 1	Quarter 2	Quarter 3	Quarter 4
2001	$1,455,000	$ 584,000	$1,322,000	$2,571,000
2002	$1,827,000	$2,761,000	$1,270,000	$2,586,000
2003	$2,440,000	$1,422,000	$1,086,000	N/A
2004	$3,996,000	$4,253,000	$5,963,000	$2,227,000
2005	$3,388,000	$4,443,000	$5,122,000	$4,469,000

In order to reduce its first quarter 2002 earnings, which had exceeded analysts' EPS expectations, Rand fraudulently increased the land inventory expense recorded for homes sold during the quarter.

On January 8, 2002, after the end of the first quarter, Rand e-mailed a target earnings amount to the relevant financial personnel in numerous Beazer divisions with instructions not to exceed the target by a certain amount. The distributed target for each division was less than each division's previously expected quarterly results. Rand advised the divisions to review their land inventory accounts in order to increase expenses and reduce earnings. In one particular e-mail, Rand instructed the Florida division to provide "more than adequate land allocations in communities closing out this year" as a means to reduce its earnings.

On January 10, 2002, Rand, via e-mails, directed certain divisions to, "[s]et aside all the reserves you reasonably can . . . the quarter is too high." This was followed by a series of e-mails in which Rand specified the amounts by which certain divisions should increase their reserves, along with targets for their EBIT (earnings before interest and taxes). The divisions substantially carried out his directions, and Rand was able to reduce Beazer's quarterly EPS from $2.60 to $2.47 a share, which exceeded analysts' consensus of $2.00 per share. In total, Beazer recorded approximately $1.827 million in excess land inventory costs for that quarter, or approximately 8 percent of its reported net income.

By increasing land inventory expenses, Rand caused Beazer to understate its net income by a total of $56 million ($33 million after tax effect; approximately 5 percent of reported net income) between 2000 and 2005. Beginning in the first quarter of 2006, Rand began to reverse the reserves existing in the land inventory accounts, which increased then-current period earnings. The credit balances in land inventory accounts were debited (i.e., zeroed out), and a cost of sales expense credited (i.e., reduced). These reversals improperly reduced expenses and increased Beazer's earnings. During all four quarters of 2006, Rand caused Beazer to release these land inventory reserves, boosting then-current period earnings by approximately $100,000 in the first quarter of 2006, approximately $301,000 in the second quarter of 2006, approximately $14,278,000 in the third quarter of 2006, and approximately $10,816,000 in the fourth quarter of 2006.

Manipulation of "House Cost-to-Complete" Reserves

Under its accounting policies, Beazer recorded revenue and profit on the sale of a house after the close of the sale of that house to a homebuyer. In the journal entries to record the sale, Beazer typically reserved a portion of its profit earned on the house. This reserve, called a "house cost-to-complete" reserve, was established to cover any unknown expenses that Beazer might incur on the sold house after the close, such as minor repairs or final cosmetic touch-ups. Although the amount of this reserve varied by region, it was typically $1,000 to $4,000 per house.

Beazer's policy was to reverse any unused portion of the house cost-to-complete reserve within four to nine months after the close, taking any unused portion into income at that time. As specified below, in various quarters between 2000 and 2005, Rand over-reserved house cost-to-complete expenses. Rand then took steps to maintain these reserves beyond the typical four to nine months and until increased earnings were required in future periods.

The following table shows the over-expensing of the cost-to-complete expense from 2000 to 2005.

	Over-Expensing of the Cost-to-Complete Expense			
Year	Quarter 1	Quarter 2	Quarter 3	Quarter 4
2000	N/A	$610,000	$ 5,000	$2,288,000
2001	$1,138,000	$543,000	N/A	N/A
2002	$2,184,000	$813,000	N/A	N/A
2003	$1,380,000	N/A	N/A	N/A
2004	$1,057,000	N/A	$1,137,000	$2,051,000
2005	N/A	$805,000	$1,427,000	N/A

Beginning in 2006, Beazer began reversing some of the excess cost-to-complete reserves that it had previously recorded. As a result of Rand's directives, Beazer reduced its cost of sales expense by approximately $1.5 million by reducing the cost-to-complete reserve to zero on a number of houses. The following shows the amount of reversal of excess cost-to-complete reserves as earnings of the period that were previously recorded fraudulently.

Additionally, at Rand's instruction certain Beazer divisions, in order to report more income, failed to establish a house cost-to-complete reserve on house sales closing during the quarter. Beazer's Las Vegas division failed to record any cost-to-complete reserve for approximately 85 houses sold during December 2005. This resulted in an improper recognition, in violation of GAAP, of more than $200,000 of income for the period. All totaled, the additional income due to cost-to-complete reserve accounting added approximately $0.03 to Beazer's EPS.

Reversal of Excess Cost-to-Complete Reserves

Year	Quarter Ended	Amount of Reversal
2006	March 31	$ 183,000
2006	September 30	$2,130,000
2006	December 31	$ 209,000
2007	March 31	$1,549,000

Deloitte & Touche

Beazer's auditor, Deloitte & Touche, specifically advised Rand via e-mail that Beazer's appreciation rights in the homes represented a continuing interest that, pursuant to GAAP, precluded Beazer from recognizing revenue when the homes were sold to GMAC. In an attempt to circumvent GAAP, and to deceive Deloitte, Rand caused the final, written versions of the sale-leaseback agreements to omit any reference to Beazer's continuing profit participation. Rand then directed, by e-mail, his subordinates to record revenue at the time the model homes were initially sold to the GMAC investor pools. Rand provided Deloitte with copies of the sale-leaseback agreements that intentionally omitted the provisions relating to the continuing profit participation by Beazer. Rand also failed to disclose the side agreements to Deloitte.

Additionally, on January 18, 2006, Rand provided to Deloitte a memo that specifically stated Beazer would not "participate in the appreciation" of the leased assets (model homes). Based on Rand's concealment and misrepresentations, Deloitte agreed that immediate revenue recognition was proper.

As reported by *CFO Magazine* and summarized in the following paragraphs,[2] a class-action lawsuit filed against Deloitte was settled on May 7, 2009. The agreement said that the audit firm should have considered the homebuilder's "make the numbers" culture to be a red flag as the housing market tanked. Deloitte agreed to pay investors of Beazer Homes nearly $1 million to settle the claim.

The investors had accused Beazer of managing earnings, recognizing revenue earlier than allowed under generally accepted accounting principles, improperly accounting for sale-leaseback transactions, creating "cookie-jar" reserves, and not recording land and goodwill impairment charges at the proper time.

The investors accused Deloitte of turning "a blind eye" to the myriad of "red flags" that should have alerted the firm to potential GAAP violations. These warning signs included the "excessive pressure" employees were under to meet their higher-ups' sales goals, tight competition in Beazer's market, and weak internal controls. Accusing the auditor of "severe recklessness," the shareholders alleged, for example, that Deloitte should have noticed that Beazer was likely overdue in recording impairments on its land assets, as the real estate market began to decline, among the other alleged accounting violations.

"Deloitte either knowingly ignored or recklessly disregarded Beazer's wide-ranging material control deficiencies and material weaknesses during the class period," according to the shareholders' complaint. "For example, Deloitte was specifically aware that financial periods were regularly held open or re-opened because it had access to Beazer's detailed financial and accounting information via, among other means, access to Beazer's JD Edwards software."

In the Beazer settlement, Deloitte denied all liability and settled to avoid the expense and uncertainty of continued litigation, according to a spokeswoman.

Restatements of Financial Statements

Due to Beazer's material noncompliance with the financial reporting requirements of the federal securities laws,

[2]Sarah Johnson, *CFO,* "Deloitte to Pay $1M in Beazer Suit," Available at: http://ww2.cfo.com/accounting-tax/2009/05/deloitte-to-pay-1m-in-beazer-suit/.

Beazer was required to issue accounting restatements. On May 12, 2008, Beazer filed accounting restatements for the fiscal year 2006. In various reports filed that day, Beazer restated its financial statements for fiscal 2006 and each of the first three quarters of fiscal 2006. Beazer admitted to the improper accounting with the following statement:

> During the course of the investigation, the Audit Committee discovered accounting and financial reporting errors and/or irregularities that required restatement resulting primarily from: (1) inappropriate accumulation of reserves and/or accrued liabilities associated with land development and house costs ("Inventory Reserves"), and (2) inaccurate revenue recognition with respect to certain model home sale-leaseback transactions.

In the filings, Beazer further acknowledged material weaknesses in its internal control over financial reporting including in its control environment and the design of accounting policy, procedures, and controls—"specifically related to the application of GAAP in accounting for certain estimates involving significant management judgments."

As set forth in those filings, Beazer acknowledged that its material weaknesses had several impacts on the Company's financial reporting, including "[i]nappropriate reserves and other accrued liabilities [being] recorded relating to land development costs, house construction costs and warranty accruals" and "[t]he accounting for certain model home sale and leaseback agreements [being] not in compliance with GAAP. . . [as the] Company's arrangement for certain sale and leaseback transactions."

Those filings went on to state that Beazer had "terminated our former Chief Accounting Officer who we believe may have caused, or allowed to cause, the internal control breakdown"; and that Beazer "believe[d] his termination has addressed concerns about the internal control deficiencies that we believe he caused or permitted to occur."

According to a separate filing by the SEC against Ian McCarthy,[3] former CEO of Beazer Homes, during the 12-month period following Beazer's filing of its inaccurate financial statements in 2006, and before any restatement or correcting disclosure by Beazer, McCarthy received bonuses and incentive- and equity-based compensation and profits from his sale of Beazer stock. In fiscal year 2006, McCarthy received a bonus of $7.1 million, of which he received $5,706,949 in cash. During fiscal year 2006 and the first quarter of fiscal 2007, McCarthy also realized total profits of $7.3 million dollars through his sale of Beazer stock. During this same time period, McCarthy was awarded 157,526 shares of restricted Beazer common stock, which were to vest in various subsequent years upon the achievement of certain performance criteria or continued employment. Of these amounts, 78,763 shares failed to vest as the result of Beazer failing to meet required performance criteria.

McCarthy had not reimbursed Beazer for the bonuses and incentive- and equity-based compensation and profits from his sale of Beazer stock received from Beazer during the relevant statutory periods, as required under the Sarbanes-Oxley Act and its clawback provision.

In July 2009, a federal bill of information was filed in U.S. District Court charging Beazer with, among other things, participation in the conspiracy and securities fraud with Rand. Beazer accepted responsibility for those charges and, in a deferred prosecution agreement, agreed to pay restitution of $50 million. Rand was indicted by a federal grand jury in August 2010.

On July 18, 2014, a federal jury convicted Rand of conspiracy and obstruction of justice charges stemming from the federal investigation into the seven-year accounting fraud and related conspiracy at Beazer. On April 30, 2015, U.S. District Judge Robert J. Conrad Jr. sentenced Rand to 120 months in prison and to three years of supervised release on conspiracy and obstruction of justice charges in connection with the investigation.[4]

---

[3]SEC, SEC Obtains Settlement with CEO to Recover Compensation and Stock Profits he received during Company's Fraud, Mar 3, 21011, Available at: https://www.sec.gov/news/press/2011/2011-61.htm.

[4]U.S. Attorney's Office Western District of North Carolina, " Federal Judge Hands Down 10-Year Sentence to Former Chief Accounting Officer for Beazer Homes USA, Inc.," Available at: https://www.fbi.gov/charlotte/press-releases/2015/federal-judge-hands-down-10-year-sentence-to-former-chief-accounting-officer-for-beazer-homes-usa-inc.

A statement released by the U.S. Attorney's Office quotes John A. Strong, the special agent in charge for the Charlotte Division of the FBI:

> The U.S. Attorney's Office is committed to safeguarding the integrity of our financial markets from corporate executives like Rand, who put profits ahead of duty. Rand's actions breached his obligation to the investors and the public and jeopardized the stability of the housing industry. Today's verdict should send a clear message that corporate fraud, in this case cooking the books, will not be tolerated and you engage in such frauds at the risk of your freedom.[5]

Questions

1. What role did organizational ethics play in the Beazer Homes fraud? Is this something the auditors of Deloitte should have been more conscious of? Explain.

2. Evaluate Beazer's accounting for cost-to-complete reserves from a GAAP perspective. Was the initial accounting for the reserve in conformity with GAAP? What was the company trying to achieve with its accounting?

3. Categorize the accounting devices used by Beazer into one the financial shenanigan groupings. Include a discussion of how earnings were managed in each case.

4. Assume you were hired to analyze the information in this case and write a two- to three-page report on your findings. Discuss each element of the fraud and why Beazer, Rand, and/or Deloitte violated ethical and professional standards.

---

[5]U.S. Attorney's Office Western District of North Carolina, "Charlotte Jury Finds Former Chief Accounting Officer for Beazer Homes USA Inc. Guilty of Accounting Fraud and Obstruction of Justice in Second Trial," July 18, 2014, Available at: https://www.fbi.gov/charlotte/press-releases/2014/charlotte-jury-finds-former-chief-accounting-officer-for-beazer-homes-usa-inc.-guilty-of-accounting-fraud-and-obstruction-of-justice-in-second-trial.

Chapter

8

Ethical Leadership and Decision-Making in Accounting

Learning Objectives

After studying Chapter 8, you should be able to:

LO 8-1 Explain the characteristics of ethical leaders.
LO 8-2 Distinguish between types of leaders.
LO 8-3 Discuss how moral intensity and organizational culture influences leadership in accounting.
LO 8-4 Explain the implications of ethical leadership failure on whistleblowing.
LO 8-5 Describe the role of GVV on ethical leadership.
LO 8-6 Describe the characteristics of competent leaders.

Ethics Reflection

Failed Leadership at Andersen

The Introduction to Chapter 2 addresses the collapse of Enron and the failed audit by Andersen. The firm did not meet its professional responsibilities to protect the public interest for a variety of reasons including: (1) It uncritically relied on management's representations; (2) failed to exercise due care and professional skepticism; (3) got too close with the client and allowed its judgment to be compromised by relationships including providing lucrative consulting services; (4) lacked independence from the client; and (5) was just careless in its approach to the audit.

Andersen's capitulation to Enron and its management touched all levels of the audit. How could the firm stand idly by while Andy Fastow, the chief financial officer, managed off-balance-sheet partnerships during the time when Enron did business with it? The conflict of interest should have raised a big red flag, and the related party transactions were superficially addressed in the audit report.

We believe the underlying cause of the audit problems experienced by Andersen can be linked to failed ethical leadership by firm management and governance including those in charge of the Enron audit and former Andersen Worldwide CEO Joseph F. Berardino. The firm failed to act on issues that were raised by its own personnel with respect to the honesty and trustworthiness of the management at Enron and the operational effectiveness of its internal controls and accounting systems. It seemed not to want to know what was happening at the company, perhaps for fear of losing a $52 million client. It closed its eyes to the red flags all around.

The following discussion is taken from a PBS interview with Joseph Berardino on May 1, 2002.[1] In February 2001, Andersen worried about Enron's aggressive accounting and was actively debating whether to retain Enron as a client. Meanwhile, Andersen's audit team at Enron was having increasingly heated internal conflicts. A senior Andersen partner, Carl E. Bass, who had been sent in to monitor the high-risk audit, strongly objected to Enron's accounting. Bass was a member of Andersen's Professional Standards Group, sometimes referred to as "The Keeper of the Holy Grail," an internal team of accounting experts that reviewed and passed judgment on tricky accounting issues facing local offices.

In a December 18, 1999, e-mail, Bass documented a conflict over how Enron should account for the sale of options owned by one of the partnerships managed by Andrew S. Fastow. If the Andersen team had accepted Bass's advice, it would have resulted in a $30 million to $50 million charge to Enron's earnings. An Andersen practice director in Houston, however, overruled Bass, who continued to object to other accounting transactions over the next couple of months. Andersen was the only one of the then-Big Five where a local partner could overrule the Professional Standards Group.

In the interview with PBS, Berardino was asked why Bass was removed from his oversight role after raising issues of concern, and he answered it was coincidence. Berardino paid a call on Enron CEO Jeffrey K. Skilling and Chief Accounting Officer Richard A. Causey that same month Bass issued his initial warnings at Enron's Houston headquarters. Berardino said it was strictly a meet-and-greet, that he didn't confer with the Andersen audit team on the Enron account before the visit, didn't know about the conflicts over the accounting, and never discussed them with Enron. He says it's a coincidence that within weeks of his visit Bass was removed.

When asked about memos sent by Bass from 1999–2001 that said there was no substance to the partnerships that Enron was setting up off-books, Berardino claimed ignorance of the memos. When the PBS reporter probed further, perhaps out of disbelief, Berardino responded testily:

> Well, it didn't come to me. I've not read those memos. I've heard about them. There were disagreements. At the end of the day, what has happened is, if you look at the restatements that we agreed to on Enron, there were two restatements of some $500 million of earnings over a five-year period. In one instance, representing about 80 percent of that restatement. Frankly, we didn't have all the facts. Whether it was withheld from us purposefully or not, we didn't have all the facts. In the second instance—roughly 20 percent of the restatement—we did have the facts, and we made a bad judgment call. . . . At the end of October, when we reviewed the transaction, we realized our people had the information they needed to make a judgment call and they made the wrong call.

Pressed on why Bass was removed, Berardino explained:

> [I]t was very unusual that we would remove somebody. I was not consulted on that decision, I don't know all the factors that went into it. But at times, frankly, we have people who don't perform, and at times we have people who do perform, and clients object to both. You've got to make a judgment call.

Berardino talked about gaining trust of the client. He explained that the client wants to feel that the firm is understanding the client's business problem, that it is understanding what they're trying to accomplish with their accounting for business transactions. What he said next is nothing short of unbelievable in the context of the ethical standards of auditors:

> If you have people that either don't have the bedside manner, don't have the capability, don't have the expertise to get in a client's shoes to understand it, clients react negatively. OK? Then we've got to make a judgment call as to whether they're objecting to that service for the right reason or the wrong reasons. It's very rare that we remove somebody. Obviously, this was one of those rare situations.

We find it quite astounding that a managing partner of a global firm such as Andersen would admit that the firm deferred to the client's wishes on a technical accounting matter and removed its technical director who complained about the accounting under the guise of not having the proper bedside manner.

Andersen failed in its audit of Enron in so many basic ways that it has become the poster child for failed leadership. It is astounding that Berardino would concede that the Andersen auditors didn't have all the facts they needed; made the wrong judgment calls; and Berardino didn't know why the technical partner was removed.

It is apparent that Berardino didn't know what he should have known; didn't want to know; didn't want to act on his knowledge; and/or was simply blind to the ethical issues that existed at Enron and that carried over to Andersen's management of the audit.

Ethical leadership is the foundation of an ethical organization. Ethical leaders create a culture of respect, trust, and accountability and always strive to do the right thing. Ethical leaders model ethical values such as honesty and integrity and communicate those values throughout the organization. Ethical leaders lead by example and earn the right to expect others to do so as well.

Leaders who lead ethically are role models, communicating the importance of ethical standards and holding their employees accountable to those standards. Leadership is the most important lever in an ethical system designed to support ethical conduct.

As you read this chapter, reflect on the following: (1) What are the characteristics of a moral manager? (2) How can moral managers create an ethical culture built on values-based leadership? (3) What is the role of moral intensity in ethical decision making? (4) How does ethical leadership influence the judgments and decisions made by accounting professionals?

Good actions give strength to ourselves and inspire good actions in others.

Plato

Plato is credited with this quote that emphasizes leading by doing. Do good deeds. In doing so, repeatedly, we begin to strengthen ourselves and it becomes a habit and part of the core of our being. From that, leaders can inspire others to do the same.[2] Leaders also lead by example. When they do good, they help build a positive character, which then shows others that doing well can motivate or encourage goodness in others.

What Is Ethical Leadership?

LO 8-1
Explain the characteristics of ethical leaders.

The ethical leader understands that positive relationships built on respect, openness, and trust are critical to creating an ethical organization environment. The underlying principles of ethical leadership are: integrity, honesty, fairness, justice, responsibility, accountability, and empathy. Covey addresses a principle-centered leadership approach to one's personal life and organization development. He emphasizes that principle-centered leadership occurs when one's internal values form the basis of external actions. Principle-based leaders influence the ethical actions of those in the organization by transforming their own behavior first. Covey encourages principle-centered leaders to build greater, more trusting and communicative relationships with others in the workplace.[3]

Ethical leaders strive to honor and respect others in the organization and seek to empower others to achieve success by focusing on right action. An ethical organization is a community of people working together in an environment of mutual respect, where they grow personally, feel fulfilled, contribute to a common good, and share in the internal rewards, such as the achievement of a level of excellence common to a practice as well as the rewards of a job well done. By emphasizing community and internal rewards, ethical leaders commit to following a virtue-oriented approach to decision making based on a foundation of values-based leadership.

John Maxwell, the internationally recognized leadership expert, said, "A leader is one who knows the way, goes the way, and shows the way."[4] Leaders lead by example. They set an ethical tone at the top.

They lead with an attitude of "Do what I say as well as what I do." Ciulla argues that what is distinctive of leadership is the concept of vision: "Visions are not simple goals, but rather ways of seeing the future that implicitly or explicitly entail some notion of the good."[5]

Lawton and Paez developed a framework for ethical leadership built on three interlocking questions: First, who are leaders and what are their characteristics? Second, how do ethical leaders do what they do? Third, why do leaders do as they do and what are the outcomes of ethical leadership?[6] They suggest that the three factors will not necessarily form discrete areas of ethics. For example, auditors need to be virtuous and exhibit the characteristics of honesty, integrity, objectivity, and professional skepticism. These traits are also essential in auditors' relations with clients because they enable professional judgment and ethical decision making in client relationships. They also facilitate the kind of probing audits and targeted inquiries of management that should be conducted selflessly and in the public interest, not that of the client or even self-interest.

Lawton and Paez state that virtues cannot be separated from the context within which they are practiced. This is certainly true of accounting professionals and the accounting profession. They also opine that different virtues will be appropriate to the different roles that leaders play. We agree that context is important. As leaders within their firms, partners must exhibit moral imagination through ethical perception of what it means to be ethical, professional, and successful. In dealing with conflicts in relationships with clients, auditors should demonstrate courage and moral imagination. Here, ethical judgment and ethical decision-making skills become critically important.

Ethical problem solving is part of the role of being an accounting professional. Ethical leadership entails building an environment where those in the organization feel comfortable in talking to others to share perspectives of the importance of finding an ethical solution to problems. Internal accountants and auditors may possess ethical values, but it will mean nothing unless a supportive organization exists to help develop the courage to put those values into action. Voicing one's values when conflicts exist creates challenges that can be exacerbated by an indifferent leader and culture that operates by rationalizing unethical actions. Pressures imposed by top management to go along with financial wrongdoing under the guise of "It is expected practice around here" or "You need to be a team player" challenges a protagonist who must counter those reasons and give voice to one's values.

Moral Person and Moral Manager

It has been claimed that part of the role of leadership includes creating the "moral organization," promoting development in others, and institutionalizing values within the organization's culture.[7] Trevino et al. discuss building ethical leadership through two pillars of character: moral person and moral manager. The executive as a moral person is characterized in terms of individual traits such as honesty and integrity. As a moral manager, the executive (i.e., CEO) creates a strong ethics message that gets employees' attention and influences their thoughts and behaviors. Both are necessary for moral leadership. To be perceived as an ethical leader, it is not enough to just be an ethical person. An executive ethical leader must also attend to cultivating the ethics and values and infuse the organization with principles that will guide the actions of all employees.[8]

The "moral person" pillar forms the basis of a reputation for ethical leadership and challenges the leader to convey that substance to others in the organization. The perception that a leader is an ethical person means that people think of the leader as having certain traits, engaging in certain behaviors, and making decisions based on ethical principles. A moral person exhibits the virtues of leadership and encourages followers to do the same.

The traits of character that inform ethical leadership can be traced back to the ancient Greek philosophy of virtue. In Chapter 1 we discussed the role of integrity as encompassing the wholeness of an ethical person and enabling that person to be honest and trustworthy and act with courage.

Building trust is a critical component of moral managers and is demonstrated through consistency, credibility, and predictability in relationships. Openness, respect, and fair treatment of others in relationships creates an environment where actions and decisions can be questioned in the interests of ethical decision making.

Moral leaders strive not only to do the right thing but do so for the right reason and communicate to others that the right thing is going to happen at all times. The right reason is not to maximize profits or increase share price, but, instead, to build an ethical culture that creates the kind of environment that supports both short-term and long-term ethical decision making.

A moral manager serves as a role model for ethical conduct in a way that is visible to employees. A moral manager communicates regularly and persuasively with employees about ethical standards, principles, and values. Moral managers use reward systems to hold employees accountable to ethical standards. They understand that doing the right thing is more than having a code of conduct but also requires carrying through ethical intent with ethical action. Moral managers are at a postconventional reasoning level in Kohlberg's model and have translated ethical judgments into ethical decision making consistent with Rest's model.

A distinguishing characteristic of many of the accounting frauds discussed in this book is that short-term factors were allowed to compromise long-term ethical decision making in the interest of creating the illusion that earnings were strong and sustainable. CFOs and CEOs acted based on non-ethical values, such as enhancing share prices and creating personal wealth. Those on the front line "held their nose" and carried out unethical orders that led to managed earnings. "Leaders" such as Jeff Skilling at Enron, Bernie Ebbers at WorldCom, and Dennis Kozlowski at Tyco created a hands-off environment that sent the message "all is well" while the company was collapsing around them.

Building a reputation for ethical leadership means to enable ethics and values to shine through the fog of beating the competition and meeting financial projections. During the accounting scandals, the mantra was to meet or beat analysts' earnings expectations. All kinds of financial shenanigans were used to accomplish the goal, as explained in Chapter 7. Some companies even turned to non-GAAP measures of earnings, such as EBITDA, to project the image of exceeding expectations.

Authentic Leaders

LO 8-2
Distinguish between types of leadership.

Authentic leaders are focused on building long-term shareholder value, not in just beating quarterly estimates. Authentic leaders are individuals "who are deeply aware of how they think and behave and are perceived by others as being aware of their own and others' values/moral perspectives, knowledge, and strengths; aware of the context in which they operate; and confident, optimistic, resilient, courageous, and of high moral character. Authentic leaders acknowledge the ethical responsibilities of their roles, can recognize and evaluate ethical issues, and take moral actions that are thoroughly grounded in their beliefs and values.[9]

Authentic leaders hold altruistic values and are concerned with achieving a common good for the group or organization for which they are responsible. Authentic leadership produces a number of positive ethical effects in followers that significantly influence the creation of an ethical organization environment and helps to promote values-based decision-making. Followers are likely to emulate the example of authentic leaders who set a high ethical standard. They are empowered to make ethical choices on their own without the input of the leader. They become moral agents of the organization.

Transformational Leadership

The need for good leaders to be ethical in their leadership is embedded within definitions of transformational leaders. Transformational leadership is defined as a leadership approach that causes change in individuals and social systems. In its ideal form, it creates valuable and positive change in the followers with the end goal of developing followers into leaders. Enacted in its authentic form, transformational leadership enhances the motivation, morale, and performance of followers through a variety of mechanisms. These include connecting the follower's sense of identity and self to the mission and the collective identity of the organization; being a role model for followers that inspires them; challenging followers to take greater ownership for their work; and understanding the strengths and weaknesses of followers, so the leader can align followers with tasks that optimize their performance.[10]

Transformational leadership is more effective than transactional leadership, where the appeal is to more selfish concerns. An appeal to social values thus encourages people to collaborate, rather than working as individuals. Transformational leadership is an ongoing process rather than the discrete exchanges of the transactional approach.

Transformational leaders raise the bar by appealing to higher ideals and values of followers. In doing so, they may model the values themselves and use appealing methods to attract people to the values and to the leader.

Followership and Leadership

The flip side of leadership is followership. First introduced by Hollander and Webb, the term *followership* is characterized as an independent relationship in which the leader's perceived legitimacy can affect the degree to which followers allow themselves to be influenced.[11] This early work emphasizes the reciprocal relationship in which followers play an active role not only by receiving but also exerting influence.

Servant leadership advocates a perspective that leaders have a responsibility to serve their followers by helping them achieve and improve by modeling leaders' ethical values, attitudes, and behaviors that influence organizational outcomes through the fulfillment of followers' needs. The basic premise of servant leadership is leaders should put the needs of followers before their own needs. Servant leaders use collaboration and persuasion to influence followers rather than coercion and control. They understand their stewardship role and are accountable for their actions. Servant leadership helps to create an ethical, trusting organizational climate.

Trust is a key component in developing successful relationships between leaders and followers. A trusting relationship is built on shared values, respect, open communication, and accountability. Trevino et al.'s pillars of ethical leadership are the relevant behaviors that leaders can employ to demonstrate integrity to followers and build trust. The pillars are antecedents to trust and include role-modeling through visible action, the use of rewards and discipline, and communicating about ethics and values.[12]

Followership, servant leaders, and authenticity all share one common characteristic: *leader ethicality*. De Cremer and Tenbrunsel define leader ethicality as the intention to demonstrate normatively appropriate conduct and to create an environment within which others will be encouraged to act ethically and discouraged from acting unethically. Demonstrating normatively appropriate conduct is in part determined by follower perceptions, thus leader intent is important. Moreover, this definition takes into consideration the importance of moral perspectives and underscores the notion that ethical behavior is to some extent defined by how it is construed within the context of social prescriptions.[13] In other words, the public interest ideal is the context within which leaders model ethical behavior to nourish the perception that the accounting profession is an ethical profession with norms and values.

The social perception of a leader's legitimacy may play an important role in determining how the leader's morally relevant actions are interpreted and the influence leaders have on followers. The social context created by followers' normative expectations is a significant determinant of leader legitimacy, and violations of such expectations can cast doubt on the leader's position, authority, status, and influence. Imagine, for example, if a controller was pressured by the CFO, who paid no regard to the ethical standards of the profession but allowed personal goals to influence professional values. The followers would be less likely to embrace the actions of such a leader.

De Cremer and Tenbrunsel posit that, due to the socially construed nature of leader legitimacy, leaders are vulnerable to follower judgments. Leaders may gain legitimacy from followers when they allow themselves to receive follower influence and behave in accordance with followers' normative expectations.[14] It stands to reason that if leadership is important to performance, followership must have something to do with it too. Organizational dissidence is best controlled when both parties strive for high ethics in their behavior and decision making.

Social Learning Theory

Social learning theory has been used to understand how leaders influence followers more generally. Social learning theory holds that individuals look to role models in the work context, and model or imitate their behavior. Modeling is acknowledged to be one of the most powerful means for transmitting values, attitudes, and behaviors. Employees learn what to do, as well as what not to do, by observing their leaders' behavior and its consequences. Leaders become role models by virtue of their assigned role, their status and success in the organization, and their power to affect the behavior and outcomes of followers.[15] Through social learning, people may adopt ethical behaviors, as evidenced by the impact of ethical leadership[16] or antisocial behaviors.[17]

Leaders who engage in unethical behaviors create a context supporting what Kemper calls "parallel deviance," meaning that employees observe and are likely to imitate the inappropriate conduct.[18] If leaders are observed "cooking the books," or enriching themselves at the expense of others, as did Skilling, Ebbers, and Kozlowski, followers learn that such behavior is expected. If leaders are rewarded for unethical conduct, the lesson for followers becomes particularly strong and we might expect them to emulate such behavior especially if no consequences exist for wrongful actions.

The social learning approach suggests a mostly instrumental understanding of what drives unethical behavior in organizations. It argues that because of leaders' authority role and the power to reward and punish, employees will pay attention to and mimic leaders' behavior, and they will do what is rewarded and avoid doing what is punished in the organization. The rewards and punishments need not be direct but also can be learned by observing how others in the organization are rewarded and disciplined.

A good example of antisocial behavior in what might be called a game of corporate survivor was at Enron where a policy nicknamed "rank and yank" had employees give one another annual ratings, with the bottom 15 percent being fired. Every year, all employees were rated from 1 (best) to 5 (worst). The more money you made for the company, the better your rating. Skilling was fond of saying that money was the only thing that motivated people. Skilling mandated that between 10 and 15 percent of the employees had to be rated as 5s. And to get a rating of 5 meant that you were fired.

Unethical cultures that foster antisocial behavior are not limited to large corporations. An often overlooked aspect of cultural deviance in the accounting profession is the negative influence of leadership in accounting firms as described in the Introduction to this chapter. Joseph Berardino established a culture at Andersen that can best be characterized as "see no evil, hear no evil, and speak no evil." One could hardly claim that he was an authentic leader who encouraged followers to follow the ethical path in auditing Enron. In fact, his inability or unwillingness to perceive the ethical issues in the Enron audit and their moral intensity opened the door to antisocial behaviors by audit personnel.

Moral Intensity

We first discussed Thomas Jones' moral intensity model in Chapter 3. Jones conceptualized his model such that moral intensity might influence each of the components of Rest's Four Component Model of Moral Behavior. It starts with ethical awareness. The more intense the ethical issues, the more likely the decision maker will be aware of the ethical implications of her intended actions.

Jones argued that ethical decisions are primarily contingent upon the characteristics of the issue at stake so that judgments of ethicality would involve a systematic evaluation of the moral intensity of the characteristics of the issue. Factors need to be evaluated for moral intensity, including the magnitude of the consequences of the moral act; the degree of social consensus that the moral act is unethical; the feelings of proximity of the moral agent to the moral act; the likelihood that the moral act would take effect; the temporal immediacy of the effect of the moral act; and the concentration of the effect. Jones's model predicts that the perceived overall intensity of a moral issue would influence the decision maker's moral judgment and, moral intent, as well as subsequent moral action.[19]

The moral intensity of issues in an organization play a role in whether whistleblowing will occur. The predictor of whistleblowing and that of empathy corresponds directly to the two moral intensity dimensions of seriousness of issue and proximity. The degree of social consensus that the moral act is unethical is greatly influenced by the culture of the organization and whether ethical leadership exists. Thus, an ethical leader is more attuned to the magnitude of consequences and can use that in the pre-action decision stage to mitigate any bystander effect.

Taylor and Curtis studied whistleblowing among public accounting seniors and found that moral intensity is one of three significant factors affecting the intention to report wrongdoing, where intention to report is measured as the likelihood of reporting and perseverance in reporting. The other two factors were professional identity and locus of commitment (organization versus colleague). The authors found that while high levels of professional identity increase the likelihood that an auditor will initially report an observed violation, the auditor's commitment to the organization drives perseverance in reporting. Auditors were more likely to report and to persevere when moral intensity is high.[20] More will be said about this study later on.

Moral awareness and moral leadership go hand in hand. A moral leader is more likely to have her radar up and notice when ethical issues exist than one who is not attuned to the ethical dimension of decisions. A moral leader knows that ethical judgments must be made to resolve ethical conflicts in a morally appropriate way.

A greater degree of harm or benefit results in an increase in moral intensity because more stakeholders are at risk and the potential negative effects of unethical actions are more serious. We could equate moral intensity with materiality issues in accounting where differences of opinion over proper accounting become more significant/intense as the amount involved increases and/or qualitative characteristics increase moral intensity—such as when an item in question masks a change in earnings or other trends.

The Role of Moral Intensity, Organizational Culture, and Ethical Leadership in Accounting

LO 8-3
Discuss how moral intensity and organizational culture influences leadership in accounting.

At an organizational level, ethical leaders build trust through actions and relationships with others. They set the tone that the value system is more important than producing numbers. In an interview with *Fraud Magazine,* Sherron Watkins characterizes the leadership of Ken Lay at Enron as follows:

> Ken Lay was setting the wrong tone. He was in effect letting his managers know that once you get to the executive suite, the company's assets are there for you to move around to yourself or your family. In some perverse way, Andy Fastow . . . could justify his behavior, saying to himself, "Well, my creative off-balance-sheet deals are helping Enron meet its financial statement goals. Why can't I just take a million here and there for myself as a 'structuring fee,' just like Lay has been taking a little Enron money and transferring it to his sister for all these years?"[21]

Watkins followed up by saying the CEO "must have pristine ethics if there is to be any hope of ethical behavior from the employees." She also suggested that CEOs must have a zero tolerance policy for ethically challenged employees, otherwise the internal control system will eventually be worthless.[22]

Ethical Leadership and Audit Firms

Personal ethical skills are primarily managed by the organizational structure of audit firms, and rules and processes have been developed with the sole aim of limiting the audit risk and guaranteeing audit quality. Ethical competencies are managed indirectly and promoted by the idea of responsible leadership and incentives to promote exemplary behaviors. Personal and professional ethics have roles to play in cultivating responsible leadership by management of audit firms. The promotion of responsible leadership is seen within audit firms as a way to improve audit quality.[23]

Responsible leadership in audit firms is essential to create an ethical environment within the firm. It is a critical component of setting the proper tone and encouraging members of the organization to ask probing questions when management's representations are unclear or unsubstantiated. Responsible leadership is an integral part of ethical leadership, although the latter also entails the ability to reason through ethical dilemmas and resolve conflicts in a morally appropriate way.

The ethical environment within an accounting firm is created through espoused values and management practices. The culture of the firm results from leadership style and may be the most important deterrent to unethical behavior.[24] Authentic (partner) leaders gain the confidence of audit staff and managers and create a foundation for ethical decision making.

Research by Ponemon found that leaders of accounting firms set the tone of their organizations, promoting those whose personal attributes more closely reflected the leaders' perceptions and moral reasoning development. He hypothesized there is a correlation between the organizational culture created by leaders of the accounting firms and the subordinates' personal characteristics and decision-making styles.[25]

Prior research has indicated that audit seniors' perceptions of their firm leaders and firm culture impact auditor behavior. Personal characteristics have an impact on individual behaviors. Shaub et al. found mixed evidence of "the ability of an accounting firm to either change an auditor's ethical orientation to match its own, or to provide an environment that closely matches an auditor's norms."[26]

The dissidence that is created when individual values do not fit into the expectations of the firm might lead the individual to alter behavior to conform to firm norms, the firing of the individual from the firm, or her voluntary departure. Ponemon confirmed the existence of a selection-socialization mechanism operating to control ethical reasoning in public accounting firms. The selection-socialization bias causes a firm to hire and promote individuals who fit into the prevailing firm culture and causes individuals unable to fit into that culture to leave.[27]

Douglas et al. studied the influence of ethical orientation and ethical judgment in situations of high and low moral intensity and found that ethical orientation is related to ethical judgments in high (but not low) moral intensity situations, which appears to support Jones' issue-contingent argument. They also found that perceived organizational culture is indirectly related to ethical judgments, as ethical culture affects individual values (i.e., idealism) and idealism affects judgments.[28]

Morris studied the influence of authentic leadership and ethical firm culture on auditor behavior. She used the definition of authentic leadership provided by Avolio and Gardner as follows:[29]

> A pattern of leader behavior that draws upon and promotes both positive psychological capacities and a positive ethical climate, to foster four constructs: greater self-awareness, an internalized moral perspective, balanced processing of information, and relational transparency on the part of leaders working with followers, fostering positive self-development.

Morris gathered data from 120 practicing senior auditors representing the Big Four firms, other international firms, large regional firms, and local firms. Participants were asked to indicate the frequency of selected dysfunctional behavior among audit seniors. Morris hypothesized that perceptions of authentic leadership are negatively related to the frequency of dysfunctional audit behaviors. The behaviors identified include under-reporting of time worked on an engagement, premature sign-off on audit procedures, and other dysfunctional behaviors.[30]

The results indicate that a typical audit senior at these firms more frequently under-reports time than prematurely signing off on audit work. The results also indicate there was a significant negative correlation between all measures of authentic leadership and dysfunctional audit behaviors with few exceptions. With respect to ethical culture, there was a negative relationship between the audit seniors' perceptions of their firms as ethical, and instances of dysfunctional audit behavior. The findings support the mediation of perceptions of authenticity in leaders on the auditors' perception of ethical firm culture and on auditors' instances of dysfunctional behavior. The results seem to indicate that the four constructs of authentic leadership, whether taken individually or in combination, have influence over the employee's perception of the ethical content of a firm's organizational culture.[31]

The takeaway from the Morris study is that authentic leaders can help to promote an ethical culture and reduce the instances of dysfunctional auditor behavior. Authentic leaders seek to eliminate ethical dissonance. As we discussed in Chapter 3, ethical (authentic) leaders commit to a high person-organization fit where organizational ethics are high and the culture promotes high individual ethics (High-High). Any other combination may jeopardize ethical decision making and sacrifice the public trust in the audit profession—at least in that instance.

Consider what might have happened at Andersen if Joseph Berardino were an authentic leader who placed ethical values ahead of non-ethical values. The culture within the firm would have been quite different. The message sent would have been that the red flags raised by Carl Bass about accounting for the off-balance-sheet partnerships had to be dealt with, not swept under the rug. Perhaps Berardino's biggest fault was in not balancing processing of information; instead, the negative aspects of what was happening at Enron were shoved in the background and hidden from view.

Gender Influence on Decision Making of Public Accounting Professionals

In a study published in *Behavioral Research in Accounting*, Bobek et al. describe the results of an investigation of how professional role (auditor or tax professional), decision context (an audit or tax issues), and gender influence public accounting professionals' ethical decision making. Participants were asked to respond to hypothetical sets of facts about contentious client conflicts for which they were asked to recommend whether to concede to the client's wishes, and to indicate their own behavioral intentions. The decision context (an audit or tax environment) was manipulated to explore individual attributes in contexts with different types of professional responsibility.[32]

The results of the study may have implications for leadership in CPA firms because the factors that influence how males and females see their role as accounting professionals differ. Males were less likely to recommend conceding, and less likely themselves to concede, in an audit condition versus a tax condition. This is not surprising given the role of a tax accountant as an advisor with an advocacy relationship, whereas an accounting professional's audit role is that of an independent judge of the fairness of the financial statements.

Looking at the responses of females, there was no significant difference based on either condition or professional role. However, it was found that females appeared to use a different decision-making process than males. Females may be more likely to use an intuitionist approach. This implies a more deliberative approach may not be used, nor one that relies more heavily on systematic ethical reasoning to resolve conflicts. If so, the implications for resolving ethical dilemmas in dealing with clients may be significant. Another surprising result was that perceptions of moral intensity were seen as a factor that might mediate context in decision making in males but not females. Thus, the results show that professional role, context, and moral intensity potentially affect male decision making in a significant way but not female decision making.

The results of the study are one snapshot in time and limited by the choice of subjects studied. It will be interesting to see if the results are duplicated in other environments. Nevertheless, they do point out that leaders of audit firms need to pay attention to gender differences in designing decision systems to ensure audit quality.

Ethical Leadership and the Internal Audit Function

Chambers identifies seven attributes of internal audit leadership as a standard for ethical behavior including honesty, courageousness, accountability, empathy, trustworthiness, respect, and proactiveness. These are important qualities for internal auditors who are on the front lines of dealing with financial fraud.[33]

Studies of ethical leadership have relied on manipulating variables such as integrity and ethical standards (i.e., high versus low), treatment of employees (i.e., fair versus not fair), and holding of employees accountable for ethical conduct (i.e., held accountable versus not held accountable).[34] The internal audit function has been conceptualized as a multi-dimensional construct with a position within the corporate governance structure of a company based on to whom the internal audit function reports (i.e., audit committee versus chief financial officer); the primary role of the internal audit function within the company (i.e., assurance versus consulting); and the work product produced (i.e., history of finding versus missing deficiencies).[35]

Internal auditors can sometimes be bullied by CFOs, or at least an attempt to do so occurs, which makes it more difficult for them to carry out their ethical obligations. This occurred at WorldCom where Cynthia Cooper was consistently pressured by Scott Sullivan to not act on the improper accounting. An internal auditor with a weak character might go along, but Cooper demonstrated strong ethical leadership skills in working with her team to uncover the scope of the fraud. She wouldn't take no for an answer and went to the audit committee first, then to the outside auditors, and persisted in her efforts to correct the wrongdoing.

When deciding whether to record a questionable journal entry (i.e., any entry for which a reasonable business case can be made for either recording it or not recording it), auditors may take their cue from executive management's behavior, especially if such behavior is the social norm and has been rewarded in the past.[36] In addition, a high-quality internal audit function can reinforce the tone at the top and provide guidance for decision makers by monitoring internal control and management's actions. For instance, accountants may hesitate to record a questionable entry if they know that internal audit is likely to detect inappropriate financial reporting practices. Prawitt et al. discovered from their study of earnings management that a quality internal audit function is associated with moderation in the level of earnings management using abnormal accruals and the propensity to meet or beat analysts' earnings forecasts as proxies.[37]

Arel et al. studied the impact of ethical leadership, the internal audit function, and moral intensity on a decision to record a questionable entry. The authors found that the joint influence of ethical leadership and internal audit quality on accountants' willingness to book a questionable accrual entry is fully mediated by participants' perception of the moral intensity of the issue. Specifically, a strong internal audit function and weak ethical leadership combined to alter accountants' perception of the moral intensity of the issue. As a result, accounting professionals who perceive greater moral intensity associated with the controller's request to record a questionable entry are less willing to book the questionable entry.[38]

The Arel study also found that a strong internal audit function may cause accountants to question the appropriateness and ethicalness of an undocumented journal entry when combined with weak ethical leadership. Conversely, a weak internal audit function removes the most important internal control to help prevent and detect financial statement fraud. A case in point is at HealthSouth. Maron Webster, a former internal auditor at HealthSouth, testified that CEO Richard Scrushy had fired him in 1989 after he questioned accounting at a company operation in Miami. Webster said he raised concerns about improperly booked receivables and was told by Scrushy that "we're under certain pressures to make certain numbers. We have an obligation to stockholders and shareholders."[39]

Former chief internal auditor Teresa Rubio Sanders, who was hired by Scrushy in 1990 and quit in late 1999, testified that her office wasn't allowed to see the general ledger, where previous testimony showed a $2.7 billion earnings overstatement occurred from 1996 through 2002. Under questioning from defense lawyer Jim Parkman, Sanders testified she never complained to HealthSouth directors about the lack of access to corporate records. She also said she rarely met with directors or the audit committee.[40] Her lack of concern for the welfare of the company or its shareholders speaks volumes about the importance of ethical leadership to the internal audit function. Internal auditors, like Sanders, who bury their head in the sand while fraud occurs not only fail in their ethical leadership role, but make it more difficult for the external auditors to uncover what is still hidden under the surface.

Ethical Leadership and Tax Practice

Studies have shown a disconnect exists between the perceptions of organizational ethics between higher and lower levels of an organization. Employees at higher levels perceive organizational ethics at a higher level.[41] In accounting, Bobek et al. found a disconnect exists between tax partners and nonpartner tax practitioners with respect to perceptions of organizational ethics when they described a self-identified ethical dilemma. On average, they found tax partners rated the ethical environments of their firms as stronger than nonpartner tax practitioners, especially with respect to firm leadership. While tax partners were more likely to describe an actual ethical dilemma than nontax practitioners, the group who described a dilemma rated the ethical environment as weaker, and this discrepancy was more pronounced for nontax practitioners.[42] This raises a question whether the ethical expectations of tax professionals are being met by their firms.

In a later study, Bobek et al. probed the reasons for the difference in perceptions of tax partners and nonpartner tax practitioners. They found that, when nonpartners believe they have a meaningful role in shaping and maintaining the ethical environment of their firms and/or have strong organizational fit with the firm, they are more likely to perceive the ethical environment as strong and perceive it similarly to firm leaders. They also found that among firm leaders (i.e., tax partners), the sense of having a stronger public interest responsibility and a higher frequency of receiving mentoring are both associated with stronger perceptions of the ethical environment.[43]

Earlier in this chapter and in Chapter 3 we discussed the relationship between organizational fit and ethical culture. It is not surprising that a strong (ethical) fit positively influences perceptions of an ethical culture. Beyond that, an important issue is what steps a firm can take to provide a meaningful role to nonpartners in shaping the ethical environment of their firm. Studies indicate that the weakest part of the ethical environment appears to be outcomes (e.g., rewards and sanctions) and "explicitly rewarding (and punishing) ethical (unethical) behavior is a tangible way to encourage nonleaders to participate in maintaining a strong ethical environment for the firm."[44]

The Role of CFOs

The CFOs at HealthSouth uniformly allowed themselves to be influenced by Scrushy, even bullied into recording improper entries to make things look better than they really were. Aaron Beam recounted his experiences at HealthSouth in an interview with the *Business Report.* He used some colorful language to describe what had happened at the company. When asked what led him to cook the books at HealthSouth, he stated:

> It's a process. When you're the CFO of a publicly traded company, you're under a lot of pressure to deliver good numbers. I think over time, just the culture of Wall Street, you learn to "put lipstick on the pig." You're careful not to say anything negative. Over time, there's a possibility you learn how to be deceptive, because you want to protect the price of the stock. We were starting to not quite make our numbers for Wall Street...[45]

Assuming Beam knew of Webster's position, it did not influence him to question the ethicalness of the accounting pushed hard on him by Scrushy. Here, there was no ethical leadership by the internal auditors to raise the level of moral intensity to a degree that could have influenced the accounting. Exhibit 8.1 further details the glaring lapses in ethical leadership and corporate culture at HealthSouth.

EXHIBIT 8.1 *Ethical Leadership and Corporate Culture at HealthSouth*

The following is largely drawn from a story in the University of Chicago Booth School of Business News following a presentation at the College by HealthSouth's former CFOs, Aaron Beam and Weston Smith.[46] The HealthSouth story took place in the 1990s and early 2000s and is about a corporate network of rehabilitation hospitals that skyrocketed up Wall Street and then plunged off a cliff. It's a story about sketchy ethics, tyrannical leadership, and crossing the line so often that boundaries disappeared.

Founded in 1984 by Beam and Richard Scrushy, the company's former chairman and CEO, HealthSouth went public two years later, after Scrushy impressed a group of Wall Street investors with a presentation on the company's potential. By 1995 the company had health centers in all 50 states, plus 40,000 employees, 10 to 12 jets, and a spot on the Fortune 500 list. Beam spent his millions on cars, condos, and a collection of French neckties that equaled an entry-level salary. It sounds a lot like what Dennis Kozlowski did at Tyco.

All the while, Beam said he was allowing Scrushy to bully him and other HealthSouth executives into manipulating financial reports to reflect the numbers Scrushy promised investors. During a meeting in 1996, Beam told Scrushy they would have to finally report a bad quarter. Scrushy said no, and they devised a way to hide the earnings shortfall.

"I should have had the courage to stand up and say, 'No, we can't cross this line,'" Beam said. Scrushy promised to deny everything if Beam reported the fraud and accused Beam of not being a team player. In 1997, Beam retired from HealthSouth, selling his company stock and walking away from a half-million-dollar annual salary. He thought the deception was behind him—until March 2003 when he heard on national television that a massive fraud had been uncovered at HealthSouth.

The $2.7 billion HealthSouth fraud involved recording fake revenues on the company's books over six years, and correspondingly adjusting the balance sheets and paper trails. Methods included overestimating insurance reimbursements, manipulating fixed-asset accounts, improperly booking capital expenses, and overbooking reserve accounts.[47]

(Continued)

According to the testimony of former CFOs Beam, Smith, Michael D. Martin, William T. Owens, and Malcolm McVay, each one realized the error of his ways, but most felt helpless to blow the whistle or even leave the company. Scrushy "managed greatly by fear and intimidation," according to Owens, who served as HealthSouth's third CFO from 2000 to 2001. Second CFO Martin testified that he tried to quit at least three times during his 1997 to 2000 tenure. "[Scrushy] said, 'Martin, you can't quit. You'll be the fall guy.'"

Apart from the organizational culture, what made the fraud possible on a structural level was Scrushy's elevation of so many decisions to the executive level, which limited checks and balances along the way. The accounting systems in the field did not interface with the corporate enterprise resource planning software, making it necessary for results to be consolidated by hand at the corporate level. That made it easy to fudge numbers, since the internal-audit staff was directed to review only the field numbers, not the consolidated numbers. In fact, Ernst & Young auditors noted in 2001 that "management is dominated by one or a few individuals without effective oversight by the board of directors or audit committee." EY also observed that the internal-audit function was understaffed, undertrained, and lacking in independence.

HealthSouth maintained impeccable corporate policies—on paper. A confidential whistleblowers' hotline had been set up in 1997. The company's nonretaliation policy gave the compliance director direct access to the board of directors.

Many employees of HealthSouth, particularly those who worked at medical centers in other parts of the country, thought they worked for an ethical company. A former regional manager who oversaw finances for facilities in several states says that the message from headquarters never conflicted with her personal values. "They were always stressing honesty in what we did, and that was how we ran it in the field," she says. "We had no reason to think they did any different."

HealthSouth is a case study in how a seemingly ethical company, at least one that had the trappings of an ethical consciousness, bowed to the unethical intentions and behaviors of its CEO and ignored the very systems that were put into place to build an ethical culture. It is a case study in how unethical leaders can corrupt the ethical culture and drag others, willingly or unwillingly, into a financial fraud that destroys a company and ruins lives along the way.

What happened at HealthSouth was not an uncommon occurrence, although the direct involvement of the CEO in pressuring other executives to execute the fraud was unusual. In most other cases (i.e., Enron and WorldCom), it was the CFOs who masterminded the fraud and carried it out. They exerted the pressure, perhaps so that the CEOs had "plausible deniability."

Ethical Leadership Failure

LO 8-4
Explain the implications of ethical leadership failure on whistleblowing.

Ethical leadership failure occurs for many reasons. Linda Thornton identifies a variety of individual and organizational factors. Individual ones include ignoring ethical boundaries within a company (i.e., ethics codes); prominent personal values (i.e., ignoring what is allowed and acting out of self-interest); and a lack of moral compass (i.e., it is not specifically prohibited so it is fine for me to do it). Organizational factors include lack of clarity (i.e., uncertain what is and is not ethical); lack of positive role models (no one does what is "expected"); and no accountability (no one suffers the consequences of their actions).[48]

Price points out that leaders characteristically make exceptions for themselves—exemptions from generally accepted moral standards—and they sometimes get it wrong and are guilty of ethical failure. He claims that these ethical failures in leaders are typically cognitive rather than volitional, a matter of false belief rather than bad desire. He opposes the view that leaders characteristically go wrong in acting selfishly because, having great power, they can get away with it. Instead, to be morally justified it is not enough for leaders to put collective interests ahead of their own interests because self-interest is not the problem. Leaders are characteristically oriented to the ends so that they share with their followers that they face cognitive challenges, which are of two sorts. First, they may fail to note the ethical constraints on the means they use to achieve their ends. Second, they may ignore the interests of parties outside their group of followers.[49]

When we examine the volitional account, we see that moral failure is about knowing what is right and not doing it, while on a cognitive level, it is a matter of being mistaken either about the content of some moral requirement or about its scope. Applying an ends-justifies-the-means approach to ethical reasoning, Price associates the volitional account primarily with egoism, but he acknowledges that a leader might cast aside moral constraints for the good of the group as well as selfish reasons. He argues that leaders in particular typically go wrong not because they want to use their position to take advantage of their followers, but because they are committed to the intrinsic value of group ends and therefore believe that goal achievement justifies moral costs to followers and outsiders.[50]

Implications for Whistleblowing in Accounting

According to Mesmer-Magnus and Viswesvaran, organizational employees have three options to address an unsatisfactory situation faced within an organization: (1) exit the organization, (2) voice discontent (i.e., blow the whistle), or (3) remain silent.[51] Employees with greater organizational commitment may prefer voicing discontent to exiting. Near and Miceli suggest that internal reporters will demonstrate high levels of firm loyalty in their initial decision to report.[52]

Sims and Keenan studied organizational and interpersonal values as predictors of external whistleblowing. They found employees were more likely to engage in external whistleblowing if they had the support of their supervisor or they perceived company policies suggested that such behavior was acceptable. The study also reported that external whistleblowing channels would be used only if would-be whistleblowers believed internal whistleblowing would be ineffective. The desire to use internal channels to report wrongdoing puts the ball in the court of companies to develop ethical systems to facilitate such reporting.[53]

The locus of organizational commitment represents the strength of employees' identification with and involvement in a particular organization, a strong belief in organizational goals and values, and a willingness to exert considerable effort on behalf of the organization.[54] In public accounting, organizational commitment is heavily emphasized through identification with the ethical systems, quality controls, and firm leadership.

Commitment to the organization contrasts with colleague commitment, with the latter dependent on a sense of responsibility and readiness to support colleagues within the organization. Auditors may choose to act on behalf of their colleagues, mindless of the welfare of the firm as a whole. Thus, unlike professional identity, which exists independent of organizational affiliation, organizational colleague commitment and firm commitment are linked together in many cases with one sustaining the other, and in other circumstances, such as when a colleague performs an unethical act, they create conflicting allegiances.[55]

In their study of whistleblowing, Taylor and Curtis examined the complex relationships in accounting firms that influence an individual's decision to report an ethical violation. They conceive of the environment of the firm as a series of concentric circles with the accounting profession as the outermost layer. An auditor can think of her professional identity as her affinity for and identification with the audit profession. Within the profession are public accounting firms. Auditors can be committed to the firm and the profession, neither one, or one or the other. Individuals also vary in their commitment to colleagues within the organization. At the center of these potentially conflicting layers of commitment is the ethical violation itself and the individual's personal reaction to it. Even if an auditor is committed to the profession and the firm, she may choose not to report an unethical or illegal event because it is deemed as not being a critical event. On the other hand, the auditor may show evidence of low commitment to the profession and the firm, but the event is so egregious that she feels she must act. Individuals must weigh all of these influences and weigh their significance in arriving at their reporting intention.[56]

Taylor and Curtis theorize that, when assessing whether to report, an individual will weigh the harm to the organization from not reporting against the harm to the colleague from reporting, and those with greater colleague commitment would demonstrate lower reporting intentions. They expected individuals with greater organizational commitment to exhibit greater reporting intentions. However, the locus of commitment and likelihood of reporting were not significantly related, although locus of commitment and perseverance of reporting are significantly related. Thus, it would appear that the longer an individual persists in attempting to resolve an issue, the more likely one's commitment to a colleague versus the organization becomes an influencing factor in determining whether to report.[57] Examining persistence as a virtue, we can see that it is likely to reflect one's commitment to ethical standards (i.e., due care and professional skepticism), and it reflects a strong sense of professional identity.

Personal responsibility for reporting is also an important consideration. Senior auditors have been found to be more likely to report a manager's ethical violation when they perceived personal costs of disclosure were low or when personal responsibility for reporting was perceived to be high. A correlation exists between the likelihood of audit seniors reporting audit staff for premature sign-off behavior based on whether the audit step was a necessary (unnecessary) step, and the staff member had a good (poor) performance history. Senior auditors were more likely to report a manager's ethical violation when they perceived personal costs of disclosure were low or when personal responsibility for reporting was perceived to be high.[58]

Brennan and Kelly studied some of the factors that influence propensity or willingness to blow the whistle among trainee auditors. The factors studied include audit firm organizational structures, personal characteristics of whistleblowers, and situational variables. The authors found that formal structures for whistleblowing and internal (versus external) reporting channels increase the likelihood of the subjects' reporting of an ethical violation by an audit partner. Their findings indicate that audit firms should examine their structures for reporting suspected or actual wrongdoing and, where necessary, improve such structures by encouraging staff to voice their concerns internally. A key issue is whether the firms have in place a system of quality controls to report internally. This is important because the respondents showed a reluctance to report externally. Brennan and Kelly's results have potentially significant implications for whether auditors use external reporting mechanisms, such as those of Dodd-Frank, if internal reporting has not resolved the differences between the auditor and firm management.[59]

Miceli et al.[60] studied the whistleblower intentions of internal auditing directors and found those directors less likely to report incidents of wrongdoing "when they did not feel compelled morally or by role prescription to do so." The authors note that these feelings of moral compunction and role prescriptions form the basis of the moral intensity of the situation.

Graham suggests that the positive contextual motivations toward reporting the unethical acts of others are a combination of the perceived seriousness of an unethical behavior and the perceived responsibility to act on this behavior. These two individual constructs are highly correlated with the seriousness of an issue generating increased feelings of responsibility to respond.[61] The more serious the matter (i.e., high moral intensity), the more likelihood it will be reported. In such instances, the professional identity of the person reporting takes precedence over organizational and colleague commitment.

Whistleblowing can be perceived as an effective response to an organization's failure to establish accountability mechanisms internally. For auditors, the act of whistleblowing is internally required when differences exist on accounting issues with management because of their compliance obligations. External auditors have a similar obligation and additional reporting requirements to the SEC under Section 10(A) of the Securities Exchange Act of 1934, as discussed in Chapter 3.

Notwithstanding Dodd-Frank requirements, external auditors have to wrestle with their conscience when differences with management on financial reporting matters exist. They have to choose between confidentiality requirements and their public interest obligation, all the while evaluating the moral intensity of the issue.

A Case Study in Ethical Leadership

A good example of where an auditor acted based on her sense of right and wrong and identity as a professional is the case of Diem-Thi Le. She was faced with an ethical dilemma where her values and beliefs contradicted the values and beliefs of her employer, the Defense Contract Audit Agency (DCAA). Le was a senior auditor and had performed an accounting system audit at the corporate office of a contractor when she found that the accounting system was inadequate because the contractor was misallocating and mischarging costs to the government. Le's supervisor (regional audit manager) concurred with her audit findings; however, subsequently, the supervisor told Le that their branch manager disagreed with her.

The regional audit manager told Le that because the branch manager was the one who signed the audit report, her opinion took precedence over Le's. Essentially, the person performing the audit had no say in the final audit report opinion. Moreover, the regional manager instructed Le's supervisor to put Le's working papers in the "superseded work paper folder." Her supervisor then deleted the audit findings from Le's working papers and, without performing any additional audit work, represented those changed working papers as Le's original working papers to support the change in the audit opinion from an inadequate accounting system to an adequate system. Shortly afterward, the audit report was issued, and the contractor accounting system was deemed adequate. Consequently, the contractor did not have to propose or implement any corrective actions to eliminate its accounting system deficiencies, which resulted in misallocating and mischarging costs to the government contracts.

Le did try to find an answer internally as to why her working papers were set aside and her audit opinion changed. Was it an anomaly or systemic problem? To satisfy her curiosity and give her branch manager the benefit of the doubt, she went to the office common drive that contained other audits and reviewed some system audits. She discovered a pattern of branch managers changing auditors' opinions, but Le did not know why these branch managers were doing it. She found out the reason after consulting with other supervisory auditors of other offices. By making the contractor systems and related internal controls adequate, less audit risk would be perceived and, consequently, fewer audit hours would be incurred on other audits. Because one of the DCAA's performance metrics was productivity rate, which measures the hours incurred versus the dollar examined, having fewer audit hours incurred for the same amount of dollars examined would increase the productivity rate. The productivity rate was one of the factors on which a branch manager's annual performance review was based.

On September 10, 2008, Le testified before the U.S. Senate Committee on Homeland Security and Governmental Affairs, which was investigating the DCAA, that an audit opinion she had developed on the audit of a contractor receiving funds from the U.S. government had been changed by a branch manager without her knowledge or approval. Ultimately, Le was responsible for a ruling by the U.S. Office of the Special Counsel that the DCAA violated the Whistleblower Protection Act when it retaliated against Le for blowing the whistle on fraudulent practices.

In reflecting on the incident in an interview with the *Orange County Register*, Le admitted to struggling with her conscience for weeks, trying through sleepless nights to get the courage to report the bad audits. She said, "I got to live with myself when I look in the mirror at the end of the day." She told the interviewer that management viewed her as the enemy, and even sympathetic coworkers were afraid of being associated with her: "When [I] walked into the break room, everybody walked out."[62]

A summary of Le's actions as a whistleblower and subsequent testimony before the U.S. Senate Committee on Homeland Security and Governmental Affairs appears in Exhibit 8.2.

EXHIBIT 8.2   *Diem-Thi Le and Whistleblowing at the DCAA*[63]

Diem-Thi Le testified before the U.S. Senate Committee on Homeland Security and Governmental Affairs on September 10, 2008. She told the committee that, because of the emphasis on the increase of the productivity rate, DCAA auditors, including herself, were pressured by management to perform audits within certain numbers of budgeted hours. Given the change in audit opinions by management without performing additional audit work or without discussing it with the auditors whose opinions were altered, she concluded that it was a lack of due professional care, at best, and negligent and fraudulent, at worst. She confided with other colleagues about her findings and was told she had no choice but to call the Department of Defense Inspector General (DoD IG) Hotline. She did so in November 2005.

Le said she never imagined that she would call the hotline and make an allegation against her management. She became disillusioned when she found out the complaint was sent back to her own agency for investigation. The independent process of review and determination of action by DoD IG personnel had been compromised. She followed up on her complaint several times, and in February 2006, she was told that it might take a long time for someone to work on her case due to limited staff. She then decided to contact the local office of the Defense Criminal Investigative Services (DCIS) and met with a special agent on March 4, 2006. She also found out that her complaint had been referred to DCAA headquarters, and that the referral included specific personal identifying information about her, such as her name and cell phone number, as well as details of the accounting system audit that triggered the hotline complaint. She concluded that her identity as a whistleblower had not been adequately protected; therefore, she suffered reprisal from DCAA management.

She made the following points about her experiences in her testimony:

- In September 2005, my management overruled my audit findings. In October 2005, I was transferred to another team. In the November 2005 Staff Conference, the regional audit manager stated that if we auditors did not like management's audit opinion, we should find another job.

- In early July 2006, I was transferred to another team. In late July 2006, my management was interviewed by the DCIS special agent. In October 2006, I found out that I was the only auditor with an "Outstanding" performance rating who did not get a performance award.

- In early April 2007, the Office of Special Counsel (OSC) investigator contacted DCAA Western Region management to inform them of my OSC complaint. Shortly after that happened, my supervisor told me that I should seek mental health counseling because of the stress I was under. She gave me an Employee Assistance Form and asked that I sign it.

- In August 2007, I was given my annual performance evaluation for the period of July 2006 through June 2007. I was downgraded from an "Outstanding" rating to a "Fully Successful" rating (two notches down). Also, my promotion points came down from 78 (out of a maximum of 120) to 58 points. Please note that prior to this job performance evaluation, I had been an outstanding auditor for several years.

- On August 31, 2007, I was given a memorandum signed by my supervisor and prepared by the DCAA headquarters' legal counsel. The memo instructed me that I was not allowed to provide any documents generated by a government computer, including e-mails and job performance evaluations, to any investigative units, including the OSC.

(Continued)

- On September 10, 2007, my supervisor advised me to read the 18 USC 641, Theft of Government Property. My supervisor stated that the unauthorized distribution of agency documents is theft, and it does not matter if the purpose is to respond to a hotline or OSC complaint.
- In August 2008, I was given my job performance evaluation for the period of July 2007 through June 2008. I remained at "Fully Successful," which is one notch above the rating that one would be put on a Performance Improvement Plan (PIP). My promotion points came down to 53.

Le concluded her testimony by stating that it was her opinion that DCAA management had become so metric driven that the quality of its audits and independence had suffered. Audits were not dictated by audit risks, but rather by the established budgeted hours and due dates. The pressure to close out audits and to meet the productivity rate was so intense that it often prevented auditors from following their instincts in questioning the contractor costs, reporting internal control deficiencies, and evaluating any suspected irregular conduct. In the end, contractors were "getting away with murder" because they knew that DCAA was so metric driven. She also pointed out that DCAA management had reduced the number of audit staff and created layers of personnel who did nothing but monitor metrics. She had hoped the culture would change and enable auditors to perform high-quality audits in accordance with generally accepted government auditing standards in order to protect the government's interest and taxpayers' money.

It is not easy to put everything on the line by questioning decisions and actions of your colleagues and the organization you work for. Diem-Thi Le's experience stands as an example of when doing the right thing can lead to right results, at least in the end, and that acting on one's conscience and a sense of professional identity can lead to positive results.

Accounting Leaders Discussed in the Text

We have identified at least three accounting professionals in this book who demonstrated leadership qualities and were successful in putting an end to wrongdoing in their organizations. Back in Chapter 1 we discussed the case of Cynthia Cooper at WorldCom. In Chapter 3 we discussed the case of Anthony Menendez at Haliburton. Finally, in this chapter we examined the experiences of Diem-Thi Le at DCAA. These three share certain qualities of behavior. They had a strong set of ethical values that informed their actions. They were persistent in searching for truth. And they were courageous and willing to put their own positions' in jeopardy to serve the public that expected only the best from them as accounting professionals.

We also discussed many who got caught up in the moment; those who gave in to the pressure of superiors and typically set aside their own values in order to do what they were told to do: Be a team player; just go along with it this one time. In these cases the common thread was fear, and intimidation was used to keep those with accounting responsibilities in line. Two examples come to mind. First, Betty Vinson at WorldCom who rationalized that if her boss, Scott Sullivan, said the accounting was acceptable, then it must be acceptable. She compromised her values and was blind to the ethical issues. Then, there were any number of CFOs at HealthSouth, as we discussed in this chapter, who lacked the courage to stand up to a bullying CEO, Richard Scrushy.

Leadership in accounting is different than leadership in most other organizations because of the public interest dimension. True leaders in the accounting profession have committed to this ideal and expect nothing less from their followers.

Values-Driven Leadership

LO 8-5

Describe the role of GVV in ethical leadership.

The starting point of a values-driven organization is the individual leader. A leader needs to connect with organizational values. Leaders must ask what they stand for and why. Leaders must consider why others would want to follow them. The goal is to get in touch with what motivates one's actions and how best to motivate those in the organization who look to the leader for direction. Values-based leadership is best summed up by Kouzes and Posner in *The Leadership Challenge:* "Clearly articulating and, more importantly, demonstrating one's values, forms the basis of a leader's credibility—and credibility in leadership is character-based."[64]

A values-based foundation is a critical element of making ethical decisions. The Six Pillars of Character discussed in Chapter 1 represent those values. Values-based decisions should start with a question: What are the values that should drive my decision making? From there, an ethical leader considers the stakeholders and their interests; weighs alternative courses of action; applies ethical reasoning to conflict situations; and decides what action should be taken given that the leader chooses to model ethical behavior in the organization.

The Giving Voice to Values (GVV) approach to decision making that was first discussed in Chapter 2 considers values to be the first pillar of the methodology. It sets the stage for the rest of the foundation including choices one makes and the purpose of deciding. Having a sense of purpose and shared values begins at the top and should filter throughout the organization to guide responses to ethical dilemmas.

GVV distinguishes between organizational values and individual values. Organizational values link to the mission of an organization and guide relationships with stakeholders. They set the tone for those in the organization and serve as standards of ethical behavior. While organizational values should be highly visible within the organization, individual values are internal to the very being of an individual. When organizational values and actions differ from what one truly believes in, then a way should be found to voice one's values with the intent of changing hearts and minds.

Ethical organizations encourage employees to voice their values. Ethical leaders know that if employees feel comfortable speaking up about matters of concern in a supportive environment, then problems will not fester and the likelihood of whistleblowing activity is lessened.

Consider the following situation: Amy is an auditor at Black and White, LLP, a mid-sized accounting firm in New York City. Amy has identified what may be a major fraud at a client entity. It seems the client engaged in a "sell-through" product agreement whereby an apparent sale to another party included a side agreement that obligated that party to resell the merchandise prior to paying for the "acquisition." Thus, a contingency existed that should have delayed the recording of the sales revenue but did not. Amy has already spoken to Pat, the audit manager, who instructed her to leave the transaction alone. It seems the client has exerted a great deal of pressure on the firm to go along with its accounting because the revenue involved is sufficient to change a loss for the year into a profit.

Amy is disappointed in Pat and what may be the firm's position on the matter. She knows the firm has a core set of values that do not square with the intended accounting. In fact, she joined the firm because the firm's values were consistent with hers. It seems as though Amy may be facing an instance of organizational dissidence in that the way in which she expected the organization to act is not the way that it did act. She wants to find a way to give voice to her values but is not sure how to go about it. What are the key issues for Amy to consider? What road should she take?

Values-based leadership cuts both ways. Amy may be disappointed in the firm's leadership but if she envisions herself as a leader (or potential leader), then she wants to demonstrate leadership instincts in deciding how to handle the matter. Perhaps she can influence the actions of the firm if she is successful in voicing her values. The GVV framework calls for consideration of the following issues.

- What are the shared values that should drive my actions?

- With whom do I need to speak to enable voicing my values?

- What do I need to say to most effectively express my point of view?
- What are the likely objections or pushback and, then,
- What should I say next?

Amy should evaluate the reasons and rationalization she needs to address. One may be that the leader(s) in the firm she decides to approach may "play the loyalty card" or insist that they "keep the client happy."

We could imagine developing a script to deal with Amy's ethical dilemma, as we explained in Chapter 3, which could entail a role-play exercise. However, here we are more interested in the facets of leadership Amy would want to cultivate in developing her game plan. First, she wants to be true to her personal and professional values. Her professional identity is tied up with how she handles the matter. Second, she needs to work within the system and identify potential supporters in the organization who might be open to hearing and supporting her point of view. Identifying leaders as potential supporters can strengthen her position. Next, she needs to carefully consider how others might react to what she plans on saying or doing. She needs to anticipate how she will respond to the objections they might make and pressures they apply. Finally, she needs to ask herself: What if I don't act and voice my values? How will I feel about myself? Would I be proud for others to know about it, including family members? What will happen if I do nothing and get blamed for inaction down the road? How will I feel if I do nothing and the organization implodes?

Ethical Leadership Competence

LO 8-6
Describe the characteristics of competent leaders.

Ethical Leadership Competence refers to the ability to handle all kinds of moral problems that may arise in an organization. It means to develop the problem-solving and decision-making skills to make difficult decisions. Leaders might try to deal with a moral problem in an automatic way, essentially using their authority for the basis of decision making. However, this System 1 approach is fraught with danger because the interests of all stakeholders may not be adequately considered; subtle moral issues may go unnoticed; and expediency is emphasized instead of thought and deliberation. As we have pointed out throughout the text, what is needed is to develop the competency to reason through ethical conflicts in a systematic way. There is no shortcut to making ethical decisions. It requires judgment and reflection on what the right thing to do is.

Thornton identifies five levels of ethical competence: personal, interpersonal, organizational, professional, and societal.[65] On a personal level, accounting professionals should internalize the values of the profession, including objectivity, integrity, diligence, and duty to society. Auditors work in teams so how they deal with others (i.e., showing respect, fair-mindedness) is a critical component of ethical competence. As members of an accounting firm, auditors should follow the ethics codes and expectations of their organizations, but they should never compromise their professional identity.

Kelly and Earley developed three measures called *The Ethical Leadership Scales,* which provide a measure of personal ethical competence, ethical leadership, and ethical organization. We have found the scales useful in teaching ethical leadership because they enable students to self-evaluate their leadership skills. Beginning with the understanding that effective ethical leadership depends on personal ethical competence, the *Ethical Competence Scale* provides a measuring stick of whether one's values consistently direct behavior. Questions to ask yourself include: Are you reliable and dependable? Are you willing to admit mistakes? Are you true to your word? Are you worthy of confidence? Do you keep promises and commitments?[66]

The *Ethical Leadership Scale* fits nicely with GVV methodology. It engages participants in reflecting on specific leadership qualities that can support voicing one's beliefs when conflicts exist in an organization and when interacting with others in organizational relationships. In discussing the usefulness of the Scales, Kelly and Earley point out that techniques of role-playing, simulation, and scenario writing can be used to enhance the experience.

The perception that followers have of managers in an organization, whether they are viewed as ethical leaders, depends on whether they are seen as moral persons and moral managers. Being a moral person is not enough to encourage ethical behavior of followers because of the distance between both parties. Moral managers gain legitimacy only if employees believe they are principled and caring, and say what they will do and do what they say.

Consistency in words and actions underlies ethical leadership. Followers must be comfortable that, if they follow the ethical path, they will be rewarded for doing so. In most of the companies that we have discussed in this book, the opposite was the case. Still, there are ethical organizations out there and leaders truly committed to doing the right thing.

When people face a moral problem they sometimes have great difficulties in not confusing moral goals, values, feelings, and emotions with the problem-solving and decision-making processes and the methods adopted for the solution of the problem. By now you know these skills can be learned but require practice, commitment, reflection, and a continuous cycle of re-examining whether you need to adjust your thinking to match the ethical demands of a situation. We suggest that a worthwhile goal is to strive to eliminate any cognitive dissonance so that your behaviors match your values and beliefs.

We end this section with a quote from Shakespeare's Hamlet: "To thine own self be true, and it must follow, as the night the day, thou canst not then be false to any man [or woman]."

Concluding Thoughts

We began this book by discussing Aristotle and the ancient Greek ethics of virtue. It is fitting that we end it by discussing the Socratic Method. The philosophical position of ethics as a choice, which focuses on the way choices are made and the skills involved, starts from the Socratic dialogue. The goal is not so much to impart knowledge, as teachers, about what is the "truth." Instead, it is to help you discover the truth for yourselves through a collaborative process of asking questions. In this way we have tried to develop critical thinking skills in our discussions and assignments. The bottom line is that as students you are more likely to value knowledge if you discover it for yourselves than if we, as teachers, just tell you what it is. As Benjamin Franklin famously said, "Tell me and I forget, teach me and I may remember, involve me and I learn."

Our emphasis on the GVV methodology has been to engage you directly in discussions that can provide a pathway to the truth and stoke the fire of integrity that burns in the souls of good people. It is now up to you to summon up the courage to do the right thing; act the right way; and influence others to do so as well, which is the true test of leadership.

Discussion Questions

1. Choose someone from the business or accounting world who you think is an authentic leader and explain why you believe that to be true.
2. Why might a moral person who is not viewed as a moral manager fail to establish an ethical culture in an organization?
3. Distinguish between authentic leadership, transformational leadership, and servant leadership. Are all necessary to change individuals and social systems within an organization?
4. Identify three reasons why there may be ethical leadership failures and explain why failed leadership occurs.
5. Values-driven leadership as envisioned in the Giving Voice to Values technique poses the following question: Once I know what is right, how do I get it done and get it done effectively? Discuss how an authentic leader would go about addressing this question.
6. Are accountants and auditors moral agents of corporations and society? Explain.
7. How might moral intensity influence the decisions made by accounting professionals?
8. Describe the role of professional judgment in ethical leadership as it pertains to accountants and auditors.
9. How does the nature of the internal audit function, strength of ethical leadership, and level of moral intensity influence whether an auditor will record questionable and undocumented journal entries?
10. How might an accounting firm influence whether non–tax practitioners view a contentious issue with a client as having been handled ethically?
11. How does an auditor's commitment to the firm, the profession, and to colleagues influence whether she will blow the whistle on financial wrongdoing?
12. Evaluate the moral intensity of the issues faced by Diem-Thi Le in her whistleblowing experience at DCAA.
13. How does organizational dissonance influence ethical leadership and decision making?
14. Why do you think studies show that no single factor has a bigger impact on the ethicality of a firm's culture than the personal examples set by firm leaders?
15. Audit firms are expected to establish and maintain a system of quality control. PCAOB inspections often cite the lack of quality controls as a deficiency of audit firms. What role does leadership play in developing the kind of quality control system that supports ethical decision making in audits?
16. Explain how the circumstances under each of the following might reflect failed leadership by auditors and the audit firm:

    - Under-reporting of time on an engagement
    - Premature sign-off on audit procedures
    - Accepting weak client explanations for accounting

17. What is the role of leadership in auditor assessments of the likelihood of fraud in the context of the fraud triangle?

18. Bruns and Merchant found that managers did not agree on the types of earnings management activities that are acceptable.[67] Refer to the definitions of earnings management in Chapter 7. Explain how leadership traits influence how managers might perceive the acceptability of earnings management.

19. Moral legitimacy refers to the generalized perception or assumption of observers that the actions of an entity are desirable, proper, or appropriate within some socially constructed system of norms, values, and beliefs. Explain how moral legitimacy might be applied to assess the actions of audit firms.

20. The American writer, Robert McKee, is quoted as saying, "True character is revealed in the choices a human being makes under pressure." Explain what you think this means in the context of moral intensity and ethical leadership of organizations.

Endnotes

1. "Interview with Joseph Berardino,"*Frontline,* PBS, May 1, 2002, Available at: http://www.pbs.org/wgbh/pages/frontline/shows/regulation/interviews/berardino.html.

2. Philosiblog, "Good Actions Give Strength to Ourselves and Inspire Good Actions in Others," April 3, 2011, Available at: http://philosiblog.com/2011/04/03/good-actions-give/.

3. Stephen Covey, *Principle-Centered Leadership* (New York: NY, Simon and Schuster, 1991).

4. John C. Maxwell, *Leadership 101: What Every Leader Needs to Know* (Nashville, TN: Thomas Nelson, 2002).

5. Joanne Ciulla, "The State of Leadership Ethics and the Work that Lies Before Us," *Business Ethics: A European Review,* Vol. 14, No. 4 (2005), pp. 323–335.

6. Alan Lawton and Iliana Paez, "Developing a Framework for Ethical Leadership," *Journal of Business Ethics,* Vol. 130 (2015), pp. 639–649.

7. See, for example, Chester I. Bernard, *The Functions of the Executive* (Cambridge, MA: Harvard University Press, 1971); and James MacGregor Burns, *Leadership* (New York, NY: Harper & Row, 1978).

8. Linda Klebe Trevino, Laura Pincus Hartman, and Michael Brown, "Moral Person and Moral Manager: How Executives Develop a Reputation for Ethical Leadership," *California Management Review,* Vol. 42, Issue 4 (Summer 2000), pp. 128–142.

9. Bruce J. Avolio and William L. Gardner, "Authentic Leadership Development: Getting to the Root of Positive Forms of Leadership," *The Leadership Quarterly,* Vol. 16 (2005), pp. 315–338.

10. James MacGregor Burns, *Leadership* (New York, NY: Harper & Row, 1978).

11. Edwin P. Hollander and Wilse B. Webb, "Leadership, Followership, and Friendship," *The Journal of Abnormal and Social Psychology,* Vol. 50, No. 2 (1955), pp. 163–167.

12. Trevino et al.

13. David De Cremer and Ann E. Tenbrunsel, *Behavioral Business Ethics* (New York, NY: Taylor & Francis Group LLC, 2012).

14. De Cremer and Tenbrunsel, pp. 84–88.

15. Trevino et al.

16. Michael Brown, Linda Klebe Trevino, and David A. Harrison, "Ethical Leadership: A Social Learning Perspective for Construct Development and Testing," *Organizational Behavior and Human Decision Processes,* Vol. 97, Issue 2 (July 2005), pp. 117–134.

17. Sandra L. Robinson and Anne M. O'Leary-Kelly, "Monkey See, Monkey Do: The Influence of Work Groups on the Antisocial Behavior of Employees," *The Academy of Management Journal,* Vol. 41, No. 6 (December 1998), pp. 658–672.

18. Theodore D. Kemper, "Representative Roles and the Legitimization of Deviance," *Social Problems,* Vol. 13 (1966), pp. 288–298.

19. Thomas M. Jones, "Ethical Decision Making by Individuals in Organizations: An Issue-Contingent Model," *Academy of Management Review,* Vol. 16 (1991), pp. 366–395.

20. Eileen Z. Taylor and Mary B. Curtis, "An Examination of the Layers of Workplace Influences in Ethical Judgments: Whistleblowing Likelihood and Perseverance in Public Accounting," *Journal of Business Ethics,* Vol. 93 (2010), pp. 21–37.

21. Dick Carozza, "Interview with Sherron Watkins: Constant Warning," *Fraud Magazine,* January/February 2007, Available at: http://www.fraud-magazine.com/article.aspx?id=583.

22. Carozza.

23. Cathy Krohmen and Christine Noel, "Responsible Leadership for Audit Quality: How Do the Big Four Manage the Personal Ethics of their Employees?" Unpublished Manuscript by the University of Provence, France, Available at: http://sites.univ-provence.fr/ergolog/Bibliotheque/noel/responsible_leadership_for_corporate_responsability.pdf.

24. Patricia Casey Douglas, Ronald A. Davidson, and Bill N. Schwartz, "The Effect of Organizational Culture and Ethical Orientation on Accountants' Ethical Judgments," *Journal of Business Ethics,* Vol. 34 (2001), pp. 101–121.

25. Larry A. Ponemon, "Ethical Judgments in Accounting: A Cognitive-Developmental Perspective," *Critical Perspectives on Accounting,* Vol. 1 (1990), pp. 191–215.

26. Michael K. Shaub, Donald W. Finn, and Paul Munter, "The Effects of Auditors' Ethical Orientation on Commitment and Ethical Sensitivity," *Behavioral Research in Accounting,* Vol. 5 (1993), pp. 145–169.

27. Ponemon, pp. 199–201.

28. Douglas et al.

29. Avolio and Gardner, pp. 320–325.

30. Jan Taylor Morris, "The Impact of Authentic Leadership and Ethical Firm Culture on Auditor Behavior," *Journal of Behavioral Studies in Business,* Vol. 7 (September 2014), pp. 1–32.

31. Morris.

32. Donna D. Bobek, Amy M. Hageman, and Robon R. Radtke, "The Effects of Professional Role, Decision Context, and Gender on the Ethical Decision Making of Public Accounting Professionals," *Behavioral Research in Accounting,* Vol. 27, No. 1 (2015), pp. 55–78.

33. Richard Chambers, "Seven Attributes of the Ethical Internal Audit Leader," *Internal Auditor,* April 1, 2013, Available at: https://iaonline.theiia.org/seven-attributes-of-the-ethical-internal-audit-leader.

34. Brown et al. (2005).

35. Audrey A. Gramling, Mario J. Maletta, Arnold Schneider, and Bryan K. Church, "The Role of the Internal Audit Function in Corporate Governance: A Synthesis of the Extant Internal Auditing Literature and Directions for Future Research," *Journal of Accounting Literature*, Vol. 23 (2004), pp. 194–244.

36. David M. Mayer, Maribeth Kuenzi, Rebcca Greenbaum, Mary Bardes, and Rommel (Bombie) Salvador, "How Does Ethical Leadership Flow? Test of a Trickle-Down Model," *Organizational Behavior and Human Decision Processes,* Vol. 108 (2009), pp. 1–13.

37. Douglas F. Prawitt, Jason L. Smith, and David A. Wood, "Internal Audit Quality and Earnings Management, *The Accounting Review,* Vol. 84, No. 4 (2009), pp. 1255–1280.

38. Barbara Arel, Cathy A. Beaudoin, and Anna M. Cianci, "The Impact of Ethical Leadership and Internal Audit Function, and Moral Intensity on a Financial Reporting Decision," *Journal of Business Ethics,* Vol. 109, No. 3 (2012), pp. 351–366.

39. *The New York Times,* "Fifth Chief Financial Officer at HealthSouth to Admit Fraud," April 25, 2003, Available at: http://www.nytimes.com/2003/04/25/business/fifth-chief-financial-officer-at-healthsouth-to-admit-fraud.html.

40. *SEC v. HealthSouth Corporation and Richard Scrushy, Defendants,* United States District Court for the Southern Division of Alabama, 261 F. Supp. 2d 1298 (May 7, 2003), Available at: http://law.justia.com/cases/federal/district-courts/FSupp2/261/1298/2515723/.

41. See, for example, Linda Klebe Trevino, Gary R. Weaver, and Michael E. Brown, "It's Lovely at the Top: Hierarchical Levels, Identities, and Perceptions of Organizational Ethics," *Business Ethics Quarterly,* Vol. 18, No. 2 (2008), pp. 233–252; and Jill M. D'Aquila, "Financial Accountants' Perceptions of Management's Ethical Standards,"*Journal of Business Ethics,* Vol. 31, No. 3 (June 2001), pp. 233–244.

42. Donna D. Bobek, Amy M. Hageman, and Robin R. Radtke, "The Ethical Environment of Tax Professionals: Partner and Non-Partner Perceptions and Experiences," *Journal of Business Ethics,* Vol. 92 (2010), pp. 637–654.

43. Donna D. Bobek, Amy M. Hageman, and Robin R. Radtke, "The Influence of Roles and Organizational Fit on Accounting Professionals' Perceptions of Their Firms' Ethical Environment," *Journal of Business Ethics,* Vol. 126 (2015b), pp. 125–141.

44. Donna D. Bobek and Robin R. Radtke, "An Experiential Investigation of the Ethical Environment of Tax Professionals," *Journal of American Tax Association,* Vol. 29, No. 2 (2007), pp. 63–84.

45. David Jacobs, "Aaron Beam, Who Served Time in Jail after the HealthSouth Scandal, Opens Up about the Wrongdoing and His New Work," *Business Report,* July 22, 2015, Available at: https://www.businessreport.com/business/aaron-beam-served-time-jail-healthsouth-scandal-opens-wrongdoing-new-work.

46. Kadesha Thomas, "From Wall Street to Prison: The HealthSouth Story," May 31, 2011, Available at: http://www.chicagobooth.edu/news/2011-05-31-healthsouth.aspx.

47. Alix Stuart, "Keeping Secrets: How Five CFOs Cooked the Books at HealthSouth," *CFO Magazine,* June 1, 2005, Available at: http://ww2.cfo.com/human-capital-careers/2005/06/keeping-secrets/.

48. Linda Fisher Thornton, "When Problems Happen, Scapegoats Are Quickly Fired (Instead of

Learning from Mistakes and Fixing the Culture)," January 15, 2013, Available at: http://leadingincontext.com/2014/01/15/understanding-and-preventing-ethical-leadership-failures/.

49. Terry L. Price, *Understanding Ethical Failures in Leadership*, (Cambridge, UK: Cambridge University Press, 2006).

50. Price.

51. Jessica R. Mesmer-Magnus and Chockalingam Viswesvaran, "Whistleblowing in Organizations: An Examination of Correlates of Whistleblowing Intentions, Actions, and Retaliation," *Journal of Business Ethics,* Vol. 62, No. 3 (2005), pp. 277–297.

52. Janet P. Near and Marcia P. Miceli, "Organizational Dissidence: The Case of Whistle-blowing," *Journal of Business Ethics,* Vol. 4, No. 1 (1985), pp. 1–16.

53. Randi L. Sims and John P. Keenan, "Predictors of External Whistleblowing: Organizational and Intrapersonal Variables," *Journal of Business Ethics,* Vol. 17 (1998), pp. 411–421.

54. Lyman W. Porter, Richard M. Steers, Richard T. Mowday, and Paul V. Boulian, "Organizational Commitment, Job Satisfaction, and Turnover among Psychiatric Technicians," *Journal of Applied Psychology*, Vol. 59, No. 5 (October 1974), pp. 603–609.

55. Linda Klebe Trevino and Bart Victor, "Peer Reporting of Unethical Behavior: A Social Context Perspective," *The Academy of Management Journal*, Vol. 35, No. 1 (March 1992), pp. 38–64.

56. Taylor and Curtis.

57. Taylor and Curtis.

58. Bobek et al. (2010).

59. N. Brennan and J. Kelley, "A Study of Whistleblowing among Trainee Auditors," *The British Accounting Review,* Vol. 39 (2007), pp. 61–87.

60. Marcia P. Miceli, Janet P. Near, and Charles R. Schwenk, "Who Blows the Whistle and Why?" *Industrial and Labor Relations Review,* Vol. 45, No. 1 (October 1991), pp. 113–130.

61. Jill W. Graham, "Principled Organizational Dissent: A Theoretical Essay," *Research in Organizational Behavior,* Vol. 8 (December 1985), pp. 1–52.

62. Tony Saavedra, "This Whistleblower Saved You Money," *Orange County Register,* August 21, 2013, Available at: http://www.ocregister.com/articles/agency-325266-whistleblower-defense.html.

63. Statement of Diem-Thi Le, DCAA Auditor, before the Senate Committee on Homeland Security and Governmental Affairs, September 10, 2008, Available at: http://www.hsgac.senate.gov /download/091008le.

64. James M. Kouzes and Barry P. Posner, *The Leadership Challenge,* 4th ed. (San Francisco: Jossey-Bass, 2008).

65. Thornton.

66. Patrick T. Kelly and Christine E. Earley, "Ethical Leaders in Accounting," in Anthony H. Catanach Jr. and Dorothy Feldmann (eds.), *Advances in Accounting Education: Teaching and Curriculum Innovations, Vol. 12* (Bingley, U.K.: Emerald, 2011), pp. 53–76.

67. William J. Bruns Jr. and Kenneth A. Merchant, "The Dangerous Morality of Managing Earnings," *Management Accounting,* Vol. 72, No. 2 (1990), Available at: https://www.researchgate.net /publication/265235024_The_Dangerous_Morality_of_Managing_Earnings.

Chapter 8 Cases

Case 8-1 Research Triangle Software Innovations (a GVV case)

Research Triangle Software Innovations is a software solutions company specializing in enterprise resource planning (ERP) business management software. Located in the Research Triangle Park, North Carolina, high-tech area, Research Triangle Software Innovations is a leader in ERP software.

Oak Manufacturing is located in Raleigh, North Carolina. Oak is a publicly owned company that produces oak barrels for flavoring and storage of wine products. As the largest company of its kind in the Southeast, Oak Manufacturing serves all 50 states and other parts of North America.

Tar & Heel, LLP, is a mid-sized professional services firm in Durham, North Carolina. It provides audit, assurance, and advisory services to clients, many of whom are in the Research Triangle area. The firm audits the financial statements of Oak Manufacturing and was just contacted by the client to assist in selecting and implementing an ERP system so the company can improve its collection, storage, management, and interpretation of data from a variety of business activities.

Steve Michaels is Tar & Heel's advisory manager in charge of the Oak Manufacturing engagement. He is reviewing the criteria used for software selection as follows:

- Alignment with client's needs
- Operations integration
- Software reliability
- Vendor support
- Scalability for growth
- Pricing

Everything seems in order for the criteria. However, Steve is concerned about the selection of the ERP software of Research Triangle Software Innovations, for one, because Research Triangle is also an audit client of the firm. Given that Research Triangle is the major client in the Durham office, Steve worries about perceptions if the firm selects its client's software product. Moreover, he knows his firm's partnership is pushing for sales of its own software and this might be an occasion to do so.

Steve calls Rosanne Field into his office to discuss her selection. This is Rosanne's first job as the lead advisory staff member on a software selection decision. She has great credentials having graduated with a bachelor's degree from the University of North Carolina, a masters from North Carolina State, and a computer science doctorate from Duke University. She has five years of experience in advisory services and has received glowing evaluations.

Rosanne explains that there were four ERP software products that made it to the "final four." From that list she paired down the selection to three packages—Research Triangle Software Innovations, Longhorn Software Systems in Austin, Texas, and Tar & Heel's own product.

Steve asks Rosanne to explain why Research Triangle Innovations was selected. She goes through the ranking of the criteria. It seems the firm's total score was slightly below Research Triangle's but higher than Longhorn Software's.

Steve asks Rosanne a few pointed questions about the selection process including: (1) Is she aware that Research Triangle is an audit client of the firm? (2) Did she consider management's desire to push the firm's own software? (3) Did she consider that the selection of the firm's software would enable it to fine-tune the product with the experience and feedback from Oak Manufacturing and enhance future sales?

Rosanne listens attentively and asks Steve whether she is expected to alter the rankings and recommend the firm's product. Steve is surprised by Rosanne's candor. He tells Rosanne that the firm would never order her to change a recommendation, so long as she paid due attention to all considerations in making the software selection, including that the firm's own package could do the same things as that of Research Triangle.

Rosanne asks for time to review her work and evaluations of the software products and discuss the matter with Steve in two days. Steve agrees.

Rosanne carefully considers what she is being asked to do. Steve was not very subtle in making his expectations known. Rosanne knows if she is going to make a strong case for staying with the Research Triangle selection, she had better be able to counter Steve's arguments.

Rosanne decides to speak with Rebecca Chang, her best friend who happens to be on the audit engagement of Research Triangle. Rebecca isn't sure whether she should share the information she has about the client with Rosanne. However, they are best friends and their siblings are married to each other. In the end she figures it's a case of "no harm, no foul."

What Rosanne learns troubles her deeply. It seems Research Triangle had been given a going concern alert in the audit report prepared by Tar & Heel, LLP. Rosanne asks why and is told it was due to questions about the company's ability to generate sufficient cash flows from earnings to continue its operations. In addition, it has already been turned down by venture capitalists and banks for additional funding.

Rosanne asks Rebecca what she would do if she were faced with the ethical dilemma. Rebecca suggests that Rosanne should speak to Vivian Snow, the advisory services partner, who is Rebecca's mentor in the firm. Rosanne likes that idea and thanks Rebecca for the advice.

Questions

1. What are the ethical issues in this case? Discuss the obligations of Tar & Heel to its stakeholders.

2. Characterize the kind of leadership demonstrated by Steve Michaels.

3. Evaluate moral intensity issues and how they might influence the actions and decisions of Rosanne.

4. Assume Rosanne decides to speak to her mentor. From past experience, she knows Vivian is a team player and has always encouraged Rosanne to do the same. Consider the following, if you were in Rosanne's position, in developing a plan to give voice to your values.

   - What is at stake for the key parties, including those who disagree with you?
   - What are the likely objections or pushback from Vivian and others?
   - How will you counter those positions? Are there any levers you can use to influence those who disagree with you?
   - What is your most powerful and persuasive response to the reasons and rationalizations you need to address?

Case 8-2 Cumberland Lumber

"It's impossible! There is no justification for ignoring these entries." These are the words spoken by Jackie Bauman at a meeting with the CFO of the company, Glen Donner.

Cumberland Lumber is a regional company and privately owned by members of the Simon family. Jackie is the chief internal auditor at Cumberland Lumber, a large lumber liquidator in the Cumberland Valley of Pennsylvania. While she does not report directly to Glen Donner, the culture of the company is such that Glen makes the final call on accounting issues because he has CEO Larry Simon's ear.

The issue being discussed between Jackie and Glen is whether a variety of year-end accruals should be recorded. These include:

1. Accrual for future vacation pay of $50,000.
2. Allowance for repairs and maintenance, $70,000.
3. Reserve for inventory obsolescence, $80,000.

The total amount of $200,000 is 25 percent of earnings for the year.

Jackie provides the following reasons for recording these amounts:

1. The accrual for vacation pay is based on a commitment to employees to pay these amounts so long as they use their vacation hours by the end of the following calendar year.
2. The allowance for repairs is an annual adjustment to reserve for future repair costs on machinery and equipment.
3. The reserve for inventory obsolescence is a new item but reflects the failure of the company to get rid of certain lumber products that have been on the books for almost two years.

Glen counters Jackie's explanation as follows.

1. Employees may not take vacation time next year because the employment market is tight and there is an economic recession, so they may not want to leave, even for a week or two, for fear of losing their job.
2. Repairs and maintenance are discretionary expenditures, and there is no reason to accrue for them.
3. The "obsolete" inventory will be sold to a buyer who is willing to take it off the company's hands so Glen suggests waiting until it is sold at that time for scrap value.

As a CPA, Jackie feels comfortable with her knowledge of the accounting rules. She tries to discuss her differences with Glen using this perspective. She also explains her ethical obligations. Glen simply tells Jackie to make the entries if she wants to keep her job.

Questions

1. Discuss the appropriateness of making the accrual entries based on the perspectives of Jackie and Glen. What do you believe to be the intent of Glen in this matter? Explain.
2. Characterize the leadership style of Glen and the culture of the company.
3. How does professional identity influence what Jackie might do in this case?
4. What would be most important to you in deciding what to do in this case if you were in Jackie's position? What would you do and why? Be sure to consider the culture of the company and leadership style in crafting a response.

Case 8-3 Parmalat: Europe's Enron[1]

After the news broke about the frauds at Enron and WorldCom in the United States, there were those in Europe who used the occasion to beat the drum: "Our principles-based approach to accounting standard-setting is better than your rules-based approach." Many in the United States started to take a closer look at the principles-based

[1]The facts of this case are taken from U.S. District Court Southern District of New York, *In re Parmalat Securities Litigation,* May 21, 2004, Available at: http://www.parmalatsettlement.com/docs/Parmalat%20Stipulation%20Settlement%20Agreement.pdf.

approach in the European Community and that is used in International Financial Reporting Standards (IFRS), which relies less on bright-line rules to establish standards, as is the case in the United States, but may have loopholes making it relatively easy to avoid the rules. In the end, it was not the approach to setting rules that brought down Parmalat. It was a case of greed, failed corporate leadership, and sloppy auditing.

Background

Parmalat began as a family-owned entity founded by Calisto Tanzi in 1961. During 2003, Parmalat was the eighth-largest company in Italy and had operations in 30 countries. It was a huge player in the world dairy market and was even more influential within Italian business circles. It had a network of 5,000 dairy farmers who supplied milk products and 39,000 people who were directly employed by the company. The company eventually sold shares to the public on the Milan stock exchange. The Tanzi family always held a majority, controlling stake in the company, which in 2003 was 50.02 percent. Tanzi family members also occupied the seats of CEO and chair of the board of directors. The structure of Parmalat was primarily characterized by the Tanzi family and the large amount of control that it wielded over company operations. It was not unusual for family members to override whatever internal controls existed to perpetrate the accounting fraud.

The Parmalat scandal broke in late 2003, when it became known that company funds totaling almost €4 billion (approximately $5.64 billion) that were meant to be held in an account at the Bank of America did not exist. On March 19, 2004, Milan prosecutors brought charges against Parmalat founder Calisto Tanzi, other members of his family, and an inner circle of company executives for their part in the Parmalat scandal. After three months of investigation, the prosecutors charged 29 individuals, the Italian branches of the Bank of America, and the accountants Deloitte & Touche and Grant Thornton. The charges included market rigging, false auditing, and regulatory obstruction following the disclosure that €15 billion (approximately $21.15 billion) was found to be missing from the bank accounts of the multinational dairy group in December 2003. Former internal auditors and three former Bank of America employees have been jailed for their roles in the fraud. The judge also gave the go-ahead for Parmalat to proceed with lawsuits against the auditors. Parmalat's administrator, Enrico Bondi, is also pursuing another lawsuit against Citigroup in New Jersey state courts. Despite all its troubles, Parmalat has recovered and today is a thriving multinational food group with operations in five continents through either a direct presence or through license agreements.

U.S. Banks Caught in the Spotlight

Parmalat had induced U.S. investors to purchase bonds and notes totaling approximately $1.5 billion. In addition, in August 1996 Parmalat sponsored an offering of American Depositary Receipts (ADRs) in the United States, with Citibank, N.A., headquartered in New York City, as depositary. Parmalat actively participated in the establishment of the ADR program. This activity made Parmalat subject to SEC rules. The SEC's inquiries focused on up to approximately €1.05 billion ($1.5 billion) of notes and bonds issued in private placements with U.S. investors. The banks investigated included Bank of America, JP Morgan Chase, Merrill Lynch, and Morgan Stanley Dean Witter. Parmalat's administrator, Enrico Bondi, helped the authorities identify all the financing transactions undertaken by Parmalat from 1994 through 2003. During the investigation, it was noted that Parmalat's auditor from 1990 to 1999, Grant Thornton, did not have copies of crucial audit documents relating to the company's Cayman Islands subsidiary, Bonlat. The emergence of a €5.16 billion (approximately $7.28 billion) hole at Bonlat triggered the Parmalat collapse. The accounting firm has since handed over important audit documents to investigators.

Accounting Fraud

One of the most notable fraudulent actions was the creation of a completely fictitious bank account in the United States that supposedly contained $5 billion. After media reports exposing the account surfaced, the financial institution at which the deposit supposedly existed (Bank of America) denied any such account. The company's management fooled auditors by creating a fictitious confirmation letter regarding the account. In addition to misleading the auditors about this bank account, the company's CFO, Fausto Tonna, produced fake documents and faxed them to the auditors in order to hide the fact that many of the company's dealings were completely fictitious.

Parmalat's management also used "nominee" entities to transfer debt and sales in order to hide them from auditors and other interested parties. A *nominee entity* is a company created to hold and administer the assets or securities of the actual owner as a custodian. These entities were clearly controlled by Parmalat and most existed only on paper.

Using nominee entities, the Parmalat management created a method to remove uncollectible or impaired accounts receivable. The bad accounts would be transferred to one of the nominee entities, thus keeping the bad debt expense or write-off for the valueless accounts off the Parmalat income statement. The transfers to nominee entities also avoided any scrutiny of the accounts by external or statutory auditors (in this case, Italian-designated auditors under the country's laws).

Creating revenues was another scheme in which the nominee or subsidiary entities were used; if a non-Italian subsidiary had a loss related to currency exchange rates, management would fabricate currency exchange contracts to convert the loss to a profit. Similar activities were undertaken to hide losses due to interest expense. Documents showing interest rate swaps were created to mislead the auditors or other parties. Interest rate swaps and currency exchange contracts are both instruments usually used to hedge on the financial markets, and sometimes to diversify the risk of certain investments. Parmalat abused these tools by creating completely fictitious contracts after the fact and claiming that they were valid and accurate. The understatement of debt was another large component of the Parmalat fraud, as was hidden debt. On one occasion, management recorded the sale of receivables as "non-recourse," when in fact Parmalat was still responsible to ensure that the money was collectible.

There were many debt-disguising schemes in relation to the nominee entities. With one loan agreement, the money borrowed was touted as being from an equity source. On another occasion, a completely fictitious debt repurchase by a nominee entity was created, resulting in the removal of a liability from the books, when the debt was still in fact outstanding. Parmalat management also incorrectly recorded many million euros' worth of bank loans as intercompany loans. This incorrect classification allowed for the loans to be eliminated in consolidation when they actually represented money owed by the company to outsiders.

The fraud methods did not stop at creating fictitious accounts and documents, or even with establishing nonexistent foreign nominee entities and hiding liabilities. Calisto Tanzi and other management were investigated by Italian authorities for manipulating the Milan stock market. On December 20, 1999, Parmalat's management issued a press release of an appraisal of the Brazilian unit. While this release appeared to be a straightforward action, what Tanzi and others failed to disclose were the facts relating to the appraisal itself. The appraisal came from an accountant at Deloitte Touche Tohmatsu and was dated July 23, 2008, nearly 19 months prior to the press release. This failure to disclose information in a timely and transparent manner demonstrates yet another way that Parmalat was able to exert influence and mislead investors.

Missing the Red Flags

The fraud that occurred at Parmalat is a case of management greed with a lack of independent oversight and fraudulent financial reporting that was taken to the extreme. As an international company, Parmalat management had many opportunities to take advantage of the system and hide the fictitious nature of financial statement items. As with many frauds, the web of lies began to untangle when the company began to run out of cash. In a discussion with a firm in New York regarding a leveraged buyout of part of the Parmalat Corporation, two members of the Tanzi family revealed that they did not actually have the cash represented in their financial statements.

At the beginning of 2003, Lehman Brothers, Inc., issued a report questioning the financial status of Parmalat. Ironically, Parmalat filed a report with Italian authorities claiming that Lehman Brothers was slandering the company with the intention of hurting the Parmalat share price.[2] Financial institutions failed to examine the accusations thoroughly and continued to loan money to Parmalat due to the supposed strength and power wielded by the company throughout the world. As Luca Sala, former head of Bank of America's Italian corporate finance division, observed, "When you have a client like Parmalat, which is bringing in all that money and has industries all over the world, you don't exactly ask them to show you their bank statements."[3]

[2]Leonard J. Brooks and Paul Dunn, *Business and Professional Ethics for Executives, Directors, and Accountants,* 6th ed. (Cincinnati, OH: South-Western Publishing, 2011).

[3]"Banker says 'Parmalat tricked me'", January 11, 2004, Available at: http://news.bbc.co.uk/2/hi/business/3386811.stm.

Failure of Auditors

The external auditor during the fraud, primarily Grant Thornton, SpA, failed to comply with many commonly accepted auditing practices and thus contributed to the fraud. The largest component of Parmalat's fraud that ultimately brought the company down was the nonexistent bank account with Bank of America. The auditors went through procedures to confirm this account, but they made one fatal mistake: They sent the confirmation using Parmalat's internal mail system. The confirmation request was intercepted by Parmalat employees and subsequently forged by Tonna or an agent acting on his behalf. The forgery consisted of creating a confirmation and printing it on Bank of America letterhead and then sending it back to the auditors.

Parmalat accused Grant Thornton and Deloitte Touche Tohmatsu of contributing to its €14 billion collapse in December 2003. Parmalat filed suit against the auditors and other third parties, seeking $10 billion in damages for alleged professional malpractice, fraud, theft of assets, and civil conspiracy. Parmalat argued that the headquarters for both Grant Thornton and Deloitte had "alter ego" relationships with their Italian subsidiaries that tied them inextricably to the alleged fraud. According to the complaint, the relationships were highlighted by the firms' own claims to being "integrated worldwide accounting organizations." Judge Lewis Kaplan in U.S. District Court for the Southern District of New York granted a motion by Deloitte USA to dismiss Parmalat's first amended complaint due to Parmalat's failure to show that poor auditing of Parmalat USA was equivalent to fraud at Parmalat in Italy.

The frauds continued for many years due, in large part, to the failures of the auditors. Italian law requires both listed and unlisted companies to have a board of statutory auditors, as well as external auditors. Parmalat's statutory board should have become suspicious of what might be happening when two CFOs departed within a six-month period during the fraud. Also, analysts were puzzled by the increasing debt levels. Yet the board just stood idly by even though it had received information about the scope of the problems. The board never reported any irregularities or problems, despite receiving complaints, because of the influence of the Tanzi family. After the fraud was discovered and resolution of the issues began, it became clear that the statutory audit board did nothing to prevent or detect the fraud.

Resolution of Outstanding Matters

Following an investigation, the founder of Parmalat, Calisto Tanzi, was sentenced in Milan to 10 years in prison in December 2008 for securities laws violations in connection with the Italian dairy company's downfall in late 2003. Tonna, the CFO, was sentenced to 30 months in jail following a trial in 2005, and other officers reached plea bargain deals. Bank of America settled a civil case brought by Parmalat bondholders for $100 million.

Bondholders in the United States and Italy had alleged the U.S. bank knew of Parmalat's financial troubles, but nevertheless sold investors Parmalat bonds that ultimately soured—allegations Bank of America denied. Both sides said the agreement cleared the way for future business between the companies. In a statement following the settlement, Bank of America stated that the record of court rulings in the case "makes it clear that no one at Bank of America knew or could have known of the true financial condition of Parmalat. We have defended ourselves vigorously in these cases and are satisfied with this outcome today."

After the accounting and business problems surfaced, a court battle ensued regarding who was responsible for the audit failures. The umbrella entities of Deloitte and Grant Thornton, Deloitte Touche Tohmatsu, and Grant Thornton International, along with the U.S. branches of both firms, were included in a lawsuit by Parmalat shareholders. Questions were raised as to whether or not the umbrella entities could be held liable for the failures of a country-specific branch of their firm. The courts held that due to the level of control that the international and U.S.-based branches wielded over the other portions of the firm, they could be included in the lawsuit.[4]

[4]Thomas M. Beshere, "Questions For International Accounting Firm Networks," *Law360,* August 20, 2009, Available at: https://www.mcguirewoods.com/news-resources/publications/Questions%20For%20International%20Accounting%20Firm%20Networks.pdf.

Legal Matters with Bank of America

On February 2, 2006, a U.S. federal judge allowed Parmalat to proceed with much of its $10 billion lawsuit against Bank of America, including claims that the bank violated U.S. racketeering laws. Enrico Bondi was appointed as the equivalent of a U.S. bankruptcy trustee to pursue claims that financial institutions, including Bank of America, abetted the company in disguising its true financial condition. Bondi accused the bank of helping to structure mostly off-balance-sheet transactions intended to "conceal Parmalat's insolvency" and of collecting fees that it did not deserve.

The lawsuit against Bank of America was dismissed. Parmalat appealed the dismissal of its lawsuits, accusing Bank of America and Grant Thornton of fraud. Bondi filed notice of Parmalat's appeal to the U.S. Court of Appeals for the Second Circuit in New York. Bondi and the Parmalat Capital Finance Ltd. unit had accused Grant Thornton of helping set up fake transactions to allow insiders to steal from the company. Parmalat Capital made similar claims in a lawsuit against Bank of America. On September 18, 2009, U.S. District Judge Lewis Kaplan said Parmalat should not recover for its own fraud, noting that the transactions also generated millions of euros for the company. "The actions of its agents in so doing were in furtherance of the company's interests, even if some of the agents intended at the time they assisted in raising the money to steal some of it," Kaplan wrote. A Bank of America spokesman said in a statement: "It has been our view all along that Parmalat Capital Finance, a participant in the fraud, was not entitled to seek damages from Bank of America, which had no knowledge of the fraud and was damaged by it. We are pleased that the court has agreed."[5]

The SEC Charges

The SEC filed an amended complaint on July 28, 2004, in its lawsuit against Parmalat Finanziaria SpA in U.S. District Court in the Southern District of New York. The amended complaint alleged that Parmalat engaged in one of the largest financial frauds in history and defrauded U.S. institutional investors when it sold them more than $1 billion in debt securities in a series of private placements between 1997 and 2002. Parmalat consented to the entry of a final judgment against it in the fraud.

The complaint includes the following amended charges:

1. Parmalat consistently overstated its level of cash and marketable securities by at least $4.9 billion at December 31, 2002.

2. As of September 30, 2003, Parmalat had understated its reported debt by almost $10 billion through a variety of tactics, including:

   a. Eliminating about $6 billion of debt held by one of its nominee entities.

   b. Recording approximately $1.6 billion of debt as equity through fictitious loan participation agreements.

   c. Removing approximately $500 million in liabilities by falsely describing the sale of certain receivables as non-recourse, when in fact the company retained an obligation to ensure that the receivables were ultimately paid.

   d. Improperly eliminating approximately $1.6 billion of debt through a variety of techniques including mischaracterization of bank debt as intercompany debt.

3. Between 1997 and 2003, Parmalat transferred approximately $500 million to various businesses owned and operated by Tanzi family members.

4. Parmalat used nominee entities to fabricate nonexistent financial operations intended to offset losses of operating subsidiaries; to disguise intercompany loans from one subsidiary to another that was experiencing operating losses; to record fictitious revenue through sales by its subsidiaries to controlled nominee entities at

[5]Chad Bray, "2nd Update: Judge Dismisses Parmalat Suits vs. Auditor, BofA," *Dow Jones Newswires,* September 18, 2009, Available at: http://www.advfn.com/news_2nd-UPDATE-Judge-Dismisses-Parmalat-Suits-Vs-Audi_39538791.html.

inflated or entirely fictitious amounts; and to avoid unwanted scrutiny due to the aging of the receivables related to these sales: The related receivables were either sold or transferred to nominee entities.

In the consent agreement, without admitting or denying the allegations, Parmalat agreed to adopt changes to its corporate governance to promote future compliance with the federal securities laws, including:

- Adopting bylaws providing for governance by a shareholder-elected board of directors, the majority of whom will be independent and serve finite terms and specifically delineating in the bylaws the duties of the board of directors.
- Adopting a Code of Conduct governing the duties and activities of the board of directors.
- Adopting an Insider Dealing Code of Conduct.
- Adopting a Code of Ethics.

The bylaws also required that the positions of the chair of the board of directors and managing director be held by two separate individuals, and Parmalat must consent to having continuing jurisdiction of the U.S. District Court to enforce its provisions.

Accounting in the Global Environment

Accounting and auditing standards and regulation of the accounting profession often are country specific. In addition to complying with any locally applicable rules, however, Deloitte firms follow general professional standards and auditing procedures promulgated by Deloitte Touche Tohmatsu. Member firms regularly cross-check each other's work to ensure quality, and they cooperate and join together under the direction of a single partner to provide audit services for international clients.

Accounting firms often assert that their foreign affiliates are legally separate, thus limiting the asset pool available to investors who file suit. They typically argue that you can't pursue the worldwide organization because one unit fails to meet its audit responsibilities. However, a closer look at what is done in reality presents a different view.

Partners and associates of member firms participate in global practice groups and attend Deloitte Touche Tohmatsu meetings. Although disclaimers on the firm's website assert the legal separateness of Deloitte Touche Tohmatsu and its members, Deloitte Touche Tohmatsu's goal is known to be to provide clients with consistent seamless service across national boundaries. Similar to other Big Four international firms, member firms use the Deloitte name when serving international clients in order to project the image of a cohesive international organization.

Questions

1. What were the failings of ethical leadership and corporate governance by management of Parmalat? How do you think these deficiencies contributed to the fraud?

2. Explain the accounting and financial reporting techniques used by Parmalat to commit accounting fraud with respect to Schilit's financial shenanigans.

3. Do you believe the auditors should have detected the accounting manipulations described in question 2? Critically evaluate whether the firms adhered to generally accepted auditing standards given the information in the case. Was this a case of "poor auditing," as characterized by Judge Kaplan, or fraud?

4. Given our discussion in Chapter 5 of the PCAOB's desire to gain access to audit workpapers of Chinese units of U.S. firms that audit Chinese companies listing in the United States, does it seem reasonable for a U.S. firm such as Deloitte to argue it has no liability for the actions of a network firm in Parmalat? What common characteristics might you look for in these alliances to assess overall firm liability?

Case 8-4 KPMG Tax Shelter Scandal

In Chapter 4 we discussed the artificial tax shelter arrangements developed by KPMG LLP for wealthy clients that led to the settlement of a legal action with the Department of Treasury and the Internal Revenue Service. On August 29, 2005, KPMG admitted to criminal wrongdoing and agreed to pay $456 million in fines, restitution, and penalties as part of an agreement to defer prosecution of the firm. In addition, nine members of the firm were criminally indicted for their role in relation to the design, marketing, and implementation of fraudulent tax shelters.

In the largest criminal tax case ever filed, KPMG admitted it engaged in a fraud that generated at least $11 billion dollars in phony tax losses, which, according to court papers, cost the United States at least $2.5 billion dollars in evaded taxes. In addition to KPMG's former deputy chairman, the individuals indicted included two former heads of KPMG's tax practice and a former tax partner in the New York City office of a prominent national law firm.

The facts of the tax shelter arrangement are complicated so we have condensed them for purposes of this case and present them in Exhibit 1.

EXHIBIT 1   Summary Of Tax Shelter Transactions Developed By Kpmg[1]

KPMG developed tax shelters to generate losses of $11.2 billion dollars for 601 wealthy clients that enabled them to avoid paying $2.5 billion in income taxes. KPMG mainly used four methods to help the wealthy clients avoid their tax liabilities or tax charges on capital gains. The shelters implemented were the Foreign Leveraged Investment Program (FLIP), Offshore Portfolio Investment Strategy (OPIS), Bond Linked Issue Premium Structure (BLIPS), and Short Option Strategy (SOS/SC 2). These shelters were designed to artificially create substantial phony capital losses through the use of an entity created in the Cayman Islands (a tax haven) for the purpose of the tax shelter transactions. The client purportedly entered into an investment transaction with the Cayman entity by purchasing purported warrants or entering into a purported swap. The Cayman entity then made a prearranged series of purported investments, including the purchase from either Bank A, which at the time was a KPMG audit client, or Bank D or both using money purportedly loaned by Bank A or Bank D, followed by redemptions of those stock purchases by the pertinent bank. The purported investments were devised to eliminate economic risk to the client beyond the cost to develop the tax shelters.

In the implementation of FLIP and OPIS, KPMG issued misleading opinion letters with assistance from its co-conspirators. The opinion letters were misleading because KPMG knew that the tax positions taken were more likely than not to prevail against the IRS, and the opinion letters and other documents used to implement FLIP and OPIS were false and fraudulent in a number of ways: For instance, the opinion letters began by falsely stating that the client requested KPMG's opinion regarding the U.S. federal income tax consequences of certain investment portfolio transactions, while the real fact is that the conspirators targeted wealthy clients based on the clients' large taxable gains and offered to generate phony tax losses to eliminate income tax on that gain as well as to provide a "more likely than not" opinion letter.

The "more likely than not" opinion letters provided an ambiguous and confusing view of the tax shelters to the users, but it brought an income of $50,000 to KPMG for each such opinion letter. In addition to that, the opinion letter continued by falsely stating that the investment strategy was based on the expectation that a leveraged position in the foreign bank securities would provide the investor with the opportunity for capital appreciation, when in fact the strategy was based on the expected tax benefits promised by certain conspirators in the tax frauds.

[1]The facts are taken from the Report Prepared by the Minority Staff of the Permanent Subcommittee on Investigations of the Committee on Governmental Affairs of the United States Senate, titled "U.S. Tax Shelter Industry: The Role of Accountants, Lawyers and Financial Professionals—Four KPMG Case Studies: FLIP, OPIS, BLIPS, and SC2," November 18 and 20, 2003, Available at: http://www.gpo.gov/fdsys/pkg/CPRT-108SPRT90655/html/CPRT-108SPRT90655.htm.

Back in Chapter 4 we discussed the "realistic possibility of success" standard in taking tax positions under the Statements on Standards for Tax Services of the AICPA. This is a high standard to meet. Generally, there would need to be a 70–80 percent of prevailing if a tax position were challenged by the IRS. The "more likely than not" standard appears in Treasury Circular 230, which covers rules of conduct for those who practice before the IRS, including CPAs, attorneys, and enrolled agents. A tax preparer who fails to comply with Circular 230 will likely be subject to penalties and possibly other sanctions if she advises a client to take a position on a tax return or a document that does not meet the applicable tax reporting standard.

The three standards for tax positions in Treasury Circular 230, ranked from lowest to highest, are reasonable basis, substantial authority, and more likely than not. A description of each of these standards appears in Exhibit 2.

EXHIBIT 2 Circular 230 Tax Positions and Compliance Standards[2]

Reasonable basis: Reasonable basis is the minimum standard for all tax advice and for preparation of all tax returns and other required tax documents to avoid a penalty under Section 6694 for the underpayment of taxes. If a return position is reasonably based on at least one relevant and persuasive tax authority cited, the return position will generally satisfy this standard.

Substantial authority: Substantial authority for the tax treatment of an item exists only if the weight of the tax authorities (Internal Revenue Code, Treasury regulations, court cases, etc.) supporting the treatment is substantial in relation to the weight of authorities supporting contrary treatment. All authorities relevant to the tax treatment of an item, including the authorities contrary to the treatment, are taken into account in determining whether substantial authority exists. This standard may be measured as a greater than 40 percent likelihood of being sustained on its merits.

More likely than not: More likely than not is "the standard that is met when there is a greater than 50 percent likelihood of the position being upheld." This is the standard for tax shelters under Section 6694 and reportable transactions.

KPMG admitted that its personnel took specific deliberate steps to conceal the existence of the shelters from the IRS by, among other things, failing to register the shelters with the IRS as required by law; fraudulently concealing the shelter losses and income on tax returns; and attempting to hide the shelters using sham attorney-client privilege claims.

The information and indictment alleged that top leadership at KPMG made the decision to approve and participate in shelters and issue KPMG opinion letters despite significant warnings from KPMG tax experts and others throughout the development of the shelters and at critical junctures that the shelters were close to frivolous and would not withstand IRS scrutiny; that the representations required to be made by the wealthy individuals were not credible; and the consequences of going forward with the shelters—as well as failing to register them—could include criminal investigation, among other things.

As we noted in Chapter 4, an unusual aspect to the case is the culture that apparently existed in KPMG's tax practice during the time the shelters were sold, which was to aggressively market tax shelter arrangements targeting wealthy clients by approaching them with the deals rather than the clients coming to KPMG. Back in the late 1990s, the stock market was booming and the firm sought to take advantage of the increasing number of wealthy clients by accelerating its tax services business. The head of KPMG's tax department at the time, Jeffrey M. Stein, and its CFO, Richard Rosenthal, created an environment that treated those who didn't support the "growth at all costs" effort as not being team players.

---

[2]*Regulations Governing Practice before the Internal Revenue Service, Title 31 Code of Federal Regulations, Subtitle A, Part 10, published June 12, 2014, Treasury Department Circular No. 230 (Rev. 6-2014),* Available at: http://www.irs.gov/pub/irs-pdf/pcir230.pdf.

Once it became clear that the firm faced imminent criminal indictment over its tax shelters, KPMG turned to its head of human resources, Timothy Flynn, to somehow persuade the government not to indict. He knew that criminal charges against the firm would probably kill it, as they did Arthur Andersen after the Enron scandal.

KPMG had for years stoutly denied any impropriety, calling its tax advice legal. But Flynn took a gamble and met with Justice Department officials and acknowledged that KPMG had engaged in wrongdoing. He got no promises in return, and the admission could have sunk the firm. Instead, it provided flexibility to the prosecutors, who were aware that the collapse of one of only four remaining accounting giants could harm the financial markets. Two months later, the government gave KPMG a deferred-prosecution deal, holding off indicting if KPMG paid a $456 million penalty and met other conditions.

The agreement between KPMG and the IRS required permanent restrictions on KPMG's tax practice, including the termination of two practice areas, one of which provided tax advice to wealthy individuals; and permanent adherence to higher tax practice standards regarding the issuance of certain tax opinions and the preparation of tax returns. In addition, the agreement banned KPMG's involvement with any prepackaged tax products and restricted KPMG's acceptance of fees not based on hourly rates. The agreement also required KPMG to implement and maintain an effective compliance and ethics program; to install an independent, government-appointed monitor to oversee KPMG's compliance with the deferred prosecution agreement for a three-year period; and its full and truthful cooperation in the pending criminal investigation, including the voluntary provision of information and documents.

Questions

1. What are the ethical obligations of tax practitioners under the AICPA Code? What are their obligations with respect to taking tax positions?

2. Evaluate the characteristics of ethical leadership with respect to the actions taken by KPMG as described in the case. Link your discussion to the tax standards discussed in your response to question 1.

3. Given that KPMG completely lost sight of its public interest obligations in the tax shelter case, and its actions cost American taxpayers at least $2.5 billion in evaded taxes, do you believe some kind of inspection process for tax advisory/consulting engagements should be established, similar to the one of the PCAOB for audits of public companies? Explain.

Case 8-5 Krispy Kreme Doughnuts, Inc.[1]

On March 4, 2009, the SEC reached an agreement with Krispy Kreme Doughnuts, Inc., and issued a cease-and-desist order to settle charges that the company fraudulently inflated or otherwise misrepresented its earnings for the fourth quarter of its FY2003 and each quarter of FY2004. By its improper accounting, Krispy Kreme avoided lowering its earnings guidance and improperly reported earnings per share (EPS) for that time period; these amounts exceeded its previously announced EPS guidance by 1 cent.

The primary transactions described in this case are "round-trip" transactions. In each case, Krispy Kreme paid money to a franchisee with the understanding that the franchisee would pay the money back to Krispy Kreme in a prearranged manner that would allow the company to record additional pretax income in an amount roughly equal to the funds originally paid to the franchisee.

There were three round-trip transactions cited in the SEC consent agreement. The first occurred in June 2003, which was during the second quarter of FY2004. In connection with the reacquisition of a franchise in Texas, Krispy Kreme increased the price that it paid for the franchise by $800,000 (i.e., from $65,000,000 to

---

[1]Unless otherwise indicated, the facts of this case are taken from Securities and Exchange Commission, *Accounting and Auditing Enforcement Release No. 2941, In the Matter of Krispy Kreme Doughnuts, Inc.*, March 4, 2009, Available at: https://www.sec.gov/litigation/admin/2009/34-59499.pdf.

$65,800,000) in return for the franchisee purchasing from Krispy Kreme certain doughnut-making equipment. On the day of the closing, Krispy Kreme debited the franchise's bank account for $744,000, which was the aggregate list price of the equipment. The additional revenue boosted Krispy Kreme's quarterly net income by approximately $365,000 after taxes.

The second transaction occurred at the end of October 2003, four days from the closing of Krispy Kreme's third quarter of FY2004, in connection with the reacquisition of a franchise in Michigan. Krispy Kreme agreed to increase the price that it paid for the franchise by $535,463, and it recorded the transaction on its books and records as if it had been reimbursed for two amounts that had been in dispute with the Michigan franchisee. This overstated Krispy Kreme's net income in the third quarter by approximately $310,000 after taxes.

The third transaction occurred in January 2004, in the fourth quarter of FY2004. It involved the reacquisition of the remaining interests in a franchise in California. Krispy Kreme owned a majority interest in the California franchise and, beginning in or about October 2003, initiated negotiations with the remaining interest holders for acquisition of their interests. During the negotiations, Krispy Kreme demanded payment of a "management fee" in consideration of Krispy Kreme's handling of the management duties since October 2003. Krispy Kreme proposed that the former franchise manager receive a distribution from his capital account, which he could then pay back to Krispy Kreme as a management fee. No adjustment would be made to the purchase price for his interest in the California franchise to reflect this distribution. As a result, the former franchise manager would receive the full value for his franchise interest, including his capital account, plus an additional amount, provided that he paid back that amount as the management fee. Krispy Kreme, acting through the California franchise, made a distribution to the former franchise manager in the amount of $597,415, which was immediately transferred back to Krispy Kreme as payment of the management fee. The company booked this fee, thereby overstating net income in the fourth quarter by approximately $361,000.

Additional accounting irregularities were unearthed in testimony by a former sales manager at a Krispy Kreme outlet in Ohio, who said a regional manager ordered that retail store customers be sent double orders on the last Friday and Saturday of FY2004, explaining "that Krispy Kreme wanted to boost the sales for the fiscal year in order to meet Wall Street projections." The manager explained that the doughnuts would be returned for credit the following week—once FY2005 was under way. Apparently, it was common practice for Krispy Kreme to accelerate shipments at year-end to inflate revenues by stuffing the channels with extra product, a practice known as "channel stuffing."

Some could argue that Krispy Kreme auditors—PwC— should have noticed a pattern of large shipments at the end of the year with corresponding credits the following fiscal year during the course of their audit. Typical audit procedures would be to confirm with Krispy Kreme's customers their purchases. In addition, monthly variations analysis should have led someone to question the spike in doughnut shipments at the end of the fiscal year. However, PwC did not report such irregularities or modify its audit report.

In May 2005, Krispy Kreme disclosed disappointing earnings for the first quarter of FY2005 and lowered its future earnings guidance. Subsequently, as a result of the transactions already described, as well as the discovery of other accounting errors, on January 4, 2005, Krispy Kreme announced that it would restate its financial statements for 2003 and 2004. The restatement reduced net income for those years by $2,420,000 and $8,524,000, respectively.

In August 2005, a special committee of the company's board issued a report to the SEC following an internal investigation of the fraud at Krispy Kreme. The report states that every Krispy Kreme employee or franchisee who was interviewed "repeatedly and firmly" denied deliberately scheming to distort the company's earnings or being given orders to do so; yet, in carefully nuanced language, the Krispy Kreme investigators hinted at the possibility of a willful cooking of the books. "The number, nature, and timing of the accounting errors strongly suggest that they resulted from an intent to manage earnings," the report said. "Further, CEO Scott Livengood and COO John Tate failed to establish proper financial controls, and the company's earnings may have been manipulated to please Wall Street." The committee also criticized the company's board of directors, which it said was "overly deferential in its relationship with Livengood and failed to adequately oversee management decisions."

Krispy Kreme materially misstated its earnings in its financial statements filed with the SEC between the fourth quarter of FY2003 and the fourth quarter of FY2004. In each of these quarters, Krispy Kreme falsely reported that it had achieved earnings equal to its EPS guidance plus 1 cent in the fourth quarter of FY2003 through the third quarter of FY2004 or, in the case of the fourth quarter of FY2004, earnings that met its EPS guidance.

The SEC cited Krispy Kreme for violations of Section 13(a) of the Exchange Act and Rules 12b-20, 13a-1, and 13a-13 thereunder, which require every issuer of a security registered pursuant to Section 12 of the Exchange Act to file with the commission all the necessary information to make the financial statements not misleading. The company was also sanctioned for its failure to keep books, records, and accounts that, in reasonable detail, accurately and fairly reflect its transactions and dispositions of its assets. Finally, Krispy Kreme was cited for failing to devise and maintain a system of internal accounting controls sufficient to provide reasonable assurances that transactions were recorded as necessary to permit preparation of financial statements in accordance with GAAP.

On March 4, 2009, the SEC reached agreement with three former top Krispy Kreme officials, including one-time chair, CEO, and president Scott Livengood. Livengood, former COO John Tate, and CFO Randy Casstevens all agreed to pay more than $783,000 for violating accounting laws and fraud in connection with their management of the company.

Livengood was found in violation of fraud, reporting provisions, and false certification regulations. Tate was found in violation of fraud, reporting provisions, record keeping, and internal controls rules. Casstevens was found in violation of fraud, reporting provisions, record keeping, internal controls, and false certification rules. Livengood's settlement required him to pay about $542,000, which included $467,000 of what the SEC considered as the "disgorgement of ill-gotten gains and prejudgment interest" and $75,000 in civil penalties. Tate's settlement required him to return $96,549 and pay $50,000 in civil penalties, while Casstevens had to return $68,964 and pay $25,000 in civil penalties. Krispy Kreme itself was not required to pay a civil penalty because of its cooperation with the SEC in the case.

SEC Charges against PricewaterhouseCoopers[2]

In a lawsuit brought on behalf of the Eastside Investors group against Krispy Kreme Doughnuts, Inc., members of management, and PricewaterhouseCoopers, a variety of the fraud charges leveled against the company were extended to the alleged deficient audit by PwC. These charges were settled and reflect the following findings.

PwC provided independent audit services and rendered audit opinions on Krispy Kreme's FY2003 and FY2004 financial statements. The firm also provided significant consulting, tax, and due diligence services. Specifically, PwC provided consulting services for employee benefit audits; business acquisitions; accounting consultations including on joint ventures; tax compliance services; tax advice and planning services; services for a cost segregation study prepared by PwC; and actuarial services in connection with the company's insurance plans. Of the total fees received during this period, 66 percent (FY2003) and 61 percent (FY2004) were for nonaudit services. The lawsuit alleged that PwC was highly motivated not to allow any auditing disagreements with Krispy Kreme management to interfere with its nonaudit services.

PwC was charged with a variety of failures in conducting its audit of Krispy Kreme. These include: (1) failure to obtain relevant evidential matter whether it appears to corroborate or contradict the assertions in the financial statements; (2) failure to act on violations of GAAP rules with respect to accounting for franchise rights and the company's relationship with its franchisees; and (3) ignoring numerous red flags that indicated risks that should have been factored into the audit and in questioning of management. These include:

- Unusually rapid growth, especially compared to other companies in the industry;

- Excessive concern by management to maintain or increase earnings and share prices;

- Domination of management by a single person or small group without compensating controls such as effective oversight by the board of directors or audit committee;

- Unduly aggressive financial targets and expectations for operating personnel set by management; and

---

[2]Material in this section was taken from United States District Court Middle District North Carolina, No. 1:04-CV-00416, *In re Eastside Investors v. Krispy Kreme Doughnuts, Inc., Randy S. Casstevens, Scott A. Livengood, Michael C. Phalen, John Tate, and PricewaterhouseCoopers, LLP,* 2005, Available at: http://securities.stanford.edu/filings-documents/1030/KKD04-01 /2005215_r01c_04416.pdf.

- Significant related-party transactions not in the ordinary course of business or with related entities not audited or audited by another firm.

The legal action against PwC referenced Rule 10b-5 of the Securities Exchange Act of 1934 in charging the firm with making untrue statements of material fact and omitting to state material facts necessary to make Krispy Kreme's financial statements not misleading. The company wound up restating its statements for the FY2003 through FY2004 period.

Questions

1. Explain the dimensions of ethical leadership that did not exist in the Krispy Kreme case both on the part of company management and PwC.
2. Evaluate the corporate governance at Krispy Kreme during its financial statement fraud including management's stewardship responsibility to owners.
3. Do you believe PwC violated its independence obligation in its relationship with Krispy Kreme and audit of its financial statements? What about other ethical requirements? Explain.
4. Using the Fraud Triangle, analyze the incentives, motivations, and/or pressures that existed and how management took advantage of its opportunities to commit the fraud.

Case 8-6 Rhody Electronics: A Difficult Client (a GVV case)

Denise Norris is a manager at Fitch & Jones, LLP, a regional audit firm in Providence, Rhode Island. Norris is preparing for a meeting with Alan Morse, the controller of Rhody Electronics, a publicly held company in Providence. The meeting concerns a variety of questions raised by the controller about the audit as follows.

- Why wasn't $1 million revenue recorded in 2016 for a December 31, 2016, transaction whereby Rhody agreed to sell $1 million of software to Ocean State Electronics in return for a stock issuance of that company? Ocean State, in return, agreed to sell $1 million of similar software to Rhody on January 5, 2017, in return for a stock issuance from Rhody.
- Why does the firm need to do additional testing of the collectability of receivables beyond that included in the original audit plan?
- Why has the firm hired a consultant to help with the audit of the company's information systems?

Norris has decided to use the occasion to raise a few issues with Morse as follows:

- Documents are not being provided in full or on a timely basis, thereby requiring extra time and effort to complete the audit.
- Inquiries are being ignored; answers are often unhelpful; and some staff in the accounting department seem to resent those questions.
- Why did Morse request a staff member be removed from the audit team citing irreconcilable "personality" differences?

Questions

1. What role should the client have in raising issues related to auditors' planning and execution of the engagement? Support your answer using ethical reasoning.

2. Assume the controller is very defensive and fails to provide acceptable responses to the questions raised by Norris. Norris is concerned about the ability of the firm to complete the audit on time and under budget. She knows she has to do something to alleviate the tension that has developed with the controller and ensure that the audit comes to a successful conclusion. However, she is not sure how best to get it done. Answer the following questions:

   - What role does ethical leadership play in the way Norris deals with the conflict? Consider how the way she handles the matter might influence the behavior of members of the firm.

   - What levers can Norris use to convince the controller of the need for better cooperation to ensure successful completion of the audit?

   - What are the most persuasive arguments Norris can make of the reasons and rationalizations that may be provided by the controller in discussing/defending his positions?

Major Cases

The following major cases can serve as detailed reviews of major issues discussed in the text. We use these cases for comprehensive written assignments, final projects, and group discussions.

Major Case 1: Adelphia Communications Corporation
- Audit risk
- Auditing standards
- Financial shenanigans
- Earnings management

Major Case 2: Royal Ahold N.V. (Ahold)
- Ethical reasoning
- Auditing standards and procedures
- PSLRA
- Legal liability (optional)

Major Case 3: Madison Gilmore's Ethical Dilemma (a GVV case)
- Values
- Stakeholder analysis
- Ethical reasoning
- Earnings management

Major Case 4: Cendant Corporation
- Income smoothing
- Fraud Triangle
- Professional judgment/AICPA Code
- Corporate governance

Major Case 5: Vivendi Universal
- Ethical leadership
- Internal controls
- Accruals
- EBITDA

Major Case 6: Waste Management
- Ethical leadership and organizational ethics
- Professional judgment/AICPA Code
- Financial shenanigans
- Fraud detection

Major Case 1

Adelphia Communications Corporation

On July 24, 2009, the U.S. Court of Appeals for the District of Columbia upheld the finding of the SEC that Gregory M. Dearlove, a certified public accountant and formerly a partner with the accounting firm Deloitte & Touche LLP, engaged in improper professional conduct within the meaning of Rule of Practice 102(e). Dearlove served as the engagement partner on Deloitte's audit of the financial statements of Adelphia Communications Corporation, a public company, for the fiscal year ended December 31, 2000. The SEC confirmed its original ruling that Adelphia's financial statements were not in accordance with generally accepted accounting principles, and that Dearlove violated generally accepted auditing standards. The administrative law judge (ALJ) also found that Dearlove was a cause of Adelphia's violations of the reporting and record-keeping provisions of the Exchange Act. The ALJ permanently denied Dearlove the privilege of appearing or practicing in any capacity before the commission.

The opinion for the court was filed by Judge Douglas H. Ginsburg of the U.S. Court of Appeals for the D.C. Circuit Court. The opinion states that the SEC concluded that Dearlove engaged repeatedly in unreasonable conduct resulting in violations of applicable accounting principles and standards while serving as Deloitte's engagement partner in charge of the 2000 audit of Adelphia. Dearlove had argued that the SEC committed an error of law, misapplied the applicable accounting principles and standards, and denied him due process. Because the SEC made no error of law, and substantial evidence supports its findings of fact, the court denied the petition.

Background Issues

John Rigas had founded Adelphia, the Greek word for brothers, in 1952, and Rigas and his children were the controlling shareholders in 2000. By the year 2000, Adelphia was one of the largest cable television companies in the United States. It had doubled the number of cable subscribers that it served by acquiring several other cable companies in late 1999. Although its assets were growing, Adelphia's debt grew substantially as well. The SEC found that, prior to 2000, Adelphia, its subsidiaries, and some Rigas-affiliated entities entered as coborrowers into a series of credit agreements. By 1999, Adelphia and the entities had obtained $1.05 billion in credit; in 2000, they tripled their available credit and drew down essentially all the funds available under the agreements.

Deloitte audited Adelphia's financial statements from 1980 through 2002, with Dearlove as the engagement partner. Dearlove and the Deloitte team described the 2000 audit, like many prior audits of Adelphia, as posing "much greater than normal risk" because Adelphia engaged in numerous transactions with subsidiaries and affiliated entities, many of which were owned by members of the Rigas family.

Deloitte issued its year 2000 independent auditor's report of Adelphia—signed by Dearlove—on March 29, 2001. In January 2002, in the wake of the Enron scandal, the SEC released a statement regarding the disclosure of related-party transactions. In March, Adelphia disclosed its obligations as co-debtor with the Rigas entities. Its share price declined from $30 in January 2002 to $0.30 in June, when it was delisted by the National Association of Securities Dealers (NASDAQ). In September 2002, the U.S. Department of Justice (DOJ) brought criminal fraud charges against Adelphia officials, including members of the Rigas family, and Adelphia agreed to pay $715 million into a victims' restitution fund as part of a settlement with the government. In April 2005 the SEC brought and settled civil actions against Adelphia, members of the Rigas family, and Deloitte.

SEC Charges

In September 2005, the SEC charged Dearlove with improper conduct resulting in a violation of applicable professional standards, including his approval of Adelphia's method of accounting for transactions between itself and one or more Rigas entities (i.e., related-party transactions). The matter was referred to the ALJ, who presided at an administrative trial-type hearing to resolve the dispute between the SEC and Adelphia. The ALJ determined Dearlove had engaged in one instance of "highly unreasonable" conduct and repeated instances of "unreasonable" conduct, and permanently denied Dearlove the right to practice before the SEC. Upon review of the ALJ's decision, the SEC held Dearlove had engaged in repeated instances of unreasonable conduct as defined under Rule 102 and denied him the right to practice before the SEC, but provided him the opportunity to apply for reinstatement after four years. Dearlove petitioned for review of that decision, which was denied by the U.S. Court of Appeals.[1]

SEC Rule 102(e) provides the SEC may "deny, temporarily or permanently, the privilege of appearing or practicing before [the SEC] in any way to any person who is found by the Commission . . . to have engaged in unethical or improper professional conduct." The rule defines three classes of "improper professional conduct" for accountants: (1) "intentional or knowing conduct, including reckless conduct, that results in a violation of applicable professional standards," (2) "a single instance of highly unreasonable conduct that results in a violation of applicable professional standards," and (3) "repeated instances of unreasonable conduct, each resulting in a violation of applicable professional standards, that indicate a lack of competence to practice before the Commission." The court supported the SEC's determination that Dearlove repeatedly engaged in unreasonable conduct.

While most of the alleged fraud at Adelphia took its form in hidden debt, the trial was also notable for examples of the eye-popping personal luxury that has marked other white-collar trials such as at Tyco.

In the court case, prosecutor Christopher Clark led off his closing argument by saying John Rigas had ordered two Christmas trees flown to New York, at a cost of $6,000, for his daughter. Rigas also ordered up 17 company cars and the company purchase of 3,600 acres of timberland at a cost of $26 million to preserve the pristine view outside his Coudersport, Pennsylvania, home. Timothy Rigas, the CFO, had become so concerned that he limited his father to withdrawals of $1 million per month.

Deloitte's Audit

Deloitte served as the independent auditor for Adelphia, one of its largest audit clients, from 1980 through 2002. The audits were complex. Several of Adelphia's subsidiaries filed their own Form 10-K annual reports with the SEC. For several years, Deloitte had concluded that the Adelphia engagement posed a "much greater than normal" risk of fraud, misstatement, or error; this was the highest risk category that Deloitte recognized. Risk factors that Deloitte specifically identified in reaching this assessment for the 2000 audit included the following:[2]

- Adelphia operated in a volatile industry, expanded rapidly, and had a large number of decentralized operating entities with a complex reporting structure.
- Adelphia carried substantial debt and was near the limit of its financial resources, making it critical that the company comply with debt covenants.
- Management of Adelphia was concentrated in a small group without compensating controls.
- Adelphia management lacked technical accounting expertise but nevertheless appeared willing to accept unusually high levels of risk, tended to interpret accounting standards aggressively, and was reluctant to record adjustments proposed by auditors.
- Adelphia engaged in significant related-party transactions with affiliated entities that Deloitte would not be auditing.

[1]Securities and Exchange Commission, *Accounting and Auditing Enforcement Release No. 2779, In the Matter of Gregory M. Dearlove, CPA,* January 31, 2008, Available at: www.sec.gov/litigation/opinions/2008/34-57244.pdf.

[2]*Securities and Exchange Commission v. Adelphia Communications Corp., et al.,* Civil Action File No. 02-CV-5776 (PKC) (SDNY), Litigation Release No. 20795, October 30, 2008, Available at: www.sec.gov/litigation/litreleases/2008/lr20795.htm.

To help manage the audit risk, Deloitte planned, among other things, to increase Deloitte's management involvement at all stages of the audit "to ensure that the appropriate work is planned and its performance is properly supervised." It also proposed to heighten professional skepticism "to ensure that accounting estimates, related-party transactions, and transactions in the normal course of business appear reasonable and are appropriately identified and disclosed."

On March 29, 2001, Deloitte issued its independent auditor's report, signed by Dearlove, which stated that it had conducted its audit in accordance with GAAS and that such audit provided a reasonable basis for its opinion that Adelphia's 2000 financial statements fairly presented Adelphia's financial position in conformity with GAAP.

Charges against Rigas Family and Deloitte

In the wake of Adelphia's decline, the DOJ brought criminal fraud charges against several members of the Rigas family and other Adelphia officials. The DOJ declined to file criminal charges against Adelphia as part of a settlement in which Adelphia agreed to pay $715 million in stock and cash to a victims' restitution fund once the company emerged from bankruptcy.

The SEC brought several actions related to the decline of Adelphia. On April 25, 2005, Adelphia, John Rigas, and Rigas's three sons settled a civil injunctive action in which the respondents, without admitting or denying the allegations against them, were enjoined from committing or causing further violations of the anti-fraud, reporting, record-keeping, and internal controls provisions of the federal securities laws.[3] The next day, the commission instituted and settled administrative proceedings against Deloitte under Rule 102(e). Without admitting or denying the commission's allegations, Deloitte consented to the entry of findings that it engaged in repeated instances of unreasonable conduct with respect to the audit of Adelphia's 2000 financial statements. Deloitte also consented to a finding that it caused Adelphia's violations of those provisions of the Securities and Exchange Act that require issuers to file annual reports, make and keep accurate books and records, and devise and maintain a system of sufficient internal controls. Deloitte agreed to pay a $25 million penalty and to implement various prophylactic policies and procedures. The commission also settled a civil action, based on the same conduct, in which Deloitte agreed to pay another $25 million penalty. Senior manager William Caswell consented to commission findings that he committed repeated instances of unreasonable conduct and agreed to a bar from appearing or practicing as an accountant before the commission with a right to apply for reinstatement after two years.[4]

Violation of GAAS: General, Fieldwork, and Reporting Standards

In determining whether to discipline an accountant under Rule 102(e)(1)(iv), the commission has consistently measured auditors' conduct by their adherence to or deviation from GAAS. Certain audit conditions require auditors to increase their professional care and skepticism, as when the audit presents a risk of material misstatement or fraud. When an audit includes review of related-party transactions, auditors must tailor their examinations to obtain satisfaction concerning the purpose, nature, and extent of those transactions on the financial statements. Unless and until an auditor obtains an understanding of the business purpose of material related-party transactions, the audit is not complete. These standards can overlap somewhat, and one GAAS failure may contribute to another.

Dearlove asked the court to compare the reasonableness of his conduct to a standard used by New York state courts in professional negligence cases, that the standard for determining negligence by an

---

[3]*Securities and Exchange Commission v. Adelphia Communications Corporation, John J. Rigas, Timothy J. Rigas, Michael J. Rigas, James P. Rigas, James R. Brown, and Michael C. Mulcahy,* 02 Civ. 5776 (SDNY) (KMW), Litigation Release No. 17837, November 14, 2002, Available at: www.sec.gov/litigation/litreleases/lr17837.htm.

[4]*Accounting and Auditing Enforcement Release No. 2237, In the Matter of Deloitte & Touche LLP,* April 26, 2005, Available at: www.sec.gov/litigation/admin/34-51606.pdf.

accountant should be based on whether the respondent "use[d] the same degree of skill and care that other [accountants] in the community would reasonably use in the same situation." Dearlove believed that his actions should be judged in the context of the large, complex Adelphia audit and to determine whether he exercised the degree of skill and care, including professional skepticism, that a reasonable engagement partner would have used in similar circumstances. Dearlove contended that this analysis "necessarily includes . . . conclusions previously reached by other professionals," a reference to the Adelphia audits that Deloitte conducted from 1994 through 1999. Dearlove asserted that he could place some reliance on audit precedent. Moreover, in his view, the fact that prior auditors reached the same conclusions was "compelling evidence" that Dearlove acted reasonably. The court rejected any suggestion that the conduct of prior auditors should be a substitute for the standards established by GAAS, ruling that "these standards apply to audits of all sizes and all levels of complexity and describe the conduct that the accounting profession itself has established as reasonable, provid[ing] a measure of audit quality and the objectives to be achieved in an audit." The court, therefore, declined to create a separate standard of professional conduct for auditors that depends in each case on the behavior of a particular auditor's predecessors.

The SEC found that prior Deloitte audits offered little support for the conclusions reached in the 2000 audit. The record did not describe how the audits of prior financial statements were performed or what evidential matter supported those audit conclusions. Moreover, Dearlove's expert, while arguing that partner rotation does not require the new auditor to perform a "de novo audit of the client," nevertheless explained that an engagement partner "would perform . . . new audit procedures or GAAP research and consultation . . . to address changed conditions or professional standards." In 2000, Dearlove was presented with markedly different circumstances from those presented to prior teams: Since 1999, Adelphia had tripled its coborrowed debt, doubled its revenues and operating expenses, and acquired more cable subscribers. The changes implicated areas of the Adelphia audit that Deloitte had specifically identified as posing high risk—namely, its rapid expansion, substantial debt load, and significant related-party transactions. Therefore, the court rejected Dearlove's argument that the similarity of prior audit conclusions lent reasonableness to his own audit and found no reason to reject GAAS as the standard by which we judge all audits.

Violation of Accounting and Reporting Standards

Having determined that Dearlove's conduct was unreasonable, the SEC turned to the applicable professional accounting and reporting standards. The GAAS required that when an audit posed greater than normal risk—as Dearlove had determined the Adelphia audit did—there must be "more extensive supervision by the auditor with final responsibility for the engagement during both the planning and conduct of the engagement." The SEC found no evidence in the audit workpapers or elsewhere in the record that Dearlove gave any consideration to the propriety of at least three separate transactions: (1) offsetting of receivables and payables, (2) reporting of coborrowed debt, and (3) direct placement of stock transactions.

Offsetting Receivables and Payables

Accounting Principles Board Opinion No. 10 states that "it is a general principle of accounting that the offsetting of assets and liabilities in the balance sheet is improper except where a right of setoff exists." Rule 5-02 of the commission's Regulation S-X requires that issuers "state separately" amounts payable and receivable. Interpretation 39, Offsetting of Amounts Related to Certain Contracts, defines a right of setoff as "a debtor's legal right, by contract or otherwise, to discharge all or a portion of the debt of another party by applying against the debt an amount that the other party owes to the debtor. The Interpretation is consistent with Rule 5-02.

The court had concluded that Adelphia's presentation of a net figure for its related-party payables and receivables violated GAAP. Because Adelphia netted the accounts payable and receivable of its various subsidiaries against the accounts payable and receivable of various Rigas entities on a global basis, it did not comport with Interpretation 39's basic requirement that netting is appropriate only when two unrelated parties are involved.

The SEC held Adelphia violated GAAP because its netting involved more than two parties: "Adelphia netted the accounts payable and receivable of its various subsidiaries against the accounts payable and receivable of various Rigas Entities on a global basis . . . [and] netting is appropriate only when two parties are involved."

The SEC analyzed the record and determined that Dearlove's conduct was unreasonable in the circumstances and that it resulted in a violation of professional standards—both GAAS and GAAP. Because GAAS focuses upon an auditor's performance and requires him to exercise due professional care, the commission rejected Dearlove's attempt to fault the SEC for marshaling the same evidence to show that his conduct was unreasonable and that he failed to exercise due professional care in performing the audit.

Coborrowed Debt

Between 1996 and 2000, several Adelphia subsidiaries and some of the Rigas entities had entered as coborrowers into a series of three credit agreements with a consortium of banks. Although the agreements differed in the amount of credit available, their terms were substantially the same: each borrower provided collateral for the loan; each could draw funds under the loan agreement; and each was jointly and severally liable for the entire amount of funds drawn down under the agreement, regardless of which entity drew down the amount. By year-end 2000, the total amount of coborrowed funds drawn under the credit agreements was $3.751 billion, more than triple the $1.025 billion borrowed at year-end 1999. Of this amount, Adelphia subsidiaries had drawn approximately $2.1 billion, and Rigas entities had drawn $1.6 billion.

Generally, an issuer must accrue on its balance sheet a debt for which it is the primary obligor. However, when an issuer deems itself to be merely contingently liable for a debt, *Statement of Financial Accounting Standards (SFAS) 5* provides the appropriate accounting and reporting treatment for that liability. *SFAS 5* establishes a three-tiered system for determining the appropriate accounting treatment of a contingent liability, based on the likelihood that the issuer will suffer a loss—that is, be required to pay the debt for which it is contingently liable. If a loss is *probable* (i.e., likely) and its amount can be reasonably estimated, the liability should be accrued on the issuer's financial statements as if the issuer were the primary obligor for the debt. If the likelihood of loss is only *reasonably possible* (defined as more than remote but less than likely), or if the loss is probable but not estimable, the issuer need not accrue the loss but should disclose the nature of the contingency and give an estimate of the possible loss or range of loss or state that such an estimate cannot be made. The issuer still must disclose the "nature and amount" of the liability, even if the likelihood of loss is only *remote* (slight).[5] From 1997 through 1999, Adelphia had included in the liabilities recorded on its balance sheet the amount that its own subsidiaries had borrowed, but it did not consider itself the primary obligor for the amount that the Rigas entities had borrowed and therefore did not include that amount on its balance sheet. Instead, Adelphia accounted for the amounts borrowed by the Rigas entities by making the following disclosure in the footnotes to its financial statements:

> Certain subsidiaries of Adelphia are coborrowers with Managed Partnerships (i.e., Rigas entities) under credit facilities for borrowings of up to [the total amount of all coborrowed debt available to Adelphia and the Rigas entities that year]. Each of the coborrowers is liable for all borrowings under this credit agreement, although the lenders have no recourse against Adelphia other than against Adelphia's interest in such subsidiaries.

---

[5]*Statement of Financial Accounting Standards (SFAS) 5,* Accounting for Contingencies, Available at: www.fasb.org.

Deloitte had approved this treatment in the audits it conducted from 1997 to 1999.

Dearlove knew that Adelphia considered the Rigas entities's debt to be a contingent liability for which its chances of suffering a loss were merely remote, making accrual on the balance sheet unnecessary pursuant to *SFAS 5*. Deloitte created no workpapers documenting its examination of Adelphia's decision. However, from the record, it appears that Deloitte considered the matter and focused its review on the likelihood, as defined by *SFAS 5*, that Adelphia would have to pay Rigas entities's share of coborrowed debt.

Dearlove also believed that, although the Rigas family was not legally obligated to contribute funds in the event of a default by the coborrowers, the family would be economically compelled to protect their Adelphia holdings by stepping in to prevent a default by the entities. Dearlove did not, however, conduct any inquiry into whether the family would, in fact, use their personal assets to prevent a default by Adelphia. Dearlove estimated the value of the Rigas family's holdings of Adelphia stock by multiplying the number of shares the Rigases owned by the price per Class A share, resulting in a figure of approximately $2.3 billion, which he concluded was by itself ample to cover the debt and conclude his *SFAS 5* analysis. However, Dearlove did not determine if these Rigas family assets were already encumbered by other debt; he saw no financial statements or other proof of the family's financial condition other than local media reports that the Rigases "were billionaires." Dearlove testified that he "never asked them: Are you worth $2 billion, $3 billion, or $10 billion?" Dearlove also did not consider whether disposing of some or all of the family's stock in Adelphia might result in a downward spiral in the stock's value or in a change in their control of the company, in the event of a default by the entities under the coborrowing agreements.

Dearlove testified that, at the end of the 2000 audit, he spoke to senior manager Caswell for about 15 minutes regarding the requirements of *SFAS 5*. During this meeting, they concluded that "the assets of the cable systems and the Adelphia common stock that the Rigases owned exceeded the amount of debt that was on the coborrowed entities, and the overhang . . . exceeded the coborrowing by hundreds of millions if not billions of dollars." Dearlove testified that, although other assets could have been included in an *SFAS 5* analysis, these two assets alone were sufficient to allow the auditors to conclude that Adelphia's contingent liability was remote. Deloitte therefore approved Adelphia's decision to exclude Rigas entities's $1.6 billion in coborrowed debt from its balance sheet and to instead disclose the debt in a footnote to the financial statements.

When it reviewed the adequacy of the note disclosure that Adelphia planned to use (which was identical to the language it had used in previous years), the audit team initially believed the disclosure should be revised. During the 2000 quarterly reviews, audit manager Ivan Hofmann and others had repeatedly encouraged Adelphia management to disclose the specific dollar amount of Rigas entities's coborrowings, but Adelphia continually ignored Deloitte's suggestions. Although Deloitte was unaware of it at the time, Adelphia management was working purposefully to obfuscate the disclosure of Rigas entities's coborrowed debt.

In November 2000, at a third-quarter wrap-up meeting attended by Dearlove, Caswell, and Hofmann, Adelphia management (including Adelphia's vice president of finance, James Brown) agreed to make disclosures regarding the amounts borrowed by the Rigas entities under the coborrowing agreements. Caswell and Hofmann subsequently suggested improvements to the note disclosure in written comments on at least six drafts of the 10-K; they proposed adding language that would distinguish the amount of borrowings by Adelphia subsidiaries and Rigas entities, such as the following: "A total of $—— related to such credit agreements is included in the company's consolidated balance sheet at December 31, 2000. The [Rigas] entities have outstanding borrowings of $—— as of December 31, 2000, under such facilities."

At the end of March 2001, as Deloitte was concluding its audit of the 2000 financials, Brown—despite his agreement in November 2000 to disclose the amount of Rigas entities's borrowing—informed the audit team that he did not think that the additional disclosure was necessary. Instead, Brown proposed adding a phrase explaining that each of the coborrowers "may borrow up to the entire amount available under the credit facility." Brown argued that his proposed language was more accurate than Deloitte's proposal because the lines of credit could fluctuate and, as a result, it would be better to disclose Adelphia's maximum possible exposure. Caswell agreed to take Brown's language back to the engagement team, but he told Brown that he did not agree with Brown and did not think that Deloitte would accept his proposed language.

Notwithstanding Caswell's reaction, Brown soon afterward presented his proposed language to the audit team, including Dearlove, Caswell, and Hofmann, during the audit exit meeting on March 30, 2001. Brown claimed that his proposed disclosure language had been discussed with, and approved by, Adelphia's outside counsel. Although Dearlove characterized the disclosure issue as "really one of the more minor points that [the audit team was] trying to reconcile at that point," the ALJ did not accept this testimony. Dearlove testified that he was "concerned" about "making it clear to the reader how much Adelphia could be guaranteeing," and that Brown's language was "more conservative" but "wasn't necessarily what we were attempting to help clarify." Dearlove also testified that he told Brown, "I don't understand how that [proposed change] enhances the note" but that, after "an exchange back and forth relative to that," Dearlove "couldn't persuade him as to what he wanted." Nevertheless, Dearlove told Brown that he agreed with the proposal and approved the change. Caswell and Hofmann also indicated their agreement.

Adelphia's note disclosure of the coborrowed debt, as it appeared in its 2000 Form 10-K with Brown's added language, read as follows:

> Certain subsidiaries of Adelphia are coborrowers with Managed Entities under credit facilities for borrowings of up to $3,751,250,000. Each of the coborrowers is liable for all borrowings under the credit agreements, and may borrow up to the entire amount of the available credit under the facility. The lenders have no recourse against Adelphia other than against Adelphia's interest in such subsidiaries.

Adequacy of the Note Disclosure of Adelphia's Contingent Liability

The SEC also considered whether Adelphia's footnote disclosure of Rigas entities's coborrowings was appropriate under GAAP. Adelphia disclosed the total amount of credit available to the coborrowers ("up to" $3.75 billion) without indicating whether any portion of that available credit had actually been drawn down, much less that all of it had. This disclosure was inadequate to inform the investing public that Adelphia was already primarily liable for $2.1 billion and a guarantor for the remaining $1.6 billion that had been borrowed by Rigas entities. Therefore, it did not comply with the requirement in *SFAS 5* to disclose the amount of the contingent liability.

The SEC concluded that Dearlove acted unreasonably in his audit of Adelphia's note disclosure, resulting in several violations of GAAS. In high-risk audit environments such as that presented by the Adelphia engagement, GAAS specifically recommend "increased recognition of the need to corroborate management explanations or representations concerning material matters—such as further analytical procedures, examination of documentation, or discussion with others within or outside the entity" when audit risk increases. The accounting for Adelphia's coborrowed debt implicated the extensive related-party transactions and high debt load that were part of the basis for Deloitte's high-risk assessment for the Adelphia audit. Management's insistence on its own accounting interpretation was precisely the behavior identified by the audit plan as presenting a much higher than normal risk of misstatement in the audit.

Moreover, Dearlove knew that the audit team believed that the footnote disclosure in previous years was inadequate and had urged additional disclosure that would have made clear the extent of Rigas entities's actual borrowings and Adelphia's resulting potential liability. Dearlove did not think that Brown's language helped achieve Deloitte's goal of clarifying the extent of Rigas entities's debt and Adelphia's obligation as guarantor. Yet Dearlove accepted Brown's language without probing his reasons for the change, without understanding Adelphia's reasons for rejecting Deloitte's language, and without discussing the issue with the concurring or risk review partners assigned to the audit. This unquestioning acceptance of Brown's proposed disclosure language was a clear—and at least unreasonable—departure from the requirements of GAAS to apply greater than normal skepticism and additional audit procedures in order to corroborate management representations in a high-risk environment. Dearlove's conduct resulted in violations of applicable professional standards.

Dearlove asserted that disclosure of the amount that Rigas entities could theoretically borrow (up to $3.75 billion) was more conservative than disclosure of the $1.6 billion that it had actually borrowed. The SEC concluded that the footnote disclosure was materially misleading to investors: "Materiality depends on the significance the reasonable investor would place on the withheld or misrepresented information." If "there is a substantial likelihood that a reasonable investor would consider the information important in making an investment decision," the information is material. A reasonable investor would think it significant that the footnote disclosure spoke only in terms of potential debt when, in fact, the entire line of credit had been borrowed and $1.6 billion of it was excluded from Adelphia's balance sheet but potentially payable by Adelphia. It was especially important for this information to appear in Adelphia's financial statements because investors had no access to the financial statements of the privately held Rigas entities. The SEC rejected Dearlove's argument that Adelphia's note complied with *SFAS 5*'s requirement to disclose the amount of debt that Adelphia guaranteed.

Debt Reclassification

After the end of the second, third, and fourth quarters of 2000, Adelphia's accounting department transferred the reporting of approximately $296 million of debt from the books of Adelphia's subsidiaries to the books of various Rigas entities. In exchange, Adelphia eliminated from its books receivables owed to it by the respective Rigas entities in the amount of debt transferred. The three transfers were in the amounts of $36 million, approximately $222 million, and more than $38 million, respectively. In each instance, the transaction took place after the end of the quarter, and each transfer involved a postclosing journal entry that was retroactive to the last day of the quarter.

A checklist prepared by Deloitte in anticipation of the 2000 audit showed that Deloitte was aware of a significant number of related-party transactions that had arisen outside the normal course of business and that past audits had indicated a significant number of misstatements or correcting entries made by Adelphia, particularly at or near year-end. An audit overview memorandum recognized as a risk area that "Adelphia records numerous post-closing adjusting journal entries" and provided as an audit response, "[Deloitte] engagement team to review post-closing journal entries recorded and review with appropriate personnel. Conclude as to reasonableness of entries posted." An audit planning memorandum provided that "professional skepticism will be heightened to ensure that . . . related party transactions . . . are appropriately identified and disclosed" and that auditors should "increase professional skepticism in [areas] where significant related party transactions could occur."

Dearlove testified that Deloitte had identified the Rigas family's control of both Adelphia and Rigas entities as posing a special risk. Dearlove also testified that he believed that it was important to know whose debt was whose, concerning Adelphia and Rigas entities. He testified that he was "generally aware the debt was audited," but that he did not review the debt workpapers directly. He also testified: "I don't recall [debt] being [a] particularly sensitive area, . . . I don't recall issues raised to me of difficulties we had. I don't recall any particular conversation I had with the team" concerning the audit of the debt. The record does not show that Dearlove knew of the three journal entries involving debt reclassification at the time of the audit.

Statement of Financial Accounting Standards (SFAS) 125, Accounting for Transfers and Servicing of Financial Assets and Extinguishment of Liabilities, permits a debtor to derecognize a liability "if and only if it has been extinguished." *SFAS 125* provides that a liability is extinguished if either (1) the debtor pays the creditor and is relieved of its obligation for the liability, or (2) the debtor is legally released from being the primary obligor under the liability, either judicially or by the creditor.[6]

When the Adelphia subsidiaries posted the debt in question to their books, they acknowledged their primary liability for the amounts posted. They could not remove the debt properly from their books without first satisfying the requirements of *SFAS 125* that either the Adelphia subsidiaries repaid the debt to the creditor during the relevant reporting periods or a creditor had released the subsidiaries from their liability for repayment. The evidence does not show, and Dearlove did not contend, that either of these events occurred. Adelphia's attempt to extinguish the debt unilaterally merely by shifting the reporting to Rigas entities violated GAAP and rendered its financial statements materially misleading by making Adelphia's debt appear less than it was.

Dearlove did not dispute that "certain debt which had been posted to Adelphia was later posted to a Rigas entity." However, focusing on the statement in the initial decision that "once Adelphia's subsidiaries had posted this debt to their books they became primary obligors for the amounts posted," Dearlove argued that *SFAS 125* does not define the circumstances under which an entity recognizes debt that may be derecognized only under the *SFAS 125* criteria. He claimed that the initial decision of the commission improperly "assumed without analysis" that the posting of debt in a ledger is such a circumstance. Dearlove argued that the application of *SFAS 125* is complex where entities are jointly and severally liable for an obligation, and it did not apply where an entity is secondarily or contingently rather than primarily liable. He asserted that Adelphia was arguably not required to recognize debt in cases where coborrowed funds were intended to be used by other coborrowers. He stopped short, however, of saying that the funds at issue were so intended, and our review of the record yields nothing to support such a contention. The record did not establish that all the reclassified debt was coborrowed debt, and the ALJ correctly concluded that the impropriety of Adelphia's debt reclassification was unaffected by the question whether the debt was coborrowed. In addition, Dearlove cited no authority to support his contention that *SFAS 125* is applicable only where primary obligors were required to recognize a liability, and we are aware of none.

The crucial question for the *SFAS 125* analysis is whether the debt was extinguished in one of the enumerated ways. If the debt was not extinguished as provided in *SFAS 125,* the debtor may not derecognize it. The SEC found that the debts were recognized when booked and that, because there was no evidence that the debts were extinguished under *SFAS 125,* the accounting treatment violated GAAP.

With respect to the direct placement of stock transactions, on at least four occasions corresponding with public offerings by Adelphia, Adelphia removed a portion of Co-Borrowing Credit Facility Debt from its books as part of sham transactions in which a Rigas Entity non-co-borrower received Adelphia securities and a Rigas Entity co-borrower "assumed" debt of Adelphia. In each instance, Adelphia claimed in Commission filings and other public statements that Adelphia had applied some or all of the proceeds from these securities transactions actually to pay down debt, when—in fact—these transactions were shams with no bona fide proceeds, and resulted only in the transfer of Adelphia's debt to the books of Rigas Entity co-borrowers.

The commission also found that Dearlove's conduct in his audit of Adelphia's accounting for debt was at least unreasonable, resulting in several GAAS violations. As explained, Dearlove knew that Adelphia had a large number of decentralized operating entities with a complex reporting structure, carried substantial debt, and engaged in significant related-party transactions with affiliated entities that

---

[6]*Statement of Financial Accounting Standards No. 125,* Accounting for Transfers and Servicing of Financial Assets and Extinguishment of Liabilities, Available at: www.fasb.org.

Deloitte would not be auditing. He also knew that Adelphia management tended to interpret accounting standards aggressively. Moreover, the audit plan specifically required that postclosing journal entries be examined in particular detail and that the audit team draw conclusions as to their reasonableness. Dearlove knew that these factors, together with others, led Deloitte to identify the Adelphia audit as posing a "much greater than normal" risk of fraud, misstatement, or error. In addition, Dearlove knew that Adelphia management netted its affiliate accounts payable and receivable and sought to reduce the amount of related-party receivables that it reported.

In this context, GAAS required Dearlove to consider the "much greater than normal" risk of the audit in determining the extent of procedures, assigning staff, and requiring appropriate levels of supervision. In addition, he was required to "direct the efforts of assistants who [were] involved in accomplishing the objectives of the audit and [to] determin[e] whether those objectives were accomplished." He was required to exercise "an attitude that includes a questioning mind and a critical assessment of audit evidence," "to obtain sufficient competent evidential matter to provide . . . a reasonable basis for forming a conclusion," and, after identifying related-party transactions, to "apply the procedures he consider[ed] necessary to obtain satisfaction concerning the purpose, nature, and extent of these transactions and their effect on the financial statements."

The reclassified debt involved postclosing journal entries of a magnitude significant enough to require the auditors to confront management and request an explanation, as required by Deloitte's audit planning documents. After discussing the entries with appropriate Adelphia personnel, Deloitte should have documented management's explanation and Deloitte's conclusions as to whether the accounting treatment was reasonable in the audit workpapers. The record did not show that any of these steps was taken. The failure to take them was, at the very least, unreasonable.

The SEC concluded that Dearlove had acted at least unreasonably in signing an unqualified audit opinion (i.e., unmodified) stating that Deloitte had conducted its audit in accordance with GAAS and that such audit provided a reasonable basis for its opinion that Adelphia's 2000 financial statements fairly presented Adelphia's financial position in conformity with GAAP.

Postscript

On April 21, 2005, it was announced that Time Warner and Comcast were buying bankrupt cable company Adelphia Communications in a $17.6 billion cash-and-stock deal. As a result of a settlement of actions against Adelphia and members of the Rigas family for securities fraud and other violations, and a related criminal forfeiture action, the U.S. Department of Justice and the U.S. Securities and Exchange Commission obtained a recovery consisting of cash of approximately $729 million. The funds were distributed to eligible claimants who suffered a financial loss as a direct result of the circumstances surrounding the Adelphia fraud.

Deloitte did not fare well in the investor lawsuits. On April 5, 2010, Deloitte & Touche LLP agreed to pay up to $210 million as part of a larger $455 million amount. Also, a number of banks, including Bank of America, Citigroup, JPMorgan Chase, Wachovia, and 35 others, agreed to pay to settle an investor lawsuit. Earlier, in 2005, Deloitte had paid the SEC $50 million to settle claims that it had incorrectly audited Adelphia's 2000 financials. Not surprisingly, the defendants, Deloitte and the banks, admitted no wrongdoing, but Deloitte spokesperson Deborah Harrington said, "Deloitte & Touche believes it has no liability for the fraud by Adelphia and its former management. Deloitte & Touche also believes, however, that it was in the best interests of the firm and its clients to settle this action rather than to continue to face the expense and uncertainty of protracted litigation."[7]

As usual, the lawyers made out well in this case, landing a 21 percent share of the settlement (or about $94 million).

[7] "Deloitte Pays $210 million to Settle Adelphia Case: 45% of Total Sum," December 10, 2006, Available at: http://www.big4.com/deloitte/deloitte-pays-210-million-to-settle-adelphia-case-45-of-total-sum-249/.

Questions

1. Dearlove and Deloitte had identified the audit as posing much greater risk than normal. Describe the risk factors in the case that most likely would have led to this conclusion.

2. Classify each of the accounting issues in the case into the financial shenanigans identified by Schilit in Chapter 7. Are there any accounting procedures that do not fit into one of the shenanigans? If not, make up a category to describe such procedures in a general way as did Schilit. Comment on the earnings management effects as well.

3. Describe each of the auditing standards and procedures the auditors failed to adhere to given the facts of the case. How did the failure of the auditors to follow them violate Deloitte's ethical standards as evidenced by the deficiencies in the work of Dearlove and other members of the audit engagement team?

4. Analyze the actions of Deloitte and Dearlove from an ethical reasoning perspective.

Major Case 2

Royal Ahold N.V. (Ahold)

Summary of Court Ruling

The U.S. Court of Appeals for the Fourth Circuit affirmed the lower court ruling in the case *Public Employees' Retirement Association of Colorado; Generic Trading of Philadelphia, LLC v. Deloitte & Touche, LLP* that Deloitte defendants lacked the necessary scienter to conclude that they knowingly or recklessly perpetrated a fraud on Ahold's investors.

This class action securities fraud lawsuit arose out of improper accounting by Royal Ahold N.V., a Dutch corporation, and U.S. Foodservice, Inc. (USF), a Maryland-based Ahold subsidiary. The misconduct of Ahold and USF was not disputed in this appeal. The main issue is the liability of Ahold's accountants, Deloitte & Touche LLP (Deloitte U.S.) and Deloitte & Touche Accountants (Deloitte Netherlands), for their alleged role in the fraud perpetrated by Ahold and USF. Under the Private Securities Litigation Reform Act of 1995 (PSLRA), plaintiffs must plead facts alleging a "strong inference" that the defendants acted with the required scienter. As explained by the Supreme Court in *Tellabs, Inc. v. Makor Issues & Rights, Ltd.*, a strong inference "must be more than merely plausible or reasonable—it must be cogent and at least as compelling as any opposing inference of non-fraudulent intent."

The Appeals Court found that Deloitte, like the plaintiffs, were victims of Ahold's fraud rather than its enablers. In its decision, the court relied on the PSLRA and the decision in *Tellabs*. Circuit Judge Wilkinson wrote the conclusion for the court.[1] The court ruling will be explained later on.

ERISA Class Action Settlement

Class action lawsuits are common in cases such as Ahold where dozens of separate private class action securities are combined. In this case the Employee Retirement Income Security Act of 1974 (ERISA) actions were filed against Ahold, Deloitte, and other defendants. On June 18, 2003, the Judicial Panel on Multidistrict Litigation transferred these actions to the U.S. District Court for the District of Maryland, *In re Royal Ahold N.V. Securities & ERISA Litigation*. Following the certification of the class

---

[1]U.S. Court of Appeals for the Fourth Circuit, *Public Employees' Retirement Association of Colorado; Generic Trading of Philadelphia, LLC v. Deloitte & Touche, LLP*, January 5, 2009, Available at: http://classactiondefense.jmbm.com/deloitte_class_action_defense_pslra_opn.pdf.

action lawsuit, the U.S. District Court in Maryland ruled in favor of the ERISA plaintiffs on November 2, 2006, and awarded them $1.1 billion in the securities fraud case against Royal Ahold.[2]

Summary of Accounting Fraud

Beginning in the 1990s, and continuing until 2003, Ahold and USF perpetrated frauds that led it to overstate its earnings on financial reports significantly:

- Ahold improperly "consolidated" the revenue from a number of joint ventures (JVs) with supermarket operators in Europe and Latin America. That is, for accounting purposes, Ahold treated these JVs as if it fully controlled them—and thus treated all revenue from the ventures as revenue to Ahold—when in fact, Ahold did not have a controlling stake. Under Dutch and U.S. GAAP,[3] Ahold should have consolidated only the revenue proportionally to Ahold's stake in the ventures.

- USF falsely reported its income from promotional allowances (PAs). Also known as *vendor rebates,* PAs are payments or discounts that manufacturers and vendors provide to retailers like USF to encourage the retailers to promote the manufacturers' products. To increase its stated income, USF prematurely recognized income from PAs and inflated its reported PA income beyond amounts actually received.

- On February 24, 2003, Ahold announced that its earnings for fiscal years 2001 and 2002 had been overstated by at least $500 million as a result of the fraudulent accounting for promotional allowances at USF, and that Ahold would be restating revenues because it would cease treating the joint ventures as fully consolidated. After this announcement, Ahold common stock trading on the Euronext stock exchange[4] and Ahold American Depositary Receipts[5] trading on the NYSE lost more than 60 percent of their value. Subsequent to the February 2003 announcement, Ahold made further restatements to its earnings totaling $24.8 billion in revenues and approximately $1.1 billion in net income.

Ahold Fraud—Joint Ventures

With respect to the JV fraud, both Deloittes advised Ahold on the consolidation of the joint ventures. Five joint ventures were at issue in this litigation: JMR, formed in August 1992; Bompreço, formed in November 1996; DAIH, formed in January 1998; Paiz-Ahold, formed in December 1999; and ICA, formed in February 2000. Ahold had a 49 percent stake in JMR and a 50 percent share of each of the other ventures at their respective times of formation. Prior to Ahold's entering into the first joint venture, Deloitte Netherlands and Deloitte U.S. gave Ahold advice about revenue consolidation under Dutch and U.S. GAAP. A memo explained that control of a joint venture is required for consolidation of the venture's revenue and discussed what situations are sufficient to demonstrate control. The memo

---

[2]*In re Royal Ahold N.V. Securities & ERISA Litigation,* 461 F.Supp.2d 383 (2006), Available at: http://www.leagle.com/xmlResult.aspx?xmldoc=2006844461FSupp2d383_1796.xml.

[3]Starting in 2005, members of the European Union (EU), including the Netherlands, adopted International Financial Reporting Standards (IFRS) as the only acceptable standards for EU companies when filing statements with securities regulators in the European Union.

[4]NYSE Euronext is the result of a merger on April 4, 2007, between the NYSE and stock exchanges in Paris, Amsterdam, Brussels, and Lisbon, as well as the NYSE Liffe derivatives markets in London, Paris, Amsterdam, Brussels, and Lisbon. NYSE Euronext is a U.S. holding company that operates through its subsidiaries, and it is a listed company. NYSE Euronext common stock is dually listed on the NYSE and Euronext Paris under the symbol NYX.

[5]An American Depositary Receipt (ADR) represents ownership in the shares of a non-U.S. company and trades in U.S. financial markets. The stock of many non-U.S. companies trade on U.S. stock exchanges through the use of ADRs. ADRs enable U.S. investors to buy shares in foreign companies without the hazards or inconveniences of cross-border and cross-currency transactions. ADRs carry prices in U.S. dollars, pay dividends in U.S. dollars, and can be traded like the shares of U.S.-based companies.

indicated that control could be shown by a majority voting interest, a large minority voting interest under certain circumstances, or a contractual arrangement.

Ahold began consolidating the joint ventures as they were formed. The various JV agreements did not indicate that Ahold controlled the ventures. For example, the JMR joint venture agreement specified that decisions would be made by a board of directors, "deciding unanimously," and that the board would consist of three members appointed by Ahold and four members appointed by JMH, Ahold's partner in the venture. However, Ahold represented to Deloitte Netherlands that it nonetheless possessed the control requisite for consolidation. Deloitte Netherlands initially accepted these representations for the consolidation of JMR and Bompreço. But as consolidation continued, Deloitte became concerned that Ahold lacked the control necessary to consolidate these first two joint ventures.

On August 24, 1998, Deloitte Netherlands partner John van den Dries sent a letter to Michiel Meurs, Ahold's chief financial officer (CFO), advising him that Ahold's representations of control would no longer suffice—that Ahold would need to produce more evidence of control in order to justify continuing consolidation of joint venture revenue under U.S. GAAP, and that without such evidence, a financial restatement would be required. In response to Deloitte Netherlands's requests, Ahold drafted a "control letter" addressed to BompreçoPar S.A., its partner in the Bompreço joint venture. The letter stated that the parties agreed that if they were unable to reach a consensus on a particular issue, "Ahold's proposal to solve that issue will in the end be decisive." After reviewing the draft letter, Deloitte Netherlands advised Ahold that if countersigned by the JV partner, the letter would be sufficient evidence to consolidate the venture. The letter was signed by Ahold and BompreçoPar in May 1999. By late 2000, Ahold had obtained similar countersigned control letters for the ICA, DAIH, and Paiz-Ahold joint ventures. Based on these letters and other evidence, Deloitte Netherlands concluded that consolidation was appropriate. However, in October 2002, Deloitte learned of a "side letter" sent to Ahold in May 2000 by one of Ahold's ICA joint venture partners, Canica. The letter stated that Canica did not agree with the interpretation of the shareholder agreement stated in the ICA control letter.

At this point, Deloitte Netherlands and Deloitte U.S. began trying to get Ahold to obtain an amendment to the shareholder agreement in order to justify ongoing consolidation. At a February 14, 2003, meeting, Deloitte Netherlands and Deloitte U.S. told Ahold that Ahold lacked the necessary control for consolidation. On February 22, 2003, Ahold revealed to Deloitte Netherlands side letters contradicting the Bompreço, DAIH, and Paiz-Ahold control letters. Two days later, Ahold announced that it had consolidated its joint ventures improperly and would be restating its revenues.

USF Fraud—Promotional Allowances

Ahold acquired USF in early 2000. Prior to the acquisition, Deloitte U.S. participated in Ahold's due diligence on USF. In a February 2000 memo, Deloitte U.S. noted that USF's internal system for recording promotional allowances received was weak because it heavily relied on vendors' figures, and that the system could "easily result in losses and in frauds." Deloitte U.S. also noted in the memo that USF's use of value-added service providers, special-purpose entities that bought products from vendors and then resold them to USF for a higher price, needed to be evaluated for their "tax and legal implications and associated business risks."

After Ahold's acquisition of USF was finalized, Deloitte U.S. became USF's external auditor. When performing an opening balance sheet audit of USF, Deloitte U.S. discovered that a USF division in Buffalo, New York, had been fraudulently accounting for PA income. This fraud required a restatement of $11 million of PA income. USF also downwardly adjusted its income by $90 million as a result of Deloitte U.S.'s advice that it be less aggressive in its method for recognizing PA income. USF used at interim periods a method known as the "PA recognition rate" to estimate promotional allowance income, in which PAs were estimated as a percentage of USF's total sales. The rate used by USF was 4.58 percent at the time of Ahold's acquisition of USF, but it rose as high as 8.51 percent in 2002. When

USF booked final numbers, Deloitte U.S. in its audits tested USF's recognition of PAs by requesting written confirmation of PA amounts from vendors and by performing cash receipt tests. Using this confirmation process, Deloitte U.S. was able to test between 65 and 73 percent of PA receivables in its audits for 2000 and 2001.

Auditing Issues

Because USF lacked an internal auditing department, in April 2000, Ahold hired Deloitte U.S. to perform internal auditing services at USF. The internal auditors did not report to the Deloitte U.S. external auditors.[6] Instead, they reported initially to Ahold USA's internal audit director and, later, to USF's internal audit director after he was hired. The audit was managed by Jennifer van Cleave under the supervision of Patricia Grubel, a Deloitte U.S. partner. One of the internal audit's objectives was to determine whether USF's tracking of PAs was adequate. In van Cleave's attempt to verify USF's PA numbers, she requested a number of documents from USF management, including vendor contracts. Management refused to produce a number of the requested documents. Several members of management also refused to meet with van Cleave when she asked to conduct exit meetings. Van Cleave was thus unable to complete all the audit's objectives.

In a February 5, 2001, draft report, van Cleave described how management's failure to produce requested documents resulted in her inability to complete some of the goals of the audit. Grubel instructed van Cleave to soften the report's language, and the version submitted to Michael Resnick, director of USF's Internal Audit Department, simply stated that Deloitte U.S. "was unable to obtain supporting documentation for some of the promotional allowance sample items," without more specifically detailing management's failures and lack of cooperation.

In its February 2003 external audit for 2002, Deloitte U.S. discovered through the PA confirmation process that USF had been inflating its recorded PA income. An investigation ensued. Ultimately, USF's former chief marketing officer (CMO), Mark Kaiser, was convicted on all counts of a federal indictment that alleged that he had induced USF's vendors to report PA income amounts and receivable balances falsely to Deloitte U.S., and that he had concealed the existence of written contracts with USF vendors from Deloitte U.S. Two other USF executives pled guilty to federal securities fraud charges; in their plea statements, they admitted that USF lied to and deceived Deloitte U.S., and that they induced vendors to sign false audit confirmation letters that falsely overstated PA payments. In addition, 17 individuals associated with USF vendors pled guilty to various charges and admitted that they signed false audit confirmation letters in order to conceal the PA fraud from Deloitte U.S.

PSLRA: Fraud and Scienter

In passing the PSLRA in 1995, Congress imposed heightened pleading requirements for private securities fraud actions. As a general matter, heightened pleading is not the norm in federal civil procedure. Frequently stated reasons include protecting defendants' reputations from baseless accusations, eliminating unmeritorious suits that are brought only for their nuisance value, discouraging fishing expeditions brought in the slight hope of discovering a fraud, and providing defendants with detailed information in order to enable them to defend effectively against a claim. When "alleging fraud or mistake," plaintiffs "must state with particularity the circumstances constituting fraud or mistake."

The PSLRA imposed a number of requirements designed to discourage private securities actions lacking merit. Among them is the requirement that in a private securities action "in which the plaintiff may recover money damages only on proof that the defendant acted with a particular state of mind, the complaint shall, with respect to each act or omission . . . , state with particularity facts giving rise to a

---

[6]Under the professional standards then in effect, an auditing firm could provide both internal and external auditing services to the same client. The Sarbanes-Oxley Act of 2002 (SOX) subsequently prohibited internal audit services for external audit clients because of independence concerns.

strong inference that the defendant acted with the required state of mind." Complaints that do not plead scienter adequately are to be dismissed.

Because the PSLRA did not define "a strong inference," the courts of appeals disagreed on how much factual specificity plaintiffs must plead in private securities actions. The Supreme Court resolved that issue in *Tellabs,* in which the Court prescribed the following analysis for Rule 12(b)(6) motions to dismiss Section 10(b) actions:

- First, courts must, as with any motion to dismiss for failure to plead a claim on which relief can be granted, accept all factual allegations in the complaint as true.
- Second, courts must consider the complaint in its entirety, as well as other sources that courts ordinarily examine, when ruling on Rule 12(b) motions to dismiss. The inquiry, as several Courts of Appeals have recognized, is whether *all* the facts alleged, taken collectively, give rise to a strong inference of scienter, not whether any individual allegation, scrutinized in isolation, meets that standard.
- Third, in determining whether the pleaded facts give rise to a "strong" inference of scienter, the court must take into account plausible opposing inferences. The strength of an inference cannot be decided in a vacuum. The inquiry is inherently comparative. The inference of scienter must be more than merely "reasonable" or "permissible"—it must be cogent and compelling, thus strong in light of other explanations.

Legal Reasoning

The "strong inference" requirement and the comparative analysis of inferences still leave unanswered the question of exactly what state of mind satisfies the scienter requirement of a 10b-5 action. In *Ernst & Ernst v. Hochfelder,*[7] the Supreme Court held that a plaintiff must show that the defendant possessed the "intent to deceive, manipulate, or defraud" in an action brought under Rule 10b-5 of the Securities and Exchange Act of 1934. However, the Court never made clear what mental state suffices to meet this requirement. ("We need not address here the question whether, in some circumstances, reckless behavior is sufficient for civil liability under Rule 10b-5."). The U.S. Court of Appeals held in *Ottman v. Hanger Orthopedic Group, Inc.,* that "a securities fraud plaintiff may allege scienter by pleading not only intentional misconduct, but also recklessness."[8] The court defined a reckless act as one "so highly unreasonable and such an extreme departure from the standard of ordinary care as to present a danger of misleading the plaintiff to the extent that the danger was either known to the defendant or so obvious that the defendant must have been aware of it" (quoting *Phillips v. LCI Int'l, Inc.*).[9] A showing of mere negligence, however, will not suffice to support a 10(b) claim.[10]

Thus, the court ruled, the question is whether the allegations in the complaint, viewed in their totality and in light of all the evidence in the record, allow us to draw a strong inference, at least as compelling as any opposing inference, that the Deloitte defendants either knowingly or recklessly defrauded investors by issuing false audit opinions in violation of Rule 10b-5(b) or 10b-5(a) and (c). On the other hand, if it found the inference that defendants acted innocently, or even negligently, more compelling than the inference that they acted with the requisite scienter, it must affirm the lower court's ruling. Plaintiffs must show that defendants actually made a misrepresentation or omission in their audit opinions on which investors relied.

---

[7]U.S. Supreme Court, *Ernst & Ernst v. Hochfelder,* 425 U.S. 185 (1976).

[8]U.S. Court of Appeals, *Ottman v. Hanger Orthopedic Group, Inc.,* 353 F.3d 338, 344 (4th Cir. 2003).

[9]U.S. Court of Appeals, *Phillips v. LCI Int'l, Inc.,* 190 F.3d 609, 621 (4th Cir. 1999).

[10]*Ernst & Ernst v. Hochfelder.*

In light of the foregoing standards, the court considered first the JV fraud. The plaintiffs alleged that Deloitte U.S. and Deloitte Netherlands allowed Ahold to consolidate the joint ventures despite knowing, or being reckless with regard to the risk, that Ahold lacked the control required for consolidation. The thrust of their argument was that the control letters and Ahold's oral representations were insufficient evidence of control under Dutch and U.S. GAAP. Thus, they argued, the defendants were complicit in the fraud. According to the plaintiffs, the secret side letters, in which the JV partners contradicted Ahold's interpretations of the JV agreements in the control letters, were irrelevant because the control letters themselves did not amend the JV agreements. The plaintiffs' arguments did not provide a basis for a strong inference that either Deloitte U.S. or Deloitte Netherlands acted knowingly or recklessly in relation to the JV fraud. The most plausible inference that one can draw from the fact that Ahold concealed the side letters from its accountants is that the accountants were uninvolved in the fraud. Ahold produced letters attesting to Ahold's control countersigned by Ahold's partners for the ICA, Bompreço, DAIH, and Paiz-Ahold joint ventures at the Deloitte defendants' request, all the while concealing the side letters from those same defendants. These facts led to a strong inference that the Deloitte defendants were attempting to ensure that Ahold had sufficient control over the joint ventures for consolidation and that Ahold was determined to prevent them from discovering otherwise. With perfect hindsight, one might posit that the defendants should have required stronger evidence of control from Ahold. Indeed, as the district court noted, it may have been negligent for the defendants to accept as the only evidence of control Ahold's repeated representations that it controlled JMR, the one joint venture for which Ahold never produced a control letter.[11] Nonetheless, the evidence as a whole leads to the strong inference that defendants were deceived by their clients into approving the consolidation. Ahold would not have needed to go out of its way to produce false evidence of control had Deloitte been complicit in the fraud, or had they been so reckless in their duties that their audit "amounted to no audit at all," as the Southern District of New York has described the standard in *SEC v. Price Waterhouse*.[12]

To establish a strong inference of scienter, plaintiffs must do more than merely demonstrate that defendants should or could have done more. They must demonstrate that Deloitte was either knowingly complicit in the fraud, or so reckless in its duties as to be oblivious to malfeasance that was readily apparent. The inference that we find most compelling based on the evidence in the record is not that the defendants were knowingly complicit or reckless, but that they were deceived by their client's repeated lies and artifices. Perhaps their failure to demand more evidence of consolidation was improper under accounting guidelines, but that is not the standard, which "requires more than a misapplication of accounting principles."[13]

The court then examined the PA fraud. The plaintiffs argued that Deloitte U.S. was knowingly complicit in the fraud when it ignored several red flags, including USF's lack of internal controls to track PA income and USF management's obstruction of the internal audit and the facts and the circumstances of USF CFO Ernie Smith's resignation. With respect to USF's problems with tracking income with PAs, it is not the case that Deloitte U.S. simply ignored the weak internal controls, as the plaintiffs alleged. Rather, Deloitte U.S. raised this issue numerous times with Ahold and USF management.

Deloitte U.S. designed a confirmation process to verify USF's reported PA income in which it contacted third-party vendors and received letters from them confirming PA amounts. The plaintiffs described the confirmation process as one that "confirmed nothing." Yet instead of merely relying on USF representations, as the plaintiffs asserted, Deloitte U.S. obtained corroboration from vendors for the figures provided by USF. Deloitte U.S. would not have attempted to verify USF's figures with third

---

[11]U.S. Court of Appeals, *In re Royal Ahold*, 351 F.Supp. 2d.

[12]*SEC v. Price Waterhouse,* 797 F.Supp. 1217, 1240 (S.D.N.Y. 1992) [citing *McLean v. Alexander,* 599 F.2d 1190, 1198 (3d Cir. 1979)].

[13]*SEC v. Price Waterhouse.*

parties if it were complicit in the scheme, nor can it be said that it was anything but proper to attempt to check the accuracy of representations made by USF management.

The plaintiffs attempted to suggest that the confirmation process was unsound because, for example, Deloitte U.S. accepted confirmation letters via fax and the letters were sent to brokers or sale executives instead of financial officers. But even if the confirmation process was somewhat flawed—which the defendants contested—the larger fact remains that the PA fraud went undetected initially only because USF and its vendors conspired to lie to Deloitte U.S. and to conceal important documents. Indeed, it was Deloitte U.S.'s confirmation process itself that ultimately revealed the fraud. In the course of the 2002 audit, Deloitte U.S. learned in early 2003 from a vendor from which it had requested PA confirmations that employees had signed inaccurate confirmation letters.

Shortly thereafter, Ahold authorized an internal investigation that revealed the extent of the fraud. No doubt it would have been better had the fraud been discovered earlier, but the strongest inference that one can draw from the evidence is that the fraud initially went undetected because of USF's collusion with the vendors, not because of wrongdoing by Deloitte U.S. As to the internal audit, the internal auditors reported not to the Deloitte U.S. external auditors but to USF, as was consistent with professional standards.[14]

The rest of the supposed red flags pointed to by the plaintiffs also failed to create a strong inference of scienter. With respect to the plaintiffs' allegations that Smith told Deloitte U.S. about the vendor rebate fraud, the district court twice concluded that this claim had no support in the record, and we see no reason to disagree with its conclusion. The plaintiffs alleged that facts like the high CFO turnover at USF and USF's rapid growth should have alerted Deloitte U.S. that there was fraud afoot, but they failed to explain why this was the only conclusion that Deloitte could make.

Conclusion

"Seeing the forest as well as the trees is essential." With respect to both frauds, the plaintiffs pointed to ways that the defendants could have been more careful and perhaps discovered the frauds earlier. But the plaintiffs could not escape the fact that Ahold and USF went to considerable lengths to conceal the frauds from the accountants and that it was the defendants that ultimately uncovered the frauds. The strong inference to be drawn from this fact is that Deloitte U.S. and Deloitte Netherlands lacked the requisite scienter and instead were deceived by Ahold and USF. That inference is significantly more plausible than the competing inference that defendants somehow knew that Ahold and USF were defrauding their investors.

The court reiterated that it is not an accountant's fault if its client actively conspires with others in order to deprive the accountant of accurate information about the client's finances. It would be wrong and counter to the purposes of the PSLRA to find an accountant liable in such an instance. The court concluded that it had found no version of the facts that would create a strong inference that the Deloitte defendants had the scienter required for a cause of action under Section 10(b); the district court rightly denied the plaintiffs' motion for leave to amend their complaint.

Questions

1. The court found that Deloitte should not be held liable for the efforts of the client to deprive the auditors of accurate information needed for the audit and masking the true nature of other evidence. Still, the facts of the case do raise questions about whether Deloitte compromised its ethical and professional responsibilities in accepting evidence and explanations provided by the client for the

---

[14]Institute of Internal Auditors, Standards for the Professional Practice of Internal Auditing, *Statement on Internal Auditing Standards 1–18.*

joint venture and promotional allowance transactions. Identify those instances and explain why you believe ethical and professional standards *may have been* violated.

2. Evaluate the decisions made by Deloitte from an ethical reasoning perspective including the effects of its decisions on the stakeholders.

3. The Ahold case is an example of how the courts have, sometimes, ruled more liberally with respect to auditors' legal obligations since the passage of the PSLRA. In the wake of Enron, WorldCom, Adelphia, and other high-profile securities frauds, critics suggest that the law made it too easy to escape liability for securities fraud and thus created a climate in which frauds are more likely to occur. Comment on that statement with respect to the fraud at Royal Ahold. Do you support the more liberal interpretation of proportional liability under the PSLRA versus the previous stricter standard under joint-and-several liability?

Optional Question

4. Explain the legal liability of auditors under SEC regulations and the *Telltabs* ruling relied on by the Court. Include in your discussion how scienter is determined. Do you agree with the commission's conclusion that the Deloitte auditors did not violate their *legal obligations* to shareholders? Why or why not ?

Major Case 3

Madison Gilmore's Ethical Dilemma (a GVV Case)

South City Electronics is involved in printed circuit board assembly (PCBA) dealing with the assembly of complex electronic system processes. The electronics company, based in the city of South San Francisco, is publicly owned with three other locations in the San Francisco Bay Area. Josh Goldberg is the chief executive officer of the company.

Ethical Dilemma

It's March 30, 2017 and Madison Gilmore, controller for South City Electronics, has just gotten off the phone with her supervisor, South City's CFO David Levin, who reiterated the points he made in a face-to-face meeting with her earlier that day—that the company would be in default on a $10 million loan if its cash flow and earnings for the quarter ended March 31, 2017, did not meet set goals in the loan agreement.

Right now the company's cash flow is $620,000 and the earnings are $160,000. This is $380,000 and $240,000, respectively, below prescribed levels. Gilmore knows her boss wants her to agree to revenue treatment for an arrangement with Victor Systems to prepay revenue on a scheduled $1.2 million sale that would put the company above the debt covenant requirements. The goods are scheduled to be sent to an offsite distribution warehouse on March 31, 2017. The sale is scheduled to be completed and goods shipped to the customer on April 5, 2017.

Gilmore is agonizing about what she should do. She knows it would be wrong to record the transaction as revenue in the first quarter of 2017. However, she is under a great deal of pressure to do so. Her boss said it was a one-time request and that she needed to be a team player in this instance.

Facts of the Case

Levin and Gilmore's face-to-face meeting featured an acrimonious dispute over whether to record the $1.2 million as revenue:

"Madison, we have fallen below debt covenant requirements," Levin said. "The only option is to accelerate the sale to Victor Systems. I've already spoken to Bob Victor, and he has agreed to the transaction and cash payment by the close of business tomorrow so long as we discount the sale by 10 percent. Even with that discount we will be above debt covenant requirements."

"The accounting rules are quite clear on this matter," Gilmore said. "Generally accepted accounting principles require us to record the transactions as of March 31 as deferred revenue because the sale will not be completed until April 5."

"I understand your concerns, Madison, and respect your position. I am a CPA as well and am quite clear on the GAAP rules. However, there is an extra feature in this arrangement that justifies the recording of revenue this quarter."

"What's that?"

"We are going to ship the merchandise to an off-site distribution warehouse that we oftentimes use as a holding facility until a customer asks for goods to be sent to its location."

"Is it our warehouse or Victor Systems' warehouse?" Gilmore asked.

"Neither. The warehouse is owned by Kelly Electronics, a company located next door to Victor. So you see, Madison, we can record the sale as if it went to Kelly, and that company will sell it to Victor."

"Who is the end user?" Gilmore asked.

"Victor Systems."

"In my mind that means we still can't record the revenue this quarter."

"Can you point to any specific accounting standard that supports your opinion?" Levin asked.

"Maybe not a specific opinion, but it is my professional judgment that the entry should be recorded as deferred revenue and a footnote added to the quarterly statements describing the warehouse holding arrangement."

"That's not going to happen. There is no way Josh will agree. Asking him to defer the revenue is bad enough, but throwing in a footnote disclosure will not only place us in default on the loan terms but also will unnecessarily create some doubt in the mind of others who might read that note and wonder about our accounting practices. Besides, this is simply an operational decision and not an accounting manipulation."

At that point Levin received a call from Bob Victor, who wanted to review the terms of the shipment. Levin excused himself and told Gilmore they would talk later in the day—the follow-up phone call referred to above.

As Gilmore contemplates the phone call and meeting earlier that day with Levin, Sue Block, the assistant controller, drops by and asks if Gilmore had heard about the phone call between Levin and Bob Victor. Gilmore says she hasn't. She figures Block has dropped by her office because she had shared her concerns with Block earlier about what she was being asked to do after the meeting with Levin.

Block fills Gilmore in in on the details of the conversation. Gilmore asks how Block knows the details. Block says she overheard a conversation in the office of Josh Goldberg between the CEO and Levin. Figuring the less she knows the way Block found out about that conversation, the better, Gilmore changes the topic.

Gilmore brings Block up to date on the follow-up phone conversation with Levin and asks Block for her advice. Block reminds her that she has always preached acting on one's values. Gilmore nods, adding "I know. That has been my mantra for the past five years since I joined the company." Block says this might be one of those times in life when Gilmore should act on her conscience regardless of the consequences. Gilmore seems to understand quite well what she has to do.

After the discussion with Block, Gilmore starts to prepare for a 5:00 p.m. meeting between Josh Goldberg, David Levin, and herself to resolve the matter of accounting for revenue on the Victor sale. She is trying to develop a game plan to voice her values and convince Levin and Goldberg why the company should not record the revenue in the March 31, 2017, quarter.

Questions

1. Is the accounting for revenue in the Victor transaction a case of operational earnings management or accounting earnings management? Explain. Briefly address auditing challenges of this kind of transaction.

2. Who are the stakeholders in this case and what are their interests? Use ethical reasoning to evaluate the appropriateness of Levin's request.

3. Assume you are in Madison Gilmore's position. Answer the following questions as you prepare for the meeting with Levin and Goldberg.

   - What are the main arguments you are trying to counter?
   - What is at stake for the key parties, including those who disagree with you?
   - What levers can you use to influence those who disagree with you?
   - What is your most powerful and persuasive response to the reasons and rationalizations you need to address?

Assume the meeting concludes and nothing has changed. Gilmore failed to change the minds of Levin and Goldberg.

4. At this point would you recommend to Gilmore that she should go to the audit committee with her concerns? Explain your reasoning.

Assume Gilmore goes to the audit committee and nothing changes. The revenue was recorded as earned revenue as of March 31. The goods were shipped to the warehouse on that day. The sale was completed on April 5. A refinancing of the $10 million loan was made shortly after April 5.

5. If you were in Madison Gilmore's position, would you blow the whistle on what you perceive to be the manipulation of the earnings for the quarter ended March 31? Under what circumstances might you blow the whistle? Who would you contact to inform them of what you consider to be earnings manipulation?

Major Case 4

Cendant Corporation[1]

The Merger of HFS and CUC

HFS Incorporated (HFS) was principally a controller of franchise brand names in the hotel, real estate brokerage, and car rental businesses, including Avis, Ramada Inn, Days Inn, and Century 21. Comp-U-Card (CUC) was principally engaged in membership-based consumer services such as auto,

---

[1]The information for this case comes from a variety of litigation releases on the SEC Web site, including www.sec.gov/litigation/admin/34-42935.htm (June 14, 2000); www.sec.gov/litigation/admin/34-42934.htm (June 14, 2000); www.sec.gov/litigation/admin/34-42933.htm (June 14, 2000); www.sec.gov/litigation/litreleases/lr16587.htm (June 14, 2000); and www.sec.gov/litigation/complaints/comp18102.htm (April 24, 2003).

dining, shopping, and travel "clubs." Both securities were traded on the NYSE. Cendant Corporation was created through the December 17, 1997, merger of HFS and CUC. Cendant provided certain membership-based and Internet-related consumer services and controlled franchise brand names in the hotel, residential real estate brokerage, car rental, and tax preparation businesses.

Overview of the Scheme

The Cendant fraud was the largest of its kind until the late 1990s and early 2000s. Beginning in at least 1985, certain members of CUC's senior management implemented a scheme designed to ensure that CUC always met the financial results anticipated by Wall Street analysts. The CUC senior managers used a variety of means to achieve their goals, including:

- Manipulating recognition of the company's membership sales revenue to accelerate the recording of revenue.
- Improperly using two liability accounts related to membership sales that resulted from commission payments.
- Consistently maintaining inadequate balances in the liability accounts, and on occasion reversing the accounts directly into operating income.

With respect to the last item, to hide the inadequate balances, senior management periodically kept certain membership sales transactions off the books. In what was the most significant category quantitatively, the CUC senior managers intentionally overstated merger and purchase reserves and subsequently reversed those reserves directly into operating expenses and revenues. CUC senior management improperly wrote off assets—including assets that were unimpaired—and improperly charged the write-offs against the company's merger reserves. By manipulating the timing of the write-offs and by improperly determining the nature of the charges incurred, the CUC senior managers used the write-offs to inflate operating income at CUC. As the scheme progressed over the course of several years, larger and larger year-end adjustments were required to show smooth net income over time. The scheme added more than $500 million to pretax operating income during the fiscal years ended January 31, 1996; January 31, 1997; and December 31, 1997.

SEC Filings against CUC and Its Officers

SEC complaints filed on June 14, 2000, alleged violations of the federal securities laws by four former accounting officials, including Cosmo Corigliano, CFO of CUC; Anne M. Pember, CUC controller; Casper Sabatino, vice president of accounting and financial reporting; and Kevin Kearney, director of financial reporting. The allegations against Corigliano included his role as one of the CUC senior officers who helped engineer the fraud, and he maintained a schedule that management used to track the progress of their fraud. Corigliano regularly directed CUC financial reporting managers to make unsupported alterations to the company's quarterly and annual financial results. The commission alleged that Corigliano profited from his own wrongdoing by selling CUC securities and a large number of Cendant securities at inflated prices while the fraud he helped engineer was under way and undisclosed.

The commission alleged that Pember was the CUC officer most responsible for implementing directives received from Corigliano in furtherance of the fraud, including implementing directives that inflated Cendant's annual income by more than $100 million, primarily through improper use of the company's reserves. According to the SEC, Pember profited from her own wrongdoing by selling CUC and Cendant stock at inflated prices while the fraud she helped implement was under way and undisclosed.

Sabatino and Kearney, without admitting or denying the commission's allegations, consented to the entry of final judgments settling the commission's action against them. The commission's complaint alleged that Sabatino was the CUC officer most responsible for directing lower-level CUC financial reporting managers to make alterations to the company's quarterly financial results.

In the first of the three separate administrative orders, the commission found that Steven Speaks, the former controller of CUC's largest division, made or instructed others to make journal entries that effectuated much of the January 1998 income inflation directed by Pember. In a second separate administrative order, the commission found that Mary Sattler Polverari, a former CUC supervisor of financial reporting, at the direction of Sabatino and Kearney, regularly and knowingly made unsupported alterations to CUC's quarterly financial results.

In a third administrative order, the commission found that Paul Hiznay, a former accounting manager at CUC's largest division, aided and abetted violations of the periodic reporting provisions of the federal securities laws by making unsupported journal entries that Pember had directed. Hiznay consented to the issuance of the commission's order to cease and desist from future violations of the provisions.

In a fourth and separate administrative order the commission found that Cendant violated the periodic reporting, corporate record-keeping, and internal controls provisions of the federal securities laws, in connection with the CUC fraud. Among other things, the company's books, records, and accounts had been falsely altered, and materially false periodic reports had been filed with the commission, as a result of the long-running fraud at CUC. Simultaneous with the institution of the administrative proceeding, and without admitting or denying the findings contained therein, Cendant consented to the issuance of the commission order, which ordered Cendant to cease and desist from future violations of the provisions.

On February 28, 2001, the SEC filed a civil enforcement action in the U.S. District Court for the District of New Jersey against Walter A. Forbes, the former chair of the board of directors at CUC, and E. Kirk Shelton, the former vice chair, alleging that they directed a massive financial fraud while selling millions of dollars' worth of the company's common stock. For the period 1995–1997 alone, pretax operating income reported to the public by CUC was inflated by an aggregate amount of over $500 million. Specific allegations included:

- Forbes, CUC's chair and CEO, directed the fraud from its beginnings in 1985. From at least 1991 on, Shelton, CUC's president and COO, joined Forbes in directing the scheme.

- Forbes and Shelton reviewed and managed schedules listing fraudulent adjustments to be made to CUC's quarterly and annual financial statements. CUC senior management used the adjustments to pump up income and earnings artificially, defrauding investors by creating the illusion of a company that had ever-increasing earnings and making millions for themselves along the way.

- Forbes and Shelton undertook a program of mergers and acquisitions on behalf of CUC in order to generate inflated merger and purchase reserves at CUC to be used in connection with the fraud. Forbes and Shelton sought out HFS as a merger partner because they believed that the reserves that would be created would be big enough to bury the fraud. To entice HFS management into the merger, Forbes and Shelton inflated CUC's earnings and earnings projections.

- Forbes and Shelton profited from their own wrongdoing by selling CUC and Cendant securities at inflated prices while the fraud they had directed was under way and undisclosed. The sales brought Forbes and Shelton millions of dollars in ill-gotten gains.

- After the Cendant merger, Forbes served as Cendant's board chair until his resignation in July 1998. At the time of the merger, Shelton became a Cendant director and vice chair. Shelton resigned from Cendant in April 1998.

Specific Accounting Techniques Used to Manage Earnings

Making Unsupported Postclosing Entries

In early 1997, at the direction of senior management, Hiznay approved a series of entries reversing the commissions payable liability account into revenue at CUC. The company paid commissions to certain institutions on sales of CUC membership products sold through those institutions. Accordingly, at the time that it recorded revenue from those sales, CUC created a liability to cover the payable obligation of its commissions. CUC senior management used false schedules and other devices to support their understating of the payable liability of the commissions and to avoid the impact that would have resulted if the liability had been properly calculated. Furthermore, in connection with the January 31, 1997, fiscal year-end, senior management used this liability account by directing postclosing entries that moved amounts from the liability directly into revenue.[2]

In February 1997, Hiznay received a schedule from the CUC controller setting forth the amounts, effective backdates, and accounts for a series of postclosing entries that reduced the commissions payable account by $9.12 million and offsetting that reduction by increases to CUC revenue accounts. Hiznay approved the unsupported entries and had his staff enter them. They all carried effective dates spread retroactively over prior months. The entries reversed the liability account directly into revenues, a treatment that, under the circumstances, was not in accordance with GAAP.

Keeping Rejects and Cancellations Off-Books: Establishing Reserves

During his time at CUC, Hiznay inherited, but then supervised, a longstanding practice of keeping membership sales cancellations and rejects off CUC's books during part of each fiscal year. Certain CUC membership products were processed through various financial institutions that billed their members' credit cards for new sales and charges related to the various membership products. When CUC recorded membership sales revenue from such a sale, it would allocate a percentage of the recorded revenue to cover estimated cancellations of the specific membership product being sold, as well as allocating a percentage to cover estimated rejects and chargebacks.[3] CUC used these percentage allocations to establish a membership cancellation reserve.

Over the years, CUC senior management had developed a policy of keeping rejects and cancellations off the general ledger during the last three months of each fiscal year. Instead, during that quarter, the rejects and cancellations appeared only on cash account bank reconciliations compiled by the company's accounting personnel. The senior managers then directed the booking of those rejects and cancellations against the membership cancellation reserve in the first three months of the next fiscal year. Because rejects and cancellations were not recorded against the membership cancellation reserve during the final three months of the fiscal year, the policy allowed CUC to hide the fact that the reserve was understated dramatically at each fiscal year-end. At its January 31, 1997, fiscal year-end, the balance in the CUC membership cancellation reserve was $29 million; CUC accounting personnel were holding $100 million in rejects and $22 million in cancellations off the books. Failing to book cancellations and rejects at each fiscal year-end also had the effect of overstating the company's cash position on its year-end balance sheet.

Accounting and Auditing Issues

Kenneth Wilchfort and Marc Rabinowitz were partners at Ernst & Young (EY), which was responsible for audit and accounting advisory services provided to CUC and Cendant. During the relevant periods, CUC and Cendant made materially false statements to the defendants and EY about the company's true financial results and its accounting policies. CUC and Cendant made these false statements to mislead the defendants and EY into believing that the company's financial statements conformed to GAAP. For example, as late as March 1998, senior Cendant management had discussed plans to use over $100 million of the Cendant reserve fraudulently to create fictitious 1998 income, which was also concealed from the defendants and EY. CUC and Cendant made materially false statements to the defendants and

---

[2] *Post-closing journal entries* means entries that are made after a reporting period has ended, but before the financial statements for the period have been filed, and that have effective dates spread retroactively over prior weeks or months.

[3] Rejects resulted when the credit card to be charged was over its limit, closed, or reported as lost or stolen. Chargebacks resulted when a credit card holder disputed specific charges related to a particular membership program.

EY that were included in the management representation letters and signed by senior members of CUC's and Cendant's management. The statements concerned, among other things, the creation and utilization of merger-related reserves, the adequacy of the reserve established for membership cancellations, the collectability of rejected credit card billings, and income attributable to the month of January 1997.[4]

The written representations for the calendar year 1997 falsely stated that the company's financial statements were fairly presented in conformity with GAAP and that the company had made available to EY all relevant financial records and related data. Those written representations were materially false because the financial statements did not conform to GAAP, and, as discussed further, the company's management concealed material information from the defendants and EY.

In addition to providing the defendants and EY with false written representations, CUC and Cendant also adopted procedures to hide its income-inflation scheme from the defendants and EY. Some of the procedures that CUC and Cendant employed to conceal its fraudulent scheme included (1) backdating accounting entries; (2) making accounting entries in small amounts and/or in accounts or subsidiaries the company believed would receive less attention from EY; (3) in some instances ensuring that fraudulent accounting entries did not affect schedules already provided to EY; (4) withholding financial information and schedules to ensure that EY would not detect the company's accounting fraud; (5) ensuring that the company's financial results did not show unusual trends that might draw attention to its fraud; and (6) using senior management to instruct middle- and lower-level personnel to make fraudulent entries. Notwithstanding CUC and Cendant's repeated deception, defendants improperly failed to detect the fraud. They were aware of numerous practices by CUC and Cendant indicating that the financial statements did not conform to GAAP, and, as a consequence, they had a duty to withhold their unqualified opinion and take appropriate additional steps.

Improper Establishment and Use of Merger Reserves

The company completed a series of significant mergers and acquisitions and accounted for the majority of them using the pooling-of-interests method of accounting.[5] In connection with this merger and acquisition activity, company management purportedly planned to restructure its operations. GAAP permits that certain anticipated costs may be recorded as liabilities (or reserves) prior to their incurrence under certain conditions. However, here CUC and Cendant routinely overstated the restructuring charges and the resultant reserves and would then use the reserves to offset normal operating costs—an improper earnings management scheme. The company's improper reversal of merger and acquisition–related restructuring reserves resulted in an overstatement of operating income by $217 million.

The EY auditors provided accounting advice and auditing services to CUC and Cendant in connection with the establishment and use of restructuring reserves. The auditors excessively relied on management representations concerning the appropriateness of the reserves and performed little substantive testing, despite evidence that the reserves were established and utilized improperly.

One example of auditor failures with reserve accounting is the Cendant reserve. Cendant recorded over $500 million in merger, integration, asset impairment, and restructuring charges for the CUC-side costs purportedly associated with the merger of HFS and CUC. The company recorded a significant portion of this amount for the purpose of manipulating its earnings for December 31, 1997, and subsequent periods, and, in fact, Cendant had plans, which it did not disclose to defendants and EY, to use a material amount of the reserve to inflate income artificially in subsequent periods.

---

[4]Available at: www.sec.gov/litigation/complaints/comp18102.htm.

[5]*Statement of Financial Accounting Standards (SFAS) 141, Business Combinations,* which eliminated the pooling methods for business combinations. The purchase method now must be used for all acquisitions.

In the course of providing accounting and auditing services, the auditors failed to recognize evidence that the company's establishment and use of the Cendant reserve did not conform to GAAP. For example, CUC and Cendant provided EY with contradictory drafts of schedules when EY requested support for the establishment of the Cendant reserve. The company prepared and revised these various schedules, at least in part as a result of questions raised and information provided by the defendants. The schedules were inconsistent with regard to the nature and amount of the individual components of the reserve (i.e., component categories were added, deleted, and changed as the process progressed). While the component categories changed over time, the total amount of the reserve never changed materially. Despite this evidence, the auditors did not obtain adequate analyses, documentation, or support for changes that they observed in the various revisions of the schedules submitted to support the establishment of the reserves. Instead, they relied excessively on frequently changing management representations.

The company planned to use much of the excess Cendant reserve to increase operating results in future periods improperly. During the year ended December 31, 1997, the company wrote off $104 million of assets that it characterized as impaired as a result of the merger. Despite the size and timing of the write-off, the defendants never obtained adequate evidence that the assets were impaired as a result of the merger and, therefore, properly included in the Cendant reserve. In fact, most of the assets were not impaired as a result of the merger.

Cash Balance from the Membership Cancellation Reserve

CUC and Cendant also inflated income by manipulating their membership cancellation reserve and reported cash balance. Customers usually paid for membership products by charging them on credit cards. The company recorded an increase in revenue and cash when it charged the members' credit card. Each month, issuers of members' credit cards rejected a significant amount of such charges. The issuers would deduct the amounts of the rejects from their payments to CUC and Cendant. CUC and Cendant falsely claimed to EY auditors that when it resubmitted the rejects to the banks for payment, it ultimately collected almost all of them within three months. CUC and Cendant further falsely claimed that, for the few rejects that were not collected after three months, it then recorded them as a reduction in cash and a decrease to the cancellation reserve. The cancellation reserve accounted for members who canceled during their membership period and were entitled to a refund of at least a portion of the membership fee, as well as members who joined and were billed, but never paid for their memberships.

At the end of each fiscal year, the company failed to record three months of rejects (i.e., it did not reduce its cash and decrease its cancellation reserve for these rejects). CUC and Cendant falsely claimed to the defendants and EY that it did not record rejects for the final three months of the year because it purportedly would collect most of the rejects within three months of initial rejection. According to CUC and Cendant, the three months of withheld rejects created a temporary difference at year-end between the cash balances reflected in the company's general ledger and its bank statements. The rejects were clearly specified on reconciliations of the company's numerous bank accounts, at least some of which were provided to EY and retained in its workpapers. CUC and Cendant falsely claimed to the defendants and EY that the difference between the general ledger balance and bank statement balance did not reflect an overstatement of cash and understatement in the cancellation reserve since it collected most rejects. In fact, the majority of rejects were not collected. By not recording rejects and cancellations against the membership cancellation reserve during the final three months of each fiscal year, CUC and Cendant dramatically understated the reserve at each fiscal year-end and overstated its cash position. CUC and Cendant thus avoided the expense charges needed to bring the cancellation reserve balance up to its proper amount and the entries necessary to record CUC and Cendant's actual cash balances.

The rejects, cancellation reserve balance, and overstatement of income amounts for the period 1996 to 1997 are as follows:

Date	Rejects	($ in millions)	
		Cancellation Reserve Balance	Understated Reserve/Overstated Income
01/31/96	$72	$37	$35
01/31/97	$100	$29	$28
12/31/97	$137	$37	$37

The EY defendants did not adequately test the collectability of these rejects and the adequacy of the cancellation reserve and instead relied primarily on management representations concerning the company's successful collection history and inconsistent statements concerning the purported impossibility of substantively testing these representations.

Membership Cancellation Rates

The company also overstated its operating results by manipulating its cancellation reserve. The cancellation reserve accounted for members who canceled during their membership period. A large determinant of the liability associated with cancellations was CUC and Cendant's estimates of the cancellation rates. During the audits, CUC and Cendant intentionally provided EY with false estimates that were lower than the actual estimated cancellation rates. This resulted in a significant understatement of the cancellation reserve liability and an overstatement of income. To justify its understated cancellation reserve, CUC and Cendant provided to EY small, nonrepresentative samples of cancellations that understated the actual cancellation rates. The defendants allowed the company to choose the samples. EY did not test whether the samples provided were representative of the actual cancellations for the entire membership population.

Audit Opinion

EY issued audit reports containing unqualified (i.e., unmodified) audit opinions on, and conducted quarterly reviews of, the company's financial statements that, as already stated, did not conform to GAAP. The Securities Exchange Act requires every issuer of a registered security to file reports with the commission that accurately reflect the issuer's financial performance and provide other information to the public. For the foregoing reason, the firm aided and abetted violations of the securities laws.

Legal Issues

SEC Settlements

Between Hiznay's arrival at CUC in July 1995 and the discovery of the fraudulent scheme by Cendant management in April 1998, CUC and Cendant filed false and misleading annual reports with the commission that misrepresented their financial results, overstating operating income and earnings and failing to disclose that the financial results were falsely represented.

The commission's complaint alleged that Sabatino, by his actions in furtherance of the fraud, violated, or aided and abetted violations of, the anti-fraud, periodic reporting, corporate record-keeping, internal controls, and lying to auditors provisions of the federal securities laws. Sabatino consented to entry of a final judgment that enjoined him from future violations of those provisions and permanently barred him from acting as an officer or director of a public company.

Kearney consented to entry of a final judgment that enjoined him from future violations of those provisions, ordered him to pay disgorgement of $32,443 in ill-gotten gains (plus prejudgment interest of $8,234), and ordered him to pay a civil money penalty of $35,000. Kearney also agreed to the issuance of a commission administrative order that barred him from practicing before the commission as an accountant, with the right to reapply after five years.

Corigliano, Pember, and Sabatino each pleaded guilty to charges pursuant to plea agreements between those three individuals and the SEC. Pursuant to his agreement, Corigliano pleaded guilty to a charge of wire fraud, conspiracy to commit mail fraud, and causing false statements to be made in documents filed with the commission, including signing CUC's periodic reports filed with the commission and making materially false statements to CUC's auditors. Pember pleaded guilty to a charge of conspiracy to commit mail fraud and wire fraud. Sabatino, pursuant to his agreement, pleaded guilty to a charge of aiding and abetting wire fraud.

In another administrative order, the commission found that Hiznay aided and abetted violations of the periodic reporting provisions of the federal securities laws, in connection with actions that he took at the direction of his superiors at CUC. Among other things, the commission alleged that Hiznay made unsupported journal entries that Pember had directed. Additional orders were entered against lower-level employees.

The commission found that Cendant violated the periodic reporting, corporate record-keeping, and internal controls provisions of the federal securities laws, in connection with the CUC fraud in that the company's books, records, and accounts had been falsely altered, and materially false periodic reports had been filed with the SEC.

On December 29, 2009, the SEC announced a final judgment against Forbes, the former chair of Cendant, arising out of his conduct in the Cendant fraud.[6] The commission alleged that Forbes orchestrated an earnings management scheme at CUC to inflate the company's quarterly and annual financial results improperly during the period 1995 to 1997. CUC's operating income was inflated improperly by an aggregate amount exceeding $500 million.

The final judgment against Forbes, to which he consented without admitting or denying the commission's allegations, enjoined him from violating relevant sections of the securities laws and barred him from serving as an officer or director of a public company.

Class Action Lawsuits

A class action suit by stockholders against Cendant and its auditors, led by the largest pension funds, alleged that stockholders paid more for Cendant stock than they would have had they known the truth about CUC's income. The lawsuit ended in a record $3.2 billion settlement. Details of the settlement follow.

By December 1999, a landmark $2.85 billion settlement with Cendant was announced that far surpassed the recoveries in any other securities law class action case in history. Until the settlements reached in the WorldCom case in 2005, this stood as the largest recovery in a securities class action case, by far, and clearly set the standard in the field. In addition to the cash payment by Cendant, which was backed by a letter of credit that the company secured to protect the class, the Cendant settlement included two other very important features. First, the settlement provided that if Cendant or the former HFS officers and directors were successful in obtaining a net recovery in their continuing litigation against EY, the class would receive half of any such net recovery. As it turned out, that litigation lasted another seven years—until the end of 2007—when Cendant and EY settled their claims against each other in exchange for a payment by EY to Cendant of nearly $300 million. Based on the provision in the Cendant settlement agreement and certain further litigation and a court order, in December 2008, the class received another $132 million. This brought the total recovered from the Cendant settlement to $2.982 billion.

Second, Cendant was required to institute significant corporate governance changes that were far-reaching and unprecedented in securities class action litigation. Indeed, these changes included

[6]*Securities and Exchange Commission v. Walter A. Forbes et al.,* District Court N.J., filed February 28, 2001.

many of the corporate governance structural changes that would later be included within the Sarbanes-Oxley Act of 2002 (SOX). They included the following:

- The board's audit, nominating, and compensation committees would be comprised entirely of independent directors (according to stringent definitions, endorsed by the institutional investment community, of what constituted an independent director).
- The majority of the board would be independent within two years following final approval of the settlement.
- Cendant would take the steps necessary to provide that, subject to amendment of the certificate of incorporation declassifying the board of directors by vote of the required supermajority of shareholders, all directors would be elected annually.
- No employee stock option could be "repriced" following its grant without an affirmative vote of shareholders, except when such repricings were necessary to take into account corporate transactions such as stock dividends, stock splits, recapitalization, a merger, or distributions.

The Settlement with EY

On December 17, 1999, it was announced that EY had agreed to settle the claims of the class for $335 million. This recovery was and remains today as the largest amount ever paid by an accounting firm in a securities class action case. The recovery from EY was significant because it held an outside auditing firm responsible in cases of corporate accounting fraud. The claims against EY were based on EY's "clean" (i.e., unmodified) audit and review opinions for three sets of annual financial statements, and seven quarterly financial statements, between 1995 and 1997.

The district court approved the settlements and plan of allocation in August 2000, paving the way for Cendant and EY to fund the settlements. Approximately one year later, in August 2001, the settlements and plan of allocation were affirmed on appeal by the U.S. Third Circuit Court of Appeals. And in March 2002, the U.S. Supreme Court determined that it would not hear any further appeals in the case.

Questions

1. Cendant manipulated the timing of write-offs and improperly determined charges in an attempt to smooth net income. Is income smoothing an ethical practice? Are there circumstances where it might be considered ethical and others where it would not? What motivated Cendant to engage in income smoothing practices in this case?

2. Analyze the actions taken by the company and its management from the perspective of the Fraud Triangle.

3. Describe the role of professional judgment in the audits by EY. Did the firm meet its ethical obligations under the AICPA Code?

4. Trust is a basic element in the relationship between auditor and client. Explain why and how trust broke down in the Cendant case, including shortcomings in corporate governance.

Major Case 5

Vivendi Universal[1]

"Some of my management decisions turned wrong, but fraud? Never, never, never." This statement was made by the former CEO of Vivendi Universal, Jean-Marie Messier, as he took the stand in November 20, 2009, for a civil class action lawsuit brought against him, Vivendi Universal, and the former CFO, Guillaume Hannezo. The class action suit accused the company of hiding Vivendi's true financial condition before a $46 billion three-way merger with Seagram Company and Canal Plus. The case was brought against Vivendi, Messier, and Hannezo after it was discovered that the firm was in a liquidity crisis and would have problems repaying its outstanding debt and operating expenses (contrary to the press releases by Messier, Hannezo, and other senior executives that the firm had "excellent" and "strong" liquidity); that it participated in earnings management to achieve earnings goals; and that it had failed to disclose debt obligations regarding two of the company's subsidiaries.[1] The jury decided not to hold either Messier or Hannezo legally liable because "scienter" could not be proven. In other words, the court decided it could not be shown that the two officers acted with the intent to deceive other parties.

The stock price of the firm dropped 89 percent, from €84.70 (about $111) on October 31, 2000, to €9.30 (about $13) on August 16, 2002, over the period of fraudulent reporting and press releases to the media.

As you read the case, consider whether Messier was accurate in his belief that fraud was not committed and whether this was an ethics failure.

Background

Vivendi is a French international media giant, rivaling Time Warner Inc., that spent $77 billion on acquisitions, including the world's largest music company, Universal Music Group (UMG). Messier took the firm to new heights through mergers and acquisitions that came with a large amount of debt.

In December 2000, Vivendi acquired Canal Plus and Seagram, which included Universal Studios and its related companies, and became known as Vivendi Universal. At the time, it was one of Europe's largest companies in terms of assets and revenues, with holdings in the United States that included Universal Studios Group, UMG, and USA Networks Inc. These acquisitions cost Vivendi cash, stock, and assumed debt of over $60 billion and increased the debt associated with Vivendi's Media & Communications division from approximately €3 billion ($4.32 billion) at the beginning of 2000 to over €21 billion ($30.25 billion) in 2002.

In July 2002, Messier and Hannezo resigned from their positions as CEO and CFO, respectively, and new management disclosed that the company was experiencing a liquidity crisis that was a very different picture than the previous management had painted of the financial condition of Vivendi Universal. This was due to senior executives using four different methods to conceal Vivendi Universal's financial problems:

- Issuing false press releases stating that the liquidity of the company was "strong" and "excellent" after the release of the 2001 financial statements to the public.

- Using aggressive accounting principles and adjustments to increase EBITDA and meet ambitious earnings targets.

---

[1]*SEC v. Vivendi Universal, S.A., Jean-Marie Messier, and Guillaume Hannezo,* United States District Court Southern District of New York, December 23, 2003, Available at: https://www.sec.gov/litigation/complaints/comp18523.htm.

- Failing to disclose the existence of various commitments and contingencies.
- Failing to disclose part of its investment in a transaction to acquire shares of Telco, a Polish telecommunications holding company.

Earnings Releases/EBITDA

On March 5, 2002, Vivendi issued earnings releases for 2001, which were approved by Messier, Hannezo, and other senior executives, that their Media & Communications business had produced €5.03 billion ($7.25 billion) in EBITDA and just over €2 billion ($2.88 billion) in operating free cash flow. These earnings were materially misleading and falsely represented Vivendi's financial situation because, due to legal restrictions, Vivendi was unable unilaterally to access the earnings and cash flow of two of its most profitable subsidiaries, Cegetel and Maroc Telecom, which accounted for 30 percent of Vivendi's EBITDA and almost half of its cash flow. This contributed to Vivendi's cash flow actually being "zero or negative," making it difficult for Vivendi to meet its debt and cash obligations. Furthermore, Vivendi declared a €1 ($1.44) per share dividend because of its excellent operations for the past year, but Vivendi borrowed against credit facilities to pay the dividend, which cost more than €1.3 billion ($1.87 billion) after French corporate taxes on dividends. Throughout the following months before Messier's and Hannezo's resignations, senior executives continued to lie to the public about the strength of Vivendi as a company.

In December 2000, Vivendi and Messier predicted a 35 percent EBITDA growth for 2001 and 2002, and, in order to reach that target, Vivendi used earnings management and aggressive accounting practices to overstate its EBITDA. In June 2001, Vivendi made improper adjustments to increase EBITDA by almost €59 million ($85 million), or 5 percent of the total EBITDA of €1.12 billion ($1.61 billion) that Vivendi reported. Senior executives did this mainly by restructuring Cegetel's allowance for bad debts. Cegetel, a Vivendi subsidiary whose financial statements were consolidated with Vivendi's, took a lower provision for bad debts in the period and caused the bad debts expense to be €45 million ($64.83 million) less than it would have been under historical methodology, which in turn increased earnings by the same amount. Furthermore, after the third quarter of 2001, Vivendi adjusted earnings of UMG by at least €10.125 million ($14.77 million) or approximately 4 percent of UMG's total EBITDA of €250 million ($360.15 million) for that quarter. At that level, UMG would have been able to show EBITDA growth of approximately 6 percent versus the same period in 2000 and to outperform its rivals in the music business. It did this by prematurely recognizing revenue of €3 million ($4.32 million) and temporarily reducing the corporate overhead charges by €7 million ($10.08 million).

Financial Commitments

Vivendi failed to disclose in its financial statements commitments regarding Cegetel and Maroc Telecom that would have shown Vivendi's potential inability to meet its cash needs and obligations. It was also worried that if it disclosed this information, companies that publish independent credit opinions would have declined to maintain their credit rating of Vivendi. In August 2001, Vivendi entered into an undisclosed current account borrowing with Cegetel for €520 million ($749.11 million) and continued to grow to over €1 billion ($1.44 billion) at certain periods of time. Vivendi maintained cash pooling agreements with most of its subsidiaries, but the current account with Cegetel operated much like a loan, with a due date of the balance at December 31, 2001 (which was later pushed back to July 31, 2002), and there was a clause in the agreement that provided Cegetel with the ability to demand immediate reimbursement at any time during the loan period. If this information would have been disclosed, it would have shown that Vivendi would have trouble repaying its obligations.

Regarding Maroc Telecom, in December 2000, Vivendi purchased 35 percent of the Moroccan government–owned telecommunications operator of fixed line and mobile telephone and Internet services for €2.35 billion ($3.39 billion). In February 2001, Vivendi and the Moroccan government entered into a side agreement that required Vivendi to purchase an additional 16 percent of Maroc Telecom's shares in February 2002 for approximately €1.1 billion ($1.58 billion). Vivendi did this in order to gain control of Maroc Telecom and consolidate its financial statements with Vivendi's own because Maroc carried little debt and generated substantial EBITDA. By not disclosing this information on the financial statements, Vivendi's financial information for 2001 was materially false and misleading.

Stakeholder Interests

The major stakeholders in the Vivendi case include (1) the investors, creditors, and shareholders of the company and its subsidiaries—by not providing reliable financial information, Vivendi misled these groups into lending credit and cash, and investing in a company that was not as strong as it seemed; (2) the subsidiaries of Vivendi and their customers—by struggling with debt and liquidity, Vivendi borrowed cash from the numerous subsidiaries all over the globe, jeopardizing their operations; (3) the governments of these countries—because some of Vivendi's companies were government owned (such as the Moroccan company Maroc Telecom), and these governments have to regulate the fraud and crimes that Vivendi committed; and (4) Vivendi, Messier, Hannezo, and other senior management and employees—Messier was putting his future, the employees of Vivendi, and the company itself in jeopardy by making loose and risky decisions involving the sanctity of the firm.

In the Fair Funds provisions of SOX, Congress gave the SEC increased authority to distribute ill-gotten gains and civil money penalties to harmed investors. These distributions reflect the continued efforts and increased capacity of the commission to repay injured investors, regardless of their physical location and their currency of choice.

On August 11, 2008, the SEC announced the distribution of more than $48 million to more than 12,000 investors who were victims of fraudulent financial reporting by Vivendi Universal. Investors receiving checks resided in the United States and 15 other countries. More than half bought their Vivendi stock on foreign exchanges and received their Fair Fund distribution in euros.

Failure of Ethical Leadership

In his analysis of the fraud at Vivendi, Soltani points to failures in ethical practice, corporate governance, and leadership as the root cause of the failure at Vivendi. He characterizes the actions of Messier as motivated by egoism, using one's authoritative position to influence others to ignore ethical practices, failure to set an ethical tone at the top, and failed corporate governance. What follows is an analysis of the points he makes in dissecting the fraud.[2]

- Use of company funds for personal benefit, including to enhance lifestyle choices.
- Failure to conceptualize core values and ethical standards in the company.
- Lack of internal control mechanisms to prevent and detect fraud.
- Ineffective control environment to prevent and detect fraud.
- Excessive risk taking.
- Opportunistic behavior.
- False earnings announcements.
- Aggressive earnings management.
- Use of loopholes in financial reporting standards to alter numbers as far as possible to achieve a desired goal.

[2]Bahram Soltani, "The Anatomy of Corporate Fraud: A Comparative Analysis of High Profile American and European Corporate Scandals," *Journal of Business Ethics*, Vol. 120 (2014), pp. 251–274.

- Lapses in accountability.
- Inability of external auditors to exercise their functions in an independent manner and detect material misstatements and fraudulent financial reporting.

It is clear that the culture at Vivendi enabled the fraud to occur and prevented the company from dealing with the crisis as it unfolded.

Questions

1. Analyze the actions taken by Messier in the case from the perspective of the discussion of ethical leadership in Chapter 8.
2. Explain how internal controls can facilitate ethical behavior and help prevent financial impropriety. What was the role of internal controls in the Vivendi fraud?
3. Why do financial analysts look at measures such as EBITDA and operating free cash flow to evaluate financial results? How do these measures differ from accrual earnings? Do you believe auditors should be held responsible for auditing such information?

Major Case 6

Waste Management

Case Overview

This case focuses on improper accounting and management decision making at Waste Management, Inc., during the period of its accounting fraud from 1992 to 1997, and the role and responsibilities of Arthur Andersen LLP (Andersen), the Waste Management auditors, with respect to its audit of the company's financial statements. The case illustrates the kinds of financial statement frauds that were common during the late 1990s and early 2000s.

The key accounting issue was the existence of a series of Proposed Adjusting Journal Entries (PAJEs) recommended by Andersen to correct errors that understated expenses and overstated earnings in the company's financial statements. These were not recorded even though the company had promised to do so. Andersen developed a "Summary of Action Steps" that was designed to change accounting in the future in order to comply with GAAP but did not require retroactive adjustments to correct past errors. In essence, it was an agreement to do something in the future that should have been done already, with no controls or insistence by Andersen that the proposed changes would in fact occur. According to SEC Litigation Release 17435:

> Management consistently refused to make the adjustments called for by the PAJEs. Instead, defendants secretly entered into an agreement with Andersen fraudulently to write off the accumulated errors over periods of up to ten years and to change the underlying accounting practices, but to do so only in future periods.

The action steps were not followed by Waste Management. The company promised to look at its cost deferral, capitalization, and reserve policies and make needed adjustments. It never followed through, however, and the audit committee was either inattentive to the financial reporting implications or chose to look the other way. According to Litigation Release 17435, writing off the errors and changing the underlying accounting practices as prescribed in the agreement would have prevented the company from meeting earnings targets and defendants from enriching themselves. Defendants got performance-based bonuses based on the company's inflated earnings, retained their high-paying jobs, and received stock options. Some also received enhanced retirement benefits based on the improper bonuses, and some received lucrative employment contracts. Dean Buntrock, the CEO and chair of the board; Philip Rooney, director, president, and chief operating officer (COO); and James Koenig, executive vice president and CFO, also avoided losses by cashing in their Waste Management stock while the fraud was ongoing. Just prior to the public disclosure of the accounting irregularities, Buntrock enriched himself by obtaining a tax benefit by donating inflated company stock to his college alma mater to fund a building in his name.

Waste Management today is a leading international provider of waste management services, with 45,000 employees serving over 20 million residential, industrial, municipal, and commercial customers, and it earned about $15 billion of revenues in 2012. It was ranked number 203 in the 2012 *Fortune* 500 listing of the largest companies in the United States. Here is a brief description of how and why the company committed fraud.

Dean Buntrock founded Waste Management in 1968 and took the company public in 1971. During the 1970s and 1980s, Buntrock built a vast waste disposal empire by acquiring and consolidating local waste hauling companies and landfill operators. At one point, the company was performing close to 200 acquisitions a year. It experienced tremendous growth in its first 20 years. From the IPO in 1971 until the end of 1991, Waste Management enjoyed 36 percent average annual growth in revenue and 36 percent annual growth in net income. The company grew from $16 million in revenue in 1971 to become the largest waste removal business in the world, with revenue of more than $7.5 billion in 1991.

Despite being a leader in the industry, Waste Management was under increasing pressure from competitors and from changes in the environmental industry. Its 1996 financial statements showed that, even though its consolidated revenue for the period from December 1994 to 1996 increased 8.3 percent, its net income declined during that period by 75.5 percent. The truth was that the income numbers had been manipulated to minimize the declines over time.

The term *ill-gotten gains* refers to amounts received either dishonestly or illegally. Litigation Release 17345 identifies the following "ill-gotten gains" at Waste Management:

Name	Positions	Amount
Buntrock	CEO and chair of the board	$ 16,917,761
Rooney	Director, president, and COO	$ 9,286,124
Koenig	Executive vice president and CFO	$ 951,005
Thomas Hau	Vice president, controller, and CAO	$ 640,100
Herbert Getz	Senior vice president, general counsel, and secretary	$ 472,500
Bruce Tobecksen	Vice president of finance	$ 640,100

These ill-gotten gains were included in a lawsuit filed by the SEC on March 26, 2002, against the six former top officers of Waste Management, Inc., charging them with perpetrating a massive financial fraud lasting more than five years. The complaint, filed in U.S. District Court in Chicago, charged that defendants engaged in a systematic scheme to falsify and misrepresent Waste Management's financial results between 1992 and 1997.

According to the complaint, the defendants violated, and aided and abetted violations of, anti-fraud, reporting, and record-keeping provisions of the federal securities laws. The SEC successfully sought injunctions prohibiting future violations, disgorgement of defendants' ill-gotten gains, civil money penalties, and officer and director bars against all defendants.

The complaint first identified the roles played by top management. Buntrock set earnings targets, fostered a culture of fraudulent accounting, personally directed certain of the accounting changes to make the targeted earnings, and was the spokesperson who announced the company's phony numbers. Rooney ensured that required write-offs were not recorded and, in some instances, overruled accounting decisions that would have a negative impact on operations. He reaped more than $9.2 million in ill-gotten gains from, among other things, performance-based bonuses, retirement benefits, and sales of company stock while the fraud was ongoing. Koenig was primarily responsible for executing the scheme. He also ordered the destruction of damaging evidence, misled the company's audit committee and internal accountants, and withheld information from the outside auditors. He profited by more than $900,000 from his fraudulent acts.

Hau was the principal technician for the fraudulent accounting. Among other things, he devised many *one-off* accounting manipulations to deliver the targeted earnings and carefully crafted the deceptive disclosures. The explanation of these manipulations is that to reduce expenses and inflate earnings artificially, management primarily used adjusting entries to conform the company's actual results to the predetermined earnings targets. The inflated earnings of prior periods then became the floor for future manipulations. The consequences created what Hau referred to as the one-off problem. To sustain the scheme, earnings fraudulently achieved in one period had to be replaced in the next. Hau profited by more than $600,000 from his fraudulent acts. Tobecksen was enlisted in 1994 to handle Hau's overflow. He profited by more than $400,000 from his fraudulent acts. Getz was the company's general counsel. He blessed the company's fraudulent disclosures and profited by more than $450,000 from his fraudulent acts.

The defendants fraudulently manipulated the company's revenues, because they were not growing enough to meet predetermined earnings targets, by manipulating current and future asset values, failing to write off asset impairments, using reserve accounting to mask operating expenses, implementing improper capitalization policies, and failing to establish reserves (liabilities) to pay for income taxes and other expenses.

Overview of Accounting and Financial Reporting Fraud

Improper Accounting Practices

The accounting fraud involved a variety of practices, including improperly eliminating or deferring current-period expenses in order to inflate earnings. For example, the company avoided depreciation expenses by extending the estimated useful lives of its garbage trucks while at the same time making unsupported increases to the trucks' salvage values. In other words, the more the trucks were used and the older they became, the more the defendants said they were worth. Other improper accounting practices included:

- Making unsupported changes in depreciation estimates.
- Failing to record expenses for decreases in the value of landfills as they were filled with waste.
- Failing to record expenses necessary to write off the costs of impaired and abandoned landfill development projects.
- Improper capitalization of interest on landfill development.
- Establishing inflated environmental reserves (liabilities) in connection with acquisitions so that the excess reserves could be used to avoid recording unrelated environmental and other expenses.
- Netting one-time gains against operating expenses.
- Manipulating reserve account balances to inflate earnings.

In February 1998, Waste Management announced that it was restating its financial statements for the five-year period 1992–1996 and the first three quarters of 1997.[1] The company admitted that through

---

[1] The amount for the first three quarters of 1997 is $180,900.

1996 it had materially overstated its reported pretax earnings by $1.43 billion and that it had understated certain elements of its tax expense by $178 million, as reported in *Accounting and Auditing Enforcement Release (AAER) 1405:*

Vehicle, equipment, and container depreciation expense	$ 509
Capitalized interest	192
Environmental and closure/postclosure liabilities	173
Purchase accounting related to remediation reserves	128
Asset impairment losses	214
Software impairment reversal	(85)
Other	301
Pretax total	$1,432
Income tax expense restatement	$ 178

Andersen audited and issued an unqualified (i.e., unmodified) report on each of Waste Management's original financial statements and on the financial statements in the restatement. In so doing, Andersen acknowledged that the company's original financial statements for the periods 1992 through 1996 were materially misstated and that its prior unqualified reports on those financial statements should not be relied upon. In the restatement, the company admitted that it had overstated its net after-tax income as follows:

	Net Income		
Year	Reported (thousands)	Restated (thousands)	Percent Overstated
1992	$850,036	$739,686	15
1993	$452,776	$288,707	57
1994	$784,381	$627,508	25
1995	$603,899	$340,097	78
1996	$192,085	$ (39,307)	100+

Netting

Top management concealed their scheme in a variety of ways, including making false and misleading statements about the company's accounting practices, financial condition, and future prospects in filings with the SEC, reports to shareholders, and press releases, and using an accounting manipulation known as *netting* to make reported results appear better than they actually were. The netting eliminated approximately $490 million in current-period operating expenses and accumulated prior-period accounting misstatements by offsetting them against unrelated, one-time gains on the sale or exchange of assets.

Andersen repeatedly issued unqualified audit reports on the company's materially false and misleading annual financial statements. At the outset of the fraud, management capped Andersen's audit fees and advised the Andersen engagement partner that the firm could earn additional fees through "special work." Andersen nevertheless identified the company's improper accounting practices and quantified much of the impact of those practices on the company's financial statements. Andersen annually presented company management with PAJEs to correct errors that understated expenses and overstated earnings in the company's financial statements.

PAJEs

Management consistently refused to make the adjustments called for by the PAJEs, and Andersen accepted management's decision even though the firm knew (or should have known) that it was not in accordance with GAAP. To placate management and ease its conscience, Andersen entered into an agreement with top management to write off the accumulated errors fraudulently over periods of up to 10 years and to change the underlying accounting practices, but to do so only in future periods. The four-page agreement or "treaty," called a Summary of Action Steps, identified improper accounting practices and prescribed 32 "must-do" steps for the company to follow to change those practices. The action steps constituted an agreement between the company and Andersen to cover up past frauds by committing additional frauds in the future. It was the smoking gun proving that Andersen knowingly participated in a fraudulent act in violation of securities laws.

Over time, the fraudulent scheme unraveled. An internal review in mid-July 1997 identified improper accounting and led to the restatement of the company's financial statements for 1992 through the third quarter of 1997. In its restated financial statements in February 1998, the company acknowledged that it had misstated its pretax earnings by approximately $1.7 billion. At the time, the restatement was the largest in corporate history.

As news of the company's overstatement of earnings became public, Waste Management's shareholders (other than the top management, who sold company stock and thus avoided losses) lost more than $6 billion of the market value of their investments when the stock declined following the public disclosure of fraud.

SEC Sanctions against Andersen and Waste Management Officers

As for the Andersen auditors, the SEC found that the firm and four of its auditors violated the anti-fraud provisions of Rule 10b-5 of the Securities Exchange Act of 1934. These provisions make it unlawful for a CPA to (1) employ any device, scheme, or artifice to defraud; (2) make an untrue statement of material fact or omit a material fact; and (3) engage in any act, practice, or course of business to commit fraud or deceit in connection with the purchase or sale of the security.

Litigation Release No. 17039 details the charges against four Andersen partners:

Partner	Position
Robert E. Allgyer	Partner in charge of Waste Management audit
Edward G. Maier	Risk management partner and engagement concurring partner
Walter Cercavschi	Partner on the Waste Management engagement
Robert G. Kutsenda	Central Region audit practice director

The SEC charged that Kutsenda knew or should have known that the netting violated GAAP, that prior misstatements that he knew about would not be disclosed to investors, that the impact of the netting on the company's 1995 financial statements was material, and that an unqualified audit report was not warranted.[2]

On August 29, 2005, the SEC issued Litigation Release 19351, announcing that the U.S. District Court for the Northern District of Illinois entered final judgments as to defendants Dean L. Buntrock, Phillip B. Rooney, Thomas C. Hau, and Herbert A. Getz, all of whom consented to the judgments without admitting or denying the allegations. The judgments permanently barred Buntrock, Rooney, Hau, and Getz from acting as an officer or director of a public company, enjoined them from future violations of the anti-fraud and other provisions of the federal securities laws, and required payment of $30,869,054

[2]Available at: http://www.sec.gov/litigation/admin/34-44448.htm.

in disgorgement, prejudgment interest, and civil penalties. The specific provisions of the securities acts that were violated include Rules 10b-5, 12b-20, 13a-1, and 13a-13 of Sections 10(b) of the Securities Exchange Act of 1934 and Section 17(a) of the Securities Act of 1933.[3]

The distribution of the penalty was as follows:

- Buntrock—$19,447,670 total, comprised of $10,708,032 in disgorgement, $6,439,638 of prejudgment interest, and a $2,300,000 civil penalty.
- Rooney—$8,692,738 total, comprised of $4,593,764 in disgorgement, $2,998,974 of prejudgment interest, and a $1,100,000 civil penalty.
- Hau—$1,578,890 total, comprised of $641,866 in disgorgement, $507,024 of prejudgment interest, and a $430,000 civil penalty.
- Getz—$1,149,756 total, comprised of $472,500 in disgorgement, $477,256 of prejudgment interest, and a $200,000 civil penalty.

On November 7, 2001, Connecticut attorney general Richard Blumenthal and treasurer Denise L. Nappier announced a $457 million settlement with Waste Management in a class action securities fraud case that provided monetary benefits for shareholders; it was the third-largest securities class action settlement in U.S. history at the time. Waste Management agreed to institute important changes in its corporate governance structure, including greater independence for the company's audit committee and enhanced accountability for shareholders with respect to corporate management. Members of the audit committee were required to be five years removed from employment with the company, rather than the current three years. The company also agreed to recommend to shareholders that their entire board of directors be elected annually, replacing the current system of staggered terms, with one-third of the board being elected each year.[4] The corporate governance changes are consistent with requirements of SOX that calls for greater independence for the audit committee and meaningful involvement in financial reporting oversight.

On June 19, 2001, the SEC announced a settlement with Arthur Andersen and the four partners in connection with the firm's audits of the annual financial statements of Waste Management for the years 1992 through 1996. The commission had alleged that Andersen and its partners failed to stand up to company management and betrayed their ultimate allegiance to Waste Management's shareholders and the investing public by sanctioning false and misleading audit reports. Thus, the firm violated its public interest obligation. As for top management at Waste Management, it failed in its fiduciary responsibilities to safeguard company assets and knowingly condoned fraudulent financial reporting.

Details of Andersen's Involvement in the Fraud

As previously mentioned, in order to conceal the understatement of expenses, top officials resorted to an undisclosed practice known as netting. They used one-time gains realized on the sale or exchange of assets to eliminate unrelated current-period operating expenses and accounting misstatements that had accumulated from prior periods. These one-time gains were offset against items that should have been reported as operating expenses in current or prior periods, and thus concealed the impact of their fraudulent accounting and the deteriorating condition of the company's core operations. Although Andersen advised company management that the use of " 'other gains' to bury charges for balance sheet clean-ups . . . and the lack of disclosure . . . [was] an area of SEC exposure," the practice persisted. In fact, Andersen prepared a PRJE (post-reclassification journal entry) to reduce pretax income from continuing operations, but the company refused to record it. Over the course of the fraud, Waste

---

[3]Available at: http://www.sec.gov/litigation/litreleases/lr19351.htm.
[4]Available at: http://www.ct.gov/ag/cwp/view.asp?A=1776&Q=283444.

Management used netting secretly to erase approximately $490 million in current-period expenses and prior-period misstatements. The netting procedure effectively acknowledged that the company's accounting practices were wrong and that the netted prior-period items were, in fact, misstatements.[5]

Andersen's Relationship with Waste Management

The SEC was very critical of Andersen's relationship with Waste Management. Litigation Release 17039 notes that the firm had audited Waste Management since before it became a public company in 1971 and considered the client its "crown jewel." Until 1997, every CFO and CAO in Waste Management's history as a public company had previously worked as an auditor at Andersen. During the 1990s, approximately 14 former Andersen employees worked for Waste Management, most often in key financial and accounting positions. Andersen selected Allgyer to be the managing partner of the Waste Management audit because he had demonstrated a "devotion to client service" and had a personal style that "fit well with Waste Management officers." During the time of the audit, Allgyer held the title of "Partner in Charge of Client Service" for Andersen's Chicago office and served as "marketing director." He coordinated marketing efforts of the office including, among other things, cross-selling non-attest services to audit clients. Shortly after Allgyer's appointment as engagement partner, Waste Management capped Andersen's corporate audit fees at the prior year's level but allowed the firm to earn additional fees for "special work." Andersen reported to the audit committee that it had billed Waste Management approximately $7.5 million in audit fees. Over the seven-year period, while Andersen's corporate audit fees remained capped, Andersen also billed the company $11.8 million in other fees. A related entity, Andersen Consulting, also billed Waste Management approximately $6 million in additional non-audit fees, $3.7 million of which were related to a strategic review that analyzed the company's overall business structure. The firm ultimately made a recommendation on implementing a new operating model designed to "increase shareholder value." Allgyer was a member of the steering committee that oversaw the strategic review, and Andersen Consulting billed his time for these services to the company. In setting Allgyer's compensation, Andersen took into account, among other things, the firm's billings to Waste Management for audit and non-audit services.[6]

SEC Charges and Sanctions against Andersen and Partners

Allgyer was charged in connection with Andersen's audit of Waste Management's 1992 financial statements. The SEC alleged that he knew or was reckless in not knowing that the firm's audit report on the company's 1992 financial statements was materially false and misleading because, in addition to quantified misstatements totaling $93.5 million, which, if corrected, would have reduced the company's net income before accounting changes by 7.4 percent, there were additional known and likely misstatements that had not been quantified and estimated. Allgyer further knew that the company had netted, without disclosure, $111 million of current-period expenses and prior-period misstatements against a portion of a one-time gain from an unrelated IPO of securities, which had the effect of understating Waste Management's 1992 operating expenses and overstating the company's income from operations. The SEC further alleged that Allgyer engaged in similar conduct in connection with the 1993 through 1996 audits. That is, he knew or was reckless in not knowing that Andersen's unqualified audit report for each of the years 1993 through 1996 was materially false and misleading.[7]

Allgyer, the partner responsible for the Waste Management engagement, consented (1) to the entry of a permanent injunction enjoining him from violating Section 10(b) of the Exchange Act and Rule 10b-5 thereunder and Section 17(a) of the Securities Act of 1933; (2) to pay a civil money penalty of $50,000;

[5]Available at: http://www.sec.gov/litigation/litreleases/lr18913.htm.
[6]Available at: https://www.sec.gov/litigation/litreleases/lr17039.htm.
[7]SEC, *In the Matter of Robert E. Allgyer, CPA,* Release Nos. 33-7986, 34-44445, June 19, 2001, Available at: https://www.sec.gov/litigation/admin/33-7986.htm.

and (3) in related administrative proceedings pursuant to Rule 102(e), to the entry of an order denying him the privilege of appearing or practicing before the SEC as an accountant, with the right to request his reinstatement after five years.

The SEC charged that Kutsenda, the central region audit practice director responsible for Andersen's Chicago, Kansas City, Indianapolis, and Omaha offices, engaged in improper professional conduct within the meaning of Rule 102(e)(1)(ii) of the commission's rules of practice with respect to the 1995 audit. During that audit, he was informed of the non-GAAP netting of a $160 million one-time gain against unrelated expenses and prior-period misstatements and that the amount represented 10 percent of Waste Management's 1995 pretax earnings. Although not part of the engagement team, Kutsenda was consulted by two of the engagement partners and, therefore, he was required under GAAS to exercise due professional care so that an unqualified audit report was not issued on financial statements that were materially misstated.[8] Kutsenda consented in administrative proceedings pursuant to Rule 102(e) to the entry of an order, based on the commission's finding that he engaged in improper professional conduct, that denied him the privilege of appearing or practicing before the SEC as an accountant, with the right to request reinstatement after one year.

AAER 1410 was issued on June 19, 2001, and details the sanctions against Andersen and its partners. The following discussion describes the sanctions imposed on the firm.[9]

The SEC complaint against Andersen charged that the firm knew of Waste Management's exaggerated profits during its audits of the financial statements from 1992 through 1996 and repeatedly pleaded with the company to make changes. Each year, Andersen gave in and issued unqualified opinions on the company's financial statements even though they did not conform to GAAP. A summary of the findings against Andersen follows:[10]

- Knowingly or recklessly issuing false and misleading unqualified audit reports on Waste Management's annual financial statements for the years 1993 through 1996.
- Failing to quantify and estimate all known and likely misstatements due to non-GAAP accounting practices.
- In 1995, knowing but doing nothing about the fact that Waste Management did not implement the action steps and continued to utilize accounting practices that did not conform with GAAP.
- Determining the materiality of misstatements improperly; failing to record or disclose information about such transactions; issuing an unqualified audit report.
- Written recognition in a memorandum prepared by Andersen of the company's improper netting practices and identification of SEC exposure; monitored continuing practice but failed to adequately disclose the effect on current earnings.

Andersen consented to (1) a permanent injunction enjoining it from violating Section 10(b) of the Securities Exchange Act of 1934 and Rule 10b-5 thereunder; (2) payment of a civil penalty of $7 million; and (3) in related administrative proceedings, the entry of an order pursuant to Rule 102(e) censuring it based upon the SEC's finding that it engaged in improper professional conduct and the issuance of the permanent injunction. The ink on the agreement barely had time to dry when, on December 2, 2001, Enron, Andersen's most infamous client, filed for Chapter 11 protection in the United States after getting embroiled in its own financial scandal.

---

[8]SEC, *In the Matter of Robert G. Kutsenda, CPA*, Release No. 34-44448, June 19, 2001, Available at: https://www.sec.gov /litigation/admin/34-44448.htm.

[9]Available at: http://www.sec.gov/litigation/litreleases/lr17039.htm.

[10]Available at: http://www.sec.gov/litigation/litreleases/lr17435.htm.

Corporate Governance at Waste Management

The fraud at Waste Management was perpetrated by top management. The board of directors either did not know about it or chose to look the other way. Members of top management had signed agreements with Andersen that included action steps to correct for past improper accounting by adjusting future income and adopting proper accounting procedures. Top management failed to live up to any of its agreements.

As the Waste Management fraud progressed over the years, the inflated earnings of prior periods became the floor for future manipulations—one-time adjustments made to achieve a number in one period had to be replaced in the next—and created the one-off accounting problem. In early 1997, Hau explained to the audit committee that "we've had one-off accounting every year that has to be replaced the next year. We've been doing this long enough that the problem has mounted. . . ."[11] Essentially, the company created a fiction of inflated earnings and had to duplicate the fiction in subsequent years. Perhaps not surprisingly, greed ruled the day, and the company wasn't simply satisfied with meeting fictitious earnings levels in subsequent years. Instead, there needed to be a higher earnings level to keep the stock price growing and enhance stock option values for top company officials each year. In essence, the company took the first step down the ethical slippery slope in 1992 and couldn't (or wouldn't) find its way back up to the high road. It hit rock bottom in 1997, when the fraud eventually unraveled. In mid-1997, the company's board of directors brought in a new CEO, who ordered a review of the accounting and then resigned after barely four months because, reportedly, he thought that the accounting was "spooky." At that time, the proverbially red flag was raised for the public to see, and Andersen's negligence came to the forefront.

In February 1998, Waste Management acknowledged "past mistakes" and announced that it would restate its financial statements for the period 1992–1996 and the first three quarters of 1997. It concluded that, for this period, the company had overstated its reported pretax earnings by approximately $1.7 billion and understated certain elements of its income tax expense by approximately $190 million. In restating its financial statements, the company revised every accounting practice identified in the action steps—practices that defendants had agreed, but failed, to change four years earlier.

As news of the company's overstatement of earnings became public, Waste Management's shareholders lost over $6 billion in the market value of their investments when the stock price plummeted from $35 to $22 per share. Although shareholders lost billions of dollars, top company officials profited handsomely from their fraud.

Questions

1. Characterize the ethical leadership at Waste Management and how it influenced organizational ethics.

2. The SEC charged Andersen with failing to quantify and estimate all known and likely misstatements due to non-GAAP practices. Describe the failings of the firm with respect to professional judgment and ethical expectations under the AICPA Code.

3. Classify each of the accounting techniques described in the case that contributed to the fraud into one of Schilit's accounting shenanigans. Include a brief discussion of how each technique violated GAAP.

4. Do you believe auditors should be expected to discover fraud when a client goes to great lengths, as did Waste Management, to withhold evidence from the auditors and mask the true financial effects of transactions? Explain.

---

[11]Available at: http://www.sec.gov/litigation/complaints/complr17435.htm.

Name Index

Note: Page numbers followed by n indicate notes.

Subject Index

Note: Page numbers followed by n indicate notes.